ENCYCLOPEDIA of MODERN ART AUCTION PRICES

ENCYCLOPEDIA of MODERN ART AUCTION PRICES

MICHÈLE BÉRARD

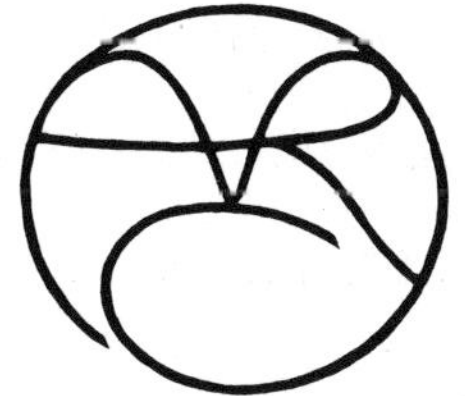

ARCO PUBLISHING COMPANY, Inc.
New York

Acknowledgment

I wish to thank Clotilde de Lavigne who
kindly contributed to the biographical chronologies.
My thanks also go to Monique Cudraz who helped me
to do this work in the English language.

Published by ARCO PUBLISHING COMPANY, INC.
219 Park Avenue South, New York, N.Y. 10003

Library of Congress Catalog Number 79-161210

ISBN 0-668-02493-3

Printed in the United States of America

CONTENTS

INDEX OF ARTISTS

FOREWORD

In the last two decades the interest in works of art of all kinds has expanded immeasurably. With the spread of wealth, a whole new section of the post-war world finds itself able to own paintings, sculptures and works of art, a pleasure that formerly belonged to the very rich. The rise of this new buying power combined with a widening reaction against the anonymity of mass production and the increasing impersonality and complexity of modern life has led to an upsurge in the demand for works of original art.

The market has, of necessity, broadened to meet the new demand, and whole new areas of interest to collectors have opened up. In the field of nineteenth and twentieth century paintings this is more evident than elsewhere. It is still necessary to be very rich to buy a major painting by Monet, Renoir or Cézanne; those collectors, therefore, who are less affluent or more adventurous have developed different tastes. Some are content with relatively less expensive works by pupils or followers of the leading artists; others prefer to buy second-rate examples by first-rate painters in the belief that it is preferable to have an inferior work by a creative genius than the masterpiece of a second-rate talent. Again, others choose to buy in newer fields and search out for themselves movements that are less widely acclaimed where the prices are still within reach. And then again there are those who endeavour to recognize talent in the work of a contemporary artist whose reputation is still little known, and try courageously to distinguish lasting genius from passing fashion.

Nowhere can the evolving tastes of the buying public be seen more clearly than in this book. It covers the years from 1961 to 1969 which probably encompassed the greatest changes in the history of art collecting of any decade in this century. Although paintings and drawings of the nineteenth and twentieth centuries represent only a small proportion of the art market as a whole, it is the area which is the most sensitive to change and wherein such changes can be most accurately compared.

It should not, however, be thought that this book is of interest only to the student of fashion. Collectors, dealers, auctioneers—in fact, anybody remotely concerned with the buying, owning or selling works of art of this period—will find it invaluable. An examination, for instance, of the pages which cover the sales of paintings by Magritte, Brauner or Dali, will show the recent spectacular rise in the demand for works by the surrealist painters, or similarly that the prices being paid in 1969 for works by Derain or Rouault were not far different from the prices being paid in 1961. Again, no *annual* index can give such a clear idea of the relative rarity with which works by a given artist appear at auction. A collector hoping to buy a painting by Franz Marc or August Macke can see from this index that his choice will be very limited in comparison, say, with the opportunities for acquiring a Kirchner or a Klee. For the auctioneer or the dealer this encyclopedia will be a basic reference work and an essential tool of his profession.

DAVID NASH
Vice President, Parke-Bernet Galleries

ENCYCLOPEDIA of MODERN ART AUCTION PRICES

INTRODUCTION

Since the end of World War II the number of collectors of modern painting has been steadily increasing. No doubt the various magazines, books, reproductions, and exhibitions dealing with art in general contributed to modern painting's becoming more widely known—as did the spectacular increase of prices paid. Between the aesthete and the speculator there is a growing number of people who wish to acquire paintings for their own pleasure while making a safe investment.

Attracted by love and enthusiasm for painting, these new collectors are generally little aware of its financial aspect. Indeed, the very idea of setting a price on a work of art makes the true art lover a little uneasy. But browsing from one gallery to another, attending an auction sale, reading newspapers, he soon comes face to face with reality and discovers that a painting considered as "a piece of merchandise" may be worth, to take extremes, from as little as one hundred to more than a million dollars. Here is a matter to think about. One purpose of this book is to make things easier for new buyers (and even the more experienced ones). The author's intention is to put things into place for the reader concerning the prices paid for modern painting during the 1960's. For it is too often ignorance of the financial value of paintings and fear of blundering that prevent the art lover from starting a collection.

By modern painters we mean all painters since the Impressionists.[1] It is understood, however, that those who went on using a style that preceeded the pictorial revolution of Impressionism, although contemporary with the movement, have not been taken into account. Nor have the artists whose careers were indissolubly bound to artistic phenomena taking place around 1960, such as Pop-Art, Op-Art,[2] and so on—their works are too recent to allow a satisfactory appreciation of the evolution of their financial value.

Within these limits, a further selection was made by the author, who thought it impossible to include all modern artists in this book. So a method of selection had to be adopted. As it was untenable to base it on purely aesthetic grounds, the only way to solve the difficulty was to base it on

[1] Including direct forerunners of the movement such as Manet, Boudin, and Jongkind.

[2] Besides, by the very nature of their production, the works of these movements can hardly take place in such a traditional category as painting.

financial ones. It was decided that this book would take into account only those artists who had at least one of their paintings auctioned for not less than $2,000 during the period we are interested in—that is to say, between September 1961 and July 1969.[3] Only drawings, watercolors, gouaches, pastels, oils, collages, and so on, made by the artist's hand and existing only as an original work are catalogued here. Prints are excluded, for collecting prints poses other problems, which could be the subject of another volume.

The author did her best to assemble all the artists whose paintings reached the sum of $2,000 and apologizes if some painters have escaped her research. Being concerned to give only correct information, she met with a new problem regarding some painters. Indeed, some of their paintings did reach $2,000 once or twice in 1961, 1962, or 1963; but immediately afterward the prices fell. As in most of these cases it could be assumed that they were artificially and episodically supported by some art dealer, she has thought it reasonable not to take these artists into account. This cannot be construed as prejudice because the method of selection rests not on aesthetic but on financial value.

If our method of selection of two hundred eighty-two artists has the great advantage of including the most famous painters of the century, it involves nevertheless two main drawbacks. First, as everybody knows, time contributes greatly to increase the value of painting. Therefore, some second-rate artists who followed important movements at the beginning of this century are included here, whereas a small number of very talented contemporary painters are not. Second, only prices reached at auction are considered here—thus rare artists whose paintings are almost never presented at auction cannot be taken into account. This is notably true of the first-rate American painter Morgan Russell.

But indeed a book mentioning only prices fetched by paintings would have appeared somewhat scanty and apt to divert the attention of the reader from art to speculation. That is why this book aims at being a kind of encyclopedia of painting. It includes, for each painter, a short biography summarizing the main events of his life. Through these biographies, and especially those of the leaders of different movements, the steps of modern painting are schematically retraced. They may serve as an introduction for the beginner as well as an *aide-mémoire* for the experienced collector.

★　　★　　★

The reader will find it easy to use this book. For each painter there is a biography followed by a sales list. The sales list includes works classified according to the three following groups: (1) drawings; (2) watercolors, gouaches, tempera, pastels, and so on; (3) paintings.

[3] This approach has been made considerably easier by the existence of yearly lists of auction prices such as, in particular, *L'Annuaire International des Ventes* by Mayer, Paris.

In each group prices follow one another from September 1961 to July 1969.

Each work is described in this order: title; date (in parentheses when approximate); dimensions in inches (the first figure of the dimensions is the height).

As for the works executed on paper (the first two groups), the nature of the medium used is indicated—pencil, ink, gouache, and so forth. The mount is specified only when it is other than paper.

As for the paintings, the medium is oil on canvas unless otherwise stated.

Every entry in addition includes a bold-face key number in parentheses referring to the Index of Sales at the end of the book. The key number reveals when, by whom, and where the work was sold.

The auction price in dollars is given in the right-hand column.

Additional information, such as dedications (in the original language) and prices reached at a previous auction when the work was sold twice during the relevant period, is footnoted.

★　　★　　★

No doubt these long price lists may seem forbidding at first sight. However, they will impart a lot of information to those willing to study them.

Insofar as auction sales are the most faithful reflection of the market, the lists in this book disclose what is available and what simply exists. They also give a good idea of what are the artist's favorite media and subjects. For instance, it will appear that the Impressionists almost never used gouache; that among them Pissarro frequently used watercolor; and that there are few pastels by Monet, a few more by Sisley and Renoir, and a greater number by Guillaumin.

Aware of available works on the market, the collector will be able to recognize and acquire the work missing in his collection. Every collection is usually built on a single idea which is its compass and charm—works by one painter, about one subject, in one technique, of one period.

This book intends mainly to give the amateur and professional collector a better understanding of the financial value of painting to enable him to buy and sell in full knowledge of the facts. For a collection is not a gathering of insignificant objects left to be covered by dust; whether large or small, it is a living thing—the privileged and sustained work of a lifetime. And like all living things, it moves and develops. One may tire of certain works, either because one's taste gains in refinement or because it changes. Besides, perfecting a collection is for many collectors much more thrilling than amassing one. To buy and sell at the appropriate price, the concern of every

3

tradesman, is also—although in a different perspective—that of every collector.

The first criterion involved in the appraisal of a work of art (authentic, of course) is the painter's signature (or the stamped signature). Beyond the formal signature are the style and manner, which are the genuine signature of a work of art. Knowing simply the name of the painter amounts only to associating the price of a painting with its creator's current rate. The price varies a great deal when it concerns a master, a follower, or a more-or-less successful artist. That is why it is necessary to know how to place every artist in the history of painting.[4] Too many collectors go on thinking that a signature is enough to give a painting value. Many other factors have to be taken into account.

After the signature comes the subject matter—figurative paintings are the most numerous. It is easy to understand that the most popular subjects and the ones that reach the highest prices at auction are the most "pleasant": landscapes, seascapes, celebrated towns, figures whose poses or costumes are decorative, fruits, and flowers. Subjects dealing with the harshness of life (anxiety, illness, death, poverty, violence), or engaged themes (religion, politics, "aggressive" eroticism) are less in demand by a public not really willing to hang them at home. Of course, when a very rare painting comes up for sale, even though the subject may not be very attractive, the price offered for it is high because of its rarity. But a rare painting with a pleasant subject will fetch a comparatively higher price.

For instance, three of Frédéric Bazille's paintings were sold during the period we are interested in. One of them, entitled "L'Ambulance improvisée" was sold, despite its title, for $19,000. But the two others, "Moresque" and "The Ramparts of Aigues-Mortes," because of their clearly less forbidding subjects, were sold respectively for $30,400 and $55,000.

These general remarks on this subject matter involve some exceptions—especially when one starts to consider artists whose talent can be expressed only through unpopular subjects or perhaps common-looking ones, the treatment of which may render the approach somewhat difficult. As long as these paintings are "typical" of their creators and as long as they win a following, they encourage a large audience whose taste is contrary to the general liking of the public. The dramatic themes of Picasso (distorted figures, skulls of animals, evocations of war); the troubled atmosphere of Pascin's paintings; the sacred compositions of Rouault; and the Expressionist paintings, distressing as they may be—all these have many admirers and not simply because of the fame of their creators.

Another aspect to consider is that subjects in demand may be over-

[4] Besides the indications given in the text, the collector can use the bibliography as a base for all that concerns painting.

4

looked in the work of painters noted for other specialties. Take flowers. Utrillo's landscapes are far more popular than his flowers, as are Van Dongen's portraits of women and society life. Flowers, therefore, are not considered representative of these painters' work.

Let us contrast Vlaminck. Though a landscape painter above all, he painted a number of flower pictures. Unlike those of Utrillo and Van Dongen, however, Vlaminck's are appreciated on the same level as his other work for the simple reason that they are as representative of his manner as are his landscapes.

All this tends to prove that the more typical of its creator a painting is and the more it resembles the idea the public has in mind the more appreciated it is.

This also is true of our third criterion: the period. A painter's work is generally divided into several periods marking a change in style. Experts on painting generally single out one period they consider the most successful. For most painters this period can be easily singled out.

The works of the Impressionists, for instance, painted before the recognition of the movement are distinct from the later ones. These, of course, command a higher price.[5]

This standard applies even more to the Neo-Impressionists. (Indeed, a Renoir painted before Impressionism would certainly be more appreciated than a non-Pointillist Signac.) For some years collectors have been fascinated by the pearly lighted mosaics painted by the Neo-Impressionists. For instance, after Seurat's untimely death, Signac became the leader of this group, and so the double influence of these two masters—different as their tempers were—helped to give the movement the amazing unity of style which made it a success. Here, more than in any other movement, the manner of second-rate but highly talented painters is close to that of the masters.

The criterion of period is a little different as it applies to the Nabis group. The paintings of Maurice Denis, Roussel, and Sérusier are preferred as period works above the others of the group. But the works of Bonnard and Vuillard by their genius escape criteria and maintain their values.

The Expressionists do not form a group per se. Many worked alone—Ensor, Münch, Soutine—and their "expressionism" is more imaginatively constructed than mere pictorial research. Their most popular paintings are the most representative of their inner dispositions, and the themes occur throughout their careers.[6]

As for the artists connected with Fauvism, Cubism, abstract art, the Dada group, or Surrealism, there is no doubt that the group-connected

[5] The paintings of the followers of the movement, being mainly assimilative, are interesting only as "Impressionist" paintings.

[6] Of the German Expressionists, the prestige of "Die Brücke" is particularly high.

paintings are much more valuable than the others. To take an extreme example: The price for Henri Hayden's fine compositions painted after the Cubist manner (1914-19) very often exceed $10,000, whereas later paintings returning to realism can hardly be sold for a tenth of this figure. (Some artists, of course, participated in several of these movements. Braque is a famous case, executing both Fauvist and Cubist paintings.)

But within every generation and every movement the artist evolves the expression that suits him best. This is why Braque has given the full measure of his genius within Cubism and this is why his Cubist paintings are more highly regarded than his later ones.

This is also true of Picasso, another creator of Cubism. But of all the painters engaged in the great movements of modern art, Picasso is perhaps the only one who created a personal style of a surprising maturity, even before participating in any of these movements. He can rightly be called an exception. Several years before Cubism, he elaborated powerful and original manners called Blue Period and Rose Period (1901-6). These works, ranked among the finest of the century, are even more highly appreciated than his Cubist paintings.

Paintings produced outside these movements may achieve an equal degree of excellence and a much more personal style. Dufy, Vlaminck, and Marquet, for instance, created their own style after Fauvism. But the historical importance of the well-known movements gains high prestige and higher prices for paintings associated with them. For instance, a Fauve Vlaminck may fetch from five to ten times the price of a later painting.

But certainly the reader has noticed that this schematic survey of the main pictorial tendencies of our time does not take into account certain artists who have evolved a unique form of expression. Consider Cézanne, Gauguin, Van Gogh, Toulouse-Lautrec, and other Post-Impressionists; independents such as Modigliani, Utrillo, Chagall, Rouault, and Gromaire. Every one of these artists has progressively created his own independent style—his best work is expressive of his inner vision.

The dimensions of a painting and the medium used have little to do with an appraisal of its value. However, in terms of decoration, it has to be said that a large canvas may hardly find a place in small apartments and a very small canvas may pass unnoticed in a large house. Paintings of an average size are generally the most pleasing.

As for the medium, if it is obvious that an oil painting is, with very few exceptions, always more expensive than a watercolor, gouache, pastel, or drawing, it goes without saying that a fine watercolor should always be preferred to a poor oil.[7]

[7] Degas' pastels, for example, perfectly representative of his art, usually surpass the prices of his oils.

This leads us directly to our last, but decisive, criterion: the quality of the work. These are, in short, the guidelines to the appraisal of quality—the ability to distinguish rich inspiration from inner sterility, the completion of harmony from inexpressive nullity, the appreciation of the architecture of a composition, the correspondence of form and color, the comprehension of invention. They may be summed up as taste—seldom inborn and capable of being educated, cultivated, and refined.

The innate excellence of a work always adds to its value. Unfortunately, intrinsic value is quite often unrelated to commercial value—especially for some painters of average ability. Some beautifully executed paintings because of the abstract handling of the subject matter never attain the prices they should. Works painted in subdued tones, for example, are not as popular as colorful ones. Color exerts great appeal and will usually be chosen over content.

★　★　★

The spectacular increase of bids on modern painting in the 1950's created passionate interest and confidence in modern art as an investment. Those who now have the same attitudes may have the expectation of being as lucky as most of their predecessors.

Earlier, only the great names were considered a really safe investment, but under the pressure of sustained demand other artists came into the limelight. Several of these have become sound financial investments as creators of genuinely artistic work. Others are more debatable as artists. These two groups include painters whose works have not followed the generally sustained, though irregular, increase of prices—some prices have remained unchanged and others have even decreased.

The 1960's witnessed the triumph of the painters commonly called the "Post-Impressionists," although they are more or less bound to earlier movements such as Impressionism, Neo-Impressionism, and the Nabis group.[8] The infatuation for these paintings of uneven quality but of easy intellectual approach and the trust in their commercial value were such that even mediocre works fetched a comparatively high price.

At present, the vogue for Post-Impressionism is fading, and the public seems to be attracted to more contemporary painters. Perhaps this is only one aspect of the increased sensitivity and eclecticism of the lover and collector of art.

[8] The real Post-Impressionists, of course, are the great independents who succeeded the Impressionists.

Basadella Afro

(1912–   )

Birthplace: Udine, Italy.

1924-28 Studies art in Venice and Florence. Exhibits in his native town.

1929 Wins the regional prize for painting, which enables him to go to Rome.

1932 Participates in an exhibition at the Galleria del Milione, Milan.

1934-36 Executes murals for the ONB College, Udine. Exhibition at the Galleria La Comete, Rome.

1937-38 Trip to Paris, where he becomes interested in French Impressionism and starts painting in this style.

1940-44 Discovers Cubism.

1947-48 Turns to abstract painting after being deeply impressed by a show of Klee's works.

1949 Meets Catherine Viviano and exhibits with other Italian artists at her gallery in New York.

1950 One-man show at the Viviano Gallery, New York, where his works are scheduled to be exhibited every two years. Spends a year in the U.S.

1951-52 Returns to Rome. One-man show at the Galleria della Palma. Participates in an exhibition of Italian art at the Museum of Modern Art, New York. Begins to be a very successful painter. Wins a prize at the Venice Biennial.

1954 Participates in the exhibition "New Decade" at the Museum of Modern Art, New York.

1955 Wins the international prize for painting at the São Paulo Biennial and exhibits in Rio de Janeiro. Becomes a member of the Carnegie Prize Jury, Pittsburgh.

1958 Teaches at Mills College, Oakland, California. Executes an important picture for UNESCO, Paris.

1960 Works exhibited in a room of honor at the Venice Biennial. Awarded national prize at the Carnegie Foundation, Pittsburgh.

1961 Exhibition at the Galerie de France, Paris.

Resident in Rome.

Sales

WATERCOLORS

1961-1962
Garden of Hope, gouache, 19¾ x 26 . . . . (88) $1,328

1965
El Liron, watercolor and gouache, 19 x 13 . . . . (494)   300
Young Lady Playing Cards, 1947, watercolor,
18¼ x 12¼ . . . . (583)   493

PAINTINGS

1961-1962
Still Life, 16¾ x 17½ . . . . (70)   711
To El Greco, 1951, 47 x 27¾ . . . . (129)   1,648
Green Landscape, 1955, 27¾ x 39½ . . . . (20)   3,318

1963
Procida, 1951, 27¾ x 19¾ . . . . (316)   3,250

1964
Still Life, 1941, 19¾ x 15¾ . . . . (435)   528
Monte Fumaiolo, 1955, 57¼ x 69 . . . . (372)   3,750

Composition, 1957, 31½ x 50¼ . . . . (372) $2,900
Compositon, on cardboard, 19½ x 25¼ . . . . (380)   1,033

1965
Crucifixion, 1949, 47 x 31½ . . . . (637)   3,500
Ciaccona, 1951, 25 x 16¼ . . . . (583)   290

1966
Mountainous Landscape, 1955, 47½ x 31½ . . . . (665)   1,800
Chicago Waterfront, 1953, 29¼ x 25¾ . . . . (701)   1,750

1967
Composition, 1947, 17¾ x 14 . . . . (882)   704

1968–July 1969
Cowboy, 1952, 43½ x 43¼ . . . . (1018)   3,700

Josef Albers

(1888–   )

Birthplace: Bottrop, in the Ruhr district, Germany.

1908 Visits Munich and its art galleries, seeing pictures by Cézanne and Matisse for the first time. Meets Rohlfs.

1913-15 Attends the Royal Art School, Berlin. Executes his first abstract pictures.

1916-20 Attends the Kunstgewerbeschule, Essen. Executes his first lithographs. Attends the Academy of Art of Munich.

1920-23 Studies at the Bauhaus at Weimar. Designs and executes stained-glass windows.

1925-33 Teaches at the Bauhaus at Dessau. Designs furniture. Travels in Europe.

1929 Shows glass paintings at the exhibition of the Bauhaus masters (with Feininger, Kandinsky, Klee, and Schlemmer) at the Kunsthalle, Basel, and at the Kunstgewerbemuseum, Zurich.

1933-49 Leaves Germany and settles in the U.S. Teaches at Black Mountain College, North Carolina. Trip to Mexico.

1936-41 Lectures at Harvard University. Several one-man shows of the Bauhaus-period glass paintings and of new oils, in American Galleries such as J. B. Neumann's New Art Circle, New York; Earl Stendhal's, Los Angeles; Nierendorf's, New York; and at the San Francisco Art Museum.

1946 One-man show at the Egan Gallery, New York.

1950 Teaches at Yale University, New Haven. Appears as a main figure in geometrical abstraction, as well as a highly influential painter. Starts his famous series of variations on the theme "Homage to the Square."

1956 Retrospective exhibition at the Yale University Art Gallery.

1960 Designs murals for the Time-Life Building, New York.

1961	Retrospective exhibition at the Stedelijk Museum, Amsterdam.
1962	Becomes Doctor of Fine Arts, Yale University.
1964	Executes "Repeat and Reverse," a stainless-steel sculpture, for the Art and Architecture Building, Yale University. Resident in New Haven.

Sales

PAINTINGS

1963

Proto-Form B, 1938, on panel, 27¾ x 23¾ .... (272) $1,100

1965

Homage to the Square: Nocturne, 1951, on panel,
31½ x 31½ .... (489) 1,600

Homage to the Square, 1959, on panel,
48¼ x 48¼ .... (592) 6,000

1966

Mirage, 1940, 27¼ x 31 .... (651) 1,500

Study for "Homage to the Square," 1962, on
panel, 24 x 24 .... (651) 2,800

1967

Homage to the Square, 1961, on panel, 32 x 32 ... (907) 1,599

Ivan Albright

(1897-   )

Birthplace: North Harvey, Illinois, U.S.

1915-16	Studies architecture. Executes surgical drawings for a medical unit during World War I.
1918-28	Participates in group shows at the Art Institute of Chicago.
1919	Travels to France, where he attends the regional fine arts school, Nantes.
1920-23	Studies at the Art Institute of Chicago.
1930	One-man show at the Walden Book Shop, Chicago. His work offers a peculiar image of reality, tinged with moral intentions and morbid overtones. Though he cannot be called an orthodox Surrealist, he has a genuine sense of unreality.
1930-31	One-man show at the Art Institute of Chicago. Awarded successively silver and gold medals by the Society of Contemporary American Art.
1943	The Chicago Society of Arts commissions two pictures: "The Portrait of Dorian Gray" and "The Temptation of St. Anthony."
1946	One-man show at the American Academy of Arts, Chicago.
1948	Wins the first prize of the Art Institute of Chicago.
1958	Participates in the art exhibition of the World's Fair, Brussels.

1964	Retrospective exhibition at the Art Institute of Chicago. Resident in Chicago.

Sales

WATERCOLORS

1968–July 1969

Trees, Trees, and Trees Again, 1939, watercolor
and gouache, 14 x 20 .... (1215) $2,500

Albert André

(1869-1954)

Birthplace: Lyons, France.

1889	Attends the Académie Julian, Paris. Meets Valtat and Ranson.
1894	Takes part in the Salon des Indépendants, Paris. Renoir notices his pictures and becomes his friend. Thanks to Renoir, Durand-Ruel shows interest in André's painting and becomes his dealer; he remains so until André's death.
1900	Meets the artists working at the *Revue Blanche*—Bonnard, Vuillard, Roussel, and Valloton. Travels to Germany, England, Spain, and Holland. Visits Signac at St. Tropez.
1904	Participates in the Salon d'Automne, Paris, where he continues to exhibit.
1918	Writes a monograph on Renoir. Becomes curator of the museum of Bagnols-sur-Cèze, Gard district, France, where several contemporary pictures are shown.
1919	Illustrates several works by Claude Farrère, Charles Maurras, and Stendhal.
1927	Mermillon writes a monograph on André.
1928	Delivers lectures about Renoir and his models at the "Heures Lyonnaises."
1937	Writes a monograph on Monet.
1947	Settles in Paris again after a long stay at Laudun, France.
1954	Died, Laudun, France.
1955	Retrospective exhibition at the Salon d'Automne, Paris.

Sales

DRAWINGS

1961–1962

The Operating Table, 13½ x 10 .... (168) $ 31

1965

Landscape with a River, India ink, 7¼ x 10¾ ..... (581) 64

1968–July 1969

Seascape, pencil, 7½ x 10¾ .... (1228) 36

WATERCOLORS

1964

Boulogne Beach, watercolor, 10¼ x 14¾ . . . . (351) $ 80
The Walk Along the Road, gouache, 11½ x 15½ . . (351)   140

1968–July 1969

Young Woman Peeling an Orange, watercolor,
    8 x 5¼ . . . . (1066)   84

PAINTINGS

1961–1962

A Shop in Marseilles by Night, 1917, 26 x 19¾ . . . (114)   1,400
Interior of a Yard at Laudun, 1921, 21¼ x 25¾ . . . . (71)   760
Highway at Laudun, on panel, 18¼ x 21¾ . . . . (56)   680
The Road to Nîmes, 1928, 19½ x 25½ . . . . (152)   300
Fruit on a Table, Fruit Stand, and Tray,
    21 x 25½ . . . . (111)   1,000
Still Life with Fruit, 12¼ x 15 . . . . (124)   420
The Laid Table, 10¾ x 13¾ . . . . (125)   1,420
Young Woman at the Piano, 11¾ x 18¾ . . . . (35)   510
Uzès, 1930, 18¼ x 25¾ . . . . (114)   800

1963

An Old Street at Laudun, 1922, 25½ x 20¾ . . . . . . (225)   1,250
Le ravin de la fausse monnaie, 21¼ x 25¾ . . . . (278)   1,120
Vase of Flowers, 18¼ x 21¾ . . . . (278)   840
Vase of Flowers, 18¼ x 21¾ . . . . (232)   429
Still Life with Fruit, 13 x 21¾ . . . . (186)   380
Bunch of Tulips, 15 x 18¼ . . . . (155)   700
Bust of a Woman, 1934, 16¼ x 13 . . . . (155)   500
Port-Mahon Beach, 1926, 23¾ x 29 . . . . (155)   1,500

1964

The Cornice Road at l'Estaque, in the Evening,
    26 x 32 . . . . (459)   2,260
The Tub, 1918, on cardboard laid down on
    cradled panel, 21¼ x 15 . . . . (336)   350
Young Woman with a Mandolin, on panel,
    31½ x 25¾ . . . . (394)   320
Villa at Roquemaure, 18¼ x 21¼ . . . . (365)   726
Port-Mahon Beach, 23¾ x 29 . . . . (371)   1,600

1965

Woman Sewing Before a Fireplace, 21¼ x 25¾ . . . (524)   380
The Haystack, 1894, 21¾ x 18¼ . . . . (613)   760
Woman Taking Off Her Stockings, on panel,
    13½ x 10 . . . . (538)   540
Model Resting, 24 x 20½ . . . . (505)   1,320
Still Life with Apples, 18¼ x 15½ . . . . (621)   286
Interior, 23¾ x 19¼ . . . . (542)   1,100

1966

Young Woman Combing Her Hair, 25¾ x 21¼ . . . (685)   360
Seated Nude, 21¼ x 17¾ . . . . (669)   660
Young Girl with a White Beret, 1927,
    19½ x 23½ . . . . (757)   332
Still Life with Apples, 14¾ x 17¾ . . . . (760)   813
Still Life with Flowers, (1930), 24½ x 24½ . . . . . . (784)   2,000
Houses in a Landscape, 17¾ x 19 . . . . (706)   440
The Highway to Laudun, 1943, on panel,
    18¼ x 21¾ . . . . (742)   500
Vase of Flowers, 18¼ x 15¼ . . . . (809)   720

1967

The Arcades, 21¼ x 25¾ . . . . (852)   1,440
Lively Landscapes, 1893, two pictures, each
    14¼ x 30¼ . . . . (928)   3,955

Still Life in a Garden, 25¾ x 32 . . . . (857) $ 280
Bystreet in Marseilles, 1917 . . . . (914)   2,460
Apples on a Plate, on panel, 12¼ x 16¼ . . . . (912)   1,200
Still Life with Apples, 12¾ x 16¼ . . . . (842)   318
Peaches and Grapes, 1939, 11 x 12¼ . . . . (876)   580

1968–July 1969

Le ravin de la fausse monnaie, 1917, 21¼ x 25¾ . (1210)   3,000
The Tub, 1918, on panel, 21¼ x 15 . . . . (1187)   2,714
Young Woman in a White Toque, 1921,
    19½ x 23½ . . . . (1187)   944
Woman in a Brown Hat, 20 x 17¾ . . . . (1070)   1,086
Peaches and Grapes, 1939, 11 x 12¼ . . . . (1153)   650
The Highway at Laudun, on panel, 18¼ x 21¾ . . (1117)   1,040
Bathers: The Catalans, Marseilles, oil on paper
    laid down on board, 38 x 44¼ . . . . (1145)   1,750
Vase of Flowers, 24¼ x 19¾ . . . . (1184)   2,420
Interior, 24 x 19¾ . . . . (1231)   1,400
Bathers: The Catalans, Marseilles, on paper laid
    down on canvas, 37 x 44 . . . . (1240)   2,880
Village of Provence, 14¾ x 21½ . . . . (1255)   1,800
Still Life with Almonds, on cradled panel,
    12½ x 16¼ . . . . (1255)   1,600
The Vase of Roses, 16¾ x 13½ . . . . (1256)   2,200
Roses, 12¾ x 14¼ . . . . (1258)   2,000
Still Life, 11 x 12¼ . . . . (1268)   1,044

Karel Appel

(1921-   )

Birthplace: Amsterdam, Netherlands.

1940-43   Studies at the Royal Academy of Fine Arts, Amsterdam.

1946   Takes part in an exhibition at the Stedelijk Museum. First one-man show at Croningen.

1948   With other painters, joins the "Cobra" experimental group. His pictures are exhibited for the first time in Paris in an avant-garde group show at the Jean Bard Gallery.

1949   Takes part in the first exhibition of international artists at the Stedelijk Museum—experimental avant-garde artists and Cobra group.

1950   Settles in Paris and takes part in the Cobra exhibition at the Librairie 73.

1951   Second Cobra international exhibition of experimental art at the Palais des Beaux-Arts, Liége, Belgium. Exhibition, "Signifiants de l'informel," at the Galerie Facchetti, Paris.

1953   Seventeenth Biennial Watercolor Exhibition at the Brooklyn Museum. One-man show at the Palais des Beaux-Arts, Brussels.

1953-54   Eleventh Biennial of São Paulo, Brazil. "Younger European Painters" exhibition at the Solomon R. Guggenheim Museum, New York. Wins the UNESCO prize. First one-man show in New York at the Martha Jackson Gallery.

1956-60   Several exhibitions in European cities such as London, Paris, Zurich, and Venice; in New York; and in his native country.

Sales

DRAWINGS

1963
Landscape, 1959, pencil and gouache, 12¾ x 15½ .... (290) $ 225

1964
Figures, charcoal heightened with gouache, 18¼ x 25¾ .... (401)   140

1966
Composition, 14 x 10½ .... (666)   80

1968–July 1969
Composition, India ink and pastel, 10¼ x 6¾ .... (1068)   283

WATERCOLORS

1961–1962
Head in the Storm, gouache, 22 x 29¾ .... (85)   500
The Secret, 1957, gouache, 19¾ x 25 .... (152)   475
Composition, 1956, gouache, 19 x 24 .... (75)   442
Composition, 1957, gouache, 19½ x 25¼ .... (143)   486
Two Figures, 1958, gouache, 22¼ x 30¾ .... (107)   467
Composition, 1958, gouache 20 x 25 .... (149)   379
Composition, 1959, gouache, 21¾ x 29 .... (149)   379
Flying Bird, 1959, gouache, 19 x 25 .... (31)   330
Startled, 1960, gouache, 29¾ x 22 .... (151)   320
Clown's Head, gouache, 25¾ x 19¾ .... (113)   176
Composition, 1955, watercolor, 18¾ x 25 .... (18)   542

1963
Yellow Figure, gouache, 30 x 22 .... (283)   384
Woman, Bird, 1955, gouache, 19¾ x 25¾ .... (232)   565
Clown's Head, 1957, gouache, 25¾ x 19¾ .... (299)   350
Human Landscape, 1959, gouache, 21¼ x 29 ..... (275)   275
Composition, 1959, gouache, 21½ x 29 .... (179)   400
Composition, 1959, gouache, 17¾ x 22 .... (249)   270

1964
Composition, 1956, gouache, 19¾ x 25¾ .... (467)   246
Composition, 1957, gouache, 19¾ x 25 .... (438)   300

1965
Face No. 2, 1960, gouache, 13 x 10 .... (507)   250
A Little Cat; A Fish, two pastels with gouache, each 10¾ x 17¼ .... (617)   475

1966
Composition, gouache, 13 x 14¾ .... (666)   150
Red Woman, 1958, gouache, 25 x 20½ .... (671)   218
Composition, 1961, gouache and colored chalk, 31½ x 47¼ .... (732)   678
Sorrowful People, 1966, gouache, 21¾ x 29¾ ..... (747)   280

1967
Maternity, gouache and collage, 25¾ x 19¾ ...... (941)   240

1968–July 1969
Bird and Fish, 1958, gouache, 22½ x 31 .... (1174)   506
Animal and Child, gouache .... (1065)   1,800
Figure, gouache, 14¾ x 13¼ .... (1138)   310
Composition, 1954, watercolor, 18¾ x 24½ ...... (1230)   260
Composition, 1959, gouache, 20½ x 28½ .... (1237)   600
Composition, 1959, gouache, 20½ x 28½ .... (1237)   750
Composition, 1960, mixed media, 21¾ x 29½ .... (1272)   504

PAINTINGS

1961–1962
Lucie and Animal, 47½ x 63¼ .... (145) $3,476
Portrait of Alvard, 1956, 45¾ x 32½ .... (164)   1,208
Figure and Sun, 1958, 31½ x 39¼ .... (96)   1,813
Fiery Woman, 1958, 50¾ x 78¼ .... (129)   1,922
Blazing Cries in Spring, 1959, 50¾ x 63 .... (37)   3,500

1963
The Little Boy, 1951, 43 x 29¾ .... (255)   686
Camilla, 1953, 56 x 43½ .... (316)   2,000
Farm on Fire, 1958, 51½ x 77¼ .... (249)   1,600
Head, Brown Background, 1959, 9 x 7¼ .... (255)   165
Rolling Landscape, 1961, 51½ x 77¼ .... (249)   2,000
The Hunting Bird, 1961, 51½ x 77¼ .... (249)   1,900
Birds, 50½ x 37½ .... (275)   1,700
Composition, 1961, 51½ x 77¼ .... (249)   2,000

1964
Sun Head, on an oval-shaped canvas, 50¼ x 39½ .... (386)   2,000
Head, 9½ x 7½ .... (455)   193
Little Boy in a Garden, 1953, 45¾ x 35¼ .... (431)   2,300
Fiery Woman, 1958, 51½ x 77¼ .... (401)   900
Head in Space, 1960, 51½ x 35¼ .... (480)   800
The Hunting Bird, 1961, 51½ x 77¼ .... (401)   1,600

1965
Flying Birds, 1958, 30 x 21½ .... (539)   800
Composition, 1958, 10¾ x 18¼ .... (622)   340
Figures in Red, 1958, 51½ x 38 .... (520)   1,160
Flower, 14 x 10¾ .... (567)   904
Two Shattered Heads, 1959, 51¼ x 74 .... (624)   1,658
Mineral Flowers, 1961, 44¾ x 57¼ .... (539)   1,700

1966
Great Head, 26 x 20 .... (689)   470
Head, 1954, 37¼ x 22 .... (812)   1,244
Etienne Martin, Portrait, 1956, 76¼ x 51¾ .... (678)   7,500
Composition, 1959, 77¼ x 38½ .... (811)   700
Composition, 1959, 16¼ x 13 .... (698)   816
Tragic Head, 1960, 36¾ x 45¾ .... (648)   1,500
Composition, 1961, 51½ x 63¾ .... (745)   2,599
Composition, 1961, 51½ x 63¾ .... (798)   1,356
Devil Woman, 1963, 51 x 38 .... (823)   2,040
Clown, 1963, 39½ x 32 .... (808)   3,192

1967
Composition, 1953, 56 x 43¾ .... (979)   2,176
Bird Woman, 1957, 45¾ x 35¼ .... (871)   1,240
Hell with Its Joys, 1958, 51½ x 77½ .... (888)   2,902
Dancing in White Space, 1959, 51¼ x 77¼ .... (864)   3,250

1968–July 1969
Composition, Red Background, 1955, 23¾ x 32 .. (1200)   800
Head, 1958, 16¾ x 13 .... (1099)   621
Blue Head, 1962, 45½ x 35¼ .... (1145)   1,300
Man's Face .... (1065)   2,400
Flower, 14 x 10¾ .... (1127)   920
Composition, 21¼ x 25½ .... (1237)   1,500
Blue Head, 1952, 45½ x 35 .... (1237)   1,900
Flower, 14 x 10¾ .... (1268)   1,021
Two Children and a Bird, 1952, 25¾ x 52¾ ...... (1268)   3,248
Animals and Sun, 1952, 38 x 51½ .... (1268)   2,900

Alexander Archipenko

(1887-1964)

Birthplace: Kiev, Russia.

1902-05	Studies painting and sculpture at the Kiev art school.
1906	Goes to Moscow, where he participates in different group shows.
1908	Goes to Paris and studies for a short time at the Ecole des Beaux-Arts and then at the Louvre Museum.
1910-12	Opens his own art school in Paris. Participates in the Salon des Indépendants and the Salon d'Automne. Becomes a member of the Section d'Or.
1913	One-man show at Der Sturm Gallery, Berlin. Takes part in the Armory Show, New York.
1914-18	Settles in Nice, France, during World War I.
1920	One-man show at the Venice Biennial.
1921	One-man show at the Société Anonyme, Museum of Modern Art, New York. Opens an art school in Berlin. Marries Angelica Schmitz, a German woman.
1923	Opens an art school in New York. Works are shown throughout the U.S. Invents mobile paintings known as "Archipentura."
1928	Becomes an American citizen.
1935-37	Takes up residence in California and exhibits in several western cities.
1939	Returns to New York.
1948	One-man show—his sixty-ninth—at the Associated American Artists Gallery, New York, where he shows his invention in sculpture—modeling of light (carved plastic).
1952	Lectures at many universities in the U.S. Exhibitions in South America.
1954	One-man show—his hundred and tenth—at the Associated American Artists Gallery, New York.
1955-56	Tour of one-man shows in six German cities.
1957	One-man show—his hundred and eighteenth—at the Perls Gallery, New York.
1959	Wins the Medaglia d'Oro at the XIIIth Biennale d'Arte Trivenata, Padua, Italy.
1960	His book, *Archipenko, Fifty Creative Years 1908-1958,* is published by Tekhne.
1962	Elected to the Art Section of the National Institute of Arts and Letters.
1964	Died, New York.
1967-69	Retrospective exhibitions organized by the UCLA Galleries throughout the U.S.

Sales

DRAWINGS

1961-1962

Standing Woman in the Nude, black lead,
17¾ x 8¼ . . . . (105) $ 429

Endless Dream, 1948, India ink and colored
pencil, 13 x 10¾ . . . . (143) 215

1963

Seated Woman in the Nude, pencil, 19 x 12¾ . . . . (216) 178

1964

Two Figures, (1920), India ink, 15½ x 9 . . . . (381) 407

Mother and Child, charcoal and colored pencil,
22¼ x 14 . . . . (374) 325

1965

Nude, (1915), colored pencil, 17¾ x 9¾ . . . . (618) $ 935

1967

Nude, (1911), wash and red chalk, 12¼ x 9½ . . . . . (987) 1,120

Laocoön, ink and charcoal, 11 x 19¼ . . . . (893) 200

Nude, (1949), pencil, 25¾ x 19¼ . . . . (914) 615

1968–July 1969

Nude, (1911), red chalk and wash, 12¼ x 9½ . . . . (1106) 760

Study of a Nude, black and red pencil,
22½ x 16¾ . . . . (1216) 500

Standing Nude, pencil, 12¾ x 10 . . . . (1090) 211

Study of a Bust, 1916, pencil and red pencil,
13½ x 10 . . . . (1272) 1,200

WATERCOLORS

1963

Two Nudes, 1919, gouache, 27¼ x 20 . . . . (283) 949

1964

Seated Nude, tempera, 14 x 10¾ . . . . (321) 250

1965

Oriental Dancer, 1935, gouache, 27¾ x 21¾ . . . . . . (489) 700

1968–July 1969

Kneeling Nude, watercolor, 12¼ x 9¼ . . . . (1268) 2,320

PAINTINGS

1961-1962

Vase of Flowers, oil on board, 13½ x 12¼ . . . . (20) 6,636

1964

The Bather, 39½ x 19½ . . . . (453) 1,658

Jean Arp

(1887-1966)

Birthplace: Strasbourg, France.

1904	First stay in Paris, where he becomes acquainted with modern painting.
1904-05	Studies at the Academy of Weimar.
1908	Studies at the Académie Julian, Paris.
1911	Participates in the first exhibition of "Modern Bund," in Lucerne, Switzerland.
1909-13	Meets Kandinsky and Klee and takes part in "Der Blaue Reiter," Munich.
1914	Second stay in Paris where he meets Max Jacob, Modigliani, Picasso, and Apollinaire.
1915	Exhibition of his first abstract works at the Tanner Gallery, Munich.
1916-19	With Tzara, Ball, and Janco, he founds the Dada movement.
1919-20	With Max Ernst, participates in the Dada publication *Die Schammade,* Cologne.

1925	Settles in Paris and takes part in the first Surrealist exhibition at the Galerie Pierre.
1926–30	Becomes a member of the Surrealist group, of "Cercle et Carré," and of "Abstraction-Création."
1948	First monograph on the artist is published by Wittenborn, New York.
1949–50	First stay in the U.S. Executes a monumental relief for Harvard University.
1954	Wins the sculpture prize at the Venice Biennial.
1956	Important retrospective exhibition in Bern.
1966	Died.

Sales

DRAWINGS

1961–1962

Couronne de Grasse, 1942, pencil, 11¾ x 8¼ ..... (143) $ 362
Twin Shape, 1917, brush and India ink, 7 x 5¼ ... (105) 339

1965

Abstraction, pencil and watercolor, 19½ x 14 ..... (541) 275
Composition, stick of greasepaint, 9 x 11¾ .... (617) 385
Composition, pencil, 12¼ x 10¾ .... (627) 240

1966

Composition, 18¼ x 12¾ .... (749) 460
Project for a Drawing, two drawings, India ink,
  5¾ x 3¼ .... (732) 90

1967

Balance-Outline, 1958, India ink, 24½ x 12 .... (918) 1,198

1968–July 1969

Drawings of the Dada Period, (1916), three
  drawings, ink and pencil, each 7¼ x 8¾ ..... (1096) 759
Germs, 1957, pencil, 15 x 10¾ .... (1214) 1,200
Balance-Outline, (1958), India ink, 24½ x 12 .... (1174) 1,265
Balance-Outline, (1958), India ink, 24½ x 12 .... (1268) 1,578

WATERCOLORS

1961–1962

A Brush's Life, 1944, gouache and India ink,
  10 x 6½ .... (105) 520
Cloud Contemplation, 1942, gouache, 12¼ x 10 ... (143) 1,356
Composition, watercolor and collage, 11¼ x 7¼ .. (110) 1,000
Siege of the Atmosphere, collage on watercolor,
  8¼ x 6½ .... (105) 475

1963

Composition, watercolor, 11½ x 8¾ .... (257) 400
The Man with Whiskers, gouache, 10½ x 8¼ ..... (315) 960

1965

Composition, watercolor, 11¾ x 7¼ .... (627) 440

1966

Composition, gouache .... (821) 580

1968–July 1969

Composition, (1964), watercolor, 4¾ x 6½ .... (1268) 278

PAINTINGS

1961–1962

In Memory of 1929, collage, 12¾ x 17¾ .... (106) 723
Composition,[1] 1948, collage, 12¾ x 10 .... (85) 1,250

[1] Inscribed "En souvenir d'une écriture cufique."

1963

Plant-Battlemented Threshold, 1959, on copper,
  28½ x 17¾ .... (249) $1,900
The Man with Whiskers, 1925, on panel,
  21¾ x 19½ .... (217) 4,633
Sailboat in the Forest, 1958, on panel,
  24½ x 21¾ .... (232) 3,390

1964

According to the Law of Luck, 1933, 6½ x 6¾ .... (377) 362
Drowsy Planet, oil and collage, 13½ x 9¼ .... (471) 1,627

1965

Ghost Scenting a Navel, 31½ x 23¾ .... (526) 10,000
Blue and Yellow Outline, torn paper,
  18¼ x 13½ .... (617) 1,130
A Tribute to Rastelli, 1956, collage, 19½ x 11¼ ... (527) 1,100
Composition with Clouds, 1959, collage,
  10 x 8¼ .... (527) 1,100
Collage, 1960, 10 x 8¾ .... (561) 700

1966

Outline, 1926, 23 x 26¼ .... (676) 9,000
Head, collage, 12¼ x 9½ .... (678) 3,100
Plant Anatomy, 1961, collage with watercolor,
  24 x 7¼ .... (798) 2,486

1967

Collage, 1960, collage, 10 x 8¾ .... (925) 429
Outline, 1962, cut-out picture mounted on panel,
  27¼ x 22 .... (925) 904

1968–July 1969

Interregnum, 1959, on cardboard, 28½ x 21 ...... (1125) 6,900
Blue and Yellow Outline, (1953), oil and collage,
  18¼ x 13¾ .... (1127) 1,840
Composition on a Blue Background, collage,
  13 x 9¼ .... (1019) 620
Figure, pencil, watercolor, collage, and frottage,
  11¾ x 7¼ .... (1099) 920
Vertical Composition, 1961, collage, 19½ x 6¾ ... (1099) 874

Jean Atlan

(1913–1960)

Birthplace: Constantine, Algeria.

1930	Arrives in Paris and studies at the Sorbonne University.
1941–44	Arrested by the Nazis, he shams madness and enters the psychiatric hospital of St. Anne, Paris.
1944	Participates in the Salon des Surindépendants, Paris. Exhibition at the Galerie Denise René, Paris.
1945–46	Works in the lithograph studio of Mourlot, Paris.
1947	Exhibition at the Galerie Maeght, Paris.
1948	First foreign exhibition at the Art Club, Vienna.
1949	First exhibition in Germany at the Egon Günther Gallery, Mannheim.

1949-55 A period of great financial difficulty.

1951 French art critic Michel Ragon publishes a book about the work of Atlan, *L'Architecte et le magicien.*

1953 Sends two pictures to Tokyo for an exhibition and scores a big success.

1955-60 Renewed outbreak of activity. Executes the poster for the exhibition "Ecole de Paris" at the Galerie Charpentier, where his works are shown yearly.

1956 First one-man show since 1947 at the Galerie Bing, Paris.

1958 Settles at Villiers-sur-Tholon, Yonne district, France.

1958-60 Exhibitions in Brussels, at the Kaplan Gallery in London, and at the Galerie Bing, Paris.

1960 Died, of cancer.

Sales

DRAWINGS

1961-1962

Composition, 1952, charcoal and colored chalk, 14¾ x 10¾ .... (57) $ 260

Composition, violet wash, 6¾ x 5¼ .... (110) 60

Composition, colored pencil, 19½ x 12¼ .... (130) 600

1963

Composition, charcoal and pastel, 21¼ x 17¾ .... (249) 1,000

1964

Composition, charcoal and pastel, 10 x 12¾ ...... (351) 440

1965

Composition, 1957, charcoal and gouache, 40½ x 28½ .... (503) 890

1966

Composition, 1956, pencil and pastel, 23 x 19 ..... (805) 425

WATERCOLORS

1961-1962

Composition, pastel, 9 x 23¾ .... (71) 400

Composition, pastel, 21¼ x 17¾ .... (30) 680

Composition, pastel, 21¾ x 18¼ .... (167) 780

Composition, pastel, 20½ x 17 .... (155) 1,100

Composition, Blue Background, 18¼ x 21¾ ...... (167) 900

Composition, gouache, 17¾ x 21¼ .... (13) 700

1963

Composition, 1947, pastel and pencil, 20½ x 25 ... (283) 588

Abstract Composition, gouache, 12¼ x 10 .... (255) 110

Composition, 1956, pastel, 11 x 15 .... (232) 678

Composition, 1956, pastel, 11 x 15½ .... (299) 490

Composition, pastel and charcoal, 18¼ x 21¼ .... (299) 820

Composition, gouache, 21¾ x 18¼ .... (287) 1,000

1964

Composition, pastel, 21¼ x 17¾ .... (375) 600

1965

Composition, pastel, 21¾ x 17¾ .... (564) 460

Composition, 1947, pastel, 9 x 12¼ .... (619) 180

Sagittarius, 1958-59, pastel, 41 x 29¾ .... (634) 787

Composition, pastel, 17¾ x 21¼ .... (627) 600

1966

Composition, pastel, 21¼ x 18 .... (672) 620

Composition, 1945, pastel, 10¾ x 9½ .... (730) 230

Composition, pastel, 10 x 12¼ .... (745) $ 429

Composition, 1952, pastel, 9 x 11¾ .... (826) 420

Composition with a Cup, pastel, 21¼ x 17¾ ...... (723) 320

1967

Red Calypso, 1959, pastel, 23¾ x 20 .... (898) 880

Composition, 1952, pastel, 14¾ x 10¾ .... (996) 500

Composition on a Red and Yellow Background, watercolor and pastel, 27¾ x 24 .... (976) 640

Composition, 1947, pastel, 12¼ x 9½ .... (897) 120

1968–July 1969

Composition, pastel and gouache, 19¾ x 23 ..... (1121) 800

Composition, pastel, 12¼ x 9½ .... (1162) 280

Composition, 1952, pastel, 25¾ x 19 .... (1043) 680

Composition, 1952, pastel and stick of greasepaint, 10 x 14 .... (1078) 500

Composition, 1956-57, pastel, 12¼ x 9½ .... (1185) 660

Composition, 1957, watercolor, gouache and pastel, 28½ x 40½ .... (1175) 800

Composition, 1958, gouache and pastel, 47 x 31½ .... (1127) 1,150

Composition, 1959, pastel, 12¾ x 9½ .... (1177) 480

Composition, 1959, pastel, 21 x 17½ .... (1117) 1,020

Composition, 1959, pastel, 17¾ x 21 .... (1129) 570

Composition, 1959, pastel, 21¾ x 18¼ .... (1116) 600

Composition, 1959, pastel, 9½ x 12¼ .... (1175) 540

The Little Bird of the Islands, watercolor, 12¾ x 10 .... (1153) 140

Composition, pastel, 22¼ x 16¾ .... (1225) 760

Composition, 1956, pastel, 17¾ x 21¼ .... (1230) 1,040

Composition, charcoal and pastel, 14½ x 10¾ ... (1244) 280

Composition, pastel, 21¾ x 18¼ .... (1254) 660

Composition, pastel, 21¾ x 15¾ .... (1254) 760

Sourate de l'Arbre, 1959, distemper and pastel, 21¼ x 32 .... (1256) 1,620

Composition, pastel, 22 x 17 .... (1264) 780

Composition, pastel, 21½ x 17¾ .... (1268) 1,508

PAINTINGS

1961-1962

Cambodia, 45¾ x 29 .... (2) 3,200

Madagascar, 1958, 32 x 21¼ .... (120) 1,720

Composition, 1952, on panel, 21¼ x 25¾ .... (155) 1,220

Zen Dance, 36¼ x 23¾ .... (13) 2,600

Czardas, 32 x 25¾ .... (59) 2,120

Composition, 21¼ x 32 .... (39) 1,620

Composition, 21¼ x 32 .... (89) 2,600

February, 1958, 32 x 21¼ .... (153) 2,000

Euphrates, 1958, 20 x 29 .... (114) 1,400

1963

Composition, 1949, 25¾ x 21¼ .... (249) 840

Composition, 1952, on panel, 21¼ x 25¾ .... (280) 790

The Caribbean, 25¾ x 21¼ .... (258) 1,600

Composition, 1956, oil and pastel on paper, 18¼ x 20¼ .... (299) 840

Circus Parade, 1958, 28½ x 45¾ .... (232) 4,068

1964

Arabia, 23¾ x 36½ .... (335) 2,000

Composition, 1956, oil on paper, 17½ x 21 .... (378) 678

Orpheus, 1957, 51½ x 32 .... (450) 1,200

Tarot, 1957, 45¾ x 29 .... (398) 1,600

Dybbuk, 45¾ x 29 .... (426) 1,240

Alpha and Omega, 1959 .... (401) $ 840
The Southern Birds, 1960, 36½ x 23¾ .... (472) 1,900

1965

Composition, 51½ x 35¾ .... (516) 2,200
Composition, 25¾ x 21¼ .... (552) 480
Alpha and Omega II, 1959, 21¼ x 32 .... (569) 1,921
Composition, on panel, 7¼ x 5¾ .... (640) 190
Composition, 21¾ x 18¼ .... (494) 550

1966

Chaldea, 46¼ x 35½ .... (666) 1,260
Salome, 32 x 21¼ .... (711) 920
Composition, 23¾ x 36¾ .... (691) 1,000
Composition, 1959, 21 x 31½ .... (689) 442
Harlem, 1957, 51½ x 32 .... (701) 2,200
Lilith, 45¾ x 29 .... (701) 1,900

1967

Composition, 1956, 32¼ x 51 .... (989) 1,250
Tishri, 1958, 19¾ x 25¾ .... (941) 1,100
Islam III, 1959, distemper and pastel, 21¼ x 32 ... (978) 1,340

1968–July 1969

Composition, 1945, 15 x 18¼ .... (1109) 700
Composition, 1957, 25¾ x 39½ .... (1132) 1,888
Composition, 36½ x 21¼ .... (1043) 1,160
The Southern Bird, 1959, distemper and pastel,
    36¾ x 23¾ .... (1175) 1,740
Composition, 39½ x 25¼ .... (1117) 1,900
Composition, 15 x 18 .... (1237) 1,000
Abstract Figure, 36 x 23½ .... (1241) 1,890
Babylon III, 1958, 32 x 21¼ .... (1256) 2,700
Diptych, two pictures, distemper, each 31½ x 21 . (1256) 3,600

Milton Avery

(1893–1964)

Birthplace: Altmar, New York, U.S.

1913   Briefly attends the Connecticut League of Art Students, Hartford.

1926   Marries Sally Michel, an illustrator.

1928   One-man show at the Opportunity Gallery, New York.

1929   Wins an award from the Art Institute of Chicago.

1930   Wins an award from the Connecticut Academy of Fine Arts.

1932   One-man show at the Gallery 144, New York. Influenced by Fauvism. His fascination with Matisse's work leads him to elaborate a style depicting flattened figures and landscapes executed with great economy.

1935–41   One-man shows at the Curt Valentine Gallery, New York.

1944–50   Several one-man shows at the P. Rosenberg Gallery, and at the Durand-Ruel Gallery, New York.

1948   Wins the second prize at the Boston Arts Festival.

1949   Wins the first prize of the Baltimore Museum of Art.

1950   A portfolio of his drypoints is published and exhibited by the Laurel Gallery.

1952   In the summer, visits Europe for the first time.

1960   Retrospective exhibition of his work is organized by the American Federation of Arts.

1962   One-man show at the Waddington Gallery, London.

1964   Died.

1965–66   Retrospective exhibition at the Museum of Modern Art, New York.

Sales

WATERCOLORS

1963

Forest in Spring, 1954, pastel, 24¼ x 18½ .... (208) $ 800

1966

Portrait of a Man, gouache on black paper,
    18¼ x 12¼ .... (665) 525

1967

Horsewoman, gouache on black paper, 12 x 18 ... (870) 700

1968–July 1969

Bird, 1950, gouache, 10 x 8 .... (1030) 525

PAINTINGS

1961–1962

The Pack of Cards, 1945, 49¾ x 33½ .... (96) 3,750
The Walk by the Seaside, 1951, 23¾ x 17¾ .... (85) 800
Nude, 1954, on panel, 8¾ x 5¾ .... (111) 225
Twilight Sea, 1958, oil on canvas on board,
    15¾ x 19¾ .... (111) 1,100

1963

Seated Woman, oil on paper laid down on board,
    10¾ x 16½ .... (179) 400
The Quarry, 1940, 23¾ x 35½ .... (272) 800

1964

Teen-Agers, on canvas laid down on board,
    17¾ x 14 .... (374) 500
Portrait of Mrs. Avery, 1944, 48 x 32¼ .... (416) 5,528
Dune Bush, 1958, on canvas laid down on board,
    17¾ x 23¾ .... (363) 800

1965

Portrait of Mrs. Avery, 1944, 48 x 32¼ .... (539) 7,000
Young Woman's Head, 1944, on board, 20 x 16 ... (624) 470
Three Seated Women, 1947, 38 x 50 .... (610) 8,000
Trees in Blossom, on board, 5¾ x 15 .... (494) 500

1966

The Man with a Red Beret, 20 x 15¾ .... (665) 1,800
Dead Trees, 1944, 30 x 36 .... (707) 4,500
Blue Nude, 1947, 32 x 47½ .... (790) 6,000
The Three Clowns, 50 x 38 .... (710) 6,250
Sleeping Bather, 1963, on canvas, 24 x 36½ .... (651) 3,500

1967

Boats Around a Sandbank, 1957, 40½ x 49½ ..... (860) 6,000
Young Artist, (1938), 36 x 28 .... (864) 2,750
Landscape with Fishermen, on panel, 24 x 30¼ ... (841) 2,000
The He-Goat, 1950, 24 x 36¼ .... (940) 4,063

1968–July 1969

Young Lady with a Mandolin, on canvas laid
   down on board, 24 x 18 . . . . (1062) $2,200
Seaside, (1936), 17¾ x 23¾ . . . . (1035)   2,400
The Worktable, 1944, 28¼ x 36¼ . . . . (1160)   3,750
End of Summer, 1954, on board, 18¼ x 24½ . . . . . (1018)   2,700
Young Woman in a Bathing Costume, on canvas,
   12 x 16 . . . . (1145)   2,100
Back View of a Nude, 1958, oil on paper,
   15¾ x 12 . . . . (1088)   525
Gardening, 16 x 20 . . . . (1229)   1,900
Woman, 1955, on canvas board, 12 x 16 . . . . (1231)   2,000

Francis Bacon

(1909-   )

Birthplace: Dublin, Ireland. His family is distantly
related to the Elizabethan philosopher Francis
Bacon.

1915   Moves to London and later to Berlin and Paris.
Lives in these cities for two years.

1926   A visit to a Picasso exhibition in Paris inspires him
to become a painter. Also influenced by Léger,
Lurçat, and the Surrealists.

1928   Returns to London and gains some success as a designer of modern furniture and rugs.

1944   Takes up painting again but destroys his former
work.

1946   Participates in the Exposition internationale de
peinture contemporaine at UNESCO, Paris.
Often draws inspiration from Muybridge's
photographs.

1953   Velasquez' portrait of Innocent I inspires his series
of popes.

1954   One-man show at the Venice Biennial.

1955   One-man show at the Institute of Contemporary
Art, London. Participates in "The New Decade,"
Museum of Modern Art, New York.

1956   Takes part in "Masters of British Painting
1800-1950," Museum of Modern Art, New York.

1962   One-man show at the Tate Gallery, London.

1964   Retrospective exhibition at the Guggenheim Museum, New York.

Resident in London.

Sales

WATERCOLORS

1961-1962

Abstract Composition, 1934, pastel, 9¼ x 14 . . . . . . (118) $1,373

PAINTINGS

1963

Sphinx, 1954, 59¼ x 45½ . . . . (189) $10,000
Reclining Nude, 1959, 77¼ x 55½ . . . . (202)   4,750

1964

Study for a Pope's Portrait, 1955, 59¼ x 45½ . . . . . (444)   15,961
Study for a Portrait, 1955, 24 x 20 . . . . (461)   8,000

1965

Man in Blue, 1954, 59¼ x 39½ . . . . (605)   9,867
Study for Figure V, 1956-57, 63¼ x 46¾ . . . . (584)   11,609
Painting,[1] 1958, 78¼ x 56½ . . . . (643)   14,373

1966

Head, 1962, on canvas laid down on board,
   15¾ x 16¾ . . . . (825)   6,634
Three Studies of Henrietta Moraes, 1966, each
   14 x 11¾ . . . . (751)   16,584

1967

Head of a Man, 1948-49, 31 x 25 . . . . (945)   4,422
Seated Figure, 1960, 59¼ x 46¼ . . . . (945)   20,730

1968–July 1969

Two Figures, 1961, 79¾ x 65¼ . . . . (1149)   32,500

Giacomo Ballà

(1871-1958)

Birthplace: Turin, Italy.

1895   Visits Rome with his mother. Exhibits yearly at the
"Società degli Amatori e Cultori di Belli Arti."

1900   Spends seven months in Paris. Returns to Italy and
meets Boccioni, Severini, and Sironi, who regard
him as their master. Still works in the manner of
Italian Divisionism.

1909-28   Exhibits frequently at the "Società degli Amatori e
Cultori di Belli Arti," Rome.

1910   Signs the "Manifesto of Futurist Painters," together
with Boccioni, Carrà, Russolo, and Severini.

1912   Executes typical Futurist works of high importance,
but does not feel ready to take part in the Paris
Futurist exhibition. His name is, however, included in the catalog.

1920   Appears as the leader of the second Futurist generation and also as Futurism's most abstract painter.

1933   Reverts to figurative painting.

1950   One-man show at the Galleria Origine, Rome.

1954   Exhibition at the Rose Fried Gallery, New York.

1957   Exhibition at the Galerie des Cahiers d'Art, Paris.

1958   Died, Rome.

[1]Original title: *The Pope with Two Owls.*

Sales

DRAWINGS

1966

Dinamismo all'aqua di seltz, colored pencil,
5¼ x 12¾ .... (802) $ 240

1968–July 1969

Balla futurista, India ink, 10 x 15 .... (1136) 960

WATERCOLORS

1961–1962

Linee forze di paesaggio, 1916, tempera and oil
on canvas, 8¾ x 11 .... (149) 2,844

Balletto futurista, 1925, gouache, 8¾ x 11¾ .... (70) 2,370

1964

Mercury Passing Before the Sun, 1914, tempera
on paper laid down on canvas, 54¼ x 38¼ .... (453) 20,730

Fleurs-Espace, 1914, tempera on paper laid down
on canvas, 26 x 25 .... (453) 4,146

Composition, 1920, tempera, 8¾ x 8¾ .... (437) 640

1968–July 1969

Composition, 1916, tempera and charcoal,
7¾ x 8¼ .... (1214) 1,280

The Garden, (1918), tempera on canvas,
76¾ x 19¾ .... (1187) 1,180

PAINTINGS

1961–1962

Ritmo compenetrato, 30½ x 30½ .... (69) 3,476

Rhythmic Movement, 30½ x 30½ .... (145) 5,056

1964

Vortice della vita, 1929, 39¼ x 29¾ .... (453) 2,073

1965

Flowers and Space, 1914, on panel laid down on
canvas, 26 x 25¼ .... (616) 3,840

Compenetrazioni irridescenti, on panel, 1912,
7½ x 18½ .... (575) 2,902

1966

Voiture roulant, 1913, oil on paper, 19¾ x 26 ..... (665) 3,200

Linea di velocità vortice, 1913, 27¾ x 31 .... (676) 15,000

Compenetrazioni irridescenti, 1912, on panel,
7½ x 18½ .... (689) 1,244

Piazza di Spagna, 29¼ x 45¼ .... (802) 1,120

1967

Atraverso le forze, 15¾ x 11¾ .... (870) 2,000

Speeding Car, 1913, 23 x 26 .... (962) 4,480

1968–July 1969

The Tennis Players, 1920, on panel, 14 x 19¼ .... (1187) 6,608

André Bauchant

(1873–1958)

	Birthplace: Châteaurenault, France.
1915	Lives in Châteaurenault until World War I. Fights in the Dardanelles and discovers Crete and the sea.
1919	Devotes himself to painting.
1921	Sends sixteen pictures to the Salon d'Automne, Paris. Executes a stage design for Diaghilev.
1937	Takes part in the exhibition "Les maîtres populaires de la réalité," Paris, where he gains great success.
1949	One-man show at the Galerie Charpentier, Paris.
1958	Died, Montoire.

Sales

PAINTINGS

1961–1962

The Shepherdess in the Storm, 18¾ x 26 .... (26) $ 580

The Herd at the Watering Place, 21¼ x 25¾ ...... (30) 1,000

The Fortified Castle, 1949, on panel, 10¾ x 14 ..... (68) 230

The Declaration, 1942, on board, 17¾ x 21¼ ...... (80) 620

Flowers in a Landscape, 1944, on panel,
17¾ x 21¼ .... (90) 1,260

Flowers, 1928, 29 x 21¼ .... (95) 590

Rest, 1928, 39½ x 25¾ .... (120) 620

Village Fair in Touraine, 24 x 19¾ .... (123) 720

Landscape, 1935, oil on panel, 10¾ x 14 .... (124) 400

1963

The Artist's House, 1923, on panel, 10¾ x 14¼ ... (224) 300

Vase of Flowers in a Landscape, on panel,
11¾ x 15 .... (258) 640

The Earthly Paradise, 1929, 19¾ x 25¾ .... (190) 500

The Cascade, 1931, canvas laid down on panel,
17½ x 15 .... (293) 340

The Pharisee and the Publican, 1933,
18¼ x 21¾ .... (306) 420

Portrait of Mermoz on a Marine Background,
1938, on panel, 19½ x 15¾ .... (242) 56

Monsieur de La Roque, 1938, 18¼ x 15 .... (222) 92

The Parade, 1942, on panel, 23 x 30 .... (258) 1,100

The Basket of Flowers, 1943, on panel,
18¼ x 24 .... (276) 440

Before the Storm, 1945, 39½ x 29 .... (283) 1,966

Azay-le-Rideau, 1949, 18¼ x 23¾ .... (287) 287

Flowers in a Landscape, 1953, 18¼ x 15 .... (232) 565

The Encounter, 25¾ x 34¾ .... (298) 1,200

1964

Three Figures, 1928, 8¼ x 12¾ .... (454) 663

The Wreck, 1932, on panel, 12¼ x 17 .... (472) 440

The Rocks, Seaside, 1939, on panel, 20 x 29 ...... (408) 400

Bunch of Flowers, 1943, on panel laid down on
canvas, 24 x 15 .... (451) 620

Nymphs in the Woods, 1944, 10¼ x 13 .... (454) 498

Vase of Flowers, 1945, on panel, 18¼ x 15 .... (480) 620

The Rendezvous in the Country, 1947, 10 x 14 .... (338) 500

Montoire, 1949, on panel, 19¾ x 15½ .... (355) 100

Sully-sur-Loire Castle, 1949, 19¾ x 24 .... (366) 90

Romantic Landscape, 1949, on panel, 10¾ x 14 ... (321) 300

Women on the Mountain, 1953, 15 x 18¼ .... (351) 192

Country Pleasures, 1954, 25¾ x 19¾ .... (378) 1,469

1965

Seascape, Côte d'Azur, 1928, 32 x 39¼ .... (624) $ 829

Gathering Fruit, 1929, on panel, 23¾ x 15½ ...... (547)   560

Flowers on a Pink Background, 1929, 45¾ x 29 ... (561)   1,430

Flowers, 1932, 21¼ x 13 .... (528)   580

The Black Rocks, 1939, 16¼ x 24 .... (523)   660

Flowers in a Field, 1941, 10 x 10¼ .... (582)   608

The Parade, 1942, on panel, 23 x 30 .... (530)   420

Landscape with Two Young Girls in Red, 1943, on panel, 13 x 18¼ .... (552)   390

Norman Women at the Fountain, 1944, on panel, 14¾ x 13½ .... (567)   1,220

Landscape with a River, 1946, 9½ x 12¾ .... (523)   220

The Vase by the Lake, 1948, 17¾ x 21 .... (507)   1,150

Landscape, 1950, 15 x 18¼ .... (541)   400

Flowers, 1955, on panel, 13 x 16¼ .... (617)   1,130

1966

Still Life with Pears, 1942, on panel, 14 x 10¾ .... (798)   678

The Gray Mountain, 1939, 22¾ x 29 .... (798)   1,243

Woman Fleeing from the Storm, 18¼ x 21¾ ...... (789)   640

The Lake .... (702)   530

Rustic Scene, 8¼ x 8¾ .... (796)   320

Flowers, 24½ x 19¾ .... (797)   1,808

Flowers in a Vase, 1931, 18¼ x 13 .... (811)   700

Bucolic Landscape, 1936, 12¾ x 15½ .... (689)   608

Mountainous Landscape, 1937, 8 x 12¾ .... (692)   140

The Parade, 1942, on panel, 23 x 29¾ .... (685)   800

Landscape, 1946, 9½ x 13 .... (672)   460

A Walk in the Woods, 1947, 7½ x 11½ .... (726)   360

Blois Castle, 1949, 21 x 23¾ .... (818)   755

Azay-le-Rideau Castle, 1949, 18¼ x 24 .... (756)   400

A Road in the Mountain, 1950, 14¾ x 17¾ ...... (691)   300

The Refuge in the Mountain, 1950, 14¾ x 17¾.... (653)   260

The Shepherdesses, 1950, on panel, 7½ x 10¼ .... (670)   600

Landscape, 1952, 13¾ x 17¼ .... (815)   580

1967

Landscape, 1922, 15¾ x 19¾ .... (965)   1,469

Mountain Flowers, 1928, 39¼ x 31¼ .... (985)   1,778

The Return of the Prodigal Son, 1922, 25¾ x 38¼ .... (985)   1,422

Dahlias, 1933, on canvas laid down on panel, 17¾ x 14 .... (963)   325

A Bunch of Flowers in a Landscape, 1936, on panel, 9¾ x 14¼ .... (873)   380

Bucolic Landscape, 1936, on panel, 13 x 15¾ ..... (885)   871

A Bunch of Flowers in a Landscape, 1936, on panel, 9¾ x 14¼ .... (961)   420

Pastorals, 1938, two panels, 9 x 12¾ .... (989)   600

The Hunter's Rest, 1944, 8¼ x 12 .... (923)   680

Figures in the Woods, 1944, 15 x 18¼ .... (978)   1,200

Flowers, Giant Asters, 1944, 21¾ x 18¾ .... (918)   1,695

Flowers, 1945, on panel, 18¼ x 15 .... (919)   1,853

Mother and Child in a Forest, 1947, 7½ x 11½ .... (907)   344

Bunch of Flowers, 1947, on panel, 23 x 30½ ...... (912)   3,000

A Vase of Flowers on the Edge of the Marsh, 1948, 17¾ x 21¼ .... (935)   600

The Ile-aux-Moines, Morbihan, 1949, 11¾ x 20½ .... (940)   871

Seascape, 1949, 21¾ x 13 .... (942)   1,130

Cheverny Castle, 1949, 12¾ x 23 .... (1000)   340

The Hermit, 28½ x 43½ .... (925)   2,034

1968–July 1969

Landscape, 14¾ x 23¼ .... (1127) $1,196

The Bridge, 1911, 18 x 12¾ .... (1174)   621

The Great Trees, 1923, on panel, 45¾ x 30 ...... (1109)   1,400

The Idyll, 1924, 12 x 8¾ .... (1200)   420

The Postman, 1925, 17¾ x 14½ .... (1070)   1,180

Portrait of My Niece, 1926, oil on canvas laid down on board, 27¾ x 19 .... (1109)   600

Beasts in the Forest, 1927, 8¼ x 10 .... (1187)   590

Gathering Fruit, 1929, on panel, 23 x 13½ ...... (1078)   640

The Couple, 1929, on panel, 10½ x 16¾ .... (1203)   1,140

Agar in the Desert, 1930, 29 x 39½ .... (1043)   2,700

The Bunch of Wild Flowers, 1933, 17¾ x 12¾ ... (1202)   780

The Peasant Family, 1933, on cardboard, 10¾ x 14 .... (1135)   400

At the Seaside, 1942, 15 x 18¼ .... (1174)   1,725

Figures in a Landscape, 1944, on panel, 9 x 13 ... (1019)   400

Flowers, 1945, on cardboard, 18¼ x 15 .... (1127)   2,070

The Descent from the Cross, 1945, on cradled panel, 19½ x 25¾ .... (1117)   1,440

Flowers, 1946, 10 x 16 .... (1061)   650

Women at the Seaside, Hendaye, 1947, 20¼ x 34½ .... (1070)   1,841

Valençay Castle, 1949, 21¾ x 29½ .... (1030)   1,000

Seascape, 1949, 21¼ x 25¾ .... (1066)   1,060

The Fruiterer, 1950, 42 x 60 .... (1208)   7,000

In the Rocks, 1950, 17 x 14 .... (1051)   700

Flowers in a Landscape, 1953, 23¾ x 27¼ .... (1113)   1,600

The Birds, 1953, on panel, 15 x 18¼ .... (1088)   700

Country Scene, on panel, 9½ x 13 .... (1060)   1,040

The Pagoda of Nara, 17¾ x 21 .... (1225)   420

Flowers, 1929, 45¾ x 35 .... (1231)   2,000

View of a Castle, 18½ x 26 .... (1231)   1,750

The Poachers, 1944, on panel, 20½ x 25 .... (1241)   2,270

The Shepherd at the Fountain, 1925, 15¾ x 19½ . (1243)   440

Walk Amid the Rocks, on cardboard, 1926, 14¾ x 21 .... (1243)   260

Portrait of a Woman, on cardboard, 1926, 12¾ x 9 .... (1243)   140

The Wild Boars, on panel, 1923, 15¾ x 25 .... (1243)   260

Flowers in a Pink Vase, 1928, 40 x 28¾ .... (1248)   3,500

Vase of Flowers, 1946, 13½ x 23¾ .... (1249)   1,960

The Weasel, 1944, oil on canvas laid down on board, 7¼ x 9 .... (1254)   580

The Bush in Blossom, 1928, 39½ x 28¾ .... (1255)   2,400

Girls Bathing, 1938, 13½ x 17¾ .... (1256)   1,700

The Fifth Day of Creation, on cardboard, 23¾ x 36 .... (1258)   5,100

Fishing at Dusk, 1943, 17 x 21 .... (1258)   900

Portrait of a Seated Man, 1946, 21 x 18¼ .... (1264)   760

The Tempest, 25¼ x 35½ .... (1264)   400

Walk on the Rocks, 1928, 24½ x 38½ .... (1264)   720

The Heirs at the Notary's, 1940, 31¼ x 43 ...... (1268)   7,540

Landscape, 18¼ x 22 .... (1268)   1,972

The Gamekeeper, 1926, 19¾ x 25 .... (1268)   3,387

Biarritz Rocks, 1949, 19¾ x 25¾ .... (1268)   1,972

The Bridge, 1911, 18¼ x 13 .... (1268)   1,288

Various Flowers, 19¼ x 23½ .... (1273)   2,520

Willi Baumeister

(1889–1955)

Birthplace: Stuttgart, Germany.

1905 Studies at the Academy of Fine Arts of Stuttgart.

1912 Makes his first trip to Paris but does not meet any of the French artists.

1913 Participates in the "Herbstsalon" at Der Sturm Gallery, Berlin.

1914 Short stay in Paris with Schlemmer.

1919 Develops a constructivist trend in his pictures. Exhibition at Der Sturm Gallery, Berlin.

1924 Returns to Paris.

1927 Takes part in an exhibition at the Galerie d'Art Contemporain, Paris.

1928 Becomes a professor at the Art School of Frankfurt.

1930 Exhibition at the Galerie Bonaparte, Paris. Becomes a member of "Cercle et Carré" and of "Abstraction-Création." Exhibitions in Frankfurt and Berlin.

1933 Suddenly dismissed by the Art School of Frankfurt. In Germany, his paintings are regarded as "degenerate" by the government and removed from the museums.

1938 Sends sixty paintings to Switzerland to protect them.

1939 Exhibition at the Galerie Jeanne Bûcher, Paris.

1939–44 Studies scientific techniques of painting. Writes *Das Unbekannte in der Kunst.*

1946 Lectures at the Academy of Art, Stuttgart. Several exhibitions in Germany.

1949 Exhibition at the Galerie Jeanne Bûcher, Paris.

1951 Wins the São Paulo Biennial prize.

1955 Died.

Sales

DRAWINGS

1963

The Tempest, (1947), charcoal, 9½ x 12½ .... (228) $ 89

1964

Composition, charcoal and colored chalk, 16¾ x 21¾ .... (467)   329

Homage to Hieronymus Bosch, 1952, charcoal, 9 x 12¼ .... (381)   176

1965

The Artist, charcoal, black lead, and colored pencil, 16½ x 11¾ .... (543)   311

Lines, 1933, pencil, 8¾ x 10½ .... (565)   68

1966

Dancer, (1912), ink, 11¾ x 8 .... (716)   148

The Tennis Party, 1934, pencil and wash, 15¾ x 11¾ .... (716)   541

Metamorphosis, 1946–47, charcoal, 18¾ x 24¼ ... (716)   738

1967

Floating Shapes, 1938, pencil and pastel, 17¾ x 12 .... (925)   452

Composition, 1935, pencil, 11¾ x 14 .... (997)   443

1968–July 1969

Figure aux trois taches blanches, 1932, black pencil with red lights, 17½ x 13½ .... (1090)   397

Composition, 1946, charcoal, 5¾ x 6¾ .... (1112) $ 84

Metaphysical Landscape, 1948, charcoal, 12½ x 19¼ .... (1112)   645

Forms, (1952), charcoal, 8¾ x 12¼ .... (1094)   74

WATERCOLORS

1961–1962

Der Lebensraum, 1954, tempera, 12¾ x 18¼ .... (16)   679

1966

Two Faces, (1919), gouache, 12¾ x 14¾ .... (716)   443

Composition, 1925, gouache, 14¼ x 12 .... (716)   2,460

1968–July 1969

Composition, 1947, watercolor on charcoal, 12¾ x 19 .... (1209)   744

Composition, (1949), tempera, 12¾ x 19¾ .... (1174)   1,380

PAINTINGS

1961–1962

The Telephone, 1931, 25¾ x 18¼ .... (149)   2,212

Landscape, the Bodensee, on cardboard, 15¼ x 18¾ .... (106)   316

Metaphysical Landscape, 1955, oil on cardboard, 13½ x 17½ .... (88)   2,952

Composition, 1937, 25¾ x 18¼ .... (106)   949

Gymnast, 21¼ x 17½ .... (88)   1,525

Artist with a Palette, 25¾ x 18¼ .... (88)   3,124

1963

Landscape at the Bodensee, (1911), oil on cardboard, 15¾ x 18¾ .... (217)   249

1964

Kneeling Figure, 1912, on cardboard, 25¾ x 18¾ .... (381)   260

Ideogram in Green, 1947, on panel, 21 x 17¾ ..... (380)   1,476

Blue, 1954, on board, 11¾ x 15½ .... (321)   300

1965

Bathers, 1911, on cardboard, 14 x 10¾ .... (543)   509

Forms, 1937, oil on paper, 17¾ x 14 .... (565)   542

Landscape, 1947, on cardboard, 21 x 25¾ .... (616)   5,120

Composition, 1948, on cardboard, 14 x 18 .... (634)   1,033

1966

M 2 on Gray, 1922, oil and pencil on canvas, 24 x 16¾ .... (816)   2,460

Schemen, 1936, 39½ x 29 .... (716)   2,214

Composition, 1938, 17¼ x 13½ .... (732)   949

Cats' Heads, 1941, on cardboard, 14 x 18¼ .... (792)   1,230

Allegretto, 1948, on cardboard, 31¾ x 39½ .... (738)   3,690

Montaru 2, 1954, oil and sand on cardboard, 21¼ x 18¼ .... (716)   2,952

1967

Bathers in a Grotto, (1910–11), on cardboard, 10¾ x 13½ .... (907)   492

Standing Football Player, 1924, oil and sand on canvas, 32 x 16¼ .... (907)   1,353

Football Player, 1924, 32 x 16¼ .... (986)   492

Relief Frieze, 1952, on panel, 10 x 19¾ .... (907)   1,722

Composition, 1948, on cardboard, 19¾ x 21¼ ..... (910)   1,378

Isib, 1953, on cardboard, 13½ x 9¼ .... (970)   1,599

Black Forms on a White Background, 1954, on cardboard, 14 x 17¾ .... (962)   1,280

1968–July 1969

Composition, 1953, on panel, 14 x 17¾ .... (1127)	$2,300
The Painter, 1931, 25¾ x 18¼ .... (1018)	1,700
Composition, 1938, 14 x 11 .... (1112)	1,116
Composition with a White Oval, 1939, 20 x 23¼ . (1112)	2,480
Fish Rising, 1951, on panel, 25¾ x 32 .... (1194)	2,976
Composition, 1951, on masonite, 18½ x 24 ...... (1248)	1,000

Jean Bazaine

(1904–   )

Birthplace: Paris, France.

1925 Takes his degree in letters at the Sorbonne University, Paris. Studies sculpture and painting at the Ecole Nationale des Beaux-Arts, Paris.

1941 Exhibition at the Galerie Jeanne Bûcher, Paris. Organizes "Vingt peintres de tradition française" at Braun's—an exhibition which reveals the originality of nonfigurative painting and sets it apart from abstract art.

1942-48 Exhibits frequently at the Galerie Louis Carré, Paris. Carries out one of his most perfect series of paintings. Avoiding representational art, he nevertheless proceeds from nature to execute his works.

1948 Participates in the Venice Biennial. Writes *Notes sur la peinture d'aujourd'hui* (published by Floury, Paris).

1949 One-man show at the Galerie Maeght, Paris.

1951 Executes an important ceramic mural for Audincourt church. Participates in the exhibition "Sur quatre murs" at the Galerie Maeght, Paris, together with Braque, Chagall, Picasso, Rouault, and others.

1952 Participates in the Venice Biennial.

1954 One-man show at the Galerie Maeght, Paris.

1965 Major retrospective exhibition at the Musée National d'Art Moderne, Paris. Executes a series of stained-glass windows for St. Séverin church, Paris.

Resident in Paris.

Sales

DRAWINGS

1963

Drawing, 1955, pencil, 12¾ x 9½ .... (217)	$ 186

1966

Seascape, 1958, pen, 8¼ x 10½ .... (747)	64

WATERCOLORS

1961-1962

Foliage, 1944, watercolor and pastel, 14 x 17¼ .... (143)	1,130
The Acrobats, 1953, watercolor, 9½ x 6½ .... (149)	711
Composition, 1954, gouache, 4¼ x 8½ .... (156)	310

1963

Composition, watercolor, 4½ x 7 .... (205)	$ 600
Composition, 1954, gouache, 4¾ x 5 .... (249)	280
Composition, 1954, gouache, 4¼ x 8½ .... (249)	330

1964

Composition, 1954, pastel, 4¼ x 8½ .... (441)	520

1965

Morning Bath, 1939, watercolor, 14½ x 19¾ ...... (573)	332

1967

Composition, 1957, gouache, 3¼ x 6¾ .... (919)	791

PAINTINGS

1964

Composition, 1964, 10½ x 6¼ .... (386)	1,500
Morning in the Woods, 1954, 56¾ x 45 .... (431)	13,000

1965

Composition, 1950 .... (503)	5,000
The Suburban Bride, 1944, 24¼ x 15¼ .... (573)	1,327
Still Life with a Spoon, 16 x 7½ .... (583)	639
The Beer Glass, 1943, 12¾ x 15¾ .... (632)	800

1968–July 1969

Walking in the Garden, 1944, 21¼ x 32 .... (1121)	4,000
Joan of Arc, 1944, 36½ x 24 .... (1174)	11,500

Frédéric Bazille

(1841–1870)

Birthplace: Montpellier, France.

1859 Studies medicine in his native town.

1862 Arrives in Paris to finish his studies but prefers to attend the studio of Gleyre, where he meets Monet, Renoir, and Sisley.

1863 Like Monet, he chooses to work in the open and often goes to the forest of Fontainebleau.

1864 Stays at Honfleur with Monet, Boudin, and Jongkind.

1865 Lives with Monet in Paris and paints "La robe rose," the famous portrait of his cousin (Louvre Museum, Paris).

1867 Spends the summer at Aigues-Mortes in the south of France.

1868 Shows "The Family Meeting" at the Salon, Paris.

1870 Died at the battle of Beaune-la-Rolande. (His early death precluded him from participating in the first Impressionist exhibition in 1874. Several of his pictures are kept in the Musée Fabre, Montpellier.)

Sales

PAINTINGS

1963

Aigues-Mortes Ramparts, 1867, 23¾ x 39½ ...... (254)	$55,000

1967

Moresque, 1869, 39¼ x 23 .... (924)	30,400
L'Ambulance improvisée, 1865, 18¾ x 25¼ .... (924)	19,200

André Beaudin

(1895–   )

Birthplace: Mennecy, France.

1915   Attends the Ecole des Arts Décoratifs, Paris, for some time, but has to give up his studies because of World War I.

1921   Travels to Italy; meets André Masson and Juan Gris, who exert a great influence on him.

1923   First one-man show at the Galerie Percier, Paris. (Catalog preface by Max Jacob.) Studies sculpture.

1932   First one-man show in London at the St. George Gallery.

1936-37   Executes etchings to illustrate Virgil's *Bucolics.* Period of his dancing nudes, horses, and bulls.

1945-46   Illustrates works by Paul Eluard and Georges Hugnet. Paints portraits.

1949   First exhibition in New York. (Catalog preface by Paul Eluard.) Often paints the banks of the river Seine.

1950-52   Illustrates works by Francis Ponge.

1953   Retrospective exhibition of his pictures, sculptures, and book illustrations at the Kunsthalle, Bern. (Catalog preface by D. H. Kahnweiler.)

1957   Retrospective exhibition at the Galerie Louise Leiris, Paris.

Sales

DRAWINGS

1963

Trees, 1938, India ink and watercolor, 19 x 25 .... (217) $ 104

1964

The Law Court, 1949, pen, 25¾ x 19¾ .... (460)   160

1965

Portrait of Max Jacob, 1923, 15½ x 12½ .... (615)   600

Composition, 1946, double sided, India ink, 14¼ x 10 .... (1180)   124

Shadow, 1953, heightened drawing, 16 x 25½ ..... (615)   260

1966

The Rider, 1931, ink and watercolor, 11¾ x 9 ..... (703)   80

The Young Lady, 1951, India ink, 17¾ x 13 ...... (801)   140

1967

Nudes, 1947, India ink, 16 x 19¾ .... (975)   240

1968–July 1969

Pipe and Glass, 1921-22, 12¾ x 15½ .... (1189)   100

Tiny Angels, 1934, charcoal, 18¼ x 24½ .... (1138)   149

The Young Lady, 1951, India ink, 18 x 12¾ ..... (1026)   150

Calligrapher, 1959, 10¼ x 8¼ .... (1264)   64

Angels and Putti, 1934, black chalk, 18¼ x 24¼ .. (1273)   106

WATERCOLORS

1964

Suzanne Roger Drawn with a Blue Pencil, watercolor, 21¾ x 18¼ .... (460)   320

Rainbow, 1964, watercolor, 11½ x 8¼ .... (447)   100

1965

The Sun, 1941, watercolor, 14½ x 11¾ .... (615)   460

Lise with Green Hair, 1943, watercolor, 21¾ x 18¼ .... (615)   700

1966

Two Trees, 1943, watercolor, 32 x 21¼ .... (801) $ 700

The White Pebbles, 1961, watercolor, 10 x 12¾ ... (696)   130

1967

Tanned Lise, 1944, watercolor, 21¾ x 18¼ .... (975)   150

PAINTINGS

1961–1962

Nudes Dressing, 18¼ x 15 .... (43)   450

The Mushrooms, 1930, 14 x 10¾ .... (105)   226

Composition, 10¾ x 14 .... (106)   249

1963

The Cross, 29 x 23¾ .... (236)   203

The Black Mirror, 25¾ x 21¼ .... (194)   560

1964

The Daggers, 1929, 39½ x 32 .... (460)   560

Dawn, 1937, 51½ x 38½ .... (460)   2,800

The Studio, 1941, on panel, 11 x 8 .... (480)   140

Two Blue Flowers, 1948, 17¾ x 10¾ .... (375)   220

Two Figures, 1949, 14¾ x 17¾ .... (416)   415

1965

The Path, 1928, 21¾ x 13 .... (615)   620

The Three-Colored Bouquet, 1932, 28¼ x 36 ..... (598)   720

The Escape, 1932, 8¼ x 4½ .... (503)   720

The Players and the Hoop, 1934, 38½ x 51½ ..... (615)   1,400

A Head at the Window, 1943, 21¾ x 17¾ .... (503)   400

Portrait of Balzac, 1946, on paper, 18¼ x 13 ...... (630)   110

The Palace, 1956, 25¾ x 32 .... (518)   700

The Wake, 1956, 39½ x 29 .... (518)   1,100

Le bateau de soir, 1956, 38½ x 51½ .... (615)   3,800

1966

Reclining Head, 32 x 21¼ .... (772)   600

Maternity, 1925, 32 x 21¼ .... (801)   700

Reclining Head, 1928, 30½ x 21 .... (689)   332

The Park, 1928, 15¾ x 12½ .... (741)   600

Bouquet in a Glass, 1932, 29 x 36½ .... (801)   1,100

Bacchanal with a Hoop, 1934, 38½ x 63¾ .... (801)   3,100

A Head at the Window, 1943, 21¾ x 18¼ .... (718)   330

The Pont St. Michel, 1948, 25¾ x 32 .... (801)   3,600

Le pont de la nuit, 1955, 37¾ x 51¼ .... (815)   1,106

1967

The Ball Players, 1926, 51½ x 32 .... (848)   450

The Hand with a Bouquet, 1928, 16¼ x 13 .... (975)   500

The Inquisitive Horses, 1938, 32 x 25¾ .... (975)   1,300

The Ox, the Cobweb, and the Red Sun, 1939, 39½ x 32 .... (975)   1,600

The Nymph and the Shepherd, After Titian, 1955, 32 x 39½ .... (975)   1,420

1968–July 1969

The Tree and the House, 1945, 18¼ x 10¾ ...... (1051)   170

The Flags, 1931, 23¾ x 29 .... (1106)   600

Three Young Nudes, 1926, 32 x 25¾ .... (1049)   640

Nude Figures Playing by the Riverside, 1932, 23¾ x 29 .... (1118)   600

Snow Bird, 1945, on cardboard, 11 x 8¾ .... (1106)   180

The Red Bird, 1945, on cardboard, 11 x 8¾ .... (1189)   240

The Unicorn and the Animals, 1949, 21¼ x 25¾ .. (1200)   600

The Friends, 1957, 18¼ x 13 .... (1189)   460

Landscape, 1948, 25¾ x 21¼ .... (1230)   1,200

The Couple, 1957, 18 x 12½ .... (1231)   425

Lise in the Sun, 1943, 21¾ x 18¼ .... (1254) $ 600
The Bouquet, 1931, 32 x 25¾ .... (1254)   800
The Lady at the Window, 1945, 9 x 7½ .... (1264)   200
Composition, 1950, 31½ x 51½ .... (1268)   1,972

Max Beckmann

(1884–1950)

Birthplace: Leipzig, Germany. Begins to paint at the age of thirteen.

1900   Attends the Academy of Fine Arts in Weimar.

1903   Visits the Louvre Museum, Paris.

1904   Stays in Florence.

1905   Influenced by the German Impressionists and by Cézanne.

1906   Wins the Florenz Preis in Weimar. Marries.

1909–11   Executes several lithographs.

1914–18   His style of painting takes on a violent aspect.

1925   Teaches painting at the School of Fine Arts, Frankfurt. Marries again.

1929–32   Awarded second prize, Carnegie International. Exhibits at the Galerie de la Renaissance and the Galerie Bing, Paris. Retrospective exhibition at the Basel Museum.

1937   Flees to Amsterdam, where he remains until 1947.

1939   Wins first prize of the Golden Gate International Exhibition, San Francisco.

1947   Travels to the U.S. Teaches painting at the School of Fine Arts, Washington University. Illustrates Milton's *Paradise Lost.*

1950   Died, New York.

Sales

DRAWINGS

1961–1962

Woman with a Fur, ink and watercolor,
9½ x 12¾ .... (106) $1,582

1964

Seaside, 1910, 6¾ x 9¼ .... (428)   135
Young Girl Reading, (1946), India ink,
10¼ x 12¼ .... (392)   1,550

1965

Man in the Nude, 1911, India ink, 12¾ x 10¼ .... (597)   394
Golgotha, 1909, pencil, 10 x 8¾ .... (565)   904

1966

Wounded Waiting in an Operating Theater,
pencil and wash, 8 x 10¾ .... (732)   746
Portrait of Peter, Son of the Artist,[1] 1917, India
ink, 10½ x 12¼ .... (732)   1,627

[1] On the reverse, portrait of Lilly Schnitzler.

1967

Two Wrestlers, (1923), pencil, 6¾ x 6½ .... (925) $ 215
Soldiers Showering at Courtrai, (1914), India ink
and wash, 11¾ x 14 .... (970)   1,919

1968–July 1969

Young Girl at the Window, 1912, pencil,
6½ x 4½ .... (1099)   218
Bathers on the Beach, 1928, charcoal,
39½ x 28¼ .... (1083)   7,564
Market Scene, pencil, 6½ x 4½ .... (1209)   372

WATERCOLORS

1965

Carnival (with Self-Portrait), 1925, watercolor,
13½ x 9 .... (634)   1,476

1968–July 1969

The Fishing Boats, 1930, watercolor, 14 x 19¼ ... (1069)   6,576

PAINTINGS

1961–1962

Green Still Life with Dry Corn, 1943,
33½ x 25¾ .... (106)   9,492
Eagle Peak, 1938, 27¾ x 35½ .... (88)   12,300

1963

Landscape, (1905), 15¾ x 19¾ .... (228)   1,476
Afternoon, 1946, 36¼ x 53½ .... (210)   8,500
Portrait of John Newberry, 1947, 28¾ x 20½ ..... (277)   7,678

1964

Seated Nude, 1946, 23 x 11¼ .... (367)   4,699

1965

Adam and Eve, 1917, 31½ x 22½ .... (565)   12,204
Landscape, (1905), 15¾ x 19¾ .... (618)   2,608
The Beach, 1930, 14¼ x 9 .... (637)   9,000

1966

The Woman with a Muff, 1944, 23¾ x 15¾ .... (716)   13,530

1968–July 1969

Riders on the Beach, 1946, 21¼ x 34¼ .... (1126)   23,415
Portrait of W. Frommel, 1949, 37½ x 22 .... (1126)   19,824
The Sea in the Evening, 19¾ x 24 .... (1194)   3,472
Landscape Near Wangerooge, 27¾ x 31½ ...... (1248)   4,000
Landscape, 1924, 23¾ x 23¾ .... (1270)   21,600

Hans Bellmer

(1902–   )

Birthplace: Katowice, Poland.

1923-24 Settles in Berlin to study engineering at the Technische Hochshule, which he soon leaves to take up illustrating. Meets Grosz.

1924-25 Spends three months in Paris. Discovers Pascin and admires his drawings.

1926-32 Becomes an industrial advertisement designer.

1928 Marries in Berlin.

1935 *Le Minotaure* publishes his work "Variations sur le montage d'une mineure articulée".

1937 Participates in the Surrealist exhibitions in Paris, Chicago, and Japan. Death of his wife.

1938 Settles in Paris. Meets André Breton, Jean Arp, Marcel Duchamp, Man Ray—and Paul Eluard and Tzara in 1943.

1939 Incarcerated with Max Ernst in the south of France.

1941 Gives up German citizenship.

1947 Participates in the exhibition "Le Surréalisme" at the Galerie Maeght, Paris.

1949 New edition of his book *Les jeux de la poupée,* done in collaboration with Paul Eluard.

1957 Issues *Anatomie de l'image.*

1963 Important exhibition at the Galerie Daniel Cordier, Paris.

1966 Drawings first exhibited in Germany at the Museum of Ulm.

Sales

DRAWINGS

1961-1962
Composition, 1960, 9 x 9 . . . . (299) $ 200

1968–July 1969
Two Women, 1939, pencil, 5 x 3¾ . . . . (1112)   645
Composition, pencil heightened with gouache,
    11¾ x 10 . . . . (1194)   496
Chimera, pencil, 8¾ x 4½ . . . . (1268)   371

WATERCOLORS

1968–July 1969
Composition, 1958, gouache, 12¾ x 10 . . . . (1200)   620

PAINTINGS

1967
Portrait of Mr. X . . ., 25¾ x 25¾ . . . . (962)   4,160

Thomas Hart Benton

(1889–   )

Birthplace: Neosho, Missouri, U.S.

1907 Studies at the Art Institute of Chicago.

1908-11 Attends the Académie Julian, Paris.

1913 Returns to the U.S. and comes under the influence of Cubism.

1916 Executes Synchromist abstractions shown at the Forum exhibition.

1918-19 Works as an architectural draftsman in the U.S. Navy.

1920 Travels in the U.S., sketching American scenes, particularly plantations and corn fields. Unsympathetic to the trends of his time, he returns to contrived representational painting. Appears as the leader of the Regionalist group and attacks modern art as typifying the shortcomings of the modern way of life.

1926-36 Teaches at the Art Students League, New York.

1930 Executes murals on the theme of American life for the New School of Social Research.

1933 Executes murals for the state of Indiana. Awarded gold medal by the Architectural League, New York.

1934-35 One-man show at the Ferargil Galleries, New York.

1939 Retrospective exhibition at the William Rocknill Nelson Gallery of Arts, New York.

1947 Executes murals for the Harzfeld department store, Kansas City.

1952-54 Retrospective exhibition at the University of Kansas City.

Resident in Kansas City.

Sales

WATERCOLORS

1964
Picking Cotton, gouache and watercolor,
    8¾ x 10¾ . . . . (324) $1,200
Still Life with Flowers and an Apple, 1944,
    tempera on panel, 16¾ x 12¾ . . . . (363)   3,000

1965
Picking Cotton, gouache and watercolor,
    8¾ x 10¾ . . . . (489)   1,900

1968–July 1969
Landscape of the Missouri, watercolor,
    12¾ x 19½ . . . . (1035)   2,750

PAINTINGS

1961-1962
West Kansas Plains, 15¾ x 23¾ . . . . (3)   2,500
The Field Workers, 1945, oil on paper, 8 x 12¾ . . . (111)   1,250

1963
People of Chilmark, 1922, 68¼ x 77¼ . . . . (225)   3,500

1964
The Wrestler, 1931, grisaille on metal,
    18¾ x 14¾ . . . . (363)   550

1965
Pony Express, 1939, on panel, 7 x 15¾ . . . . (489)   2,000
Still Life, 1952, 29¾ x 21 . . . . (610)   4,000

1967

Picking Cotton, 1939, on canvas laid down on
  panel, 31¼ x 38¼ .... (860) $17,000

1968–July 1969

Arts of the West: Study for a Mural, on board,
  9½ x 14½ .... (1229) 5,500

Arts of the South: Study for a Mural, on board,
  8½ x 14 .... (1229) 5,500

T.P.'s Beach at Gay Head, Martha's Vineyard,
  Mass., 1950, on board, 12 x 16 .... (1229) 10,000

Emile Bernard

(1868–1941)

Birthplace: Lille, France.

1881   Settles in Paris with his family and attends the Collège Sainte Barbe.

1884–86   Despite his father's opposition, attends the Ecole
des Beaux-Arts (studio of Cormon), where he
meets Toulouse-Lautrec. But he appreciates the
Impressionists and Cézanne above all.

1887   Works with Van Gogh. First attempt at
"Cloisonnisme."

1888   Works with Gauguin at Pont-Aven.

1889   Takes part in the exhibition of the Pont-Aven group
called "Groupe impressionniste et synthétiste," at
the Café Volpini, Paris. Affected by a deep mysti-
cal crisis.

1890   Returns to Paris. Death of his friend Van Gogh.
Writes *Les hommes d'aujourd'hui* about Van Gogh
and Cézanne. Shows great interest in medieval
works of art.

1891   Falls out with Gauguin. Spends the summer in Brittany. Participates in the Salon des Indépendants,
Paris. Takes part in an exhibition of the Nabis
group at the Galerie Le Barc de Boutteville, Paris.

1892   Organizes the first retrospective exhibition of Van
Gogh at the Galerie Le Barc de Boutteville, Paris.

1893   Publishes his correspondence with Van Gogh in *Le
Mercure de France.*

1894–03   Travels to Italy, Spain, Constantinople, Samos, and
Egypt, where he marries. Abandons the Nabis
group's ideas.

1901   One-man show at the Galerie Ambroise Vollard,
Paris.

1905–14   Sets up the review *La Rénovation Esthétique.* Travels
to Holland and Italy. Paints "Le cycle humain" in
Venice.

1930–40   Stays at Pont-Aven in Brittany.

1941   Died.

Sales

DRAWINGS

1963

Notre-Dame de la Joie, wash, double sided,
  14¾ x 11 .... (314) $ 60

1964

Genoa, sepia, 12¾ x 10 .... (412) $ 120
Old Geneva, sepia, 14 x 10¾ .... (483) 60
The Old Castle, sepia wash, 13 x 16¾ .... (329) 275

1965

The Little Bridge, 1930, India ink and ink wash,
  14¾ x 11 .... (582) 41
The Girl Friends, sepia wash, 7¼ x 11½ .... (547) 110
Siena, sepia wash, 11¾ x 16¾ .... (547) 140

1966

Le Canet, wash, 15 x 18 .... (691) 160
Le Castel, sepia wash, 9½ x 11¾ .... (702) 90
Genoa, sepia wash, 13 x 9 .... (665) 250
Chambery, 10 x 12¾; *Venice,* 14 x 11, sepia
  wash .... (784) 575

1967

Silenus, 1888, ink, 10 x 21½ .... (881) 221
Old Houses in Tonnerre, 1906, wash,
  13½ x 10½ .... (937) 160

1968–July 1969

Bathers, pen and India ink wash, 8 x 10 .... (1099) 161
Nudes, double sided, 7½ x 11½ .... (1042) 140
Genoa, wash, 12¾ x 10 .... (1078) 112
The Athlete, sepia wash, 10 x 8 .... (1089) 90
Landscape with Rocks, 1913, ink, 11¾ x 18¾ .... (1128) 76
The Park of Versailles, wash, 10¾ x 14½ .... (1084) 260
View of Torcello, sepia, 9 x 11½ .... (1224) 100
The Cymbals Player, India ink, 11½ x 8¾ .... (1228) 60
Cicci, sepia wash, 11 x 14¼ .... (1231) 250
Landscape at St. Botolph, pen, sepia ink, and
  brown washes, 9½ x 12¾ .... (1241) 126
Three Figures, pen, sepia ink, and brown washes,
  8½ x 6½ .... (1241) 164
The Road, wash, 10½ x 13¾ .... (1243) 44
Torcello Church, pen and sepia wash, 9 x 11½ ... (1244) 50
Bust of Homer, Marseilles, sepia, 12¾ x 9¾ .... (1248) 375
Nude, wash, 10 x 7½ .... (1266) 76
Three Figures on the Quay, ink and watercolor,
  16 x 11 .... (1273) 479

WATERCOLORS

1961–1962

The Breton Women, watercolor, 7½ x 6 .... (119) 240
The Ile de la Jatte, 1889, watercolor, 12½ x 9½ .... (18) 610
The Ile de la Jatte, 1889, watercolor, 12¾ x 9½ ... (167) 360

1963

Landscape of Pont-Aven, (1886), watercolor,
  11¾ x 7¾ .... (283) 791

1964

Landscape, (1886), watercolor, 7¾ x 11¾ .... (377) 723

1966

The Walk, watercolor, 16¼ x 12¼ .... (745) 1,175
Landscape of Brittany, watercolor, 7¼ x 11½ .... (794) 300

1967

Composition, gouache, 15¾ x 11¾ .... (919) 904

1968–July 1969

The Embarkation, 1893, watercolor, 15¾ x 10¾ .. (1213) 136
Three Women in Cairo, 1893, watercolor,
  9¾ x 14 .... (1231) 425
Constantinople, 1893, watercolor and pastel,
  21¾ x 31½ .... (1234) 300

Street Scene, watercolor, 16 x 12 .... (1240) $ 600

The Goose Girl,[1] watercolor, 4¾ x 7¼ .... (1256) 820

Fisherman, Pilgrim, and Head of the Christ,
pencil and watercolor, 9½ x 12¼ .... (1272) 360

PAINTINGS

1961–1962

A Walk in the Meadows, 21¾ x 18¼ .... (68) 760

The Meadow, 18¼ x 21¾ .... (25) 1,000

Noyers, Yonne, 24½ x 29¼ .... (90) 230

St. Briac, (1887), 17½ x 21¼ .... (143) 3,842

The Woods of Love at Pont-Aven, 1892,
28¾ x 38¾ .... (84) 12,357

1963

Young Lady with a Shawl, 1930, on cardboard,
39½ x 28½ .... (234) 104

1964

Women Coming Out of the Bath, 1893, on panel,
33¾ x 25¾ .... (405) 1,306

Portrait of the Artist's Son, 23 x 17 .... (454) 166

View of Tonnerre, 18¼ x 21¾ .... (471) 1,808

Seated Woman (recto), *Nude* (verso), 1929, on
panel, 41½ x 31¼ .... (336) 230

1965

The Washerwomen, 1888, 8¾ x 13¼ .... (612) 2,800

Self-Portrait, 1897, 36½ x 23¾ .... (556) 20

Breton Countryside, 33¾ x 27¼ .... (647) 800

Portrait of a Woman, 1928, on board,
39½ x 29¾ .... (507) 750

Nude, 1932, on cardboard, 31¾ x 23¾ .... (612) 310

The Couple, 26 x 19 .... (503) 360

The Letter, on panel, 42 x 29¾ .... (559) 330

Young Lady in Brittany, 1940, on cardboard,
24 x 18¼ .... (598) 40

Still Life with Apples, on cardboard laid down on
panel, 20¾ x 14¼ .... (632) 290

Still Life with a Jug, 23 x 31 .... (604) 344

1966

The Water Carriers, 34½ x 30½ .... (742) 700

Religious Scene, 23 x 29 .... (757) 1,382

Banks of the River Seine at Asnières, 1885,
12¾ x 16¼ .... (809) 1,200

The Cliffs, (1887), on cardboard, 13 x 20½ .... (653) 1,840

Breton Landscape, on panel, 11½ x 15½ .... (793) 1,800

Bathers, 1889, 35¼ x 27¾ .... (808) 9,867

View of Tonnerre: The Mill of Hell, 1904,
24 x 13 .... (808) 1,886

Women in the Nude Lying in a Landscape, 1910,
68½ x 63¼ .... (778) 740

The Harbor, 1929, on cardboard, 29¾ x 40 .... (655) 660

The Park, on panel, 18¼ x 12½ .... (655) 126

Reclining Nude, 1929, 33¾ x 51½ .... (653) 164

Landscape, 25¾ x 32 .... (784) 700

1967

The Banks of the River Seine at Asnières, 1885,
12¼ x 15¾ .... (982) 3,081

Meadow at St. Briac, 1887, 18¼ x 21½ .... (880) 4,975

Bathers Under a Tree, 1890, 12¾ x 16¼ .... (993) 1,460

Women Gathering Oysters, 1891, 22 x 15¼ .... (992) 3,390

Landscape of Burgundy, (1904), 39½ x 27¾ ...... (940) $ 987

View of Tonnerre, 27 x 37¼ .... (855) 600

Senlis, 38½ x 48 .... (995) 400

Fashionable Lady with a Rose, 1926, on
cardboard, 39½ x 28½ .... (920) 90

Still Life, 1927, on cardboard, 23 x 19¾ .... (850) 300

Still Life, on board, 23¾ x 18 .... (989) 550

Still Life with a Melon, on cradled panel,
21¾ x 25¾ .... (870) 900

The Quai Bourbon, Ile St. Louis, 1929,
31½ x 23¾ .... (861) 300

Portrait of M. Tampier, 1935, on panel,
19¾ x 15½ .... (943) 66

The Pietà, 1935, on panel, 31¼ x 48¼ .... (985) 995

Self-Portrait,[2] on board, 16 x 13¼ .... (985) 758

1968–July 1969

Landscape, 38 x 31½ .... (1127) 989

Still Life with Lemons, 1890, on cardboard,
15 x 18¼ .... (1053) 6,200

The Musicians, 1892, 22½ x 30 .... (1126) 2,726

Wine Harvest in Burgundy, (1904), 34¾ x 33¾ .. (1138) 991

*Two Breton Women on the Bank of the Aven at
Pont-Aven,* 35¼ x 38¾ .... (1179) 840

Young Woman in a Pink Bodice, 1926, on
cardboard, 25¼ x 21¼ .... (1154) 140

Landscape of Brittany, 30 x 26½ .... (1039) 1,500

Landscape of Brittany, on cardboard,
39½ x 29¼ .... (1186) 720

The Brook, on board, 39½ x 27 .... (1070) 1,133

Water Carriers, 35½ x 31 .... (1078) 800

Portrait of Tampier, 1934, on cardboard,
41½ x 32½ .... (1211) 90

Young Woman with a Beret, 1937, on cardboard,
42 x 32¾ .... (1161) 72

Portrait of a Woman, on cardboard, 31½ x 23¾ .. (1213) 56

Portrait of a Parisian, on cardboard, 31 x 21¾ ... (1060) 2,080

The Refugees, 1939, on cardboard, 19½ x 25¼ ... (1015) 66

Landscape with Ruins, 39½ x 29¾ .... (1088) 325

Farmyard at Pont-Aven, 1940, 41½ x 28 .... (1187) 540

Palace by the Grand Canal, Venice, on
cardboard, 27¼ x 20½ .... (1224) 1,100

The Bathers, 1889, 36½ x 29 .... (1224) 26,400

Landscape of Provence, 1904, on canvas laid
down on board, 39 x 27 .... (1240) 912

Still Life with an Earthenware Dish, on cardboard
laid down on canvas, 15 x 21¾ .... (1244) 300

Marseilles Harbor, 1929, 30½ x 42 .... (1248) 4,000

Marseilles Harbor, 40¼ x 29¾ .... (1253) 1,500

Reclining Woman in the Nude, on cardboard,
29 x 39¼ .... (1254) 2,400

Breton Women on the Heath, Near the Sea,
21¼ x 29 .... (1255) 3,800

Marseilles Harbor, (1929), 30½ x 42¼ .... (1268) 1,972

Seaside, Cancale, Brittany, 1886, 18 x 21½ ..... (1270) 7,200

Portrait of the Artist's Grandmother, Asleep,
1889, 22 x 18 .... (1271) 1,560

The Birth of Venus, 30 x 24¾ .... (1271) 480

---

[1]Inscribed "Specimen d'Art. Procédé inventé par Boch. Dessin sur verre etc...."

[2]This is Bernard's last self-portrait.

Renato Birolli

(1906–1959)

Birthplace: Verona, Italy. Studies art at the Academia Cignaroli.

1928 Settles in Milan.

1936 Stays in Paris.

1937-38 Returns to Italy and takes part (with other painters) in the creation of the antifascist group "Corrente." Jailed.

1943-45 Participates in the Italian Resistance and executes drawings entitled "Italia 1944."

1947 Short stay in Paris. With the Italian avant-garde, takes part in the Fronte Nuovo delle Arti. Joins the group called "Eight Italian Painters."

1951 Wins an award at the São Paulo Biennial.

1955 Given an award by the Carnegie Foundation, Pittsburgh.

1955-58 Exhibits at the Viviano Gallery, New York. Often participates in the Venice Biennial, where he wins various prizes.

1959 Died.

1960 Retrospective exhibition at the Venice Biennial.

Sales

DRAWINGS
1961-1962
The Resistance Movement, 1944, 6 x 7½ . . . . (15) $ 79

1968–July 1969
Seated Woman, 1930, charcoal, 11 x 9 . . . . (1214) 224

WATERCOLORS
1961-1962
Composition, 1956, pastel, 11¾ x 15¾ . . . . (16) 205

1964
The Bridges, 1937, gouache, 18¾ x 26½ . . . . (439) 240

PAINTINGS
1961-1962
Still Life, 13½ x 19 . . . . (14) 442
Barconi at La Trinité-sur-Mer, 1948, 20½ x 25 . . . . (15) 996
Analogia sul Rosso, 1955, 21¼ x 27¾ . . . . (16) 664
Analogia sul Rosso, 1955, 21¼ x 27¾ . . . . (70) 711

1964
Still Life, 1948, 33¼ x 22½ . . . . (435) 800

1966
The Red Taxi, 1932, 23¾ x 23 . . . . (802) 7,200

1967
Landscape, 1942, 27¾ x 22 . . . . (882) 1,680

Roger Bissière

(1888–1964)

Birthplace: Villeréal, France.

1905 Attends the Academy of Fine Arts, Bordeaux.

1910-11 Settles in Paris. Takes part in the Salon des Artistes Français.

1920 Participates in the Salon d'Automne and the Salon des Indépendants, Paris.

1922 Meets Braque, who leads him toward Cubism—a style he soon gives up. Exhibition at the Galerie Léonce Rosenberg, Paris.

1923-30 Exhibition at the Galerie Druet, Paris.

1925-38 Becomes a professor at the Académie Ranson, Paris.

1937 Takes part in the exhibition "Les maîtres de l'art indépendants" at the Musée du Petit Palais, Paris.

1939 Settles in the Lot district, France. An eye disease forces him to give up painting for four years.

1945 "Hommage à Bissière" at the first Salon de Mai, Paris.

1947 Exhibition of his pictures and tapestries at the Galerie René Drouin, Paris.

1951 Exhibition, "Images sans titres," at the Galerie Jeanne Bûcher, Paris.

1952 Wins the Grand Prix des Arts.

1954-55 Several exhibitions in Europe, in the U.S., and one in São Paulo.

1959 Important retrospective exhibition at the Musée National d'Art Moderne, Paris.

1964 Died.

Sales

DRAWINGS
1961-1962
The Woman with a Hat, red chalk, 14¾ x 14¼ . . . . (147) $ 30
1963
Nude with Drapery, red chalk, 21¼ x 18¾ . . . . (254) 260
1964
Two Women, 10 x 14¾ . . . . (451) 90
1965
Nude in a Landscape, black pencil, 16 x 12½ . . . . . (580) 52
1966
Interior with a Man and a Woman, 23¾ x 18¾ . . . (742) 280
1968–July 1969
The Cliffs, pencil, 8¼ x 11¾ . . . . (1240) 120
The Cliffs, 8 x 11¾ . . . . (1245) 120

WATERCOLORS
1961-1962
The Model, gouache, 12¾ x 6 . . . . (144) 230
Composition, 1952, watercolor, 9½ x 12¾ . . . . (75) 790
1965
Composition, 1954, watercolor, 10 x 15¾ . . . . (567) 791
Women at the Balcony, watercolor, 9½ x 7½ . . . . . (580) 76
1966
Standing Nude, Combing Her Hair, gouache,
12¼ x 5¾ . . . . (702) 400
Cubist Still Life, gouache, 9¼ x 5 . . . . (757) 387

PAINTINGS

1961-1962

Still Life with a Decanter, 19 x 21¾ .... (43) $ 310

Landscape, 1946, on paper mounted on canvas,
25¾ x 39½ .... (88)   4,969

Resting by the Seaside, 19¾ x 31 .... (136)   260

Composition, 1955, 15¾ x 26 .... (149)   1,844

Composition, 1955, 21¼ x 25¾ .... (88)   3,592

Composition, 1957, 13 x 18¼ .... (156)   1,020

Nocturnal, 1957, 29 x 36½ .... (156)   2,800

Landscape, 1957, 39½ x 32½ .... (149)   5,056

Landscape, on cardboard, 8 x 13 .... (156)   870

Two Women, 1921, 45½ x 32 .... (156)   560

1963

Interior with a Woman, 15 x 21¾ .... (238)   204

Sitting Model, 29 x 21¼ .... (254)   560

St. Jacques Church, on cardboard, 17 x 11¾ ..... (280)   116

Bather, 21¼ x 32 .... (185)   300

Young Girl with a Basket of Fruit, (1919),
42¾ x 25¾ .... (306)   720

Two Women with a Still Life, 1921, 45 x 32 ...... (299)   600

Composition, 1949, on panel, 25¾ x 19¾ .... (249)   3,020

Abstract Composition, 1955, 26½ x 43 .... (249)   3,800

Composition, 1955, 18½ x 30 .... (249)   2,100

Composition, 1955, 13 x 28½ .... (249)   1,300

Morning, 1957, on paper, 18¼ x 14¼ .... (249)   1,300

Composition, 1957, 19¾ x 25¾ .... (200)   3,200

Landscape, 1957, 39½ x 32 .... (200)   4,200

Composition on a Black Background, 1957, on
board, 17 x 21¼ .... (283)   2,260

Gray, 1958, 15 x 19 .... (249)   1,100

1964

Flowers and Red Tablecloth, 1923, 26 x 13½ ..... (346)   330

Composition, 1952, 14¾ x 18¾ .... (377)   1,898

Abstract Composition, 1955, 26½ x 43 .... (351)   180

Morning, 1957, on paper, 18¼ x 14¼ .... (351)   1,100

Composition, 1957, on panel, 16¾ x 22½ .... (386)   2,000

Young Ladies at the Seaside, 19¾ x 31 .... (335)   300

Woman with a Newspaper, 29 x 23¾ .... (404)   400

1965

Women with a Still Life, 1921, 35¼ x 45¾ .... (612)   760

Woman Leaning on Her Elbow, 1923, 32 x 39½ ... (627)   800

Two Nudes, 1926, 18¼ x 14¾ .... (561)   1,040

Bare-Breasted Woman with a Gray Skirt,
45¾ x 32 .... (599)   680

Woman in the Park, on panel, 21¾ x 25 .... (533)   320

Two Figures, on cardboard, 18 x 21 .... (624)   276

Back View of a Nude, Blue Scarf, 10¾ x 16¼ .... (632)   280

Seated Woman, on panel, 21¾ x 16¼ .... (567)   678

Composition, 1952, 23¾ x 28½ .... (561)   3,600

The Village Across the Trees, 19 x 30½ .... (647)   300

Composition, 1956, 21¾ x 18¼ .... (518)   1,200

Still Life with a Gray Jug, 51 x 32 .... (529)   1,960

1966

Still Life in a Landscape, 20½ x 30 .... (741)   700

Reclining Woman, 10¾ x 15¾ .... (749)   2,020

Woman Seated in a Landscape, 31 x 24½ .... (656)   1,040

Still Life with Pomegranates, 18¼ x 21¾ .... (742)   300

Still Life, 10¾ x 18¼ .... (718)   920

The Garden Table, 28 x 36 .... (724)   1,000

The Artist's House, on cardboard, 9 x 16¼ .... (781) $ 800

Landscape, on cardboard, 14 x 25¾ .... (798)   1,040

Still Life with a Shell, two frescoes, each
93¾ x 29¾ .... (826)   1,600

Sitting Young Woman, Leaning on Her Elbow,
28½ x 21¼ .... (670)   860

Composition, 1960, 14 x 17½ .... (745)   1,763

Silver Wedding, on panel, 43½ x 29¾ .... (685)   4,400

Composition, 1957, 23¾ x 29 .... (811)   1,560

1967

Still Life with a Violin, on panel, 27¼ x 22 .... (923)   1,000

Still Life, on panel, 20½ x 27¾ .... (909)   230

Still Life with Watermelons, 1925, 19¾ x 29 ...... (905)   800

Lunch in the Garden, on cardboard, 18¾ x 21¾ ... (926)   660

Landscape, (1930), on cardboard, 23 x 32¾ .... (984)   840

Houses in the Country, 19¾ x 29 .... (857)   680

Resting in the Forest, on panel, 21¾ x 25¼ ...... (976)   800

Composition on a Black Background, 1957, on
paper mounted on canvas, 17 x 21¼ .... (918)   1,898

Abstract Composition, 32 x 39½ .... (1000)   3,400

1968-July 1969

Portrait of a Woman, 21¼ x 16¼ .... (1127)   736

Young Lady in Gray, 63¾ x 38½ .... (1116)   900

Young Woman with a Hat, 29 x 23¾ .... (1116)   480

Girl Sleeping in the Woods, 19 x 30½ .... (1131)   810

Reclining Nude, on panel, 14 x 25¾ .... (1170)   690

Bather, 24 x 36½ .... (1129)   1,000

The Artist's Wife, 34 x 21¼ .... (1181)   1,160

Woman with a Mandolin, 18¼ x 15 .... (1053)   760

The Country Concert, on cardboard, 9¾ x 13 .... (1042)   320

Still Life with Guitar, 1940, on board,
21½ x 25¾ .... (1174)   1,196

Composition, 30 x 45 .... (1117)   3,500

Composition in Green and Brown, (1957),
36 x 29¼ .... (1125)   6,900

Landscape, 1931, 13 x 18¼ .... (1224)   640

The Siesta, 21¼ x 31½ .... (1227)   590

Composition No. 395, 1958, 16 x 21½ .... (1237)   850

Seated Woman Wearing a Green Bodice,
21¼ x 28½ .... (1256)   1,100

Umberto Boccioni

(1882-1916)

Birthplace: Reggio di Calabria, Italy.

1901   Visits Rome, where he meets Severini and Ballà.

1902   First trip to Paris.

1904   Stay in Petrograd, Russia.

1910   With Carrà, Russolo, Ballà, and Severini, signs the
"Manifeste des peintres futuristes."

1911   Stays in Paris, where he meets Picasso, Braque, and
Dufy. Paints "Moods: Farewell."

1912   First exhibition of Futurism at the Galerie Bernheim-Jeune, Paris. The Futurists publish the "Manifeste technique de la sculpture futuriste." (Boccioni is also a sculptor.)

1913   Exhibition of futurist sculptures at the Galerie de la Boétie, Paris.

1916   Died, Verona.

Sales

DRAWINGS

1966

Sonno, (1910–12), pencil, 6½ x 9½ .... (689) $ 193

1967

Study of Hands, (1907), pencil, 11¾ x 9 .... (925)   147

Study for "The Football Player," 1913, pen,
4 x 5¼ .... (925)   904

Reclining Nude, (1914), India ink on a pencil
preparation, 10 x 12¼ .... (925)   3,074

1968–July 1969

Two Heads, pencil and pen, 13 x 15¾ .... (1214)   3,360
Head, 1912, charcoal, 14¾ x 13 .... (1214)   3,360

WATERCOLORS

1964

Portrait of the Artist's Sister, 1909, pastel,
17½ x 13½ .... (461)   2,400

PAINTINGS

1961–1962

Woman's Head, 1910, on cardboard, mounted on
canvas, 11¾ x 9½ .... (149)   4,108
Quelli che vanno, 1911, 15 x 21¾ .... (21)   25,280

1964

Portrait of Mrs. Busoni, 1915, 21¼ x 29¼ .... (461)   6,400
Horses Under the Storm, 25 x 20 .... (405)   1,103

1967

Sitting Woman, 1908, 29 x 25¾ .... (940)   1,886

Camille Bombois

(1883–   )

Birthplace: Venarey-lès-Laumes, Côte-d'Or district, France.

1899   Starts to draw rustic scenes.

1903   Supports himself as a wrestler in a circus, which gives him authentic material for paintings on circus themes.

1907   Lives in Paris, working at night in a printing plant to earn his living and painting in the daytime.

1922   Shows his pictures on Montmartre pavements. The famous German critic Wilhelm Uhde takes an interest in his work, which enables him to devote himself entirely to painting. Settles in a studio and elaborates his own "naïve" style.

1937   Takes part in the exhibition "Les maîtres populaires de la réalité," Paris.

1952   Takes part in various exhibitions in Dortmund; at the Stedelijk Museum, Amsterdam; and at the Palais des Beaux-Arts, Brussels.

1956   Exhibits at the Kunsthalle, Basel, with Bauchant, Séraphine de Senlis, and Vivin.

1958   Exhibits at the Perls Galleries, New York, together with Vivin.

1960   Takes part in the exhibition "La peinture naïve française du Douanier Rousseau à nos jours," Paris.

1964   Participates in the exhibition "Le monde des naïfs" at the Musée National d'Art Moderne, Paris.

Sales

PAINTINGS

1961–1962

The Bather, 6¼ x 8¾ .... (111) $ 350
Flowers, 15¾ x 13 .... (3)   925
A Wrestling Match, 12¾ x 15¾ .... (152)   1,050

1963

The Mill, 7½ x 10¾ .... (179)   900
A Field of Flowers, 10¾ x 15¾ .... (225)   1,200
The Fisherman, 7½ x 10¾ .... (255)   740
A Walk in the Park, 6½ x 8½ .... (293)   400

1964

Bather, 6¼ x 8¾ .... (374)   550
Portrait of Damia, 17¾ x 15 .... (438)   775
Woman by the Waterside, 14 x 10¾ .... (451)   420

1965

Three Clowns, 21½ x 18¼ .... (567)   2,147
Charlot, 13½ x 9 .... (567)   791
A Young Lady, 16¼ x 13 .... (561)   300
The Waste Land, 21¼ x 25¾ .... (499)   1,800

1966

Still Life, 21 x 25¾ .... (784)   3,700
A Bridge Over the Stream Dordogne, (1950),
7½ x 10¾ .... (784)   3,250

1967

Boats on the River, 6½ x 9½ .... (1002)   1,160
The Riverside, 19¾ x 29¾ .... (963)   7,500
The Farmer's Three Daughters, 18¼ x 25¾ ...... (978)   4,800
Young Lady with a Butterfly, 21 x 17¾ .... (989)   2,900
Portrait of Charles Trenet, 21¾ x 18¼ .... (967)   1,808
Beby the Clown, 13½ x 9 .... (912)   1,600
The Gipsy, 28½ x 23 .... (841)   3,750
Landscape, 31½ x 25 .... (841)   4,750
Still Life, on panel, 9¼ x 13¼ .... (989)   1,800

1968–July 1969

Landscape with a Dam, 7¾ x 10¾ .... (1145)   3,400
Washerwomen on the Banks of the River Marne,
10¼ x 13½ .... (1187)   5,192
St. Cucufa Pond, 21¼ x 25¾ .... (1018)   3,250
The Wood of St. Cucufa, 18¼ x 25¾ .... (1113)   1,900
Walk Around a Pond, on panel, 6¼ x 10 .... (1043)   1,540

A Pregnant Servant, on board, 7¾ x 4½ . . . . (1042) $ 710
Village Street, 10¼ x 14 . . . . (1159) 1,320
A Farm Through the Trees, on panel, 6½ x 10 . . . (1215) 1,900
The Beach, on cradled panel, 10 x 13¼ . . . . (1080) 2,750
Bather, on panel, 5¼ x 3¾ . . . . (1203) 1,363
Beby the Clown, 13½ x 9 . . . . (1060) 1,920
Woman Gathering Crabs, 9½ x 7½ . . . . (1177) 2,100
Still Life, on panel, 9¼ x 13¼ . . . . (1231) 1,600
The Fishermen, 7¾ x 10¾ . . . . (1248) 4,250
River Scene, 21¾ x 18 . . . . (1248) 800
By the Riverside, 24 x 28 . . . . (1248) 7,500
The Old Mill, 15 x 22 . . . . (1268) 6,496
The Washerwomen, 17¾ x 24½ . . . . (1271) 4,320

Pierre Bonnard

(1867–1947)

Birthplace: Fontenay-aux-Roses, near Paris, France.

1886–87 Studies law in Paris and takes his degree.

1888–89 Attends the Académie Julian and later the Ecole des Beaux-Arts, where he meets M. Denis, P. Sérusier, K. X. Roussel, and Edouard Vuillard, with whom he becomes very friendly. Devotes himself entirely to painting. Sérusier sets up the group called the Nabis (the Prophets).

1891 With the Nabis, participates in the Salon des Indépendants, Paris. Paints in clear shades.

1894 Designs the famous poster of "La Revue Blanche." Has also done various prints for book illustration. Meets the famous art dealer Ambroise Vollard. His palette darkens, taking on brown and gray shades.

1896 First one-man show at the Galerie Durand-Ruel, Paris.

1906 Important exhibition at the Galerie Bernheim-Jeune, Paris. (Bernheim has been his dealer since 1899.)

1910 Begins to work steadily in the South of France at towns like St. Tropez, Grasse, Antibes, and Cannes, where he meets Renoir and Signac again. His palette brightens considerably.

1913 Drawing and pictural constructions become more important, more adaptive to his colors, more forceful.

1921 Retrospective exhibition at the Galerie Druet, Paris.

1922–23 Participates in the Venice Biennial.

1925 Marries.

1926 As a member of the Carnegie Jury, stays for a short time in the U.S.

1928 Important exhibition at de Hauck's, New York. Becomes a complete master of dazzling color.

1932 Important Bonnard-Vuillard exhibition at the Kunsthaus, Zurich.

1934 Exhibition at Wildenstein's, New York.

1936 Awarded second prize, Carnegie International.

1938 Bonnard-Vuillard exhibition at the Art Institute of Chicago.

1939 Retires to his villa, "Le Bosquet," at Le Cannet. Does not return to Paris until the end of World War II.

1942 Death of his wife Marthe.

1946 Important exhibition at Bernheim's, Paris. Retrospective exhibition at the Museum of Modern Art, New York. Participates in the Salon d'Automne, Paris.

1947 Died, Le Cannet, France. (Had just finished his last picture, "The Almond Tree in Blossom.") Important retrospective exhibition at the Musée de l'Orangerie, Paris.

Sales

DRAWINGS

1961–1962

The Seated Toilette, charcoal, 11 x 8¾ . . . . (106) $1,130
Bather, black lead, 10½ x 6½ . . . . (106) 1,220
Two Figures, India ink, 10 x 5¼ . . . . (143) 2,712

1963

Woman with a Dog, pencil, 11¾ x 7½ . . . . (232) 1,582
Woman with a Dog, pencil, 11¾ x 7½ . . . . (283) 1,220
Café de la Gare, colored pencil, 6½ x 11 . . . . (202) 700
At the Café, black lead, 6¾ x 5¼ . . . . (280) 100
The Table on the Terrace, black lead, 6½ x 6¾ . . . (204) 210
Two Musicians, black lead, 6½ x 6¾ . . . . (218) 150
Street Scene, charcoal, 8¼ x 6½ . . . . (255) 2,194
Study of a Nude Model, pencil, 8 x 5 . . . . (208) 475
Nudes, black lead, double sided, 5¼ x 8 . . . . (290) 450
Landscape of the South of France, pencil,
10 x 13 . . . . (315) 987
Sketch of Flowers, pencil and watercolor,
6 x 8¼ . . . . (202) 2,100
Mischievousness and Mandolin, two drawings
(recto-verso), India ink and pencil, 10 x 6¾ . . . (179) 1,300

1964

Portrait of Monsieur Dolbeau, 1885, pencil,
6½ x 7½ . . . . (454) 553
Woman with a Dog, pencil, 11¾ x 7½ . . . . (441) 904
Figure with a Basket, black lead, 6½ x 4¾ . . . . (471) 670
Back View of a Nude, ink and watercolor,
12¼ x 7½ . . . . (354) 850
Seated Nude, Side View, blue pencil, 10¼ x 7¾ . . (394) 700
Presumed Portrait of Madame Bonnard, pencil,
9¼ x 11¾ . . . . (408) 180
The Baby, pencil, 8 x 6¾ . . . . (329) 200
Singer (recto), *Study for "The Movement"*
(verso), pencil and wash, 8¼ x 10½ . . . . (453) 1,133
Study for "The Woman with Ducks," charcoal on
canvas, 58½ x 19½ . . . . (464) 3,000
Pont des Arts, colored pencil, 16¾ x 10¼ . . . . (378) 3,616

1965

Interior, colored pencil, 11½ x 9 . . . . (547) 1,840
Sketch for a Fan, wash, 10 x 13 . . . . (582) 1,382
Sensitive Octave, pencil, ink, and watercolor,
7½ x 10¼ . . . . (541) 425
Nude, pencil, 6¾ x 5¼ . . . . (617) 588
Nudes, pencil, double sided, 5¼ x 8¼ . . . . (606) 275

1966

The Little Girl, pencil, 6 x 4½ .... (711) $ 240
Couple, India ink, 15 x 10 .... (797)   2,486

1967

Coming Out of the Bath, pencil, 11½ x 9 .... (923)   1,000
Girl with a Mirror, (1902), pencil, 6¼ x 5¼ .... (970)   886
Hamlet, 1895, study for a poster, pen and
     watercolor, 12¼ x 7½ .... (951)   1,596
Woman and Cab, (1899), charcoal, 12 x 7¼ .... (951)   813
Study for "Le petit solfège illustré," pen and
     wash, 7¼ x 10¼ .... (881)   691
Study for "Le petit solfège illustré," pencil and
     India ink wash, 6¾ x 10¼ .... (995)   640
Woman Washing Herself, (1916), charcoal,
     13 x 10 .... (951)   2,467
Fishermen at Dory, brush and ink, 4½ x 9 .... (951)   377
Bust of a Nude, (1920-25), pen, 8¼ x 10¾ .... (951)   492
The Lesson of Solfeggio, black lead, bister, and
     India ink wash, diameter 3 .... (929)   270
The Breakfast, black lead, 5½ x 4 .... (965)   1,921
The Pont Neuf, charcoal and colored pencil,
     10 x 16¼ .... (912)   1,360
Nude in the Bath, black lead, double sided,
     6½ x 4¾ .... (918)   2,305

1968–July 1969

The Laundress, (1898), charcoal, 15 x 11¾ ...... (1059)   595
Two Heads, (1898), pen and sepia wash, 4 x 4½ .. (1126)   545
Standing Young Lady in the Nude, (1900), pencil,
     4¾ x 3 .... (1191)   1,416
Standing Nude, (1900), pencil, 5¾ x 4½ .... (1059)   347
Street Scene, Paris, (1900-10), pencil, 8 x 5¼ ... (1059)   644
Couple Lying on the Grass, (1910), pen,
     5¼ x 7½ .... (1059)   545
The Palm Tree, (1930), black chalk, 5¾ x 4¼ .... (1059)   223
Trouville Harbor, 1936, pencil, 4½ x 6 .... (1174)   2,070
The Little Window, (1940), pencil, 6¾ x 5¼ ..... (1174)   1,840
The Orchard, (1930-40), pencil, 5½ x 8¼ .... (1059)   595
Landscape, (1930-40), pencil, 4¾ x 6½ .... (1059)   545
Portrait of a Young Lady, (1940), charcoal,
     18½ x 12¼ .... (1126)   2,230
Nudes in the Forest, charcoal, 12 x 8¾ .... (1127)   3,450
Two Children on a Bench, colored pencil,
     6¾ x 5 .... (1061)   550
Still Life, black lead, 5 x 6½ .... (1127)   1,564
The Rabbits, fan-shaped drawing, wash, 11 x 21 . (1117)   2,200
The Walk, pencil and watercolor, 6½ x 4¾ ...... (1127)   4,600
Study for the Poster "La Revue Blanche," (1894),
     pencil, sepia ink, and gouache, 11½ x 9 ..... (1239)   8,400
Two Heads, (1898), brush, black ink, and sepia
     wash, 4 x 4½ .... (1241)   1,310
Landscape, black lead, 4¼ x 6¾ .... (1268)   1,926
Village in a Landscape, black chalk, 4¼ x 7 ..... (1272)   816
Hairdressing (recto), *Nude Drying Her Leg*
     (verso), pencil, 6¼ x 4¾ .... (1272)   1,008
The Harpoon, reed pen and India ink, 10½ x 8 .. (1273)   277

WATERCOLORS

1961–1962

After the Lunch, gouache and media,
     12¾ x 19½ .... (137)   28,000
Landscape with Red Roofs, gouache, 12¾ x 8¾ ... (114)   3,040
Landscape of the South of France, pencil and
     gouache, 19½ x 12¾ .... (106)   7,910

Le Cannet, 1935, gouache, 10¾ x 13 .... (70) $6,636
"Petit solfège illustré" by C. Terrasse, 1893, 72
     watercolors, drawings, or sketches .... (92)   10,000

1963

Le Cannet, gouache and watercolor on paper laid
     down on canvas, 10 x 12 .... (210)   4,387

1964

Landscape with Red Roofs, gouache, 12¾ x 8¾ ... (340)   4,000
The Idlers, watercolor, 45½ x 29¾ .... (409)   1,720

1965

Boulevard Scene, Paris, (1890), 4¾ x 5¼ .... (569)   2,938
Street Scene, (1891-92), tempera on canvas,
     30 x 20 .... (624)   7,739
*Landscape at Vernon, Seen from the Artist's
     Window,* (1932-35), watercolor, 12¾ x 9¼ ... (624)   7,739
Le Cannet, 1935, gouache, 10¼ x 13 .... (559)   1,760
The Woman with a Little Dog, watercolor,
     9 x 7¼ .... (553)   3,760
Landscape, Boulodrome, watercolor,
     25½ x 19¾ .... (569)   28,928

1966

The Fireplace, gouache on paper laid down on
     canvas, 19¾ x 25¾ .... (730)   12,000

1967

Basket of Fruit on a Red Tablecloth, (1930),
     watercolor, 20 x 29¾ .... (938)   20,730
Street Scene, (1899), tempera on canvas, panel of
     a folding screen, 29¾ x 19½ .... (988)   6,966
Two Women on a Bicycle, watercolor, 5¼ x 5¼ ... (890)   2,020

1968–July 1969

Seascape, watercolor and gouache, 10 x 12¼ .... (1113)   7,000
The Young Schoolgirls' Walk, 1891, watercolor
     and gouache, 9½ x 14 .... (1068)   44,840
Landscape of Vernon, (1920), watercolor,
     4¾ x 6¾ .... (1174)   7,130
The Beach, watercolor, 7¼ x 10½ .... (1109)   6,400
Flowers, gouache, 15 x 22½ .... (1125)   21,850
Basket of Fruit, gouache laid down on canvas,
     12¼ x 9 .... (1268)   16,240
The Garden, gouache, 9 x 12¾ .... (1268)   22,736
Cup of Fruit, gouache, 21¼ x 30 .... (1268)   25,520

PAINTINGS

1961–1962

Florist's Shop, 1894, 9 x 9¼ .... (8)   17,000
Grandmother and Child, 1897, 14¾ x 14¾ .... (83)   24,714
The High Mirror, (1914), 48½ x 32¼ .... (8)   101,000
St. Tropez, (1914), 16¾ x 21½ .... (164)   18,123
The Terrasse Family in Their Garden, 1915,
     25¼ x 32 .... (112)   27,460
Bonnard's Kitchen, 20½ x 14¼ .... (116)   30,200
Interior with a Seated Woman, 23¾ x 29 .... (18)   53,788
Nude in False Light, 48 x 21¼ .... (64)   50,000
Faun and Nymph, on cardboard, 25¾ x 28 .... (93)   16,950
Nude with Tub, 17¾ x 19½ .... (125)   33,160
The Rue Tholozé, 22½ x 15 .... (143)   17,854
The Herd by the River, 18¼ x 25¾ .... (114)   20,000
Farmyard, on cradled panel, 17½ x 19 .... (71)   10,600
Woman with a Hat, on cradled panel, 26 x 13½ ... (114)   32,400

1963

Woman with a Dog, 1891, 16¼ x 13 .... (254)   38,000
At the Embroiderer's, (1896), on panel,
     13¾ x 16 .... (247)   16,452

The Duck Pond, on panel, 13 x 16¼ .... (318) $16,200
Farm at Vernon, 1932, 25 x 29¾ .... (241) 56,000
The River Seine at Vernon, 21¾ x 25 .... (241) 19,000
Children Picking Fruit in a Garden, 1912,
   65¾ x 51½ .... (309) 29,552
Foliage and Fruit, 14¼ x 30 .... (309) 11,865
Meadow at Vernon, 30 x 20 .... (243) 50,000
Buttercup with Blue Vase, 23 x 19½ .... (243) 50,400
Woman in Red Before a Bunch of Flowers,
   23¼ x 19¾ .... (243) 57,200
Woman with Mimosas, 1922, 19 x 24½ .... (279) 55,000
Woman and Nymph, on cardboard, 25¾ x 28 ..... (232) 16,478
Portrait of Mademoiselle Dupuis de Fraynel,
   16¾ x 14½ .... (245) 27,420
Solfeggio, 19¾ x 15¾ .... (296) 15,200
The Place Clichy, on cradled cardboard,
   21¼ x 27¼ .... (243) 62,000
Woman in a White Dress, 25¾ x 21¼ .... (243) 27,000
Flowerpot with Face, 30 x 20¼ .... (243) 70,000

1964
The Snowballs, 1891, 15¾ x 12¾ .... (416) 22,112
Bathers on the Outskirts of a Wood, 1899,
   19¾ x 17¾ .... (458) 15,961
The Capstan, on cardboard, 14¾ x 14¾ .... (401) 16,600
The Toilette, (1908), 30 x 18¼ .... (454) 58,044
Faun and Nymph, on board, 26 x 28 .... (339) 7,000
Fair-Haired Nude, 1913, 24 x 18¼ .... (416) 67,718
View from the Terrace, Vernon, 1920, 11½ x 9 .... (394) 10,400
St. Tropez Harbor, 1925, 14¼ x 26½ .... (458) 42,079
The River Seine at Vernon, (1932), 16 x 25¾ ..... (378) 19,888
Basket and Fruit, 1933, 28 x 13¾ .... (453) 46,988
Young Boy with a Purse, on panel, 18¾ x 14¾ ... (458) 34,824
Young Lady in a Pink Bodice, 13 x 18¼ .... (471) 30,732
In the Park, on board, 14¾ x 17½ .... (458) 12,188
Cannes Harbor, 1935, 17¾ x 21¾ .... (347) 27,600
Flowers in a Vase, 27¾ x 18¾ .... (347) 56,000
Landscape of the South of France, (Bonnard's
   house), 1936, 19 x 25½ .... (431) 52,500
Basket of Fruit on a Table, 17¾ x 24 .... (474) 58,000
Young Woman with a Cup of Coffee, 16¾ x 20 ... (474) 22,000
Basket of Peaches, 1939–45, 12¼ x 15½ .... (416) 41,460
Red Poppies with Stone Jug, 28 x 21¼ .... (340) 56,000

1965
The Snowballs, 1892, 15¼ x 12 .... (624) 10,227
The Tipcart, 1894, 12 x 9½ .... (522) 19,901
Going Out, (1898), on panel, 27 x 19¼ .... (575) 49,752
The Pont de la Jatte, (1908), 51 x 63¼ .... (575) 52,516
Study for the Portrait of E. Vuillard, (1910), on
   panel, 18¼ x 15 .... (594) 5,000
Woman with a Hat, 1910, on panel, 26½ x 13¾ ... (575) 37,314
St. Tropez Cove, 1912, 17½ x 22 .... (629) 30,471
The White Ship in the Harbor, on panel, 9 x 6½ .. (617) 13,334
The High Mirror,[1] (1914), 49¼ x 32¾ .... (526) 155,000
The Capstan, Brittany, 1915, 14¾ x 14½ .... (522) 19,348
The Walk, 1917, 18¼ x 25¾ .... (594) 50,000
The Bathers of the Happy Island, (1919), on oval-
   shaped canvas, 26 x 38½ .... (594) 50,000
Interior, on cardboard, 21¼ x 14 .... (569) 31,301
Wintry Landscape at Vernon, (1920), 15¾ x 24 ... (569) 40,228
View from the Terrace at Vernon, 9½ x 11¾ ..... (553) 11,800

[1]Sold in New York in October 1961 for $101,000.

Landscape Near Giverny, (1924), 19½ x 24½ ..... (522) $27,640
My House at Vernon, 19½ x 25 .... (526) 60,000
Houses at the Seaside, 1927, on cradled panel,
   15¾ x 18¾ .... (637) 27,500
The River Seine at Vernon, 1932, 21¾ x 25 .... (559) 8,400
The Red House, 21¼ x 17¾ .... (645) 6,256
Fashionable Ladies on the Pont Neuf, 14 x 19¾ .. (547) 39,200
Portrait of Madame Dupuy, 18¼ x 14¾ .... (583) 21,765
Cannes Harbor and the Estérel, on panel,
   9 x 6½ .... (553) 10,400
Landscape, 19¾ x 24 .... (628) 17,992
Woman Combing Her Hair, on cardboard,
   21¾ x 14¾ .... (564) 17,800
The Departure, 11¼ x 16¾ .... (633) 13,000

1966
The Woman with Ducks, 1892, peinture à la colle,
   61 x 25¾ .... (741) 10,000
Venetian Shutters, (1895), 16¼ x 8¾ .... (819) 14,000
*In the Country: Mother and Little Boy, Father
   and Little Girl,* two pictures, each
   39½ x 12¾ .... (686) 46,988
Lively Landscape, (1913), 51½ x 86½ .... (694) 12,000
Tea Time in the Garden, Yellow Table,
   25¾ x 17½ .... (797) 30,736
Snowy Landscape at Vernon, (1920), 15¾ x 24 .... (797) 45,652
Fluvial Landscape, 17 x 20½ .... (797) 41,132
The Breakfast, 1922, 16¾ x 20 .... (750) 33,168
Young Woman in a White Dress, (1925),
   25¾ x 21¼ .... (812) 23,494
Interior with Mimosas, (1925–30), 23 x 19½ ...... (686) 38,696
Bust of a Woman, on panel, 5½ x 3¾ .... (797) 4,520
Landscape of Provence, 13½ x 16¾ .... (753) 31,922
The Wells, Seaside, 28½ x 21¼ .... (750) 51,134
Landscape, 14¾ x 23¾ .... (744) 24,182

1967
Seated Young Lady with a Rabbit, 1891, 38 x 17 .. (988) 47,272
At the Café, on cradled panel, 11¾ x 18¼ .... (987) 46,000
Children on the Village Road, 1895, on cardboard
   laid down on board, 11¼ x 9 .... (987) 12,200
Holiday, (1900), 9½ x 15½ .... (982) 25,359
The Large Garden, 1900, 66¼ x 87 .... (852) 60,200
Street Scene, (1902), 21¼ x 27¾ .... (988) 57,224
The Ball Game, 1905, 21¼ x 29¾ .... (880) 71,864
Interior with a Woman, 1910, 32 x 25¾ .... (938) 30,404
Lively Landscape, (1913), 51½ x 76¾ .... (880) 85,684
Wintry Landscape at Vernon, (1916–20),
   15¾ x 24 .... (911) 37,000
Portrait of P. Sérusier, on panel, 18¼ x 14¾ ..... (982) 9,480
Basket of Fruit in the Sun, (1927), 23¾ x 17½ .... (880) 63,572
Sailboats on the Sea (St. Tropez Cove), (1936),
   20 x 31¼ .... (938) 82,920
Venetian Shutters, on cardboard, 16¾ x 9 .... (918) 19,436
*The Lady with a Muff (Portrait of Madame
   Bonnard),* 17¾ x 14¾ .... (965) 41,584

1968–July 1969
Riverside, 18 x 17¾ .... (1106) 18,400
The Red Roof, 22½ x 14¾ .... (1176) 15,000
The Red-Roofed House, on panel, 9 x 10¾ .... (1187) 36,580
The Street, 1889, 21¾ x 15 .... (1187) 96,760
Table Corner and Cat, (1897), on cradled
   cardboard, 20¼ x 7¾ .... (1173) 21,160
The Woman with a Muff, on cardboard laid down
   on canvas, 17¾ x 14¾ .... (1173) 38,180

The Farm in the Evening, (1903), on cardboard,
17½ x 19 ....(1200) $ 9,600
Young Lady Threading a Needle, 1905, 24 x 22 .. (1193) 54,516
Woman Drying Herself (Madame Bonnard),
1909, 27¾ x 14 ....(1187) 94,400
Landscape with Bathers, 1910, 22½ x 37¾ ......(1068) 29,264
The Strawberries, 1910, 25 x 20 ....(1176) 115,000
Young Lady with a Green Dress, 1910,
23¼ x 15½ ....(1126) 32,214
Portrait of Madame Dupuy, (1916), 18¾ x 15 .... (1057) 18,500
Mimosas, White Lilacs, and Red Poppies, 1917,
21 x 16¾ ....(1132) 35,400
Vase of Flowers, 17½ x 12¾ ....(1132) 87,320
Interior with a Standing Nude or The Toilette,
1921, 48¼ x 22 ....(1187) 202,960
Nude Dressing, (1923-24), 18¾ x 13¾ ....(1056) 47,500
Beach and Sailboats, (1930-35), on board,
13 x 9¼ ....(1187) 37,760
The Farm at Vernon, 1932, 25 x 29¾ ....(1049) 42,000
Landscape, Le Cannet, (1935), 29 x 26 ....(1056) 82,500
Nude with a Dog, (1940), 47½ x 19¾ ....(1132) 122,720
Teatime, 25¾ x 17½ ....(1125) 32,200
Cannes Harbor, 15½ x 27 ....(1125) 53,360
The Long-Haired Young Lady, (1901),
13½ x 8½ ....(1235) 14,000
Nude with a Tub, (1917), 13¾ x 12 ....(1239) 45,600
Vase of Flowers, 14¾ x 22¼ ....(1239) 28,800
The Farm in the Evening, (1903), on cardboard,
17½ x 19 ....(1254) 14,000
Madame Claude Anet at Home, 32½ x 25¾ .....(1255) 44,000
Landscape, (1925), 8¾ x 13 ....(1270) 19,200

Francisco Bores

(1898–   )

Birthplace, Madrid, Spain.

1915 Attends a private academy of painting, Madrid.

1922 Exhibits at the Salon Nacional, Madrid.

1925 Participates in the Salon de Artistos Ibericos, Madrid. Stays in Paris, where he meets Juan Gris, Miró, Picabia, and Matisse, who will encourage him a great deal. Cubism exerts a brief influence on him.

1927 First one-man show at the Galerie Percier, Paris. Many one-man shows in Paris follow—including those at the Galerie Léonce Rosenberg, the Galerie Pierre, the Galerie de France, and the Galerie Kahnweiler.

1952 Participates yearly in the Salon de Mai, Paris.

1954 Participates yearly in the exhibition "Ecole de Paris" at the Galerie Charpentier, Paris. Also exhibits abroad in London, New York, Chicago, Brussels, Geneva, Stockholm, and other important cities.

1954-62 Exhibits at the Galerie Louis Carré, Paris.

1962 Exhibits at the Crane Kalman Gallery, London. Resident in Paris.

Sales

DRAWINGS

1961–1962

Nude, 1930, pencil, 11 x 8½ ....(105) $ 77

WATERCOLORS

1961–1962

Plate on a Square Tablecloth, 1960, gouache,
19½ x 25¾ ....(129) 220
Still Life, gouache, 9½ x 12¾ ....(59) 232

1963

Bust of a Woman, 1959, watercolor, 25¾ x 19¾ ... (238) 160

1964

Reclining Nude, 1942, pastel, 9½ x 12¾ ....(375) 110

1965

Still Life, 1955, watercolor, 10 x 11½ ....(547) 340

1966

Still Life, 1955, watercolor, 9½ x 11½ ....(730) 360

1967

Still Life with Bananas, 1960, gouache,
19¾ x 26 ....(881) 166
Corrida, gouache, 12¾ x 11¹ ....(986) 142

1968–July 1969

Plate on a Checked Tablecloth, 1960, gouache,
19½ x 25¾ ....(1138) 211
Stranded Boat, 1933, watercolor, 8¾ x 10¾ .....(1162) 120
Blue Flowers, 1959, gouache, 19¾ x 25 ....(1072) 320

PAINTINGS

1961–1962

Winter Still Life, 1929, 29 x 23¾ ....(80) 660
Still Life with Bananas, 1929, 29 x 23¾ ....(110) 1,340
The Black Bottle, 1939, 15 x 18¼ ....(143) 768
Bathers, 15 x 18¼ ....(39) 500
Water Polo, 13 x 18¼ ....(35) 640
Seated Dancer, 39½ x 32 ....(79) 600
The Man with a Cock, 45¾ x 35¼ ....(108) 712
A Walk, 13 x 16¼ ....(93) 452

1963

The Poet, 1929, 38½ x 51½ ....(306) 480
The Winding Stairs, 1929, 31½ x 23 ....(216) 206
Crowd in the Sun, 1930, 63¾ x 51½ ....(237) 940
Plate and Knife, 15 x 18¼ ....(299) 280
Still Life with a Cock, 29 x 36½ ....(180) 420
Still Life with a Fish, 1948, 18¼ x 21¾ ....(287) 330
Still Life with Bananas, 1949, 21¼ x 25¾ ....(249) 460
Still Life, 15 x 21¾ ....(249) 400

1964

Fruit in a Dish, 1927, 23¾ x 29 ....(460) 1,100
Interior with a Figure, 1929, 32 x 23¾ ....(441) 497
Landscape, 1930, 15 x 18¼ ....(375) 240
The Card, 1935, 46 x 35¼ ....(460) 1,720
Picnic, 1943, on panel, 8¾ x 10¾ ....(475) 300

Red Still Life with a Blue Fruit Stand, 1942,
25¾ x 32¼ .... (401) $ 440

Grapes with a Glass of Wine, 54 x 65 .... (337)   700

The Bath, (1949), 14 x 10¾ .... (441)   181

Still Life with Biscuits, 1951, 21¼ x 25½ .... (368)   663

Still Life with a White Fish, 1954, 31½ x 39½ ..... (368)   553

Still Life with Windflowers, 1954, 32 x 39½ .... (386)   1,100

1965

Cards, 1928, 8¾ x 10¾ .... (615)   560

Composition, 1929, 32 x 23¾ .... (563)   460

Red Flowers, 1935, 51½ x 38½ .... (615)   2,900

Metallic Still Life, 1938, 25¾ x 32 .... (615)   1,400

"1987," 8¾ x 10¾ .... (494)   85

Yellow Interior, 1955, 57¾ x 45 .... (518)   1,120

Nature-Morte aux attributs de parfumerie,
25¾ x 32 .... (513)   380

1966

Restaurant by the Waterside, 35¼ x 45¾ .... (742)   640

Three Little Girls, 1927, 26 x 31½ .... (701)   400

Three Men and a Woman Sitting at a Table,
1931, 45 x 77¼ .... (674)   440

Still Life with Red Wine, 1933, 23¾ x 29 .... (801)   1,300

Still Life with a Lemon, 1934, 36½ x 51½ .... (801)   2,000

Pourville Beach, 1933, on cardboard, 9 x 10¾ ..... (801)   460

The Skinned Rabbit, 1935, 32 x 39½ .... (745)   1,130

Playing at Dice, 1936, 46 x 35¼ .... (730)   1,200

Clear Day, 1937, 18¼ x 15 .... (741)   500

The Music Lesson, 1938, 38 x 51½ .... (784)   1,100

Composition in Front of the Window, 1944, on
panel, 25¾ x 19¾ .... (791)   400

Still Life, 1947, 35¼ x 46 .... (770)   1,420

Bust of a Child, 1948, 18¼ x 15 .... (811)   300

Interior with a Young Girl, 1951, 35¼ x 46 .... (681)   1,040

Boys, 1954, 14 x 10¾ .... (781)   240

By the Waterside, 1956, 46 x 35¼ .... (809)   1,260

Young Lady in White, 1958, 63½ x 51¼ .... (678)   2,600

Composition in Green and White, 1959,
29 x 36½ .... (789)   600

1967

Still Life with a Cock, 28½ x 36 .... (995)   500

Card Players, 1928, 36½ x 29 .... (993)   440

Women at the Café, 1928, 39½ x 32 .... (975)   1,100

At the Café, 1929, 29¾ x 23¾ .... (975)   1,600

Still Life with Pears, 1929, 18¼ x 21¾ .... (975)   700

Still Life with an Inn, 1931, 32 x 39½ .... (975)   800

Interior with a Vase of Flowers, 1940,
21¼ x 25¾ .... (993)   320

Flowers in a Vase, 1944, 13 x 18¼ .... (849)   300

Composition in Front of the Window, 1944, on
panel, 25¾ x 19¾ .... (934)   350

Still Life with Lemons, 1947, 21 x 25½ .... (985)   332

Still Life with Flowers, 1948, 21¼ x 25¾ .... (854)   460

Vase and Fruit Stand, 1958, 29 x 36½ .... (852)   800

Still Life with a Bowl, 1958, 23¾ x 29 .... (950)   800

Flowers, 18¼ x 21¾ .... (973)   300

1968–July 1969

Houses, 1948, 21¾ x 18¼ .... (1051)   500

Apples, 1927, 18¼ x 21¾ .... (1012)   200

Basket of Cherries, 1934, 23 x 28¾ .... (1203)   892

Games, 1938, 15 x 18¼ .... (1020)   409

Flowers, 1939, 18¼ x 21¾ .... (1042)   330

Landscape, 13 x 16¼ .... (1078) $ 240

Still Life, 21¼ x 25¾ .... (1026)   940

Men at a Café, 45½ x 35 .... (1054)   1,240

Woman with a Corset, 57¾ x 45½ .... (1259)   1,400

Still Life with a Decanter, 35¼ x 46 .... (1259)   900

Eugène Boudin

(1824–1898)

Birthplace: Honfleur, France.

1844   Works in a bookshop in Le Havre, where he is able to exhibit his favorite painters: Isabey, Troyon, Couture, and Millet.

1847-48   Stay in Paris. A trip to Belgium gives him the opportunity to study Flemish and Dutch masters.

1851-54   A scholarship enables him to study painting in Paris. Meets Courbet and Baudelaire. Exhibits at the Société des Amis des Arts, Paris. Returns to Le Havre, where he meets Monet and Jongkind.

1861-63   Returns to Paris. Meets Corot, who later calls him "the king of skies."

1864   After a stay in Honfleur, he returns again to Paris, exhibiting yearly at the Salon.

1867   Stay in Brittany.

1869   Executes a mural for Boudainville Castle.

1870   Becomes a successful painter, frequently commissioned. Trip to Anvers.

1874   Participates in the first exhibition of the Impressionist group, Paris.

1880   Meets Durand-Ruel and signs a contract with his gallery.

1882   One-man show at the Galerie Durand-Ruel, Paris.

1884   Acquires a house at Deauville.

1889   One-man show at the Galerie Durand-Ruel, Paris.

1890   Takes part in the exhibition at the Société Nationale des Beaux-Arts, Paris.

1892   Awarded the rank of Chevalier of the Legion of Honor.

1895   Undermined by illness, visits the south of France for a while and then settles in Venice.

1897   Returns to Brittany.

1898   Died, Deauville. (Regarded as the direct precursor of Impressionism.)

Sales

DRAWINGS

1961–1962

Fishing Boats Alongside a Quay, charcoal,
11½ x 7½ .... (68) $ 220

The Pasture, pencil, 5¼ x 5¾ .... (73)   80

Study of Cows, black pencil, 5¼ x 5¾ . . . . (119) $ 50

Crinolines on Deauville-Trouville Beach, pencil and watercolor, 7 x 12¼ . . . . (84)   8,238

Crinolines on Deauville Beach, pencil and watercolor, 6 x 10¼ . . . . (164)   2,609

The Beach Hut, pencil and watercolor, 5½ x 4 . . . . (128)   1,098

Harbor Scene, pencil and watercolor, 8½ x 12½ . . (174)   220

Market Scene, pencil and watercolor, 6½ x 7½ . . . . (96)   2,100

Sailors' Rest, charcoal and pastel, 5¾ x 7½ . . . . . . (177)   270

1963

The Beach, pen and watercolor, 5½ x 8½ . . . . (255)   1,371

Sailors' Rest, pencil and pastel, 5¾ x 7½ . . . . (275)   400

A Young Fisherman Lying on the Beach, pencil and watercolor, 4 x 6½ . . . . (307)   340

Harbor Scene, colored pencil, 7½ x 11½ . . . . (216)   110

Crinolines on the Beach, pencil and watercolor, 5¾ x 9¾ . . . . (202)   4,100

1964

Four Women in Crinolines in Trouville, 1865, pencil and watercolor, 4½ x 9 . . . . (416)   11,332

Figures with Sunshades on the Beach, 1867, pencil and watercolor, 4½ x 8 . . . . (458)   1,306

Seascape, pencil and watercolor, 6¾ x 8¾ . . . . (471)   1,085

Breton Women in Plougastel, pencil and watercolor, 5¾ x 8¼ . . . . (367)   1,658

A Quay with Figures, colored chalk heightened with white, 5¼ x 8 . . . . (420)   232

Sailors' Meal, black lead, 4½ x 6¼ . . . . (338)   90

Fishermen, 3 x 4¼ . . . . (477)   120

1965

Reclining Figures, black pencil, 5¾ x 8½ . . . . (612)   140

1966

Seated Woman, drawing heightened with watercolor and gouache, 4¼ x 5¾ . . . . (706)   460

Harbor Scene, on gray paper, 7 x 11 . . . . (665)   425

A Group on the Beach, drawing with watercolor . . . . (650)   3,400

Figures on Deauville Beach, 1867, pencil and watercolor, 5¾ x 7¾ . . . . (750)   3,455

Fishermen and Boat, pencil, 5¾ x 5¼ . . . . (666)   160

Study of a Landscape, pencil and watercolor, 4 x 6½ . . . . (648)   300

Children in Front of a Hospital, pencil and watercolor, 5 x 8¼ . . . . (813)   967

1967

Crinolines on Trouville Beach, (1865), pencil and watercolor, 6½ x 10¼ . . . . (982)   7,110

Pardon in Brittany, black pencil and wash heightened with watercolor and gouache, 8 x 10¾ . . . . (987)   800

Fishing Boats, black pencil, 3¾ x 5¾ . . . . (1002)   130

The Entrance of the Harbor, wash, 4 x 6 . . . . (976)   600

Fishwives, pencil and watercolor, 6½ x 8½ . . . . . . (881)   1,061

1968–July 1969

Figures Walking in Trouville, 1864, pencil and watercolor, 5 x 7½ . . . . (1132)   9,440

Fishing Boats, black pencil and watercolor, 4½ x 8¼ . . . . (1189)   900

On the Beach, 1866, pencil and watercolor, 3¾ x 6¾ . . . . (1174)   1,150

Sailboats, black lead heightened with watercolor, 4¾ x 8 . . . . (1137)   1,040

Fishing Sailboats and Rowboat, black pencil, 5¼ x 8 . . . . (1212) $ 440

Douarnenez Cove, pencil and watercolor, 9¾ x 14½ . . . . (1134)   1,062

The Three-Masted Ship, pencil and wash, 5 x 6 . . (1224)   1,000

Figures and Animals, black lead, 3 x 5 . . . . (1227)   74

Studies of Hands, drawing heightened with chalk, 11½ x 8¾ . . . . (1230)   120

Seated Woman, 11½ x 8¾ . . . . (1230)   270

Fishermen on the Beach, pencil and watercolor, 4 x 5¾ . . . . (1240)   1,320

The Departure, pencil, 4 x 6 . . . . (1240)   480

Interior of a Farmhouse, pencil and watercolor, 6¾ x 9¼ . . . . (1240)   1,440

Sailors' Rest, charcoal and pastel on gray paper, 5¾ x 7½ . . . . (1241)   655

WATERCOLORS

1961–1962

Fishing Boats, watercolor, 6¾ x 8¼ . . . . (156)   1,160

Fishermen Offshore, watercolor, 8¼ x 11 . . . . (160)   1,820

The Estuary, pastel, 5¾ x 8¼ . . . . (128)   1,181

Antwerp Harbor, watercolor, 5 x 7½ . . . . (26)   1,000

Antwerp Harbor, watercolor, 8 x 11½ . . . . (125)   2,200

Rotterdam, watercolor, 6¾ x 8¼ . . . . (156)   1,060

Fishermen on the Roads of Brest, watercolor, 5¼ x 9 . . . . (143)   1,627

Women in Crinolines on the Beach, and Boats, watercolor, 6 x 10½ . . . . (76)   700

A Couple on Deauville Beach, watercolor, 6½ x 11¾ . . . . (128)   3,295

Figures on the Beach, watercolor, 4¼ x 8½ . . . . . . (119)   780

Crinolines on Trouville Beach, 1865, watercolor, 6 x 9 . . . . (58)   4,000

A Beach with Crinolines, Trouville, 1869, watercolor, 5 x 7¾ . . . . (137)   7,500

A Beach with Crinolines, Trouville, 1869, watercolor, 5 x 8 . . . . (137)   7,500

Trouville Beach, 1874, watercolor, 5¾ x 7½ . . . . . . (102)   1,160

Seascape, Washerwomen in Trouville, pastel, 7¼ x 10 . . . . (84)   686

A House in Normandy, watercolor, 5¼ x 5¾ . . . . . . (73)   200

Peasants in the Country, watercolor, 8¾ x 11½ . . . (117)   460

Harvesters, watercolor, 5¾ x 7½ . . . . (12)   320

1963

Figures on Trouville Beach, 1865, watercolor, 6½ x 10¾ . . . . (316)   4,500

Fervaques, 1897, pastel on paper on board, 13¾ x 16¾ . . . . (202)   4,250

Seaside Scene, pastel, 5¾ x 8¾ . . . . (208)   875

Deauville Beach with Figures, watercolor, 5¼ x 9 . . . . (256)   1,356

Berck Beach with Figures, 1863, watercolor, 11¾ x 19½ . . . . (256)   124

In Front of a Church, watercolor, 8 x 10½ . . . . (258)   560

Study of the Sky, pastel, 5¾ x 5¾ . . . . (223)   720

Breton Fisherman on the Strand, watercolor, 3½ x 5¾ . . . . (301)   700

The Market of the Canal in Rotterdam, watercolor, 8 x 9½ . . . . (258)   2,400

1964

The Opening of the Grand Salon of the Casino de Trouville, 1865, watercolor and pencil, 9½ x 16½ . . . . (416)   20,454

Trouville Beach, watercolor, 4¾ x 9½ . . . . (471)   7,006

The Seashore, Capri, (1865), watercolor,
5½ x 8¼ .... (448) $1,700

Seascape, pastel, 6 x 8¼ .... (341) 500

The Rest, pastel, 6 x 7½ .... (398) 260

A Beach with Figures, watercolor, 4¾ x 8¼ ...... (399) 1,400

Church Square, watercolor, 9 x 8 .... (473) 620

The Child's Meal, Mother and Child, two
watercolors, each 5¾ x 7¼ .... (473) 400

Village Street, watercolor, 8¾ x 8 .... (329) 1,200

1965

The Beach Huts, 1865, pencil and watercolor,
6 x 9 .... (575) 4,975

Figures on the Beach, (1865), watercolor,
4¾ x 7¾ .... (624) 2,211

*A Couple in Front of Figures and Beach Huts on
Trouville Beach*, 1865, watercolor, 5¾ x 10 ... (613) 3,800

Fishing Boats in Scheveningen, 1876, watercolor,
8¾ x 13 .... (564) 5,200

Sailboats on the Sea at Sunset, pastel, 4¾ x 7¼ .. (612) 520

Sunset, pastel, 5¾ x 8¼ .... (518) 240

A Beach, pastel, 7¼ x 11 .... (581) 1,460

The Seaside, watercolor, 7¼ x 11¾ .... (583) 2,322

1966

Woman in Blue Seated on the Beach, 1865,
watercolor, 5¼ x 7½ .... (744) 4,972

Woman Seated on the Beach, 1865, watercolor,
5¼ x 7½ .... (797) 4,746

Trouville Beach with a Rider, (1865), pastel,
7½ x 11½ .... (813) 2,764

Trouville Beach, 1869, watercolor and black lead,
6 x 9 .... (681) 2,720

The Beach, watercolor, 5¼ x 7½ .... (672) 3,140

Seascape, pastel, 6¾ x 10¾ .... (726) 880

Berck Women, watercolor, 5¼ x 8¾ .... (741) 1,640

Study of the Sky, pastel, 5¾ x 8½ .... (829) 420

1967

On the Beach, the Blue Crinoline, 1863,
watercolor and pencil, 4¾ x 7½ .... (940) 5,224

Beach Scene, 1867, watercolor, 5¾ x 8¼ .... (911) 5,200

Beach Scene, 1869, watercolor and pencil,
4¾ x 9½ .... (889) 6,500

Shrimper, pastel, 5¾ x 8¼ .... (849) 720

Men and Women of Brittany, watercolor,
4¾ x 8¾ .... (978) 940

1968–July 1969

Trouville Beach with Figures, 1867, pencil and
watercolor, 6 x 10 .... (1068) 8,260

Trouville Beach, 1870, watercolor, 5¼ x 10¾ .... (1125) 17,250

Figures on the Beach of Trouville, 1870, pencil
and watercolor, 6½ x 13 .... (1176) 17,500

Bretons at Plougastel, 1870, watercolor and
gouache, 10 x 8¼ .... (1137) 800

Crinolines on the Beach, 1879, pencil and
watercolor, 4½ x 7¼ .... (1191) 4,012

Crinolines on the Beach, watercolor, 3¾ x 5¾ ... (1189) 3,000

Study of Fishermen Careening a Boat,
watercolor, 5¾ x 8½ .... (1189) 800

Figures on a Beach, watercolor, 6¼ x 9¼ .... (1050) 3,400

Fishing Boats Alongside the Quay, watercolor,
6½ x 4½ .... (1078) 600

Seascape, pastel, 4½ x 5¾ .... (1134) 1,180

Sailboat, watercolor, 4½ x 6½ .... (1138) 1,858

Sailboats, watercolor, 7¼ x 8¾ .... (1039) 380

Fair Day at Argentan, watercolor, 8¾ x 10 ...... (1140) $ 800

Sailboat in Honfleur Outer Harbor, (1860),
pastel, 8¼ x 11 .... (1239) 9,120

Bathing Time on Trouville Beach, 1867,
watercolor and pencil, 6 x 9 .... (1239) 11,520

Women Seated on the Beach, watercolor and
pencil, 4¼ x 10¼ .... (1239) 10,080

Figures on Trouville Beach, 1868, 5¾ x 3¾ ...... (1239) 10,080

Crinolines on the Beach, pencil and watercolor,
5 x 8½ .... (1240) 3,600

Seascape, Sunset, pastel, 4 x 5¾ .... (1244) 900

Fishwife, watercolor, 4¼ x 7¼ .... (1262) 330

Study of the Sky, pastel, 7¼ x 5¾ .... (1262) 4,700

Fishermen, watercolor, 11 x 4 .... (1268) 1,710

Figures on Trouville Beach, 1867, watercolor and
pencil, 5½ x 7¾ .... (1272) 4,800

Beach Scene, 1866, watercolor and pencil,
6 x 8¾ .... (1272) 4,320

Figures with Sunshades on the Beach, 1865,
watercolor and pencil, 6 x 8¾ .... (1272) 4,320

Sunset over the Sea, pastel, 7 x 10¾ .... (1272) 720

Beach and Sailboats at Honfleur, watercolor and
pencil, 5 x 7¾ .... (1272) 840

PAINTINGS

1961–1962

The Market in Rotterdam, on panel, 1876,
10 x 13 .... (32) 5,800

Honfleur, the Square with the Old Well, on
paper, 9 x 12¾ .... (32) 1,640

Le Havre Harbor, 1889, 26 x 35¾ .... (29) 21,200

Antwerp Harbor, 1872, 21¾ x 35¼ .... (29) 31,000

The Cap D'Antibes, 18¼ x 25¾ .... (33) 760

Sailboats and Fishing Boats in Le Havre Harbor,
1892, on panel, 13 x 16¼ .... (80) 9,200

View of Rouen, 1895, 18½ x 25½ .... (137) 28,000

Marseilles Harbor, 10¾ x 14 .... (69) 4,266

The River Loire, on panel, 8 x 16 .... (128) 10,160

Moon Effect, 19½ x 29 .... (64) 18,000

The End of the Mass, on panel, 10¾ x 8¼ .... (32) 5,000

A Vase of Flowers, 12¾ x 9¾ .... (109) 2,000

Wedding in Brittany, on panel, 11½ x 18¼ .... (76) 6,200

A Farmyard, 9½ x 12¾ .... (52) 720

The Meadow, on panel, 9½ x 13 .... (154) 500

A Meadow, Morning Effect, 1880, 14¾ x 18¼ ..... (71) 3,000

The Pasture, on panel, 7 x 9 .... (158) 520

Cows in Pasture, on panel, 6¾ x 9 .... (124) 280

Cows in Pasture, 1880, 16¼ x 21¾ .... (171) 1,640

Oxen Resting, 14½ x 18½ .... (167) 1,840

The River Touques Valley, Cows in Pasture, on
panel, 10¾ x 15¾ .... (124) 920

A Pasture on the Bank of the River Touques,
1870, 15 x 18¼ .... (90) 1,750

*Fishing Boats, Fishermen, and Ducks on the
Strand*, on panel, 11 x 14 .... (32) 4,400

Camaret, 1873, 21¼ x 35 .... (27) 7,400

Portrieux Rocks, 1873, 14¾ x 23 .... (71) 2,600

Boats, 1876, 14¼ x 23 .... (156) 7,000

Deauville Pond, 1885, 19 x 29 .... (128) 19,771

View of Trouville Harbor, on panel, 10 x 14 ...... (164) 7,414

The Dune at Berck, 21¼ x 29¼ .... (156) 2,900

The Banks of the River Touques, Trouville, 1890,
20 x 29¾ .... (156) 6,900

The River Touques in the Moonlight, 1890,
15¾ x 21¾ .... (22) $8,362

The Harbor, St. Valéry, 1886, 15¾ x 22 .... (29) 4,600

The River Touques in Trouville, 18¼ x 25¾ .... (29) 8,000

The Banks of the River Loques, Calvados, 1886,
on panel, 18½ x 29¾ .... (83) 13,730

The Ferry at Plougastel, on panel, 6½ x 10 .... (34) 1,900

Seaside Scenery, on panel, 10 x 14½ .... (150) 113

***Father and Daughter on Deauville-Trouville
Beach,***[1] on canvas on board, 8¾ x 10¾ ...... (112) 14,279

Fishermen's Wives on the Beach, 4¾ x 9 .... (137) 6,000

Fishermen's Wives on the Beach,[2] 4¾ x 10 .... (137) 7,500

1963

Roebucks' Cover, 1869, a decorative panel
executed for Boudainville Castle, 79 x 87 ..... (299) 1,700

Camaret, Finistère, 1872, 15½ x 25 .... (202) 10,500

Seascape, on board, 9 x 14 .... (232) 9,831

Pasture Land, 1873, 14¼ x 23 .... (241) 2,000

Oxen in Pasture, 14¾ x 18¼ .... (198) 2,000

Cows in Pasture, on panel, 8 x 10¾ .... (257) 470

The Ship in the Harbor, Rotterdam, 1875, on
panel, 21¾ x 29¾ .... (259) 18,400

Lormont Harbor, Bordeaux, 1875, 19½ x 31½ .... (247) 22,484

A Market in the Harbor, on panel, 15 x 18¼ ..... (293) 2,160

Fishermen's Wives on the Beach, Berck, 1875, on
panel, 6 x 9½ .... (259) 13,200

***Berck, Fishermen's Wives Near a Boat; Berck,
Fishermen's Wives,*** two panels, each
4¾ x 6½ .... (198) 14,000

Boats, 1876, 14½ x 23½ .... (254) 6,100

Le Havre Harbor, 1877, on panel, 10 x 13¼ ...... (277) 8,226

Honfleur Harbor, 17¾ x 23¾ .... (202) 10,000

Sailboats in the Bay, 1880, 17¾ x 25¾ .... (224) 22,100

Berck Beach, 1882, 21 x 28 .... (247) 20,839

Le Havre Harbor, 1885, on panel, 10½ x 13½ .... (261) 9,323

Sailboats in the Harbor, 1886, on panel,
10¾ x 14 .... (303) 10,600

Sailboats, 17¾ x 25¼ .... (298) 12,300

Inshore Pilots, 1884, 25¾ x 36¾ .... (259) 13,800

Camaret, the Harbor, 21¼ x 35¼ .... (198) 22,000

The Outlet of St. Valéry-en-Caux Harbor, 1889,
16 x 22 .... (277) 12,065

Moored Boat, on board, 13 x 9½ .... (277) 6,581

Cows in a Meadow, 1888, 12¾ x 18¾ .... (258) 1,400

The Park, 20 x 24½ .... (283) 6,328

Etaples, 1890, on board, 14 x 18¾ .... (210) 10,968

Trouville Harbor, on panel, 12½ x 15¾ .... (245) 17,000

The Outlet of Trouville Harbor, 1890, on panel,
16¼ x 13 .... (243) 12,000

Sailboats, 17¾ x 25¼ .... (298) 12,300

A Beach, 16¼ x 25¾ .... (199) 24,400

Three Women on a Beach, 4½ x 8½ .... (255) 1,645

Walking by the Waterside Near a Sailboat,
11¾ x 18¾ .... (258) 15,600

Dunkirk, 1890, 14 x 22¾ .... (241) 14,400

Apples and Plums, 6½ x 9½ .... (190) 1,160

Still Life with Shellfish, 29 x 39¼ .... (235) 1,700

The Breakers, Antibes, 1893, 29 x 19½ .... (210) 16,452

The Coast Near Benneville, 1897, 21 x 35¼ ...... (277) 13,710

Still Life with Eggs, 21¼ x 29 .... (313) 720

[1]Inscribed "A Mademoiselle Jeanne, 1892."
[2]Inscribed "Berck."

1964

The Mouth of the River Escaut, 15¾ x 25¾ ...... (400) $13,000

Around Quimper, 1857, on panel, 15¾ x 23¼ ..... (416) 5,528

Sailboat in the Harbor, 17½ x 23¾ .... (398) 6,600

The Entrance of Le Havre Harbor, 1866,
21¼ x 29 .... (371) 16,400

Le Havre Harbor, 1866, 17¼ x 21¼ .... (425) 18,400

Dunkirk, the Harbor Under Snow, 1870,
14 x 22 .... (416) 1,935

Sunrise, Camaret, 1871, 15½ x 25¼ .... (405) 10,447

View of a Fishing Harbor by Moonlight, 1873,
12¾ x 17¾ .... (353) 4,000

Seashore, Cows in Pasture, 14¾ x 18½ .... (474) 1,200

Le Havre Harbor, 1877, on panel, 9½ x 12¾ ..... (474) 8,000

Berck Beach, 1880, 17¾ x 25¾ .... (367) 12,162

Trouville Harbor, 1881, 12¾ x 18¼ .... (416) 8,016

Boarding Quay at Boulogne, on cradled panel,
9½ x 12¾ .... (409) 3,900

Sailboats, on panel, 8¾ x 10¾ .... (471) 9,040

View of Trouville, 1886, 17¾ x 23¾ .... (453) 11,056

Deauville, the Shore at Low Tide, 1890,
19¾ x 29¼ .... (408) 5,600

Le Crotoy, 1891, on panel, 13½ x 18¾ .... (347) 11,600

The Meadow by the Riverside, on panel,
8¼ x 16¼ .... (347) 2,000

Sluice Gate of a Brook in the Orne, 17 x 25¾ .... (354) 13,500

Cattle Quenching Their Thirst, 21¾ x 34½ .... (472) 8,300

Quillebeuf, 1892, 19¾ x 29¼ .... (463) 17,600

Landscape with a Meadow, 1894, on panel,
8¼ x 10¾ .... (433) 542

The Outlet of Trouville Harbor, on panel,
12¾ x 10¼ .... (341) 10,200

Berck Beach, on panel, 8 x 12¾ .... (340) 6,800

Study of Cows, on panel, 11 x 14¾ .... (367) 8,568

Flowers, 12¾ x 9½ .... (399) 2,500

Fécamp Dock, Sunset, 1894, 18¼ x 25¾ .... (416) 14,925

The Dock of La Barre, Le Havre, 1894, on panel,
12¼ x 15¾ .... (458) 8,416

Trouville, the Entrance of the Harbor, 1885, on
panel, 15¼ x 12 .... (416) 14,096

Fishing Boats, 1897, on panel, 10¾ x 8¼ .... (354) 5,750

1965

The Quarantine Dock in Le Havre, 1869,
12¾ x 18¼ .... (613) 8,600

Le Toulingue, Finistère, 1872, 21¾ x 31¼ .... (614) 13,000

Fishermen's Wives on Trouville Beach, 1875;
Washerwomen in Trouville, two panels,
6 x 9½ and 5¾ x 8¾ .... (564) 27,000

Seascape, 1875, on panel, 8¾ x 12¾ .... (575) 9,674

***The Valley of the River Touques (Cows in
Pasture),*** 1881, 24½ x 35¼ .... (624) 9,674

Study of Cows, on panel, 8¼ x 13 .... (624) 1,244

Cows in Pasture, 15¾ x 25¼ .... (491) 900

Trouville Seen From Deauville, 1881,
15¾ x 21¾ .... (624) 13,544

The River Touques, 1883, 20½ x 28 .... (583) 13,059

Dordrecht, 1884, on panel, 15 x 18¼ .... (583) 10,157

Trouville in the Morning, Low Tide, 1889,
18¾ x 25¾ .... (624) 9,121

Deauville, the Beach, (1890), 14¾ x 23 .... (594) 19,000

Brigs Nearing the Harbor, 1894, 17½ x 25 .... (624) 20,730

Fishing Boats Leaving a Harbor, 1896, on panel,
10 x 8 .... (522) 7,739

Sailboats, 14¼ x 23 .... (553) $8,000

Washerwomen by the Seaside, on panel,
  8¼ x 12¾ .... (617) 18,871

Washerwomen, on panel, 9½ x 14 .... (518) 37,000

The Mouth of the River Landerman, 16 x 25¼ .... (569) 6,102

Seascape, Antwerp, on panel, 8¾ x 12¾ .... (569) 6,780

A Market in Brittany, on panel, 10 x 13 .... (559) 4,640

The Walk in the Forest, 29 x 23 .... (640) 1,900

Honfleur Harbor, 21¼ x 25¾ .... (641) 1,440

Honfleur Harbor, on panel, 12¾ x 16½ .... (575) 12,182

Berck Beach, 14¾ x 23 .... (583) 43,530

1966

Dordrecht Tower, 1870, on panel, 14 x 17½ ...... (686) 12,714

Fishermen's Wives by the Seaside, 1872, on
  panel, 15½ x 22 .... (749) 38,000

View of Trouville, 1875, on panel, 8 x 16 .... (750) 8,845

Sailboats Lying at Anchor, Deauville Dock, 1880,
  on panel, 12¾ x 16 .... (812) 14,373

The Banks of the River Touques, 1881,
  19 x 29¾ .... (809) 3,400

Berck Beach, 24½ x 20 .... (800) 13,200

The Quai de la Marine, Villefranche, 1890,
  19¾ x 24 .... (776) 20,000

St. Valéry-en-Caux, 1890, 15¼ x 21 .... (727) 11,400

Le Havre Harbor, 14¾ x 18¼ .... (744) 12,430

Trouville Beach, 1890, 18¼ x 30 .... (797) 39,550

The Entrance of the Harbor, on panel,
  10¾ x 8½ .... (753) 5,514

Dunkirk Harbor, 1891, on panel, 12¾ x 16 ...... (713) 14,500

Crinolines on the Beach, on panel, 6½ x 11¾ ..... (741) 34,000

The Mountains of the Estérel, 1893, on cradled
  panel, 10½ x 16¼ .... (741) 6,200

The Banks of the River Touques, 1895,
  19½ x 28¾ .... (686) 11,609

Yachts in Deauville Dock, 1896, on panel,
  14¾ x 18¼ .... (812) 24,876

Raz de Seine, Brittany, 1897, 25 x 35¾ .... (686) 19,348

The Bay of the River Somme, on board,
  10½ x 8¼ .... (749) 5,200

The Calvary by the Church, on panel,
  16¼ x 12¾ .... (814) 6,000

Washerwomen on the Bank of a River, on panel,
  8¼ x 10¼ .... (808) 14,510

Cows by the Pond, on panel, 9¼ x 12¾ .... (666) 1,100

Haymaking Time, 20¼ x 29 .... (689) 1,935

Sunset, on cardboard laid down on cradled panel,
  6½ x 9½ .... (758) 560

1967

Sailboats in the Harbor, 1869, 18¼ x 25¾ .... (903) 17,600

Sailboats Lying at Anchor, 1870, 18 x 25½ .... (965) 20,340

The Trading Dock in Brussels, 1871, on panel,
  11 x 27 .... (988) 57,224

Camaret Harbor, 1872, 21¾ x 35½ .... (993) 20,000

Portrieux, the Bay, 1873, 14¼ x 23 .... (852) 4,400

The Entrance of Portrieux Harbor, 1875,
  14¼ x 22¾ .... (880) 15,478

Rotterdam Harbor, 1876, on panel, 9 x 12¾ ...... (938) 11,056

Boats at Low Tide, 1879, 11¾ x 18¼ .... (940) 6,675

Trouville Harbor, 1888, on panel, 13 x 16½ ...... (982) 12,324

Trouville Beach, 1889, 21½ x 35¼ .... (880) 82,920

The Mouth of the River Touques, on panel,
  12¾ x 16¼ .... (901) 13,000

The Valley of the River Touques, 21¾ x 34½ ..... (995) 8,000

Ducks in a Harbor, 12¾ x 18 .... (938) 3,870

Villefranche, the Citadel, 1892, 19 x 28¾ .... (938) $11,332

Trouville Piers, 1893, on panel, 10½ x 8¾ .... (864) 13,000

Pasture on the Bank of the River Touques,
  25¾ x 32 .... (900) 1,560

Tunny-Fishing Vessel Leaving Trouville Harbor,
  12¼ x 14¼ .... (923) 11,200

Fécamp Dock, 1894, on panel, 10¾ x 8½ .... (940) 4,063

Washerwomen on the Bank of the River Touques,
  1894, on panel, 9½ x 14 .... (993) 29,400

Walk in the Forest, 29 x 23 .... (854) 2,100

View of Venice, 1895, on board, 12¾ x 18¼ ...... (923) 18,000

The Entrance of Trouville Harbor, 1895, on
  panel, 10¾ x 8¼ .... (911) 11,000

Washerwomen, 1896, on panel, 5¾ x 9½ .... (902) 18,600

Sailboats in Honfleur, 1896, on panel, 15 x 18¼ ... (978) 18,800

The Entrance of the Harbor, on panel,
  12 x 15½ .... (940) 11,318

Towing on the Canal, on panel, 10¾ x 16¼ .... (993) 18,500

Cows at the Watering Place, on panel,
  8¼ x 12¾ .... (993) 1,560

1968–July 1969

Camaret, 1872, 21½ x 35¼ .... (1200) 38,000

Sailboats in the Harbor, 1873, on panel, 13 x 9 .. (1106) 14,400

Berck Fisherwomen, 1875, on cradled panel,
  11¾ x 19 .... (1190) 38,000

Recollection of Portrieux, 1872, 14½ x 22½ ..... (1044) 15,200

Trouville Harbor, (1878), on panel, 7¾ x 10 ..... (1068) 12,980

Trouville Harbor, 1878, on panel, 11 x 16¼ ...... (1068) 25,488

Honfleur Harbor, 18¾ x 25¾ .... (1173) 17,480

Dieppe Harbor, a View from Le Pollet,
  18¼ x 25¾ .... (1053) 28,500

The Beach, Stormy Sky, 1885, 17¾ x 25¼ ...... (1193) 71,862

Deauville Dock, 1887, on panel, 14 x 10½ .... (1106) 14,400

Tunny-Fishing Vessel Leaving Trouville Harbor,
  12¼ x 18¼ .... (1053) 9,800

Sunset, 1888, on panel, 4½ x 6¼ .... (1070) 3,304

Stranded Boats in the Estuary, 1890, on panel,
  12¼ x 15½ .... (1044) 9,200

Etretat, 1890, 14¼ x 23 .... (1126) 17,346

The Strand at Ste. Adresse at Dusk, 1890,
  21¾ x 32 .... (1047) 4,600

Sailboats on the Beach, Low Tide, Etaples, 1890,
  on panel, 13½ x 18½ .... (1187) 22,420

La Touques, 1891, 19¾ x 23½ .... (1049) 8,300

Washerwomen in Trouville, Low Tide, 1891, on
  panel, 13 x 17¼ .... (1126) 27,258

On the Beach, on panel, 5 x 8¾ .... (1027) 22,000

Boats at Low Tide, 1892, on panel, 10¾ x 8¾ .... (1027) 6,200

Venice, the Entrance of the Grand Canal, 1894,
  on panel, 14¾ x 18¼ .... (1187) 59,000

Fécamp Dock, 1894, on panel, 14¾ x 17¾ .... (1057) 16,000

Fécamp Dock, Fog Effect, 1894, on panel,
  15 x 18¼ .... (1050) 10,800

Quay of the Dogana, Venice, 1895, on panel,
  10¼ x 13¾ .... (1126) 39,648

Harbor in Brittany, 8¾ x 15¼ .... (1109) 13,400

View of Antibes, 20 x 29¾ .... (1068) 35,400

Entrance of the Harbor at Low Tide, on panel,
  9¼ x 12¾ .... (1132) 22,420

The Timber Dock at Harfleur, on panel,
  18½ x 15 .... (1113) 18,000

The Harbor, Fishing Boats, and Washerwoman,
  on panel, 10¾ x 8¾ .... (1132) 25,960

Dunkirk Under Snow, 14¼ x 23 .... (1113) 6,000

Cows by the Seaside, 20 x 29	(1174)	$8,050
Landscape with a White Horse, 16½ x 21¾	(1106)	3,200
The Herd, 16¼ x 25¾	(1119)	1,400
Breton Oxen, on cardboard, 9½ x 13	(1139)	780
St. Valéry, 1891, 14½ x 23	(1224)	18,400
Le Havre, Sunset, 1882, 21¼ x 29¼	(1226)	17,600
Tourgéville Dunes, 1890, 21¾ x 35¼	(1226)	32,000
The River Touques During the Great Tides, 1891, 19¾ x 29¼	(1226)	27,000
Fountain, Flowers, and Birds, 1869, 158 x 75	(1226)	22,000
Sunset, on panel, 10¾ x 8½	(1226)	7,600
Trouville Harbor, High Water, 1894, on panel, 10½ x 16	(1235)	20,000
Entrance of Trouville Harbor, Low Tide, 1893, 13¼ x 10¼, on panel	(1235)	18,000
Washerwomen by the River Touques, 1895, on panel, 10¾ x 16	(1235)	46,000
Trouville Scenery, 1884, 14¾ x 18¼	(1235)	17,000
Cow Lying Down,[3] 1875, 5¾ x 7½	(1238)	600
Still Life with Game, 1853, 36¾ x 56	(1239)	9,120
Venice, the Palace, and the Campanile, 19½ x 29	(1239)	124,800
Fisherwomen on the Sands at Berck, 1875, on panel, 11¾ x 19	(1239)	52,800
The Roadstead of Brest, (1870), 16½ x 25½	(1239)	38,400
Moonlight, on panel, 10½ x 8¼	(1239)	7,200
Seascape (recto), *At Low Tide* (verso), on panel, 7 x 9¼	(1239)	8,400
Sailboats in a Harbor, on panel, 9¼ x 13	(1239)	18,000
The Canal of St. Valéry-en-Caux, Moon Effect, 1891, 15¼ x 21¼	(1239)	24,000
The Entrance of Trouville Harbor, 1894, 13 x 9¼	(1239)	10,800
Farmyard Near Honfleur, 1859-60, on board, 7½ x 7½	(1241)	7,560
Cows in Pasture, 25¼ x 35¼	(1241)	3,530
Fishermen on the Beach: Sunset, oil on paper laid down on panel, 9 x 6	(1241)	907
An Ox in a Meadow, with the Sea in the Background, on panel, 5¾ x 8½	(1255)	1,400
Deauville: Sailboats Alongside the Quay, 1878, 12¼ x 8½	(1258)	21,600
Sailboats Alongside a Quay, on panel, 9 x 12¾	(1258)	12,600
Fishermen's Wives on the Strand, 1870, 18¼ x 26	(1258)	16,000
Plougastel, 1874, on panel, 9 x 12¾	(1261)	17,600
Deauville Dock, (1888), 8½ x 10¾	(1268)	17,400
Fishermen, 10¾ x 14¼	(1268)	4,408
View of Dordrecht, 1884, 17¾ x 25	(1270)	34,800
La Canche at Etaples, Low Water, 1886, 14¼ x 23	(1270)	33,600
Trouville Bridge, 1881, 15¾ x 21½	(1270)	24,000
Bordeaux Harbor: Sailboat on the Stocks, 1874, 21 x 34¾	(1270)	38,400
St. Vulfran Church Square, Abbeville, 1894, 17½ x 14½	(1270)	36,000
A Street of Abbeville with St. Vulfran Church in the Background, 1894, 17½ x 14½	(1270)	31,200
Sunset at Deauville, 1893, 21½ x 13⅓	(1270)	28,800
Cows in Pasture, on paper laid down on canvas, 12 x 17¾	(1271)	6,240
The Mountains of the Estérel, 1893, on panel, 10¼ x 15¾	(1273)	13,100
Cows in Pasture, 1877, 15½ x 21	(1273)	7,560

[3]Dedicated to C. P. Rainouard.

Georges Braque

(1882–1963)

Birthplace: Argenteuil, near Paris, France.

1890 Family settles in Le Havre, where he studies at the local fine arts school.

1900 Studies painting in Paris.

1902-04 Settles in Montmartre. Attends the Académie Humbert—and the Ecole des Beaux-Arts for a short time. Abandons the academies and starts to work by himself.

1905-06 Exhibits at the Salon des Indépendants, Paris. Trip to Antwerp with Friesz, who converts him to Fauvism.

1907-08 Meets Matisse, Derain, and Vlaminck. Signs a contract with the art dealer Kahnweiler, who introduces him to Apollinaire and Picasso. Executes his first Cubist (or rather "pre-Cubist") painting, "Nude." (Cuttoli Collection.) Exhibition at the Galerie Kahnweiler, Paris.

1910 His favorite subject matter is still life; he will be called the "Chardin of Cubism."

1912 Introduces the first "collages" to the final stage of Cubism; also mixes sand with oil paint and imitates marble, wood, etc. Marries Marcelle Lapré.

1915 Seriously wounded during World War I, he takes a long time to recover.

1917 Léonce Rosenberg becomes his dealer.

1919 Exhibition at the Galerie Léonce Rosenberg, Paris.

1920 Executes his first sculpture and woodcuts.

1922 Settles in Montparnasse. Beginning of his so-called neoclassic period. The Salon d'Automne assigns a whole room to his work.

1924 Exhibits at the Galerie Paul Rosenberg, Paris.

1930 Reverts to a clearer representational painting, renewing his usual creativeness.

1933 First major retrospective exhibition at the Kunsthalle, Basel, and afterward exhibitions in the chief cities of the world.

1937 Given an award by the Carnegie Institute, Pittsburgh.

1945 Becomes seriously ill.

1946 With Rouault, exhibits at the Tate Gallery, London.

1947 Exhibits at the gallery of his new dealer, Maeght, in Paris.

1948-49 Wins first prize for painting at the Venice Biennial. Retrospective exhibition in Cleveland and New York.

1956 Starts his famous series "The Bird." Retrospective exhibition in Edinburgh and London.

1963 Died. (Besides paintings, Braque executed stage decorations, tapestries, murals, stained-glass windows, jewels, etchings, and lithographs.)

Sales

DRAWINGS

1963

Fish, 9½ x 12¾	(190)	$1,200
Woman with a Mask, charcoal and India ink, 4¾ x 4	(217)	542

1964

Flowers, ink and watercolor, 17¼ x 12¼ .... (378) $4,407

Portrait of a Woman, pen and watercolor,
4¾ x 3¾ .... (398)   190

Woman in Profile, pen and watercolor,
8½ x 9¼ .... (354)   2,800

1965

"Les Fâcheux," 1924, pencil and watercolor,
8 x 8½ .... (637)   1,200

1966

Head, pencil and ink, 12¼ x 9½ .... (757)   1,050

Bird, 1953, India ink and gouache, 10½ x 7¾ ..... (798)   3,616

1967

Self-Portrait, 1955, pen, 15½ x 12¼ .... (951)   2,031

The Lamp, 1918, pen, 4 x 4½ .... (939)   1,382

Composition with a Guitar, 1920, pencil, gouache,
and collage, 6¾ x 10 .... (1004)   7,750

1968–July 1969

The Teapot, pen, 12 x 9¾ .... (1106)   1,700

Lemons, India ink, 11 x 18 .... (1080)   3,250

Stage Costume, pen, 9¾ x 7½ .... (1142)   661

Cover Design for "Les Fâcheux," 1924, pencil
and watercolor, 7¾ x 8½ .... (1248)   1,200

Birds, 1955, India ink, 9½ x 6¾ .... (1256)   940

Face in Profile, 1955, India ink wash, 10¼ x 7¼ . (1256)   860

WATERCOLORS

1961–1962

Still Life, 1929, pastel, 15¾ x 7¼ .... (21)   16,590

Winged Bulls, 1958, watercolor on checked paper,
7¼ x 5½ .... (143)   938

1963

Still Life, (recto), 9¼ x 7, *Composition,* (verso),
7¼ x 10, 1925, gouache .... (283)   8,927

Still Life, 1942, gouache, 10½ x 14¾ .... (283)   5,921

Two Apples, pastel on blue-gray paper, 7 x 11 .... (309)   3,461

Vase of Flowers, gouache, 17½ x 12¼ .... (263)   5,000

1964

The Bird, watercolor, 18½ x 24½ .... (341)   5,400

The Bird, 1956, gouache on newsprint,
21½ x 18½ .... (454)   1,050

Fish in a Jar, watercolor, 16¾ x 17½ .... (354)   6,500

1965

Still Life with a Guitar, 1913, gouache and
charcoal, 11 x 16¾ .... (633)   13,500

Anemones, 11½ x 13¾ .... (583)   6,384

The Dialogue of the Animals, watercolor and
gouache, 18½ x 24½ .... (564)   4,000

Bird on a Blue Background, pencil and
watercolor, 10 x 7½ .... (597)   2,952

1966

Bird Facing a Cloud, gouache, 8¼ x 10¾ .... (741)   2,800

1967

"Les Fâcheux," 1924, watercolor, 8¼ x 8 .... (965)   1,808

The White Bird, gouache and oil on canvas,
8 x 10¾ .... (918)   5,424

Buffoon's Costume, watercolor, 8¼ x 5¼ .... (922)   1,161

1968–July 1969

Dove on a Red Background, gouache on paper
laid down on canvas, 10 x 14 .... (1125)   6,670

The Bird, watercolor, 18¾ x 24½ .... (1113)   10,400

The Bird of Prey, 1961, watercolor and collage,
12¾ x 5¾ ....(1099) $2,530

*Project for a Stage Decoration for "Tartuffe" by
Molière,* gouache and collage, 21 x 30 ......(1200)   2,000

The White Bird, gouache on paper laid down on
canvas, 8 x 10¾ ....(1268)   6,728

PAINTINGS

1961–1962

La Calanque, 1907, 23¼ x 28½ .... (8)   47,000

Boats by the Shore, 10 x 15¾ .... (20)   25,280

Still Life with Apples, on panel .... (102)   6,600

The Glass of Absinthe, (1910-11), 11¼ x 9 .... (129)   21,968

Apples and Pears, 1928, on panel, 5¾ x 8¾ .... (8)   12,500

Still Life: Glass and Newspaper, 1913, on oval
canvas, 14¼ x 21 ....(129)   74,142

Still Life with Grapes, 1919, 12 x 18¼ .... (31)   10,984

A Glass, a Pipe, and a Lemon, 1929, 12¼ x 25¾ ... (69)   44,240

A White Pot, Bread, and Matches, 21½ x 15 ..... (120)   19,600

The Yellow Aquarium, (1934-35), 21½ x 15½ ...... (96)   21,000

Still Life, (1935), 7¼ x 13 .... (143)   19,210

The Lamp on the Table, 1952, 25½ x 31½ .... (8)   61,000

1963

Flowers, 6¾ x 12¾ .... (232)   8,814

Bunch of Yellow Flowers, 15¾ x 10¾ .... (232)   14,690

Still Life, 1918, 9¾ x 12¾ .... (200)   15,600

Landscape, the Road, 1928, 11½ x 29 .... (210)   17,823

Still Life with a Pipe, 1931, 10 x 14 .... (200)   14,400

The Glass of Absinthe, 11¾ x 8¾ .... (194)   14,000

Fish in a Jar, on paper laid down on canvas,
18½ x 12¼ .... (296)   18,000

Europa, 1950, oil on plaster, 12 x 9¼ .... (210)   7,677

Red Dahlias, 1956, 18¼ x 15 .... (279)   24,500

Still Life, 14 x 18½ .... (283)   37,742

1964

Seashore in the South of France, 1907,
16 x 19¾ ....(340)   12,600

Still Life with a Pipe, 7¼ x 12¾ .... (398)   10,000

Bathers, 1929, 7¾ x 13¾ .... (341)   9,000

Glasses and Cut Pear, 1929, 9¼ x 16 .... (367)   16,031

A Cup of Fruit and a Glass, 7¼ x 10¾ .... (463)   8,000

The Pot, collage on cardboard, 14 x 10¾ .... (460)   9,000

Landscape, (1932), 11¾ x 29¼ .... (471)   18,984

Still Life, (1938-39), 19¾ x 25¾ .... (471)   61,472

Still Life with a Small Decanter, 1938,
14¾ x 18¼ .... (405)   1,016

A Bunch of Flowers and a Spiny Lobster, 1942,
12¼ x 25¼ .... (367)   27,640

The Blue Pond, 1942, 23¾ x 31¾ .... (416)   63,572

Teapot and Lemons, 1943, oil on cardboard and
cradled sandpaper, 8¾ x 15¾ .... (465)   4,200

Still Life with the Ace of Clubs, 9¾ x 12¾ .... (465)   10,600

The Lobster, 1944, 13 x 21½ .... (454)   18,795

Daisies on a Chair, 1946, 31½ x 23 .... (416)   72,970

1965

A Walk lined with Olive Trees, 1907, 15 x 18¼ .... (565)   36,386

Fishing Boats (Leperrey), 1909, 36¼ x 29 .... (633)   67,500

A Candlestick and a Glass of Absinthe, 1910,
13 x 9½ .... (575)   20,730

Woman with a Mandolin, (1910), 32 x 21¼ .... (615)   66,000

The Glass, 1912, collage and charcoal,
20¼ x 28¼ .... (633)   19,000

The Daily (Violin and Pipe), 1912, collage and
charcoal on paper, 28½ x 42 . . . . **(615)** $34,000

The Man with a Guitar, 1914, 51½ x 29 . . . . **(615)** 312,000

Still Life with Grapes and Lemons, 1921,
25¾ x 8 . . . . **(575)** 41,460

Woman's Head, 1928, 18¼ x 15 . . . . **(594)** 27,000

Baluster and Skull, 1939, 18¼ x 20½ . . . . **(594)** 45,000

Yellow Still Life, 1955, 13¼ x 25¾ . . . . **(561)** 14,400

The Poet, 1958, collage, ink, and gouache,
7 x 20½ . . . . **(522)** 5,528

Still Life with Fruit, 10¾ x 26 . . . . **(613)** 31,200

1966

A Gray Bird on a Turquoise Background, oil on
paper laid down on canvas, 20½ x 13 . . . . **(744)** 10,170

The Mandola, 1909-10, 28¾ x 23¾ . . . . . **(751)** 93,976

Still Life: Pipe and Glass, (1913), oil, pastel, and
charcoal, oval shape, 10¼ x 13¼ . . . . **(694)** 18,500

Still Life with a Teapot, (early work),
18¼ x 21¾ . . . . **(814)** 2,100

Mandolin, oil on paper laid down on canvas,
18½ x 21¾ . . . . **(749)** 19,000

A Bottle of Rum, 1918, 38¼ x 27 . . . . **(676)** 120,000

Still Life, (1920), 28¼ x 35½ . . . . **(713)** 55,000

Front and Side View, 1942, 19¾ x 19 . . . . **(808)** 29,020

Teapot and Apple, (1945), on panel, 7½ x 8¼ . . . . . **(797)** 17,628

Bunch of Yellow Flowers, 1952, 25¾ x 12 . . . . **(753)** 40,628

Birds, on board, 13 x 21¾ . . . . **(797)** 16,950

1967

The Black Jug, 7½ x 13 . . . . **(923)** 5,800

Boat Alongside a Quay, (1904), 18¼ x 21½ . . . . **(982)** 15,405

The Candlestick, 1911, 18½ x 15 . . . . **(982)** 68,730

Reclining Nude in a Landscape, (1925), 11 x 16 . . . **(864)** 14,000

The Cut Pear, 1935, 7½ x 13 . . . . **(880)** 14,373

*Still Life with a Spiny Lobster on a Checked
Tablecloth*, (1943), 16½ x 36½ . . . . **(965)** 77,970

Daisies in a Decanter, on panel, 15¾ x 12¼ . . . . . . **(923)** 11,000

Thésée, 8¾ x 12¾ . . . . **(993)** 5,800

Mauve Teapot on a Striped Tablecloth, 1953,
7½ x 12¾ . . . . **(938)** 8,292

Gray Bird on a Green Background, 1961-62, oil
and gouache on paper laid down on canvas,
13¼ x 21 . . . . **(954)** 10,500

1968–July 1969

The Canal St. Martin, 1906, 19¾ x 24½ . . . . **(1126)** 128,756

Fishing Boats (Leperrey),[1] 1909, 36¼ x 29 . . . . . . **(1056)** 132,000

A Tribute to J.S. Bach, 1912, 21¼ x 28¾ . . . . **(1068)** 271,400

Collage, 1912, collage and charcoal, 24 x 18¾ . . . **(1064)** 40,120

Glass and Card, 1918, 14 x 18¾ . . . . **(1057)** 40,000

Fruit in a Dish, 1924, 12 x 20½ . . . . **(1064)** 40,120

Fisherwoman (Head II), 1928, 18¼ x 15 . . . . **(1057)** 35,000

Jug, Glass, and Apples, 1933-34, 11 x 28½ . . . . . . **(1068)** 69,620

The Hulk, 1937, 7½ x 13 . . . . **(1173)** 20,700

Boat on Varengeville Beach, 1937, on panel,
10¾ x 16¾ . . . . **(1132)** 18,800

Two Lemons, 1939, 7½ x 12¾ . . . . **(1125)** 18,630

The Green Wash Bowl, 1942, 25¾ x 32 . . . . **(1126)** 49,560

Sunflowers, 1943, 12¼ x 10¼ . . . . **(1126)** 34,692

Fields, 1956, 10¾ x 18¼ . . . . **(1106)** 11,600

Boat on the Strand, 8¾ x 14 . . . . **(1050)** 14,400

The Pot, collage on cardboard, 14 x 10¾ . . . . **(1118)** 7,000

[1] Sold in New York in December 1965 for $67,500.

Figure and Vase,[2] painted and engraved plaster,
20 x 21½ . . . . **(1053)** $11,000

Allegorical Composition,[3] single enamel, in blue,
12¼ x 9 . . . . **(1109)** 2,300

Bird on a Red Background, gouache and oil on
canvas, 10¼ x 14½ . . . . **(1241)** 7,560

Swifts in the Rain, (1961), oil on paper laid down
on canvas, 11¾ x 16¾ . . . . **(1268)** 15,312

Still Life with a Jug, 18¼ x 21¾ . . . . **(1268)** 26,680

Still Life with Jugs, 1906, 20¾ x 25 . . . . **(1270)** 120,000

Victor Brauner

(1903–1966)

Birthplace: Pietra-Naemtz, Romania.

1924 Exhibition at the Mozart Gallery, Bucharest.

1934 Exhibition at the Galerie Pierre, Paris. Becomes a
successful painter, his works being shown in the
main galleries of Europe and America. Takes part
in the exhibitions of the Surrealist group.

1938 Takes part in the Exposition Internationale du Surréalisme, Paris, at the Galerie des Beaux-Arts.

1953 Works are shown regularly at the Galerie Alexandre Iolas, Paris.

1952 Exhibition at the Hanover Gallery, London.

1954 Exhibition in Milan.

1960-61 Takes part in the exhibition "Surrealist Intrusion in
the Ancestors' Domain," New York; and in the
Venice and São Paulo Biennials.

1966 Died.

Sales

DRAWINGS

1965

Composition, 1931, pen, 10¼ x 11½ . . . . **(491)** $ 96

Man, 1949, white chalk on black cardboard,
10 x 6 . . . . **(634)** 123

Portrait, 1957, India ink, 25 x 19½ . . . . **(627)** 300

Mystère du Double, ink and watercolor, 9 x 5¾ . . **(494)** 350

1967

Composition, 1958, colored pencil, 4¼ x 3¾ . . . . . . **(970)** 148

1968–July 1969

Constructivist Composition, (1925), three
drawings in India ink, each 14 x 10 . . . . **(1096)** 874

Sttting Figure, 1947, ink and wax on paper,
8¾ x 6¼ . . . . **(1203)** 496

WATERCOLORS

1963

Conversation, 1941, watercolor and ink wash,
21¼ x 14¼ . . . . **(179)** 325

Composition, 1961, gouache, 25 x 19¾ . . . . **(249)** 640

[2] Frame also executed by Braque.
[3] Executed in Ligugé's studio.

1964

Composition, gouache, 21¾ x 29¾ .... (413) $ 600

1965

The Flame, watercolor and gouache, 18½ x 16¼ .. (627) 680

1968–July 1969

Sketch for "The Forsaking," 1961, watercolor,
19¾ x 25 .... (1053) 2,400
Fantastic Bestiary, 1963, gouache, 19¾ x 25 ..... (1185) 8,000

PAINTINGS

1961–1962

The Escape, 1938, 24¾ x 19¾ .... (152) 550
The World, 1950, 26 x 33 .... (145) 3,160

1963

The Tragic Story of Mr. K,[1] 1933, 25½ x 17¾ ..... (275) 1,300
"Kabiline" in Movement, 1933, 36½ x 29 .... (306) 5,600
Blood Flower, 1943, 25¾ x 21¼ .... (316) 4,600
Standing Man, 1956, on panel, 9½ x 7½ .... (258) 720
The Trees, 1957, 35¼ x 45½ .... (249) 1,700
Material Achievement of Delight, 1960,
32 x 25¾ .... (249) 2,000
Inclusion Morphogène, 1960, 32 x 25¾ .... (249) 1,800
The Tree of Sensual Delight, 1961, 39½ x 32 ..... (249) 1,900
Spirit Space, 1961, 35¼ x 45½ .... (249) 2,800

1964

Attacked by the Winds, 1958, 23¾ x 28½ .... (386) 2,100
Extrait du Radian Symbolique, 1962, 36½ x 29 ... (401) 1,600
Forms Attacked by Counterforms, 1961,
46 x 35¼ .... (401) 1,900

1965

Tête à tendance, 1944, 22 x 18¼ .... (616) 3,840
Figure, 1953, 25¾ x 19¾ .... (561) 840
Cocktail, 1955, 28½ x 23¾ .... (561) 1,360
The Violet Hat, 1957, wax, 25¾ x 21¼ .... (617) 4,294
The Boyard, 1958, colored wax on canvas,
32 x 25¾ .... (512) 2,100
Aggregation II, 1958, 32 x 25¾ .... (543) 1,556
La Formatrice, 1962, 51½ x 38¼ .... (512) 5,200

1966

The Ages of Man, 1934, on panel, 17 x 23 .... (809) 3,800
Composition, wax and candle on paper laid down
on canvas, 24 x 19¾ .... (798) 1,808
Flowers, Sun, 1953, 8¾ x 10¾ .... (727) 980
Surprise Box, 1954, wax on paper, 22 x 29 .... (701) 4,000
Man and Bird, 1954, wax on paper, 20¼ x 30 ..... (701) 3,250
The Tree of Sensual Delight, 39½ x 32 .... (672) 6,200
Mineral Spirit, 1961, 39½ x 32 .... (808) 5,514

1967

Dawn, 1956, 46 x 35¼ .... (923) 8,000
Additivité d'une figure dans l'espace, 1956,
18¼ x 21¾ .... (864) 700
Composition, wax on canvas, 24½ x 19¾ .... (996) 1,440
Full-Length Figure, 1959, wax on canvas,
25¾ x 19½ .... (962) 1,920

1968–July 1969

Surrealist Figures, 1929, on canvas, 19½ x 13¼ .. (1061) 750
Portrait, 1951, 21¼ x 25¾ .... (1174) 11,040
Portrait with Flowers, 1953, 21¼ x 25¾ .... (1127) 10,810

[1]K refers to Kafka.

The Monster, 1954, encaustic on paper,
19¾ x 25¾ .... (1208) $8,500
Fish of Honor, 1948, 29 x 36½ .... (1053) 11,400
Forlorn, 1958, wax paint on paper, 30½ x 22½ ... (1109) 11,600
Devouring Generation, 1964, 32 x 25¾ .... (1200) 12,200
Portrait with Flowers, 21¼ x 25¾ .... (1268) 16,240

Maurice Brianchon

(1899–   )

Birthplace: Fresnay-sur-Sarthe, France.

1918 Attends the Ecole des Arts Décoratifs, Paris.

1922 Becomes a member of the Salon d'Automne.

1924 Wins the Blumenthal prize.

1925 Executes several stage designs for the Opéra, Paris. Exhibition at the Galerie Devambez, Paris.

1927 Exhibition at the Galerie "Le Portique," Paris. Often draws inspiration from the circus, the music hall, and the ballet.

1930–32 Exhibitions at the Galerie Bernheim, Paris.

1934 Takes part in the exhibition "Artistes de ce temps" at the Musée du Petit Palais, Paris. Participates in the Venice Biennial.

1937 Becomes a professor at the Ecole des Arts Décoratifs and later at the Ecole Nationale des Beaux-Arts, Paris. Executes several stage designs.

1942 Designs tapestries for the famous factory of Aubusson, France. Exhibition at the Galerie Louis Carré, Paris.

1951 Retrospective exhibition at the Musée des Arts Décoratifs, Paris. Exhibition at the Wildenstein Gallery, London.

1956 Exhibition at the Tooth Gallery, London.

1959 Travels to the U.S. Exhibition at the Findlay Gallery, New York.

1962 Exhibition at the Galerie des Beaux-Arts, Paris.

Sales

DRAWINGS

1961–1962

River Banks, pen, 18½ x 12¼ .... (35) $ 80
The Dead Trees, India ink, 12¾ x 18¼ .... (154) 70

1963

Seascape, pen .... (276) 160

1964

Reception at the Elysée, pencil and watercolor,
4 x 5¼ .... (441) 316

1965

The Dead Tree, pen, 12 x 18¼ .... (529) 76

1966

The Beach, Deauville, pencil and watercolor,
14¼ x 21 .... (757) $ 580

1968–July 1969

View of a Town, pencil, watercolor, and gouache,
10 x 16 .... (1070)   130

WATERCOLORS

1961–1962

Still Life with a Red Tablecloth, pastel,
24½ x 18½ .... (32)   520

Still Life with a Red Tablecloth, pastel,
25¾ x 15¾ .... (123)   840

Still Life with Shrimps, gouache, 13 x 17¾ .... (160)   400

On the Beach, watercolor and gouache,
16¾ x 19¾ .... (98)   520

1963

Aubade, watercolor, 16 x 21¾ .... (309)   396

On the Beach, watercolor, 6½ x 4¾ .... (280)   76

Village in Winter, watercolor, 16¾ x 10¼ .... (281)   757

1964

Stage, gouache heightened with pastel,
12¾ x 21¾ .... (449)   560

The Pier, watercolor, 10¾ x 14¾ .... (441)   452

Figures on the Beach, gouache, 9 x 8½ .... (416)   1,935

1965

The Pier, gouache, 17½ x 14½ .... (523)   500

In the Harbor, gouache, 13¾ x 19¾ .... (548)   480

Sylvia, pastel, 18 x 12¾ .... (518)   600

1966

Sylvia, Ballet, pastel, 12¾ x 18 .... (741)   380

The Dancer with the Bunch of Flowers, pastel,
14¼ x 16¾ .... (819)   230

Diane Sleeping, gouache, 16½ x 21¾ .... (798)   701

Village in Winter, watercolor, 10¼ x 16¾ .... (745)   452

Aubade, Sketch for a Decoration, watercolor,
16 x 21¾ .... (671)   139

1967

Landscape, gouache, 20½ x 17 .... (870)   1,200

La Baule: The Beach Huts, (1945), watercolor,
10 x 16¾ .... (987)   600

Le Ranelagh, (1945), watercolor and gouache,
7¼ x 10¼ .... (901)   600

At the Casino, gouache, 23¾ x 25¾ .... (874)   380

Snowy Landscape, watercolor, 10 x 16¼ .... (926)   600

Nude with a Pink Sofa, gouache, 10 x 11¼ .... (919)   452

On the Beach, watercolor, 7 x 5¼ .... (956)   44

1968–July 1969

Autumn Bouquet, pastel, 18¾ x 11¾ .... (1075)   270

The Apples, pastel, 6¾ x 18¼ .... (1162)   280

The Pink Shrimps, gouache, 13¼ x 17¾ .... (1174)   920

At the Beach, watercolor, 6¾ x 5¼ .... (1066)   50

Sailboats in Provence, gouache, 14 x 19¾ .... (1200)   1,000

Riverside, watercolor, 21¼ x 17½ .... (1203)   1,041

Landscape, gouache, 21 x 17 .... (1061)   650

PAINTINGS

1961–1962

Landscape, 21¼ x 29 .... (9)   540

1963

Landscape, 1931, 17½ x 21¼ .... (246) $ 220

Snow Effect, 21¼ x 29 .... (251)   230

Seashore, 13 x 21¾ .... (258)   860

Couple of Dancers, 21¾ x 13 .... (198)   820

On the Beach, 25¾ x 32 .... (79)   3,254

1964

The Harbor, 1929, on cardboard, 13 x 21¾ .... (404)   210

An Estate at Chevreuse, on board, 9½ x 13 .... (471)   1,017

The Departure, 1948, 32 x 39½ .... (354)   4,000

The Towboat, 26 x 40½ .... (395)   640

1965

Nude with a Hat, 1927, on panel, 13 x 9½ .... (532)   280

Nude Seated on an Armchair, 32 x 39½ .... (564)   2,800

The Pontoons, 1929, 18¼ x 22 .... (628)   435

The Pleasure Boat, 13 x 18¼ .... (532)   360

View of a Harbor, on board, 16 x 9 .... (535)   608

Beach, 13 x 21¾ .... (567)   1,356

Winter Landscape, 23¾ x 32 .... (552)   290

The Republican Guard at the Racecourse,
23¾ x 29 .... (617)   3,277

1966

On the Beach, 25¾ x 32 .... (798)   2,599

Landscape, 25¾ x 32 .... (798)   2,034

1967

The Two Girl Friends, on cardboard, 13 x 18¼ .... (987)   1,400

At the Races, 18¼ x 21¾ .... (873)   520

At the Races, 17½ x 25 .... (1006)   1,194

The Banks of the River Seine, 13 x 18¼ .... (1007)   320

Still Life with a Fir Cone, 23¼ x 35½ .... (888)   1,382

The Floods, (1964), 32¼ x 39½ .... (841)   3,300

1968–July 1969

Still Life with Pineapples, 31¼ x 25 .... (1187)   1,227

Still Life with Pineapples, 32¼ x 25¾ .... (1018)   1,000

Still Life with a Lemon, 15 x 21¾ .... (1127)   2,093

The Regattas, 24 x 24 .... (1037)   1,420

On the Beach in Normandy, on cardboard,
10¾ x 14¼ .... (1084)   190

The Clown, on cardboard, 16¼ x 12¾ .... (1131)   300

Orpheus, on cardboard, 16¼ x 9½ .... (1200)   340

Model Resting, 15½ x 24½ .... (1109)   960

Reclining Nude, 1944, 28¾ x 36½ .... (1208)   6,500

Composition, wax paint on canvas, 24 x 19¾ .... (1230)   1,160

Fair-Haired Model, 1942, 25½ x 21½ .... (1231)   750

On the Beach, 32 x 25¾ .... (1238)   1,000

Dance, on cardboard, 16¾ x 9½ .... (1238)   520

Bernard Buffet

(1928–   )

Birthplace: Paris, France. Begins to paint at the age of ten.

1944 Attends the Ecole des Beaux-Arts. First exhibition is organized by the bookkeeper Guy Weelen.

1946 Takes part in the Salon des Moins de Trente Ans, Paris.

1947 Takes part in the Salon des Indépendants, Paris.

1948 Wins the Prix de la Critique. Exhibition at the Galerie St. Placide, Paris. A contract with David, the art dealer, leads to a rise in the price of his paintings. Paints the "Passion" scenes and the "Horrors of War." Leaves Paris to stay in Brittany and Vaucluse.

1949 Exhibition at the Galerie Drouant-David, Paris, where he gains a great success.

1950 Exhibition at the Kleemann Gallery, New York.

1952 Exhibition at the Knoedler Gallery, New York.

1954 Exhibition at the Drouant-David Gallery, Paris ("Nudes" and "Bestiary").

1957 Several exhibitions in Europe in London, Nuremberg, Dusseldorf, and Paris. Retrospective exhibition at the Niveau Gallery, New York.

1958 Retrospective exhibition at the Galerie Charpentier, Paris.

1959 Exhibits "Landscapes of New York" at the Galerie David et Garnier, Paris. Exhibition at the Findlay Gallery, Chicago.

1966 Retrospective exhibition at the Galerie Isy Brachot, Brussels.

1968 Shows "The Beaches" series at the Galerie David et Garnier, Paris. Produces *Le Cirque,* an important book of lithographs.

Sales

DRAWINGS

1961–1962

Standing Man, India ink, 25¾ x 19 . . . . (124) $ 96
Christ on the Cross,[1] 1954, black lead, 20½ x 27 . . . (158) 200
Sketch for the Passion, 1954, 21¼ x 29¼ . . . . (102) 390
The Horrors of War, two drawings, each
    69¼ x 39½ . . . . (2) 340

1963

Still Life, 1950, India ink, 20 x 26½ . . . . (208) 800

1964

Study for the Passion, 1953, 30 x 22 . . . . (449) 250
Study for "Le Sindon," 22 x 30 . . . . (449) 260
Thrush, pencil, 5 x 8¼ . . . . (455) 97

1965

Head, (1951), pencil, 8 x 6 . . . . (624) 359
Woman's Head, 1953, black stone and colored
    pencil, 27¾ x 21¾ . . . . (524) · 300
Sketch for "The Passion," 1954, pencil,
    29¼ x 18½ . . . . (541) 450
Christ, charcoal, 10¾ x 18½ . . . . (611) 420
The Sleeping Child, 1959, India ink, 19¾ x 25¾ . . . (559) 100
Landscape with a Cypress, pen, 19½ x 19½ . . . . . . (508) 220

[1] Inscribed "Sketch for the Passion."

1966

Self-Portrait, 1954, pen, 14¼ x 11¼ . . . . (648) $ 450
Still Life with a Bottle, 1948, India ink, 23 x 25 . . . (742) 330
The Lighthouse, 1952, black lead, 25½ x 19½ . . . . . (703) 1,000
Fishermen's Houses in Brittany, 1963, pen and
    watercolor, 19 x 25 . . . . (757) 2,073

1967

Still Life, 1951, India ink on paper laid down on
    canvas, 25¾ x 19¾ . . . . (893) 650
The Lighthouse, 1952, pencil, 25¼ x 39½ . . . . (985) 758
The Hanged Man, pencil, 11½ x 4¼ . . . . (967) 497
Nude with an Owl, 1954, charcoal, 71¼ x 51½ . . . . (926) 200
Street Scene, 1955, pencil, 19¾ x 25¾ . . . . (831) 400
Self-Portrait, 1955, pen, 15½ x 12 . . . . (951) 5,224
The Blue Coffepot, 1960, pen and watercolor,
    25 x 19¼ . . . . (963) 1,000
The Clown, 1967, India ink heightened with
    watercolor, 31 x 20¾ . . . . (986) 738

1968–July 1969

Scene in a Street, 1952, India ink, 18¾ x 25 . . . . . (1145) 375
Nude with an Owl, 1954, charcoal, 71¼ x 51½ . . . (1026) 600
Head of a Man, 20 x 10¾ . . . . (1054) 110
Head of a Man with a Basque Beret, India ink,
    16¼ x 10¼ . . . . (1205) 320
Portrait of a Man, pencil, 8¼ x 6¼ . . . . (1145) 225
Vase of Flowers, pencil, 6¾ x 3½ . . . . (1154) 110
The Beach, 9 x 13 . . . . (1223) 140
Woman's Head, 1953, colored pencil,
    19¾ x 25¼ . . . . (1227) 500
Woman Dressing, black pencil, 6½ x 4¾ . . . . (1243) 116
The Church, 1955, 25¾ x 19¾ . . . . (1268) 1,206
Tulips, 1958, India ink, 15 x 11 . . . . (1268) 580

WATERCOLORS

1961–1962

Clown, 1955, watercolor, 25¾ x 19¾ . . . . (93) 1,311
Still Life, 1960, gouache on paper mounted on
    canvas, 19½ x 25 . . . . (152) 1,700

1963

Still Life with Eggs, watercolor, 19¾ x 25¾ . . . . . . (311) 700

1964

Still Life with a Saucepan, 1955, watercolor,
    19½ x 25 . . . . (329) 1,100
The Fried Eggs, 1955, 19½ x 25¼ . . . . (366) 800
Portrait of Annabel, 1960, gouache, 25 x 19½ . . . . . (340) 1,040
Normandy, 1963, tempera, 19¾ x 25¼ . . . . (321) 1,200

1965

*Sunflowers in a Vase with a Melon Slice on a Red
    Background,* 1955, watercolor, 25¾ x 19½ . . . (602) 1,944
The Christmas Tree, watercolor and India ink,
    17 x 12¾ . . . . (559) 260

1966

Les Baux, gouache, 10 x 13 . . . . (824) 70

1967

Landscape, watercolor and India ink, 6¾ x 11¾ . . (919) 633

1968–July 1969

The Flying Ship of Jules Verne, watercolor,
    29 x 21 . . . . (1145) 350
Tulips in a Vase, colored pencil and gouache,
    25¾ x 19½ . . . . (1258) 1,200

PAINTINGS

1961–1962

Still Life, 35¼ x 51½ .... (30) $1,600
Still Life with a Jug, 1948, 18¼ x 13 .... (93) 1,426
Still Life, 1952, 9½ x 16¼ .... (71) 660
Flowers, 1954, 22 x 13 .... (18) 859
Flowers in a Blue Vase, 1961, 25¼ x 19¾ .... (64) 3,500
The Blue Orris, 1958, 31¾ x 25½ .... (8) 5,000
Still Life with a Skate, 21¼ x 25¾ .... (76) 2,300
Still Life with a Coffeepot, 1955, 38¼ x 50¼ .... (37) 5,800
Still Life with a Pike, 1955, 38¼ x 50¼ .... (64) 3,750
The Pan, 1953, 46 x 29 .... (76) 1,600
Glasses, Bottles, and Heads, 1952, 35¼ x 57¾ .... (171) 1,300
Landscape, 1951, 46¾ x 59¼ .... (93) 4,520
Riviera Scene, 1957, 38 x 21 .... (96) 7,500
Arc Castle, 1958, 38 x 51 .... (96) 4,000
Beaulieu-sur-Mer, 1958, 37¾ x 50¾ .... (8) 12,000
The Lighthouse, 25¾ x 39¾ .... (39) 780
The Lighthouse, 25¾ x 39¾ .... (95) 700
New York, 1958, 64 x 31¼ .... (96) 3,000
Silent Life, 19 x 27 .... (30) 840
The Forgotten Suicide, 1952, 25¼ x 21 .... (85) 1,700
The Eiffel Tower, 25¾ x 17¾ .... (142) 1,700
Libellula, 1959, 20¼ x 24¾ .... (111) 1,000
Front View of a Great Nude, 1948, 76¾ x 36¾ .... (111) 750
Portrait of a Man, 51½ x 38½ .... (213) 500
Toreador, 1958, 50½ x 37½ .... (64) 6,500

1963

Still Life, 1948, 17¾ x 13 .... (226) 1,349
Back View of a Nude, 1948, 79 x 38 .... (285) 1,696
Self-Portrait, 1949, 36½ x 25¾ .... (285) 1,243
Happy New Year, 1950, 19¼ x 29 .... (225) 1,750
Daisies in a Vase, 1951, oil on paper laid down on
    canvas, 25¼ x 19 .... (216) 1,508
Still Life with Vegetables, 1952, 9 x 15½ .... (208) 650
Vase of Flowers, 1954, 24 x 15 .... (299) 960
Skulls and Bowl, 1954, 38 x 76¾ .... (293) 1,200
Cheese, 1956, 39¼ x 31¾ .... (315) 3,016
The Ram, 1956, 19¾ x 25¾ .... (318) 300
Still Life (Plate, Wine Glass, and Flowers), 1957,
    21¼ x 17½ .... (275) 2,050
Portrait of Kiki, 1957, 46¼ x 35½ .... (312) 3,500
Still Life with Oranges, 1958, 25¼ x 17¾ .... (275) 1,900
Torero, 1960, 51 x 37½ .... (202) 5,000
Flowers, 1961, 25¼ x 21¼ .... (202) 4,000
Butterfly, 15¼ x 23¾ .... (183) 860

1964

Still Life with Two Bottles and a Revolver, 1949,
    23¾ x 31¾ .... (329) 600
Still Life with Butterflies, 1951, 25¾ x 29¾ .... (374) 2,300
Still Life with Artichokes, 1953, 31¾ x 39½ ...... (341) 2,120
The Tree, 1954, 77½ x 39 .... (399) 1,600
Flowers in a Gray Vase, 1954, 25¾ x 17¾ .... (329) 2,200
Still Life with a Backgammon Board, 1956,
    34¾ x 45½ .... (329) 2,000
Still Life with Flowers, Pistol, and Candle, 1956,
    28½ x 19¾ .... (438) 1,100
Seated Nude, 46 x 32 .... (337) 1,000
Still Life with Fish, 1957, 25¾ x 21¼ .... (472) 1,240
Still Life with Eggs, 1957, 23¾ x 36½ .... (378) 2,712

Portrait, 1958, 46 x 35½ .... (340) $1,500
Flowers, 1961, 25¾ x 20½ .... (448) 3,700
Roses, 1963, 21¼ x 25¾ .... (386) 1,800

1965

The Artist in His Studio, 1947, 59¼ x 79 .... (606) 4,250
Portrait of Camilo Aldao, 1949, 21½ x 14¾ ...... (624) 1,437
Still Life with a Decanter, 1949, 19¾ x 25¾ ..... (528) 1,160
The Farm, 1952, 32 x 39½ .... (552) 620
The Studio, 1955, 51½ x 38¼ .... (561) 3,000
The Beach, 1955, 19¾ x 25¾ .... (543) 2,263
Church Square, 1955, 35¼ x 58 .... (561) 4,000
Still Life, 25¾ x 21¼ .... (602) 3,209
The Clown, 1955, 59¼ x 39½ .... (613) 3,200
Blue Orris, 1958, 32 x 26 .... (637) 2,800
Still Life with Bread and Wine, 1960,
    21¼ x 31½ .... (606) 2,800
Flowers, 1961, 38¾ x 25¾ .... (494) 2,000

1966

Still Life with Fish, 1949, 18¼ x 25¼ .... (798) 2,260
Still Life with Melon, 1950, 18¼ x 25¾ .... (721) 950
The Fish Seller, 1951, 51½ x 64 .... (805) 1,000
Still Life, 19¾ x 25¾ .... (665) 1,800
Still Life with a Wild Boar's Head, 1952,
    34½ x 57¼ .... (784) 1,600
Still Life, 1952, 35¼ x 57¾ .... (811) 1,360
Still Life with a Cup of Fruit, 1954, 23¼ x 28 ..... (815) 1,437
Still Life with Flowers, 1955, 38¾ x 51½ .... (784) 1,600
Vase of Flowers, 1955, 36½ x 29¼ .... (681) 1,900
The Circus (The Wild Beast's Cage), 1955,
    122½ x 53 .... (744) 8,362
Bunch of Flowers, 1959, 25¾ x 19¾ .... (814) 1,720
Parliament, London, 1960, 31½ x 50¾ .... (760) 4,788
Rio di Palazzo, Venice, 1962, 39½ x 25¾ .... (816) 6,150

1967

Model in the Studio, 1949, 36¾ x 24 .... (939) 1,161
Still Life, 1952, 57¾ x 77 .... (967) 3,164
Still Life with Fish, 1952, 58½ x 76¼ .... (989) 2,500
Still Life with Fish, 18¼ x 25¼ .... (919) 1,582
Seated Woman in the Nude, 1953, 38 x 51½ ...... (976) 1,040
Big Boy, 1955, 29¼ x 36½ .... (963) 1,600
Two Women of Brittany, 1956, 51½ x 77 ...... (858) 1,800
View of Beaulieu, 1957, 34¾ x 50¾ .... (864) 7,000
The Parrot, 1958, 25 x 17¾ .... (870) 1,800
Vase of Flowers, 1958, 25¾ x 18 .... (870) 2,200
Arums in a Vase, 23¾ x 32 .... (901) 2,000

1968–July 1969

Still Life, 1948, 19 x 25 .... (1088) 800
Still Life with a Coffeepot, 1949, 29½ x 39½ ..... (1030) 1,250
Landscape, oil on paper, 19¾ x 25¾ .... (1127) 805
Bust of a Woman, 1950, on panel, 25¾ x 19¾ .... (1066) 1,100
Still Life, 1950, 9½ x 12¼ .... (1026) 840
Notre-Dame de Paris, 1952, 57½ x 45 .... (1066) 700
Still Life, 1952, 34¾ x 57¼ .... (1117) 960
Fish and Lemons, 1953, 19¾ x 25¾ .... (1200) 980
Skull with a Rosary, 1953, 25¾ x 18¼ .... (1127) 690
The Model in the Studio, 1953, 45¾ x 29 .... (1139) 920
Orris, 1955, 29 x 23¾ .... (1189) 2,000
Self-Portrait, 1955, 51 x 38½ .... (1145) 3,900
Café Scene, 1956, 51½ x 76¼ .... (1018) 2,500
Beaulieu Harbor, 1957, 34¾ x 50¾ .... (1126) 6,938

Still Life, 1957, 23¾ x 36½ .... (1127) $1,725
Still Life, 58½ x 77¼ .... (1174) 4,025
The Lighthouse, 1959, 25¾ x 39½ .... (1174) 1,978
Seated Young Lady, 1959, 62¼ x 31½ .... (1080) 2,750
BullFighter, 1961, 39½ x 32 .... (1174) 3,680
Mountain Ste. Victoire, 1963, 34¾ x 51 .... (1193) 4,956
Seated Nude, 36½ x 29 .... (1113) 2,000
Sprouted Onions and Empty Basket,
  23¾ x 36½ .... (1225) 2,600
Flowers, 1961, 25½ x 21½ .... (1248) 3,750
Still Life with Melons, 1953, 21¼ x 25½ .... (1248) 2,000
Landscape with Lighthouse, 1954, 41½ x 53½ ... (1268) 3,480

1968–July 1969
Landscape, 1916, pencil, 19½ x 13½ .... (1229) $ 800

WATERCOLORS

1964
Field in December, 1932, watercolor, 25 x 38½ ... (363) 2,700
The Old House, 1939, watercolor, 20½ x 24½ .... (329) 2,200
Autumn Landscape, watercolor, 25¾ x 31 .... (324) 3,500

1966
Yellow Violets, 1961–63, watercolor, 49 x 31 ...... (707) 4,500

1967
The Old Farm, 1931, watercolor, 14¾ x 21¼ ..... (860) 1,400

Charles Burchfield

(1893–1967)

Birthplace: near Salem, Ohio, U.S.

1912 Attends the Cleveland Institute of Art. (He has one-man shows here in 1916, 1917, 1921, and 1944.)

1916 First one-man show at the Sunwise Turn Bookshop, New York.

1918 After World War I, returns to Salem and works as a mill clerk. Turns his back on modernism and paints local landscapes in a rather conventional manner.

1920-30 Settles in Buffalo, New York, with his wife and his five children, working as a wallpaper designer. (Though he does not belong to the Regionalist group, he has often been regarded as one of them.)

1930 "Winter Twilight," one of his few oils, brings him fame and the opportunity to devote himself entirely to painting.

1930-64 Several one-man shows at the Rehn Galleries, New York.

1946 Given an award by the Carnegie Institute, Pittsburgh.

1949 Teaches at the University of Minnesota, Duluth.

1949-52 Teaches at the Art Institute of Buffalo, New York. Becomes a member of the American Academy of Arts and Letters and of the National Academy of Design.

1956 Major retrospective exhibition at the Whitney Museum of American Art, New York.

1963 One-man show at the State University of New York, Buffalo.

1967 Died.

Sales

DRAWINGS
1961-1962
The New Moon and the Old House, 1960, pencil
  and watercolor, 10½ x 16¾ .... (111) $ 800

Gustave Caillebotte

(1848–1894)

Birthplace: Paris, France. Inherits an important fortune at his father's death.

1873 Attends the Ecole Nationale des Beaux-Arts, Paris, in Bonnat's studio.

1875 Joins the Impressionist group.

1876-82 Participates in the second Impressionist exhibition and in the following ones in 1877, 1879, 1880, and 1882. Like all the Impressionists, prefers to work in the open but, unlike them, he is also interested in indoor scenes.

1882-94 Alters his style and withdraws from public activity. Stays in Normandy, painting still lifes and landscapes.

1887 Settles at Gennevilliers, near Paris, where he receives his friends Sisley, Monet, and Renoir.

1894 Died. (Caillebotte owned several Impressionist pictures and intended to donate them to the Musée du Luxembourg, Paris, but the state refused them. Part of this donation was to enter the Musée du Luxembourg many years later [in 1929], thanks to Clémenceau.)

Sales

WATERCOLORS
1964
Portrait of a Young Man, pastel, 17¾ x 15¾ ..... (329) $1,300

PAINTINGS
1961-1962
The Canal, 15¾ x 23¾ .... (114) 2,000

1963
The Park, on panel, 10¾ x 14 .... (310) 226
The Manor House and Its Garden, (1880-85),
  21½ x 26 .... (277) 3,839

Paris Under Snow, 18¼ x 25¾ . . . . (258) $1,000
The Boatman from Argenteuil, 25¾ x 21¼ . . . . (243) 900

1964
The Surroundings of Argenteuil, 21½ x 29¼ . . . . . . (461) 3,840
The Country House, on panel, 10 x 13½ . . . . (454) 276

1965
The Park, on panel, 10¾ x 14 . . . . (576) 339
Portrait of a Seated Woman, 1882, 32 x 25¾ . . . . (594) 8,250
A Boat on the River Seine, 19¾ x 25¾ . . . . (612) 3,800

1966
The Banks of a River, 1887, 25¾ x 21¼ . . . . (666) 5,600
The Blooming Rose Bush, 21¾ x 15 . . . . (666) 900
The Man with the Top Hat, (1870-75),
   21½ x 15 . . . . (686) 4,975
Child on a Sofa, 1885, 29 x 23¾ . . . . (811) 1,000
Portrait of Paul Hugo, 1878, 79 x 38½ . . . . (811) 3,360
The Painter Morot in His Studio, 17½ x 21¼ . . . . . (808) 5,804

1967
Still Life with Lobster, 23 x 28½ . . . . (940) 2,902
Vase of Lilacs, 25¾ x 21¼ . . . . (880) 9,950

1968–July 1969
The Artist in His Studio, 18 x 21¾ . . . . (1057) 10,000
Boats Near a Bridge, 15 x 18 . . . . (1080) 1,750
Riverside, 29 x 23¾ . . . . (1080) 5,500
The Sea, Seen From Villerville, 1882, 23¾ x 29 . . (1183) 5,000
View of a River, 28¾ x 23½ . . . . (1239) 12,480
The Park Alley, 1886, 32 x 25¾ . . . . (1254) 6,000

Alexander Calder

(1898-   )

Birthplace: Lawton, Pennsylvania, U.S.

1915-19 Enters the Stevens Institute of Technology, Hoboken, New Jersey.

1923 Attends the Art Students League, New York, for two years.

1926 Visits London and Paris. Attends the Atelier de la Grande Chaumière, Paris. Visits Latin America and India.

1927 Returns to the U.S.

1928 Back in Paris, he meets Pascin and exhibits at the Salon des Indépendants.

1929 Meets Louisa James (his future wife) on his return to the U.S.

1930 In Paris, visits Mondrian's studio and then starts his first experiments in abstraction. Meets Van Doesburg, Léger, Einstein, and Le Corbusier. Joins the Abstraction-Création group, Paris.

1932 First exhibition of his mobiles at the Galerie Vignon, Paris. Exhibits at Julian Levy's Gallery, New York. Returns to Paris via Spain, where he meets Miró.

1934-43 Exhibits yearly at the Pierre Matisse Gallery, New York.

1940 First exhibition of jewelry at the Marian Willard Gallery, New York.

1943 Exhibition at the Museum of Modern Art, New York.

1946 Exhibition at the Galerie Louis Carré, Paris.

1948 Travels to Brazil and exhibits in Rio de Janeiro and São Paulo.

1950 One-man shows at the Galerie Maeght, Paris, and at the Gallery of Contemporary Arts, Washington, D.C.

1952 Wins an award at the Venice Biennial.

1954 Exhibits his gouaches at the Cahiers d'Art, Paris.

1955 Retrospective exhibition at the Curt Valentin Gallery, New York.

1958 Creates mobiles for the Brussels World's Fair, for UNESCO in Paris, and for Idlewild International Airport, New York.

1959 Exhibits large stabiles at the Galerie Maeght, Paris.

1962 One-man show at the Perls Galleries, New York. Exhibition at the Tate Gallery, London.

1964 Exhibition at the Guggenheim Museum, New York.

1965 Exhibition at the Musée National d'Art Moderne, Paris.

1966-68 Exhibitions of his gouaches at the Perls Galleries, New York.

The artist usually spends six months at Roxbury, Connecticut, and the other half of the year in his house at Saché, France.

Sales

DRAWINGS

1963
Symbols, 1961, India ink, 14¾ x 22 . . . . (216) $ 247

1965
The Circus, 1932, ink, 29¾ x 21¾ . . . . (541) 900

1966
Composition, 1941, India-ink wash, 18¾ x 25 . . . . . (651) 450
Pyramids, 1953, India ink, 29 x 42¾ . . . . (689) 553

1967
On Paul's Cathedral Grows a Tree, 1944, India
   ink, 11¼ x 10¼ . . . . (889) 650

1968–July 1969
Composition, 1953, pen and color wash,
   29¾ x 40 . . . . (1059) 1,115
Composition, 1933, India ink and gouache,
   31 x 23 . . . . (1096) 1,380
Red Sun, 1965, India ink and gouache,
   29¾ x 42¾ . . . . (1134) 944
Composition in Black, Yellow, and Red, 1967,
   India ink and gouache, 23 x 31 . . . . (1134) 944

WATERCOLORS

1961-1962
Moon and Stars, 1947, watercolor and gouache,
   22¾ x 30¾ . . . . (111) 475
Abstraction, 1946, watercolor, 18½ x 15 . . . . (152) 400
Composition, 1953, gouache, 30 x 42 . . . . (75) 790
Composition in Black, Red, Yellow, and Green,
   gouache, 29¼ x 43 . . . . (70) 869

Composition, gouache, 30¾ x 22¼ .... (129) $ 494
Constellations, gouache, 15 x 22 .... (129) 494
Composition, 1961, gouache, 29¾ x 41¼ .... (129) 961

1963
Aboriginal Figure, 1944, gouache, 30¾ x 22¾ ..... (290) 325
Composition in Blue and Black, 1953, gouache,
  29¼ x 40 .... (315) 494
Abstraction, 1961, gouache, 28¾ x 41½ .... (272) 500
Butterfly, 1961, gouache and India ink, 15 x 22 ... (217) 283
Pagoda, 1961, gouache and India ink, 22 x 30 ..... (217) 384

1964
Figs, 1964, gouache, 29¾ x 42¼ .... (386) 420
Red Poppies, gouache, 29¾ x 42¼ .... (480) 240

1965
Composition in Red and Black, 1961, watercolor,
  21½ x 30 .... (582) 442
Red on Black, 1961, gouache, 23 x 30 .... (624) 691
Composition, watercolor, 19¾ x 26 .... (627) 300

1966
Dream Figments, 1964, gouache, 29¾ x 42¾ ...... (751) 967
Gril with Black Moon, 1965, gouache,
  41½ x 29¾ .... (747) 360
Constellations, 1964, gouache, 22 x 29¾ .... (689) 442

1967
The Universe, 1961, gouache and watercolor,
  29¾ x 41¾ .... (985) 830
The Creation, 1961, gouache and watercolor,
  29¾ x 41¾ .... (985) 853
Composition, 1964, watercolor, 42¼ x 29¼ .... (923) 600

1968–July 1969
Composition, 1953, gouache and India ink,
  42 x 28¾ .... (1189) 760
Composition, 1963, tempera, 11¾ x 9½ .... (1214) 608
Constellations, 1964, gouache, 22 x 29¾ .... (1145) 650
Black Disks, 1964, gouache, 29½ x 41½ .... (1134) 826
Planets, 1965, watercolor and India ink,
  29¾ x 43 .... (1185) 1,040
Composition, watercolor, gouache, and India ink,
  21¾ x 29 .... (1255) 1,140
Black and Red Composition, 1955, gouache,
  brush, and India ink, 24 x 18 .... (1272) 672

PAINTINGS

1966
Yellow Snake, 1966, 41½ x 29¾ .... (747) 640

1967
Splotchy, 27¼ x 53½ .... (963) 2,500

1968–July 1969
Smeary, 48¼ x 70½ .... (1080) 1,900
Circus Scene, 25¾ x 25¾ .... (1145) 2,000
Composition, 47¼ x 52½ .... (1018) 3,000

Charles Camoin

(1879–1965)

Birthplace: Marseilles, France. His inclination to paint is encouraged by his father (a decorator).

1898-99 Travels to Paris after his father's death. Attends the Ecole des Beaux-Arts, in Gustave Moreau's studio, and meets Matisse, Manguin, Marquet, and Rouault.

1899-02 Meets Cézanne and keeps up a correspondence with him until his death.

1903 Exhibition at the Galerie Berthe Weil, Paris.

1905 Pictures are shown in the famous Fauves' room at the Salon d'Automne, along with those of Matisse, Vlaminck, Derain, Marquet, and Van Dongen. Thanks to Signac, discovers St. Tropez (a fishing harbor in the south of France) and buys a house in the village.

1910 One-man show at the Shames Gallery, Frankfurt.

1912-13 Travels through Morocco with Matisse and Marquet. Takes part in the Armory Show, New York.

1914-18 Comes under the influence of Renoir and Bonnard. Spends summers at St. Tropez and winters in his Montmartre studio, Paris.

1945 One-man show at the Galerie Charpentier, Paris. (Catalog preface by Colette.)

1955 Wins the Prix du Président de la République at the Menton Biennial.

1958 Retrospective exhibition at the Galerie Bernheim, Paris.

1960 Takes part in the exhibition "Contemporary French Masters 1960," Chicago.

1965 Died, Paris.

1966 Retrospective exhibition at the Musée des Beaux-Arts, Marseilles.

Sales

DRAWINGS

1963
Portrait of a Young Lady, charcoal, 11¾ x 8¾ .... (188) $ 130

1965
Nude Combing Her Hair, pen, 10¼ x 8 .... (547) 290

1968–July 1969
The Ornamental Lake, black lead, 5¼ x 6¾ ..... (1227) 120
Young Man with a Red Scarf, 11¾ x 8¾ .... (1234) 100
The Park .... (1238) 186

WATERCOLORS

1961–1962
Young Lady on a Sofa, pastel, 12¼ x 16 .... (9) 300
The Moulin de la Galette, watercolor, 19 x 12¼ ... (157) 160

1963
The Woman with a Necklace, pastel, 11¾ x 9 ..... (242) 90

1964
Bust of a Young Lady, pastel, 4¾ x 3¾ .... (323) 56
Head of a Woman, pastel, 11½ x 8¾ .... (379) 190
Vase of Flowers, pastel, 6¼ x 7¾ .... (466) 320

1965

Woman on a Sofa, pastel, 12¼ x 16 . . . . (611) $ 640

The Flower Beds, pastel, 7½ x 10¼ . . . . (516) 320

1966

Bare-Breasted Young Woman, Her Arms Raised,
    pastel, 23¾ x 17¾ . . . . (819) 1,300

Portrait of a Woman, watercolor, 9½ x 8 . . . . (687) 66

Young Lady with an Easel, pastel, 5¼ x 6¾ . . . . . . (758) 146

Le Poilu, pastel, 8 x 6 . . . . (669) 190

Path in the Country, pastel, 9½ x 13 . . . . (742) 400

The Woman with the Necklace, pastel, 9 x 11¾ . . . (824) 440

1967

The Woman with the Necklace, (1915), pastel,
    12 x 9¼ . . . . (912) 860

The Young Lady in a Blue Hat, pastel,
    12¼ x 9½ . . . . (935) 350

St. Tropez, watercolor, 4¼ x 7¼ . . . . (961) 240

1968–July 1969

Young Woman with Arms Folded, pastel,
    18¾ x 23 . . . . (1115) 660

Portrait of a Woman, pastel, 19 x 15 . . . . (1119) 500

Bust of a Young Woman, pastel, 10¼ x 9½ . . . . . . (1172) 340

The Harbor, pastel, 8 x 10¾ . . . . (1220) 380

The Footbridge, pastel, 11¾ x 9 . . . . (1238) 1,620

PAINTINGS

1961–1962

Bathers on the Beach, 18¼ x 25¾ . . . . (56) 1,240

Window Open, Looking Out to the Harbor, on
    paper, 13 x 10 . . . . (68) 560

A Julot, 6½ x 9 . . . . (12) 100

The Place Clichy, 25¾ x 32 . . . . (71) 860

*Portrait of Marie Pesson (Actress at the Odeon
    Theater),* 24 x 19¾ . . . . (35) 120

Young Girl Seated, 32 x 25¾ . . . . (80) 800

Near St. Tropez, 25¼ x 31½ . . . . (44) 1,300

Landscape, 29 x 36¼ . . . . (143) 859

The Estérel, 1954, 36¼ x 29 . . . . (93) 1,266

1963

The Village, 1902, 10 x 13¼ . . . . (255) 548

The Bay of St. Tropez, 19¾ x 24 . . . . (293) 1,040

Open Window, Looking Out to the Harbor,
    14 x 10¾ . . . . (192) 630

The Creek, 24 x 27¾ . . . . (199) 1,840

River in a Park, 8¾ x 14 . . . . (258) 1,200

Still Life with Fruit, on cardboard, 7 x 9 . . . . (281) 407

Still Life with Table, 17½ x 21 . . . . (315) 713

1964

Flowers and Fruit, 21¼ x 25¾ . . . . (341) 2,100

Landscape at Oletta (Corsica), 18¼ x 21¾ . . . . . . (450) 720

*Interior with Madame Chantin and Madame
    Camoin,* 1920, 17¾ x 21 . . . . (454) 1,244

Springtime at Les Canubiers, 19¾ x 18¼ . . . . (373) 1,500

Landscape, 25¾ x 32 . . . . (401) 1,600

Still Life with Apples, 21¼ x 25¾ . . . . (380) 1,476

Landscape in Provence, 13 x 18¼ . . . . (441) 1,763

1965

The Square in the Sun, (1907), 25¾ x 32 . . . . (598) 2,140

The Square in the Sun, (1907), 25¾ x 32 . . . . (563) 1,300

Sailboat in the Harbor, (1908), 25¾ x 32 . . . . (553) 3,040

Harbor in the South of France, 21¾ x 18¼ . . . . . . (507) 1,100

Marseilles, 25¾ x 32 . . . . (532) 4,000

Surroundings of Nice, 25¾ x 32 . . . . (543) 2,122

The Garden of Pigonnet, 23¾ x 32 . . . . (613) 1,700

Bust of a Reclining Nude, on canvas laid down on
    panel, 5¾ x 6¼ . . . . (547) $ 500

Flowers in a Jug, 17½ x 14½ . . . . (582) 1,271

Vase of Flowers, 10¾ x 6¾ . . . . (627) 290

The Turkish Woman, 21¾ x 18¼ . . . . (563) 640

Still Life, 21¾ x 25¾ . . . . (526) 3,500

1966

Woman Reading, (1906-07), 29¾ x 25¾ . . . . (672) 1,100

Flowers in a Vase, 13 x 9½ . . . . (745) 904

Suburban Landscape, (1910), 12¾ x 19¼ . . . . (666) 1,000

Harbor in Provence, 15 x 21¾ . . . . (681) 1,500

Nude with a Green Shawl, 1926, 24 x 18¼ . . . . . . (824) 1,440

Under the Hedgerow, 25¾ x 32 . . . . (685) 2,200

Martigues Harbor . . . . (749) 1,900

Le Pilon du Roi at Aix-en-Provence,
    19¾ x 25¾ . . . . (798) 2,825

1967

The Child's Meal, 18¼ x 21¾ . . . . (857) 2,900

Lola Camoin and a Friend in a Provençal House,
    19¾ x 25¾ . . . . (976) 2,200

The Woman with a Green Shawl, 1926,
    24 x 18¼ . . . . (912) 1,820

Young Ladies with a Sunshade, 21¼ x 25¾ . . . . . . (919) 1,808

Menton Harbor, 25¾ x 32 . . . . (864) 2,850

Village at the Seaside, 20¾ x 25 . . . . (888) 2,764

St. Tropez Harbor, 25¾ x 32 . . . . (986) 3,198

St. Tropez Harbor, 23¾ x 29 . . . . (978) 5,500

St. Tropez Harbor, 10¾ x 18¼ . . . . (967) 1,989

The Vase of Windflowers, 21¾ x 15 . . . . (850) 1,560

Still Life, 15 x 21¾ . . . . (911) 1,400

Still Life, 25¾ x 32 . . . . (978) 4,400

Les Santons, on cardboard, 10¾ x 14 . . . . (1007) 460

Sitting Nude, 16¼ x 13 . . . . (874) 580

1968–July 1969

Gathering Apples, 21¼ x 25¾ . . . . (1174) 3,220

Landscape at Gassin, 28½ x 41½ . . . . (1127) 4,830

Landscape of the Estérel, 18¼ x 21¾ . . . . (1113) 2,000

Marseilles, the Old Harbor, 21¾ x 38 . . . . (1049) 5,000

Fishing Boat in the Harbor, 26 x 32 . . . . (1208) 6,000

Surroundings of St. Tropez, 16¼ x 25¾ . . . . (1127) 5,865

Landscape, 19¾ x 24 . . . . (1028) 2,300

Nude with a Green Scarf, 1926, 24 x 18¼ . . . . . . (1060) 2,560

Nude with a Scarf, 1937, 36½ x 23¾ . . . . (1049) 2,500

Smiling Little Girl in a Blue Bodice, 14 x 10¾ . . . (1196) 300

Portrait of a Child, 8¼ x 6½ . . . . (1213) 500

Young Woman Sleeping, 21¼ x 25¾ . . . . (1117) 4,800

The Woman in a White Dress, 35½ x 23 . . . . (1116) 2,200

Back View of a Nude, 24 x 18¼ . . . . (1115) 1,500

Nude in a Landscape, 9½ x 13 . . . . (1189) 1,140

Nude with a Red Cushion, 32 x 25¾ . . . . (1116) 2,800

Portrait of a Woman, 25¾ x 19¾ . . . . (1019) 840

Still Life with Fruit, 13 x 16¼ . . . . (1127) 1,886

Still Life with a Basket of Flowers, 16¼ x 13 . . . . (1051) 2,000

Vase of Flowers, 21 x 14¾ . . . . (1213) 1,960

Jug with Flowers and Fruit Stand, 25¾ x 21¾ . . . (1184) 3,640

Windflowers in a Blue Vase, 10¾ x 8¾ . . . . (1051) 1,900

Vase of Windflowers, 19¾ x 14½ . . . . (1113) 2,300

Still Life with a Spanish Jug, 25¾ x 32 . . . . (1117) 3,600

Still Life, 25¾ x 32 . . . . (1181) 4,100

Still Life with a Teapot, 22 x 17¾ . . . . (1221) 2,160

*Still Life with Fruit and Flowers ("Mauve
    Harmony"),* 25 x 31¼ . . . . (1226) 4,600

Still Life with Fruit, 27½ x 9 .... (1231) $5,750
Woman Reading, (1905), 25½ x 19¼ .... (1235)   13,500
Gathering Mimosa, 21¼ x 25¾ .... (1262)   5,000
In the Garden, 21¾ x 18¼ .... (1262)   4,100
Bunch of Flowers, (1919), 18¼ x 15 .... (1268)   3,944

Massimo Campigli

(1895–1971)

Birthplace: Florence, Italy.

1919   Sent to Paris by an Italian newspaper, he lives in the city for nine years and begins to paint under the influence of Cubism.

1928   Returns to Italy. Visits the Etruscan Museum of the Villa Giulia. Executes a series of "rustic" pictures painted in Romania.

1929   One-man show at the Galerie Jeanne Bûcher, Paris. Many exhibitions follow—in Paris, Milan, New York, Venice, London, and in Holland.

1931   Executes a mural in Milan, Italy, where he spends several years. Frequent trips to Paris and New York.

1937   Settles in Paris for a time.

1939   Executes a fresco at the University of Padua.

1940   After a stay in Milan, settles in Venice during World War II.

1946   Exhibition in an Amsterdam museum.

1948   The Venice Biennial assigns an entire room to his work.

1957   Exhibits at the Galerie de France, Paris.

1971   Died, St. Tropez, France.

Sales

DRAWINGS

1961–1962

Two Young Girls with Flowers, 1950, pencil, 13 x 17 .... (20) $ 600

Young Woman, Her Hands Crossed, 1959, India ink, 14¾ x 10¾ .... (110)   240

1963

Two Young Ladies, 1952, charcoal, 17¾ x 13 ..... (208)   275

1968–July 1969

Self-Portrait in Chinese Costume, 1942, pencil, 15½ x 9 .... (1214)   480

PAINTINGS

1961–1962

Weavers, 26 x 32 .... (149)   8,848

Composition on a Light Background, 1961, 32 x 39½ .... (149)   4,108

Head of a Little Girl, 12¾ x 16¾ .... (14) $1,422
The Labyrinth, 31½ x 39¼ .... (145)   4,740
The Boat, 1931, 31 x 42¼ .... (20)   13,430
Vine Harvest, 1940, 14 x 20½ .... (69)   4,266
Woman's Head, 1941, fresco, 10¼ x 13 ...... (69)   2,212
Two Seated Women, 1947, 25¾ x 19½ .... (96)   2,800
Walk, 1951, 21¼ x 25¾ .... (14)   2,686
Women on a Sofa, 1952, 34¾ x 45½ .... (70)   8,690
Women by the Staircase, 1955, 12¾ x 19¾ .... (44)   950
Walk, 1956, 25¾ x 36½ .... (69)   3,634
Decorated Dress, 1956, 35½ x 15 .... (88)   4,945

1963

Two Women Fetching Water, 1929, 28½ x 23¾ ... (217)   6,780
Figure with a Vase, 28 x 17½ .... (180)   1,700
Woman, 1962, 16¾ x 15 .... (202)   1,700

1964

Biography, 1931, 50¼ x 38½ .... (367)   6,357
Woman at the Fountain, 1925, 25 x 20½ .... (368)   4,146
Portrait of Signora Campigli, 24½ x 19½ .... (479)   2,285
The Seven Women and the Chair, 1956, 22 x 15¾ .... (435)   2,560
The Russian Mountain, 1958, 48 x 63¾ .... (437)   8,800
Composition with a Figure, 1963, 15 x 18¼ .... (439)   1,760

1965

The Staircase, 1964, 21¼ x 24 .... (616)   3,040
Four Women's Heads, 1954, 19½ x 14¾ .... (535)   1,520

1966

Self-Portrait, 1927, 18½ x 15 .... (802)   7,040
Figure, 1965, 15¼ x 21¼ .... (802)   3,200
Standing Woman, 1957, oil and gouache on paper, 19½ x 9 .... (734)   339
Two Figures, 1960, 13 x 16¼ .... (698)   2,720

1967

Woman Playing the Guitar, 1927, 37½ x 29 .... (882)   10,880
Composition with Figures, 1959, 26½ x 19¾ ...... (882)   4,800
Woman on a Red Background, 1963, 36¾ x 29 .... (962)   6,400

1968–July 1969

Spectators at a Bullfight, 1931, 32 x 39½ .... (1231)   6,000

Carlo Carrà

(1881–1966)

Birthplace: Quargnento, Italy. From the age of twelve earns his living by doing decorative paintings. Attends the Brera Art School, Milan.

1900   First trip to Paris. Does decorative paintings for the World's Fair, Paris.

1909   Meets Marinetti and Boccioni.

1910   With Boccioni, Russolo, Ballà, and Severini, signs the "Manifeste des peintres futuristes."

1911	Second trip to Paris, where he meets Apollinaire, Modigliani, and Picasso. Comes under the influence of Cubism.
1912-13	Participates in the Futurist exhibitions of Paris, London, and Berlin. Meets Stravinsky and Diaghilev.
1915	Parts from the Futurists. Meets Di Chirico in Ferrara and is influenced by him.
1917	Joins Di Chirico's Metaphysical painting.
1919	Writes the book *La Pittura Metafisica*.
1925	Participates in the third Rome Biennial.
1932	Trips to Munich, Prague, and Dresden.
1937	Trips to Algiers, Malta, and Palermo.
1950	Participates in the Venice Biennial.
1966	Died.

Sales

DRAWINGS

1968–July 1969

The Model, 1917, pen, 4¾ x 7¾ . . . . (1214) $1,040
The Model, 1917, charcoal, 15¾ x 10¾ . . . . (1214) 3,680

WATERCOLORS

1961–1962

Venice, watercolor, 10 x 15½ . . . . (69) 395

PAINTINGS

1961–1962

Zinnie, 1939, 22½ x 18¼ . . . . (149) 5,056
Landscape in Blue, 20½ x 27 . . . . (145) 3,950
Snow in Paris, 1934, 17¾ x 23¼ . . . . (75) 4,266
A Boy on the River, 1935, 14 x 19 . . . . (69) 695
A House at the Seaside, 1950, 15¾ x 19¾ . . . . (14) 2,449
Landscape, 1954, 20 x 23¾ . . . . (69) 2,054
Little Stream, 1956, 19¾ x 27¾ . . . . (15) 1,817

1964

The Riders of Revelation, 1908, 14½ x 37¼ . . . . (453) 4,422
The Seashore with Boats, 11 x 13 . . . . (454) 691
Seascape, 1960, 24 x 19¾ . . . . (435) 2,560

1965

Suburban Café, 1914, collage, 18¼ x 12¾ . . . . (616) 12,000
Landscape, 1931, on board, 14½ x 20¾ . . . . (525) 6,800
Seascape, 1954, 19¾ x 27¾ . . . . (616) 6,720
Lacustrine Landscape, 1922, 13½ x 19¾ . . . . (616) 7,600

1966

Bathers, 1944, 15¾ x 19¾ . . . . (802) 7,040
Seascape, 1961, 15¾ x 19¾ . . . . (802) 4,480
Seascape, (1963), 12¾ x 19¾ . . . . (665) 1,100

1967

Dervio Lake, 1943, 15 x 21¼ . . . . (962) 7,040
Seascape, 1962, 19¾ x 23¾ . . . . (962) 6,080
Landscape at San Gaudenzio di Varallo, 1927,
  27¾ x 35½ . . . . (882) 14,400

Felice Casorati

(1886–1963)

Birthplace: Novara, Italy.

1907	Studies music and painting in Padua. Exhibits a portrait of his sister at the Venice Biennial.
1908-11	Stay in Naples. Comes under the influence of modern art and joins the Italian Neo-Classicist group.
1918	With other artists, including Carrà and Russolo, sets up an art school in Turin.
1920	Takes part in the activity of the Italian avant-garde and devotes himself to pictural construction and color problems.
1937	Laureate of the Carnegie Foundation, Pittsburgh.
1963	Died, Turin.

Sales

WATERCOLORS

1961–1962

Woman Asleep, tempera, 9½ x 13½ . . . . (14) $ 213

1964

The Milky Way, 1914, tempera, 69 x 53¾ . . . . (461) 6,720
Nude with a Landscape, tempera, 23¾ x 19¾ . . . . . (435) 1,920

1966

The Movies, 1953, tempera on canvas,
  34¼ x 25¾ . . . . (802) 8,000

PAINTINGS

1961–1962

Nude, 15¾ x 30½ . . . . (14) 2,528
Still Life, 21¾ x 29¾ . . . . (69) 3,792
Nude, 14½ x 30 . . . . (70) 3,476
Nude on a Blue Background, 19¾ x 26½ . . . . (145) 2,212
The Siesta, 1926, on cardboard, 20½ x 16¾ . . . . . . (149) 5,056

1963

Landscape of Tuscany, 1925, on board,
  11 x 11¾ . . . . (184) 548

1964

Nude with a Fur, 1930, on panel, 20½ x 14½ . . . . . (461) 5,600
The Sleepers in Blue, 29¾ x 35½ . . . . (437) 7,200

1965

Sitting Nude, (1945), on board, 19¾ x 15¾ . . . . (616) 7,200

1966

Woman Thinking, 1952, on cardboard,
  19½ x 14½ . . . . (802) 4,800
Le Torri (Reclining Nude), 1956, 51½ x 35½ . . . . . (802) 14,400
The Green Apples, 1962, 19¾ x 15¾ . . . . (802) 8,000

1967

Nude with Cards, 1954, 20¼ x 31½ . . . . (962) 11,200

Mary Cassatt

(1845–1926)

Birthplace: Pittsburgh, Pennsylvania, U.S.

1851 Travels through Europe with her parents.

1856-65 Studies at the Pennsylvania Academy of Fine Arts.

1872 Stays in Italy, Spain, Holland, and Belgium. Sends her picture "At the Balcony" to the Salon, Paris.

1877 Settles with her family in Paris. Degas invites her to join the Impressionist group.

1879 Her Impressionist pictures are shown in the U.S. at the Associated American Artists Gallery, New York. Participates in the exhibitions of the Impressionist group, except for the one of 1882.

1883 Slightly influenced by Japanese art.

1886 Participates in the eighth and last Impressionist exhibition, together with Degas, Gauguin, Guillaumin, Pissaro, Signac, Seurat, and the rest.

1890 With Degas, visits an exhibition of Japanese prints and is strongly influenced by Japanese art.

1891 First one-man show at the Galerie Durand-Ruel, Paris.

1892 Stays at Cap d'Antibes in the south of France.

1893 Exhibition at the Galerie Durand-Ruel, Paris.

1898-99 Stay in the U.S.

1904 Made Chevalier of the Legion of Honor.

1914 Wins the Gold Medal of Honor of the Pennsylvania Academy.

1914-18 Spends World War I at Grasse in the south of France. Failing sight forces her to give up painting.

1926 Died, Mesnil-Théribus, Oise.

Sales

DRAWINGS

1961–1962

Figures, pencil, 4 x 7¼ .... (97) $ 50
Portrait of a Young Lady, red chalk, 11 x 8¾ ...... (85)   675

1963

At the Theater, 3¾ x 5½ .... (186)   210
Woman Wearing a Hat, 1895, black lead, 12 x 9 .. (186)   370
Dog's Head, black lead, 4 x 7¼ .... (278)   64
Maternity, pencil, 9 x 8 .... (305)   230

1964

Women's Heads, pencil, 4 x 7 .... (438)   275
Head of a Young Lady, colored pencil,
    11¾ x 9¼ .... (354)   1,250
The Two Friends, black lead, 5¼ x 7½ .... (376)   300

1965

Mother and Her Children, charcoal, 33¾ x 27¼ .. (489)   1,900
Portraits of Women, two drawings, pencil,
    5¾ x 3¼ and 8¾ x 5¾ .... (494)   250
Espalier, pencil and pastel, 11 x 10 .... (541)   2,800

1966

Woman and Child, 7¾ x 4½ .... (711)   220
Portrait of a Young Lady, black pencil, 9 x 6¾ ... (829)   140
Woman's Head, (1880), pencil, 5 x 7½ .... (721)   350
Heads, pencil, 7 x 6½ .... (805)   225
Maternity, charcoal, 17¾ x 21¼ .... (665)   600

1967

Mother and Her Child, (1899), pencil and
    watercolor, 9 x 7¼ .... (881) $1,050

1968–July 1969

Mother and Child, pencil, 7 x 4½ .... (1231)   450
Child's Head, pastel, 8 x 8¼ .... (1234)   2,280
Study for "The Hairdressing," (1890–91),
    8½ x 5½ .... (1240)   2,400
Mother and Child, pencil on buff paper,
    7¾ x 6¼ .... (1248)   300
Studies of Women, two drawings, pencil,
    14¾ x 2¾ and 3¾ x 3¼ .... (1248)   300
Studies of Women, two drawings, 6 x 5 and
    3¾ x 5¼ .... (1248)   475
Mother with Her Child, (1895), pencil, 8¼ x 6 ... (1272)   7,680

WATERCOLORS

1961–1962

The Two Sisters, pastel, 25¾ x 32 .... (167)   21,200
Woman and Child, watercolor, 13½ x 19¼ .... (167)   1,840
Maternity, (1890), watercolor, 12¾ x 9 .... (93)   2,396
Maternity, (1893), watercolor, 18¼ x 13½ .... (93)   2,147
A Mother, Her Little Daughter, and Her Baby,
    1895, pastel, 36½ x 29 .... (156)   10,000
Study for a Woman, Puffed Red Bodice, 1895,
    pastel, 27 x 20½ .... (71)   8,800
*Side View of the Bust of a Woman Carrying a
    Child in Her Arms,* 1905, pastel, 21¼ x 25¾ .. (167)   930
Two Young Ladies, 1910, pastel, 18¼ x 18¼ .... (73)   4,400
*A Young Lady Wearing a Blue Bodice and a
    Little Girl Wearing a Red Dress,* 1913, pastel,
    30¼ x 25¾ .... (156)   7,620

1963

The Jardin du Luxembourg, watercolor, 18 x 15 .. (284)   1,230
Portrait of Suzanne, 1891, pastel on paper
    mounted on board, 16¾ x 11½ .... (277)   14,258
Portrait of a Little Girl, pastel on gray paper,
    17½ x 14¼ .... (245)   15,081
Maternity, pastel, 24 x 16¾ .... (245)   9,316
A Mother and Her Child, pastel, 32 x 25¾ .... (277)   8,226
Portrait of a Woman, watercolor, 10½ x 7½ ...... (202)   1,500
Baby Stretching, watercolor, 11½ x 9½ .... (253)   400
Child's Head, pastel, 24 x 18 .... (186)   800
A Mother and Her Child, pastel, 32 x 25¾ .... (186)   1,600

1964

The Reading (A Mother and Her Child), 1898,
    pastel, 18 x 25 .... (453)   20,730
A Mother and Her Child, pastel, 28 x 23¼ .... (416)   11,609
Seated Young Lady, pastel, 25¼ x 19¾ .... (416)   6,081
A Mother and Her Child, watercolor, 17¾ x 13 ... (377)   3,051
The Woman in a Green Hat, watercolor,
    18½ x 12¾ .... (324)   850

1965

A Mother and Her Child, watercolor, 17¼ x 13 ... (489)   1,850
Maternity, pastel, 18¼ x 23¾ .... (546)   34,550
A Mother and Her Child, pastel, 28¾ x 22 .... (624)   38,696
The Woman with a Veil, pastel, 22 x 17½ .... (522)   4,700
The Little Girl with the White Hat, pastel,
    21 x 17 .... (633)   17,000

1966

Young Lady Holding a Little White Dog, pastel
    on gray paper laid down on canvas, 29 x 24 ... (776)   26,000

*Young Lady Wearing a Blue Bodice and Little
    Girl Wearing a Red Dress,* (1912-13), pastel,
    30 x 25 .... (776) $27,000
Dark-Haired Little Girl, pastel, 19¾ x 19 .... (686) 9,674
Naked Child, watercolor, 11¾ x 10 .... (742) 600
Portrait of Suzanne, 1891, pastel on paper laid
    down on board, 16¾ x 11½ .... (713) 14,500

1967
Woman and Child, watercolor, 16¼ x 11 .... (939) 3,870

1968–July 1969
Little Girl Seated in a Yellow Easy Chair, pastel,
    23 x 20 .... (1132) 21,240
Mother and Baby, 1899, pastel, 26 x 20½ .... (1068) 54,280
Maternity, (1881), pastel, 23¾ x 18¼ .... (1057) 84,000
Figure, 18 x 12½ .... (1248) 400

PAINTINGS

1961–1962
Little Girl Dressed in Pink, 25¾ x 21 .... (31) 7,689
Seated Woman Dressed in White, 1877,
    31¼ x 25¾ .... (128) 27,714
Woman's Head and Baby, 15 x 18¼ .... (71) 2,100
Side View of a Woman, 29 x 23¾ .... (156) 14,140

1963
Reading, 1898, 15 x 19½ .... (245) 7,678
The Lady with Gloves, 1900, 14 x 11 .... (210) 15,904
The Little Girl with the Japanese Doll,
    23¼ x 19 .... (277) 6,032

1964
Little Girl Coming Out of Her Bath, 25¾ x 20 .... (454) 13,820
Bust of a Child, 13¼ x 10¼ .... (416) 10,503

1965
Portrait of Madame Cordier, 1874, on panel,
    19 x 15¾ .... (539) 7,250
Maternity, 14½ x 16½ .... (553) 2,200
Little Girl with a Doll, 24 x 19¾ .... (553) 10,000
Bunch of Lilacs, 24 x 20 .... (610) 9,000

1966
Woman Holding a Little Girl on Her Knees,
    28½ x 23 .... (753) 49,334

1967
Two Women Painting in a Landscape, 1892,
    30¼ x 25 .... (860) 7,500
Portrait of a Young Girl, (1875), on canvas laid
    down on board, 15¾ x 12¾ .... (1006) 3,483
Vase of Lilacs, (1889), 23¾ x 18½ .... (940) 13,059
The Young Girl in a White Hat, 1908,
    24½ x 19¾ .... (954) 32,500

1968–July 1969
The Scottish Nurse, (1874), on panel, 12¾ x 10 .. (1187) 5,900
Woman's Head, (1900), 14 x 10¾ .... (1132) 6,608
Mother and Child, (1908), 27¾ x 23¾ .... (1176) 42,500
Study of a Woman, 14¾ x 16¼ .... (1138) 6,195
Portrait of a Little Girl, 1909, 18¼ x 15 .... (1176) 16,000
The Sewer, 21¼ x 21¼ .... (1224) 33,600
Woman's Head, (1900), 13½ x 10½ .... (1248) 4,800

Paul Cézanne

(1839–1906)

Birthplace: Aix-en-Provence, France.

1852-58 Studies at the Collège de Bourbon, where he meets
Emile Zola.

1859 Studies law at the university of Aix-en-Provence.
His father, a successful banker, buys a country
house called Le Jas de Bouffan.

1861 His father finally accepts the fact that Cézanne will
devote himself to painting. Settles in Paris and
attends the Académie Suisse, where he meets Pissarro and Guillaumin. As he is not admitted to
the Ecole des Beaux-Arts, he returns to Aix.

1862-64 Second stay in Paris. Meets Bazille, Monet, Sisley,
and Renoir, but still appreciates Delacroix and
Courbet above all.

1864-70 Spends half his time in Paris and the other half in
Aix. The Salon refuses his pictures every year.

1873-74 Comes under the influence of Pissarro and paints
many landscapes. Takes part in the first exhibition of the Impressionist group, thanks to
Pissarro.

1878 Unable to hold to the ideas of the Impressionists, he
leaves the movement.

1882 Settles down at Le Jas de Bouffan.

1886 Marries Hortense Fiquet. End of his friendship with
Zola. Inherits an important fortune at his father's
death.

1891 First attack of diabetes.

1892 Paints the famous series "Card Players," "Bathers,"
and "Mont Ste. Victoire."

1895 First one-man show at the Galerie Ambroise Vollard, Paris.

1899 Sells Le Jas de Bouffan but remains in Aix. Participates in the Salon des Indépendants, Paris.

1900 Begins to be famous in France and even abroad.

1904 Several of his pictures are shown in the Salon d'Automne, Paris. It is a triumph.

1905 Takes part in the Salon d'Automne and the Salon
des Indépendants, Paris. Finishes "Les Grandes
Baigneuses," one of his major works.

1906 Died, Provence.

Sales

DRAWINGS

1961–1962
Bull and Bullfighter, pencil, 8 x 4¾ .... (33) $ 330
Mont Ste. Victoire, pencil, 11¾ x 18½ .... (64) 2,600
Mont Ste. Victoire, pencil and watercolor,
    11¾ x 17½ .... (112) 11,533
Trees and Houses in Provence, (1883–87), pencil
    and watercolor, 10½ x 14 .... (128) 12,082

1963
Likely Study for "St. Anthony's Temptation,"
    pencil and watercolor, 6¾ x 7 .... (293) 1,440
Bust of a Woman, black lead, 5 x 3½ .... (293) 980
Nude, pencil, 9 x 5¼ .... (283) 1,650
Back View of a Seated Nude, (1862–68), charcoal,
    23¾ x 18¼ .... (277) 2,468
Men Angling, sepia ink, double sided, 7½ x 11¾ .. (277) 2,742
The Glade, pencil and watercolor, 12 x 19 .... (316) 5,500

1964

Study of Bathers, black lead, 8 x 5¼ . . . . **(466)** $1,100

Study of a Woman's Profile, (1871-72), black lead, 8 x 5 . . . . **(454)**   1,990

The Great Pine, black chalk and watercolor, 9½ x 16¼ . . . . **(458)**   4,933

Trees, pencil, 10 x 12¼ . . . . **(448)**   1,200

Fantastic Scene (recto), sepia ink, *Group of Figures* (verso), pencil, 4½ x 8 . . . . **(387)**   884

Portrait of Madame Cézanne and Studies of Clothes, pencil, 10½ x 8 . . . . **(454)**   6,634

1965

The Gully (recto), *Trees and Rocks* (verso), (1895-1900), watercolor and pencil, 11 x 18 . . . **(624)**   4,975

Studies for Trees, pencil and watercolor, double sided, 11 x 17½ . . . . **(629)**   4,643

Trees and Greenness, 1890-96, black chalk and watercolor, 16¾ x 12 . . . . **(629)**   20,314

The Trees, pencil and watercolor, 11 x 17 . . . . **(583)**   1,509

The Trees, pencil and watercolor, 11 x 17 . . . . **(617)**   1,107

Trees, pencil, 10 x 12 . . . . **(606)**   1,050

Study of a Landscape, pencil, 8¾ x 15 . . . . **(507)**   375

Fantastic Scene (recto), ink, *Group of Figures,* (verso), pencil, 4½ x 8 . . . . **(582)**   608

Book on a Table, Head of Cézanne's Son on the Right (recto), *Head of Cézanne's Son, About 12 Years Old* (verso), 4¾ x 8½ and 4½ x 6¾ . . . . **(512)**   1,220

Diana the Huntress, double sided, 7½ x 4½ . . . . . . **(512)**   760

Head of Little Paul Cézanne (recto), *Bather with His Arms Spread Out* (verso), 8½ x 4¾ . . . . . . **(512)**   1,620

1966

Bather with His Right Arm Raised, black lead, 11 x 6 . . . . **(741)**   900

Tree at Le Jas de Bouffan, black chalk and blue and yellow wash, 9 x 11¾ . . . . **(738)**   8,364

Tree at Le Jas de Bouffan, (1883-87), pencil and watercolor, 9 x 11¾ . . . . **(812)**   5,528

1967

Study of a Man's Head, (1886-68), charcoal, 11¾ x 9¼ . . . . **(985)**   2,086

Study of a Standing Man, (1865-70), charcoal, 11¼ x 7½ . . . . **(939)**   1,797

Landscape with Trees, (1895), pencil, 12 x 16¾ . . . **(889)**   1,200

1968–July 1969

Milon de Crotone, After Puget, pencil, 8½ x 5¼ . . . . **(1099)**   1,748

The Venus of Milo, pencil, 8 x 4 . . . . **(1099)**   2,806

Flowers and Fruit,[1] black lead, 12¼ x 19 . . . . **(1178)**   620

The Valley of the Arc, pencil and watercolor, 19 x 11¾ . . . . **(1216)**   7,500

Study of a Standing Man, Leaning Forward, (1865-70), charcoal, 11¼ x 7½ . . . . **(1117)**   1,300

Study for "St. Anthony's Temptation," sepia ink and pencil, 8 x 4¾ . . . . **(1088)**   2,500

Study of a Man in the Nude, charcoal, 18¼ x 11 . . . . **(1193)**   2,354

The Oak, (1885-90), pencil and watercolor, 15½ x 11¾ . . . . **(1134)**   11,800

Man's Head, (1889), pencil heightened with watercolor, 5 x 8¼ . . . . **(1240)**   2,400

Landscape with Trees, Jas de Bouffan, pencil, 12 x 16½ . . . . **(1246)**   1,400

[1]On the reverse, studies of animals.

Bather, His Right Arm Raised, black lead, 9 x 6 . **(1258)** $3,800

Study for "Harvest Time" (recto), pencil and watercolor, *The Man with a Scythe* (verso), pencil, 4¾ x 8½ . . . . **(1272)**   35,760

WATERCOLORS

1961-1962

Landscape, a Path Amid the Trees, watercolor, 8½ x 6 . . . . **(125)**   5,620

The Glade, watercolor, 12½ x 19½ . . . . **(143)**   4,633

Landscape Near Vichy, 1897, watercolor, 11½ x 18¼ . . . . **(20)**   22,910

Still Life, watercolor, 11½ x 14 . . . . **(75)**   9,480

1963

Landscape of Aix-en-Provence,[2] 1897, watercolor, 16¼ x 12 . . . . **(243)**   13,600

Path, Trees, and Greenness, watercolor, 16¾ x 11¾ . . . . **(293)**   11,200

Study of Trees, watercolor, double sided, 11 x 17½ . . . . **(210)**   4,113

1964

The Alley of Le Jas de Bouffan, (1870-71), gouache, 9½ x 12¼ . . . . **(448)**   8,500

1965

The Entrance of the Garden, (1872-77), watercolor, 18¼ x 11¾ . . . . **(594)**   37,000

A Boat, Lake of Annecy, 1896, pencil and watercolor, 8½ x 18½ . . . . **(594)**   19,000

1967

Trees, watercolor, 4¼ x 7½ . . . . **(1004)**   7,500

Landscape, watercolor, 5¾ x 7¼ . . . . **(993)**   2,500

Still Life: Milk Jug, Sugar Basin, Kettle, and Seven Apples, (1895-00), watercolor, 18¼ x 24¼ . . . . **(880)**   400,780

1968–July 1969

The Geranium Pots, (1888-90), watercolor, 12¼ x 10¾ . . . . **(1187)**   158,120

The Shanty in the Woods, (1895-00), pencil and watercolor, 17½ x 11½ . . . . **(1068)**   51,920

The Murder in the Gully of l'Estaque, watercolor, 4¾ x 7½ . . . . **(1183)**   6,600

Untitled, watercolor, 5¾ x 7¼ . . . . **(1252)**   6,800

Trees and Greenness, watercolor, 17 x 12¼ . . . . . **(1268)**   38,976

PAINTINGS

1961-1962

The Road, (1865-67), on panel, rounded at the top and at the bottom, 14 x 6½ . . . . **(50)**   3,020

House in the South of France, (1860-65), 10¼ x 13 . . . . **(50)**   10,000

The Path in the Rocks, 15¾ x 12¾ . . . . **(124)**   17,000

Lively Landscape with Figures, (1860), 15 x 18¼ . . . . **(32)**   6,000

1963

Cottages at Auvers, Autumn, 1873, 27¾ x 22½ . . . **(245)**   104,196

The Toilette, (1895-00), 14 x 10¾ . . . . **(247)**   32,904

Bathers Resting, (1875-76), 15 x 18¼ . . . . **(277)**   113,793

Romantic Landscape, 10¼ x 13 . . . . **(262)**   1,200

1964

The Glade, (1867-69), 8 x 15½ . . . . **(450)**   12,400

Les Grandes Baigneuses,[3] 51½ x 77 . . . . **( )**   1,388,000

[2]Dedicated "A mon cher ami Guillemet."
[3]Sold directly to the National Gallery, London, in November 1964.

1965

Houses at l'Estaque, (1882-85), 25¾ x 32 .... **(594)** $ 800,000

Landscape, (1865-67), 9½ x 15 .... **(512)** 4,400

Mediterranean Landscape, 1870, 8¾ x 12¼ ...... **(561)** 5,800

The Glade, (1867), 9 x 15½ .... **(569)** 15,142

1966

Le Jas de Bouffan, (1885-87), 29¼ x 21¾ .... **(713)** 350,000

1967

*Portrait of the Artist's Father, Sitting and
    Reading His Newspaper,* (1865), 66¾ x 45 ... **(954)** 250,000

Portrait of a Man, (1875-77), 18¼ x 14½ .... **(954)** 20,000

Apples, (1878), 5 x 10¼ .... **(954)** 40,000

Portrait of the Artist's Son, (1880), 8¾ x 5¼ ...... **(954)** 55,000

Underwood, (1895-00), 32 x 25¾ .... **(880)** 248,760

Chinese People Adoring the Sun, 11 x 8¾ .... **(901)** 3,000

1968–July 1969

Farmyard, (1860-65), 10¼ x 13 .... **(1018)** 11,000

Self-Portrait, (1862-64), 17½ x 12¾ .... **(1126)** 17,346

Italian Crockery, (1873-74), 16¾ x 21¾ .... **(1057)** 96,000

Neighborhood of Le Jas de Bouffan, (1875),
    14¼ x 20½ .... **(1126)** 64,428

Bellevue House, (1882-85), 21 x 25¼ .... **(1187)** 365,800

Le Jas de Bouffan, (1885-87), 17¾ x 21 .... **(1068)** 96,760

The Mill at l'Huile, (1870-71), 14¾ x 17¾ .... **(1068)** 82,600

*Thatch-Roofed Cottage Amid the Trees at
    Auvers,* 1873, 23½ x 19¼ .... **(1235)** 220,000

Satyrs and Nymphs, 9 x 11¾ .... **(1268)** 33,640

Marc Chagall

(1887-   )

Birthplace: Vitebsk, Russia.

1907 Attends the Imperial Fine Arts School, Petrograd.

1908-09 Enters the Zvanseva School and discovers modern painters—Cézanne, Gauguin, Van Gogh.

1910-11 Visits Paris and settles at La Ruche. Meets Cendrars (who will become one of his best friends), Max Jacob, Apollinaire, La Fresnaye, Delaunay, Léger, Modigliani, and Lhote. Participates in the Salon des Indépendants, Paris.

1914 First one-man show at Der Sturm Gallery, Berlin. Returns to Russia.

1915 Marries Bella Rosenfeld.

1918-19 During the Russian Revolution, he is made head of the Vitebsk Fine Arts Department, but soon resigns. Participates in the first official exhibition of revolutionary art, in Petrograd, where he gains a large success.

1921 Falls out of favor with the regime. Begins to write his autobiography.

1923-24 Settles in Paris and travels in France.

1926 Exhibits for the first time in New York at the Reinhart Galleries.

1930-31 Ambroise Vollard commissions him to do illustrations of the Bible. Visits Palestine, Egypt, and Syria. Issues his book *Ma Vie.*

1933 Retrospective exhibition at the Kunsthalle, Basel. Travels in Italy, Spain, England, and Holland.

1939 Deeply moved by the violence spreading over the world, he turns to more dramatic themes. Given an award by the Carnegie Institute, Pittsburgh.

1941 Invited by the Museum of Modern Art, New York, he settles in the U.S. with his wife.

1945-46 Stage decoration and costumes for the ballet *Fire Bird,* with music by Stravinsky. Retrospective exhibitions at the Museum of Modern Art, New York, and the Art Institute of Chicago.

1947-48 Returns to France and settles in Orgeval. Retrospective exhibition at the Musée National d'Art Moderne, Paris; at the Stedelijk Museum, Amsterdam; and at the Tate Gallery, London. Wins the first prize for engraving at the Venice Biennial.

1950-51 First Ceramics. First sculptures. Settles at Vence in the South of France. Trip to Israel.

1952 Marries Valentine Brodsky.

1955 Begins his series called "Message Biblique."

1957 Visits Israel. Issues his book *La Bible.* Executes two murals and stained-glass windows for the Church of the Plateau d'Assy, Savoy.

1959 Retrospective exhibition at the Pavillon de Marsan, Paris.

1962 Goes to Israel for the inauguration of his stained glass in Jerusalem.

1963 Retrospective exhibition in Tokyo and Kyoto. Begins the ceiling of the Paris Opéra. Executes stained-glass windows for Metz Cathedral, France.

1964-65 Goes to New York. Executes stained glass for the Dag Hammarskjold Memorial at the UN. Paints murals for the new Metropolitan Opera at Lincoln Center, New York.

1966 Executes mosaics, tapestry designs, and twelve murals for the Parliament of Jerusalem.

1967 Exhibition, "Message Biblique," at the Louvre Museum, Paris. The Maeght Foundation, St. Paul de Vence, pays him homage.

1968 Exhibition at the Pierre Matisse Gallery, New York.

1969 Important retrospective exhibition at the Grand Palais, Paris.

Resident mainly in the south of France.

Sales

DRAWINGS

1961–1962

Russian Village, 1910, pencil, 4½ x 6¼ .... **(129)** $2,334

The Basket of Fruit, 1950, India ink and wash,
    17½ x 21 .... **(96)** 3,750

*The Artist and His Wife in a Fancied Landscape
    Above Vence,* 1953, wash, 25¾ x 19¾ .... **(80)** 3,400

The Artist with His Palette,[1] ink, gouache, and
    colored pencil, 9 x 12¾ .... **(164)** 769

[1] Inscribed "En bon souvenir."

1963

The Drinker, 1913, India ink with pen and brush,
pencil, white heightening, 8¾ x 11¼ . . . . (217) $5,085

The Violinist, 1914, ink, 6½ x 3¼ . . . . (315)   1,152

Face in Profile, ink, 7¾ x 6½ . . . . (233)   270

The Basket of Fruit, 1950, sepia ink and wash,
17½ x 21¼ . . . . (202)   2,800

Recollection of Vence, 1957, pen, 6½ x 3¼ . . . . (179)   200

1964

The Violinist, 1914, India ink, 6¾ x 3¼ . . . . (378)   1,808

The Painter (recto), ***Flying Figure*** (verso),
1918-19, pencil, 10 x 14 . . . . (454)   1,382

The Cock and the Lovers,[2] 1947, pen and
gouache, 13½ x 10½ . . . . (378)   3,051

A Cock, 1950, pen, 8¾ x 6¼ . . . . (377)   791

The Couple, 1951, ink and watercolor, 14¾ x 11 . . (354)   3,800

Couple in a Garden Before a House, 1956, India
ink wash, 12¾ x 9½ . . . . (381)   1,944

1965

Lovers, India ink and colored pencil, 11 x 17¼ . . . (561)   2,400

The Painter with His Easel, (self-portrait),
colored pencil and gouache, 13½ x 8½ . . . . (561)   1,360

The Flying Soul, ink, 17½ x 9½ . . . . (588)   800

Musician Clowns, pen-and-ink wash, 30½ x 22 . . . (539)   5,750

The Parade, (1963-64), ink, watercolor, and wash,
29½ x 21¾ . . . . (526)   10,500

1966

Bird with a Couple, 1947, pencil and watercolor,
13½ x 10¼ . . . . (798)   2,893

Springtime, pen, 13½ x 9½ . . . . (802)   960

The Angel with a Violin, India ink, 14¾ x 9¾ . . . . . (816)   1,599

In the Wind of Arles, 1959, India ink and pastel,
14 x 9½ . . . . (826)   1,160

1967

The Birth, 1910, pen, 6¾ x 6¼ . . . . (918)   3,616

Self-Portrait, 1911-12, wash and watercolor,
12¾ x 9¼ . . . . (1004)   3,500

The Jewish Wedding, 1911, pen and wash,
4½ x 7 . . . . (1004)   2,900

The Soul of the City, 1943, ink and watercolor,
19¾ x 14 . . . . (1004)   8,250

Couple of Lovers, (1955), pen, 14 x 8 . . . . (927)   373

Self-Portrait, 1955, ink and brush, 15½ x 12 . . . . . . (951)   2,175

The Violinist and His Family, charcoal and pastel,
19½ x 12¾ . . . . (881)   3,870

1968–July 1969

Angel and Violinist, (1938-39), India ink,
12¾ x 9½ . . . . (1099)   1,288

Lovers, 1946-47, India ink and pastel, 8¾ x 5¾ . . (1030)   1,600

The Three Blacks, 1950, wash, 16 x 20 . . . . (1018)   4,000

Woman Reading, with a Bird,[3] 1951, India ink
and colored pencil, 7¼ x 5¼ . . . . (1134)   472

The Painter Before His Easel,[4] 1946, India ink
and colored pencil, 8¼ x 6¼ . . . . (1134)   1,062

The Woman with a Bunch of Flowers,[5] 1946, India
ink and colored pencil, 8¼ x 6 . . . . (1134)   1,534

The Rendezvous of Love, 1951, India ink,
10¾ x 8½ . . . . (1134)   2,596

Lover with a Bunch of Flowers, ink and white
gouache on rice paper, 30 x 20 . . . . (1057) $6,500

Interior II, 1911, pencil and pen, 4½ x 8 . . . . (1216)   4,500

Half Title Page from a Book,[6] 1959, pencil,
14½ x 9¾ . . . . (1231)   900

Portrait of a Man, 1926, India ink on tracing
paper with white heightening, 7¼ x 5½ . . . . (1241)   655

Musician Clowns, India ink and wash, 30½ x 22 . (1246)   8,250

The Model and the Violinist, India ink wash,
10¾ x 8 . . . . (1256)   1,720

King David, India ink, 14 x 4 . . . . (1256)   900

The Dancer, India ink, 10¾ x 8 . . . . (1256)   1,640

The Artist at His Easel,[7] 1946, colored ink,
10 x 7 . . . . (1272)   720

WATERCOLORS

1961–1962

Nude Seated on a Red Chair, watercolor,
6 x 4¾ . . . . (106)   3,164

The Green Church, oval watercolor, 9 x 11½ . . . . . (106)   7,910

Goats in the Garden, 1918, gouache and
watercolor, 10½ x 14 . . . . (106)   6,441

Angel with a Violin, tempera, 10 x 15 . . . . (14)   1,659

Lovers on a Swing, gouache, 12¾ x 10 . . . . (31)   5,629

The Open Window, watercolor, 10¾ x 8 . . . . (120)   760

The Somnambulist,[8] 13¼ x 9½ . . . . (129)   4,943

Study of Figures, watercolor, 11¼ x 8 . . . . (155)   3,620

The Beauty and Her Horse, gouache, 12¾ x 9¾ . . (109)   820

Lunch in Front of the Window, watercolor and
gouache, 10½ x 8 . . . . (167)   860

The Window at Payra-Cava, (1923), gouache,
24½ x 19 . . . . (93)   12,430

The Dinner, 1924, gouache, 20¼ x 16½ . . . . (18)   13,334

The Offering, 1924, gouache, 20¼ x 16½ . . . . (18)   13,334

The Donkey Wearing the Lion's Skin, 1926,
gouache, 16¼ x 20 . . . . (69)   13,430

Woman and Child, 1935, gouache, 7½ x 10 . . . . . . (145)   9,480

Happy New Year, 1950, watercolor and gouache,
8 x 10½ . . . . (44)   2,000

The Basket of Oranges, 1950, watercolor,
19¾ x 25½ . . . . (106)   5,650

About the Cock, 1955, watercolor, distemper, and
ink, 41½ x 29¾ . . . . (20)   20,540

Landscape, 1957, watercolor, 9 x 7½ . . . . (143)   1,537

The Cock, 1958, gouache and watercolor, on
Japanese vellum, 26 x 21 . . . . (164)   7,963

Composition, 1958, gouache, 15½ x 20½ . . . . (18)   14,690

The Artist's Muse, 1958-59, gouache and pastel,
24 x 18½ . . . . (93)   10,170

La Fontaine Fables, gouache, 20½ x 16¾ . . . . (93)   11,074

Biblical Scene, gouache, 31¼ x 23 . . . . (26)   6,220

The Crucifixion, gouache on cardboard,
11 x 12¾ . . . . (31)   4,943

1963

The Donkey Wearing the Lion's Skin, (1925),
gouache, 20¼ x 16¾ . . . . (232)   8,927

The Donkey Wearing the Lion's Skin, gouache,
20¼ x 16¾ . . . . (306)   7,400

Girl Coming Back From the Village, 1926,
gouache on brown paper, 23¼ x 16¼ . . . . (309)   8,570

[2]Dedicated "A Léon Degaud, Merci."
[3]On the flyleaf of *Chagall* by Charles Estienne.
[4]On the flyleaf of *Chagall* by René Schwob.
[5]On the flyleaf of *Chagall* by René Schwob.

[6]Dedicated "Pour Monsieur et Madame Liebskind, en bon souvenir."
[7]Dedicated "Pour Lady Clerk, souvenir amical."
[8]Inscribed "A Paris, La Ruche, 1911-12."

The Fox and the Grapes, 1926, gouache and
  watercolor, 19¾ x 15¾ .... (254) $7,200
Ormine and the Idol of the Woods, gouache,
  19¾ x 16¼ .... (312)   5,000
The Man with the Torah, (1930), gouache, pastel,
  and oil on paper, 23 x 18¼ .... (210)   17,275
The Artist in His Studio, (1930), gouache,
  25¾ x 21½ .... (210)   18,646
The Blue Violinist, watercolor and gouache,
  24 x 19½ .... (277)   16,315
Woman and Child, 1935, gouache on paper,
  9½ x 7¼ .... (255)   5,484
The Tree in Blossom, gouache, 25 x 19 .... (206)   14,100
Sunset, 1952, gouache, 27¼ x 21¾ .... (202)   7,000
Lovers, gouache, 11½ x 16¼ .... (255)   3,565
Roses and Mimosas, 1952, gouache and pastel,
  16¼ x 17½ .... (202)   6,500
A Yoke of Oxen, gouache, 19½ x 25¼ .... (199)   16,600
The Woman with the Bunch of Flowers, 1958,
  gouache, 10 x 8¼ .... (241)   4,000

1964

The Rabbi, watercolor, 16¾ x 13½ .... (354)   9,000
The Somnambulist, 1911-12, gouache, 13 x 8½ ... (474)   8,200
The Student, 1925, gouache, 25 x 19 .... (416)   16,584
In the Forest, gouache, 20½ x 16¼ .... (471)   12,769
The Madonna, (1935), gouache, 18¼ x 10¾ ...... (335)   12,500
Nude in a Field, 1937-39, gouache, 19 x 24½ ..... (453)   12,438
Orgeval Steeple, gouache and pastel, 31¼ x 23 ... (465)   24,000
Ormine and the Idol of the Woods, gouache,
  19¾ x 16¼ .... (408)   6,100
The Orchids, watercolor and gouache, 22 x 17¾ .. (340)   6,400
Flowers, gouache, 39½ x 25¾ .... (399)   21,000
Lovers Under a Tree, 1947, tempera, watercolor,
  and pencil, 8 x 8¼ .... (381)   4,520
Flowers, 1949, watercolor and gouache, 25 x 19 ... (474)   11,000
The Dancer, 1950, gouache and watercolor,
  25 x 19¾ .... (367)   12,438
Lovers, 1953, watercolor on paper laid down on
  canvas, 24 x 18¼ .... (458)   5,804
Eliah and the Fire Chariot, gouache and
  watercolor, 14 x 10¼ .... (458)   6,384
The Dream, 1959, watercolor and gouache,
  26 x 19¾ .... (354)   12,000
The Donkey Wearing the Lion's Skin, gouache,
  20¼ x 16¾ .... (378)   10,396

1965

The Sacrifice of Abraham, (1911-12), watercolor
  and pencil, 7¼ x 6½ .... (565)   4,068
The Synagogue, 1917, watercolor, 15½ x 13½ .... (634)   12,792
The Goose, 1926, gouache, 25¾ x 19¾ .... (628)   7,545
The Hen with the Eggs, (1927), gouache,
  19¾ x 16¼ .... (583)   8,700
Man and Cock, watercolor, 24¼ x 18¾ .... (486)   11,968
The Fire Chariot, 1935, gouache and watercolor,
  14 x 10¼ .... (559)   5,000
The Russian Priest, gouache and watercolor
  heightened with pastel, 15½ x 18½ .... (575)   8,845
Vitebsk, watercolor and gouache, 12¾ x 17 ...... (561)   9,800
The Red Cock, 1947, gouache, 13½ x 10¼ .... (583)   1,886
Boat at St. Jean, 1949, gouache, 30½ x 22¼ ...... (526)   42,500
Vase of Flowers, 1950, watercolor and India ink,
  29¼ x 20¼ .... (512)   5,520
Lovers, 1950, watercolor and gouache with pastel
  heightening, 25¼ x 19½ .... (552)   13,000

The Painter's Inspiration, watercolor, 20 x 14 .... (612) $10,000
Nude, gouache, 12½ x 9½ .... (567)   2,373
Reclining Woman, gouache, 19 x 23¾ .... (636)   9,800
Lovers Fleeing at Dawn, watercolor, 10 x 13½ .... (617)   6,102

1966

A Tribute to Apollinaire, 1912, watercolor, 9 x 8 .. (734)   4,520
Male and Female Peasants, (1925), gouache and
  watercolor, 25 x 19 .... (776)   19,000
A Jewish Wedding (The Violinist on the Roof),
  (1925-26), gouache and pastel, 21¼ x 25¾ .... (776)   31,000
The Miller, His Son, and the Donkey, 1926,
  gouache, 19¾ x 15½ .... (694)   23,000
Circus Scene, 1926, gouache, 24 x 18½ .... (694)   29,000
The Drunkard and the Woman, (1926-27),
  gouache, 19½ x 15½ .... (812)   9,398
The Lovers and the Moon, 1927, gouache on
  bister paper, 25 x 19 .... (694)   24,000
The Russian Pope, gouache and watercolor
  heightened with pastel, 15¾ x 18½ .... (784)   7,000
Lovers with the Russian Village, (1945),
  watercolor, 10¼ x 14 .... (734)   3,729
Vase of Flowers, (1949), watercolor and gouache,
  25¼ x 19¾ .... (797)   19,888
Bunch of Flowers, gouache and oil on paper,
  16¾ x 21 .... (744)   21,922
Woman and Cock, gouache, 23¼ x 18½ .... (808)   2,177

1967

The Violinist, (1910-13), pencil, watercolor and
  gouache, 5¾ x 4½ .... (927)   3,277
Golgotha, 1912, gouache, 18¾ x 23¼ .... (938)   29,022
The Cowherd, 1926, gouache, 22 x 25¾ .... (841)   6,250
A Nose and a Ladder, (1926-27), gouache,
  25¼ x 18 .... (954)   30,000
The Bow (The Acrobat with the Red Horse),
  1927, gouache on paper laid down on canvas,
  36 x 26¾ .... (864)   30,000
Clown and Equestrienne, gouache, 19½ x 25¼ .... (987)   16,000
At the Circus, gouache, 26½ x 20¼ .... (987)   25,000
Violinist on the Snow, (1930), gouache and
  watercolor, 19¾ x 25¾ .... (954)   37,500
The Reverie, (1930), gouache, 18½ x 25 .... (940)   9,867
The Bride and the Groom, 1949, gouache,
  25¾ x 19½ .... (864)   27,000
The Bride, gouache, 23½ x 19½ .... (954)   25,000
The Bride, 1950, gouache, 25¼ x 20 .... (982)   34,365
Still Life, 1950, gouache and watercolor,
  19½ x 25¼ .... (889)   12,500
Maternity, watercolor, 12¾ x 9¾ .... (965)   9,492
Self-Portrait, 1957, pastel and watercolor,
  9¼ x 7 .... (870)   950
The Fantastic Dream, (1958), pastel, watercolor,
  and gouache, 18 x 11¼ .... (918)   10,170
The Cock with the Violin, gouache and
  watercolor on paper laid down on canvas,
  37½ x 27¼ .... (864)   15,000
Lovers with a Bunch of Flowers, watercolor,
  12¼ x 9½ .... (978)   7,200
The Hand (Self-Portrait), 1963, gouache,
  29¾ x 21½ .... (938)   15,202

1968–July 1969

The Painter and the Angel, 1925-26, gouache,
  24½ x 19 .... (1173)   19,320
Circus Horse, 1926, watercolor and gouache,
  25¾ x 19¾ .... (1176)   22,500

The Oak and the Reed, 1926, gouache laid down
on canvas, 19½ x 15½ .... (1176) $13,500

A Nose and a Ladder, (1926-27), gouache,
25¼ x 18 .... (1132) 23,600

The Dog, (1927-31), gouache, 20 x 16 .... (1216) 12,000

Musician Clown, (1937-38), gouache, 26 x 18½ .. (1176) 31,000

An Old Woman and Two Girls, watercolor,
15 x 11 .... (1138) 3,965

The Siren with a Bunch of Flowers, 1953,
watercolor, 24 x 19 .... (1181) 8,000

Lovers, 1954, watercolor and gouache, 25 x 19½ . (1117) 16,000

The Peasant and the Well, 1954, gouache and
watercolor, 24 x 18 .... (1208) 6,500

Lovers of Vence, 1955-56, gouache on paper laid
down on canvas, 25¾ x 19½ .... (1056) 16,000

Flowers, gouache and pastel, 25¾ x 19¾ .... (1173) 28,750

The Angel with a Bunch of Flowers, gouache,
6¾ x 5¾ .... (1051) 3,340

Maternity with Flowers, watercolor and India
ink, 7¼ x 4 .... (1113) 2,800

Composition, pastel and gouache, 26 x 20 .... (1125) 8,970

In the Forest, gouache, 20½ x 16¼ .... (1125) 14,030

La nuit: femme cheval, gouache, 34¼ x 25½ ..... (1068) 14,160

Self-Portrait with a Hand, 1963, gouache,
29¾ x 21¾ .... (1173) 16,100

Lovers with the Eiffel Tower, watercolor,
24½ x 19 .... (1235) 12,500

Flowers, 1959, gouache and pastel .... (1252) 44,000

Two Vases of Flowers, 1958, 25¼ x 19½ .... (1254) 25,400

The Poetical Garden, pastel, 19¾ x 14¾ .... (1256) 13,000

Flowers,[9] watercolor, 7¼ x 5¼ .... (1268) 3,828

Lovers with a Bunch of Flowers, watercolor,
11¼ x 7½ .... (1268) 9,512

The Fiancés in the Moonlight, gouache,
29¼ x 21¼ .... (1268) 25,984

The Violinist's Family, pastel, 12¾ x 19½ .... (1268) 17,400

The Lamplighter, 8¼ x 12½ .... (1270) 19,200

Lovers and Vase of Roses, (1958-59), 20 x 14½ .. (1270) 14,480

The Jewish Wedding, gouache, 19 x 19 .... (1270) 27,840

The Bride and the Ass, (1953), 10½ x 8¼ .... (1270) 18,000

PAINTINGS

1961–1962

Lovers: Memories of My Father, (1928), oil,
gouache, and watercolor on paper,
20¼ x 25 .... (129) 23,341

The Tree in Blossom, 1956, oil and gouache on
paper, 25 x 20¼ .... (143) 20,340

Still Life, (1925), 17¾ x 21½ .... (96) 20,000

Peyra-Cava (The Fir Cones), 1930, 28½ x 23¾ .... (8) 33,000

Still Life with Pineapple, 15 x 24 .... (18) 18,758

Nocturnal, 1941, 34¾ x 24¼ .... (128) 41,190

Lovers, 1937-43, 52¼ x 39 .... (8) 77,500

1963

Still Life, (1925-30), 18½ x 13¼ .... (210) 18,646

Two Lovers and the Moon, 1930, 16 x 12 .... (247) 19,194

Bunch of Flowers, 1937, 39¼ x 28 .... (210) 41,130

A Tribute to Paris: Notre-Dame, 1953-54,
30 x 39½ .... (279) 52,500

Dream of Russia, 1956, oil and gouache,
25¼ x 19½ .... (202) 8,500

Lovers and Flowers, oil and gouache on paper,
24½ x 19¾ .... (283) 21,244

Basket of Fruit with a Ribbon, 26 x 22 .... (312) 23,820

1964

The Artist's Sister, 1908, 24 x 20½ .... (416) $15,216

Russian Peasant, 1912, 26½ x 22 .... (416) 35,932

Young Soldiers, 1914, peinture à l'essence on
paper laid down on board, 19 x 14½ .... (453) 8,292

A Woman and Flowers, on canvas laid down on
board, 11¼ x 9 .... (475) 8,600

The Annunciation, 21¾ x 18½ .... (378) 36,516

The Beautiful Red-Haired Girl, 1949, 44¾ x 36 ... (416) 70,482

Married People and the Eiffel Tower,
25¼ x 19¾ .... (340) 15,000

1965

The Somnambulist, 1911-12, on cardboard,
14 x 8¾ .... (634) 12,546

Fir Cones, Peyra-Cava,[10] 1930, 29 x 24 .... (594) 41,000

The Madonna of the Village, 1938-42,
39¾ x 39¼ .... (526) 82,500

Allegory of the Crucified Painter, 21 x 16¼ ...... (553) 9,000

The Bride Under the Baldachin, 1949,
45½ x 37¼ .... (594) 78,000

The Flute Player, 1958, oil and gouache,
26½ x 21¼ .... (617) 16,950

The Wedding, 1959-61, on cardboard,
20½ x 25¼ .... (561) 31,000

Pink Nude and Bunch of Flowers, 32 x 25¾ ...... (569) 32,612

1966

The Carrousel of the Louvre, 1954, 17¾ x 14¾ ... (808) 13,349

1967

The Shepherd, oil, chalk, and India ink on
Japanese vellum, 25¾ x 20½ .... (911) 12,400

The Shepherd, 1958, oil, chalk, and India ink on
Japanese vellum, 25¾ x 21 .... (965) 19,888

The Bread Seller, 1910, 25¾ x 29¾ .... (864) 70,000

The House Is Burning, (1917), 22½ x 24 .... (880) 82,920

Self-Portrait, 1939-40, 31¼ x 25¼ .... (923) 43,600

Crucifixion, (1940), 19 x 14¼ .... (954) 24,000

Ste. Chapelle, 1953, 39½ x 32¼ .... (982) 78,210

Fiancés with a Bunch of Flowers, 21¾ x 18 .... (987) 32,000

1968–July 1969

Still Life on the Roofs, (1923), 18¼ x 21½ .... (1132) 59,000

Bella with a Book and a Vase of Flowers, 1926,
18¼ x 25¾ .... (1068) 44,840

Fiancés, (1927-30), 58 x 36 .... (1187) 173,460

Self-Portrait with Bella, 1939-40, 32 x 25¾ ...... (1057) 56,000

Village Scene with a Clock, (1952), on board .... (1056) 52,500

Flowers, (1930), 30½ x 23¼ .... (1057) 27,500

*Mother and Child on the Bank of the River
Seine,* 1953, oil on silk, 11 x 8¾ .... (1132) 70,800

The Flowery Cock, 1955, oil on paper laid down
on canvas, 38¼ x 57¾ .... (1173) 64,400

The Violinist, canvas laid down on board,
9 x 5¾ .... (1125) 10,120

The Violinist, 31¼ x 21 .... (1056) 42,000

Flowers in a Vase, 14 x 10¾ .... (1049) 18,000

The Artist's Studio with a Vase of Sword Lilies,
32 x 23½ .... (1235) 62,500

Tulips, 25¾ x 19¾ .... (1268) 41,760

---

[9]Dedicated "En bon souvenir, pour Monsieur et Madame Sussman."

[10]Sold in New York in October 1961 for $33,000.

Victor Charreton

(1864–1936)

Birthplace: Bourgoin, France. Studies law at the University of Grenoble and establishes himself as a solicitor in Lyons.

1894   As far as his profession permits it, devotes himself to painting and exhibits for the first time at the Salon Lyonnais, Lyons. Visits several museums during journeys to Spain, Italy, Africa, and Corsica.

1898   Participates in the Salon des Artistes Français, Paris. His favorite subject matter is landscape.

1902   Devotes himself entirely to painting.

1913   Wins the Gold Medal at the Salon des Artistes Français, Paris. Member of the Academies of Sciences, Letters, and Arts of Clermont-Ferrand. Participates in the foundation of the Salon d'Automne, Paris.

1936   Died, Clermont-Ferrand.

1960   Inauguration of the Musée Victor Charreton in his native town of Bourgoin.

1968   Retrospective exhibition entitled "Victor Charreton et son époque," at the Musée de Montmartre, Paris.

Sales

PAINTINGS

1963

The Village, 23¾ x 29 . . . . (254) $ 520

The Countryside Near Royat, Snow Effect,
29 x 36½ . . . . (215)   280

The Park, 23¾ x 28½ . . . . (191)   200

1964

Autumn Effect, 25¾ x 32 . . . . (351)   520

Murols Village Under Snow, on cardboard,
23¾ x 29 . . . . (338)   220

Snow, on cardboard, 14¼ x 18¼ . . . . (441)   475

The Fisherman, 23¾ x 29¼ . . . . (454)   553

1965

The Suburban Garden, on cardboard, 17¾ x 22 . . . (647)   400

Sun on the Orchard, 23¾ x 29 . . . . (611)   360

Murols Village Under Snow, 23¾ x 29 . . . . (499)   360

1966

Village Under Snow, on cardboard, 15 x 23 . . . . (699)   86

Seaside, on cardboard, 14¾ x 17¾ . . . . (828)   90

The Woman in the Garden, on cardboard,
17½ x 22 . . . . (733)   170

Orchard in Spring, on board, 23 x 28¾ . . . . (689)   193

1967

Seascape, on cardboard, 13½ x 16¾ . . . . (935)   40

Snowy Landscape, 15 x 18¼ . . . . (972)   176

Landscape, on cardboard, 11 x 13½ . . . . (1000)   220

Landscape of Pont-Aven, 23¾ x 29 . . . . (955)   280

1968–July 1969

The Castle of St. Amand-Tallande Under Snow,
36½ x 29¼ . . . . (1117)   2,100

Snowy Landscape in the Mountains, 15 x 18¼ . . . (1066)   480

The Village Under Snow, on cardboard,
23¾ x 29 . . . . (1210)   1,200

The Barn Under Snow, on cardboard,
14¾ x 18¼ . . . . (1014)   650

The Farm Under Snow, on cardboard,
28½ x 35½ . . . . (1014) $1,420

Trees in Blossom, 23¾ x 29 . . . . (1014)   840

Underwood Alley at Douelan, on cardboard,
13 x 16¼ . . . . (1077)   280

The Vase of Windflowers, on cardboard,
15¾ x 12¼ . . . . (1038)   60

Vase of Roses, 29 x 36½ . . . . (1117)   1,400

Landscape, 19¾ x 29 . . . . (1220)   600

Parc du Luxembourg, on cardboard, 18 x 14¾ . . . (1225)   360

The Castle of St. Amand-Tallande, 19¾ x 24 . . . . (1253)   2,100

The Village by the River, 12¾ x 16¼ . . . . (1253)   1,300

The Sunny Fountain, 23¾ x 29 . . . . (1256)   2,400

Village Under Snow, 23¾ x 29 . . . . (1256)   2,400

Autumn Landscape, 51½ x 35¼ . . . . (1267)   860

Giorgio di Chirico

(1888–   )

Birthplace: Volo, Greece, of Italian parents. Attends the Academy of Fine Arts in Athens for two years.

1905   Visits Italy and reproduces several works of Italian Renaissance painters such as Ucello, Botticelli, and della Francesca. Influenced by Nietzsche and Wagner.

1909-10   Paints his first "metaphysical" pictures of empty towns.

1911   Settles in Paris, where he meets Picasso, Apollinaire, Max Jacob, and Paul Guillaume.

1914   First paintings showing statues and geometrical elements.

1915   Returns to Italy and in Ferrara meets Carlo Carrà, upon whom he will exert a great influence.

1919   Joins the "Valori Plastici" group.

1924   Returns to Paris and joins the Surrealist group.

1925   Participates in the first Surrealist exhibition at the Galerie Pierre, Paris.

1926   In Rome, executes stage decorations for *Morte di Niobe,* a play by Alberto Savinio.

1929   Publishes *Hebdomeros,* a dream novel. Stage decorations for the Ballets Russes de Monte Carlo.

1930   Stage decorations for *The Life of Orestes,* an opera by Křenek, at the Kroll-Oper, Berlin. Illustrations for Apollinaire's *Calligrammes.*

1933   Executes frescoes at the Palazzo della Triennale, Milan. Turns to an academic style in succeeding years.

Resident near Rome, Italy.

Sales

DRAWINGS

1961–1962

The Two Ages, pencil and watercolor, 10 x 6½ . . . (152) $ 350

1963

Study of a Man in the Nude, 1920, pen,
14¼ x 9¾ .... (291) $ 130

Young People, pencil, 11 x 27¾ .... (255)   96

Horses by the Seashore, pencil, 6¼ x 9½ .... (216)   274

1964

"Bosco," pencil, 6¾ x 6 .... (439)   208

1965

The Gladiators, black pencil .... (613)   260

1966

Figures Under the Moon, pencil, 10¾ x 8¼ ...... (672)   600

1967

The Trophy, 1926, India ink, 2½ x 5¾ .... (927)   452

1968–July 1969

Landscape with Riders, pencil and wash,
9½ x 12¾ .... (1214)   720

The Archaeologist, 1926, colored pencil,
20½ x 11½ .... (1184)   4,000

Metaphysical Drawing, pencil and sepia ink,
12 x 9¼ .... (1191)   1,180

WATERCOLORS

1961–1962

The Resting Warrior, watercolor, 9¼ x 8¾ .... (159)   1,154

1963

Manikins, (1933), gouache, 10 x 12½ .... (208)   800

The Stadium, gouache, 9½ x 12¾ .... (290)   500

1964

The Warrior's Son, gouache on board,
10¼ x 13¼ .... (454)   940

1965

Mythological Figure, watercolor and gouache,
14 x 7¼ .... (541)   450

1966

New York, (1936), gouache and ink, 5¼ x 11 ..... (784)   1,600

1967

Still Life with Peaches, (1940), tempera on board,
9¼ x 13 .... (962)   2,080

1968–July 1969

Nurses on the Beach, watercolor, 12¾ x 9½ ..... (1246)   2,300

The Masterpiece in the Studio, gouache,
16¼ x 22 .... (1255)   7,200

PAINTINGS

1961–1962

Metaphysical Landscape with a White Tower,
1914, 23½ x 15½ .... (88)   6,199

Interno Metafisico, 19¾ x 23¾ .... (14)   3,318

Metaphysical Family, 1926, 36½ x 28 .... (21)   15,800

The House in the House, 29 x 21¼ .... (30)   1,300

The Mysterious Bath, 1929, 14¼ x 10½ .... (20)   4,424

Man and Horse, 14½ x 22 .... (14)   1,100

Horsemanship Lesson, on canvas laid down on
cardboard, 21½ x 21¾ .... (114)   2,000

The Departure of the Knight Errant, 8 x 11¾ ...... (75)   711

Two Horses by the Seashore, 23¾ x 31½ .... (131)   4,108

Horses, 19¾ x 23¾ .... (145)   3,792

Horses on the Beach, 28¾ x 35½ .... (152)   1,000

Piazza d'Italia, 1921, 25¾ x 32 .... (69)   6,794

Piazza d'Italia, 21½ x 30¾ .... (96)   6,250

Landscape, 11½ x 16¼ .... (15) $ 537

Venetian Freak in the Style of Veronese, 1951,
106¼ x 152¼ .... (128)   2,059

Portrait of Maria Lani,[1] 21¾ x 18¼ .... (158)   250

Warrior, on panel, 25¼ x 21 .... (44)   1,000

Self-Portrait, 6 x 8 .... (69)   790

Self-Portrait, 1919, 20 x 24½ .... (75)   8,690

Self-Portrait, 1936, 16¼ x 21 .... (149)   3,476

1963

Mythological Scene, 13½ x 22¼ .... (202)   4,000

The Landscape Painter, 1918, 39½ x 31½ .... (316)   7,800

Horses by the Seashore, 1929, 14¼ x 20¼ .... (224)   2,020

Horse by the Seashore, 14¼ x 17½ .... (216)   2,194

Still Life with Tomatoes and Cucumbers,
14¾ x 21¾ .... (316)   2,200

1964

Venice, 19¾ x 27¾ .... (435)   5,120

Spatial Architecture, 14 x 11¾ .... (329)   2,800

Il Trovatore .... (435)   5,440

Still Life, 19¾ x 27¾ .... (439)   5,440

Self-Portrait, on panel, 11½ x 8 .... (454)   829

Two Horses in a Landscape, 15½ x 19½ .... (387)   1,935

Horses by the Seashore, 39½ x 28½ .... (437)   11,200

Horse, on board, 10 x 12½ .... (374)   850

1965

The Coast of Thessalia, 37¼ x 29¼ .... (526)   10,000

Classical Landscape, 1926, 23¾ x 23¾ .... (539)   4,000

Horse and Zebra by the Seashore, 1928,
19¾ x 27¾ .... (616)   8,800

Three Horses on the Beach, 29 x 36 .... (583)   4,353

The Gladiators, 1929, 13 x 17¾ .... (494)   2,400

Seated Manikin, 1930, 36 x 25¼ .... (522)   8,292

View of St. Viet Church, Prague, 13¼ x 19½ ..... (543)   1,528

Still Life, 21¼ x 29 .... (539)   3,000

1966

The Grand Canal, Venice, 26½ x 38¾ .... (671)   4,933

The Centaur, 1910, 46¾ x 29¾ .... (802)   12,800

The Studio, 1917, 17 x 13½ .... (753)   8,706

Composition with a Streamer, 13 x 10½ .... (701)   850

Stage Decoration for the Ballet "The Jug,"
(1924), on board, 12½ x 18¼ .... (701)   3,250

The Warriors, 31½ x 25¾ .... (802)   11,200

Riders, 15¾ x 19¾ .... (802)   3,200

Seated Manikin, 23¾ x 19¾ .... (802)   8,000

Seated Manikin, 1926, 18¼ x 14¾ .... (753)   6,384

Seated Manikin, 1926, 36¼ x 28¾ .... (750)   7,739

Woman's Head, 23 x 23¼ .... (701)   1,950

Gladiators, 1927, 63¼ x 37½ .... (802)   17,600

Resting Gladiators, (1927), 63¼ x 37½ .... (802)   19,200

Mythological Scene, Gods and Horses, (1930–35),
on board, 47¼ x 95 .... (694)   6,500

Metaphysical Figure, 29 x 20½ .... (665)   8,000

Riders and Warriors, 31½ x 25 .... (757)   4,422

Still Life, 52½ x 40¼ .... (749)   3,000

Il Trovatore Solitario, 31½ x 23¾ .... (776)   8,500

1967

Oreste e Pilade, 36 x 25¾ .... (882)   8,800

Interno Metafisico, 23¾ x 16¾ .... (882)   5,280

Ettore ed Andromaca, 15¾ x 11¾ .... (940)   4,933

[1]Dedicated "A Maria Lani."

Piazza d'Italia, 23¾ x 19¾ .... (962) $6,400
Manikin, 1916, 21¼ x 15 .... (962) 13,600
The Great Tower, 22 x 14 .... (954) 6,500
Still Life,[2] 1926, 14 x 10¾ .... (912) 3,100
Underwood, 1927, 19¾ x 23¾ .... (962) 7,200
Boboli Gardens, on panel, 15¾ x 27 .... (841) 3,500
Horses on the Beach, 19¾ x 24½ .... (940) 2,612
Two Horses, 11 x 15 .... (888) 2,073
Horse Facing the Sea, 15½ x 18¼ .... (923) 2,800

1968–July 1969
The Asymptote, 18¼ x 21¾ .... (1057) 7,500
Classical Scene, (1920), 20 x 24½ .... (1208) 6,000
Piazza d'Italia, 15¾ x 19¾ .... (1174) 8,050
Man and Horse, oil on paper laid down on
    canvas, 15½ x 19¼ .... (1070) 2,714
Horses in a Landscape, on board, 7¾ x 11 ...... (1187) 2,124
The Chariot of the Sun, 13 x 16¼ .... (1125) 3,700
Venice: S. Giorgio Island, (1943), 16 x 20 .... (1235) 8,500
Cavallo Fuggente, 1940, 16 x 20 .... (1241) 5,540
Rovine Classiche, 1926, 23 x 23 .... (1241) 13,860

Sir Winston Churchill

(1874–1965)

Birthplace: Blenheim Palace, Oxfordshire, England. Renowned as soldier, statesman, writer, and artist.

1895 Enters the Army. Also works for an important London newspaper as a war correspondent.

1900 Elected to Parliament.

1908-11 Becomes successively President of the Board of Trade, Home Secretary, and First Lord of the Admiralty.

1915 Begins to paint in his leisure hours.

1918-21 Serves as Secretary for War and Air Minister.

1924-29 Serves as Chancellor of the Exchequer.

1939 Issues two essays on painting in *Thoughts and Adventures.* Becomes First Lord of the Admiralty for the second time.

1940-45 Serves as Prime Minister.

1947 Exhibits at the Royal Academy, London.

1948 Writes *Painting as a Pastime.*

1951-55 Serves as Prime Minister for the second time.

1953 Awarded the Nobel Prize for Literature. His work includes *Life of Lord Randolph Churchill, World Crisis, Marlborough,* and *The Second World War.*

1959 Retrospective exhibition at the Royal Academy, London.

1965 Died, London.

[2]Dedicated to Jean Cocteau.

Sales

PAINTINGS

1965
Canal Scene, (1938), 19¾ x 23¾ .... (526) $26,000
Mimizan, Landes, (1925), 25 x 29¾ .... (605) 27,569
The Water Mill, (1936-39), 29¾ x 25 .... (643) 13,820
The Gate of Marrakech, 1943, 19½ x 24¼ .... (633) 13,000
The Palladian Bridge at Wilton, 23¾ x 17½ ...... (637) 26,000
Menaggio, Lake Como, 19¾ x 29¼ .... (546) 38,696

1966
View of the Thames at Taplow, 25 x 30 .... (776) 16,000
Black Swans, 27¾ x 22 .... (681) 10,000
Landscape, Mimizan, 1920, 25 x 30 .... (776) 12,000
The Coast Near Antibes, (1925), 24 x 30 .... (785) 19,734
Blenheim Lake, (1926-29), 19¾ x 23¾ .... (713) 14,000
Antibes, 1930, 19¾ x 23¾ .... (693) 12,714
Ightham Moat, 19¾ x 23 .... (693) 22,112
La Dragonnière, Cap Martin, 24 x 29¾ .... (693) 5,528
The Coast in Amsterdam, 1938, 13 x 19¼ .... (709) 17,412
The Park of the Castle at St. George,[1] 14 x 10 .... (693) 1,382

1967
Seaside, 1930, 19½ x 23¼ .... (893) 2,000

1968—July 1969
*Randolph Churchill and Lady Castlerosse on the
    Terrace of Horizon Castle,* (1935), on canvas
    laid down on board, 14 x 19¾ .... (1149) 6,000
The Beguinage, Bruges, 1946, 25 x 30¼ .... (1165) 17,346
Landscape of the South of France, (1920),
    19½ x 29¾ .... (1025) 2,974

Antoni Clavé

(1913-   )

Birthplace: Barcelona, Spain. Attends the local fine arts school for six years.

1935 Period of collages.

1939 Visits France and soon settles in Paris. Executes his first lithographs. Comes under the influence of Picasso's Blue Period. Participates in the Salon d'Automne, Paris—until 1948.

1940 One-man show at the Galerie du Sans Pareil, Paris.

1942 Works by Vuillard and Bonnard exert a strong influence on him. Exhibits at the Ecole Nationale des Beaux-Arts, Paris. Illustrates *Lettres d'Espagne* by Mérimée.

1944 Meets Picasso.

[1]This picture was begun by Churchill and finished by Dunoyer de Segonzac, Paul Maze, Simon Lévy, and Ivor Balsan.

1946	Trip to Czechoslovakia. One-man show at the Galerie Delpierre, Paris. Illustrates *The Queen of Spades* by Pushkin and executes stage decorations.
1950	Takes a great interest in the Middle Ages. Illustrates *Gargantua* by Rabelais.
1954	Gives up theatrical and illustrative works to devote himself exclusively to painting. Wins the prize for engraving at the Venice Biennial.
1956	Reverts to collages.
1957	One-man show at the Tooth Gallery, London. One-man show at Stephen Silagy's, Los Angeles. Given an award by the São Paulo Biennial.
1960	Executes metal sculptures. One-man show at the Galerie Creuzevault, Paris.
1967	Exhibition of tapestries at the Musée Picasso, Antibes.
1968	One-man show at the Galerie Creuzevault, Paris. Resident in France.

Sales

DRAWINGS

1964

The Cyclist, India ink, 15 x 10¾ .... (377) $ 249

1965

The Cyclist, India ink, 15 x 10¾ .... (567)   249

1966

Animals, India ink, 14¼ x 10¼ .... (798)   283

1968–July 1969

Carmen, 1944, India-ink wash heightened with gouache, 6¼ x 8 .... (1110)   224

Candide, 1948, wash and gouache, 11¾ x 8¾ .... (1110)   242

Warrior No. 32, 1959, pencil, ink, and collage, 11 x 9 .... (1095)   125

WATERCOLORS

1961–1962

Decoration for the Ballet "Carmen," two gouaches, 20¼ x 23¾ and 18½ x 24¼ .... (152)   1,000

Fish, gouache, 21¾ x 30 .... (18)   1,288

The Man with a Pipe, watercolor, 12¾ x 9½ ...... (68)   460

Portrait,[1] gouache and collage, 14½ x 11 .... (110)   280

1963

Two Warriors, gouache, 29¾ x 21¾ .... (257)   660

A Cup of Fruit and a Jug, gouache, 22 x 18¼ ..... (315)   494

1964

Stage Decoration, gouache, 10¼ x 15 .... (375)   166

Woman Painting, watercolor and gouache, 14½ x 21½ .... (480)   960

The Family, 1962, varnished gouache, 25¼ x 31½ .... (480)   260

Composition, gouache, 22 x 30 .... (413)   900

1965

Face, watercolor and gouache, 14½ x 9¾ .... (503)   270

Decoration for "Carmen," gouache, 8¾ x 6 ...... (523)   210

Don José, gouache, 8¼ x 6¼ .... (523)   170

The King, 1958, watercolor, 12½ x 9½ .... (627)   440

Face, watercolor and gouache, 12½ x 9¾ .... (598)   200

Young Lady with a Ribbon, watercolor, 25 x 19 ... (547)   1,160

[1] Dedicated "Pour mon ami Sapone."

1966

Figure, gouache, 25¼ x 18¼ .... (798) $1,898

Model for "Gargantua," gouache, 8 x 10 .... (796)   220

The Cock, gouache, 10¾ x 8¾ .... (826)   280

Composition, gouache, 20¼ x 29 .... (671)   435

1967

Composition, gouache and collage on pavatex, 30¼ x 22½ .... (919)   1,017

Composition, gouache, 29¾ x 21¾ .... (967)   1,356

Portrait of a Boy, gouache and collage, 21¾ x 13 .... (893)   375

Harlequin No. 9, 1950, gouache and collage, 19¼ x 14 .... (957)   829

1968–July 1969

Angevine-Mâconnaise, two watercolors, each 10 x 6¾ .... (1116)   110

Man and Bird, watercolor, 6½ x 9 .... (1230)   640

The Clown, gouache, 6½ x 5¾ .... (1245)   104

PAINTINGS

1961–1962

Woman with a Veil, 1955, 28 x 17¾ .... (149)   1,343

Little Girl with a Cat, 31½ x 25½ .... (37)   2,750

The King, 29¾ x 22 .... (37)   2,000

The King, on cardboard mounted on canvas, 8¾ x 7¼ .... (120)   1,000

The King with a Pipe, on paper, 27¾ x 19¾ ...... (143)   1,130

The Cock, 18¼ x 13 .... (34)   720

Anglers, on panel, 12¾ x 21¼ .... (71)   600

Woman with a Flowery Hat, on paper laid down on canvas, 25¾ x 19¾ .... (72)   1,350

Composition, 1957, 21¼ x 29 .... (70)   2,133

1963

Still Life with a Fish, oil and collage on board, 32 x 39½ .... (316)   1,750

Still Life with Slices of Watermelon, 34 x 34 ...... (315)   1,042

King No. 16, on board, 19½ x 4¾ .... (179)   375

The Public Garden, 1943, on cardboard, 25¾ x 32 .... (296)   1,020

Carmen, the Cat, on panel, 18¼ x 24 .... (281)   791

Landscape, 1949, 25¾ x 21¼ .... (232)   1,469

The Red King, (1957), on paper mounted on canvas, 29¾ x 22 .... (202)   1,700

Fish, 1959, on cardboard, 21 x 30½ .... (232)   904

Still Life, oil and gouache on paper laid down on canvas, 22½ x 30 .... (236)   1,175

1964

The King, on panel, 31½ x 25¼ .... (398)   1,500

The King, 30¼ x 22½ .... (377)   1,243

King, collage, 21¾ x 29¾ .... (386)   600

Interior Scene, 1941, on panel, 18¼ x 15 .... (325)   320

The Woman with a Cock, 1946, on panel, 29 x 19¾ .... (409)   1,100

Portrait of a Child, on board, 17 x 14 .... (374)   1,100

Little Girl's Head, on cardboard, 18¼ x 15 .... (445)   780

Harlequin with a Guitar, 21¾ x 15 .... (467)   1,107

Still Life, 1949, 20¼ x 25¾ .... (336)   960

Still Life, 1957, on cardboard, 23¾ x 32 .... (377)   2,260

The King with the Big Red and Blue Head, 1959, oil and collage, 41½ x 29¾ .... (448)   4,100

1965

Still Life: Fish with Carpet, 1958, oil and collage
on panel, 47½ x 47½ .... (526) $3,250

The King, collage and oil on paper laid down on
panel, 30 x 22 .... (637) 2,750

Still Life, 23¾ x 28½ .... (541) 2,750

Man and Bird, collage and gouache, 30¼ x 22¼ .. (516) 1,300

Still Life, 23¾ x 29 .... (634) 1,722

Still Life, 29 x 36½ .... (613) 1,800

1966

Paddock, 1945, on panel, 7½ x 9½ .... (685) 620

Clown's Head, on paper, 27 x 19 .... (798) 1,130

The King, 1958, on panel, 41½ x 29¾ .... (670) 3,600

The King, 39½ x 31½ .... (665) 2,000

Cyclists, on board, 19½ x 25½ .... (701) 900

Warrior, 1961, 41½ x 29¾ .... (747) 1,440

1967

Still Life, 29 x 36¼ .... (893) 2,000

Still Life on a Table, 8¼ x 12¼ .... (917) 360

Cup with Fish, 39½ x 39½ .... (919) 2,147

The King, 39½ x 35¼ .... (870) 2,000

1968–July 1969

A Young Lady and a Cat, 29 x 19¾ .... (1030) 900

The Queen, on panel, 42 x 26¼ .... (1145) 1,750

The King, on panel, 32 x 25¾ .... (1118) 2,460

Blue Landscape, 32 x 39½ .... (1118) 2,000

Figures, 19¾ x 24 .... (1078) 800

Portrait of a Young Lady, 1949, on canvas,
18¼ x 15 .... (1078) 600

Still Life, 1957, on cardboard, 23¾ x 32 .... (1174) 2,070

Interior with a Woman, on panel, 36 x 44¾ ...... (1168) 2,100

Fish, (1946), 21¼ x 29 .... (1268) 2,900

Lucie Cousturier

(1876–1925)

Birthplace: Paris, France. Very little is known about
her.

1901　Participates for the first time in the Salon des Indépendants, Paris. Also participates in the exhibitions of the Neo-Impressionist group.

1919　Trip to North Africa.

1925　Died, Paris. (Author of monographs on Paul Signac
and Henri-Edmond Cross.)

Sales

WATERCOLORS

1963

Landscape of the South of France, watercolor,
11¾ x 16 .... (194) $ 600

1964

African Scene, watercolor, 8 x 10½ .... (450) $ 104

Landscape of Sénégal, watercolor, 7½ x 11¾ ..... (379) 250

1966

La Bièvre, 1913, watercolor, 14¼ x 10 .... (706) 280

Pine Trees by the Seaside, 1927, watercolor,
8¾ x 11¾ .... (683) 460

Flowers, watercolor, 10½ x 13¾ .... (745) 271

1967

Still Life with Fruit and Flowers, pastel,
22 x 17¾ .... (858) 460

Little Girl Seated, watercolor, 10¼ x 12¾ .... (858) 400

Parasol Pine by the Seaside, watercolor,
17¾ x 22 .... (886) 300

1968–July 1969

Niampara: Guerzé Village, watercolor, 10¾ x 8 .. (1073) 60

Niampara: Guerzé Village, watercolor,
13½ x 11½ .... (1116) 150

The Parasol Pine, pastel, 17 x 21¼ .... (1184) 660

African Man, watercolor, 10¾ x 8¼ .... (1220) 76

West Indian Girl in a Deck Chair, watercolor,
8¾ x 6½ .... (1234) 100

Pines by the Seaside, watercolor, 8¾ x 11 .... (1265) 1,000

PAINTINGS

1961–1962

Vase of Flowers and Still Life, 25¾ x 19¾ .... (116) 2,040

St. Tropez, 9½ x 13 .... (125) 1,100

1963

Flowery Table, 19¾ x 25¾ .... (190) 900

The Pine, 18¼ x 13 .... (194) 760

1964

Woman's Head in Profile, 16¼ x 13 .... (466) 300

Still Life with a Bust, 1901, 25¾ x 19¾ .... (408) 100

Flowers in a Pot, 1909, 18¼ x 13 .... (450) 1,660

Mediterranean Shore, 15 x 18¼ .... (379) 2,320

1965

Mediterranean Landscape, 19½ x 17 .... (612) 2,200

Woman's Head in Profile, 16¼ x 13 .... (540) 264

1966

Landscape of the South of France, 24¼ x 20 ..... (742) 3,800

Flowers and Fruit, 24 x 18¼ .... (689) 1,797

Cleared Table, 1899, 19½ x 25 .... (669) 1,600

Portrait of a Young Woman, 24 x 20 .... (758) 820

1967

The Cup of Coffee, 1901, 26 x 21¼ .... (858) 1,000

Portrait of an African, 23¾ x 32 .... (919) 1,356

Woman: Pink and Blue, 36½ x 29¼ .... (988) 4,976

Little Girl Seated, 19½ x 16¾ .... (886) 320

Mediterranean Landscape, on cardboard,
14¾ x 18¾ .... (858) 1,500

Still Life with Sweet Peppers and Pomegranates,
19¾ x 24 .... (912) 2,500

1968—July 1969

Teatime Under the Arbor, 1901, 31½ x 23¾ ..... (1110) 920

Landscape, 10¾ x 8¾ .... (1106) 920

Still Life with Flowers, on panel, 14 x 10¼ ...... (1181) 1,520

*Still Life with a Vase of Flowers and Fruit
Stands,* 29 x 36½ .... (1116) 2,800

St. Tropez, 21¼ x 25¾ .... (1225) 5,200

Self-Portrait, 9½ x 7½	(1231)	$ 700	*Landscape,* black lead, 6 x 9	(377)	$ 113

Self-Portrait, 9½ x 7½ .... (1231) $ 700
St. Tropez Landscape, 21½ x 25¾ .... (1249) 4,700
Flowers, 18¼ x 13 .... (1252) 4,060
Yellow Daisies, 1901, 25¾ x 21¼ .... (1253) 1,440
Nude with a Red Cushion, 23¾ x 29 .... (1256) 4,600
Still Life, 1903, on canvas laid down on board,
   23 x 31¼ .... (1271) 3,720
Still Life: Pots and Vegetables, 17 x 21½ .... (1273) 2,770

Henri-Edmond Cross

(1856–1910)

Birthplace: Douai, France. Family name is Delacroix.

1883 His family settles in Paris, but as they are not sympathetic to his projects, he soon decides to live by himself. Enters the studio of Bonvin, who advises him to take the pseudonym of Cross.

1884 Takes part in the foundation of the Salon des Indépendants and in its first exhibition, Paris. Exhibits in this salon until 1891. Comes under Impressionist influence and lightens his palette.

1886 Settles in his own studio in Paris. Joins the group of Seurat, Signac, Angrand, and Luce and embraces the divisionist theories of Neo-Impressionism.

1891 Settles in the south of France, at Cabasson and later at Le Lavandou, living and working by himself and seeing only Signac and Van Rysselberghe.

1904 Travels through Italy, producing some of his most beautiful paintings and several watercolors. His colors get brighter and brighter.

1910 Died, St. Clair, Var district.

1913 Retrospective exhibition at the Galerie Bernheim-Jeune, Paris.

Sales

DRAWINGS

1961–1962

Landscape with a Church, black lead and colored
   pencil, 6½ x 5¾ .... (164) $ 82
Bathers, blue pencil, 18¼ x 16¼ .... (114) 3,600

1963

La Ronde, blue pencil, 18¼ x 16¾ .... (209) 42
Les Champs-Elysées, 1898, colored chalk .... (297) 233
The Angels, colored pencils, 7¼ x 5¼ .... (278) 192

1964

Young Woman in the Nude, Conté pencil,
   12¼ x 8¼ .... (398) 520
Nude on the Beach, colored pencil, 7½ x 10¼ .... (441) 475
Reclining Woman, Conté pencil, 6 x 8¾ .... (378) 452

Landscape, black lead, 6 x 9 .... (377) $ 113
Trees in the Country, colored pencil, 4 x 2¾ ..... (338) 48
Three Scabious, pen and watercolor, 7¼ x 7 ...... (368) 193

1965

Studies of Nudes, blue ink, 11½ x 9 .... (497) 170
The Harbor, pencil and watercolor, 5¼ x 6 .... (631) 410

1966

Hilly Landscape, colored pencil, 5½ x 8½ .... (691) 104
Back View of a Nude, charcoal, 25¾ x 13½ ...... (809) 620

1967

Young Girl Reclining, pencil, 6 x 11¼ .... (927) 249
Child Playing, Conté pencil, 8¾ x 11¾ .... (898) 200
Summer Morning, colored pencil, 6½ x 5¾ ...... (843) 230
The Parasol Pine, charcoal, 11½ x 9 .... (883) 460
The Parasol Pine, 1901, colored pencil,
   8¾ x 11½ .... (978) 2,600

1968–July 1969

Mountainous Landscape, charcoal, 8¾ x 14½ ... (1127) 230
Mediterranean Landscape, colored pencil,
   9 x 12¾ .... (1191) 1,652
Landscape with Figures, black chalk, 6 x 8¾ .... (1099) 1,702
Landscape of the South of France, colored pencil,
   6½ x 9¾ .... (1084) 180
Bridge on the River Seine, black lead and colored
   pencil, 4 x 4¾ .... (1068) 153
Branches in Blossom, two drawings, pencil and
   watercolor, 7¼ x 5¾ and 7¼ x 4¼ .... (1088) 225
The Flight of the Nymphs, charcoal, 8¼ x 10¼ .. (1087) 230
Study of the Sky, colored pencil, 5¾ x 9 .... (1168) 300
Landscape, charcoal, 9 x 11¾ .... (1117) 600
Seated Figures, colored pencil, 4¾ x 6¼ .... (1106) 144
Portrait of Madame Cross, black pencil,
   23½ x 18¼ .... (1183) 600
Landscape, colored pencil, 28¾ x 37 .... (1241) 2,270
Study of Two Men, pencil, 18½ x 13½ .... (1248) 600
Strolling Fisherman, pencil, 13 x 9¼ .... (1248) 350
Pine, colored chalk, 7¼ x 10 .... (1273) 189
Fishing Boats, two drawings, pencil, each
   2¾ x 4 .... (1273) 63
Hindu Woman Seated, pencil, 3¼ x 5½ .... (1273) 151
Sheet of Studies of Women and Children, black
   and colored chalk, 7½ x 4½ .... (1273) 70

WATERCOLORS

1961–1962

The Eucalyptus, St. Clair, watercolor, 4¾ x 6¼ ... (156) 700
The Bather, St. Clair, watercolor, 5¼ x 8¼ .... (156) 800
The Sower, watercolor, 4½ x 7¼ .... (72) 360
Female Peasant, watercolor, 10¾ x 8¼ .... (72) 420
Bather at St. Clair, watercolor, 6¾ x 9¾ .... (29) 2,000
Sunset at St. Clair, watercolor, 4 x 6¾ .... (29) 800
Landscape, watercolor, 10¾ x 15½ .... (29) 1,100
Landscape of Provence, watercolor, 11 x 14½ ..... (68) 980
The Ball of the 14 Juillet at St. Tropez,
   watercolor, 10¼ x 8¼ .... (40) 1,800
Landscape, watercolor, 6¾ x 9½ .... (106) 542
House in the Pine Grove, watercolor, 6¼ x 8¼ ... (123) 680
The Hammock, watercolor, 4½ x 6¼ .... (171) 400
Cabasson, pencil and watercolor, 5¾ x 9¼ ...... (156) 640
Antibes, watercolor, 8¾ x 10¾ .... (116) 1,440
Venice, watercolor, 4½ x 17½ .... (125) 620

1963

Woman in a Landscape, 1903, watercolor,
10 x 15½ . . . . (241) $ 240

Landscape of the South of France, watercolor,
6¾ x 10 . . . . (293)   1,400

The Pines, watercolor, 4¾ x 6½ . . . . (420)   713

Bormes, watercolor, 11¾ x 14 . . . . (232)   2,034

Pines on the Seashore, watercolor, 4¾ x 6¾ . . . . . (283)   701

1964

Venice, watercolor, 4½ x 5¼ . . . . (399)   1,000

Underwood, charcoal and watercolor,
14½ x 22¾ . . . . (454)   981

The Bathers at St. Clair, watercolor, 6¾ x 9¾ . . . . (340)   1,500

Socrate's House at St. Clair, watercolor, 7 x 10 . . . (340)   1,700

Child Playing, pencil and watercolor, double
sided, 5¼ x 3¾ . . . . (441)   429

The Towboat, watercolor, 4½ x 6¼ . . . . (412)   102

Mediterranean Harbor, watercolor, 6¾ x 9½ . . . . . (401)   1,360

Maritime Landscape, watercolor, 6¾ x 9½ . . . . (409)   840

1965

Village in Holland, gouache on board, 8¾ x 9 . . . . . (526)   2,500

View of a Little Harbor, watercolor, 5¼ x 6 . . . . . . (488)   400

Branches in Blossom, watercolor, 7¼ x 9½ . . . . (567)   237

Figure at Le Lavandou, watercolor, 7 x 9¾ . . . . . . (1418)   720

Landscape, watercolor, 5¾ x 11 . . . . (499)   1,440

The Pointe de la Fossette, watercolor, 6¾ x 8¾ . . (547)   380

1966

Tree and Figures, watercolor, 6 x 5¼ . . . . (745)   542

Landscape of Le Lavandou, watercolor, 7 x 9¾ . . . (702)   440

Under the Parasol, the Côte d'Azur, watercolor
on paper laid down on board, 10¾ x 15½ . . . . (753)   1,161

Mediterranean Landscape, watercolor,
6¾ x 9¾ . . . . (653)   1,400

Landscape at Sunset, watercolor, 4¾ x 7 . . . . (814)   400

Garden at the Seaside, watercolor, 10 x 12¾ . . . . . (819)   2,900

The Trees, watercolor, 7¼ x 7½ . . . . (742)   1,800

Landscape of Provence, watercolor, 6¾ x 9½ . . . . . (689)   3,179

San Trovaso Bridge, Venice, (1903-05),
watercolor, 6¾ x 9½ . . . . (681)   2,000

1967

Maritime Pines, watercolor, 6¾ x 9½ . . . . (978)   1,640

Garden Corner, watercolor, 5¾ x 6¾ . . . . (911)   660

Landscape, pastel, 9¾ x 12¾ . . . . (995)   1,800

Maritime Landscape, pastel and colored pencil,
4½ x 5¼ . . . . (1007)   320

Roses, watercolor, 8 x 10¾ . . . . (1002)   200

1968–July 1969

Landscape, 1909, watercolor, 11½ x 14 . . . . (1125)   4,255

Sailboat, 1902, watercolor, 4¼ x 6¼ . . . . (1061)   300

Seaside, watercolor, 5¼ x 8¾ . . . . (1089)   120

The Bay, watercolor, 6¼ x 10 . . . . (1153)   170

Seascape in Provence, watercolor, 7¼ x 10 . . . . . . (1180)   4,620

The Sailboat, watercolor, 7¼ x 6 . . . . (1039)   740

Landscape at St. Clair, pastel, 9 x 11¾ . . . . (1202)   2,000

The House in the Trees, watercolor, 9¾ x 8¼ . . . (1200)   700

Nurses in the Woods, watercolor, 5¼ x 5¾ . . . . . . (1026)   860

The Orchid, watercolor and gouache, 5¾ x 3¼ . . (1118)   70

The Hydrangeas, watercolor, 4¾ x 7 . . . . (1026)   400

Landscape of the South of France, watercolor,
9 x 12¼ . . . . (1252)   3,000

Venice, watercolor, 7½ x 5¾ . . . . (1265)   1,260

Landscape, watercolor, 6½ x 11¾ . . . . (1268)   3,480

PAINTINGS

1961–1962

Canal in Venice, 21 x 17½ . . . . (128) $4,394

1963

The Green Arbor, 16¾ x 23¼ . . . . (198)   2,100

Wine Harvest, 21¼ x 25¾ . . . . (258)   9,600

1964

The Grand Canal in Venice, 14½ x 23¾ . . . . (398)   18,000

Landscape of the Creuse, on cardboard,
9 x 12¾ . . . . (345)   1,420

The Flowery Terrace, on panel, 9½ x 13 . . . . (371)   7,200

In the Park, 15 x 24 . . . . (471)   13,334

The Little Girl in a Red Dress, 36½ x 25¾ . . . . . . (378)   13,560

1965

Bathers in a Landscape, 1896, 31½ x 25¾ . . . . . . (515)   30,000

Under the Arbor, 17¾ x 23¼ . . . . (516)   2,800

The Orchard, (1888-90), 25¾ x 32 . . . . (575)   6,495

*Woman at the Foot of a Tree (Study for "The
Glade"),* 1906, on panel, 6½ x 9¼ . . . . (624)   1,161

1966

Maritime Landscape, 15 x 21½ . . . . (666)   14,000

Flowers on the Beach, on panel, 9½ x 5¾ . . . . (819)   3,200

The Arbor, 18 x 23¼ . . . . (814)   4,000

Orris and Zinnias, on panel, 5¾ x 9 . . . . (685)   1,200

Nymphs, 1906, 32 x 39½ . . . . (750)   27,640

1967

Venice, (1904), 15 x 23¾ . . . . (965)   22,148

Hilly Landscape, 1904, 13½ x 21¾ . . . . (982)   7,821

The Farm in the Morning, 1892, on cradled panel,
9 x 12¾ . . . . (911)   5,000

Bather, oil on paper laid down on canvas,
10¾ x 14 . . . . (858)   4,620

1968–July 1969

Woman in Violet, 1896, 24 x 21½ . . . . (1152)   24,000

Fishing-Net Haulers, (1899), 21 x 32 . . . . (1152)   40,000

The Road Near the Coast, (1907), 29 x 36½ . . . . . (1056)   56,000

The Bridge, 18 x 21 . . . . (1080)   3,250

The Tuileries, on paper, 6¾ x 9½ . . . . (1144)   620

The Fairies' Round, on panel, 5¾ x 6 . . . . (1144)   510

Landscape, on panel, 6½ x 10 . . . . (1109)   520

Two Women in a Landscape, oil on paper laid
down on canvas, 11 x 14 . . . . (1109)   6,600

Landscape of Provence, on panel, 8 x 11½ . . . . . . (1187)   6,136

*The Sculptor's Studio; The Print Lover; The
Painter; Corot Drawing in His Garden at
Ville d'Avray;* four oils on paper, 9½ x 12¼
and 9 x 12¾ . . . . (1050)   620

Study for "Wine Harvest," on panel, 5½ x 9¼ . . . (1051)   2,000

Courtyard Under Snow, on cardboard, 8¾ x 6¼ . (1183)   480

The Parasol Pines, on cradled panel, 9½ x 12¾ . . (1180)   6,020

Antibes in the Morning, 1908, 32¼ x 25¾ . . . . . . (1152)   70,000

Self-Portrait, on panel, 19 x 12¼ . . . . (1116)   820

Old Hotel Under Snow, on cardboard, 8½ x 6¼ . (1225)   800

Near the Lake, on panel, 8¾ x 10¾ . . . . (1233)   2,140

Venice: Sailboats in Front of the Dogana,
(1903-05), 14½ x 23¾ . . . . (1235)   26,000

The Pointe de la Galère, 1892, 25 x 36 . . . . (1239)   218,400

The False Pepper Plant, Provence, 1907,
29 x 36¼ . . . . (1239)   91,200

The Gas Burner, (1885-90), 6¾ x 10½ . . . . (1239)   7,200

Algeria: Villa and Park, 9¼ x 13½ . . . . (1241)   3,780

The Stream at Harvesttime, on board, 13 x 9¼ .. **(1241)** $4,280
Village in Verdure, on board, 9¼ x 6¾ .... **(1241)** 2,770
Portrait of Madame Van Rysselberghe, 10¾ x 9 . **(1258)** 2,600
The River Seine at the Pont-Neuf, 8¼ x 6¾ ..... **(1260)** 900
Mediterranean, East Wind, (1902), 23 x 32 ...... **(1270)** 39,600
The Grand Canal, Venice, on board, 9¼ x 12¾ .. **(1270)** 3,960

Salvador Dali

(1904–   )

Birthplace: Figueras, Spain.

1913–14 Executes his first paintings at Cadaqués. Discovers Impressionism through the works of a friend of his father.

1919–22 Discovers Cubism. Enters the Madrid School of Fine Arts. Meets Lorca and Buñuel. Exhibits for the first time at the Dalmau Galleries, Barcelona.

1923 Takes a great interest in Di Chirico's "Metaphysical" painting.

1925 First one-man show at the Dalmau Galleries, Barcelona.

1927–28 Arrives in Paris. Meets Miró, Picasso, and André Breton, leader of Surrealism. Executes "Le Sang plus doux que le miel," which is regarded as his first Surrealist work. Issues the "Manifeste Croc." Participates in the international exhibition of painting at the Carnegie Institute, Pittsburgh. Collaborates in Buñuel's film, *Le Chien Andalou.*

1929 Meets Paul Eluard and Gala, his future wife. One-man show at the Galerie Goemans, Paris. Buys a house at Port-Lligat, near Cadaqués. Collaborates in Buñuel's film, *L'Age d'or.*

1931–32 Issues *L'Amour et la mort* and *Babaou,* Paris.

1932–38 Illustrates Surrealist books by Breton, Eluard, and Tzara.

1933 One-man show at the Julian Levy Gallery, New York. Illustrates *Chants de Maldoror* by Lautréamont (published by Skira).

1934 One-man show at the Zwemmer Gallery, London. Falls out with Breton and is excluded from the Surrealist group. Travels to New York.

1935–37 Paints the famous "Girafe en Feu" (Kunsthalle, Basel). Second trip to New York, where he is received enthusiastically. Issues *La Conquête de l'irrationnel* and *La Métamorphose de Narcisse* (Paris and New York).

1937–38 Trip to Italy. Takes a new interest in the Renaissance and Baroque. Strongly impressed by Palladio. Through Stefan Zweig, meets Sigmund Freud in London.

1939 Settles in the U.S. during World War II.

1941–42 First major retrospective exhibition at the Museum of Modern Art, New York. Issues *The Secret Life of Salvador Dali,* New York.

1943 One-man show at the Knoedler Gallery, New York.

1944–48 Active in book illustration.

1948–49 Returns to Spain and Port-Lligat. Turns to religious subject matters.

1951–52 Executes 102 watercolors for the illustration of Dante's *Divina Comedia.*

1955–56 Executes "La Cène" (National Gallery, Washington, D.C.) Writes *Les Cocus du vieil art moderne* (Paris and New York).

1959 Wins the gold medal of the City of Paris. Executes his first historical painting, "The Discovery of America by Christopher Columbus."

1964 Important retrospective exhibition in Tokyo, Japan. Issues his *Journal d'un Génie* (Paris).

1966 Creates Pop objects. Produces an important lithographic work.

Resident in Paris, with frequent stays in Spain.

Sales

DRAWINGS

1961–1962

Studies for "The Creation of Monsters," two drawings, pencil, each 13¾ x 9⅜ .... **(111)** $ 600

The Virgin and the Child with St. John the Baptist, black and brown ink, tempera, and watercolor, 14 x 14¼ .... **(67)** 1,136

Portrait of Edward Wasserman, pencil, 8 x 10 .... **(164)** 165

Presumed Portrait of Paul Eluard, pencil 8¼ x 10¼ .... **(49)** 280

Metamorphosis, pencil, 8¾ x 12¼ .... **(102)** 90

Gala in the Nude, 1932, pencil, 9¼ x 12 .... **(31)** 467

The Dance; The Song, two drawings, pen and pencil on a silver background, each 10¾ x 7¾ .... **(64)** 800

1963

Lobster Telephone, 1933–1962, colored pencil, 10½ x 8 .... **(179)** 325

The Man with the Cigarette, 1934, India ink heightened with gouache, 19½ x 15 .... **(243)** 1,000

1964

The Flower Woman, 1937, colored pencil, 11½ x 8¼ .... **(483)** 310

Allegory of Hunger, 1939, pen and wash, 18½ x 24½ .... **(420)** 1,161

Study for "The Madonna": Head, ink and watercolor, 16¾ x 7¾ .... **(454)** 1,437

Allegory, 1943, India ink and watercolor, 22 x 28 .... **(329)** 2,300

Composition, pen and colored pencil, 12¾ x 19¾ .... **(480)** 700

Study of a Nude, 1950, red pencil and ink, 14 x 10¾ .... **(416)** 663

Allegorical Composition, 1958, sepia ink and wash heightened with white, 39½ x 29¼ ..... **(448)** 3,000

Landscape, 1958, pen and sepia wash, 19 x 29¼ ... **(448)** 2,000

Rhinoceros, 1959, ink and wash, 33½ x 23 .... **(420)** 1,451

Octopus Attack, 1963, pen and wash, 18¾ x 22 ...**(420)** 551

1965

Surrealist Composition, 1923, pen and colored pencil, 12¾ x 16¾ .... **(553)** 1,080

Cannibalism of Things, 1936, pencil, 42 x 30¾ .... **(512)** 3,200

Study of Figures, 1939, pen, 24 x 19 .... **(629)** 1,886

The Horseman of the Apocalypse, 1944, ink and gouache, 20 x 20¼ .... **(624)** 4,699

Plumed Figure, ink, 17 x 13 . . . . **(507)** $1,300
Riders' Fight, pen, 11 x 16¾ . . . . **(617)** 1,085
Riders, pen, 11½ x 16¾ . . . . **(500)** 400
Two Faces of the Artist, 1961, ink, 6 x 8 . . . . **(612)** 360
Study of Two Nudes, 1961, charcoal, 24 x 18¼ . . . . **(535)** 1,520
Nude, pencil, 8¼ x 6 . . . . **(550)** 791
The Recital, pencil, 7¾ x 10 . . . . **(588)** 220

1966
*Design for the Cover of "Bulletin du
    Surréalisme," No. 4,* 1936, ink and blue and
    red chalk, 11¾ x 8¼ . . . . **(760)** 290
Caprice, Faringdon Park, 1938, pen and
    watercolor, 22½ x 31 . . . . **(808)** 4,063
Allegory of Hunger, 1939, pencil and wash,
    19 x 25 . . . . **(753)** 1,741
Femme aux seins, pen, 6 x 6 . . . . **(653)** 150

1967
The Couple, 1929, pen, 10 x 6 . . . . **(839)** 262
Woman and Mirrors, 1933, colored pencil,
    11¾ x 8¾ . . . . **(963)** 400
Study for Mae West's Portrait, pencil,
    11½ x 14 . . . . **(881)** 249
*Project for the Surrealist Demonstration at
    Trafalgar Square,* 1936, red and blue pencil
    with India ink, 12 x 8½ . . . . **(881)** 442
Hercules, charcoal, 39½ x 25¼ . . . . **(855)** 320
The Grave of Mausole, (1950), pencil and red ink
    on gray paper, 11¾ x 31 . . . . **(831)** 750
Study for "La Vierge autosodomisée," 1953, pen,
    17½ x 10 . . . . **(940)** 2,902
Chronos the Giant, 1965, pen and watercolor,
    29¾ x 21¼ . . . . **(988)** 2,985
The Tragic Corrida,[1] 1966, blue ink, 11½ x 15 . . . **(1006)** 1,493
The Mountain of Peace, 1966, ball-point pen and
    watercolor, 10¼ x 7 . . . . **(1006)** 746

1968–July 1969
"Cubico," ball-point pen, 11¾ x 17¾ . . . . **(1030)** 750
Landscape, 1923, pencil, 9¾ x 12¾ . . . . **(1099)** 460
The Devil's Hand, black pencil, 8¾ x 6¾ . . . . **(1084)** 164
Et le ruisseau de nuit qui bercera sous terre, 1934,
    India ink, 11¾ x 9 . . . . **(1214)** 1,760
Caryatids, pen and watercolor, 16 x 12½ . . . . **(1026)** 1,200
Angel's Head Blowing Up, 1952, ball pen and
    pen, 22 x 17 . . . . **(1216)** 3,500
Composition, 1965, India ink, 8¼ x 11¼ . . . . **(1127)** 966
Composition, 1965, pen and watercolor,
    29¾ x 21¼ . . . . **(1174)** 4,600
Sheet of Studies, pen, 11¾ x 7¼ . . . . **(1240)** 336
Bacchanal, Ballet to Wagner, (1936), charcoal,
    19 x 23 . . . . **(1248)** 1,600
Hands, 1952, wash, 16¼ x 11½ . . . . **(1254)** 3,400

WATERCOLORS
1961–1962
Orlando, 1948, gouache, 18½ x 9 . . . . **(152)** 525
Spanish Dancer, 1949, watercolor, 13½ x 9¾ . . . . . . **(49)** 1,280
Spanish Dancer, 1949, watercolor, 13½ x 10 . . . . . . **(164)** 659
The Resurrection, 1953, gouache, 6¾ x 10¼ . . . . **(14)** 711
Snakes and Pianos, watercolor, 10¼ x 7¼ . . . . **(96)** 1,500
The Blue Door, watercolor, 10¼ x 7¼ . . . . **(96)** 1,000

[1] Inscribed "Viva Picasso."

1964
Figures in Space, 1949, watercolor, 12¼ x 9¼ . . . . **(354)** $2,500
1965
The Guitar Player, 1922, watercolor, 8¼ x 5¾ . . . **(550)** 633
Composition with Flowers, 1953, watercolor,
    40¼ x 30 . . . . **(485)** 11,500
Boceto de la batalla de Tetuan, 1961, gouache
    and oil, 14¼ x 11 . . . . **(539)** 4,500

1966
Fantastic Landscape: Morning, 1942, tempera on
    canvas, 100 x 99½ . . . . **(694)** 1,700
Fantastic Landscape: Noon, 1942, tempera on
    canvas, 100 x 91 . . . . **(694)** 2,500
Fantastic Landscape: Evening, 1942, tempera on
    canvas, 100 x 100¾ . . . . **(694)** 2,750

1967
Three Seated Figures, (1923), watercolor,
    18¾ x 10 . . . . **(881)** 1,050
Purgatory, 1941, gouache, 16¼ x 11½ . . . . **(883)** 1,140
The Good Fairy, 1950, watercolor, 15½ x 11 . . . . . . **(996)** 2,040
Hell, 1951, watercolor, 17 x 12¼ . . . . **(996)** 1,720
Shattered Engine, 1963, watercolor and pencil,
    6 x 9½ . . . . **(862)** 270

1968–July 1969
The Apparition of the Cross, 1926, gouache and
    watercolor, 19 x 15 . . . . **(1138)** 3,469
Interior, 1939, watercolor and gouache,
    12¾ x 19¾ . . . . **(1080)** 2,000
Purgatory Song, watercolor, 18¼ x 12¼ . . . . **(1197)** 2,800
Christmas Stockings, 1946, watercolor and
    collage, 15 x 12 . . . . **(1241)** 6,550
Israel's Rebirth, watercolor, 22 x 15 . . . . **(1246)** 3,750
The Lamp; The Peacock, two gouaches, each
    4 x 3¼ . . . . **(1268)** 1,206
Fauns, 1950, gouache, 18½ x 12½ . . . . **(1268)** 6,496

PAINTINGS
1961–1962
For Frederico Garcia Lorca, 1926, 39½ x 39½ . . . . **(149)** 11,850
The Crucifixion, 1958, tryptich on canvas, center
    66 x 51, side parts 66 x 17 . . . . **(128)** 989

1964
*Folding Screen Decorated with Chinese Figures,
    Peacocks, and Butterflies,* four paper panels
    laid down on canvas, each 67¼ x 21¾ . . . . **(365)** 464

1965
Portrait of the Artist's Sister, Anne-Marie, 1925,
    16¾ x 16¾ . . . . **(539)** 3,400
The Knight of Death, 25¾ x 21 . . . . **(526)** 10,000

1966
Composition, 1930, on board, 15½ x 12¼ . . . . **(694)** 11,500
Appearing of the City of Delft, on panel,
    12¼ x 13¾ . . . . **(808)** 11,318

1968–July 1969
Carnival Nostalgia, 18½ x 18½ . . . . **(1193)** 16,107
Bust of a Woman, oil and sand on panel,
    16¼ x 13 . . . . **(1184)** 2,800
The Victory, 1944, 13 x 9¾ . . . . **(1126)** 10,408
Composition, 9½ x 6½ . . . . **(1224)** 11,800
Gradiva retrouve les ruines d'anthropomorphes,
    25¾ x 21¼ . . . . **(1224)** 43,200
Ossification matinale du Cyprès, 32½ x 26 . . . . . . **(1224)** 82,000

Stuart Davis

(1894–1964)

Birthplace: Philadelphia, U.S.

1909 Attends Robert Henri's art school in New York.

1910 As one of Henri's students, takes part in the Independents' exhibition on West 35th Street, New York.

1913 Participates in the Armory Show, New York, where he discovers Cubism through the French pictures exhibited here. Calls it "the greatest single influence I have experienced." Starts to work as a cartoonist and illustrator.

1917 Unlike most American artists after World War I, does not revert to mere representational painting. Works hard to elaborate his own style, according to the demands of modernism.

1921 Executes his "Labels" series.

1927 First series of abstract works.

1928-29 Travels to Paris.

1931 Teaches at the Art Students League, New York.

1933-39 Works for the Federal Art Project. From 1938, gradually turns toward the abstract.

1944-51 Given awards by the Carnegie Institute, Pittsburgh; the Pennsylvania Academy of Fine Arts; the Art Institute of Chicago; and the American Art Exhibition.

1945 Retrospective exhibition at the Museum of Modern Art, New York.

1952 The Venice Biennial assigns an entire room to his work.

1955 Participates in the exhibition "Cinquante Ans d'art moderne aux Etats-Unis" at the Musée National d'Art Moderne, Paris.

1956 Becomes a member of the National Institute of Arts and Letters.

1957 Retrospective exhibitions at the Whitney Museum of American Art, New York, and the San Francisco Museum of Art.

1964 Died. It is increasingly acceptable to consider Davis as "the first American artist to appropriate successfully the means of French art toward the end of making distinctively American pictures" (B. Rose).

Sales

DRAWINGS

1965
Boats, 1917, pencil, 16¼ x 14¼ .... (507) $ 300

1966
Springtime, 1917, 14 x 18¾ .... (665)   300

1967
The Cove, 1917, pencil, 14 x 17¾ .... (963)   350

1968–July 1969
Street Scene, 1917, pencil, 14 x 16¾ .... (1035)   425
Landscape, 1917, pencil, 14 x 17¾ .... (1062)   250
Town View, 1917, pencil, 14 x 16½ .... (1231)   175

WATERCOLORS

1961-1962
Country Town, 1917, watercolor, 14 x 15 .... (152)   300

1963
View of a Country Town, 1917, watercolor,
    13¾ x 15¾ .... (208) $ 425

1966
The Summer Villas, 1913, watercolor,
    10¾ x 14¼ .... (648)   550

PAINTINGS

1961-1962
The Petrol Pump, 20¼ x 13½ .... (85)   2,600

1963
Seascape, 1919, 23¾ x 29¾ .... (179)   400
Windy Day, 1911, 29¾ x 37½ .... (272)   1,000

1964
Portrait of a Man, 1914, 24¾ x 20¾ .... (329)   450

1965
Landscape, 1912, 30 x 36¾ .... (610)   900

1966
Composition, 1922, on canvas laid down on
    board, 14 x 10 .... (651)   1,700

1967
New York-Paris, 1931, 39½ x 51½ .... (952)   28,000

1968–July 1969
Washhouse No. 2, 1929, 17¼ x 23¾ .... (1035)   14,000

Edgar Degas

(1834–1917)

Birthplace: Paris, France. His father, a bank manager, highly appreciates music and painting.

1852 Changes a room into a studio in his father's apartment.

1855-58 Attends the Ecole Nationale des Beaux-Arts, Paris. Travels to Italy to perfect his study of painting; stays in Rome, Naples, and Florence.

1860 Turns to historical and mythological subject matter. Starts a long series of portraits.

1862-65 Encounter with Manet and the future Impressionists causes him to alter his style and give up his former subject matter.

1872 Attends ballet rehearsals at the Paris Opéra. Also shows much relish for race-course scenes. Stay in New Orleans.

1874 Participates in the first exhibition of the Impressionist group at Nadar's, Paris. Takes part in all the succeeding shows of the group, except for the one of 1882.

1881 First sculptures. The medium of pastel becomes more and more important in his work.

1882 Series of "Ironers" and "Milliners."

1885 Paints mostly dancers and nudes. His sight begins to fail seriously.

1886 Participates in the last exhibition of the Impressionist group, Paris.

1889 Stays in Spain and Morocco.

1893 Exhibits at the Galerie Durand-Ruel, Paris.

1898 Almost blind, he devotes himself to sculpture. Very little is known about his last years, which are lived out in almost complete retirement.

1912 His works fetch high prices at auction.

1917 Died, Paris.

Sales

DRAWINGS

1961–1962

Young Woman in the Nude, 1857, 12¼ x 8 . . . . (167) $ 360

After the Bath, Woman Drying Herself, 19¾ x 20½ . . . . (167) 5,000

Standing Woman, 12¼ x 9 . . . . (71) 1,800

Seated Nude, 21¼ x 14¼ . . . . (40) 1,240

Portrait of Madame Ducros, (1857), pencil, 12¼ x 8¾ . . . . (84) 5,767

Copy After an Italian Marble, 1859, black lead, 11¼ x 7¼ . . . . (60) 48

Studies After Michelangelo, black lead, 9 x 6¼ . . . (147) 150

Dancer, Her Arm Raised, black pencil, 12¼ x 9 . . . (17) 2,400

Drawing After a Greek Low Relief, pencil, 10 x 9 . . . . (106) 203

Studies After Michelangelo, pencil, 10 x 8 . . . . (106) 237

Bather, charcoal and pastel, 25 x 15¾ . . . . (106) 7,910

Dancer, charcoal, 21 x 14½ . . . . (106) 2,712

Woman at a Balustrade, charcoal on gray-blue paper, 19½ x 30 . . . . (31) 2,197

Three Dancers, charcoal, 24 x 19¼ . . . . (18) 9,605

Dancer at the Bar, charcoal, 11¼ x 8¼ . . . . (164) 3,295

Woman Drying Herself, color print touched up by the artist, 23¾ x 20 . . . . (156) 1,960

Study for a Nude, charcoal, 11¾ x 8¾ . . . . (156) 780

After the Bath, Woman Drying Herself, charcoal on tracing paper, 34 x 28¾ . . . . (171) 1,900

After the Bath, Seated Woman in the Nude, charcoal, 19¾ x 12¾ . . . . (84) 6,865

After the Bath, (1894), charcoal, heightened with white, 22½ x 24 . . . . (128) 11,533

Woman Dressing, charcoal, 29 x 19½ . . . . (140) 4,394

Dancer at Ease, stick of greasepaint, 11¼ x 8¾ . . . . (80) 580

Study for a Dancer, print with color lights, 14¼ x 9½ . . . . (80) 5,600

Bust of a Monk, pen, 8¼ x 5½ . . . . (51) 50

Standing Nude, Dressing, brush wash . . . . (77) 1,700

Woman Wearing a White Apron, pencil and watercolor, 13½ x 7¼ . . . . (152) 2,850

Portrait of Madame Edmond Morbilli (Born Thérèse Degas), charcoal heightened with colored pencil, 11½ x 9 . . . . (140) 7,689

Two Studies of Little Fourteen-Year-Old Dancer, (1879-80), black and white chalk and pastel on gray paper, 18¼ x 22½ . . . . (128) 19,771

1963

Study of the Hindquarters of a Horse, black chalk, 7¼ x 9¼ . . . . (219) $ 373

A Cavalry Clash, After Ucello, 1859, pencil, 9¾ x 15½ . . . . (195) 1,050

Rider, charcoal, 9¾ x 7¼ . . . . (225) 1,200

Portrait of a Monk in Profile, black lead, 8½ x 4½ . . . . (235) 220

Fame, stick of greasepaint, 49½ x 39½ . . . . (293) 640

Marguerite Degas Embroidering, 1858-60, pencil with white lights, 14 x 10 . . . . (277) 6,032

Study of Nudes (Four Figures), (1900), charcoal, 20¼ x 17½ . . . . (210) 3,565

Study of Nudes, charcoal, 22¾ x 15½ . . . . (195) 400

Standing Woman, 21 x 13 . . . . (257) 900

Standing Man: Study for "The Rape," black lead, 12¾ x 7½ . . . . (208) 800

Studies of a Young Man Sleeping, black lead on pink paper, 9¼ x 7¼ . . . . (222) 260

After the Bath, Woman Drying Herself, charcoal on tracing paper, 34¼ x 28¾ . . . . (258) 1,400

After the Bath, Woman Drying Herself, charcoal on tracing paper, 34¼ x 28¾ . . . . (291) 20,000

Dancers, charcoal, 19¾ x 14 . . . . (202) 2,500

Dancers, charcoal, 24½ x 14 . . . . (296) 3,400

Seated Dancer, black lead, 18½ x 11½ . . . . (315) 1,097

Dancer, Her Arms Raised, charcoal, 16¾ x 13 . . . . (210) 3,839

Three Dancers in Tights, charcoal on tracing paper, 24¾ x 20¾ . . . . (293) 15,000

1964

Portrait of René Degas, 1855, black lead, 11¾ x 9 . . . . (452) 8,600

Study for the Injured Jockey, charcoal heightened with chalk, 10 x 13½ . . . . (452) 8,400

Marguerite Degas, black lead on pinkish paper, 10½ x 8¼ . . . . (452) 3,200

Woman Reading, 1880, charcoal with white lights on gray paper, 19 x 12¼ . . . . (416) 11,056

Pruner on a Tree, charcoal, 23½ x 18¼ . . . . (354) 2,200

After the Bath, Woman Drying Herself, charcoal, 34 x 28½ . . . . (354) 3,600

Angel Sounding the Trumpet, black lead heightened with watercolor, 11½ x 11½ . . . . . . (399) 700

Standing Nude in Profile, charcoal, 11¾ x 9 . . . . . . (401) 1,600

Seated Dancer, black pencil, 18½ x 11½ . . . . (454) 1,106

Head in Old Finery, pencil, 10¼ x 7¼ . . . . (383) 294

Study of the Muscles of the Right Hand, pencil and red chalk, 15 x 8 . . . . (383) 158

Dancer Looking to the Right, charcoal, 17 x 10 . . . (383) 4,520

Dancer with a Fan, charcoal, 23¾ x 17 . . . . (453) 9,950

Dancer Refastening Her Shoulder Strap, charcoal with pastel lights, 23¾ x 14½ . . . . (452) 20,200

Woman Coming Out of Her Bath, charcoal, 24 x 21 . . . . (341) 5,800

Coming Out of the Bath, charcoal, blue chalk, and wash, 9¼ x 12 . . . . (458) 9,286

Nude Adjusting Her Slipper, charcoal and chalk, 22 x 13 . . . . (354) 4,250

The Ironer, charcoal on tracing paper, 21 x 15¾ . . (452) 14,200

1965

Dancer at Ease,[1] (1880-90), charcoal, 16¾ x 10¼ . . . . (624) 5,528

[1]Dedicated "A M. Charpentier."

Dancers at Ease, charcoal, 34½ x 32½ . . . . **(561)** $6,240

Dancer Refastening Her Shoulder Strap, colored chalk, 17 x 11½ . . . . **(522)** 16,584

Three Dancers, charcoal, 25 x 21 . . . . **(522)** 9,398

Study of Dancers, charcoal and brown chalk, 22 x 19 . . . . **(522)** 15,202

After the Bath: Woman Drying Herself, charcoal, 37¼ x 21 . . . . **(575)** 24,876

Study of Wrapped Figures, 1856, pencil and ink, 10¼ x 8 . . . . **(575)** 4,699

Man's Head, charcoal, 8¾ x 6¾ . . . . **(644)** 700

Naked Man, charcoal, 17½ x 9¾ . . . . **(624)** 884

Racehorses, black lead, 10 x 15 . . . . **(624)** 3,870

Figures, pencil, 9 x 5¾ . . . . **(577)** 220

Study of Men and Women in the Nude, double sided, 17¾ x 11 . . . . **(499)** 1,200

Study for "Alexandre et le Bucéphale," black lead, 11¾ x 6 . . . . **(567)** 1,356

1966

Houses at Le Mont St. Michel, 1885, charcoal, 14½ x 10 . . . . **(749)** 800

Two Warriors, (1857), pencil, 8¾ x 5½ . . . . **(689)** 332

Horse and Rider Group, black lead on onionskin paper, 8½ x 6 . . . . **(668)** 80

Study of a Horse, pencil, 5¼ x 5½ . . . . **(734)** 283

Horse, charcoal, 12¾ x 8 . . . . **(703)** 7,500

Study of a Dancer, black pencil with pastel lights, 12 x 8½ . . . . **(703)** 6,750

Three Studies of a Dancer, (1873-76), pencil, 12¼ x 8¼ . . . . **(812)** 4,689

Standing Dancer, charcoal, 12½ x 9¼ . . . . **(750)** 6,081

Four Dancers, charcoal with heightening, 17½ x 27 . . . . **(745)** 7,910

Dancers, black lead, 23¼ x 18¼ . . . . **(797)** 7,232

Four Dancers, charcoal with heightening, 21¼ x 14¾ . . . . **(744)** 9,040

Four Dancers, two drawings, charcoal and wash, each 17½ x 27 . . . . **(819)** 16,000

Dressing After the Bath, (1882-85), charcoal, 26½ x 15¾ . . . . **(686)** 17,137

Dancer, black pencil heightened with gouache on pink paper, 11 x 9 . . . . **(681)** 26,400

1967

Studies of Classical Sculpture, (1853-58), double sided, 17½ x 11½ . . . . **(1089)** 884

Landscape, black lead, 12 x 10¼ . . . . **(965)** 1,401

The Conversation, on tracing paper, 11¾ x 15¾ . . **(912)** 300

Dressing After the Bath, 1890, charcoal, 23¼ x 22 . . . . **(938)** 23,494

Study of a Seated Nude, charcoal, 25 x 19½ . . . . . **(1004)** 12,500

After the Bath, charcoal, 27¾ x 34¾ . . . . **(988)** 16,172

Dance Figures, charcoal, 17½ x 23½ . . . . **(978)** 12,000

Ballet Girl, charcoal, 12¼ x 9½ . . . . **(987)** 3,000

Dancer on Stage,[2] pencil, 9¼ x 6¼ . . . . **(889)** 3,300

Bather Holding Her Foot, charcoal, 27¾ x 23 . . . . **(982)** 14,457

Study of a Standing Nude, charcoal, 12¾ x 10 . . . **(1004)** 4,500

Study of a Naked Warrior, pencil, 9 x 6 . . . . **(927)** 294

Study of Horses, black pencil, 9¼ x 8 . . . . **(849)** 760

1968–July 1969

Portrait of Monsieur de Broutelles, charcoal, 13¾ x 8¾ . . . . **(1199)** 12,400

After the Bath, charcoal, 29 x 23 . . . . **(1199)** $27,600

Woman Drying Her Hair, charcoal and pastel, 39½ x 43½ . . . . **(1199)** 27,000

Dancer, Her Right Arm Raised, pencil, 13¼ x 8¾ . . . . **(1216)** 9,000

Study of a Dancer, charcoal, 21¾ x 13¾ . . . . **(1018)** 4,250

Woman Leaning on Her Elbow, pencil, 9 x 6 . . . . **(1088)** 1,650

Young Dancer Refastening Her Shoulder Strap, charcoal and pastel with white lights, 17 x 9¼ . . . . **(1176)** 26,000

Study of a Nude, charcoal, 19 x 9 . . . . **(1111)** 4,464

After the Bath, Woman Drying Herself, (1900), charcoal, 17½ x 19¾ . . . . **(1187)** 18,880

Back View of a Woman Dressing, charcoal and wash, 12¼ x 9 . . . . **(1200)** 1,160

Three Dancers in Motion, charcoal, 24 x 34 . . . . . **(1113)** 12,000

Three Dancers in Motion, charcoal, 19 x 28 . . . . . **(1132)** 17,700

Fall of the Curtain, Dancer in Profile, charcoal, 18¼ x 23¾ . . . . **(1125)** 16,100

Study of Horses, 8¾ x 7½ . . . . **(1117)** 820

Horse, charcoal, 7¼ x 10 . . . . **(1193)** 6,443

The Illness of Stratonis, pencil, 6½ x 9 . . . . **(1116)** 1,100

Study of Two Hands, charcoal, 10¼ x 16¾ . . . . . . **(1099)** 3,795

Study of a Nude, (1900), charcoal, 21¼ x 14 . . . . . **(1239)** 6,720

Bust of a Dancer, charcoal heightened with white, 16¼ x 16¼ . . . . **(1239)** 7,200

Three Dancers in Motion,[3] charcoal, 24 x 34¼ . . . **(1239)** 28,800

Ballet Scene, (1890-95), charcoal, 14½ x 2½ . . . . . **(1239)** 30,000

Dancer Leaning on Her Right Knee, charcoal heightened with pastel, 20¾ x 13¼ . . . . **(1254)** 2,800

Child's Head, black pencil, 9½ x 6½ . . . . **(1262)** 720

Study of Hands, black pencil, double sided, 6 x 5¾ . . . . **(1262)** 500

Study of Anatomy, black pencil and red chalk, 5¾ x 2¾ . . . . **(1262)** 210

Sheet of Studies of Classical Sculptures, 1853-58, double sided, pencil, 17½ x 11½ . . . . **(1272)** 528

Horse at Stable, (1885-89), charcoal, 9¼ x 12 . . . **(1272)** 11,280

Dancer, red chalk, 12¼ x 8¾ . . . . **(1272)** 44,400

Dancer, brown pencil slightly heightened with pink pastel, 13¼ x 9 . . . . **(1272)** 15,600

Four Dancers, charcoal, 12¼ x 19¼ . . . . **(1272)** 30,000

WATERCOLORS

1961–1962

Beach at Low Tide, pastel, 11¾ x 17¾ . . . . **(80)** 3,000

Moors of the River Somme, pastel, 9½ x 16¼ . . . . **(114)** 3,000

Head of a Red-Haired Woman,[4] (1888), pastel, 15½ x 15½ . . . . **(164)** 13,730

Woman Wiping Her Back, (1895), pastel, 27¼ x 23¼ . . . . **(8)** 78,000

Dancer in Pink, pastel, 36¾ x 29 . . . . **(29)** 72,000

La Danseuse étoile, (1887-90), pastel, 16 x 15¾ . . . **(137)** 90,000

The Conversation, 1895, pastel on paper on board, 25¾ x 19¾ . . . . **(112)** 65,904

1963

Dancer Swinging (Green Dancer), (1879), pastel, 26 x 12¼ . . . . **(245)** 287,910

Path in the Meadow, (1890-93), pastel, 11¾ x 15½ . . . . **(255)** 2,194

Landscape, pastel, 10¾ x 16¾ . . . . **(194)** 2,600

[2]Inscribed "Degas, un peu honteux."

[3]Sold in Versailles in June 1968 for $12,000.
[4]Presumed portrait of Mademoiselle Dobigny.

Russian Dancers, 1895, pastel, 19 x 26½ .... (247) $126,132
Russian Dancers, pastel, 29¼ x 24 .... (206) 10,200
Dancer with a Fan, 1898, pastel, 19¾ x 14 .... (241) 18,800
Coming Out of the Bath, (1900-05), pastel,
  35½ x 31¼ .... (210) 24,678
The Rouart Family, pastel, 40¾ x 47½ .... (254) 16,000

1964

Café Concert Singer, 1880, fan-shaped gouache
  on silk, 7½ x 23¾ .... (399) 2,500
Woman Scratching Herself, (1883), pastel,
  12¾ x 9½ .... (453) 17,966
Dancer at the Bar, 1885, pastel, 24½ x 19 .... (453) 55,833
Russian Dancers, 1895, pastel, 21 x 27¾ .... (399) 29,000
Three Dancers, (1896), pastel, 21 x 19 .... (416) 66,889
The Cup of Chocolate, pastel, 36½ x 31¼ .... (452) 45,000
The Hairdressing, pastel, 29¾ x 20½ .... (452) 18,600
Woman Drying Her Feet, (1893), pastel, 21 x 25 .. (416) 33,168
Bather by the Waterside, pastel, 41½ x 36½ ...... (340) 30,000
Dancer with a Fan, pastel, 20 x 14½ .... (471) 25,312
Olinde et Sophronie, pastel, 21¼ x 16½ .... (452) 4,600
Unhappy Nelly, pastel, 24½ x 18¾ .... (416) 60,808

1965

Ballet Rehearsal, 1875, gouache and pastel,
  21¾ x 26¾ .... (526) 410,000
Rider and Amazon, (1881-85), pastel, 11 x 9 ...... (624) 11,609
Dancer Refastening Her Shoulder Straps,
  1896-99, pastel, 24 x 18 .... (624) 38,696
Woman Dressing, (1897), pastel, 16¾ x 13 .... (575) 41,460
Seated Dancer, (1898), pastel and charcoal on
  paper laid down on board, 21 x 19½ .... (594) 22,000
Three Standing Dancers, (1900), pastel, 28 x 22 ... (526) 40,000
Dancers, pastel, 29¾ x 24 .... (522) 33,168
Three Dancers, pastel, 25¾ x 19¾ .... (546) 52,280
Dancers in Pink Ballet Skirts, pastel, 36 x 19 ..... (617) 39,550
*Madame Alexis Rouart and Her Children in a
  Park*, pastel, 39¾ x 48 .... (522) 38,696
Dancer, fan-shaped watercolor, 13 x 21¼ .... (561) 1,900

1966

Standing Dancer, (1880), pastel, 17¾ x 20¼ ...... (750) 27,640
Woman Dressing, (1897), pastel and charcoal,
  24½ x 32¾ .... (750) 42,842
Bather by the Waterside, pastel, 42 x 36¼ .... (812) 49,752
Landscape, pastel, 10¼ x 16 .... (689) 2,626
Two Dancers, Their Arms Raised, (1900), pastel,
  28 x 15 .... (694) 31,000

1967

Three Dancers Before Training, (1880), pastel,
  24 x 18¼ .... (857) 62,000
Woman Combing Her Hair, pastel, 21¾ x 25¾ ... (978) 34,000
Reclining Woman in the Nude, pastel, 12¾ x 16 ... (940) 34,824
Nude, (1894), pastel, 32¾ x 20¼ .... (954) 32,500
A Woman and Two Children in a Park,[5] pastel,
  43¾ x 49½ .... (965) 84,750

1968–July 1969

Coming Out of the Bath, (1884), pastel,
  19¾ x 25¼ .... (1056) 72,500
*Two Dancers Shown to the Waist, Refastening
  Their Shoulder Straps*, (1897), pastel,
  22½ x 16¾ .... (1187) 153,400
Dancer in Red, (1897), pastel, 25¼ x 19¾ .... (1068) 35,400

[5]Madame Rouart and her children.

Group of Dancers, (1899), pastel and charcoal,
  27 x 24 .... (1187) $61,360
Study of a Nude and of a Dancer, (1902), pastel,
  37 x 19½ .... (1187) 56,640
Four Dancers, (1903), pastel, 33¼ x 29 .... (1176) 185,000
Dancer, Yellow Bodice, pastel, 28½ x 21¼ ...... (1189) 144,000
Three Dancers, pastel, 18¼ x 21¼ .... (1126) 44,604
Woman Combing Her Hair, charcoal and pastel,
  33½ x 34½ .... (1126) 56,994
Moors of the River Somme, pastel, 11½ x 17 .... (1019) 1,600
Blue Dancer (Before the Class, Three Dancers),
  pastel, 21¼ x 19¾ .... (1239) 240,000
Three Red Dancers, (1896), pastel, 25¾ x 20¾ ... (1239) 134,400
Dancers, Pink Skirts, 38¼ x 25½ .... (1241) 171,000
Landscape, pastel, 10 x 17¼ .... (1262) 1,620
Two Dancers at the Foyer (The Dance School),
  1875, pastel and gouache, 11¾ x 8¼ .... (1270) 148,800
Nude, (1879), pastel over monotype, 5½ x 8 ..... (1270) 42,720

PAINTINGS

1961–1962

Copy After a Fresco by Titian, 32 x 18½ .... (76) 1,160
Café Concert Singer, 1880, peinture à l'essence
  on silk, 11½ x 23¾ .... (71) 3,700
Study of a Nude, 1896, 30½ x 32¾ .... (112) 197,712
Portrait of Filippo Lippi, 11¼ x 14½ .... (70) 1,501

1963

Portrait of a Young Woman After Pontormo,
  1858, 25 x 17½ .... (277) 15,081
Landscape of Italy, 7¾ x 12¼ .... (194) 1,200
Portrait of a Student, (1865-68), 13¾ x 11 .... (245) 26,049
Paul Valpinçon, (1868-72), oil on paper laid down
  on canvas, 12½ x 9½ .... (245) 23,581
Portrait of a Young Lady, (1878), 15½ x 12¼ ..... (245) 43,872
The Rehearsal on Stage: Five Dancers, 1889,
  29¼ x 31¾ .... (245) 150,810
Jockey, on panel, 10¼ x 8 .... (245) 101,454

1964

Portrait of Marguerite Degas, (1856-57),
  12¼ x 9¼ .... (454) 17,690
Landscape of Italy, 17 x 24 .... (397) 2,000
The Child in Blue, on paper laid down on canvas,
  15 x 5¾ .... (452) 3,560
Portrait of René Degas, 15½ x 12¾ .... (452) 15,200
Doctor Camus, (1868), 16 x 12¾ .... (416) 11,056
Portrait of Jerôme Ottoz, (1868-72), 18¼ x 15 .... (454) 8,292
Portrait of a Seated Man, 14¼ x 11½ .... (465) 7,000
The Ballet, Three Dancers, (1873), 18¼ x 24 ..... (367) 41,460
Dancer on Stage, 1880, on panel, 20 x 22 .... (431) 41,905

1965

The Tired Dancer .... (493) 90,000
Landscape of Italy, 17 x 24 .... (532) 840

1966

*St. Anthony Resuscitating a Woman Killed by
  Her Husband*, (1858), after
  Titian, 31¾ x 18½ .... (750) 6,910
Portrait of Madame Gaujelin, 1867, 10¾ x 8¾ .... (750) 12,714
Doctor Camus, (1868), 15¾ x 12¾ .... (812) 8,292
At the Café Chateaudun, 1869, peinture à
  l'essence on paper, 9¼ x 7¼ .... (686) 37,314
The Jockey, (1866-72), peinture à l'essence,
  12¾ x 9¼ .... (812) 66,336

1968–July 1969

Ironer in Back Lighting, (1883), 31½ x 25 .... (1132) $ 342,200
Reclining Nude Man, (1856), 14¼ x 24½ .... (1113) 10,000
Young Woman and Ibis, 1861, 38¾ x 29¼ .... (1187) 59,000
Portrait of Alfred Niaudet, (1877), 18¼ x 12¾ ... (1049) 140,000
Jephtha's Daughter, 14 x 10¾ .... (1126) 19,824
Village Street, 1895-98, 32 x 27¼ .... (1189) 40,000
Landscape of Italy, 19½ x 24 .... (1184) 1,040

Robert Delaunay

(1885–1941)

Birthplace: Paris, France.

1902-04 Begins to paint during his holidays in Britanny, coming under the influence of Gauguin and the Ecole de Pont-Aven.

1905 Devotes himself entirely to painting. Meets Metzinger and, like him, comes under the influence of Neo-Impressionism. Also meets the Douanier Rousseau, whose painting he highly appreciates.

1908 Discovers and greatly admires Egyptian and Chaldean arts. Comes under Cézanne's influence, which will lead him toward Cubism.

1909-10 Starts his series of "Cities" and "Eiffel Towers." His mastery asserts itself in these thoroughly original compositions, showing his tremendous passion for color and his great lyricism, which introduces not only bright color but dynamism into Cubism. Proceeding from Cubism, he alters this style so much as to turn finally to genuine abstraction. Marries Sonia Terk.

1911 Takes a great interest in sports themes. At the invitation of Kandinsky, takes part in the first exhibition of the "Blaue Reiter," Munich. Meets Gleizes. Starts his series of "Windows" (in abstract).

1912 Takes part in the second exhibition of the "Blaue Reiter." Exerts his own influence upon Macke, Franz Marc, and Klee during their stay in Paris. Executes his large composition, "City of Paris," shown at the Salon des Indépendants, Paris. Exhibits at the Galerie Barbazanges, Paris. Apollinaire in one of his poems, calls Delaunay's manner "orphic." Besides Delaunay and his wife, Orphism includes Kupka, Morgan Russell, and Macdonald-Wright. Series of his "Simultaneous Disks."

1913 Trip to Berlin, where he participates in the first Herbstsalon at Der Sturm Gallery.

1914-18 Trip to Spain, where he remains during World War I. Meets Diaghilev and Stravinsky. Reverts to representation. Stage decoration for Diaghilev's *Cleopatra.* Portrait of Stravinsky.

1921 Returns to Paris, living in his house at Neuilly. Meets the Surrealist poets.

1922 Major retrospective exhibition at the Galerie Paul Guillaume, Paris.

1924-25 Paints many landscapes of Paris. Executes the mural "City of Paris" for the Exposition Internationale des Arts Décoratifs, Paris.

1930 Returns permanently to abstraction. Produces his series of "Rhythms."

1937-38 Executes an important decoration for the Paris World's Fair. With Gleizes, Villon, Lhote, and Sonia Delaunay, executes murals for the Room of Sculpture at the Salon des Tuileries, Paris. Meets Kandinsky. (Previously knew him only through letters.) Bad health forces him to give up his work.

1939 Organizes the first exhibition of "Réalités Nouvelles," at the Galerie Charpentier, Paris.

1940 After the German invasion, stays in the Auvergne and later at Mougins.

1941 Died, Montpellier, in the south of France.

Sales

DRAWINGS

1965

Study for "Portuguese Still Life," 1915-16, ink, 10 x 12 .... (494) $ 275

1968–July 1969

Portuguese Still Life, 1915, pen, 8¼ x 10¾ ...... (1068) 2,596

WATERCOLORS

1963

Rainbow, 1913, watercolor, 19 x 23¼ .... (316) 6,750

1965

Young Nude Reading, (1915), oval-shaped watercolor, 24 x 19¾ .... (637) 7,000

1966

Relief Disks, 1936, gouache and sand on paper, 21¼ x 38 .... (678) 9,500
Portuguese Still Life, 1915-16, pastel, 29 x 40¾ ... (753) 15,961

1967

Football, watercolor on cardboard laid down on canvas, 31½ x 22½ .... (923) 7,600

1968–July 1969

Football, 1924, pastel, 17¾ x 14¼ .... (1026) 6,020
Football, 1924, pastel, 17¾ x 14¼ .... (1125) 7,590
Paris Lovers, 1923, pastel, 17 x 13½ .... (1216) 1,000

PAINTINGS

1961-1962

Portrait of Jean Metzinger, on cardboard, 21¾ x 16¾ .... (40) 4,000
Portrait of Madame Mandel,[1] (1923), 19½ x 24 ... (164) 1,318
Nude Reading, 18¼ x 15 .... (160) 10,100
Landscape, 1925-27, 15 x 21¾ .... (69) 6,952
Portuguese Still Life, 1916, wax medium on paper, 37½ x 30 .... (164) 7,689
Succulent, on panel, 10¾ x 8¾ .... (95) 1,100
Motion of a Line, 21¾ x 71¼ .... (145) 6,320
Still Life with a Red Carpet, colored relief composition on cement, 16¼ x 19½ .... (70) 10,270

1963

Circular Forms (Moon No. 2),[2] 1913, 32 x 25¾ ... (316) 14,000
Sprinters, 7½ x 9½ .... (298) 3,300

[1]On the reverse of an unfinished abstract composition.
[2]On the reverse, a study for the towers of Laon.

1964

Portrait of Jean Metzinger, (1906), on paper laid
down on canvas, 20¼ x 16¾ .... (354) $14,000

Nude Reading, 1915, 37¼ x 30 .... (354)   9,000

The Andalusian with a Yellow Mantilla, encaustic
on panel, 15½ x 11¾ .... (335)   1,440

1965

Begonias, (1909), on cardboard, 21¼ x 14¼ ...... (553)   1,200

Nude Reading,[3] 1915, wax on canvas, 18¼ x 15 ... (553)   7,800

Portuguese Still Life, oil and gouache,
28½ x 36¾ .... (485)   11,000

Landscape of Paris: The Tower, 1924, 66 x 33¼ .. (637)   18,000

Landscape, (1925), on board, 14¾ x 21½ .... (617)   14,238

Landscape, (1925-27), on panel, 15 x 21½ .... (575)   6,910

Sprinters, 1930, 44¼ x 57¼ .... (575)   22,112

Rhythm Helix, 1936, 63¾ x 51¼ .... (553)   10,000

Air, Iron, and Water, (1936-37), 38¼ x 59¾ ...... (485)   10,000

Still Life with a Hen Parrot, on panel,
10¼ x 8¾ .... (627)   2,400

Red Fish, on cardboard, 10¼ x 7¾ .... (627)   2,000

1966

Portuguese Still Life, 1916, wax on paper laid
down on canvas, 37½ x 29¾ .... (797)   22,600

View of Paris and the Eiffel Tower, 1925,
82¼ x 20½ .... (814)   23,200

The Andalusian with a Mantilla, on canvas laid
down on panel, 16¼ x 12¼ .... (830)   1,020

1967

Simultaneous Windows, 1912, 18 x 14¾ .... (880)   38,696

1968–July 1969

Woman at the Marketplace, Portugal, 1915, wax
on canvas, 32 x 39½ .... (1175)   8,400

Nude Reading, Madrid, 1915, wax on canvas,
18¼ x 15 .... (1175)   8,200

The Spanish Girl, 16¼ x 12½ .... (1113)   720

Flowers, on board, 19¼ x 12½ .... (1018)   1,800

Rhythm Helix, (1936), 63¾ x 50½ .... (1068)   11,800

Sonia Delaunay

(1885-   )

Birthplace: Ukraine, Russia. Studies fine arts in
Petrograd and later in Germany.

1906   Settles in Paris and marries the famous German critic Wilhelm Uhde. Exhibits in his gallery the following year.

1910   Marries the French painter Robert Delaunay and
begins to play a great part in the evolution of his
work.

1913   Becomes an important abstract painter. Executes
great canvases entitled "Rythmes Simultanés."

[3] Sold in Versailles in December 1962 for $10,100.

1914   Paints the famous "Prismes Electriques."

1914-19   Stays in Spain and Portugal.

1920   Turns to fashion and decoration.

1925   Exhibition of printed fabrics at the Arts Décoratifs,
Paris.

1939   Participates in the exhibition "Réalités Nouvelles"
at the Galerie Charpentier, Paris.

1945   Exhibition, "Art Concret," Paris.

1946   Takes part in the Salon des Réalités Nouvelles, Paris, as well as in several exhibitions all over the
world—London, Vienna, Belgium, South
America.

1949   Takes part in the exhibition "Premiers Maîtres de
l'art abstrait" at the Galerie Maeght, Paris.

1954   One-man show at the Galerie Bing, Paris.

Resident in Paris.

Sales

DRAWINGS

1965

Simultaneous Dress No. 603, pencil and wax,
15½ x 10½ .... (574) $ 90

1968–July 1969

Compositions, two drawings, 1942-43, pencil,
10¾ x 8¼ .... (1116)   260

WATERCOLORS

1961–1962

Woman, watercolor, 7¼ x 4¾ .... (153)   220

Spirals, 1936, watercolor, 4½ x 9¾ .... (110)   100

Colored Rhythm, 1942, gouache, 9¼ x 7½ .... (156)   550

Colored Rhythm, 1948, gouache, 15¾ x 15¼ ..... (149)   506

1963

Composition, 1916, gouache, 13 x 8¾ .... (249)   620

1964

Woman with a Parasol: Simultaneous Contrasts,
1914, watercolor, 19 x 12 .... (387)   774

Colored Rhythm, 1958, gouache, 18¾ x 15¾ ...... (386)   700

Rhythm, Color, gouache, 21¾ x 23¾ .... (413)   340

1965

Colored Rhythm, 1956, gouache, 11¾ x 8¾ .... (543)   453

Simultaneous Contrasts: Woman With a Parasol,
1914, gouache and watercolor, 19 x 12 .... (535)   498

1966

Composition, 1956, gouache, and black pencil,
12¾ x 17½ .... (770)   369

1967

Composition, 1942, watercolor, ink, and pencil,
7½ x 5 .... (889)   400

Abstract Composition, 1960, 21¾ x 29¾ .... (890)   977

Composition, 1960, watercolor, 21¾ x 23¼ ...... (1009)   330

Colored Rhythm, 1960, gouache, 13½ x 12¼ ...... (965)   633

1968–July 1969

Composition, 1914, pastel, 14 x 6 .... (1129)   400

Composition No. 98, 1925, watercolor, 10¼ x 14 . (1191)   1,298

Composition, watercolor, 8¼ x 8¼ .... (1078)   300

Colored Rhythms, 1952, gouache, 17¾ x 14 ...... (1175)   340

Colored Rhythm, 1959, gouache, 26¼ x 22 ...... (1175)   1,500

Colored Rhythm, 1959, gouache, 27½ x 22¼ ..... (1099)   1,104

Composition, 1961, gouache, 25¾ x 19½ .... **(1155)** $ 528
Colored Rhythm, 1950, gouache, 9½ x 8¼ .... **(1268)** 812
Composition, 1952, gouache, 17¾ x 13 .... **(1268)** 974

PAINTINGS

1963

Composition with Circles, 1915, peinture à la
   colle on canvas, 9 x 7¼ .... **(253)** 760

1966

Composition, 1956, on silk, 72¼ x 77¼ .... **(749)** 780

1967

Composition, 1954, 31½ x 39½ .... **(958)** 1,188

1968–July 1969

Seated Portuguese, 1916, wax on canvas,
   31 x 38 .... **(1175)** 3,000
Self-Portrait, Portugal, 1916, wax on paper,
   12 x 9¼ .... **(1175)** 820

Paul Delvaux

(1897–   )

Birthplace: Antheit, Belgium.

1920-24 Attends the Brussels Academy of Fine Arts.

1930 Comes under the influence of the Expressionists—Permeke, De Smet, Ensor, and others.

1933 Exhibits at the studio La Grosse Tour, Brussels.

1934 Participates in the exhibition of *Le Minotaure* at the Palais des Beaux-Arts, Brussels, together with Di Chirico, Magritte, and others. Introduces Surrealism into his own style of painting, but only to a certain extent.

1936 One-man show at the Palais des Beaux-Arts, Brussels.

1938 Participates in the International Exhibition of Surrealism at the Galerie des Beaux-Arts, Paris.

1939 Exhibits "Les Phases de la Lune" at the Museum of Modern Art in New York.

1940 Participates in the International Exhibition of Surrealism, Mexico.

1944-45 Retrospective exhibition at the Palais des Beaux-Arts, Brussels.

1948 One-man show at the Galerie Drouin, Paris. Participates in the Venice Biennial. Henri Storck's film *Le Monde de Paul Delvaux* wins the first prize at the Venice Film Festival.

1950 Teaches at the Ecole Nationale Supérieure d'Art et d'Architecture, Brussels.

1952 Executes a mural for the Kursaal, Ostend.

1957 Participates in the São Paulo Biennial.

1962 Retrospective exhibition at the Musée des Beaux-Arts, Ostend.

1965-67 Executes three panels for the Transeurope Express. Paul Hassaert assigns a large part of his film *La Clef des chants surréalistes* to Delvaux's work. Fills an important post at the Académie Royale de Belgique, in the Fine Arts department.

1968 His works fill an entire room at the Montreal World's Fair.

1969 Retrospective exhibition at the Musée des Arts Décoratifs, Paris.

Resident in Brussels.

Sales

DRAWINGS

1965

The Dialogue, 1936, ink and watercolor,
   21¾ x 30¾ .... **(624)** $1,658

1967

Women in a Street, 1965, pencil and wash,
   24¼ x 19½ .... **(927)** 1,256
Bust of a Young Lady, 1948, India ink wash,
   9½ x 13 .... **(883)** 740

1968–July 1969

Lovers, India ink and wash, 8¼ x 10¾ .... **(1145)** 1,000
Lovers, 1947, ink and pencil, 9 x 11 .... **(1215)** 1,900
The Garret, 1944, pen and wash, 13 x 9¼ .... **(1145)** 650
Two Seated Women, pen and wash with gouache
   lights, 8¼ x 6¾ .... **(1203)** 743
The Encounter, 1965, on tin, 27¾ x 21¾ .... **(1268)** 6,960

WATERCOLORS

1961-1962

Landscape, 1936, watercolor, 21¾ x 31½ .... **(75)** 411

1966

On the Terrace, 1946, watercolor, 23 x 19½ ...... **(767)** 2,200
Regissa Station, watercolor, 23¼ x 25¾ .... **(767)** 1,800

1967

View of Huy, 1934, watercolor, 27¾ x 35¼ .... **(867)** 1,400

1968–July 1969

The Valley, 1926, watercolor, 14¼ x 19½ .... **(1022)** 880
The Conversation, 1953-54, watercolor,
   15¾ x 19¾ .... **(1268)** 7,772

PAINTINGS

1965

The Little Path, 48¼ x 47¾ .... **(520)** 6,600

1967

Penelope, 1946, on panel, 47½ x 69½ .... **(864)** 9,250
Young Roman Ladies, 5¼ x 6¾ .... **(947)** 320

Charles Demuth

(1883–1935)

Birthplace: Philadelphia, U.S.

1905 Attends the Pennsylvania Academy of Fine Arts.

1907-12 Makes two trips to Paris, where he attends the Académie Colarossi and the Académie Julian.

1915 Comes under the influence of modern art, mainly Cézanne's. His favorite medium is watercolor. First one-man show at the Daniel Gallery, New York, where his works are shown until 1926.

1916-17 Following the example of European masters, he attempts, like Shamberg and Sheeler, to adapt machine imagery to painting. Impressed by Cubism, but unable or unwilling to assimilate it thoroughly, he creates from it a simplified and stylized manner in keeping with modernism yet still closely linked to the clearest representational painting. (This manner is called Precisionism or Cubism-Realism.)

1919 Begins to work in oil.

1926 One-man show at the Stieglitz Gallery, New York.

1927 Paints "My Egypt," a picture showing grain elevators.

1935 One-man show at the Whitney Museum of American Art, New York. Died.

1949 Retrospective exhibition at the Museum of Modern Art, New York.

Sales

DRAWINGS

1963

Still Life with Apples, pencil and watercolor,
7¼ x 7¼ . . . . (208) $ 500

Roses, pencil and watercolor, 11¾ x 17¾ . . . . (225) 700

WATERCOLORS

1965

Houses, pastel, 23¼ x 17¾ . . . . (489) 1,500

1967

Street Scene, watercolor, 12¾ x 7¾ . . . . (952) 4,500

PAINTINGS

1963

Landscape No. 6, on panel, 11¾ x 15¾ . . . . (290) 200

Maurice Denis

(1870–1943)

Birthplace: Grandville, France. Spends his youth with his family in St. Germain-en-Laye, near Paris.

1888 Attends the Académie Julian, Paris, where he meets Bonnard, Ranson, and Sérusier.

1889 Setting up of the Nabis group (the Prophets). Denis appears not only as one of them, but as the theorist of the movement.

1891 Participates in the Nabis' exhibition at the Galerie Le Barc de Boutteville, Paris.

1893 Produces stage decorations and costumes for the Théâtre de l'Oeuvre, Paris. Illustrations for André Gide's work *Le Voyage d'Urien.*

1895 First trip to Italy. Reverts to the humanist and classical tradition.

1897 Second trip to Italy.

1899 Decorations for the chapel Sainte-Croix, Le Vésinet.

1900 Paints "A Tribute to Cézanne."

1903 Ambroise Vollard publishes 216 engravings intended to illustrate *L'Imitation de Jésus-Christ.*

1905 Trip to Spain.

1906 With K. X. Roussel and E. Bernard, calls on Cézanne in Aix-en-Provence.

1907-08 Stays in Italy. Teaches at the Académie Ranson.

1909-28 Travels to Moscow, Switzerland, Siena, Algeria, Tunisia, Jerusalem, Greece, Italy, the U.S., and Canada.

1911 Illustrates Verlaine's *Sagesse,* published by Vollard.

1912 Decorations for the Théâtre des Champs-Elysées, Paris.

1913 Publishes his work *Théories* (Paris).

1919 With the painter Desvallières, sets up the "Ateliers d'Art Sacré," wishing to give a new impulse to religious painting.

1921 Publishes his work *Nouvelles Théories* (Paris).

1924-25 Decorations for the Musée du Petit-Palais, Paris.

1927 Decorations for St. Louis Church, Vincennes.

1939 Decorations for the palace of the Society of Nations, Geneva. Publishes his work *Histoire de l'Art Religieux* (Paris).

1943 Died, in an automobile accident.

1945 Retrospective exhibition at the Musée d'Art Moderne, Paris.

Sales

DRAWINGS

1963

Maternity, India ink and wash, 8 x 6 . . . . (232) $ 316

Bacchant, 1913, charcoal and pastel, 26½ x 17½ . . (305) 225

Parsifal. 1913, pen and colored pencil, 5½ x 3¾ . . . (219) 77

Study for St. Paul, 1916, pencil, 12 x 9 . . . . (280) 30

The Good Shepherd, charcoal, 17¾ x 14¾ . . . . (262) 44

1964

Allegory of Work, charcoal and pastel,
12¼ x 9¼ . . . . (339) 40

Self-Portrait, 1935, pen, 6¼ x 8¼ . . . . (343) 44

1965

Landscape of the South of France, 1922, pencil
and gouache, 5 x 8 .... (582) $ 318

1966

Allegory, pencil, 16¾ x 43¾ .... (652)   56
Communicants, heightened drawing, 11¾ x 11 .... (756)   48
Quartet in the Park, India ink and wash,
5½ x 15½ .... (720)   26

1967

Three Women Seated on the Ground, pencil
heightened with pastel, 11¼ x 17¾ .... (923)   220
Study of Dancers, charcoal heightened with
pastel, 27¼ x 23 .... (873)   100
Dancer, colored chalk, 18½ x 13½ .... (986)   738

1968–July 1969

Seated Woman, pencil, 19½ x 12¼ .... (1084)   56
Biblical Scene, pencil and red chalk, 8 x 7½ ..... (1172)   84
Study for Eloa, 1916, slightly heightened drawing,
19½ x 21 .... (1032)   120

WATERCOLORS

1963

Still Life with Brushes, gouache, 22½ x 17¾ ...... (238)   76

1964

On the Beach, 1906, watercolor and India ink,
10½ x 16 .... (383)   701
Maternity, watercolor, 10¼ x 6¼ .... (441)   203
Design for Stained Glass, watercolor, 17 x 6¾ .... (355)   40

1965

The Lagoon in Venice, watercolor, 5½ x 9¼ ...... (598)   104

1968–July 1969

Study for the Decoration "St. Georges," tempera,
19 x 27¼ .... (1118)   130
Bather with Her Child, watercolor, 6½ x 8 ...... (1223)   154
Landing, two gouaches, 15½ x 12¼ and 15 x 12 .. (1262)   500
Four Young Girls Near a Pond, 1892-95,
watercolor, pen, brush, and India ink,
16½ x 12½ .... (1272)   528

PAINTINGS

1963

Adam and Eve, 1890-94, 27¾ x 38 .... (219)   1,695
The Water Carriers, 1903, 23 x 29 .... (254)   1,060
Statue of a Saint, on cardboard, 9½ x 6¼ .... (209)   67
Beach with Boat, 1924, 38¼ x 49½ .... (235)   400
The Music Lesson, on cardboard, 45¾ x 39½ ..... (258)   220
The Procession at Gruyère, 27¼ x 18¼ .... (182)   200

1964

Calvary, 1889, 16¼ x 13 .... (457)   440
Procession Under the Trees, 1892, 22 x 32 .... (332)   2,300
The Apparition of Christ, 1917, on cardboard,
10¾ x 14¾ .... (347)   700
Visitation, Venice, 1922, 20¼ x 29 .... (347)   1,200
Interior of a Church, 20¼ x 14¼ .... (428)   541
Rome: La Trinità dei Monti, 1928, 11½ x 18¾ .. (350)   270
The Wonderful Distribution, on board, 14 x 17 ... (420)   638
Delphes, 1929, on cardboard, 16¾ x 24½ .... (332)   240

1965

A Walk in the Country, 1897, 15½ x 23 .... (612)   800
Nausicaa, 1909, 37½ x 51½ .... (553)   3,200
Hope, 1915, on cardboard, 28½ x 9½ .... (556)   1,400

Little French Garden, 1921, on cardboard,
19¾ x 14¾ .... (690) $ 290
Madame Mellerio and Her Children, on board,
9 x 12¼ .... (541)   800
La Trinità dei Monti, Rome, 1928, 11½ x 18¼ .... (583)   871
Pilgrimage in Brittany, 26 x 19¾ .... (505)   640
The Temple of Wisdom, on panel, 17¾ x 23¾ .... (632)   260
Farms on the Beach, 1933, 19½ x 23¾ .... (629)   1,219
Bather by the Riverside, 17¾ x 11½ .... (645)   2,176

1966

The Yellow Cat, 1915, on cardboard, 18 x 19 ..... (749)   1,900
Holy Week Procession, 1900, on board,
12¼ x 10 .... (808)   929
The Olive Trees, 1907, on panel, 16¾ x 25¾ ...... (823)   1,686
Allegory, on cardboard, 10¾ x 7½ .... (781)   280
Two Young Girls in the Garden, on panel,
11¾ x 18½ .... (808)   1,016
The Beach, 21¼ x 25¾ .... (671)   145
The Triumphal Arch at St. Rémy de Provence, on
cardboard, 15 x 21 .... (810)   400

1967

Place des Terreaux in Lyons, on cradled panel,
17 x 24½ .... (852)   500
The Baby's Meal, 1903, 20½ x 16¾ .... (888)   1,244
Bullfight, (1905), on board, 9½ x 12¾ .... (967)   1,627
Aquatic Games, 1908, 37½ x 30½ .... (888)   4,699
The White Hind, on cardboard, 12¾ x 10 .... (949)   330
Italian Garden, 21¾ x 19¾ .... (877)   300
Rowing, 1924, on board, 14¼ x 19¼ .... (940)   1,393
New York Harbor, on cardboard, 29 x 42 .... (909)   520
Orpheus and Eurydice, 45¼ x 65¼ .... (923)   2,000
Hilly Landscape, 1929, 16½ x 24¼ .... (855)   500
View of Rouen, on cardboard, 10 x 19¾ .... (987)   600

1968–July 1969

The Windmill at La Bernerie, on cardboard,
13¾ x 20½ .... (1075)   460
St. Sebastian, 1893, 15½ x 12¾ .... (1187)   7,788
The Pipes of Pan, 1914, on cradled panel,
19¾ x 29¾ .... (1117)   1,760
Self-Portrait of the Artist with his Family,
Perros-Guirrec, 1923, 39¼ x 48½ .... (1126)   1,982
The Spanish Steps and La Trinità dei Monti,
1928, 29¾ x 19½ .... (1126)   4,460
Maternity, 1925, 18½ x 21¾ .... (1119)   600
Allegory of Sea (Mosaic Project), 32¾ x 56 ..... (1031)   312
Christ, on cardboard, 9¾ x 6¼ .... (1210)   240
Branch of Fruit, on cardboard, 10¼ x 11¾ ...... (1174)   2,185
Here Is the Holy Lamb, 1928, 25¾ x 36½ .... (1222)   1,560
The Shepherds and the Magi, 10¾ x 14 .... (1233)   400
New York Harbor, 1927, on board, 28¼ x 42 .... (1235)   3,000
Landscape in Greece, 1929, on board,
15¾ x 23¾ .... (1240)   1,320
Bank of the Nile at Luxor, 1929, on board,
20 x 14½ .... (1240)   600
Siena Cathedral, 1907, 12½ x 14½ .... (1240)   2,640
The Waves, 1909, 29¾ x 55¼ .... (1240)   1,152
*Game of Battledore and Shuttlecock on the
Beach,* 1914, 19 x 23 .... (1247)   2,360
Caravanserai at Biskra, on cradled panel,
16¾ x 22 .... (1268)   1,763
Landscape, 1914, 19¾ x 29¾ .... (1268)   4,176
The Via Appia, Rome, 1903, 18¾ x 25 .... (1271)   1,320
Constantine Arch, Rome, 1928, 14¼ x 21½ ...... (1271)   1,200

André Derain

(1880–1954)

Birthplace: Châtou, near Paris, France.

1895 Begins to paint.

1898-99 Attends the Académie Carrière in Paris, where he meets Matisse. Meets Vlaminck, who also lives at Châtou.

1901-02 Visits the Van Gogh exhibition, where he introduces Vlaminck to Matisse. Works with Vlaminck in the same studio at Châtou.

1904 Attends the Académie Julian, Paris.

1905 Follows Matisse to the south of France. Ambroise Vollard buys all his pictures. Participates in the Salon d'Automne with the other "Fauves"—Matisse, Rouault, Vlaminck, and Manguin. Exhibition at the Galerie Berthe Weil, Paris.

1907 Signs a contract with the dealer Kahnweiler. Produces engravings and sculptures.

1908 Produces ceramics. Comes under the influence of Cézanne and Cubism, and completely falls out with Fauvism.

1909 Illustrates *L'Enchanteur pourrissant* by Apollinaire.

1910 Stay at Cagnes in the south of France. Trip to Spain, where he meets Picasso again. First series of still lifes.

1912 Returns to Paris. Beginning of his so-called "Gothic" period, marked by stylization.

1914 Paints "Le Samedi," one of his major works. His picture, "La Cène," shows the end of the Cubist influence.

1916 First one-man show at Paul Guillaume's, Paris.

1919 Stage decoration for Diaghilev's ballet *La Boutique Fantasque*, Paris.

1920-30 Travels through the south of France.

1928 Wins the Carnegie prize for his picture "La Chasse" (Pittsburgh Museum).

1931 Important exhibition at Paul Guillaume's, Paris.

1945 Illustrations for Rabelais' *Pantagruel* (published by Skira).

1954 Died, in an automobile accident at Garches, near Paris.

Sales

DRAWINGS

1961-1962

Seated Woman, 17 x 23¾ .... (70) $1,422
Dancing Nude, 14¼ x 9 .... (25) 116
Virgin,[1] black lead, 21 x 14¼ .... (51) 520
Seated Nude, Front View, black lead, 10¼ x 8 .... (177) 130
Back View of a Seated Woman, stumped pencil,
    17½ x 13¾ .... (76) 200
Nude, stick of greasepaint, 12¼ x 9 .... (82) 278
Still Life, red chalk and pencil, 18¼ x 24 .... (156) 360
Landscape, pencil, on paper, 9½ x 12¼ .... (156) 260
Group of Figures, colored pencil, 6 x 7¾ .... (124) 126
Seated Nude, charcoal, 15 x 16¾ .... (172) 124
Portico with Bathers, pen 20½ x 27¼ .... (98) 340
Landscape with Steeple, sepia, 14¼ x 21¾ .... (130) 500

[1]After Raphael.

Russian Ballet Character, India ink, 10¼ x 8¼ .... (53) $ 190
Dancer,[2] ink and watercolor, 12½ x 10 .... (164) 824
The Shepherd, pen and watercolor, 7½ x 4½ ..... (140) 275
Theater Scene, wash and watercolor,
    18¼ x 23¼ .... (141) 5,000
Back View of a Woman's Head, red chalk,
    13½ x 9½ .... (141) 360
Walking Nude, red chalk, 24½ x 18¼ .... (141) 500
Three-Quarter View of a Seated Nude, red chalk,
    23¼ x 17¾ .... (141) 280
The Cretan Bull, red chalk, 8¾ x 13 .... (53) 120
Woman's Face, red chalk, 15 x 12¾ .... (32) 180
Seated Woman, red chalk, 24¼ x 18 .... (85) 450

1963

Woman's Head, on the Right, (1914), red chalk,
    14¼ x 10½ .... (219) 339
The Virgin with the Goldfinch (After Raphael),
    charcoal, 21¾ x 18¼ .... (232) 429
Portrait of the Artist's Mother, blue ink,
    22½ x 17½ .... (216) 210
Woman with a Dog, 13½ x 8 .... (254) 260
Standing Nude, Front View, pencil, 11¾ x 8 ..... (300) 240
Nude, red chalk, 8 x 12¼ .... (265) 330
Study of a Nude, (1920), red chalk, 23¾ x 16¼ ... (255) 247
Bare-Breasted Woman, red chalk, 22½ x 16¾ .... (607) 800
Seated Nude, pencil, 25¾ x 14 .... (232) 497
Nudes in a Landscape, pen, watercolor, colored
    pencil with gouache lights, 10¾ x 15¾ .... (258) 300
Hilly Landscape, wash, 6 x 9 .... (224) 400
Still Life, red chalk and pencil, 18¼ x 24 .... (254) 420

1964

The Banks of the River Lot, (1912-13), pencil,
    19½ x 24 .... (416) 1,106
Still Life, red chalk and pencil, 18¼ x 24 .... (351) 480
The Cup of Fruit, black pencil, 17¾ x 21¾ .... (393) 240
Walk in the Forest, pencil, 10 x 14 .... (392) 246
Landscape, pencil, 9½ x 14 .... (441) 328
Hunting, bister and brownish red wash,
    9½ x 12¼ .... (401) 600
Portrait of May Dauriac, red chalk, 14½ x 17 .... (374) 250
Back View of a Nude, 1927, charcoal .... (433) 181
Reclining Nude, pen, 8¾ x 11½ .... (329) 300
Standing Nude, red chalk, 24 x 15¾ .... (399) 380
Nude, red chalk, 22½ x 17½ .... (321) 475
Young Nude, charcoal, 24½ x 17¾ .... (368) 498
Seated Nude, red chalk, 10¼ x 14¼ .... (322) 350
Woman in Profile, black pencil, 8¾ x 9¾ .... (466) 180
Woman's Head, red chalk, 17 x 11¾ .... (460) 700

1965

Seated Woman, pencil, 18½ x 24 .... (582) 553
Seated Nude, red chalk, 23 x 17½ .... (516) 600
Back View of a Standing Nude, red chalk,
    25 x 19 .... (565) 396
Seated Nude, red chalk, 23¼ x 17½ .... (538) 470
Nude with a Rock, red chalk, 15 x 12 .... (507) 250
Two Nudes, red chalk, 18¼ x 24¼ .... (624) 332
Landscape, pencil, 10 x 14 .... (597) 283
The Studio, India ink, 21¾ x 16¾ .... (512) 520

[2]Costume design for Diaghilev's ballet *La Boutique Fantasque*, 1919. Inscribed "Madame Lopokowa."

1966

Landscape (Study for "Le Bosquet" 1912), red
chalk, 25¼ x 19¾ .... (801) $3,400
Seated Nude, (1925), black pencil, 24 x 17 .... (703)   2,100
Nude, 15¾ x 23¼ .... (655)   430
The Model, red chalk, 20½ x 13¾ .... (829)   360
Reclining Nude, black pencil, 8¼ x 10¾ .... (796)   120
Seated Nude, red chalk, 18¾ x 15¾ .... (671)   319
Seated Dancer, charcoal, 24 x 18¾ .... (757)   829
Woman's Head, red chalk, 17 x 11½ .... (685)   500
Head of a Young Girl with Long Hair, charcoal,
21¾ x 17 .... (734)   1,040
Side View of a Young Lady, red chalk,
23¾ x 19 .... (798)   723
Landscape, pencil, 16 x 21 .... (784)   400
The Village, black pencil, 17¾ x 23¼ .... (743)   1,160

1967

Six Characters of "La Boutique Fantasque,"
series of 6 drawings, pen and watercolor, with
make-up information, each 6½ x 4½ .... (922)   2,211
Young Girl's Head, black lead, 23¾ x 18½ .... (893)   950
Seated Nude, red chalk, 18½ x 25¾ .... (1004)   2,000
Standing Woman in the Nude, red chalk,
25 x 18¼ .... (898)   560
Nude, pencil, 12½ x 9 .... (956)   380
Standing Nude, red chalk, 24½ x 18 .... (889)   1,000
Seated Nude, red chalk, 12¼ x 9¼ .... (881)   553
Seated Nude, charcoal, 12½ x 9¼ .... (926)   250
Reclining Nude, India ink, 11¾ x 15¾ .... (967)   339
The High Trees, (1910), charcoal and red chalk,
24½ x 18½ .... (984)   460
Underwood, charcoal, 18 x 24 .... (918)   904

1968–July 1969

Nude, red chalk on paper laid down on canvas,
67¼ x 23¾ .... (1018)   4,000
Seated Nude, India ink, 14 x 9 .... (1088)   550
Nude in Profile, India ink, 7¾ x 10½ .... (1026)   500
Bust of a Nude, red chalk, 23¾ x 18½ .... (1094)   620
Standing Nude, pencil, 10 x 6¼ .... (1172)   340
Standing Nude, pencil, and black chalk,
11½ x 8¾ .... (1138)   297
Reclining Nude; Reclining Nude, two drawings,
pencil and ink, 13¼ x 17¼ and 11¾ x 15¾ ... (1183)   840
Nude, red chalk, 23 x 18¾ .... (1061)   650
Bathers, black lead and colored pencil,
4½ x 4¼ .... (1099)   414
Model in Profile, red chalk, 24 x 17½ .... (1134)   472
Reclining Nude, pencil, 15½ x 20¼ .... (1205)   240
Nude in a Landscape, pencil and green chalk,
18½ x 12¼ .... (1193)   1,982
Still Life with a Stone Jug, 1910, pencil and
watercolor, 5½ x 4½ .... (1068)   2,006
Still Life with a Pedestal Table, pen, 11¾ x 8 .... (1019)   530
Portrait of a Woman, India ink, 25¼ x 19½ ..... (1026)   800
Heads, pencil and watercolor, 14 x 9 .... (1221)   150
Young Woman's Head, pen, 14 x 9½ .... (1223)   260
Study of a Nude, India ink, 8 x 11 .... (1224)   660
Seated Nude, red chalk, 25¼ x 18¾ .... (1225)   800
Ballerina, 23 x 18¼ .... (1227)   590
Nude in Profile, 15½ x 23¼ .... (1227)   260
Long-Haired Nude, black lead, 24½ x 23¼ ...... (1227)   340

Landscape, pencil, 10½ x 15 .... (1231) $ 450
Seated Woman in the Nude, red chalk,
18½ x 24 .... (1231)   375
Sheep Carriers, pen and ink, 11¾ x 15½ .... (1231)   425
Nude on a Sofa, red chalk, 16¾ x 23 .... (1234)   960
Landscape, (1920-25), brown chalk, 18½ x 24¾ .. (1240)   480
Woman's Head, brown chalk, 23 x 17½ .... (1240)   336
Landscape with Trees, sepia washes, 14¾ x 20¼ . (1241)   605
Seated Nude, charcoal, 12½ x 9½ .... (1241)   479
Seated Woman in the Nude, India ink,
14½ x 11¼ .... (1246)   1,000
Standing Woman in the Nude, charcoal on buff
paper, 17¼ x 15¾ .... (1246)   850
Nude Man, Back View, red chalk, 25 x 18 ..... (1248)   800
Bust of a Young Man, charcoal, 24¾ x 18¾ ..... (1248)   750
Nude, pencil, 25 x 17½ .... (1248)   500
Reclining Woman, pencil, 16 x 24 .... (1248)   550
Bust of a Woman, pencil, 12½ x 10¼ .... (1248)   250
Reclining Woman, Conté pencil, 12 x 17 .... (1248)   300
Theater Character: Woman, (1942), black pencil,
8½ x 6½ .... (1265)   400
Theater Character: Man, black pencil, 8½ x 6½ . (1265)   400
Venus with a Fur, (1930), colored pencil, 8 x 6¼ . (1265)   500
Standing Nude, pencil, 13 x 9½ .... (1268)   394
Portraits, three drawings, black lead, 4½ x 5¼ ... (1268)   534
Portrait of a Young Woman, India ink,
25¼ x 19¼ .... (1268)   719
Studies, pencil with heightening, 13¾ x 8½ ..... (1273)   189
Study for Pantagruel, pencil, 13¾ x 8½ .... (1273)   139

WATERCOLORS

1961–1962

Study, gouache, 7 x 14 .... (18)   712
Table with Fruit, pastel, 14¾ x 20¼ .... (141)   620
Horse Dealer Leading His Horses, (1905),
watercolor, 16¾ x 23 .... (102)   3,000
Woman in Profile, gouache, 14 x 9¾ .... (158)   150
The Wild Dance, 1906, watercolor and gouache,
19¾ x 24½ .... (20)   11,850
Ballet Character, watercolor, 11½ x 8¾ .... (52)   320
Dancer in a Blue and Green Garment,[3] gouache,
14¼ x 10 .... (114)   300
Harlequins, gouache, 14¼ x 11¾ .... (71)   1,760

1963

The Wrestlers, (Fauve period), watercolor,
18¾ x 12¼ .... (232)   2,441
Fishing Boats, 1905, watercolor and colored
pencil, 19¾ x 24½ .... (309)   14,832
Sunset Over the Thames, 1905, watercolor,
19¾ x 25 .... (225)   11,500
Lost Eden, (1909), gouache, 14¾ x 18¼ .... (255)   1,097
Landscape, (1910), watercolor, 13 x 18¾ .... (179)   450
Landscape, watercolor, 14¾ x 20½ .... (241)   420
Bust of a Woman, Back View, 1920, pastel,
24 x 18 .... (277)   1,782
Stage Decoration, gouache, 10¼ x 14¼ .... (227)   200
Louis XIV Feminine Costume, watercolor,
10¾ x 8 .... (281)   768

1964

Nudes on the Beach, (1904-05), watercolor,
19¾ x 25¾ .... (354)   22,000
The Wrestlers, (1905), watercolor, 19 x 11¾ ...... (371)   2,400

[3]Costume design for *Les Soirées de Paris,* La Cigale, 1921.

Fishing Boats, 1905, gouache and watercolor,
24½ x 19¾ .... (378) $17,628

Nudes (recto), (1907), *Woman and Landscape,*
(verso), watercolor, 19 x 25 .... (454) 387

Young Ladies Dancing, (1907), watercolor,
25¾ x 32 .... (378) 18,080

The Towboats, watercolor, 7½ x 11½ .... (378) 3,616

The Stagecoach, watercolor, 19½ x 25¼ .... (471) 7,006

The Cup of Fruit, gouache, 9 x 12 .... (460) 1,040

Mask with a Turban, gouache, 10¾ x 8¾ .... (321) 275

Dark-Haired Girl with Blue Eyes, pastel,
18¼ x 15¾ .... (335) 1,660

Under the Arbor, gouache and watercolor,
13¼ x 11 .... (351) 780

Ballet Design, gouache, 6¼ x 13¾ .... (368) 1,050

The Landing Place, watercolor, 18¾ x 24 .... (471) 9,492

1965

Scene on a Quay, (1903-05), watercolor,
18¼ x 23¼ .... (633) 6,500

The Cabs, 1905, watercolor, 19 x 24 .... (617) 14,690

The Soldiers of the Republic, 1899, watercolor,
11 x 13 .... (548) 1,440

The Swans' Pond, gouache, 6 x 15½ .... (567) 1,921

Boats in the Cove, watercolor, 7½ x 11½ .... (518) 1,800

Bathers Amid the Rocks, gouache, 13 x 10¼ ..... (515) 13,020

At the Café, gouache, 18¼ x 23¾ .... (569) 12,995

1966

*Nude Woman Beneath an Eagle and Near a
Bush,* watercolor and India ink, 15½ x 18½ .. (727) 3,520

Two Bathers, gouache, 10 x 12¾ .... (815) 977

Landscape, (1921), watercolor on paper laid down
on canvas, 12 x 16¾ .... (784) 1,500

Stage Character, watercolor, 8 x 6¼ .... (745) 678

Stage, watercolor, 18½ x 24 .... (797) 6,780

Still Life, pastel, 15½ x 19 .... (798) 4,068

Basket of Flowers, gouache, 11½ x 17 .... (801) 5,400

1967

The Soldiers of the Republic, 1899, watercolor,
11 x 13 .... (918) 4,407

Bust of a Woman, 1920, pastel, 23½ x 17½ ...... (985) 758

Woman's Head, (1928-30), pastel, 21¼ x 18 ..... (1004) 2,000

Reclining Nude, watercolor, 7 x 10 .... (996) 420

1968-July 1969

The Charge, (1904), watercolor, 18¼ x 22½ ..... (1173) 14,720

Hilly Landscape, gouache, 12½ x 19¾ .... (1145) 1,400

Woman and Landscape, (recto), (1907), *Nude,*
(verso), watercolor, 19 x 25 .... (1187) 5,900

Stage Costume for "Les Joyeuses Commères,"
watercolor and gouache over a pencil sketch,
10¾ x 8 .... (1142) 708

Bust of a Young Lady, pastel, 17¾ x 14¼ .... (1117) 3,300

Figures, watercolor, 11 x 19 .... (1174) 1,725

Etruscan Scene, watercolor, 12¼ x 18¼ .... (1202) 700

The Sylphs' Dance, watercolor laid down on
canvas, 12 x 17 .... (1018) 1,800

Boats at Collioure, watercolor, 10 x 12½ ...... (1023) 7,400

Still Life with a Jug, pastel, 15¼ x 18¼ ...... (1246) 3,500

Theater Design, gouache, 14½ x 20 .... (1248) 1,000

The Blue Bird, (1921), watercolor, 5¾ x 8 ..... (1265) 600

Theater Character, (1945), watercolor, 7¼ x 8¾ . (1265) 560

Standing Woman, watercolor, 10¾ x 8 .... (1268) 650

Woman in a Crinoline, watercolor, 10¾ x 8 ..... (1268) 696

Valet, watercolor, 10¾ x 8 .... (1268) $ 742

The Blue-Eyed Brunette, 1936, pastel,
17¾ x 14½ .... (1272) 4,080

The Birth of Venus, pencil, ink, and watercolor,
5½ x 13 .... (1272) 1,296

PAINTINGS

1961-1962

Interior, (1903), 13 x 16¼ .... (143) 6,554

Landscape, (1905), oil on cardboard, 8¾ x 10¾ .... (18) 15,142

Underwood (St. Maximilien), 36½ x 29 .... (18) 18,984

Landscape with Tall Trees, 15 x 18¼ .... (114) 6,000

Landscape of the South of France, 8¾ x 13 ...... (69) 1,896

Landscape at Aix-en-Provence, 9½ x 16¼ .... (150) 12,656

View of Cahors, 15¾ x 17¾ .... (141) 2,800

Landscape of the South of France, 8¾ x 13 ...... (26) 1,620

Landscape at Castelgandolfo, (1921),
24½ x 29¾ .... (88) 12,054

Landscape, 11 x 8¼ .... (155) 1,000

Underwood, 32 x 39½ .... (93) 9,718

The Path in the Forest, 1931, 13 x 15¾ .... (164) 6,865

La Ciotat, (1930-32), 12 x 16 .... (31) 9,336

Dance, 1905, 20½ x 25 .... (31) 17,025

Madame Germaine Carco, 23½ x 18¾ .... (37) 1,800

Head of a Young Gipsy, 12¼ x 10 .... (53) 1,120

Young Lady in Profile, 13¾ x 9½ .... (80) 2,100

Woman's Head, 12¼ x 10 .... (33) 1,300

Woman's Head, 14½ x 11¼ .... (167) 1,560

Portrait of a Woman, 13¾ x 10¾ .... (76) 1,300

Bather, 6¾ x 11¾ .... (143) 768

Reclining Bather, 7½ x 12¾ .... (160) 1,240

Reclining Nude, 11¾ x 17 .... (68) 2,000

Seated Woman in the Nude, 22½ x 13½ .... (155) 2,300

Bust with a Flower, 23¾ x 22 .... (64) 5,000

Bunch of Flowers, 15½ x 21 .... (122) 1,356

Flowers, oil on canvas laid down on board,
8¼ x 6½ .... (143) 1,966

Still Life with a Cup of Fruit, (1912), 32¼ x 18¼ ... (88) 8,856

Still Life with a Dog, 4½ x 11 .... (26) 820

Still Life with a Violin, 32 x 23¾ .... (29) 3,200

Still Life, on an oval cardboard, 16¾ x 12¾ ...... (20) 13,430

1963

Portrait of a Woman, 18¼ x 15 .... (262) 1,620

The Set Table, 1921-22, 38½ x 64½ .... (277) 19,194

The Plate of Fruit, 16¼ x 23¾ .... (198) 5,600

St. Cyr: The Road, (1922), 17½ x 21 .... (277) 7,129

The Beach, (1925), 6½ x 12 .... (210) 3,290

The Bathers, 4 x 5¼ .... (224) 850

The Bathers, 10¼ x 15¾ .... (318) 1,600

The Bathers, 8 x 12¼ .... (296) 3,000

Apples and Pears, 1925, 13 x 21½ .... (210) 3,565

Still Life, 18¼ x 21¾ .... (206) 4,100

Still Life, 25¾ x 32 .... (283) 9,492

Head of a Red-Haired Woman, (1925),
10¾ x 13 .... (299) 440

The Smile, 15¾ x 12½ .... (316) 2,250

Portrait of a Woman, 12½ x 12¼ .... (296) 3,600

Bust of a Young Girl, 13 x 8¾ .... (242) 1,180

The Woman with the Blue Collarette,
25¾ x 21¼ .... (318) 8,200

Nude, 10 x 8 .... (179) 575

Landscape, 8 x 10¾ .... (179) 1,100

Villeneuve-lès-Avignon by Night, 1925, 21 x 25 ... (309) $7,251
The Basilica of St. Maximin, 24½ x 29 .... (243) 21,000
The Gypsy, 18¼ x 15 .... (243) 8,200
Still Life with Apples, Pears, and Grapes, (1930), 12 x 23¼ .... (277) 6,581
The Public Garden, 17¾ x 17½ .... (254) 5,200
Hunting Scene, 7½ x 13 .... (283) 4,294
Landscape of the South of France, 19¾ x 25¾ .... (283) 10,396
Bathers, 6¾ x 11¾ .... (283) 701
The Olive Trees, 25¾ x 32 .... (258) 6,000
Seated Nude, 19¾ x 18¼ .... (243) 3,000
Landscape with Clouds, 15 x 18¼ .... (312) 2,240
Portrait of a Young Woman, 18 x 14¾ .... (202) 6,250
Little Girl with a Scarf, 25¾ x 21¼ .... (243) 7,600
Nude with Green Drapery, 25¾ x 21¼ .... (232) 9,718

1964
The Artist's Studio, (1903), 13 x 16¼ .... (378) 10,283
Boats on the River Thames, 1905, 21¼ x 25¾ ..... (378) 48,364
Don Quixote and Sancho Panza, 1905, 39½ x 29 .... (471) 34,352
Landscape, (1907-08), 8 x 10 .... (367) 8,292
The Artist's Dog, (1913-15), 27¾ x 38¾ .... (416) 2,488
Seated Nude, 1921, 46¼ x 34¾ .... (454) 2,764
Still Life with a Basket of Fruit, (1921-22), 16¾ x 21¼ .... (367) 7,739
Horse, (1924), 35¾ x 15¾ .... (416) 4,975
Landscape by Night, Villeneuve-lès-Avignon, 1925, 21 x 25 .... (405) 5,224
View of Cadaqués, 1927, 15 x 18¼ .... (368) 7,186
Three Figures on the Grass, 13½ x 16¼ .... (378) 17,402
Le Bateau ivre, distemper on paper laid down on canvas, 27¾ x 37½ .... (398) 2,800
Landscape, 20¼ x 24¼ .... (354) 5,250
Ollioules Woods, Toulon, 23¼ x 28¼ .... (458) 9,286
Bather, 10¼ x 20½ .... (347) 2,200
Reclining Nude, 29¾ x 25¾ .... (371) 6,100
Nude with a Chair, 12¼ x 10¼ .... (340) 1,300
Portrait of Madame Coquiot, 24 x 19¾ .... (397) 700
Reclining Nude with a Chair, 11¾ x 17 .... (335) 2,300
Seated Nude, 36 x 32½ .... (399) 4,800
Pears, on panel, 6¾ x 10½ .... (399) 1,260
Still Life with Fish, 13¾ x 20½ .... (395) 3,000
Still Life with a Ewer, 10 x 12 .... (474) 1,500
Still Life with a Jug and Lemons, 16¼ x 13 .... (398) 1,560
Still Life with Fish, 18¼ x 21¾ .... (471) 3,390
Vase of Dahlias, 19 x 21¼ .... (453) 11,056
Tree, 13¾ x 7½ .... (347) 1,300
Flowers, 18¼ x 15 .... (460) 4,400

1965
Dance, (1905-06), 73 x 80 .... (594) 70,000
The Thames, (1905-06), 25¾ x 29¾ .... (573) 82,920
The Artist's Dog, (1913-15), 27¾ x 36¾ .... (624) 2,211
The Harbor, (1920), 23¾ x 30 .... (628) 4,933
The Olive Trees, 25¾ x 32 .... (564) 10,000
Seated Woman in the Nude, 1921, 45½ x 35¼ .... (547) 3,800
Portrait of a Woman, 13 x 10¼ .... (497) 1,060
Woman's Head, 12¾ x 12¾ .... (526) 5,750
The Woman with a Coral Necklace, 21½ x 17½ ... (522) 5,528
Douarnenez Harbor, 1936, 17½ x 21¼ .... (575) 16,584
Naiads, 15 x 18¼ .... (561) 3,900
The Dead Tree, 8¾ x 12¼ .... (583) 3,192
Nude, 11¾ x 10¾ .... (539) 4,750

Portrait of a Man, 18¼ x 20¼ .... (561) $10,000
Reclining Nude, 12 x 16¾ .... (553) 2,400
Fair-Haired Young Woman, 12¼ x 10 .... (561) 900
Young Girl's Head, 20¼ x 16 .... (637) 6,000
Nude on Her Bed, 17¾ x 21¼ .... (624) 4,975
Portrait of Madame Coquiot, 24 x 19¾ .... (532) 360
Still Life with Bread, 25¾ x 32 .... (569) 10,057
Still Life with Fruit, 10 x 16¾ .... (617) 3,955
Still Life with a Basket, on canvas laid down on panel, 9½ x 7¼ .... (569) 3,164
Still Life with a Ewer, 10 x 12 .... (613) 2,400

1966
The Suburbs of Collioure, 1905, 23¾ x 29 .... (801) 100,000
Landscape of St. Maximin, 1912, 13 x 16¼ .... (811) 6,620
Near Sanary, 17½ x 21¼ .... (808) 13,349
Seated Blond Nude, 24½ x 21¾ .... (797) 6,102
Woman's Head, 21½ x 18¼ .... (701) 3,500
The Italian Girl, 1914, 27¾ x 12¼ .... (750) 4,146
Head, 13¾ x 13 .... (701) 3,250
Landscape of Provence, (1922), 24 x 19¾ .... (713) 6,500
Snowy Landscape, on panel, 9¾ x 12¾ .... (808) 3,192
The Roman Bridge, (1930), 18¼ x 21¾ .... (744) 6,328
Reclining Nude, 11 x 14 .... (784) 3,000
Landscape with Blue Sky, 30 x 38½ .... (666) 8,000
Picnic on the Grass, 8¾ x 10¾ .... (797) 9,944
Nude, Back View, 12½ x 8¾ .... (786) 900
Still Life, 7¼ x 7¼ .... (744) 3,610
Still Life with Pears and Grapes, 12½ x 15¼ ..... (738) 4,428

1967
Basket of Fruit, 11¾ x 14¼ .... (923) 4,600
Underwood at Châtou, 1905, 31½ x 39½ .... (918) 61,020
The Bridge at Châtou, 1908, 16¼ x 13 .... (965) 14,464
Basket of Fruit, (1912), 14¾ x 14¾ .... (982) 4,266
Figure, 1913, 36¼ x 29¼ .... (993) 10,600
The Gipsy, 19½ x 21¼ .... (893) 5,500
Still Life, 1920-22, 23¾ x 17¾ .... (938) 4,975
Still Life with Tomatoes, 7¼ x 8¼ .... (940) 4,351
Still Life, 7¼ x 7¼ .... (919) 4,068
Reclining Woman in the Nude, 1921, 47 x 35¼ .... (918) 10,057
Portrait of a Woman, 18½ x 14¼ .... (852) 2,800
Portrait of a Woman, (1923), 16 x 16¾ .... (888) 2,349
Reclining Blond Nude, 38¾ x 58 .... (984) 9,600
Still Life, (1928), 29 x 37 .... (864) 8,000
Still Life with Fruit, 9 x 13 .... (918) 5,085
Still Life with Fruit, 21 x 21¾ .... (987) 14,600
Head of a Red-Haired Woman, (1928-30), 8¼ x 6 .... (988) 2,737
Reclining Nude, 10¼ x 17½ .... (850) 2,400
Seated Blond Nude, 24 x 11¾ .... (912) 4,300
Woman's Head (Madame Careo), on panel, 12¾ x 10¾ .... (870) 2,500
Young Lady's Head, 18½ x 14½ .... (841) 2,750
Landscape, on panel, 8½ x 11 .... (864) 3,500
Landscape at Camiers, 16 x 12¾ .... (963) 4,250
A Path in the Forest, 21¼ x 25¾ .... (989) 4,000
Bacchanal (Project for a Fresco), 7¼ x 17¾ .... (938) 2,764

1968–July 1969
Landscape of the Ile de France, (1904), 15½ x 20½ .... (1068) 61,360
Parliament and Westminster Bridge, London, 1906, 29 x 36¼ .... (1068) 14,160

The Banks of the Thames, 1906, 26 x 39¼ . . . . **(1132)** $141,600
The Orchard, (1907), 21¼ x 25¾ . . . . **(1187)** 41,480
Bathers, (1908), on canvas laid down on panel,
12¼ x 15½ . . . . **(1187)** 6,136
Landscape of the South of France, (1909), on
board, 19½ x 23¼ . . . . **(1193)** 4,956
Seated Urchin, (1921), 29 x 23½ . . . . **(1176)** 10,000
The Forest at Saint-Cyr-lès-Lecques (Var), 1921,
29 x 36¼ . . . . **(1187)** 38,940
Bust of a Dark-Haired Young Lady, 18¼ x 15 . . . **(1117)** 5,400
Head of a Woman with a Veil, 14¾ x 11 . . . . **(1053)** 2,000
Head of a Sleeping Woman, 10 x 12 . . . . **(1060)** 3,000
Bust of a Seated Woman, 36¼ x 29 . . . . **(1106)** 10,200
Woman's Head, 10½ x 8¾ . . . . **(1132)** 1,416
Nude, on board, 6 x 8¼ . . . . **(1127)** 4,140
Reclining Nude, 7¾ x 12¾ . . . . **(1026)** 1,800
Standing Nude, Her Arm Raised, 8¼ x 4¾ . . . . . . **(1219)** 1,100
Portrait of Lady Abdy, 45¾ x 34¾ . . . . **(1117)** 12,900
The Comedian, 29 x 23¾ . . . . **(1121)** 6,750
The Picnic, on board, 8¾ x 10¾ . . . . **(1132)** 3,540
Fontainebleau Forest, 32 x 39½ . . . . **(1125)** 9,200
Landscape of Italy, 36¼ x 25¾ . . . . **(1200)** 9,600
Still Life, 31¼ x 39¼ . . . . **(1187)** 8,260
Vase of Flowers, 14½ x 12 . . . . **(1145)** 5,000
Seated Nude, 24 x 18¼ . . . . **(1224)** 6,400
Le Bateau ivre, tempera on canvas, 27¼ x 37¼ . . **(1225)** 5,620
Woman's Head, 14 x 15 . . . . **(1235)** 3,250
The Bridge at Châtou, (1906), 15½ x 12½ . . . . **(1235)** 18,000
The Pond, (1931-33), 19½ x 25½ . . . . **(1235)** 6,500
Trees, l'Estaque, (1906), 18¼ x 15 . . . . **(1239)** 80,400
Still Life, (1911-13), 18 x 22½ . . . . **(1239)** 7,680
La Mappemonde, 1914, 41 x 29 . . . . **(1239)** 22,800
Young Girl's Head, (1912-13), on canvas laid
down on board, 16 x 10¼ . . . . **(1240)** 2,280
Young Girl, 17½ x 15 . . . . **(1248)** 3,500
Head of a Tzigane, 12½ x 10 . . . . **(1248)** 4,250
Portrait of a Woman (The Belgian Refugee),
18½ x 16 . . . . **(1248)** 3,250
Seated Blond Nude, 24 x 21¾ . . . . **(1254)** 6,400
Fontainebleau Forest, 32 x 39½ . . . . **(1268)** 10,440
Still Life, 7¼ x 14¾ . . . . **(1268)** 3,573
The Model, 24 x 19¾ . . . . **(1268)** 11,600
Landscape, 19¾ x 25¾ . . . . **(1268)** 19,488
Le Bateau ivre, (1907-08), tempera on canvas,
27¼ x 37¼ . . . . **(1268)** 1,624
Landscape, (1904), 15¾ x 21¾ . . . . **(1268)** 74,240
Underwood at Leques, 1925, 25½ x 32 . . . . **(1270)** 8,400
Woman with a Coral Necklace, 21½ x 17½ . . . . . . **(1270)** 6,720
Figures, with Trees in the Background,
8½ x 10½ . . . . **(1271)** 1,008
Portrait of a Woman with Her Dog, (1947), on
panel, 10¼ x 5½ . . . . **(1271)** 3,640

François Desnoyer

(1894–   )

Birthplace: Montauban, France.

1912-14 Attends the Ecole des Arts Décoratifs, Paris.

1922 Participates in the Salon des Indépendants and in the Salon d'Automne, Paris.

1924 Wins the Blumenthal prize. Exhibits yearly in the main Parisian salons and has two one-man shows at the Galerie Drouant-David and at the Galerie Guiot, Paris.

1936 Teaches at the Ecole des Arts Décoratifs for twelve years.

1937 Wins the gold medal at the International exhibition, Paris.

1950 Wins the first prize of contemporary painting, Paris. Awarded the rank of Officer in the Legion of Honor.

1951 Settles permanently at Sète in the south of France.

1955 Wins the first prize at the Menton Biennial.

1958 Wins the gold medal at the International Exhibition, Brussels.

1960 One-man show at the Musée des Beaux-Arts, Paris.

Sales

DRAWINGS

1963
Young Woman's Head, 19½ x 14 . . . . (254) $ 50

1966
Seated Nude, black pencil, 10¼ x 7¾ . . . . (794)   70

1968–July 1969
Reclining Woman, black pencil, 8 x 10¾ . . . . (1110)   80

WATERCOLORS

1963
Windflowers in a Vase, watercolor, 13 x 9½ . . . . . . (296)   360
Reclining Young Woman, watercolor, 8¾ x 11¾ . . (296)   160
The Village, watercolor, 10¼ x 13¾ . . . . (311)   260

1964
Dax, watercolor, 10¼ x 14 . . . . (355)   370

1965
Vase of Flowers, watercolor, 17¾ x 11¾ . . . . (588)   120
Fun Fair, gouache, 8¼ x 10¾ . . . . (508)   110
The Church, gouache, 8¼ x 12 . . . . (509)   240

1966
Jormier, gouache, 8¼ x 12 . . . . (692)   200

1967
Rest in the Country, watercolor, 8½ x 11¾ . . . . (980)   60
Young Woman Lying on the Grass, watercolor,
8½ x 11¾ . . . . (857)   160

1968–July 1969
Flowers in a Blue Vase, watercolor, 18¾ x 12½ . . (1051)   240
On the Beach, watercolor, 8¾ x 12¼ . . . . (1200)   520
View of Hostingues, watercolor, 9¾ x 15½ . . . . . . (1029)   160
Three Young Girls, watercolor, 12¼ x 10 . . . . (1089)   56

PAINTINGS

1961–1962

Antibes Harbor, 24 x 19¾ .... (102) $1,320
The Standing Model, 21¼ x 13 .... (157)   160
The Arrival of the Fleet, on panel, 18¼ x 21¾ ..... (76)   800

1963

The Garden by the Sea, 21¼ x 25¾ .... (238)   300
The Harbor, 39½ x 32 .... (298)   970
The Harbor, on panel, 13 x 16¼ .... (276)   1,120
Arbonne, on panel, 9½ x 13 .... (296)   700
Landscape, 23¾ x 31½ .... (232)   859
Landscape, 23¾ x 31½ .... (281)   904

1964

Seated Woman, on panel, 13 x 9½ .... (355)   200
The Model in the Studio, on panel, 21¾ x 13 ..... (393)   160

1965

Sète Harbor, 21¾ x 18¼ .... (619)   1,110
The Harbor, 39½ x 32 .... (598)   1,300
Canal Boat, on panel, 8¾ x 13 .... (552)   1,800
Underwood at Fontainebleau, on panel,
    8¼ x 10¼ .... (631)   200
Landscape, 23¾ x 31½ .... (617)   283

1966

The Ball, 18¼ x 21¾ .... (672)   660
Gemenos Near Aubagne, Winter 1938, 15 x 24 ... (811)   840
Group of Executed Men, on panel, 29 x 20½ ..... (652)   200
The Ice-Cream Man, 10¼ x 18¾ .... (809)   900

1967

The Ice-Cream Man, 10 x 18¾ .... (995)   1,200
The Market, on cardboard, 13 x 16¼ .... (912)   1,300

1968–July 1969

The Reading, 39½ x 31½ .... (1202)   1,300
The Model, 36½ x 23¾ .... (1043)   520
Sète Harbor, on panel, 13 x 18¼ .... (1213)   700
Back View of a Young English Lady, 21¾ x 15 .. (1183)   720
Woman Reading, 39½ x 19¾ .... (1221)   1,040
Sparenburg, 1951, 77¼ x 51½ .... (1258)   2,400
Landscape, on panel, 9½ x 13 .... (1266)   560
Landscape, 9½ x 13 .... (1266)   500

Preston Dickinson

(1889–1930)

Birthplace: New York, U.S.

1905-10   Attends the Art Students League, New York.
1910-14   Travels to Europe, where he studies art.
1915   Exhibits at the Daniel Gallery, New York.
1924   Exhibits at the Pennsylvania Academy of Fine Arts.
1926   Discovers the Quebec scenes which he relishes.
1930   Died, Hendaye, France.

Sales

WATERCOLORS

1967

Still Life, pastel, 17¾ x 19¾ .... (952) $1,500

1968–July 1969

Landscape, pastel, 7¾ x 12 .... (1035)   850
Still Life with Fruit and Pottery, 1930, pastel,
    24¾ x 18¾ .... (1035)   3,600

PAINTINGS

1961–1962

Village Near the Sea, on board, 11¾ x 15¾ ...... (111)   475

Otto Dix

(1891–   )

Birthplace: Gera, Germany.

1910-14   Studies painting in Dresden and then in Düsseldorf.
1919-22   Participates in the foundation of the "Secession" group, Dresden.
1922-25   Executes a series of etchings on the theme of World War I. Travels to Italy and Paris.
1926   Retrospective exhibition at the Neumann-Nirendorf Gallery, Berlin, and at the Tannhaüser Gallery, Munich.
1927-33   Teaches at the Academy of Dresden. Works are shown at the Nazi "Exhibition of Degenerate Art," Dresden and Munich.
1935   Exhibits at the Museum of Modern Art, New York, and at the Carnegie Institute, Pittsburgh.
1945-46   Turns toward religious subject matters.
1951-52   Participates in group shows in Mannheim, Essen, Freiburg, and Karlsruhe.
1957   Participates in the exhibition "German Art of the 20th Century," New York.
1958   Participates in the exhibitions "Cinquante ans d'art moderne," Brussels, and "Contemporary German Graphic Art and Sculpture," London.

Sales

DRAWINGS

1961–1962

A Life, black and brown chalk, 15¾ x 15 .... (106) $ 339
Bust of a Woman Leaning to the Right, 1929, red
    chalk on green paper, 16½ x 14¾ .... (105)   90

1963

Woman Reading, India ink, 8¾ x 9½ .... (219)   90

1964

Woman at Her Window, 1932, charcoal
    heightened with white, 23 x 18¾ .... (428)   209

1965

Young Woman's Head, 1921, pencil, 17½ x 12¾ .. **(543)** $ 396
Young Lady in a Blouse, 1921, pencil, 17 x 12¼ ... **(616)**   640
Landscape with Trees, black chalk, 11 x 10¾ ..... **(634)**   197

1966

Mother Country, 1919, India ink, 14 x 17½ .... **(816)**   443
Eastern Harbor, 1922, pen and watercolor,
19¾ x 14¾ .... **(812)**   691

1967

Self-Portrait Surrounded with Heads and Nudes,
1922, pencil and watercolor, 17¼ x 14 .... **(927)**   1,718
Nude, (1921), pencil, 16¼ x 21¼ .... **(962)**   608
Reclining Nude, (1922), pencil, 17½ x 19½ .... **(910)**   677
Nude, 1932, charcoal heightened with white,
21¼ x 15 .... **(970)**   664
Young Woman in Red, 1930, colored chalk,
19¾ x 15½ .... **(907)**   640
Portrait of the Historian Ferdinand Schmidt,
pencil, 25¾ x 18¼ .... **(986)**   369
Reclining Nude, red chalk, 17½ x 23 .... **(859)**   456
Christ's Head, 1956, colored chalk and gouache,
13 x 9 .... **(998)**   202

1968–July 1969

Murder, (1919), India ink, 16¾ x 13 .... **(1099)**   218
A Fair Couple, 1921, black lead and colored
pencil, 17¼ x 13½ .... **(1099)**   437
Portrait of Nelly, the Artist's Daughter, 1924,
pen, 7½ x 6 .... **(1030)**   160
Seated Nude, 1921, pencil, 16¾ x 10¼ .... **(1194)**   223
Young Girl's Head, 1930, red chalk, 11¾ x 17¾ .. **(1209)**   595

WATERCOLORS

1961–1962

The Valet, oil and watercolor on paper,
22¼ x 15½ .... **(105)**   395
Grosser Dirnenkopf, charcoal and watercolor,
22½ x 19 .... **(105)**   208

1965

Portrait of Mutzli, 1922, pencil and watercolor,
19¾ x 14¾ .... **(597)**   763
Head of a Bearded Man, (1917), pastel,
10¾ x 11 .... **(634)**   738

1966

Woman with a Hat, in Left Profile, 1922, pen and
watercolor, 12¾ x 10 .... **(712)**   787

1967

The Last Rose, 1923, watercolor, 19¾ x 14¾ ..... **(882)**   1,600
Ethel, 1929, pen and watercolor, 20 x 14 .... **(970)**   1,550
Horses Grazing, gouache, 15½ x 16¼ .... **(927)**   791
Self-Portrait with an Easel, 1947, pastel, 15 x 10 .. **(910)**   394
Autumn Landscape, 1953, watercolor, 6¼ x 9 ..... **(998)**   177

1968–July 1969

The Newborn, 1922, pencil and watercolor,
19½ x 18½ .... **(1090)**   446
Beach Scene, 1923, watercolor, 15¼ x 20 .... **(1041)**   1,710
The Caf' Conc' Singer, 1923, pen and watercolor,
8¼ x 8 .... **(1112)**   918
The Bearded Man, 1923, watercolor, 14¾ x 11 ... **(1099)**   805
Christ's Head, pastel, 13¼ x 10 .... **(1145)**   225
Underwood, 1943, pastel, 24¾ x 19¼ .... **(1194)**   372
Autumn Landscape, Bodensee, 1953, watercolor,
13½ x 19½ .... **(1090)**   670

PAINTINGS

1961–1962

Felix Müller's Family, 1919, 29¾ x 35½ .... **(88)** $2,165

1965

Portrait of the Photographer Hugo Erfurth, 1919,
on panel, 31 x 39¼ .... **(543)**   4,809

1966

Flowers, 1911, 24½ x 14¼ .... **(816)**   394
The Newborn, on cardboard, 10 x 14¾ .... **(816)**   1,328

1968–July 1969

Souche Tal, France, (1916), on paper mounted on
canvas, 15½ x 16½ .... **(1232)**   7,500

Kees van Dongen

(1877–1968)

Birthplace: Delfshaven, in the suburbs of Rotterdam, Netherlands.

1894-95   Enters the Rotterdam Academy of Fine Arts. Executes his first portraits. Longs to visit Paris.

1900-03   Settles in Paris. Marries Augusta Preitinger, a young Dutch woman. Executes illustrations for such reviews as *L'Assiette au Beurre, Le Rire, L'Indiscret,* and *La Revue Blanche.*

1904   Participates in the Salon des Indépendants and the Salon d'Automne, Paris. First one-man show at the Galerie Ambroise Vollard, Paris. His pictures already show his fondness for violent colors and the artificial shades of night places.

1905   Exhibits in the Fauves room at the Salon d'Automne, Paris. Unlike the other Fauves, he will always paint in pure colors. Exhibits at the Galerie Druet, Paris.

1906   Moves to the Bateau-Lavoir in Montmartre, where he meets Picasso and Max Jacob. Later settles in Montparnasse.

1908   Kahnweiler (his dealer since 1907) organizes two exhibitions of his works, one at the Flechtheim Gallery, Düsseldorf, and the other at his Rue Vignon gallery, Paris. Signs a contract with the Galerie Bernheim-Jeune, Paris.

1911-14   Has several exhibitions all over Europe: in Paris, London, Brussels, Berlin, Petrograd, Spain and Holland. Also exhibits in Morocco. Meets Countess Cassati (Jasmy) with whom he leads a sophisticated life until 1934.

1918   Exhibits at Paul Guillaume's, Paris. (Catalog preface by Apollinaire.)

1920   Becomes an extremely successful painter and a fashionable personality. Starts a long series of portraits of Parisian personalities such as Boni de Castellane, Anna de Noailles, Anatole France, and Maurice Chevalier.

1927   Exhibits at the Stedelijk Museum, Amsterdam.

1929	Becomes a French citizen.
1931	Organizes the exhibition "Trente Ans de peinture" in his own studio, Paris.
1937	Exhibits at the Palais des Beaux-Arts, Brussels; at the Gimpel Gallery, New York; and at the Carnegie Institute, Pittsburgh. Retrospective exhibition at the Musée Galliéra, Paris.
1942	Retrospective exhibition at the Galerie Charpentier, Paris. (Catalog preface by Sacha Guitry.)
1953	Exhibits at the Wildenstein Galleries, New York.
1965	Exhibits at the Leonard Hutton Galleries, New York.
1967	Important retrospective exhibition at the Musée National d'Art Moderne, Paris.
1968	Died, Monaco.

Sales

DRAWINGS

1961–1962

The Guitar Player, charcoal and watercolor, 11¾ x 9½ .... (26) $ 680

The Guitar Player, charcoal and watercolor, 11¾ x 9½ .... (53) 620

Woman at Her Toilette, (1903), pencil, ink, and watercolor, 18¼ x 10¾ .... (93) 3,616

Monte Carlo, the Gardens, pen and watercolor, 10¾ x 14 .... (128) 302

Seated Woman with Dog, Wearing a Red Necklace,[1] pen and watercolor, 21¾ x 13½ .... (64) 2,000

1963

Young Man, (1900), black pencil, 4½ x 6½ .... (281) 192

Relaxation, (1905), charcoal and pastel, 26½ x 34½ .... (277) 4,113

Figures, (1905), pencil and pastel, 11½ x 9 ...... (232) 1,085

Study for "Le Compliment," 1905, black pencil, 5¼ x 8¼ .... (283) 226

Reclining Nude, (1906), India ink, 21 x 28 .... (277) 823

The Siesta, (1906), charcoal, 11 x 17½ .... (255) 1,097

Bust of a Young Woman, black pencil, 6 x 3¾ .... (300) 200

Napoleon Bonaparte, blue pencil and India ink, 10¾ x 9 .... (179) 450

Tea Dance, 1920, black pencil, 8 x 5¼ .... (283) 565

Standing Nude, 17½ x 10¾ .... (254) 1,260

1964

The Horse, wash, 19¾ x 25¼ .... (399) 900

Cow in a Meadow, colored pencil heightened with watercolor, 6½ x 6½ .... (441) 215

Two Cronies, (1900), India ink and colored pencil, 12½ x 16¼ .... (377) 1,220

Two Cronies, (1900), India ink, 12¾ x 16¼ .... (472) 700

Street at Montmartre, charcoal and watercolor, 10¾ x 16¾ .... (454) 387

Study of Nudes, charcoal heightened with watercolor, 17½ x 11 .... (401) 620

Rosy Dolly, colored pencil, 13 x 10 .... (366) 580

The Woman with a Necklace, pencil heightened with watercolor, 18¼ x 10¼ .... (418) 1,100

Design of a Poster for the Deauville-Amsterdam Twinning, pencil heightened with watercolor and blue pencil, 7¼ x 6½ .... (333) 130

The Parade, India ink and watercolor, 23¾ x 14¾ .... (465) 2,100

[1] Inscribed "En souvenir du 14 Juillet 1919, cordialement."

1965

Portrait of a Man, 1900, India ink on bister paper, 10¾ x 17¾ .... (561) $ 520

Woman with a Sunbonnet, India ink, 23¾ x 17½ .... (534) 760

The Wedding Dance, pen, 5¼ x 7½ .... (632) 200

Seated Woman, Her Arms Crossed Behind Her Head, India ink, 14¼ x 10 .... (503) 560

The Omnibus, pencil, 4 x 6¾ .... (581) 240

Standing Woman, charcoal and watercolor, 17½ x 10¾ .... (585) 367

The Dance Lesson, pencil, 7½ x 5¾ .... (611) 460

On the Nile at Aswân, pencil and watercolor, 12 x 18¼ .... (535) 1,050

The Blue Hour; The Cup of Tea, 12¾ x 17¾ and 11¾ x 16¼ .... (582) 857

The Street Singers, charcoal with white lights, 17½ x 10¾ .... (564) 1,000

1966

A Feat of the Apaches; Chaud les marrons!; Misery and Philanthropy; Valets; India ink, each 12¾ x 19¼ .... (757) 1,935

The Street Singers, charcoal and watercolor, 17½ x 10¾ .... (706) 1,400

The Wedding Dance, wash, 5¼ x 7½ .... (672) 410

Woman's Head, pencil, 13 x 10 .... (703) 850

Mademoiselle Bibi, 1950, ink, 8¼ x 6 .... (721) 220

Street at Montmartre, charcoal and watercolor, 10¾ x 16¾ .... (689) 415

The Young Lady with a Lotus, colored pencil, 7½ x 5¾ .... (718) 370

Woman with a Fan, pen and wash, 17½ x 13½ .... (808) 813

The Walk, colored pencil, 8 x 4½ .... (798) 904

1967

In the Street, charcoal and colored pencil, 11½ x 9 .... (976) 640

Street Scene, pencil, 4¾ x 6 .... (963) 275

Chaud les marrons!, India ink, 12 x 18¾ .... (889) 825

Spanish Girl with a Red Rose, ink and watercolor, 24¾ x 18 .... (982) 8,295

Fashionable Ladies, colored pencil, 8 x 4½ ...... (883) 1,160

The Young Lady with a Necklace, wash and gouache, 11½ x 9½ .... (987) 900

The Woman with a Parasol, colored pencil, 8¼ x 6½ .... (949) 820

Misery and Philanthropy, pencil and India ink, 11¾ x 17¾ .... (870) 900

1968–July 1969

Café Lena, Dorpstraat, Rotterdam, 1895, India ink and watercolor, 21 x 25 .... (1173) 9,430

Illustration for a Tale of "The Arabian Nights," 1918, India ink, 10¾ x 7¼ .... (1161) 330

Study of a Seated Nude, 1919, India ink heightened with watercolor, 17½ x 10 ...... (1134) 1,038

Dance, blue pencil heightened with watercolor, 17½ x 10¼ .... (1134) 944

Portrait of a Woman, 1928, pen and watercolor, 19 x 11½ .... (1068) 1,369

White Oxen Under the Yoke, pencil and watercolor, 10¾ x 17¾ .... (1210) 800

Women in Housecoats, India ink and watercolor, 17 x 10¼ .... (1113) 1,640

On a Visit, India ink and blue pencil heightened with white, 11½ x 17¾ .... (1051) 960

Portrait of a Woman, ink and watercolor,
17½ x 13¼ .... (1134) $ 944
Young Dancer, pencil and watercolor, 6 x 4¾ ... (1172)   520
Woman and Horse, 13½ x 10¼ .... (1065)   3,000
Flowers, pen, 10 x 8 .... (1078)   370
The Blue Hour, India-ink wash, 12½ x 17¾ ..... (1078)   1,160
At the Marketplace, black lead, 5 x 8 .... (1030)   275
Seated Woman, black pencil, 5¾ x 3¾ .... (1088)   275
La Grimaldi, wash heightened with watercolor,
24½ x 18¾ .... (1226)   5,000
The Conversation, wash, black and blue pencil,
12¾ x 16¼ .... (1262)   1,020
Back View of a Seated Woman, black lead,
5¾ x 3¾ .... (1268)   1,183
Front View of a Nude, India ink, 26 x 16¼ ...... (1268)   6,032

WATERCOLORS

1961-1962

Dutch Carters, watercolor, 5¾ x 4½ .... (124)   280
Living Picture, watercolor, 5¾ x 4½ .... (124)   340
Street Scenes, (1905), watercolor, 18¼ x 14¾ ...... (93)   4,068
Fun Fair Booth, (1923), pastel, 10½ x 17¾ .... (143)   2,441
The Model, (1920), watercolor laid down on
panel, 24½ x 19¼ .... (143)   3,684
Orchids, gouache, 17¾ x 14 .... (30)   900
The Kiosk, watercolor, 21¾ x 29¾ .... (116)   4,600
The Sandwich Man, gouache, 24½ x 9 .... (160)   1,620
Absinthe, watercolor, 10¼ x 8 .... (80)   2,400
Three Cronies, watercolor and charcoal,
10¼ x 5¼ .... (133)   370
The Café Terrace, watercolor, 10½ x 8 .... (27)   1,960
The Little Girl with a Rose, watercolor,
27¾ x 20½ .... (76)   1,600
Maternity, watercolor, 27¾ x 21¾ .... (157)   720

1963

The Model, gouache, 23 x 18¼ .... (194)   3,200
The He-Goat, 1923, watercolor, 6½ x 8¾ .... (281)   723
The Caravan, watercolor, 16¾ x 21¼ .... (252)   1,100

1964

Street Scene, (1905), watercolor and gouache on
gray paper, 18¼ x 14¼ .... (354)   4,600
The White Sailboat, (1922), watercolor,
10½ x 12 .... (377)   1,130
Riders at the Bois, watercolor, 12¼ x 19 .... (401)   2,400
Woman with a Bunch of Flowers, watercolor and
India ink, 19¾ x 13¼ .... (380)   935
The Woman with a Mauve Dress, watercolor,
24¾ x 19¼ .... (398)   3,200
The Parade, watercolor, 25 x 15½ .... (340)   2,900

1965

Circus Parade, watercolor, 19¼ x 25 .... (645)   4,352

1966

Venice: Leda and the Swan, watercolor and
gouache, 19 x 14 .... (798)   2,599
The Mystery of Zilda, pastel, 10¾ x 17¾ .... (798)   2,034
Portrait of Maud Sweeny, watercolor, 26 x 18¼ .. (830)   2,400
Seated Woman in a Fur Coat, watercolor,
10¼ x 7¼ .... (670)   1,700
Halle aux Vins, watercolor, 24 x 14 .... (789)   1,260
Young Woman's Head, watercolor, 14¼ x 10¼ ... (824)   1,000
Portrait of a Woman, watercolor, 18¼ x 13½ ..... (745)   1,085

Hindu Woman, watercolor, 14 x 10¾ .... (703) $2,700
Young Woman with a Necklace, gouache and
paint on paper, 23¾ x 16¼ .... (726)   6,900

1967

Portrait of a Woman, 1900, gouache,
16¼ x 13¼ .... (1004)   7,750
Salome, pastel heightened with ink, 23 x 16¾ ..... (979)   1,088
Place Blanche, watercolor, 8¼ x 10¾ .... (918)   3,616
Young Woman in Profile, watercolor, 14¾ x 10¾ . (898)   2,040
Moroccan Rider, watercolor, 5¾ x 9 .... (996)   880
Greyhounds, watercolor, 5¼ x 8 .... (876)   510
At the Casino, watercolor, 19¾ x 12¼ .... (911)   4,200

1968–July 1969

Nini Lying Down, watercolor, 10¾ x 17¾ .... (1173)   2,185
Fun Fair Booth, 1903, pastel, 10½ x 17¾ .... (1181)   2,800
The Spanish Girl, (1910), watercolor,
24½ x 18¼ .... (1132)   5,192
Leda and the Swan in Venice, watercolor,
8 x 13¾ .... (1068)   1,699
Portrait of Madame Agnelli, gouache, 25¾ x 20 . (1127)   7,130
Fun Fair Booth, pastel, 10½ x 17¾ .... (1127)   1,840
The Dutch Milk Maid, ink and watercolor,
26½ x 21½ .... (1246)   6,000
Fashionable Lady, watercolor, 18¼ x 11 .... (1252)   3,800
Baroque House, watercolor, 17¼ x 10¼ .... (1262)   700
The Swede, 1933, watercolor, 18¼ x 11¾ .... (1268)   3,898
Young Woman in Profile, watercolor, 61¾ x 33 .. (1268)   8,004
The Parisian, gouache, 15½ x 12¾ .... (1268)   6,264
Portrait of Madame Agnelli, gouache, 25¾ x 20 . (1268)   6,264
Red-Haired Woman in a Hat, pastel and
charcoal, 25¾ x 20 .... (1268)   37,120
Gennep Mill, 1884, watercolor, 12 x 18¼ .... (1272)   16,800

PAINTINGS

1961-1962

Seated Nude, (1907), 19¾ x 25¾ .... (71)   22,000
Portrait of a Woman, 21¾ x 18¼ .... (143)   10,961
Half-Length Portrait of a Woman, 21¾ x 18¼ ..... (68)   4,000
Portrait of a Woman, 19 x 22½ .... (34)   2,400
Sleeping Beauty, 25¾ x 21¼ .... (116)   6,400
Woman in Green Tights, 21¾ x 18¼ .... (116)   16,000
Eve Francis, 55½ x 45½ .... (31)   8,787
Portrait of Eve Francis, 1923, 57¾ x 45 .... (120)   5,220
The Paddock, (Fauve period), 29 x 21¼ .... (120)   16,200
Portrait of Madame X . . ., 21¾ x 15 .... (114)   6,200
Ida Rubinstein and Anna Pavlova,[2] 1909,
21¼ x 25¾ .... (143)   19,888
Portrait of Madame Utrillo-Valore, (1920),
57¾ x 45 .... (93)   27,120
Portrait of a Woman with a Medallion,
18¼ x 13 .... (109)   4,000
Portrait of William Powell, 15¾ x 12¾ .... (95)   1,320
Spagbola, Sivigliana, 1910, 19¾ x 25¾ .... (69)   18,960
Deauville: The Parasols, 16¼ x 13 .... (160)   6,400
On the Beach at Deauville, 21 x 25¼ .... (30)   6,700
Riders at the Bois, 21¼ x 32 .... (116)   7,000
Le Petit Black, 6½ x 8¾ .... (167)   1,800
The Lion, (1907), 58½ x 33¼ .... (171)   1,500
The Pink Camellia, (1925), 21¾ x 13¼ .... (93)   11,413
Roses and Daisies, 25¾ x 21½ .... (156)   5,600

[2]Recollection of the Russian Opera season.

1963

The Man in a Gray Waistcoat, 39½ x 32 . . . . (241) $1,400

Dancers, (1906), 35½ x 28¼ . . . . (202) 25,000

Portrait of a Woman, 21½ x 13 . . . . (216) 3,565

The Wild Girl, 16¼ x 13 . . . . (248) 1,800

The Trench, 32 x 39½ . . . . (232) 35,256

The Singer, 1920, 27¾ x 19½ . . . . (210) 8,226

Jasmy at Garches, (1922), 29 x 19¾ . . . . (232) 14,464

At the Circus: White Horse and Black Horse,
    18¼ x 21¾ . . . . (312) 2,600

Le Petit Black, 6¾ x 8¾ . . . . (238) 580

The Red House, 32 x 39½ . . . . (318) 22,000

1964

Houses in Amsterdam, 10¾ x 8¾ . . . . (371) 2,600

Boat at Scheveningen, (1900), 38¾ x 28 . . . . (367) 8,845

The Acrobat, (1906–08), 28 x 19½ . . . . (416) 20,454

The Blue Hat, Kiki de Montparnasse, (1906–08),
    39½ x 32 . . . . (416) 19,901

Restaurant in Venice, (1920), 35½ x 28 . . . . (454) 20,454

Horses on Deauville Beach, (1921), 13 x 15¾ . . . . . (454) 9,950

The Streetwalkers, 51½ x 32 . . . . (472) 16,000

The Café Concert, 16¼ x 10¾ . . . . (409) 6,020

Two Americans Feeding the Sea Gulls, Cannes,
    1920, 25 x 30½ . . . . (367) 11,609

*The Pont Alexandre III and the Dome of the
    Invalides*, 1922, 31¼ x 39¼ . . . . (367) 17,966

A Street (recto), *Study of a Horse* (verso), on
    cardboard, 8¾ x 12¼ . . . . (341) 2,700

Orchids, 1930, 21½ x 18¼ . . . . (367) 6,634

The Nile at Aswân, 1931, 21 x 14 . . . . (367) 7,186

Nude with a Rose, 39½ x 32 . . . . (371) 17,600

Woman on a Sofa, 18¼ x 21¾ . . . . (347) 22,000

The Lighthouse, 15 x 24 . . . . (340) 6,200

Reclining Woman, Her Breast Bare, 39½ x 32 . . . . (340) 26,000

Game of Draughts, 22 x 19¾ . . . . (340) 6,400

The Bunch of Roses, 29 x 23¾ . . . . (399) 15,000

Sleeping Beauty, 25¾ x 21¼ . . . . (399) 9,000

Nude in an Armchair, 14¼ x 14¼ . . . . (399) 1,760

The Artist's Son, a Pipe in His Mouth, 1943,
    24 x 18¼ . . . . (354) 15,000

Fashionable Lady with a Red Scarf, 63¼ x 38¾ . . . (371) 8,700

The Lady with a Siamese Cat, 51½ x 51½ . . . . (474) 7,760

The Hussar,[3] 39½ x 32 . . . . (340) 30,000

The Bed, 39½ x 32 . . . . (340) 23,000

1965

The Woman with a Tie, (1903–04), 25¾ x 19¾ . . . . (553) 11,800

Nude on a Black Background, 1905, 39½ x 31¾ . . . (553) 32,000

*The Red Poppy (or: Madame Does Not Want
    Any Children)*, (1906), 21½ x 18¼ . . . . (522) 38,696

Clouds, 1907, 25 x 21 . . . . (640) 4,500

Place de la Concorde, 32¾ x 39½ . . . . (539) 13,500

Bar in Cairo, 1920, 25¾ x 21¼ . . . . (522) 27,087

The Music Hall, 16¼ x 10¾ . . . . (640) 7,000

Orchids, 1930, 21½ x 18¼ . . . . (575) 6,219

Basket of Flowers, 32 x 39½ . . . . (617) 21,018

Kaia Metis the Polynesian, on panel,
    21¾ x 18¼ . . . . (561) 9,600

Woman with a Hat, 25¾ x 19¾ . . . . (561) 18,400

The Man with a Top Hat, 36½ x 29 . . . . (553) 25,200

Lucie the Mulatto, 39½ x 32 . . . . (624) 17,966

[3]Dutch night club.

The Lady with a Siamese Cat . . . . (634) $ 20,910

Portrait of Madame Diamant, on cardboard laid
    down on cradled panel, 24 x 17¾ . . . . (516) 9,000

Madame Simone Berriau, 63¾ x 48¾ . . . . (617) 16,950

The Blue Cow, 15 x 21¾ . . . . (547) 3,400

The Sacré-Coeur in the Morning, 31¼ x 25¼ . . . . . (522) 3,870

In the Bois de Boulogne, 1952, on board,
    16 x 13 . . . . (624) 10,503

1966

Young Lady in a Blue Hat, 17½ x 13¾ . . . . (698) 2,856

The Acrobat, 1904, on cradled panel,
    31¼ x 20½ . . . . (797) 18,532

The Woman with a Necklace, Red Backround,
    1905, 39¼ x 31¼ . . . . (694) 47,000

Equestrienne, (1905), 29 x 36½ . . . . (823) 6,800

Portrait of a Woman, 9½ x 7½ . . . . (727) 3,700

Portrait of the Virgin, 13 x 9½ . . . . (780) 2,856

Cannes, (1907–08), 19 x 25 . . . . (744) 18,984

Portrait of a Woman, (1910), 40¼ x 28 . . . . (707) 6,000

The Parisian, 21¾ x 18¼ . . . . (797) 18,758

The Studio, 1917, 25¾ x 21¼ . . . . (750) 17,137

Caille sur Canapé, (1922), 11 x 31½ . . . . (750) 16,584

Seated Young Woman in the Nude, 67¾ x 31½ . . . (811) 18,000

Place Vendôme, (1925–30), 21¼ x 25¼ . . . . (776) 8,500

The Arabian Nights, 13 x 10¼ . . . . (797) 2,938

Still Life with Roses, 18¼ x 21¼ . . . . (776) 12,000

Woman with Cats, 55½ x 55½ . . . . (722) 22,000

1967

Harvesttime, 20½ x 25¼ . . . . (880) 19,348

Lola, (1906), 21½ x 18¼ . . . . (880) 8,292

Dancer, (1906), 25 x 20¾ . . . . (880) 20,730

Mika, Nude on a Sofa, 1908–10, 21¼ x 25¾ . . . . . (923) 28,400

The Spanish Dancer, 1910, 39½ x 32½ . . . . (864) 55,000

The Circus Horses, (1910–12), 17¾ x 21¼ . . . . (938) 9,674

Portrait of Madame Claudine V . . ., 1911,
    25¾ x 21¼ . . . . (850) 8,000

Horsewoman and Bather on the Beach, (1925),
    25¾ x 21¼ . . . . (938) 17,966

Trees in Upper Egypt, 1928, 51½ x 99 . . . . (965) 22,148

Races at Deauville, 25¾ x 39½ . . . . (923) 40,000

Portrait of a Woman, 1938, 25¼ x 21 . . . . (982) 9,717

The Parisian, 21¾ x 18¼ . . . . (965) 15,820

Walk in the Bois de Boulogne, on cardboard,
    16¼ x 16¼ . . . . (976) 9,000

Cock and Hens, on cardboard, 9½ x 11 . . . . (978) 2,100

The Orange Seller, oil and gouache, 24½ x 19 . . . . (901) 7,000

1968–July 1969

The Country of Jongkind, 18¼ x 21¾ . . . . (1180) 11,800

Woman's Head, (1903–04), 18¼ x 14¾ . . . . (1132) 21,240

Batignolles-Odéon Bus, (1903–05), 18 x 26 . . . . . . (1056) 44,000

The Pigs' Merry-Go-Round, 1904, oil on paper
    laid down on canvas, 25 x 19¼ . . . . (1187) 9,912

View of Paris, and the Eiffel Tower, (1903–04),
    16¾ x 20 . . . . (1068) 12,980

Portrait of Maud Loti, (1906–08), 32 x 39½ . . . . . (1068) 54,280

The Milliner, (1910), 30½ x 14¼ . . . . (1125) 28,980

Great Nude (Zita), 1911, 51½ x 38¼ . . . . (1152) 66,000

Woman with a Large Hat, (1912), 28½ x 23¾ . . . . (1152) 40,000

Oriental Woman, (1913), 45½ x 38 . . . . (1125) 81,650

The Allée des Acacias at the Bois, (1920),
    21¾ x 26 . . . . (1056) 30,000

The Pond of Latone at Versailles, (1920),
    32 x 39½ . . . . (1152) 17,500

Bather Seated on a Beach, (1920), 7¼ x 9¼ . . . . . **(1070)** $4,720
Race Course, Deauville, 1920, 36¾ x 29¼ . . . . **(1152)** 49,000
The Paddock, Deauville, 1920, 32 x 39½ . . . . **(1109)** 32,000
The Tails, Deauville, 1920, 29 x 24 . . . . **(1152)** 33,000
Montparnasse Blues,[4] (1920-23), 39½ x 31½ . . . . **(1152)** 78,000
Night Feasts, Venice, 1921, 29 x 36½ . . . . **(1187)** 24,780
The Picnic at Le Louvard, 1924, 32¼ x 39½ . . . . . **(1152)** 65,000
The Piebald Horse, Normandy, 18¼ x 21¾ . . . . . **(1049)** 7,000
At Shepheard's Restaurant, Cairo, 1928,
    39½ x 32 . . . . **(1152)** 40,000
Mademoiselle Alanova, (1930), 19½ x 14¼ . . . . . . **(1126)** 6,443
Anatole France, 72¼ x 45 . . . . **(1152)** 80,000
The Acrobat, on cardboard, 24 x 16 . . . . **(1189)** 37,000
Equestrienne at the Bois, 1938, 51¾ x 77¼ . . . . . . **(1173)** 57,500
Cocolina, 29 x 24 . . . . **(1152)** 40,000
Princess Zeitoun, 29 x 23¾ . . . . **(1152)** 14,000
The Woman with Jewels, 38¼ x 51½ . . . . **(1173)** 69,000
Boulevard de Jardin Botanique at Monte Carlo,
    21¼ x 25¾ . . . . **(1053)** 33,000
Rainy Day at Monte Carlo, 21¼ x 25¾ . . . . **(1053)** 33,000
The Art Critic, 39½ x 32 . . . . **(1113)** 6,300
Flowers, 21 x 17¾ . . . . **(1125)** 14,950
La Mallorquina, 39½ x 32 . . . . **(1224)** 33,600
The Black Turban, 21¾ x 18¼ . . . . **(1224)** 27,600
Three Gigantic Rosebuds on a Turquoise-Blue
    Background, 36½ x 29 . . . . **(1225)** 10,000
At the Moulin de la Galette, 21¼ x 17¾ . . . . **(1228)** 32,000
The Female Clown, 25½ x 18 . . . . **(1235)** 30,000
Luisa, 1920, 21¾ x 18¼ . . . . **(1235)** 18,000
Miss Toni Chase, (1920), 25½ x 21½ . . . . **(1235)** 15,000
Surroundings of Overschie, Holland, on board,
    9¾ x 12½ . . . . **(1235)** 4,000
The Piebald Horse, Normandy, 17¾ x 21¼ . . . . . **(1239)** 10,800
The Singer, 1920, 27¾ x 19¾ . . . . **(1241)** 35,300
Eve Francis, (1923), 55½ x 45½ . . . . **(1254)** 30,000
The Avenue du Bois, 18¼ x 21¾ . . . . **(1256)** 28,600
Gathering Hay, (1920), 19¾ x 25¾ . . . . **(1265)** 28,000
Great Vase of Chrysanthemums, 51½ x 35 . . . . . . **(1270)** 36,000

1910   His first experiments in abstract art are among the earliest in the U.S. First one-man show at Stieglitz's 291 Gallery, New York.

1914   Participates in the National Arts Club Annual, New York. Always proceeds from nature to reach abstraction, as is shown in the work "Nature Symbolized."

1917   Participates in the exhibition of the Society of Independent Artists, New York.

1926   Participates in the International Exhibition of Modern Art organized by the Société Anonyme at the Brooklyn Museum, New York.

1926-29   Several exhibitions at Stieglitz's Intimate Gallery, New York.

1929   Participates in the exhibition "Paintings by 19 Living Americans," New York.

1930-46   Exhibits yearly at An American Place Gallery, New York.

1938   Participates in the exhibition "Trois Siècles d'Art aux Etats-Unis," at the Musée du Jeu de Paume, Paris.

1946   Died.

1947   Retrospective exhibition at the Downtown Gallery, New York.

Sales

WATERCOLORS

1967

Centreport Series No. 16, (1941), watercolor,
    6 x 9 . . . . **(952)** $3,250

PAINTINGS

1964

The Clay Wagon, 1935, 20 x 28 . . . . **(454)** 1,935

1966

Green, Black, Gray, (1942), 18¼ x 26 . . . . **(707)** 4,250

1967

Sunrise IV, 1937, 10 x 14 . . . . **(952)** 6,000
The Flash of Lightning, (1939-40), oil and wax on
    canvas, 20½ x 32¼ . . . . **(952)** 16,000

Arthur Dove

(1880-1946)

Birthplace: Canandaigua, New York.

1903   Studies at Cornell University.

1903-07   Supports himself as an illustrator, gaining fame.

1907-09   Goes to Europe with Alfred Maurer and Arthur Carles, studying painting in France and Italy. Participates in the Salon D'Automne, Paris.

Albert Dubois-Pillet

(1846-1890)

Birthplace: Paris, France. Senior member of the Neo-Impressionist group. Very little is known about his life.

1877-79   Some of his works are exhibited at the Salon, Paris. By profession commander in the Gendarmerie (constabulary), he had started painting as a dilettante.

---

[4]Formerly in the Poiret Collection.

1884   Takes part in the foundation of the "Société des Artistes Indépendants" and becomes its vice-president.

1886-87   Abandons his dark shades and thoroughly embraces Neo-Impressionism, with its light and divided colors. Thwarted by Degas, he is not admitted to the last exhibition of the Impressionist group. Participates in the Salon des Indépendants, Paris.

1890   Died, Le Puy, France, of smallpox.

1891   Retrospective exhibition of his work at the Salon des Indépendants includes 64 pictures—portraits, still lifes, harbor scenes, and above all landscapes, his favorite subject matter.

Sales

DRAWINGS

1965

The Quays Behind Notre-Dame, (1888), pen, two colors, 6 x 6¼ .... (598) $1,200

1968-July 1969

The Transporting Bridge in Rouen, stippled wash, 8¾ x 10¾ .... (1225)   1,500

The Ferryman, stippled wash, 8¾ x 8¼ .... (1225)   2,600

PAINTINGS

1961-1962

Le Puy in Winter, 1889, 14¾ x 19¾ .... (31)   3,295

1965

An Old Street in Rouen, on cardboard, 17½ x 11¾ .... (612)   7,000

1966

Le Puy: The Sunny Square, 32 x 23¼ .... (819)   11,000

1967

Cliffs at Yport, 10¼ x 16¼ .... (976)   10,200

1968-July 1969

The Channel, 1885, 17¾ x 12¾ .... (1117)   1,600

View of Paris: The Quai St. Michel, The Quai du Marché Neuf, and Notre-Dame, 38½ x 70 .. (1225)   67,000

Jean Dubuffet

(1901-)

Birthplace: Le Havre, France.

1918   Attends the Académie Julian, Paris.

1919   Meets Dufy, Max Jacob, and Suzanne Valadon.

1924-30   Gives up painting and sets up a wholesale wine company.

1933   Starts painting again.

1937   Gives up painting a second time and turns again to business.

1942   Reverts to painting for good.

1944   First exhibition at the Galerie René Drouin, Paris.

1946   Writes *Prospectus aux amateurs de tout genre.*

1947   Stay in Africa, at El Golea. Exhibitions in New York and Chicago (organized by Pierre Matisse). Founds the "Art brut" group.

1949   Executes his "Grotesque Landscapes" during a stay in the Sahara. Writes *L'Art brut préféré aux arts culturels.*

1950   Paints the famous series "Corps de dames."

1951-52   Stay in New York.

1955-57   Does his first "Assemblages d'empreintes."

1955-61   Settles at Vence in the south of France.

1960   Retrospective exhibition at the Musée des Arts Décoratifs, Paris.

1961   Leaves Vence from time to time to stay in Paris.

1962   Retrospective exhibition at the Museum of Modern Art, New York.

1966   Retrospective exhibitions at the Tate Gallery, London; the Guggenheim Museum, New York; and the Stedelijk Museum, Amsterdam.

Resident mainly in Paris.

Sales

DRAWINGS

1961-1962

Corps de Dame, 1950, pen, 10¾ x 8½ .... (152) $ 700

Figure in a Landscape, 1956, India ink and collage, 35½ x 19¾ .... (129)   2,471

D 74 Drawing, 1960, pen, 12½ x 9¾ .... (85)   700

1963

Portrait of Jean Paulhan, 1947, India ink, 10¼ x 7¾ .... (299)   340

Arab and Palm Trees Beneath the Sun, 1948, colored pencils, 9½ x 19 .... (249)   440

African Tale, 1948, colored pencil, 12¾ x 9 .... (225)   850

Remembrance of North Africa, 1948, colored pencil, 12¼ x 9 .... (299)   560

Landscape, 1952, India ink, and watercolor, 23¼ x 18¾ .... (255)   1,782

Visit of the Estate, 1954, ink wash and collage, 19 x 25¾ .... (189)   3,000

Abstract Figure, 1961, India ink, 10 x 13¼ .... (216)   274

1964

The Arab and the Camel, 1948, India ink and colored chalk, 12½ x 9 .... (435)   800

Arab and Palm Trees Beneath the Sun, 1948, colored pencil, 9½ x 19 .... (351)   560

Blue-Eyed Figure, 1948, pencil and charcoal, 13½ x 10 .... (453)   1,106

Landscape, 1952, ink and watercolor, 23¼ x 18¼ .... (372)   2,700

Exuberant Landscape, 1954, impresses gathering and India ink, 19½ x 23¾ .... (378)   1,446

Citroën 45 YZ 75, 1961, pen, India ink and wash, 11 x 12½ .... (383)   418

Composition, 1963, colored pencil, 8 x 5 .... (377)   226

1965

M. Paulhan, St. Moritz, 1945, black lead, 8 x 5 ... (494)   525

Figures in a Landscape, 1948, colored pencil, 10 x 13½ .... (567)   339

Arab in the Palm Grove, 1948, colored chalk,
13 x 10 ...... (582) $ 681

Corps de Dame, 1950, pen, 10¾ x 8¾ ...... (494) 650

Boum au vin rouge, 1952, pen, 15½ x 11¾ ...... (565) 588

Base of the Wall with Wet Ground, 1955, ink and
collage, 40 x 25¼ ...... (561) 2,320

L'Arbre de barbe, 1959, wash, ink, and collage,
10½ x 15 ...... (567) 2,034

Head, 1960, ink, 11¾ x 8¾ ...... (507) 600

1966

Figure in a Landscape, 1960, India ink,
12¾ x 10 ...... (734) 904

Corps de Dame, 1950, pen, 10¾ x 8¼ ...... (784) 1,000

Corps de Dame, 1950, pen, 10¾ x 8¼ ...... (805) 850

Landscape, 1952, ink and watercolor,
23¼ x 18¼ ...... (665) 2,700

Disheveled Dog, 1960, pen, 8¼ x 3¾ ...... (811) 260

Composition, 1952, India ink, 12½ x 9¼ ...... (745) 678

1967

Boat III, 1964, colored ink, 10¾ x 8¼ ...... (939) 691

1968–July 1969

Drawing for Oukiva Sebot, 1958, India ink,
7¼ x 7¼ ...... (1214) 960

Woman's Head, (1943), colored chalk,
11¼ x 9¾ ...... (1099) 667

Figure, 1948, colored pencil, 12¾ x 9½ ...... (1127) 1,150

Topography, 1959, ink and collage on canvas ...... (1208) 2,750

Boat III, 1964, colored ink, 10¾ x 8¼ ...... (1191) 1,298

Arab with Palm Trees, 1948, pencil, 12¼ x 9 ...... (1246) 4,750

Barrow XVIII, 1964, felt pen with red and blue
ball-point pen, 10½ x 8½ ...... (1273) 856

Assemblage, collage, 15½ x 17¼ ...... (1224) 3,100

Topography, 1959, India ink and collage laid
down on canvas, 18¼ x 23½ ...... (1268) 1,021

The Two Clouds, 1954, collage and India ink,
18½ x 18¾ ...... (1270) 11,040

WATERCOLORS

1961–1962

Composition, 1952, gouache, 18¾ x 23¾ ...... (75) 2,212

Composition, 1951, gouache, 9¾ x 13 ...... (93) 2,034

The Oasis, pastel, 13 x 10 ...... (59) 1,600

Landscape at Les Colias, gouache, paper and
butterfly wings, 14 x 9 ...... (88) 4,182

1963

The Desert, 1947, gouache, 12¼ x 16¼ ...... (258) 800

Composition, 1952, gouache, 23¼ x 18¾ ...... (283) 1,695

Landscape with Figures, 1957, watercolor,
9 x 12¾ ...... (275) 750

1964

Arab Musicians, gouache, 12¼ x 16¼ ...... (393) 360

Three Arabs, 1947, watercolor, 10½ x 8½ ...... (453) 1,106

The Camel, 1948, pastel, 13 x 10 ...... (437) 880

The Cow, 1954, watercolor, 10 x 19 ...... (454) 2,073

1965

Still Life with a Pack of Cards, 1928, watercolor,
25 x 18¼ ...... (508) 210

Arab, 1948, watercolor and gouache, 17¾ x 21¾ ...... (539) 1,750

The Fecundation of Palm Trees, 1948, gouache,
17 x 19 ...... (561) 1,020

Algerian Village, 1948, gouache, 17½ x 22½ ...... (637) 2,200

Two Figures, 1949, gouache, 9½ x 11¾ ...... (567) 1,539

Bust of a Man, 1962, gouache, 26½ x 18 ...... (512) 1,100

1966

Arab with a Palm Tree, 1948, watercolor,
17 x 21¼ ...... (811) $1,200

El Golea, 1948, gouache, 17 x 21¼ ...... (784) 3,750

1967

Birds in the Palm Trees, with Roses, 1949,
watercolor, 10 x 13 ...... (1004) 2,000

Goat, 1949, gouache, 9¼ x 12¾ ...... (919) 1,695

Walkers Crossing One Another, 1962, gouache,
35½ x 26½ ...... (965) 3,955

1968–July 1969

Landscape, 1943, gouache, 6¼ x 10¼ ...... (1125) 2,990

Palm Trees and Arabs, 1948, gouache,
15¾ x 12¾ ...... (1125) 3,335

Four Figures and the Sky, 1946, gouache,
12¼ x 9½ ...... (1126) 4,460

Landscape, 1943, watercolor, 6½ x 10 ...... (1224) 1,560

PAINTINGS

1961–1962

Landscape with a Garden, 1944, 32 x 25¾ ...... (88) 11,070

Portrait of Edith Boisonnas, 1947, 12¼ x 19 ...... (69) 4,266

L'Homme au teint ramagé, 1950, 25¾ x 21½ ...... (164) 3,844

L'Expansion des solitudes, 1952, oil on canvas on
board, 21¼ x 24½ ...... (129) 5,492

Time Squanderers, 1955, 23¾ x 28¾ ...... (31) 5,767

Topography with Saltpetre, 1957, on canvas
mounted on canvas, 31 x 31 ...... (120) 3,800

Urgencies, 1957, 31½ x 39¼ ...... (164) 4,668

Figure with Blemishes, 1957, collage, paper and
oil, 49¾ x 31¼ ...... (164) 7,689

The Contemplative Person, 1958, 36¼ x 29 ...... (149) 9,164

Clear Median Area, 1959, collage on canvas,
19½ x 30 ...... (29) 2,800

Clear Median Area, 1959, collage on canvas,
19½ x 29¾ ...... (145) 3,692

1963

Side View, Aztec Style,[1] 1945, 25¾ x 21¾ ...... (279) 9,500

Three Bedouins of El Golea, 1948, peinture à la
colle on paper, 17¾ x 21¾ ...... (224) 940

Grotesque Landscape, 1949, 35¼ x 45¾ ...... (279) 13,000

Landscape with Bushes, 1949, 45¾ x 35¼ ...... (210) 7,403

Portrait of Antonin Arthaud, 1950, on panel,
25¾ x 21¼ ...... (299) 3,920

Olympia, 1950, 35¼ x 45¾ ...... (279) 17,000

Urgencies, 1957, 32 x 39½ ...... (200) 4,000

The Bare Table, 1957, 38¾ x 51¼ ...... (249) 6,400

Areas and Progresses, 1957, 32 x 39½ ...... (299) 5,100

Allurement of the Ground, 1958, 35¼ x 46¼ ...... (299) 2,800

L'Homme au teint ramagé, 25¾ x 21¼ ...... (200) 3,100

The Contemplative Person, 1958, 36¼ x 29 ...... (200) 4,800

Texturology LVIII, Bright Earth Sheet, 1958,
45 x 57¾ ...... (249) 4,100

1964

Small Green Nude, 1944, on board, 24½ x 16¾ ...... (416) 4,699

Summer Noon, 1952, on board, 32 x 36¼ ...... (453) 6,910

Landscape, 1954, 8 x 8 ...... (377) 2,034

Silver-White Head, 1954, 10 x 7½ ...... (448) 3,000

Le Jardin de casse repique, 1956, 22½ x 25¾ ...... (431) 7,500

Texturology LVIII, Bright Earth Sheet, 1958,
45 x 57¾ ...... (351) 2,300

[1]Dedicated "A Germaine et Jean, Bonne Année 1946."

1965

Vue de Paris aux piétons furtifs, 1944,
35¼ x 44¾ .... (573) $26,258

Head with Flaws, 1951, on board, 32 x 25¾ .... (539)   6,250

Site aux errances, 1955, 32 x 39½ .... (561)   4,000

Sparkling on the Path Soil, 1957, impresses
gathering and collage, 51¾ x 25¼ .... (539)   2,000

Topography, Crumbs, and Pavement, 1958,
44¾ x 57¼ .... (575)   12,438

Trotte la houle, 1964, 35¼ x 45½ .... (637)   10,000

1966

French Farm, 1944, 45¼ x 35¼ .... (776)   15,000

Wall with Inscriptions, 1945, 39¼ x 32 .... (678)   26,000

Pink Face Like a Bamboo Apple, pavatex,
21¾ x 18 .... (744)   10,170

Cows in the Meadow, 1954, 39½ x 32 .... (686)   19,901

Site aux errances, 1955, 32 x 39½ .... (808)   7,545

Astravagale, 1956, oil and collage, 28½ x 16¾ .... (678)   23,000

The Mail, 1955, 25 x 31½ .... (678)   13,000

Woman, 1957, oil and collage, 26 x 19¼ .... (707)   4,500

Barbe de Voyana, 1959, collage, 19¾ x 13 .... (811)   1,600

Median Area, 1959, on paper laid down on
canvas, 19¾ x 30 .... (685)   1,600

The Bus, 1961, 35¼ x 45¾ .... (751)   18,795

Figure, 45¾ x 35¼ .... (797)   9,718

Colloquy Beneath the Trees, 22¾ x 45¼ .... (749)   5,800

Figure in a Cocked Hat, 28 x 30 .... (749)   7,200

1967

Desnuda, 1945, 29 x 21¼ .... (880)   8,292

The Violinist, 1953, 57¾ x 45 .... (864)   22,500

The Donkey at Work, 1955, 29 x 36¼ .... (864)   17,000

The Theater of Flesh (New Corps de Dame),
1955, 45½ x 35¼ .... (938)   8,845

Biste au bec, 1955, 25 x 19½ .... (982)   11,850

Corps de Dame, 1957, oil and collage, 19¾ x 13 ... (870)   2,600

1968–July 1969

Lippeur de vin clairet, 1945, 29 x 24 .... (1064)   37,760

Il Flûte sur la bosse, 1947, 45¾ x 35¼ .... (1064)   47,200

The Gipsy, 1954, 36¼ x 29¼ .... (1176)   36,000

The Steward, 1954, 51½ x 35¼ .... (1132)   29,500

Landscape No. 114, 1954, impresses gathering and
collage, 25¼ x 19½ .... (1113)   2,000

Chassé-Croisé, 1961, 32 x 39½ .... (1187)   36,580

Marcel Duchamp

(1887–1968)

Birthplace: Blainville, near Rouen, France. Brother of sculptor Raymond Duchamp-Villon and painters Jacques Villon and Suzanne Duchamp. Attends the Académie Julian, Paris.

1910 Early works show the influence of Cézanne.

1911 Joins the Section d'Or group. Paints the first studies of his "Nude Descending a Staircase."

1912 His "Nude Descending a Staircase" is shown at the Section d'Or exhibition, Paris.

1913 The same picture creates a scandal at the Armory Show, New York.

1914-15 His first "ready-mades" dumbfound the public. Visits the U.S., where he becomes the central figure of the Stieglitz group—with Man Ray, Picabia, and others. Embraces an "anti-art" attitude, like the Dadaists of Zurich.

1915-23 Paints the monumental work (on glass) "La Mariée mise à nu par ses célibataires même."

1916 Participates in the foundation of the Society of Independent Artists, New York.

1917 Publishes the reviews *The Blind Man* and *Wrong Wrong.*

1920 Takes the pseudonym of Rose Sélavy in order to sign some of his works. With Katherine Dreier, sets up the Société Anonyme, New York, to extend modern art throughout the U.S.

1926 Takes part in *Anemic Film* with Man Ray and Marc Allégret. Organizes an exhibition of the Société Anonyme, New York.

1941 With André Breton, organizes a Surrealist exhibition in New York.

1942 With Breton and Ernst, publishes the review *V V V* in New York.

1950 His works have entered several American collections.

1955 Becomes an American citizen.

1957 Retrospective exhibition of his and his brothers' work in New York and Houston.

1968 Died.

Sales

DRAWINGS

1968–July 1969

The Crab: Study for a Pennant, 9 x 14½ .... (1237) $ 450

PAINTINGS

1965

Nude Over Nude, (1911), on board mounted on
cradled panel, 25¾ x 19¾ .... (594)   24,000

1968–July 1969

Church at the Seaside, Le Tréport, (1903-04),
20¾ x 29 .... (1208)   6,500

Landscape with Trees, 1908, 18¼ x 23¼ .... (1056)   13,000

Charles Dufresne

(1876–1938)

Birthplace: Millemont, France.

1887 Goes to Paris and attends the Ecole des Beaux-Arts in the studio of Hubert Ponscarme, a medal engraver, but is soon attracted to painting.

1903 Exhibits at the Salon de la Société Nationale, Paris. Becomes a friend of Dunoyer de Segonzac.

1905 Meets the engraver Lespinasse. Participates in the Salon des Indépendants, Paris.

1908 Trip to Italy with Lespinasse.

1910 Winning a two-year scholarship, he stays at the Villa Abd-el-Tif, Algiers. Greatly admires Delacroix and, as this master did in his time, draws his inspiration from the exotic flavor of local scenes, painting some of his most beautiful pictures.

1912 Settles in Paris. Starts painting in brownish shades. Participates in the Salon des Indépendants and in the exhibition of the Société Nationale des Beaux-Arts, Paris.

1914 Slightly influenced by Cubism.

1921 Designs stage decorations and costumes for the ballet *Antar* at the Paris Opéra.

1922 One-man show at the Galerie Barbazanges, Paris.

1923 With other artists, sets up the Salon des Tuileries, Paris.

1925 Exhibits at the Musée des Arts Décoratifs, Paris. Wins the third Carnegie prize.

1930 Turns to religious subject matters.

1937 Does two large panels showing "Le Théâtre de Molière," at the Palais de Chaillot, Paris.

1938 Important murals for the Ecole de Pharmacie, Paris. Died, La Seyne, Var district, France.

Sales

DRAWINGS

1965

The Departure, ink gouache, and pastel, 11¾ x 11¾ .... (535) $ 498

1967

Nude in a Hammock, pen and wash, 8¾ x 6¾ ... (1004) 300

1968–July 1969

At the Café, At the Theater, three drawings in one frame .... (1234) 180

WATERCOLORS

The Arena, 1904, pastel, 16¼ x 25¼ .... (40) 540
Horse and Rider, watercolor, 15 x 10 .... (20) 758
The Fortune-Teller, gouache, 9 x 7¼ .... (32) 310
The Village, 1917, watercolor, 19 x 15¾ .... (68) 400
French Convalescent Playing the Piano at Oscar's in Amiens in Front of English Officers, 1917, watercolor, 16¾ x 16¼ .... (84) 384

1963

Home Scene, gouache, 7 x 9½ .... (232) 350
Bucolic Scene, watercolor, 7½ x 10 .... (296) 280

1964

The Onagers, 1919, gouache, 16¼ x 19¾ .... (395) 220
Algerian Landscape, watercolor, 9 x 10¼ .... (472) 380

The Mountebanks, gouache, 16¼ x 13 .... (463) $ 920
Landscapes, gouache, 13¼ x 16¾ .... (408) 320

1965

The Musicians, gouache, 15 x 12¼ .... (613) 840
The Mountebanks, gouache, 16¼ x 13 .... (632) 660
Landscape in Upper Provence, gouache, 13 x 16¾ .... (560) 300

1966

The Open Window, gouache, 12 x 10¾ .... (745) 1,062
Riders, gouache, 14½ x 11¾ .... (781) 340

1967

At the Theater, gouache, 17½ x 24¼ .... (961) 150
La Rue aux femmes, gouache, 4½ x 11¼ .... (951) 551

1968–July 1969

The Rape of Europe, gouache, 12 x 18½ .... (1077) 660
At the Circus, gouache, 19¾ x 25 .... (1230) 620
Lion Hunting, gouache, 8¾ x 11 .... (1249) 1,400
Musicians and Figures in Red, gouache .... (1263) 600
The Parade, watercolor and gouache, 11¾ x 14 .. (1265) 640
Nude, gouache and collage on yellow paper, 8 x 8 .... (1268) 696

PAINTINGS

1961–1962

Nativity, 27¼ x 67½ .... (76) 1,820
Lion Hunting, 25¾ x 32 .... (157) 1,840
The Cabaret, 7¼ x 7¼ .... (154) 1,960
The Mountebanks, on paper, 13½ x 18¾ .... (143) 723

1963

Lion Hunting, 23¾ x 29 .... (283) 3,051
Hunting Scene, 14 x 10¾ .... (232) 1,746
At the Hotel, Olympia (Nude), 38¼ x 51½ .... (232) 7,458
Crucifixion, 36¾ x 39½ .... (315) 2,057

1964

Mythological Scene, on cardboard laid down on canvas, 9 x 19½ .... (471) 814
The Temptation of St. Anthony, 33 x 51½ .... (471) 3,277
Country Scene, on paper laid down on canvas, 13 x 15 .... (377) 1,469
The Lion and the Stag, on board, 14¼ x 11½ ..... (405) 580
Young Woman, Front View, 25¾ x 19¾ .... (466) 320
Flowers and Plaster, 24 x 19¾ .... (399) 1,400

1965

The Boat, on paper, 12¼ x 11¾ .... (567) 904
The Guitar Player, on paper laid down on panel, 14¼ x 11¾ .... (516) 500
Paul et Virginie, 27¼ x 67¾ .... (569) 3,616
Paul et Virginie, on paper .... (635) 960

1966

Exotic Landscape, 49½ x 46¼ .... (744) 5,537
Reclining Nude, 15¾ x 21¾ .... (702) 1,440
Moses Rescued from Water, on board, 11¼ x 19 .... (757) 1,161

1967

Still Life with Shells, 16¼ x 16¼ .... (901) 600
Exotic Landscape, on paper, 12¾ x 15½ .... (934) 660
Landscape of the Isles, 25 x 29 .... (978) 1,400
Venus, 32 x 39½ .... (984) 2,040

1968–July 1969

The Dufresne Family at Bormes, 32 x 39½ ...... (1049) $4,200
Country Meal, 9¼ x 11½ .... (1117) 960
Hell, (1932), 9¾ x 16 .... (1187) 1,463
The Turkish Hunter, 43 x 43 .... (1181) 11,400
The Earthly Paradise, 39½ x 39½ .... (1181) 6,200
Still Life with Fruit, 9½ x 13 .... (1121) 700
Still Life, 21½ x 18¼ .... (1184) 1,800
Bunch of Flowers, 39½ x 30 .... (1213) 5,200
The Return of Christopher Columbus,
  38½ x 57¾ .... (1235) 3,750
Portrait of Madame Dufresne, 39½ x 32 .... (1256) 6,220
Lion Attacking a White Horse, ... (1263) 720
Still Life with Fruit, 39½ x 32 .... (1265) 6,000
Vase of Flowers and Cup of Fruit, 24 x 19¾ ..... (1265) 3,400

Jean Dufy

(1888–1964)

Birthplace: Le Havre, France. Brother of Raoul Dufy.

1906 Attends the Fine Arts School of Le Havre.

1919 Settles in Montmartre, Paris.

1922 Marries in Paris. Participates in the Salon d'Automne, Paris.

1936-37 Collaborates with Raoul Dufy in the decoration of the Pavillon de l'Electricité, at the Paris World's Fair.

1939 Settles at Preuilly-sur-Claize, Indre-et-Loire district.

1943-44 Settles at Boussay, near Preuilly-sur-Claize.

1964 Died, Boussay, France (a few months after his wife).

Sales

DRAWINGS

1963

Two Women, heightened drawing, 14¼ x 20¼ .... (180) $ 100

1965

The Harbor, 1939, pen, 16¼ x 21¼ .... (529) 170
Paris, pen, 8¼ x 7½ .... (611) 240

1966

Verdun, 1916, pencil and watercolor, 11¾ x 7¾ ... (665) 550

1967

Horses, Riders, and Horsewoman, wash and
  watercolor, 21 x 30 .... (883) 660
The Sacré-Coeur, pencil, 13 x 8 .... (876) 100
The Orchestra, wash, 21¼ x 30½ .... (1000) 512
In Front of the Palace, pen, 9 x 12½ .... (870) 225

1968–July 1969

Woman Playing with a Cat, India ink and pencil,
  18¾ x 14 .... (1088) $ 400
House Amid the Trees, black lead, 10¾ x 14¾ ... (1213) 160
Young Man, pencil, 12½ x 9½ .... (1231) 400
Portrait of a Woman, pen, 21½ x 17 .... (1248) 550
Woman Ironing, 1924, pen, 18 x 12½ .... (1248) 600
Seated Woman, blue pencil, 12¼ x 9¾ .... (1248) 200

WATERCOLORS

1961–1962

The Moulin Rouge, gouache, 18¼ x 24½ .... (157) 520
The Circus, watercolor, 17 x 23 .... (27) 820
Equilibrists, gouache, 14 x 8¼ .... (141) 210
The Trapezist, watercolor and gouache,
  23¼ x 16¾ .... (17) 700
Riders in the Bois, watercolor, 17 x 20½ .... (36) 210
Regattas, 1926, watercolor, 18¼ x 24¼ .... (98) 300
Harvesttime, 1926, watercolor, 18¼ x 24¼ .... (98) 300
The Country House, watercolor, 21¼ x 18¼ .... (47) 350
A Bunch of Flowers, watercolor, 52 x 42 .... (109) 460
Venice, The Grand Canal, gouache, 18¾ x 23¾ ... (174) 206
Nude, watercolor, 23¾ x 17¾ .... (19) 320

1963

Interior with a Vase of Flowers, 1920, watercolor
  and gouache, 21¼ x 19½ .... (202) 1,250
Jetée de fleurs, gouache, 24 x 17¾ .... (293) 900
Seascape, 1924, watercolor, 16½ x 23¾ .... (225) 1,000
Venice, gouache, 16¾ x 24½ .... (290) 1,050
The Fishing Harbor, 1930, watercolor,
  18½ x 25¼ .... (258) 700
Harbor Scene, gouache, 16½ x 24½ .... (208) 1,450
The Grand Palais in Paris, gouache, 16¾ x 24¾ .. (179) 900
Landscape (Preuilly-sur-Claize), watercolor,
  19 x 25¾ .... (242) 420
The Cowboys' Entrance, watercolor and gouache,
  15¾ x 23 .... (248) 820
Vase of Flowers, 1961, gouache, 8¼ x 5½ .... (253) 156

1964

In the Fields, 1924, watercolor, 15½ x 21¾ .... (404) 422
Bust of a Woman, 1925, watercolor, 21 x 17 ...... (384) 69
The Quays of the Harbor, 1930, watercolor,
  20½ x 16¾ .... (336) 260
Harbor Scene, watercolor, 16¾ x 21¾ .... (374) 1,100
The Spanish Dance, gouache, 10¾ x 8 .... (393) 260
Hackney Coaches, watercolor, 12 x 18¼ .... (330) 530
Harvesttime, watercolor and gouache,
  17¾ x 23¾ .... (438) 1,250
The Bois, watercolor, 17¾ x 24 .... (366) 670
Still Life with Flowers, watercolor and gouache
  on paper laid down on canvas, 24¾ x 18¾ .... (374) 1,100
View of Paris, tempera on paper on canvas,
  19 x 25¼ .... (321) 2,000

1965

Roses, 1919, watercolor, 12¾ x 9½ .... (547) 400
Springtime Bouquet, 1920, watercolor, 25 x 18¾ .. (543) 962
Still Life with a Black Cat, 1922, watercolor,
  16¾ x 20¼ .... (541) 550
The Torchlight Tattoo, 1922, watercolor,
  21¼ x 16¾ .... (647) 1,140
14 Juillet, watercolor, 17¾ x 21¼ .... (541) 2,350
Harvesttime, 1923, watercolor, 18¾ x 25 .... (606) 1,700
The Serenade, watercolor, 8¼ x 5½ .... (599) 190

Flowers, watercolor, 19 x 20½ .... (599) $ 860
Place de la Concorde, gouache, 17¾ x 23¾ ...... (507) 2,150
The Circus, watercolor and gouache, 17¾ x 23 ... (494) 1,500
The Cab and the Rider, 1954, gouache, 6 x 9¼ .... (597) 787
Avenue du Bois, gouache, 16¼ x 23¾ .... (518) 1,020
The Harbor, watercolor and gouache,
19½ x 25¼ .... (598) 1,140

1966
Still Life with Flowers, watercolor, 17 x 22½ ..... (659) 900
Soldier Riding, 1916, watercolor, 10 x 8 .... (702) 220
Vase of Flowers, 1921, watercolor, 13½ x 16¾ .... (702) 540
La Goulue, gouache on newsprint, 6¾ x 8 .... (726) 330
The Guitar Player, 1925, watercolor, 22½ x 18½ .. (798) 1,582
Spanish Dance, watercolor and gouache,
13½ x 19½ .... (824) 800
The Villa by the Waterside, 1926, watercolor,
19¾ x 23¾ .... (810) 700
Landscape, watercolor, 15¾ x 20 .... (718) 750
Verdun, watercolor and pencil, 11 x 15 .... (805) 500
The Pond, watercolor, 16 x 20 .... (718) 750
Landscape of Provence, watercolor, 18¾ x 24 .... (665) 1,500
The Pont-Neuf, watercolor, 17¼ x 22 .... (711) 1,400
Cabs at the Bois, 1951, gouache, 5 x 7¾ .... (817) 200
*Vase of Flowers with a Balcony Looking Out
Over the Town,* watercolor and gouache,
17¼ x 19½ .... (727) 1,100
The Ballet of Katherine Dunham, gouache and
watercolor, 18¾ x 24½ .... (772) 1,000

1967
The Green Plant in Front of the Window, 1919,
watercolor, 19¾ x 15 .... (852) 500
Verdun, 1916, watercolor, 10 x 7½ .... (950) 240
Fluvial Landscape, 1920, watercolor, 12¼ x 17¾ .. (870) 1,500
Circus Scene, 1924, watercolor, 13 x 19½ .... (893) 1,000
At the Circus, watercolor and gouache,
17½ x 23 .... (995) 2,400
The Quadrille's Entrance into the Arena,
gouache, 23¾ x 18½ .... (919) 1,808
Woman's Head, gouache and watercolor on
paper laid down on canvas, 12½ x 8¾ .... (870) 350
Venice, gouache, 16¾ x 25 .... (841) 1,750
Landscape in Provence, gouache, 17¾ x 23¼ ..... (967) 949
The Harbor, watercolor, 16¾ x 20½ .... (911) 840
View of Munich, 1956, watercolor and gouache,
12½ x 19 .... (998) 3,075

1968–July 1969
Flowers, 1916, watercolor, 12½ x 9½ .... (1154) 280
Seascape, 1924, watercolor, 16¾ x 24 .... (1145) 1,300
Vase of Flowers, 1925, watercolor, 18 x 14¼ ..... (1116) 480
Bunch of Flowers, gouache and watercolor,
17 x 13 .... (1061) 600
Bunch of Flowers, watercolor, 21¾ x 18¼ .... (1196) 1,080
Flowers in a Vase, watercolor and gouache,
19¾ x 15½ .... (1103) 1,420
Vase of Flowers, watercolor, 27 x 22½ .... (1183) 1,700
Sailboats Racing, 1925, watercolor, 14¾ x 22¾ .. (1184) 1,100
Venice, 1926, watercolor, 15 x 19¾ .... (1051) 980
The Côte d'Azur, watercolor and gouache,
19¾ x 25¾ .... (1061) 1,750
The Harbor, watercolor, 20½ x 17 .... (1014) 620
A West Indian Ball, gouache .... (1119) 1,260

The Ballet, gouache, 16¾ x 21¼ .... (1168) $ 860
At the Circus, watercolor and gouache,
19¾ x 25¼ .... (1103) 2,080
Circus Scene, gouache and watercolor on paper
mounted on board, 23¾ x 30¼ .... (1088) 1,450
Circus Scene, watercolor, 17½ x 21¼ .... (1028) 900
Interior with a Violoncello, gouache, 25¼ x 19½ . (1113) 2,100
Street with Figures, watercolor, 14 x 16 .... (1203) 1,115
Village Street, watercolor, 16½ x 21¾ .... (1210) 1,100
The Moulin de la Galette, watercolor,
17½ x 21¼ .... (1200) 1,800
The Moulin Rouge, gouache, 18½ x 24½ .... (1189) 2,600
The Esplanade des Invalides, gouache and oil on
paper laid down on canvas, 19¾ x 25 ...... (1088) 2,500
View of Paris with Notre-Dame, watercolor,
18½ x 24 .... (1213) 1,440
The City, watercolor, 15½ x 15 .... (1031) 330
Blue Roofs, watercolor, 16¾ x 10 .... (1030) 500
Reclining Nude, watercolor and ink, 23 x 17¾ ... (1030) 950
River Scene, watercolor, 17 x 22 .... (1088) 1,200
Le Havre Harbor, watercolor, 18¼ x 23 .... (1220) 860
Fishing Boats, watercolor, 19½ x 25 .... (1222) 620
Sailboats, watercolor, 14¾ x 22½ .... (1224) 800
Regattas, watercolor, 19¼ x 25 .... (1227) 980
Woman with a Necklace, pen and watercolor on
paper mounted on canvas, 20 x 16 .... (1231) 600
Flowers and Shell, watercolor and gouache,
23½ x 18 .... (1231) 2,250
Versailles, 1943, watercolor, 18¼ x 23½ .... (1231) 1,700
Woman's Head, pastel, 14 x 10½ .... (1231) 350
Paris Scene, gouache and watercolor, 18 x 24 ... (1231) 2,600
Place de la Concorde, gouache and watercolor,
17½ x 23 .... (1231) 2,500
Honfleur, watercolor, 1944, 16¾ x 19½ .... (1237) 1,130
Haymaking Time, 19 x 21¾ .... (1247) 1,700
On the Balcony, watercolor, 20¾ x 16½ .... (1248) 1,300
Soldier on Horseback, watercolor, 12 x 7½ ...... (1248) 800
Still Life, watercolor, 18½ x 15¾ .... (1248) 2,000
The Harbor, watercolor, 17½ x 22½ .... (1252) 2,900
Sailboats in the Harbor, watercolor, 15 x 20¾ ... (1255) 1,000
Church Square, watercolor, 25 x 19 .... (1256) 980
The Pond, 1922, watercolor, 21¾ x 16½ .... (1258) 1,300
Walkers, watercolor, 14¼ x 15¾ .... (1258) 1,100
Landscape, 1933, watercolor, 21 x 16¾ .... (1268) 928

PAINTINGS
1961–1962
The Symphony Orchestra, 23¾ x 29 .... (26) 1,400
Two Musician Clowns, 15¾ x 17¾ .... (152) 900
Portrait of a Young Woman, 1928, 10¾ x 8¾ ...... (52) 130
Still Life, 1926, 23¾ x 29 .... (102) 960
Corn Harvest, 1925, 14½ x 21 .... (128) 137
Country Scene, 1928, 18¼ x 24 .... (68) 820
Road by the Waterside, 1921, 32 x 25¾ .... (120) 900
The Piazza di Spagna in Rome, 19½ x 23¾ .... (44) 1,400
The Gare des Invalides, 1930, 17¾ x 21½ .... (64) 1,900
The Grand Palais and the Invalides, 18¼ x 21¾ .. (109) 1,000
An Afternoon at the Bois de Boulogne,
18½ x 25 .... (2) 1,500

1963
Interior with a Woman, 1923, 24 x 18¼ .... (266) 470
Still Life with Flowers and Fruits, 1928,
21¼ x 17½ .... (208) 1,050

Interior with a Nude, 1928, 32¼ x 25¼ .... (208) $1,100
The Pont des Arts, 1929, 21¼ x 29 .... (286) 620
Paris, 21¼ x 25¾ .... (314) 1,000
The Invalides, 19½ x 25 .... (275) 2,000
Bunch of Flowers, 1930, 17 x 21¼ .... (246) 960
Bunch of Flowers, 25¾ x 19¾ .... (236) 1,853
The Harbor, 1934, 18¼ x 15 .... (306) 800
Sailboats, 16¼ x 9½ .... (223) 480
Landscape, 21¼ x 29 .... (303) 1,700
Riders at the Bois de Boulogne, 19½ x 25¼ ...... (275) 2,200
At the Circus, 19½ x 23¾ .... (275) 1,850
Shells, 12¾ x 18¾ .... (290) 600
Still Life, ... (298) 1,560

1964
The Tuileries, 1924, 20¾ x 24¾ .... (374) 2,600
Flowers, 1930, 21¾ x 18 .... (321) 1,600
Bunch of Flowers, 25¾ x 21¼ .... (371) 1,700
Yen Island, 1930, 11 x 18¾ .... (329) 1,200
Horse Races, 19½ x 15¾ .... (321) 1,600
Cabs, 19¾ x 29 .... (335) 1,160
The Circus, 13¾ x 10¼ .... (438) 1,550
The River Seine by the Institut, 21¼ x 32 .... (399) 2,200
The Louvre, 8 x 14½ .... (329) 2,200
View of a Village, 18½ x 25¾ .... (467) 984

1965
A Team, Riders, and Walkers, 14¾ x 32½ .... (564) 2,600
Rue Laffitte, 15 x 18¼ .... (543) 2,263
A Teapot and a Cup of Fruit in Front of a Mirror,
  1923, 21¼ x 25¾ .... (603) 1,220
Portrait of Madame Dufy, 1925, 21¾ x 18¼ ...... (547) 1,360
Walking Along the River Seine, 1929,
  23¾ x 28½ .... (634) 3,198
Still Life, 11¾ x 15¾ .... (572) 560
Window with a Bunch of Flowers, on cradled
  cardboard, 21 x 14¾ .... (599) 800

1966
Flowers Behind the Open Window, on cradled
  panel, 21 x 14¾ .... (731) 1,300
The Invalides, Paris, 19¾ x 25 .... (648) 2,300
Venice, 1926, 28½ x 39½ .... (784) 2,300
Glasgow, on paper laid down on canvas,
  19½ x 25 .... (784) 2,700
The Juggler, 1928, 21¾ x 18¼ .... (798) 2,712
Still Life with Roses and Lemons, 1928,
  18¼ x 21¾ .... (685) 1,300
Tulips, on paper laid down on canvas,
  25¾ x 19¾ .... (805) 1,500
The River with the Stone Bridge, 23¾ x 29 ...... (659) 1,640
The Pont du Commerce, 1927, 23¾ x 29 .... (923) 2,900
The Orchestra, 1927, 17¾ x 14¾ .... (870) 2,300
The Harbor, 1931, on cradled panel, 22 x 15 ...... (978) 1,560
Landscape, 25¾ x 18 .... (989) 3,250
View of Paris, 23¾ x 31½ .... (963) 7,000
Circus, 20¼ x 23 .... (917) 1,840
Notre-Dame, 13 x 9½ .... (918) 1,243
The Entrance of the Harbor, 25¾ x 21¼ .... (976) 3,000
Wild Flowers, 14 x 10¾ .... (848) 760

1968–July 1969
Village on the Banks of a Stream, 1920,
  15 x 18½ .... (1030) 3,000
Peonies, 1922, 32¼ x 25¾ .... (1030) 4,000
Trapezists, 1927, 25¾ x 21¼ .... (1113) 2,840

Clowns and Orchestra, 17½ x 21 .... (1138) $1,611
The Circus, 21¼ x 29 .... (1061) 2,850
Harvest in the Oise, 1927, 25¾ x 32 .... (1159) 3,400
Harvesttime, 29 x 36½ .... (1183) 4,200
The Woman with a Bouquet, 1928, 24 x 18¼ ..... (1051) 1,600
At Medrano Circus, 1929, 23¾ x 28½ .... (1085) 1,984
View of a Harbor, 1930, 18¼ x 21¾ .... (1200) 2,160
Place Blanche, 18¼ x 21¾ .... (1200) 3,500
*Landscape of the Ile-de-France; Farmhouse in
  the Ile-de-France,* two panels, 5¾ x 13 and
  6¾ x 12¾ .... (1183) 1,200
Woman's Face, on cradled panel, 20¼ x 15¾ .... (1089) 340
Landscape, 25¾ x 19¾ .... (1228) 2,600
The Circus, 21¼ x 6 .... (1231) 3,500
Montmartre Scene, mixed media on paper,
  mounted on canvas, 19 x 25½ .... (1231) 2,400
Place Pigalle, mixed media on canvas,
  18½ x 21½ .... (1231) 3,700
Bridges Over the River Seine, 11 x 13¼ .... (1248) 2,200
The Harbor, 18¼ x 13 .... (1266) 1,220
Village Near a Lake, (1919–20), 13 x 18 .... (1271) 1,800

Raoul Dufy

(1877–1953)

Birthplace: Le Havre, France.

1900   Attends the Ecole des Beaux-Arts in the studio of Bonnat, Paris. Discovers the Impressionists at Durand-Ruel's and Cézanne at Ambroise Vollard's.

1901   Exhibits at the Salon des Artistes Français, Paris. The Van Gogh exhibition at Bernheim's exerts a great influence on him.

1903   Sends his first pictures to the Salon des Indépendants, Paris.

1905   Visits the Salon d'Automne and is deeply impressed by Matisse's "Luxe, Calme, et Volupté."

1906   First one-man show at the Galerie Berthe Weil, Paris. Takes part in the Salon d'Automne, Paris.

1907–11   Abandons pure color and darkens his palette, producing severe compositions.

1911–12   Produces fabric designs for the famous couturier Poiret and for the firm Bianchini in Lyons.

1920–21   Stay in Vence, in the south of France. Produces ceramics and tapestries.

1922   Trip to Sicily.

1923–25   Draws inspiration from horse races. Trip to Morocco.

1926   Exhibition at the Galerie Bernheim-Jeune, Paris. Illustrations of Apollinaire's *Le Poète assassiné.*

1927   Pictures and watercolors done in Nice are regarded as a new assertion of his style.

1936-37   Important decoration for the Palais de l'Electricité at the Paris World's Fair is his largest work.

1940   Settles in the south of France.

1943   Important exhibition at the Palais des Beaux-Arts, Brussels.

1949   Important exhibition at the Louis Carré Gallery, New York.

1950   Trip to Boston. Stage decoration for Jean Anouilh's play *Ring Around the Moon.*

1952   Wins the first prize at the Venice Biennial. Very important exhibition at the Musée d'Art et d'Histoire, Geneva.

1953   Died, Forcalquier, France. Exhibition at the Ny-Carlsberg Glyptotek, Copenhagen. Retrospective exhibition at the Musée d'Art Moderne, Paris.

Sales

DRAWINGS

1961-1962

Standing Nude, black lead, 25¾ x 17¾ .... (171) $ 320

Seated Woman in the Nude, (1905), charcoal, 21 x 17 .... (102)   800

Female Nude, pencil, 21¾ x 16¾ .... (124)   300

Nude Model, (1925), pencil, 19½ x 23¾ .... (85)   850

Drowsy Woman, pen, 19 x 24 .... (80)   620

Bust of a Woman, wash, 23¼ x 17¾ .... (124)   1,000

Standing Man in the Nude (Study for "La Fée Electricité"), ink, 25¼ x 19½ .... (136)   290

Horses and Figures, India ink, 10¼ x 4½ .... (136)   140

Harvest and Horses, blue ink, 20¼ x 15½ .... (95)   1,000

The Wheat Field, India ink, 15½ x 25¼ .... (102)   1,800

The Birds, India ink, 17 x 23¾ .... (85)   1,100

The Quays of the River Seine, wash with heightening, 18¼ x 24 .... (30)   1,300

Maritime Allegory, India ink, 14¼ x 18 .... (155)   620

The Outlet of the Harbor, charcoal, 16¾ x 21¼ ... (177)   380

View of a Harbor, pencil, 17¾ x 23¾ .... (32)   500

Seascape, blue-ink wash, 17½ x 21¼ .... (76)   760

St. Léger en Yvelines, black chalk and watercolor, 16¾ x 21¾ .... (96)   2,400

1963

The Sledge, wash, 9 x 12¼ .... (258)   340

Still Life with a Guitar, black lead, 9 x 11 .... (258)   200

Study for the Orchestra of the Theater in Le Havre, 1902, charcoal heightened with white, 12¾ x 18½ .... (255)   2,204

The Violinist, India ink, 25¼ x 19½ .... (299)   1,000

The Violoncellist, India ink, 23½ x 18 .... (232)   452

Seaside, pencil, 16¾ x 21 .... (283)   904

The Outlet of the Harbor, charcoal, 16¾ x 21¼ ... (275)   600

Seascape, charcoal, 16¾ x 20¾ .... (225)   600

Ste. Adresse Beach, pencil and wash, 15 x 11½ ... (199)   4,000

A Woman at Her Window, Nice, ink, 11½ x 9¾ .. (208)   400

The Olive Tree, pencil, 18¼ x 24 .... (194)   440

Reclining Nude, black lead, 17¼ x 21¼ .... (242)   80

Standing Nude, charcoal heightened with white, 24½ x 17½ .... (262)   180

Still Life with a Landscape in the Background, India ink, 6½ x 7½ .... (186)   280

1964

Procession of Belgian and Foreign Delegations at the Funeral of King Albert I in Brussels in 1934, pen, 19½ x 25¼ .... (401)   410

Carnival Characters Before the Casino de la Jetée in Nice, (1938), pen, 19½ x 25¼ .... (401) $ 800

Aboard the "Queen Mary," 1937, pen with heightening, 25¾ x 19¾ .... (377)   1,537

Seaside Scene, pen, 10 x 14 .... (374)   400

La Croisette, pencil, 16¾ x 20½ .... (454)   1,050

View of Deauville, pencil, 21¼ x 29 .... (321)   250

Harvesttime, pen and grayish-blue wash, 20 x 15½ .... (401)   840

The Wheat Field, pen, 19 x 25 .... (453)   1,050

Portrait of a Woman, India-ink wash, 25¾ x 18¼ .... (453)   691

Bust of a Man, black lead, 23¾ x 18½ .... (376)   190

Marche Militaire, ink, 19 x 24½ .... (354)   2,000

The Hill with Olive Trees, charcoal, 18¼ x 23¾ ... (322)   560

Landscape, red chalk, 16¾ x 21 .... (441)   1,175

Place de la Concorde, pencil, 11¼ x 9¼ .... (383)   226

Réunion Musicale, black lead, 19 x 24½ .... (472)   900

1965

View of a Beach on the Côte d'Azur, pencil, 17 x 21 .... (507)   425

Woman Thinking, 24 x 18¼ .... (559)   320

Nude, wash and India ink, 21 x 16¼ .... (598)   330

Woman's Head, pencil, 21¾ x 7¼ .... (644)   375

Still Life with a Coffeepot, India-ink wash, 19 x 25 .... (586)   680

The Violoncellist, pen, 15¾ x 11 .... (586)   920

The Wheat Field, ink, 19½ x 25¾ .... (582)   1,437

The Studio in Vence, Conté pencil, 19 x 25 .... (590)   700

Amphitrite (Sketch for a Tapestry), pencil, 18¾ x 25 .... (582)   1,271

1966

Seated Nude, 1929, pen, 19 x 25 .... (672)   1,170

L' Estaque, (1908), pencil and watercolor, 10 x 11¾ .... (689)   829

Bois de Boulogne, black lead, 19½ x 25¼ .... (745)   1,311

St. Léger en Yvelines, black chalk and watercolor, 17 x 22 .... (707)   4,250

Odalisque, pen, 19¾ x 26 .... (703)   4,250

Portrait of Madame R. D., India ink, wash, and watercolor, 25¼ x 19½ .... (798)   927

1967

Bateaux-Lavoirs Along the River Seine, wash and watercolor, 17¾ x 23¾ .... (912)   1,200

Aboard a Ship, pen, 14¼ x 18 .... (919)   1,130

Fishing on the High Seas, black pencil, 17½ x 21½ .... (879)   420

The Fishermen, 17 x 21¼ .... (978)   560

The Helm, India ink, 14 x 17¾ .... (967)   994

Portrait of a Woman, brush and India ink, 25¾ x 19¾ .... (905)   400

Young Lady Seated, India-ink wash, 23½ x 18¾ .... (995)   820

The Violinist, pen heightened with white gouache, 25¾ x 19¾ .... (984)   700

Orchestra, India ink and watercolor, 8¼ x 10¾ ... (918)   2,938

1968-July 1969

Au Bistro, (1898), pencil and watercolor, 10¾ x 13¾ .... (1070)   2,360

Barges Near the Pont Marie, 1904, pencil and wash heightened with white gouache, 14¼ x 19½ .... (1191)   6,136

House in a Park, (1909), pencil and watercolor, 10 x 12¾ .... (1075)   640

The Artist's Wife, 1910, 24 x 17¾ . . . . (1051) $ 400

Portrait of Madame Dufy, 1910, black chalk,
25¼ x 18¾ . . . . (1191)   1,770

The Orchestra, pen and watercolor, 8¼ x 10¾ . . . (1113)   2,800

Landscape, India ink, 14 x 3 . . . . (1174)   253

Les Saintes Maries, pen, 9¾ x 7¼ . . . . (1106)   560

The Troika, wash, 8¾ x 11¾ . . . . (1162)   760

Young Girls Riding, India ink, 19¾ x 25¾ . . . . . . (1125)   2,875

Grooming Horses in a Farmyard, black lead,
13½ x 22 . . . . (1023)   380

The Artist's Dog, pen and wash, 14¼ x 19½ . . . . . (1168)   160

Woman with a Necklace, India ink, 17½ x 4¾ . . . (1127)   1,150

Standing Nude, pencil, 26 x 19¾ . . . . (1060)   880

Reclining Nude, India ink, 19 x 25 . . . . (1066)   520

In the Drawing Room, 4 x 6½ . . . . (1154)   72

A Tribute to Lyautey in Nancy, pen, 19¾ x 26 . . . (1203)   3,221

The Reception in Honor of Dufy in London, India
ink, 19¾ x 25¾ . . . . (1088)   1,750

Amphitrite (Sketch for a Tapestry), pencil,
10¾ x 24¾ . . . . (1080)   1,800

*Study of a Statue and an Egyptian Temple—The
Ox Apis,* double sided, black lead, 6½ x 9½ . (1225)   440

Study of Costumes, black lead, 5¼ x 7¾ . . . . (1227)   90

The Musicians, black lead, 5¼ x 7¾ . . . . (1227)   150

Huygens, pen, 25¾ x 14¼ . . . . (1234)   520

The Forest, pen and ink, 19 x 25 . . . . (1240)   2,520

Near Vence, pencil, 16½ x 20½ . . . . (1240)   1,320

Fishermen with Nets, pen, 10 x 15½ . . . . (1241)   856

The Outlet of the Harbor, black chalk,
17 x 21½ . . . . (1241)   907

Study of a Costume, 5¼ x 8 . . . . (1245)   80

Study of Costumes for a Show, 8 x 5¼ . . . . (1245)   76

Pierrots, 5¼ x 8 . . . . (1245)   50

The Violinist, 8 x 5¼ . . . . (1245)   82

Landscape at St. Jeannet (Near Vence), black
pencil, 17½ x 21½ . . . . (1246)   1,100

Banks of the River Marne, Boating, India ink,
17¾ x 22 . . . . (1253)   1,500

Studies of Figures, pen, 19 x 23 . . . . (1253)   640

Seated Nude, pen, 19¾ x 13½ . . . . (1254)   2,800

The Parade, India ink, 19¾ x 25¾ . . . . (1265)   1,820

The Great Oak, pencil, 19½ x 25¼ . . . . (1272)   1,560

The Seaman, pen and black ink, 14 x 18 . . . . (1273)   1,386

WATERCOLORS

1961–1962

Cup of Fruit on a White Tablecloth, 1941,
watercolor and gouache, 20¼ x 24 . . . . (114)   4,000

A Butterfly is a Flying Flower, watercolor,
19¾ x 12¼ . . . . (157)   1,440

Windflowers and Tulip, watercolor, 19¾ x 25¼ . . . (34)   4,200

Ste. Adresse, watercolor, 19¾ x 25¾ . . . . (18)   4,520

Honfleur Harbor, 1898, watercolor, 10 x 12 . . . . . . (65)   610

Seascape, "Souvenir du Havre," watercolor,
17¾ x 25 . . . . (75)   1,343

Marseilles Harbor, 1925, watercolor,
19¾ x 25¾ . . . . (156)   3,540

Nice, 1930, watercolor, 19 x 25 . . . . (69)   5,372

Monte Carlo Ballet, watercolor, 14 x 20½ . . . . (18)   3,526

The Terrace in Front of the Church in Taormina,
1922, watercolor, 19¾ x 25¾ . . . . (80)   3,700

The Bridge Over the River Arno in Florence,
watercolor, 19¾ x 25¾ . . . . (80)   3,200

The River Thames, watercolor, 19½ x 25 . . . . (68)   3,220

The British Parliament and the Thames,
watercolor, 19¾ x 23¾ . . . . (30) $4,100

View of Spain, 1949, watercolor, 19¾ x 25¾ . . . . . . (93)   5,424

The Threshing Machine, 1912, watercolor,
9½ x 12¾ . . . . (143)   1,582

Country Landscape, watercolor, 19½ x 25 . . . . (70)   2,370

Landscape with Trees, 1934, watercolor,
19 x 25¼ . . . . (156)   2,700

The Orchestra, gouache, 15¾ x 9 . . . . (71)   6,600

At the Restaurant, 1950, watercolor and gouache,
19½ x 25 . . . . (96)   3,500

Nymphs Bathing, pastel and watercolor,
18½ x 25¼ . . . . (26)   2,220

Window Looking Out on the Sea, gouache,
21¼ x 19½ . . . . (143)   3,842

Seaside with Boats, watercolor, 19¾ x 25 . . . . (6)   4,520

Fountain on the Harbor, watercolor, 10 x 13½ . . . . (162)   1,160

Les Régattes au Grand Pavois, watercolor,
19½ x 25¼ . . . . (171)   2,720

The Regattas, 1934, watercolor, 18¼ x 25¼ . . . . . (171)   1,280

Paddock Scene, (1930), gouache, 18¾ x 23¾ . . . . . (8)   12,500

At the Races: To the Starting Post, gouache,
19½ x 25 . . . . (71)   7,840

The Races, watercolor, 19½ x 25 . . . . (96)   4,000

1963

Canal de la Marne at St. Maurice, 1903, pastel,
15 x 15¾ . . . . (199)   4,200

The Carrousel Court, 1904, pastel, 17 x 21¼ . . . . . (199)   8,000

Cannes, (1924), watercolor, 19½ x 25 . . . . (210)   7,129

Circus Scene, 1924, watercolor and gouache,
19 x 25¼ . . . . (254)   7,200

The Thames in London, 1930, watercolor,
19¾ x 25¾ . . . . (225)   3,000

Minnie the Bitch, 1934, watercolor, 18¾ x 25 . . . . . (210)   4,661

The Alsatian, watercolor, 19 x 21 . . . . (262)   340

The Races, (1935), watercolor, 20¾ x 28 . . . . (232)   6,328

Horse Races, watercolor, 19¾ x 25¾ . . . . (281)   6,102

The Races, watercolor, 8 x 25¾ . . . . (283)   3,503

The Red Table, 1936, watercolor, 24 x 17½ . . . . . . (283)   4,746

*Project for the Decoration of the Palais de la
Lumière,* watercolor, 19¾ x 24 . . . . (298)   6,100

Brochure for an Exhibition Stand, watercolor,
12¾ x 19¾ . . . . (299)   1,560

The Sea at Le Havre, (1938), gouache,
20¼ x 27¼ . . . . (208)   4,100

Pompeii, (1938), watercolor, 19¾ x 25¾ . . . . (279)   4,000

Village with Horses, watercolor, 17¾ x 23¾ . . . . . (318)   3,500

*Rough Sketch for a Stage Decoration: Two
Characters and Musicians,* watercolor,
14¼ x 23¾ . . . . (306)   400

The Rowers, watercolor, 15½ x 29 . . . . (296)   4,200

The Wicker Sofa Before the Window, 1942,
watercolor, 19½ x 25¾ . . . . (296)   7,400

St. Tropez, watercolor, 16¾ x 21¼ . . . . (179)   6,000

1964

The Baie des Anges in Nice, (1928), gouache,
20 x 23¾ . . . . (372)   5,250

Reclining Nymph, (1930), watercolor and
gouache, 19¾ x 25¼ . . . . (329)   2,600

Seaside, watercolor and gouache, 21¾ x 29 . . . . . (377)   6,780

Children in the Park at Hardrancourt, 1932,
watercolor, 19¾ x 25¾ . . . . (465)   3,800

The Start at the Races, watercolor, 21¾ x 29¾ . . . (340)   6,000

The Corn Field, watercolor and gouache,
21¾ x 26½ . . . . (340)   5,300

The Races, 1935, watercolor, 8 x 25½ . . . . (335) $3,400

The Butterflies, watercolor, 16¼ x 21 . . . . (335) 1,900

The Viaduct, watercolor, 25 x 19 . . . . (335) 1,180

Reception in the Great Drawing Room at the Palais de l'Elysée, (1938), gouache, 15¼ x 23½ . . . . (401) 3,700

The Reception, gouache and watercolor, 22½ x 29¾ . . . . (354) 6,800

Portrait of Madame D., watercolor, 25¼ x 19½ . . . (441) 1,356

Venice, 1938, gouache, 19½ x 25 . . . . (416) 7,186

Racecourse in Deauville, gouache, 19 x 25¾ . . . . . . (368) 10,503

The Actor William Gilbert, watercolor, 25 x 19½ . . . . (439) 4,160

Le Bistro, gouache, 19½ x 25¾ . . . . (367) 5,528

Still Life with a Cup of Fruit, 1940, watercolor, 19¾ x 25¾ . . . . (347) 3,800

Amélie-les-Bains, 1940, watercolor, 25¾ x 19½ . . . (378) 6,102

Still Life with a White Tablecloth, 1941, watercolor, 19½ x 25 . . . . (394) 3,580

The Murdered Poet, watercolor, 11½ x 8¼ . . . . . . (448) 2,200

La Madeleine, oval-shaped gouache, 16¾ x 14 . . . . (471) 3,503

Still Life Before a Landscape, watercolor, 19½ x 25¼ . . . . (426) 2,100

Nude by the Seaside, watercolor, 27 x 20½ . . . . (405) 2,902

Golfe-Juan, watercolor and gouache, 20¼ x 24½ . . . . (354) 4,500

The Windflowers,[1] 1953, watercolor, 17½ x 21¼ . . . (378) 6,328

The Butterflies, gouache, 12¾ x 19½ . . . . (347) 2,200

The Races, gouache, 11¼ x 25¼ . . . . (471) 12,091

1965

The Wrestlers, watercolor and gouache, 19½ x 25¼ . . . . (526) 5,000

The Quay, 1901, gouache, watercolor, and charcoal, 17½ x 22½ . . . . (629) 5,804

The Sonata, 1902, pastel, 18½ x 24½ . . . . (582) 967

Nude on a Sofa, watercolor, 19¾ x 25¾ . . . . (561) 1,900

Cannes, 1929, watercolor, 18¾ x 24½ . . . . (567) 5,650

Nude, 1929, gouache, 24¾ x 16 . . . . (616) 5,760

The Old Harbor in Marseilles, watercolor, 19½ x 25 . . . . (632) 6,400

The Olive Trees, watercolor, 17¾ x 21¼ . . . . (503) 1,740

Landscape with Olive Trees, watercolor heightened with gouache, 21¼ x 17 . . . . (586) 2,000

Requisition of Horses, watercolor and pencil, 19¾ x 23¾ . . . . (526) 6,500

The Models of Monsieur Poiret, (1931), gouache, 8¾ x 16¾ . . . . (569) 3,277

Dufy's Vestibule in Perpignan, watercolor, 20¼ x 25¾ . . . . (624) 3,179

Regattas in Henley, 1933, gouache and watercolor, 19 x 25 . . . . (522) 6,081

At the Races, the Paddock, watercolor, 16¾ x 20½ . . . . (553) 4,800

Races in Deauville, gouache and watercolor, 19½ x 25¼ . . . . (539) 10,750

Epsom, gouache and watercolor, 19½ x 21¼ . . . . . . (539) 8,700

The Paddock, 1935, watercolor, 20½ x 28 . . . . (559) 5,800

At the Races, to the Starting Post, watercolor, and gouache, 19½ x 25¼ . . . . (569) 12,204

The Pier in Deauville, watercolor, 19½ x 25¼ . . . . (526) 7,000

Walkers at the Seaside, watercolor, 4¾ x 23¾ . . . . (617) 1,989

St. Germain, (1935), watercolor, 19¾ x 25¾ . . . . . . (561) 2,500

[1]Dedicated "A Emilienne."

The Viaduct, watercolor and pencil, 25¼ x 19 . . . . (503) $1,400

Amboise, watercolor, 19¾ x 25¾ . . . . (539) 5,750

View of New York, 1937, gouache, 19½ x 25¾ . . . . (624) 2,902

Arizona Flowers, watercolor, 19½ x 25 . . . . (617) 9,379

Figure, gouache, 25¾ x 19½ . . . . (567) 3,503

La Piazzetta in Venice, (1938), gouache and watercolor, 19½ x 25¼ . . . . (539) 3,900

La Salute, Venice, watercolor, 18¾ x 24½ . . . . (617) 3,978

Amélie-les-Bains,[2] 1940, watercolor, 25¾ x 19¾ . . . (559) 3,820

Reclining Nude, watercolor, 19¼ x 25 . . . . (612) 2,900

The Alsatian,[3] watercolor, 19½ x 24 . . . . (577) 480

Bunch of Daisies, 1941, gouache, 19¾ x 26 . . . . . . (569) 6,215

Still Life with a Cup of Fruit, watercolor, 19½ x 25 . . . . (516) 2,400

Open Window with a Map of the World, watercolor, 19¾ x 25¾ . . . . (561) 3,800

The Circus, gouache, 21 x 26¾ . . . . (602) 7,006

1966

The Park of Marseilles, 1903, watercolor, 10 x 15 . . . . (784) 2,000

The Casino in Nice, watercolor, 19½ x 25½ . . . . . . (744) 6,215

Circus Scene, 1924, watercolor and gouache, 19¾ x 25¾ . . . . (801) 8,000

Amphitrite, (1925), gouache on paper mounted on board, 30 x 26¼ . . . . (701) 5,750

Women in Morocco, 1926, watercolor, 19 x 25 . . . . (749) 2,200

Standing Woman in the Nude, 1929, gouache, 24¾ x 16 . . . . (745) 5,424

Sailboats, (1929-30), watercolor, 19½ x 25 . . . . (802) 5,760

Bridge over the River Loire, watercolor, 19¾ x 25¼ . . . . (797) 3,051

The Admiralty Ball, (1930), gouache, 19 x 25¾ . . . . (797) 7,684

The Models of Monsieur Poiret, 1931, gouache, 8¾ x 17 . . . . (666) 4,400

The Models of Monsieur Poiret, gouache, 8¾ x 17 . . . . (798) 2,983

Horse Races, gouache, 19½ x 25 . . . . (797) 13,560

At the Races: Goodwood 1935, watercolor and gouache, 19½ x 25½ . . . . (808) 13,349

Horse Races, watercolor, 19¼ x 25¼ . . . . (703) 5,500

A Fair Summer, watercolor and gouache, 15½ x 23 . . . . (744) 5,311

The Sideboard, (1937), gouache and watercolor, 19 x 25¼ . . . . (776) 6,500

The Master's House (Called Farmyard and Castle), watercolor, 19¾ x 25¾ . . . . (741) 3,400

Balcony Looking on Amélie-les-Bains, 1940, watercolor, 19¾ x 25¾ . . . . (741) 6,000

Window with a Green Shutter, watercolor, 25¾ x 19½ . . . . (681) 3,040

Front of the Ecole Militaire, watercolor, 19½ x 25¼ . . . . (681) 2,500

Venus and the Organ Player (After Titian), gouache and watercolor, 19 x 25¼ . . . . (776) 5,000

Window Looking Out on Paris: The Opera, gouache, 28 x 16¼ . . . . (811) 1,820

Lunch in Front of the Sea, watercolor, 19¼ x 24½ . . . . (727) 3,600

The Cup of Figs, watercolor, 13¾ x 17½ . . . . (685) 800

Still Life with a Cup of Fruit, watercolor, 19¾ x 25¾ . . . . (814) 2,200

Still Life with Peaches, watercolor, 16¾ x 21¼ . . . (745) 4,045

[2]Sold in Geneva in May 1964 for $6,102.
[3]Sold in Paris in June 1963 for $340.

1967

Country Party, watercolor, 24 x 29¼ . . . . (857) $3,600

The Paddock, 1925, watercolor and gouache,
19¼ x 25 . . . . (1004)   9,500

The Farm, 1925, watercolor, 19¾ x 25¾ . . . . (1004)   3,250

Ascot: Before the Race, 1928, watercolor,
15 x 19¼ . . . . (988)   14,928

Standing Nude, 1929, gouache, 24 x 15 . . . . (970)   6,888

View of Westminster, 1930, watercolor,
19½ x 25¼ . . . . (940)   6,384

Epsom Derby, 1933, watercolor, 19¾ x 26 . . . . (938)   10,227

Tennis Players and Riders, watercolor,
18½ x 24 . . . . (993)   4,600

The Paddock, gouache and watercolor,
19½ x 25¼ . . . . (1004)   13,000

Saumur, 1937, watercolor, 19 x 25¼ . . . . (889)   5,000

Chenonceaux Castle, watercolor and gouache,
19¼ x 25¼ . . . . (988)   6,469

La Fée Electricité, watercolor, 19 x 25¼ . . . . (911)   5,800

Bunch of Roses, 1941, watercolor, 19½ x 25¼ . . . . (938)   4,975

Flowers, watercolor, 23¼ x 18½ . . . . (1007)   800

Still Life with Fruit, watercolor, 17½ x 21¾ . . . . . . (949)   1,000

Wild Flowers, watercolor, 19¾ x 25¾ . . . . (941)   3,000

Still Life with a Cup of Fruit, watercolor,
17 x 21¾ . . . . (976)   7,000

The Studio on the Rue Séguier, watercolor,
10 x 12¼ . . . . (965)   1,695

Glassy Bay, watercolor, 25¾ x 19¾ . . . . (978)   1,440

Toulon, watercolor and gouache, 19½ x 25¼ . . . . . (918)   6,554

Boats and Sailboats on the High Seas,
watercolor, 19 x 24½ . . . . (881)   2,764

Bather, Back View, gouache and watercolor,
25 x 20¼ . . . . (841)   2,000

View of Vence, watercolor, 16¾ x 20¼ . . . . (985)   2,725

Circus, gouache on blue paper, 19¾ x 25¼ . . . . (864)   5,250

1968–July 1969

Rowers on the River Marne, 1920, watercolor,
19¾ x 25¾ . . . . (1117)   4,600

Vence, watercolor, 19½ x 25¼ . . . . (1193)   9,416

Nude, 1929, gouache, 24¾ x 16 . . . . (1173)   6,670

Seated Nude, Her Arm Raised, gouache,
25¼ x 18½ . . . . (1066)   2,200

View of Westminster, 1930, watercolor,
19½ x 25¼ . . . . (1193)   11,151

Ascot, 1938, gouache and watercolor,
19¾ x 25¾ . . . . (1056)   15,000

The Concert, watercolor, 19¾ x 25¾ . . . . (1053)   9,600

View of Ste. Adresse, 1942-43, watercolor,
22½ x 28¼ . . . . (1173)   6,900

Apartment for Rent, watercolor, 25¾ x 19¾ . . . . . (1173)   4,600

The Sea at Ste. Adresse, (1943), gouache,
22 x 28 . . . . (1112)   6,200

At the Races, watercolor and gouache, 19 x 24 . . . (1049)   3,600

The Farmyard, watercolor and gouache,
19¾ x 25¾ . . . . (1049)   4,500

The Races, watercolor, 19 x 25¼ . . . . (1053)   4,900

Paddock, watercolor, 19¾ x 26 . . . . (1109)   10,200

Paddock, watercolor, 20 x 26 . . . . (1125)   14,030

Paddock, watercolor, 21¼ x 25¾ . . . . (1125)   9,430

Paris, watercolor, 22½ x 19¾ . . . . (1117)   6,000

Chenonceaux, watercolor, 18½ x 25 . . . . (1126)   5,947

The Boats, watercolor, 18½ x 24 . . . . (1039)   3,600

Harbor Scene, watercolor and gouache,
19¾ x 25¾ . . . . (1176)   16,500

Nude Seated on the Beach, watercolor and
gouache, 27 x 21½ . . . . (1125) $4,370

Around the Table, watercolor, 19¼ x 25 . . . . (1189)   5,200

Closed Venetian Shutters, watercolor,
19½ x 25¾ . . . . (1187)   9,912

Village in the Trees, watercolor, 4¾ x 8 . . . . (1213)   1,240

Underwood,[4] watercolor, 8¾ x 11¾ . . . . (1230)   960

The Birth of Venus, (1930), gouache, 20¼ x 13¾ . (1235)   7,000

On the Coast, watercolor, 18½ x 24¾ . . . . (1240)   6,240

Sailboats and Liners, watercolor, 19 x 23¾ . . . . . . (1241)   4,790

Still Life with a Fruit Stand, India ink,
watercolor, and gouache, 16¾ x 21½ . . . . (1246)   4,250

Composition: Still Life with Boats, watercolor,
19½ x 24½ . . . . (1246)   5,500

The Country House by the River, watercolor,
19 x 24½ . . . . (1255)   5,900

Bather, Boats, and Shells, watercolor,
19½ x 12¾ . . . . (1256)   9,160

Landscape, watercolor and gouache, 15 x 18¼ . . . (1258)   2,600

The Siren, watercolor, 21¼ x 29¼ . . . . (1261)   4,000

*Parvis Church with Mountains in the
Background,* watercolor . . . . (1263)   3,900

Deauville: Tennis Players and Riders, watercolor,
18½ x 23¾ . . . . (1265)   7,000

Front View of a Seated Man,[5] 1905, watercolor,
23¾ x 26½ . . . . (1265)   3,000

Seated Woman, gouache, 25¾ x 17 . . . . (1268)   7,192

The Threshing Machine, (1910), watercolor,
19¾ x 24¼ . . . . (1268)   6,264

Paddock, watercolor, 19¾ x 25¾ . . . . (1268)   17,400

Paddock, watercolor, 19½ x 25¼ . . . . (1268)   17,864

Landscape, watercolor, 18¾ x 25 . . . . (1268)   7,888

Still Life, watercolor, 19¾ x 25 . . . . (1268)   7,656

Cup of Fruit, 1948, gouache, 19½ x 25 . . . . (1268)   5,612

Games on the Beach, gouache and watercolor,
19¾ x 26¼ . . . . (1272)   4,800

Paddock, (1928-30), watercolor and gouache,
15½ x 20¾ . . . . (1272)   7,200

Fruit, watercolor, 18¼ x 23¾ . . . . (1273)   2,520

PAINTINGS

1961–1962

Trains in the Approaches to the Gare St. Lazare,
18¼ x 15 . . . . (9)   3,160

Street Decked with Flags (Le 14 Juillet), 1906,
21½ x 17¾ . . . . (8)   28,500

Composition, 1909, 19¾ x 24 . . . . (69)   5,056

Banks of the River Seine, (1902), 35½ x 46 . . . . . . (109)   18,200

Le Havre Harbor, 1902, 19¾ x 24 . . . . (27)   7,800

Landscape of Falaise, (1902), 31¾ x 25¾ . . . . (8)   15,000

St. Paul de Vence, 25¾ x 32 . . . . (120)   7,000

The Casino at Nice, 15 x 18¼ . . . . (143)   6,328

Before the Casino, 21¾ x 18¼ . . . . (166)   6,800

St. Paul de Vence, 1920, 20½ x 16½ . . . . (128)   9,611

The Regattas, 18¼ x 21¾ . . . . (29)   6,400

Ste. Adresse Beach, (1909), 18¼ x 21¾ . . . . (93)   8,362

Ste. Adresse Bay, 1924, 25¼ x 32 . . . . (31)   11,808

Bois de Boulogne, 1910, 25¼ x 31½ . . . . (88)   11,070

The River Seine at St. Cloud, on board,
10 x 23¾ . . . . (18)   10,396

Nautical Festival, 29 x 23¾ . . . . (18)   19,436

[4]Dedicated "A Monsieur Bourguin."
[5]Inscribed "Souvenir Amical."

Bathers, on panel, 7½ x 15 . . . . (95) $2,310

Bathers, 1939, on panel, 9½ x 16¼ . . . . (114)   8,000

Reclining Nude, 6¾ x 10 . . . . (76)   2,000

Reclining Nude, 7¼ x 10¼ . . . . (5)   3,000

Seated Model, Back View, 32 x 25¾ . . . . (116)   780

Studio with Torso and Blue Cardboard,
    18¼ x 21¾ . . . . (160)   13,320

Dr. Paul Viard, 1949, 17½ x 14¾ . . . . (84)   769

The Corn Field,[6] 17¾ x 21½ . . . . (64)   6,500

The Farm, 18½ x 22 . . . . (30)   7,300

The Garden, 35¼ x 25¾ . . . . (171)   6,900

A Basket and Strawberries on a Red Background,
    17¾ x 54½ . . . . (64)   3,500

Roses, 1939, on panel, 15¾ x 12¾ . . . . (143)   9,040

1963

The Studio, 1904, 18¼ x 15 . . . . (228)   1,525

The Studio at 19 Rue Jeanne d'Arc in Perpignan,
    18¼ x 21¾ . . . . (298)   9,000

Ste. Adresse Beach, 1908, 18¼ x 21¾ . . . . (306)   7,210

The Bather, 18 x 14¾ . . . . (202)   6,000

Seaside, 13 x 21¾ . . . . (258)   7,200

The Casino in Nice, 1927, 18¼ x 21¾ . . . . (210)   11,242

Seated Woman in Profile, 18¼ x 15 . . . . (271)   400

Landscape, 1930, 15 x 18¼ . . . . (254)   3,000

Landscape, on panel, 10 x 23¾ . . . . (283)   8,701

The Javanese, 1930, 31½ x 25¾ . . . . (309)   6,592

Nude on a Sofa, 6¾ x 10 . . . . (181)   1,440

The Reception, 23 x 35½ . . . . (309)   14,832

The Regattas at Henley, 1931, 29 x 23¾ . . . . (312)   16,600

Corn Fields, 19½ x 23¾ . . . . (202)   6,250

Seated Nude, 1939, on board, 11 x 19¾ . . . . (296)   3,400

Seated Nude, 32 x 25¾ . . . . (283)   1,966

The Birth of Venus,[7] 1939, 14¾ x 17¾ . . . . (210)   5,484

Orpheus, on panel, 24 x 16¼ . . . . (312)   12,020

Still Life with Jug and Apples, 7¼ x 14 . . . . (257)   600

The Fishermen, 23¾ x 29 . . . . (318)   2,300

Bringing in the Hay, 13 x 16¼ . . . . (232)   7,345

1964

Ste. Adresse Beach, (1904), 25¾ x 32 . . . . (340)   18,400

Ste. Adresse Beach, 13 x 16¼ . . . . (378)   7,458

Le Havre Beach, 1906, 25 x 31½ . . . . (416)   46,988

Foul Weather, Le Havre, 1907-08, 21 x 25¼ . . . . . (394)   12,000

St. Vincent Church in Le Havre, 1907-08,
    32 x 23¾ . . . . (367)   15,202

The Trees, 14¾ x 17½ . . . . (458)   4,643

Landscape, 1908, 16¼ x 10¾ . . . . (399)   2,120

The Model in the Studio, 15 x 18¼ . . . . (340)   6,800

The Three Bathers, 25¾ x 21¼ . . . . (371)   11,600

The Painter and His Model, 1909, 32 x 25¾ . . . . . (475)   7,000

The Roofs, 14 x 10¾ . . . . (401)   1,200

Bather with Beach Huts, 20¼ x 16¾ . . . . (401)   7,600

The Walk in Trouville, (1922), 25¾ x 32 . . . . (354)   9,000

Pink Roofs, 21¼ x 25¾ . . . . (371)   11,000

Seaside, (1922-23), 12½ x 21 . . . . (416)   8,292

Houses and Cliffs, 18 x 15 . . . . (419)   2,000

The Basin, (1927), 32 x 39½ . . . . (448)   11,000

Interior with a Yellow Pier Table, 18¼ x 21¼ . . . . (378)   14,012

The Javanese, 1930, 32½ x 26 . . . . (372)   8,500

Landscape, 1930, 15 x 18¼ . . . . (351)   2,800

[6] Dedicated "A Madame R. Thorliman."
[7] After Botticelli.

Gala at the Opera, 21¼ x 25¾ . . . . (347) $16,000

Three People Having Tea, 14¾ x 17¾ . . . . (416)   7,739

Young Woman with a Red Scarf, 21¾ x 23¾ . . . . . (346)   1,580

Harvesttime, 21½ x 25¾ . . . . (372)   9,000

The Park, (1936-39), 21¼ x 25½ . . . . (431)   5,750

The Rowers, 23 x 31 . . . . (367)   13,820

Back From Hunting, 13 x 16 . . . . (453)   5,528

The Desks, The Rehearsal, 23¾ x 21¾ . . . . (377)   5,650

The Quintet, 1941, 10¼ x 13½ . . . . (368)   7,739

St. Paul de Vence, 25¾ x 32 . . . . (394)   12,030

Ste. Adresse, 1951, 8¾ x 19¾ . . . . (416)   9,398

1965

L'Estaque, 1908, 18¼ x 15 . . . . (617)   9,492

The Rue Lepic, 1904, 25¾ x 21½ . . . . (624)   6,634

The River, 25¾ x 32 . . . . (628)   23,796

The Studio, 1909, 32 x 25¾ . . . . (628)   13,930

The Fountain in Avignon, 1913, 29 x 23¾ . . . . . . (561)   5,800

The Mechanical Piano, (1915), 18¼ x 21¾ . . . . . . (526)   17,000

The Regattas, (1920-22), 25¼ x 31½ . . . . (526)   17,000

The Sea, 1921-22, 51½ x 64 . . . . (561)   10,000

Fishermen Amid the Rocks, (1921-23), 36 x 28½ . . (583)   23,216

Regattas at Cowes, 1929, 52¼ x 64¼ . . . . (573)   69,111

The Model in the Studio, (1930), 21¾ x 18¼ . . . . . (539)   8,750

The Painter and His Model, 32 x 25¾ . . . . (569)   9,944

Juan-les-Pins, 14¾ x 17¾ . . . . (522)   9,674

Deauville Dock, 1935, 25¾ x 32 . . . . (594)   28,000

Seascape, 32 x 25¾ . . . . (569)   20,792

The Model in the Studio, 1939, on panel,
    16¼ x 13 . . . . (518)   4,400

The Fleet, 1939, on panel, 8½ x 14¾ . . . . (575)   3,870

Black Cargo, 16½ x 14½ . . . . (567)   8,588

Nude with Black Boats, on panel, 6 x 11½ . . . . . . (547)   1,800

Studio with Carpet and Picture, (1942),
    14¾ x 18¼ . . . . (594)   125,000

The Golden Orchestra, 1942, 18¼ x 24 . . . . (573)   19,348

Studio with Palette, 1943, 18¼ x 21¾ . . . . (561)   14,000

Portrait of Dr. Viard, 1949, 17½ x 14¾ . . . . (539)   1,400

The Orchestra, 1951, on panel, 16¾ x 24½ . . . . . . (594)   17,000

The Threshing Machine, 13 x 16¼ . . . . (564)   4,700

The Open Window, 29 x 36½ . . . . (561)   12,400

1966

Interior with a Nude, 21¾ x 18¼ . . . . (670)   5,800

The Rowers, (1907), 21¼ x 25¼ . . . . (776)   34,000

Landscape, (1908), 25¾ x 21¼ . . . . (802)   16,000

Still Life with Pears, (1909), 18¼ x 21¾ . . . . (797)   16,272

Cubist Landscape, 18 x 21¾ . . . . (727)   14,000

Landscape of Vence, 1922, 28 x 36¼ . . . . (84)   7,600

Harvest at Langres, 19¾ x 29 . . . . (711)   18,000

The Little Town, (1922-25), 21¼ x 26 . . . . (784)   4,500

Amphitrite, 1936, 74¼ x 63¼ . . . . (750)   60,808

Corn in Normandy, 13 x 32½ . . . . (798)   8,814

The Avenue du Bois, 14¾ x 18¼ . . . . (713)   8,750

On the Pier, 19¾ x 24 . . . . (797)   13,221

Seascape, 28½ x 36 . . . . (694)   22,000

The Fountain in Avignon, 28¾ x 23¾ . . . . (749)   6,400

Fishermen on Trouville Pier, 25¾ x 32 . . . . (727)   16,000

Mexican Orchestra, 18¼ x 21¾ . . . . (744)   11,978

Landscape in Vence, 25¾ x 32 . . . . (742)   12,200

Nude on a White Background, 13 x 16¼ . . . . (753)   9,867

Blue and Red Symphony, 1952, 23¾ x 29 . . . . (776)   20,000

1967

View of Paris from the Artist's Studio, Rue Corton, (1903), 21¼ x 25¾ .... (912) — $7,800
Rough Weather, Le Havre, (1907-09), 21 x 25 .... (864) — 8,500
Landscape of l'Estaque, 1908, 18½ x 15 .... (954) — 9,000
View of Munich, 1909, 17¾ x 21¾ .... (940) — 8,415
The Painter and His Model (Madame Dufy), 1909, 32 x 25¾ .... (938) — 8,292
Acrobat, 1910, 16¼ x 12½ .... (993) — 5,600
Landscape, 1911, 14¾ x 18 .... (982) — 7,110
The Gardener, 1915, 32 x 17¾ .... (988) — 16,172
Reclining Nude, 21¾ x 18¼ .... (911) — 8,400
Landscape of Vence, 1922, 28 x 36½ .... (965) — 17,176
Paddock, 13 x 16¼ .... (965) — 18,532
Ste. Adresse Beach, 1925, on panel, 16¼ x 19¾ ... (918) — 9,718
Little Nude, (1942), 10 x 11¾ .... (841) — 2,500
Seated Great Nude, 51½ x 33½ .... (911) — 11,000
Reclining Woman in the Nude, 18¼ x 21¾ .... (989) — 5,500
Three People Having Tea, 14¾ x 17¾ .... (954) — 15,000
Still Life with a Cup of Fruit, 25¾ x 33½ .... (905) — 3,000
Still Life with a Cup of Fruit, 25¾ x 32 .... (954) — 9,500
Woman with a Parasol, 21¼ x 25¾ .... (923) — 16,000
Self-Portrait, on cardboard, 14 x 10¼ .... (971) — 1,100

1968–July 1969

Young Woman Seated in the Pine Grove, (1901), 15 x 18¼ .... (1133) — 3,820
Coming Out of the Church and the Market Place, Le Havre, 1902, on panel, 17½ x 21 .... (1187) — 4,956
The Canal, Marseilles, (1902), 21¼ x 25 .... (1152) — 14,000
Les Martigues, 1903, 14¾ x 17¾ .... (1132) — 4,720
Old Houses on the Dock, Honfleur, (1905-06), 23¾ x 29¾ .... (1152) — 100,000
The Three Parasols, 1906, 23 x 29¼ .... (1152) — 140,000
The Painter and His Model, (1909), 32 x 25¾ .... (1125) — 9,890
The Ball of the 14 Juillet at Antibes, (1910), 21¾ x 25 .... (1152) — 40,000
The Lady in Pink, Portrait of Madame Dufy, 1918, 46 x 35¼ .... (1187) — 56,640
The Fountain of Vence, 1921, 32 x 25¾ .... (1173) — 19,780
Vence, 25¾ x 32 .... (1173) — 17,710
Nice: The Baie des Anges, 15 x 18¼ .... (1126) — 19,824
The Paddock, 1925, 34 x 49¾ .... (1181) — 59,000
The Eiffel Tower Seen from the Seine, 1925, 21½ x 25¾ .... (1057) — 15,000
Casino de la Jetée, Nice, (1928), 24 x 29¾ ...... (1152) — 24,000
At the Races, Ascot, 1930, 21¼ x 25¾ .... (1152) — 45,000
The Horse Races in Deauville, (1931), 25¾ x 32 .. (1152) — 52,000
Caudebec Harbor, 23 x 28¾ .... (1068) — 21,240
Nude Seated on a Stool, (1932), 49½ x 34¼ ..... (1018) — 10,000
Nude Model in the Studio, 29 x 23¾ .... (1152) — 20,000
Regattas at Henley, (1933-34), 25¾ x 32 .... (1152) — 25,000
Portrait of Madame Roudinesco, 1934, 57¾ x 38¼ .... (1152) — 15,000
Deauville Dock, (1935), 25¾ x 32 .... (1056) — 29,000
Yachts in Deauville Harbor, (1938), 23¾ x 29 .... (1152) — 42,000
Orpheus, (1939), 28½ x 22½ .... (1152) — 20,000
Ste. Adresse, 14¼ x 18¼ .... (1053) — 12,000
Ste. Adresse Harbor, 13 x 16¾ .... (1018) — 6,000
Seascape, 32 x 25¾ .... (1125) — 25,300
Reclining Nude, 6 x 11¾ .... (1132) — 4,248
Portrait of Madame Laval, 1943, 21¾ x 18¼ .... (1200) — 7,200
Young Woman on a Pink Sofa, 38¼ x 29 .... (1159) — 8,300

Still Life with a Coffeepot and a Round Table, 32 x 25¾ .... (1225) — $20,000
The Cubist Village, 1912, 18¼ x 21¼ .... (1226) — 10,200
Ascot: The Races, (1932), 15 x 18 .... (1235) — 24,000
Nude on a Bed, (1939), 10 x 15 .... (1235) — 13,000
Le Havre, 14 x 18 .... (1235) — 16,000
The Trapezist, (1910), 15½ x 12½ .... (1239) — 9,120
The Farm, on cardboard, 10¼ x 13½ .... (1252) — 5,700
Boats, 13 x 15¾ .... (1258) — 13,200
Siesta in the Fields, on panel, 6¾ x 17 .... (1266) — 7,000
Martigues Harbor .... (1268) — 9,280
Interior, 13 x 32 .... (1268) — 19,720
Landscape, 15 x 18¼ .... (1268) — 15,080
In the Trees, on panel, 17¾ x 21¼ .... (1268) — 8,166
Window with Colored Panes, (1906), 32 x 25½ ... (1270) — 72,000

André Dunoyer de Segonzac

(1884-   )

Birthplace: Boussy-St.-Antoine, Seine-et-Oise district, France.

1905 Fails the entrance examination of the Ecole Nationale des Beaux-Arts, Paris. Attends L.O. Merson's studio, Paris.

1907-08 Attends the Académie de la Palette, Paris. Participates in the Salon d'Automne, Paris. Discovers St. Tropez and executes his first landscapes of the south of France.

1909-10 Participates in the Salon des Indépendants, Paris. Executes a series of drawings of Isadora Duncan. (His work relies on drawing.) Paul Poiret buys his picture "Les Buveurs" and introduces him to Raoul Dufy, Max Jacob, and Vlaminck. Also meets Apollinaire.

1910-14 Trips to Italy, North Africa, and Spain.

1912 Participates in the Salon de la Section d'Or at the Galerie de la Boétie, Paris. The art critic C.R. Marx takes a great interest in his work.

1914 First one-man show at the Galerie Lévêque, Paris.

1918 Gradually appears as the most sincere enemy of modernism and of all the theories of the European avant-garde. Rejects Impressionism, Fauvism, and Cubism as well, remaining true to the old French tradition. Has been called "the anti-Picasso."

1920 One-man show at the Independent Gallery, London.

1923 Watercolor becomes one of his favorite media and he shows much relish for "painting in water" on large sheets of paper.

1924 Exhibition at the Galerie Barbazanges, Paris.

1925-28 Frequent stays at St. Tropez.

1929 First trip to the U.S.—at the invitation of the Carnegie Institute, Pittsburgh.

1933	Wins the first prize at the Carnegie Institute, Pittsburgh.
1934	First one-man show in New York at Brummer's. Given an award by the Venice Biennial.
1937	Important exhibition of his prints at the Bibliothèque Nationale, Paris.
1938	Exhibits at the Women's Art Club, Chicago.
1939	One-man show at Carrol Carstairs' Gallery, New York, and at Wildenstein's, London.
1939–44	Stays at Chaville and at St. Tropez during World War II.
1947	Becomes a member of the Royal Academy, London.
1948	Retrospective exhibitions at the Galerie Charpentier, Paris, and at the Kunsthalle, Basel. Becomes a member of the Académie Royale, Brussels. Publishes *Les Géorgiques* by Virgil, which includes his most brilliant series of etchings. (Has devoted a great amount of time to illustration from the beginning of his career.)
1951	Retrospective exhibition at the Musée d'Art et d'Histoire, Geneva.
1955	Appointed member of the National Institute of Arts, U.S.
1960	Retrospective exhibition at the Galerie Charpentier, Paris.
	Resident in Paris.

Sales

DRAWINGS

1961–1962

Reclining Nude With a Blouse, wash, 10¼ x 24 ... (126) $ 400

Three Figures in a Walk, pen and watercolor, 45 x 19½ .... (64)   5,500

The Hen and Her Chicks, pen, 8¼ x 12¾ .... (27)   270

Boxing, pen, 13 x 10¼ .... (71)   720

The Pont des Arts and the Institut de France, pen, ... (119)   640

St. Tropez, a Boat in the Harbor, (1952), India ink, 12½ x 10 .... (143)   407

St. Anne Hill, pen and wash, 22½ x 31¼ .... (164)   1,867

1963

Le Poilu, 1917, India ink, 7½ x 5¾ .... (276)   80

The Stretcher Bearer, ink, 8¼ x 6¾ .... (218)   160

The Trench, (1920), India ink, pen, and brush, 8 x 5¼ .... (219)   167

Portrait of Courteline, pen, 9 x 8¾ .... (283)   305

Young Woman, Her Breast Bare, 1925, India-ink wash, 19 x 12¼ .... (232)   565

Bust of a Woman, wash, 8 x 6¾ .... (238)   110

Nude, pen, 8¾ x 7½ .... (179)   235

Reclining Nude, ink, 9¾ x 12¾ .... (210)   603

Model Resting, pen and wash, 19½ x 25¼ .... (258)   1,440

The Rest, pen, 17 x 21¼ .... (198)   1,100

Model Resting, pen and wash, 19½ x 25¼ .... (291)   1,260

The Grand Trianon, pen and charcoal, 14½ x 24¾ .... (224)   1,060

St. Loup de Naud, 1948, India ink, 11½ x 18½ .... (219)   610

Landscape, India ink, 16¾ x 24½ .... (247)   494

The River, pen, 14 x 20¼ .... (255)   3,702

The Bouillabaisse Beach, wash, 8¾ x 10¾ .... (257)   320

St. Tropez: The Citadel Hill, pen and wash, 15 x 22 .... (277) $1,645

St. Tropez Cove, pen and India-ink wash, 13¾ x 19 .... (222)   1,040

1964

Landscape of the Ile-de-France, (1932), pencil, 7¼ x 12¾ .... (335)   1,100

The Valley, pen, 11¾ x 18¼ .... (399)   900

The Steeple with Willows, India ink, 12¼ x 9 .... (398)   400

Landscape, pen and wash, 11¾ x 18½ .... (374)   200

The Church, pen and watercolor, 18¾ x 12¾ .... (448)   2,100

Seated Woman, pen, 18¼ x 12¼ .... (409)   1,200

Hilly Landscape, pen, 13½ x 18½ .... (409)   420

St. Tropez, pen and wash, 8¾ x 10¾ .... (418)   290

Bather Drying Herself, pen and wash, 18½ x 24 .... (466)   1,300

Kneeling Nude, pen, 15¾ x 15 .... (466)   1,200

Standing Bacchant, Front View, pen, 12¼ x 10 .... (376)   380

Nude, pen and watercolor, 19½ x 12¾ .... (448)   2,600

Model Resting, pen and wash, 19½ x 25¼ .... (474)   1,240

Nude with Cushions, India ink and wash, 12¾ x 19 .... (371)   1,300

Reclining Nude, pen and wash, 16¾ x 24 .... (368)   553

The Towboat, (1960), pen and India-ink wash, 14¼ x 19½ .... (383)   1,695

1965

The Couple, pen and wash, 12 x 19 .... (540)   260

Landscape of the South of France, India-ink wash, 21¾ x 30 .... (617)   4,294

Presumed Portrait of Maud Loty, pen, 8 x 10¼ .... (499)   280

The Boxer, pen and wash, 10½ x 7½ .... (535)   152

Les Permissionaires, ink, 8¾ x 16¼ .... (541)   325

The Harbor, India ink and wash, 14 x 18½ .... (617)   949

The Street, India ink, 12¼ x 10 .... (567)   881

Landscape, pen and wash, 13½ x 19 .... (624)   2,764

The Trees, ink and watercolor, 15 x 11½ .... (582)   1,382

1966

Nude in a Landscape, pen, 12¼ x 10 .... (745)   452

Les Poilus, pen, 9½ x 6½ .... (654)   100

Seated Man, pen and India-ink wash, 16¾ x 23¼ .... (703)   2,300

Seated Nude, (1923), pen, 16½ x 10 .... (689)   332

Riverside, India ink, 14 x 19½ .... (734)   1,085

Nude with a Parasol, pen and India-ink wash, 9 x 14½ .... (794)   200

Lovers, India ink, 10¼ x 17 .... (665)   650

Bather Drying Herself, pen and wash, 18¾ x 24 .... (652)   840

Nude in a Landscape, pen, 18½ x 12¾ .... (666)   1,200

The Approaches to Ville-d'Avray, (1955), pen and watercolor, 21¼ x 29¾ .... (808)   6,384

The Outskirts of St. Tropez, (1957), ink and watercolor, 21¼ x 29¾ .... (808)   6,384

1967

Woodcutter at Villiers-Adam, 1910, pen, 16½ x 10½ .... (911)   400

Young Woman on a Sofa, 1911, pencil, 10½ x 14½ .... (999)   400

Girl at a Bar, 1929, pen and India-ink wash, 8¼ x 6¼ .... (927)   163

Seated Nude, pen and wash, 17¾ x 12¼ .... (987)   520

The Beach, (1936), charcoal and watercolor, 24 x 17¾ .... (1004)   3,250

Quays, pen, 12 x 19 .... (855)   1,100

Knockout, ink, 10¾ x 13½ .... (898)   480

Reclining Nude, pen and India-ink wash, 19 x 24 .... (857)   1,040

View of a Monastery, pen and wash, 15 x 22½ ... (1004) $2,250
Fagots, pen, 19¾ x 14¼ .... (937) 840
The Journalist, India ink, 10 x 8 .... (845) 270
Landscape of the Ile-de-France, pen and wash,
 19 x 14¼ .... (985) 901

1968–July 1969
The Lake, pen and wash, 14¾ x 22½ .... (1068) 2,832
Landscape of Provence, pen and wash,
 14¾ x 22¼ .... (1068) 2,360
Landscape, pen, 10¾ x 16¾ .... (1042) 920
Chapel in Provence, pen and wash, 14 x 19 ...... (1189) 1,200
Grimaud Hill, pen and wash, 15¾ x 23 .... (1191) 3,304
View of St. Tropez, pen and wash, 10¾ x 13½ ... (1102) 966
Vineyards and Mulberry Trees, pen and India-ink
 wash, 15½ x 23 .... (1134) 2,360
Cypresses and Parasol Pines, (1946), India ink
 and watercolor, 22½ x 30½ .... (1216) 12,500
Study for "L'Education Sentimentale," pen,
 8 x 4 .... (1145) 200
Trees, pen and wash, 17 x 11½ .... (1138) 495
The Hamlet, pen, 8¾ x 12 .... (1144) 200
Landscape with a Monastery, India ink and wash,
 14¾ x 22¾ .... (1080) 2,750
The Vert-Galant, India ink and wash, 14 x 19½ .. (1051) 1,400
Christiane, pen and wash, 12 x 11½ .... (1061) 850
Denise, pen, 8 x 7 .... (1030) 425
Rugby, 8¾ x 5¾ .... (1128) 280
Landscape, India ink, 10 x 14¼ .... (1223) 320
The Rugby Player, pen and wash, 7¼ x 6 ...... (1223) 290
Reading, pen and wash, 11¾ x 19½ .... (1226) 1,360
Chennevières, India ink, 9½ x 13¾ .... (1227) 550
110ème Haies, 8½ x 9½ .... (1231) 350
A Boxer, pen and wash, 7 x 8¼ .... (1231) 225
The Two Doves, India ink, 5¼ x 12¼ .... (1238) 116
Springtime at St. Tropez, India ink and gray
 wash, 15½ x 23 .... (1240) 3,240
Seated Nude, India ink, 11½ x 13¾ .... (1240) 768
Portrait of a Lawyer, pen, brush, and India ink,
 9¾ x 11¾ .... (1240) 432
At Work, pen and India ink, 12 x 18¼ .... (1240) 960
Fields in Front of the Village, pen, 9 x 12 ...... (1241) 856
Portrait of a Woman, pen, 7¼ x 7 .... (1241) 479
A Crane, Jardin des Plantes, pen, 10¼ x 7¾ .... (1248) 175
Seated Women, pen, 8¾ x 7 .... (1248) 275
Rugby, two drawings, pen, 5 x 3½, and 4 x 2¾ ... (1248) 190
Landscape, India-ink wash, 8¼ x 11 .... (1268) 1,021
Landscape, India ink, 14 x 19¾ .... (1268) 1,577
The Rower, India-ink wash, 13¾ x 18¾ .... (1268) 1,856
Grimaud Hill, brush, pen, and India ink,
 15 x 22½ .... (1272) 3,840
View of the Valley, pen, India ink, and wash,
 15½ x 23 .... (1272) 1,920

WATERCOLORS
1961–1962
The River Marne at Chennevières, watercolor,
 20½ x 30½ .... (53) 9,000
The Village Steeple, watercolor, 24½ x 18½ ...... (116) 3,000
Landscape of the South of France, watercolor,
 15¾ x 29¼ .... (143) 7,684
Landscape Seen from the Window,[1] watercolor,
 11½ x 8¾ .... (93) 1,808
Anse de Pampelone, watercolor, 21½ x 30 .... (18) 8,588

[1]Inscribed "Pour la Treille Muscate."

1963
The Swiss Pond in Versailles, watercolor,
 18¾ x 24½ .... (277) $3,428
Still Life, watercolor, 14 x 17½ .... (224) 4,400
The Woman with the Armchair, watercolor,
 17½ x 17 .... (198) 2,400
Landscape, 1939, watercolor, 11¾ x 19¾ .... (208) 400
Landscape in Provence, watercolor, 10 x 18½ .... (215) 3,600
Landscape of St. Tropez, watercolor,
 15¾ x 29¼ .... (283) 8,588
St. Tropez, watercolor, 17½ x 30 .... (296) 8,040

1964
The Swiss Pond in Versailles, watercolor,
 19 x 25 .... (337) 6,700
The Grand Morin Near Dammartin, watercolor,
 27¼ x 20¼ .... (465) 7,600
St. Tropez Beach, watercolor, 10¾ x 9½ .... (321) 450
St. Tropez, watercolor, 31 x 19¾ .... (471) 9,492
Evening on the Estérel, gouache, 12¼ x 18¾ ... (335) 3,760
Hilly Landscape, watercolor, 20¼ x 30½ .... (371) 8,200
Still Life with Flowers, watercolor, 21¾ x 30 ..... (378) 9,718

1965
Moret-sur-Loing, watercolor, 20½ x 28½ .... (569) 8,588
The Village by the River, watercolor, 21 x 27½ ... (553) 7,600
Still Life with Antique Plaster, watercolor,
 11¾ x 11¾ .... (567) 2,712
Reclining Nude, watercolor, 7 x 10¾ .... (561) 580
Landscape of St. Tropez, watercolor, 20 x 30¼ ... (617) 6,328
Evening on the Estérel, watercolor and gouache,
 11½ x 18¾ .... (503) 240
Vase of Carnations on the Terrace at St. Tropez,
 watercolor and pen, 23 x 31¼ .... (624) 12,714
Still Life with Flowers, watercolor .... (569) 9,944

1966
Still Life with Antique Plaster, watercolor,
 11¾ x 11¾ .... (798) 2,712
House in a Landscape, watercolor, 18¼ x 24¼ ... (814) 2,900
On the Beach, 1952, watercolor, 8 x 12¼ .... (795) 620
Still Life with a Hat, watercolor, 9½ x 12¼ ...... (829) 820

1967
The Morin at Serbonne, 1934, watercolor,
 21¾ x 28½ .... (912) 7,720
Landscape, watercolor, 19¼ x 28 .... (918) 9,266
Evening on the Estérel, gouache, 12¼ x 18½ ..... (995) 2,000
Still Life, pen and watercolor, 22 x 25 .... (895) 8,500

1968–July 1969
Landscape with a River, watercolor, 20¾ x 27½ . (1113) 7,800
Young Vintagers (St. Tropez), 1930, watercolor,
 9½ x 8¾ .... (1154) 720
The Windmill at Quinte Joie on the Morin,
 (1937), watercolor 21½ x 30¼ .... (1187) 8,968
Landscape of St. Tropez, pen and watercolor,
 20¼ x 30¾ .... (1176) 12,000
The Bridge, (1924), pen and watercolor,
 14½ x 19½ .... (1138) 5,947
Still Life, watercolor, 11¾ x 11¾ .... (1127) 3,910
Still Life, watercolor, 21¾ x 29¾ .... (1068) 11,328
The Statuette, watercolor, 14½ x 20 .... (1200) 900
Couple on the Beach, watercolor, 7½ x 11¾ .... (1225) 1,300
The Footbridge, pen and watercolor, 14 x 20 .... (1241) 5,540
St. Tropez Beach, watercolor, 10½ x 9½ .... (1248) 625
The Table with Flowers, watercolor, 21¾ x 30 ... (1249) 15,200

Village Church, watercolor, 21¾ x 29¾ . . . . (1249) $10,000
Mediterranean Coast, watercolor, 16¼ x 22½ . . . (1254) 5,600
Evening on the Estérel, watercolor and gouache,
11 x 18½ . . . . (1255) 2,600
The Bunch of Flowers, watercolor and gouache,
21¼ x 29¾ . . . . (1258) 16,000
Still Life with a Grapefruit, watercolor, 30 x 22 . . (1268) 12,528
Vase of Windflowers on the Table, pen, India ink,
and watercolor, 21½ x 29½ . . . . (1272) 14,400

PAINTINGS

1961–1962
Boatmen on the Morin, 1924, 79 x 83 . . . . (116) 33,000

1963
Landscape: The Grand Morin, 25¾ x 31½ . . . . (225) 9,500
The Church, on panel, 8¼ x 10¼ . . . . (247) 1,974
The Chalets, 25¾ x 19¾ . . . . (198) 4,000

1964
Reclining Nude, (1925), 10¾ x 18¼ . . . . (454) 4,422
On the Beach, on panel, 13 x 16¼ . . . . (371) 3,400
Autumn Landscape, 1932, 18¼ x 25¾ . . . . (347) 6,000
Landscape, 18¼ x 21¾, 19¾ x 25¾ . . . . (474) 11,300
Nude with a Turban, 19¾ x 25¾ . . . . (474) 5,000
Still Life, Lemons and Eggs, 20½ x 34½ . . . . (347) 10,600

1965
The Bather, (1922), 25¼ x 17½ . . . . (624) 3,870
Bathers, 12¾ x 14 . . . . (494) 2,800
The Bridge on the River, Villiers-sur-Morin,
1924, 25¾ x 36¼ . . . . (628) 12,188
Springtime, 21¼ x 17 . . . . (575) 4,975
The Red Carpet, 1926, 39½ x 32 . . . . (637) 32,000
The Bouillabaisse Beach, St. Tropez, (1935), on
panel, 13 x 16¼ . . . . (561) 3,400

1966
Reclining Nude, (1922), 12¾ x 21¼ . . . . (808) 3,192
Still Life, (1931-32), 18¾ x 24 . . . . (689) 3,317
Landscape, 18¼ x 53¾ . . . . (776) 8,500

1967
Poplars, 25¼ x 31½ . . . . (982) 3,318
Landscape with an Olive Tree, 21¼ x 32 . . . . (912) 8,000
Bathers, (1923), 23¾ x 29 . . . . (880) 9,674
Cows in Pasture, 29 x 36¾ . . . . (858) 5,600

1968–July 1969
Suburban Spring, (1922), 19¾ x 29 . . . . (1057) 18,000
*The Farm with a Threshing Floor, St. Tropez
Cove,* 1926, 38¼ x 76¾ . . . . (1109) 16,800
Reclining Nude, 11 x 18¼ . . . . (1126) 3,965
Vase of Flowers, 21¾ x 18½ . . . . (1018) 15,000
Squatting Bather, 19 x 24¾ . . . . (1268) 18,560
View of Paris, 27 x 25 . . . . (1268) 15,080
Autumn Landscape at St. Tropez, 18¼ x 25¾ . . . (1268) 15,080

James Ensor

(1860–1949)

Birthplace: Ostend, Belgium.
1877-79 Attends the Fine Arts Academy of Brussels.
1879 Returns to Ostend, where he remains for the rest of his life.
1880 Starts elaborating his own style.
1881 Member of the art society "Chrysalide."
1882 Member of the "Essor" group.
1883 Leaves this group and joins the XX group.
1884 First exhibition of the XX group in Brussels.
1886 First etchings.
1888 Executes his most famous work, "L'Entrée du Christ à Bruxelles."
1891 Takes part in the "Libre Esthétique" group.
1899 Retrospective exhibition at the Palais des Beaux-Arts, Brussels.
1900 Discovers African art.
1930 King Albert I raises him to the rank of baron. Exhibition at the Galerie des Beaux-Arts, Paris.
1949 Died.
1954 Retrospective exhibition at the Musée d'Art Moderne, Paris.

Sales

DRAWINGS

1961–1962
Profiles, black lead, 8¾ x 6¾ . . . . (154) $ 170
Chinese Conductor, 1937, sepia ink, 8¾ x 6¾ . . . . . (111) 250
My Houris, colored pencil with white lights,
11½ x 7¾ . . . . (106) 701
Le Miracle des pains et des pêches, colored
chalk, 15 x 19 . . . . (128) 220

1963
Ensor Surrounded with Masks, colored drawing,
10¾ x 12¼ . . . . (317) 380
Puppets, 1911-12, colored pencil, 5¾ x 9 . . . . (299) 200
Still Life with a Vase of Flowers, (1932) . . . . (179) 325

1964
Portrait of Leo Tolstoi, Seated, 5¼ x 5 . . . . (383) 610
Pituition, 1911, colored pencil, 9½ x 6¾ . . . . (328) 280
Three Characters in Costumes, 1912, colored
pencil, 9 x 11¾ . . . . (455) 415
My Darling Aunt, 1916, pencil and pen
heightened with white, 6¾ x 8¼ . . . . (374) 125

1965
Laziness: The Sleepers, chalk, 6¾ x 9 . . . . (597) 332
The Fisherman of Ostend, 1880, red chalk,
29¼ x 23 . . . . (536) 880
Study of Dogs, charcoal, 9 x 6¾ . . . . (565) 181

1966
Man in the Nude, Back View, charcoal,
6¾ x 5¾ . . . . (734) 147
Henri Degraux Playing Billiards, colored chalk
with white gouache lights, 9½ x 11½ . . . . (734) 3,955
Portrait of a Young Man, 1882, red chalk,
8¾ x 6¾ . . . . (782) 600
Portrait of Jean Breydel, 1899, black chalk,
5¼ x 7¼ . . . . (738) 492

Puppets, 1911, 5¼ x 9 . . . . (749) $ 420
Marion, 1911, colored pencil, 10 x 7¼ . . . . (811) 290
Mourned Deceased, 1916, colored drawing,
   11 x 17½ . . . . (767) 800
Study of Heads, 7¼ x 6, double sided . . . . (786) 140

1967
Marion, Friend of Miamia, 1911, colored pencil,
   9¼ x 6¾ . . . . (939) 498
Still Life, black lead, 8¾ x 6¾ . . . . (967) 203
Three Masks, 9¼ x 12¼ . . . . (965) 723
The Urchin, charcoal and wash, 28¼ x 21½ . . . . . . (889) 850
Figures, pencil, pen, and watercolor, 10 x 13 . . . . . (927) 1,017
The Piano Sconce, 8¾ x 6¾ . . . . (846) 140

1968–July 1969
Study Sheet: Fireplace, Head, and Man,
   charcoal and stump, 8¾ x 6½ . . . . (1099) 575
Orchestra and Stage, colored chalk, 8½ x 11 . . . . (1099) 1,610
My Darling Aunt, 1916, pencil heightened with
   white, 6¾ x 8¼ . . . . (1145) 500
The Dance of Dawn, 1931, pen and colored chalk,
   18½ x 23¾ . . . . (1068) 1,770
Witch in Ostend, 29 x 23¾ . . . . (1965) 2,800
Project for a Playbill for the Ostend Theater,
   ink . . . . (1046) 290
Woman's Head, (1882), pencil, 8¼ x 6½ . . . . (1240) 816
The Artist and His Family, 1886, pencil and
   brown chalk, 8½ x 11½ . . . . (1240) 2,040
Sketch for Chess: The Queen, a Rook, a Pawn,
   black lead and colored pencil, 7½ x 11 . . . . . . (1268) 3,016

PAINTINGS
1961–1962
The Waves, 1876, 8 x 10¾ . . . . (31) 549
Infâmes Vivisecteurs (With a Self-Portrait), 1925,
   24½ x 31¼ . . . . (88) 7,872
Card of Giocco, 1940, 26½ x 40 . . . . (69) 3,160
The Cab . . . . (165) 340

1963
The Love Scale,[1] 1912, 37¼ x 47½ . . . . (210) 8,226
Park with Birds, 19½ x 23½ . . . . (202) 5,000

1964
Seated Urchin, 1880, 29 x 22½ . . . . (373) 640
The Cathedral, 1892, on panel, 19 x 23¾ . . . . (416) 9,121
Tulips and Cornflowers, 1903, 25¼ x 20¾ . . . . (416) 3,317
Infâmes Vivisecteurs, 24½ x 31¼ . . . . (341) 6,100
The Puppets, 1916, 36¾ x 46¾ . . . . (471) 8,362
Fantastic Ballet, 1918, 32 x 39½ . . . . (471) 9,040
Recollections, 1926, 27¾ x 24 . . . . (471) 8,362
Cosmic Fantasy, 11¾ x 19¾ . . . . (427) 840

1965
On the Coast,[2] (1875-76), 19½ x 33½ . . . . (624) 663
The Violin, 1883, 19¾ x 32¾ . . . . (593) 3,200
Accessories, on cardboard, 9½ x 6¾ . . . . (636) 900
The Call of the Siren, 1891, on board,
   14¾ x 18¼ . . . . (616) 4,960
Bathing in Ostend, 1920, 15¼ x 18½ . . . . (520) 5,400
The North Sea, 15¾ x 19¾ . . . . (611) 2,400
Recollections (With a Self-Portrait), 1926,
   27¾ x 24 . . . . (616) 12,000
Still Life, on cardboard, 9½ x 6¾ . . . . (636) 1,400

[1] Inscribed "Décor pour mon ballet Flirt des Marionnettes."
[2] Executed at the age of fifteen.

1966
The Puppets, 38 x 46½ . . . . (798) $8,023
Masks and Clowns, 24 x 19¾ . . . . (798) 3,887
Surroundings of Ostend, on cardboard,
   7¼ x 9½ . . . . (782) 2,200
Still Life, 6¼ x 8¼ . . . . (782) 2,800
China and Fans, on panel, 9 x 12½ . . . . (698) 3,046

1967
Romantic Walk, 12¾ x 9½ . . . . (947) 3,400
A Boy on a Chair, 29¾ x 21¼ . . . . (947) 4,400
Landscape Near Ostend, 15 x 21¾ . . . . (979) 1,360
The Winds, (1910-12), 19¾ x 24 . . . . (938) 7,186

1968–July 1969
Pink Carnations, on panel, 8¾ x 6½ . . . . (1173) 6,440
Seascape, on panel, 7¼ x 9 . . . . (1150) 1,500
Seascape, 23¾ x 29¼ . . . . (1065) 2,000
Seascape, 6½ x 8½ . . . . (1268) 4,222
Flowers, on panel, 8¾ x 6½ . . . . (1268) 6,844
*Study for the Bridge Competition "The Four
   Queens,"* 1940, on board, 8¼ x 10½ . . . . (1271) 2,880

Max Ernst

(1891–   )

Birthplace: Brühl, Germany. Studies philosophy at the University of Bonn.

1913 Exhibits at the first Herbstsalon, Berlin. First stay in Paris.

1914 Meets Arp in Cologne at the "Werkbund" exhibition.

1920 Publishes *Die Schammade* with Baargeld in Cologne. Dada exhibition at the Winter Brauerei, Cologne. First exhibition of collages at the Galerie "Au Sans Pareil," Paris.

1922 Goes to Paris. Illustrates *Répétitions* and *Les Malheurs des Immortels* by Eluard. First experiments in automatic writing with Breton, Eluard, and Picabia.

1924 Joins the Surrealist group in Paris.

1925 First "frottages." Participates in the first exhibition of the Surrealists at the Galerie Pierre, Paris. Stage decoration for *Romeo and Juliet* for the Ballets Russes.

1929-34 His "collage novels"—*La Femme aux cent têtes* and *Une Semaine de bonté*—are published by the Galerie Jeanne Bûcher, Paris. Paints a large fresco for the "Mascotte-Bar," Zurich.

1937 Stage decoration for Jarry's play *Ubu enchainé* at the Théâtre des Champs-Elysées, Paris.

1938-39 Decorates his house at St. Martin de l'Ardèche with sculptures and frescoes.

1939-40 Arrested and taken to a concentration camp in France.

1941	Journey to the U.S.
1942	Participates in the review *VVV* with Breton and Duchamp.
1945	Takes part in Richter's film *Dreams that Money Can Buy.*
1947	Illustrations for *A l'Intérieur de la vue* by Eluard.
1948	Returns to Paris.
1950	Important exhibition at the Galerie Drouin, Paris.
1954	Wins the first prize at the Venice Biennial.

Sales

DRAWINGS

1961–1962

Fabulous Animal, pencil and frottage, 7½ x 10¼ .. **(106)** $ 791

Leaves,[1] 1925, frottage, charcoal, and white chalk, 10 x 17 **(140)** 1,510

Painting on an Easel, 1930, frottage and pen, 12 x 9 **(164)** 522

The Gallant Sheep, 10, 1948-49, India ink and collage, 9¾ x 8¼ **(105)** 678

1963

Nude with Flowers, pencil, 6¾ x 4¼ **(275)** 325

Left Side of a Man's Head, (1930), colored pencil, 12½ x 9¾ **(179)** 600

Two Figures, 1959, colored pencil, 10 x 8 **(255)** 768

1964

Study for "L'Histoire naturelle," 1925, pencil, 14¼ x 10 **(461)** 1,200

The Three Graces, (1923), pen, 6¾ x 5¾ **(383)** 338

The Eye of Silence, 1925, pencil, 10¼ x 8 **(368)** 995

Restaurant Scene, pencil and watercolor, 3½ x 5½ **(467)** 197

1965

The Bell Ringer, 1950, pencil, 4¾ x 3¾ **(618)** 689

The Haunted House, India ink, 8¼ x 6¼ **(565)** 475

1966

Nimbler Than the Moon, 1925, black lead and frottage, 8¼ x 6¼ **(668)** 600

Bird,[2] (1925), black and red chalk, 10 x 7¼ **(816)** 1,722

The Leaf,[3] pencil and watercolor, 16¾ x 10 **(703)** 3,500

Frottage, pencil and frottage, 14¼ x 9¾ **(734)** 814

The Bride of the Wind, 1940, pencil, 10 x 8 **(757)** 442

Composition, (1951), drawing and collage, 11¾ x 17¾ **(745)** 418

1967

Bird,[4] black and red chalk, 10 x 7¼ **(907)** 1,230

The Haunted House, (1922), India ink, 8¼ x 6½ .. **(927)** 486

The Beautiful Assyrian, 1949, India ink and collage, 5½ x 4½ **(927)** 305

Automatic Study for Nothing, 1951, pencil and collage, 17¾ x 11½ **(970)** 787

1968–July 1969

Mechanical Drawing, (1919), on a photograph with India-ink lights, 10¼ x 15½ **(1096)** 2,760

"Ça me fait pisser," (1919), on a photograph with India-ink lights, 20 x 8¼ **(1096)** 1,725

[1]Drawing for *L'Histoire naturelle.*
[2]Series *L'Histoire naturelle.*
[3]Series *L'Histoire naturelle.*
[4]Series *L'Histoire naturelle.*

The Horse Falls, the Night Too, 1925, pencil and frottage, 8 x 6½ **(1099)** $1,886

Loplop Présente, 1932, frottage, collage, and pencil, 26 x 20¼ **(1096)** 3,795

Portrait of the Poet Artaud, 1937, stick of greasepaint, 7¾ x 4¾ **(1174)** 1,595

Surrealist Composition, 1949, ink, oil, and collage **(1134)** 2,360

Composition, drawing with heightening, 10¼ x 17 **(1109)** 1,320

Metamorphosis, colored pencil, 12½ x 8 **(1134)** 826

Starfish, pencil and frottage, 4 x 7¾ **(1134)** 472

Couple of Birds, India ink and colored chalk, 13½ x 9¾ **(1194)** 2,232

Horses, pen, 4¼ x 7¾ **(1214)** 640

The Forest, pencil and frottage, 9 x 10¼ **(1240)** 2,520

WATERCOLORS

1961–1962

Composition, pastel, 19¾ x 14 **(143)** 1,593

1963

Figures, (1921-24), gouache and frottage, 10½ x 8¼ **(277)** 2,194

Barbarians Marching Westward, 1935, gouache, 9 x 12¼ **(219)** 3,503

Study for Surrealism and Painting, 1942, pastel, 21½ x 17½ **(255)** 2,194

1964

Composition, gouache, 10 x 12¾ **(351)** 1,640

1965

The Cormorants, 1920, watercolor on the photograph of a collage, 10¾ x 9 **(604)** 1,620

"2 holoeder sulfate silicate picastrate u. zwillinge nach meiner wahl mit stabchen," (1919), gouache, India ink and pencil, 4½ x 6½ **(522)** 2,266

Game, pastel, 9 x 7¼ **(567)** 497

Blue Element, gouache, 9¼ x 7¼ **(567)** 1,266

1966

Shell Flowers, (1929), gouache, 9¾ x 14 **(744)** 4,746

1968–July 1969

Standing Woman, on a Yellow Background, gouache, 7¼ x 5¾ **(1174)** 4,370

Dancer, 1951, pastel, 25¾ x 19¾ **(1268)** 8,816

PAINTINGS

1961–1962

Love Forever! or Charming Country, 1923, 51½ x 38½ **(88)** 8,856

The Forests Age, 1926, 36 x 23¾ **(88)** 14,760

The Trees, 32 x 39½ **(32)** 14,200

Landscape, 1930, 4 x 5¼ **(39)** 2,212

The Waves, 10¾ x 28½ **(160)** 2,000

Barbarians Marching Westward, 1935, on paper on board, 9 x 12¼ **(31)** 4,394

Chinese Walls, 1935, on paper on board, 9½ x 13 **(164)** 4,805

Composition with Birds, 1946, 12¾ x 14¾ **(85)** 4,250

Happy New Year, 1948, 24 x 21 **(84)** 10,709

Birds and Ocean (recto), *Arizona* (verso), 1949-54, 53½ x 60½ **(88)** 37,392

The Frog's Song, 1953, 25¾ x 36¼ **(88)** 19,188

Rare Bird, 1955, 36¼ x 29 **(88)** 15,744

The Three Cypresses, 1951, 40¼ x 40¼ . . . . (156) $14,000

The Birds, 7¼ x 10 . . . . (160) 2,400

Bird's Head, 1948, on a lozenged pane,
20¼ x 20¼ . . . . (129) 4,943

The Two Owls, 1952, on paper on canvas,
15¼ x 11 . . . . (105) 6,441

Yellow Birds, 1957, 63½ x 50½ . . . . (31) 19,222

New Mexico, 1956, 25¾ x 32 . . . . (29) 10,000

Galapagos, 1955, 32 x 39½ . . . . (149) 13,430

Pink Figures, 1958, on panel, 10¾ x 14 . . . . (149) 5,372

1963

Heaven's Army, 1925, 32 x 39½ . . . . (309) 21,424

*Portrait of the Poet Johannes-Theodor
Kuhlemann*, on glass, 16¾ x 13½ . . . . (316) 2,600

Monuments with Birds, (1927), 6½ x 8¾ . . . . (219) 2,147

Prince Consort, 1931, collage and pen on paper,
25¾ x 19¾ . . . . (277) 3,290

Loplop, 1932, 39½ x 31½ . . . . (247) 8,226

Lonely Tree and Conjugal Trees, 1942, 31 x 39 . . . (247) 30,162

Jardin Gobe-Avions, 1934, 23 x 28¼ . . . . (277) 8,226

The Year 1939, ink and collage, 24¼ x 18½ . . . . . . (283) 4,068

Pink Figures, 10¾ x 14 . . . . (200) 4,500

Maternity, 15 x 15 . . . . (200) 3,000

Galapagos, 1955, 32 x 39½ . . . . (200) 9,800

A School for an Equilibrist, 18¼ x 15 . . . . (200) 4,500

Fancied Landscape, on panel, 5 x 6¾ . . . . (316) 1,500

Glade, 1958, 24 x 19¾ . . . . (279) 6,250

1964

The Bride of the Wind II, 1926, 32 x 39½ . . . . (367) 24,876

The Great Lovers, 1926, 39 x 31¼ . . . . (454) 11,056

Forest, Bird, and Sun, 1927, 31¼ x 39 . . . . (454) 16,584

The Engadine, 9 x 7¼ . . . . (454) 3,317

The Shadow of the Dove, oil on canvas and
collage, 21¾ x 13 . . . . (474) 5,500

Marie-Berthe, (1932-34), 25¾ x 21 . . . . (454) 5,528

Small Landscape, 1934, 7½ x 9½ . . . . (383) 2,825

The Bird I, fresco, 21 x 15 . . . . (448) 3,000

Composition, paint and frottage, 16¼ x 25 . . . . (448) 4,750

Composition, 7½ x 9½ . . . . (351) 1,920

The Dancer of the Marsh, 1955, on cardboard,
23¾ x 14¼ . . . . (401) 3,800

While the Earth Sleeps, 1956, 35¼ x 45¾ . . . . (416) 19,348

1965

The Eye, (1925), frottage, 10 x 7¾ . . . . (624) 1,797

Inside the Sight: The Egg, 31½ x 24 . . . . (629) 18,863

The Dove Was Right, 1926, on board inlaid with
a bird cage, 16 x 13 . . . . (522) 4,975

The Castle, Cologne, on panel, 10¾ x 14 . . . . (624) 1,935

Frogs, (1927-29), 10¾ x 14 . . . . (624) 5,804

Figures, One with No Head, 1928, oil and sand
on canvas, 67¼ x 51½ . . . . (629) 31,922

Forêt-Arêtes,[5] (1928), 10 x 8 . . . . (522) 3,040

Bérénice, 1935, 7¾ x 9½, frame decorated by the
artist . . . . (632) 4,000

Child Minerva, 1956, 51¼ x 35¼ . . . . (637) 22,500

Composition, 1962, on panel, 8¾ x 6¼ . . . . (616) 2,880

1966

Forest, 7¼ x 9¼ . . . . (802) 6,400

Early, on cardboard, 10 x 8 . . . . (802) 2,720

Little Girl Seated, 1911, on cardboard,
19¾ x 15½ . . . . (763) $ 950

The Great Lover, 1924, 39½ x 32 . . . . (809) 9,000

Bird in a Cage, 1928, oil and bars, 19¼ x 16½ . . . . (816) 6,150

Forêt-Arêtes, (1928), 10 x 8 . . . . (689) 2,902

Shells, (1930), 25 x 31½ . . . . (686) 20,454

L'Ange du foyer, 1937, 15 x 18¼ . . . . (713) 7,500

Window, 1943, 20¼ x 16 . . . . (776) 6,000

Landscape, 1951, 14 x 14¾ . . . . (812) 6,081

Sun Spots, 1957, 17¾ x 14¾ . . . . (757) 4,422

A Fixed Idea of Neptune, 1961, 10¾ x 8¾ . . . . (738) 2,952

After Velàzquez, 1955, oil and collage on panel,
11¾ x 9½ . . . . (747) 2,400

*The Moon Was Full and Bright in My Black
Soul*, 1966, 29 x 36¼ . . . . (751) 11,056

Composition, 7½ x 9½ . . . . (811) 1,900

Butterflies, frottage, 25 x 31¼ . . . . (694) 10,000

1967

Figures, One with No Head, (1928), 63¼ x 51½ . . (882) 35,200

Composition, 49 x 46½ . . . . (882) 20,800

The Sun and the Sea, (1926-29), paint on glass,
21¼ x 17¾ . . . . (880) 8,568

Shell, (1927), 15 x 18¼ . . . . (880) 9,674

Flowers and Birds in a Landscape, 1928,
19½ x 24 . . . . (880) 14,373

Landscape and Figure, 1931, collage and pencil,
25½ x 19½ . . . . (962) 3,040

Chimeras in the Mountain, 1940, 8 x 13 . . . . (938) 7,739

Mask, 1947, oil on paper, 12 x 18 . . . . (841) 3,750

Collage, 1949, collage and ink, 10¾ x 8 . . . . (939) 857

Bird No. 12, oil and relief on board, 7½ x 8½ . . . . . (986) 3,690

The Plums, 12¾ x 18¼ . . . . (940) 6,965

1968–July 1969

Composition with a Horse, 1913, 14 x 19¾ . . . . . . (1125) 26,910

Composition, 22 x 24¾ . . . . (1125) 23,000

Bird, 1920, collage, 4½ x 5¾ . . . . (1096) 1,380

Fantastic Monsters, 1927, on paper, 9½ x 13 . . . . (1112) 8,432

Shell Flower, 1927, 7½ x 9½ . . . . (1132) 8,496

The Sea, (1927-29), 17¾ x 14¼ . . . . (1187) 11,328

Sunset, 1929, 39½ x 32¼ . . . . (1068) 19,352

The Starry Castle, 1937, colored frottage,
12¾ x 10 . . . . (1214) 1,120

Untitled, 1951, on board, 9 x 9 . . . . (1132) 4,484

Composition, on paper laid down on canvas,
15¾ x 11 . . . . (1117) 4,100

Project for "Une Semaine de bonté," 6¼ x 4½ . . . (1138) 595

The Laughing Child, 1954, 11½ x 15½ . . . . (1070) 7,080

Flakes, kama-mère, 20¼ x 14¼ . . . . (1189) 8,000

Birds in the Mirror, kama-mère, 21¾ x 18¼ . . . . . (1189) 12,000

Sleeping Eskimo, 1948, 28 x 24 . . . . (1235) 27,000

The Octopus, (1925-26), 25 x 31½ . . . . (1270) 43,200

The City, (1955-56), oil and frottage on paper laid
down on canvas, 8¼ x 11¼ . . . . (1270) 7,200

---

[5]Dedicated "A la tante Wanda, l'oncle Tonnerre."

Georges d'Espagnat

(1870-1950)

Birthplace: Melun, France.

1888 Goes to Paris and studies art by himself, working, for instance, at the Louvre Museum. Trip to Italy. Deeply impressed by the Venetian painters.

1892-93 Back in France, he remains true to the manner of the romantic painters. Participates in the Salon des Indépendants, Paris.

1894 First one-man show at the Galerie Le Barc de Boutteville, Paris. Produces several prints, including engravings and lithographs.

1898 Journeys to Morocco, Great Britain, Belgium, Germany, Switzerland, and Italy.

1899-03 Meets Valtat, Albert André, Bonnard, Vuillard, and Maurice Denis. Alters his style, which shows a slight Impressionist influence.

1900 Decorations for Durand-Ruel's apartment in the Rue de Rome, Paris.

1905 Takes part in the foundation of the Salon d'Automne, Paris.

1905-10 Stay in the south of France with Valtat and Renoir. Travels through Europe.

1910-14 Paints several portraits. Exhibits steadily at the Galerie Durand-Ruel, Paris.

1921-28 Exhibitions at the Galerie Druet, Paris.

1929 Exhibition at the Galerie Georges Ginoux, Brussels.

1931 Exhibition at the Durand-Ruel Gallery, New York.

1935 Starts to teach at the Ecole des Beaux-Arts, Paris.

1937-38 Series of decorations for the Palais de la Découverte, Paris; the Palais de Justice, Toulouse; and the Palais du Luxembourg, Paris.

1950 Died.

Sales

DRAWINGS

1966

Reclining Nude, Back View, red chalk, 11½ x 23¾ .... (702) $ 160

Child Reading, pencil and watercolor, 6¾ x 6¾ ... (784) 425

1968–July 1969

Woman Reading, red chalk, 9 x 6 .... (1015) 58

WATERCOLORS

1961–1962

The Flute Player, pastel, 7 x 9 .... (68) 120

Garden Corner, watercolor, 8¼ x 10¼ .... (154) 190

1964

La Rochelle: The Harbor, watercolor, 8¾ x 11½ .... (332) 180

Mother and Child, watercolor, 8¼ x 9½ .... (404) 90

Hilly Landscape, watercolor, 11¾ x 8 .... (441) 118

1965

The Gathering, watercolor, 10 x 9½ .... (491) 160

The Gardener, watercolor, 10¼ x 6¾ .... (612) 180

1966

The Sailboats, pastel, 7¼ x 9¼ .... (711) 230

Woman in a Landscape, watercolor, 10¼ x 6¾ ... (772) 264

The Banks of the River Marne, in the Springtime, watercolor, 10 x 11¾ .... (723) 260

Hilly Landscape, watercolor, 6¾ x 8¾ .... (809) $ 192

The Yellow Hill, watercolor, 8¼ x 11 .... (691) 120

Gathering Fruit, two works, pencil and watercolor, 10 x 9 and 10 x 8 .... (648) 850

1967

Sailboats in the Harbor, watercolor, 8¾ x 11¾ ... (874) 240

The Harbor, watercolor, 9 x 11¾ .... (971) 170

1968–July 1969

Bucolic Scene, watercolor, 7½ x 10 .... (1089) 104

Mediterranean Harbor, watercolor and gouache, 9 x 11¾ .... (1212) 700

Landscape, watercolor, 10¾ x 13 .... (1220) 250

Reverie, watercolor, 11½ x 8¾ .... (1238) 260

PAINTINGS

1961–1962

Two Vases of Windflowers, 25¾ x 21¾ .... (50) 1,040

Still Life with Windflowers, 18¼ x 21¾ .... (76) 1,600

Garden of Beaulie-la-Tour, 38¼ x 51¾ .... (114) 3,600

Riverside, 21¼ x 29 .... (161) 1,060

Red-Haired Woman Reading, 24 x 19¾ .... (2) 440

1963

Young Girl Seated, 29 x 23¾ .... (262) 400

Young Woman Undressing Herself, 32 x 25¾ ..... (234) 400

Brother and Sister, 23¾ x 29 .... (235) 300

The Cup of Fruit, 24 x 19¾ .... (303) 920

The Bunch of Roses, 15¾ x 12¾ .... (276) 720

Vase of Flowers on a Table, 25¾ x 32 .... (224) 1,460

Children in the Country, 23¾ x 29 .... (198) 840

Bust of a Woman, 16¼ x 13 .... (209) 80

Sailboats in the Harbor, 23¾ x 29 .... (241) 1,000

Woman and Child Seated by the Seaside, 32 x 39½ .... (306) 2,800

On the Beach, two paintings, 55¼ x 15¾ .... (318) 2,800

1964

Gathering Apples, 1896, 29 x 36¼ .... (371) 2,400

The Terrace, 1899, 51½ x 38¼ .... (465) 2,200

Children Walking, 15¾ x 12¾ .... (339) 500

The Sleeper, 14¾ x 21¼ .... (440) 320

Quai Malaquais, (1920), 18¼ x 21¾ .... (358) 443

The Reading, 1927, 13 x 18¼ .... (480) 460

The Fishing Boat on the High Seas, 23¾ x 29 .... (474) 1,600

Nude with a Blue Scarf, 18¼ x 15 .... (332) 1,100

Young Girl Playing with a Dog, 52½ x 38¾ ..... (359) 460

A Bunch of Carnations, 29¼ x 23¾ .... (394) 1,700

Still Life with Fruit, Flowers, and Rouen Crockery, 32 x 39½ .... (391) 2,420

1965

Vase of Flowers, on panel, 14¾ x 18¼ .... (523) 820

The Model in the Studio, 19¾ x 24 .... (518) 1,000

Madame d'Espagnat in Her Garden, 16¾ x 19¼ .. (534) 410

Sailboats Entering the Harbor, on canvas laid down on panel, 13 x 16¼ .... (588) 610

Madame d'Espagnat and Her Son Jean-Noël, (1919-20), 36¾ x 29¼ .... (553) 1,300

Surroundings of Cagnes, 25¾ x 32 .... (524) 1,072

The Garden of Beaulieu-sur-Mer, 38¼ x 51½ .... (553) 2,200

The Reader, 23¾ x 29 .... (628) 1,451

Woman and Child at the Seaside, 29 x 36¼ ...... (617) 4,294

1966

Woman in a Blue Dress, 21¼ x 28½ . . . . (745) | $1,808
Portrait of Madame X. . ., 1924, 21¾ x 18¾ . . . . . . (781) | 1,100
Sleep, 32 x 25¾ . . . . (706) | 420
Still Life, 21¾ x 18¼ . . . . (648) | 1,750
Field of Flowers, 24 x 19 . . . . (798) | 859
Still Life with Flowers and Fruit, on cardboard,
   16¼ x 20½ . . . . (820) | 340
Fishing, 67¾ x 51¾ . . . . (814) | 1,000
The Bird Trap, 67¼ x 48½ . . . . (814) | 900
Little Girls in a Garden in Bloom, 63½ x 23 . . . . . . (819) | 1,600
Vase of Flowers, 21¼ x 25¾ . . . . (749) | 2,000

1967

Interior with a Seated Woman, 18½ x 15¼ . . . . (923) | 600
Vase of Flowers, 21¾ x 18¼ . . . . (923) | 1,500
Vallée du Loup, (1900), 29 x 36¼ . . . . (963) | 3,500
Juziers Hills, 23¾ x 29 . . . . (1000) | 840
In the Garden, 15 x 18¼ . . . . (887) | 700
The Nap, 25¾ x 36¼ . . . . (934) | 500
Still Life with Dahlias and Fruit, on cardboard,
   16¼ x 20½ . . . . (920) | 260
Vase of Flowers, on panel, 21¾ x 18¼ . . . . (978) | 1,020
The Red Body, 21¼ x 25¾ . . . . (971) | 940
The Arab Rider, on cardboard, 12½ x 15½ . . . . (875) | 560
Woman and Child in a Landscape, 29 x 23¾ . . . . . . (861) | 970
Fishing Harbor, 15 x 18¼ . . . . (857) | 560
Young Girl Reading, 25¾ x 21¾ . . . . (926) | 780
The Young Artist, 23¾ x 29 . . . . (993) | 1,040
The Sewer, 21¼ x 18¼ . . . . (911) | 1,160

1968–July 1969

La Pointe de l'Aiguillon, on cardboard laid down
   on cradled panel, 15½ x 18½ . . . . (1106) | 2,400
Sailboats Alongside a Quay, (1905-07),
   17½ x 21 . . . . (1187) | 4,012
La Rochelle Harbor, 24 x 31 . . . . (1162) | 4,100
Seascape, 13 x 21¾ . . . . (1051) | 860
The Farm, 24 x 18¼ . . . . (1075) | 1,420
Landscape, 21¼ x 25¾ . . . . (1127) | 3,680
The Walk, on cardboard, 13 x 9½ . . . . (1026) | 500
A Path Along the Bank of the River Seine,
   23¾ x 29 . . . . (1183) | 2,500
Sleeping Woman, 25¾ x 36¼ . . . . (1119) | 880
Portrait of a Young Woman in Profile, 1925,
   16¼ x 13 . . . . (1060) | 672
The Open Shirt, 32 x 25¾ . . . . (1039) | 950
The Rest, 21¼ x 29 . . . . (1202) | 2,200
Seated Woman, 30¼ x 25 . . . . (1061) | 950
Interior with a Seated Young Lady, 18¼ x 15 . . . . (1115) | 830
Reclining Nude, 23¾ x 29¼ . . . . (1030) | 2,750
The Drawing Lesson, 36¼ x 29 . . . . (1089) | 1,300
Fruit and Vase of Flowers, 32 x 25¾ . . . . (1184) | 5,100
Flowers and Fruit, 29 x 23¾ . . . . (1014) | 2,840
Still Life, 25¾ x 21¾ . . . . (1170) | 2,070
Flowers, 23¾ x 29 . . . . (1113) | 3,100
Still Life, 13 x 18¼ . . . . (1088) | 1,600
Still Life, 21¾ x 18½ . . . . (1088) | 2,600
Vase of Flowers, 24¼ x 20 . . . . (1026) | 1,200
Vase of Roses and Two Apples, 24 x 19¾ . . . . (1029) | 2,200
Portrait of Pablo Casals, 15¾ x 12¾ . . . . (1211) | 300
The Bunch of Flowers, 25¾ x 21¼ . . . . (1221) | 3,200
The Quai Conti in Paris, 18¼ x 21¾ . . . . (1221) | 2,700
Still Life with Apples and Flowers, 18¼ x 15 . . . . (1221) | 1,450

Bunch of Red Flowers, 21¼ x 25¾ . . . . (1226) | $4,000
The Vase of Flowers, 24 x 19¾ . . . . (1227) | 2,300
Young Woman Awaking, 25¾ x 36½ . . . . (1230) | 1,000
The Red-Roofed Village, 15 x 18¼ . . . . (1234) | 1,080
The Wood, 15 x 18¼ . . . . (1234) | 860
The Red-Roofed Cottage, 10¾ x 14 . . . . (1234) | 560
Landscape . . . . (1245) | 2,050
Women by the Waterside, 18¼ x 24 . . . . (1249) | 8,700
Flowers, on cardboard, 21¾ x 18¼ . . . . (1252) | 3,100
Reclining Young Girl in the Nude, 25¾ x 39½ . . . (1255) | 3,240
Young Nude, Dressing, 51 x 33½ . . . . (1261) | 3,400
Mother Teaching Her Little Boy How to Write,
   23¾ x 29 . . . . (1261) | 3,400
Flowers and Fruit, on cradled panel, 18¼ x 15 . . . (1262) | 2,600
Still Life with a Jug, 14¾ x 18¾ . . . . (1265) | 1,300

Maurice Estève

(1904–   )

Birthplace: Culan, France. Attends various private academies in Paris.

1923   Spends a year in Spain, managing a design studio in a fabric factory.

1924–27   Works at the Académie Colarossi, Paris.

1929   Participates in the Salon des Surindépendants, Paris, where he exhibits yearly.

1930   One-man show at the Galerie Yvangeot, Paris.

1937   With Robert Delaunay, decorates the Pavillon de l'Aviation et des Chemins de Fer at the World's Fair of Paris.

1938   Exhibits at the Galerie de l'Equipe, Paris.

1941–44   Participates in the Salon d'Automne and many other group shows in Europe.

1948   Important exhibition at the Galerie Louis Carré, Paris. Exhibits yearly at the Salon de Mai, Paris.

1953   Takes part in the Sâo Paulo Biennial.

1954   Takes part in the Venice Biennial and in the exhibition of the Carnegie Foundation, Pittsburgh.

1955–56   One-man shows at the Galerie Villand et Galanis, Paris. Retrospective exhibition at the Royal Museum, Copenhagen.

Resident in Paris, working in his Montmartre studio.

Sales

DRAWINGS

1961–1962

Seated Nude, black lead, 17¾ x 11 . . . . (155) | $ 240
Composition, 1955, charcoal and pencil,
   14¾ x 18½ . . . . (153) | 540

1967

Breakfast, 1936, India ink, 10 x 7½ . . . . (996) $ 180

Evening, 1938, pencil and watercolor, 9½ x 12¼ . . (996)   240

Composition, 1955, charcoal, 12½ x 16 . . . . (967)   384

1968–July 1969

Pâques de guerre, 1940, wash, two drawings, each
8¾ x 6¼ . . . . (1043)   140

Maternity, 1934, 12¾ x 10 . . . . (1225)   200

Maternity, 1935, 6¾ x 5¼ . . . . (1230)   560

WATERCOLORS

1961–1962

Composition, (1950), watercolor, 15¾ x 12¼ . . . . . . (149)   1,422

Composition, watercolor, 19¾ x 14¾ . . . . (59)   1,900

Composition, watercolor, 17½ x 22½ . . . . (110)   1,500

1963

Composition, 1948, gouache, 14 x 8¼ . . . . (287)   900

Composition, watercolor, 13½ x 8 . . . . (194)   820

Composition, watercolor, 19¾ x 14¾ . . . . (299)   1,420

1964

The Studio, watercolor, 14¾ x 19¾ . . . . (377)   1,808

Composition, watercolor, 15 x 20 . . . . (408)   400

Still Life, 1962, watercolor, 19¾ x 25¼ . . . . (450)   1,000

Watercolor No. 747, watercolor, 15½ x 23¾ . . . . . . (413)   1,560

1965

Composition, watercolor, 20 x 14¾ . . . . (553)   1,000

1966

Composition, 1948, gouache, 13½ x 8 . . . . (696)   820

1967

Composition, watercolor, 17 x 12¼ . . . . (890)   1,993

1968–July 1969

The Couple, 1932, watercolor, 8 x 12¼ . . . . (1043)   400

Composition, 1935, watercolor, 8¼ x 9½ . . . . (1129)   440

Composition, 1964, watercolor, 19½ x 24 . . . . (1185)   1,600

PAINTINGS

1961–1962

Still Life with a Salad Shaker, 1942, 32 x 23¾ . . . . (149)   8,216

Composition, 18½ x 21¾ . . . . (69)   4,424

1963

The Ancient, 1951, 36 x 29 . . . . (232)   14,012

Composition, 1957, 8¾ x 10¾ . . . . (283)   2,260

Piling, 1957, 10¾ x 16¼ . . . . (232)   4,407

L'Arnée, 1958, 9½ x 13¾ . . . . (232)   3,164

1965

Evening at Trenay, 1945, 25¾ x 19¾ . . . . (583)   1,741

The Norman Farm, 1945, 25¾ x 31¾ . . . . (573)   3,317

The Apprentices, 1945, 25¾ x 32 . . . . (569)   5,650

Sicilian Chair, 1953, 24 x 19¾ . . . . (552)   1,800

1966

The Attic, 1945, 25¾ x 32 . . . . (797)   4,520

Jean Fautrier

(1898-   )

Birthplace: Paris, France. Spends his youth in London.

1912   Attends the Royal Academy of Arts, London.

1914   Returns to France.

1923-24   So-called "chestnut-color" period.

1925-27   Paul Guillaume is interested in his work and organizes an important exhibition at the Galerie Bernheim-Jeune, Paris. So-called "black" period.

1939   His lithographs are shown at the Galerie de la N.R.F., Paris.

1945   Exhibition at the Galerie René Drouin, Paris.

1951   Participates in the exhibition "Signifiants de l'Informel" at the Galerie Facchetti, Paris.

1954   Devotes himself entirely to painting.

1955-56   Exhibition at the Galerie Rive Droite, Paris. Exhibits also in New York at the Alexandre Iolas Gallery and at the Hugo Gallery.

1959   Travels through Europe. Exhibition at the Hanover Gallery, London.

1960   Wins the first prize at the Venice Biennial.

Resident at Chatenay-Malabry near Paris.

Sales

DRAWINGS

1961–1962

Standing Nude, 1926, black pencil and wash,
17 x 10 . . . . (115) $ 90

Composition, 1961, India ink and wash,
12¾ x 18¾ . . . . (110)   320

1963

Nude, 1924, red chalk, 40¾ x 28½ . . . . (300)   600

Seated Nude, charcoal and red chalk,
20½ x 14¾ . . . . (291)   100

Composition, 1956, 11¾ x 19 . . . . (249)   120

Composition, wash, 14 x 21 . . . . (249)   170

1964

Bust of a Woman, red chalk, 25¼ x 19 . . . . (466)   210

Standing Nude, Front View, (1926), charcoal and red chalk, 12½ x 8¼ . . . . (376)   80

Variations on a Nude, 1960, ink on blotting paper,
19½ x 25 . . . . (351)   600

Composition, 1960, ink on blotting paper with pencil and pen lights, 9¾ x 6¼ . . . . (401)   260

Composition, 1961, ink and chalk, 19½ x 25¼ . . . . (370)   140

1965

Nudes, two drawings, each 8¾ x 13 . . . . (612)   220

Standing Nude, red chalk, 10¾ x 8¼ . . . . (631)   212

1967

Head, colored chalk and gouache, 16¾ x 13¾ . . . . (986)   221

1968–July 1969

Reclining Nude, 1944, India ink, two drawings,
each 11¾ x 13½ . . . . (1129)   380

Woman's Face, pastel, 17½ x 11¾ . . . . (1222)   320

WATERCOLORS

1961–1962

Head, 1926, pastel, 17½ x 14 . . . . (85)   125

Composition, gouache, 19¾ x 25¾ . . . . (16)   711

Composition, gouache, 19½ x 25¼ .... (30) $1,100
Composition, 1958, gouache, 19¾ x 25¾ .... (75)   869
Composition, 1957, gouache, 19½ x 25¼ .... (116)   240
Composition, 1959, gouache, 19¾ x 25¾ .... (156)   700
Composition, 1959, gouache, 19¾ x 25¾ .... (156)   720
Composition, watercolor, 18¼ x 15 .... (27)   560
Composition, 1943, watercolor, 3¾ x 5¼ .... (153)   280

1963
Composition, 1959, gouache, 19¾ x 25 .... (299)   470
Blue and Pink Nude, gouache, 19 x 25 .... (249)   540
Composition, gouache, 17¾ x 25¼ .... (205)   420

1964
Composition, watercolor, 12¾ x 18½ .... (394)   170

1965
Composition, 1958, gouache on blotting paper,
    19½ x 25¼ .... (561)   340
Composition, 1960, gouache, 19½ x 25½ .... (567)   836

1966
Figures Seated at Table, 1924, watercolor,
    8 x 11¾ .... (745)   1,153
Composition, watercolor and gouache,
    17¾ x 23½ .... (718)   340
Abstract Composition, 1958, gouache, 18¼ x 15 ... (666)   290

1967
Flowers, gouache, 15 x 16¼ .... (919)   1,808
Abstract Composition, 1943, gouache, 3¾ x 5¼ ... (854)   340
Composition, 1943, gouache, 3¾ x 5¼ .... (898)   260
Standing Nude, watercolor, 25¼ x 18½ .... (996)   400

1968–July 1969
Cups of Flowers, watercolor, 14¾ x 16½ .... (1183)   1,000
Head, pastel, 17¼ x 14 .... (1224)   1,040
Composition, 1958, gouache, 15 x 18¼ .... (1226)   560
Flanders, gouache, 12¾ x 19¾ .... (1245)   160
Nude, gouache, 21¼ x 29 .... (1268)   812

PAINTINGS

1961–1962
The Fish, 13½ x 16¼ .... (110)   1,540
Nude, 1926, 13 x 16¼ .... (70)   1,264
Portrait in One's Shirt Sleeves, 1929, 24 x 19¾ .... (9)   280
Flowers, 1939, oil on paper laid down on canvas,
    25 x 23¼ .... (80)   1,960
Still Life, oil on paper laid down on canvas,
    16¼ x 22 .... (80)   1,000
Waves, 1956, oil on paper on canvas, 18¼ x 24 ... (149)   5,056
Chipie, 1956, 29 x 21¼ .... (156)   7,400
Composition, 1957, 8¾ x 10¾ .... (69)   2,054
Colored Lines II, 1958, 25¾ x 39½ .... (88)   7,872

1963
Waves, 1956, 18¼ x 24 .... (200)   3,560
La Grenouillère, 1956, 13 x 18¼ .... (200)   3,000
Vase of Flowers, 39½ x 32 .... (198)   1,600
Tureen with Fruit, 21¾ x 25¾ .... (254)   1,000
Pineapple, 29¾ x 23¾ .... (318)   1,300
Blotting Paper Applied on Canvas, 19½ x 25¼ ... (263)   640

1964
Fish in a Basket, 25¾ x 32 .... (401)   2,100
Flowers in a Vase, 21¾ x 18¼ .... (425)   960
Flowers, 19¾ x 24 .... (466)   540

1965
Hostage's Head, No. 11, 1943, on board,
    14 x 10¼ .... (485) $4,250
Vase of Flowers, 18 x 14¾ .... (632)   560
Composition, 35¼ x 57¼ .... (617)   11,752
Partisan's Head, plaster and oil on canvas,
    10¾ x 8½ .... (512)   1,000
The Three Trees, 1944, plaster and oil on canvas,
    23¾ x 36¼ .... (512)   6,300
Vase of Flowers, 21¾ x 18¼ .... (512)   1,120

1966
Portrait of a Woman, 14 x 10¾ .... (711)   500
Vase of Flowers, 1925, 21½ x 18¼ .... (676)   1,500
Fish, 25¾ x 32 .... (811)   3,400
Roses, 1928, oil on paper, 26 x 32½ .... (811)   3,000
The Hanging Rabbit, 39½ x 32 .... (681)   1,560
Waves, 1956, 18¼ x 23¾ .... (749)   1,440
Endless Lines, 1957, 31¼ x 38¾ .... (701)   2,250
Mujeres, 1957, oil and plaster on canvas,
    44¼ x 57¼ .... (678)   5,000
Composition, 1957, on paper laid down on
    canvas, 10¾ x 14¼ .... (829)   1,200
Small Colored Squares, 1958, 18¼ x 21½ .... (678)   2,300
Composition, paint on paper laid down on
    canvas .... (784)   325

1967
Standing Woman, 29¼ x 21¾ .... (919)   3,390
Seaweed, 1956, 21¼ x 31½ .... (982)   4,740

1968–July 1969
Bust of a Woman, 29 x 21¼ .... (1183)   1,900
The Fish, 13 x 16¼ .... (1124)   1,020
Abstract Composition, 1956, 21¼ x 32 .... (1173)   11,500
Nude, 13¼ x 9½ .... (1222)   460
Young Picard, 1925, 39½ x 28½ .... (1226)   2,000
House by the Riverside, 16¼ x 13 .... (1238)   820
Mountainous Landscape, 21¼ x 25¾ .... (1238)   500
The Basket of Fish, 25¾ x 32 .... (1254)   4,000
Grapes, 7½ x 9½ .... (1268)   1,392

Lyonel Feininger

(1871–1956)

Birthplace: New York, U.S. Studies music with his father and plays the violin very early in life.

1887-93   Journey to Germany, Belgium, and France. Decides to give up music and become a painter. Attends the Kunstgewerbeschule, Hamburg; the Berliner Kunstakademie; the Collège St. Servais, Liége; and the Académie Colarossi, Paris.

1893-06   Stay in Berlin. Works for several newspapers as illustrator and caricaturist.

1906-08   Stay in Paris. Meets Pascin and Robert Delaunay. Devotes himself entirely to painting.

1911	Participates in the Salon des Indépendants, Paris. Discovers Cubism and Cubists.
1913	Invited by Franz Marc to exhibit with the Blaue Reiter group at the first Herbstsalon, Berlin.
1918-24	Meets Gropius. Teaches at the Bauhaus. With Jawlensky, Kandinsky, and Klee, sets up the "Blue Four" group.
1929	Exhibition at the Museum of Modern Art, New York.
1931-32	Retrospective exhibition at the National Gallery, Berlin. One-man shows in Hanover, Leipzig, and Hamburg.
1936	Returns to the U.S. and teaches at Mills College, Oakland, California. Stay in Berlin.
1937	Settles permanently in New York.
1938	Executes murals for the 1939 World's Fair, New York.
1941-54	Exhibits steadily at the Curt Valentin Gallery, New York.
1944	Retrospective exhibition at the Museum of Modern Art, New York.
1947	Elected president of the Federation of American Painters and Sculptors.
1949	Feininger-Villon exhibition at the Institute of Contemporary Art, Boston.
1950	First one-man show in Paris at the Galerie Jeanne Bûcher.
1951	One-man show at the Cleveland Museum of Art.
1954	Retrospective exhibition at the Bayerische Akademie der Schönen Künste, Munich.
1956	Died, New York.
1959-61	Retrospective exhibitions in the U.S., Great Britain, and Germany.

Sales

DRAWINGS

1961-1962

International Society of Peace, 1907, India ink, 6¾ x 10¼	(106)	$ 145
Benz VI, 1914, charcoal, 8½ x 10	(37)	1,700
Vorstadthäuser, 1921, pen and watercolor, 10¾ x 8½	(84)	1,977
Gelmeroda, 1927, pen and wash, 14½ x 11	(84)	1,648
Coastal Scene, charcoal and wash, 11¾ x 18	(64)	1,700
Three Sailboats, India ink and watercolor, 6¼ x 10¼	(106)	1,446
Boat with Flag, pen and watercolor, 6¾ x 10¾	(111)	1,500
Shipping, 1939, pencil and watercolor, 8¾ x 11	(44)	2,300
Old Gables, 1941, charcoal, 18¼ x 12¼	(105)	1,808
Stranded, 1942, pen, 7¾ x 10¾	(151)	836
Boats at Sea, 1947, pen and watercolor, 7¾ x 11½	(37)	2,600
Five Figures, 1955, pen and watercolor, 3 x 5¾	(107)	209

1963

Draga and Alexander, 1909, India ink and gouache, 8¾ x 7½	(216)	384
Boats in the Harbor, 1921, India ink and watercolor, 7½ x 9½	(219)	2,147
Dune VII, 1925, ink and watercolor, 11 x 17¾	(272)	1,550
Treptow an der Rega, 1925, India ink and watercolor, 14¾ x 11¼	(219)	2,305
Landscape, 1934, India ink, 7¾ x 9¼	(228)	443

Church and Town, 1939, India ink and watercolor, 8 x 11	(219)	$1,989
Calamity Bay, 1940, pen, 11¾ x 7¾	(225)	850

1964

The Great Houses, 1910, pen, 10 x 7¾	(428)	1,476
Gross Gromsdorf, 1914, charcoal, 9½ x 7¼	(383)	1,030
Four Children, India ink and watercolor, 3¼ x 6¼	(467)	541
Mellingen V, ink and watercolor, 9¼ x 11	(354)	3,000
Freighter I, 1943, ink and watercolor, 12 x 18¾	(454)	3,040
Composition, 1954, pen and watercolor, 6 x 4	(374)	400

1965

The Country Road, 1913, pencil, 6¼ x 8	(565)	158
Village in Thuringia, 1917, pencil, 6½ x 7½	(535)	553
Seascape, 1940, ink and watercolor, 19 x 26¼	(637)	6,000
Yachts, 1950, pen and wash, 11 x 18¼	(539)	1,200
Hildesheim I, 1952, black ink and watercolor, 11¾ x 9	(583)	1,161

1966

Gnomes, India ink and colored chalk, 5¾ x 4½	(734)	565
Old Houses, 1926, India ink and watercolor, 10¾ x 13	(738)	2,706
Christmas Greeting Cards, 1954, pen and watercolor, 5¾ x 4	(805)	450

1967

Regamündung, 1930, India ink and watercolor, 11¼ x 17¾	(927)	3,616
The Violinist, 1918, pen and color wash, 9½ x 12	(940)	2,612
Caricature of Theodore Roosevelt, 1904, pencil, gouache, and watercolor, 10 x 7½	(1004)	800
A Mystery, India ink, 3¼ x 6½	(927)	226
Steamer, 1931, ink and watercolor, 11¾ x 17¾	(1004)	3,500
Sardine Nets in Brittany, 1931, India ink and watercolor, 8¾ x 16½	(970)	2,460
Sailboats, 1932, pen and watercolor, 9 x 13¼	(986)	2,214
Sailboats, 1934, ink and watercolor, 9¼ x 12¾	(889)	2,200
Seaside, 1935, colored chalk, 5 x 8¼	(998)	861

1968–July 1969

The Bicycle Racer, pencil and pen, 9½ x 7½	(1099)	690
Landscape, 1921, pencil, 5¾ x 8	(1214)	560
Sunset, 1926, India ink and watercolor, 10½ x 17½	(1112)	3,472
Fliehende Schiffe II, 1934, pen and watercolor, 11½ x 14¾	(1094)	3,174
Four Children, pen and watercolor, 3 x 5¾	(1138)	669
Freiherr von Rheinbaben (Caricature), India ink, 9¾ x 7¼	(1090)	248
Village, 1954, pen and pencil heightened with watercolor, 6 x 9¾	(1061)	1,300
The Pond, 1917, charcoal, 9 x 12	(1240)	4,080

WATERCOLORS

1961-1962

Park III, 1916, watercolor, 12½ x 9¾	(88)	1,624
The Village Church, 1920, watercolor, 10¾ x 10	(88)	2,460
Oberweimar VII, 1920, watercolor, 9¼ x 12¼	(149)	2,844
The Towboat, 1929, watercolor, 12¼ x 19	(149)	2,528
Floating in Space, watercolor and India ink, 12½ x 18¾	(106)	1,853
The Sailor, 1934, watercolor and pen, 5 x 7	(24)	566
Blaue Marine, 1941, watercolor, 12¼ x 19	(149)	2,844

Boats at Sea, 1947, watercolor and pen,
7¾ x 11½ .... (37) $1,500
Yellow Sky, 1950, watercolor, 8¼ x 11¾ .... (129)   1,373
Landscape, 1950, watercolor, 12¼ x 18¾ .... (75)   2,370

1963
Sailboats, 1932, watercolor and pen, 10¾ x 16¾ .. (228)   3,001

1964
Swinemünde, 1933, watercolor, 8 x 11½ .... (461)   3,040
Seascape, 1937, watercolor, 8 x 11½ .... (471)   2,034

1965
House on Fire, 1918, India ink and watercolor,
9¼ x 9 .... (565)   2,034
Romance at the Seaside, 1943, pen and
watercolor, 9 x 12 .... (597)   2,583
Freighter I, 1943, watercolor and pen,
12¼ x 18¾ .... (616)   2,880
St. Guénolé, 1952, pastel, 9 x 11¾ .... (567)   2,124

1966
Oberweimar VII, 1920, watercolor and India ink,
8¾ x 11½ .... (792)   3,936
Clippers, 1946, watercolor, 11¾ x 18¼ .... (707)   4,600
Composition, 1949, pastel, 9¼ x 10¾ .... (798)   1,672
St. Guénolé, 1952, pastel and India ink,
8¾ x 11¾ .... (734)   2,034

1967
Street in Quimper, 1931, India ink and
watercolor, 6½ x 9¼ .... (927)   2,124
Derelicts, 1941, watercolor, 13¼ x 18¾ .... (864)   3,750
Village Street, 1944, watercolor, 10¾ x 18 .... (952)   3,250
The Tower III, 1948, watercolor, 18 x 12 .... (952)   4,500

1968–July 1969
The Sardine Fishers II, 1932, 12 x 18¾ .... (1209)   4,960
The Quay, 1932, pen and watercolor,
15¾ x 11½ .... (1112)   6,696
The Sailboat, 1933, pen and watercolor,
8½ x 10 .... (1112)   3,720
Gaberndorf, 1934, watercolor and India ink,
8 x 11½ .... (1090)   3,224
Niedergrunstadt VII, 1916, India ink and
watercolor, 9½ x 12½ .... (1246)   3,750
Tanker, 1933, pen and watercolor, 9¼ x 12 ...... (1246)   2,700

PAINTINGS

1961–1962
The Messenger, 1912, 19 x 15¾ .... (140)   6,041
The Fishing Fleet, 1912, 15¾ x 19 .... (88)   13,284
People, Moon, and Stars, 1916, 19 x 16 .... (84)   5,767
Architecture II, 39½ x 31½ .... (149)   23,700
Ship of Stars, 1937, 19¾ x 28¾ .... (88)   22,386
Mirage I (Isles in the Sky), 1942, 12 x 27 .... (88)   14,268

1963
Seaside, 1924, 11¾ x 18¾ .... (202)   6,250
Village, 1953, 13 x 19¾ .... (202)   9,000

1964
The Tunnel, 1949, 17¼ x 28¼ .... (461)   23,200
The Red Clown, 1919, 29 x 26¼ .... (461)   27,200
The Town Hall in Treptow, 1930, 17¼ x 30¾ ..... (383)   20,340
Gaberndorf, 1921 .... (380)   29,520

1966
Houses and Figures, 1909, 20½ x 18¼ .... (750)   19,901
Ruins by the Sea, 1930, 26½ x 42¾ .... (750)   34,826
The Farm, Lobbe, 1907, 15¼ x 25 .... (738)   2,460

1967
Thatch-Roofed Cottage in a Landscape, Lobbe,
1907, 14¾ x 24¼ .... (880) $5,528
Cammin, 1934, 23½ x 19¾ .... (864)   10,000

1968–July 1969
The Stranded Ship, 1924, 12 x 18¾ .... (1235)   17,000

Tsugouharu Léonard Foujita

(1886–1968)

Birthplace: Edogawa, Japan.

1907-12 Enters the Fine Arts School, Tokyo.

1913 Journey to Paris. Greatly admires the Impressionists and knows nothing about modern art of the time. Though he does not speak French, makes friends with the Montparnasse artists, including Van Dongen, Picasso, and Modigliani.

1914 Lives and works with Modigliani and Soutine—and like them suffers extreme poverty.

1917 Discovered by the art dealer Chéron, he is given an important exhibition at his gallery in the Rue de la Boétie, Paris.

1919 Participates in the main Parisian salons.

1923 Becomes a very famous painter.

1926 Awarded the rank of Chevalier in the Legion of Honor.

1929 Travels around the world.

1931 Trip to the U.S., South America, and Cuba.

1933 Returns to Japan, where he remains with his family until 1939.

1939 Stay in Paris.

1940 Spends World War II in Japan and exhibits all over the Far East.

1949 Settles permanently in Paris. Takes an interest in every artistic technique.

1955 Becomes a French citizen. Later becomes converted to Roman Catholicism, taking Léonard as his Christian name.

1968 Died.

Sales

DRAWINGS

1961–1962
Young Japanese Girl with a Child, India ink and
watercolor, 10½ x 8¼ .... (61) $ 152
Young Lady Reading, 1924, pen and wash,
13 x 17½ .... (152)   375
Woman Leaning on Her Elbow, pencil,
15½ x 14 .... (73)   200
Standing Woman in the Nude, 23 x 14¾ .... (130)   180

Mademoiselle Edith Farès, wash and watercolor, 14¾ x 10 . . . . (147) $ 44

Self-Portrait, 1926, wash, 7¼ x 4½ . . . . (72) 120

Lesbos, 1927, pencil and watercolor, 18¾ x 12 . . . . . (44) 900

Bust of a Young Woman in the Nude, 1930, pen and pencil, 15¾ x 12¾ . . . . (51) 124

Head of a Chinese Wrestler, 1934, ink and watercolor, 14 x 11 . . . . (128) 192

Head of a Cat, pen and wash, 1954, 7¼ x 5¾ . . . . . (141) 220

1963

Sleep, pen, India-ink wash, and watercolor heightening, 11½ x 15½ . . . . (295) 170

Seated Young Lady, 1925, black lead, 28 x 41 . . . . . (246) 70

Seated Nude, 1926, pen, 20 x 16 . . . . (255) 219

Portrait of a Young Woman, 1926, pen and stump, 13 x 9 . . . . (318) 500

Woman's Head, 1930, pencil, 15 x 12 . . . . (315) 494

Portrait of Florence Fels, pen, 4¾ x 4½ . . . . (179) 125

Nude Model, 1932, ink and watercolor, 23¾ x 16 . . . . (208) 725

Maternity, 1950, pencil, 12¼ x 8½ . . . . (232) 497

1964

Lesbos, 1927, pencil and watercolor, 18¾ x 12¼ . . (321) 600

Yvonne, 1928, ink and charcoal, 12 x 9 . . . . (438) 525

The Fall of Phaeton, 1928, black lead and stump on tracing paper laid down on canvas, 37½ x 32 . . . . (376) 200

The Pole Jumper, pencil, 43½ x 27¾ . . . . (359) 430

Side View of a Woman, pen, 6¾ x 5¾ . . . . (377) 305

Portrait of a Young Woman, 1929, wash, 11 x 8 . . (329) 500

Two Nudes, pencil, 49 x 13 . . . . (426) 400

Self-Portrait, pen, 5¼ x 4 . . . . (418) 150

Nude with an Apple, pencil, 49 x 13¼ . . . . (426) 200

1965

Portrait of a Woman, 1930, pen and wash, 16¼ x 12 . . . . (523) 550

The Two Girl Friends, 44¾ x 20¼ . . . . (604) 488

Portrait of Youki, 50½ x 19¾ . . . . (588) 340

Nude Leaning on Her Elbow, 1928, pencil, 13¼ x 15 . . . . (516) 440

Portrait of a Chinese Wrestler, 1934, ink and watercolor, 15 x 11¾ . . . . (541) 450

Reclining Nude, pencil on silvered paper, 9¼ x 18¼ . . . . (497) 340

1966

Portrait of a Young Woman, 1925, pen and wash, 14 x 10¾ . . . . (665) 475

Reclining Young Woman, 1925, pencil and white stone, 25 x 37½ . . . . (691) 1,080

The Little Girl with a Ball, 1925, pencil heightened with watercolor, 14 x 11 . . . . (757) 276

Woman's Head, black pencil, 8¾ x 10¼ . . . . (829) 100

Male Nude, 38 x 32 . . . . (711) 240

Standing Nude, on tracing paper, 49 x 17¾ . . . . . . (706) 70

Study of a Woman in the Nude, pencil, 49½ x 17¾ . . . . (828) 224

Woman's Head, pen, 7¼ x 5½ . . . . (749) 100

Self-Portrait, ink, 5¾ x 3¾ . . . . (793) 120

1967

Bust of a Woman, Her Hands Crossed on Her Chest, 1924, pen and India-ink wash, 15¾ x 11 . . . . (929) 560

Anna de Noailles, 1924, black lead, 54 x 19¾ . . . . . (879) 220

Woman's Head, 1926, pencil and ink, 10¼ x 7¼ . . (939) $ 415

Two Nudes, pencil heightened with pastel, 42¼ x 26 . . . . (873) 340

Seated Woman, pencil, 42¼ x 23¾ . . . . (841) 575

Portrait of the Artist's Father, pencil heightened with white chalk, 47½ x 27 . . . . (961) 190

The Virgin and the Child, 1940, 10½ x 8¼ . . . . (838) 710

Woman Turned to the Left, India ink, 13½ x 8 . . . . (855) 540

Montparnasse Bridge, 10¾ x 10 . . . . (1007) 290

Young Lady with a Bird, pen and watercolor, 26¼ x 19¾ . . . . (963) 1,700

1968–July 1969

Portrait of a Young Woman in Profile, 1930, pen, 15 x 11½ . . . . (1019) 440

Portrait of a Woman, 1925, pen and wash, 11½ x 9¼ . . . . (1216) 1,100

Portrait of a Woman, 1926, pen, 10¼ x 7 . . . . (1030) 800

Kiki de Montparnasse, 1927, pencil and charcoal, 25 x 36¾ . . . . (1210) 1,400

Self-Portrait, ink, 5½ x 4½ . . . . (1210) 480

Model Resting, 1927, black pencil on tracing paper, 15½ x 32½ . . . . (1168) 840

Nude, 1928, pen and wash, 12¼ x 10 . . . . (1145) 850

Sleeping Young Woman, 1928, ink, 8¾ x 10¾ . . . (1183) 1,100

Woman's Head, pencil and India-ink wash, 7¾ x 10 . . . . (1178) 1,040

Portrait of a Woman, 1929, pen and stump, 12½ x 8 . . . . (1082) 560

Woman's Head, 1932, pencil and watercolor, 10¾ x 7½ . . . . (1191) 991

Man's Head in Profile, 1934, bamboo and watercolor . . . . (1120) 800

Geisha, ink, 5¼ x 4¼ . . . . (1128) 78

La Môme Moineau et son felin, ink, 6¾ x 9 . . . . . (1116) 600

On the Norman River, pencil and watercolor, 14¼ x 9 . . . . (1098) 356

The Chapel, 12¾ x 9 . . . . (1154) 184

Indian of Bolivia, pencil and watercolor, 34½ x 18½ . . . . (1216) 3,800

Standing Man, 49½ x 28½ . . . . (1228) 440

The Athletes, 23¾ x 48¼ . . . . (1230) 1,040

Bust of a Young Girl, 9½ x 7¼ . . . . (1230) 360

Le Grand Vefour, pencil, watercolor, and gouache, 1951, 12 x 9¾ . . . . (1240) 840

Portrait of a Young Girl, 10 x 7¼ . . . . (1245) 600

The Two Friends, 1928, charcoal, 40¼ x 26½ . . . . (1245) 600

Little Girl with a Cat, India-ink wash, 20½ x 13½ . . . . (1254) 3,400

The Little Girl, black lead, 17¼ x 9½ . . . . (1262) 1,300

Portrait of Madame A., 1931, drawing heightened with watercolor . . . . (1265) 1,200

Young Lady in Her Bed, 1925, India-ink wash, 12¾ x 15 . . . . (1268) 3,016

Hen with Golden Eggs, pen and ink, 5 x 3¾ . . . . . (1273) 756

WATERCOLORS

1961–1962

The Woman with a Cat, watercolor, 5¾ x 7¼ . . . . . . (86) 152

1964

Japanese Woman Combing Her Hair, watercolor and gouache, 12¼ x 15½ . . . . (325) 190

Woman with a Red Mantilla, watercolor, 8¾ x 6¾ . . . . (343) 260

1965

Mother and Child, 1917, watercolor, 18¾ x 15 .... (612) $2,000

Woman with a Bird, 1917, watercolor,
15¾ x 12¾ .... (561)   780

The Man with a Bowler Hat, watercolor,
7 x 6¼ .... (599)   180

The Conversation, 1926, watercolor, 8¾ x 6½ .... (621)   170

Japanese Woman Dressing, watercolor,
12¼ x 15½ .... (547)   800

1966

Portrait of a Young Woman, watercolor and
pencil, 48¼ x 19¾ .... (692)   380

Three Dancers, watercolor, 15¼ x 11¼ .... (698)   680

Dancers, watercolor, 15 x 11½ .... (726)   1,200

1967

Portrait of a Young Lady, 1928, pastel,
11¾ x 10 .... (976)   380

Bust of a Woman, 1928, pastel, 11¾ x 9½ .... (934)   260

1968–July 1969

The Temptation of Buddha, (1918), watercolor
and gouache on a golden background,
14 x 23 .... (1109)   3,300

Woman's Head, 1917, watercolor, 10¼ x 8 ...... (1145)   1,100

The Dancer, 1917, watercolor, 19¼ x 7¼ .... (1145)   1,000

Le Chien de Fô, watercolor, 16¾ x 11½ .... (1140)   140

The Dragon, watercolor, 5¼ x 24 .... (1140)   220

The Eye, 1948, watercolor and wash, 18 x 20 .... (1145)   300

Poster Project, watercolor, 11½ x 10¼ .... (1238)   600

Aquatic Birds, gouache, 8¼ x 6¾ .... (1262)   1,200

PAINTINGS

1961–1962

Old House, 25¾ x 22½ .... (166)   900

The Broca Hospital, 10¾ x 18¼ .... (160)   960

1963

The Two Children, 1918, 31½ x 25 .... (315)   2,934

The Two Girl Friends, 1926, 36¾ x 24½ .... (315)   1,919

Bust of a Child, 13 x 9½ .... (298)   2,200

Bust of a Young Woman, 13 x 9½ .... (298)   3,000

Thinking, on panel, 8 x 6 .... (208)   1,600

Oliver Twist, 1958, 10 x 8 .... (208)   1,800

1964

Still Life with a Watch, 1926, 9½ x 13 .... (440)   920

Woman's Head, 1928, peinture à l'essence,
7½ x 9½ .... (440)   1,162

1965

The Public Park, 1917, 18 x 21¾ .... (553)   2,400

Landscape, 1917, 25¾ x 32 .... (617)   1,921

Head of a Young Lady, 1950, 10 x 8 .... (494)   1,700

Little Girl with a Cat, 1950, 13 x 7¾ .... (494)   2,800

Two Little Girls with Cats, 10¾ x 14 .... (503)   4,900

The Little Girl with Potatoes, 13 x 10 .... (494)   3,000

Dog, 1959, paint with India-ink lights, 15 x 18¾ .. (621)   880

1966

Still Life with a Crab, 1922, 14 x 10¾ .... (685)   1,600

Green Plant, 25¾ x 21¼ .... (781)   580

Reclining Nude, 1927, 24 x 32¼ .... (784)   3,000

Reclining Nude, 6½ x 10¾ .... (670)   800

Young Woman with a Little Dog, 29 x 40 .... (819)   10,400

Portrait of a Young Indonesian, oil on paper,
14 x 10 .... (665)   725

The Girls of the Castle, 1951, 15 x 18¼ .... (707) $8,000

Maternity, 21¾ x 18¼ .... (744)   8,588

1967

Maternity, 6¾ x 5¾ .... (901)   5,000

Portrait of Jeanne Hébuterne, 13 x 9½ .... (898)   2,800

Portrait of a Little Girl, 1939, 13 x 9½ .... (838)   2,530

The Triumph of Life Over Death, 63¼ x 73½ ..... (984)   10,000

1968–July 1969

Reclining Nude, 1927, 24 x 32¼ .... (1030)   3,600

The Dream, 1939, 9½ x 13 .... (1067)   3,400

The Waif, 7 x 5½ .... (1231)   3,800

Hôtel Ostreicole, on masonite, 9 x 12¾ .... (1231)   3,500

Head of a Young Woman, 1926, mixed media on
canvas, 10¾ x 8¾ .... (1240)   3,000

Foxes and Dogs, on silk, 38½ x 57¾ .... (1250)   12,800

Samuel Lewis Francis

(1923-   )

Birthplace: San Mateo, near San Francisco, California, U.S.

1941–43   Studies medicine and psychology at Berkeley University, California.

1945–46   Decides to be an artist and studies painting at the California School of Fine Arts, San Francisco.

1947   Executes his first abstract pictures.

1948–50   Studies art history at Berkeley University, California, where he receives a degree.

1950   First trip to Paris. Joins the group of American painters who work under the artistic leadership of the French painter Jean-Paul Riopelle, and becomes very friendly with him.

1952   First one-man show at the Galerie du Dragon, Paris.

1955–56   Exhibitions at the Galerie Rive Droite, Paris. Also exhibits at the Martha Jackson Gallery, New York. Participates in the exhibition "Twelve Americans" at the Museum of Modern Art, New York.

1957–58   Travels around the world. Exhibition at Kornfeld and Klipstein's, Bern.

1958   Executes a large mural for the Kunsthalle, Basel. Exhibits with S. Jaffe and K. Smith at the Centre Culturel Américain, Paris. Takes part in the exhibition "Cinquante Ans d'art moderne" at the World's Fair, Brussels.

1959   One-man show at Kornfeld and Klipstein's, Bern. Second journey around the world. Executes a large mural for the Chase Manhattan Bank, Park Avenue, New York.

1960   Returns to Paris. Takes an interest in lithographs.

1961 Becomes seriously ill. Exhibition at the Galerie Jacques Dubourg, Paris. Executes his series of "Blue Balls." Returns to the U.S.

1962-66 Settles in Santa Monica, California. Exhibition at Kornfeld and Klipstein's, Bern. Executes a series of colored lithographs.

Resident in Santa Monica, California.

Sales

DRAWINGS

1963

Black, 1950, India-ink wash, 18 x 17 . . . . (219) $ 542

1965

Composition, 1949, India ink, 10¾ x 8¼ . . . . (565) 407

Abstraction, wash, 12¾ x 10 . . . . (507) 275

WATERCOLORS

1961-1962

Composition, watercolor, 26½ x 40 . . . . (69) 2,370

Composition, watercolor, 12¼ x 16¾ . . . . (93) 1,085

Composition, 1960, watercolor, 21 x 14¾ . . . . (143) 1,243

Composition, watercolor, 12½ x 14¾ . . . . (93) 802

Composition, watercolor, 21¾ x 17 . . . . (164) 1,428

Gouache, 1957, gouache on paper, 40 x 27 . . . . (106) 3,503

Composition, 1958-59, watercolor, 11¼ x 8¾ . . . . . . (18) 904

Composition, 1958, watercolor, 19½ x 12½ . . . . (143) 1,085

Composition, New York, 1958-59, gouache,
11 x 8¾ . . . . (143) 791

Vertical Red, 1960, gouache, 12¾ x 17 . . . . (70) 869

Composition, Blue on White, 1960, tempera,
40½ x 27¼ . . . . (20) 3,318

1963

Blue II, 1956, watercolor, 27¼ x 40¼ . . . . (316) 2,600

Composition, gouache, 8 x 3 . . . . (232) 452

Untitled, watercolor, 13½ x 10 . . . . (219) 1,898

Untitled, 1959, gouache, 8¾ x 6 . . . . (219) 836

Black, Blue, and Yellow, 1959, gouache, 6 x 4½ . . . (255) 329

1964

Composition, 1950, gouache, 21½ x 17 . . . . (368) 774

Painting No. 28, gouache and watercolor,
23 x 15¾ . . . . (405) 2,177

Painting-Black Surge, watercolor, 10¾ x 14¾ . . . . (405) 1,306

Untitled, 1954, gouache and watercolor,
40¾ x 27¼ . . . . (383) 4,294

Untitled, 1955, watercolor, 14 x 17½ . . . . (383) 1,130

Tokyo, 1957, watercolor, 25¾ x 38¾ . . . . (383) 3,526

Blue, Black, and Yellow, 1958, gouache,
21¾ x 29½ . . . . (387) 1,936

Composition, 1960, gouache, 11 x 7½ . . . . (471) 859

Composition, gouache, 11¾ x 9 . . . . (351) 580

1965

Composition, 1950, gouache, 20½ x 16¼ . . . . (489) 425

Painting, 1957, watercolor, 29¾ x 42¼ . . . . (522) 1,382

Painting, watercolor, 21¾ x 17½ . . . . (624) 1,382

Composition, 1958, watercolor, 30 x 22 . . . . (583) 2,467

Painting on paper, (1958), gouache and
watercolor, 40 x 27 . . . . (565) 3,616

Composition, 1958, tempera on paper,
39½ x 26½ . . . . (567) 1,808

Composition, (1958), gouache and watercolor,
29¾ x 22 . . . . (618) $2,952

Green-Red, 1960, gouache, 29¾ x 21¼ . . . . (575) 1,935

1966

Composition in Blue, Red, and Yellow,
watercolor, 55¼ x 42¾ . . . . (651) 2,750

Blue, Red, and Yellow, 1956, watercolor,
25 x 19 . . . . (815) 1,382

Untitled Watercolor, 1957, watercolor, 8¾ x 6¼ . . (734) 452

1967

Red on Black, 1954, gouache, 7¾ x 5¾ . . . . (927) 610

Blue Balls, (1964), watercolor, 30 x 22½ . . . . (927) 452

Untitled, gouache and tempera, 30¼ x 22 . . . . (1004) 2,250

Composition in Blue, 1961, watercolor,
25¾ x 30 . . . . (881) 2,073

1968-July 1969

Untitled, 1959, watercolor and tempera,
45½ x 27 . . . . (1099) 3,795

Composition, tempera, 12¾ x 10 . . . . (1080) 850

Composition, watercolor, 22 x 17¾ . . . . (1080) 1,700

Composition, watercolor, 12¾ x 19¾ . . . . (1018) 600

Abstraction, watercolor, 19¾ x 12¾ . . . . (1030) 600

Blue and Blue, gouache, 14 x 11¾ . . . . (1174) 782

Composition in Red and Yellow, (1956),
watercolor, 22 x 36¼ . . . . (1268) 2,784

Composition, gouache and collage, 6 x 4 . . . . (1268) 510

PAINTINGS

1961-1962

Blue and Red, 1954, 31½ x 23¾ . . . . (106) 7,910

Composition, (1959), on paper on cardboard,
30 x 22 . . . . (88) 2,952

1963

Blue White, 1952, 81¾ x 76 . . . . (219) 9,492

Abstract Composition, 1953, 57¼ x 37½ . . . . (189) 10,000

Painting, 1956, 51¼ x 38¼ . . . . (247) 9,597

1964

Composition, 1951, oil and gouache on paper,
10¼ x 8¼ . . . . (368) 1,106

Red No. 2, 1954, 76¼ x 45 . . . . (431) 16,500

Composition 5809 E, 1958, 11¾ x 9 . . . . (461) 2,080

Composition, 1958, 23¾ x 35½ . . . . (367) 5,528

1966

Deep Blue, Yellow, and Red, 1956, 64 x 51½ . . . . . (734) 9,944

Tiny Blue, (1960), 18¼ x 13 . . . . (738) 2,460

Composition, oil and gouache, 29¾ x 22 . . . . (745) 3,277

1968-July 1969

Composition, 1954, 32 x 25¾ . . . . (1268) 9,280

Otto Freundlich

(1878–1943)

Birthplace: Stolp, Pomerania, Poland. Studies art history in Munich and Florence.

1905 Starts painting and sculpturing.

1908 Begins to paint in broad patches of pure color.

1909 Goes to Paris. Meets Picasso. With the Cubists, participates in many exhibitions throughout Europe.

1919 Paints his first entirely abstract pictures.

1930 Member of "Cercle et Carré" and of "Abstraction Création."

1943 Died, Poland, to which he had been deported by the Nazis.

1954 Retrospective exhibition at the Galerie Rive Droite, Paris.

Sales

DRAWINGS

1968–July 1969
Die Hervorragende II, pencil, 1913, 6¾ x 4 ..... (1240) $ 408

PAINTINGS

1961–1962
The Mother, 1921, 47½ x 39½ .... (31)   2,197
Composition, 1936, on board, 8¼ x 8¼ .... (13)   1,800
Mosaic, 7¼ x 7¼ .... (59)   540

1968–July 1969
Abstract Composition, 1931, 21½ x 18 .... (1099)   2,852

Emile Othon Friesz

(1879–1949)

Birthplace: Le Havre, France.

1895-96 With his friend Raoul Dufy enters the School of Fine Arts, Le Havre.

1897 A scholarship enables him to go to Paris.

1898 Attends the Ecole des Beaux-Arts, in the studio of Bonnat, Paris. (Dufy rejoins him here in 1900.) Soon leaves Bonnat to enter Gustave Moreau's studio, where he meets Matisse, Marquet, and Rouault. Discovers the Impressionists at Durand-Ruel's. Executes copies of the great masters of the past in the Louvre Museum, Paris.

1900 Participates in the Salon des Artistes Français, Paris.

1901 Becomes very friendly with Pissarro and spends some time with him in the Creuse district, where he meets Guillaumin.

1903 Participates in the Salon des Indépendants, Paris.

1904 Participates in the Salon d'Automne, Paris. Works at Cassis, near Marseilles.

1905 Participates in the Salon d'Automne with Matisse, Marquet, Manguin, Vlaminck, Derain, and Van Dongen—in the famous "Cage aux Fauves."

1906 Trip to Anvers. Stay at La Ciotat in the south of France with Braque.

1907 The art dealer Druet shows a great interest in his work and reserves all his forthcoming pictures. (Falls out with Druet in 1912.)

1909-11 Trips to Munich, Italy, and Portugal.

1913 Successful exhibition at the Paul Cassirer Gallery, Berlin.

1914 Teaches at the Académie Moderne, the Académie Scandinave, and the Académie de la Grande Chaumière, Paris.

1919 Several stays in Toulon and elsewhere in Provence.

1925 Wins the Carnegie prize.

1935 Executes tapestry designs for the famous Manufacture des Gobelins, near Paris.

1937 With Dufy, executes "La Seine," a mural for the Palais de Chaillot.

1938 As a member of the Carnegie Foundation Jury, makes a trip to the U.S.

1949 Died, Paris.

Sales

DRAWINGS

1961–1962
Bigot Mill, pen, 9 x 8¾ .... (106) $ 118
Landscape at l'Estaque, black chalk, 6½ x 8½ .... (106)   181
View of a Harbor, 1906, ink and charcoal, 9½ x 12½ .... (152)   275
The Loggia, colored pencil, 12½ x 19½ .... (154)   76
Figures, pen, 2½ x 3¾ .... (168)   16
Seated Nude, 1929, pencil, 13 x 9½ .... (143)   47
Standing Nude, Front View, charcoal and red chalk, 18½ x 12¼ .... (177)   64
Standing Nude, charcoal, 14 x 9½ .... (84)   69
Reclining Nude, 1930, charcoal, 11 x 16¼ .... (102)   100
Lion Asleep, red chalk, 6¾ x 9½ .... (18)   72
Composition, pencil, 13¾ x 10 .... (93)   77

1963
The Couple, blue pencil and bister wash, 7¼ x 6 .. (295)   76
The Roadstead of Toulon, colored pencil, 4½ x 13½ .... (242)   60
The Village, charcoal, 9 x 8½ .... (255)   96
Mechanic, charcoal, 8¾ x 11 .... (232)   47
Study for a Landscape, pencil, 12¾ x 16¾ .... (232)   68

1964
Studies of Figures, 8¾ x 10¼ .... (386)   180
Seated Woman Holding Her Knee, 12¾ x 15½ ... (401)   120
Standing Woman, Front View, pen, 5½ x 3¼ ..... (338)   20
Landscape of l'Estaque, black chalk, 6½ x 8½ .... (467)   148
Standing Woman, red chalk, 16¼ x 9¾ .... (378)   99
Still Life, India ink, 11 x 17¾ .... (441)   57
The Water Carrier, pencil, 12½ x 8½ .... (418)   50

1965
The Terrace; Nude, two drawings, 10¾ x 8¾ and 6¾ x 8¾ .... (488)   140
Stage Business, pencil, 6¼ x 8½ .... (612)   40

Chaville Woods, pencil, 10¾ x 8 . . . . (612) $ 30

Nude, 15½ x 10 . . . . (612)   140

The Village, black lead, 11¾ x 10 . . . . (577)   60

Adam and Eve, red chalk, 14¼ x 13½ . . . . (559)   80

The Harbor, pencil, 6¼ x 10½ . . . . (497)   140

Landscape at l'Estaque, 1907, black chalk,
6½ x 8½ . . . . (565)   208

1966

The Three-Masted Ship, pencil, double sided,
7¾ x 5 . . . . (653)   26

Cliff, 1907, ink and pencil, 7 x 8¾ . . . . (648)   275

Female Nude, 16¼ x 10¾ . . . . (672)   124

Seated Nude, 19¾ x 11 . . . . (781)   78

The Model, black lead, 9½ x 12¼ . . . . (696)   90

Seated Woman, pen, 10¾ x 11 . . . . (681)   200

Portrait of a Woman, ball-point pen, 5¼ x 4½ . . . . (674)   16

Mother and Child, 9½ x 6¼ . . . . (788)   40

Seated Nude, 17½ x 11 . . . . (824)   112

Silhouettes of Women, pencil, 9½ x 12¾ . . . . (718)   120

The Tree, 9 x 11¾ . . . . (663)   48.

Houses in a Landscape, pen, 11¾ x 17¾ . . . . (758)   96

1967

Two Bathers, red chalk, 8¼ x 6¼ . . . . (845)   40

Standing Nude, pencil, 14¾ x 10¾ . . . . (948)   30

Model Resting, black pencil, 9 x 17 . . . . (835)   70

Seated Nude, Front View, black lead, 13½ x 8 . . . . (879)   120

Peasant, red chalk, 8¼ x 6¼ . . . . (950)   28

Still Life with Fruit, blue wash, 6¾ x 8 . . . . (1007)   160

1968–July 1969

Front View of a Seated Nude, pencil, 14½ x 10 . . (1026)   104

Seated Nude, pencil, 12 x 9 . . . . (1084)   26

Seated Nude, Her Arms Raised, black pencil,
14¼ x 10 . . . . (1075)   1,000

The Lighthouse, red chalk, 12 x 18¼ . . . . (1048)   130

Ste. Adresse, pencil, 7¾ x 9¾ . . . . (1016)   28

Landscape, India ink, 9½ x 12¼ . . . . (1066)   52

Elephants Fighting, black pencil, 5 x 10 . . . . (1134)   28

Bust of a Woman, pencil, 15½ x 11½ . . . . (1221)   62

Seated Nude, charcoal on paper laid down on
canvas, 51½ x 38¼ . . . . (1224)   400

Studies, blue ink, 8 x 10 . . . . (1230)   80

Landscape with Trees, charcoal heightened with
color, 13¼ x 9 . . . . (1233)   76

Seated Young Woman, charcoal, 24½ x 18¼ . . . . (1233)   90

Bobino Music Hall, India ink and colored pencil,
6¾ x 10¼ . . . . (1234)   170

Standing Nude, 15¾ x 10¾ . . . . (1253)   100

Queen at the Court of Assyria, pencil and ink,
18¾ x 14 . . . . (1266)   50

Allegory, India ink, 2¾ x 4¾ . . . . (1266)   20

Study of a Landscape, 8¾ x 11 . . . . (1266)   22

The Forest, stick of greasepaint, 6¾ x 7½ . . . . . . (1266)   22

WATERCOLORS

1961–1962

Landscape of Lourdes, 1918, watercolor,
7¼ x 14¾ . . . . (18)   1,130

The Two Roads of the Côte-d'Or, watercolor,
8 x 10½ . . . . (58)   190

Le Havre Harbor, gouache, 27 x 21¼ . . . . (35)   600

Reclining Woman, gouache, 14¼ x 10¼ . . . . (124)   230

Standing Nude, pastel, 18¼ x 26 . . . . (34)   340

1963

Coast of Grâce, Honfleur, watercolor, 19 x 25¼ . . (254) $1,240

Landscape, watercolor, 6¼ x 14 . . . . (232)   791

1964

Nudes on the Beach, watercolor, 12½ x 19½ . . . . . (347)   2,100

Landscape of Italy, 1920, watercolor, 9½ x 11¾ . . . (405)   203

Standing Nude, Left-Side View, 1930, watercolor,
22½ x 13 . . . . (401)   320

Landscape, watercolor, 8 x 11 . . . . (321)   275

Picnic, watercolor, 12¼ x 19 . . . . (398)   400

Landscape, watercolor, 24½ x 18 . . . . (329)   950

1965

Landscape, 1907, watercolor, 8 x 10 . . . . (516)   1,680

Leda and the Swan, watercolor, 12¼ x 19½ . . . . . (617)   678

1966

Landscape of Cassis, watercolor, 10¼ x 15 . . . . . . (809)   420

Landscape, 1901, watercolor, 9½ x 14¾ . . . . (669)   244

The Mulatto, watercolor, 18½ x 8¼ . . . . (828)   80

1967

Landscape, 1939, watercolor, 17½ x 16¾ . . . . (923)   1,100

The Neighborhood of Cassis, watercolor,
12¼ x 10¼ . . . . (911)   560

Regattas, watercolor, 19 x 10 . . . . (985)   1,185

1968–July 1969

Model Resting, 1930, watercolor, 18¼ x 23¾ . . . . (1168)   240

Reclining Nude, watercolor, 17¾ x 24 . . . . (1174)   276

Seascape, (1905), watercolor, 19¾ x 25 . . . . (1060)   2,400

The Liner, watercolor, 20¼ x 23 . . . . (1200)   800

The Red Sail, watercolor, 14¼ x 19¾ . . . . (1039)   1,460

The Vine Arbor, watercolor and gouache,
13½ x 22 . . . . (1075)   520

The Jar, watercolor, 20½ x 25 . . . . (1193)   2,230

Landscape, watercolor, 8¾ x 12¼ . . . . (1221)   290

La Roche-Percée: The Bathers, watercolor,
9 x 12¼ . . . . (1238)   840

The Washboard, pastel, 15½ x 18¼ . . . . (1238)   200

The Trees on the Terrace, watercolor,
17¼ x 11¼ . . . . (1260)   360

Vase of Roses,[1] 1918, watercolor on paper laid
down on board, 22¼ x 15½ . . . . (1272)   1,920

PAINTINGS

1961–1962

La Rochelle, 13 x 18¼ . . . . (71)   1,680

The Road to l'Estaque, 1906, 18¼ x 15 . . . . (72)   3,320

Antwerp Harbor, 1906, 19¾ x 24 . . . . (102)   4,350

Honfleur Dock, 21¼ x 29 . . . . (39)   2,500

Landscape of Toulon, 1924, 20½ x 24 . . . . (6)   1,763

The Old Harbor, 21¼ x 25¾ . . . . (155)   2,900

The Model, 29¾ x 36¼ . . . . (71)   4,600

Bathers, 29 x 36¼ . . . . (120)   3,300

The Woman with a Jade Necklace, 1928,
21¾ x 18¼ . . . . (73)   780

Seated Woman in the Nude, 1928, 21¾ x 18¼ . . . . (155)   1,320

Nude with Blue Drapery, 1930, 29 x 23¾ . . . . (147)   600

Bathers on the Coast of Grâce, 1946, 15 x 18¼ . . . . (32)   1,200

Great Standing Nude,[2] 1934, on paper laid down
on canvas, 45 x 31½ . . . . (29)   1,220

[1] Inscribed "Souvenir du réveillon de la paix."
[2] Study for "La Paix" for the Palais des Nations, Geneva.

Landscape with Bathers .... (147) $1,800
Portrait of Jacqueline, 1922, 18¼ x 15 .... (143)   994
Portrait of Monsieur Paquereau, 1924, 8¼ x 6¼ ... (49)   600
Underwood, 25¾ x 21¼ .... (33)   1,420
Vase of Flowers, 5¼ x 27 .... (33)   1,640
The Gardener, 21¾ x 18¼ .... (9)   560
Rocks, 1913, 19¼ x 14¼ .... (67)   2,571
The Wine Harvest, 1920, 36¼ x 29 .... (76)   1,200
Springtime, 1929, 38¼ x 51½ .... (167)   3,800
Springtime, Toulon, 1931, 32 x 25¾ .... (116)   1,620
Rest Under the Trees, 1937, 25¾ x 32 .... (80)   3,100
Summer Delights, 1948, 40¼ x 51½ .... (73)   6,000
The Hammock, 1912, 39¼ x 59¼ .... (29)   4,800
Composition, 138¼ x 47½ .... (143)   5,650

1963
Model Resting, 1897, 15 x 18¼ .... (235)   210
Nude with Blue Drapery, 29 x 23¾ .... (262)   600
The Harbor, 1905, 23¾ x 29 .... (243)   16,000
A Bunch of Flowers, (1914), 36¼ x 29 .... (283)   4,520
Rodin's Garden Behind the Couvent des Oiseaux,
   1919, 12¾ x 17¾ .... (315)   1,371
The Garden, the Woman, and the Bird, 1922,
   46 x 35¼ .... (312)   3,400
The Terrace, 25 x 31½ .... (210)   2,104
The Wine Harvest, 1924, 25¾ x 32 .... (258)   2,500
Study for Leda, 1927, 10¾ x 17¾ .... (179)   400
Seated Young Lady, 1928, 21¾ x 18¼ .... (280)   700
The Garden, 1931, 39½ x 32 .... (232)   4,407
Rocks on La Bruyère de Noron in Normandy,
   21¼ x 25¾ .... (221)   900
Banks of a River, 1933, 21¼ x 25 .... (315)   2,468
Little Harbor, Honfleur, 1933, 17¾ x 22¼ ...... (202)   3,300
St. Malo, 1938, 15 x 18¼ .... (306)   1,420
The Road in Provence, 32 x 23¾ .... (198)   2,800
Fruit, Peaches, and Grapes, 1943, 15 x 18¼ .... (296)   1,500
Honfleur: The Estuary, 1948, 23¾ x 29 .... (318)   2,600
Tree in Blossom, 25¾ x 32 .... (640)   2,800
Standing Nude in a Landscape, 14 x 8¾ .... (188)   420
Standing Woman in the Nude, 32 x 21¼ .... (237)   800
Seated Nude, 32 x 25¾ .... (241)   1,200

1964
Country House,[3] 1892, on cardboard, 6¼ x 8¾ .... (441)   181
Seaweed Harvest, 1899, 31½ x 59 .... (401)   1,200
Antwerp Harbor,[4] 1906, 19¾ x 24 .... (409)   5,400
A Harbor, 1906, on canvas laid down on panel,
   17¾ x 12¼ .... (399)   4,000
Bathers in a Landscape, 25¾ x 32 .... (399)   2,900
St. Malo, the Harbor, 19½ x 24 .... (454)   1,244
Blue Bird, on panel, 5¼ x 11½ .... (377)   723
Portrait of His Cousin Lesieutre, 19¾ x 31½ .. (377)   1,695
Landscape, 21¼ x 25¾ .... (354)   2,100
Head of a Young Peasant of the Piedmont, 1920,
   on panel, 15¾ x 12½ .... (325)   270
Woman with a Fan, 15¼ x 18¼ .... (393)   660
Bust of a Young Woman, 1923, on canvas laid
   down on panel, 18¼ x 13 .... (399)   800
Toulon, Domaine des Jarres, 1923, 19¾ x 19¾ ... (343)   1,200
Sailboats at Honfleur, on paper laid down on
   canvas, 9½ x 14 .... (366)   860
Shed of the Moranes, 18¼ x 21¾ .... (379)   510

Grapes and Peaches, 1929, 23¾ x 29 .... (347) $1,760
Daffodils in a Vase, 18¼ x 13 .... (471)   960
The Big Jar, 25¾ x 29¼ .... (459)   1,921
A Garden Near Toulon, 1933, 19¾ x 24 .... (419)   2,000
La Ciotat, 15 x 18¼ .... (458)   3,482
Two Women Resting in the Open, 1935,
   20½ x 25¼ .... (405)   1,016
The Birds, 43 x 42¾ .... (378)   2,034
Honfleur Harbor, 21¼ x 25¾ .... (394)   4,600
House by the Riverside, (1936), 23¾ x 29 .... (441)   2,938
Auction Sale in Normandy, 17½ x 12¾ .... (416)   3,040
The Tree Planter, Honfleur, 1939, 18¼ x 15 .. (347)   1,560
The Crossroads, 1939, 25¾ x 32 .... (325)   900
Nude with Blue Drapery, 29 x 23¾ .... (382)   360
The Roofs, 17½ x 14¾ .... (405)   3,192
Landscape of the South of France, on panel,
   10½ x 14 .... (374)   850
Landscape, 21¾ x 15 .... (432)   1,280
Peace: Study for a Tapestry Design, 25¼ x 19¾ .. (393)   620

1965
Entrance of Honfleur Harbor, 21¼ x 25¾ .... (561)   2,400
Banks of the River Seine, Auteuil, 1899, on panel,
   16¼ x 24 .... (561)   7,100
The Pont-Neuf, 1903, 51 x 59¾ .... (512)   15,600
Laziness, 1909, 32 x 39½ .... (628)   8,126
Cassis,[5] (1910), 19 x 23¼ .... (598)   1,520
The Skaters, 1920, 25¾ x 27¾ .... (628)   2,612
Fishing Harbor, 15 x 17¾ .... (632)   2,600
The Bathers, 7¼ x 13½ .... (632)   1,000
Pot of Hydrangeas, 1922, 32 x 25¾ .... (532)   300
Vase of Flowers, 25¾ x 21¼ .... (553)   2,100
Springtime in Toulon, 31½ x 25¾ .... (516)   2,200
Nude with a Basket of Oranges, 10¾ x 7½ .. (516)   480
The Bathers, on cardboard, 24 x 19¾ ...... (512)   1,960
Toulon Garden, 1931, 39½ x 32 .... (564)   3,200
Bather on the Edge of a Lake, 1932, 13 x 23¾ ... (518)   3,600
Mignonne, allons voir si la rose. . . , 36¼ x 25¾ ... (511)   3,200
Portrait of a Woman, 1935, 25¾ x 21¼ ...... (567)   814
Interior with a Woman, 29 x 23¾ .... (559)   780
Garden in Honfleur, 1945, 18¾ x 16¾ ...... (507)   1,350
Honfleur, the Outlet of the Harbor, 21¼ x 25¾ ... (515)   4,600
Landscape at St. Léonard (Sarthe), 25¾ x 32¼ ... (553)   4,600
Antwerp Harbor, on canvas laid down on panel,
   17¾ x 12¼ .... (553)   5,000
The Harbor, 18¼ x 24 .... (617)   3,616
La Rochelle Harbor, 1947, 21¼ x 25¼ ...... (503)   4,400
St. Malo Harbor, 19½ x 24 .... (582)   1,437
Composition with a Bird and Fruit, 42 x 54½ ... (617)   1,424
A Bunch of Flowers, 23¾ x 29 .... (569)   4,068

1966
Ste. Anne (Provence), 1901, 18 x 23¾ .... (742)   1,040
Landscape, 1901, 22½ x 27¾ .... (701)   2,600
Village Roofs, 1904, 29 x 21¼ .... (808)   4,063
The Farmyard, 23¾ x 31½ .... (681)   3,000
Honfleur Harbor, 1905, 14¾ x 7¾ .... (812)   6,910
Presumed Portrait of Fernande Olivier, (1906),
   29 x 23¾ .... (745)   4,972
Antwerp Harbor, (1906), 20¾ x 29 .... (713)   7,500
The Harbor, 1906, 23¾ x 29 .... (686)   24,600
Landscape, 1908, 21¾ x 18 .... (784)   2,000

[3] Inscribed "Premier essai de peinture."
[4] Sold in Paris in May 1962 for $4,350.

[5] On the reverse, a sketch of the Fauve period.

Landscape, on panel, 16¼ x 13 . . . . (772) $ 700

Landscape, (1909), 11½ x 14 . . . . (745)   1,808

Landscape of Paris, (1911), 32 x 25¾ . . . . . (744)   2,486

The Forest, Jura, 1919, 32 x 25¾ . . . . . . (797)   4,294

Three Young Girls in a Garden, (1920-23),
25 x 31¼ . . . . (757)   2,764

Suzanna and the Old Men, (1924), 17½ x 13 . . . . (758)   680

Landscape of the Jura, (1925), 29 x 23¾ . . . . (815)   2,073

The Glade, 18¼ x 15 . . . . (781)   620

Window Looking Out on the Harbor, Toulon,
(1927), 25¾ x 21½ . . . . (742)   2,760

Wrapped Nude on a Sofa, 23¾ x 29 . . . . . . (811)   1,400

Toulon Harbor, 1929, 23¾ x 29 . . . . (815)   4,422

View of Toulon, 25¾ x 32 . . . . (814)   3,500

Toulon Harbor, 27½ x 16 . . . . (711)   2,620

Little Mediterranean Harbor, oil on paper,
14 x 19¾ . . . . (666)   500

Mediterranean Village, 19¾ x 24 . . . . (685)   6,020

Landscape at La Rocca Parvera (Piedmont),
21 x 25¼ . . . . (701)   2,100

La Rochelle Harbor, 21 x 25¾ . . . . (798)   5,876

St. Malo, 25 x 31¾ . . . . (808)   3,773

The Creek, on cardboard, 13 x 15¾ . . . . . . (793)   860

The Fisherman, 21 x 25¼ . . . . (809)   1,900

The Angler, 19¾ x 24 . . . . (724)   800

Fishing Harbor, 30 x 32½ . . . . (727)   5,100

Flowers in a Vase, 18¼ x 15 . . . . (758)   900

1967

Norman Farm, 1939, 25¾ x 32 . . . . (901)   3,000

Landscape, 1905, 12¼ x 17¾ . . . . (965)   9,492

The Regattas, 1906, 23 x 32½ . . . . (864)   23,000

Landscape, (1909), 11½ x 14 . . . . (918)   3,616

Rocks, Toulon, 1913, 19½ x 24¼ . . . . (1006)   1,742

House on the Outskirts of a Forest, 1919,
25 x 31¼ . . . . (985)   1,896

The Cypresses, 1924 . . . . (986)   1,476

Flowers in a Vase, 31½ x 25¾ . . . . (893)   4,000

Reclining Nude on a Green Sofa, 1927,
21¼ x 26 . . . . (934)   700

Bather, 25¾ x 21 . . . . (989)   3,250

Young Woman on a Green Sofa, 23½ x 29 . . . . (912)   1,760

Toulon Harbor, 1935, 23¼ x 28½ . . . . (888)   3,179

Boats at Sea, 15 x 21¾ . . . . (923)   2,200

St. Malo, 1938, 15 x 18¼ . . . . (898)   2,200

Honfleur Dock, 25¾ x 32 . . . . (911)   7,600

Sodom and Gomorrah, 15¾ x 11¾ . . . . (995)   720

Bathers in a Landscape, 1939, 25¾ x 32 . . . . (987)   3,800

The Crossroads, 1939, 25 x 31½ . . . . (888)   2,488

Fellow Student, 21¾ x 15 . . . . (848)   700

Flowers and Fruit on a Red Background, 1940, on
panel, 16¼ x 22½ . . . . (862)   110

Still Life, 8¼ x 10 . . . . (926)   384

Nude with a Japanese Vase, 1944, 21¾ x 18¼ . . . (943)   460

Nude with a Mirror, on canvas laid down on
panel, 21 x 14¼ . . . . (865)   550

The House Amid the Trees, 21½ x 25¾ . . . . . (912)   4,000

Harbor Scene, 19¾ x 25¾ . . . . (841)   1,500

Bathers in a Landscape, 29 x 23¾ . . . . (935)   1,800

Garden in Honfleur, 1945, 18½ x 16½ . . . . . (935)   840

Seated Nude, 22 x 18¼ . . . . (912)   900

The Fountain, 31½ x 25¾ . . . . (985)   1,090

Reclining Nude, 21¼ x 25¾ . . . . (967)   1,130

Interior with Women, 19¾ x 24 . . . . (995)   3,700

1968–July 1969

Landscape of the Creuse Valley, (1905), (recto),
Snowy Landscape, (1903), (verso),
25¾ x 33½ . . . . (1173) $11,960

The Red Cart, 23¾ x 32 . . . . (1173)   4,600

Roofs of a Little Town, 1904, 29 x 21¼ . . . . . (1126)   3,965

The Rocks at Crozant, 1902, 32¾ x 23¾ . . . . (1109)   900

Antwerp Harbor, (1906), 15 x 17¾ . . . . . . (1125)   15,640

Pinnaces, Antwerp Harbor, 1906, 23½ x 29 . . . (1152)   33,000

Landscape of Portugal, (1907), 11½ x 14¼ . . . . (1117)   4,600

Seaside: The Walk, 1914, 21¼ x 29 . . . . . . (1189)   7,400

Bathers on the Beach, 7½ x 10¾ . . . . (1210)   760

The Skaters, 1920, 25¾ x 32¼ . . . . (1187)   3,068

Bathers, Le Havre, 1921, on panel, 13 x 16¼ . . . (1200)   4,000

Portrait of Monsieur Paquereau, 1923,
58½ x 49¾ . . . . (1077)   1,000

Bathers, 1924, 45¾ x 35¼ . . . . (1060)   7,680

Seated Nude, 1924, 13½ x 10¾ . . . . (1070)   1,888

Bathers, 29 x 36¼ . . . . (1106)   2,620

Nude with a Mirror, on canvas, 20½ x 14¼ . . . (1042)   160

The Veranda, 1928, 25¾ x 32 . . . . (1049)   3,800

Toulon Harbor, 1929, 18¼ x 14¼ . . . . (1121)   5,200

Toulon, Cronstadt Quay, 1929, 23¾ x 29 . . . . (1157)   6,700

Resting in the Garden, Toulon, 32 x 26½ . . . . (1053)   3,800

Toulon Harbor, 19¾ x 25¾ . . . . (1053)   700

Nude in Front of an Open Window, 29 x 23¾ . . . (1138)   1,982

Toulon Harbor, 1929, 18¼ x 21¾ . . . . (1138)   2,726

The Woman with a Green Hat, (1930), 32 x 23½ . (1126)   991

House in Provence, 23¾ x 29 . . . . (1116)   800

Figures in a Garden, 1930, 23 x 28½ . . . . . (1132)   1,062

St. Malo Harbor, 1935, 21¼ x 25¾ . . . . . . (1202)   6,400

St. Malo Harbor, 1938, 25 x 31½ . . . . (1070)   6,608

St. Malo, 15 x 18¼ . . . . (1026)   2,520

Landscape, on cardboard, 10½ x 14 . . . . . . (1078)   290

Honfleur Harbor, 19¾ x 24 . . . . (1125)   5,750

Garden in Honfleur, 1945, 17¾ x 16½ . . . . . (1019)   720

Honfleur Harbor, 25¾ x 32 . . . . (1200)   8,000

Battleships in Toulon Harbor, 28¾ x 36¼ . . . . (1057)   6,000

La Roccasparuera, 21 x 25½ . . . . (1113)   2,000

Mandolin, Skull, and Shell, 23 x 28½ . . . . . (1187)   590

Buddha, 25¼ x 19 . . . . (1051)   1,200

Still Life with Chrysanthemums, 18¼ x 15 . . . . (1147)   800

Still Life, 46½ x 54½ . . . . (1018)   1,250

Aquarium, 29 x 23¾ . . . . (1174)   2,760

The Gully, 18 x 13¼ . . . . (1225)   560

Bathers, 29 x 36½ . . . . (1226)   2,400

The Open Window, 29 x 23¾ . . . . (1228)   2,800

Seated Nude, 21¾ x 15 . . . . (1235)   3,100

*Still Life: Watermelon, Eight Peaches, and a
Vase,* 19¼ x 23½ . . . . (1240)   1,920

Bridge in a Landscape, (1910), 10½ x 13½ . . . . (1240)   1,800

Roofs, 17½ x 14½ . . . . (1241)   4,030

The Shepherd, 21 x 25½ . . . . (1241)   35,300

The Dahlias, 18¼ x 14¾ . . . . (1245)   1,040

Portrait of a Woman, 15¾ x 12½ . . . . (1245)   184

Still Life, on panel, 12¾ x 19 . . . . (1247)   820

Portrait of a Woman, 18¼ x 14¼ . . . . (1247)   820

Still Life, on board, 16 x 13 . . . . (1248)   850

The Creuse at Crozant, 1901, 21¼ x 29 . . . . . (1252)   10,220

The Harbor Seen from the Hill, 25¾ x 32 . . . . (1255)   6,800

La Roccasparuera, Italy, 1920, 21¼ x 25½ . . . . (1255)   2,820

St. Malo Roofs and Harbor, 1938, 21¼ x 25¾ . . . (1255)   3,200

Sailboats in the Harbor, 18¼ x 25¾ . . . . . . (1255)   2,300

Nude Seated on a Sofa, 36½ x 25¾ . . . . (1255) $1,400
The Hill with Olive Trees Near Toulon,
   23¼ x 28½ . . . . (1255)   2,000
Honfleur: The Entrance of the Harbor,
   18¼ x 24 . . . . (1258)   6,820
Oriental Garden, 25¾ x 32 . . . . (1258)   2,500
The Italian Girl, 18¼ x 15 . . . . (1258)   560
Village at the Bottom of the Mountains, 1902,
   19¾ x 23¾ . . . . (1260)   1,400
Roses, 24½ x 19¾ . . . . (1260)   600
Honfleur Dock, 25¾ x 32 . . . . (1261)   6,600
Bather, 29 x 23¾ . . . . (1262)   4,200
The Pond, (1891), on cardboard, 13½ x 11½ . . . . . (1268)   1,299
Nude, 17½ x 17 . . . . (1268)   1,160
Flowers, 1926, 25¾ x 19½ . . . . (1268)   3,944
Roses, on cradled panel, 23½ x 17 . . . . (1268)   1,694
Flowers, 15 x 14¼ . . . . (1268)   6,728
Landscape at Cassis, (1906-07), 24½ x 31½ . . . . . (1270)   13,920
Honfleur Harbor, (1911), 23¾ x 29¼ . . . . (1273)   7,060

Paul Gauguin

(1848-1903)

Birthplace: Paris, France.

1865   Enlists in the navy.

1871   Works with a stockbroker in Paris and meets Schuffenecker, who is to be his backer in times of
trouble.

1873   Marries Mette-Sophie Gad, a Danish woman.

1874   Starts painting as a hobby and acquires an important collection of Impressionist pictures.

1876   Meets Pissarro.

1880-82   Participates in the fifth, sixth, and seventh Impressionist exhibitions, Paris.

1883   Decides to give up his work and devote himself entirely to painting.

1886   Reduced to a state of extreme poverty. First stay at
Pont-Aven, Brittany. Participates in the last Im-
pressionist exhibition, Paris. Meets Van Gogh in
Paris.

1887   Travels to Panama and the West Indies.

1888   Second stay in Pont-Aven, where he meets Emile
Bernard; they set up Synthesism and Cloisonism.
First one-man show at Boussod and Valadon, Paris. Follows his friend Van Gogh to Arles in the
south of France. Subsequently they have a falling
out. Returns to Paris.

1889   Exhibition of the Impressionist and Synthesist
group at the Café Volpini, Paris. This exhibition
exerts a great influence on the Nabis. Third stay
in Pont-Aven.

1891   Decides to leave for Tahiti and spends some time
there, working very hard.

1893   Lack of money and poor health cause him to return
to France. Exhibits at Durand-Ruel's, Paris.

1894   Fourth stay in Pont-Aven.

1895   Second journey to Tahiti. Despite extreme depression, even to the point of attempted suicide, he
paints most of his masterpieces.

1900   Settles in the Marquesas Islands.

1903   Died.

Sales

DRAWINGS

1961-1962

Study of Women and a Horse, charcoal,
   10¾ x 9 . . . . (85) $ 180
Studies of Young Boys' Heads, charcoal, double
   sided, 6 x 4½ . . . . (57)   104
Trees on a Beach in Tahiti (recto), *Men and Pigs*
   (verso), pencil and watercolor, 4½ x 6½ . . . . . (128)   769
Head of a Tahitian,[1] charcoal, 10 x 7¼ . . . . (128)   1,922
Maori Head[2] (recto), *Back View of a Tahitian*
   (verso), pencil, 6¼ x 4 . . . . (102)   580
Tahitians, red chalk and pastel, cut into an
   irregular shape at the top, 10 x 8¼ . . . . (50)   1,640

1963

*Study Sheet: Harvesttime and Head of a Young
   Breton Lady,* black and colored pencil with
   watercolor, 10¾ x 7¼ . . . . (219)   1,808
Fishermen's Wives, charcoal, 11¾ x 8 . . . . (226)   568
Study of Animals, pencil and watercolor, double
   sided, 6¼ x 11¾ . . . . (296)   320
Study of a Landscape, and Hands, black pencil,
   double sided, 6 x 4½ . . . . (291)   320
Peasant and Her Child, pencil and watercolor,
   10 x 7½ . . . . (255)   823
Portrait of Ingeborg Taulow,[3] bister ink, 2 x 3 . . . . (265)   224
The Woodcutter, 1891, ink, 12¾ x 8½ . . . . (210)   3,016
Study of a Landscape, Figures, and Hands, black
   pencil, double sided, 6 x 4½ . . . . (221)   290
Maori Head, pencil, 6¼ x 4 . . . . (190)   420
Two Tahitian Women, (1894), pen and pencil,
   9¼ x 7¾ . . . . (210)   2,742
Two Tahitians with Idols, ink, 10 x 7½ . . . . (210)   1,234
Parau no te varua ino; Tahitian Legend, (1892),
   two drawings on the same sheet, pencil,
   6 x 3¾ . . . . (210)   2,331

1964

Study of Animals, double sided, charcoal, 15 x 9 . . (339)   400
Study of Cows, double sided, pencil, 4½ x 6 . . . . . . (329)   475
Child Leaning on a Chair, charcoal on mauve
   paper, 10¼ x 8 . . . . (321)   1,200
Tahiti Notebook, double sided, 6½ x 4¼ . . . . (383)   859
Study of Tahitians: Three Heads (recto), *One
   Head* (verso), pencil, 6¼ x 3¾ . . . . (368)   829
Squatting Tahitian, charcoal, 9½ x 7¼ . . . . (416)   884

1965

Study of Men and Animals, red chalk,
   15¼ x 20¾ . . . . (630)   1,120
*Aline, the Artist's Daughter, Putting On Her
   Socks,* black chalk, 10¼ x 12¼ . . . . (623)   710

---

[1] Inscribed "Mon cher David."
[2] Page of the Tahiti notebook.
[3] Gauguin's sister-in-law.

Heads of Tahitians, double sided, on a notebook
   sheet, 6¼ x 4 . . . . **(598)** $ 500
Dancer, 2¾ x 2½ . . . . **(577)**   160
Tahitian's Head, (1896), (recto), ink and wash,
   (verso), pencil and red chalk, 5¼ x 4½ . . . . **(535)**   3,317
Peasants, charcoal, 10¾ x 9 . . . . **(606)**   1,300

1966

A Laundress in Profile, 1888, (recto), *Bust of a*
   Young Boy (verso), colored pencil, 6½ x 4 . . . **(681)**   800
Village Street with Figures in Brittany, 1888,
   (recto), *Two Geese, a Peasant, a Small*
   Breton (verso), colored pencil, 6½ x 4 . . . . **(681)**   1,200
Little Breton with a Jug, 1888, (recto), *Little*
   Breton Filling a Jug at the Fountain (verso),
   colored pencil, 6½ x 4 . . . . **(681)**   1,220
Children and Women's Heads (recto), *Man*
   Fighting a Bear (verso), 6½ x 4 . . . . **(681)**   560
Studies of Children's Heads, a Woman, and
   Silhouettes of Figures, pen, double sided,
   6½ x 4 . . . . **(681)**   900
Study of Cows, charcoal, 12¼ x 8 . . . . **(734)**   226
Portrait of a Man,[4] *and Head of Poppi the Dog*
   (recto), *Two Men's Heads* (verso), black
   pencil . . . . **(681)**   360
Two Tahitians, (1895-01), blue pencil, black lead,
   and monotype, double sided, 25 x 20¼ . . . . **(686)**   30,404
Tahitian's Head (recto), *Self-Portrait* (verso), pen
   and color wash, 12 x 7½ . . . . **(812)**   3,317

1967

Study for the Tahitian Nativity, (1902), charcoal
   and colored pencil, 10¼ x 8 . . . . **(881)**   3,040
Tahitian: Study of a Hand, pencil, charcoal, and
   wash, 12 x 8 . . . . **(951)**   580

1968–July 1969

Study of a Tahitian, pencil, double sided,
   14¼ x 10¾ . . . . **(1113)**   2,000
Squatting Woman, charcoal, 10 x 7 . . . . **(1080)**   1,700
Bust of a Woman, 1901, 12¼ x 10 . . . . **(1181)**   1,040
Portrait of Mette Gauguin, charcoal on gray-blue
   paper, 5½ x 4½ . . . . **(1138)**   793
Study of a Tahitian; Study of a Hand Holding a
   Mandolin, black pencil and India ink,
   12 x 8 . . . . **(1240)**   960
Study of Naked Children, black lead, double
   sided, 11¾ x 9 . . . . **(1256)**   640

WATERCOLORS

1961–1962

Landscape: Martinique, 1887-88, gouache,
   12¾ x 19¾ . . . . **(88)**   13,530
Childhood in Brittany, 1889, watercolor,
   10 x 14¾ . . . . **(125)**   17,600
Brittany, fan-shaped watercolor, 4¾ x 16¾ . . . . . . **(125)**   3,000
View of Notre-Dame de Paris, watercolor and
   pencil, 7¾ x 10¼ . . . . **(106)**   1,266
Tahitian's Head, watercolor, 3 x 1¾ . . . . **(97)**   200
Tahitian Leaning to the Right, Her Hands on Her
   Knees, irregular-shaped watercolor, 8¾ x 4 . . . **(50)**   3,700
Ictus, watercolor heightened with oil, 16 x 21¾ . . . **(116)**   5,400

1964

A Farm at Pont-Aven, watercolor, 10¾ x 6¾ . . . . . **(371)**   7,600
Tahitian's Head, watercolor, 9¼ x 7¾ . . . . **(378)**   3,390
The Fagot Gatherer, pastel and charcoal,
   18¼ x 15 . . . . **(458)**   13,059

1965

Portrait of Richard Lund, pastel, 9½ x 7½ . . . . **(629)** $4,146

1966

Landscape of Brittany, (1888-90), watercolor,
   7½ x 11½ . . . . **(812)**   3,455
Woody Path, watercolor, 13½ x 10 . . . . **(770)**   2,769

1967

Aline and Pola, 1885, pastel, 28 x 20½ . . . . **(982)**   60,435

1968–July 1969

Young Girl with a Mandolin, 1885, fan-shaped
   gouache on silk, 5¾ x 21¼ . . . . **(1049)**   15,600
Portrait of Clovis, (1882), pastel, 11 x 10 . . . . **(1176)**   18,000
Landscape, gouache, 10 x 6¾ . . . . **(1097)**   2,838
Ictus, watercolor slightly heightened with oil,
   16 x 21¾ . . . . **(1109)**   5,000
Decorative Design for a Piece of Furniture,[5]
   watercolor and gouache, 16¼ x 23½ . . . . **(1258)**   10,000

PAINTINGS

1961–1962

Still Life with Oysters, 1876, 21 x 36¾ . . . . **(76)**   27,000
Vase of Flowers, 1885, 13¼ x 10¼ . . . . **(112)**   19,222
Landscape Near Rouen, 1884, 23½ x 28½ . . . . **(137)**   47,500
Landscape of Brittany, Cow in a Meadow, 1885 . . **(128)**   21,968
The Rue de Vaugirard, 21¾ x 19¼ . . . . **(114)**   24,000
Portrait of the Painter Roy, 16 x 12¾ . . . . **(116)**   12,600
Village of Martinique, 1887, 17½ x 27¼ . . . . **(128)**   9,611
Girl of Martinique Squatting in the Grass,
   10¾ x 8¾ . . . . **(26)**   12,000
Tahitian with a Yellow Skirt, 4¾ x 8¼ . . . . **(70)**   13,430
Standing Tahitian, (1898-99), on a door with
   panes, 39½ x 21¼ . . . . **(83)**   35,698

1963

Le Petit Laveur,[6] 1887, 17¾ x 12¾ . . . . **(210)**   30,162
The Dance of the Three Breton Girls, 1888,
   28 x 34½ . . . . **(245)**   205,650
The Laundress, (1894), 35¼ x 29 . . . . **(279)**   110,000
Still Life with a Cup of Fruit and a Jug,
   12¾ x 18¼ . . . . **(241)**   5,200
Farm in Brittany, 17¾ x 12¼ . . . . **(254)**   14,000
Landscape of Brittany, on panel, 18¾ x 25 . . . . . . **(243)**   12,400
Landscape of Brittany, 13½ x 10¼ . . . . **(247)**   19,194
The Road, 24 x 19¾ . . . . **(194)**   18,000

1964

Landscape of Brittany, 1879, 11¾ x 17¾ . . . . **(458)**   13,059
Brook, Brittany, 1883, 15 x 18¼ . . . . **(464)**   15,600
The Entrance of the Village, 1889, 21 x 13¼ . . . . . **(340)**   15,000
Tahitian with a Boy, 1899, 36¾ x 23 . . . . **(453)**   248,760
"Heureux les pauvres d'esprit, car le Royaume
   des Cieux leur appartient," on panel,
   24½ x 12¼ . . . . **(405)**   871
Still Life with Three Peaches, 17¾ x 21 . . . . **(369)**   5,822

1965

Landscape of Brittany, 1873, 9½ x 13½ . . . . **(496)**   4,970
A Glade, 15 x 18¼ . . . . **(551)**   1,200
Houses in the Country, 1874, 10¼ x 13 . . . . **(629)**   5,524
Landscape of Viroflay, 1875, on canvas laid down
   on board, 18½ x 12¾ . . . . **(624)**   11,056

---

[4] Schuffenecker on Gauchi-Taylor.

[5] Inscribed "Gauguin Stupidit."
[6] Martinique.

The Garden of the Rue Carcel at Vaugirard, 1879,
22 x 18 .... (575) $38,696
Emile Gauguin, 8¼ x 6¼ .... (583) 5,514
The Square Pond, 1884, 21¼ x 25¾ .... (539) 32,500
Bathing in Front of Pont-Aven Harbor, 1886,
32 x 23¾ .... (526) 62,500
Joan of Arc, 1889, fresco mounted on panel,
46 x 23 .... (594) 65,000
"La Maison du Pan Du," 1890, 19½ x 23¾ .... (522) 77,392
Hina Maruru (Fête à la lune), 1893, 36¾ x 27¾ ... (594) 275,000

1966

Bathing at the Mill of Bois-d'Amour, Pont-Aven,
1886, 23¾ x 29 .... (812) 95,358
The Wave, 1888, 23¾ x 28¾ .... (713) 150,000
Christmas Eve (The Blessing of the Oxen),
28 x 32¼ .... (808) 139,296

1967

The Horse Pond, 1885, 17¾ x 21¾ .... (954) 30,000

1968–July 1969

Sailboats Alongside a Quay, 29 x 23½ .... (1106) 66,000
Little Girl Lying in a Meadow, 1884, 29 x 23¾ ... (1057) 57,500
The Boat, 1896, 19¾ x 14¼ .... (1132) 51,920

Gen-Paul
(Eugène Paul)
(1895–   )

Birthplace: Montmartre, Paris, France.

1918 Seriously wounded during World War I, he returns to Paris. Works as a cornetist at the Cirque Bouglione, Paris. (Always shows much relish for musical instruments.) Decides to devote himself to painting and studies by himself. Meets painters such as Suzanne Valadon, Utrillo, Leprin, and Jean Dufy.

1923–24 Gradually elaborates his own style, grounded in incisive drawing and akin to Expressionism. His favorite subject matters are musicians, clowns, horse races, portraits, and views of Montmartre. Works mostly in colored pencil, gouache, and oil. Visits France and Spain. Exhibits at the Breckpod Gallery, Antwerp. Exhibits at the Saville Gallery, London. First trip to the U.S.—to which he returns in 1934 and 1937.

1926 First one-man show in Paris at the Galerie Bing. Participates in the Salon d'Automne, Paris. Executes a series of engravings for the Galerie Guiot, Paris. Meets Vlaminck, Derain, Marcel Aymé, and Francis Carco. Also makes friends with a great number of renowned actors and musicians.

1927 Participates in the Salon des Indépendants, Paris.

1928 Signs a contract with the Galerie Bernheim-Jeune, Paris.

1940 Stays in Marseilles.

1947 Stays in the U.S., to which he frequently returns. Starts to execute colored lithographs.

1952 Retrospective exhibition at the Galerie Drouant-David, Paris.

1953 Birth of his son Gen Paul.

1965 Exhibition at the Galerie Chalom, Paris.
Resident in Montmartre, Paris.

Sales

DRAWINGS

1961–1962

Creixmans and His Friend, 1929, black lead,
9½ x 6 .... (58) $ 60
Moulin de la Galette, colored pencil, 10¾ x 15 .... (25) 160
Place du Tertre, colored pencil, 9½ x 12¾ .... (177) 116
La Java, charcoal and watercolor, 16¾ x 10¼ .... (154) 130
Musician Clown, colored pencil, 16¼ x 10¾ ...... (168) 120
Riders, colored pencil, 11¾ x 16¼ .... (79) 120
Flowers, 1954, colored pencil, 11½ x 8¼ .... (52) 60
Portrait of Sidney Bechet, colored pencil,
17 x 11¾ .... (27) 330

1963

Flowers, colored pencil, 16 x 10 .... (251) 100
Horse Races, colored pencil, 10¾ x 15 .... (234) 142
Horse Races, colored pencil, 15¾ x 11½ .... (281) 136
The Saxophonist, 1957, colored pencil, 15 x 11 ... (314) 120
Musician Clown, colored pencil, 15 x 10¼ .... (287) 300
The Musician, colored pencil, 15 x 8¼ .... (276) 1,300

1964

Horse Races, colored pencil, 11¾ x 15¾ .... (370) 150
Races, colored pencil, 11¾ x 8¼ .... (414) 74
Corrida Scene, colored pencil, 18¾ x 23¾ .... (426) 200
Card Players, pencil, 8¼ x 10¼ .... (441) 108
Flowers, colored pencil, 16¼ x 11 .... (409) 110
Accordionist Clown, colored pencil, 16 x 12 ...... (376) 110
The Flutist, colored pencil, 11½ x 8¼ .... (375) 140
The Théâtre de l'Atelier, colored pencil,
10¼ x 10 .... (430) 130

1965

Card Players, colored pencil and India ink,
17½ x 17¾ .... (564) 360
Races, colored pencil, 16¼ x 20½ .... (529) 150
Rue Lepic, 1953, colored pencil, 14 x 17½ .... (563) 120
The Picador, colored pencil, 15¾ x 11¾ .... (548) 96
Woman at Her Toilette, 1955, colored pencil,
11¼ x 7¾ .... (512) 130
The Violoncellist, colored pencil, 19½ x 12¾ ..... (567) 565
Bunch of Flowers, 1961, colored pencil,
16¼ x 11 .... (534) 80

1966

Card Players, ink and colored pencil,
26½ x 19¾ .... (742) 220
Café Scene, (1923–24), charcoal with gouache
lights, 19 x 25¾ .... (757) 498
Christ on the Cross, wash, 16 x 10 .... (655) 100
Alma Railway, colored pencil, 18¾ x 25¼ .... (793) 200
The Musician, colored pencil heightened with
gouache, 16 x 11 .... (762) 140
The Clarinet Player, colored pencil, 15¾ x 10¼ ... (674) 100
The Violinist, ink and colored pencil,
14¼ x 10¼ .... (796) 220
Races, colored pencil, 16¼ x 21 .... (798) 249
Vase of Flowers, colored pencil, 19 x 12¼ .... (788) 80
Woman's Head, colored pencil. .... (827) 130

1967

Flowers, colored pencil, 17¾ x 12¾ .... (832) 80
Vase of Flowers, colored pencil, 15 x 10¾ .... (879) 42

The Street, 1924, watercolor, 11¾ x 17¾ . . . . **(887)** $ 300

The Quartet, gouache, 19½ x 25¼ . . . . **(995)**   380

Rider, watercolor, 19¾ x 26 . . . . **(967)**   791

1968–July 1969

Montmartre d'hier à aujourd'hui, gouache,
20¼ x 12¾ . . . . **(1012)**   110

The Game of Cards, pastel and India ink,
25 x 19 . . . . **(1174)**   299

The Legionnaire, 1929, watercolor, 24¼ x 19 . . . . **(1179)**   680

The Quartet, watercolor and gouache, 19½ x 25 . **(1026)**   260

Cyclists in Cannes, gouache, 18¼ x 23¾ . . . . , **(1059)**   119

Marseilles, watercolor, 19 x 24½ . . . . **(1115)**   230

A Ride, watercolor, 18¾ x 28½ . . . . **(1213)**   260

Christ, watercolor, 16¾ x 11 . . . . **(1213)**   70

Notre-Dame and the Banks of the River Seine,
watercolor, 18¾ x 24½ . . . . **(1162)**   270

Horsemen Riding, varnished gouache, 19 x 25 . . . **(1118)**   800

The Accordionist and the Guitar Player, gouache,
25 x 19½ . . . . **(1196)**   600

Street Decked with Flags, gouache, 14¼ x 20¼ . . **(1103)**   440

Geneva, watercolor, 19 x 25¼ . . . . **(1183)**   210

Horse Races, watercolor and gouache,
18¼ x 24½ . . . . **(1220)**   180

The Moulin Rouge, watercolor, 17¾ x 25 . . . . **(1223)**   220

Card Players, gouache, 25 x 19 . . . . **(1225)**   240

Walking in the Bois, gouache, 19 x 25 . . . . **(1226)**   640

The Equestrienne, gouache, 19¼ x 25¼ . . . . **(1226)**   840

Fishing Harbor, watercolor and gouache,
19½ x 25 . . . . **(1226)**   900

Cannes, gouache, 19¾ x 25¾ . . . . **(1228)**   640

Horse Races, watercolor, 19½ x 24½ . . . . **(1228)**   310

Rue Lepic, watercolor, 19½ x 24½ . . . . **(1228)**   580

Musician Clowns, gouache, 25 x 19 . . . . **(1233)**   240

Robinson, gouache, 14 x 12½ . . . . **(1238)**   440

At the Horse Races: Jumping Over the River,
19 x 25 . . . . **(1243)**   700

Montmartre Under Snow, gouache, 19½ x 25½ . . **(1244)**   940

Longchamp: The Paddock, gouache and
watercolor, 17¾ x 23½ . . . . **(1246)**   750

Horse Races, gouache, 19¾ x 25¾ . . . . **(1247)**   590

The Game of Bowls, watercolor, 18¼ x 15 . . . . . . **(1247)**   320

Card Players, India ink heightened with colored
pencil, 25¾ x 19¾ . . . . **(1247)**   220

A Rider, Avenue du Bois, watercolor, 19 x 25¾ . . **(1262)**   820

The Pont-Neuf: Equestrian Statue of Henri IV,
gouache, 19 x 25 . . . . **(1262)**   230

The Moulin Rouge, gouache, 19 x 25 . . . . **(1262)**   240

The Artist's Studio, 1928, gouache, 19¾ x 26 . . . . **(1265)**   1,060

Place Pigalle, 1930, gouache, 19¾ x 26 . . . . **(1265)**   960

PAINTINGS

1961–1962

The Black Train, 28½ x 35½ . . . . **(30)**   2,440

Cars, 23½ x 33½ . . . . **(111)**   700

Vase of Flowers, 21¾ x 13 . . . . **(25)**   440

Clown, on panel, 21¾ x 13 . . . . **(154)**   640

The Flutist, on cardboard, 21½ x 13 . . . . **(60)**   900

The Saxophonist, 36½ x 23¾ . . . . **(29)**   2,600

Portrait of a Little Boy, 16¼ x 9½ . . . . **(39)**   700

Horse Races, 18¼ x 21¾ . . . . **(109)**   960

Races, 19 x 25¼ . . . . **(152)**   968

Cyclists, 35½ x 23¼ . . . . **(152)**   1,500

Street with a Cyclist, 25¾ x 32 . . . . **(32)**   3,020

At the Café, 25¾ x 32 . . . . **(32)**   2,060

The Guinguette and the Bowls Players,
29 x 36½ . . . . **(160)** $2,600

Jockeys on Horseback, 16¼ x 10¾ . . . . **(43)**   260

Races in Auteuil, 19¾ x 25¾ . . . . **(26)**   1,160

Self-Portrait with a Cornet, 21¾ x 13 . . . . **(117)**   180

Portrait of the Artist Disguised, 21½ x 18¼ . . . . . **(144)**   1,210

1963

Violoncellist, on panel, 14 x 9 . . . . **(234)**   320

Violoncellist, on panel, 21½ x 12¾ . . . . **(179)**   575

Violinist, on panel, 13½ x 8¼ . . . . **(281)**   633

Clown Playing the Violin, on panel, 14 x 8¾ . . . . . **(295)**   360

The Clown, 21¾ x 13 . . . . **(254)**   360

Chez Léon, 32 x 25¾ . . . . **(232)**   1,469

The Place du Tertre, 25¾ x 32 . . . . **(241)**   1,160

Portrait of Frank Will, 29 x 23¾ . . . . **(293)**   780

The Parisian, oil on pavatex, 16¼ x 10¾ . . . . **(281)**   1,220

Portrait of a Child, 21¾ x 13 . . . . **(185)**   600

Races, 17¾ x 25¾ . . . . **(251)**   420

Racehorses, 19¾ x 26 . . . . **(314)**   620

Cyclists, 29 x 36½ . . . . **(276)**   2,300

The Beach at Cette, 25¾ x 32 . . . . **(318)**   2,800

1964

Maisons-Laffitte Station, 1928, 29 x 36½ . . . . **(399)**   1,640

The Saxophonist, 21¾ x 13 . . . . **(412)**   520

Violinist Clown, 1946, peinture à l'essence on
paper laid down on canvas, 13 x 9¾ . . . . **(351)**   310

Portrait of Frank Will, 29 x 23¾ . . . . **(379)**   1,220

Races, 19¾ x 25¾ . . . . **(382)**   620

The Violinist, 36 x 23¾ . . . . **(438)**   850

St. Paul in Montmartre, 23¾ x 31½ . . . . **(427)**   1,300

Rue Lepic, 24 x 29¼ . . . . **(471)**   3,729

St. Raphael, 29 x 36½ . . . . **(366)**   1,700

Bois-Colombes Station, 32 x 25¾ . . . . **(341)**   1,800

Woman with a Green Pullover, on pavatex,
16¼ x 10¾ . . . . **(377)**   1,243

Vase of Flowers, 25¾ x 21¼ . . . . **(371)**   2,000

1965

The Café-Tabac of Old Montmartre, 1914,
21¼ x 25¾ . . . . **(516)**   1,800

The Violinist, (1925), 36½ x 23¾ . . . . **(503)**   2,000

Musician Clown, 36½ x 23¾ . . . . **(621)**   960

Musician Clown, on panel, 21¾ x 13 . . . . **(599)**   400

Rue Lepic, 23¾ x 29 . . . . **(537)**   4,181

Riverside at Tourtoirac, Dordogne, 29 x 36½ . . . . **(572)**   620

The Harmonica Player, on panel, 25¾ x 13 . . . . . **(619)**   800

A Horse and His Jockey, on board, 15¾ x 10 . . . . **(624)**   636

Flowers and Fruit, 21¾ x 18¼ . . . . **(513)**   800

Young Lady with a Doll, 27¾ x 23 . . . . **(589)**   1,000

1966

Little Girl Seated, 1924, 29 x 23¾ . . . . **(798)**   2,034

Vase of Flowers, (1927), 21¾ x 18¼ . . . . **(727)**   1,420

Child with a Pink Pullover, 1928, 21¾ x 18¼ . . . . **(745)**   2,260

Woman's Head, on panel, 18¼ x 12¾ . . . . **(796)**   460

Flowers in a Vase, 1937, gouache, 25¾ x 19½ . . . . **(829)**   400

The Moulin de la Galette in Winter, 23¾ x 29 . . . . **(731)**   920

Musician, on panel, 21¾ x 13 . . . . **(809)**   700

Rider, 21 x 12¼ . . . . **(659)**   460

Start of the Races, 1950, 19¾ x 25¾ . . . . **(820)**   520

Flowers in a Vase, 24 x 15 . . . . **(814)**   600

LaGamine, 21¾ x 14¾ . . . . **(742)**   360

Long Live Toulouse-Lautrec, 1965, 36½ x 29 . . . . . **(729)**   440

1967

Place du Tertre, 21¼ x 26 . . . . (919)	$1,921
Chez Léon, 25¾ x 32 . . . . (919)	2,260
The Moulin Rouge, 26 x 31½ . . . . (867)	1,900
Montfort l'Amaury, 1926, 22 x 18½ . . . . (967)	2,034
The Musician, on panel, 21¼ x 13 . . . . (971)	840
The Musician, on panel, 21¾ x 13 . . . . (995)	700
The Trumpeter, on panel, 13¼ x 9¼ . . . . (935)	160
Young Lady, 17¾ x 13 . . . . (947)	480
Woman and Child, 32 x 23¾ . . . . (934)	920
The Child with a Vase of Flowers, 29 x 19¾ . . . . . . (923)	1,000
Vase of Flowers, 29 x 23¾ . . . . (950)	800
Vase of Flowers, 29 x 23¾ . . . . (912)	1,200

1968–July 1969

The Violinist, 36½ x 25¾ . . . . (1212)	1,520
Woman and Child, 32 x 23¾ . . . . (1026)	1,400
Portrait, 21¾ x 13 . . . . (1042)	530
Chez Léon, 1945, 25¾ x 32 . . . . (1060)	1,920
At the Races, 8¾ x 10¾ . . . . (1168)	320
Riders, 19¾ x 25¾ . . . . (1127)	782
The Horse Race, 19¾ x 25¾ . . . . (1110)	600
At the Races, 18¼ x 21¾ . . . . (1019)	620
A Horse and His Jockey, on panel, 16¼ x 10¾ . . (1145)	500
The Square, 21¼ x 25¾ . . . . (1039)	1,500
Montmartre in Winter, 21 x 25¾ . . . . (1022)	1,280
Montfort l'Amaury: Rue de Paris, 18¼ x 21¾ . . . (1159)	1,240
Montfort l'Amaury: La Montière, 13 x 18¼ . . . . . (1159)	1,160
Vase of Flowers, on panel, 18¼ x 14¾ . . . . (1104)	500
The Fish, 21¼ x 32 . . . . (1238)	700
Christ, 16½ x 13 . . . . (1254)	560
The Clown, 16¼ x 13 . . . . (1254)	1,020
Street of Montmartre, on panel, 16¼ x 10¾ . . . . . (1266)	660
Two Clowns, 24 x 15 . . . . (1267)	600
Portrait of J. P. Granval, 1928, 21¾ x 18¼ . . . . . . (1268)	2,668
Horses, (1962), 19¾ x 25¾ . . . . (1268)	1,206

Paul-Elie Gernez

(1888–1948)

Birthplace: Onnaing, near Valenciennes, France.

1901 Studies drawing at the Academy of Valenciennes.

1903 Works at Onnaing Crockery. Decides to devote himself to painting.

1906 First trip to Paris. Attends the Ecole Nationale des Beaux-Arts but soon leaves to work by himself, making frequent visits to the Louvre Museum. Has a natural gift—for pastel in particular.

1908 Returns to Valenciennes and teaches at the local lycée.

1911 Teaches at Honfleur. Executes his first important compositions. Discovers Boudin and the Impressionists. Makes friends with Valloton.

1917 Exhibits at the Galerie Bernheim-Jeune, Paris. Bonnard and Vuillard highly appreciate his work for its personal and sensitive qualities. Exhibits at the Galerie Druet, Paris. His picture "View of Honfleur Pier" is bought by the state.

1922-24 Exhibits at the Galerie Druet and the Galerie Berthe Weil, Paris. Participates yearly in the Salon d'Automne and the Salon des Indépendants, Paris.

1925-34 Several exhibitions at the galleries of Drouant, Bernheim, Druet, and Durand-Ruel, Paris. From 1931 on, participates yearly in the Salon des Tuileries, Paris.

1932 Promoted to the rank of Chevalier of the Legion of Honor—and to the rank of Officer in 1947.

1947 Exhibits at the Galerie Charpentier, Paris.

1948 Died. Robert Rey produces the first monograph on Gernez.

Sales

DRAWINGS

1966

Landscape, charcoal, 9¼ x 15¾ . . . . (706) $	44

1967

Honfleur; Honfleur Neighborhood, two drawings, charcoal, 10 x 15¾ . . . . (850)	560

1968–July 1969

Seated Nude, charcoal, 19¾ x 14¾ . . . . (1202)	200
Le Havre Harbor, charcoal, 10 x 17 . . . . (1110)	140
Honfleur, stick of greasepaint and charcoal, 17½ x 24 . . . . (1162)	210
Sailboats in a Harbor, charcoal, 10 x 16¼ . . . . . . (1230)	240
Honfleur Harbor, 1938, charcoal, 19¾ x 29¼ . . . . (1265)	360

WATERCOLORS

1961-1962

Nude with Blue Cushions, 1924, pastel, 20¼ x 27¾ . . . . (102)	500
Nude in a Landscape, pastel, 23¼ x 28 . . . . (30)	1,160
Back View of a Reclining Nude, pastel, 12¾ x 20¼ . . . . (108)	540
Reclining Nude, pastel, 19¾ x 29 . . . . (108)	210
Woman Powdering Her Face, pastel, 13 x 17½ . . . . (5)	156
Marie Delaunay Sewing, pastel, 21¼ x 14¾ . . . . (48)	440
Still Life: Virgin and Shells, 1929, pastel, 21 x 28½ . . . . (34)	880
Entrance of Honfleur Harbor, 1926, pastel, 17 x 35½ . . . . (58)	400
Entrance of Honfleur Harbor, watercolor, 12¼ x 19 . . . . (81)	320
Honfleur, 1928, pastel, 13½ x 14¼ . . . . (55)	194
Boats in the Harbor, pastel, 9½ x 12¼ . . . . (25)	200
Sailboats in Honfleur, pastel, 15 x 25¾ . . . . (26)	600

1963

Harbor Decked with Flags, pastel, 11¾ x 17½ . . . . (280)	264
Flowers, pastel, 29 x 23¾ . . . . (215)	1,080
Marie Delaunay Sewing, pastel, 14½ x 21¼ . . . . . . (281)	712
Bunch of Flowers, pastel, 27¾ x 23 . . . . (298)	1,800

1964

Still Life with a Bunch of Flowers, pastel,
23¾ x 17½ .... (335) $ 640

Deauville Beach, 1926, gouache, 15¾ x 28¾ ...... (401)   660

Seated Nude, Back View, 1927, pastel,
17¾ x 14¾ .... (404)   360

Honfleur, la Commanderie, 1938, watercolor,
14¼ x 22 .... (394)   420

1965

Les Martigues, 1925, pastel, 13½ x 19½ .... (627)   660

Nude, 1932, pastel, 21¼ x 32 .... (516)   1,500

Reclining Nude, pastel, 17½ x 27¼ .... (523)   370

Nude with a Fan, pastel, 17½ x 25¼ .... (523)   400

Woman at Her Toilette, pastel, 26½ x 14¾ .... (619)   370

Honfleur, la Lieutenance, watercolor,
13½ x 20½ .... (524)   650

Bunch of Flowers, pastel and gouache,
31¼ x 25¼ .... (563)   1,120

The Beach, watercolor, 14 x 21¼ .... (563)   260

On the Beach, pastel, 14 x 23¾ .... (611)   900

The Circus Horse, pastel, 14¼ x 8 .... (503)   300

Flowers, pastel, 22 x 20½ .... (504)   800

1966

The Beach, pastel, 12¾ x 21¼ .... (809)   660

Seated Young Woman in the Nude, pastel,
19½ x 25¼ .... (711)   440

Deauville Beach, 1935, watercolor, 11 x 18¼ ..... (824)   500

The Trees, 1915, pastel, 24¾ x 19½ .... (718)   290

Intimacy, 1923, pastel, 20½ x 13 .... (655)   200

La Roque Cliffs, 1925, pastel, 19 x 28 .... (670)   620

Sunset, pastel, 9 x 11¾ .... (699)   84

Young Woman Sewing, 1928, pastel, 28 x 23 ...... (814)   1,200

Nude with Red Drapery, 19½ x 10¼ .... (781)   200

Honfleur, watercolor, 12¼ x 19 .... (772)   290

Seated Young Woman in the Nude, pastel,
19½ x 25¼ .... (759)   340

1967

Flowers in a Vase, pastel, 28½ x 23¾ .... (923)   1,320

Landscape, 1915, pastel, 25 x 19½ .... (894)   242

Seaside, gouache, 16¾ x 19½ .... (967)   791

Reclining Nude, 1926, gouache, 11½ x 19 .... (1000)   400

Deauville Plain, watercolor, 11 x 21¼ .... (1000)   380

On the Beach, pastel, 19¾ x 23¾ .... (911)   700

The Beach, 1926, pastel, 25¼ x 36 .... (901)   800

Honfleur, watercolor, 9½ x 12¾ .... (883)   340

Reclining Nude, pastel, 18¼ x 24½ .... (978)   140

Back View of a Nude Facing a Folding Screen,
1954, pastel, 14½ x 20¼ .... (926)   250

Trouville Beach, watercolor, 9 x 11¾ .... (964)   290

1968–July 1969

Sailboats in the Harbor, 1920, pastel,
13½ x 19½ .... (1157)   900

Maritime Landscape, pastel, 23¼ x 28 .... (1117)   1,420

Sailboats, 1921, watercolor, 14 x 15¾ .... (1172)   560

Honfleur Harbor, watercolor, 13½ x 20½ ...... (1121)   600

La Lieutenance à Honfleur, pastel, 12¼ x 18¼ ... (1210)   840

Honfleur Harbor, 1921, gouache, 19¾ x 25 ...... (1202)   1,760

The Beach, 1937, watercolor, 11¾ x 18¾ .... (1181)   720

Nude Dressing, 1924, pastel, 16¼ x 8 .... (1117)   1,000

Standing Nude, Her Arms Raised, 1924, pastel,
28½ x 19 .... (1039)   400

Woman in Green, pastel, 17½ x 12¾ .... (1042)   440

Back View of a Nude, pastel, 23¾ x 19½ .... (1078) $ 420

Interior with Two Nudes, pastel, 20½ x 31¼ ..... (1113)   900

Nudes in Front of the Sea, pastel and gouache,
21¾ x 35½ .... (1109)   1,000

Reclining Nude with a Seascape Background,
pastel, 38¾ x 21¾ .... (1189)   1,560

The Forest, pastel, 23¾ x 19½ .... (1038)   260

Sewing, pastel, 29 x 23¾ .... (1172)   1,300

The Model with Black Stockings, pastel,
17¾ x 21 .... (1220)   760

The Estuary of the River Seine, Honfleur, pastel,
13½ x 26½ .... (1225)   1,300

Women Under a Tree, 1918, pastel, 9 x 12 ...... (1245)   450

Two Vases of Flowers, pastel, 24 x 19¾ .... (1255)   3,100

Vase of Flowers, pastel, 29 x 23¾ .... (1256)   6,100

Honfleur Harbor, watercolor, 14 x 12¼ .... (1256)   1,100

The Harbor, watercolor, 8 x 19 .... (1260)   530

The Hill Above the Harbor; Sailboats, two
watercolors, 9 x 12¼ .... (1260)   840

Entrance of Honfleur Harbor, 1921, watercolor,
12¼ x 18¼ .... (1265)   740

View of Honfleur, (1938), watercolor, 17 x 25¼ .. (1265)   900

PAINTINGS

1961–1962

Trees and Clouds, 1907, 29 x 23¾ .... (124)   760

Young Nude Getting Up, 38¼ x 34 .... (146)   260

Still Life with Apples, 1918, on cardboard,
25¾ x 21 .... (76)   240

Bathers and Shells in Front of Honfleur,
23¾ x 28½ .... (30)   1,100

Sailboats in Honfleur, 14 x 10¾ .... (26)   560

Boat Leaving the Pier, 13 x 21¾ .... (35)   400

The Deck Seen from the Buoys, on cardboard,
10¾ x 14 .... (155)   740

1963

The Regattas, 23¾ x 32 .... (224)   780

The Close in Normandy, 1915, 17¾ x 23¾ .... (262)   120

Boats Entering Harbor, 12 x 18¼ .... (188)   560

Honfleur, 1919, 29 x 36½ .... (160)   600

Honfleur Beach, 1925, 23¾ x 32 .... (215)   1,000

The Pine Trees (Honfleur Neighborhood), on
cardboard, 8 x 4¾ .... (209)   80

Three Bathers, 17¾ x 21¼ .... (185)   660

Honfleur Harbor, 1928, 13 x 21¾ .... (238)   320

Honfleur Harbor, on panel, 21¼ x 32 .... (295)   1,860

Honfleur, the Harbor, on cardboard, 23¾ x 32 ... (258)   2,100

1964

Landscape, 17¾ x 23¾ .... (418)   260

Ste. Catherine Market in Honfleur, 1901, on
cardboard, 18¼ x 21¾ .... (401)   480

Honfleur, 24 x 29 .... (366)   920

Bathers, 1916, on panel, 22 x 18¼ .... (355)   400

The Lighthouse, 1923, 19¾ x 29 .... (409)   340

Honfleur, 1925, 13 x 21¾ .... (339)   620

Country Pleasures, 1930, 32½ x 50¼ .... (450)   800

Nude and Shell, 22 x 27¾ .... (337)   1,160

1965

Tennis Court and Seaside, 1927, 19¾ x 25¾ ..... (640)   430

Honfleur, 1915, on canvas laid down on panel,
23¾ x 28 .... (647)   800

The Bunch of Flowers, 18¼ x 15 .... (553)   1,340

1966

Herd of Cows and Sheep, on cardboard,
19¾ x 29¾ .... (653) $ 380
Tree with Heather, on cardboard, 7½ x 9½ .... (655) 162
Street in Honfleur, 1912, 23¾ x 16 .... (764) 500
Sailboats in Honfleur .... (679) 440
Boulevard Carnot in Honfleur, 1914, on
cardboard, 25 x 31½ .... (670) 700
The Entrance of Honfleur Harbor, 21¼ x 32 ..... (819) 1,400
Towboat Alongside a Quay, 18¼ x 21¾ .... (824) 320
Nymphs and Faun, on cardboard, 23¾ x 18¼ ..... (702) 180
Nude with a Pink Skirt, 10¾ x 8¾ .... (752) 310

1967

Landscape of the Val de la Reine, on cardboard,
21¼ x 25¾ .... (934) 400
The Path of the Mont-Joli, 21¼ x 32 .... (836) 400
Fishing Boat in the Harbor, 13 x 15¾ .... (1002) 660
Nude with a Fan, 33¾ x 54½ .... (875) 380
Reclining Nude, Mauve Background,
19½ x 25¾ .... (926) 380
Nude with Shells, on cardboard, 19½ x 23¾ ...... (921) 600
Two Nudes in Front of the Fireplace,
21¾ x 18¼ .... (1000) 820
Bunch of Flowers, 21¼ x 17¾ .... (911) 1,400

1968–July 1969

Towboat in Honfleur, 18 x 21¾ .... (1026) 700
Sailboat Near the Harbor, 23¾ x 32 .... (1210) 2,100
Trees in Honfleur, on panel, 7½ x 4½ .... (1210) 200
The Quai St. Etienne in Honfleur, 34½ x 38 ..... (1172) 2,400
Honfleur, 1925, 25¾ x 45½ .... (1213) 3,900
The Estuary, 1918, 18¼ x 24 .... (1066) 440
Seascape, 18¼ x 21¾ .... (1042) 740
Moonlight Over the Sea, on panel, 8¼ x 12½ ... (1014) 240
Sailboats at Sea, on panel, 10¾ x 18¼ .... (1109) 1,800
The Pier, on panel, 10¾ x 18¼ .... (1039) 1,020
The Torrent, 21¼ x 25¾ .... (1078) 580
Standing Woman in the Nude, 13 x 7½ .... (1115) 300
Reclining Nude, on cardboard, 7¼ x 9 .... (1038) 440
Nude Seated on a Red Sofa, on cardboard,
12¾ x 17¾ .... (1172) 760
Flowers and Fruit, 1927, 8¾ x 10¾ .... (1048) 190
Still Life: The Painter's Tools, 21¼ x 29 .... (1196) 650
Still Life: Tureen and Green Glass Jar, 1917,
24 x 19¾ .... (1211) 1,000
Nosegay in a Green Pot, (1930), 18¼ x 15 .... (1053) 2,300
Flowers, Nudes, and a Shell by the Sea, 1931, on
cradled panel, 32 x 25¾ .... (1181) 4,800
Honfleur Harbor, 18¼ x 24 .... (1223) 1,360
Still Life with a Tureen and a Green Bottle, 1917,
24 x 19¾ .... (1227) 470
Honfleur Harbor, 13 x 18¼ .... (1234) 900
Vase of Flowers with Parrots, 1918, 21¾ x 18¼ .. (1245) 300
Books on a Chest of Drawers, 29¾ x 25¾ .... (1245) 360
Nude in a Landscape, 1933, 16¼ x 13 .... (1247) 580
Nudes in a Landscape, 1918, 25¾ x 19¾ .... (1253) 1,320
Landscape, on cardboard, 17½ x 25 .... (1253) 1,200
Still Life, 24 x 19¾ .... (1253) 1,040
The Entrance of Honfleur Harbor, 1918,
10¾ x 14 .... (1255) 1,400
Nudes in a Landscape, 1918, 15¼ x 18¼ .... (1255) 1,200
Landscape with a Woman Wearing a Blue Apron,
oil on canvas, laid down on cardboard,
10¾ x 14 .... (1255) 920

The Breton Village, 23¾ x 29 .... (1255) $ 620
The Beach, on panel, 8¼ x 10¾ .... (1256) 2,640
Roofs in the Rain, 1913, on cardboard, 17 x 12¾ . (1260) 520
*The Steeple and Ste. Catherine Market in
Honfleur,* on board, 14 x 10¾ .... (1264) 960
Orchard in Normandy, on canvas laid down on
panel, 14¾ x 17¾ .... (1264) 640
White Houses in Brittany, (1918), 25¾ x 36½ .... (1264) 600

Alberto Giacometti

(1901–1966)

Birthplace: Stampa, Switzerland. Son of a painter, he starts to carve and paint very early.

1919 Decides to devote himself to art. Enters the Arts and Crafts School of Geneva, where he studies sculpture.

1920-21 Stays in Italy, where he copies several pictures.

1922 Arrives in Paris. Attends the Académie de la Grande Chaumière. African art, Cycladic sculpture, the works of Laurens and Lipchitz, and Cubism in general exert a great influence on him. Takes part in the Salon des Tuileries.

1926-30 Executes abstract sculptures and begins his open-work statues. Meets Aragon, Breton, and Dali, and joins the Surrealist movement. Exhibits at the Galerie Pierre, Paris, together with Miró and Arp.

1932 One-man show at the Galerie Pierre Colle, Paris.

1934 First one-man show in New York at the Julian Levy Gallery. Reverts to figurative sculpture.

1936 Takes part in the exhibition "Fantastic Art, Dada, and Surrealism" at the Museum of Modern Art, New York.

1948-50 Starts to paint some of his elongated figures. Creates a series of skeletal figures in motion. Important exhibition at the Pierre Matisse Gallery, New York.

1951 Exhibition at the Galerie Maeght, Paris.

1953-55 One-man show at the Art Club, Chicago. Exhibits at the Pierre Matisse Gallery, New York, and the Galerie Maeght, Paris. Retrospective exhibition at the Solomon R. Guggenheim Museum, New York, and the Arts Council of Great Britain, London.

1957-61 Included in many group shows in Europe as well as in the U.S.

1962 Wins the first prize for sculpture at the Venice Biennial.

1964 His work is prominently displayed at the opening of the Fondation Maeght, at St. Paul de Vence in the south of France.

1966 Died.

Sales

DRAWINGS

1961–1962

Still Life, 1954, pencil, 19¾ x 12¾ . . . . (149) $1,027
Still Life on a Sideboard, pencil, 18¾ x 18¼ . . . . . . (129) 824
Head, 1956, sepia, 14¼ x 9¼ . . . . (129) 824
In the Village, 1955, pencil, 13 x 19¾ . . . . (156) 840

1963

Interior, 1949, pencil, 19¾ x 14¾ . . . . (283) 1,198
The Studio, 1952, pencil, 18¼ x 11½ . . . . (219) 881
Palm Tree and Birds, 1952, ink, 8 x 5¼ . . . . (216) 192
Still Life, 1954, pencil, 15¾ x 11½ . . . . (299) 760
Nude, 1954, pencil, 18¼ x 11 . . . . (299) 1,000
Tables in Front of the Café, 1956, ink, 14 x 10 . . . . (283) 904
Studio Corner, 1957, 19¾ x 12¾ . . . . (249) 780
Portrait of Stravinsky Conducting His Orchestra,
   1957, pencil, 12¾ x 19¾ . . . . (299) 840
Still Life, 1958, pencil, 12¼ x 19½ . . . . (232) 1,469

1964

Standing Woman (recto), *Two Heads* (verso),
   pencil, 13 x 8¾, ... (461) 1,280
Still Life, 1958, pencil, 19 x 12¼ . . . . (416) 1,106

1965

Bunch of Flowers, 1949, 10¾ x 8½ . . . . (616) 1,440
The Chair, (1940), black lead, 12½ x 9¼ . . . . (617) 1,853

1966

Annette Sewing, (1955), black lead, 19¾ x 13 . . . . . (744) 2,373
Still Life, 1949, pencil, 11½ x 8¾ . . . . (757) 1,106
Annette, 1949, pencil, 23 x 11½ . . . . (750) 2,073
Vase of Flowers, 1952, pen, 11¾ x 8 . . . . (815) 691
Portrait of Peter Watson, 1953, pencil,
   18¾ x 12 . . . . (751) 2,211

1967

Boughs, 1951, pencil, 12 x 9¼ . . . . (870) 650
Still Life, 1952, pen, 9 x 6½ . . . . (889) 950
Interior, Annette Sewing, 1954, pencil, 20 x 14 . . . (982) 3,792
Bust of a Woman, 1959, pencil, 19½ x 12½ . . . . (982) 853

1968–July 1969

Standing Nude, 1923-24, pencil, 12¼ x 4½ . . . . . . (1099) 2,392
Silvio at His Desk, 1955, stump and pencil,
   16¾ x 11¾ . . . . (1099) 4,830
Still Life, black lead, double sided, 7¼ x 4½ . . . . . (1127) 1,265
Still Life, 1959, pencil, 19¾ x 12¾ . . . . (1173) 4,485
Diego, blue ball-point pen, double sided, 6½ x 4 . (1145) 1,000
Diego, (1963), red ball-point pen, 4½ x 5¾ . . . . . . (1145) 650
Fruit Stand (recto), *Woman Reading* (verso),
   1954, pencil, 17¾ x 12¾ . . . . (1246) 3,750
Figure, 1942, pencil, 11¼ x 4 . . . . (1268) 1,972
Reclining Woman, 1959, ink, 10 x 14½ . . . . (1268) 2,784
Seated Figures, 1951, black lead, double sided,
   16¾ x 10¼ . . . . (1268) 4,640

WATERCOLORS

1963

Valle Onsernone, 1919, pastel, 5 x 5 . . . . (179) 450

1964

Landscape of Switzerland, 1934, watercolor,
   9 x 14 . . . . (438) 450

1968–July 1969

Valle Onsernone, 1919, 4½ x 5 . . . . (1232) 1,400

PAINTINGS

1961–1962

Figures Seated at Table, 1956, 20 x 15 . . . . (164) $5,492
Annette: Seated Portrait, 1958, 36½ x 30½ . . . . (149) 13,430

1963

Portrait No. C 1780, 1947, 22 x 10¾ . . . . (279) 4,500

1965

Head on a White Background, 1948, 13 x 7½ . . . . . (485) 7,500
Standing Nude, (1948), 11½ x 4¾ . . . . (566) 4,113
Diego: Seated Portrait, 1949, 32 x 21¾ . . . . (573) 30,404
Portrait of Annette II, 1951, 37 x 29¼ . . . . (573) 23,218
Black Head, 1957, 32 x 25¾ . . . . (637) 11,500
Bust of Diego, 1957, 16¼ x 13 . . . . (616) 11,200

1967

Still Life with Apples, 1924, 10 x 11¾ . . . . (970) 4,428
Portrait, 1947, 22 x 10¾ . . . . (962) 12,800
Still Life with Bottles, (1950), 18¾ x 17 . . . . (864) 22,000

Wilhelm Gimmi

(1886–1965)

       Birthplace: Zurich, Switzerland. Becomes a teacher.

1908–11 Settles in Paris. Attends the Académie Julian and visits the Louvre Museum.

1911 Trip to Italy. Is especially fond of Masaccio's and della Francesca's frescoes. Comes under the influence of Cézanne.

1911–40 Still lives in Paris but often stays in the south of France.

1919 Participates in the Salon d'Automne, Paris.

1940 Settles in Switzerland, by Lake Geneva.

1942 Wins a prize for his illustration of G. Keller's *Romeo and Juliet in the Village.* Executes decorations for the Federal Polytechnic School of Zurich.

1965 Died.

Sales

DRAWINGS

1966

Woman Reading, pencil, 13¾ x 10¼ . . . . (734) $ 212

1968–July 1969

Kneeling Model, black pencil, 12¼ x 8¾ . . . . (1128) 80

WATERCOLORS

1961–1962

Landscape, Cahors, 1926, watercolor,
   12½ x 18¾ . . . . (93) 136

1966

Studio Scene, gouache, 19 x 24 . . . . (798) 339

1968–July 1969

The Woman with the Black Stockings, 1914,
 watercolor, 10 x 12¾ . . . . (1127) $ 966
A French in Switzerland, pencil and watercolor,
 8¾ x 6 . . . . (1170)   299

PAINTINGS

1961–1962

Box at the Theater, on panel, 10¾ x 8½ . . . . (106)   167

1963

Seated Nude, 15 x 18¼ . . . . (282)   814

1964

Seated Nude, 16¼ x 13 . . . . (383)   531
Woman Reading, 17¾ x 15 . . . . (451)   190
Woman Combing Her Hair, 1923, 25¾ x 21¼ . . . . (336)   120

1965

Bather, 18¼ x 15 . . . . (523)   146
The Harlequin, 15¾ x 12¾ . . . . (503)   160
Side View of a Nude, Brick-Red Drapery, 1925,
 18¼ x 15 . . . . (632)   210
Model with Black Stockings, 1922, 21¾ x 18¼ . . . . (532)   280
View of Provence, 21¼ x 25¾ . . . . (532)   300

1966

Fortifications in Paris, 15 x 18¼ . . . . (745)   701
Back View of a Nude, Reading, 10¾ x 14 . . . . (798)   814

1967

Albi Cathedral, 18¼ x 15 . . . . (995)   250
Landscape with a Church, 29 x 21¾ . . . . (919)   1,130
Bust of a Woman, 16¼ x 13 . . . . (1009)   230
The Model, 1923, 13 x 9½ . . . . (876)   120
Windflowers in a Vase, 16¼ x 13 . . . . (837)   280

1968–July 1969

Still Life, 18¼ x 21¾ . . . . (1127)   920
Houses Amid the Trees, 1913, 18¼ x 21¾ . . . . (1127)   4,600
Standing Harlequin, 25¾ x 21¼ . . . . (1107)   1,380
Still Life with a Shell, 1927, 23¾ x 29 . . . . (1099)   1,058
The Underwood, 18¼ x 21¾ . . . . (1174)   2,990
Portrait of a Woman, 16¾ x 13 . . . . (1127)   368
Front View of a Seated Nude, 1923, 16¼ x 13 . . . (1026)   210
Nude in a Green Armchair, 12¼ x 10¾ . . . . (1223)   280
The Terrace, 14¾ x 11½ . . . . (1223)   280
Two Women, on panel, 10¾ x 8¾ . . . . (1268)   464
Houses Amid the Trees, 1913, 18¼ x 21¾ . . . . (1268)   3,828

Albert Gleizes

(1881–1953)

Birthplace: Paris, France.

1901   Begins to paint in the Impressionist style.

1910   Comes under the influence of Cubism, which plays a cardinal part in the elaboration of his own style. With Metzinger and Le Fauconnier, participates in the Salon d'Automne.

1911   Participates in the Salon des Indépendants and the Salon d'Automne, which demonstrate the acceptance of Cubism in exhibitions. Apollinaire introduces him to Picasso.

1912   Takes part in both the foundation and the exhibition of the Section d'Or group, Paris. With Metzinger, writes the first book dealing with Cubism, entitled *Du Cubisme.*

1913   Takes part in the Armory Show, New York. Also takes part in the first Herbstsalon, Berlin.

1915   Journey to New York.

1937   Participates in the exhibition "Les Maîtres de l'art indépendant," Paris.

1939   Retires to St. Rémy de Provence in the south of France.

1947   Important retrospective exhibition in Lyons.

1950   Exhibition of religious art in the Vatican, Rome. Illustrates *Les Pensées* by Pascal.

1953   Exhibition, "Les Elèves de Gleizes," at the Ecole des Beaux-Arts, Paris. Died, Paris.

Sales

DRAWINGS

1961–1962

Woman Reading, 1904, pencil, 8¼ x 6½ . . . . (161) $ 46
Clown's Head, 1915, pen, 7½ x 7 . . . . (152)   550
Composition, 1915, pen, 7¼ x 10¾ . . . . (110)   180
Cubist Composition, pen, 11 x 8½ . . . . (106)   239

1964

Woman Reading, 1904, pencil, 8¾ x 6¾ . . . . (357)   130
The Meal Under the Trees, 1908, sepia wash,
 8¾ x 13½ . . . . (375)   104

1965

Man Amid Shadows and Symbols, India ink,
 6¼ x 5¾ . . . . (566)   194
Landscape at Nanterre, 1905, pen and wash,
 7 x 8 . . . . (491)   200

1966

Hotel Garden, 1909, wash, 13¼ x 15¾ . . . . (692)   220

1967

*Motion Pictures at the Café Excelsior, Porte
 Maillot,* 1903, wash, 12½ x 16 . . . . (857)   480
Landscape of Montreuil, 1914, wash and gouache,
 4½ x 6 . . . . (926)   256
Seated Man, pencil, 10 x 7½ . . . . (1007)   90

1968–July 1969

Rowing Along the Banks of the River Seine, 1903,
 sepia wash, 11¾ x 15¾ . . . . (1110)   302
Figure, 1944, India ink, 6½ x 3¼ . . . . (1110)   110
Castle Court, 1909, sepia wash, 14 x 15¾ . . . . (1244)   240

WATERCOLORS

1961–1962

Composition, 1923, gouache, 6½ x 4¾ . . . . (93) $ 407

Cubist Composition, 1923, tempera, 13 x 7¾ . . . . . . (106) 678

Portrait of a Painter, gouache, 13½ x 8 . . . . (44) 950

The Village, gouache, 11¾ x 14 . . . . (59) 1,490

Meeting in the Garden, pastel and gouache,
8¼ x 10¼ . . . . (157) 200

Seated Figure, watercolor, 8¾ x 6¾ . . . . (110) 620

1964

The Blessing of the Bishop, watercolor and
gouache, 12¾ x 10 . . . . (337) 560

1965

Bagnères-de-Bigorre, 1908, watercolor and
gouache, 4 x 6½ . . . . (574) 170

Composition, 1922, gouache, 9 x 5¾ . . . . (490) 200

Composition, 1923, gouache, 10 x 7½ . . . . (503) 400

Composition, 1929, gouache, 5¾ x 6¼ . . . . (523) 340

Composition, 1937, gouache, 14 x 10½ . . . . (618) 1,476

Resting Under a Tree, watercolor, 7½ x 11¾ . . . . . (499) 248

1966

Landscape, 1909, watercolor, 9¼ x 14½ . . . . (798) 768

Resting in the Garden, 1909, watercolor and
gouache, 8½ x 10¼ . . . . (718) 400

Young Woman and Her Child, 1916, watercolor,
10¼ x 6 . . . . (702) 130

Vase of Flowers, 1933, gouache, 11 x 8¾ . . . . (681) 700

Composition, 1938, gouache, 14¾ x 18¾ . . . . (713) 1,000

1967

Still Life, 1922, tempera, 8¾ x 5¾ . . . . (927) 814

Composition, 1924, gouache, 6¼ x 3 . . . . (897) 320

Composition, 1934, gouache, 8 x 6 . . . . (926) 520

Composition, 1943, gouache, 5¾ x 4½ . . . . (926) 400

Portrait of a Man, gouache, 17¾ x 13½ . . . . (988) 871

Composition, gouache, 10¾ x 24½ . . . . (973) 460

1968–July 1969

Composition, 1919, gouache, 11 x 8 . . . . (1049) 800

Landscape, 1909, watercolor, 9 x 14 . . . . (1174) 1,495

Composition, 1921, gouache, 10¾ x 13½ . . . . (1161) 660

Seated Woman, 1921, watercolor, 8 x 6 . . . . (1181) 2,600

Composition, 1922, gouache, 9 x 5¾ . . . . (1026) 660

The Family, 1924, watercolor, 9 x 7½ . . . . (1030) 650

Composition, 1926, gouache, 15¾ x 10 . . . . (1213) 780

Composition, 1928, gouache, 10 x 7½ . . . . (1026) 880

Composition, 1930, gouache, 10¼ x 5¼ . . . . (1078) 600

Cubist Composition, 1932, gouache, 5¾ x 10¾ . . . (1180) 600

Still Life, 1937, gouache, 14 x 11 . . . . (1194) 942

Three-Color Composition, 1937, gouache,
10¾ x 24¾ . . . . (1106) 800

Composition, 1939, gouache, 4½ x 2 . . . . (1078) 340

At Court, 1942, gouache on board, 23¼ x 16¾ . . . (1134) 1,416

Still Life, 1943, gouache, 24¼ x 18¾ . . . . (1134) 1,227

Composition on Three Themes, 1923, gouache,
17½ x 11¾ . . . . (1241) 2,020

Composition, 1934, gouache, 8 x 5¾ . . . . (1241) 806

Composition, gouache, 7½ x 4¾ . . . . (1245) 366

Composition, 1942, gouache, 12¼ x 8¾ . . . . (1245) 670

Composition with a Bird, 1921, 8¼ x 12¼ . . . . . . (1255) 1,220

Seated Figure, (1921), watercolor, 6 x 4¾ . . . . . . (1256) 2,200

Cubist Composition, watercolor, 11½ x 7½ . . . . . (1256) 2,800

Cubist Composition, gouache, 8¾ x 6½ . . . . (1268) 1,392

Landscape, 1909, gouache, 13¾ x 18½ . . . . (1273) 756

PAINTINGS

1961–1962

Composition: Christ in Glory, 35½ x 28½ . . . . (120) $1,640

Paris Bridges, 1912, 23¾ x 29 . . . . (88) 12,054

Cubist Portrait of a Woman, 1913, 15¾ x 12¾ . . . . . (96) 2,600

The Sea Gull, 1921, on panel, 25¾ x 36¾ . . . . (13) 4,100

Abstraction, 1921, on board, 36½ x 28¾ . . . . (140) 3,295

Fancied Still Life, 1924, on cardboard, 39½ x 32 . . . (58) 3,800

Woman in a Green Armchair, 1932, 32 x 25¾ . . . . . . (72) 1,740

Composition, 31½ x 23 . . . . (30) 3,000

Woman Seated in a Green Armchair, 32 x 25¾ . . . . (30) 2,000

1963

Threshing Corn, on cardboard laid down on
board, 20½ x 24¾ . . . . (258) 3,200

The Town Under Snow, 1902, 18¼ x 21¾ . . . . (209) 400

Abstract Composition, 1930, 31½ x 35¼ . . . . (189) 2,400

Composition,[1] 1937, on panel, 10 x 47½ . . . . (249) 1,120

1964

Landscape, 1933, on paper, 5¾ x 7¼ . . . . (409) 300

Still Life, 1921, on panel, 10¾ x 8¼ . . . . (372) 850

1965

Banks of the River Seine, Nanterre, 1909,
10¼ x 15½ . . . . (574) 560

Composition, 1912, 16¼ x 10¾ . . . . (561) 1,800

Composition, (1923), 25¾ x 32 . . . . (516) 2,620

The Village, 41¼ x 29¼ . . . . (583) 6,965

Composition: The Woman in Green, 1923,
26 x 21½ . . . . (637) 3,250

Triptych, Left Side, 1930-31, 63¼ x 26 . . . . (637) 7,500

Triptych, Right Side, 1930-31, 63¼ x 26 . . . . (637) 7,500

The Martyrdom of St. Sebastian, on cardboard,
25¾ x 20½ . . . . (599) 640

Composition, 1934, on paper, 8 x 5¾ . . . . (589) 320

1966

Landscape with a Tree, 1914, 39½ x 31½ . . . . (753) 16,832

1967

Mont Valérien, 1901, 21¼ x 25¾ . . . . (926) 820

Landscape, 1919, 17½ x 14¾ . . . . (888) 1,520

Woman in the House, 1921, 25½ x 21¼ . . . . (910) 1,501

Landscape, 12¾ x 18¼ . . . . (950) 400

1968–July 1969

The Cart, 1907, 12¾ x 17¾ . . . . (1059) 595

St. Sebastian, on cardboard, 25¾ x 20½ . . . . (1140) 740

Composition, 1917, 18 x 15 . . . . (1125) 4,140

Object Picture, 1920, 36¼ x 29 . . . . (1132) 4,956

Still Life with a Guitar, 1921, on board,
36¼ x 25¾ . . . . (1173) 8,050

Cubist Composition, 25¾ x 32 . . . . (1117) 4,300

Composition, 1930, 53¾ x 42 . . . . (1121) 3,900

Composition, 1930-31, 63½ x 57¼ . . . . (1184) 4,920

Light, 1936, 54¾ x 37¼ . . . . (1125) 7,820

Light, 1936, 54¾ x 37¼ . . . . (1049) 4,200

Composition, Gray Circle, 1947, on panel,
21¼ x 31¼ . . . . (1121) 1,360

*Composition with Two Elements: Cadences and
Rhythms,* (1924), 52 x 35¼ . . . . (1232) 7,500

Serrières Composition, 1923, 86½ x 49¼ . . . . (1232) 8,500

[1]Executed with Léger and Survage for the World's Fair, Pavillion de l'Union des Artistes Modernes.

Blue and Yellow Composition, (1921), 79 x 43¼ .. (1232) $8,500

Rocky Landscape with a Bridge, on board laid
    down on panel, 1910, 23½ x 26½ .... (1239)   11,040

View of a Village with Trees in Blossom, 1922,
    15 x 18 .... (1273)   4,790

Edouard Goerg

(1895–1969)

Birthplace: Sydney, Australia. (Of French parentage.)

1900   His family settles in Paris.

1912   Attends the Académie Ranson in the studios of Maurice Denis and Sérusier. Develops a great interest in such painters as Bosch, Goya, Daumier, and Rouault.

1913   Travels to Italy and India.

1920   Participates in the Salon des Indépendants, Paris.

1924   Participates in the Salon des Indépendants and the Salon d'Automne, Paris.

1925   First one-man show at the Galerie Berthe Weil, Paris.

1926   Meets the famous art dealer Paul Guillaume. Exhibits at the Art Institute of Chicago.

1927   Exhibition at the Galerie Bernheim-Jeune, Paris.

1934   Trip to Belgium and Holland. Exhibition at the Galerie Jeanne Castel, Paris.

1935–40   Executes highly imaginative pictures characterized by a strange and poetical atmosphere.

1945   Illustrates Baudelaire's poems *Les Fleurs du Mal*. His engravings, intended for such books, hold an important place in his work.

1947   Important exhibition at the Galerie Drouant-David, Paris.

1949   Wins the first Halmark prize.

1950   In Lugano, wins the first prize for etching.

1954   Participates in the Venice Biennial. Exhibits at the Museum of Art, São Paulo. Also exhibits at Jacques Helft's, Buenos Aires.

1957   Exhibition at the Galerie Drouant-David, Paris. Buys a house at Callian in the south of France.

1969   Died, Callian, Var district.

Sales

DRAWINGS

1961–1962

The Parisian, 1944, black lead, 17¾ x 11¾ .... (56) $ 250

Portrait of a Woman, pen, 12¼ x 9½ .... (119)   120

Group of Figures with Two Nudes, India ink
    wash, 14¼ x 10¼ .... (143)   124

1963

The Little Girl with a Basket, 1945, India ink,
    12¾ x 9 .... (224) $ 320

1964

Two Nudes, pen heightened with wash,
    14¾ x 10¾ .... (466)   340

Midinette, 1948, pen, 13 x 10 .... (355)   104

The Musicians, India ink, 16¼ x 9½ .... (345)   260

1965

Interior with a Seated Nude, pen and wash,
    11 x 15 .... (503)   240

Three Portraits, 1953, pen, 11¼ x 9½ .... (619)   160

The Brook, pen, 9½ x 12½ .... (504)   40

Four Faces, 1963, wash, 11½ x 8¼ .... (611)   180

1966

Society People, India ink, 9½ x 15½ .... (656)   250

Seated Nude, pen and wash, 11½ x 15¾ .... (666)   360

Many Happy Returns of the Day, India-ink wash,
    11¾ x 19½ .... (726)   240

Ange du Bizarre, India ink, 12¾ x 9½ .... (810)   150

1967

The Birthday, wash, 12¼ x 19½ .... (1007)   200

Landscape, pen, 10 x 13 .... (894)   200

Ange du Bizarre, wash, 12¼ x 9¼ .... (995)   100

1968–July 1969

Young Girl with a Butterfly, pencil, 12¾ x 9½ ... (1195)   122

Head of a Young Girl, 1944, charcoal .... (1262)   260

WATERCOLORS

1961–1962

Child with Flowers, gouache, 19 x 12¾ .... (173)   290

The Piano Lesson, gouache, 14 x 9¾ .... (141)   290

1963

Young Girl with a Nosegay, gouache,
    19½ x 12¾ .... (190)   670

Garden Party, 1942, gouache, 25¼ x 19 .... (296)   760

1964

Bathers, varnished gouache, 12¼ x 19½ .... (333)   400

Portrait of a Young Girl, gouache, 15 x 11½ ...... (419)   420

1967

Two Fashionable Ladies, gouache, 12¼ x 15½ .... (974)   580

1968–July 1969

Reclining Woman and Flowers, pastel, 14¾ x 22 . (1028)   480

Fisherwoman, gouache .... (1263)   1,040

Two Young Girls with a Bunch of Flowers,
    gouache .... (1263)   1,060

PAINTINGS

1961–1962

The Earthly Paradise, 1928, 39½ x 29 .... (109)   1,900

The Little Dancer and Her Friends, 1950,
    25¾ x 19¾ .... (71)   1,200

Red-Haired Woman Amid Flowers, 25¾ x 21¼ .... (30)   1,760

The Flower Girl, 25¾ x 19¾ .... (136)   2,010

The Nymphets, 21¾ x 25¾ .... (39)   1,400

Red-Haired Woman Amid Flowers, 25¾ x 21¼ ... (160)   1,600

Valentin in Montparnasse, 39½ x 25¾ .... (90)   2,000

Ondines, 1953, 24 x 19¾ .... (155)   1,240

Overalls and Blue Jeans, 36½ x 29 .... (109)   2,160

The Tzigane in Love, 1960, 27¾ x 39¼ .... (155)   1,800

1963

The Earthly Paradise, 1928, 39½ x 29 . . . . (194)	$1,760
Fancied Portrait, 1940, 14 x 10¾ . . . . (258)	460
Flowers for the Flower Girl, 1958, 25¾ x 22 . . . . . . (206)	1,120
The Sisters, 1959, 25¾ x 21¼ . . . . (206)	1,520
The Race Course, 1959, 25¾ x 21¼ . . . . (258)	1,500
Suburban Figures, 21¾ x 18¼ . . . . (306)	1,440
At the Flower Girl's, 29 x 36¼ . . . . (198)	2,300
The Two Rivals, 16¼ x 13 . . . . (198)	920
Woman in the Woods, 2 x 13 . . . . (290)	375
Little Nude with a Straw Hat, 18¼ x 10¾ . . . . (254)	1,440
Nude with a Branch, 21¾ x 25¾ . . . . (254)	1,500
The Flower Girl with a Blue Pot, 32 x 25¾ . . . . (224)	2,600

1964

The Rivals, 1932-33, 21¾ x 13¼ . . . . (475)	1,760
The Window, 39½ x 32 . . . . (399)	2,800
Interior with a Nude (The Accordionist in Love with My Maid), 36¼ x 29 . . . . (466)	1,800
Flowery Town, 32 x 25¾ . . . . (398)	1,820
The Return of the Prodigal Son, 18¼ x 24 . . . . (409)	640
Woman with Flowers, 19¾ x 12¾ . . . . (401)	380
Angling Nymph, 1950, 18¼ x 13 . . . . (472)	600
To Each His Guardian Angel, 29¼ x 23¾ . . . . (371)	2,160
Too Much to Choose From, 29 x 36¼ . . . . (351)	2,900

1965

The Subway, 1931, 25¾ x 32 . . . . (524)	2,520
Love in Bloom, 32 x 25¾ . . . . (510)	1,900
The Bride, 25¾ x 19¾ . . . . (532)	˙920
The Newborn, 32 x 25¾ . . . . (530)	560
The Flower Girl, 25¾ x 21¼ . . . . (529)	2,200

1966

Young Girl with Flowers, 20¼ x 13 . . . . (701)	525
Portrait of Willy, 29¾ x 21¾ . . . . (719)	600

1967

Nude with a Black Cat, 21¼ x 25¾ . . . . (900)	1,900
The Little Breton Girl Has Won the Beauty Prize, 21¾ x 18¼ . . . . (861)	1,620
The Young Eunuch, 1925, 29 x 36¼ . . . . (921)	1,600
Willy and His Dog, 29 x 21¼ . . . . (884)	1,000

1968–July 1969

One Thing at a Time, 31½ x 44¼ . . . . (1117)	2,000
It Is a Holiday, 1948, 24 x 19¾ . . . . (1200)	2,000
The Tiny Gray Cap, 1953, 16½ x 10¾ . . . . (1026)	1,300
Ophelia, 1954, 18¼ x 15 . . . . (1183)	1,610
Clear Profile, 1955, 13 x 10 . . . . (1200)	760
A Pretty Girl in Grasse, 1958, 21¾ x 18¼ . . . . (1210)	2,300
Fashionable Ladies, on paper, 12¼ x 15½ . . . . (1220)	1,600
Bathers, 32½ x 39½ . . . . (1254)	4,400
The Lovers, 1958, pencil and gouache, 14 x 10¼ . (1254)	4,800
Nudes: Three Young Girls and a Child with a Bunch of Flowers, 1949, 24 x 17¾ . . . . (1255)	2,240
Seaside Baths: Women and Boats, 1948, 21¾ x 17¾ . . . . (1255)	1,620
Three Nudes, 1943, 36½ x 25¾ . . . . (1262)	3,100
Reading to the Model, (1930), 25¾ x 32 . . . . (1268)	3,480

Vincent van Gogh

(1853–1890)

Birthplace: Groot-Zundert, Netherlands. (Son of a pastor.)

1869-75	Works in the Goupil Galleries in The Hague, Brussels, London, and Paris.
1872	Starts to keep up a correspondence with his brother Théo.
1876-78	Dismissed by the Goupil Galleries. Goes to Amsterdam to study theology. Does not carry on his studies.
1879-80	Stay in the Borinage, Belgium, as a pastor. Gives up religion and decides to become a painter. Lives in extreme poverty and depression.
1880-81	Settles in Brussels to study painting and meets the painter Van Rappard. Théo begins to back him, which he does until the end.
1882-83	Stay in The Hague. Executes his first oil paintings. Sets up a studio in his father's house at Nuenen, where he works very hard.
1885	Death of his father. Attends the Academy of Fine Arts, Antwerp.
1886	Goes to Paris, where Théo lives. Attends Cormon's studio, where he meets Toulouse-Lautrec. Visits the Louvre Museum. Meets the Impressionists and, coming under their influence, lightens his palette.
1887	Becomes very friendly with Emile Bernard. Executes many pictures.
1888	Settles in Arles, in the south of France. Discovers the Mediterranean. Gauguin joins him, and they live and work together. Van Gogh paints many masterpieces. Shortly there is a hostile confrontation and Gauguin returns to Paris. Van Gogh spends two weeks in the hospital, having attempted to cut off his ear.
1889	First hallucinations. Commits himself to the asylum in Arles and later in Saint Rémy. Continues to paint until the end.
1890	His picture "La Vigne rouge" is sold at the exhibition of the XX, Brussels (the only picture sold in his lifetime). Returns to Paris and meets Théo again. Settles at Auvers-sur-Oise and becomes very friendly with his doctor, Gachet. Shoots himself on July 27th and dies two days later.
1891	Retrospective exhibition at the Salon des Indépendants, Paris.

Sales

DRAWINGS

1963

The Coffee Drinker, 1882, pencil, 12¾ x 10 . . . . . . (219)	$3,842
Peasant Digging (Nuenena), 1884, charcoal, 10½ x 8¼ . . . . (277)	3,565
Postcard Addressed to Anton Kerssemakers-Simonis in Eindhoven: Two Peasants Digging, 1885, ink, 3¾ x 5½ . . . . (210)	6,892

1964

Willows, colored chalk, 19 x 11¾ . . . . (458)	13,349
The Sower, 1881, pen and India-ink wash heightened with white gouache, 24 x 15¾ . . . . (401)	15,600

VAN GOGH

1966

In Holland, charcoal, 5¼ x 8¼ . . . . (734) $7,684
The Thistles, 1863, black chalk, 7¼ x 5¾ . . . . (757)   829
Sorrow,[1] 1882, pencil and charcoal, 17¾ x 10¾ . . . (753)   31,922
Couple Walking (recto), 1890, **Glass, Tin Pot, Faces, etc.** (verso), pencil, 11 x 17 . . . . (750)   3,593

1968–July 1969

The Sower, 1882, pencil, 19½ x 9¾ . . . . (1191)   16,048
The Park of the Institut St. Paul at St. Rémy, sepia ink and black chalk, 18½ x 24 . . . . (1194)   39,680

WATERCOLORS

1964

Woman Picking Up Linen, 1881-83, watercolor, 10 x 15¾ . . . . (479)   7,616
Agricultural Labor, watercolor, 12 x 19½ . . . . (458)   15,090

1965

The Weaver, 1884, watercolor, 11¾ x 17 . . . . (522)   13,820

1967

Peasant Digging, 1883-85, watercolor heightened with white, 10¼ x 17½ . . . . (927)   20,340

1968–July 1969

Woman Picking Up Linen, (1881-83), watercolor, 10½ x 16¼ . . . . (1099)   16,100
The Weaver, watercolor, 12¼ x 17¾ . . . . (1106)   20,000
Old Peasant, watercolor, 10 x 7¼ . . . . (1125)   23,460

PAINTINGS

1961-1962

Peasant's Head, Nuenen 1885, on panel, 19 x 14 . . . . (31)   21,968
Left-Side View of a Peasant's Head, 1885, 9¾ x 7¼ . . . . (88)   6,396
Still Life: Lemons and Blue Gloves, Arles 1889, 18¾ x 24½ . . . . (112)   219,680
The Confines of Paris, 1886-88, 18 x 21¼ . . . . (137)   90,000

1963

Peasant Digging, 1881, 23¼ x 17½ . . . . (247)   28,791
A Mill in Montmartre, 1887, 17½ x 14¼ . . . . (245)   42,501
Unloaders, Arles, 1888, 21¼ x 25¾ . . . . (247)   123,390
View of the Asylum and of the Chapel at St. Rémy, 1889, 17¾ x 23¾ . . . . (210)   252,264

1964

Peasant at Work, (1883), on panel, 12¼ x 11¾ . . . . (340)   15,000
Child's Head and Orris on a Mosaic Background, 23¾ x 13½ . . . . (371)   6,200
Peasant Walking Along the Fields,[2] 1889, 18¼ x 15 . . . . (416)   69,100
Auvers: View of the Village, 1890, 17¼ x 20¼ . . . . (274)   132,672

1965

Peasant of Nuenen Picking Potatoes, 1885, on canvas laid down on panel, 17 x 12¼ . . . . (583)   24,667
Unloaders, 1888, 21¼ x 25¾ . . . . (526)   240,000
Pietà (After Delacroix), 1889-90, 16 x 13¼ . . . . . . (624)   110,560
The Harvester, 31½ x 25¾ . . . . (493)   250,000

1966

The Water Mill, 22¾ x 31 . . . . (698)   25,840
The Water Mill, 1884, on canvas laid down on panel, 17 x 22¼ . . . . (686)   20,730

---

[1]"Comment se fait-il qu'il y ait sur terre une femme seule—délaissée. Michelet."
[2]After J. F. Millet.

The Walk in Autumn, 1885, on canvas laid down on panel, 25½ x 34¼ . . . . (686) $26,258
Landscape at Nightfall, 1855, on canvas laid down on board, 14 x 17 . . . . (750)   30,404
The Pont d'Asnières, (1887), 21 x 28½ . . . . (713)   140,000
Light Effect in the Branches, 1890, 12¾ x 9½ . . . . . (750)   39,249
Portrait of Mademoiselle Ravoux, 1890, 29¼ x 21½ . . . . (753)   435,300

1967

The Water Mill, (1884), 23¾ x 31½ . . . . (864)   32,500
Ginger Pot Filled with Chrysanthemums, (1885), on canvas laid down on panel, 15¾ x 11½ . . . . (864)   8,000
Standing Woman, (1885-86), 15 x 11 . . . . (880)   10,277
The Confines of Paris, (1886-88) 18½ x 21¾ . . . . . (988)   129,376
Vase of Flowers, 1885, on canvas laid down on panel, 12¼ x 9 . . . . (918)   19, 210
Peasant Harvesting, 1889, 15½ x 9½ . . . . (918)   115,712
Vase of Peonies, 1889, 21¼ x 17¾ . . . . (938)   49,752

1968–July 1969

Portrait of the Artist's Mother, 15½ x 12¼ . . . . . . (1126)   272,580
House Near a Church, La Haye, (1882), on canvas laid down on panel, 13½ x 10 . . . . (1176)   9,500
The Dunes, 1882, on panel, 14¼ x 23¼ . . . . (1021)   19,180
The Dunes, Surroundings of La Haye, 1883, on panel, 13 x 19 . . . . (1187)   15,340
After the Storm, 1884, 26½ x 49¾ . . . . (1068)   44,840
Still Life, 1884-85, on canvas laid down on panel, 12 x 15¾ . . . . (1132)   30,680
Landscape of the Brabant, 1885, 8¾ x 14¾ . . . . . . (1069)   16,988
Landscape of the Brabant, 1885, 9 x 14¾ . . . . (1193)   54,516
The Presbytery Garden in Nuenen, 1885, 20¼ x 30½ . . . . (1176)   45,000
The Thistles, 1888, 21¾ x 17¾ . . . . (1126)   84,252
Peasant's Head, 15 x 12 . . . . (1193)   32,214
The Sower, 1888, Arles, 13¼ x 16 . . . . (1241)   189,000
Ecumenism, 29 x 36½ . . . . (1247)   1,040

Nathalie Gontcharova

(1881-1961)

Birthplace: Russia.

1898   Studies art in Moscow. Meets Larionov.

1906   Takes part in the exhibition of Russian painting organized by Diaghilev at the Salon d'Automne, Paris. Takes part in the Crown Exhibition, Moscow.

1910-14   Joins Larionov's Rayonism. Retrospective exhibitions in Moscow and Petrograd. Settles in Paris. Exhibition, together with Larionov, at the Galerie Paul Guillaume, Paris. (Catalog preface by Apollinaire.)

1918   Exhibition with Larionov, "L'Art décoratif moderne," Paris. Takes a great interest in stage decoration and nearly stops painting.

1928 Participates in the "International Theatre Exhibition" at the Whitechapel Art Gallery, London, and in the exhibition of contemporary Russian art at the Ruskin Gallery, Birmingham.

1938 Becomes a French citizen.

1948 Stage decorations for *Le Barbier de Séville* by Beaumarchais, at the Cambridge Theatre, London. Participates in the retrospective exhibition of Rayonism at the Galerie des 2 îles, Paris.

1952 With Larionov, exhibits at the Galerie de l'Institut, Paris. Participates in the exhibition "L'Oeuvre du XXème Siècle" at the Musée d'Art Moderne, Paris.

1956 Important exhibition at the Galerie de l'Institut, Paris.

1960 Participates in the exhibition "Les Sources du XXème Siècle" at the Musée d'Art Moderne, Paris.

1961 Died, Paris.

Sales

DRAWINGS

1965

Rain, (1908), pencil, charcoal, and colored pencil, 12 x 8¼ . . . . (582) $ 304

1967

Japanese Art, (1913), black and red pencil, 10 x 7¼ . . . . (881) 276

1968–July 1969

Chinese Costume, 1922, India ink, 19¾ x 12¾ . . . (1142) 260

Portrait of Igor Stravinsky, pencil, 13½ x 10 . . . . (1142) 826

Bunch of Flowers, India ink, 27¼ x 22 . . . . (1191) 425

Oriental Character, 12¾ x 8¾ . . . . (1223) 64

Landscape of Russia, 10 x 14¾ . . . . (1223) 104

Allegory, watercolor, 14 x 10 . . . . (1223) 140

Character of the Middle Ages, 8 x 6½ . . . . (1227) 84

Rayonist Composition, (1913), colored pencil heightened with gouache, 12¼ x 8¼ . . . . (1240) 1,008

Rayonist Composition, (1914), pencil, 5½ x 8¼ . . (1240) 480

Vase of Flowers, pen, 15 x 11½ . . . . (1240) 360

Landscape; Room Decoration, two drawings, black pencil, 10¼ x 15 and 10½ x 17 . . . . (1240) 360

Side View of a Woman, 16¼ x 12¼ . . . . (1253) 60

Rayonist Landscape, (1914), pencil, black and brown pencil, heightened with green, 10¼ x 8 . . . . (1272) 480

Portrait of a Woman, pencil, 5¾ x 4 . . . . (1273) 139

WATERCOLORS

1961–1962

Flowers, watercolor, 11 x 7¾ . . . . (164) 302

1963

Effect I, gouache, 4 x 8 . . . . (210) 219

Composition, watercolor, 42¾ x 50¾ . . . . (233) 360

1964

Rayonist Watercolor, 1908, watercolor, 15 x 10 . . . (416) 1,797

1965

The Tulips, watercolor, 13¼ x 10 . . . . (492) 140

1966

Costume Study for "The Fire Bird," watercolor and gouache, 14 x 7½ . . . . (829) 200

Young Woman with a Hat, (1917), gouache, 15½ x 11 . . . . (757) $ 498

Roses in a Cup, watercolor, 10¾ x 17¾ . . . . (741) 350

The Spanish Girl, pastel and charcoal, 24 x 18¼ . . (805) 800

1967

Trees, (1912), watercolor, 14 x 10 . . . . (985) 308

Costume for a Seraph, watercolor and collage, 21 x 15 . . . . (922) 2,349

1968–July 1969

Flowers on a Blue Background, 1912, watercolor, 10 x 6½ . . . . (1138) 322

Project for the Curtain of "Le Coq d'Or," (1913-14), pencil and watercolor, 22½ x 29 . . (1142) 2,596

Peasant Costume for "Le Coq d'Or," pencil and gouache, 15 x 10¾ . . . . (1142) 991

Decoration for "Renard," 1921, gouache, 7¾ x 9 . . . . (1142) 991

Landscape, gouache, 10½ x 6¾ . . . . (1134) 307

The Trees, pastel, 14¼ x 10 . . . . (1087) 196

The Brown River, watercolor, 42¾ x 50¾ . . . . (1126) 2,106

Flowers, gouache, 7½ x 4¼ . . . . (1240) 384

Flowers and Sky, watercolor and gouache, 10¼ x 6¼ . . . . (1241) 370

Decorative Composition, watercolor, 10¼ x 6¼ . . (1241) 428

Composition, watercolor, 14¾ x 10 . . . . (1253) 120

The Spanish Girl, stencil, 18¼ x 10¾ . . . . (1253) 100

Seated Woman, watercolor, 14 x 10 . . . . (1253) 70

PAINTINGS

1964

Fishermen, 1909, 46¾ x 41¼ . . . . (416) 3,040

The Loom, 1912-13, 61 x 39¼ . . . . (367) 4,699

Portrait of Larionov, 1913, 41½ x 31 . . . . (367) 2,764

1965

Bunch of Flowers in a Vase, 14¼ x 11¼ . . . . (492) 420

The Cab, 1905, 26 x 31½ . . . . (582) 1,713

Peaches and Red Flowers, 1907, on canvas laid down on board, 35½ x 28 . . . . (624) 1,106

Composition, 1913, 41½ x 34½ . . . . (634) 9,348

Spanish Dancer, 1916, 78¼ x 34½ . . . . (522) 3,731

Bunch of Roses, 18¼ x 15 . . . . (538) 284

1966

Bathers, 1912-13, 91 x 60 . . . . (815) 2,349

Spanish Dancer, 1916, 78¼ x 34½ . . . . (815) 1,243

White Tulips, 16¼ x 8¾ . . . . (815) 498

Vase of Flowers, 9¾ x 7½ . . . . (655) 280

Flowers in a Vase, 23¾ x 18¼ . . . . (741) 650

Magnolias, (1924), on cardboard, 32 x 22½ . . . . . . (681) 1,380

1967

Spanish Woman in Gray, 1916, 77½ x 38¾ . . . . (888) 1,520

Fishing, 1909, 44¼ x 39½ . . . . (888) 4,146

The Fagot Gatherer, 36¼ x 26 . . . . (985) 995

Flowers in a Vase, 23¾ x 18¼ . . . . (1002) 420

Flowers in a Vase, 23¾ x 18¼ . . . . (887) 400

Vase of Windflowers, 10¾ x 8¾ . . . . (926) 160

Vase of Flowers, 9¾ x 7½ . . . . (874) 180

Spanish Girls, folding screen including five panels, each canvas 93 x 29¾ . . . . (929) 2,600

1968–July 1969

Composition, 41½ x 31 . . . . (1125) 7,360

Bather, 1912, 55 x 37¾ . . . . (1126) 3,965

Composition, 1926, on panel, 17½ x 14¾ . . . . **(1043)** $ 800
Still Life, 1926, on board, 18¼ x 15 . . . . **(1132)** 826
Vase of Windflowers, 9 x 15¾ . . . . **(1187)** 590
Flowers in a Vase, 23¾ x 18¼ . . . . **(1168)** 400
Bunch of Flowers,[1] (1921), on board, 6¼ x 8¾ . . . **(1232)** 1,700
Woman with a Kimono, 25¼ x 20 . . . . **(1240)** 432
Space, 1952, 39¼ x 25½ . . . . **(1240)** 1,560
Wine Harvest, 1907-10, 46 x 36¾ . . . . **(1240)** 4,560
Still Life with Flowers, Two Fish, and Grapes,
    31½ x 23 . . . . **(1241)** 1,890
Still Life, 32 x 21 . . . . **(1248)** 1,200
The Pink House in Moscow, (1904), 21 x 27¾ . . . **(1268)** 6,264
Constructive Figure,[2] 1913, 41¼ x 30¾ . . . . **(1270)** 12,240
Spanish Woman, (1916), 41 x 18¼ . . . . **(1271)** 2,280
Bottle, 16 x 9½ . . . . **(1273)** 655

Arshile Gorky

(1904-1948)

Birthplace: Armenia.

1920   Settles in the U.S. Attending Brown University, begins to paint as a hobby.

1925   Goes to New York. Dismissed by three art schools, one after the other. Prefers to study contemporary masters in the museums and galleries. Influenced by Picasso, Léger, and Miró, he regards Cubism as the modern tradition, from which a painter can draw as from the old masters.

1929   Begins to turn to a colorful abstract style.

1940   Elaborates his own abstract expressionist style. Meets André Breton and is the last artist to be accepted by the Surrealists as a member of their group. Also meets Calder, Matta, and Ernst.

1944   Paints his brilliant picture, "The Liver Is the Cock's Comb," from carefully prepared drawings, according to his habit.

1946   About thirty pictures and several drawings are destroyed when his studio burns out.

1948   Died, New York, a suicide (after a cancer operation and a car crash).

1950   Important retrospective exhibition at the Whitney Museum, New York.

Sales

DRAWINGS

1961-1962
Studio, pen and pastel, 8¼ x 10¾ . . . . **(69)** $2,054

1963
Composition, pencil and colored chalk,
    8½ x 10¾ . . . . **(179)** 350

[1]Dedicated "A notre cher ami Monsieur Ernest Szamstorski."
[2]Dedicated "A Madame Florence Bank amicalement."

1964
Cascades, (1941), colored pencil and black lead,
    14 x 11 . . . . **(372)** $1,800
The Orchard, (1942), colored pencil and ink,
    11¾ x 15¾ . . . . **(372)** 2,200
Study for "Death Agony," 1946, pen and pastel,
    10 x 11¾ . . . . **(461)** 1,920

1965
Portrait and Studies of Figures, four drawings,
    pencil, each 8¾ x 6¾ . . . . **(489)** 1,550
Opening, pen, wash, and colored chalk, 8 x 10¾ . . **(583)** 406
Composition, (1944), 10 x 12¾ . . . . **(494)** 550

1966
Composition, (1931), pencil, 24½ x 18¼ . . . . **(651)** 1,600
Double Portrait, pen, 10½ x 7½ . . . . **(672)** 200
Study II, (1946), charcoal and colored pencil,
    18¾ x 25 . . . . **(751)** 2,764

1967
Composition, (1946), pencil and pastel,
    11½ x 15¼ . . . . **(889)** 1,800

1968–July 1969
Untitled, (1936-37), ink, 13 x 8 . . . . **(1030)** 350
Abstraction, pencil, 14 x 10¾ . . . . **(1145)** 150
The Table, 10½ x 7½ . . . . **(1237)** 300

WATERCOLORS

1965
Improvisation, 1932, gouache, 22 x 30 . . . . **(485)** 4,000

1961-1962
Still Life with Yellow and Red Fruit, 24¾ x 30¼ . . **(152)** 2,200
Composition with Vegetables, 27¾ x 35½ . . . . **(152)** 3,300

1963
Abstract Still Life, 32½ x 22½ . . . . **(189)** 3,500

1965
Composition in Yellow, Green, Gold, and Red,
    1946, 11¾ x 14¾ . . . . **(489)** 2,750
Dialogue of the Egg, (1946), 31½ x 40¾ . . . . **(489)** 15,750
Terracotta, 1947, 48¼ x 56¼ . . . . **(592)** 18,000

1966
Abstraction, (1934), on panel, 25¾ x 10 . . . . **(651)** 1,700

Adolph Gottlieb

(1903-   )

Birthplace: New York, U.S.

1919   Enters the Art Students League, New York.

1920-22   Goes to Europe and settles in Paris. Attends the Académie de la Grande Chaumière, Paris. Admires modern French masters such as Cézanne, Matisse, and Léger.

1930   One-man show at the Dudensing Gallery, New York. Works for the Federal Art Project.

1934	With Mark Rothko, takes part in the foundation of "The Ten," a group of American painters.
1935–40	Participates in the exhibitions of "The Ten," New York. Influenced by Klee and Miró.
1944–45	Becomes president of the Federation of American Painters and Sculptors.
1947-54	Exhibits yearly at the Kootz Gallery, New York.
1950	Abandons abstract expressionism for a kind of chromatic abstraction.
1957	Retrospective exhibition at the Jewish Museum, New York.
1959	One-man show at the Galerie Rive Droite, Paris. Participates in Documenta II, Kassel.
1964	One-man show at the Marlborough-Gerson Gallery, New York.
1967	Exhibits at the Chicago Art Club.
1968	Exhibits at the Whitney Museum of American Art and the Guggenheim Museum, New York.
	Resident in New York.

Sales

WATERCOLORS

1961–1962

Centrifugal, 1961, gouache, 14¾ x 10 . . . . (111) $ 475

1966

Composition, 1954, watercolor, 10 x 14 . . . . (651)   325

1968–July 1969

Movement West, 1956, gouache, 20¾ x 29¾ . . . . . (1246)   750

Heavy Sky, 1956, gouache, 20¼ x 29 . . . . (1246)   750

Open Forms, 1956, 20¼ x 29 . . . . (1246)   750

PAINTINGS

1963

Still Life, 29¾ x 39½ . . . . (275)   725

Plutomania, 1951, 36 x 48¼ . . . . (316)   3,700

Four Red Clouds, 1956, 49½ x 59¼ . . . . (189)   5,500

1964

The Articled Alchemist, 1946, 24 x 30 . . . . (372)   1,400

Night Swirl No. 5921, 1959, 90¾ x 72¼ . . . . (431)   7,000

Levitation, 1959, 90 x 60¼ . . . . (372)   7,000

1965

Composition, 35½ x 47½ . . . . (489)   2,250

Prismatic, 1959, 72¼ x 91¼ . . . . (592)   7,000

Crimson Spinning No. 1, 1959, 88½ x 71¼ . . . . (526)   12,000

Levitation, 1960, 87¾ x 6¾ . . . . (526)   8,000

1967

Blast III, 1958, 69¼ x 40¼ . . . . (864)   4,250

1968–July 1969

Double Disks, 1967, acrylic on paper mounted on board, 8 x 15 . . . . (1237)   1,800

Orange Blast, 1967, acrylic on paper mounted on board, 20 x 15 . . . . (1237)   900

John Graham

(1881–1961)

	Birthplace: Kiev, Russia.
1911	Studies law at the University of Kiev.
1920	Emigrates to the U.S. and becomes an American citizen.
1921	Attends the Art Students League, New York.
1926	First one-man show at the Baltimore Museum of Art.
1929	One-man show at the Galerie Zborowski, Paris.
1931	One-man show at the Société Anonyme, New York.
1937	Writes *System and Dialectics of Art.*
1954	Exhibits at the Stable Gallery, New York.
1961	Died, London.

Sales

PAINTINGS

1968–July 1969

Fantastic Landscape, 1931, 18 x 24 . . . . (1145) $ 275

Woman in Blue, 1943, 30¼ x 24 . . . . (1062)   5,500

Abraham, 38½ x 22 . . . . (1062)   700

Houses, 15 x 18 . . . . (1231)   200

Figure in Lavender, 30 x 24 . . . . (1237)   1,950

Morris Graves

(1910-   )

	Birthplace: Fox Valley, Oregon, U.S.
1929-30	Leaves school to ship out on a vessel, visiting ports like Tokyo, Shanghai, and Hong Kong. Takes a great interest in Far Eastern civilization.
1931	Returns to the U.S. Works on his earliest sketchbooks.
1932	After a trip to Beaumont, Texas, and New Orleans, returns home and begins to paint.
1933	Wins a prize at the Seattle Museum of Art.
1936-39	Works for the Federal Art Project. Alters his style, which takes on a surrealistic quality. Starts his series of "Birds." First one-man show at the Seattle Museum of Art.
1942	Participates in the exhibition "Americans 42" at the Museum of Modern Art, New York.
1942-59	Exhibits yearly at the Willard Gallery, New York.
1943	One-man show at the Chicago Art Club.
1948	Retrospective exhibition at the California Palace, San Francisco.
1956	Retrospective exhibition at the Whitney Museum of American Art, New York.
1957	Takes part in a group show at the Institute of Contemporary Art, London.

Sales

DRAWINGS
1966
Still Life, 1947, charcoal, 23 x 17 . . . . (721) $ 375
Studies of Birds, (1943), pen and wash,
21¼ x 27 . . . . (776)   500
Goose, 1953, ink, 42¾ x 24½ . . . . (776)   2,600

1968–July 1969
The Owl, 1957, ink, 20 x 29¾ . . . . (1018)   600

WATERCOLORS
1965
Composition, 1948, gouache, 25 x 10 . . . . (489)   900

1966
Surfbird, (1940), tempera and watercolor,
23 x 27¾ . . . . (776)   6,000
In the Night, 1943, watercolor and wash,
27¼ x 25¼ . . . . (776)   3,500
Joyous Young Pine, (1944), tempera on paper laid
down on canvas, 13¾ x 27 . . . . (776)   2,500

1967
Feather, (1945-50), tempera on paper laid down
on canvas, 52½ x 26½ . . . . (893)   800
Oh Outrages Nest, 1950, watercolor and wash,
18¾ x 25 . . . . (889)   700

1968–July 1969
Bird, 1953, tempera and watercolor, 14 x 24¼ . . . (1030)   1,100
Mandala, (1945-50), gouache, watercolor, and
gold leaf, 12¾ x 12¾ . . . . (1018)   200
Woodpeckers, tempera and watercolor,
11¾ x 19½ . . . . (1246)   2,300

Juan Gris

(1887–1927)

Birthplace: Madrid, Spain.

1902   Attends the Arts and Crafts School of Madrid.

1904   At the beginning, is influenced by Art Nouveau. Changes his own name of José Victoriano Gonzalès to the pseudonym of Juan Gris.

1906   Goes to Paris. Settles at the Bateau-Lavoir, where Picasso lives. Meets Apollinaire, Max Jacob, and André Salmon. Does illustrations for papers such as *L'Assiette au Beurre.*

1907   Becomes very friendly with the art critic Maurice Raynal. Meets the dealer Kahnweiler.

1910-11   Devotes all his energies to painting and sells a few pictures.

1912   Participates in the Salon des Indépendants and the exhibition of the Section d'Or, Paris. First collages. Signs a contract with Kahnweiler.

1913   Stay at Céret with Picasso. Thickens his colors with sand and ashes.

1914   Spends the summer at Collioure in the south of France and becomes very friendly with Matisse.

1915   Illustrates Pierre Reverdy's *Poèmes en Prose.* Executes several other illustrations in the coming years—for Max Jacob, Salacrou, Tzara, and Radiguet.

1917   Signs a contract with the dealer Rosenberg.

1920   One-man show at Rosenberg's, Paris. Participates in the Salon des Indépendants, Paris, where the last Cubist group show takes place.

1921   Executes lithographs. Meets Diaghilev in Monte Carlo.

1922-23   Executes several stage decorations for Diaghilev's ballets.

1923   One-man show at Kahnweiler's, Paris.

1924   Delivers his lecture "Sur les Possibilités de la peinture" at the Sorbonne University, Paris.

1925   Exhibition at Flechtheim's, Berlin.

1927   Died, Paris.

Sales

DRAWINGS
1961–1962
Still Life with a Book, Fruit, and a Glass, black
lead, 12¼ x 12½ . . . . (106) $3,616
The Fruit Stand, (1915-16), pencil, 15 x 10¾ . . . . . (164)   4,119
Still Life with Cigarettes,[1] black lead, 6½ x 8¾ . . . . (36)   880
The Conversation,[2] India ink, 12¾ x 11 . . . . (128)   384
The Beauty and the Handsome Athlete, India ink
and colored pencil, 14¼ x 8¾ . . . . (117)   196
Why I Shall Never Become Your Mistress, pen,
13½ x 11 . . . . (111)   300
In the Bedroom, India ink and colored pencil,
9½ x 9¼ . . . . (143)   542
Flirt, India ink and gouache, 13½ x 12¼ . . . . (51)   280
The Cocktail, India ink, 16¾ x 12 . . . . (31)   659
Guillaume II as a Doctor of Molière, heightened
drawing, double sided, 15¾ x 12¾ . . . . (68)   200
Master of the Masters, drawing heightened with
gouache, 13¾ x 11 . . . . (168)   270
In the Colonies, India ink and gouache,
11¾ x 12¼ . . . . (5)   110
I Am a Gentleman, India ink, 13½ x 11 . . . . (108)   232

1963
The Departure of the Aviator, 1908, charcoal,
black chalk, and watercolor, 13¾ x 10¾ . . . . . . (219)   271
Three Children Playing, (1908), India ink
heightened with white, 16¾ x 11 . . . . (219)   407
The Hunter and the Peasant,[3] ink and gouache,
12 x 8¼ . . . . (255)   356
The Franco-German War, wash and blue pencil,
11¼ x 9½ . . . . (271)   60
At the Café, ink and colored pencil, 11½ x 9 . . . . . (251)   260
The Couple, pencil, 16 x 11 . . . . (216)   205
The Letter, ink, 18 x 10¼ . . . . (216)   439
The Bay, 1924, colored pencil, 8¾ x 11½ . . . . (255)   877

[1] Inscribed "Arec mes voeux pour 1920."
[2] Study for *L'Assiette au beurre.*
[3] For *L'Assiette au beurre.*

1964

***A Fashionable Woman Admired by Three Men in
Tailcoats***, (1908), India ink, 16¼ x 12 . . . . (383) — $ 158

***She Can Be Sure that Tomorrow Will Have
Enough to Pay Me!***, pencil, 15¾ x 12¼ . . . . . (346) — 190

***That Marix Has to Be Prosecuted for Unfair
Competition***, 1908, India ink, blue chalk, and
white lights, 13¾ x 11 . . . . (383) — 124

Illustration for "L'Assiette au Beurre," (No. 474,
1910), ink heightened with white, 15 x 10½ . . . (368) — 221

The Smoker: Portrait of Frank Haviland, 1912,
colored pencil, 28 x 23 . . . . (405) — 9,286

Pushing Person, India ink and blue and black
pencil, 10 x 9½ . . . . (455) — 249

Gifts, pencil and watercolor, 12¾ x 10 . . . . (329) — 500

In the Drawing Room, pen, 12¾ x 11 . . . . (374) — 500

The Cove, blue and brown pencil, 8¾ x 11¾ . . . . . (405) — 1,016

Cubist Composition, charcoal, 8¾ x 11¼ . . . . (471) — 1,130

1965

Still Life with Apples, After Cézanne, pencil,
11 x 12¾ . . . . (586) — 1,000

Street Scene in Paris, ink and blue pencil,
12¾ x 20½ . . . . (507) — 725

At the Airport, charcoal heightened with white,
14 x 10¾ . . . . (644) — 375

Still Life with a Guitar, 1923, ink, 8 x 11 . . . . (633) — 4,000

Pierrot with a Mandolin, pencil heightened with
chalk, 11½ x 8¾ . . . . (516) — 1,620

1966

Guitar and Newspaper, 1913, charcoal and
colored pencil, 35½ x 23 . . . . (753) — 14,510

In a Bar, pencil and charcoal, 12¼ x 11¼ . . . . (793) — 350

Still Life, (1923–24), charcoal heightened with
chalk, 7¼ x 10¾ . . . . (812) — 2,488

Still Life, colored chalk, 4¾ x 4½ . . . . (816) — 738

The Letter, ink and gouache, 17 x 11¾ . . . . (703) — 3,250

Project for a Stage Curtain, pencil, 7½ x 9½ . . . . . (757) — 111

1967

The Stag, the Hunter, and the Hind, India ink
heightened with gouache, 11 x 11 . . . . (898) — 600

The Moon, (1910), India-ink wash, charcoal, and
blue pencil, 15 x 9½ . . . . (929) — 360

Guitar and Fruit Stand, 1923, charcoal, ink, and
gouache, 6¼ x 9¾ . . . . (1004) — 3,750

10 to 1, charcoal, blue pencil, and white gouache,
14½ x 12¼ . . . . (929) — 360

1968–July 1969

The Man with a Top Hat, 1912, charcoal,
19 x 12½ . . . . (1064) — 11,800

Fashionable Woman, India ink, 8 x 4½ . . . . (1088) — 375

The Rendezvous,[4] pencil heightened with white,
11¾ x 8¾ . . . . (1018) — 1,200

Still Life with a Fruit Stand, 1921, pencil, 7¼ x 11 (1068) — 2,242

At the Café, gouache, 12¾ x 12¾ . . . . (1221) — 820

The Walk, pencil, pen, brush, and ink, 1908,
13¼ x 11¼ . . . . (1272) — 960

WATERCOLORS

1961–1962

The Shipwreck, watercolor and gouache, 10 x 8 . . . (155) — 300

Toilette, gouache, 11¾ x 8¾ . . . . (30) — 620

Rider,[5] watercolor, 12 x 9½ . . . . (164) — 1,373

[4]Illustration for *L'Assiette au beurre*.
[5]Costume design for Diaghilev's ballet *Temptations*, 1923. Dedicated "A
Grigoriew, amicalement."

1963

The Bedroom, pastel and India ink, 9½ x 9¼ . . . . . (232) — $ 406

The Interrogatory, gouache, 8¼ x 8 . . . . (187) — 140

The National Assistance, watercolor, 10 x 8¼ . . . . (178) — 200

The National Assistance Office, gouache,
10 x 8¼ . . . . (315) — 548

1964

The Interrogatory, watercolor and pencil,
10 x 8 . . . . (472) — 310

1965

Still Life, 1918, semicircle-shaped gouache,
3¾ x 9½ . . . . (583) — 2,177

The Toilette, gouache, 11½ x 8½ . . . . (497) — 190

The Toilette, gouache, 11½ x 8½ . . . . (586) — 360

1966

The Gentleman,[6] 1924, oval-shaped watercolor,
7½ x 5¼ . . . . (784) — 650

The Stag Hunt, gouache, 11 x 11 . . . . (718) — 212

1967

Swans, gouache and India ink, 16¾ x 21¼ . . . . . . (975) — 3,200

1968–July 1969

The Stag, the Hind. . .and the Hunter, gouache,
10¼ x 10¼ . . . . (1225) — 1,160

PAINTINGS

1961–1962

Still Life with a Cup, 1913, 18½ x 10¾ . . . . (129) — 20,595

Still Life, 1915, on cardboard, 11¾ x 7¾ . . . . (80) — 8,400

Newspaper and Pipe, 1917, on panel,
10½ x 13½ . . . . (140) — 8,787

Glass, Bottle, and Newspaper, 1919, 28 x 21¼ . . . (140) — 28,833

Still Life, 1923, on panel, 7¼ x 10¼ . . . . (20) — 12,640

***Still Life With a Pipe, a Pocketknife, and a
Green Apple on an Open Book***, 1924,
9¼ x 12¾ . . . . (64) — 6,000

Book and Violin, 1926, 13 x 16¼ . . . . (31) — 16,476

1963

Landscape, 1917, on panel, 45½ x 18¾ . . . . (277) — 17,823

Composition with a Glass, 1919, 13¼ x 7½ . . . . . (210) — 7,678

Harlequin with a Guitar, 1919, 45½ x 35¼ . . . . . (309) — 72,512

The Pedestal Table, 1921, 24 x 18¼ . . . . (247) — 23,307

1964

The Two Pierrots, 1922, 39¼ x 25 . . . . (416) — 27,640

Still Life with the Ace of Clubs, 1917, on board,
15¾ x 10 . . . . (460) — 16,700

The Fruit Stand, 1920, 10¾ x 14 . . . . (460) — 10,400

House in Provence, 1924, 8 x 13½ . . . . (405) — 5,514

1965

Still Life with Grapes, 1914, collage, pencil, and
gouache on canvas, 32 x 23¾ . . . . (615) — 56,000

Still Life with a Lamp, 1914, collage,
21¾ x 18¼ . . . . (615) — 39,000

Still Life with a Newspaper, 1916, on board,
32 x 17¾ . . . . (615) — 64,000

Still Life, 1918, 18½ x 21½ . . . . (624) — 19,348

Harlequin Guitar Player, 1918, 39½ x 25¾ . . . . . (615) — 41,000

Fruit Stand and Newspaper, 1918, 36½ x 25¾ . . . (615) — 48,000

Still Life with a Pear, on panel, 6½ x 10¾ . . . . . . (583) — 3,773

Still Life with Cards, 1926, 10 x 13¾ . . . . (522) — 13,820

Red Carpet, Fruit Stand, and Decanter, 1926,
25¾ x 32 . . . . (615) — 31,000

[6]Costume design for *The Temptations of the Shepherdess*, 1924.

1966

Still Life, (1911), oval-shaped picture, 7¾ x 10 . . . . **(694)** $7,750

The Musician's Table, 1914, collage and paint on
paper mounted on canvas laid down on
cradled panel, 31½ x 23½ . . . . **(676)**   45,000

Pipe and Decanter, 1917, on board, 26¼ x 9½ . . . . **(801)**   12,200

The Jug, 1920, 18¼ x 13 . . . . **(801)**   26,000

The Scotswoman, 1918, 36½ x 25¾ . . . . **(801)**   23,000

Crosswords, 1925, 15 x 18¼ . . . . **(801)**   14,000

1967

Still Life with a Cup, 1913, 18½ x 11 . . . . **(982)**   28,440

Still Life, 1919, 18¼ x 10½ . . . . **(880)**   38,706

Fruit Stand and Flask, 1920, 23¾ x 29 . . . . **(975)**   24,000

1968–July 1969

The Bottle of Bordeaux Wine, 1913, oil and
collage on canvas, 21½ x 12¾ . . . . **(1064)**   84,960

The Bottle of Rosé Wine, 1914, oil and collage,
17½ x 10¼ . . . . **(1064)**   40,120

L'Intransigeant, 1915, 25¼ x 17¾ . . . . **(1064)**   7,670

Still Life with a Poem,[7] 1915, 31¾ x 25¾ . . . . **(1056)**   120,000

Landscape, Loches, 1916, on panel, 21¾ x 15 . . . . **(1068)**   2,832

Fruit Stand and Glass, 1924, 9 x 12¾ . . . . **(1068)**   21,240

Bowl and Fruit Stand, 1925, 18¼ x 21¾ . . . . **(1187)**   38,940

Marcel Gromaire

(1892–1971)

Birthplace: Noyelles-sur-Sambre, France.

1900-10   Goes to Paris. Gives up his law studies to devote himself to painting. Attends many academies of Montparnasse. Meets Matisse.

1914-20   Expressionism exerts a great influence on his own style. His favorite subject matter is the world of peasants and workmen. Appreciates Cézanne and Seurat above all the modern masters.

1925   Participates in the Salon des Indépendants, Paris, showing his important work, "La Guerre."

1933   Retrospective exhibition at the Kunsthalle, Basel.

1937   Executes decorations for the World's Fair, Paris.

1939   With Lurçat and Dubrcuil, promotes a tapestry revival, working at the Manufacture des Gobelins and at Aubusson.

1947   One-man show at the Galerie Louis Carré, Paris.

1949   One-man show at the Galerie Louis Carré, New York.

1952   Wins first prize, Carnegie International.

       Resident in France.

1971   Died.

[7]The poem is by Pierre Reverdy.

Sales

DRAWINGS

1961–1962

Landscape, 1919, charcoal, 9¼ x 12¼ . . . . **(143)** $ 226

Landscape, 1923, pen and sepia wash,
12¾ x 9¾ . . . . **(152)**   350

Reclining Nude, 1923, drawing in two colors,
24½ x 19¾ . . . . **(168)**   1,000

Towboat at Bougival, 1927, India ink, 9¾ x 11¾ . . **(115)**   202

Fishing Boats, India ink, 12¼ x 9½ . . . . **(26)**   360

Washerwoman, India ink, 9½ x 12 . . . . **(106)**   158

Reclining Woman, black lead, 12¾ x 10 . . . . **(147)**   180

Two Women, 1931, pen and watercolor,
18½ x 14 . . . . **(151)**   1,023

The Dyke, 1938, India ink and watercolor,
12¾ x 16¾ . . . . **(52)**   560

Bust of a Young Woman, 1941, ink and
watercolor, 12 x 9½ . . . . **(96)**   1,100

Reclining Nude, 1955, India ink, 9½ x 13 . . . . **(72)**   330

Back View of a Kneeling Nude, 1958, pen,
13 x 10 . . . . **(102)**   400

1963

*Reclining Nude, Her Hands at the Nape of Her
Neck,* 1923, black heightened with pastel,
19¾ x 24½ . . . . **(278)**   1,040

Nude Dressing, 1924, India ink, 12¼ x 9 . . . . **(276)**   420

Towboat at Bougival, 1927, pen, 10 x 11¾ . . . . **(318)**   340

Seated Nude, pencil and watercolor, 12½ x 9½ . . . **(194)**   720

Seated Nude, 1927, pen and watercolor,
11¾ x 10¾ . . . . **(283)**   678

Motorcyclists, 1930, pen, 9½ x 12¾ . . . . **(315)**   274

Nude, 1945, India ink, 13 x 10 . . . . **(283)**   610

Study for a Nude, 1950, ink, 13 x 10 . . . . **(179)**   425

Study of a Nude, 1952, India ink, 13 x 10 . . . . **(219)**   271

The Beach, 1957, pen and watercolor,
19¾ x 12¾ . . . . **(208)**   950

1964

Reclining Young Woman in the Nude, 1924, pen,
8½ x 11¼ . . . . **(398)**   350

Woman, 1925, India ink, 13½ x 10 . . . . **(346)**   200

The Vagrant, 1925, pen, 12½ x 9¾ . . . . **(471)**   429

Reclining Nude, 1929, India ink, 8¾ x 11½ . . . . . . **(441)**   610

Nude, pen, 10 x 12¾ . . . . **(329)**   550

Motorcyclists, 1930, pen, 9¼ x 12¼ . . . . **(335)**   340

Motorcyclists, 1930, India ink, 9¼ x 12½ . . . . **(378)**   678

Nude Leaning on Her Elbow, 1931, pen,
12¼ x 9¼ . . . . **(377)**   497

Landscapes, 1934, two drawings, India ink, each
4¾ x 6½ . . . . **(409)**   220

Reclining Nude, 1935, pen, 9½ x 12¼ . . . . **(466)**   340

Reclining Nude, 1940, pen, 10 x 12¾ . . . . **(466)**   320

Reclining Nude, 1944, pen, 10 x 12¾ . . . . **(366)**   400

Nude, 1949, pen, 12¾ x 9½ . . . . **(408)**   320

Nude with an Armchair, 1952, pen, 12¾ x 9½ . . . . **(474)**   340

Reclining Nude, 1952, India ink, 25 x 12¾ . . . . **(335)**   640

Reclining Nude, 1956, pen, 9½ x 12¾ . . . . **(472)**   340

Reclining Nude, 1959, pen, 10 x 12¾ . . . . **(401)**   360

Nude, 1963, pen, 10 x 13 . . . . **(386)**   560

1965

Interior Scene, 1923, pen and wash, 9 x 12½ . . . . . **(503)**   720

Reclining Nude, 1925, India ink, 9¾ x 12¾ . . . . **(503)**   340

Nude with a Tub, 1925, India ink, 9¾ x 12 . . . . **(567)**   396

Seated Nude, 1926, India ink, 12¾ x 9½ . . . . **(634)**   295

Nude with a Phonograph, 1931, pen, 12 x 9¼ . . . . . **(607)** $ 440

Seated Nude, 1945, India ink, 13 x 10 . . . . **(567)**   418

Nude in an Armchair, 1952, pen, 12¾ x 9½ . . . . **(540)**   360

Nude, 1954, pen, 12¾ x 10 . . . . **(523)**   364

Reclining Nude, 1956, pen, 9½ x 12¾ . . . . **(523)**   336

1966

The Ploughman, 1923, pen, 12¼ x 9 . . . . **(815)**   387

Reclining Nude, 1923, ink, 18½ x 25 . . . . **(689)**   663

Nude Washing Herself, 1925, ink, 9 x 12 . . . . **(703)**   650

Nude, India ink, 10 x 12¾ . . . . **(805)**   525

Nude, ink, 10 x 12¾ . . . . **(648)**   400

Composition, 1946, ink and watercolor,
12¾ x 17¾ . . . . **(713)**   1,600

Seated Model, 1953, pen, 13 x 10¼ . . . . **(770)**   568

Reclining Nude, pen, 10 x 13 . . . . **(718)**   480

Reclining Nude, 1958, pen, 10 x 12¾ . . . . **(809)**   580

1967

Portrait of a Woman, 1925, India ink and
watercolor, 25 x 18¾ . . . . **(921)**   1,400

The Musicians, 1925, pen and watercolor,
9¼ x 12¼ . . . . **(1004)**   2,700

Little Fishing Harbor, India ink, 10¾ x 11½ . . . . . . **(986)**   295

Bathers at the Seaside, 1926, pen and watercolor,
10 x 12¾ . . . . **(1004)**   2,000

Portrait of Bernheim Jr., 1927, pen, 11½ x 10 . . . . . **(966)**   290

Reclining Nude, 1938, India ink, 13 x 10 . . . . **(958)**   422

The Bar, 1926, India ink, 9¾ x 6½ . . . . **(927)**   305

Seated Nude, 1949, India ink, 13 x 10 . . . . **(967)**   316

Standing Nude, 1952, pen, 13 x 10 . . . . **(978)**   560

Cooking Scene, ink and watercolor, 15¾ x 12 . . . . **(889)**   1,000

Reclining Nude, 1958, India ink, 10 x 13 . . . . **(995)**   640

Standing Nude, 1957, pen, 18¾ x 13 . . . . **(881)**   470

Reclining Nude, 1960, pen, 9 x 12 . . . . **(893)**   550

Seated Woman in the Nude, 1962, ink,
13¼ x 10 . . . . **(898)**   500

1968–July 1969

Cubist Landscape, 1913, colored pencil, 8 x 9 . . . . **(1110)**   180

Reclining Nude, 1923, pen, 18¾ x 25 . . . . **(1145)**   500

Landscape, 1923, pen, 9½ x 12¼ . . . . **(1154)**   300

Nude, 1925, pen, 14¾ x 10 . . . . **(1121)**   340

The Man with an Upset Glass, 1925, India ink,
10¼ x 7¾ . . . . **(1161)**   280

Young Woman with a Scarf, 1929, pen,
12¾ x 10 . . . . **(1213)**   300

Reclining Nude, 1935, India ink and watercolor,
15 x 21¾ . . . . **(1183)**   1,940

Seated Nude, 1939, India ink, 12¾ x 10 . . . . **(1174)**   460

Reclining Nude, 1945, pen, 10 x 13 . . . . **(1026)**   500

Seated Nude, 1954, India ink, 13½ x 9½ . . . . **(1127)**   483

The Coifs of Pont-Aven, 1954, pen and
watercolor, 12¾ x 17 . . . . **(1030)**   1,500

Seated Nude, 1955, pen, 13½ x 10 . . . . **(1078)**   390

Reclining Nude, 1957, pen, 10 x 13 . . . . **(1026)**   470

Reclining Nude, 1957, India ink, 10¼ x 13¼ . . . . . **(1099)**   736

Reclining Nude, 1961, pen, 10 x 12¾ . . . . **(1119)**   460

Standing Nude, 1963, pen, 13½ x 10¼ . . . . **(1051)**   380

Standing Nude, 1965, 13 x 9½ . . . . **(1216)**   550

The Vault, pen, 12¾ x 10 . . . . **(1220)**   270

Reclining Nude, Turned to the Left, 1945, pen,
10 x 12¾ . . . . **(1224)**   600

Standing Nude, India ink, 1925, 14¾ x 10¼ . . . . . **(1247)**   320

Seated Nude, 1926, pen, 10¼ x 7½ . . . . **(1262)**   700

Reclining Nude, 1957, India ink, 10 x 12¾ . . . . . . **(1268)**   580

Seated Nude, 1957, India ink, 13 x 10 . . . . **(1268)**   580

Reclining Nude, 1957, India ink, 10 x 13 . . . . **(1268)** $ 684

Seated Nude, 1926, India ink and wash,
9½ x 11¾ . . . . **(1268)**   777

WATERCOLORS

1961–1962

Two Women in a Boat, 1928, watercolor and pen,
12¾ x 16¼ . . . . **(75)**   1,264

Reclining Nude, 1924, watercolor, 18¾ x 24¾ . . . . . **(98)**   820

Reclining Nude, watercolor, 18½ x 24½ . . . . **(160)**   1,300

Football Players, watercolor, 16¾ x 12¾ . . . . **(170)**   700

At the Movies, 1935, gouache, 16¾ x 12¾ . . . . **(18)**   1,288

The Three Hills, 1941, watercolor, 12½ x 17 . . . . . . **(34)**   780

The Sailboat, 1959, watercolor, 19½ x 13 . . . . **(143)**   1,220

1963

At the Café, 1926, watercolor, 15¾ x 12¼ . . . . **(238)**   740

Woman Knitting, 1926, watercolor, 15 x 12¼ . . . . . **(238)**   740

The Carrousel, 1933, watercolor, 13½ x 16¼ . . . . . **(232)**   1,808

The Drinkers, 1946, gouache, 12 x 16½ . . . . **(208)**   2,600

Composition, 1947, watercolor, 12¼ x 9½ . . . . **(232)**   1,085

1964

Nude, 1925, watercolor, 24 x 18¼ . . . . **(472)**   1,400

The Sandwich Man, 1925, watercolor and pen,
18¾ x 12¼ . . . . **(378)**   1,763

Reclining Nude, 1926, pen, 11½ x 10¼ . . . . **(399)**   320

Bathing, 1930, watercolor, 17 x 13 . . . . **(371)**   1,300

At Dessert, 1942, watercolor, 12¼ x 9½ . . . . **(409)**   920

Haarlem, 1951, watercolor, 12¾ x 17½ . . . . **(361)**   1,060

1965

Models in the Studio, 1931, watercolor,
15¾ x 11¾ . . . . **(627)**   1,170

The Potter, 1948, watercolor, 17 x 12¼ . . . . **(573)**   1,050

Interior, 1948, watercolor, 12¼ x 17 . . . . **(573)**   1,880

1966

Garden Entrance, 1927, watercolor and India ink,
9¼ x 12¼ . . . . **(798)**   1,107

Bullfight, 1929, watercolor and India ink,
16¼ x 12¾ . . . . **(784)**   1,400

Football Players, 1930, watercolor, 16¾ x 12¾ . . . **(681)**   1,120

Sailors and Sailboats, 1952, watercolor, 13 x 10 . . . **(811)**   760

1967

Roofs, 1952, pen and watercolor, 12¾ x 19½ . . . . . **(831)**   700

Two Fair-Haired Bathers, 1960, watercolor,
13 x 17½ . . . . **(838)**   1,440

1968–July 1969

The Village, 1932, watercolor, 9¼ x 12¼ . . . . **(1104)**   700

Bust of a Young Woman, 1943, watercolor,
12¾ x 9½ . . . . **(1043)**   1,800

The Town, 1945, watercolor, 10 x 12¾ . . . . **(1051)**   1,200

The Forest, 1946, watercolor, 13 x 10¾ . . . . **(1127)**   1,058

Landscape, 1952, watercolor, 12¾ x 17¼ . . . . **(1053)**   1,600

Landscape, 1956, watercolor, 12¾ x 16¾ . . . . **(1127)**   1,840

The Harbor in Brittany, 1962, watercolor,
13 x 17¼ . . . . **(1026)**   1,300

Blond Bather on a Rock, 1953, watercolor,
17½ x 13 . . . . **(1254)**   2,160

PAINTINGS

1961–1962

The Flemish Milkmaid, 1922, 21¾ x 18¼ . . . . **(171)**   840

Splendor of Woman, 32 x 25¾ . . . . **(109)**   11,200

Standing Nude, 25¾ x 21¼ . . . . **(160)**   5,500

Sailboats Entering the Harbor, Finistère, 1927,
  25¾ x 32 . . . . (102) $4,900
Peasant with Pieces of Furniture, 1930,
  32 x 25¾ . . . . (102)   4,200
Little Nude, 1934, 16¼ x 13 . . . . (72)   3,340
Autumn Road, 1940, 18¼ x 21¾ . . . . (76)   1,600

1963
The Vegetable Woman, 32 x 25 . . . . (298)   7,000
Noyelles Church, 1923, 25¾ x 32 . . . . (255)   3,016
The Shed, 1927, 39½ x 32 . . . . (303)   9,000
Boats, 1930, 17¾ x 20¾ . . . . (208)   3,000
The Ash Track, 1930, 32¼ x 39½ . . . . (303)   9,000
Gathering Flowers, 1931, 39½ x 32 . . . . (258)   7,400
The Sea Gulls' Cliff, 1937, 25¾ x 32 . . . . (255)   2,057
Clouds on the Mountain, 32 x 39½ . . . . (194)   8,200
Nude on a Red Sofa, 1960, 14¾ x 17¾ . . . . (202)   4,500
Interior with a Nude, 25¾ x 21¼ . . . . (298)   6,000

1964
Bust of a Reclining Man, 1922, 21¾ x 18¼ . . . . (480)   680
Small Reclining Nude, 1927, 13 x 18¼ . . . . (408)   4,200
Back View of a Nude, on panel, 16¼ x 12¾ . . . . . . (475)   3,000
Seated Nude, 21¾ x 18¼ . . . . (337)   4,600
The Red-Haired Model, 1938, 18¼ x 21¾ . . . . (341)   6,200
The Red-Haired Model, 1938, 21¾ x 18¼ . . . . (472)   5,600
Blond Nude on a Red Stool, 1958, 25¾ x 21¼ . . . . (371)   6,560

1965
Seated Nude, 1928, 21¾ x 18¼ . . . . (516)   6,500
Rocky Landscape, 1943, 15 x 18¼ . . . . (564)   2,700
Small Flemish Bridge, 1946, 18½ x 15 . . . . (573)   4,975
Nude Under a Tree, 1950, 31¼ x 38¾ . . . . (573)   7,739
The Brook Flows into the Sea, 1960, 25¾ x 32 . . . . (559)   5,600
Landscape with Three Nudes, 1962, 21¼ x 25¾ . . . (559)   7,900

1966
Still Life, 1913, 25 x 20½ . . . . (698)   1,768
Three Bathers, 1932, 39¼ x 32 . . . . (678)   17,000
Cliff with Sea Gulls, 1937, 25 x 31¼ . . . . (753)   5,514
The Earth, 1938, 29 x 39½ . . . . (819)   10,400

1967
Marché aux Puces, 1927, 51½ x 37½ . . . . (901)   12,000
The Red-Haired Model, 1938, 18¾ x 22 . . . . (921)   6,000
Around the Lamp, 1939, 32 x 39½ . . . . (940)   10,447
The Purple Roof, 1945, 29 x 19¾ . . . . (1000)   1,960
Patch of a Pond, 1947, on cradled panel,
  16¼ x 13 . . . . (978)   1,900
The Path with a Gas Burner, on canvas laid down
  on cardboard, 13¾ x 10¼ . . . . (987)   1,920
Interior with a Gray Pot, 1955, 25¾ x 32 . . . . (993)   7,200
The Seine Flows Through Paris, 32 x 39½ . . . . (993)   9,600
Interior with a Gray Pot, 1955, 25¾ x 32 . . . . (918)   10,848
St. Jacques Tower, 1956, 32 x 25¾ . . . . (918)   7,797
The Flower Market at La Madeleine, 1956,
  32 x 39½ . . . . (988)   5,473

1968–July 1969
Suburban Sunday, 1927, 63¼ x 51½ . . . . (1187)   9,440
Smugglers, 1930, 32 x 39½ . . . . (1049)   5,700
The Thatch-Roofed Cottage, 1942, on paper laid
  down on canvas, 15 x 18¼ . . . . (1106)   1,800
Manhattan Headland, 1951, 18 x 21¾ . . . . (1080)   4,250
Blond Nude on a Red Stool, 1958, 25¾ x 21¼ . . . (1117)   6,700
The Brook Flows into the Sea, 1960, 25¾ x 32 . . . (1113)   6,000
The Fruit Seller, 1953, 31½ x 38½ . . . . (1235)   13,000
Nude in a Garden Armchair, 1931, 21½ x 18 . . . . (1270)   9,320

Georges Grosz

(1893–1959)

Birthplace: Berlin, Germany.
1912   Begins to draw.
1917   Participates in the earliest Dada events in Berlin.
1920-30   Executes a series of drawings and caricatures showing life in Berlin during World War I, dis-
playing his natural gift for caustic and witty expression in art.
1932   Invited by the U.S. to teach art at the Art Students
League, New York.
1951   Returns to Europe.
1959   Died, Berlin.

Sales

DRAWINGS

1961–1962
At Night, India ink, 19½ x 14 . . . . (106) $ 316
Street Scene, India ink, 20¾ x 14 . . . . (106)   316
Maid with Three Visitors, pen, 6¼ x 7¼ . . . . (105)   118
Lady Hamilton, 1928, India ink, 23¾ x 15¾ . . . . . . (37)   1,100
The Encounter, (1928), pen and watercolor,
  24¼ x 19 . . . . (85)   1,200
Almsgiving, 1933, India ink, 22¼ x 16¾ . . . . (111)   400
Portrait of Hitler, India ink and brush,
  22½ x 15¾ . . . . (106)   181

1963
Nude, pencil, 7½ x 8 . . . . (219)   127
Street Scene, 1917, India ink, 18¾ x 14 . . . . (219)   305
The Prostitute's Room; Murder at the Zoo, wash,
  8½ x 10½ and 8½ x 10¾ . . . . (208)   350
Two Men and Two Women in Evening Dress,
  India ink, 25¼ x 20 . . . . (284)   443
The Wreck, (1925), India ink and watercolor,
  20½ x 25¾ . . . . (228)   541

1964
Standing Nude, with Head Missing, pen,
  11½ x 7 . . . . (383)   86
The Encounter, 1923, India ink, 19¾ x 15¾ . . . . . . (467)   246
Varnishing Day, India ink, 20½ x 25¾ . . . . (461)   640

1965
I Love You, India ink, 23¾ x 18¼ . . . . (597)   455
The Kiss, pen, 22½ x 17¾ . . . . (629)   813
The Maid and the Three Customers, (1914), ink
  and wash, 6¼ x 7¼ . . . . (566)   226
The Street, (1915), ink and colored pencil,
  8¾ x 10 . . . . (522)   829
The Belly Dance, (1919), pen, 14¾ x 10 . . . . (522)   691
Old Street in Marseilles, 1927, pen, 25¼ x 19½ . . . (634)   344

1966
Figures, (1922), (recto), *Studies of a Man and a
  Woman* (verso), 20¼ x 16 . . . . (686)   5,804
Nightclub, pen and watercolor, 19¾ x 15¼ . . . . . . (815)   691

1967
Café Trocadéro, 1915, pen, 8¼ x 6¾ . . . . (927)   452
Reclining Girls, 1915, India ink and colored
  pencil, 8 x 11¾ . . . . (970)   689
Couple, 1918, pen, 18¾ x 13 . . . . (882)   480
Two Drinkers, 1920, pen, 12¾ x 8¾ . . . . (998)   357

Tartarin de Tarascon, 1920, India ink,
16¼ x 11¾ .... **(907)** $ 615

The Quarrel, (1922), ink, 21 x 17½ .... **(910)**   664

Standing Nudes, (1922), India ink, 20½ x 13½ .... **(970)**   738

Emma Sitting For Romney, 1923, India ink,
15 x 10¾ .... **(927)**   655

Woman with a Straw Hat, 1924, pen and
watercolor, 14 x 9½ .... **(986)**   836

Two Women, (1924), pen, 11½ x 8¼ .... **(962)**   480

Street Scene in Paris, 1925, India ink,
12¼ x 9½ .... **(906)**   418

The Dream of Tartarin de Tarascon, (1926), India
ink, 17½ x 11¾ .... **(927)**   859

The Equilibrist, colored pencil, 11½ x 8¾ .... **(962)**   448

The Road Song, pen, 25 x 19 .... **(985)**   664

Two Men Watching Two Soldiers Passing By,
India ink, 19¾ x 14¼ .... **(859)**   456

The Beer Drinkers, pen, 8¾ x 16¼ .... **(915)**   812

Scene in a Brothel, India ink, 23¼ x 18 .... **(963)**   900

"Gottes sichtbare Segen ruht auf uns" (Schiller),
pen, 20 x 19½ .... **(885)**   813

1968–July 1969

At the Café, (1915), pen and colored chalk,
11 x 8¾ .... **(1099)**   621

Back View of a Nude, 1916, charcoal, 9 x 10½ ... **(1041)**   190

Street Scene, (1922), India ink, 24 x 18¾ .... **(1191)**   1,227

At the Café, (1924), India ink, 22½ x 17½ .... **(1134)**   472

Camel Following a Caravan, pen, 12¾ x 19¾ .... **(1094)**   248

"Brandung," Street Scene, (1926), India ink,
25½ x 20¾ .... **(1094)**   620

No More War!, India ink, 25 x 19½ .... **(1209)**   794

Portrait of Wieland Herzfelde, 1926, pencil,
23¼ x 17¾ .... **(1209)**   546

The Prostitute and the Civil Servant, (1930), pen,
22¾ x 12¾ .... **(1105)**   342

Reclining Nude, 1945, pencil and pastel,
17¾ x 23¾ .... **(1061)**   1,200

The Kiss, India ink, 22¼ x 18 .... **(1145)**   700

Morning, pencil, 8¾ x 11¼ .... **(1068)**   614

Three Figures, India ink, 19 x 14¾ .... **(1214)**   608

Brothel, 1925, pen, brush, and India ink,
25 x 19¼ .... **(1240)**   960

Café Denis, 1914, ink and colored pencil,
11¼ x 8¼ .... **(1246)**   4,100

At the Café Schmidt, (1926-28), 25 x 20¼ .... **(1273)**   1,008

WATERCOLORS

1961–1962

"Beauty, It Is You I Want to Enjoy," 1919-20,
watercolor, 16¾ x 11¾ .... **(88)**   1,353

Die Serviertochter, watercolor, 24 x 18¾ .... **(105)**   362

Interior of a "Gasthaus" in Berlin, 1927,
watercolor, 17¾ x 23¼ .... **(64)**   2,750

The Shadows of the World, watercolor,
19 x 25¾ .... **(64)**   1,000

The Private, 1937, watercolor, 22 x 15½ .... **(129)**   824

In Front of the Barracks, India ink and
watercolor, 16¼ x 20¼ .... **(106)**   791

1963

Fog, 1934, watercolor, 23½ x 17 .... **(225)**   700

Berlin by Night, watercolor, 24¼ x 17¾ .... **(208)**   900

Seated Nude, watercolor, 23¾ x 15¾ .... **(290)**   900

The Glass of Rhine Wine, watercolor, 15 x 18¾ ... **(281)**   475

1964

In the Bus, (1932), watercolor, 26¼ x 19¼ .... **(461)** $ 720

The Refugees, 1940, watercolor, 17¾ x 26¾ ...... **(324)**   1,000

Beginning of Spring No. 4, watercolor,
23¾ x 18¼ .... **(416)**   1,520

1965

The Stroll Family, watercolor, 24½ x 18¼ .... **(489)**   1,050

The Café, 1925, watercolor, 26 x 38 .... **(637)**   4,500

Street Scene in New York, 1932, watercolor,
23¾ x 17¾ .... **(489)**   900

1966

Seaside, watercolor on paper laid down on board,
15 x 19¾ .... **(790)**   800

1967

The Glutton and the Poor, 1936, gouache and
watercolor, 17¾ x 23 .... **(889)**   2,600

Scene in a Café, Berlin, watercolor, 17¾ x 23 .... **(889)**   4,250

Young Lady Undressing, 1929, watercolor,
24 x 17 .... **(881)**   1,437

Squatting Nude, watercolor, 24 x 19½ .... **(841)**   1,800

The Milkman, watercolor, 19 x 15 .... **(1004)**   1,400

Burlesque, 42nd Street, New York, 1932,
watercolor, 25 x 19¼ .... **(986)**   1,353

1968–July 1969

Two Women Carrying Baskets, 1932, watercolor
and red ink, 12 x 9 .... **(1090)**   694

American Street, (1940), watercolor, 17½ x 14 ... **(1090)**   992

The "Decent" Woman, (1930), watercolor,
23¾ x 18¼ .... **(1041)**   1,216

Scene in a Street, (1933), watercolor,
25¾ x 17¾ .... **(1112)**   1,141

Brown Shirts, 1934, watercolor, 24½ x 18¾ ..... **(1216)**   1,700

PAINTINGS

1961–1962

Seated Nude, 39½ x 31½ .... **(106)**   1,401

1963

Recollection of the Sea, 1937, 11¾ x 14 .... **(179)**   550

1967

Still Life with a Fish, 23 x 39½ .... **(969)**   1,600

1968–July 1969

Self-Portrait, 1938, 47½ x 33¼ .... **(1160)**   9,000

Back View of a Nude, 1942, on panel,
28¼ x 19¾ .... **(1160)**   5,000

The Carp, 1930, 8¾ x 15½ .... **(1112)**   893

Portrait of Otto Korschwitz, 1938, 25½ x 19½ ... **(1229)**   800

Nude, 19½ x 15 .... **(1229)**   2,750

Francis Gruber

(1912–1948)

Birthplace: Nancy, France.

1916 His family settles in Paris. Decides to become a painter. Meets Braque and Bissière.

1920-28 Greatly admires the German and Dutch masters of the past.

1928 Attends the Académie Scandinave, where he works with Friesz and Dufresne.

1930 Participates in the Salon d'Automne and the Salon des Tuileries, Paris.

1935 Exhibition of drawings at the Académie Ranson, Paris.

1936-37 Executes murals for the Lycée Lakanal, Sceaux. Executes a stained-glass window entitled "Les Sports et les loisirs" for the World's Fair, Paris.

1938 Executes a stained-glass window entitled "Hommage à la sculpture" for the Musée d'Art Moderne, Paris.

1940 Has to spend some time in the mountains because of an attack of tuberculosis.

1942 Teaches at the Académie Ranson, Paris. Works by himself.

1945 One-man show at the Galerie Roux-Henschel, Paris, where he exhibits his famous picture "Job." Illustrates some of Baudelaire's works. Trip to England.

1947 Stay at La Trinité-sur-Mer, Brittany. Takes part in the exhibition "Contemporary French Painting" at the Whitney Museum, New York.

1948 Died, Paris.

1950 Retrospective exhibition entitled "Hommage à Gruber" at the Musée d'Art Moderne, Paris.

Sales

DRAWINGS

1961-1962
Study of a Man, 1946, pencil, 19½ x 24½ .... (27) $ 360

1966
Standing Nude, 1940, 24½ x 17 .... (742) 280
Seated Nude, 1946, pencil, 24½ x 18¼ .... (809) 800

1967
Seated Nude, 1945, 25¾ x 19½ .... (874) 700

1968–July 1969
Figures, 24 x 18¼ .... (1115) 420

WATERCOLORS

1961-1962
The Village in the Valley, watercolor, 9¾ x 12½ ... (2) 390

1966
The Village in the Valley, 1933, watercolor,
9½ x 13½ .... (682) 450

PAINTINGS

1961-1962
Mother and Child, 1944, 16¼ x 12¾ .... (20) 6,952
Still Life, 32 x 25¾ .... (114) 2,040

1963
Still Life with a Bird, 1937, 25¾ x 32½ .... (206) 1,160

1964
Still Life, 1947, 32 x 26 .... (461) $2,400
The Model in the Studio, 1938, 21¾ x 18¼ .... (474) 1,300
A Dam on the River Seine, 1942, 17¾ x 21¼ ..... (476) 1,700

1965
The Storm, 1938, 39½ x 39½ .... (518) 5,400
Still Life with Lilacs, 1942, 39½ x 32 .... (518) 5,600
The Armchair in Front of the Fireplace,
16¼ x 13 .... (552) 1,320

1967
Landscape, 1945, 36½ x 29 .... (852) 4,020

1968–July 1969
Sunday Desires, 32 x 25¾ .... (1256) 7,800

Armand Guillaumin

(1841–1927)

Birthplace: Paris, France.

1861 Attends the evening classes of the Académie Suisse, Paris, where he meets Cézanne and Pissarro.

1863 Takes part in the Salon des Refusés, Paris.

1874 Participates in the first Impressionist exhibition at Nadar's, Paris. Participates in all the following exhibitions of the Impressionist group, except for those of 1876 and 1879.

1887 Discovers the Creuse region, where he executes a great number of his works. Meets Van Gogh.

1891 Trip to the south of France.

1893 One-man show at the Galerie Durand-Ruel, Paris, where he exhibits again in 1895 and 1897. Executes a series of landscapes of Crozant, Creuse.

1904 Trip to Holland.

1927 Died, Paris.

Sales

DRAWINGS

1961-1962
The Pine Trees, 1911, charcoal, 17¾ x 23¾ .... (99) $ 100
The Banks of the River Seine, 1882, 16¾ x 24 ..... (72) 160
Landscape with a Cart, 1886, charcoal,
18½ x 24½ .... (60) 176

1963
The Plough, charcoal, 18¼ x 23¾ .... (314) 150

1964
Landscape, 1872, charcoal, 11 x 17½ .... (393) 50
Quay Along the River Seine, 1885, charcoal,
12 x 18¾ .... (393) 64
The Village, 1884, black chalk, 15½ x 21¼ .... (362) 202
The Artist's Daughter, colored pencil,
18¼ x 20¼ .... (401) 1,000

1965

Landscape, 1878, 7¼ x 10¾ . . . . **(611)** $ 180
Washerwomen, charcoal, 8 x 11 . . . . **(582)** 124

1966

Landscape, 1871, Conté pencil, 11 x 17 . . . . **(798)** 147
The Old Olive Tree, charcoal, 11¼ x 8½ . . . . **(777)** 150

1967

The Little Girl with Red Socks, 1890, pencil
   heightened with pastel, 9 x 6¾ . . . . **(935)** 400

1968–July 1969

Study of a Woman Reading, charcoal,
   14½ x 11½ . . . . **(1241)** 454
Study of a Young Lady, charcoal, 15 x 10¾ . . . . . **(1241)** 706

WATERCOLORS

1961–1962

Bust of a Young Lady, 1879, pastel, 15¾ x 11¾ . . . **(124)** 520
Villeneuve-sur-Yonne, pastel, 18¼ x 23¼ . . . . **(124)** 1,020
Pontcharra, Near Grenoble, pastel, 23 x 17½ . . . . **(124)** 800
Landscape, pastel, 10 x 12¼ . . . . **(106)** 610
The Banks of the River Seine, Unloading Sand,
   pastel, 23 x 31¼ . . . . **(76)** 570
Unloading Barges, 1880, pastel, 14 x 20½ . . . . **(102)** 780
The Banks of the River Seine, Quai de Bercy,
   1885, pastel, 19¾ x 25¼ . . . . **(120)** 1,140
Landscape at St. Chéron, pastel, 18¾ x 24¼ . . . . . . **(46)** 520
Apple Trees in Damiette, 1884, pastel, 18½ x 24 . . . **(46)** 144
Landscape at Crozant, (1885), pastel,
   18½ x 22¾ . . . . **(85)** 1,100
Landscape in Normandy, pastel, 23 x 30 . . . . **(164)** 1,098
Haystacks, 1892, pastel, 19½ x 25¼ . . . . **(6)** 1,030
Landscape of the Creuse, pastel, 19 x 23 . . . . **(32)** 1,400
The Farm, pastel, 19½ x 25¼ . . . . **(109)** 860
Apple Trees, pastel, 18¼ x 23¾ . . . . **(173)** 220
Baby Sleeping, 1896, pastel, 10 x 14 . . . . **(47)** 240
Sewing in the Garden, pastel, 1898, 18¼ x 23 . . . . . **(32)** 2,800
Portrait of a Little Girl, pastel, 1898, 24 x 19 . . . . . . **(32)** 800
Madame Guillaumin Writing, pastel, 18¼ x 15½ . . . **(42)** 840
Madame Guillaumin Reading, 1905, pastel,
   18½ x 23 . . . . **(85)** 700

1963

The Child and His Food, 1894, pastel, 18¼ x 17 . . . **(262)** 120
Landscape with a Bridge, 1910, pastel,
   17¾ x 23¾ . . . . **(306)** 500
Landscape, pastel, 12 x 10¾ . . . . **(232)** 452
Banks of the River Seine, pastel, 9½ x 14½ . . . . **(276)** 700
Village Scene, pastel, 23¼ x 18½ . . . . **(202)** 1,600
The Actor Chamart as Jodelet, pastel, 24½ x 57 . . **(201)** 180
Portrait, pastel, 15½ x 11¾ . . . . **(224)** 620

1964

The Banks of the River Seine, 1868, pastel,
   11 x 12¼ . . . . **(426)** 480
The Caravans, 1889, pastel, 19 x 24¼ . . . . **(454)** 1,797
Caravan in Epinay, 1889, pastel, 19 x 24 . . . . **(418)** 500
Barges on the River Seine, 1893, pastel,
   25¾ x 32 . . . . **(335)** 600
The Boats, pastel, 11 x 12¾ . . . . **(329)** 600
Banks of the River Seine, pastel, 11 x 12¼ . . . . **(426)** 480
Banks of the River Seine, pastel, 9½ x 14¼ . . . . **(409)** 280
Seaside at Agay, 1914, pastel, 18¼ x 23¾ . . . . **(341)** 1,440
Landscape at Agay, Var, pastel, 18 x 24¼ . . . . **(454)** 1,050

Landscape at Crozant, pastel, 17¼ x 22½ . . . . **(450)** $ 800
Landscape at Gif, pastel, 18½ x 24 . . . . **(399)** 1,560

1965

The Path of St. Chéron at Miregaudon, 1893,
   pastel, 19¾ x 25¾ . . . . **(518)** 940
The Bay of Agay-Anthéor, 1914, pastel,
   19 x 24½ . . . . **(559)** 1,600
Crozant, pastel, 16¾ x 22 . . . . **(632)** 1,260
Pine Trees Near the Sea, pastel, 17¾ x 24 . . . . **(577)** 740
The Lane, pastel, 21 x 15 . . . . **(612)** 1,000
Landscape of the Creuse, pastel, 18¼ x 21¾ . . . . . . **(599)** 1,500

1966

Landscape, 1912, pastel, 18¾ x 24 . . . . **(741)** 1,300
The Child and His Food, 1894, pastel, 18¼ x 17 . . . **(749)** 640
Portrait of Jodelet, 1900, pastel, 24 x 17¾ . . . . **(718)** 760
Young Woman Reading, pastel, 11¾ x 14¾ . . . . . . **(648)** 2,600
Gully of the Sedelle, 1916, pastel, 11½ x 14¾ . . . . . **(702)** 920
Seaside, pastel, 18 x 24¼ . . . . **(815)** 1,327
Landscape with a Stream, pastel, 7½ x 12¼ . . . . . . **(828)** 302
Vase of Flowers, watercolor, 8½ x 11½ . . . . **(734)** 723
Landscape, pastel, 19¼ x 23 . . . . **(745)** 1,243
Cartage on the Bank of the River Seine, pastel,
   19 x 25 . . . . **(669)** 1,800

1967

Towboats, 1869, pastel, 10 x 16¾ . . . . **(976)** 1,040
Damiette, 1886, pastel, 10¼ x 16¾ . . . . **(911)** 1,200
The Coast Road of St. Palais-sur-Mer, 1894,
   pastel, 13 x 23¾ . . . . **(986)** 1,279
St. Palais Beach, pastel, 15¾ x 23¾ . . . . **(905)** 600
Pontgibaud, 1895, pastel, 18¼ x 24½ . . . . **(858)** 2,320
View of a Valley, pastel, 18 x 23¾ . . . . **(985)** 995
Young Woman at the Piano, 1909, pastel,
   24 x 17¾ . . . . **(987)** 1,600
Breakfast, pastel, 20½ x 14¼ . . . . **(987)** 1,040
The Sleeping Girl, pastel, 17½ x 19¾ . . . . **(935)** 1,400
The Child Near the Table, pastel, 14¾ x 17½ . . . . . **(935)** 320
Landscape of the Creuse, pastel, 18¼ x 24½ . . . . . . **(901)** 600
The Barge on the River Seine, pastel, 14 x 18¼ . . . **(886)** 150
Crozant, pastel, 18¼ x 24 . . . . **(911)** 820
Agay, pastel, 24 x 18¼ . . . . **(967)** 1,017

1968–July 1969

Sunrise Over the Creuse, pastel, 12 x 18½ . . . . . . **(1075)** 940
Quai de la Rapée, Paris, 1869, pastel, 17½ x 23 . . **(1174)** 3,565
Quai de la Rapée, 1869, pastel, 17¾ x 23¼ . . . . . . **(1116)** 820
The Lighter, 1874, pastel, 15¾ x 24 . . . . **(1060)** 3,520
The Moored Boat, pastel and gouache,
   17½ x 21 . . . . **(1026)** 2,000
The Sewer (Garden at Epinay), (1886), pastel,
   19½ x 25 . . . . **(1152)** 7,750
Woman Reading on a Cliff, 1893, pastel and
   gouache, 17½ x 21¼ . . . . **(1134)** 3,776
Child Eating, 1894, pastel, 18½ x 17 . . . . **(1068)** 4,012
Young Ladies, pastel, 19¾ x 25¾ . . . . **(1159)** 1,820
The Creuse, pastel, 17¾ x 21¼ . . . . **(1018)** 3,250
Banks of the Creuse, pastel, 17¾ x 23¾ . . . . **(1039)** 2,240
The Valley of the Sedelle, pastel, 17¾ x 24 . . . . . . **(1117)** 2,800
Landscape at Crozant, pastel, 32 x 39½ . . . . **(1051)** 1,520
Landscape, pastel, 18 x 24 . . . . **(1127)** 1,265
Landscape of the Creuse, pastel, 16¾ x 23¾ . . . . . **(1055)** 560
Village Street, pastel, 20¼ x 26 . . . . **(1200)** 6,000
Trees on the Coast, pastel, 18 x 24½ . . . . **(1231)** 2,000

The Sand Screener, pastel, 20 x 27½ .... (1231) $2,500
The River at Crozant, 1898, pastel, 18 x 24 ...... (1241) 3,780
The Beach at St. Palais, 1893, pastel,
   15½ x 23½ .... (1241) 4,030
The Main Street at Eragny (Oise), pastel, 9 x 9 .. (1245) 340
Landscape, pastel and charcoal, 16¾ x 22½ ..... (1246) 3,250
Landscape, pastel, 17¾ x 22 .... (1268) 5,306
The Old Well, Crozant, 1903, pastel, 18¼ x 20½ . (1268) 5,800

PAINTINGS

1961–1962

Crozant on a November Morning, 1893,
   25¾ x 36½ .... (32) 3,800
Seascape, 23½ x 20¾ .... (32) 1,200
Rocks on the Côte d'Azur, (1890), 23¾ x 28½ ..... (96) 3,250
Landscape of the South of France, 21¾ x 25¾ .... (150) 1,130
La Perrière, High Tide, 1893, 21¼ x 25¾ .... (124) 970
The Sea at Agay, Var, 1893, 29 x 36½ .... (116) 10,000
Surroundings of Agay, 21¼ x 25¾ .... (168) 2,300
Agay, 9½ x 13 .... (134) 800
Rocks at Cap Lunny and Castel d'Agay, 1893,
   23¾ x 29 .... (76) 1,220
The Pont Marie, (1890), 19 x 25 .... (164) 5,492
The River Seine at Ivry, 1900, 15½ x 25¾ .... (119) 2,000
La Pierrière at St. Palais, 29¼ x 36½ .... (39) 2,900
Landscape, 21¼ x 25¾ .... (143) 2,486
Pasture, 21¼ x 25¾ .... (7) 640
Pasture, 21¼ x 25¾ .... (147) 280
La Folie in the Morning, Dull Weather,
   18¼ x 21¾ .... (76) 3,200
Landscape of the Creuse, 25 x 31¼ .... (171) 4,600
Haystacks, Morning Effect, (1890), 25¾ x 32 ..... (32) 2,800
Landscape with a Barrier (Crozant), 32 x 25¾ ..... (32) 3,600
Crozant, Landscape Under Snow, 18¼ x 21¾ ..... (76) 2,560
Crozant, 1906, 23¾ x 28¾ .... (164) 4,393
Crozant, 23¾ x 32 .... (156) 4,420
Snow Effect at Crozant, Creuse, 32 x 25¾ .... (80) 2,420
Crozant, La Sédelle in Autumn, 23¾ x 29 .... (177) 2,000
Crozant, Lock of Génétin, 1907, 19¾ x 23¾ ...... (138) 5,989
Landscape of the Creuse, 23¾ x 36½ .... (69) 3,160
Landscape of the Creuse, 29 x 36½ .... (76) 2,820
The Banks of the River Creuse, 13 x 16¼ .... (155) 720
View of the Creuse in Winter,[1] 13 x 17½ .... (50) 3,500
Banks of the River Creuse, 1905, 25¾ x 36½ ...... (71) 4,400
Young Woman Sewing, 18¼ x 15¼ .... (150) 441

1963

Landscape with Haystacks, 1891, 29¼ x 40 .... (258) 4,000
The Bridge over the Sédelle at Crozant, 1903,
   15¼ x 18½ .... (259) 2,300
Landscape: First Days of October, 25¾ x 32 ..... (312) 3,200
The Road at Crozant: Fog and White Frost,
   21¾ x 25¾ .... (262) 2,000
Landscape of the Creuse, 25 x 31½ .... (210) 3,839
August Evening at St. Palais, 1909, 23¼ x 28 ..... (247) 6,032
Pointe de la Baumette, Near Agay, Var,
   14¾ x 17½ .... (245) 5,484
*Landscape of the Creuse, Old Path in the
   Evening*, 1921, 18¼ x 21¼ .... (318) 1,800
Red Rocks, 21¼ x 25¾ .... (278) 1,800
Landscape of the Vallée de Chevreuse,
   21¾ x 18¼ .... (198) 5,000

Pasture, 21¼ x 25¾ .... (221) $ 460
The Farmyard, 27 x 13 .... (280) 262
Still Life with Apples, 7½ x 9½ .... (215) 600
Vase of Flowers, 11½ x 12¼ .... (254) 2,900
Carolles, 19¾ x 27¾ .... (225) 4,000

1964

Le Trayas, 17¾ x 25¾ .... (378) 2,079
The Coast at St. Palais, 1909, 21¼ x 25¾ .... (354) 4,000
Landscape: Banks of the River Creuse,
   36 x 26½ .... (344) 4,500
The Creuse, 21½ x 25¾ .... (372) 3,250
Crozant: The Sun Over the River, 23¾ x 29 ..... (397) 3,000
Landscape of the Creuse, 25¾ x 32 .... (398) 3,800
Landscape of the Creuse in Winter, 23 x 28 ..... (395) 3,000
The Seine at Ivry, 15½ x 25¾ .... (337) 3,000
Boats on the River Seine, 12¾ x 15¾ .... (405) 2,177
Banks of the River Seine, Snow Effect,
   20 x 26½ .... (401) 2,600
Seaside, 29 x 36½ .... (341) 4,000
Banks of the River Creuse, 23¾ x 29 .... (341) 4,400
The Scholar, 21¼ x 17½ .... (354) 3,500
Apple Trees in Blossom, 25¾ x 32 .... (399) 4,600
Girl Reading in the Country, 14 x 10¾ .... (378) 4,294
Ploughman in a Field, 21¾ x 27¾ .... (416) 6,081
Twilight, 24 x 29¼ .... (448) 3,500
The Sunday Walk, 9½ x 13 .... (398) 2,300
Rocks at the Seaside, 25¾ x 32 .... (472) 3,400
Landscape with a Farm, 31½ x 25¼ .... (458) 4,643
Banks of the River Marne, 23¼ x 28½ .... (354) 5,000
The Old Path, (1921), 18¼ x 21 .... (448) 2,850
Still Life with a Nosegay, 29 x 23¾ .... (450) 5,300

1965

Portrait of Martinez in the Studio, 1878,
   35½ x 29¾ .... (594) 45,000
Orchard at Miregaudon, 1892, 25¾ x 32 .... (518) 4,000
Banks of the River Creuse in the Morning,
   16¼ x 29 .... (567) 3,164
Crozant-lès-Ravines, 1898, 21¼ x 25¾ .... (553) 3,760
*The River Creuse in the Neighborhood of
   Crozant*, 21¾ x 25¾ .... (559) 4,000
Boigneville-lès-Carnaux, 31¼ x 25¼ .... (583) 2,757
Rising Sun at Crozant, 23¾ x 29 .... (617) 3,616
Moulin Bouchardon, Creuse, 1906, 19 x 23 .... (613) 7,400
The Quiet Stream, 25¾ x 32 .... (628) 8,126
The Coast of the Val André, (1907), 23¾ x 32 ..... (539) 3,000
Landscape Under Snow, 12¾ x 16 .... (582) 1,658
Banks of the River Seine, 12¾ x 15¾ .... (583) 1,015
Landscape of Brittany, 17½ x 24½ .... (553) 1,200
Artist, Resting,[2] 19½ x 23¾ .... (495) 3,420

1966

Landscape of the Creuse, 25¾ x 32 .... (759) 5,000
Landscape of the Creuse Under Snow, 19 x 23 .... (814) 2,520
Landscape of the Creuse, 21 x 28¼ .... (721) 3,250
*Crozant, End of September, in the Morning,
   White Frost*, 21 x 29 .... (776) 5,000
The Puy Barion (Creuse), 25¾ x 32 .... (711) 4,800
Autumn Landscape, 19¾ x 23¾ .... (784) 3,750
Peasants Sowing Beans, 1888, 16¾ x 23 .... (686) 9,398
Thatched Cottages at St. Evroult, 1893,
   23¼ x 28½ .... (812) 5,252

---

[1] Inscribed by the artist on the reverse "Crozant, l'hiver petit givre, 1904."

[2] Presumed portrait of Cézanne.

Haystacks, 21¼ x 32 ....(749) $3,800
Agay, 15 x 18¼ ....(762) 2,100
The Solidor Tower at St. Servan, 23¾ x 29 ......(814) 6,400
Oléron Island, 21¾ x 24 ....(814) 3,400
Young Lady in a Pink Dress, 32 x 25¾ ....(808) 6,384

1967

The Quays of the River Seine, 13 x 18¼ ....(911) 1,600
The Mills, 23¾ x 29 ....(978) 6,800
Snowy Landscape, 24 x 19¾ ....(967) 5,650
Landscape of the Creuse, 19¾ x 24 ....(919) 4,294
The Mountain Path, 13 x 16¼ ....(976) 1,600
The Dale at Pontgibaud, 25¾ x 32 ....(976) 4,200
The Estérel, 21¼ x 25¼ ....(849) 2,500
Autumn Landscape, 25¾ x 32 ....(995) 4,200
Landscape of the Creuse, 21¾ x 25¾ ....(901) 6,200
Landscape of the Creuse, 29 x 36½ ....(954) 8,500
Landscape of the Creuse Under Snow, 19 x 23 ....(873) 3,000
Still Life with Peaches, 18¼ x 15 ....(912) 3,000
Plum Tree in Blossom, 1895, 23¾ x 29 ....(988) 9,454

1968–July 1969

Woman and Child in a Landscape, 1890,
    32 x 25¾ ....(1189) 23,000
Mistral Blowing at Le Trayas, 1907, 29 x 39½ ...(1189) 8,000
Rocks at the Seaside in the Evening, (1906),
    23¾ x 29¼ ....(1152) 18,000
Rocks at the Seaside, 25¾ x 32 ....(1106) 3,700
Rocks at St. Palais, 29 x 36½ ....(1057) 7,000
St. Palais-sur-Mer, 19¾ x 25¾ ....(1080) 6,500
Rouen Harbor, 15 x 27 ....(1127) 4,370
Agay, 21¼ x 25¾ ....(1113) 2,800
Daybreak, 1874, 21 x 25 ....(1068) 44,840
Bâteau-Lavoir at the Pont Marie, 17¾ x 24 .....(1049) 10,600
Autumn in the Creuse, 23¾ x 29 ....(1049) 4,400
The Bench in the Garden, 18 x 21¾ ....(1184) 2,800
Haystacks, (1886), 30¾ x 43¾ ....(1187) 14,632
The Old Path at Crozant, 1907, 24 x 29 ....(1183) 10,400
Landscape at Crozant, 23¾ x 29 ....(1060) 8,640
Banks of the Creuse, 25¾ x 32 ....(1093) 7,000
The Creuse at Génétin, 15 x 21¾ ....(1187) 6,136
Orange Rocks, 28½ x 23¾ ....(1193) 11,151
Woman Reading, 25¾ x 32 ....(1152) 37,000
Autumn: Landscape of the Creuse, 9¾ x 12½ ...(1225) 5,600
Riverside, 23¾ x 29 ....(1226) 13,600
Landscape with a Cove, (1885), 29½ x 39½ .....(1235) 13,500
Windmills by the Canal: Villeneuve, 1902,
    15 x 18½ ....(1235) 22,000
The Coast of the Estérel, 21½ x 26 ....(1235) 12,000
Crozant in Autumn, 21 x 28½ ....(1239) 12,000
White Frost at Crozant, 29 x 39 ....(1239) 22,800
Windmills and Boats in Holland, 21 x 26 ....(1239) 24,000
Unloading on the Bank of the River Seine, 1873,
    20½ x 25 ....(1239) 13,200
Cliffs at St. Palais, 22¼ x 27½ ....(1241) 13,860
Banks of the River Creuse, (1906), 21¾ x 21¼ ...(1252) 16,020
Crozant: A March Morning in 1900, La
    Fondbonne, 25¾ x 31½ ....(1258) 16,000
St. Sauves: Snow Effect, (1910), 23¾ x 29 ......(1258) 7,600
The River Seine in Paris, 49¾ x 71¼ ....(1261) 90,000
Red Rocks at Agay, 25¾ x 32 ....(1262) 11,000
Banks of the River Seine, Ivry, 13 x 16¼ ....(1268) 6,264
The Quiet River, 25½ x 31¾ ....(1270) 21,600
Quai de Bercy: Bathing of Horses, 13 x 16 ......(1270) 13,200

Fishermen and Sailboats, Junction of the Seine
    and the Marne, Ivry,[3] 1891, 18 x 21½ ....(1270) $21,600
Riverside, 27½ x 33½ ....(1270) 13,600
Reading: Portrait of Madame Guillaumin,
    32 x 25½ ....(1270) 21,600
Agay Coast, 17½ x 21 ....(1273) 8,560

Philip Guston

(1913-   )

Birthplace: Montreal, Canada.

1930 Studies at the Otis Art Institute, Los Angeles.

1945 First one-man show at the Midtown Gallery, New York.

1948-50 Abandons representational elements and begins to paint large abstract pictures.

1955 Participates in the exhibition "Cinquante Ans d'art moderne aux Etats-Unis" at the Musée National d'Art Moderne, Paris. Regarded as one of the major abstract expressionists in America.

1956 Participates in the exhibition "Twelve Americans" at the Museum of Modern Art, New York.

Resident in New York.

Sales

DRAWINGS

1966

Composition with Black Lines, 1961, India-ink
    wash, 26 x 40¼ ....(651) $ 400

1968–July 1969

Composition, 1960, India ink, 18¼ x 24 ....(1030) 325

WATERCOLORS

1965

Signs, 1958, gouache, 15 x 20½ ....(541) 650

PAINTINGS

1965

Wintry Flower, 1959, on board, 31¼ x 40¾ ....(592) 3,500
Uru, 1957, 68½ x 60¾ ....(526) 10,000
Mercator, 1958, 68½ x 72½ ....(526) 7,000

1967

Number II, (1952), 48¾ x 50¾ ....(870) 7,000

1968–July 1969

Garden of M., 1960, 67¼ x 77¼ ....(1018) 5,000
Painting I, 1963, on board, 30 x 40 ....(1237) 3,200

[3]Dedicated "A. M. Hayashi."

Robert Gwathmey

(1903–   )

Birthplace: Richmond, Virginia, U.S.

1926-30 Attends the Pennsylvania Academy of Fine Arts. Travels to Europe, where he studies art.

1931-37 Teaches at Beaver College, Pennsylvania.

1938-52 Teaches at the Carnegie Institute of Technology.

1940 First one-man show at the ACA Gallery, New York. Wins first prize at the San Diego Exhibition of Watercolors.

1943 Wins second prize at the Carnegie Institute, Pittsburgh.

1946 Receives the American Academy of Arts and Letters grant. One-man show at the ACA Gallery, New York.

1949 One-man show at the ACA Gallery, New York.

Resident in New York.

Sales

DRAWINGS

1968–July 1969

Seated Old Woman, black lead and colored pencil, 17¾ x 11¾ . . . . (1062) $ 450

WATERCOLORS

1965

The Reaper, watercolor, 17 x 11¾ . . . . (489) 450

1967

The Clam Gatherer, watercolor, 21 x 14 . . . . (870) 550

PAINTINGS

1963

The Cotton Planter, 36½ x 43½ . . . . (272) 3,200
The Attentive Young Boy, 17¾ x 12¾ . . . . (272) 875

1968–July 1969

Dirt Farmer, 50 x 34 . . . . (1229) 6,500
Man Singing, 12 x 10 . . . . (1248) 1,600

Marsden Hartley

(1877–1943)

Birthplace: Lewiston, Maine, U.S. Studies in New York.

1908 Early works are influenced by the Italian Impressionist Segantini.

1910 Participates in a group show at Stieglitz's famous "Photo-Secession," New York, together with Weber, Dove, and Carles.

1912 Travels to Paris, where he meets the Cubists.

1913 First stay in Germany. Participates in an exhibition with the "Blaue Reiter" group, Munich. Exhibits in the first Herbstsalon, Berlin. At this time, his landscapes are reminiscent of Kandinsky's works. Short trip to the U.S. Takes part in the Armory Show, New York.

1914-16 Second stay in Germany. Turns to abstraction and paints a series of abstract landscapes on the theme "Amerika," and also a series of brilliant still lifes.

1916 Returns to the U.S. and participates in several exhibitions. Abandons the hot expressionist palette and paints in clear shades.

1918-20 Reverts to figuration, to which he remains true for the rest of his life.

1926 Stay in Aix-en-Provence, France, Cézanne's native town.

1932-33 Stay in Mexico. Starts painting in the primitive manner that marks his late style.

1943 Died, Ellsworth, Maine.

Sales

DRAWINGS

1963

Figure, pencil, 11¾ x 8½ . . . . (208) $ 175

1964

Seated Man, pencil, 11¾ x 9 . . . . (374) 125

1966

Seated Young Man, pencil, 11¾ x 9 . . . . (648) 225
Cobbs Camp 2, charcoal, 14 x 11 . . . . (805) 200

WATERCOLORS

1965

Seated Athlete, pastel, 18¼ x 23 . . . . (507) 400

PAINTINGS

1961-1962

Landscape of New Mexico, (1920-21), 23¾ x 23¾ . . . . (44) 1,300

1963

Musical Theme, (1912-13), on canvas laid down on panel, 25¾ x 21 . . . . (279) 5,000
The Basket of Fruit, (1922-23), 13½ x 25¼ . . . . (272) 2,500

1965

Landscape, 19¾ x 24 . . . . (489) 1,800
Landscape of Vence, (1925), 19¾ x 24 . . . . (610) 2,400
Mexican Landscape, 1922, on canvas laid down on panel, 26 x 31½ . . . . (610) 2,500

1967

Mexican Landscape, 1932, on board mounted on panel, 25 x 33½ . . . . (952) 6,250

1968–July 1969

New England Landscape, (1934-35), on panel, 24 x 20 . . . . (1229) 4,000

Hans Hartung

(1904–   )

Birthplace: Leipzig, Germany.

1914–32 Goes to Basel, then to Dresden, and begins to paint. Is mainly influenced by Kokoschka, Nolde, and Franz Marc.

1922 Turns to abstraction.

1925 Meets Kandinsky.

1924–28 Attends the Academies of Fine Arts of Leipzig, Dresden, and Munich. Reverts to representative painting for a while.

1931 First exhibition at the Heinrich Kühl Gallery, Dresden.

1933–34 Stay in Spain.

1935 Forced to leave Germany, he goes to Paris, where he meets Kandinsky again, and Mondrian and others.

1937 Takes part in the Salon des Surindépendants and in the exhibition "De Cézanne à nos jours" at the Musée du Jeu de Paume, Paris.

1938 Takes part in the exhibition showing twentieth-century German art, London.

1939 Enlists as a volunteer in the French Foreign Legion, which takes him to North Africa. Loses his right leg when wounded in 1944.

1945 Becomes a French citizen.

1946 Takes part in the Salon des Réalités Nouvelles and the Salon de Mai, Paris.

1947 First one-man show at the Galerie Lydia Conti, Paris. Appears as an outstanding figure in abstract painting.

1950 Participates in the exhibition "Advancing French Art," organized by Louis Carré and shown in New York, San Francisco, and Chicago.

1956 Participates in the exhibition "Abstrakte Malerei," at the Beyder Gallery, Basel.

1957 Participates in the exhibition "Peintres d'aujour-d'hui France-Italie," Turin.

1959 Several one-man shows all over Europe.

1960 Wins first prize at the Venice Biennial.

Resident in Paris.

Sales

DRAWINGS

1961–1962

Composition, 1952, colored chalk on paper on canvas, 19 x 25 ....(129) $ 879

Composition, India ink, 15 x 12¼ ....(33) 440

Composition, 1957, charcoal and pastel, 19 x 25 ...(110) 800

Composition, 1958, colored chalk, 19¾ x 25¾ ....(149) 632

Composition, 1960, black and colored pencil, 28 x 18¼ ....(120) 540

Composition, 1960, colored pencil, 28 x 18¼ ......(171) 300

1963

Composition, 1952, charcoal, 19 x 25¾ ....(299) 440

Abstract Composition, 1958, colored chalk and pencil, 18½ x 17 ....(219) 271

Composition, 1958, colored pencil, 19½ x 25¼ ....(283) 723

1965

Composition, 1947, black chalk and gouache, 17¾ x 24¼ ....(566) $ 283

Composition, ink, 25¼ x 19 ....(508) 204

Composition, 1952, chalk and ink, 19¼ x 25¾ ....(634) 369

Composition, colored pencil and wash, 20¼ x 15¾ ....(553) 760

Composition, 1961, wash and colored pencil, 19½ x 28½ ....(540) 300

1966

Composition, 1957, colored pencil, 20¼ x 15¾ ....(727) 640

Composition, 1949, charcoal and oil on paper, 19¾ x 15¾ ....(791) 600

Composition, 1958, charcoal and pastel, 19¾ x 25 ....(721) 650

Composition, 1958, pencil, 19½ x 24½ ....(805) 350

1967

Composition, 1953, charcoal and pastel, 19½ x 25¾ ....(996) 420

Composition, 1958, charcoal and pastel, 19¾ x 25 ....(963) 950

Composition, 1960, pencil, 19½ x 24½ ....(831) 450

Composition, colored drawing, 18¾ x 28 ....(907) 664

1968–July 1969

Composition, 1958, colored pencil, 19¾ x 25¾ ...(1088) 300

Composition, 1959, charcoal, 17½ x 21¾ ....(1174) 322

Composition, 1960, black pencil and pastel, 19½ x 25 ....(1061) 575

Composition, 1960, black pencil and pastel, 24½ x 19 ....(1200) 500

Composition, 1960, charcoal and colored pencil, 19 x 29 ....(1031) 360

Composition, 1957, stick of greasepaint and pastel, 25¾ x 19¾ ....(1268) 812

WATERCOLORS

1961–1962

Metamorphosis, pastel, 19¾ x 25¼ ....(75) 1,185

Ventaglio, pastel, 19 x 23¾ ....(16) 790

Composition, pastel, 20 x 15¾ ....(59) 1,300

Composition, 1957, pastel, 25¾ x 19¾ ....(93) 1,130

Composition, 1957, pastel, 25¼ x 19½ ....(156) 700

Composition, 1958, pastel, 19¾ x 25¾ ....(155) 800

Composition, 1958, pastel, 19½ x 25¼ ....(64) 900

Composition, 1960, gouache, 18¼ x 28 ....(110) 900

Composition, 1960, pastel, 29 x 19 ....(143) 633

1963

Composition, watercolor and stick of greasepaint, 21¼ x 15 ....(281) 1,379

Composition, 1957, pastel, 25¼ x 19½ ....(249) 520

Composition, 1958, pastel, 19¾ x 25 ....(299) 520

Composition, 1959, pastel, 19½ x 25 ....(249) 440

Composition, 1959, pastel, 21¼ x 17 ....(241) 440

Composition, 1961, pastel, 32 x 24 ....(255) 686

1964

Composition, 1959, pastel, 19½ x 25 ....(351) 440

Composition, 1961, pastel, 19¾ x 29 ....(236) 800

Composition, 1957, watercolor and stick of greasepaint, 21¼ x 15 ....(617) 407

Composition, 1961, pastel, 23¾ x 31½ ....(541) 800

1966
Composition, gouache and pastel, 24¾ x 18¾ ..... (745) $ 723

1967
Composition, 1959, pastel and charcoal,
17½ x 21½ .... (881)   912
Composition, pastel, 25 x 18¾ .... (967)   407

PAINTINGS

1961–1962
Composition, 1955, 18¾ x 31½ .... (129)   4,394

1963
Composition, 1955, 63½ x 47½ .... (279)   13,000
Composition, 1951, 21¾ x 18¼ .... (249)   3,800

1964
Canvas, 1954, 15 x 39½ .... (431)   3,750
Composition, 1963, 14 x 59¼ .... (386)   3,600

1965
*Canvas, Black Circle on a Light Green
Background,* 1948, 38¼ x 52¼ .... (573)   8,845
Composition, 1950, 25¼ x 31½ .... (512)   2,000
Composition, 1950, on cardboard, 19¾ x 29 ...... (512)   1,100
Painting, 1950, 38½ x 51½ .... (637)   6,250
Composition in Blue, 1961, 25¼ x 36¼ .... (522)   3,040
Composition, 1962, 31½ x 23¾ .... (616)   3,840

1966
Composition, 1943, oil and sand on cardboard,
37½ x 33¾ .... (798)   5,876
Composition T, 1957, 63½ x 48¼ .... (678)   3,750
K 14, 1963, 25¾ x 36½ .... (802)   4,320

1967
Painting, 1950, 38½ x 50½ .... (963)   5,000
Painting, 1950, 19¾ x 29 .... (885)   1,451
Composition, 1957, 18 x 21¾ .... (870)   1,000
Composition, 1962, 36½ x 29 .... (919)   1,695
Composition, 38¼ x 51½ .... (868)   3,040
Composition, 1964, 25¾ x 41½ .... (841)   3,500

1968–July 1969
Composition, 1952, 19¾ x 25¾ .... (1200)   3,400
Composition, 1955, 39¼ x 32¼ .... (1080)   2,750
Composition, 1961, 23 x 36 .... (1187)   2,124
Composition, 1962, 36½ x 29 .... (1132)   2,360
Untitled, 1953, mixed media, 18¾ x 25 .... (1237)   950
Untitled I, 1957, 31¾ x 21¼ .... (1271)   2,040
Untitled II, 1961, 24 x 18 .... (1271)   1,488

Henri Hayden

(1883-   )

Birthplace: Warsaw, Poland.

1902   Attends the Fine Arts School, Warsaw.

1907   Settles in Paris. Discovers modern French painting.

1909-10   Participates in the Salon d'Automne, Paris. Trip to Brittany, where he spends several summers.

1911   First one-man show at the Galerie Druet, Paris. Comes under Cézanne's influence.

1912-14   Participates in the Salon des Indépendants, Paris. Meets the dealer Charles Malpel.

1915   Turns to Cubism. Meets Juan Gris, Metzinger, Severini, and Picasso. Signs a contract with the dealer Léonce Rosenberg.

1923-32   Falls out with Cubism and reverts to a more representational painting. Signs a contract with the dealer Zborowski. Participates in the Salon des Tuileries, Paris. Organizes exhibitions at Bernheim's, Drouant's, and other galleries. Becomes a French citizen.

1940-44   Spends World War II at Mougins with Robert Delaunay.

1955   One-man show at the Galerie Suillerot, Paris.

1958   One-man shows at the Galerie Bénézit, Paris (works in the manner of Cézanne and Cubism), and at the Galerie Suillerot, Paris (recent paintings).

1960   Important retrospective exhibition, Lyons.

1961   One-man show at the Waddington Gallery, London.

Resident in Paris.

Sales

DRAWINGS

1963
Road Lined with Trees, India ink, 10 x 11½ ...... (242) $ 18

1966
The Suspension Bridge, 1948, India ink,
12¼ x 19 .... (670)   76

1967
The Suspension Bridge, 1948, India-ink wash,
12¼ x 18¾ .... (834)   44

WATERCOLORS

1965
Seaside, 1916, watercolor, 9 x 11½ .... (599)   96

1966
Still Life with a Pedestal Table, 1917, gouache,
12¾ x 10 .... (753)   1,596
Cherbourg Harbor, 1953, watercolor,
14¼ x 20½ .... (781)   180
Landscape, 1955, watercolor and gouache,
12½ x 19½ .... (718)   320

1967
Basket and Pink Shell, 1963, gouache, 15 x 21 ... (1006)   647
The Castle, gouache, 11 x 16¼ .... (955)   64

1968–July 1969
Still Life with a Bottle, watercolor, 10 x 7¼ ..... (1162)   260
Fields, 1961, gouache, 12¾ x 19 .... (1140)   170
Landscape, 1961, gouache, 12¾ x 19 .... (1078)   210

PAINTINGS

1961–1962

Portrait of Kisling (with a Guitar), 1914,
   32 x 17¾ .... (40) $1,400
Seaside: Le Pouldu, 1908, 18¼ x 25¾ .... (120)   1,200
Cubist Composition, 1917, 36½ x 25½ .... (9)   2,400
Woman with a Basket of Peaches, 1928,
   29 x 21¼ .... (9)   310
Landscape, 17½ x 20 .... (155)   300
Creyssel Church, 1929, 25¾ x 21¼ .... (47)   144
"14 Juillet" in Brittany, Douelan, 25 x 27 .... (167)   340
Sanary Harbor, 15 x 18¼ .... (161)   200
Landscape: Mareuil, on cardboard, 13 x 16¼ ...... (52)   180
Cubist Composition with Fruit Stand, 23¾ x 29 ... (157)   1,500
The Garden, oil on board, 18¼ x 16 .... (164)   192

1963

Still Life with Apples, 1910, 17 x 24 .... (224)   700
Still Life, (1919), 36 x 23 .... (279)   5,500
Still Life, 1948, 19¾ x 25¾ .... (242)   160
Still Life, 10¾ x 14 .... (188)   400
Still Life with Tulips, 36½ x 25½ .... (178)   200
Vase of Flowers, 29 x 23¾ .... (278)   250
Seated Nude, 31½ x 23½ .... (271)   180
Young Woman Dressing, 31½ x 23½ .... (233)   260
The Alpilles, 13 x 16¼ .... (236)   124
Landscape, 23¼ x 28½ .... (314)   300

1964

Landscape, on cardboard, 16¼ x 13 .... (370)   160
"14 Juillet" at Douelan, 1907, 25 x 27 .... (441)   520
Sunset, on panel, 13 x 18¼ .... (346)   260
View of Provence, 1935, 23¼ x 27¼ .... (365)   232
Landscape of Provence, 12¾ x 17¾ .... (412)   200
The Little Merry-Go-Round, on panel,
   13 x 18¼ .... (483)   180
Model in the Studio, 29 x 23¾ .... (404)   140
The Pont Neuf, 10¾ x 16¼ .... (401)   176
The Green Hamlet, 1960, 21¼ x 29 .... (351)   800

1965

Still Life with Pipe and Newspaper, (1914),
   18¼ x 25¾ .... (624)   1,658
Woman in an Armchair, 1917, on board,
   16¼ x 12¾ .... (624)   2,488
In the Wood, 21¼ x 29 .... (538)   260
Reclining Nude, 10¾ x 16¼ .... (631)   180
Still Life with Fruit and Bread .... (586)   300
Mountainous Landscape, on cardboard,
   15 x 18¼ .... (530)   96
Island at St. Jean, 1958, 21¼ x 25¾ .... (561)   760
Landscape, 1958, 21¼ x 25¾ .... (632)   860

1966

Surroundings of Toulon, 19¾ x 25¾ .... (672)   400
Still Life with Pipe and Newspaper, (1914)
   18¼ x 25¾ .... (815)   1,382
Seated Nude, 29 x 23¾ .... (656)   260
The Saxophonist, 1921, 39½ x 29 .... (753)   3,482
Mandolin and Bowl of Fruit, 1922, 43½ x 19½ .... (815)   2,764
Still Life with Fish, 18¼ x 25¾ .... (723)   160
Still Life, 25¾ x 32 .... (749)   900
Young Woman in the Bloom of Youth, 1932,
   29 x 23¾ .... (711)   540
Seated Nude with Blue Drapery, 26 x 36 .... (781)   200

Portrait of a Woman, 29 x 21¼ .... (674) $ 240
Still Life, 1946, 15 x 24 .... (674)   600
Landscape Oil, on paper laid down on canvas,
   14¼ x 19 .... (714)   140
Vase of Flowers, 29 x 23¾ .... (670)   500
Flowers in a Blue Vase, 13 x 16 .... (760)   580

1967

Sanary, 1925, oil on paper laid down on canvas,
   15 x 18¼ .... (935)   110
Surroundings of Toulon, 1925, 22 x 25¾ .... (858)   280
Still Life, 1944, 18¼ x 21¾ .... (874)   120
Entrance of a Village, on board, 14½ x 18¼ ...... (888)   207
The River Dordogne at Meyronne, 13 x 16¼ ..... (834)   250
Landscape of Provence, 15 x 18¼ .... (873)   104
Still Life, on panel, 15 x 21¾ .... (941)   190
*Still Life with a Cup of Fruit, a Bottle, and a
   Loaf,* 21¼ x 29 .... (956)   140
River Bank, 1952, on board, 12¾ x 18¼ .... (985)   166
Still Life with a Pink Shell, 1963, à la colle
   painting on board, 15 x 21 .... (888)   819

1968–July 1969

Village at the Seaside, 1903, 25¾ x 36½ .... (1045)   2,440
View of Paris, 1914, 36½ x 29 .... (1157)   5,300
Cassis, Seen from Ramatuelle, 13 x 18¼ .... (1210)   680
Landscape, 21¼ x 29 .... (1039)   140
Landscape of Sanary, 21¼ x 25¾ .... (1213)   360
Green Landscape, 19¾ x 24 .... (1144)   360
Landscape, on panel, 15 x 18¼ .... (1019)   96
Bunch of Flowers, on panel, 13½ x 17¾ .... (1167)   400
Still Life with a Guitar, on panel, 6¼ x 12½ ..... (1072)   164
Vase of Flowers, 29 x 23¾ .... (1060)   1,440
Reclining Woman in the Nude, 26 x 36 .... (1211)   424
The Dale, 15 x 21¾ .... (1225)   800
Fair-Haired Young Woman, 18¼ x 13 .... (1227)   400
Surroundings of Sanary, 21¼ x 25¾ .... (1230)   760
Vase of Flowers, 13 x 16¼ .... (1230)   280
Still Life with a Guitar on a Pedestal Table, 1922,
   43 x 19½ .... (1241)   7,810
Still Life with a Violin .... (1251)   4,600
Still Life with a Red Curtain, 1914, 25½ x 31¾ ... (1271)   6,240
Woman Seated at Table .... (1251)   5,400
The Three Pierrots, 1914, 121 x 100 .... (1268)   9,976
Landscape and Church, on board, 12½ x 15¾ ... (1273)   529

Erich Heckel

(1883–   )

Birthplace: Däbeln, Germany.

1897-04 Studies art at Chemnitz. Meets Schmidt-Rottluff.

1904-05 Also studies architecture in Dresden. Becomes very friendly with Kirchner and Bleyl.

1905 With Kirchner and Bleyl, sets up the famous group "Die Brücke."

1906 Meets Nolde and Pechstein.

1909-10 Stays in Rome and Berlin. Makes friends with Müller.

1911 Settles in Berlin.

1912 Exhibits at the Sonderbund exhibition, Cologne. Meets Lyonel Feininger.

1913 Dissolution of "Die Brücke." One-man show at the Fritz Gurlitt Gallery, Berlin.

1914 Exhibits at the Werkbund exhibition, Cologne. Trips to Belgium and Holland.

1915-18 Enlists as a volunteer in the Red Cross in Flanders. Meets Beckmann and Ensor.

1919 Becomes very friendly with Paul Klee.

1921-36 Travels all over Europe.

1937 Like most German artists of his time, he sees his works exposed as "degenerate" by the Nazis and withdrawn from the museums.

1944 Settles in Hemmenhagen.

1949-55 Teaches at the Akademie für bildende Künste, Karlsruhe.

Resident in Hemmenhagen.

Sales

DRAWINGS

1961-1962

Young Girl on the Beach, drypoint, 9¼ x 7 .... (106) $ 29

1965

Woman Reading, 1908, colored chalk, 18¼ x 14¼ .... (543) 537

Siddi Heckel Seated, (1914), charcoal and watercolor, 12¾ x 11½ .... (566) 1,288

Woman, 1936, charcoal and watercolor, 20 x 16 ... (618) 369

1966

Woman's Head, colored chalk, 5¾ x 3¾ .... (738) 246

1967

Young Girl Seated on a Red Cushion, 1910, charcoal and color, 14 x 17½ .... (927) 1,672

Perpetual Snow, 1921, pencil and watercolor, 14¾ x 17½ .... (910) 590

Landscape Near Berchtesgaden, 1922, pencil, 8 x 15½ .... (915) 153

1968-July 1969

Woman's Head, 1913, India ink, 9 x 5¾ .... (1099) 379

The Artist's Wife, 1920, pencil and watercolor, 26 x 19¾ .... (1068) 708

Hilly Landscape, 1923, colored chalk, 17¾ x 23¾ .... (1114) 521

WATERCOLORS

1961-1962

Woman Reading, watercolor, 23¾ x 19¾ .... (105) 215

Brandung, watercolor, 23¾ x 17¾ .... (106) 203

The House by the Sea, 1909, watercolor, 14 x 18¾ .... (149) $ 664

Young Girl Dancing Before a Mirror, 1910, watercolor, 19¼ x 23½ .... (24) 652

Red-Roofed House and Trees, 1912, watercolor and pencil, 14¼ x 17½ .... (88) 738

1963

The Bar, 1910, watercolor, 19¼ x 19½ .... (284) 1,009

Fishing Harbor, 1929, watercolor, 22 x 27¼ ...... (284) 738

1964

The Bridge, 1914, watercolor, 19¼ x 15 .... (383) 768

Bathers, 1919, gouache, 13 x 11 .... (455) 221

Alpine Scenery, 1922, watercolor and chalk, 21¼ x 25½ .... (383) 294

Still Life with Flowers, 1926, watercolor, 27 x 21¼ .... (467) 836

Landscape with Trees, 1944, watercolor, 18¾ x 24 .... (428) 689

1965

Reclining Woman, 1914, watercolor, 19½ x 15½ .. (543) 481

The Storm, 1920, watercolor, 26 x 19¾ .... (597) 984

The Caf' Conc' Dancers, 1921, watercolor, 16½ x 13 .... (634) 689

Still Life with Fruit, 1937, watercolor, 24 x 18½ ... (618) 910

Young Boys on the Beach, 1937, watercolor, 18 x 14¾ .... (514) 684

Vase of Flowers, 1946, watercolor and gouache, 19½ x 13½ .... (582) 608

1966

Young Girl with a White Shirt, 1910, pencil and watercolor, 11 x 12½ .... (734) 407

Two Bathers, 1925, charcoal and watercolor, 25 x 20½ .... (712) 787

Landscape of Provence, 1929, pencil, watercolor, and colored chalk, 19¾ x 26¾ .... (792) 984

Vase of Flowers, 1939, watercolor, 27 x 21¾ ...... (712) 1,033

Chestnut-Tree Flowers in a Gray Vase, 1940, watercolor, 27¼ x 21¾ .... (738) 566

1967

Head of a Young Girl with a Hat, 1909, pencil and watercolor, 5½ x 4½ .... (927) 215

Standing Nude, 1919, watercolor, 17¾ x 12½ ..... (986) 935

Seaside, 1919, watercolor, 19 x 25 .... (998) 738

Two Nudes in a Forest, 1924, charcoal and watercolor, 18¾ x 23¾ .... (998) 959

Hilly Landscape, 1949, watercolor and colored chalk, 19 x 25 .... (970) 787

Flowers, 1963, watercolor, 27¾ x 22 .... (907) 1,107

1968-July 1969

Landscape, 1921, watercolor, 18¼ x 23½ .... (1094) 546

The Boat, 1912, watercolor, 12¾ x 11 .... (1041) 836

Still Life with Flowers, 1921, watercolor, 22 x 18½ .... (1114) 397

Woman Reading, 1924, watercolor, 23¾ x 19¾ .. (1099) 333

Mountain Stream, 1925, watercolor and black chalk, 27 x 19¾ .... (1090) 1,190

Still Life, 1926, watercolor, 26 x 21 .... (1194) 1,736

Landscape, 1935, watercolor and gouache, 22 x 27¼ .... (1085) 1,538

Ostseekueste, 1911, watercolor, 10½ x 13¼ ..... (1232) 3,000

A Boy and a Young Lady, 1910, watercolor, 8½ x 11 .... (1232) 2,750

Vorm Kliff, 1925, watercolor, 24½ x 20½ .... (1232) 2,000

PAINTINGS

1961–1962

Two Women on the Beach, 1921, 32 x 27¾ . . . . (88) $2,214

1964

The Mad Soldier, 1916, 20 x 16¼ . . . . (467)   1,476
Blooming, 1907, 27 x 30 . . . . (383)   9,718

1965

Yellow Dahlias, 1922, 31¼ x 27¾ . . . . (624)   4,837

1966

Bather with a Rock, 1914, 39½ x 26½ . . . . (738)   8,364

1968–July 1969

Yellow Dahlias, 1922, 31½ x 27¾ . . . . (1194)   8,432

Auguste Herbin

(1882–1960)

Birthplace: Quievry, France.

1901-02 Attends the Fine Arts School of Lille.

1903 First stay in Paris.

1905-07 Takes part in the Salon des Indépendants and the Salon d'Automne, Paris. Works under the influence of Cubism.

1917 Exhibits at the Galerie Léonce Rosenberg and the Galerie de l'Effort, Paris.

1926 Abandons representational painting.

1931 With Vantongerloo, founds the Abstraction-Création group.

1949 Elaborates his own abstract manner, which he explains in his work *L'Art non-figuratif non-objectif* (published by Lydia Conti, Paris). Exhibits at the Salon des Réalités Nouvelles, Paris; becomes its manager and remains so until 1955. Also exhibits at the Galerie René, Paris.

1956 Retrospective exhibition at the Palais des Beaux-Arts, Brussels, and at the Museum of Fribourg-en-Brisgau.

1959 Several works of his are shown at the exhibition "Peintres d'aujourd'hui France-Italie," Turin.

1960 Died, Paris.

Sales

DRAWINGS

1961–1962

Composition, 1919, pencil and watercolor,
12½ x 9½ . . . . (174) $ 88

1963

Cup of Fruit, 5½ x 12¼ . . . . (286)   110

1964

Fruit Stand, pencil, 9 x 11¾ . . . . (377) $ 215
Composition, 1938, colored pencil, 4¾ x 11 . . . . (375)   76
Trees by the Riverside, charcoal, 22 x 17½ . . . . . . (328)   96

1965

Composition, 1910, 19 x 14¼ . . . . (503)   160

1966

Composition, 1920, India ink and watercolor,
12¾ x 8¾ . . . . (734)   1,017

WATERCOLORS

1961–1962

Abstract Composition, 1917, watercolor,
17¾ x 11¾ . . . . (106)   723
Composition, watercolor, 14¾ x 9½ . . . . (115)   160
Composition, 1925, watercolor, 13¼ x 10 . . . . (27)   150
Composition, 1941, gouache, 13½ x 10¾ . . . . (143)   407
Portal, watercolor, 14¾ x 10¾ . . . . (110)   300
Life, watercolor, 10¼ x 13½ . . . . (153)   300
Love, gouache, 14¾ x 11 . . . . (154)   240
Bird, gouache, 8¾ x 13½ . . . . (154)   280

1963

Composition, 1922, gouache, 19½ x 12¼ . . . . (241)   520
Landscape at Céret, watercolor, 11 x 15 . . . . (314)   152
Composition, gouache, 12¾ x 10 . . . . (249)   280
Composition, 1939, gouache, 4¾ x 11 . . . . (219)   463

1964

Half-Length Portrait of a Young Woman,
watercolor, 22¼ x 14¾ . . . . (467)   172
The Village, watercolor, 9 x 13 . . . . (359)   160
Composition, watercolor, 12 x 9 . . . . (441)   745

1965

Composition, (1930), gouache, 9 x 12½ . . . . (566)   520
Arabesque, gouache, 12¾ x 9½ . . . . (621)   192

1966

Moon, 1945, gouache, 10¾ x 8¾ . . . . (672)   460
Landscape, watercolor, 11 x 14¾ . . . . (718)   340
Composition with Spirals, watercolor,
11¾ x 9½ . . . . (669)   320
Composition, watercolor, 10 x 7¼ . . . . (730)   340

1967

Composition, 1917, watercolor, 19 x 11¾ . . . . (795)   960
Abstract Composition, 1917, watercolor,
17¾ x 11½ . . . . (927)   1,130
The Sailboats, watercolor, 17½ x 21¾ . . . . (911)   640
Composition, 1938, gouache, 12¾ x 9 . . . . (1004)   900
The Harbor, watercolor, 10¾ x 14¾ . . . . (996)   320
Green, 1946, gouache, 13½ x 10¼ . . . . (907)   861
Composition, gouache, 13 x 11 . . . . (919)   1,130

1968–July 1969

Circles, gouache, 11¾ x 9 . . . . (1202)   800
Arabesques, gouache, 13½ x 9 . . . . (1202)   1,100
Geometrical Composition, 1919, gouache,
27½ x 14 . . . . (1184)   1,600
Composition, watercolor, 9¼ x 11½ . . . . (1078)   400
The Terrace, watercolor, 10¾ x 14¾ . . . . (117)   800
Twirls, watercolor, 6 x 8¼ . . . . (1153)   410
Composition, watercolor and gouache, 10¼ x 7 . . (1078)   400
Landscape, Céret, watercolor, 11 x 15 . . . . (1059)   595
Composition, watercolor, 9 x 11¾ . . . . (1238)   520
Composition, watercolor, 10¼ x 7¼ . . . . (1238)   490

Composition, 1920, gouache, 12¼ x 9 .... (1240) $1,800
Composition, (1925-30), gouache, 11½ x 8¼ ..... (1240) 1,800
Composition, gouache on canvas, 21¾ x 15 ...... (1244) 2,500
Composition, 1920, gouache, 11½ x 8¾ .... (1247) 1,240
Composition, 1920, gouache, 21¼ x 17¾ .... (1255) 1,800
Composition, 1920, 12¾ x 8¼ .... (1255) 1,230
Composition, 1931, gouache, 15½ x 10¾ .... (1255) 1,160
Composition, 1941, watercolor, 17¾ x 12¾ ...... (1265) 1,280
Composition, gouache, 10 x 1¾ .... (1268) 812
Still Life, watercolor, 29 x 20½ .... (1268) 2,250

PAINTINGS

1961-1962

Paris: The Pont-Neuf, 1912, 23¾ x 29 .... (136) 800
Geometrical Figure, 1920, 25¾ x 32 .... (120) 820
The Moulin Rouge, 1926, 45½ x 35¼ .... (140) 1,153
Composition, 1927, 36¼ x 25 .... (140) 714
Composition, 21¼ x 25¾ .... (35) 680
Spiritual Reality, 1939, 19 x 44¼ .... (13) 660
Mother, 1943, 21¾ x 18¼ .... (35) 800
La Ronde, 39½ x 32 .... (153) 1,100
Riverside, 1956, 22 x 17½ .... (153) 360

1963

Condé-sur-Aisne, 1914, 24 x 15 .... (299) 1,200
Construction, 1919, 39¼ x 31¼ .... (189) 1,200
Composition for Motion Pictures No. 2, 1930,
   60 x 23¾ .... (309) 2,637
Man, Woman, 1944, 57¼ x 35¼ .... (309) 3,461
Projection, 1945, on panel, 9½ x 14 .... (234) 140
Village in the Mountains, 18¼ x 21¾ .... (238) 280
Landscape in the Valley, 23¾ x 32 .... (299) 400
Cubist Landscape, 21 x 12½ .... (255) 740
Mediterranean Landscape, 21¼ x 25¾ .... (262) 520
Composition, 16¼ x 13 .... (205) 640
Country Landscape, 23 x 28½ .... (283) 1,130

1964

The Farm, 1912, 34 x 26 .... (458) 2,322
Willow at Valdencourt, 29¾ x 25¾ .... (375) 2,000
Composition, 1918, 28½ x 21¼ .... (471) 4,972
The Lake, 1923, 21 x 31½ .... (329) 325
Composition, 9½ x 16¼ .... (414) 240
Twirls, 1929, 36½ x 29 .... (471) 4,520
Composition, 1931, 39½ x 32 .... (401) 1,000
Notre-Dame de Paris, 23¾ x 19½ .... (405) 1,335

1965

The Village, 32 x 46 .... (561) 1,300
Composition, 1934, 18¼ x 10¾ .... (561) 460
The Garden of a House, 23¼ x 28½ .... (583) 2,322
Park, 12¾ x 15¾ .... (645) 1,478

1966

The Coffeepot, 16¼ x 12¾ .... (741) 1,760
Still Life with Apples and Red Flowers, (1906),
   29 x 23¾ .... (808) 2,177
Portrait of a Man, (1915), 21 x 17½ .... (757) 1,797
Composition, 1920, 28¾ x 23¾ .... (727) 2,000
Composition, 59¾ x 23¾ .... (698) 1,741
Composition, 50¼ x 62½ .... (776) 3,000
Luna, 1945, 24 x 16 .... (816) 1,845
Landscape with a Stream, 31½ x 25¼ .... (708) 1,000
Boats Alongside the Quay, 17½ x 21 .... (823) 2,448
The Towboat, 20¾ x 25 .... (823) 1,414

1967

Landscape, 25¾ x 32¼ .... (870) $2,750
Vases of Flowers, 1905, 28 x 35½ .... (870) 2,500
Hillsides Along the River Seine, 1907, 29 x 23¾ ... (898) 740
The Pont Marie, (1911), 25¾ x 32 .... (975) 3,700
Composition, 1919, 36½ x 25¾ .... (907) 4,920
Landscape at Monthier, 1922, 31½ x 25 .... (940) 1,683
Composition, 1930, oil on paper laid down on
   canvas, 21¾ x 18¼ .... (965) 4,520
Cow Lying Down, on cardboard, 6 x 9 .... (968) 164

1968-July 1969

Composition, 29 x 23¾ .... (1173) 2,990
Hillsides Alongside the River Seine, 1906,
   28½ x 23¾ .... (1051) 900
View of a Harbor I, Corsica, (1907), 21 x 25 ..... (1070) 4,012
View of a Harbor II, Corsica, (1907), 20¾ x 25 .. (1070) 6,372
Hamburg Harbor, (1908), 23½ x 29 .... (1114) 2,282
Landscape of Luxembourg,[1] 1908, 21¼ x 17½ ... (1202) 3,200
Flowers and Fruit, 1908, 21¾ x 13 .... (1174) 4,370
Woman's Head, 1912, 17¾ x 15 .... (1109) 1,500
Composition, 1919, 36½ x 25¾ .... (1125) 6,555
Still Life with Fruit and a Basket of Eggs, 1925,
   34¾ x 45½ .... (1059) 2,478
Composition, 1930, 36¼ x 28¾ .... (1057) 3,750
Composition, 1938, 25¾ x 32 .... (1026) 2,800
Flowerpot, on cardboard, 25 x 20½ .... (1118) 520
Still Life with a Coffeepot, 16¼ x 13 .... (1043) 1,700
Composition, 29 x 36½ .... (1224) 4,800
Landscape, 23½ x 32 .... (1231) 1,500
Composition, 1938, 21¾ x 18¼ .... (1268) 5,336
House by the Riverside in Spring, (1903-05),
   17¾ x 21 .... (1271) 4,680

Morris Hirshfield

(1872-1946)

Birthplace: a small Polish town close to the German border.

1890   Emigrates to the U.S., where he earns his living working in a shop.

1936-37   Lives in Brooklyn, New York. Executes his first pictures.

1939   Participates in the exhibition "Unknown American Painters" at the Museum of Modern Art, New York.

1941   Exhibition, "They Taught Themselves," at the Museum of Art, San Francisco.

1943   Takes part in the exhibition "American Primitive Painters of Four Centuries." One-man show at the Museum of Modern Art, New York.

1944   One-man show at the Julian Levy Gallery, New York.

1946   Died.

[1]On the reverse, *The Haystacks*.

Sales

PAINTINGS

1968–July 1969
Young Lady with a Dog, 1943, 45¾ x 35½ .... (1208) $18,000

Ivon Hitchens

(1893–   )

Birthplace: London, England.

1909 Trip to New Zealand. Studies at St. John's Wood School and the Royal Academy, London.

1921–35 Produces several schemes of decoration (St. Paul's, Dorking; All Souls' Free Church, Golders Green).

1925 First one-man show at the Mayor Gallery, London.

1929 Becomes a member of the London Artists Association.

1934 Participates in the exhibition "Objective Abstraction" at the Zwemmer Gallery, London.

1944 Exhibits at the Leicester Galleries, London.

1945–48 Retrospective exhibitions in Leeds and Sheffield.

1956 Participates in the Venice Biennial.

1959 Executes murals for the Senior Common Room, Nuffield College, Oxford.

1962 One-man show at the Waddington Galleries, London.

1963 Executes murals for the University of Sussex, Brighton. Exhibits at the Arts Council, Tate Gallery, London.

Sales

WATERCOLORS

1968–July 1969
The Orchard, (1915), watercolor, 6¼ x 9¾ ...... (1141) $ 566

PAINTINGS

1962
Narcissus and Lilies No. 1, (1951), 14 x 26½ .... (74) 989
Trees and Water, 17½ x 42 .... (118) 2,197
Summer Flower in a Green Vase, 20 x 31½ .... (148) 1,785

1963
The River, 15½ x 29 .... (304) 1,316
Flowers No. 1, 1946, 22¾ x 27¾ .... (207) 877
Flowers in a Jug, 1943, 29 x 17¾ .... (207) 1,590
The Path to the Lake, 21¼ x 23¼ .... (309) 1,813
Fawley Valley, 19 x 29 .... (213) 1,121
Figure in the Shadow No. 2, 1959, 19¼ x 29 ...... (268) 1,371

1964
Springtime, 1933, 28½ x 39½ .... (444) 1,161
The Garden, 19¾ x 40½ .... (421) 1,797

1965
Flowers, 1948, 31½ x 38½ .... (584) $1,382
Flowers, 16¾ x 29¼ .... (605) 1,103
A Storm in June, 19¾ x 33 .... (605) 2,177
April Brilliance No. 2, 1952, 20 x 51½ .... (643) 2,349

1966
Interior with Flowers, 23¾ x 19¾ .... (709) 755
Bathers in a Landscape, 1934, 21¾ x 23 .... (693) 608
Sunflower and Blue Vase, 1947, 25¾ x 21¾ ...... (761) 2,073
Trees in Autumn, 1948, 16¾ x 29¼ .... (818) 1,219
Woody Landscape, 1951, 16¾ x 49¾ .... (761) 2,211
Autumn Ride No. 2, 1951, 17¾ x 42¼ .... (693) 1,935
Garden, 1957, 19¾ x 41½ .... (825) 1,520
Firwood Ride No. 11, 1958–59, 15¾ x 42¼ .... (825) 1,658
Composition in Green No. 4, 1961, 17 x 56½ ...... (709) 1,596
Cars in Green, 1961, 17 x 56½ .... (785) 1,886
September Water, 1961, 17 x 55½ .... (693) 1,658

1967
Landscape of Sussex, 1933, 21 x 23 .... (869) 1,050
Landscape, 16¾ x 43 .... (1003) 1,896
Flowers in a White Vase No. 1, 1944, 19¾ x 23¾ .... (957) 1,106
Flowers and Landscape, 27 x 33 .... (945) 1,382
Fallen Log No. 2, 20 x 40½ .... (945) 1,382
Nude, Violet and Yellow, 20 x 40½ .... (944) 1,596

1968–July 1969
Carnations and Lilacs, 16¾ x 29½ .... (1025) 1,090
Drive Gates, 1943, 19¾ x 38½ .... (1074) 4,012
Tangled Pool No. 4, 1947, 15¼ x 29 .... (1206) 2,124
Sleeping Woman No. 2, 1950, 22¼ x 27½ .... (1074) 1,180
Reclining Nude No. 4, 1950, 22½ x 28¼ .... (1141) 1,416
June, 1961, 24 x 55½ .... (1143) 3,469
Vase of Flowers, 24 x 20 .... (1141) 661
Trees in Winter, 20¾ x 36¾ .... (1143) 2,106

Karl Hofer

(1878–1955)

Birthplace: Karlsruhe, Germany.

1892–96 Works at a bookkeeper's in Karlsruhe. Attends the Karlsruhe Academy of Arts. Shows much relish for Buddhist sculpture and for Cézanne's paintings.

1899–01 Stay in Paris.

1902–03 Attends the Stuttgart Academy of Arts.

1903–08 Stay in Rome.

1908–13 Stay in Paris.

1909–11 Travels in India.

1913 Goes to Berlin.

1914–17 Stays in France and Switzerland.

1919	Returns to Berlin.
1923	Appointed member of the Preussischen Akademie der Künste, Berlin.
1928	Given an award by the Carnegie Institute, Pittsburgh.
1938	Excluded from the Preussischen Akademie der Künste, Berlin.
1943	His studio and a great number of his works are destroyed.
1953	Given an award by the city of Berlin.
1955	Died, Berlin.

Sales

DRAWINGS

1961–1962

Little Girl Playing with a Balloon on the Beach, pencil, 18½ x 14¼ . . . . (100) $ 133

Nude, India ink, 22¼ x 15½ . . . . (197)   114

1964

Bather, (1910), chalk, 13½ x 12¼ . . . . (389)   228

Jacob Wrestling with the Angel, (1910), chalk, 17¾ x 12¾ . . . . (349)   152

1966

Seated Nude, (1925), charcoal, 18¼ x 12¾ . . . . (734)   316

Study of a Nude, pen and wash, 23¼ x 14¾ . . . . . . (815)   387

Seated Young Woman, (1925), charcoal, 21 x 16 . . (716)   369

1967

Little Girl Playing, chalk, 18¼ x 11½ . . . . (927)   226

Marthe, 1925, pencil, 15½ x 10¼ . . . . (910)   541

Bather, black lead, 13¼ x 12 . . . . (985)   142

The Young Girl with a Cactus, 1921-22, charcoal, 19¾ x 15 . . . . (983)   380

Study of Two Nudes, black lead, 13¼ x 12 . . . . (939)   276

Two Bathers, pencil, 16 x 24¾ . . . . (915)   418

Standing Nude, pen, 15¾ x 9 . . . . (998)   123

1968–July 1969

The Insane Woman, pencil, 23 x 15¾ . . . . (1105)   285

Jacob and the Angel, chalk, 15¾ x 11¾ . . . . (1209)   161

Helena, pen, 15½ x 12 . . . . (1169)   125

Seated Nude, charcoal, 16¼ x 10¾ . . . . (1114)   248

Standing Nude, pen and ink wash, 21½ x 13 . . . . . (1272)   240

WATERCOLORS

1963

Clown, watercolor, 21¾ x 15¾ . . . . (284)   1,082

1965

Vase with a Bunch of Flowers, watercolor, 25 x 18½ . . . . (597)   935

1967

Two Heads, watercolor, 17 x 13¼ . . . . (864)   700

Reclining Woman, watercolor, 19¾ x 11¾ . . . . . . (1004)   950

1968–July 1969

Head of a Little Girl, watercolor, 20 x 14¾ . . . . . . (1114)   595

PAINTINGS

1961–1962

Back View of a Reclining Nude, 1908, 19¾ x 27¼ . . . . (107)   2,706

St. Gothard Pass, (1936), 25 x 35¼ . . . . (88)   3,075

Still Life with Fruit, 1943, 15¾ x 23¾ . . . . (94)   1,353

1963

Still Life with Peaches, 1926, 12 x 16¾ . . . . (219) $ 836

Still Life with Apples and Pears, 1921, 17¾ x 22 . . (269)   2,660

Peri, 1913, 27 x 39¼ . . . . (228)   4,182

Three Young Girls in the Nude, 38¾ x 29¼ . . . . . . (297)   2,337

1964

Autumn Flowers, 1907, 39½ x 27¾ . . . . (454)   1,106

Two Young Girls, (1920), 11¾ x 10 . . . . (428)   357

Young Girl with Fruit, 1927, 22 x 19 . . . . (380)   4,674

The Standard Bearer, 25¼ x 21 . . . . (392)   861

1965

Landscape of Tessin, 19¾ x 31½ . . . . (634)   3,198

Young Girl, on board, 13 x 8½ . . . . (624)   332

1966

Malcesine, 1937, 19¾ x 31½ . . . . (707)   3,500

The Fancied Farewell, 1952, 40¼ x 44¼ . . . . (816)   5,412

Seated Young Girl, on cardboard, 9¾ x 7¼ . . . . . . (775)   689

Head of a Young Girl, 16¾ x 15 . . . . (738)   787

1967

Still Life with Peaches, 1934, 16¼ x 23¾ . . . . (986)   1,353

Nude at the Window, 1940, 39½ x 25¾ . . . . (986)   4,428

Women at the Seaside, (1905), 26½ x 27¾ . . . . (910)   1,181

Self-Portrait with His Wife, 42 x 31¼ . . . . (915)   6,888

Landscape, 1937, 27¼ x 35½ . . . . (970)   3,936

The Friends, 40 x 25¾ . . . . (907)   1,968

1968–July 1969

Young Girls on the Beach, on canvas laid down on panel, 11½ x 17¼ . . . . (1090)   942

Autumn Flowers, 1917, 39¾ x 27¾ . . . . (1126)   2,974

Daphnis and Chloe, 1913, on board, 38½ x 27½ . . (1132)   3,304

A Boy, His Head Wrapped in a Towel, 1924, 43¾ x 31½ . . . . (1114)   10,416

Hans Hofmann

(1880-1966)

	Birthplace: Weissenburg, Germany. (Will study in Germany as well as in France.)
1910	One-man show at the Paul Cassirer Gallery, Berlin.
1915	Sets up a school of modern art in Munich.
1930	Goes to the U.S. to lecture at the University of California and at the Art Students League, New York.
1934	Becomes an American citizen. In New York, founds an art school bearing his name. Introduces the most advanced concepts of European painting to his students.
1940-45	Produces his most typical lyrical pictures, reaching an unprecedented degree of freedom in abstract style.

1947	One-man show at the Betty Parsons Gallery, New York. Exhibition at the Kootz Gallery, New York, where he will exhibit yearly.
1949	Exhibition at the Galerie Maeght, Paris.
1959	Reverts to a more structured composition. Resident in New York.
1966	Died, New York City.

Sales

DRAWINGS

1966

The Student, 1932, ink, 14¾ x 13 . . . . (665) $ 375

1967

Composition, 1934, India ink, 8 x 10¾ . . . . (841)   225

View of a Castle on a Hill, pen, 5¾ x 5¾ . . . . (872)   813

1968–July 1969

Abstraction, India ink, 8¼ x 10¾ . . . . (1030)   300

Untitled, 1947, charcoal and pastel, 8¾ x 5¾ . . . . (1088)   325

WATERCOLORS

1961–1962

Untitled, 1936, watercolor, 10 x 12¾ . . . . (164)   549

1964

Metamorphosis, 1944, watercolor, 28½ x 22½ . . . . (458)   1,596

1965

Composition, 1944, gouache, 16¾ x 14 . . . . (489)   550

PAINTINGS

1966

Succulence, 1946, on panel, 23¾ x 14¾ . . . . (651)   2,600

1967

Avis, 1959, 33 x 20¾ . . . . (864)   8,500

1968–July 1969

Summer, 1963, 40½ x 30¼ . . . . (1018)   5,000

Avis, 1959, 75 x 59¼ . . . . (1018)   7,000

Portrait of Madeleine, on board, 24 x 18¼ . . . . . . (1088)   1,300

Green Vista, 1962, on panel, 24 x 32¼ . . . . (1080)   3,500

Portrait, on board, 24 x 18 . . . . (1237)   2,200

Edward Hopper

(1882-1967)

Birthplace: Nyack, New York, U.S.

1900-06	Attends the New York School of Art.
1906-10	Visits England, Holland, Germany, Belgium, and France, painting city scenes. Returns to the U.S. and settles in New York. Exhibits at the Harmonic Club, New York.
1913	Participates in the Armory Show, New York.

1920	First one-man show at the Whitney Studio Club, New York.
1924	Exhibits watercolors and prints at Rehn's, New York.
1929	Participates in the exhibition "Paintings by Nineteen Living Americans" at the Museum of Modern Art, New York.
1930	One-man show at the Museum of Modern Art, New York.
1933	Retrospective exhibition at the Chicago Arts Club.
1937	Exhibits at the Carnegie Institute, Pittsburgh.
1940	Series of one-man shows at Rehn's, New York.
1950	Retrospective exhibition at the Museum of Fine Arts, Boston.
1952	Participates with three other American painters in the Venice Biennial.
1955	Awarded gold medal of the National Institute of Arts and Letters.
1962	Exhibition of his complete graphic work at the Philadelphia Museum of Art.
1967	Died.

Sales

WATERCOLORS

1968–July 1969

Hilly Landscape, 1924, watercolor, 14 x 20 . . . . . . (1160) $17,000

Study for "Smash the Hun," watercolor,
  9½ x 6½ . . . . (1229)   4,000

Oluf Høst

(1884-1966)

Birthplace: Svaneke, Bornholm, Denmark.

1900	Goes to sea as a sailor, making several long voyages which greatly influence his later paintings.
1905	Attends several art schools including the Academy in Copenhagen. Studies with and is especially influenced by G. Vermehren, J. Rohde, and H. Giersing.
1910-28	Lives and travels extensively in Germany, Holland, Italy, Belgium, and Denmark.
1911	Exhibits in Charlottenburg, Germany.
1929	Settles permanently in Gudhjem, on the island of Bornholm, Denmark.
1936-37	Takes part in the Exposition of Contemporary Danish Art at Muzeul Toma Stelian, Bucharest, Romania. Is subject of Helge Ernst Film, *Oluf Høst—A Painter And His Milieu.* Has paintings in many museums, including Copenhagen, Stockholm, Aarhus, Malmo, and Ronne.
1966	Died, Gudhjem, Denmark.

Sales

PAINTINGS

1961–1962
Path in the Forest, 1937, 17 x 14¾ .... (87) $ 511

1965
Little Girl in Blue in Front of a Farm, 15 x 24 ..... (623) 2,698

1966
Autumn Evening, 1945, 15 x 24 .... (771) 3,266
Snowy Landscape, 15¾ x 26 .... (661) 2,485

1967
Summer Night, 1935, 32 x 39½ .... (851) 3,300
Seaside, 21¼ x 25¾ .... (851) 1,848
The Farm, 32 x 51¾ .... (890) 4,290

Fritz Hundertwasser

(1928–   )

Birthplace: Vienna, Austria.

1943   Most of his family dies in concentration camps.

1948   Attends the Fine Arts School in Vienna. Comes under the influence of Egon Schiele.

1949   Changes his own name of Friedrich Stowasser to Fritz Hundertwasser. Trip to Italy. Comes under the influence of Paul Klee.

1950   First trip to Paris.

1951   Visits southern Europe and North Africa.

1952   Turns to abstraction.

1953–56   Second stay in Paris. Exhibits at the Galerie Paul Facchetti, Paris.

1954   Trip to Rome. Executes several watercolors. Elaborates his theory of "Transautomatismus."

1956   Provides an account of Transautomatismus in the French Art Review *Cimaise.*

1957   Buys a country house in Normandy. Spends the summer at St. Tropez.

1957–60   Signs a contract with the Galerie Kamer, Paris.

1958   Marries, but divorces his wife two years later.

1959   Given an award by the São Paulo Biennial.

1961   Visits Japan. Wins a prize at the International Art Exhibition, Tokyo.

1962   Marries his second wife, Yuuko Ikewada, in Vienna. Settles in Venice. Participates in the Venice Biennial, with an entire room assigned to his work.

Sales

DRAWINGS

1967
Untitled, 1956, ink and gouache, 14½ x 23¾ ..... (1005) $1,185

WATERCOLORS

1963
Composition in Red and Blue, 1955, watercolor, 19½ x 25¼ .... (239) $2,660

1964
Singing Boats, 1956, watercolor, 18¼ x 21¾ ...... (389) 1,900
Composition, watercolor, 6¾ x 5¾ .... (375) 100

1965
Motorcar with Red Rain, (1958), watercolor, 11¾ x 25¾ .... (514) 1,520

1966
Green Styria, watercolor, egg, and colored chalk, 19¾ x 24 .... (816) 2,460

1967
Meadow with a Cloud, 1958, gouache on silvery background, 4¾ x 5½ .... (907) 443
Composition, watercolor, 5¼ x 7½ .... (967) 271
Composition, watercolor and collage, 9 x 6 .... (927) 441
Composition, tempera, 6½ x 3½ .... (970) 492

1968–July 1969
Composition, watercolor, 7½ x 10¼ .... (1099) 379
Composition, watercolor, 7¼ x 4½ .... (1174) 460

PAINTINGS

1961–1962
Composition, 17½ x 21¾ .... (16) 442
Composition, 13 x 17½ .... (16) 474

1965
Head, 1952, painted on the bottom of a chair, 17½ x 18 .... (514) 1,140

1966
Composition, collage and watercolor, 6¾ x 6½ ... (744) 396

1967
The Garden in the Halo, 1956, 14¾ x 19½ .... (967) 3,390

Jean Jansem

(1920–   )

Birthplace: Seuleuze, Asia Minor.

1931   Goes to Paris.

1936–38   Attends the Ecole des Arts Décoratifs, Paris.

1940   Becomes a French citizen.

1942   Marries.

1944   Participates in the Salon des Indépendants, Paris.

1946   Devotes himself entirely to painting.

1950   Participates in the Salon de la Jeune Peinture, Paris.

1950–64   Visits Greece, Spain, Italy, Germany, and the U.S. Resident at Issy-les-Moulineaux, near Paris.

Sales

DRAWINGS

1963
The Laundress, India ink .... (270) $ 260

1964
Nude, ink, 25 x 19 .... (374) 400
Teatime, India ink, 25 x 18¾ .... (355) 120

1965
The Conversation, India-ink wash, 9½ x 8 .... (640) 100

1966
Nude, India ink, 25 x 17¾ .... (648) 375

1967
Squatting Nude, India ink and gouache,
   9¼ x 7¾ .... (838) 170
Squatting Nude, wash and gouache, 9½ x 8 ...... (995) 290
Village Street, India ink, 25¼ x 20¼ .... (971) 148

1968–July 1969
The Doll, India-ink wash, 9½ x 7½ .... (1154) 36
Still Life with a Basket, India ink, 19¾ x 25¾ ... (1048) 164
Squatting Woman, India ink and gouache,
   9 x 7½ .... (1238) 144

WATERCOLORS

1962
The Hobo, gouache, 18¼ x 23¼ .... (102) 380

1967
The Family, gouache, 15 x 20¼ .... (912) 620

1968–July 1969
Meeting, watercolor and gouache, 10¼ x 14¾ ... (1098) 180

PAINTINGS

1964
Still Life, 13 x 15 .... (409) 640
Spanish Scenes, 21½ x 25¾ .... (445) 800

1965
Two Seated Peasants, 18¼ x 25¾ .... (606) 850
Little Girl Having Her Hair Combed,
   25¾ x 18¼ .... (553) 1,000

1966
The Two Children, 21¾ x 18¼ .... (809) 810

1967
Fishermen, 1954, 45 x 57¾ .... (838) 1,700
Old Woman and Child, 62¼ x 37½ .... (841) 2,400
Squatting Woman in the Nude, 62¾ x 44¾ .... (893) 2,000

1968–July 1969
Still Life, 31¾ x 16 .... (1030) 1,000
Woman Washing the Floor, on metal, 4¾ x 5¾ .. (1161) 140
Woman with a Basket, 14 x 9½ .... (1078) 520
Reclining Woman, 14 x 10¾ .... (1223) 480
Seated Child, 21¾ x 18¼ .... (1228) 540
Mexican Boy, 1956, 36¼ x 25½ .... (1248) 1,800
Seated Young Girl in Blue Slacks, 39½ x 19¾ ... (1255) 1,200
Mother and Child, 35½ x 28 .... (1265) 1,200

Alexej von Jawlensky
(1864–1941)

      Birthplace: near Moscow, Russia.

1889   Enters the Academy of Fine Arts in Petrograd.

1896   Settles in Munich and attends A. Azbe's school of painting. Meets Kandinsky.

1903   First exhibition at the "Secession," Munich.

1905   Goes to France, painting in Brittany and Provence.

1909   Participates in the foundation of the New Association of Artists, Munich.

1912   Meets Nolde and Klee.

1914   Stays in Switzerland during World War I.

1917-21   Paints a series of mystic portraits. Portraiture seems to be his favorite interest and holds an important place in his work.

1920   Retrospective exhibition at the Gurlitt Gallery, Berlin.

1921   Settles in Wiesbaden, Germany.

1924   With Feininger, Kandinsky, and Klee, sets up the group "Die Blauen Vier."

1929   Important exhibition of the group "Die Blauen Vier" at the Möller Gallery, Berlin. Paints portraits influenced by Cubism.

1941   Died, Wiesbaden.

Sales

DRAWINGS

1961–1962
Seated Woman in the Nude, 1912, chalk,
   19 x 12¾ .... (94) $ 344
Seated Nude, 1912, chalk, 19 x 12¼ .... (428) 234

1965
Reclining Woman, (1910), pencil, 9 x 14¾ .... (566) 452

1967
Seated Nude, 1911-12, charcoal, 17¾ x 11¾ ...... (870) 400
Portrait of Madame Kirchhoff, 1921, pencil,
   9¼ x 7¾ .... (939) 69
Head, 1927, pencil, 6¾ x 5¾ .... (841) 175

1968–July 1969
Seated Nude, 1912, pencil, 13 x 8½ .... (1090) 322
Seated Nude, (1912), charcoal, 16½ x 12¼ ...... (1232) 1,900

WATERCOLORS

1961–1962
Composition with a Cross, 1915, watercolor,
   12¼ x 9¼ .... (105) 1,695
Blue Vases, watercolor, 4¾ x 3¾ .... (106) 145
Woman's Head, (1922), watercolor, 8½ x 6¾ ...... (24) 910

1963
The Blue Vase, 1931, watercolor, 5¼ x 3¾ .... (219) 226

1964
The Blue Vase, 1931, watercolor, 5¾ x 4½ .... (383) 215
Woman's Head, 1922, watercolor, 9 x 7¼ .... (428) 861

1965
Vase of Flowers, watercolor, 3¾ x 3¾ .... (624) 152

1966
Flowers in a Blue Vase, 1912, watercolor,
   6½ x 4 .... (808) 638
Reclining Nude, watercolor and pencil,
   3¾ x 5¾ .... (738) 836

1967

Still Life with Flowers, 1931, watercolor,
6½ x 4¼ .... **(907)** $ 467

1968

Still Life with Carnations, 1933, watercolor,
6 x 3¾ .... **(1090)**   223

Woman's Head, (1917), watercolor on paper laid
down on board, 9 x 6¾ .... **(1068)**   1,794

Still Life, 1925, pencil and watercolor, 3¾ x 5 ... **(1061)**   180

PAINTINGS

1961–1962

Still Life with a Chair and a Bunch of Flowers,
1906, on cardboard, 17½ x 13 .... **(88)**   4,034

Landscape, 1906, on cardboard, 21 x 19¾ .... **(18)**   6,102

Murnau, (1909), on panel, 13½ x 16¼ .... **(143)**   3,254

Murnau, (1909), on cardboard, 13 x 16¾ .... **(149)**   5,688

The Spaniard, 1909, on cardboard on board,
29¾ x 20 .... **(88)**   8,610

Dark-Haired Little Girl, 1910, on cardboard on
panel, 21 x 19¼ .... **(88)**   11,316

Woman's Head, 1910, on cardboard, 21 x 19½ ... **(149)**   7,268

Landscape at Murnau, (1910), on board,
20½ x 21¼ .... **(96)**   7,000

The Blue Beret, 1912, 25¾ x 21¼ .... **(106)**   9,718

The Feast of Nature, (1914), on panel, 20½ x 19 .. **(143)**   5,876

Mythical Head, 1914, on board, 21 x 19½ .... **(129)**   1,922

Reclining Head, on cardboard, 14 x 10 .... **(106)**   3,390

Landscape, 1916, 24 x 16¾ .... **(20)**   4,424

Landscape, 1916, on panel, 2½ x 14 .... **(143)**   3,119

Landscape, 1916, on cardboard, 14¾ x 10¾ ...... **(168)**   1,200

Flowers, 1917, 10¼ x 14¼ .... **(70)**   2.054

Schiefer Mund, 1917, on board, 15 x 9 .... **(31)**   2,609

Young Lady's Head, 1917, on cardboard,
11½ x 8 .... **(18)**   3,051

Portrait of a Woman, 1917, on cardboard,
15 x 9 .... **(93)**   3,571

Portrait, (1928), on cardboard, 14 x 10¾ .... **(143)**   5,198

Meditation: The Romance of the Evening, 1930,
on panel, 7 x 5¾ .... **(85)**   875

Head, 1932, on cardboard, 7¼ x 5¾ .... **(106)**   1,243

Dahlias, Chrysanthemums, and Blue Vase, 1935,
on cardboard, 20 x 14½ .... **(88)**   5,412

Es Glütet, Meditation, 1936, on cardboard,
10 x 7¼ .... **(106)**   1,356

1963

The Red Roofs, Murnau, 1910, on board,
13 x 17¾ .... **(316)**   3,300

Still Life with Oranges, on cardboard, 12 x 14¾ .. **(283)**   2,961

House and Hill, 1907, on cardboard, 21 x 19½ .... **(283)**   5,560

Landscape, 1914, on paper laid down on canvas,
14 x 10¾ .... **(247)**   2,742

Song, 1916, on board, 14 x 10¼ .... **(255)**   1,700

Variation, (1916), on paper laid down on canvas,
14 x 10 .... **(202)**   2,500

Portrait of a Woman, 1917, on cardboard,
15 x 9 .... **(232)**   2,034

Blue Eyes, 1918, on panel, 16 x 12¼ .... **(232)**   4,181

Head, 1920, on panel, 14½ x 10½ .... **(202)**   2,800

Head, 1932, on canvas laid down on cardboard,
14 x 10 .... **(219)**   1,944

Meditation in Reddish Brown, 1937, on paper,
7¼ x 10 .... **(232)**   1,582

Roses, 1937, on cardboard, 18¾ x 13½ .... **(219)**   3,616

1964

The Village in the Mountain, (1910-12), on paper
on cardboard, 19½ x 21 .... **(383)** $3,842

Breton Peasant, 1911, on cardboard, 21 x 19½ .... **(383)**   8,362

Prerow Dunes, 1911, on board, 13 x 17¾ .... **(405)**   2,031

Little Landscape, 1915, 10¼ x 15 .... **(453)**   1,658

Variations with a Yellow Church, 1916,
14¾ x 10¼; *Summer is Long in Coming,* 1919,
14½ x 10¼; *Variation,* 1916, 14¾ x 10½;
White Mass, 1918, 14½ x 10½; on canvases
laid down on board .... **(431)**   11,000

To the Guardian of the Temple, 1921, 14¾ x 11 ... **(453)**   3,870

Woman's Head, 1933, on board, 12¾ x 12¾ ...... **(354)**   4,250

Meditation No. 22, 1936, on canvas laid down on
cardboard, 10 x 7½ .... **(383)**   1,311

Meditation in Green, 1937, on board, 10 x 7¼ .... **(458)**   1,451

Meditation in Dark Red, on paper, 10 x 7¼ ...... **(433)**   1,582

Still Life with Flowers, on paper, 7¼ x 5 .... **(392)**   738

Vase with Flowers, on cardboard, 16¾ x 14 ...... **(467)**   1,968

1965

Fuessen VI, Snowy Landscape, 1905, on board,
14¾ x 19½ .... **(637)**   3,750

Landscape at Murnau, on cardboard,
12¾ x 17½ .... **(543)**   3,112

Young Lady with a Black Fan, 1911, 21¼ x 19¾ .. **(543)**   18,369

Byzantine, 1913, on cardboard, 26½ x 21¼ ...... **(616)**   15,200

Little Girl with Plaits, on canvas, 25¼ x 20½ ..... **(539)**   7,000

Varied Flowers, 1915, on board, 20 x 13½ .... **(583)**   2,177

Springtime Wind and Meadow, 1916, 13½ x 10 ... **(624)**   3,179

Portrait of a Woman, 1917, on panel,
15¾ x 11½ .... **(569)**   3,503

Woman's Head, on cradled panel, 21 x 17½ ...... **(526)**   7,000

Martyr's Head, 1921, on paper laid down on
cardboard, 15¼ x 10½ .... **(634)**   2,337

In a Good Mood, 1932, peinture à l'essence on
panel, 11¾ x 11 .... **(535)**   884

Still Life with Flowers, 1935, on cardboard,
9¼ x 7¼ .... **(543)**   1,837

Meditation, 1935, on cardboard, 6¾ x 5¼ .... **(566)**   678

Meditation, 1936, on cardboard, 10 x 7½ .... **(616)**   1,200

1966

Reclining Young Woman, (1914), on board,
12¼ x 17 .... **(776)**   4,250

Uphill Road, in the Evening, 1912, on cardboard,
17½ x 12¾ .... **(792)**   4,674

Springtime, 1916, on cardboard, 14 x 10½ .... **(734)**   2,712

Two Portraits of Women, 1917, on board, double
sided, 15½ x 11½ .... **(808)**   5,514

Saturne, 1913, on cardboard, 17 x 13 .... **(738)**   3,936

I Pray, 1936, on paper, 7¼ x 5¼ .... **(763)**   1,710

Meditation in Green, on paper, 10 x 7¼ .... **(745)**   1,853

Late Summer, on board, 14 x 10¼ .... **(753)**   3,628

Woman's Head, on paper, 14¼ x 10¾ .... **(798)**   4,746

Woman with Plaits, on cardboard, 26½ x 23¾ .... **(744)**   11,074

1967

Still Life with a Bottle, (1903), 19¾ x 24 .... **(927)**   3,390

Still Life, 1904, on cardboard, 25 x 17¾ .... **(986)**   6,396

Madame Sid, 1906, on board, 21 x 19 .... **(982)**   11,850

Yellow Clouds, (1909-10), on cardboard,
13 x 16¾ .... **(986)**   6,396

Still Life with a Round Table, 1910, on cardboard,
22 x 20 .... **(927)**   8,136

House with a Palm Tree at Ascona, 1915, on
board, 19 x 21 .... **(982)**   7,110

House in the Mountains, (1912), 19¾ x 21¼ ...... **(880)** $11,609
Woman Thinking, (1912), on board, 21¼ x 19¼ ... **(880)** 22,112
Sicilian, 1913, on cardboard, 26 x 19¾ .... **(986)** 19,680
Head of a Little Girl, 1910, on cardboard,
    21¾ x 19¾ .... **(927)** 6,554
Variation, (1916), 14 x 10¼ .... **(963)** 3,250
Landscape, 15 x 22 .... **(918)** 8,136
Woman's Head I, on board, 11¾ x 8¼ .... **(988)** 3,981
Still Life with Flowers, 1935, on cardboard,
    7¾ x 6 .... **(907)** 1,722
Vase of Flowers, (1935), on paper, 10 x 6¾ ...... **(970)** 2,952
Meditation, 1936, on cardboard, 10 x 7 .... **(970)** 1,427

1968–July 1969
Houses with Gardens, 1908, on cardboard,
    21 x 21 .... **(1114)** 9,176
Portrait of Mademoiselle Kimmel, 1910, on board,
    21 x 19½ .... **(1187)** 36,580
Trees, (1911), 14¾ x 21 .... **(1132)** 2,030
Portrait of a Woman, 1911, (recto), *Little Boy in a
    Sailor Suit* (verso), on board, 28½ x 19½ .... **(1187)** 60,180
The Red Dune, 1911, on board, 13 x 17½ .... **(1208)** 9,000
The House Amid the Trees, St. Prax, 1915, on
    board, 13 x 16 .... **(1187)** 20,060
Face, (1916–18), on canvas laid down on
    cardboard, 12¼ x 10 .... **(1099)** 4,370
Head, (1919), 14¼ x 10½ .... **(1208)** 6,500
Head, 1923, on canvas laid down on cardboard,
    16¾ x 12¾ .... **(1090)** 2,232
Woman's Head, on cardboard, 14½ x 17½ ...... **(1146)** 1,330
Kreuzritter, 1933, on panel mounted on panel,
    17½ x 14 .... **(1057)** 10,500
Meditation in Black and Orange, 1935, on
    cardboard laid down on board, 7½ x 5 ...... **(1090)** 645
Meditation, 1935, on board, 6 x 4 .... **(1088)** 1,100
Meditation, 1936, on cardboard, 10 x 7½ .... **(1114)** 1,637
View of Murnau, on cardboard, 14½ x 17½ ..... **(1041)** 1,520
The Yellow Pot, 20¾ x 23 .... **(1125)** 9,660
Portrait, on board, 15 x 11 .... **(1125)** 9,200
Divine Brightness, 1918, on canvas mounted on
    board, 16¾ x 12¾ .... **(1232)** 9,000
Small Landscape VI,[1] (1904), on board, 9 x 13½ . **(1232)** 5,250
Large Meditation III, on canvas mounted on
    glass, 10 x 7 .... **(1232)** 2,000
Large Meditation IV, on canvas mounted on
    glass, 10 x 7 .... **(1232)** 2,000
Sunrise, (1922), mounted on board, 14 x 10¾ .... **(1232)** 9,500
Still Life with a Decanter and Apples (recto),
    Field (verso), 1904, on board, 20¾ x 19¼ .... **(1235)** 14,500
Woman's Head, 1912, on board, 27½ x 19¾ ..... **(1239)** 24,000
Bildnis Lisa Kummel, 1930, 21 x 19¾ .... **(1239)** 3,360
Study for Bildnis Lisa Kummel, 1930, on board,
    17 x 13¼ .... **(1239)** 3,360
Variation, 1919, on canvas laid down on board,
    14½ x 10¾ .... **(1239)** 5,040
Head, 1936, on panel, 10 x 7 .... **(1268)** 2,900
Head, 1935, on panel, 5¾ x 7¼ .... **(1268)** 2,088
Red Gables, 1910, 13 x 17¾ .... **(1270)** 12,000

[1]Dedicated "Für Dich Lisa A. Jawlensky."

Johann-Barthold Jongkind

(1819–1891)

Birthplace: Latrop, Netherlands.

1836 Death of his father, a pastor. Studies painting in The Hague—taught by the landscape painter Schelfhout, a continuator of the Dutch Luminists.

1843 Obtains a scholarship.

1845 Meets the French painter Isabey, who takes him to Paris. Settles in Montmartre. Attends Isabey's studio.

1847-52 Several stays on the coast of Normandy with Isabey. Working in the open with his friend, Jongkind recaptures the maritime skies and winds, the vast stretch of sea and sand, and the shifting light that he enjoyed in his native country.

1848 Trip to the Netherlands. Participates in the Salon, Paris.

1850-53 Sinks into alcoholism and debauchery and seems in peril of a mental breakdown. Because of his dissolute living, he is deprived of his scholarship. Experiences a period of increasing money troubles.

1855-60 Trying to avoid destitution, returns twice to his country, living in Rotterdam. The French painter Cals brings him back to Paris where he meets Madame Fesser, a Dutchwoman, who persuades him to give up excessive drinking.

1862 Meets Claude Monet, who introduces him to Eugène Boudin. The three artists work together in Le Havre, at the "Ferme St. Siméon," and on the Norman coast.

1863 Participates in the famous Salon des Refusés, Paris, along with Manet, Pissarro, Guillaumin, Cézanne, Whistler, and others.

1863-65 Long stays in Honfleur, working with Monet and Boudin. Produces most of his masterpieces, especially in watercolor, to which he introduces a fresh, simplified technique and reaches a dazzling mastery.

1865-70 Amateurs and art dealers begin to take a great interest in his work; frequently commissioned.

1878 Settles at La Côte St. André, Isère district.

1879-83 Victim of persecution mania.

1891 Died, shortly after confinement in a Grenoble hospital. (Like Boudin, Jongkind is regarded as a direct precursor of Impressionism.)

Sales

DRAWINGS

1961–1962
Canal in Holland, charcoal, 11¾ x 9¼ .... **(36)** $ 70
The Côte St. André, 1879, pencil and watercolor,
    6¼ x 9¼ .... **(84)** 1,236
Boats in Venice, 1868, chalk with white lights,
    11½ x 9 .... **(152)** 775

1963
Boisfort, 1866, drawing heightened with wash,
    4½ x 7½ .... **(318)** 410
Brussels, 1866, wash, 7½ x 4½ .... **(258)** 900
Boats on the River, Conté pencil, 10¼ x 16¾ .... **(258)** 280
The Pont de Notre-Dame in Paris, pencil and
    wash, 7¼ x 10¾ .... **(283)** 1,469

1964

Street in Rouen, 1864, black pencil and wash,
7 x 4¼ . . . . (393) $ 190

Sailboats, 1865, sepia wash, 9 x 7¼ . . . . (368) 470

*The Harbor: Mouth of the Meuse Before
Maassluis,* 1866, pencil, 3¾ x 6½ . . . . (416) 1,520

Fluvial Scenery with Boat and Sunset, colored
chalk, 10¾ x 16 . . . . (428) 1,107

Sailboats on the Escaut, double sided, 6¼ x 9 and
6 x 8¾ . . . . (477) 560

The Outskirts of Rotterdam, charcoal,
10½ x 16½ . . . . (383) 791

Canal and Mills in Holland, charcoal and wash,
8¼ x 15½ . . . . (396) 1,160

Canal in Holland, pencil, 7½ x 6 . . . . (335) 220

Yoke of Oxen, pencil, 6¾ x 9½ . . . . (418) 440

1965

The Pond Before the Farm (recto), *The Village
Square* (verso), pencil and watercolor,
4½ x 7½ . . . . (508) 300

Lighter on a Canal in Holland, pencil and
watercolor, 8¼ x 10 . . . . (624) 1,106

The Estuary, 3¾ x 5¾ . . . . (598) 290

The Sailboat, wash and red chalk, 9 x 7 . . . . (531) 600

1966

Figures, wash and watercolor, 5¼ x 7¼ . . . . (772) 160

1967

The River Seine at Notre-Dame, black pencil and
wash, 7¼ x 12¼ . . . . (852) 1,120

Sailboats in Le Havre, charcoal, 12¼ x 10¼ . . . . . . (978) 560

Figures on the Edge of a Canal, pencil, 9 x 12¼ . . (898) 340

Landscape with Skaters, charcoal, 9½ x 12½ . . . . . (929) 96

1968–July 1969

Study of Clouds, 1871, pencil and watercolor,
6½ x 10½ . . . . (1068) 661

The Road, black lead, 5¼ x 8 . . . . (1075) 170

Study of Boats and Figures, (1846–48), (recto),
Fishing Boat Alongside a Quay (verso), India
ink and wash, 7¼ x 11½ . . . . (1240) 1,008

Shop at a Street Corner, (recto), pencil and
watercolor, *Restless Sea in a Harbor* (verso),
pencil, 3½ x 4¼ . . . . (1240) 1,008

*Quay of the River Seine, Notre-Dame in the
Background,* (recto), 1865, black chalk,
watercolor, and gouache, *Suburban Street of
Paris* (verso), pencil, 11¼ x 18½ . . . . (1240) 5,760

Street in Paris, 1878, pencil, 5½ x 9 . . . . (1272) 1,080

Sailboat, black chalk, 4¼ x 7 . . . . (1273) 504

WATERCOLORS

1961–1962

Epinay Castle, 1876, (recto), *The Côte St. André,*
1876, (verso), two watercolors, each 4 x 6¾ . . . . (29) 1,300

A Canal in Holland, watercolor, 11½ x 9 . . . . (84) 3,844

Honfleur, the Harbor, 1864, watercolor,
8¼ x 10¾ . . . . (84) 3,430

The Boulevard de Port-Royal, Snow, 1879,
watercolor, 7½ x 8 . . . . (84) 4,668

The Côte St. André, 1884, watercolor, 4¾ x 8¼ . . . . (80) 680

Skaters, 1884, gouache, 6 x 9¾ . . . . (71) 1,040

The River Meuse in Antwerp, 1866, watercolor
and gouache, 8 x 13½ . . . . (71) 3,020

Mill in Rotterdam, watercolor, 6 x 8¼ . . . . (123) 540

Road in the Isère, watercolor, 6 x 8¼ . . . . (123) $ 600

Riverside, watercolor, 4¾ x 7¾ . . . . (106) 814

Landscape with a Stream, watercolor and
charcoal, 6¾ x 10 . . . . (106) 1,040

Landscape, watercolor, 10 x 13½ . . . . (172) 340

Landscape in Nevers, watercolor, 9 x 13 . . . . (152) 1,200

The Suburbs of Lyons, watercolor, 4½ x 5¼ . . . . . . (144) 200

The Farmer,[1] watercolor, 8 x 6¾ . . . . (114) 800

November Morning, watercolor, 6 x 8¼ . . . . (30) 680

Boats in the Harbor, 1868, watercolor, 6½ x 8 . . . . . (76) 2,500

Entrance and Lighthouse of Honfleur Harbor,
watercolor, 11¼ x 14½ . . . . (76) 1,800

Snowy Road, 1885, watercolor, 5¾ x 8¼ . . . . (76) 1,040

Landscape Under Snow, 1886, watercolor
enlarged by the artist, 6½ x 9 . . . . (76) 1,440

1963

Quai de Bercy, 1862, watercolor, 5¾ x 12¼ . . . . . . (283) 4,270

Sailboat, 1865, watercolor, 5 x 5¼ . . . . (258) 1,200

*Village and Mill on the Edge of a Canal in
Holland,* 1867, watercolor, 8¾ x 12¼ . . . . (258) 2,900

The Pont-Marie in Paris, 1870, (recto), *Place
Ducale in Nevers,* 1870, (verso), watercolor,
6½ x 10½ . . . . (258) 1,500

Road at the Outskirts of Nevers, 1874, watercolor
and gouache, 4½ x 9¾ . . . . (318) 860

House on the Road, watercolor, 11 x 17½ . . . . (254) 3,400

Boulevard de Port-Royal in Paris, 1875,
watercolor, 6¼ x 15 . . . . (258) 3,620

The Côte St. André, 1877, watercolor, 6½ x 11 . . . (318) 2,700

The Farm, 1877, watercolor, 4½ x 10¼ . . . . (247) 1,508

Balbins Pass, 1879, 6¼ x 13¼ . . . . (283) 3,390

Lyons, 1883, watercolor, 4¾ x 8¼ . . . . (306) 780

Landscape, watercolor, 4 x 5¼ . . . . (224) 400

The Côte St. André, 1883, (recto), *Sasenage
Mountain Near Grenoble,* 1882, (verso),
watercolor, 6¾ x 10 . . . . (258) 3,600

The Côte St. André, 1884, double-sided
watercolor, 5¼ x 11 . . . . (258) 2,400

Grenoble, 1885, double-sided watercolor,
6½ x 9¾ . . . . (318) 1,700

1964

Marseilles, 1873, watercolor, 9¼ x 13¾ . . . . (471) 3,616

Sailboats on the River Meuse, 1871, watercolor,
11½ x 15¾ . . . . (368) 981

Road at the Outskirts of Nevers, 1874,
watercolor, 4½ x 9¾ . . . . (382) 800

The Path with Green Ruts, 1881, watercolor,
5¾ x 9 . . . . (409) 1,000

Les Chuzeaux, 1881, watercolor, 5¾ x 9 . . . . (378) 2,825

A Road in the Isère, 1882, watercolor, 6 x 9 . . . . . . (353) 1,300

On the Mountain, 1885, watercolor, 6 x 9½ . . . . . (416) 1,382

Landscape, 1885, watercolor, 4¾ x 7½ . . . . (398) 1,100

The Poplars, watercolor, 10½ x 7¼ . . . . (401) 2,100

Ste. Adresse, watercolor and pen, 4½ x 7¼ . . . . . . (348) 640

1965

Old Street in Morlaix, watercolor, 10¼ x 11 . . . . . (564) 1,800

Landscape in Nevers, 1850, watercolor, 10 x 14 . . . (614) 750

Landscape with a Pond, 1869, watercolor,
8¾ x 13¾ . . . . (642) 1,240

[1]On the reverse, *House,* watercolor, 6¼ x 9.

Harvest Scene, 1882, double-sided watercolor,
6¼ x 9¼ .... (617) $2,554

The Côte St. André, 1883, (recto), *The Thatch-
Roofed Cottage,* 1883, (verso), watercolor,
6½ x 19½ .... (522)   2,902

The Road, watercolor, 6¾ x 7½ .... (613)   1,260

1966

The Farm, watercolor and gouache, 9½ x 12¾ .... (749)   1,600

The Cart of Seaweed, 1862, watercolor, 9 x 13½ .. (741)   2,600

Honfleur, 1863, watercolor, 6 x 9 .... (744)   2,486

The Cart of Hay in Front of the Farm, 1871,
watercolor, 4½ x 7½ .... (829)   840

The Seamstress, 1872, watercolor, 8 x 11¼ .... (814)   1,800

Village at the Côte St. André, 1878, watercolor,
4 x 6½ .... (798)   735

The Côte St. André, Isère, 1880, gouache,
7¼ x 21¼ .... (686)   4,699

Landscapes with a Cart and a Goatherd, 1883 and
1884, double-sided watercolor, 4¾ x 8¼ ..... (829)   800

Mill in Holland, watercolor and gouache,
4½ x 7½ .... (706)   960

Antwerp Harbor, watercolor, 15½ x 8 .... (684)   1,680

1967

Le Chautoy, Nièvre, 1861, watercolor,
10¾ x 15¾ .... (881)   2,211

Houses by the Waterside, 1863, watercolor,
12¼ x 10¼ .... (1002)   960

The Seamstress, 1872, watercolor, 8 x 11 .... (887)   1,400

Marseilles, 1873, watercolor, 9¼ x 13¾ .... (918)   3,729

Landscape, 1882, watercolor, 5¾ x 9¼ .... (912)   1,900

The Côte St. André, 1885, double-sided
watercolor, 6¾ x 10¼ .... (938)   3,593

Village Near Grenoble, (recto), 1885, *The Road*
(verso), gouache, 6½ x 19¾ .... (982)   3,081

Entrance of a Village, watercolor, 6½ x 10½ ..... (982)   1,659

Skaters, 1885, gouache, 5 x 7¼ .... (881)   2,487

1968–July 1969

The Cart of Seaweed, 1862, watercolor, 9 x 13½ . (1106)   2,200

Nevers, the Road, 1871, watercolor, 4 x 6 .... (1044)   1,260

Ruins of Langeron, 1872, charcoal and
watercolor, 10½ x 16 .... (1099)   322

The Drac in Grenoble, 1875, watercolor,
10 x 15½ .... (1202)   4,600

The Valley of the Drac, 1883, watercolor,
6¾ x 20½ .... (1049)   3,000

The Stagecoach, 1885, watercolor, 4½ x 7¼ ..... (1044)   270

Riverside, Winter Effect, 1886, watercolor and
gouache, 4¾ x 7¼ .... (1131)   640

Winter at the Côte St. André, 1888, watercolor,
5½ x 8¼ .... (1127)   4,140

Yoke of Oxen on the Road, 1889, watercolor and
gouache, 4¼ x 7½ .... (1189)   1,560

Nero's Helmet, watercolor, 5¾ x 8¾ .... (1134)   1,062

Canal in Dordrecht, watercolor, 11¾ x 19 .... (1028)   2,100

Landscape of the Yser, 1877, watercolor, and
gouache, 7 x 11 .... (1225)   2,220

The Farm, (1861–65), pencil and watercolor,
8½ x 11¼ .... (1240)   2,040

Sailboats, Antwerp, 1866, watercolor, 8 x 11½ ... (1241)   3,780

Winter at La Côte St. André, watercolor,
5¼ x 8¼ .... (1268)   6,844

Nero's Helmet, watercolor, 5¾ x 8¾ .... (1272)   2,160

PAINTINGS

1961–1962

Seaside Landscape, on panel, 9 x 13½ .... (22) $1,266

A Street in Delft, 1858, 18¾ x 21¾ .... (164)   7,140

Banks of a Canal in Holland, 13¼ x 17 .... (162)   5,560

Boats Alongside the Quay, 20¼ x 23¾ .... (5)   1,600

Honfleur Harbor, 1865, 12¾ x 17¾ .... (128)   11,533

The Harbor in the Moonlight, 1868, 13 x 16¾ ..... (27)   1,400

Skaters at Overschie, 1876, 22 x 32¾ .... (84)   37,071

The Estuary, 1877, 9 x 12¾ .... (128)   4,119

Seascape, 1890, 8¾ x 14 .... (164)   7,140

1963

"Au Roi du Désert," 14 x 21 .... (199)   20,000

Back from Fishing, 1847, 15½ x 21 .... (306)   1,400

The Harbor, 1858, 16¾ x 23½ .... (289)   3,200

Lighter, 1859, 9½ x 12¾ .... (299)   1,400

The Road Under Snow, 1861, 16¾ x 22½ .... (258)   12,600

Sailboats and Boats on the River, 1863,
9¾ x 12¾ .... (318)   14,000

Charenton, 1868, 9½ x 12¼ .... (309)   6,262

Boulevard Montparnasse, 1870, on panel,
10½ x 15½ .... (255)   4,387

Canal in Holland, 1872, 12½ x 20½ .... (255)   6,855

1964

Moonlight Over a Canal, 1853, 21¼ x 32 .... (397)   900

The Estuary with Sailboats and Figures, 1853,
17¼ x 23¾ .... (434)   1,900

Path by the Waterside, 1862, 12¾ x 9½ .... (401)   2,040

The Towpath, 1864, 13½ x 18¼ .... (416)   49,199

View of the Bas-Meudon, 1865, 13 x 18½ .... (453)   16,584

Great Sailboats in Honfleur, 1865, 13 x 19 .... (458)   14,510

Canal in Holland, Moonlight, 1865, 23 x 14¾ ..... (401)   5,600

Skaters in Holland, 1866, 13¼ x 20¼ .... (340)   24,000

View of a Harbor, Low Tide, 1867, on board,
7 x 14¼ .... (479)   5,168

The Estuary, 1867, 12¾ x 17½ .... (416)   12,162

Castle in Holland, 1869, 13½ x 18¾ .... (382)   3,400

Overschie Village, 1875, 9½ x 12¼ .... (454)   5,528

View of the Outskirts of Delft, 1886, 17¾ x 29¾ .. (353)   3,600

Square of the Côte St. André, 1887, 8¾ x 14¼ .... (400)   17,600

1965

The Entrance of Rotterdam Harbor, 1857,
16¾ x 22 .... (602)   8,927

Skaters, 1858, 16¾ x 22 .... (518)   23,200

A Mill in Holland, on the Bank of the Canal,
11 x 16¼ .... (561)   1,920

Lock in Holland, 1866, 11½ x 18 .... (624)   7,739

Mill in Holland, 1866, 13 x 18¼ .... (512)   4,500

Sailboat on the High Seas at Night, 1867,
10½ x 13½ .... (629)   2,322

Boat on a Canal in Holland, 1868, 13 x 9¾ .... (571)   4,020

Moonlight at Delft, 1871, 13½ x 18¾ .... (617)   1,017

Landscape with a River, 1878, on cradled panel,
10 x 13 .... (614)   6,250

The Quays of the Seine, 1883, 10 x 14 .... (531)   3,100

The Pont-Neuf, 21 x 31½ .... (583)   8,706

1966

Thatch-Roofed Cottage by a Canal, 1843,
22½ x 30½ .... (765)   3,482

Old House, Normandy, (1850), 15¾ x 11¾ .... (686)   3,317

The Banks of the River Seine, in Paris, 1851,
13½ x 21¼ .... (750)   4,422

Canal in Holland, Night Effect, 1853, 17¼ x 24 ... (808) $3,773

Canal in Rotterdam, 1865, 15¾ x 21¾ .... (823)   3,808

The River Seine in Rouen, 1865, 16 x 21½ .... (753)   36,275

Delft, the Old Harbor in the Moonlight, 1868, on panel, 13 x 17 .... (808)   3,192

Rue de Paris, 1870, on panel, 9 x 12¼ .... (812)   11,056

Sailboat on the Escaut, Near Antwerp, 1871, 13 x 18¼ .... (689)   8,983

Harbor in Holland, 1876, 15½ x 18½ .... (812)   3,317

Mills, 1886, 13 x 18¼ .... (807)   4,900

1967

Moonlight Over Rotterdam, 1871, 13½ x 18¾ .... (912)   2,400

Lighter on a Canal in Holland, 1862, 16 x 21¼ .... (940)   6,965

Landscape of the Bas-Meudon, 1865, 13 x 18½ ... (880)   58,044

Dutch Harbor, 1873, 13½ x 18½ .... (987)   20,600

Skaters in Holland, 1864, 16 x 21½ .... (938)   16,584

Paris, Banks of the River Seine, 1851, 14 x 21¾ .. (852)   8,400

Interior of a Church, 1855, on panel, 18¼ x 12 .... (849)   1,500

1968–July 1969

Paris Street in the Moonlight, 1854, 10 x 15½ ... (1070)   1,298

A Canal in Holland, 1855, 9 x 12¼ .... (1070)   2,242

Boulevard Jourdan, Paris, (1865), 7½ x 9½ ..... (1132)   11,800

Beach in Normandy, 1866, 13¼ x 22 .... (1132)   22,420

Mouth of the Meuse, 1868, 12¾ x 17½ .... (1126)   17,346

A Canal in Holland, 1869, 16¼ x 25¾ .... (1190)   34,400

The River Meuse in Dordrecht, 1872, on panel, 8¼ x 12¾ .... (1071)   7,000

The River Saône in Lyons, 1874, 13 x 17¾ ...... (1163)   17,000

The Road Works on the Boulevard de Port-Royal, 1875, 12¼ x 20¼ .... (1086)   6,850

Skaters in Holland, 1875, 9¼ x 12¾ .... (1068)   7,552

View of a Harbor at Nightfall, 1876, 15¼ x 18½ .. (1069)   4,274

Canal at the Outskirts of Dordrecht, 1887, 13 x 20½ .... (1113)   2,878

Riverside in the Moonlight, on panel, 8¾ x 13 ... (1132)   2,596

Moonlight Over the Canal in Holland, 1876, 22 x 18½ .... (1254)   4,200

Ste. Adresse Beach, 1862, 9¾ x 18 .... (1270)   23,520

The Canal in the Sunset, 1872, on paper laid down on canvas, 12½ x 17½ .... (1271)   840

Washerwomen by a Canal, on panel, 14¾ x 8¾ .. (1273)   6,500

Asger Jorn

(1914–)

Birthplace: Vejrun, Denmark.

1935   Executes him first abstract composition.

1936-37   Goes to Paris, where he studies under Léger. With Le Corbusier, executes decorations for the 1937 World's Fair. Participates in the Salon des Indépendants, Paris.

1938   Returns to Denmark. Sets up the review *Helhesten* with the architect Dahlmann Olsen.

1938-48   Takes part in the groups "Host" and "Spiralen."

1945   Changes his name from Jorgensen to Jorn.

1948   One-man show at the Galerie Breteau, Paris.

1948-52   Joins the Cobra group and takes part in its exhibitions. Participates in the Salon des Surindépendants, Paris.

1949   Participates in the first exhibition of Experimental Art, Amsterdam.

1953   One-man show at the Birch Gallery, Copenhagen.

1955   Settles permanently in Paris. First trip to Italy, to which he often returns. Exhibits at the Galleria del Naviglio, Milan.

1957-60   Has many exhibitions at the Galerie Rive Gauche, Paris.

1958   Participates in the exhibition "Cinquante Ans d'art moderne" at the Brussels World's Fair. Retrospective exhibition at the London Institute of Contemporary Arts.

1959   Participates in Documenta II, Kassel.

1959-60   Participates in the exhibition "European Art Today," U.S.

1962   Participates in "Cobra et Après" at the Palais des Beaux-Arts, Brussels.

1964   Retrospective exhibition at the Stedelijk Museum, Amsterdam. Participates in "Painting and Sculpture of a Decade" at the Tate Gallery, London. Dodeigne-Jorn exhibition at the Kunsthalle, Basel.

1965   Trip to Mexico and the U.S.

Sales

DRAWINGS

1968–July 1969

Composition, 1938, colored chalk, 10 x 7¼ ...... (1024) $ 264

WATERCOLORS

1961–1962

Composition, pastel, 10 x 11¾ .... (16)   332

Composition, watercolor and gouache, 18¼ x 21¾ .... (75)   948

1963

Multicolored Composition, gouache, 15 x 20½ .... (283)   1,017

1964

Abstract Composition, 1961, gouache, 15 x 20½ ... (471)   1,130

Old Rabbit, 1961, gouache, 18¼ x 11¾ .... (387)   166

Figures, 1963, gouache, 17¾ x 12¾ .... (401)   140

1965

Old Colors, gouache and watercolor, 17½ x 13½ .... (582)   166

1967

Composition, (1961), gouache, 15 x 20½ .... (967)   949

PAINTINGS

1961–1962

A Demon, 17¾ x 14 .... (87)   653

Composition, 10 x 15 .... (16)   743

Joy of Living, 1946, 26½ x 23¼ .... (149)   2,528

The Successful Painter, 19¾ x 17¾ .... (69)   1,343

The Sleepless Night, 1938, 25¼ x 31½ . . . . (145)	$3,476
Polemicists and Witnesses, 1955, 29 x 39½ . . . . (75)	4,108
Figure, 1956, 19¾ x 23¾ . . . . (70)	1,896
Composition (Heavy Weather), 1960, 25¾ x 32 . . . (143)	1,876
Formio e Cigalette, 1961, 21¼ x 29 . . . . (156)	1,420

1963

Bird, ... (226)	639
Joy of Living, 1946, 26½ x 23¾ . . . . (200)	1,660

1964

Appeldorn, 1944, 30 x 40 . . . . (422)	824
Figure, oil on paper, 8½ x 5¼ . . . . (455)	193

1965

Composition, 32 x 25¼ . . . . (617)	2,486
Impulsive Expulsion, 24 x 19¾ . . . . (617)	1,356
Strange Animal, 1956, collage and gouache, 18¾ x 25¾ . . . . (582)	276

1966

Spatenbrau, Plenty of Beer, 1959, 31½ x 25¾ . . . . (751)	2,073
Composition with Figures and Animals, 1945, 37½ x 49¾ . . . . (771)	5,282
Cosmic Creation, 1952, 24½ x 28½ . . . . (771)	2,286
Poor Poet, 31½ x 25¼ . . . . (729)	1,020
Self-Portrait, 29¼ x 20½ . . . . (662)	2,272
Composition, 24 x 19¾ . . . . (798)	972
It Shows, 1942, 25 x 19½ . . . . (823)	2,584

1967

Witches, 1955, 25¾ x 19½ . . . . (851)	2,402
Composition with a Green Mask, 15¾ x 11¾ . . . . . (892)	871
Composition, 1965, collage, 19¾ x 25¾ . . . . (958)	594

1968–July 1969

Composition, 14¼ x 20 . . . . (1024)	726
The Cat, 1954, 36½ x 48 . . . . (1100)	2,970

Wassily Kandinsky

(1866–1944)

Birthplace: Moscow, Russia.

1886	Studies law in Moscow.
1896	Decides to go to Munich to study painting.
1900	Enters the Fine Arts Academy of Munich.
1901	Sets up the group "Die Phalanx." Exhibits at the "Secession," Berlin.
1905	Participates in the Salon d'Automne, Paris.
1906	Settles for one year in Paris, where he discovers Fauvism.
1909	With Jawlensky, sets up the New Association of Artists, Munich.
1910	Writes his famous book *Über das Geistige in der Kunst* (published in 1912). Utterly breaks away from naturalism. Makes friends with Franz Marc.
1911	With Franz Marc, founds the group "Der Blaue Reiter," whose first exhibition takes place at the Tannhauser Gallery, Munich.
1912	Retrospective exhibition at Der Sturm Gallery, Berlin. Participates in the exhibition "Moderne Bund" at the Kunsthaus, Zurich.
1913	Participates in the first Herbstsalon at Der Sturm Gallery, Berlin. Participates in the Armory Show, New York.
1914	Returns to Moscow.
1918	Teaches at the Academy of Fine Arts, Moscow.
1919-21	Founds the Academy of Arts and Sciences and twenty-two museums in the U.S.S.R. Returns to Germany.
1922	Exhibits at the Goldschmidt and Wallerstein Gallery, Berlin. Teaches at the Bauhaus at Weimar.
1924	Foundation of the group "Die Blauen Vier," which comprises Kandinsky, Klee, Feininger, and Jawlensky.
1926	Becomes a German citizen.
1928	Stage decoration and costumes for *Pictures at an Exhibition* by Moussorgsky, at Dessau.
1929	First exhibition in Paris at the Galerie Zak. Stays in Belgium, where he meets Ensor.
1930	Participates in the exhibition of "Cercle et Carré," Paris.
1931	Travels through the Middle East, to Italy, and France. Executes frescoes for the International Architecture Exhibition, Berlin.
1933	Settles in France.
1934	Meets Mondrian, Miró, Arp, Pevsner, Delaunay, and Magnelli. Exhibits at the Galerie Jeanne Bûcher, Paris.
1937	In Germany, his works are designated "degenerate" by the Nazis.
1939	Becomes a French citizen.
1944	Died, Paris.

Sales

DRAWINGS

1961–1962

Composition No. 659, India ink and watercolor on pink paper, 8¾ x 6½ . . . . (106)	$2,599

1963

With the Square, 1923, India ink and gouache, 18 x 16½ . . . . (225)	5,750
Drawing, 1930, India ink with pen and brush, 6 x 7½ . . . . (219)	791

1964

The Desert, 1916, ink and watercolor, 12¾ x 10 . . . (458)	10,157
Composition, 1925, India ink and watercolor, 14 x 9 . . . . (383)	5,763
Composition, 1934, India ink, 9 x 8¼ . . . . (368)	1,106

1965

Composition, 1927, India ink, 11¼ x 9 . . . . (618)	1,476
Composition, 1932, India ink, 9 x 7½ . . . . (597)	2,091
Drawing No. 1, 1934, pen, 14 x 9 . . . . (541)	975
Flying Dragon, 1938, ink, 19¾ x 9 . . . . (494)	1,400

1966

Drawing No. 6, 1932, ink, 14 x 8¼ . . . . (721)	750
Composition, 1927, ink, 12 x 10 . . . . (757)	1,797

1967

Composition with a Cab, (1909), ink, 7 x 10 ...... (841) $ 750
Drawing, 1930, India ink, 6 x 7¾ .... (927)   791

1968

Composition, 1927, pen, 11½ x 9½ .... (1191)   2,596
Together, 1931, colored ink and tempera,
   12¼ x 9½ .... (1099)   4,600
Composition, 1933, India ink, 10 x 14 .... (1127)   1,150
Composition, 1933, India ink, 11 x 14¼ .... (1114)   1,240
Composition, 1939, India ink, 8¼ x 6 .... (1030)   1,500
Composition, India ink, 10 x 13¾ .... (1268)   2,088

WATERCOLORS

1961–1962

Improvisation, 1918, watercolor and ink,
   10½ x 14 .... (88)   4,797
Circles in the Dark, watercolor, tempera, and
   India ink, 13½ x 13 .... (149)   3,850
Gedampfte Glut, 1928, airbrush and watercolor
   on a gouache background, 14½ x 10 .... (105)   6,102
K 357, 1929, watercolor, 19¾ x 17 .... (129)   6,041
Schwacher Bogen, 1929, watercolor on an
   airbrushed background, 19½ x 10 .... (105)   6,102
Composition with a Red Point, 1930, watercolor,
   6½ x 6¾ .... (105)   2,260
Circles Center, 1932, gouache, 13 x 19½ .... (69)   5,688
Composition, 1940, gouache, 8¾ x 6½ .... (145)   3,476
Composition with White Forms, 1940, gouache,
   12¾ x 19½ .... (88)   7,626

1964

Composition, 1924, gouache, 13½ x 8¾ .... (454)   4,699
Concentric, 1924, watercolor, 13½ x 9 .... (448)   4,250
Downward, 1925, watercolor and India ink,
   15½ x 12¾ .... (467)   2,952
Tear, 1928, gouache and ink, 19 x 12¾ .... (415)   10,503
Almost No. 492, 1930, tempera, ink, and plaster
   on cardboard, 13 x 6¼ .... (415)   8,292
Circle Center, 1932, gouache, 12¾ x 18½ .... (454)   4,422
Composition, 1932, gouache, 20¼ x 12¼ .... (386)   4,620
Composition No. 696, 1941, watercolor, 19 x 12 ... (367)   4,160
Fan Shaped, No. 707, 1943, tempera and oil on
   board, 22½ x 16¾ .... (415)   17,966
The Evening, tempera on cardboard, 12½ x 18¾ .. (380)   1,599

1965

The Princess with a Bewitched Horse, (1906),
   tempera on cardboard, 19½ x 19½ .... (566)   6,102
The Bear, (1906), tempera on cardboard,
   11¾ x 19½ .... (566)   4,181
The "Blaue Reiter" Notification, (1912–13),
   watercolor, 12¼ x 10¼ .... (485)   7,200
Improvisation, 1918, watercolor, 10¾ x 13½ ...... (575)   4,975
Transmission, 1935, watercolor, 20¼ x 19 .... (545)   5,658
Composition, 1941, watercolor, 19 x 11 .... (574)   4,600

1966

The Orange Seller, (1904–05), gouache, on a gray
   cardboard, 14 x 19¾ .... (712)   4,920
Gouache on Gray No. 661, 1940, gouache,
   25 x 8 .... (814)   2,500

1967

The Tournament, 1902, tempera on cardboard,
   18½ x 30½ .... (927)   6,780
Tears, 1928, gouache and ink, 19 x 12¾ .... (954)   11,000

Composition, 1930, tempera, 19½ x 12¾ .... (970) $4,428
Klotzig, 1931, watercolor, 13½ x 11½ .... (982)   7,820
Abstraction, 1941, gouache and watercolor,
   12¼ x 10¼ .... (889)   3,100

1968

Composition No. 696, 1941, watercolor,
   18½ x 12 .... (1216)   8,250
Three, 1928, watercolor, 13½ x 20 .... (1268)   15,544

PAINTINGS

1961–1962

Biderstein Park in the Winter, Munich, (1904), oil
   on canvas on cardboard, 9¼ x 12¾ .... (88)   5,855
Gabriele Münter at His Easel, 1908, oil on
   cardboard, 13 x 17¾ .... (88)   15,744
Murnau, 1908, on board, 11½ x 15¾ .... (31)   14,279
Keil auf Kreis, 1926, on cardboard, 16¼ x 13 ..... (149)   17,380
Composition, 1927, 20¼ x 17 .... (93)   15,494
White on Black, 1937, oil and tempera on a black
   background, 19¾ x 18½ .... (105)   4,972

1963

Autumn Landscape, Near Murnau, 1908,
   12¾ x 15¾ .... (316)   15,000
Bavarian Landscape with a Church, (1908), on
   board, 13 x 17¾ .... (279)   20,000
Church at Froshhausen, 1908, on board,
   17½ x 12¾ .... (225)   22,500
Staffelsee, (1908–09), on board, 13 x 16 .... (316)   13,000
Four Forms, 1943, oil and tempera on cardboard,
   23 x 16¾ .... (219)   8,362

1964

Kallmunz, Oberpfalz, 1903, on canvas, 9½ x 13 ... (415)   9,950
The Railway Track, 1905, on canvas laid down on
   board, 12¾ x 15½ .... (448)   7,500
Bridge in Paris, 1906, on board, 11¼ x 13½ ...... (454)   3,870
Rapallo, 1906, 9½ x 12¾ .... (415)   7,739
Ludwigskirche in Munich, 1908, on cardboard,
   26¾ x 38 .... (416)   33,168
Great Study, 1914, 39¾ x 31¼ .... (415)   110,560
Improvisation, 1914, 43¾ x 43¾ .... (415)   138,200
Accentuated Corners, 1923, 51½ x 51½ .... (415)   60,808
White Dot No. 248, 1923, 36 x 29 .... (415)   42,842
Unprotected, 264a, 1923, 38½ x 37 .... (415)   49,752
Getting Brighter, 1924, 27¾ x 23½ .... (415)   44,224
Above to the Left, 1925, on cardboard,
   27½ x 19½ .... (415)   31,786
Black Triangle, 1925, on cardboard, 31¼ x 21¼ ... (415)   17,966
Yellow Circle No. 335, 1926, on cardboard,
   27¾ x 19½ .... (415)   37,314
Tear No. 362, 1926, 40 x 32½ .... (415)   55,280
Radiant Lines No. 401, 1927, 39¼ x 29¼ .... (415)   33,168
Growing Dimness, 1927, 19¾ x 16¾ .... (989)   11,028
Lightness in Heaviness No. 457, 1929, on
   cardboard, 19½ x 19½ .... (415)   19,348
Krass und Mild, 1932, 37¾ x 47½ .... (415)   26,811
Rigid and Bowed, 1935, oil and sand on canvas,
   45 x 63¾ .... (415)   66,336
Quiet Tension No. 638, 1937, 35 x 42 .... (415)   27,640
The Right Touch No. 649, 1938, 35¼ x 45¾ ...... (415)   55,280
49 Times 49, 1942, on cardboard, 19½ x 19½ ..... (383)   10,396

1965

Oberpfalz Valley, 1903, on board, 9¼ x 12¾ ...... (526) $9,000

Kallmunz, Oberpfalz, 1903, on canvas laid down
on cardboard, 9½ x 13 .... (616) 12,800

Summer in Murnau, 1908, on board, 12¾ x 15¾ .. (624) 13,820

The Haystacks, 1908, on board, 12¾ x 17½ ...... (624) 7,186

1966

Oberpfalz Valley, 1903, on board, 9½ x 12¾ ...... (808) 12,188

Murnau, Autumn, 1908-09, on cardboard,
13 x 17½ .... (802) 12,000

Starnbergersee, 1908, on board, 12 x 15½ .... (686) 14,096

Village Street, with a Castle, 1909, on board,
19 x 25 .... (750) 38,696

Some Dots, 1925, on board, 27¾ x 19¾ .... (753) 33,373

Yellow Edge, 1930, oil, tempera, and ink,
19½ x 19½ .... (753) 11,028

1967

Street at Starnberg, 1905, on board, 9½ x 13 ..... (954) 15,000

The Rocks in Rapallo, 1906, on board, 9½ x 13 ... (988) 11,196

The Corn Field, Near Dresden, 9 x 14 .... (940) 7,545

Composition in Pink, 1928, 16¼ x 22 .... (962) 14,400

White Gate, 1928, on board, 16¾ x 12¾ .... (938) 7,739

Light Counterpressure, 1929, on board,
19½ x 19½ .... (940) 14,510

1968–July 1969

Staffelsee, 1908-09, on cardboard, 13¼ x 16¼ ... (1125) 24,150

Village Street, (1905), 10½ x 16¾ .... (1056) 16,000

Early in the Morning, 1906, 37¾ x 50½ .... (1187) 63,720

Blue Rider at the Tunisian Market, (1907),
29 x 36¼ .... (1187) 16,520

Light Counterpressure, 1929, on board,
18¾ x 18¾ .... (1057) 11,000

Village Church at Kochel, (1906-07), on canvas
mounted on board, 9 x 13 .... (1232) 25,000

Lana, (1908), on board, 13 x 16 .... (1232) 26,000

Rapallo: A Boat on the Sea, 1906, on board,
9½ x 13 .... (1232) 26,000

Hilly Landscape, on board, 16¼ x 19¼ .... (1241) 35,300

Farmyard in the Summer, on board, 9¼ x 12¾ ... (1241) 17,600

Coolness, 1941, oil and lacquer on board,
19¼ x 27½ .... (1270) 62,400

John Kane

(1860–1934)

Birthplace: West Calder, Scotland. His family name
is Caine.

1879 Follows his mother, who settles in Pennsylvania,
U.S., with her second husband. Spends several
years shuttling from job to job.

1891 Looses his left leg in an accident.

1897 Marries Maggie Halloran.

1907 Begins to support his family by enlarging and color-
ing photographs.

1910 Stay in Akron, Ohio.

1925-26 Submits pictures to the Carnegie International Exhibition, but they are rejected. However, his
scenes of the Scottish Highlands make him famous. From now until 1934, his work is included
in the Carnegie International Exhibitions.

1928 Joins the Associated Artists of Pittsburgh and exhibits steadily with this group.

1929 Given an award by the Carnegie Institute. Exhibits
at the Harvard Society of Contemporary Art.

1931 First one-man show at the Contemporary Art Galleries, New York.

1932 One-man show at Manfred Schwartz's.

1933 Wins a first prize in Pittsburgh for the work "Liberty Bridge."

1934 Died.

Sales

PAINTINGS

1963

View of Pittsburgh, 27¾ x 33¾ .... (272) $12,500

1968–July 1969

View of Philadelphia, 1928, 20 x 24 .... (1035) 12,000

Michel Kikoïne

(1892–1969)

Birthplace: Gomel, Russia.

1908-11 Attends the School of Fine Arts of Wilno with his
friend Chaïm Soutine.

1913 Goes to Paris. With Soutine, enters the Ecole Nationale des Beaux-Arts, in Cormon's studio.
Marries during World War I.

1919 Draws children's portraits to earn his living. First
one-man show at the Galerie de la Licorne, Paris.
Participates in the Salon des Indépendants, Paris.

1920 One-man show at the Galerie Bernheim Jeune,
Paris.

1921 Birth of his son, the future painter Jacques Yankel.

1923 Signs a contract with the Galerie Chéron, Paris.
Stays at Cagnes-sur-Mer in the south of France.

1925 Signs a contract with Netter. Becomes a French
citizen.

1930 One-man show at the Galerie Billet-Worms, Paris.
Buys a house in Burgundy. The Philadelphia Museum of Art buys two of his pictures.

1935 One-man show at the Galerie Emsild, Paris.

1945 Exhibits at the Galerie Chaire-Lauthier, Toulouse.

1949-50 One-man show at the Brummer Gallery, New York.
Exhibits in Jerusalem, Haifa, and Tel Aviv.

1951   Given an award by the Menton Biennial.

1955   One-man show at the Redfern Gallery, London.

1956   Works on a series of colored lithographs on the theme of the children of Israel.

1957   One-man show at the Galerie Romanet, Paris.

1969   Died.

Sales

DRAWINGS

1963

Seascape and Landscape, (recto-verso), pencil and watercolor, 12¼ x 14¾ . . . . (246) $ 116

1964

Fishing Boats, (recto-verso), colored pencil, 11 x 14 . . . . (355)   250

1965

Country House, pen, watercolor, and colored pencil, 11¾ x 8¾ . . . . (561)   320

The Conversation Under the Trees, colored pencil, 10¼ x 14¼ . . . . (630)   140

1968–July 1969

Horse, black lead, 8¾ x 11¾ . . . . (1144)   96

WATERCOLORS

1963

Sailboats in a Harbor, gouache, 14¼ x 17¾ . . . . . . (181)   160

1964

Still Life, watercolor, 12¼ x 18¾ . . . . (321)   300

Landscape, gouache, 14¾ x 21¾ . . . . (430)   184

1965

The Creek, watercolor, 10¼ x 14¾ . . . . (647)   180

Landscape, watercolor, 10 x 15 . . . . (619)   220

The Garden, varnished gouache, 9½ x 12¼ . . . . . . (642)   124

Houses in the Country, gouache and colored pencils, 9 x 11¾ . . . . (632)   160

View of Vannes, gouaches, 12 x 17¾ . . . . (507)   250

Scene in a Harbor, watercolor and gouache, 11¾ x 18¾ . . . . (507)   300

1966

Landscape, watercolor, 15¾ x 12¾ . . . . (803)   104

The House in the Forest, gouache, 10¼ x 8¼ . . . . . (820)   180

Landscape of Provence, watercolor, 7¼ x 9¾ . . . . . (764)   120

The Ile de la Cité, watercolor and gouache, 11¾ x 17¼ . . . . (655)   260

The Fishermen, watercolor and gouache, 12¾ x 15¾ . . . . (656)   280

The Little Harbor, gouache, 13½ x 18¼ . . . . (726)   190

1967

Landscape, gouache and colored pencil, 17¾ x 12¼ . . . . (876)   340

Landscape, gouache and colored pencil . . . . (1007)   170

Village of Auvergne, watercolor, 12½ x 16¾ . . . . . . (920)   220

Glints, watercolor, 15¾ x 12¾ . . . . (858)   240

Bunch of Roses, gouache, 13½ x 10½ . . . . (855)   140

1968–July 1969

Walkers in a Park, watercolor and gouache, 11¾ x 14¾ . . . . (1131)   116

On the Beach, watercolor, 9½ x 12¼ . . . . (1167)   170

Landscape with Flower Beds, varnished gouache, 19½ x 12¾ . . . . (1154)   380

Landscape of the Morvan, watercolor and gouache, 19 x 25 . . . . (1178) $ 300

Landscape, watercolor and gouache, 12¾ x 17¾ . (1171)   180

Landscape, watercolor and colored pencil, 11¾ x 9 . . . . (1078)   160

Houses of Provence, gouache, 12¾ x 8¾ . . . . (1211)   280

Still Life, watercolor and gouache, 11¼ x 14 . . . . (1098)   260

Still Life with a Fruit Stand, gouache, 11 x 14¼ . . (1161)   340

Toward the Evening, gouache, 19 x 20½ . . . . (1098)   420

Landscape of Provence, pastel, 12¾ x 8¾ . . . . (1245)   490

PAINTINGS

1961–1962

The Road, 1914, 19¾ x 24 . . . . (53)   460

Thatch-Roofed Cottages and Cypresses, 21¼ x 25¾ . . . . (53)   1,600

Little Houses Surrounded with Trees, 21¼ x 25¾ . . . . (9)   680

Portrait of a Little Boy, 21¾ x 18¼ . . . . (9)   320

Portrait of a Young Woman, 16¼ x 13 . . . . (43)   560

Underwood, 1924, 36½ x 29 . . . . (120)   960

Street of Paris, 1920, 24 x 36½ . . . . (146)   840

Flowers, 21¾ x 18¼ . . . . (143)   701

Portrait of the Artist, 1925, 39 x 25¼ . . . . (37)   1,500

Vase of Flowers, 21¼ x 25¾ . . . . (25)   550

Roses, 1928, 29 x 23¾ . . . . (136)   520

Flowers and Fruit, 25¾ x 21¼ . . . . (52)   700

Landscape, 21 x 25¼ . . . . (152)   400

1963

Hilly Landscape, 21¼ x 25¾ . . . . (238)   600

Red-Roofed House on the Outskirts of the Forest, 21¼ x 32 . . . . (306)   900

Landscape in Spring, 25¼ x 29¾ . . . . (192)   620

Fruit Stand and Fruit on Tablecloth, oil and gouache on paper, 12¾ x 18¾ . . . . (278)   220

Still Life, 16¾ x 24 . . . . (246)   430

Seated Nude, back view, 22 x 17¾ . . . . (234)   310

The Gipsy, on panel, 21¾ x 18¼ . . . . (258)   500

Bathers, 34½ x 45½ . . . . (216)   1,152

1964

Landscape, 1924, 36½ x 29 . . . . (394)   1,220

Red-Roofed Houses on the Outskirts of the Forest, 18¼ x 21¾ . . . . (475)   400

Bunches of Roses, 1928, 29 x 23¾ . . . . (346)   960

Vase of Flowers, 29 x 23¾ . . . . (478)   660

Great Trees, 1930, 31½ x 21¼ . . . . (333)   480

House in a Landscape, 23¾ x 28¾ . . . . (387)   774

Young Musicians, 39½ x 32 . . . . (404)   960

Landscape with a Village, 23¾ x 28½ . . . . (420)   493

The Mill at Aunay-sur-Serein, Yonne, 25¾ x 32 . . (436)   560

Landscape, 28½ x 36 . . . . (454)   691

Still Life with a Violin, 21¾ x 31½ . . . . (327)   600

Still Life, 45¾ x 35¼ . . . . (341)   720

Still Life, 1954, 25 x 21¼ . . . . (398)   600

Reclining Nude, 1957, 25¾ x 36½ . . . . (398)   840

Landscape of the South of France, 1963, 25¾ x 32 . . . . (450)   800

1965

Reclining Nude, 1957, 25 x 36 . . . . (534)   640

Bathers, on the Beach, 25¾ x 21¼ . . . . (559)   620

Village of Provence, 19¾ x 23¾ . . . . (559)   440

Landscape, 36½ x 29 .... (599) $1,000
Still Life with Fruit, 16¾ x 24 .... (563)   420
Still Life with a Green Jug, 21¼ x 25¾ .... (552)   400
Palette and Windflowers, 27¼ x 18¼ .... (540)   400
The Man with a Pipe, 32½ x 21¼ .... (503)   1,100

1966

The Entrance of the Village, 17¾ x 25 .... (653)   960
Landscape, 22 x 15 .... (810)   340
Landscape, 23¾ x 29 .... (742)   960
Landscape, 22½ x 33½ .... (824)   900
Landscape of the Cap d'Antibes, 25¾ x 32 .... (674)   660
Resting Under the Tree, oil on paper laid down
    on canvas, 14¾ x 10¾ .... (670)   420
Portrait of a Child, 15¾ x 12¾ .... (663)   300
Portrait of a Little Girl, 17½ x 14½ .... (689)   498
Young Woman Resting, 1957, 25 x 36 .... (793)   940
Flowers in a Vase, 21¾ x 18¼ .... (793)   370
Still Life, 27¼ x 18¼ .... (702)   420
Vase of Flowers, 18¼ x 15 .... (689)   442
Still Life with Flowers, 29 x 23¾ .... (809)   1,040

1967

Surroundings of Clamart, 1915, 21¼ x 29 .... (845)   760
Landscape, 14¼ x 30 .... (838)   500
Seascape, 24 x 19¾ .... (941)   400
Holidays, 29 x 36½ .... (898)   960
Back Home, 13 x 16¼ .... (912)   900
Flowers and Fruit, 25¾ x 21¼ .... (984)   520
Foliage, 21¼ x 29 .... (943)   400
Bunch of Flowers, 13 x 16¼ .... (1007)   230
Portrait of a Woman, 57¾ x 38½ .... (995)   440

1968–July 1969

Mountainous Landscapes, 13½ x 25¾ .... (1210)   1,100
The Faithful Praying at the Synagogue, on panel,
    25¾ x 21¼ .... (1210)   900
*Landscape with a Thatch-Roofed Cottage and
    Two Figures,* 1915, 13 x 16¼ .... (1060)   2,400
Landscape, 25¾ x 32 .... (1015)   520
The Village, 28½ x 21¼ .... (1131)   740
Entrance of the Village, 21¼ x 29 .... (1116)   860
The Harbor, 18¼ x 15 .... (1066)   500
Village of Aunay-sur-Serein, on canvas laid down
    on cardboard, 15 x 18¼ .... (1122)   540
Walk in a Park, 1930, on panel, 10¾ x 15¾ ...... (1110)   500
The Young Lady in Blue, 29 x 14¾ .... (1026)   720
Little Girl and Fish, 21¼ x 32 .... (1172)   760
Bust of a Woman, 21¾ x 18¼ .... (1230)   820
Vase of Flowers, 27 x 19 .... (1234)   1,400
Mother and Child, 45½ x 31½ .... (1265)   1,100
The Young Girl with Flowers, on canvas laid
    down on panel, 36½ x 23¾ .... (1266)   1,320

Ernst-Ludwig Kirchner

(1880–1938)

Birthplace: Aschaffenburg, Germany.

1901   Studies architecture in Dresden. Paints in his leisure hours.

1904   Meets Heckel. Executes a series of pictures in the Neo-Impressionist manner. Discovers Japanese prints and African art.

1905   Heckel introduces him to Schmidt-Rottluff. Takes his degree in architecture, but devotes himself entirely to painting. Executes his first lithographs.

1906   Meets Nolde and Pechstein. With friends, sets up the group "Die Brücke." Participates in the first and second exhibitions of "Die Brücke" in Dresden-Löbtau.

1911   Settles in Berlin. The review *Der Sturm* publishes his illustrations. With Pechstein, he founds (unsuccessfully) the "MUIM-Institut," Berlin.

1912   With Heckel, executes murals for the "Sonderbund" international exhibition, Cologne. Participates in the exhibition of "Der Blaue Reiter" at the Goltz Gallery, Munich, and at Der Sturm Gallery, Berlin.

1913   Dissolution of "Die Brücke."

1915-16   Enters a sanatorium.

1917   Settles at Davos.

1923   Exhibits at the Kunsthalle, Basel.

1925-26   Founds the group "Rot-Blau."

1937   In Germany his works are designated "degenerate" by the Nazis.

1938   Despairs of the political development of his country. Becomes seriously ill. Died, Davos, a suicide.

Sales

DRAWINGS

1961–1962

At the Restaurant, black chalk, 4¼ x 6¼ .... (106) $ 90
Back View of Seated Nude, colored chalk,
    17¾ x 14 .... (106)   768
Two Young Girls, chalk and watercolor, 4¾ x 6 ... (106)   99
Two Nudes on Fehmarn Beach, black lead,
    23½ x 17½ .... (106)   452
Young Lady Bathing, 1913, pencil and
    watercolor, 18¼ x 15 .... (135)   787
Shepherd with Cows, (1920), colored chalk,
    14 x 18¾ .... (107)   283
Forest in the Mountains, (1923), wash on chalk,
    19¾ x 13 .... (107)   332
Hilly Landscape with Cows, 1921, chalk,
    13½ x 21¼ .... (151)   295
Woman in the Nude, pencil, 21¾ x 16¼ .... (151)   246

1963

Two Models in a Studio, (1909), colored chalk,
    17 x 13¾ .... (219)   588
Two Young Girls, (1910), black chalk and
    watercolor, 4¾ x 6 .... (219)   131
Café Scene, (1912), pencil, 9¼ x 6¼ .... (219)   113
Mother and Child by the Brook, (1925), black
    chalk, 18¾ x 14¾ .... (219)   192
Pillnitz Castle in Dresden, pen and colored chalk,
    6½ x 8 .... (284)   123
Reclining Nude, India ink, 17½ x 13½ .... (179)   250

1964

The Circus, (1908-10), colored chalk, 7 x 9¼ ..... **(467)** $ 394

Negro Dancer, 1908, charcoal, 8 x 6½ .... **(428)** 91

Seated Nude, colored chalk, 13¾ x 16¼ .... **(428)** 418

Reclining Nude, (1908), colored chalk, 12¾ x 17 .. **(383)** 915

Seated Woman with a Large Hat, (1908), India ink and pastel, 35½ x 27 .... **(383)** 1,989

Boats, 1910, colored chalk, 8¼ x 11½ .... **(383)** 226

Dancing, Berlin, (1911-12), pencil and watercolor, 10½ x 13½ .... **(383)** 791

Reclining Nude, pencil, 13½ x 20¼ .... **(329)** 375

Bathers, 1933, pencil, 19¾ x 14 .... **(321)** 325

1965

Harvesttime, wash and pencil, 10 x 7¾ .... **(597)** 197

Nude with a Tub, 1912, pencil, 23 x 17½ .... **(616)** 608

Alpine Landscape, 1917, pencil and watercolor, 15 x 19 .... **(637)** 1,100

Three Women, 1918, black chalk, 18¼ x 14 .... **(566)** 294

And Pippa Dances, (1924), colored chalk, watercolor, and India ink, 14 x 18¾ .... **(545)** 792

1966

Three Women, colored chalk, 12¾ x 16½ .... **(775)** 295

Woody Landscape at Davos, 1918-19, colored chalk on green paper, 20¼ x 28 .... **(734)** 949

The Consultation, 1931, pencil, 20¼ x 13½ .... **(734)** 140

Reclining Young Girl, pen and India-ink wash, 18¼ x 23¼ .... **(754)** 407

Kneeling Nude, colored pencil, 16¾ x 13¾ .... **(806)** 418

Couple of Lovers, (1908), colored chalk, 13½ x 17 .... **(716)** 836

Standing Nude, (1928), pen, 8¾ x 5¾ .... **(677)** 144

Still Life and Model, (1907), wash, 17½ x 13½ .... **(753)** 638

Portrait of a Woman, colored chalk and pen, 18¾ x 14 .... **(712)** 1,033

Maternity, colored pencil, 18½ x 12½ .... **(763)** 456

1967

Couple of Lovers, 1903, charcoal and colored pencil, 17½ x 13 .... **(970)** 787

Couple of Lovers, 1905, pen, 17 x 13½ .... **(979)** 707

The Couple, 1907, ink, 17½ x 13¼ .... **(985)** 308

Smoker and Dancer, 1912, black chalk, 22 x 14 ... **(930)** 520

Young Girl Seated in a Garden, (1912), pencil, 11 x 13¼ .... **(946)** 494

Man's Head, 1912, pencil, 10 x 13½ .... **(998)** 308

View of Davos, 1919, pen, 7 x 8¾ .... **(859)** 266

The Villa in the Park, charcoal on yellow paper, 9½ x 13 .... **(906)** 342

Peasants Near a Well, 1922, colored chalk, 14 x 19¾ .... **(930)** 814

Hilly Landscape, 1934, charcoal, 14 x 19½ .... **(963)** 350

1968–July 1969

Two Reclining Nudes, 1904, colored chalk, 27 x 36¼ .... **(1209)** 2,034

Portrait of a Young Girl, 1906, India ink, 17 x 12¼ .... **(1114)** 645

Fluvial Landscape, 1907, colored chalk, 14 x 17 .. **(1094)** 570

The Haystacks, 1907, pen, 14¼ x 10½ .... **(1102)** 1,150

Industrial Ward in Dresden, (1908), pencil and watercolor, 10¾ x 13½ .... **(1209)** 1240

Franzi in the Studio, (1909), black and yellow chalk, 17 x 13½ .... **(1041)** 570

Nude with a Fan, (1910), charcoal, 17½ x 14 ..... **(1146)** 608

Dancer, 1910, pencil and colored chalk, 13½ x 10½ .... **(1105)** $ 304

At the Café, (1912), India ink and colored pencil, 6½ x 8½ .... **(1068)** 236

Seated Nude and Reclining Young Lady, (1913-14), black and gray chalks, 19½ x 26 .. **(1102)** 1,610

Hugo with Two Women, 1915-16, black chalk heightened with watercolor, 14¾ x 22 ...... **(1090)** 744

Dancer, 1928, pen, 10¼ x 8¼ .... **(1011)** 84

View of Berlin,[1] 1932, pen and India-ink wash, 10 x 13½ .... **(1102)** 736

Portrait of Llewelyn Powys, 1938, black chalk, 20¼ x 14¼ .... **(1102)** 782

Standing Nude, pen, 8¾ x 6½ .... **(1030)** 325

Seated Nude, charcoal, 11½ x 17 .... **(1214)** 608

Sketchbook, (including 200 sheets with sketches and drawings), pencil, pen, and India ink, 10½ x 6¼ .... **(1102)** 4,485

Seated Lady, colored pencil, pen, and India ink, 5¼ x 3½ .... **(1240)** 816

Seated Nude, pen and India ink, 10½ x 14½ .... **(1240)** 1,008

Street Scene, ink and colored pencil, 6½ x 8¼ ... **(1246)** 350

Tennis, pen and ink, 8½ x 6¼ .... **(1272)** 240

Kopf, black pencil, 7¼ x 6½ .... **(1272)** 168

Nude, pen and ink, 7 x 5½ .... **(1272)** 432

Young Girl on the Strand, colored pencil, 8 x 6½ .... **(1272)** 480

The Conversation, pencil, 6¼ x 8 .... **(1272)** 192

Der Totentanz, pencil, 6½ x 8 .... **(1272)** 240

Sketches for a Head, black pencil, 8½ x 6½ ..... **(1272)** 216

WATERCOLORS

1961–1962

Bridge in Dresden, (1909), watercolor, 6½ x 8 ..... **(44)** 700

Men and Woman, gouache, watercolor, and pencil, 14¼ x 18¼ .... **(84)** 1,373

Rower on the Muggelsee, 1910-11, watercolor, 10½ x 13½ .... **(88)** 1,476

Woman in the Nude on a Violet Background, 1913, watercolor on chalk, 17½ x 11¼ .... **(24)** 1,476

Two Men Seated at Table, (1918), watercolor, 14¼ x 20¼ .... **(24)** 1,132

Belvedere Hotel and Street in Davos, watercolor on chalk, 14¼ x 20¼ .... **(24)** 517

Partie aus Konigstein im Taunus, 1916, watercolor, 14¼ x 21¾ .... **(149)** 1,106

1963

Standing Nude, watercolor, 20½ x 13¾ .... **(232)** 1,311

Woman in the Nude in a Wood, 1920, pastel, 25 x 18¾ .... **(228)** 861

The Grand Hotel Belvedere at Davos, (1927), pencil and watercolor, 14 x 19¾ .... **(219)** 610

At the Fortune-Teller's, (1928), watercolor, 6¾ x 8½ .... **(239)** 342

1964

Standing Nude and Kneeling Nude, pastel, 17 x 13¾ .... **(467)** 1,968

Street in the Suburbs of Dresden, 1907, pastel, 10 x 13 .... **(387)** 553

Young Lady's Head, (1908), watercolor, 17¾ x 13½ .... **(383)** 1,333

At the Café, tempera and watercolor, 19½ x 14¾ .... **(467)** 1,476

The Couple, 1912, watercolor, 21½ x 15½ .... **(405)** 1,045

[1]On the reverse, *Nude,* 1910.

Alpine Village in Winter, watercolor, 14 x 19¾ ... **(405)** $1,103

Seated Woman, 1914, pencil and watercolor,
14¼ x 10¾ .... **(383)** 2,147

Palucca the Dancer, (1922), watercolor and India
ink, 19¾ x 15½ .... **(392)** 1,933

Trees in Spring, 1923, watercolor, 19¾ x 13½ ..... **(383)** 814

The Branderburger Tor in Berlin, 1929, pen and
watercolor, 14¾ x 19½ .... **(383)** 1,401

1965

Boats in the Harbor, watercolor, 13 x 17½ .... **(512)** 840

The Fir Trees, watercolor and pencil,
12½ x 17½ .... **(393)** 1,554

The Park, watercolor, 13¾ x 17 .... **(638)** 1,645

Garden, 1905, pastel, 9½ x 13½ .... **(616)** 592

1966

At the Café, 1926, watercolor, 19¾ x 14¾ .... **(792)** 2,337

Boats in the Harbor, watercolor, 13 x 17½ .... **(811)** 760

Two Nudes in the Forest, watercolor and pencil,
19½ x 14¼ .... **(738)** 1,107

1967

The Seven Deadly Sins, watercolor and India ink,
9¼ x 12¾ .... **(907)** 590

Two Reclining Nudes, 1904, pastel, 13½ x 17 ..... **(986)** 1,353

The Pine Grove, (1920), watercolor, 11 x 8½ ..... **(970)** 984

Glade, (1924), pencil and watercolor, 16 x 14 ..... **(930)** 362

Dancer, (1930), watercolor, 19¼ x 14¾ .... **(910)** 861

1968–July 1969

Street Scene, watercolor, 19½ x 14 .... **(1090)** 744

Suburbs, (1909-10), watercolor on chalk,
10¼ x 13½ .... **(1102)** 828

The Trams, Dresden, 1910-11, watercolor on
chalk, 11 x 14¾ .... **(1102)** 1,380

Dancers, (1911), pencil and watercolor, 6 x 8 .... **(1102)** 690

Garden in Bloom, 1938, pastel, 15 x 16¾ .... **(1102)** 841

Reclining Nude with a Cat, (1906), watercolor,
19¼ x 23¾ .... **(1232)** 8,000

Flowers and Figure, 1930, gouache, 18¼ x 14¼ .. **(1240)** 1,200

The Skiers, 1926, watercolor, 14 x 19¼ .... **(1246)** 3,750

PAINTINGS

1961–1962

Flower Bed, 1906, oil on cardboard, 19½ x 27¾ ... **(149)** 5,530

Japanese Theater, (1910), 45 x 45 .... **(149)** 11,850

Bagnante nel tino, 1912, 16¼ x 23¾ .... **(70)** 9,322

Two Young Ladies Chattering, 1912-13,
14 x 17¾ .... **(88)** 3,567

Seehorn, 1919, 38 x 31¾ .... **(88)** 6,150

Mountain Devil, 11 x 7¾ .... **(106)** 1,153

1963

Negro Dancers, 1905, 67¼ x 37¼ .... **(279)** 26,000

A Couple Under a Japanese Parasol, (1912),
39½ x 29¼ .... **(279)** 15,500

1964

Passers-By in a Street, at Night, 1925,
35½ x 27¾ .... **(467)** 8,610

The Galgenberg at Iéna, 1915, 27½ x 25¾ .... **(383)** 8,136

The Forge, 1917, 39½ x 29¾ .... **(372)** 7,000

The Painter and His Model, 1921, 29¾ x 23¾ .... **(416)** 6,081

Still Life with Flowers, a Bottle, and Ceramics,
31¾ x 27¼ .... **(405)** 11,028

1965

Bathers,[2] 35½ x 31½ .... **(545)** $ 24,246

Nude with a Mirror, 63¼ x 31¾ .... **(638)** 17,220

Still Life with Flowers, 31¾ x 27¼ .... **(512)** 3,800

1966

Die Schwarze Grete, 1907-08, on cardboard,
20¼ x 28¾ .... **(734)** 8,475

The Painter and His Model, 1921, 29¾ x 23¾ .... **(689)** 4,146

1967

Still Life with a Mask, 1913-14, 32 x 28 .... **(930)** 7,910

*Couple Seated at Table Under a Japanese
Parasol,* 1912-14, 39½ x 29¾ .... **(907)** 22,632

View of Davos, in Winter, 1927, 47½ x 35½ ...... **(954)** 15,000

1968–July 1969

Peasant Seated in a Landscape, 39½ x 30 .... **(1194)** 10,664

Trees on a Hill, (1895), on cardboard laid down
on canvas, 9 x 12¾ .... **(1102)** 805

Alpine Landscape, 1920, 35½ x 39½ .... **(1126)** 29,736

The Artist and His Model, 1921, 29¾ x 23½ ..... **(1145)** 7,000

Sertigberge, (1924), 47½ x 47½ .... **(1126)** 39,648

Gut Staberhoff II (Hauser in Fehmarn), (1912),
35 x 46½ .... **(1232)** 50,000

Two Nudes in the Forest, 1909, 34¼ x 47¼ ...... **(1239)** 50,400

Moïse Kisling

(1891–1953)

Birthplace: Krakow, Poland.

1906   Enters the Fine Arts Academy of Krakow.

1911   Goes to Paris on the advice of Pankevicz, his professor and friend.

1912   Meets Apollinaire, Picasso, Derain, Modigliani, Pascin, and others, at the Café de Versailles, birthplace of the Ecole de Paris.

1913   Follows Picasso to Céret. Though aware of Cubism, elaborates his own style, which is closer to naturalism—like his friends Modigliani, Pascin, and Soutine. Participates in the Salon des Indépendants, Paris.

1914-15   Enlists in the French Foreign Legion.

1919   Becomes a French citizen.

1920   First exhibition at the Galerie Druet, Paris.

1924   Exhibits at Paul Guillaume's and at Bernheim's, Paris.

1926-37   Exhibits in New York, London, Geneva, Brussels, and other cities. Settles at Sanary, in the south of France.

1940   Threatened by the Gestapo, he has to leave France. Goes to the U.S.

[2]On the reverse, *Two Nudes.*

1946	Returns to France.	
1949	Settles again at Sanary.	
1951	Exhibition at the Galerie Drouant-David, Paris.	
1953	Died, Sanary.	

Sales

DRAWINGS

1961–1962

Nude, 1930, red chalk, 13½ x 9½ . . . . (152) $ 450

1963

Circus Woman, 1919, black pencil, 15½ x 22 . . . . . (276)   172

1964

Little Girl in a Garden, black lead, 13 x 10 . . . . (412)   140

1965

Self-Portrait, pen, 13½ x 10 . . . . (491)   200
Seated Woman, pencil and charcoal, 16 x 10¼ . . . (497)   150
Nude with Folded Arms, 23½ x 12¼ . . . . (503)   236

1966

Street Corner, pen, 7½ x 6¼ . . . . (711)   64
Montmartre, 1916, 10¼ x 10¼ . . . . (655)   150
Montparnasse, 1916, pencil, 10½ x 10 . . . . (772)   140
The Café, 1916, black lead, 10 x 14 . . . . (794)   250
Seated Nude, 1916, 15¾ x 8 . . . . (781)   84
Boat Alongside the Quay, 1917, black lead,
    11 x 8 . . . . (811)   190
Yoga Posture, 1919, 15¾ x 22 . . . . (669)   150

1967

Seated Nude, 1916, 15¾ x 8¼ . . . . (950)   52
Kiki de Montparnasse, 1943, black pencil,
    10 x 7 . . . . (858)   150

1968

At the Café, 1916, 10¼ x 14 . . . . (1051)   570
The Acrobat, 1919, pencil, 15½ x 21¾ . . . . (1051)   140
Seated Nude, 1922, 19¾ x 11 . . . . (1240)   480
Seated Woman in the Nude, 1951, pencil,
    12½ x 9 . . . . (1248)   800

WATERCOLORS

1961–1962

Tulips and Orris, watercolor, 23½ x 12¾ . . . . (64)   900
Fruit Stand on the Kitchen Table, 1917,
    watercolor, 13¼ x 15½ . . . . (49)   320

1967

Woman in a Studio, watercolor and gouache,
    17 x 12¼ . . . . (852)   700
Interior, 1917, watercolor, 9 x 11½ . . . . (1004)   650

1968–July 1969

Interior, 1917, watercolor, 9 x 11¾ . . . . (1145)   450
The Sailboats, 1918, watercolor, 19 x 13 . . . . (1117)   1,400
The Sailboat, St. Tropez, 1923, watercolor,
    21¾ x 17¾ . . . . (1109)   900
Interior, 1917, 8¾ x 11½ . . . . (1241)   1,159

PAINTINGS

1961–1962

Landscape with a River, 1919, 17¾ x 21½ . . . . (120)   1,100
Vase of Flowers, 16¼ x 13 . . . . (120)   1,520
Vase of Flowers, 16¼ x 13 . . . . (33)   1,140

Vase of Flowers, 21¾ x 25¾ . . . . (85) $1,250
Bluets in a Vase, 16¼ x 13 . . . . (143)   1,311
The Skinned Wild Boar, 18¼ x 21¾ . . . . (25)   210
The Joint of Beef, 9 x 16¼ . . . . (130)   500
Landscape Near St. Tropez, 13 x 16¼ . . . . (141)   940
Bandol, the Harbor, 1948, 12¾ x 15¾ . . . . (71)   1,760
Front View of a Seated Nude, 16¼ x 13 . . . . (18)   1,153
Reclining Nude, 27¾ x 39½ . . . . (160)   3,000
Nude, 28¼ x 20¾ . . . . (111)   1,200
Bust of a Nude Young Lady, 16¼ x 13 . . . . (58)   1,100
Young Woman, 21¾ x 15 . . . . (34)   1,200
Kiki de Montparnasse, 1918, 28½ x 39 . . . . (64)   3,600
Portrait of a Young Girl, 1941, 21½ x 14¾ . . . . . . (152)   1,900
The Model, 1947, 21¾ x 15 . . . . (57)   1,380

1963

Portrait of a Woman, 29 x 21¼ . . . . (241)   1,300
Bust of a Woman, 16¼ x 13 . . . . (241)   1,200
Landscape, 1914, 18¼ x 21¾ . . . . (316)   1,400
St. Tropez, 1918, 18¼ x 21¾ . . . . (206)   1,100
Entrance of the Bois, 28¼ x 21¼ . . . . (202)   1,100
The Mediterranean Basin, 15¾ x 13 . . . . (179)   1,500
Marseilles Harbor, 25¾ x 19¾ . . . . (298)   1,500
Still Life with Fruit, 10½ x 15¾ . . . . (208)   700
Sweet Peas, 11½ x 17¾ . . . . (225)   1,500
Still Life with Fruit, 28¼ x 20¾ . . . . (202)   1,100
Fruit in a Cup, on cardboard, 14¼ x 18¼ . . . . (318)   1,000
Woman's Head, 9 x 7¼ . . . . (216)   1,042
Seated Peasant, 39 x 31½ . . . . (255)   2,413
Nude, 29 x 23¾ . . . . (191)   2,100
Young Nude, 29 x 21¼ . . . . (194)   2,000
Bare-Breasted Young Lady, 16¼ x 10¾ . . . . (252)   960
Nude, 16¼ x 13 . . . . (281)   1,089
The Half-Caste Girl, on panel, 17½ x 15¾ . . . . . . (300)   250
Bust of a Young Woman, 22 x 15½ . . . . (224)   1,600
Blond Woman, 17¾ x 12¾ . . . . (275)   1,000
The Sitting Model, 21¾ x 16¼ . . . . (258)   1,000
The Woman with a Blue Scarf, 28 x 23 . . . . (306)   2,200

1964

The Cliffs, Tyniec, 1911, 19 x 23¼ . . . . (405)   1,161
Interior: Young Man with a Dog, 1916,
    29 x 23¾ . . . . (401)   2,100
The Public Garden, 1917, on panel, 16¼ x 13 . . . . (397)   440
St. Tropez, September 1918, 29 x 23¾ . . . . (401)   1,560
Flowers, 44¼ x 34½ . . . . (341)   4,220
Portrait of a Dark-Haired Woman, 1918,
    18¼ x 13½ . . . . (341)   1,000
Landscape of Provence, (1920), 38¾ x 31½ . . . . . . (448)   5,250
Bust of a Young Nude, 29 x 21¼ . . . . (399)   1,700
Fair-Haired Young Lady with a Black Bodice,
    32 x 23¾ . . . . (371)   3,620
Portrait of Jacqueline, 1932, 17½ x 12¾ . . . . (454)   1,797
Still Life with Fruit and Pottery, 39½ x 31¾ . . . . . (448)   2,400
Mimosas, 1943, 29 x 21 . . . . (354)   5,500
Springtime, 1943, 34 x 25 . . . . (448)   4,100
The Mimosas, 1947, 16¼ x 13 . . . . (371)   1,360
Flowers in a Mauve Vase, 1947, 21¼ x 17½ . . . . . (453)   2,764
Long-Haired Nude, 29 x 21¼ . . . . (395)   1,360
Fair-Haired Young Woman, 18¼ x 13 . . . . (474)   1,000
Flowers in a Vase, 32 x 23¾ . . . . (474)   3,120

1965

Still Life with Fruit, 1914, 28¼ x 35	(591)	$2,448
The Bunch of Forget-Me-Nots, 13 x 16¼	(553)	1,600
Nude with Drapery, 1920, 21¾ x 18¼	(627)	1,500
Bust of a Young Woman with a Red Bodice, 16¼ x 13	(512)	1,300
Great Nude on a Sofa, 1933, 38¼ x 77¼	(553)	15,200
Seated Nude, 29¼ x 21¾	(526)	2,700
Back View of a Seated Nude, 21¾ x 17	(640)	3,060
Seated Nude, 29 x 21¼	(523)	880
Bowl of Orchids, 1941, 23¾ x 39½	(624)	4,561
Liliaceae in a Blue Vase, 25 x 20¼	(590)	1,356
The Rosery, 33¼ x 44¾	(553)	3,500
Vase of Flowers, 29 x 21¼	(539)	2,800
Young Girl with a Blue Bodice, 39½ x 29	(558)	4,000
Fair-Haired Young Lady with a Black Bodice, 32 x 23¾	(516)	4,840
Woman with a Collarette, 25¾ x 21¼	(628)	4,353
Portrait of a Bare-Breasted Young Lady, 16¼ x 10¾	(503)	4,040
Portrait of a Young Lady, 29¼ x 23¾	(539)	2,400
Portrait of a Seated Young Lady, 38¾ x 28	(583)	2,902
Portrait of a Young Boy, 29 x 21¼	(507)	1,800
Kiki de Montparnasse, 9 x 7½	(613)	1,000
Sailboats in the Harbor, 21¾ x 15	(518)	1,620
Surroundings of St. Tropez, 23¾ x 29	(532)	2,272
Flowers, 24 x 29	(633)	3,250

1966

Young Lady with a Necklace, 23¾ x 29	(666)	2,360
The Walker, 1916, 29 x 23¾	(800)	2,100
Green-Eyed Young Girl, 25¾ x 19¾	(727)	3,220
Seated Nude with a Red Cushion, 16¼ x 13	(819)	4,600
Kiki de Montparnasse, Back View, 28¼ x 23	(808)	1,596
Young Lady in Profile, 15¾ x 13	(701)	1,150
Bare-Breasted Young Woman, 25¾ x 21¼	(819)	2,600
Reclining Nude, 10¼ x 16¼	(784)	1,200
Portrait of Suzy Solidor, 21¾ x 15	(824)	1,780
Young Lady in the Garden, 46¼ x 35¼	(753)	4,063
Standing Nude, 25¾ x 15	(685)	1,820
Bunch of Wild Flowers, 1947, 15¾ x 12¾	(685)	2,840
Mimosa in a Vase, 10¾ x 8¾	(749)	1,200
Mimosas, 29¼ x 21¾	(805)	5,000
Vase of Flowers, 16¼ x 13	(737)	1,840
Landscape of Provence, 23¾ x 29	(784)	2,750
Resting, 35½ x 43½	(675)	4,200

1967

Vase of Orchids, 21¼ x 29	(857)	2,600
Mother and Child, 1916, 46 x 34¾	(856)	3,200
Bare-Breasted Young Woman, 1916, 28½ x 23¾	(857)	1,460
The Red-Haired Girl, 1918, 29¼ x 23¾	(898)	2,800
Paris: The Towboat Near a Bridge, 1918, on panel, 16¼ x 12¾	(852)	3,200
Mimosas,[1] 1943, 29 x 21	(963)	7,750
Portrait of a Young Dutch Lady, 1932, 43½ x 32¾	(888)	7,739
The Bunch of Roses, 29 x 21¼	(842)	2,300
Portrait of Edith Mera, 1932, 76¼ x 44¼	(888)	12,438
Flowers in a Blue Vase, 1918, 14 x 10¾	(852)	2,000

[1] Sold in New York in April 1964 for $5,500.

Violet Flowers in a Blue Vase, 8¾ x 10¾	(918)	$2,260
Flowers in a Vase, 22 x 15	(995)	4,500
Seated Little Girl, 25¼ x 16¼	(983)	1,520
Seated Nude, 39½ x 29	(993)	4,000
Reclining Nude, 15 x 21¼	(978)	1,760
Portrait of Suzy Solidor, 21¾ x 15	(912)	2,700
Bust of a Red-Haired Young Woman, Back View, 29 x 23¾	(912)	2,800
The Woman with a Green Shawl, 1947, 16¼ x 13	(909)	1,800
The Child with the Red Overcoat, 21¾ x 15	(923)	2,700
Vase of Flowers, 1951, 38¼ x 28	(846)	4,200
Flowers, 24¼ x 16	(870)	2,000
Underwood at Sanary, 39½ x 29	(963)	4,500
Landscape of Provence, 23¾ x 29	(989)	1,550
Landscape of Provence, 15 x 21¾	(923)	2,820

1968–July 1969

The Vineyard in the Valley, 1917, 10¾ x 14	(1023)	1,420
Kiki, 1918, 29¾ x 39½	(1157)	7,200
St. Tropez, 1918, 25 x 32	(1208)	5,000
Back View of a Nude, (1919), 31½ x 17¼	(1187)	3,304
Kiki de Montparnasse, Back View, 1925, 29 x 23¾	(1060)	3,520
Still Life with Lilies, 1932, 29 x 21¼	(1060)	6,720
View of Amsterdam, 1935, 14¾ x 21¼	(1132)	2,832
Standing Nude, 1935, 29 x 21¼	(1106)	6,200
The Orchids, 16¼ x 13	(1106)	2,800
Portrait of Rosine, 1938, 31 x 23	(1018)	4,750
Bunch of Mimosas, 1945, 29 x 36½	(1018)	7,250
Vase of Flowers, 16¼ x 13	(1113)	3,300
Vase of Poppies, 23¾ x 29	(1113)	4,700
The Rosery, 34 x 46	(1113)	6,000
Entrance of a Park, 33½ x 45¼	(1132)	4,484
Landscape Near Sanary, (1922), 14¾ x 21¼	(1132)	3,776
Young Lady, 22 x 15	(1139)	3,800
Reclining Nude, 15 x 21¼	(1088)	1,300
Half-Length Portrait of a Woman, 15¾ x 14	(1026)	2,800
Young Mulatto, 14 x 10¾	(1051)	880
Portrait of Aïcha, 29 x 23¾	(1030)	3,000
The Red-Haired Girl, 28½ x 21¼	(1116)	4,820
Rustic Scene, on canvas laid down on panel, 39½ x 32¼	(1030)	3,500
The Red-Haired Nude, 1949, 37½ x 65¼	(1226)	30,000
Bandol: The Harbor, 1948, 13¼ x 18¾	(1226)	5,000
Landscape, 10¾ x 16¼	(1226)	3,040
Portrait of a Young Girl, 16 x 13	(1231)	4,250
Reclining Nude, 15 x 21½	(1231)	1,000
Flowers, 16¼ x 13	(1247)	4,640
Vase of Flowers, 22 x 18	(1248)	8,000
Back View of a Nude, 1919, 31¾ x 18	(1248)	2,500
St. Tropez, on panel, 18¼ x 13	(1252)	5,600
Reclining Nude, 21¼ x 29	(1255)	2,400
Back View of a Nude with Green Drapery, 21¼ x 32	(1256)	2,900
Roses in a Vase, 18¼ x 15¼	(1258)	5,800
Young Woman with a Red Scarf, 16¼ x 13	(1258)	7,200
Bust of a Young Woman, 10¾ x 8¾	(1261)	5,200
Still Life with Oysters, 23¾ x 29¾	(1265)	4,000
Kiki de Montparnasse, 16¼ x 13	(1268)	6,032
Bust of a Naked Woman, 29 x 21¼	(1268)	6,960
Still Life with a Basket of Oranges, (1917), 28 x 20¼	(1271)	4,800

Paul Klee

(1879–1940)

Birthplace: Münchenbuchsee, near Bern, Switzerland.

1900 Goes to Munich and enters the Academy of Fine Arts.

1906 Marries. Exhibits his etchings at the "Secession," Munich.

1908 Greatly admires Cézanne, Van Gogh, and Ensor.

1909 Exhibits at the Kunsthaus, Zurich.

1911 First one-man show at the Tannhauser Gallery, Munich. Meets Kandinsky, Jawlensky, Münter, Macke, and Franz Marc.

1912 Participates in the second exhibition of "Der Blaue Reiter" at the Goltz Gallery, Munich. Trip to Paris, where he meets Picasso, Delaunay, Apollinaire, and Wilhelm Uhde. Comes under a strong Cubist influence.

1914 Participates in the foundation of the "New Secession" of Munich.

1917 Exhibits at the Dada Gallery, Munich.

1918 First monograph (*Der Sturm*, Berlin).

1920 Retrospective exhibition at the Goltz Gallery, Munich.

1921-24 Teaches at the Bauhaus at Weimar.

1923 Exhibition at the Kronprinz Palace, Berlin.

1924 First exhibition in New York, at the Société Anonyme. Foundation of the group "Die Blauen Vier" which includes Klee, Kandinsky, Feininger, and Jawlensky.

1925 Issues his book *Pädagogisches Skizzenbuch*. Exhibition at the Goltz Gallery, Munich. Takes part in the first group show of Surrealism at the Galerie Pierre, Paris.

1926 First one-man show in Paris. Keeps on teaching at the Bauhaus, which has moved to Dessau.

1929 Stay in Egypt.

1930 Exhibition at the Museum of Modern Art, New York.

1931 Leaves the Bauhaus to teach at the Academy of Fine Arts, Düsseldorf.

1933 Forced to leave Germany, he settles in Switzerland.

1935 Retrospective exhibition in Bern, Basel, and Lucerne.

1937 Alters his style, introducing a series of new signs in his work. Seems to be more interested in oil painting than ever before (his favorite media previously were pencil, pen and ink, watercolor, and gouache). His works are exposed as "degenerate" by the Nazis.

1940 Died, Muralto-Locarno, Switzerland.

Sales

DRAWINGS

1961-1962

Cosmic Revolutionist, pen on notepaper, 10 x 8¾ . . . . (105) $2,011

Cosmic-Mystic Wish, black lead, 7¾ x 2 . . . . (106) 633

Duels, ink and brush, 10 x 19¾ . . . . (105) 1,537

Bazaar, Still Life, pen, 7½ x 8¾ . . . . (106) $1,898

The Witches' Monument, pencil, 14 x 10¼ . . . . (20) 3,476

Little Girls, 1913, pen, 5½ x 8½ . . . . (105) 994

Drawing for 25 D 2, 1925, pencil, 12¼ x 8¾ . . . . . . (107) 1,795

Fünf Dynamoradiolaren, 1926, pencil, 11 x 9 . . . . . (149) 632

Your Animals, 1926, pen, 10 x 12 . . . . (31) 1,153

Old Upper Works, 1928, pen, 9½ x 12¾ . . . . (129) 3,844

Little and Great, 1929, India ink, 17¾ x 11¾ . . . . . (156) 1,040

An Abstraction of a Figure Carrying a Bundle Is Indicated by a Series of Nearly Parallel Blue Lines Overlapped by Similar Areas of Red and Green, 1930, colored pencil, 11 x 8¼ . . . . . . (37) 700

Psychogram with a Foot, 1930, pen and watercolor, 7¾ x 11½ . . . . (37) 2,600

Former Hope, 1932, ink, 18¼ x 11½ . . . . (164) 659

Namens Zweizehn. . ., 1932, charcoal and colored chalk, 18¼ x 12 . . . . (129) 2,746

Bust, Abstract Suggestion Created by Lines, 1940, charcoal, 11½ x 8 . . . . (37) 700

1963

Ganymede, 1908, pen, 6¾ x 3¾ . . . . (219) 339

Durchgeistigung Durch Primitivitat, 1909, pen and colored pencil, 12 x 9 . . . . (277) 4,113

Woman's Head, 1910, India-ink wash, 6½ x 5 . . . . (219) 1,266

Two Nudes, 1911, pen 3¼ x 6¼ . . . . (232) 1,085

Sketch of a Landscape, 1917, India-ink wash, 4½ x 8¼ . . . . (219) 701

Der Feuerbote, 1919, pencil, 4¾ x 8¾ . . . . (284) 615

The Pathetic, 1922, drawing in oil color with airbrush, 9 x 7 . . . . (219) 2,034

Dancing Witch, 1922, pen, 12¼ x 5½ . . . . (249) 700

The Witch Casting Out the Animals, 1924, pen, 4½ x 9½ . . . . (219) 768

Good Advice Needed, pencil on tracing paper, 16¾ x 11¾ . . . . (249) 580

Naval Port, 1929, 14¾ x 19¾ . . . . (299) 900

Portraits of Winds, 1931, pencil, 11¾ x 13¼ . . . . . (219) 678

Hexenfels, 1932, India ink, 18 x 12¼ . . . . (232) 1,537

Klagendes Tier, 1933, pencil, 12¾ x 8 . . . . (225) 550

View of La Vigie, 1933, bister ink, 14 x 18 . . . . (316) 2,500

Somnambulist, 1934, 1¼ x 12½ . . . . (299) 540

1964

Woman in Bed, 1908, pen and watercolor, 7½ x 6 . . . . (368) 829

Initial, 1911, ink and watercolor, 8¾ x 4½ . . . . (372) 1,800

Sketch Composition, 1912, ink and watercolor, 5¾ x 7½ . . . . (448) 2,400

Sketch No. 44, 1912, pen, 2¼ x 3¾ . . . . (392) 541

The Exasperating Animals, 1912, pen, 2½ x 9½ . . . (471) 1,537

The Harbor, 1916, ink, 8 x 6½ . . . . (453) 1,520

Prehistoric Flora, 1920, violet ink, 7¾ x 11¼ . . . . . (383) 1,424

Composition with Threads, 1922, pencil, 8¾ x 11¾ . . . . (367) 1,658

The Defender, 1929, pen, 8¾ x 4 . . . . (378) 1,130

Ansteigende Ortswege, 1930, ink, 18¾ x 11¾ . . . . . (372) 1,400

Angel Hat, 1931, charcoal and colored pencil, 9¾ x 9 . . . . (383) 1,808

Namens Zweizehn, 1932, pencil and gouache, 18¼ x 11½ . . . . (368) 2,626

Vorsicht bei Bildung, 1932, 17½ x 15 . . . . (465) 1,360

The Potter's Breakfast, 1939, pencil . . . . (383) 927

1965

Landscape with Two Horses, 1910, pen and
watercolor, 9½ x 12½ . . . . (597) $ 910

Winkelmotiv, 1917, pen and watercolor,
5½ x 3¾ . . . . (522)   2,764

Interior, 1924, pencil, 8½ x 11¼ . . . . (597)   2,263

Peevish Old Man, 1929, ink, 13 x 8¼ . . . . (526)   5,000

Last Hope, 1929, pen, 13 x 8¼ . . . . (624)   1,797

"Il n'a nul mal qui n'a le mal d'amour," 1931,
colored pencil, 8¼ x 12¾ . . . . (637)   1,200

Hands Up, 1938, drawing in grayish blue with
brush, 14 x 7¼ . . . . (566)   1,808

Child and Grotesque, 1938, blue and red pencil,
12 x 8 . . . . (494)   1,450

1966

Steamer on the Lake of Thun, 1911, pen, 3¾ x 9 . . . (734)   1,898

Self-Sacrifice, pencil, 10¼ x 6½ . . . . (738)   2,829

Group of Lions (Watch Out), 1924, ink and
watercolor, 8¼ x 15 . . . . (713)   14,500

Bei Nummer Zwei, 1928, 17¾ x 6¼ . . . . (749)   800

Head on a Table, 1929, pen, 9 x 8 . . . . (738)   3,444

Marshland People, 1932, ink and wash,
20 x 14¾ . . . . (751)   2,349

New Roots, W 12, 1932, colored pencil,
16¾ x 12¾ . . . . (802)   5,760

Wrestle, 1932, pen, 10½ x 10¾ . . . . (734)   1,175

Somnambulist, 1934, pencil, 19¼ x 12½ . . . . (734)   814

Zwei Rote in Zernst, 1936, colored pencil,
12 x 16¾ . . . . (665)   1,300

Julia, 1937, India ink, 11 x 7 . . . . (738)   2,214

1967

Nude, (1902-04), pencil, 9½ x 6½ . . . . (927)   418

Munich, the Suburb, India-ink wash, 4¾ x 7¼ . . . (927)   2,712

The Magician, India ink, 6½ x 4 . . . . (927)   1,130

Constructions, Scenes, India ink, 15½ x 12 . . . . (927)   4,972

The Passions, 1918, pen, wash, and colored
pencil, 6½ x 9½ . . . . (940)   2,175

Things Under the Rain, 1918, pencil and
watercolor, 8¼ x 6½ . . . . (889)   2,250

Das Ach Bild, 1918, ink and watercolor, 11 x 8 . . . (1004)   10,000

Composition, 1919, pen, 8 x 8½ . . . . (954)   2,750

Drawing of a Snail, 1921, violet ink, 9½ x 11¼ . . . (970)   1,919

Fluchtiges auf dem Wasser, 1929, ink and
watercolor, 10¼ x 12 . . . . (1004)   9,000

In Engelsshut Brust, 1931, ink, 25 x 17¾ . . . . (881)   2,764

Eitel, 1932, ink, 21 x 14 . . . . (982)   3,081

The Last Outbursts, 1933, pencil, 10¾ x 17½ . . . . . (970)   2,116

Diana Park, 1933, pencil, 10½ x 17½ . . . . (889)   1,750

Figure, 1939, India ink, 19¾ x 13½ . . . . (962)   4,160

1968–July 1969

Nabul oder die Hollishe Verkehrtheit, 1919, pen,
11¾ x 9¼ . . . . (1064)   2,832

Wald bei G, 1925, pen and watercolor,
12¾ x 5¾ . . . . (1132)   14,160

Behind the Thickets, 1932, wash, 13 x 8¼ . . . . (1174)   1,196

Grete, 1933, pencil, 15 x 8¼ . . . . (1099)   1,150

Uber Hohung, 1934, pencil, 19¼ x 12 . . . . (1080)   1,000

Tanzprobe, 1934, pencil, 4½ x 8 . . . . (1059)   644

Untitled,[1] pen and watercolor, 6½ x 7¾ . . . . (1239)   9,600

Ein Tish mit seltsammer Flora besetzt, 1921,
13 x 10 . . . . (1240)   2,160

[1] Inscribed "Gottfried Galston Dank zum 31 August 1919."

Wind von Links unten, 1922, pencil, 13 x 9½ . . . . (1240) $2,160

Am Faden, 1924, pen on paper mounted on
canvas, 6¾ x 6 . . . . (1246)   1,700

Landscape, 1910, ink wash, 9¼ x 10¾ . . . . (1246)   2,500

Felsgraber, 1929, charcoal, 9¾ x 13 . . . . (1246)   1,750

Zeichnung zum Sganarelle, 1921, pen, 10 x 12 . . . (1246)   5,500

Festzug auf Schienen, 1923, oil drawing on paper,
10 x 13½ . . . . (1246)   8,000

Physiognomisch-Streng, 1930, pencil, 16 x 10½ . . (1246)   5,750

Pflege der Hände, 1924, pencil on paper mounted
on board, 4¾ x 9 . . . . (1246)   5,500

Katastrophe J Vier, 1925, India ink on paper
mounted on board, 7¼ x 9¼ . . . . (1246)   6,500

Augenscheinliches Gespräch, 1929, ink,
11½ x 17½ . . . . (1246)   1,500

A Lady's Dream, 1912, pen and ink, 12 x 18 . . . . . (1272)   5,040

Initial (recto), 1917, watercolor, pen, and India
ink, 8¾ x 4½, ***Construction*** (verso), pen and
India ink, 5½ x 3¾ . . . . (1272)   3,840

WATERCOLORS

1961–1962

***View from the Window of the Paternal House,
Bern,*** black watercolor, 9½ x 8¼ . . . . (106)   3,887

The Green Watering Can, watercolor, 3¾ x 4½ . . . (106)   2,260

The Old City, watercolor, pastel, and India ink,
9¼ x 13 . . . . (106)   10,396

Ausserhalt München-Schwabing, 1910,
watercolor, 4 x 8¾ . . . . (156)   2,100

Ground Plan of a House, 1917-99, chalk and
watercolor, 8¾ x 8¾ . . . . (88)   4,182

Blue Stairs with Two Figures, 1920-87,
watercolor, 9½ x 8 . . . . (88)   14,760

Garden Still Life with a Watering Can,
watercolor, 5¾ x 4¾ . . . . (106)   3,616

J.D., chalk and watercolor, 7 x 11 . . . . (106)   7,684

Scaffolding in Blue, gouache, 12¼ x 9½ . . . . (143)   4,520

The Saint, watercolor, 8¼ x 11 . . . . (145)   11,850

Adam and Eve, watercolor, 13 x 8¾ . . . . (105)   16,724

The Lamp on the Balcony, 1925, watercolor,
8¾ x 11¼ . . . . (164)   4,119

Jacqgassen, 1929, watercolor, 11 x 8¼ . . . . (29)   2,500

Stiller Hofen, 1929, watercolor, 11 x 8¼ . . . . (29)   2,700

The Old City, watercolor, pastel, India ink,
9¼ x 13 . . . . (106)   10,396

News in October, 1930, tempera on canvas,
18¾ x 16¾ . . . . (106)   23,052

Mother and Child, 1930, gouache on paper,
12¾ x 9¾ . . . . (31)   6,865

Maasvoller auf Bau, 1930, watercolor, 14 x 10¼ . . (164)   4,668

Trees on Water, 1933, pastel, 17½ x 20½ . . . . (164)   7,140

Portrait of Mrs. Bl., 1931, watercolor,
23½ x 15½ . . . . (164)   3,295

Protectress, 1932, watercolor, 19 x 12¼ . . . . (149)   17,380

Flowers in a Vase, 1934, watercolor, 11¾ x 8¼ . . . (149)   6,952

It Is Going to Rain, 1939, watercolor, 10½ x 8¾ . . . (96)   2,250

1963

Out of Munich-Schwabing, 1910, watercolor,
4 x 8¾ . . . . (249)   1,420

Composition: Birth of Colors, 1915, watercolor,
9¼ x 5¾ . . . . (219)   3,842

Taormina (Pleasantly), 1924, watercolor and pen,
4¾ x 8¾ . . . . (219)   3,932

Brutaler Pierrot, 1927, watercolor and ink, on paper mounted on cardboard, 12¾ x 12¾ .... (277) $8,226

Maasvoller auf Bau, 1930, watercolor, 14 x 10¼ .. (200)   4,800

Prealps, gouache, 7 x 11 .... (283)   3,616

A Prick, 1931, watercolor and pen, 12¼ x 19 ..... (283)   3,955

Haim, 1932, watercolor, 25 x 19 .... (210)   6,581

Vase of Flowers, 1934, watercolor, 12¾ x 8¾ ..... (200)   4,600

The Chinese, 1937, gouache, 9½ x 6¾ .... (219)   4,746

Album Sheet for Y, 1937, blue gouache, 11 x 7¼ .. (232)   1,999

Pansies at Breakfast, watercolor, 9 x 11 .... (205)   2,400

1964

Children's Graveyard, 1918, watercolor and pen, 8¼ x 6¾ .... (378)   3,842

E, 1918, watercolor, 5¾ x 5¾ .... (453)   4,146

Composition with the Moon, 1919, gouache on canvas, 6 x 6 .... (368)   3,317

The Water Carrier, 1920, tempera and oil on brown paper, 4 x 8¼ .... (405)   2,902

Pomulaore Fresco, 1922, watercolor, 14¼ x 7¼ ... (383)   9,266

Scene with Young Ladies, 1923, watercolor, 11¼ x 8¾ .... (378)   3,164

House by the Waterside, 1930, watercolor, 13½ x 19½ .... (465)   4,000

Beschwingte Bindungen, 1930, tempera on paper, 18¾ x 24 .... (372)   6,000

Friendly Game, 1933, tempera on a plaster background, 11 x 11¾ .... (383)   29,832

Öffnung K2, 1933, tempera on a chalk background, on paper, 8¼ x 13 .... (433)   5,650

The Wind Scatters, 1934, tempera, 8¼ x 13 ...... (454)   4,422

Petite Bête de luxe, 1935, watercolor, 11 x 9½ .... (460)   1,260

Sick Young Lady, 1937, gouache, 12¾ x 8 .... (378)   4,068

Nachts und Hart, 1939, gouache, 12¾ x 8¾ ...... (454)   5,528

The Sleeping Girl, 1939, watercolor, 11 x 8¼ ..... (405)   3,482

1965

Arm of the Tenor-Bouffe, watercolor, 10¾ x 8¼ .. (615)   3,400

The Regattas, 1911-22, watercolor, 3¾ x 8 ...... (606)   1,700

Place El Halfouine in Tunis, 1914, watercolor, 9¾ x 7¼ .... (566)   11,978

The Bird, 1917, watercolor, 8 x 5¾ .... (522)   4,422

Blue and Orange Exercise, 1924, watercolor, 15 x 19¾ .... (638)   11,070

Seaside,[2] 1925, watercolor .... (522)   3,040

Trotz Mond, 1930, watercolor, 9½ x 12¼ .... (567)   7,006

A Prick, 1931, watercolor and gouache, 9½ x 12¼ .... (617)   3,955

Opening K2, 1933, gouache, 10 x 13¼ .... (567)   4,633

Seaside (Port Cros) J 17, 1933, gouache, 13¾ x 17½ .... (545)   1,271

The Ordered Car, 1935, gouache, 7¼ x 11 .... (597)   4,428

Landscape of a Park, 1937, watercolor, 11½ x 17 .... (583)   3,192

1966

View of Pinz, the Threatened Town, 1915, ink and blue and black watercolor, 5¾ x 8¾ ..... (734)   6,893

Fantastic Goddess, 1916, watercolor, 6¾ x 9½ .... (753)   7,255

Landscape in Red, 1917, gouache and watercolor on paper laid down on cardboard, 5 x 7 ...... (734)   5,650

The Snail Sign, 1921-27, watercolor and scumble, 15½ x 10¾ .... (713)   10,000

[2]Dedicated to Mademoiselle Ise Biernet.

Boat and Sailboats, 1931, watercolor and gouache, 17½ x 25 .... (678) $80,000

Head, 1935, tempera, 12¾ x 7½ .... (812)   8,845

Schweres durch ein Gesicht gezogen, 1938, gouache on newsprint, 19 x 12¾ .... (812)   4,422

1967

Group of Houses, 1912-19, watercolor, 6 x 6¼ .... (940)   2,467

Island of Flowers, 1929, watercolor, 16½ x 12½ ... (970)   10,332

The Rocks, 1931, watercolor, 17½ x 21¾ .... (927)   4,294

Geometrical Composition, 1930, watercolor, 14 x 9¼ .... (927)   7,458

Trotz Mond, 1930, watercolor, 9½ x 12¼ .... (965)   6,102

Schweres durch ein Gesicht gezogen, 1930, gouache on newsprint, 19¼ x 12¾ .... (1004)   5,250

Low and High, 1932, watercolor, 14¾ x 20¼ ..... (881)   4,146

Versuch auf was für einem Pferd, 1933, watercolor, 9¾ x 12¾ .... (864)   4,750

Two People Under an Umbrella, 1938, watercolor, 9½ x 12¼ .... (864)   8,000

1968–July 1969

Friendship of Two Young Ladies, 1913, pen and watercolor, 9½ x 6 .... (1099)   5,750

Leitungsstangen, 1913, pen and watercolor, 6½ x 6 .... (1099)   5,750

Plant in the Garden, 1915, watercolor, 9½ x 7 ... (1114)   9,920

Carnival in the Snow, 1923, watercolor, 9½ x 9¼ .... (1209)   14,384

Perspective, Scherzo, 1925-26, gouache, and watercolor, 11 x 8¾ .... (1057)   7,000

Airport, 1925, watercolor and ink, 3 x 13¾ ...... (1057)   10,500

Côte de Provence No. 2, 1927, watercolor, 10 x 12¾ .... (1064)   22,420

Forlorn Soul, 1929, pen and watercolor, 13½ x 19 .... (1114)   20,832

"Accente," 1929, watercolor, 7 x 14½ .... (1209)   10,168

Was alles hangt, 1930, watercolor, 19 x 12¾ ... (1057)   19,000

Vom Baum (The Tree), 1933, gouache, on dark gray paper, 8¼ x 12¾ .... (1208)   7,500

Two Tulips, 1933, watercolor, 19½ x 24½ .... (1174)   4,255

The Owl, 1937, tempera on newsprint, 11 x 14 ... (1114)   8,432

Landscape, 1937, watercolor, 11¾ x 17½ .... (1099)   5,750

Sextet of Genius, 1937, pastel, 14¼ x 19½ ...... (1187)   37,760

Hibernation, 1937, tempera on paper, 12¼ x 19¼ .... (1187)   27,140

Nachts und Hart, 1939, watercolor, 10½ x 8 .... (1216)   7,500

"Gebärde eines Anlitzes II," 1939, gouache, 24½ x 18½ .... (1132)   20,060

Small Wintry Landscape with a Little Girl by the Brookside, 1912, watercolor, 6¼ x 8¾ ...... (1232)   16,500

J. D. Zartes Aquarell, 1917, watercolor, 6¾ x 10¾ .... (1232)   18,000

Architecture in Red and Green, 1921, watercolor, 6½ x 10¼ .... (1232)   18,000

Vegetal Beings, 1917, ink and watercolor on paper mounted on brown paper, 8 x 7¼ ..... (1246)   17,000

Kurort, 1913, watercolor, 4¼ x 7¼ .... (1246)   5,000

Vorhang, 1924, gouache and watercolor, on linen mounted on board, 3¼ x 9 .... (1246)   6,000

Strahlen Baume, 1915, ink and watercolor, mounted on red paper, 5½ x 4½ .... (1246)   3,500

Park Anlege, 1937, gouache on board, 8½ x 5¼ .. (1246)   5,000

Blumenstocke II: Hand-Colored Lithograph, 1923, watercolor on print, 10 x 6¾ .... (1246)   10,500

Die Bucht von Mazzaro, 1924, gouache, 12¼ x 17¾ .... (1246)   5,000

Nachbar Turen, 1933, watercolor, 12½ x 13 ..... **(1246)** $5,250
Your Forefather, 1933, gouache, 22½ x 16¾ ..... **(1268)**   6,264
Fall-Sun, 1934, watercolor, 12¾ x 19 .... **(1268)**   14,384
Gebärde eines Anlitzes, 1939, gouache,
   24½ x 18½ .... **(1268)**   23,200
Gebirgs-Gärlein, 1939, gouache, 11½ x 8 .... **(1268)**   7,772
Küstenlandschaft, 1915, gray and purple wash,
   6¾ x 9¼ .... **(1272)**   2,160

PAINTINGS

1961–1962

The Orris, 1906, 25¾ x 16 .... **(128)**   549
Reed Ships, 1919, oil on paper, 12 x 15½ .... **(164)**   10,984
Dancer, 1930, oil on paper on board, 13½ x 9 ..... **(164)**   10,984
Old Trees, 1931, 12¼ x 18¼ .... **(69)**   948
Buntes Distanziert, 1932, on board, 19½ x 17½ ... **(129)**   12,357
Composition, 1934, oil and glue on cloth,
   4¾ x 12½ .... **(71)**   1,900

1963

The Fine Spot for Angling, 1923, 10 x 14 .... **(200)**   6,000
The Stairs (Hausertreppe) III, 1923, oil on paper
   mounted on board, 13½ x 10 .... **(279)**   15,000
Dancer, 1930, 13½ x 9½ .... **(200)**   9,100

1964

Writing No. 132a, 1919-20, 6½ x 8; *Writing
   Attempt No. 132b,* 1919-20, 6½ x 6 .... **(383)**   10,396
Garden in the Plain, 1920, on cardboard,
   7¼ x 10 .... **(383)**   9,492
Sea Ghost, 1933, on canvas, 18¼ x 21¾ .... **(378)**   18,080
Gruppe Macht Augen, 1938, oil and gouache on
   paper, 13 x 19 .... **(471)**   18,080

1965

The Bird, 1919, oil on paper laid down on canvas,
   7½ x 13 .... **(566)**   8,588
The Departure of the Boats, 1927, 20 x 26 .... **(575)**   60,808
Sea Ghost, 18¼ x 21¾ .... **(583)**   9,286
Clown with a Child, 1931, on board, 27 x 19¾ ..... **(615)**   15,000
Diary of Port-Cros: Mediterranean Seaside,
   1933, oil on paper, 17¾ x 14 .... **(494)**   1,100
Diary of Port-Cros: View of La Vigie, 1933, oil on
   paper, 14 x 18 .... **(526)**   1,300
Spärlich belaubt, 1934, oil and watercolor,
   12¾ x 19 .... **(616)**   19,200
Dynamics of a Head, 1934, 25¾ x 19¾ .... **(615)**   24,000

1966

Three Times Three Crosses, 1925, oil on paper
   laid down on canvas, 10 x 10¼ .... **(676)**   9,000
Artistenbildnis, 1927, on board, 25 x 16 .... **(676)**   51,000
Blumen Pfannen I, oil on paper, 8¼ x 10½ .... **(727)**   2,200
Zwei Rohre, 1932, 16 x 6½ .... **(694)**   8,000
Landscape, on cardboard, 8¼ x 13½ .... **(802)**   12,800

1967

Boats and Buoys, 1927, oil and gouache on
   canvas laid down on panel, 18½ x 26¼ .... **(864)**   26,000
Stern Glance, 1938, oil on paper, 13 x 19 .... **(918)**   17,628

1968–July 1969

With the Turning Black Sun and the Arrow, 1919,
   9¾ x 12¾ .... **(1080)**   12,000
Bust, 1922, oil and watercolor on paper,
   19½ x 12¼ .... **(1064)**   24,780
The Old Graveyard, 1925, oil on board mounted
   on panel, 14½ x 19¼ .... **(1187)**   25,960

District of Villas in Florence, 1926, on board,
   19½ x 14½ .... **(1057)** $82,500
Boats and Sailboats, 1927, oil on canvas laid
   down on panel, 18½ x 26¼ .... **(1187)**   30,680
Aquarium, 1927, oil and plaster mounted on
   panel, 14¾ x 20½ .... **(1064)**   37,760
Knight with a Spear, (1929), 21¼ x 17 .... **(1057)**   38,000
Gardens of the South, 1936, oil on paper laid
   down on cardboard, 10½ x 12¾ .... **(1064)**   84,960
Pierrette, 1937, oil on paper laid down on board,
   11¾ x 8 .... **(1132)**   7,552
Evening Fire, on cardboard, 14¾ x 14¼ .... **(1099)**   30,590
The River Rhine at Duisburg, 1937, 6¾ x 10¼ ... **(1239)**   14,400
Bühnenprobe, 1925, mixed media on board,
   19 x 11¾ .... **(1241)**   25,200
Sea Ghost, 1933, 18¼ x 21¾ .... **(1268)**   31,320

Franz Kline

(1910-   )

Birthplace: Wilkes-Barre, Pennsylvania, U.S.

1931-38   Studies art at Boston University and later at Heath-
   erly's Art School, London.

1938   Returns to New York.

1942-45   Exhibitions at the National Academy of Design.

1950   One-man show at the Egan Gallery, New York.
   Participates in many American exhibitions, in
   particular at the Sidney Janis Gallery, New York.

1952   Participates in an exhibition of American painting
   at the Galerie de France, Paris. Teaches at Black
   Mountain College. Participates in the International Exhibition of the Carnegie Institute,
   Pittsburgh.

1953-54   Teaches at the Pratt Institute, Brooklyn, and at the
   art school of the Museum of Philadelphia.

1954-56   Participates in the exhibition "New Decade" at the
   Whitney Museum of American Art, New York,
   and in "Twelve Americans" at the Museum of
   Modern Art, New York.

1956-60   Takes part in the Venice Biennial.

1957   Takes part in the São Paulo Biennial.

1958   Given an award by the Guggenheim Foundation,
   New York.

Resident in New York.

Sales

DRAWINGS

1965

Composition, (1950), India ink and gouache,
   10¾ x 8 .... **(566)** $1,356

1966

Study for "The Fortune-Teller," pencil, 8 x 11 .... **(805)**   150

WATERCOLORS

1965
Composition, 1955, gouache on paper laid down
on board, 10¼ x 13 .... (606) $1,100

1966
Circus Scene, watercolor and pen, 14 x 16¾ ...... (710)   525
Seated Woman, watercolor and chalk,
8¼ x 11¼ .... (805)   200

PAINTINGS

1961–1962
Barroom Painting, 1940, on panel, 35½ x 30¾ ..... (37)   4,500
Barroom, 1940, on panel, 35½ x 30¾ .... (96)   2,250
Composition with a Red Sign, 1956, 19¾ x 29 ...... (75)   2,054

1963
A Couple Dancing in a Bar, 1940, on panel,
35½ x 30¾ .... (272)   1,600

1964
Composition, 1953, 41¾ x 37½ .... (372)   7,000
Abstraction, 1947, on board, 17 x 31½ .... (368)   387

1965
Abstraction, oil on paper mounted on board,
13 x 18¾ .... (489)   600
Initial, 1959, 100¾ x 78 .... (592)   18,000
Still Life, 21¾ x 15¾ .... (489)   2,300

1966
Elizabeth, 1946, 20½ x 16¾ .... (651)   3,000
The "Anne May," 1941, on canvas laid down on
board, 16 x 20½ .... (805)   650
Greenwich Village: The Fortune-Teller,
19½ x 24 .... (805)   650
Dahlia, 1959, 82¼ x 67¼ .... (707)   21,000

1967
Untitled, 1958-59, oil and collage, on panel,
14¼ x 22 .... (750)   2,486
Composition, oil and collage on board, 8¾ x 10 ... (688)   2,750

1968–July 1969
Black Siena, 1960, 92½ x 67¼ .... (1057)   28,000
City Landscape, on canvas laid down on board,
9 x 11 .... (1030)   475
Landscape, 1944, on canvasboard, 11½ x 14¾ ... (1229)   1,300

Karl Knaths

(1891–1971)

Birthplace: Eau Claire, Wisconsin, U.S. Son of a
German immigrant father and an American
mother.

1912-18   Attends the Art Institute of Chicago.

1919   Settles in Provincetown, Massachusetts.

1922   Marries the pianist Helen Weinrich. Goes to Washington, where he teaches at the Phillips Memorial Gallery.

1930   First one-man show at the Daniel Gallery, New York.

1937   Teaches at Bennington College. Lectures at universities, including the Yale summer school and the American University, Washington.

1946   Wins the first prize of the Carnegie Institute, Pittsburgh. One-man show at the Paul Rosenberg Gallery, New York.

1950   Wins the first prize in the show "American Painting Today" (including 6,000 artists), at the Metropolitan Museum, New York.

1951   The Art Institute of Chicago bestows on him an honorary fine arts degree.

1971   Died.

Sales

PAINTINGS

1966
The Fisherman's Hut, 1949, 45½ x 40¼ .... (710) $3,250

Oskar Kokoschka

(1886–   )

Birthplace: Pöchlarn, Austria.

1904-06   Attends the Fine Arts School of Vienna. Becomes very friendly with Egon Schiele.

1907   Writes a play entitled *Mörder, Hoffnung der Frauen.*

1908   Illustrates his book *Die träumenden Knaben.* His first exhibition (in Vienna) shows fiercely expressionist pictures and is adversely criticized. Meets the architect Adolf Loos. Executes the portrait of Professor Forel; a long series of portraits follows this one.

1910   Goes to Berlin. Adolf Loos introduces him to the group "Der Sturm." Signs a contract with the dealer Cassirer.

1912-14   Exhibits at "Der Sturm" Gallery, Berlin.

1916   Seriously wounded during World War I.

1917   Exhibits at the Dada Gallery, Zurich.

1919   Executes stage decorations for his play *Job und Der Brennende Dornbusch,* Max Reinhardt Theater, Berlin.

1920-24   Teaches at the Academy of Dresden.

1924   Stay in Switzerland. Visits the south of France, Spain, Portugal, and Holland.

1926   First trip to London.

1927   Exhibits at the Cassirer Galleries in Berlin and Zurich.

1928-30   Visits North Africa, Italy, and the Middle East.

1931   One-man show at the Galerie Georges Petit, Paris. Settles in Vienna.

1937	First retrospective exhibition in Vienna. In Germany, his works are designated "degenerate" by the Nazis.
1938	Settles in England, where he works on the theme of the horrors of war.
1947–48	Trip to Switzerland. Exhibits at the Kunsthalle, Basel, and at the Kunsthaus, Munich. Participates in the Venice Biennial. Also exhibits in the U.S. (New York, Boston, San Francisco, and St. Louis).
1955	Settles in Switzerland. Teaches at the Fine Arts Academy of Salzburg in the summer.
1958	Retrospective exhibition in Munich.

Sales

DRAWINGS

1961–1962

Standing Nude, India ink and wash, 25¼ x 17 .... (164) — $ 879
At the Milliner's, India ink and wash, 11½ x 80 .... (24) — 123
Seated Young Girl, Her Right Arm Raised, (1920), pencil, 11¼ x 8¾ .... (24) — 133
Portrait of a Young Lady, Front View, colored chalk, 24¾ x 17 .... (106) — 5,085
Nude,[1] colored chalk, 17½ x 21¾ .... (100) — 494
Portrait of Olda in Prague, 1934, blue chalk, 17 x 14 .... (149) — 427
Portrait of a Woman, red chalk, 21½ x 15¼ ...... (159) — 923

1963

The Temptation of St. Anthony, 1906, India ink heightened with white, 9 x 7¼ .... (284) — 123
Nude with Drapery, 1914, charcoal and watercolor, 17 x 12¾ .... (255) — 1,782
Seated Nude, 1936, blue chalk, 17½ x 14 .... (269) — 304
Seated Little Girl, pencil, 13½ x 18¾ .... (460) — 791
Portrait of Webster Aitken, 1938, blue pencil, 15¾ x 20¼ .... (216) — 603
Portrait of the Violinist Webster Aitken, 1938, blue pencil, 15¾ x 20¼ .... (284) — 935

1964

Nude, (1907), pencil, 17¼ x 12 .... (428) — 1,230
Seated Nude, 1910, charcoal heightened with watercolor, 11¾ x 8½ .... (383) — 814
Young Lady Sleeping, (1920), pencil, 8¾ x 11½ ... (462) — 380
A Nude, a Horse, and Pigeons in a Landscape, 1938, blue chalk, 15½ x 17½ .... (383) — 1,243
Portrait, Right Hand Under Chin, 1939, red chalk, 15¾ x 16¾ .... (383) — 655
The Model, 1931, red chalk on paper laid down on canvas, 22 x 17½ .... (409) — 500
Portrait, 1931, red pencil, 19 x 15 .... (454) — 1,520
The Broken Red Egg, colored chalk, 8 x 10 ...... (458) — 1,596
Bird Killers, illustrated letter, pencil and colored chalk, 4½ x 7¼ .... (405) — 580

1965

Study for "The Woman in Blue," 1919, India ink, 11¾ x 15 .... (566) — 1,356
Murderers of Birds, illustrated letter, pencil and colored chalk, 4¾ x 7 .... (502) — 638
Seated Couple, pencil, 8¼ x 5½ .... (550) — 588
Portrait of Ambassador Maisky, 1942, colored pencil, 11½ x 9¼ .... (624) — 1,244

[1]Dedicated "A mon cher Matthey comme signe de mes sentiments sincères, Paris, 31."

1966

Corona I, Portrait of a Young Lady, 1917-18, black chalk, 19¾ x 14 .... (734) — $1,808
Portrait of a Woman, charcoal, 27¾ x 19½ ...... (775) — 590
Figurine, 1907, India ink and watercolor, 10¼ x 10 .... (716) — 394
Mother and Child, red chalk, 25¾ x 20¼ .... (677) — 1,140
Head of a Young Lady, pencil, 18¾ x 22 .... (751) — 1,935

1967

Portrait of a Young Lady, (1924), blue pencil, 13 x 16¾ .... (930) — 542
Standing Nude, (1919), India ink, 24 x 18¾ ...... (986) — 1,476
Sketch of a Rider, (1948), colored chalk, 7 x 10¾ .... (915) — 492
Still Life with Fruit, 1948, colored chalk, 11 x 15 .. (907) — 910

1968–July 1969

Portrait of Arthur Rossler, (1912), black chalk, 17 x 13½ .... (1099) — 851
Self-Portrait, 1911, India ink, 5¾ x 4¼ .... (1114) — 645
Young Lady Walking, 1920, pen, 27¼ x 20 ...... (1114) — 595
Half-Length Portrait of a Young Lady, 1923, blue pencil on board, 18¾ x 17½ .... (1134) — 590
Reclining Woman, pencil, 11¼ x 9 .... (1134) — 472
Three-Quarter Portrait of a Woman, 1936, pencil, 18 x 14½ .... (1099) — 1,288
Portrait of a Friend, 1938, brown chalk, 16¾ x 13½ .... (1191) — 1,062
Reclining Nude (recto), *Study of Legs* (verso), colored pencil, 10¾ x 14¾ .... (1068) — 944
Woman, pencil, 10½ x 7½ .... (1231) — 300

WATERCOLORS

1961–1962

Costume Design No. 11 for the Diamond Jubilee Procession of Emperor Franz Josef I on June 12, 1908,[2] watercolor and gouache, 9½ x 7 .... (1) — 114
Lake Geneva in Spring, watercolor, 18¼ x 24 ...... (31) — 1,648
Flowers, 1941, watercolor, 20½ x 16 .... (129) — 2,883
Portrait, 1946, watercolor, 25 x 19 .... (164) — 2,334
View of Florence, 1948, pastel, 8¼ x 12¼ .... (70) — 1,027

1963

Seated Woman, watercolor, 27¼ x 19¾ .... (205) — 1,800
The Cyclamen, watercolor, 16 x 12¾ .... (255) — 1,782
Portrait of a Young Lady, watercolor, 27 x 20¼ .. (255) — 960
Flowers, 1941, watercolor, 20½ x 16 .... (247) — 1,782

1964

Draped Figure, 1914, watercolor, 17 x 12 .... (416) — 553
Two Young Ladies Seated, (1920), watercolor and tempera, 27¼ x 20½ .... (383) — 2,712
Seated Figure, (1921), watercolor, 24 x 17¾ ...... (354) — 3,400
Three Fish, watercolor, 17½ x 23 .... (367) — 2,488
The Turkey Cock, 1942, watercolor, 17 x 22 ...... (367) — 3,317
Vase with Tulips, 1958, watercolor, 24½ x 19½ ... (428) — 2,583

1965

Young Girl Standing, watercolor, 27 x 19¾ .... (545) — 1,980
Hungarian Dancers, watercolor, 8¾ x 7½ .... (638) — 246
Portrait of a Young Lady, 1920, watercolor, 26½ x 18¾ .... (522) — 3,317

[2]Inscribed by the artist.

Portrait of a Young Lady Seated, (1920),
watercolor, 26½ x 18¾ .... (637) $3,750
Young Lady Seated at Table, (1921–22),
watercolor, 27½ x 20¼ .... (566) 4,520
Portrait of Mary Mersen, 1930, watercolor,
13¼ x 16 .... (637) 2,700
Still Life with Orris, 1964, watercolor,
20¼ x 16¼ .... (597) 1,993

1966
Seated Nude, watercolor, 27¼ x 20½ .... (712) 1,230
Portrait of a Woman, (1924), watercolor,
25¾ x 20 .... (775) 2,952
Seated Nude, watercolor, 27¼ x 20½ .... (775) 738
Seated Young Woman Holding Her Head, 1931,
watercolor, 16¾ x 13¼ .... (757) 1,244
Fields of Flowers, 1946, watercolor, 24½ x 19½ ... (753) 2,612
Bunches of Grapes, 1961, watercolor, 25 x 19¾ ... (775) 3,075

1967
Seated Young Girl, (1921), watercolor,
25¼ x 19¾ .... (930) 4,068
Portrait of Mary Mersen, (1931), watercolor,
13¼ x 16 .... (982) 1,422
Sea Gulls and Crayfish, 1942, watercolor,
19 x 24½ .... (982) 2,844
Vase of Flowers, watercolor, 19½ x 15½ .... (938) 3,593

1968–July 1969
Study of a Flower, 1967, watercolor, 23¼ x 18¾ . (1134) 3,894
Landscape with Three Figures, 1958, watercolor,
17½ x 21½ .... (1134) 1,652
Nude Holding Her Waist, pencil and watercolor,
17¾ x 11¾ .... (1209) 2,852
The Garden, 1958, watercolor, 17½ x 21½ .... (1191) 1,770
The Dead Pheasant, (1945), watercolor,
18¾ x 24 .... (1216) 3,250
A Rose with Wild Flowers, 1958, watercolor and
gouache, 23¾ x 17¼ .... (1272) 4,080

PAINTINGS

1961–1962
Seated Young Girl,[3] (1908), 30¾ x 34¾ .... (61) 1,520
Child and His Parents' Hands, 1909, 28½ x 20½ .. (164) 13,181
Mother and Child, 22 x 29¾ .... (31) 15,103
Herwarth Walden, 1910, 39½ x 27 .... (31) 63,158
The Actor Sommaruga, 1910, 39½ x 23¾ .... (106) 10,396
Scottish Coast,[4] 1942, 25 x 30 .... (88) 12,792
Capriccio, 1943, 25¼ x 30 .... (20) 18,960
Great Bunch of Flowers, 1959, 35½ x 27¾ .... (88) 29,274

1963
A Clown and a Dog, 1948, 35¾ x 23¾ .... (210) 26,049
Still Life: Flowers by the Window, 28½ x 38¾ .... (202) 26,500

1964
Roses I, 1925, 29 x 22¾ .... (454) 11,056

1965
Portrait of Emil Ludwig, 1914, 49½ x 31¼ .... (545) 22,632

1966
Portrait of Robert Freund, 1909, on canvas laid
down on board, 23¼ x 18¾ .... (686) 19,348
Roses in a Vase, 1925, 35½ x 27¾ .... (738) 22,140

[3]Unfinished painting.
[4]On the reverse, *Small Sketch,* 1946.

1967
Portrait of Countess Droghede,
(1944–47), 40¼ x 30 .... (954) $ 72,500
1968–July 1969
Vernet-les-Bains, 1925, 32½ x 45¾ .... (1057) 40,000
Portrait of an Italian Peasant, 25 x 31½ .... (1176) 42,500

Käthe Kollwitz

(1867–1945)

Birthplace: Königsberg, Germany.

1885–89 Studies in Berlin and Munich. Mostly interested in drawing and engraving.

1891 Marries Doctor Karl Kollwitz and settles in Berlin. Will have two sons: Hans in 1892 and Peter in 1896.

1902–08 Produces several works on the theme "Bauernkrieg." Her style shows a likeness to Picasso's Blue Period.

1907 Visits Italy.

1919 Appointed member of the Preussischen Akademie der Künste, Berlin.

1923 Executes a series of woodcuts entitled "Der Krieg."

1927 Visits the U.S.S.R.

1928 Appointed director of a graphic art studio at the Preussischen Akademie der Künste, Berlin.

1933 Excluded from the Preussischen Akademie der Künste, Berlin.

1934 Goes to the U.S.

1934–35 Executes eight lithographs on the theme "Vom Tod."

1940 Death of her husband.

1943 Her Berlin apartment is destroyed.

1944 Settles in Moritzburg, Germany.

1945 Died, Moritzburg.

Sales

DRAWINGS

1961–1962
Prisoners, charcoal, 12¼ x 16½ .... (106) $ 497
The Return, charcoal, 19½ x 29 .... (106) 1,153
Death Grasping a Woman, charcoal, 25 x 19 ..... (106) 1,356
Studies for "Losbruch," charcoal, 15¾ x 18¾ ..... (106) 339

1964
Standing Man and Seated Couple, (1910),
stumped charcoal, 18¼ x 19 .... (383) 791
Mother and Child, charcoal, 15 x 14 .... (383) 1,107

1965
Mother and Child, charcoal, 25 x 18½ .... (597) 1,427
Child, pencil, 21¾ x 17 .... (507) 400
Carmagnole, charcoal, 21 x 16¾ .... (541) 1,800

1966

Old Woman Peeling Potatoes, (1900), India ink,
12¾ x 8 .... (734) $1,808

Women and Children, 1918, charcoal, 13 x 18¼ ... (689)   1,382

The Workwoman, pencil and watercolor,
19 x 18¾ .... (698)   680

1967

Sketches: Folded Arms and a Hand, chalk,
18¾ x 11½ .... (930)   1,040

Self-Portrait, 1893, India ink, wash, 11¼ x 9½ .... (910)   2,706

Dead Woman and Child, 1903, charcoal
heightened with white, 17 x 19 .... (910)   2,337

Man Threatening a Woman, (1905), charcoal,
25¼ x 19½ .... (910)   2,460

Farmers, 1906, charcoal and red chalk, 8¼ x 17 ... (910)   787

Mother and Child Sleeping, (1909), pencil,
11¼ x 15¾ .... (998)   1,697

Maternity, 1910, charcoal, 20 x 18¾ .... (910)   2,583

Despair, pencil, 10¾ x 8 .... (963)   500

Mother and Child, charcoal, 23 x 18¼ .... (915)   2,017

Volunteers, 1922-23, charcoal, 19½ x 27¾ .... (910)   4,920

1968–July 1969

Study of Figures and Hands, (1897), ink and
pencil, 20 x 13½ .... (1101)   2,990

The Couple of Lovers, 1924, charcoal, 6½ x 8¼ .. (1101)   1,058

Death Pulling a Child Away from His Mother,
1910, charcoal, 22 x 18 .... (1114)   2,356

Despair, charcoal, watercolor, 14 x 22 .... (1059)   1,189

Despair, charcoal, 9½ x 7¼ .... (1088)   600

Woman with a Child in Her Lap, black pencil,
pen, brush, and India ink, 16¾ x 25½ .... (1240)   2,040

WATERCOLORS

1962

Burial Vault of Innocents, pastel, 24 x 14¾ .... (106)   927

1963

The Night Shift, watercolor, 9½ x 11 .... (265)   363

Willem de Kooning

(1904–   )

Birthplace: Rotterdam, Netherlands.

1916   Serves his apprenticeship with a house painter.

1919-24   Attends the evening classes at the Academy of Fine Arts, Rotterdam.

1926   Journey to the U.S. Works as a house painter, also supporting himself with commercial art jobs.

1934   Produces his first abstract works.

1936   Exhibits in a survey of Federal Art Projects at the Museum of Modern Art, New York.

1939   Executes a mural for the World's Fair, New York.

1948   First one-man show at the Egan Gallery, New York.

1950   Retrospective exhibition at the Venice Biennial.

1951   Participates in the exhibition "Abstract Painting and Sculpture in America" at the Museum of Modern Art, New York. One-man show at the Egan Gallery, New York.

1952   Participates in the exhibition "Regards sur la peinture Américaine" at the Galerie de France, Paris.

1952-53   Teaches at Yale University. Settles on Long Island.

1956   Exhibition at the Sidney Janis Gallery, New York.

Resident on Long Island.

Sales

DRAWINGS

1961–1962

Abstraction, India ink, 23 x 18¾ .... (111) $ 950

Study for the "Queen of Hearts," 1943-44, wash,
11 x 7½ .... (164)   439

1963

The Torso, colored pencil, 7½ x 4¾ .... (189)   900

1964

Composition, (1947-48), India ink .... (372)   3,750

Abstractions, double sided, 27¾ x 27¾ .... (372)   3,000

1966

Woman Rowing, charcoal, 9 x 6¼ .... (651)   575

1967

Woman, First Version, 1951, charcoal, pastel, and
pencil, 21½ x 16 .... (864)   6,500

1968–July 1969

Figure, pencil, 10¾ x 8¼ .... (1237)   575

WATERCOLORS

1965

Figure, black watercolor, 23 x 17¾ .... (489)   900

1967

Woman, (1952), pastel and watercolor,
16¼ x 13½ .... (889)   7,750

1968–July 1969

Composition, pastel, 11½ x 8½ .... (1237)   550

PAINTINGS

1961–1962

Untitled, (1945), oil, gouache, and pencil on
board, 20 x 23¼ .... (164)   1,785

Standing Woman, 1949, oil on paper on board,
16¾ x 6½ .... (111)   1,700

Study for "Leaves in Weehawken," 1957, on
panel, 7½ x 6¾ .... (111)   1,900

1963

Two Standing Women, (1949), on board,
29¾ x 26½ .... (279)   27,000

1964

Stenographer, 1948, oil on parchment laid down
on board, 24 x 19½ .... (372)   9,000

Gold Digger, 1949, oil on paper laid down on
board, 15 x 18¾ .... (431)   11,000

1965

Menit Parkway, 1959, 81½ x 70½ . . . . (485) $ 40,000

Woman, 1953, oil on paper laid down on canvas,
    29¼ x 21¼ . . . . (592) 24,000

Police Gazette, 1955, 43 x 50½ . . . . (592) 37,000

Reclining Figure, (1947), on panel, 14¾ x 20 . . . . . . (637) 3,500

1966

Grand Opening, oil on newsprint laid down on
    panel, 35½ x 30½ . . . . (651) 12,000

Elegy, (1940), on panel, 40½ x 48 . . . . (694) 20,000

Black and White, Rome, 1959, oil on paper laid
    down on canvas, 40½ x 28¼ . . . . (651) 4,250

Composition, (1964), oil on newsprint laid down
    on panel, 15 x 21¾ . . . . (805) 1,500

1967

Composition, (1939), on panel, 28¼ x 23 . . . . (870) 17,500

Composition in Black and White, (1951), oil on
    paper, 24 x 32½ . . . . (870) 3,000

Woman, oil on newsprint laid down on panel,
    28½ x 22½ . . . . (870) 3,700

1968–July 1969

Composition, (1937), on panel, 7¼ x 13 . . . . (1080) 5,692

Composition, oil on newsprint laid down on
    panel, 22¼ x 28½ . . . . (1018) 7,250

Study of a Woman, oil on paper mounted on
    board, 28½ x 22¾ . . . . (1237) 8,250

Walt Kuhn

(1880–1949)

Birthplace: New York, U.S.

1901 Goes to Europe. Attends the Académie Colarossi in Paris and the Academy of Fine Arts of Munich.

1908-09 Attends the New York School of Art and thereafter Robert Henri's school on upper Broadway.

1910 First one-man show at the Madison Gallery, New York.

1911 Exhibits with the Pastelists at the Madison Gallery, New York.

1912 Appointed secretary of the Association of American Painters and Sculptors, New York. With its president, Arthur B. Davies, he organizes the famous Armory Show, intended to provide a major survey of international modern painting in the U.S. To carry out this intention, he returns to Europe, carefully investigating the Sonderbund show in Cologne, the Salon des Indépendants in Paris, and the exhibition set up by Roger Fry at the Grafton Gallery, London. In Paris, Davies and Kuhn meet the Duchamp brothers and the renowned dealer Ambroise Vollard, who will loan a great number of works to the show. Back in the U.S., Kuhn becomes art advisor to his friend, the lawyer and collector, John Quinn.

1913 Participates in the Armory Show, New York. Matisse's influence seems prominent in his way of painting.

1926-27 Teaches at the Art Students League, New York.

1928 One-man shows at the Knoedler Gallery and at the Downtown Gallery, New York.

1944-48 Exhibits at the Durand-Ruel Gallery, New York.

1949 Died.

Sales

DRAWINGS

1964

The Ranch, 1928, India ink and wash, 19 x 27¼ . . . (324) $ 450

1966

The Oak, 1946, pen and wash, 23 x 19½ . . . . (784) 600

1968–July 1969

Cock, 1944, ink and watercolor, 8¾ x 8 . . . . (1062) 400

WATERCOLORS

1963

Study for Roberto, 1946, mixed media on paper,
    18½ x 11¾ . . . . (290) 3,100

1968–July 1969

Clown's Head, watercolor and ink, 4½ x 5¾ . . . . . (1229) 550

Parade, watercolor and ink, 8½ x 9½ . . . . (1229) 1,000

Circus Horses, watercolor and ink, 6¼ x 8 . . . . . . (1229) 950

Shop Talk, watercolor and ink, 6¼ x 8¼ . . . . (1229) 1,200

PAINTINGS

1967

Spring, Summer, and Autumn Flowers, (1920),
    three panels, each 31½ x 11¾ . . . . (860) 2,000

Dancer, oil on paper laid down on canvas,
    24¼ x 14 . . . . (860) 5,000

1968–July 1969

The Clown, on canvas laid down on board,
    8¾ x 6 . . . . (1062) 1,600

Yasuo Kuniyoshi

(1893–1953)

Birthplace: Okayama, Japan.

1906 Goes to the U. S. Studies at the Los Angeles School of Art and at the National Academy of Design.

1910 Attends Robert Henri's school, New York.

1914-16 Attends the Independent School of Art.

1916-20 Attends the Art Students League, New York.

1922 First one-man show at the Daniel Gallery, New York.

1925	Visits Europe.
1928	One-man show at the Daniel Gallery, New York.
1929	Participates in the exhibition "Paintings by Nineteen Living Americans" at the Museum of Modern Art, New York.
1930	One-man show at the Daniel Gallery, New York.
1931	Given an award by the Carnegie Institute, Pittsburgh. Exhibits at the National Museum of Modern Art, Tokyo.
1933	Exhibits at the Downtown Gallery, New York, until 1961.
1935	Receives the Guggenheim Foundation fellowship.
1936	One-man show at the Art Students League, New York.
1939	One-man show at the Museum of Modern Art, Baltimore.
1942	Wins the first prize at the Golden Gate International Exhibition, San Francisco.
1944	Wins the first prize at the Carnegie Institute, Pittsburgh.
1948	Retrospective exhibition at the Whitney Museum, New York.
1953	Died, New York.
1954	Retrospective exhibition at the National Museum of Modern Art, Tokyo.

Sales

DRAWINGS

1963

Nevadaville, 1941, black lead, 11¾ x 15¾ .... (272) $ 700

The Passer-By on the Bridge, India ink,
   10½ x 13½ .... (272)   375

1965

War Scene, pencil, 15¾ x 11¾ .... (494)   350

1967

Lola, 1942, India ink, 20 x 16¾ .... (889)   850

1968–July 1969

Two Churches, pencil, 10 x 14¾ .... (1062)   500

PAINTINGS

1964

Seaside, 17¾ x 23¾ .... (324)   2,500

Still Life with Flowers, 1926, 29¾ x 24 .... (324)   6,000

1965

Portrait of a Bearded Man, 7½ x 5¾ .... (610)   800

1967

Still Life with a Watermelon, 1938, 40¼ x 56 ..... (952)   12,000

1968–July 1969

Two Pears, 1931, 6 x 10 .... (1035)   2,750

Child Angling, 1921, 19¾ x 15¼ .... (1035)   6,500

The Equilibrist, on board, 27¼ x 19¼ .... (1160)   4,500

Nude on a Couch, 1922, 12 x 16 .... (1229)   3,500

Franz Kupka

(1871–1957)

Birthplace: Opocno, Czechoslovakia.

1888	Enters the Academy of Fine Arts, Prague.
1892	Continues his studies in Vienna.
1895	Settles in Paris. Exhibits at the Société des Beaux-Arts.
1906	Becomes a member of the Salon d'Automne, Paris. Very well known as an illustrator. Paints in the Neo-Impressionist manner.
1911	Suddenly turns to abstract painting.
1912	Exhibits his abstract works for the first time at the Salon d'Automne, Paris.
1913	Participates in the Salon des Indépendants and in the Salon d'Automne, Paris.
1921	One-man show at the Galerie Povolotzky, Paris.
1924	One-man show at the Galerie de la Boétie, Paris.
1946	Important retrospective exhibition at the museum of Prague.
1951	Retrospective exhibition at the Galerie Louis Carré, New York.
1957	Died, near Paris.

Sales

DRAWINGS

1961–1962

Composition, pen, 4½ x 3¼ .... (110) $ 60

A Face, black pencil, 8¼ x 8¼ .... (115)   160

1963

The Fun Fair, (1905), charcoal and stump,
   21¾ x 17¾ .... (222)   76

Study for the "Great Nude," 1908, charcoal
   heightened with white, 17¾ x 21 .... (225)   600

1964

Composition, colored pencil, 5¾ x 5¼ .... (328)   110

Composition, 1954, black pencil, 8 x 8¼ .... (450)   130

1965

Composition, pencil heightened with wash and
   blue pencil, 9 x 7½ .... (508)   260

1966

Composition No. 44, 8¼ x 8 .... (824)   84

Composition, charcoal, 13½ x 12¼ .... (809)   200

1967

Self-Portrait, 1899, pen and India-ink wash,
   9¾ x 7 .... (833)   260

Mother of Liberty, India ink, 8½ x 10¼ .... (986)   148

The Hand, colored pencil, 4½ x 7¼ .... (883)   140

Composition, 7½ x 7½ .... (834)   70

1968–July 1969

Peking (1900), India ink, 12¾ x 10 .... (1101)   115

Study for the Poster of "Nora" by Ibsen, pencil,
   gouache, and watercolor, 16¾ x 14¾ .... (1088)   250

WATERCOLORS

1961–1962

Female Form, 1909, pastel, 15 x 6 .... (71)   320

Localization of Graphic Mobiles I, 1911, pastel,
   12¾ x 12¾ .... (71)   840

Composition, gouache, 10 x 8 .... (59) $ 860
Composition, gouache, 17 x 18¼ .... (129) 686
About a Dot, (1913-18), gouache, 20½ x 22 .... (129) 1,373

1963
Composition, gouache, 12¾ x 12¾ .... (271) 190

1964
Composition, gouache, 10¾ x 10¾ .... (351) 520
Composition, 1929, watercolor .... (409) 370
Geometrical Composition, watercolor and
  gouache, 5¼ x 7¾ .... (393) 180
The Rocks of Tregastel, gouache, 8¼ x 11½ ...... (375) 820

1965
Flight, (1908), gouache, 9 x 8 .... (617) 2,373
Composition, watercolor and gouache, 7 x 5¼ .... (508) 280

1967
Composition, (1912), watercolor, 11¾ x 8¼ .... (889) 1,200
Composition, (1911), tempera, 10¾ x 10¼ .... (893) 300

1968-July 1969
Young Woman, Her Hands Behind Her Back,
  watercolor and gouache, 23¼ x 16¾ .... (1131) 310
Organic Cycle, (1915-20), gouache and
  watercolor, 8¼ x 12¾ .... (1272) 1,680
White Forms on Black, 1921, gouache, 14 x 19¼ . (1272) 1,200

PAINTINGS

1961-1962
The Dancer, 21¾ x 18¼ .... (155) 2,140
Reminiscence, Study, 1920, 32 x 23 .... (116) 3,200
Reminiscence, 1920, 32 x 23 .... (164) 2,197
Conception, 19 x 28½ .... (59) 13,600

1963
The Dancer, 1905, on cardboard, 19 x 18¼ .... (241) 1,400
Landscape, 23¾ x 19½ .... (225) 1,000
Reminiscence, Study, (1920), 31¼ x 22¼ .... (225) 4,000

1964
The Dancer with Vertical Planes, 1903, on
  cardboard, 19 x 18¼ .... (476) 1,500
The Dancer, 21¾ x 18¼ .... (399) 620

1965
Composition with a Dancer, 21¾ x 18¼ .... (598) 1,600
Composition, on cardboard, 15 x 24 .... (571) 600

1968-July 1969
Nude Dancer, 21¼ x 17¾ .... (1139) 2,000
Montmartre, (1895-96), on panel, 10 x 6½ ...... (1080) 900
Still Life with Statue and Books, 1909, 23 x 23¾ . (1271) 3,840

Roger de La Fresnaye

(1885-1925)

Birthplace: Le Mans, France.

1903 Attends the Academy Julian, Paris. Meets Dunoyer de Segonzac.

1908 Attends the Academy Ranson, working with Maurice Denis and Sérusier. Influenced by Maurice Denis for about a year.

1910 Trip to Germany and Italy.

1911 Paints landscapes at La Ferté-sous-Jouarre. Meets Gleizes, Metzinger, and Picabia at Villon's. Participates in the foundation of the Section d'Or, Paris.

1912 Produces his most important works—for instance, "L'Artillerie," "L'Architecte," and "La Conquête de l'Air"—between 1912 and 1914. Participates in the Salon des Indépendants and the Salon d'Automne, Paris. Starts to take an interest in sculpture.

1912-13 Comes under the influence of Braque and Picasso. Participates in the exhibition of the Section d'Or, Paris. Series of still lifes. Tries to elaborate a new classicism.

1914-17 Executes Cubist drawings and watercolors during World War I. Develops pneumonia and is discharged by the army. Settles at Hauteville, Ain district, and later in Grasse in the south of France.

1918 Falls out with Cubism and reverts to Naturalism.

1925 Died, Grasse, of tuberculosis.

Sales

DRAWINGS

1961-1962
Head, pencil, 9 x 8¼ .... (106) $ 45
Pierrot, black lead and watercolor, 6¾ x 10¼ ..... (106) 1,175
Still Life, charcoal and white chalk, 14 x 10¾ ..... (106) 497
Studies, black lead, 8½ x 10 .... (35) 230
Portrait, black lead, 13½ x 10 .... (143) 407

1963
The Man with a Pipe, 1917, wash, 10 x 7¾ .... (243) 1,120
Pierrot, 1921, pencil, ink, and watercolor,
  6¼ x 9¾ .... (202) 1,200
Study for the "14 Juillet," pencil and wash,
  17 x 10 .... (254) 220
Figures, 1924, India ink, 10¼ x 8 .... (254) 700
Woman in the Nude, Back View, 1925, charcoal,
  12¾ x 8¼ .... (255) 329

1964
Seated Nude, black lead, 24½ x 17¾ .... (457) 80
Bathers, black lead, 8 x 4¾ .... (483) 106
Le Poilu, 1914, pencil on red paper, 3¼ x 6½ ..... (393) 40
Woman at the Theater, pencil, 8¼ x 6¼ .... (460) 400
Bathers, pencil, 5 x 8 .... (377) 170
The Street, 1921, India-ink wash, 10 x 6½ .... (471) 814
Study of a Woman in the Nude, charcoal,
  24 x 17½ .... (430) 440
Seated Nude, charcoal, 18½ x 13 .... (441) 384

1965

Figure Leaning on His Elbow, pencil, 11½ x 8¾ .. (561) $ 240

Nude, pencil, 10 x 8 .... (507)   150

Dancers, pencil and pen, 7¼ x 4½ .... (630)   120

Study of a Man in the Nude, pencil and
    watercolor, 16¼ x 9¼ .... (567)   260

1966

Study for "Married Life," 1912, charcoal,
    18¼ x 23¼ .... (801)   3,000

The Teapot, India ink, 7½ x 9 .... (801)   1,020

Nudes in a Landscape, 10¼ x 8 .... (655)   80

View of Meaux,[1] black lead, 5 x 8¼ .... (794)   90

Women—Sketch Pages, 10¼ x 8 .... (674)   70

Nude, pencil, 8¾ x 5¾ .... (696)   182

Dancers, pencil, 8¾ x 5¾ .... (665)   250

Man's Head, 1921, pencil, 16 x 11 .... (703)   2,100

1967

Woman's Head, 1921, pencil, 12¾ x 9¼ .... (857)   720

Horse and Stableboy, 1921, black lead and white
    gouache, 9 x 6½ .... (929)   1,700

Landscape with Fortified Castle, 1922, pencil and
    stump, 13½ x 18¾ .... (909)   2,320

Seated Nude in Profile, pencil, 8¼ x 5¼ .... (975)   560

1968–July 1969

Back View of a Nude, (1905), charcoal,
    30½ x 20 .... (1134)   236

Bathers, black lead, 4½ x 5¼ .... (1077)   78

Nude, charcoal, 30 x 20½ .... (1026)   196

Seated Woman in the Nude, pencil and India-ink
    wash, 10 x 7½ .... (1178)   120

Standing Nude, pencil heightened with white
    stone, 25 x 12¾ .... (1072)   580

Young Woman in a Landscape, pencil, 3¾ x 5¾ . (1226)   200

Two Portraits; Cubist Portrait; Bust of a Figure;
    four drawings, pen and wash, 5¾ x 3¾ ...... (1226)   1,800

Still Life with Glass, wash, 3¾ x 5½ .... (1226)   700

Head of a Warrior, wash, 10 x 7¼ .... (1238)   740

Dancers, pencil, 8¾ x 5¾ .... (1248)   100

Point-Croix Street and Church, Brittany, black
    lead, 4 x 6¾ .... (1267)   116

Orchard on the Hill, Brittany, black lead,
    4 x 6¾ .... (1267)   150

WATERCOLORS

1963

The Bottle, 1920, gouache and watercolor, 9 x 6 .. (247)   2,194

1964

The Wheelbarrow, 1912, oval pastel, 19 x 13½ .... (460)   1,440

1966

Still Life with a Pipe, 1913, watercolor and
    gouache, 6½ x 13¼ .... (685)   3,700

The Hive, 1912, oval pastel, 13½ x 19 .... (801)   2,200

Figures in a Landscape, 1913, watercolor,
    9¼ x 12¾ .... (703)   2,750

1967

The Hive, 1912, oval pastel, 19¼ x 14 .... (1004)   3,500

Still Life with a Drum, 1918, watercolor,
    10¾ x 7¾ .... (930)   2,486

[1]On the reverse, studies of nudes.

Man Seated Near a Tree, 1920, watercolor,
    12¼ x 9¼ .... (857) $1,300

Reclining Nude, watercolor, 10¼ x 8 .... (926)   700

Country Works, tempera, 36¾ x 36¾ .... (918)   27,120

1968–July 1969

The Watering Can, 1912, oval pastel, 19 x 13½ .. (1212)   1,440

The Sick Person, 1922, gouache, 9½ x 6 .... (1200)   1,860

PAINTINGS

1961–1962

One of the Bacchants in the Louvre, (1909), on
    cardboard, 6½ x 9½ .... (102)   640

Self-Portrait, 29 x 23¾ .... (114)   1,580

Joan of Arc, 1912, 79 x 39½ .... (171)   25,000

1963

Eve, 42 x 26½ .... (232)   3,842

1964

Eve, (1909-10), 50¾ x 37½ .... (405)   12,188

1965

*Books on a Pedestal Table (Still Life with
    Books),* 1912, 32 x 23¾ .... (615)   27,000

The Conquest of the Air, First Sketch, 1913,
    37¼ x 28½ .... (615)   32,400

Tulips with a Red Curtain, 1909, 20 x 25¾ .... (615)   6,400

1966

The Watering Can (Emblems), 1913, 34½ x 76 .... (694)   100,000

Springtime, 1908, 42 x 31 .... (727)   26,400

Still Life with a Bunch of Radishes, 1912,
    29 x 21¼ .... (711)   12,000

1967

Still Life with a Bunch of Radishes, 1912,
    29 x 21¼ .... (864)   12,000

Front View of a Nude, (1911), 31½ x 17¾ .... (995)   4,020

Bathers, 1912, 63½ x 50¾ .... (864)   70,000

Joan of Arc, 1912, 79 x 39½ .... (901)   14,000

The Romanian, 1921, 25¾ x 21¼ .... (901)   7,000

"L'Après-midi d'un faune," oil on paper, laid
    down on canvas, 19¾ x 29¾ .... (901)   4,800

1968–July 1969

Still Life with a Bottle, on board, 22 x 28½ ...... (1126)   16,107

Still Life, 21¾ x 27¾ .... (1162)   12,600

Landscape with White Clouds, on cardboard,
    9½ x 13½ .... (1117)   2,400

Seated Nude, (1910), 19 x 15½ .... (1271)   1,200

Wilfredo Lam

(1902-   )

Birthplace: La Grande, Cuba. Son of a Chinese tradesman.

1920-23 Attends the Fine Arts Academy of Havana.

1924 Goes to Madrid, where he meets the curator of the Prado Museum.

1928 First exhibition at Vilches Gallery, Madrid.

1936 Visits for the first time an exhibition of Picasso's works, in Madrid.

1936-37 Attends the Academy of the "Quatre Gates," Barcelona.

1938 Goes to Paris. Exhibition at the Galerie Pierre, Paris. Makes friends with André Breton, Victor Brauner, Paul Eluard, Max Ernst, and Tristan Tzara. Joins the Surrealist group.

1941-45 Travels to the West Indies, visiting Cuba and Haiti.

1946 Exhibits at the Pierre Matisse Gallery, New York.

1947-52 Stays in Cuba and New York. Meets Marcel Duchamp and Gorky in New York. Visits Italy and Great Britain.

1951 Awarded first prize at the "Salone Nazionale," Havana.

1952 Returns to France and settles in Paris.

1953 Participates yearly in the Salon de Mai, Paris.

1957-58 Appointed member of the Graham Foundation for Advanced Study in Fine Arts, Chicago.

1962 Issues a series of etchings entitled "Images" (Carlo Grossetti, Milan).

1966-67 Retrospective exhibitions in Basel, Hanover, Amsterdam, Stockholm, Brussels, and Berlin.

Sales

DRAWINGS

1961-1962

Bird and Snake, 1945, India ink, 9¼ x 8 . . . . (129) $ 82
The Trophy, 1946, pen, 20 x 24½ . . . . (140)   330

1964

The Trophy, 1946, ink, 20 x 24½ . . . . (387)   193

1965

Triscalcire, 1946, pen, 20 x 24½ . . . . (624)   359

1967

Monsters, 1946, pen, 19¾ x 24½ . . . . (986)   467
Composition, 1957, stick of greasepaint,
    25½ x 19¾ . . . . (967)   249
Composition, 1958, chalk and watercolor,
    15¾ x 11¾ . . . . (970)   541

1968-July 1969

Symbol, 1953, charcoal, 19¾ x 25¾ . . . . (1101)   333
Abstraction, 1955, colored chalk, 21¾ x 27¼ . . . . (1138)   421

WATERCOLORS

1961-1962

Composition, watercolor, 11¾ x 15¾ . . . . (18)   199
Composition, gouache, 18¾ x 24 . . . . (75)   442

1963

Aquarium, 1938, pastel, 39½ x 25 . . . . (299)   720

Two Women, 1938, gouache, 40¼ x 28½ . . . . (249) $1,800
Face, 1938, watercolor, 25 x 18¾ . . . . (249)   480
Face, 1939, watercolor, 25 x 18¾ . . . . (249)   360

1966

The Couple, 1938, gouache, 41 x 29¼ . . . . (701)   600
Woman, 1939, watercolor, 28½ x 21¾ . . . . (703)   375
Seated Woman Holding a Child, 1942, gouache
    and pencil, 41½ x 32 . . . . (784)   1,300

1968-July 1969

Composition, 1958, pastel, 25 x 19 . . . . (1214)   384
Composition, pastel, 27½ x 19½ . . . . (1237)   1,400

PAINTINGS

1963

Angels and Horns, 1945, 23¾ x 29¾ . . . . (309)   1,582

1964

Standing Woman . . . . (326)   1,500
The Guest, 1964, 25¾ x 20 . . . . (386)   960

1965

Long-Haired Woman, 1939, 39½ x 29 . . . . (518)   1,200

1966

Portrait of a Seated Woman, 1939, 39½ x 29 . . . . . (797)   2,147
Seated Figure, 1939, 39½ x 28½ . . . . (751)   829
Two Faces, 1955, 25¼ x 21 . . . . (753)   1,741
White Birds, 1963, 36¾ x 28½ . . . . (802)   2,560
Two Heads, 1964, 20 x 16¼ . . . . (802)   880

1967

Composition, 11¾ x 15¾ . . . . (919)   339
Horsewoman, 1950, 42¼ x 35¼ . . . . (888)   2,349

1968-July 1969

Two Faces, 1955, 25¼ x 21 . . . . (1030)   3,750
Birds in Space, 1955, 41½ x 39½ . . . . (1080)   3,750
Good Day Mr. Lam, 1959, 29¼ x 59½ . . . . (1224)   6,200

André Lanskoy

(1902-   )

Birthplace: Moscow, Russia.

1921 Goes to France and settles in Paris. Attends the Académie de la Grande Chaumière.

1923 Takes part in a group show at the Galerie de la Licorne, Paris.

1924 Noticed by the German critic Wilhelm Uhde, who buys several of his pictures.

1925 First one-man show at the Galerie Bing, Paris.

1928 Meets R. Dutilleul, who buys a great number of his pictures.

1938 Exhibits in The Hague, Amsterdam, and Utrecht.

1939 First abstract gouaches.

1944 One-man show at the Galerie Jeanne Bûcher, Paris. Meets the dealer Louis Carré. First oils in abstract.

1948 One-man show including works from 1944 to 1948 at the Galerie Louis Carré, Paris.

1952 One-man show at the Galerie Louis Carré, Paris. Participates in the International Exhibition of the Carnegie Institute, Pittsburgh.

1954 One-man show at the Galerie Louis Carré, Paris. Exhibition, "Lanskoy Early and Recent Paintings," at the Fine Arts Associates, New York. Participates steadily in the Salon de Mai, Paris.

1959 One-man show at the Albert Loeb Gallery, New York.

1960 Participates in the exhibition "Peintres Russes de l'Ecole de Paris" at the Musée de St. Denis, near Paris. One-man show at the Albert Loeb Gallery, New York.

1965 One-man show at the Knoedler Gallery, New York. Resident in Paris.

Sales

DRAWINGS

1961–1962
Composition, charcoal, 25 x 19 . . . . (58) $ 160

1963
Composition, charcoal, 25 x 19 . . . . (232) 226
Still Life, colored pencil, 14 x 19¾ . . . . (275) 225

1965
Composition, charcoal, 39½ x 29¾ . . . . (617) 226

1967
Street Scenes of Paris, two drawings, pencil,
　7½ x 10 and 9¼ x 6¾ . . . . (870) 75

1968–July 1969
Composition, charcoal, 42½ x 29¾ . . . . (1088) 125
Still Life with Fruit, colored chalk, 14¼ x 20½ . . . (1241) 403

WATERCOLORS

1961–1962
Composition, 1948, pastel, 43 x 29 . . . . (124) 300
Composition, gouache, 10 x 12¾ . . . . (93) 463
Composition, gouache, 10 x 25¼ . . . . (110) 540
Composition, gouache, 23¼ x 18¾ . . . . (115) 360

1963
Middle-Class Interior, gouache, 15 x 21¼ . . . . (246) 120
The Meal, gouache, ... (187) 260
Composition, watercolor, 19½ x 25 . . . . (241) 440
Composition, gouache, 10 x 12¾ . . . . (236) 396
Composition, gouache, 43½ x 29¾ . . . . (283) 1,311

1964
Composition, 1958, gouache, 10 x 12¾ . . . . (386) 320
Composition, gouache, 19 x 25¼ . . . . (335) 400
Composition, watercolor, 19 x 24¾ . . . . (471) 565
Composition, gouache, 19½ x 24½ . . . . (372) 475

1965
The Meal, gouache, 19¾ x 25¼ . . . . (559) 290
Composition, gouache, 9½ x 12¼ . . . . (563) 166
Composition, gouache, 25¼ x 9½ . . . . (599) 240
Composition, 1953, gouache, 12¾ x 10 . . . . (606) 175

1966
Composition, gouache, 4 x 7 . . . . (665) $ 200
Home Scene, gouache, 15¾ x 20½ . . . . (669) 240

1967
Composition, gouache, 9½ x 12¾ . . . . (852) 220
Composition, gouache, 25 x 9¾ . . . . (919) 271

1968–July 1969
Composition, gouache, 25¾ x 10 . . . . (1153) 300
Composition, gouache, 25¾ x 10 . . . . (1174) 506
Composition, 1959, gouache, 25¾ x 10 . . . . (1116) 300
Composition, gouache, 10 x 12¾ . . . . (1175) 200
Composition, gouache, 12¾ x 10 . . . . (1114) 546
Composition, gouache, 15 x 21¼ . . . . (1127) 299

PAINTINGS

1961–1962
Interior, 29¼ x 39½ . . . . (30) 1,660
Home Scene, 23¾ x 32 . . . . (109) 820
Landscape, 39½ x 29 . . . . (171) 1,220
Violet Fog, 28½ x 21¼ . . . . (59) 960
Harlequin, 45¾ x 32 . . . . (156) 1,300
Woman in the Garden, 24¾ x 31½ . . . . (152) 600
Yellow Rain, 1955, 39½ x 29 . . . . (149) 1,580
The Chinese Proverb, 1959, 23¾ x 29 . . . . (136) 700
Composition, 31½ x 25¾ . . . . (167) 740
Composition, collage, 42¾ x 29¼ . . . . (110) 460

1963
Bust of a Young Boy, 13 x 8¾ . . . . (276) 160
Harlequin, 45¾ x 32 . . . . (299) 620
Green and Pink Composition, 45 x 57¾ . . . . (299) 1,400
Composition, collage, 29¼ x 43½ . . . . (237) 170
Harmless Landscape, 23¾ x 29 . . . . (238) 550
The Buttes Chaumont, 15 x 18¼ . . . . (293) 640
Prosaic Week, 29 x 39½ . . . . (224) 800
Bouquet, 21¼ x 29 . . . . (254) 900
Figure in a Landscape, 21¼ x 25¾ . . . . (254) 480
Composition, 16¼ x 13 . . . . (249) 490
Lulineux, 1956, 23¾ x 29 . . . . (200) 1,000
Two Harlequins, 1957, 38¾ x 57½ . . . . (279) 2,200
The Pink Snow, 1958, 23¾ x 28½ . . . . (290) 2,500

1964
Home Scene, 21¼ x 25¾ . . . . (436) 480
The Bretons, 1925, 21¼ x 32 . . . . (436) 136
Interior, 1935, 21¾ x 25¾ . . . . (346) 300
Interior, 29 x 39½ . . . . (354) 1,000
Summer at Home, 29 x 39½ . . . . (345) 450
Composition with Blue Blobs, 23¾ x 29 . . . . (351) 540
Composition, 29 x 23¾ . . . . (393) 200
Abstract Landscape, 1944, 6¼ x 7½ . . . . (374) 275
The Unsuspected Landscape, 29 x 21¼ . . . . (404) 220
Harlequin, 1956, 45¾ x 32 . . . . (328) 520
The Elevated Subway, 21¼ x 25¾ . . . . (366) 720
At the Theater, 36½ x 29 . . . . (335) 600
The Roofs of Paris, 21¼ x 25¾ . . . . (366) 560
Protected by the Blues, 1959, 39½ x 29 . . . . (372) 650
The Invisible Knot, 1959, 39½ x 29 . . . . (431) 2,200
The Harbor, 23¾ x 32 . . . . (341) 700
The Canal, 20¾ x 31¼ . . . . (321) 575
Shadows of Your Garden, 1963, 39½ x 25¾ . . . . . . (401) 460

Still Life, 21¼ x 32 . . . . (418) $ 420
Still Life with Flowers and Fruit, 13 x 16¼ . . . . (370)   360

1965
At Daybreak, 39½ x 28¾ . . . . (567)   814
Composition, 29 x 23¾ . . . . (567)   610
Portrait, 1955, 45½ x 32 . . . . (561)   780
Harlequin, 1956, 45¾ x 32 . . . . (561)   660
Presence, 39½ x 29 . . . . (583)   696
The Harvester's Display, 29 x 23¾ . . . . (518)   600
Meal in the Red Room, 15 x 18¼ . . . . (503)   420
Easily Crossed, 1961, 29 x 23¾ . . . . (566)   339
Man Dining, 31½ x 25¼ . . . . (636) 1,200

1966
The Pasture, 13 x 16¼ . . . . (718)   320
Main Street, 23¾ x 32 . . . . (745) 1,446
Meudon: Walls, Roofs, Viaduct, 1932,
   21¼ x 25¾ . . . . (795)   320
Landscape with a Hoarding, on panel,
   26½ x 17¾ . . . . (798) 1,130
Composition in Green and Blue, 23¾ x 29 . . . . (711)   480
Composition, 21¼ x 25¾ . . . . (720)   340
Protected by the Blues, 1959, 39½ x 29 . . . . (648) 1,000
The Mirror that Repeats the Tragedy, 1959,
   57½ x 38¼ . . . . (678) 2,500
Prolonged Desire, 23¾ x 29 . . . . (681)   280
Smelling Red Poppies, 39½ x 29 . . . . (809)   990
Still Life, 18¼ x 21 . . . . (772)   420
Harlequin, 46¼ x 32 . . . . (808) 2,177

1967
Suburban Landscape, 25¾ x 32 . . . . (976)   840
Pink Roofs, 19 x 25¾ . . . . (919)   723
Forewarning of the Harvest, 32 x 39½ . . . . (950)   800
Still Life, 21¼ x 32 . . . . (912) 1,500
Still Life with Fruit, 29 x 39½ . . . . (989) 1,100
Asiatic Joy, 1955, 39½ x 29 . . . . (963)   750
Composition, 1955, 45½ x 31½ . . . . (985)   569
Composition, 20½ x 25¼ . . . . (839)   230
To Set the Butterflies on Fire, 1959, 23¾ x 28¾ . . . (979)   408
The Holidays of a Phenomenon, 1959,
   57¾ x 38½ . . . . (1000)   900
Composition on a Black Background, 45 x 58 . . . . . (984) 1,400
The Three Children, 21¼ x 25¾ . . . . (967)   678

1968–July 1969
Still Life with a Bouquet, 25¾ x 21¼ . . . . (1051) 1,000
Still Life with a Siphon, 24 x 36½ . . . . (1175) 1,100
Three Figures Around a Table, 8¾ x 10¾ . . . . (1175)   280
Two Women Seated Around a Table, (1933-35),
   8¾ x 10¾ . . . . (1070)   519
Red Interior, 1946, 31½ x 45½ . . . . (1018) 1,500
Interior, 8¾ x 10¾ . . . . (1127)   575
Asiatic Joy, 1955, 39½ x 29 . . . . (1088)   775
Seated Nude, 45¾ x 29 . . . . (1042) 1,060
Children's Round in the Garden, 21¼ x 25¾ . . . . . (1177)   500
Composition, 23¾ x 32 . . . . (1043)   760
Composition, two collages, each 42 x 28½ . . . . (1129)   800
Reclining Nude, 29 x 45¾ . . . . (1220)   370
Seated Woman, 25¾ x 21¼ . . . . (1223)   560
Vase of Flowers, 18¼ x 10¾ . . . . (1230)   600
Still Life: Breakfast Table, 21¼ x 32 . . . . (1231)   550
Oyster Beds, 14 x 9½ . . . . (1237)   290
Interior with Figures, 9 x 10¾ . . . . (1268)   742
Composition, 8¾ x 10¾ . . . . (1268)   510

Charles Lapicque

(1898–   )

Birthplace: Theizé, Rhône district, France.

1909   His family settles in Paris.

1917   Attends independent academies of painting.

1919   Enters the Ecole Centrale (for engineering), Paris. Executes his first paintings.

1925   Comes under the influence of Cubism and abstract art. Meets the dealer Jeanne Bûcher.

1928   Forgoes being an engineer and gradually decides to devote himself to painting.

1929   One-man show at the Galerie Jeanne Bûcher, Paris.

1933   Takes an increasing interest in scientific investigation of color.

1938   Becomes Docteur ès Sciences.

1941   Takes part in the exhibition "Jeunes Peintres de tradition française" at the Galerie Braun, Paris. One-man show at the Galerie Jeanne Bûcher, Paris.

1942   Takes part in a group show at the Galerie Friedland, Paris, together with Bazaine, Estève, Lhote, Pignon, and Tal-Coat.

1947   One-man show at the Galerie Louis Carré, Paris.

1948   Appointed painter to the navy.

1949   Exhibition at the Galerie Van Geluwe, Brussels, and the Galerie Denise René, Paris.

1953   Wins the Raoul Dufy prize at the Venice Biennial. One-man show at the Galerie Villand et Galanis, Paris.

1956   One-man show at the Galerie Villand et Galanis, Paris.

1958   Issues *Essais sur l'espace, l'art, et la destinée* (Grasset, Paris).

1959   Participates in the exhibition "Fifteen Painters of Paris" at the Corcoran Gallery, Washington.

1961   Exhibits at the Lefevre Gallery, London.

Resident in Paris.

Sales

DRAWINGS

1961–1962
Horses, 1950, pen, 12¾ x 19¾ . . . . (104) $ 160

1963
Figure, 1947, India ink and brush heightened with
   charcoal, 21¼ x 17½ . . . . (249)   130

1967
The Engagement, 1944, colored pencil, 9 x 12¾ . . . (883)   170
Seascape, 1946, ink and pencil, 8 x 10¼ . . . . (996)   84

1968–July 1969
Calvary, 1947, ink wash, 10¼ x 8 . . . . (1129)   100
The Declaration, dated 46, 10¼ x 8 . . . . (1230)   80
The Boat, dated 52, India ink, 17½ x 21¼ . . . . (1264)   420
The Tree, dated 57, charcoal, 8¾ x 6¾ . . . . (1264)   150

WATERCOLORS

1961–1962
The Reprimand, 1944, pastel, 18¼ x 24 . . . . (110)   760

1964
Le Pioupiou, 1960, gouache, 8¾ x 6¾ . . . . (409)   140

1965

The Family, 1946, watercolor, 10 x 8¼ . . . . **(564)** $ 160
Composition, 1950, watercolor, 12¾ x 19¾ . . . . **(611)**   240

1966

Le Pioupiou, 1960, gouache, 8¾ x 6¼ . . . . **(696)**   130
Sketch for an Illustration, 1960, gouache,
    6¾ x 4½ . . . . **(730)**   144

1967

The Military Man, 1960, gouache, 7¼ x 4¾ . . . . . . **(854)**   150

1968–July 1969

Child Carrying Bread, 1960, watercolor,
    12¾ x 9 . . . . **(1129)**   330
Portraits of Children, 1960, watercolor,
    6¾ x 4½ . . . . **(1042)**   220

PAINTINGS

1961–1962

Turrets and Rocks, 25¾ x 39½ . . . . **(160)**   3,120
The Surrender of Breda, 32 x 23¾ . . . . **(160)**   2,900
Regattas in the Rocks, 25¾ x 39½ . . . . **(160)**   3,400
Still Life, 1941, 36½ x 25¾ . . . . **(104)**   5,060
The Kings of France, 1947, on paper,
    17¼ x 20½ . . . . **(104)**   600
The Semaphore of Pleubian, dated 1953,
    18¼ x 25¾ . . . . **(59)**   4,300
Night on the Lagoon, 1955, 8¾ x 13 . . . . **(155)**   1,240

1963

House of Brittany, 29 x 36½ . . . . **(224)**   3,200
Low Tide, 39½ x 32 . . . . **(224)**   2,600
House of Normandy in Autumn, 1945, 29 x 39½ . . **(224)**   2,680
Longuivy Harbor, 45¾ x 35¼ . . . . **(298)**   6,000

1964

Anthony and Cleopatra, 32 x 39½ . . . . **(371)**   2,800

1965

Fishing, 1946, 29 x 39½ . . . . **(553)**   3,000
The Strand at Pleubian, 1953, 21¼ x 29 . . . . **(561)**   3,520
Flamine, 1953, 23¾ x 15 . . . . **(547)**   1,400
Handling off Cherbourg, 1959, 25¾ x 32 . . . . **(552)**   1,260

1966

Lion en Majesté, 1962, 39½ x 29 . . . . **(727)**   2,400
The Tide Mill, 1945, 23¼ x 31½ . . . . **(789)**   1,400

1967

The Desert, 1962, 15 x 24 . . . . **(911)**   2,000
Ker dans l'intérieur, 1946, 29 x 36½ . . . . **(978)**   2,200
Lovers on the Strand, 1947, 29 x 19¾ . . . . **(978)**   1,560
Fernando Cortez, 1953, 23¾ x 32½ . . . . **(912)**   2,300
The Strand at Pleubian, 1953, 21¼ x 29 . . . . **(852)**   2,020
Venice, 1955, oil on paper laid down on canvas,
    12¼ x 17¾ . . . . **(921)**   1,220

1968–July 1969

Handling at Sunset, 1959, 32 x 45¾ . . . . **(1173)**   4,830
The Road to Nagpour, 1961, 25¾ x 32 . . . . **(1113)**   2,840
Chocolates and Mirrors, 1963, 23¼ x 36 . . . . **(1117)**   1,700
Tennis, 1965, 35¼ x 45¾ . . . . **(1181)**   2,400

Pierre Laprade

(1875–1932)

Birthplace: Narbonne, France.

1892   Goes to Paris and attends the Académie Carrière. Also reproduces works by Poussin, Delacroix, and Manet.

1901   Participates for the first time in the Salon des Indépendants, Paris. Discovers the Impressionists but does not come under their influence.

1903   Participates in the Salon d'Automne, Paris.

1907   First trip to Italy. Series of his views of Italian towns: Tivoli, Naples, Florence, and Siena. Exhibits steadily at the Salon des Tuileries and the Galerie Druet, Paris.

1932   Died, in his house at Fontenay-aux-Roses, near Paris. Major retrospective exhibition at the Galerie Druet, Paris. (Laprade produced a great number of illustrations intended for works by La Fontaine, Flaubert, Paul Valéry, Proust, Verlaine, and Géraldy.)

1939   Exhibition, "Bonnard, Laprade, Bouche," at the Galerie Durand-Ruel, Paris.

Sales

DRAWINGS

1961–1962

Woman, Her Arm Raised, India ink, 7¼ x 5¾ . . . . . **(81)** $ 40

1963

Seated Woman, charcoal, 11½ x 12¾ . . . . **(216)**   219
Interior with a Woman, charcoal, 10¾ x 9 . . . . **(281)**   429
The Park, charcoal heightened with pastel,
    9¼ x 12¼ . . . . **(293)**   300
Telling Secrets, pencil and watercolor,
    8¼ x 10¼ . . . . **(314)**   120

1964

Mantes (with the Cathedral in the Background),
    pencil and watercolor, 10¼ x 13¾ . . . . **(348)**   330
Seated Young Woman Looking at a Drawing,
    1906, charcoal, 16 x 12½ . . . . **(398)**   400

1965

Vase of Flowers Under the Arcade, pencil and
    watercolor, 8¼ x 3¼ . . . . **(492)**   160
The Woman in a Hammock, charcoal,
    11½ x 18¼ . . . . **(529)**   130

1967

Young Boy Writing, India ink, 8 x 8¼ . . . . **(919)**   124
The Scholar at Work, pen, 6¼ x 5¾ . . . . **(897)**   90
The Woman in a Hammock, charcoal,
    15½ x 18¼ . . . . **(850)**   130

1968–July 1969

Woman with a Guitar, pencil and watercolor,
    15 x 11 . . . . **(1067)**   250
Two Nudes on a Terrace, pencil and watercolor,
    9 x 7 . . . . **(1095)**   100
Young Girl with an Easel, charcoal, 20½ x 14 . . . . **(1247)**   600

WATERCOLORS

1961–1962

Picking Roses, watercolor, 6¼ x 5½ . . . . (5)   136
View of Rome, watercolor, 8¾ x 8¾ . . . . **(125)**   336

1963

A Halt in the Forest, watercolor, 5¾ x 5¼ ...... (276) $ 106
The Rest, watercolor and gouache, 6 x 14 .... (291) 260
Harlequin with Flowers, watercolor, 8 x 6 .... (238) 100
Young Girl with Her Arms Raised, watercolor,
    6½ x 5¾ .... (280) 64
Sewer at the Window, watercolor, 16¼ x 11¾ .... (318) 900

1964

The Couple in the Park, watercolor, 6 x 5¼ ...... (466) 120
At the Piano, watercolor, 17¼ x 13½ .... (466) 640
The River Arno in Florence, gouache, 6¼ x 8½ .. (398) 380
View of Naples, gouache, 6 x 9¾ .... (408) 280
Masked Harlequin, watercolor, 10¾ x 9 .... (366) 156
Window at Buzenval, watercolor, 19½ x 14 .... (361) 440
Landscape, watercolor, 12¼ x 14 .... (377) 927
The Public Garden, watercolor, 10 x 8 .... (465) 800

1965

Landscape, watercolor, 14¼ x 12¾ .... (567) 881
View of Italy, watercolor, 13 x 18¾ .... (512) 460
Interior with a Woman, pastel, 5¾ x 7¾ .... (599) 150

1966

Little Girl, watercolor, 6¼ x 8 .... (745) 791
Italian Landscape, watercolor and gouache,
    9¾ x 8½ .... (793) 440
The Statue Before the Sea, watercolor, 8 x 6 ..... (804) 106
Figures in a Park, watercolor, 10¼ x 7¼ .... (804) 242
The Park, watercolor, 11¾ x 12¾ .... (758) 300
The Archangel, gouache, 5¼ x 4 .... (824) 110
Woman Picking Flowers, watercolor, 11 x 8½ .... (655) 370
Florence, watercolor, 10¼ x 15 .... (809) 340
Woman Mending a Lamp Shade, gouache,
    7½ x 6½ .... (757) 498

1967

Open Window, watercolor, 14¾ x 13½ .... (987) 760
Pine Trees, watercolor, 10¾ x 16¾ .... (936) 420
Figures in a Park, watercolor, 17¾ x 17 .... (905) 220
Tipsiness, watercolor, 6½ x 5¾ .... (843) 180
Arabesques, gouache, 8½ x 8 .... (999) 110

1968–July 1969

Picking Flowers, watercolor, 10¾ x 7¼ .... (1117) 520
Young Woman Picking Up Roses, watercolor and
    gouache, 9½ x 6½ .... (1159) 440
The Rosery, watercolor, 9½ x 6½ .... (1075) 300
Scene in a Park, watercolor, 17 x 17¾ .... (1078) 420
The Park of Dampierre, watercolor, 12¾ x 17 ... (1034) 1,000
The Woman with a Black Velvet Mask,
    watercolor, 4¾ x 3 .... (1140) 170
The Triton, Palermo Museum, watercolor,
    19¾ x 12¾ .... (1121) 700
View of Rome, watercolor, 11¾ x 17½ .... (1200) 1,320

1968–July 1969

The Walk, stencil heightened with watercolor,
    8¾ x 7½ .... (1227) 62
Harlequin Flower, stencil heightened with
    watercolor, 8¾ x 7½ .... (1227) 86
*Pierrot Under the Green Arbor; Rest Before the
    Window*, two stencils heightened with
    watercolor, each 6¾ x 8¼ .... (1238) 104
Harlequin Greeting; Harlequin with Flowers, two
    stencils heightened with watercolor, each
    8 x 6 .... (1245) 44

View of a Park, gouache, 6¼ x 14¾ .... (1258) $ 600
*Landscape of a Garden with Roses, Seen
    Through an Open Window*, watercolor and
    gouache .... (1263) 1,360

PAINTINGS

1961–1962

Still Life: Roses in a Vase, Books, and Fan,
    25¾ x 21¼ .... (124) 1,060
Cherries in a Cup, 11½ x 9¾ .... (123) 410
Vase of Roses, 28½ x 32½ .... (30) 2,000
Rosery on the Banks of the Erdre, 45¾ x 29 ..... (162) 1,240
Vase of Roses, on panel, 18¼ x 14¾ .... (71) 2,040
Bunch of Flowers, on panel, 11 x 8¾ .... (150) 226
Still Life: Roses and Oranges, 34 x 27 .... (29) 5,200
Pierrot Under the Pergola, on cardboard,
    22½ x 27¾ .... (76) 1,500
The Woman with a Veil, 25¾ x 19 .... (90) 560
The Woman with a Veil, 25¾ x 19 .... (146) 164
Florence, 23¾ x 32 .... (40) 2,200

1963

Roses, 32 x 25¾ .... (258) 5,600
Still Life: Roses in a Vase, Book, and Fan,
    25¾ x 21¼ .... (312) 2,800
Yellow Roses, 18¼ x 15 .... (318) 3,000
Still Life with a Bouquet, 33¾ x 45 .... (198) 3,800
The Public Garden, on cardboard, 10¾ x 16¼ .... (291) 580
Guingamp, the Wash House, 32 x 25¾ .... (215) 1,600
Round of the Nymphs, peinture à l'essence on
    cardboard 24 x 23¼ .... (262) 680
The Model, on cardboard, 18¾ x 13½ .... (259) 1,200
Reclining Nude on a Blue Sofa, on canvas laid
    down on panel, 21¼ x 25¾ .... (306) 3,200

1964

The Music Lesson, 1897, 15 x 18¼ .... (471) 1,876
The Greek Temple, 20 x 18¼ .... (355) 260
Round of the Nymphs, peinture à l'essence on
    cardboard, 24 x 23¼ .... (350) 520
Pompeii, 23 x 28½ .... (341) 900
Japanese in the Garden, 25¾ x 21¼ .... (440) 1,600
Young Lady at the Piano, 25¾ x 20 .... (398) 1,600
Young Ladies with Roses, Near the Pond,
    32 x 45¾ .... (347) 2,500
Provençal Landscape, on cardboard, 20½ x 28½ .. (409) 870
Roses in a Glass, 18¼ x 15½ .... (399) 2,000
Roses, 23¾ x 19¾ .... (341) 3,000

1965

Puppets, 39½ x 32 .... (532) 1,560
Temple of Love, 21¼ x 25¾ .... (532) 700
Woman Leaning on Cushions, 21¾ x 18¼ .... (553) 3,160
Young Girl Flipping Through an Album,
    25¾ x 21 .... (524) 860
Lavena, 25¾ x 21¼ .... (553) 3,000
Provençal Landscape, on cardboard, 28½ x 20½ .. (567) 1,808
Basket of Roses, 21¼ x 25¾ .... (569) 2,260

1966

The Harlequin, 11½ x 8¼ .... (702) 560
Carnival Characters, 14 x 11 .... (810) 490
Roses in a Vase, on cardboard, 14 x 12¾ .... (811) 1,200
Roses, Masks, and Lemons, 36¾ x 29¾ .... (648) 2,750

1967

Clisson, 25¾ x 32 .... (901) — $2,900
Indolent on a Sofa, on cardboard, 17¾ x 19¾ .... (912) — 1,060
The Tapestry, 13 x 16¼ .... (984) — 1,800
Woman Adorning a Vase, 23¼ x 19¼ .... (888) — 2,764
At the Piano, 15 x 18¼ .... (911) — 3,200

1968–July 1969

*Quimper: the Towers of the Cathedral Through
   the Trees,* 24½ x 24½ .... (1049) — 1,800
Rowing, 23¾ x 29 .... (1026) — 2,320
Antwerp, the Harbor, 19¾ x 19 .... (1189) — 2,100
The River Seine in Paris, 24 x 18¼ .... (1131) — 1,640
The Forum, 13½ x 18¼ .... (1117) — 920
Young Woman in a Park, 33¾ x 22¾ .... (1043) — 1,320
Conversation in a Park, 29 x 21¼ .... (1113) — 2,020
The Solfeggio Lesson, 24 x 23 .... (1181) — 4,700
The End of the Day in Toulouse, 19¾ x 24 ...... (1226) — 4,200
Little Girls in the Tuileries, 21 x 56¾ .... (1235) — 4,250
San Miniato, Florence, 20½ x 33½ .... (1235) — 2,250
Still Life with a Doll, (1922), on board, 41½ x 8 .. (1235) — 2,500
The Fields Before the Church, 19¾ x 24 .... (1254) — 7,600
La Charité-sur-Loire, 23¾ x 29 .... (1258) — 3,400
Vase of Roses Before the Window, 29 x 21¼ .... (1265) — 5,000
Landscape, 21¼ x 25¾ .... (1268) — 8,816
The Cloister in Italy, 24 x 18¾ .... (1268) — 6,844

Michel Larionov

(1881-1964)

Birthplace: Tiraspol, near Odessa, Russia.

1898 — Enters the Moscow Fine Arts school, but works mostly in his own studio. Meets Nathalie Gontcharova.

1903 — Paints under the influence of Impressionism.

1906 — Takes part in the exhibition "The World of Art," Petrograd. Exhibits at the Union of Russian Artists, Moscow. Trip to Paris and London with Diaghilev. Participates in the exhibition of Russian Artists at the Salon d'Automne, Paris.

1907 — With David Burlink, organizes the Crown exhibition. With Gontcharova, sets up the group "The Blue Rose" and the review *The Golden Fleece.*

1908 — First exhibition of the *Golden Fleece,* Moscow, includes works by such French masters as Sisley, Pissarro, Matisse, Braque, and Marquet.

1909 — Second exhibition of the *Golden Fleece.* Becomes the leader of the Russian avant-garde. Exhibits at the Union of Russian Artists, Moscow.

1910 — Organizes the exhibition "The Jack of Diamonds," including works by Gleizes and Lhote. Elaborates the first Rayonist works.

1912 — Organizes the exhibition "The Donkey's Tail"—with Gontcharova, Malevitch, and Tatlin—in Moscow.

1913 — The first Rayonist works are shown in the exhibition "The Target," Moscow. Issues the manifesto of Rayonism, Moscow. Takes part in the first exhibition of "Der Sturm," Berlin.

1914 — Organizes the Exhibition No. 4, Moscow. Trip to Paris with Diaghilev. With Gontcharova, exhibits at the Galerie Paul Guillaume, Paris. (Catalog preface by Apollinaire.)

1915 — Follows Diaghilev to Switzerland. Takes an increasing interest in stage decoration and nearly stops painting.

1918 — Settles in Paris. Takes part in the exhibition "L'Art décoratif théâtral moderne" at the Galerie Sauvage, Paris.

1921 — Takes part in the first Russian exhibition at the Whitechapel Art Gallery, London. Participates in the Salon d'Automne, the Salon des Indépendants, and the Salon des Tuileries, Paris.

1922 — Exhibition at the Kingmore Gallery, New York.

1925 — Exhibits in Tokyo and participates in the Rome Biennial.

1930 — Takes part in the exhibition "Décors de théâtre" at the Galerie de France, Paris.

1938 — Becomes a French citizen.

1948 — Retrospective exhibition of Rayonism at the Galerie des Deux Iles, Paris.

1949 — Participates in the exhibition "Les Premiers Maîtres de l'art abstrait" at the Galerie Maeght, Paris.

1952 — Participates in the exhibition "L'Oeuvre du XXème Siècle" at the Musée National d'Art Moderne, Paris.

1954 — Participates with Gontcharova in the exhibition "Diaghilev" at London and Edinburgh.

1955 — Participates in the exhibition "L'époque héroïque" at the Galerie de l'Institut, Paris.

1956 — Retrospective exhibition of works from 1903 to 1915 at the Galerie de l'Institut, Paris. Exhibits in the chief European cities.

1963 — Major retrospective exhibition at the Musée National d'Art Moderne, Paris.

1964 — Died.

Sales

DRAWINGS

1963

Resting, bister pencil, 17¾ x 30 .... (293) — $ 400

1964

Group of Costumes for the Prussian Tales, pencil
   and watercolor, 22¼ x 17 .... (416) — 608
Portrait of a Woman, pen and colored chalk,
   8 x 6 .... (420) — 73

1966

Ballet Rehearsal: Lifar and Diaghilev, 1927, pen,
   15 x 26 .... (757) — 691
Cannes, 9½ x 16¾ .... (670) — 66

1967

Diaghilev and Massine at a Table, pen, 7½ x 11 .. (922) — 221

LARIONOV

1968–July 1969

Rayonist Study of a Dancer in Motion, 1915,
pencil and watercolor, 15½ x 11 . . . . (1142) $1,534

*A Drawing for the Program Cover of Diaghilev
Russian Ballets,* 1920, pencil and gouache,
18 x 12¼ . . . . (1142) 897

*Stravinsky Assisting Diaghilev During His
Sickness,* 1915, pencil 13 x 17 . . . . (1142) 1,237

Portrait of Guillaume Apollinaire, pen and pencil,
10¾ x 8 . . . . (1043) 400

Drunkard with a Glass of Vodka, pencil, 10 x 8 . . (1240) 336

WATERCOLORS

1961–1962

Chimera, watercolor, 13 x 17 . . . . (164) 115

1963

Winter Evocation, (1914-15), gouache on blue
paper, 19 x 13½ . . . . (255) 274

1966

The Fish, 1907, gouache, 9 x 14¾ . . . . (723) 120

1967

Dancer, 1915, watercolor and gouache,
15½ x 11¼ . . . . (1009) 560

Palm Trees, watercolor, 10 x 17¾ . . . . (911) 1,640

A Forest Under Snow, (1909), gouache,
19½ x 12¾ . . . . (881) 221

1968–July 1969

Peasant, 1912, gouache, 14¼ x 9 . . . . (1134) 142

Still Life with Flowers, watercolor, 7½ x 10¼ . . . . (1068) 165

The Tournament, watercolor, 22 x 30¼ . . . . (1191) 6,136

The Red Cloth, (1912), gouache, 9¾ x 15½ . . . . . . (1240) 1,248

*Project of Stage Decoration for the Théâtre
Marigny,* (1926), gouache, 16¼ x 22 . . . . (1244) 130

Composition, 1916, gouache, 13½ x 22½ . . . . (1268) 1,392

PAINTINGS

1964

Soldiers, 1908, 29 x 37½ . . . . (367) 4,146

Rayonism, 1913-15, 9 x 11¼ . . . . (367) 1,658

Summer, 1912, 54½ x 46¼ . . . . (416) 7,739

Autumn, 1912, 53¾ x 45 . . . . (416) 7,739

1965

Bakers, (1907), 28½ x 23¾ . . . . (624) 829

Fancied Landscape, (1908), 43 x 32¾ . . . . (624) 2,211

1966

Abstraction, 1910, 14¾ x 10 . . . . (721) 1,800

Still Life in the Major Key, 1907, 36½ x 30½ . . . . . (681) 3,200

Portrait of Gontcharova, 1907, 23¼ x 19½ . . . . . . (741) 760

Blooming Twig in a Vase, (1908), 13 x 16¼ . . . . . . (723) 280

The Flight to Egypt, 28 x 21 . . . . (749) 1,800

1967

Study for "Still Life in the Major Key," 1907,
28½ x 25¾ . . . . (985) 806

Cubist Figure, oil and gouache, 22½ x 17¾ . . . . . . (1009) 700

Two Heads of Young Ladies, 23 x 12¼ . . . . (848) 190

Soldiers, 1909, 34¾ x 40¾ . . . . (993) 3,800

1968–July 1969

Foliage, (1903), 46¼ x 51¾ . . . . (1070) 4,012

Still Life in the Morning, 19¼ x 33 . . . . (1132) 1,416

The Model, 31½ x 17¾ . . . . (1187) 897

Still Life, 23 x 31 . . . . (1240) $1,152

Fish, 1907, on board, 8¾ x 14½ . . . . (1241) 1,512

A Tribute to Delacroix, 25¾ x 19¾ . . . . (1243) 780

The Fruit Stand, 12½ x 16¼ . . . . (1243) 620

Marie Laurencin

(1885-1956)

Birthplace: Paris, France.

1905 Attends the Académie Humbert, Paris. Meets Braque, Picasso, Apollinaire, and André Salmon.

1906 Participates for the first time in the Salon des Indépendants, Paris.

1912 Private exhibition at the Galerie Barbazanges, Paris.

1913 Exhibits at Rosenberg's, Paris—until 1940.

1914 Marries Otto von Watgen, a German painter.

1916 Stay in Barcelona, where she meets Gleizes and Picabia again.

1920 Returns to Paris after a trip to Germany.

1924 Stage decorations and costumes for the Ballets Russes—*Les Biches* by Poulenc.

1926 Participates in "Trente Ans d'art indépendants 1884-1914," at the Grand-Palais, Paris.

1928 Stage decorations for *A quoi rêvent les jeunes-filles* by Alfred de Musset, at the Comédie Française, Paris.

1956 Died, Paris.

Sales

DRAWINGS

1961–1962

The Artist in a Boat with Apollinaire, India ink,
pen, and brush, 8 x 9½ . . . . (106) $ 169

The Writer Garcia Calderon, 1934, 8¼ x 7 . . . . (58) 76

1963

Salome, 1906, charcoal, 8¼ x 6¾ . . . . (209) 36

Under White Rose Trees, 1906, India-ink wash,
8¼ x 6¼ . . . . (209) 60

Seated Woman, (1906), colored chalk, 7½ x 4¾ . . . (179) 475

*Young Lady with Pigeons; Portrait of a Young
Lady,* two drawings, colored pencil, each
6¾ x 5¼ . . . . (208) 650

Women Artists, charcoal, 7½ x 4¾ . . . . (209) 60

Portrait of a Young Lady, pencil, 11 x 9 . . . . (255) 713

Portrait of a Young Lady, charcoal, 7 x 4¾ . . . . . . (284) 108

Woman's Head, pencil and watercolor,
13½ x 9¾ . . . . (309) 1,121

1964

The Siren, black lead, 6 x 4½ . . . . (404) $ 130

In a Boat (the Artist and Apollinaire), ink and pencil, 8 x 10 . . . . (374) 175

Cocaine, 1921, black lead and colored pencil, 8 x 5¾ . . . . (397) 110

Girl with Flowers, 1940, colored pencil, 16¾ x 11 . . . . (321) 675

Bust of a Young Woman, colored pencil, 11½ x 8¼ . . . . (675) 460

Young Lady with a Turban, 1942, colored pencil, 11½ x 9½ . . . . (450) 1,200

1965

Portrait of a Woman, 1906, charcoal, 11 x 8 . . . . . . (530) 320

Portrait of Guillaume Apollinaire, (1911), pencil and India ink, 8¼ x 7 . . . . (606) 475

The Poet, pencil and India-ink wash, 8¼ x 7¼ . . . . (581) 204

Portrait of Hans Heinz Ewers, 1917, black lead and blue pencil, 8¼ x 5¾ . . . . (513) 120

Leda, colored pencil, 11 x 8¾ . . . . (586) 1,000

Dancer, colored pencil, 10 x 12¾ . . . . (539) 650

I Am Sick, India-ink wash, 5¼ x 3¼ . . . . (597) 209

Little Girl Playing in a Garden, pencil, 7¼ x 10 . . . (566) 226

Woman's Head, black lead and colored pencil, 10¾ x 8¼ . . . . (541) 850

Woman's Head, blue pencil and black lead, 12 x 9 . . . . (624) 719

The Woman with a Blue Bird, wash and watercolor, on an oval panel, 6¼ x 4¾ . . . . (516) 600

1966

Portrait, 1917, 6½ x 4¾ . . . . (745) 237

Portrait of a Woman, India ink, 5¼ x 3¾ . . . . (798) 221

Three Women in a Boat, blue ink, 8 x 10¼ . . . . (720) 220

Dancer, black lead, 8 x 4¾ . . . . (726) 44

Study of Women, blue ink, 8 x 10 . . . . (796) 300

Dancer, black lead and colored pencil, 10 x 12¾ . . (665) 1,500

1967

Bust of a Seated Woman, 1903, pencil, 8½ x 6¾ . . (857) 150

The Siren, colored pencil, 10½ x 8½ . . . . (889) 1,200

Self-Portrait, 1921, black lead and red pencil, 8 x 5¾ . . . . (939) 802

Little Bridge at St. Benoit-sur-Loire, colored pencil, 7½ x 10¼ . . . . (949) 390

Head of a Young Woman, 1948, black lead and colored pencil, 19½ x 17¼ . . . . (963) 1,900

Girl Friends with a Dog, charcoal and pastel, 10¼ x 13½ . . . . (967) 768

Young Lady with a Necklace, pencil, 10¾ x 8¾ . . . (870) 350

1968–July 1969

Carnival, (1913), pencil, 7¾ x 6½ . . . . (1134) 283

Young Lady with a Laurel Wreath, pencil, 11½ x 9¾ . . . . (1209) 595

The Two Friends, black lead and colored pencil, 11½ x 10 . . . . (1184) 1,440

Young Lady with Her Dog, black lead and colored pencil, 5¾ x 4¾ . . . . (1191) 755

Young Lady with a Cat, pencil and watercolor, 12¾ x 9¼ . . . . (1088) 1,750

Seated Woman in Profile, 8 x 5¼ . . . . (1039) 800

Bust of a Woman, India ink, 7¾ x 4¾ . . . . (1127) 414

Portrait of a Young Lady, 1931, black lead, 10 x 14 . . . . (1034) 1,100

Self-Portrait, black lead, 12½ x 10 . . . . (1068) 944

Young Lady, colored pencil, 10¾ x 7½ . . . . (1226) $1,160

Young Lady with a Dog, colored pencil, 8¾ x 11 . . . . (1247) 960

The Siren, (1925), charcoal, 8 x 7½ . . . . (1268) 1,369

Head of a Young Lady, colored pencil, 13 x 9½ . . (1268) 1,740

Young Girl in Profile, (1910-12), colored pencil, 8 x 5¼ . . . . (1268) 1,902

Dancer, pencil, 8¼ x 4½ . . . . (1273) 227

WATERCOLORS

1961–1962

Young Ladies Playing, 1927, watercolor, 9¼ x 11¼ . . . . (31) 494

Two Young Ladies, watercolor, 11¾ x 9½ . . . . (136) 840

Children's Round, watercolor, 13 x 17½ . . . . (6) 1,672

Hinds, watercolor, 10¼ x 8 . . . . (51) 420

Bust of a Young Lady, 1928, watercolor, 10½ x 8 . . . . (152) 1,100

Bust of a Woman, watercolor, 11¾ x 8¼ . . . . (160) 760

Woman's Head, watercolor, 11½ x 10 . . . . (156) 860

Flowers, watercolor, 13 x 11½ . . . . (80) 560

Stage Decoration for a Theater, 1946, watercolor, 13½ x 17½ . . . . (64) 2,100

The Sheet of Water, watercolor, 13½ x 17 . . . . (64) 2,100

1963

Andalusian Horse and Rider, 1916, watercolor, 3¾ x 3¼ . . . . (209) 40

The Young Ladies and the Horse, watercolor, 9¾ x 7¾ . . . . (225) 1,500

Three Dancers, watercolor, 10½ x 13½ . . . . (275) 1,200

Two Young Ladies, watercolor, 11½ x 9½ . . . . (290) 1,700

The Young Lady with Black Eyes, watercolor, 10¼ x 8 . . . . (318) 920

1964

Three Young Ladies, watercolor, 14½ x 14½ . . . . . (340) 1,500

Young Lady with a Dog, watercolor, 12¾ x 9½ . . . (450) 1,400

La Dame aux Camélias, 1936, watercolor, 8 x 6 . . . (454) 829

Two Blue Dancers, watercolor, 14¾ x 11 . . . . (471) 1,876

The Young Dancer, watercolor, 11½ x 9½ . . . . (454) 1,382

Woman's Head, watercolor, 13 x 9¾ . . . . (372) 1,500

Young Woman with a Pink Bodice, watercolor, 13 x 10 . . . . (448) 2,300

1965

Young Lady with a Blue Turban, 1910, oval pastel, 6¼ x 5¼ . . . . (617) 746

Young Woman in a Pink Dress, watercolor, 12 x 9 . . . . (561) 1,440

Woman's Head, 1919, watercolor, 8 x 5¼ . . . . (582) 829

Young Dancers, watercolor, 9 x 12¼ . . . . (539) 1,500

Seated Little Girl, watercolor, 9½ x 7¼ . . . . (567) 836

A Walk in the Bois, watercolor, 18¾ x 23¾ . . . . . . (617) 4,407

1966

Dancers, 1940, watercolor, 13½ x 17½ . . . . (798) 3,390

Creoles, pencil, ink, watercolor, pastel, and charcoal, 8¼ x 10½ . . . . (734) 7,006

Young Lady in a Pink Bodice, (1942), watercolor, 11¾ x 10 . . . . (784) 1,750

The Two Sisters, watercolor, 13½ x 10 . . . . (787) 1,800

Dancers in Pink and Blue, watercolor, ink and pencil, 14¾ x 11 . . . . (805) 2,750

1967

Bust of a Woman, pastel, 8½ x 6¾ . . . . (857) $ 560
Spanish Girls, fan-shaped watercolor, 5¾ x 18¾ . . (968)   820
Head of a Young Lady, watercolor, 9¼ x 7¼ . . . . (1004)   2,600
Young Lady with a Nosegay, watercolor,
10¾ x 8¾ . . . . (911)   2,200
Young Woman in a Pink Hat, watercolor,
11¾ x 10 . . . . (852)   1,640
Young Ladies Dancing, watercolor, 9½ x 13 . . . . . . (995)   2,300
Hinds, watercolor, 10¼ x 14 . . . . (978)   2,620
Three Women, watercolor, 9¼ x 12¼ . . . . (912)   1,600
Dancers in the Forest, watercolor, 12¼ x 14¾ . . . . (841)   3,000
Young Ladies with a Dog, watercolor, 17½ x 14 . . (987)   4,800
The Two Friends, watercolor, 17½ x 14 . . . . (987)   7,000

1968–July 1969

Young Lady with a Mandolin, watercolor,
14½ x 11¾ . . . . (1113)   3,600
Seated Young Woman, watercolor, 12 x 8 . . . . (1080)   1,700
Two Young Ladies, 1928, watercolor, 14 x 10¼ . . (1101)   1,840
Standing Woman,[1] watercolor, 8 x 7¼ . . . . (1127)   920
"L'habit d'Arlequin," watercolor, 8 x 7¼ . . . . (1171)   740
Woman Reading, watercolor, 10¾ x 8½ . . . . (1034)   1,600
The Man with a Hat, watercolor, 7¾ x 4½ . . . . . . (1117)   640
The Athlete, tempera and oil on canvas,
82½ x 29¼ . . . . (1193)   2,478
Portrait of the Artist's Mother, watercolor,
7½ x 4¾ . . . . (1174)   1,840
Two Young Ladies Playing with Their Dogs,
pastel and wash, 13¼ x 9½ . . . . (1240)   1,920
Classical Dancer, watercolor, 10 x 7½ . . . . (1241)   353
Hinds, watercolor, 10¼ x 8 . . . . (1246)   2,000
Young Lady with a Dog, watercolor, 11½ x 9½ . . (1246)   3,000
Three Young Ladies, watercolor, 9¼ x 13¼ . . . . . (1246)   2,000
Two Young Ladies, watercolor, 11½ x 9½ . . . . (1246)   3,250
The Two Girl Friends, watercolor, 17½ x 14¼ . . . (1254)   6,000
The Two Girl Friends, watercolor, 17¾ x 14¼ . . . (1254)   6,000
Woman in Right Profile, watercolor . . . . (1263)   1,800
Young Ladies and Dog, watercolor, 14¾ x 10¾ . . (1268)   4,872
Bust of a Woman, watercolor, 10¾ x 8¼ . . . . (1268)   1,647
Portrait of a Woman, 1908, 6½ x 4¾ . . . . (1268)   3,596

PAINTINGS

1961–1962

The Poetess Marguerite Gillot, (1912),
32½ x 25¾ . . . . (88)   5,658
Young Lady with Blue Birds, (1915), on
cardboard, 24¼ x 18½ . . . . (88)   3,567
Young Gentleman Before His Castle,
10¾ x 16¼ . . . . (26)   1,340
Woman's Head, 16¼ x 13 . . . . (156)   2,500
Woman with Tulips, 17¾ x 14¾ . . . . (64)   4,000
Portait of Paul Eluard, 10½ x 8½ . . . . (26)   740
Young Dancer, 1925, 31½ x 21 . . . . (64)   6,000
Amazon, (1920–21), on panel, 11¾ x 11 . . . . (96)   2,000
Young Woman with a Fan, 1927, 31½ x 20½ . . . . . (83)   12,357
The Boat, 1926, 17¾ x 21¾ . . . . (83)   6,590
The Kiss, 31¼ x 25 . . . . (83)   10,984
Portrait of Somerset Maugham, 1936,
22½ x 19½ . . . . (83)   4,119
A Girl Called Rose, 1930, 17½ x 14¼ . . . . (67)   2,571

The Young Swede, 1934, oil on linen cardboard,
14 x 10¾ . . . . (168) $1,000
Young Woman in a Green Toque, 1936,
18¼ x 15 . . . . (71)   2,700
Young Ladies at the Balcony, 1948, on panel,
10¼ x 8¼ . . . . (68)   962

1963

Two Women, 1922, 23¾ x 19½ . . . . (202)   4,500
Young Lady in a Blue Hat, 1930, 18¼ x 15 . . . . . . (252)   2,620
*Three Young Ladies Dancing and Playing the
Banjo*, 45 x 57¾ . . . . (318)   7,600
Comedians, 36½ x 29 . . . . (243)   9,600
The Young Woman with a Yellow Scarf,
29 x 21¼ . . . . (243)   7,000
The Young Lady, 14 x 10¾ . . . . (243)   2,200
Dancer on Stage, on board, 10¼ x 8¼ . . . . (216)   1,097
Flore, 15 x 18¼ . . . . (185)   1,620
Portrait of a Woman, 14 x 10¾ . . . . (299)   680
Young Lady with an Adorned Hat, 15¾ x 12¾ . . . . (179)   2,700
Young Lady with Flowers, 15¾ x 12¾ . . . . (202)   4,000
Portrait of a Woman, 12¼ x 9½ . . . . (283)   2,712
Portrait of Paul Eluard, on board, 10½ x 8½ . . . . (236)   1,062

1964

Young Lady, (1912), 13½ x 9¾ . . . . (378)   2,938
Woman with a Dog, 1922, 24 x 19¾ . . . . (340)   4,000
Young Lady with Her Arm Raised, 16¼ x 13 . . . . . (474)   3,400
Head of a Young Lady, 1933, 17½ x 14¾ . . . . (416)   5,252
Vase of Tulips, 1933, 23½ x 19½ . . . . (416)   4,975
Still Life, on cardboard, 10¼ x 11½ . . . . (471)   1,831
The Vase of Lilies, 1934, 23½ x 19½ . . . . (367)   3,317
Woman with a Guitar, 1936, 21½ x 18 . . . . (367)   6,081
Young Lady with a Yellow Ribbon, 16 x 12¾ . . . . . (454)   2,764
Head of a Young Lady, 1937, 16 x 13 . . . . (354)   3,000
Portrait of a Young Woman, 1941, 16¼ x 13 . . . . . (482)   2,600
Portrait of a Young Lady, 21 x 17½ . . . . (405)   3,482
Woman and Flowers, peinture à l'essence, on
cardboard, 12¾ x 11¾ . . . . (401)   480
Vase of Flowers, on panel, 12¾ x 9½ . . . . (454)   829
*Models of Tapestries: Flowers, Animals, and
Garlands*, on 4 irregular cardboards,
16¾ x 16¾ . . . . (480)   540

1965

Woman's Head,[2] 10¾ x 8¾ . . . . (494)   2,600
Woman with a White Buttonhole, 1924,
25 x 19½ . . . . (535)   5,804
The Three Young Ladies, 15 x 21¾ . . . . (552)   5,400
Young Lady with a Necklace, on cradled panel,
13¼ x 10 . . . . (633)   4,750
Catherine with a Rose, 26 x 21½ . . . . (539)   3,000
Riders, 1930, 16½ x 13¼ . . . . (602)   9,944
Reading, 25¼ x 21¼ . . . . (628)   9,286
Portrait of Lady Cunard, 35½ x 27¾ . . . . (522)   8,292
The Game of Battledore and Shuttlecock,
21¼ x 25¾ . . . . (569)   4,859
The Lady with a Handkerchief, on cardboard,
23¾ x 17 . . . . (545)   3,112
Seated Young Lady, 16¼ x 13 . . . . (516)   2,420
Reclining Nude, 1941, 10½ x 16 . . . . (582)   1,935
The Two Young Ladies, 1942, 25¾ x 21¼ . . . . (515)   6,600
Juliette, 21¾ x 18¼ . . . . (629)   4,933

---

[1] Executed for *L'habit d'Arlequin*.

[2] Self-portrait?

LAURENCIN

1966

The Family, (1908), 25 x 31¼ .... (694)	$ 18,000
The Two Sisters, 22 x 18¼ .... (648)	7,000
Young Ladies in the Forest, 1920, 32 x 39½ ...... (784)	7,500
Bust of a Young Lady, 1936, 17¾ x 14¾ .... (815)	4,699
Nude, 1941, 10¾ x 16 .... (784)	3,500
Woman's Head, 1952, on cradled panel, 11 x 9 .... (665)	1,750
Bust of a Young Lady, 16¼ x 13 .... (702)	3,320
Nosegay, 19½ x 25¼ .... (689)	4,284
Self-Portrait, on panel, 14 x 12 .... (809)	1,400

1967

Amazon, (1920), on board, 11¾ x 11 .... (940)	2,467
Nosegay, 1925, 20 x 24½ .... (965)	10,509
Dancer on Stage, on panel, 10¼ x 8¼ .... (988)	3,234
Young Lady with a Dog, 1921, 46 x 35¼ .... (954)	14,000
Nosegay, 1938, 14 x 10¾ .... (918)	4,181
Portrait of Madame Alice Derain, 16¼ x 13 ...... (857)	1,640
Young Woman with a Necklace, 14 x 10¾ .... (852)	4,200
Countess Elizabeth Costa de Beauregard with Her Children, Jean and Marie-Zéphyre, 1947, 18¼ x 22 .... (982)	6,399
Portrait of a Young Lady, 18 x 15 .... (963)	7,500

1968–July 1969

Young Lady with a Brown Scarf, (1908), on panel, 32¼ x 23¾ .... (1018)	4,750
Woman with a Hat, 1911, on an oval cardboard, 14 x 10¼ .... (1109)	8,000
Flowers in a Pot,[3] 16¼ x 13 .... (1200)	2,400
Vase of Flowers and Birds, 1927, 25¼ x 20¾ .... (1132)	8,732
Nosegay, 1933, 17½ x 14¾ .... (1070)	2,832
Ophelia, 1934, 17¾ x 14¾ .... (1176)	10,500
Head of a Young Lady, 1937, 16 x 13 .... (1080)	4,300
Young Lady with a Blue and Red Hat, 15½ x 12¼ .... (1187)	6,608
Woman with a Green Ribbon, 18 x 15 .... (1152)	11,000
Young Lady with a Rose, 16¼ x 13 .... (1200)	9,400
Young Girl with a Blue Bow; Young Girl with Pink Flowers; Young Girl with a Hat; Young Girl with a Mantilla, four oval paintings on canvas laid down on cardboard, each 16¼ x 12¾ .... (1049)	11,000
Three Young Women Playing with Dogs, 14¼ x 21 .... (1132)	6,372
Young Ladies with a Dog, 16¼ x 13 .... (1200)	8,000
Two Young Ladies, 24 x 19¾ .... (1208)	9,500
Bust of a Young Lady, oval painting, 15¾ x 12¼ .... (1125)	7,820
Leda and the Swan, 36½ x 29 .... (1049)	13,600
The Reading, 31 x 25 .... (1121)	9,700
The Little Page, 10¾ x 8¾ .... (1113)	5,520
Portrait of a Man, 13 x 9½ .... (1212)	820
Young Lady with a Blue Ribbon, on an oval canvas, 15½ x 12¼ .... (1225)	8,600
Vase of Flowers, on canvas laid down on cardboard, 10¾ x 14 .... (1225)	3,000
Head of a Young Lady, (1910-12), on an oval canvas, 15¼ x 12 .... (1239)	7,920
Young Woman with a Hat, (1910-12), on an oval canvas, 15¼ x 12 .... (1239)	8,160
Young Lady with a Blue Ribbon, 16¼ x 13 ...... (1247)	8,400
The Woman in a Green Hat, 18¼ x 15 .... (1254)	9,200

[3] Collection Guillaume Apollinaire.

LAURENS

Flowers in a Vase, 10½ x 13½ .... (1255)	$2,400
Young Woman, 1952, on cradled panel, 11 x 9 ... (1262)	4,400
Bunch of Flowers, 1933, 18¼ x 15 .... (1268)	9,280
The Tulips, 25¾ x 21¼ .... (1268)	14,152
Three Young Women with Veils, 35¼ x 28 ...... (1270)	17,040
Portrait of Paul Eluard, 1942, on panel, 10½ x 8¼ .... (1273)	1,640

Henri Laurens

(1885–1954)

Birthplace: Paris, France.

1905 Marries Marthe Duverger.

1905-11 Studies sculpture by himself. Meets Braque, who brings him over to Cubism.

1913 Participates for the first time in the Salon des Indé-pendants, Paris.

1915 Makes friends with Juan Gris and Modigliani.

1916 Meets Pierre Reverdy and illustrates some of his works. Executes collages. Meets Picasso and the dealer Léonce Rosenberg. First exhibitions at the Galerie Rosenberg and the Galerie de l'Effort Moderne, Paris.

1918 Signs a contract with Léonce Rosenberg.

1924-31 Takes a great interest in architecture and decoration.

1935 Wins the Helena Rubinstein prize.

1936 Executes some works for the Paris World's Fair.

1937 First stay at the seaside. Works on the theme of the sirens.

1938 Together with Braque and Picasso, has an impor-tant exhibition in Oslo, Stockholm, and Copenhagen.

1939-44 Series of etchings entitled "Les Fusillés."

1948 Participates in the Venice Biennial.

1949 Exhibits at the Palais des Beaux-Arts, Brussels.

1950 Given an award by the Venice Biennial.

1951 Retrospective exhibition at the Musée National d'Art Moderne, Paris.

1952 Executes a monumental work for the University of Caracas.

1953 Given an award by the São Paulo Biennial.

1954 Died, Paris. (Though Laurens won fame through his sculpture, he had painted from the beginning of his career.)

Sales

DRAWINGS

1961-1962

Reclining Nude, pencil and watercolor, 10 x 15 .... (84) $ 769

1964

Young Lady, 1919, India ink, 10¾ x 8¾ .... (378) $ 316

Portrait of a Young Lady, 1919, India ink,
10¾ x 8¾ .... (394)   250

Nude, pencil, 13½ x 10¼ .... (458)   261

Squatting Woman in the Nude, (1950), charcoal
and pencil, 4½ x 11½ .... (383)   194

1967

Seated Woman, chalk, 11¼ x 9 .... (930)   350

Standing Woman, 1918, pen, 8 x 5¼ .... (975)   360

Seated Nude, pencil and charcoal, 11¼ x 6¾ ..... (870)   850

1968–July 1969

Naiad, stick of greasepaint, 4 x 9½ .... (1174)   230

Nude, black pencil, 23 x 14¾ .... (1200)   560

Seated Woman in the Nude, 23 x 14¾ .... (1026)   900

Reclining Nude, (1940), pencil, 11½ x 17¾ ...... (1114)   992

Seated Nude, black pencil, 23¼ x 14¾ .... (1244)   580

WATERCOLORS

1961–1962

Rhythmical Dance, gouache, 17½ x 14¾ .... (43)   640

Caryatid, gouache, 17½ x 14¾ .... (93)   1,243

Cubist Composition, watercolor .... (78)   800

1964

S.F.A. 1918, a Woman with Flags, watercolor,
9¼ x 6½ .... (460)   500

The Green Glass, 1915, gouache and collage,
15½ x 8¼ .... (460)   640

1965

Squatting Woman, gouache, 16¾ x 13 .... (615)   1,420

Face, 1917, gouache and collage, 20½ x 11¾ ..... (615)   4,800

Guitar and Music Paper, 1918, gouache and
collage, 16 x 23¾ .... (615)   11,000

The Racing Car, watercolor and gouache,
4¾ x 8 .... (613)   560

1966

Composition, 1918, gouache, 6¾ x 9¾ .... (801)   1,600

Seated Nude, watercolor, 10 x 15¾ .... (826)   760

Nude, watercolor and pencil, 10 x 15½ .... (727)   680

1967

L'Etang-la-Ville: The Halt, 1917, gouache and
collage, 19¾ x 13½ .... (975)   5,200

Reclining Nude, 1924, gouache, 3 x 12¾ .... (975)   620

1968–July 1969

Squatting Woman, 1950, gouache, 25¼ x 19¾ ... (1106)   1,200

Reclining Woman, gouache and plaster, 9 x 13¾ . (1109)   2,100

Sleeping Woman, 1949, watercolor, 11½ x 19½ .. (1200)   660

Woman Seated on the Ground, 1950, gouache and
black lead, 10¾ x 15¾ .... (1118)   600

PAINTINGS

1961–1962

Portrait of Josette Gris, 1917, collage and black
and white chalk, 29¼ x 20 .... (106)   3,842

Still Life: Bottle and Glass, 1917, collage and
charcoal, 23¼ x 15½ .... (140)   8,787

Woman's Head, 1917, collage and charcoal,
23 x 15½ .... (140)   6,041

Composition, 1915, collage, 7¼ x 5¼ .... (29)   800

Composition, collage, 4 x 6¼ .... (153)   600

1963

Fruit Dish and Pipe, 1918, collage and colored
chalk, 14½ x 19½ .... (219) $5,989

1964

Sculptor's Stool, 1917, collage on an oval
cardboard, 12¾ x 9 .... (460)   1,500

1965

The Hand with Dominoes, 1918, collage,
9 x 12¾ .... (615)   2,400

Woman's Head, 1918, collage and corrugated
cardboard, 24½ x 17 .... (615)   8,400

Composition, 1918, collage and gouache,
12¼ x 15½ .... (516)   2,300

1966

Still Life, collage on board, 12¾ x 15¾ .... (801)   4,800

Seated Woman, 1918, collage and oil,
38¾ x 25¾ .... (676)   9,500

Guitar and Clarinet, 1919, on cardboard,
9¼ x 14 .... (801)   4,040

1968–July 1969

Composition, 1918, collage and chalk on
cardboard, 23½ x 15½ .... (1106)   3,400

Composition, Guitar, 1918, oil and collage on
cardboard, 23¾ x 15½ .... (1049)   4,000

Woman's Head, 1917, collage, 11½ x 7¼ .... (1200)   2,100

Composition, 1943, 18¼ x 12¾ .... (1258)   3,200

Abel Lauvray

(1870–1950)

Birthplace: Rennes, France.

1895   Executes his first landscapes of Vétheuil and Brittany during vacations. Devotes the major part of his work to landscape.

1902   Makes friends with Claude Monet, who becomes his master.

1903   Exhibits at the Salon des Indépendants, the Salon d'Automne, and the Société Nationale des Beaux-Arts, Paris.

1950   Died. (Was almost completely unknown during his lifetime.)

Sales

PAINTINGS

1961–1962

The River Seine at Vétheuil, on cardboard laid
down on canvas, 19¾ x 25¾ .... (99) $ 130

1964

Banks of the River Seine at Vétheuil, on panel,
19¾ x 25½ .... (350)   620

Bank of the River Seine at Vétheuil, 15 x 21¾ .... (442)   270

Riverside, 19¾ x 29 .... (450)   600

1965

View of Avignon: The Tower of Philippe-le-Bel,
23¾ x 32 . . . . (518) $1,000

1966

Landscape of the South of France, 23¾ x 32 . . . . . (741)   1,700
Riverside, 15 x 21¾ . . . . (793)   1,400
Banks of the River Seine at Vétheuil,
19¾ x 25¾ . . . . (687)   1,340

1967

The River Seine at Vétheuil, 19¾ x 25¾ . . . . (898)   1,400
Villeneuve-lès-Avignon, 19¾ x 25¾ . . . . (858)   1,500
Landscape of the South of France, on cardboard,
10¾ x 14 . . . . (976)   360
Landscape by the River Seine at Vétheuil, on
panel, 10¾ x 14 . . . . (976)   500
Bank of the River Seine and Mantes Cathedral,
23¾ x 32 . . . . (976)   1,200
Surroundings of Vétheuil, 23¾ x 32 . . . . (976)   2,600

1968–July 1969

Village by the River Loire, on paper laid down on
canvas, 15 x 21¾ . . . . (1159)   1,320
Landscape of the South of France, 23¾ x 32 . . . . (1144)   700
Avignon: The Tower of Philippe-le-Bel,
19¾ x 29 . . . . (1189)   3,100
Landscape of the Ile-de-France, 19¾ x 25¾ . . . . . (1051)   1,220
Landscape of Touraine; Villeneuve-lès-Avignon,
two panels, each 10¾ x 14 . . . . (1051)   640
A Corner of the Artist's Studio at Vétheuil, on
panel, 19¾ x 25¾ . . . . (1116)   1,500
The River Seine and Mantes Cathedral,
23¾ x 32 . . . . (1183)   840
Landscape, 10¾ x 14 . . . . (1238)   420

Emmanuel de La Villeon

(1858–1944)

Birthplace: France.

1888   Exhibits for the first time at the Salon des Indépendants, Paris.

1890   Participates in the exhibition of the Société Nationale des Beaux-Arts, Paris.

1908   Becomes a member of the Société Nationale des Beaux-Arts, Paris. His work consists chiefly of landscapes and seascapes executed under the influence of Impressionism.

1944   Died, Paris.

Sales

DRAWINGS

1966

In the Sand Hills, pen and black and colored
pencil, 4 x 6½ . . . . (695) $ 180
Wintry Landscape, colored pencil, 14¾ x 10 . . . . . . (695)   64

WATERCOLORS

1966

The Moor, pastel, 9½ x 12¾ . . . . (695) $ 86
The Walk, 1925, pastel, 8¾ x 10¾ . . . . (695)   40
Outskirts of the Wood, watercolor, 8¾ x 11 . . . . . . (695)   52

1968–July 1969

Autumn Landscape, pastel, 9½ x 12¾ . . . . (1072)   90
In the Forest, watercolor, 28½ x 21 . . . . (1230)   130
Surroundings of Grenoble, watercolor,
7¼ x 10¼ . . . . (1266)   116

PAINTINGS

1961–1962

Parc de Floreyre, Canton de Vaud, Snow Effect,
1899, 23¾ x 36½ . . . . (9)   700
Snowy Landscape, 1900, 36½ x 23¾ . . . . (120)   1,200
Landscape with Birch Trees, 1915, 23¾ x 29 . . . . (40)   760
Surroundings of Bitry, 13 x 16¼ . . . . (9)   440
Snow at Salvar, 1929, 20½ x 25¼ . . . . (136)   620
Landscape with Pink Acacias, 25¾ x 36½ . . . . (26)   1,040

1963

Haymaking Time, 1908, 25¾ x 36½ . . . . (306)   1,360
Old Walls, Winter Morning, 1912, 23¾ x 36½ . . . . (278)   170
Landscape, 18¼ x 21¾ . . . . (241)   180

1964

The Field of Salvar Park, 19¾ x 29 . . . . (473)   680
Cherry Trees in Blossom, 18¼ x 21¾ . . . . (473)   270

1965

Figures Under the Trees, 18¼ x 21¾ . . . . (577)   330
Outskirts of the Wood, 1906, 18¼ x 21¾ . . . . (540)   270
The Walk of the Park, 1902, on cardboard,
23¾ x 36¼ . . . . (491)   1,200
Landscape Near Nevers: The Way to the Pond,
18¼ x 21¾ . . . . (599)   120
The Path of Floreyre, Switzerland, 21¾ x 18¼ . . . (497)   500
Skaters, 19¾ x 25¾ . . . . (511)   640
The Wash House, 28¾ x 23¾ . . . . (516)   780
The Walk of the Park, 23¾ x 36¼ . . . . (490)   1,200

1966

My Portrait, 1888, on board, 10¾ x 14 . . . . (695)   244
Snow Effect at Salvar, 1903, 32½ x 39½ . . . . (695)   600
A Lane Near Yverdon, 1894, 19¾ x 19¾ . . . . (695)   190
The Trees in Blossom, 1892, on panel, 13 x 23¾ . . (718)   280
Surroundings of Yverdon (Canton de Vaud),
32½ x 39½ . . . . (711)   500
Landscape, 23¾ x 36½ . . . . (809)   400
The Lane of Bitry, 18¼ x 21¾ . . . . (774)   220
Washerwoman, 23¾ x 28 . . . . (774)   260
Pink Trees, 28½ x 23¾ . . . . (774)   320
Cattle in Pasture, 1904, 23¾ x 36¾ . . . . (666)   460
A House in a Landscape, 1904, 15 x 24 . . . . (652)   240
Landscape, on cardboard, 5¾ x 8¾ . . . . (652)   96
A Study of Heather, 1940, on cardboard,
13 x 16¼ . . . . (695)   190

1967

Surroundings of Yverdon, 1892, 19¾ x 24 . . . . (911)   640
The Lake, 19¾ x 29 . . . . (950)   600
Twilight Over the Glade, 32½ x 39½ . . . . (858)   540
Hop-o'-My-Thumb, 29¼ x 39½ . . . . (976)   550
The Deep Valley, 23¾ x 29 . . . . (993)   320

The Gorges of the River Tarn, 18¼ x 13 .... (943) $ 200
The Road in the Forest, 23¾ x 19 .... (848) 130
Bunch of Flowers, 25¼ x 31½ .... (832) 180

1968–July 1969

Underwood, on cardboard, 13 x 19¾ .... (1051) 160
Landscape, 1892, 19¾ x 29 .... (1119) 680
Autumn, Valley of St. Verain, 1902, 17¾ x 21¼ .. (1026) 680
Vase of Flowers, 1916, 25¾ x 32 .... (1015) 300
Dawn of Release, on panel, 15 x 18¼ .... (1128) 316
Seascape, 1924, 21¾ x 29 .... (1095) 400
Towboat on the River Seine, 18¼ x 25¾ .... (1072) 400
A Lane, Finistère, 18¼ x 21¾ .... (1053) 560
Landscape, on panel, 13 x 16¼ .... (1223) 500
Autumn Landscape Near Yverdon (Switzerland),
   1908, 23¾ x 36½ .... (1224) 4,000
Autumn in the Nivernais, 1908, 18¼ x 21¾ ...... (1225) 1,220
The Bridge, on panel, 5¼ x 7¼ .... (1227) 170
Underwood Alley, 9½ x 14 .... (1230) 420
The Garden on the Hill, on cardboard, 9 x 11 .... (1238) 200
Surroundings of Montmuron, 1890, 23¾ x 29 .... (1252) 3,100
Landscape in Spring, 23¾ x 29 .... (1254) 1,900
Castle in the Morvan, 25¾ x 36½ .... (1256) 1,300
Pesselières Park, 25¾ x 36 .... (1256) 2,500

Henri Lebasque

(1865–1957)

Birthplace: Champigné, Maine-et-Loire district, France.

1885 Goes to Paris. Attends Bonnat's studio for two years. Begins to work in the open.

1893 Meets Luce and Signac at the Salon des Indépendants, Paris. Joins Neo-Impressionism for a short time.

1900-06 Settles near the river Marne.

1903 Becomes a member of the Salon d'Automne, Paris.

1906 Discovers the French Riviera.

1923 Sets up the Salon des Tuileries, Paris.

1924 Settles at Le Cannet in the south of France. Executes a long series of nudes.

1925 Given an award by the Carnegie Institute, Pittsburgh.

1957 Died, Le Cannet. Retrospective exhibition at the Musée des Ponchettes, Nice.

Sales

DRAWINGS

1961–1962

Marthe Lebasque Sleeping, India ink, 8 x 10¾ ... (155) $ 100
A Child, black lead, 11 x 10½ .... (56) 60
Nude, stick of greasepaint, 10 x 13½ .... (168) 120

1963

*A Child Seated in a Park; Mother and Child in a
   Landscape; The Harbor Church*, three
   drawings, pencil and pen .... (225) $ 400
Dance, red chalk, 8 x 11 .... (242) 52
Standing Nude, pen, 8¾ x 5¾ .... (264) 50
Nude Taking Off Her Blouse, charcoal
   heightened with white, 10 x 4¾ .... (295) 64
Venice, pen, 10 x 7¼ .... (236) 63

1964

Studies of Breton Women, (1898), charcoal
   heightened with chalk, 11¾ x 18¾ .... (441) 158
Young Boy in a Short Shirt, India ink, 8 x 6 ...... (418) 60

1965

Seated Nude, Conté pencil, 23¾ x 15¾ .... (571) 220
Portrait of a Woman, black lead, 15 x 12 .... (494) 250
Study of a Woman, pen, 10¼ x 11½ .... (563) 60
Seated Young Boy, pencil, 9½ x 5¾ .... (582) 55

1966

Landscape, India ink, 4¾ x 6¾ .... (798) 75
Figures, pencil, 4¾ x 7 .... (798) 79
The Model, charcoal, 18¾ x 13 .... (829) 36
The Baby's Lunch, pencil and watercolor,
   4 x 3¼ .... (653) 90

1967

Maternity, pencil and watercolor, 10¾ x 17¾ .... (939) 332
Seated Nude, 12¾ x 14¾ .... (894) 56
Standing Nude, ink and blue pencil, 13¼ x 21 .... (848) 100
Woman Sewing, India ink, 16¾ x 14½ .... (858) 220
Young Woman Reading in a Garden, pencil and
   watercolor, 8¼ x 11 .... (989) 190
Landscape of La Bocca, red chalk, 11¾ x 17¾ .... (985) 166

1968–July 1969

Youthful Gambols, pencil, 16¼ x 16¾ .... (1051) 120
Seated Nude, pen, 7 x 8 .... (1063) 76
Nude, India ink, 13½ x 9½ .... (1127) 103
Maternity, black lead, 7½ x 4½ .... (1174) 172
Two Women in a Garden, ink and watercolor,
   9¼ x 7 .... (1061) 200
Seated Nude, pencil and watercolor, 8¾ x 6½ ... (1095) 200
Young Woman with a Guitar, pencil, 7½ x 6¾ ... (1225) 220
The Little Girl, black lead, 12¾ x 8 .... (1227) 38
Seated Nude, pencil and watercolor, 11 x 9½ .... (1231) 175
Seated Young Lady, charcoal on checkered
   paper, 17 x 11 .... (1231) 350
Seated Woman, pen, 9 x 6¾ .... (1253) 82
Le Poilu, 9 x 7¼ .... (1253) 60
Model with Her Arm Raised, charcoal,
   21 x 14¼ .... (1261) 220
Reclining Nude, charcoal, 14 x 22½ .... (1266) 250
Standing Nude, charcoal, 23¾ x 10¾ .... (1268) 696

WATERCOLORS

1961–1962

Coming Out of the Bath, watercolor, 7¾ x 4 ...... (82) 96
The Beach, watercolor, 5¼ x 6 .... (117) 65

1963

Nono Lying Down, gouache, 10½ x 7¾ .... (281) 167
The Siesta, watercolor, 4¼ x 5 .... (238) 92
Interior with a Woman, pastel, 18½ x 22 .... (208) 1,600
On the Beach, watercolor, 19¾ x 14¼ .... (271) 180

Landscape, watercolor, 10¾ x 7½ .... (236) $ 122
The Swing, watercolor, 6¾ x 8¾ .... (262)   80

1964

Woman with a Parasol, watercolor, 9½ x 12¼ .... (394)   82
Portrait of a Woman, pastel, 15¾ x 14 .... (370)   160
The Harbor, watercolor, 11 x 16¾ .... (366)   350
Landscape, pastel, 11 x 14 .... (441)   203

1965

The Harbor, watercolor, 12½ x 17 .... (516)   380
Woman Reading in the Garden, watercolor and
  gouache, 6¼ x 6 .... (617)   283
Landscape, watercolor, 3¾ x 6¼ .... (492)   90
The Garden, watercolor, 10 x 12 .... (563)   280
Two Young Girls, watercolor, 10¼ x 8 .... (606)   275
Seascape, watercolor, 9½ x 12¾ .... (647)   146
The "Argentina," watercolor, 11¾ x 8¼ .... (530)   80
Model Resting, pastel, 9½ x 18¾ .... (508)   120

1966

The Portal, watercolor and pencil, 10¾ x 7¾ ..... (721)   275
Beach Huts on the Seashore, watercolor, 9 x 14 .. (745)   723
Musing at the Window, watercolor, 10¼ x 7 ...... (691)   240
The Garden, watercolor, 9½ x 11 .... (663)   280
The Harbor, watercolor and India ink,
  9½ x 12½ .... (788)   120
Red Rocks, watercolor, 10¼ x 15 .... (655)   200
A Herd on the Hill, watercolor, 7 x 11 .... (817)   70
Standing Nude, Back View, watercolor,
  11½ x 7½ .... (668)   124
Young Lady at the Seaside, watercolor, 16 x 10 ... (666)   380
Woman with a Necklace, gouache, 15 x 21 .... (655)   230
Woman with a Guitar, watercolor, 13 x 12¼ ...... (742)   180
Woman with a Parasol, watercolor, 8½ x 9¾ ..... (793)   580

1967

The River Seine at Les Andelys, watercolor,
  10 x 14¾ .... (935)   132
The Harbor, watercolor, 7¼ x 9 .... (995)   250
Compiègne Forest, watercolor, 11 x 17½ .... (999)   370
Landscapes, two watercolors, each 3¾ x 6¼ ..... (1007)   260
The Bay, watercolor, 11½ x 15½ .... (949)   140
Figures on the Seashore, watercolor, 5¾ x 11¾ ... (976)   460
*Young Woman on the Bank of the River Seine, at
  Les Andelys,* watercolor, 10 x 14½ .... (898)   130
The Model with a Blouse, watercolor,
  10¾ x 6¾ .... (1002)   140
Sleeping Nymph, watercolor, 3½ x 5¼ .... (956)   116
Nude with a Red Sofa, watercolor, 11 x 10¼ ..... (934)   72
Model Resting, watercolor, 8 x 14¾ .... (848)   290
Fantastic Garden, watercolor, 13 x 10 .... (919)   271

1968–July 1969

The Fruit Stand, watercolor on paper laid down
  on canvas, 17¾ x 22 .... (1184)   720
The Blue Sofa, watercolor, 8 x 7½ .... (1066)   230
Woman on a Sofa, watercolor, 10¼ x 8 .... (1084)   170
Young Woman Seated in a Garden, watercolor,
  12¼ x 8¾ .... (1032)   380
Young Woman Leaning Upon a Cradle. 1927,
  watercolor, 10¾ x 17¾ .... (1134)   472
Fashionable Woman with a Blue Parrot, gouache,
  15 x 12¼ .... (1202)   590
Young Ladies with a Nosegay, watercolor,
  6 x 10 .... (1042)   160

Reclining Nude, watercolor, 6½ x 13 .... (1098) $ 180
Nudes, watercolor, 11¾ x 15½ .... (1026)   530
The Bath, watercolor, 10 x 14 .... (1048)   220
After the Bath, watercolor, 10 x 7 .... (1051)   270
Road at the Seaside, watercolor, 7½ x 10 .... (1078)   116
Boats, watercolor, 11 x 14 .... (1061)   350
Rocks of the Estérel, watercolor, 9½ x 13½ ..... (1171)   190
The Harbor, watercolor, 7½ x 9 .... (1172)   300
Fashionable Young Lady, watercolor, 7¼ x 6¾ .. (1223)   80
"The Sky Always Clearer than Water,"
  watercolor, 9 x 12¼ .... (1223)   240
The Terrace, watercolor, 10¼ x 8¼ .... (1225)   280
The West Indian Girl, watercolor, 10¾ x 13½ ... (1225)   400
On the Beach, watercolor, 6½ x 8½ .... (1225)   340
Boats, watercolor, 11 x 13½ .... (1231)   400
*Marthe Lebasque with a Dove at Her Terrace,
  Ste. Maxime,* (1906-08), 31½ x 50½ .... (1239)   9,120
The Bather, watercolor, 13 x 10¼ .... (1245)   210
The Beach, watercolor, 10 x 12¾ .... (1245)   350
Women at the Window, pen and watercolor,
  14½ x 8½ .... (1248)   350
Man Seated on the Beach, watercolor, 6 x 9 .... (1253)   142
The Model and His Dog, watercolor, 6 x 8 ...... (1253)   200
Young Servant Tying Up a Scarf, watercolor,
  11 x 8¾ .... (1261)   500
The Public Garden, watercolor, 6¾ x 9½ .... (1261)   320
Little Girl on the Terrace, watercolor, 9 x 8¼ ... (1261)   500
Nude on a Sofa, Her Arm Raised, watercolor,
  9 x 8 .... (1261)   300
Woman in a Mauve Dressing Gown, 8 x 8¾ ..... (1261)   560
Landscape with a Cactus, watercolor, 8¾ x 11¾ . (1261)   700
Bathing Time, watercolor, 8 x 11½ .... (1261)   620
Reclining Nude, Back View, watercolor,
  8¼ x 12¼ .... (1261)   440
Young Woman Seated on a Beach, watercolor,
  10 x 15¾ .... (1261)   580
Seated Women Watching the Sailboats,
  watercolor, 10 x 16¾ .... (1261)   2,000
Seated Nude Combing Her Hair, watercolor,
  12¼ x 9½ .... (1261)   400
The Harbor, watercolor, 10¼ x 15¾ .... (1261)   600
Women Seated on the Pier, watercolor,
  10¼ x 15¾ .... (1261)   2,000
Woman with a Hat on the Beach, watercolor,
  10¾ x 15 .... (1261)   960
Nude Seated on a Beach, watercolor, 11¾ x 8¾ . (1261)   460
Black Sails, watercolor, 10¼ x 16¼ .... (1261)   960
Life in the Cities and Life in the Fields,
  watercolor, 21 x 14¼ .... (1261)   420
Reclining Nude with a Mirror, watercolor,
  8¼ x 12¼ .... (1261)   600
Woman in a Rocking Chair, watercolor,
  8¾ x 8¾ .... (1261)   720
Woman in the Garden, watercolor, 8¼ x 11½ .... (1261)   600

PAINTINGS

1961–1962

The Village Church, 1897, 19½ x 24 .... (95)   460
Madame Lebasque Picking Flowers, 1906,
  21¾ x 14¾ .... (96)   2,300
Théâtre aux Armées, 1917, 29 x 36½ .... (90)   300
Young Woman Sewing, 18¼ x 13 .... (125)   2,020
Young Nude with a Flower Garland, 35¼ x 46 .... (155)   360

Nude with a Blue Cushion, 15 x 18¼ . . . . (177) $ 520
Girl Reading, 5¾ x 7½ . . . . (161) 290
The Woman with a Mandolin, 33¼ x 25¾ . . . . (27) 1,200

1963
Villefranche-sur-Mer, 32 x 21¼ . . . . (306) 1,900
The Model in the Sun, 34¾ x 45½ . . . . (306) 2,700
Landscape with a Nude, 1897, 17¾ x 14 . . . . (225) 950
Home Scene, (1907), 28½ x 25¼ . . . . (225) 700
Reclining Nude on a Green Background,
    25¾ x 32 . . . . (215) 1,020
Nono Lebasque on Her Terrace, 58 x 38½ . . . . (271) 400
Flowers, 21¼ x 17¾ . . . . (185) 540
The Two Sisters on the Terrace, 29 x 36½ . . . . . . (318) 1,200
Apple Trees in Blossom, 19¾ x 24 . . . . (276) 1,700
Crows, 29 x 32 . . . . (235) 180
Still Life with Watermelons, on panel,
    12¼ x 23¼ . . . . (314) 400
Pasture, 21¼ x 25¾ . . . . (203) 1,600
Harvest Scene, 32 x 32 . . . . (291) 1,600

1964
The Terrace, 1923, 19¾ x 24 . . . . (440) 680
Landscape, 18¾ x 12¾ . . . . (329) 1,100
Landscape, 24 x 19¾ . . . . (404) 940
Landscape of the South of France, 16¼ x 18¼ . . . . (418) 510
Still Life with a Nosegay, 32 x 21¼ . . . . (450) 760
Dahlias in a Persian Vase, 33 x 26 . . . . (395) 600
Young Ladies with Baskets of Flowers, on
    cardboard, 11 x 6¾ . . . . (335) 210
Musing, 11¾ x 15½ . . . . (346) 582
Woman with a Parasol, 17½ x 21 . . . . (405) 1,596
The Chilly Nude, 29 x 19¾ . . . . (401) 480

1965
The Creek, 16¼ x 13 . . . . (559) 640
The Fishing Party, 28 x 36½ . . . . (518) 1,100
Rest, 23¾ x 29 . . . . (631) 1,300
Landscape, 1893, 20 x 25¼ . . . . (611) 1,900
Springtime, 28½ x 31½ . . . . (507) 750
Study for the Portrait of Mademoiselle Zambelli,
    22 x 19¾ . . . . (540) 100
Nono, (1900), 36½ x 29 . . . . (556) 20

1966
Rowing, 29¼ x 36½ . . . . (685) 4,300
River Bank, (1908), 36 x 29 . . . . (721) 850
The Conversation on the Stairs, 1909, 39½ x 32 . . . (809) 2,000
The River Seine at Les Andelys, 29 x 36½ . . . . (758) 260
Banks of the River Seine, 9½ x 13 . . . . (653) 380
Boats at St. Tropez, 14 x 17 . . . . (796) 520
Nude on a Sofa, 29 x 19¾ . . . . (706) 640
Nude on an Upholstered Sofa, 24¼ x 15 . . . . (728) 1,700
Women by the Waterside, 29 x 21¼ . . . . (742) 1,500
Nude on the Beach . . . . (737) 2,000
The Violin Lesson on the Terrace, 57¾ x 38¾ . . . . (727) 1,000
Young Lady with an Easel, 19 x 9 . . . . (731) 720
Woman at Her Toilette, 13 x 9½ . . . . (724) 320
Young Lady with a Goat, 28½ x 23 . . . . (764) 560
Young Lady with a Blue Belt, on paper,
    12¾ x 8¾ . . . . (829) 160
Young Nude on a Sofa, 31½ x 25¼ . . . . (666) 2,600
The Conversation Under the Trees, 15 x 18¼ . . . . . (666) 2,000
Still Life, on canvas, 12¼ x 23 . . . . (692) 344
Vase of Flowers, 15 x 18 . . . . (813) 525

1967
Nono at the Seaside, 15 x 18¼ . . . . (995) $1,700
The Little Guitar Player, 25¾ x 18¼ . . . . (987) 1,440
The Musician, 50¾ x 35¼ . . . . (989) 2,500
Woman with a Hammock, 19¾ x 24 . . . . (912) 1,960
Woman Reading on a Sofa, 15 x 18¼ . . . . (845) 900
Young Lady at Her Toilette, 25¾ x 15 . . . . (900) 1,160
Young Woman in a Green Armchair, on
    cardboard, 19 x 19 . . . . (976) 1,020
Portrait, 21¾ x 18¼ . . . . (967) 2,712
Woman in a Blouse, Squatting on an Armchair,
    on cardboard, 19½ x 19½ . . . . (912) 1,020
Seated Young Woman, 18 x 13 . . . . (893) 900
Springtime Landscape, 15½ x 17¾ . . . . (832) 700
The Terrace at the Seaside, 25¾ x 32¼ . . . . (870) 2,000

1968–July 1969
Still Life, on cardboard, 11¾ x 19 . . . . (1127) 690
Still Life with Fish, 1909, 25¾ x 32 . . . . (1116) 1,440
Still Life with Watermelons, 12¼ x 23¼ . . . . (1051) 560
Théâtre aux Armées, 1917, 36½ x 29 . . . . (1127) 1,978
Flowers Before Slatted Shutters, 1921,
    17½ x 14¼ . . . . (1132) 1,605
Vase of Flowers, on paper, 17¾ x 14¼ . . . . (1113) 1,160
The Cigarette, 21¾ x 18¼ . . . . (1157) 3,500
Still Life, 25¾ x 29 . . . . (1061) 1,800
Nosegay, 23¼ x 19 . . . . (1213) 1,800
Flowers, 18¼ x 15 . . . . (1174) 1,610
The Fair-Haired Child, 18¼ x 15 . . . . (1051) 960
Woman with a Necklace, 33½ x 23¼ . . . . (1113) 820
Bather Seated on a Pier, on canvas, 12¾ x 15½ . . (1070) 1,534
Reclining Nude, 32 x 45¾ . . . . (1037) 2,460
Seated Nude, 32 x 25¾ . . . . (1186) 3,300
Nude Dressing, 31 x 22¾ . . . . (1030) 3,400
Woman Seated on a Sofa, 28½ x 36½ . . . . (1045) 1,200
Temple of Love, 23¾ x 32 . . . . (1132) 826
Landscape: The Banks of the Stream Yaudet,
    (1897), 20 x 24¼ . . . . (1113) 6,000
Raging Sea at Morgate, 23¾ x 29 . . . . (1060) 3,520
Great Trees on the Banks of a River, 36¾ x 29 . . (1161) 1,100
Rowing, (1912-14), 32 x 48¾ . . . . (1068) 3,776
The Park, 36½ x 29 . . . . (1119) 820
Morning Effect on the River Loing, 18¼ x 21¾ . . (1078) 1,160
Landscape with a River, 15 x 18¼ . . . . (1115) 1,760
The Old Bridge, 18¼ x 21¾ . . . . (1026) 2,400
Woman with a Parasol in a Landscape,
    29 x 36¾ . . . . (1026) 3,000
On the Terrace, 18¼ x 21¾ . . . . (1222) 800
Scene in a Park, 23¾ x 29 . . . . (1224) 4,700
The Terrace, oil on paper laid down on canvas,
    18¼ x 24 . . . . (1228) 4,440
On the Balcony, 24 x 19¾ . . . . (1231) 2,200
Portrait of a Woman, 16¼ x 13 . . . . (1231) 2,000
A Street at Champigné, Maine-et-Loire District,
    1890, 15 x 20½ . . . . (1240) 2,400
The Woman in a Hammock, 10¼ x 12¾ . . . . (1248) 5,000
Still Life, 13¼ x 21 . . . . (1248) 2,000
Playing in the Surf, 22¾ x 18¼ . . . . (1248) 1,800
Côte d'Azur, 13 x 19½ . . . . (1248) 1,600
Roses in a Vase, 18¼ x 15 . . . . (1254) 120
Great Trees by the River, 29 x 36½ . . . . (1255) 1,500
The Sea Seen from the Balcony, 18¼ x 21¾ . . . . . (1255) 5,100
On the Terrace, Ste. Maxime, (1914), 25¾ x 32 . . (1261) 19,000

Great Nude with a Leopard, (Le Cannet, 1926),
38½ x 64 .... (1261) $ 13,000

The Carpet on the Balcony, (Le Cannet, 1926),
39½ x 32 .... (1261) 8,400

Dancer with a Mirror, (1913), 18¼ x 21¾ .... (1261) 2,500

Vase of Flowers, 21¾ x 18¼ .... (1261) 4,400

Seated Nude, 25¾ x 19¾ .... (1261) 5,600

Crab Fishing, on panel, 6½ x 6 .... (1261) 800

Almond Trees in Blossom at Collioure, (1921),
21¼ x 25¾ .... (1261) 6,000

The Pheasant, 25¾ x 30½ .... (1261) 1,120

Japanese in Her Garden, oil on paper laid down
on canvas, 19¾ x 26 .... (1261) 5,200

Winter at Lagny, (1906), 21¼ x 29 .... (1261) 5,620

Woman with a Pink Parasol on the Balcony, (Ste.
Maxime 1914), 36½ x 29 .... (1261) 14,200

Great Fair-Haired Nude, 32 x 39½ .... (1261) 6,200

Madame Lebasque Playing the Guitar,
19¾ x 24 .... (1261) 2,400

Interior with a Bunch of Flowers, 29 x 21¼ ...... (1261) 5,500

Lagny, View of the Quai de Pomponne, 1904,
21¼ x 25¾ .... (1261) 9,000

Woman in a Blue Dressing Gown at Morgate,
(1924), 23¾ x 29 .... (1261) 4,500

Young Girl at the Piano, oval painting,
22 x 18¼ .... (1261) 1,400

Young Woman in Green with a Coral Necklace,
18¾ x 20 .... (1261) 2,100

Reclining Nude, Her Arms Raised, Blue Cushion,
25¾ x 32 .... (1261) 6,000

Young Lady on a Terrace, at the Seaside,
19¾ x 25¼ .... (1261) 7,000

Still Life with Oranges and Lemons, 18¼ x 21¾ . (1261) 3,600

Woman with a Blue Scarf, Reading, 21¾ x 18¼ . (1261) 2,800

The Nymphs' Bath, 45½ x 59¼ .... (1261) 68,000

Little Girl Writing, 15¾ x 17¾ .... (1261) 2,000

Great Trees, 10¾ x 8 .... (1261) 1,900

Nude with Cushions, 19¾ x 29 .... (1261) 2,400

Underwood Near the Sea, on panel, 6¾ x 10¼ .. (1261) 2,200

Young Girl with a White Parasol in a Garden,
29 x 23¾ .... (1261) 6,600

Reclining Nude with Tapestry, 25¾ x 39½ ...... (1261) 4,400

Young Woman by the Waves, 16¼ x 13 .... (1261) 2,000

Young Lady in Yellow, Reading, (1921),
21¼ x 25¾ .... (1261) 7,200

Maritime Landscape, on panel, 17¼ x 10 .... (1261) 2,520

Collioure Cove, 21¼ x 25¾ .... (1261) 5,400

Child with Flowers, 19¾ x 24 .... (1261) 8,400

Interior with a Woman Reading, 15 x 18¾ ...... (1261) 3,800

Teatime on the Terrace, (1914), 42 x 76¾ .... (1261) 16,400

Women Knitting by the Seaside, 19¾ x 24 ...... (1261) 5,300

Great Nude at the Curb of the Well, 43½ x 34¾ . (1261) 4,600

The Beach, 21¼ x 29 .... (1261) 8,600

Walking in the Country, 29 x 36½ .... (1261) 7,000

Walk by the Waterside, 23¾ x 29 .... (1261) 9,600

Young Woman in a Pink Hat, 21¾ x 18¼ ...... (1261) 3,500

Great Nude with a Bedizened Cloth, 35¼ x 51½ . (1261) 10,600

Seated Nude, 15 x 21¾ .... (1265) 2,600

Reclining Nude, 31¾ x 45¾ .... (1266) 4,100

Albert Lebourg

(1849–1928)

Birthplace: Montfort-sur-Risle, Eure district, France.

1865 Serves his apprenticeship with an architect in Rouen, but soon gives up this job to devote himself to painting.

1872 Appointed teacher of drawing at the Société des Beaux-Arts, Algiers. Begins to work in the open.

1877 Settles in Paris.

1879–80 Participates in the exhibitions of the Impressionist group, Paris.

1883 Participates in the Salon, Paris.

1891 Exhibits each year at the Société Nationale des Beaux-Arts, Paris.

1895 Stays in Holland, where he works in watercolor.

1896 Returns to Paris.

1899 Exhibition at Bernheim's, Paris.

1900 Executes some works for the World's Fair, Paris.

1903 Exhibits at the Galerie Paul Rosenberg, Paris.

1918 One-man show at the Galerie Georges Petit, Paris.

1924 Paralysis forces him to stop painting.

1928 Died, Rouen.

1932 Retrospective exhibition at the Musée de Rouen.

Sales

DRAWINGS

1961–1962

Landscape, charcoal, 9 x 11½ .... (12) $ 22

Landscape, charcoal, 12 x 19 .... (143) 99

1963

Lacroix Island in Rouen, 1872, charcoal,
11 x 17½ .... (293) 180

Algiers Harbor, charcoal, 11½ x 17¾ .... (234) 24

The Pont des Arts, wash, 7½ x 11½ .... (182) 120

1964

Landscape with a Wooden Bridge, Normandy,
charcoal, 12½ x 18¼ .... (384) 48

The Pont des Arts and the Institut, black lead,
4 x 6¼ .... (411) 76

1965

Notre-Dame, charcoal, 33¾ x 45½ .... (612) 500

1966

Algiers, charcoal heightened with chalk,
11¾ x 18¾ .... (718) 200

The Quays of the River Seine in Paris, charcoal,
6½ x 11¾ .... (804) 86

Riverside, charcoal, 11 x 17½ .... (726) 120

Landscape, charcoal and pen, 11 x 17¾ .... (652) 60

1967

Quai de Seine, pencil, 6½ x 11¾ .... (843) 200

Algiers Harbor, charcoal, 10¾ x 17½ .... (897) 160

The Quays of the River Seine and Notre-Dame,
charcoal, 27¼ x 39½ .... (978) 820

1968–July 1969

The Quays in Paris, charcoal and chalk, 12 x 19 . (1196) 680

Riverside with Poplars, charcoal, 32 x 18¼ ...... (1117) 400

Banks of the River Seine, charcoal, 6½ x 10 ..... (1038) $ 170

The Old Oak, charcoal and chalk on green paper,
18¼ x 12 .... (1088)   550

The Laid Table, Lamp Effect, charcoal,
11½ x 17¾ .... (1265)   400

WATERCOLORS

1961–1962

St. Honoré-les-Bains, watercolor, 14¼ x 21 .... (90)   600

1963

Place Henri IV, watercolor, 7½ x 11¾ .... (234)   204

Bridge Over the River Seine, watercolor,
12¼ x 18¼ .... (254)   800

1964

Sailboats in La Rochelle Harbor,[1] watercolor,
9½ x 11¾ .... (341)   620

Landscape, watercolor, 6½ x 9½ .... (409)   200

Landscape, watercolor, 11¾ x 19 .... (374)   225

1965

The Lock, watercolor, 7½ x 11½ .... (559)   300

The Lock, watercolor, 7½ x 11 .... (631)   460

Boats in La Rochelle Harbor, watercolor,
8 x 11¾ .... (612)   480

Landscape, watercolor and charcoal, 20 x 13 ..... (567)   176

1967

Lerdanne, Belgium, watercolor, 11½ x 19 .... (1007)   330

La Panne, watercolor, 11¾ x 18½ .... (919)   904

Landscape, watercolor, 8 x 12¼ .... (976)   640

Riverside, watercolor, 11¾ x 19½ .... (881)   774

1968–July 1969

The Forest, watercolor and charcoal,
19½ x 12¾ .... (1127)   322

Harnessed Horse, watercolor, 9 x 11¾ .... (1183)   330

La Panne, Belgium, watercolor, 11¾ x 19½ ..... (1116)   380

The Pont Neuf and the Statue of King Henry IV,
watercolor, 7¼ x 12 .... (1202)   1,420

Notre-Dame de Paris and the River Seine, pastel,
13¾ x 19½ .... (1227)   1,280

The Stream (recto), *Three Figures in a Boat*
(verso), watercolor, 6½ x 10 .... (1240)   408

Rouen: The Harbor, watercolor, 11½ x 18¾ ..... (1255)   2,400

PAINTINGS

1961–1962

Landscape of Normandy, 1872, on cardboard,
8¾ x 10¾ .... (155)   400

A View of Rotterdam, 1895, 18¾ x 29 .... (84)   2,197

A Mill in the Surroundings of Rotterdam, 1906,
13 x 21¾ .... (120)   1,800

The River Seine in Paris, 1912, 27 x 39½ .... (124)   2,760

The Viaduct of Auteuil, 14 x 26 .... (114)   1,240

The Bridge of Argenteuil, 19¾ x 29 .... (122)   1,921

The Iton Near Hondouville, 18¼ x 24 .... (171)   2,700

The Pont Marie, 15 x 21¾ .... (33)   2,440

The Quai d'Orsay in Paris, 15½ x 21¾ .... (150)   1,695

Mills Near Rotterdam, 18¼ x 29 .... (27)   2,360

The Pré aux Loups in Rouen, 18¼ x 29 .... (32)   2,200

Banks of the River Seine, Winter Effect, 1895,
15 x 21¾ .... (32)   5,000

[1]On the reverse, a wash study of the same subject matter.

The Little Thatch-Roofed Cottage in Normandy,
18¼ x 25¾ .... (32) $2,700

Banks of the River Seine, 15¾ x 25¾ .... (26)   2,000

Banks of the River Seine at Dieppe-Dalle,
19¾ x 29 .... (26)   3,220

The River Seine at La Bouille, 18¼ x 28½ .... (147)   1,400

The River Seine at La Bouille, 19¾ x 29 .... (76)   2,600

A Bend of the River Seine at Bougival,
14 x 25½ .... (6)   3,729

Surroundings of Rouen, 15¾ x 25¾ .... (93)   972

Banks of the River Seine Near Rouen,
19¾ x 24 .... (39)   2,500

The Pont St. Michel, 19¾ x 29 .... (30)   3,700

Lighters Alongside the Quays, 15 x 21¾ .... (160)   2,400

Marshy Landscape, 5¾ x 9¾ .... (152)   375

Seascape, 24 x 19¾ .... (168)   1,100

A Square in Dieppe, 15 x 17¾ .... (164)   1,648

Quay of La Rochelle, 18¼ x 21¾ .... (176)   2,300

1963

Landscape, 15¾ x 25¾ .... (232)   2,486

Vase of Flowers, 1874, oil on paper laid down on
board, 12¾ x 10 .... (224)   800

Banks of the River Seine, 1895, 14 x 25¾ .... (257)   900

A Mill in Holland, 1896, 20¼ x 29 .... (258)   2,200

The Footbridge of the Institut, 18¼ x 30 .... (258)   3,000

The Harbor, 16¼ x 23¾ .... (258)   3,200

Fishing Harbor in Holland, 15 x 25 .... (198)   2,800

The River Seine at La Bouille, 18¼ x 33½ .... (198)   3,020

The River Seine in Paris, 15¾ x 25¾ .... (296)   5,000

Notre-Dame from the Quays, 20½ x 29 .... (259)   3,700

Banks of the River Marne at St. Maur Park,
18¼ x 33¾ .... (259)   6,040

River Bank, 18¼ x 33½ .... (285)   3,390

Floods, 16¼ x 29 .... (251)   940

Landing Stages of the Bateaux-Mouche,
18¼ x 30 .... (234)   1,460

Sunset on the Banks of the River Seine,
15¾ x 28½ .... (234)   1,620

Banks of the River Seine, 12¼ x 23 .... (235)   800

Banks of the River Seine, 18¼ x 30 .... (224)   5,000

Lighters on the River Seine, on panel,
14¾ x 14¾ .... (216)   576

The Shady Walk, 18¼ x 21¾ .... (215)   1,560

Old Street at Mont-Ferrand, 25¾ x 15½ .... (215)   1,300

Honfleur Harbor, 15¾ x 25¾ .... (262)   2,000

Landscape with a Mill, 32 x 23¾ .... (262)   4,100

In Rouen Harbor, 14 x 25¾ .... (254)   1,600

The Pré aux Loups in Rouen, 18¼ x 29 .... (182)   2,100

The Pré aux Loups in Rouen, 18¼ x 29 .... (291)   1,200

Surroundings of Rouen, 18¾ x 30 .... (190)   2,660

Landscape, on panel, 6 x 9½ .... (179)   450

1964

Sailboats Leaving the Harbor, on cardboard,
10 x 13 .... (347)   6,200

Banks of the River Seine, 15½ x 28 .... (367)   4,699

The River Seine, 15¾ x 29 .... (458)   2,612

The Rising of Waters, Paris, 1896, 18¼ x 25¾ .... (472)   2,500

The Sailboat on the River Seine, 19¾ x 24 ...... (352)   2,800

The Old Trocadéro, 1897, 14¾ x 24 .... (454)   3,317

Notre-Dame de Paris, 23¼ x 19½ .... (405)   1,741

A Church in a Landscape, 1897, 19 x 28 .... (416)   2,902

The Viaduct of Auteuil, 14 x 26 .... (332)   1,400

Notre-Dame de Paris, on panel, 13 x 10 .... (346)   520

Fog on the River Seine, 18¼ x 30½ . . . . (397) $2,100

Lighters Alongside the Quay by the Banks of the River Seine, 18¼ x 30 . . . . (351)   1,600

The River Seine in Paris, 1910, 15 x 24 . . . . (407)   2,938

View of the Mont Dore, 15¾ x 29 . . . . (395)   1,000

Hilly Landscape, 19½ x 28 . . . . (440)   1,882

Landscape, 15 x 24 . . . . (371)   1,600

Riverside, 21¼ x 29¾ . . . . (327)   2,600

Banks of the River Seine, 15¾ x 25¾ . . . . (359)   2,220

The Road at Hondouville, 21¾ x 18¼ . . . . (341)   1,700

The Iton at Hondouville, 18¼ x 30 . . . . (401)   2,500

Riverside, 18¼ x 33¾ . . . . (401)   2,200

The Cliff of St. Valéry, 15½ x 28 . . . . (405)   1,596

Rouen, 17½ x 21 . . . . (448)   1,500

Wolves' Valley, Down Ste. Catherine Slope, Rouen, 18¼ x 30 . . . . (465)   3,600

Seascape, 13½ x 26 . . . . (446)   3,700

1965

In the Harbor of La Rochelle, 19¾ x 29 . . . . (564)   2,520

View of Meudon, 1887, 23¾ x 40¼ . . . . (591)   5,222

The Start of the Ferry on the Low Seine, 29 x 39½ . . . . (612)   6,700

Banks of the River Schie at Delft, Mist Effect, 1896, 15¾ x 25¾ . . . . (612)   3,020

Windmill at Delft-Haven, 1896, 15 x 21¾ . . . . (612)   3,600

The Outlet of Dieppe Harbor, 14¼ x 25¾ . . . . (559)   3,000

Etretat Cliffs, 18¼ x 29¼ . . . . (559)   2,000

Valley of the River Seine (Carrière St. Denis), on canvas laid down on board, 18¼ x 30 . . . . (545)   2,688

A Quay Along the River Seine, 15 x 22 . . . . (539)   900

Banks of the River Seine in Paris, 15 x 24 . . . . (629)   4,498

The River Seine at Bougival, on panel, 6 x 9½ . . . . (612)   1,020

Standing Figure, on panel, 5¾ x 9 . . . . (612)   440

The Loading Dock of the Steamboat, La Bouille, 19¾ x 29 . . . . (583)   4,063

Dieppe Harbor, 14 x 25¾ . . . . (600)   7,260

The River, 18¼ x 24 . . . . (518)   3,600

The Pont de Sèvres, 15½ x 29 . . . . (521)   4,700

The River Seine in Rouen, 19¾ x 25¾ . . . . (553)   2,800

A Plain in the Sun, 15 x 24 . . . . (522)   1,520

Banks of the River Allier in Summer, 15 x 24 . . . . . (571)   1,600

Riverside, 19 x 25 . . . . (581)   3,200

The Lock of Charenton Dock, 19¾ x 29 . . . . (512)   3,100

1966

A House in a Landscape at Dawn, 15 x 28 . . . . (741)   2,200

Surroundings of Clermont-Ferrand, 1886, 9 x 15¾ . . . . (808)   1,741

The Canal St. Denis in Winter, 1891, 25¾ x 26 . . . (675)   4,700

Notre-Dame from the Quai de la Tournelle, 15¾ x 24 . . . . (814)   7,000

Sky Effect Over Rouen, 1894, 19¾ x 29 . . . . (808)   2,902

The River Seine in Rouen, 24 x 39½ . . . . (669)   5,000

Landscape at Hondouville, 1897, 15½ x 25 . . . . (689)   1,244

The Edge of Lake Geneva at St. Gingolph, 1900, 21¾ x 32 . . . . (724)   3,420

The Towpath, 1907, 19¾ x 29 . . . . (809)   4,200

The River Seine in Rouen and the Faubourg St. Sever, 1908, 19¾ x 39¼ . . . . (819)   9,600

Lake Geneva at St. Gingolph, 1911, 18¼ x 33¾ . . . (819)   2,800

View of Rouen, 14 x 25¾ . . . . (797)   4,859

Honfleur Bay, 18¼ x 34 . . . . (797)   7,006

Rustic Bridge Near Rouen, 19¾ x 28½ . . . . (713)   3,500

Riverside, 15½ x 25¼ . . . . (813) $1,714

Courbevoie in Autumn, 19½ x 25½ . . . . (666)   3,600

Banks of the River Seine Around St. Cloud, 18¼ x 30 . . . . (666)   3,000

Banks of the River Seine, 14 x 25¾ . . . . (702)   3,000

The Viaduct of Arcueil, 14 x 25¾ . . . . (685)   3,040

Lighters on a River, 12 x 21 . . . . (813)   1,161

A Quay in La Rochelle, 14¾ x 23½ . . . . (823)   3,536

The River Seine at Bougival, 19¾ x 29 . . . . (793)   3,620

The Quays of Notre-Dame, 15 x 21¾ . . . . (727)   1,440

Lighters on the River Seine at Bercy, 15½ x 28½ . . . . (711)   4,400

1967

Snow Effect at the Gates of Paris, 1890, 18¼ x 25¾ . . . . (976)   5,300

Algiers, The Market, 1874, 14¼ x 11 . . . . (976)   820

Landscape Near Annemasse, (1890), 19¾ x 29 . . . . (963)   2,750

The River Seine at the Louvre, 15 x 25¾ . . . . (935)   5,000

Riverside, on panel, 5¾ x 9 . . . . (935)   1,620

The River Seine at the Louvre, 15 x 25¾ . . . . (878)   6,200

The River Seine in Paris, 15 x 18¼ . . . . (978)   6,600

Notre-Dame de Paris, 16 x 12¾ . . . . (898)   1,370

The River Seine at Notre-Dame, 15 x 21¾ . . . . (901)   5,200

The River Seine Near Rouen, 18¼ x 25¾ . . . . (849)   2,000

Banks of the River Seine Near Rouen, 21¼ x 32 . . . . (901)   7,600

The River Seine in Rouen and the Faubourg St. Germain, 1908, 19¾ x 39¼ . . . . (967)   5,876

Rouen Harbor, on cardboard, 10½ x 16 . . . . (995)   1,600

Rouen, 19¾ x 29 . . . . (911)   3,600

Rouen Under Snow, 18¼ x 33¾ . . . . (976)   7,000

Landscape in Normandy, 17¾ x 25¼ . . . . (984)   6,600

The Slope of St. Valéry, 19¾ x 28¾ . . . . (926)   3,980

Surroundings of Pont-du-Château, 14¾ x 24 . . . . . (857)   2,500

The End of Autumn Near Hondouville, 24 x 32 . . . (912)   3,900

The Bridge, Sunset, 15 x 24 . . . . (940)   1,306

Scene on a River, 15¾ x 25¾ . . . . (870)   2,250

The Shady River, 25¾ x 21¼ . . . . (978)   2,100

The River Seine in Rouen, 1908, 19¾ x 39¼ . . . . . . (918)   6,554

1968–July 1969

Hondouville, a Bridge Over the Iton at the Entrance of the Village, 15¾ x 25¾ . . . . (1210)   5,600

Sunrise with White Frost at Hondouville, 19¾ x 25¾ . . . . (1116)   5,600

The River Seine Near Rouen, 18¼ x 33¾ . . . . (1127)   4,140

Dredger on the River Seine, 11¼ x 20 . . . . (1116)   1,240

Banks of the River Seine, 15¾ x 25¾ . . . . (1075)   4,200

Outlet of Dieppe, 14 x 25¾ . . . . (1113)   4,380

The Quays and Notre-Dame Under Snow, 12¼ x 18¾ . . . . (1219)   4,000

The River Seine Near Rouen, 18¼ x 26 . . . . (1051)   3,900

Dieppe, 10¾ x 16¼ . . . . (1051)   3,400

Banks of the River Seine at St. Cloud, 18¾ x 30 . . (1080)   3,500

The River Seine in Flood in Paris, 16¼ x 25¾ . . . . (1026)   3,820

Banks of the River Seine at St. Sever, 18¼ x 29 . . (1039)   5,200

Landscape with a Mill, 1896 . . . . (1156)   4,420

Paris: The River Seine and St. Gervais, 15 x 24 . . (1049)   4,200

The Willows, 11 x 17½ . . . . (1049)   1,400

Sailboats, on panel, 9¾ x 13 . . . . (1140)   840

Canal in Rotterdam, 17¾ x 25 . . . . (1187)   4,012

Canal in Rotterdam, 15 x 21¾ . . . . (1118)   3,600

Boats and Mills in Rotterdam, 14 x 25¾ . . . . (1106)   3,700

Surroundings of Pont-du-Château, 14¾ x 24 .... (1053) $1,420

Fluvial Landscape, Snowy Weather, 23¾ x 42¾ . (1079)   6,200

Summer Morning in Normandy, 25¾ x 36½ ..... (1183)   7,200

The Glade, 15½ x 18½ .... (1196)   2,160

Landscape, 16¾ x 27¾ .... (1026)   2,000

Village on a Hillside, 10¼ x 17¾ .... (1070)   1,558

The Mont Dore, 19¾ x 29 .... (1116)   3,500

The Bridge Over the River Rhône, St. Maurice,
    20 x 29 .... (1193)   4,708

Rue D'Alger, on panel, 16½ x 10¾ .... (1051)   500

The Mosque, 1876, 19 x 12¼ .... (1131)   1,400

On the Quays in La Rochelle, 15½ x 24 .... (1226)   18,400

The Fishing Harbor, 16¼ x 25¼ .... (1250)   12,800

Outlet of Dieppe Harbor, 1882 .... (1252)   14,000

Bank of the River Seine, 15¾ x 29 .... (1259)   10,000

Rouen Harbor, 14 x 25¾ .... (1252)   10,000

Le Havre Harbor, 15½ x 28½ .... (1252)   11,200

Rouen Harbor, 12¾ x 21¾ .... (1255)   6,400

Sunset at Andrésy, 1898, 19¾ x 29 .... (1258)   12,000

The River Seine at the Ile St. Louis, 15¾ x 25¾ . (1258)   11,200

Rouen Harbor, 21¼ x 29 .... (1258)   5,600

Fog Effect, 14¼ x 23¼ .... (1261)   7,200

The River Seine at the Louvre, 15¾ x 25¾ ..... (1262)   4,000

Sail and Mill in Rotterdam, 1896, 18¼ x 25¾ .... (1268)   6,496

La Bouille, 18¼ x 29 .... (1268)   8,584

River Bank, 15 x 21¾ .... (1268)   11,600

Le Corbusier

(1887-1965)

Birthplace: La Chaux-de-Fonds, Switzerland—as Charles-Edouard Jeanneret.

1900   Studies engraving at the local art college and becomes very much influenced by the painter l'Eplattenier, who turns him toward architecture.

1910-11   Travels to Germany, Turkey, Greece, and Italy.

1917   Settles in Paris, where he remains for seventeen years.

1918   Takes up painting—and will paint throughout his life. With his friend Ozenfant, creates "Purism."

1920   With Ozenfant, exhibits at the Galerie Druet, Paris.

1922   Participates in the Salon des Indépendants, Paris. Establishes an architect's business.

1923   Exhibition at the Galerie Léonce Rosenberg, Paris.

1922-24   Designs houses for Ozenfant and Lipchitz, among others.

1928   Decides to sign his pictures Le Corbusier, his grandfather's name.

1936   Works with the Ministry of Education and Public Health in Rio de Janeiro. Produces various projects relating to the Musée National d'Art Moderne, Paris.

1938   Retrospective exhibition of his paintings at the Kunsthaus, Zurich.

1940-49   Investigates sculpture in relation to architecture.

1953   Exhibition at the Musée d'Art Moderne, Paris.

1954   Exhibition at the Kunsthalle, Bern.

1957   Exhibition at the Kunsthaus, Zurich.

1962-63   Exhibition at the Musée d'Art Moderne, Paris.

1965   Died, in the south of France, drowned in a bathing accident.

Sales

DRAWINGS

1961-1962

Composition, 1941, pen and watercolor,
    22¼ x 17¾ .... (105) $1,243

1963

Cubist Still Life, black lead and colored pencil,
    6½ x 5¾ .... (204)   400

The "Moscophore," colored chalk and pencil,
    20 x 12 .... (255)   247

1964

Two Nudes, 1936, ink and watercolor, 8¼ x 12 .... (416)   193

1965

Composition, 1940-41, ink and watercolor,
    22½ x 16¾ .... (582)   138

1968–July 1969

Bowls, Pipes, and Rolled Papers, 1919, pencil,
    17½ x 22 .... (1269)   3,840

Glasses, Pipes, and Bottles, 1920, pencil on
    tracing paper, 23¼ x 28 .... (1269)   1,680

Violin and Violin Case, 1920, charcoal on tracing
    paper, 33¾ x 37¾ .... (1269)   7,680

Accordion and Decanter, 1926, colored pencil on
    tracing paper, laid down on board,
    17¼ x 14 .... (1269)   3,840

Siphons and Beer Glass, 1928, pencil and colored
    pencil, 10½ x 8¼ .... (1269)   1,680

The Red Hand, (1930), pencil and colored pencil,
    8¼ x 12 .... (1269)   2,280

The Oyster Gatherer of Arcachon, (1932),
    8¼ x 10¾ .... (1269)   1,920

The Two Women, 1932, colored pencil and pencil,
    12¼ x 8¼ .... (1269)   1,872

The Three Seated Women, 1940-46, charcoal,
    colored pencil, and wash, 24¾ x 19 .... (1269)   1,320

Liveliness, 1950, collage, brush and India ink on
    brown paper laid down on board, 20 x 25¾ . (1269)   2,640

The Amazons, 1958, collage, brush and India ink,
    27¼ x 40 .... (1269)   5,760

Two Women, 1938-59, brush, India ink, and white
    gouache, 17 x 13½ .... (1269)   960

Ride, 1964, colored pencil, wash, brush, India ink,
    and blue ink .... (1269)   2,040

WATERCOLORS

1963

The Woman in Blue, 1937, watercolor and
    collage, 8¼ x 12 .... (295)   224

Composition with a Violin, 1925, watercolor,
    10½ x 8¼ .... (222)   220

1964

White and Black, 1934, watercolor, 11¾ x 8 ...... (366) $ 100

Profile, 1951, watercolor, 10¾ x 8¼ .... (480)   130

1968–July 1969

Ozon 40, pen and watercolor, 10¾ x 8¼ .... (1101)   1,196

Bottles and Glasses, 1926, pastel and pencil on tracing paper, 21½ x 25½ .... (1269)   6,240

Table, Bottle, and Book, 1926, pencil and pastel, 17¼ x 13¾ .... (1269)   2,880

Study of Sculpture, 1940, pen, India ink, and watercolor on paper tablecloth, 19½ x 15½ .. (1269)   1,920

Study of a Tapestry, 1940, 19¾ x 13 .... (1269)   2,040

Carnival, watercolor, collage, pen, brush, and India ink, 1940, 8 x 10½ .... (1269)   1,800

Drunkenness, 1958, brush, India ink, and watercolor on paper laid down on board, 24¾ x 38½ .... (1269)   3,840

The Fox, 1936–58, brush, India ink, and watercolor, 24¾ x 38½ .... (1269)   4,560

Bull, 1952–61, collage, gouache, brush, and India ink, 44¼ x 27¼ .... (1269)   4,560

Vapeurs, 1924–62, collage, gouache, brush, and India ink, 19¾ x 43¼ .... (1269)   4,320

PAINTINGS

1963

The Woman in Red, 1937, collage, pen, and watercolor, 8¼ x 12 .... (222)   460

1964

Composition, 1930, on cardboard, 11½ x 9 .... (471)   2,260

1966

Composition, 1930, 39½ x 32 .... (656)   660

Composition, 1930, 39½ x 32 .... (812)   1,120

Composition, 1937, collage, 8¼ x 12¼ .... (669)   424

1968–July 1969

Violin, Glass, and Bottles, 1925, 39½ x 32 .... (1269)   21,600

The Violet Dice, 1926, 23¼ x 28½ .... (1269)   14,400

Table, Bottle, and Book, 1926, 39½ x 32 .... (1269)   12,000

Glasses and Bottles with Vermilion, 1928, 51¼ x 35 .... (1269)   21,600

The Oyster Gatherer of Arcachon, 1928, 16¼ x 13 .... (1269)   6,720

Still Life with Fork, 1929, 57½ x 44¾ .... (1269)   24,000

Lea, 1931, 57½ x 45 .... (1269)   20,400

Lively Perspective, 1932, 35 x 57½ .... (1269)   19,200

The Cart of Wood and the Bathers, 35 x 45¾ .... (1269)   20,400

Green Athlete, 1938, 51 x 32 .... (1269)   19,200

The Two Sisters, 1938, 39½ x 32 .... (1269)   15,600

Embrace, 1938, 63¾ x 51¼ .... (1269)   21,600

Hand Crossed on the Head, 1928–39, 39½ x 32 .. (1269)   18,000

Still Life with a Red Scarf, 1940, 38½ x 51¼ ..... (1269)   21,600

Bull XV, 1957, 63½ x 50¾ .... (1269)   26,400

Crossbow, 1961, enamel paint on metal, 24¾ x 34 .... (1269)   3,600

Reclining Woman, 1961, enamel paint on metal, 24¾ x 34 .... (1269)   3,600

Still Life with Several Objects, 1923-44-49-52-53, 44¾ x 57½ .... (1269)   24,000

Fernand Léger

(1881–1955)

Birthplace: Argentan, Normandy, France.

1897–99   Studies architecture in Caen.

1900   Goes to Paris, where he works with an architect.

1903   Attends the Ecole des Arts Décoratifs and the Académie Julian, Paris.

1905–06   Settles at La Ruche in Montparnasse. Comes under the influence of Impressionism and then of Cézanne. Trip to Corsica.

1909   Breaks away from Impressionism and turns to Cubism. Makes friends with Apollinaire, Max Jacob, Robert Delaunay, and Henri Rousseau.

1910   Meets the dealer Kahnweiler, who introduces him to Braque and Picasso. Meets the future "Section d'Or" group at Jacques Villon's.

1911   His "Nudes in the Forest" create a sensation at the Salon des Indépendants, Paris. Participates in the first exhibition of the "Section d'Or," Paris.

1912   Participates in the Salon d'Automne and the Salon des Indépendants, Paris. First one-man show at the Galerie Kahnweiler, Paris.

1913   Signs a contract with Kahnweiler.

1918–19   Illustrates works by Blaise Cendrars. Marries Jeanne Lohy.

1920   Meets Le Corbusier.

1921–24   Continues to elaborate his own way of painting, becoming more and more concerned to express the life of his time. Succeeds perfectly in his attempt to insert man into the world of machinery depicted in his compositions. Meets Van Doesburg and Mondrian. Designs stage decorations and costumes for a ballet by Arthur Honegger and for *La Création du Monde* by Darius Milhaud. Collaborates in films directed by Abel Gance and Marcel l'Herbier. Sets up his own academy. Produces the film *Ballet Mécanique.* Trip to Italy.

1925   Executes murals for the Exposition des Arts Décoratifs, Paris. Lectures at the Collège de France.

1928   One-man show at the Flechtheim Gallery, Berlin.

1931   First trip to the U.S.

1933   Exhibits at the Kunsthaus, Zurich.

1935   Second trip to the U.S., with Le Corbusier. Exhibits at the Museum of Modern Art, New York, and the Art Institute of Chicago.

1937   Executes a mural for the Palais de la Découverte, Paris. Exhibits at the Artek Gallery, Helsinki.

1938   Third trip to the U.S. Decorates the apartment of Nelson Rockefeller, in New York. Delivers lectures on "Color in Architecture" at Yale University.

1940–45   Spends World War II in the U.S. Teaches at Yale University and Mills College, California. Collaborates in Hans Richter's film *Dreams that Money Can Buy.* Exhibits at the Paul Rosenberg Gallery, the Valentine Gallery, and the Kootz Gallery, New York.

1946   Returns to France. One-man show at the Galerie Louis Carré, Paris. Executes a mosaic for the church of Assy, Savoie district.

1949   Retrospective exhibition at the Musée National d'Art Moderne, Paris. Designs the stage decorations for *Bolivar,* an opera by Darius Milhaud. Series of lithographs entitled "Le Cirque."

1950	Exhibits at the Tate Gallery, London. Death of his wife.
1951	Executes stained glass for the church of Audincourt, Doubs district. Exhibits his first polychrome sculptures at the Galerie Louise Leiris, Paris.
1952	Participates in the Venice Biennial. Marries his pupil, Nadine Khodessevitch. Executes a mural for the U.N., New York.
1953	Exhibits at the Museum of Modern Art, New York.
1955	Given an award by the São Paulo Biennial. Retrospective exhibition at the Musée de Lyon. Died, Gif-sur-Yvette, near Paris.
1956	Retrospective exhibition at the Musée des Arts Décoratifs, Paris.
1960	Inauguration of the Musée Fernand Léger at Biot in the south of France.

Sales

DRAWINGS

1961–1962

The Smoker, 1917, ink and brush, 20½ x 14¾ ..... (129) $4,668

Piece of Flannel, 1929, pencil, 10¾ x 8¾ .... (20) 2,212

Face, India ink and chalk, 17 x 12¾ .... (93) 1,356

Composition, India ink, 14¾ x 12¾ .... (31) 1,043

Kneeling Woman in the Nude, India ink, 12¾ x 9½ .... (76) 190

Musical Landscape, 1930, India ink, 9½ x 12¾ .... (68) 640

Composition, 1935, pencil, 12¼ x 9½ .... (149) 822

Composition, 1943, ink, pen, and brush, 8½ x 10 .. (106) 497

Bust of a Woman, 1949, India ink, 9¾ x 6½ ...... (105) 542

1963

Composition, 1930, 9 x 11¾ .... (215) 450

Section of a Stained-Glass Window, 1933, pen, 13½ x 11½ .... (283) 475

Abstract Composition, pen and wash, 10¾ x 8 .... (216) 439

Still Life, India ink, 13½ x 18¾ .... (208) 600

Woman with a Parrot, India-ink wash on tracing paper .... (270) 4,900

1964

Kneeling Woman in the Nude, 1910, pen, 13 x 10 .... (408) 180

Standing Woman in the Nude, 1910, India ink, 11¾ x 6½ .... (383) 396

The Hand and the Siphon, 1921, 9 x 5¾ .... (460) 1,600

Still Life, 1928, pencil, 11½ x 8½ .... (387) 829

Two Seated Figures, 1934, ink on red paper, 25¾ x 19¾ .... (458) 1,161

Study for "Divers," 1942, India ink, 21¾ x 29 ..... (354) 3,100

Portrait of Rimbaud, 1948, India ink on tracing paper, 10 x 8 .... (460) 380

The Clarinetist, 1948, ink and gouache, 12¾ x 9¼ .... (455) 829

Woman's Head, 1949, India ink and watercolor, 13 x 10 .... (329) 1,300

1965

Nude, (1908–10), pen, 12 x 7¼ .... (539) 750

Woman in the Nude, 1909, pen, 9¾ x 4½ .... (617) 350

Contrast of Forms, 1913, wash and gouache, 25 x 19½ .... (615) 22,000

Drawing for "The Game of Cards," 1916, pencil, wash, and oil on paper, 20¼ x 14¾ .... (624) 6,081

The City, 1916, wash, 7 x 5 .... (516) 760

The Smoker, 1917, pen and wash, 20½ x 14¾ ..... (522) $3,040

Composition, 1923, pencil, 9 x 13 .... (539) 1,600

Composition, India ink, 14¾ x 12¾ .... (567) 1,085

Root, 1932, pencil, 14½ x 10¾ .... (609) 2,600

Two Nudes, 1939, pen, 14 x 11¾ .... (616) 2,560

The Five Clowns, 1952, 15½ x 21¾ .... (615) 4,000

1966

Still Life with Pens and Pencils, pen and wash, 11½ x 9 .... (734) 949

Study of a Nude, 1909, pen, 12¼ x 9 .... (665) 375

War Landscape, (1914–15), ink and oil on paper, 8¾ x 5¾ .... (750) 3,593

Structure, 1919, India ink, 10¼ x 8 .... (703) 1,900

Woman, (1927), pencil on brown paper, 10¾ x 6¾ .... (703) 2,000

Still Life with a Statuette of Mercury, 1949, India ink and watercolor, 11 x 9 .... (738) 2,952

1967

Reclining Nude, 1909, pen, 9½ x 12¾ .... (839) 180

Tree and House, 1925, pencil, 10¼ x 7¾ .... (1005) 1,778

Still Life, 1930, pen, 9½ x 12¾ .... (939) 1,520

Composition, 1931, blue chalk heightened with white, 25 x 19 .... (982) 2,370

Black Figure, 1931, pencil and watercolor, 18 x 14 .... (940) 1,596

Two Nudes, 1939, India ink and gouache, 16 x 12¼ .... (975) 1,400

Young Woman, pencil, 14¾ x 11 .... (975) 6,000

Circus Scene, "Vive la Ste. Jeanne," 1948, pencil, India ink, and watercolor, 14 x 21 .... (930) 2,599

Portrait of Arthur Rimbaud, 1949, pen and watercolor, 25 x 19¾ .... (870) 2,250

Builders, a Study of Hands, 1951, pencil and ink, 19 x 11½ .... (881) 1,161

The Parade, 1952, India ink, 25¼ x 32½ .... (994) 2,800

Self-Portrait, 1955, wash, 20¼ x 14 .... (951) 871

1968–July 1969

Two Reclining Women, 1913, ink with gouache lights, 19½ x 25 .... (1068) 24,072

Verdun: The Roofs, 1916, pen and wash, 7½ x 5¾ .... (1212) 800

Composition, 1938, ink and gouache on pale blue paper, 10 x 12¼ .... (1018) 3,250

Moving Geometrical Element, India ink and gouache, 10½ x 9½ .... (1191) 1,298

Head of Rimbaud, 1948, India ink heightened with watercolor, 13¼ x 9¾ .... (1080) 1,500

Here Comes the Time of Murderers, 1948, India ink and red gouache, 12¾ x 9½ .... (1203) 1,487

The Dove, 1948, India ink, 12 x 17 .... (1134) 2,124

Study of Plants, 1948, pen and watercolor, 13 x 10 .... (1068) 1,180

Bust of a Woman, 1948, India ink and gouache, 13 x 9½ .... (1134) 1,888

The Beautiful Cyclist, 1949, India ink heightened with watercolor, 17½ x 13½ .... (1134) 3,540

Study of a Hand, 1951, India ink and watercolor, 22¼ x 16¾ .... (1114) 2,356

The Acrobat and the Horse, 1953, India ink and gouache, 12¾ x 17½ .... (1109) 2,500

Composition, India ink, 12¾ x 11¾ .... (1101) 1,518

Nude in Front of a Window, 1921, 15 x 12 ...... (1246) 7,750

Composition with a Compass, 1929, pen and India
  ink, 11½ x 8¾ .... (1246) $2,500
Country Rest, 1921, double sided, 14¾ x 10¼ .... (1256)   4,800
Nude Seated on the Ground, pen and sepia wash,
  10¼ x 9¼ .... (1267)   340
Still Life, 1924, black lead, 12½ x 9 .... (1268)   6,032
The Two Women, ink, 25 x 19 .... (1268)   1,728
At the Café, Fragment, (1915), pen and brown
  ink, 6½ x 9 .... (1273)   3,280
Self-Portrait,[1] gray wash, 20 x 14 .... (1273)   1,512
Departure, black and colored ink, 12¾ x 9 ...... (1273)   706

WATERCOLORS

1961–1962

Composition, 1917, watercolor in black and gray,
  15½ x 11 .... (106)   4,407
The Deck of the Towboat, 1919, watercolor,
  14 x 16¾ .... (140)   3,295
Composition,[2] (1924), gouache, 14½ x 11¾ .... (3)   1,900
Yellow Element, 1932, gouache, 20½ x 16¼ .... (18)   2,124
Composition, 1932, watercolor, 17¾ x 14¾ .... (143)   3,390
Composition, watercolor, 15¾ x 27¾ .... (145)   11,850
Cows, 1932, watercolor, 17¾ x 14¾ .... (93)   2,486
Composition with Serge Lifar, 1934, gouache,
  19¾ x 25¾ .... (70)   6,162
Two Profiles with the Aloe, 1937, gouache,
  12 x 18¾ .... (164)   3,158
Composition, (1936), gouache, 12¾ x 15 .... (93)   3,277
Composition, 1942, gouache and oil, 10¾ x 11¾ .. (106)   1,582
Stage,[3] 1946, gouache, 9½ x 12¾ .... (96)   2,000
Still Life, 1946, gouache, 12¾ x 10½ .... (116)   1,600
Plants and Flowers, gouache, 23¾ x 19¾ .... (138)   2,620
Study of a Butterfly and Flowers, gouache,
  10¾ x 15 .... (69)   1,580
Woman Holding a Bird, gouache, 7¼ x 6¾ .... (6)   1,492
Composition with a Woman's Bust, 1948,
  watercolor and gouache, 15¾ x 18¾ .... (37)   2,000
Trees and Flowers, 1948, watercolor, 13 x 10 ..... (149)   664
Composition, 1948, watercolor and gouache,
  12¼ x 8¾ .... (96)   2,100
Composition, 1948, gouache, 12¾ x 10 .... (168)   650
Deauville Beach, 1950, watercolor and gouache,
  12¼ x 15¾ .... (88)   1,427
Woman with a Flower, 1952, gouache,
  21¼ x 19½ .... (164)   1,510

1963

"J'ai seul la clé de cette parade sauvage,"
  watercolor, 13 x 10¼ .... (190)   1,040
Faces, gouache, 10 x 13 .... (236)   972
Cows, 1932, watercolor, 17¾ x 14¾ .... (236)   1,605
Aircraft Propellers, 1937, gouache, 12 x 18¾ ..... (210)   1,645
The White Hen, 1937, gouache, 12¾ x 15 .... (210)   1,508
Composition, 1938, gouache, 15½ x 11½ .... (241)   820
Composition, 1945, watercolor, 4 x 4¾ .... (232)   429
The Couple, watercolor, 19¾ x 24 .... (311)   1,000
The Theater, gouache, 7¾ x 10 .... (232)   904
Project of Decoration, watercolor, 12 x 9¼ .... (299)   1,400
Project of Stained Glass, 1954, watercolor,
  23¾ x 41 .... (200)   3,000

1964

Composition, 1927, watercolor, 10¾ x 7½ .... (378) $2,712
"The Triumph of David,"[4] gouache, 18¼ x 25 .... (416)   2,488
Man and Woman, 1944, gouache, 11¾ x 17¾ ..... (460)   1,200
The Potter, gouache, 12¼ x 15 .... (471)   1,944
Composition, 1948, watercolor, 12½ x 9¾ .... (370)   480
The Desert, 1949, watercolor, 12½ x 9½ .... (401)   820
Logs, 1950, gouache, 15¾ x 20¾ .... (448)   1,900
Woman Reading, 1950, gouache, 11 x 15½ .... (399)   760
Builders, (1950), gouache, 25¾ x 19¾ .... (378)   6,328
Composition, watercolor, 6¾ x 7¾ .... (471)   1,130
Composition, gouache, 10¾ x 5½ .... (448)   2,400
Composition, gouache, 12¼ x 9¾ .... (379)   260
Composition, 1952, tempera, 19 x 25¼ .... (439)   2,240
The Two Lovers,[5] (1952-53), gouache,
  19½ x 15½ .... (387)   2,488

1965

The Smoker (Contrast of Forms), 1913,
  watercolor and gouache, 11¼ x 9¼ .... (594)   14,000
Bathers, 1921, gouache, 15¾ x 12¼ .... (616)   2,880
Landscape, gouache, 7¼ x 6¼ .... (523)   960
Bust and Instruments, 1938, gouache, 12 x 16 ..... (526)   4,750
Woman's Head, 1947, watercolor, 13 x 10 .... (606)   2,100
Composition with a Woman's Bust, 1949,
  watercolor, 12¼ x 17 .... (637)   3,750
The Birthday, on a Yellow Background, 1950,
  gouache, 25¾ x 19¾ .... (561)   7,400
The Polychrome Tents, 1950, watercolor,
  11 x 15 .... (617)   1,853
Logs, 1952, watercolor and gouache, 25¾ x 19¼ .. (541)   3,000

1966

Study for the Staircase, 1913, gouache,
  19 x 24½ .... (801)   13,600
Two Figures, 1927, watercolor, 12 x 10 .... (801)   5,200
The Musing Poor, watercolor, 12¼ x 9 .... (802)   2,240
Landscape, (1937), gouache, 12¾ x 10 .... (798)   3,752
Roof and Trees, 1950, gouache, 11¾ x 16¾ .... (811)   620
Composition, gouache, 11¾ x 9 .... (742)   1,760

1967

Composition, 1931, gouache, 15 x 12¾ .... (982)   2,726
Contrast of Forms, 1934, watercolor and India
  ink, 21½ x 16¾ .... (1004)   2,200
Composition, 1936, gouache, 6 x 11¾ .... (975)   2,100
The Head and the Hand, 1939, gouache and India
  ink, 17¾ x 12¾ .... (975)   3,800
Study for "Builders," gouache, 23¾ x 19½ .... (975)   4,200
The Man with a Vase, 1939, gouache and ink,
  8½ x 12 .... (889)   2,850
Composition, 1946, watercolor and India ink,
  13 x 10½ .... (912)   1,600
The Road, 1948, watercolor, 11¾ x 9½ .... (996)   600
Landscape, watercolor and gouache, 7½ x 6½ .... (918)   1,062

[1] Inscribed "J'aime faire des portraits. Pourquoi pas?"
[2] Dedicated to his friend Goll.
[3] Dedicated "A Jakovski, amicalement."

[4] Costumes and stage design for the ballet created in 1936. Dedicated to
Serge Lifar.
[5] Study for "The Picnic."

1968–July 1969

The Smoker, 1911, watercolor and ink,
16¼ x 12¾ . . . . (1064) $ 17,700

Stage Costume for the Swedish Ballets, 1924,
pencil and watercolor, 10¼ x 7½ . . . . (1142)   1,888

Composition, 1938, gouache and India ink,
9½ x 12¼ . . . . (1134)   3,304

Composition, 1939, pen and watercolor,
10 x 15¼ . . . . (1101)   3,795

The Worker, (1948), gouache, 16¼ x 11¾ . . . . (1134)   1,298

Woman's Head and Flowers, 1948, watercolor
and India ink, 13¼ x 9¾ . . . . (1026)   1,420

Composition, 1948, gouache, 12¾ x 9½ . . . . (1161)   380

"J'ai seul la clé de cette parade sauvage," 1948,
watercolor, 13½ x 19 . . . . (1113)   1,440

Illumination, 1948, watercolor, 11 x 8¼ . . . . (1043)   800

*Sketch for "Les Illuminations" by Arthur
Rimbaud,* 1949, gouache and India ink,
12¼ x 9 . . . . (1026)   420

Deauville, 1950, watercolor, 11¼ x 15¼ . . . . (1183)   1,760

Summer, 1953, watercolor, 15½ x 23¼ . . . . (1117)   6,700

The Farm Girl, 1953, watercolor, 21 x 15½ . . . . . . (1121)   1,800

Composition with a Wheel, gouache, 9 x 22 . . . . . (1053)   4,200

"The Man Who Wanted to Fly," gouache,
13 x 11 . . . . (1051)   360

Composition in Yellow, Black, and Blue, 1948,
gouache, 25½ x 21 . . . . (1225)   5,000

Red Flowers and Rope, 1949, pen and watercolor,
13 x 9¼ . . . . (1241)   2,770

Composition: Leaves and Buds, 1946, brush,
black ink, and watercolor, 13¼ x 10½ . . . . . . (1241)   3,150

Sunny Landscape, watercolor, 13 x 9½ . . . . (1256)   2,040

Man in a Studio, 9 x 8 . . . . (1256)   6,000

Figure Lying in a Landscape, 1921, watercolor
and gouache, 10 x 14 . . . . (1272)   19,200

PAINTINGS

1961–1962

The Breakfast,[6] 25¾ x 19½ . . . . (129)   27,460

Mechanical Elements, 1920, 25¼ x 21 . . . . (64)   18,500

Houses, 1922, 25¼ x 21 . . . . (83)   35,698

The Rest, 1921, 19½ x 25¼ . . . . (64)   20,000

Woman Holding a Flowerpot, 25¾ x 19¾ . . . . (160)   6,960

Dancers, 21 x 25¼ . . . . (88)   7,380

Composition, 1928, 25¾ x 36½ . . . . (29)   12,400

Still Life with a Pipe, 1930, on cardboard,
14¾ x 11 . . . . (164)   1,648

The Green Tree, 1932, 23¾ x 36½ . . . . (106)   9,266

Still Life, 1938, 18¼ x 25¾ . . . . (106)   7,684

The Jacket, 1934, 25¾ x 19½ . . . . (164)   961

The Young Lady with a Still Life, 1937,
28½ x 36¼ . . . . (31)   13,730

The Blue Vase, 1937, 25¾ x 36½ . . . . (105)   18,532

The Blue Doll, 24 x 19¾ . . . . (33)   11,000

The Blue Doll, 1943, on cardboard, 24 x 19¾ . . . . . (80)   10,200

1963

Mechanical Elements, 1922, on board, 15 x 10¾ . . (279)   15,500

Still Life: The King of Cards, 1927, 21¼ x 25¾ . . . (247)   7,678

Landscape, 1929, 36½ x 29 . . . . (299)   9,200

Still Life in Red and Blue, 1939, 19¾ x 25¾ . . . . . . (232)   6,780

Bather, 25¾ x 21¼ . . . . (258)   8,500

Chinatown, 1943, 35¼ x 28 . . . . (210) $ 14,807

Mechanical Elements on a Blue Background,
1945, 25¾ x 19¾ . . . . (258)   5,100

Two Women Holding Flowers, 1954, 21¼ x 25¾ . . (258)   6,000

Great Study for "Spare Time Activities,"
26 x 36½ . . . . (296)   16,800

1964

The Profile, 1924, on cardboard, 15 x 10½ . . . . (460)   1,900

Composition with Compasses, 1932, 10¾ x 21½ . . . (401)   3,400

Composition on a Blue Background, 1937,
35¾ x 25 . . . . (405)   6,965

The Black Tree, 1937, 18¼ x 13 . . . . (401)   3,000

Still Life in Red and Blue, 1939, 19 x 25 . . . . (416)   8,845

Polychrome Composition, 1939, 36 x 29 . . . . (460)   11,000

Portrait of Eluard, 1947, 25¾ x 19¾ . . . . (399)   6,600

The Fruit Stand, 1948, 23¼ x 36 . . . . (416)   15,202

Still Life with a Yellow Vase, 1949, 25 x 19 . . . . . . (416)   8,292

Mechanical Element, 1952, 25¼ x 19½ . . . . (458)   8,126

Mechanical Element, 1952, 25¾ x 19¾ . . . . (378)   10,170

1965

Composition, on cardboard, 15 x 17 . . . . (564)   3,420

Landscape, 1914, 29 x 39½ . . . . (615)   48,400

The Scaffolding, 1919, 32 x 23¾ . . . . (615)   37,000

Mechanical Elements,[7] 1922, on board mounted
on cradled panel, 15 x 10¾ . . . . (594)   10,000

Still Life, Yellow Leaf, 1927, 29 x 36 . . . . (615)   19,000

Still Life: Composition for a Dining Room, 1930,
33¼ x 47 . . . . (624)   18,795

Composition with a Leaf, 1931, 35½ x 42 . . . . (561)   14,600

Flower and Dolls, 1937, 35¼ x 51½ . . . . (615)   27,200

Composition with an Inkwell, 1938, 36½ x 25¾ . . . (613)   9,200

Still Life with Three Leaves, 1939, 38½ x 51½ . . . . (637)   28,000

Composition, 1945, 10¼ x 14¼ . . . . (569)   2,599

Still Life with a White Vase, 1948, 25¾ x 36½ . . . . (617)   15,820

Flowers and Mandolin on a Blue Background,
1951, 25¾ x 19¾ . . . . (561)   11,200

Blue Jug and Red Carpet, 1952, 21 x 25 . . . . (573)   7,739

Study for the Camper, 1954, 36½ x 29 . . . . (561)   21,000

The Camper, 1954, 63¼ x 51½ . . . . (485)   41,000

1966

The Staircase, 1914, 34¾ x 49¼ . . . . (676)   100,000

Still Life with Compasses, 1926, 35½ x 28¼ . . . . . . (676)   30,000

Still Life with an Inkwell, 1927, 29 x 36½ . . . . (801)   15,000

Landscape, 1929, 36½ x 29¼ . . . . (808)   13,930

Still Life, 1930, 33½ x 47½ . . . . (685)   17,600

Composition with a Triangle, 1931, 25¾ x 18¼ . . . . (694)   10,000

A Face in a Medallion, (1935), 18¼ x 14¾ . . . . (734)   8,814

Figure and Plant, 1938, 29 x 36½ . . . . (801)   14,200

Chinatown, 1943, 29¼ x 36 . . . . (797)   11,300

The Blue Road (Normandy), 1947, 18¼ x 25¾ . . . . (742)   5,600

The Three Sisters, 1950–51, on canvas laid down
on panel, 50¼ x 37¼ . . . . (678)   56,000

Still Life with a Bird, 1951, 25¾ x 36½ . . . . (801)   11,200

1967

Still Life, 1918, 25¾ x 32 . . . . (982)   40,290

Two Women Dressing, 1920, 25 x 19¾ . . . . (864)   35,000

Composition with Two Faces, 1921, 19¾ x 25¾ . . . (901)   18,000

Architecture, 1923, 25¾ x 36½ . . . . (901)   22,000

Still Life with the Ace of Diamonds, 1929,
35½ x 25¾ . . . . (940)   15,961

---

[6]Inscribed on the reverse "Les deux femmes à la toilette, 1er état, F. Léger, 20."

[7]Sold in New York on October 30, 1963 for $15,500.

The Blue Spider,[8] 1938, 36 x 25¾ .... (975) $ 15,200
Composition, 1938, on panel, 15½ x 17½ .... (962) 8,800
Composition, 1939, 15 x 18¼ .... (930) 4,068
White Butterfly, 1946, 15 x 18¼ .... (965) 8,362
The Branch on a Black Background, 1948,
   36½ x 29 .... (923) 13,600
Composition with the King of Hearts, 1948,
   36½ x 25¾ .... (975) 13,000
The Three Sisters, 1950–51, on canvas laid down
   on panel, 50¼ x 37¼ .... (988) 34,832
A Bird Before Tree Trunks, 1952, 29 x 36½ ...... (994) 12,000
Young Woman with Blue Fabric, 13 x 18¼ .... (994) 5,820

1968–July 1969
The Clown, 1918, 13 x 9½ .... (1064) 29,500
Mechanical Elements, 1920, 25¾ x 21¼ .... (1056) 34,000
The Disc, 1927, 36½ x 29 .... (1125) 24,840
Woman with a Parrot, 1941, 37¼ x 25¾ .... (1018) 18,500
The Yellow Flower, 1944, 18¼ x 24 .... (1125) 11,270
White Butterfly, 1946, 15 x 18¼ .... (1173) 9,775
Composition with a Basket, 1950, 25¼ x 19¾ .... (1043) 6,800
A Face and a Vase, 1951, 36½ x 25½ .... (1184) 16,000
Woman with a Flowerpot, 1952, 25¾ x 19¾ ..... (1117) 8,400
Sunflower on a Polychrome Background, 1954,
   21¾ x 19¾ .... (1202) 10,000
Still Life with a Blue Background, on cardboard,
   17¾ x 14¾ .... (1213) 7,200
Figure: Contrast of Forms, 1912, India ink, oil,
   and charcoal on paper, 10 x 18½ .... (1235) 35,000
The Rug in the Landscape, 1949, 9¾ x 25½ ..... (1241) 16,400
Two Pink Cloths and a Saw, 1953, 21¼ x 24 ..... (1254) 13,000
The Black Bust, 1929, 15 x 21¾ .... (1268) 19,488
Composition, 1939, 14¼ x 19 .... (1268) 14,848

Georges Lemmen

(1865–1916)

Birthplace: Belgium.

1889–92 Participates in the Salon des Indépendants, Paris.
Seurat exerts a strong influence upon him.

1894–97 Becomes a member of the group "La Libre esthétique," Brussels.

1899 Executes illustrations for the review *Die Insel.*

1916 Died.

Sales

DRAWINGS

1963
The Seamstress, 1900, pencil, 9 x 12 .... (255) $ 151
The Kiss, red and black pencil, 22 x 15 .... (216) 137

[8] A poem by Paul Eluard.

1966
Head of a Little Girl, 1892, charcoal, 14¼ x 11 .... (819) $ 340
Study of Three Heads, 1892, charcoal, 13½ x 10 .. (734) 520
Portrait of Madame Georges Lemmen, 1894,
   India ink, 11½ x 8¾ .... (731) 300
Standing Nude, 1913, red chalk heightened with
   colors, 24½ x 18¾ .... (731) 220
Two Women, charcoal, 10 x 13 .... (813) 138

1967
Sewing, 1901, colored pencil, 10 x 13 .... (949) 450
Young Lady Reading, red chalk, 9½ x 6½ .... (930) 271
Portrait of Madame Lemmen, 1894, pen and
   wash, 11½ x 9 .... (939) 829
Good Night, charcoal, 22 x 15 .... (1000) 220

1968–July 1969
Young Ladies Reading, two drawings, charcoal
   and India ink, each 9¾ x 6½ .... (1101) 172
Nude, black pencil and red chalk, 19½ x 25 ..... (1110) 220
The Artist's Mother, 1886, white chalk on brown
   paper, 18¾ x 8¼ .... (1203) 136
Young Woman Dressing, 1912, red chalk, 11 x 9 . (1066) 180
Young Nude, Seated, colored pencil, 7½ x 10¾ .. (1219) 200
The Rower, colored pencil, 12¾ x 10¼ .... (1089) 300
Bather Under the Orange Tree, colored pencil,
   gouache, and distemper, 21 x 15 .... (1043) 500
The Siesta, 9½ x 12¼ .... (1220) 144
Nude in an Armchair, colored pencil, 10 x 14 .... (1220) 340
Nude with Drapery, 1913, red chalk .... (1223) 280
Seated Nude, colored pencil, 24½ x 20 .... (1223) 300
Nude with Drapery, red chalk, 17 x 19¾ .... (1223) 180
"La Famille Lemmen s'émancipe," India ink and
   wash, 5½ x 5 .... (1240) 144
On the Beach, 1891, charcoal, 9 x 11¼ .... (1241) 756
Woman Reading, 1897, Conté pencil, 28¼ x 23 .. (1246) 2,100
Madame Lemmen by the Fireplace, 1890,
   charcoal, 13½ x 10 .... (1246) 1,500

WATERCOLORS

1965
Bunch of Sunflowers, 1895, watercolor and black
   ink, 24 x 18¼ .... (556) 200
Nude, pastel, 19¾ x 25 .... (589) 360

1966
Nude Standing, Leaning on Her Elbow, 1913,
   pastel and red chalk, 24 x 17¾ .... (819) 240
Vase of Sunflowers, 1895, watercolor and India
   ink, 23¾ x 18¼ .... (718) 300
Reclining Nude, 1907, pastel, 11¾ x 18¾ .... (813) 884
Under the Lamp, watercolor, 9 x 12¼ .... (708) 360
Women at the Seaside, watercolor and gouache,
   8¾ x 11¾ .... (718) 344

1967
Reading, gouache, 14¾ x 19 .... (949) 1,220
Woman Combing Her Hair, watercolor, 14 x 8 ... (949) 330
Two Nudes, 1903, pastel and colored pencil,
   9 x 12¼ .... (978) 560
Flowers and Frogs, 1890, watercolor, 8¾ x 11¾ ... (934) 170

1968–July 1969
Sunflowers, 1895, watercolor, 24 x 18¼ .... (1187) 260
Gathering Fruit, 1904, watercolor, 11½ x 9 ...... (1154) 340
Sewing, watercolor, 14¾ x 11½ .... (1117) 560
The Toilette, After Tintoretto, 1910, watercolor,
   6¾ x 10 .... (1117) 400

Daybreak Over the Sea, 1911, watercolor,
  10¼ x 14 . . . . (1043) $ 320
Young Woman Sleeping, watercolor, 9 x 11 . . . . . (1066)   400
Young Woman Reclining, watercolor, 4½ x 6 . . . . (1089)   140
Woman Reading in an Armchair, 1892, watercolor
  and ink, 21 x 23 . . . . (1231)   180
The Sewer, 1905, ink and watercolor,
  14¼ x 11¼ . . . . (1248)   900

PAINTINGS

1961–1962
Snowy Landscape, 17¾ x 24 . . . . (95)   440

1963
Portrait of a Woman with a Red Toque,
  11½ x 13½ . . . . (235)   120
Nude, 29¾ x 21¾ . . . . (275)   1,000

1964
Woman in Profile, 1907, 18¼ x 15 . . . . (405)   696
Landscape of La Holpe, 16¾ x 23¼ . . . . (391)   320

1965
Seated Young Woman, 1911, on cardboard laid
  down on canvas, 21¾ x 29¼ . . . . (516)   1,900
Heyst, 1891, on board, 5 x 8½ . . . . (624)   1,935

1966
Woman with a Dog, 1905, on cardboard,
  8½ x 6¼ . . . . (819)   1,040
Still Life with Everlasting Flowers, (1895),
  23¾ x 32 . . . . (819)   1,840
Young Lady with a Red Ribbon, 1896, on
  cardboard, 14¼ x 11 . . . . (731)   430
Nude with a Mirror, 1907, oil on paper, 12 x 9 . . . . (813)   1,161
In Mind, 1911, on cardboard, 21¼ x 16¼ . . . . (767)   800

1967
Heyst-sur-Mer, 1892, 6¾ x 9¾ . . . . (918)   2,215
Ste. Marie Church, Dusk, 14 x 10 . . . . (871)   460
The Woman with a Red Bodice, 1907, on
  cardboard, 21¾ x 18¼ . . . . (978)   1,600
Landscape, on panel, 6 x 9 . . . . (978)   640
Seated Nude, on cardboard, 9 x 7¼ . . . . (850)   460
Self-Portrait, on panel, 16 x 10¾ . . . . (985)   995

1968–July 1969
Portrait of Madame Lemmen, 1891, on board,
  10 x 11 . . . . (1068)   6,608
Back View of a Seated Nude, 1903, on panel,
  10¼ x 7 . . . . (1132)   1,062
Model Dressing, 1904, on cardboad, 9½ x 12 . . . . (1043)   1,120
Seated Nude, 34¾ x 25 . . . . (1218)   2,400
Nude with a Red Armchair, on cardboard,
  21¾ x 18¼ . . . . (1117)   1,900
Still Life with Flowers, 1910, on cradled panel,
  35½ x 27¼ . . . . (1061)   2,300
Houses, on cardboard, 22 x 17½ . . . . (1219)   450
Bunch of Flowers, on panel, 17½ x 13½ . . . . (1218)   1,200
Still Life with Everlasting Flowers, 24 x 31½ . . . . (1113)   2,260
Portrait of a Woman, 11½ x 13½ . . . . (1042)   400
Child with a Necklace, on board, 17 x 20 . . . . (1231)   2,000
Attitudes, 1906, on board, 18½ x 14¾ . . . . (1241)   1,386
Nabi Landscape, (1901), on
  cardboard, 21¾ x 18¼ . . . . (1265)   700
Landscape, 1908, on panel, 21¾ x 27¾ . . . . (1268)   3,530
Three Vases of Flowers and a Shell, (1905),
  19 x 24 . . . . (1270)   4,320

Marcel Leprin

(1891–1933)

Birthplace: Cannes, France. An orphan, he spends his youth with his uncle in Marseilles.

1919   Returns to Marseilles after World War I. Decorates cafés to earn his living.

1921   Goes to Paris.

1922   Becomes a member of the Salon d'Automne, Paris.

1923   Exhibits at the Galerie Marseille, Paris. Participates in the Salon des Indépendants, Paris.

1924   Participates in the Salon d'Automne, Paris.

1925   One-man show at the Galerie Berthe Weil, Paris, where his landscapes of Montmartre, Belleville, and Chaville are very successful.

1926-27   One-man show at the Tooth Gallery, London. Takes part in the exhibition "Paris par ses meilleurs peintres" at the Galerie Henry, Paris.

1928   One-man show at the Galerie Druet, Paris. Takes part in the exhibition "De Lautres à Utrillo" at the Galerie Bernheim, Paris.

1930-31   Stays in Caen, Honfleur, and St. Malo. One-man show at the Galerie Druet, Paris. His work "Le Bassin de Honfleur" is bought by the Musée du Luxembourg, Paris.

1932   Returns to Paris.

1933   Died, Paris.

Sales

DRAWINGS

1963
Sailboats in the Harbor, 1932, charcoal,
  12¾ x 15¾ . . . . (287) $ 164

1966
The Salutation of the Bullfighter, colored pencil
  and gouache, 12¼ x 20 . . . . (718)   220

1968–July 1969
The Canal in Moret-sur-Loing, 9½ x 12¾ . . . . (1038)   76

WATERCOLORS

1968–July 1969
Marseilles Harbor, 1915, pastel, 17¾ x 23¾ . . . . . (1060)   2,400

PAINTINGS

1961–1962
"Au Mimosa," 25¾ x 32 . . . . (40)   700
The Detached House, 21¼ x 29 . . . . (90)   900
Honfleur: Outlet of the Harbor, 21¼ x 25¾ . . . . . . (17)   660
Village Path, 25¾ x 36½ . . . . (35)   640
Notre-Dame from the Quays, 7½ x 9½ . . . . (146)   280
Honfleur, the Harbor, 25¾ x 36½ . . . . (171)   3,300
A Street in Avallon, 29 x 36½ . . . . (171)   1,000
The Market Town, 18¼ x 25½ . . . . (171)   1,600

1963
The Artist's Studio, 29 x 21¼ . . . . (293)   700
A Street of Paris, 16¼ x 13 . . . . (271)   240
Still Life, 18¼ x 21¾ . . . . (267)   600
An Old Mill in Moret, 10¾ x 14 . . . . (182)   280

The Old Harbor, on cardboard, 10¼ x 14 .... (276) $ 680
Honfleur Harbor, 21¼ x 25¾ .... (306)   1,200
Bullfight Scene, 25¼ x 36½ .... (224)   1,580

1964

Landscape, on cardboard, 10¾ x 14 .... (450)   620
Landscape with a Barrier, 15¾ x 21¼ .... (472)   920
Landscape of Avallon, 23¾ x 32 .... (440)   740
Coming Out of the Church, 29 x 23¾ .... (393)   430
Montmartre, 25¾ x 19¾ .... (401)   250
Notre-Dame from the Quays, 18¼ x 21¾ .... (335)   800
Dunkirk Harbor, 25¾ x 36½ .... (337)   1,680

1965

Old Street in Montmartre, 29 x 23¾ .... (598)   800
The Moulin de la Galette Under Snow,
    18¼ x 21¾ .... (512)   960
Surroundings of Paris, 29 x 23¾ .... (564)   500
A Village Street, 29 x 23¾ .... (553)   1,200
The Florists of the Cours St. Louis, 24 x 19¾ ..... (554)   1,140
The Market, Rue Lepic, 18¼ x 21¾ .... (604)   600
La Commanderie, Honfleur, 18¼ x 21½ .... (523)   1,040
The Port, 21¼ x 25¾ .... (492)   1,230
The Picador in the Bull Ring, 25¾ x 36½ .... (553)   1,500

1966

The Place du Tertre, 29 x 36½ .... (809)   1,160
The Place du Tertre, 36½ x 29 .... (674)   1,320
The Quays of the River Seine in Paris,
    23¾ x 29 .... (819)   1,720
Bullfight Scene: The Killing, 21¼ x 29 .... (685)   900
The Picador, 25¾ x 36½ .... (793)   640
The Harbor, 18¼ x 21¾ .... (741)   360
The Green Portal, 23¾ x 32 .... (819)   1,800

1967

The Square in Caen, 15 x 18¼ .... (987)   1,000
The Church, 18¼ x 22 .... (935)   400
Quai de Bercy, 18¼ x 21¾ .... (911)   1,700
St. Joseph Shelter, 18¼ x 21¾ .... (901)   2,400
The Moulin de La Galette, 20½ x 25 .... (885)   551

1968–July 1969

The Covered Market in Caen, on panel,
    11½ x 16½ .... (1049)   3,000
The Tobacconist's, 29 x 23¾ .... (1049)   1,400
The Yard at Villiers-le-Bel, 21¾ x 18¼ .... (1026)   520
Landscape at Gonesse, 35¼ x 46 .... (1109)   3,200
Costermongers' Barrows, Rue Lepic,
    18¼ x 21¾ .... (1116)   720
Notre-Dame and the Quays, 21¼ x 25¾ .... (1210)   2,120
Montmartre: Rue Norvins, 32 x 25¾ .... (1106)   4,000
Montmartre: Place Blanche, 21¾ x 18¼ .... (1183)   2,100
The Guitar Player, 18¼ x 13 .... (1133)   260
The Old Walls, 15 x 21¾ .... (1104)   220
The "Brasserie du Cidre" in Honfleur,
    21¼ x 25¾ .... (1039)   2,400
Vase of Flowers and Fruit, 29 x 23¾ .... (1109)   1,040
Houses by the River Bank, 13 x 18¼ .... (1224)   1,100
Seated Woman, on cardboard, 10¾ x 7½ .... (1244)   300
St. Père Church, 45¾ x 35¼ .... (1256)   3,400
The Butte Montmartre, 21¼ x 25¾ .... (1256)   2,800
Place Pigalle, 23¾ x 29 .... (1258)   5,500
The Street .... (1263)   800

Henri Le Sidaner

(1862–1939)

Birthplace: Mauritius.

1891   Wins a medal and a scholarship at the Salon des Artistes Français, Paris. Works under the exclusive influence of Impressionism all his life, painting a great number of landscapes often shrouded in a misty atmosphere. Excels in producing twilight effects.

1900   Given an award at the Paris World's Fair.

1930   Promoted to the rank of Officer of the Legion of Honor. Becomes a member of the Académie des Beaux-Arts, Paris.

1939   Died, Versailles.

Sales

DRAWINGS

1965

A Shop in Chartres, 1903, pencil and oil on paper,
    9 x 12¾ .... (582) $ 829

1967

The Old Bridge in Nemours, (1910), black pencil
    heightened with colored pencil, 6½ x 7½ ..... (985)   119

WATERCOLORS

1964

The Gardens of Versailles, pastel, 25 x 32 .... (455)   553

1967

The Pavilion, gouache and colored pencil,
    13½ x 17¾ .... (995)   420

PAINTINGS

1961–1962

The House in the Trees, on cardboard, 9 x 10¼ .... (51)   104
The Terrace, 36 x 52¼ .... (27)   260
La Darse Harbor, Villefranche-sur-Mer,
    18¼ x 21¾ .... (90)   500

1963

Sailboats in the Harbor, 8¾ x 6½ .... (280)   180
Venice, 5¾ x 7 .... (255)   247
The Rail by the Waterside, 23¾ x 29 .... (244)   300
The Village, 24¾ x 31¼ .... (309)   3,461
Le Croisic Harbor, 32 x 39½ .... (215)   1,680

1964

Snow in Chartres, 15 x 18¼ .... (395)   240
The Pond, Surroundings of Beauvais, 21¼ x 29 ... (395)   1,000
The Small Town of Berberoy (Oise district), 1937,
    50¼ x 60½ .... (368)   1,382
The Flower Girl, (1930–39), 15 x 18¼ .... (351)   640
Nocturne, 25¼ x 31½ .... (405)   1,393
Venice, on board, 10½ x 8¼ .... (416)   1,797
In the Shade of the Branches, 31½ x 39¼ .... (367)   3,040

1965

Isola Madre, Lake Maggiore, on panel, 5¾ x 8 ... (497)   200
Houses in the Sun, on panel, 12¾ x 16 .... (575)   2,488
The Bridge Over the Canal, 35½ x 29 .... (585)   1,393
The Lighter, Bruges, 1904, 25 x 21 .... (624)   774
The Yellow Tablecloth, 27¾ x 38 .... (535)   2,764

The Terrace, Villefranche, 32 x 39¼ . . . . (583) $4,353
A House by the Waterside, on panel, 10 x 13 . . . . . (614) 525
The Stairs of the Trianon, 23 x 28 . . . . (624) 3,317
The Staircase, 23¾ x 29 . . . . (490) 700

1966

The Artist Carlos Lefebvre in His Garden, 1888,
    on panel, 7½ x 12¾ . . . . (666) 340
Young Lady in Her Garden, 19¼ x 25½ . . . . (666) 560
The Island of the Fishermen, 1909, 31¼ x 39 . . . . . (818) 2,177
Sailboat on the Open Sea, on panel, 21¾ x 25¾ . . (788) 106
The Bridge of Maines, 28½ x 23½ . . . . (760) 1,596
Flowerpots, 28½ x 35½ . . . . (760) 1,161
House by the Canal, 29¾ x 25¾ . . . . (757) 1,935
House, 29 x 36½ . . . . (724) 1,800
Small Red and Yellow Houses, on board,
    5¾ x 7½ . . . . (808) 580
A Village in the Evening, 19½ x 25¾ . . . . (757) 1,161
The Clematis, Gerberoy, 1927, 29 x 36½ . . . . (808) 2,757
Roses in a Vase, on board, 17¾ x 14¾ . . . . (813) 829
Landscape, 34¾ x 58 . . . . (810) 380
The Rue Royale, 35½ x 50½ . . . . (753) 2,612
The Lunch, 32 x 39½ . . . . (707) 3,000

1967

Young Woman in an Orchard, 1899, 19 x 25 . . . . . . (888) 663
Quimperlé: The Quai Brizieux, 25¾ x 21¾ . . . . (849) 1,100
Moonlight Over the Sea, at Villefranche,
    32 x 25¾ . . . . (849) 1,400
The Small Harbor, 25 x 31½ . . . . (939) 3,593
The Church Around the Corner, on panel,
    10¾ x 14 . . . . (940) 987
The Shop, Chartres, 1903, 9½ x 12¾ . . . . (940) 987
Hampton Court, 1906-07, oil and pencil on paper
    laid down on board, 10 x 14¾ . . . . (985) 901
The Lock, (1909), 32¼ x 39½ . . . . (870) 1,000
A Canal in Bruges, 18¼ x 24½ . . . . (897) 1,160
Nocturne, 25¼ x 31½ . . . . (885) 1,016
A View of Gerberoy in the Summertime, 1936,
    25 x 31½ . . . . (988) 3,981
The Entrance of Gerberoy Village, 25¾ x 32 . . . . . (912) 2,400
A Town by a River, on board, 12¾ x 16¼ . . . . (888) 2,902
The "Hundred Stairs," Versailles, 25¼ x 31½ . . . . (888) 1,327

1968–July 1969

Flowery Window, 23¾ x 29 . . . . (1200) 3,200
The Three Windows, 23¾ x 29 . . . . (1203) 1,858
Landscape, on board, 1890, 10¼ x 13½ . . . . (1029) 260
Young Peasant, 1890, 24 x 18¼ . . . . (1168) 280
The Horse Pond, 1890, on panel, 10¼ x 13 . . . . . . (1203) 892
The Wash House, 21¼ x 25¾ . . . . (1162) 3,200
A Patch of Garden, 32¼ x 24 . . . . (1187) 2,077
A Village by the Waterside, 23¾ x 29 . . . . (1180) 3,900
A Gray Evening Over Lisieux, 1917, on panel,
    7½ x 9½ . . . . (1210) 740
A House at Sunset, 21¾ x 17½ . . . . (1104) 776
The Trianon, on panel, 5¾ x 4 . . . . (1213) 220
In the Shade Under the Branches, Gerberoy,
    Oise, 1924, 31½ x 39¼ . . . . (1187) 12,272
The Sunny River Bank, 23¾ x 29 . . . . (1223) 8,600
The Little Canal, Venice, 31¾ x 25¼ . . . . (1240) 5,280
Little Girl Picking Flowers, 1887, 14½ x 21¼ . . . . (1240) 1,968
Dusk, 1897, 18 x 25 . . . . (1241) 1,760

The Entrance of Moret-sur-Loing, on panel,
    10¾ x 14 . . . . (1261) $4,200
Snowy Village, on panel, 10¾ x 14 . . . . (1261) 3,800
Lunch in the Woods, 59¾ x 49½ . . . . (1261) 15,200
By the Riverside, 1896, on board, 10½ x 13¾ . . . . (1271) 720
The Pavillon de Musique in the Parc du Trianon
    at Versailles in Autumn, (1920), on board,
    12 x 12¾ . . . . (1271) 2,640
Roses in a Vase, on board, 17¾ x 14½ . . . . (1271) 1,920

Jack Levine

(1915-   )

Birthplace: Boston, Massachusetts, U.S.

1924-29 Studies painting with H. Zimmerman and later with
D. Ross. Attends classes at the Boston Museum of
Fine Arts.

1935 Works for the Federal Art Project. Comes under the
influence of the Expressionists—among them
Rouault, Soutine, and Kokoschka.

1936 Exhibits at the Museum of Modern Art, New York.

1939 First one-man show at the Downtown Gallery, New
York.

1942 Settles in New York.

1947 Spends one year in Italy. One-man show at the Alan
Gallery, New York.

1953 Retrospective exhibition at the Institute of Contemporary Art, Boston.

1955 Retrospective exhibition at the Whitney Museum of
American Art, New York.

1959 Dedicates his work "1932" to his friend Georges
Grosz.

1960 Retrospective exhibition at the Museo Nacional de
Arte Moderno, Mexico.

Resident in New York.

Sales

DRAWINGS

1963

General Franco and Foster Dulles, pencil,
    7½ x 10 . . . . (208) $ 375

1965

Gideon, red chalk, 21 x 15¾ . . . . (494) 300

1967

King Solomon, pencil, 7 x 10 . . . . (952) 475
Portrait of a Woman, pencil, 14¾ x 10¾ . . . . (889) 350

1968–July 1969

Portrait of a Young Woman, pencil, 5¾ x 9 . . . . . (1088) 125
Horse and Rider, pencil, 12¾ x 9¾ . . . . (1062) 350

PAINTINGS

1965
Little Girl in Blue, 1955, 20 x 16¼ . . . . (485) $3,500

1966
Study for "Election Night," 24 x 21 . . . . (790)   3,800

1967
Apteka, (1947), 40¼ x 59¼ . . . . (952)   15,000

1968–July 1969
The Pawnshop, 1951, 59¼ x 96¾ . . . . (1160)   23,000
Nature Study, 1949, 10 x 14 . . . . (1229)   1,500

André Lhote

(1885–1962)

Birthplace: Bordeaux, France.

1898   Works at a sculptor's. Later attends the Bordeaux Fine Arts School.

1905-06   Decides to devote himself to painting.

1907   Participates in the Salon des Indépendants and the Salon d'Automne, Paris.

1908   Settles in Paris.

1909   Wins a one-year stay at the Villa Medicis, Rome— together with Raoul Dufy.

1910   First one-man show at the Galerie Druet, Paris. Greatly admires Cézanne and is strongly influenced by him.

1921   Teaches at the Académie Notre-Dame des Champs, Paris. One-man show at the Galerie Druet, Paris.

1933   Issues *La Peinture, le Coeur, et l'Esprit* (Denoël et Steele, Paris).

1936-37   Executes a decoration for the Paris World's Fair.

1938   Settles in Gordes during World War II.

1942   Teaches at the Académie de Montparnasse, Paris.

1951   Trip to Egypt. Takes a great interest in Egyptian painting.

1955   Executes three murals for the Faculté de Médecine of Bordeaux.

1957   Retrospective exhibition at the Musée National d'Art Moderne, Paris.

1958   Issues his *Traité du Paysage et de la Figure* (Bernard Grasset, Paris).

1959   One-man shows in New York and Copenhagen.

1962   Died, Paris.

Sales

DRAWINGS

1961–1962
Seated Nude, Her Arm Raised, 19½ x 12¼ . . . . (68) $ 340
Dancer Standing at Ease, 11½ x 8 . . . . (68)   60

1963
The Village, pen, 8 x 10¼ . . . . (262) $ 36
Nude Combing Her Hair, black lead, 19½ x 12¼ . . . . (234)   270

1964
Landscape of Provence, pen, 8¼ x 12¼ . . . . (409)   86
Model with a Bracelet, black lead, 11¾ x 8¼ . . . . . (382)   57
Marseilles, colored pencil and watercolor, 18¼ x 13 . . . . (365)   319

1965
Roussillon, pen, 8¾ x 12¾ . . . . (599)   160

1966
Seated Nude, black lead, 12 x 8½ . . . . (720)   180
Junon, pen, 22 x 15 . . . . (659)   170
Seated Woman, pencil, 14¾ x 9 . . . . (764)   140
A Town in Provence, pen, 14¾ x 22¾ . . . . (749)   150

1968–July 1969
Landscape of Provence, sepia wash, 15 x 22¾ . . . (1030)   275
Reclining Nude, black lead, 10¾ x 14 . . . . (1048)   160
Composition, India ink, 9½ x 13 . . . . (1227)   132
Bust of a Young Woman, pencil, 19½ x 13 . . . . . . (1234)   180
Young Woman with a Mirror, India ink, 10¼ x 8 . . . . (1238)   260
Seated Woman, India ink, 12¼ x 8 . . . . (1238)   280
The Harbor, wash, 9¾ x 13¼ . . . . (1260)   192

WATERCOLORS

1961–1962
Interior with a Young Lady Seated at a Table, gouache, 11½ x 15 . . . . (76)   350
The Harbor, 1927, watercolor, 15 x 23¼ . . . . (27)   520
Villeneuve-lès-Avignon, 1930, watercolor, 15 x 23 . . . . (12)   320
Landscape, 11 x 15 . . . . (52)   300
Landscape of Provence, 1931, watercolor, 14¾ x 22½ . . . . (124)   140
Riverside, 1932, watercolor, 14¾ x 22½ . . . . (124)   150
Reclining Nude, pastel, 11¾ x 19½ . . . . (2)   360
Biblical Scene, gouache, 12¼ x 8 . . . . (154)   150

1963
Landscape, watercolor and gouache, 11 x 15 . . . . . (241)   460
Reclining Woman, (1918), gouache, 5 x 12¼ . . . . . (280)   420
A Village, watercolor, 12½ x 19½ . . . . (234)   432
Figure in a Kitchen, 1941, gouache, 11 x 8½ . . . . . (232)   655

1964
The Conversation, 1912, watercolor and gouache, 12¼ x 9½ . . . . (419)   400
Music at Teatime, watercolor, 13½ x 17½ . . . . (345)   544
Figures, 1917, watercolor, 9½ x 12¼ . . . . (418)   640
Woman's Head, 1910, gouache, 18¼ x 14 . . . . (368)   138
Landscape, pastel, 12½ x 19½ . . . . (450)   420
The Trees, pastel, 14 x 10¾ . . . . (441)   147
The Willows, pastel, 11½ x 8¾ . . . . (384)   96
Seated Nude, pastel, 24½ x 18¾ . . . . (325)   440
Seated Nude, Legs Crossed, gouache, 13½ x 8¾ . . . . (350)   190
Man's Head, watercolor and gouache, 18 x 11¾ . . (374)   650
View of a Castle, watercolor, 21¼ x 14 . . . . (374)   275
The Tulips, watercolor, 21¼ x 14 . . . . (469)   360
Landscape of Provence, gouache, 11 x 15¼ . . . . . . (335)   430

1965

Seated Woman, gouache and pencil, 10½ x 10½ .. (523) $ 580
Seated Woman, 1954, gouache, 10¼ x 6½ .... (523)   310
Seated Nude, pastel, 24 x 18¼ .... (529)   520
The Country House, gouache, 11 x 14¾ .... (559)   240
Village on a Hill, gouache, 9 x 12 .... (582)   387
The Village, watercolor, 14¾ x 14¾ .... (491)   720
The Winter Garden, gouache, 15½ x 11 .... (555)   320
Cliffs, watercolor, 14¼ x 23 .... (523)   310
Sailboats in a Harbor, watercolor, 10¾ x 13¼ .... (632)   780
Vase of Flowers, pastel, 17¾ x 14 .... (647)   350
The Plate of Fish, watercolor and gouache,
    12¼ x 16¼ .... (577)   320

1966

Landscape of Avignon, watercolor, 13½ x 19¾ ... (796)   500
Houses in a Landscape, pastel, 9¼ x 11½ .... (758)   290
Still Life with a Candlestick, (1922), gouache,
    6½ x 9 .... (668)   320
The Village, pastel, 9¼ x 11½ .... (793)   610
The Sisters, pastel, 28½ x 23¼ .... (810)   800

1967

Exotic Landscape, 1911, gouache, 12¼ x 19½ .... (960)   396
Cubist Composition, watercolor, 14¾ x 22½ ...... (921)   240
Landscape of the South of France, 1932,
    watercolor, 14¼ x 22 .... (845)   660
Landscape, gouache, 10¾ x 15 .... (934)   260
Landscape of North Africa, gouache, 7½ x 11½ .. (937)   300
Landscape, watercolor, 12¾ x 19¾ .... (967)   542
Landscape, watercolor, 11 x 15 .... (894)   360
Landscape Near Toulon, gouache, 11 x 16¾ ...... (898)   280
Bust of a Young Woman, pastel, 29¼ x 24 ...... (858)   600
Still Life with a Fruit Stand, watercolor, 8 x 8½ .. (935)   180
"14 Juillet," watercolor, 8½ x 10¾ .... (943)   640

1968–July 1969

The Village, gouache, 14 x 21¼ .... (1131)   440
Landscape, watercolor, 12 x 12¾ .... (1134)   802
Landscape, 1927, watercolor, 14¾ x 22 .... (1172)   560
Gordes, watercolor, 15 x 22½ .... (1119)   640
The Fishermen's Meal, pastel, 21¾ x 26 .... (1117)   2,200
Seated Man, watercolor, 5¼ x 8 .... (1032)   200
Seated Nude, gouache on board, 15 x 11 .... (1061)   800
Reclining Nude with a Coffepot, gouache,
    5½ x 13 .... (1191)   944
Composition with a Table, watercolor, 4½ x 5½ . (1167)   124
Landscape at Marmande, watercolor,
    14¾ x 22¼ .... (1225)   900
Island in Venice, gouache, 15 x 11 .... (1225)   920
Marmande, 1929, watercolor, 14¼ x 22¾ .... (1225)   920
Model Resting, pastel, 11¾ x 19½ .... (1225)   1,400
Woman Seated with a Dove, 1917, 22¼ x 15¼ ... (1240)   4,560

PAINTINGS

1961–1962

The Heath Near Bordeaux, (1917), 25¼ x 27¾ .... (53)   1,960
Underwood, 24 x 19¾ .... (35)   1,060
Still Life, 1914, 9½ x 13 .... (27)   820
Notre-Dame of Paris, 13 x 18¼ .... (19)   810
Sleep, 29 x 39½ .... (76)   1,420
Seated Woman with a Blue Bodice, 33½ x 27 ...... (47)   1,200
The Woman with a Green Dress, 39½ x 19¾ ..... (155)   960

Seated Woman, 16¼ x 13 .... (155) $ 720
Cubist Landscape, 21¾ x 18¼ .... (30)   1,480
Reading on the Terrace, 1951, 25½ x 31½ .... (85)   1,600

1963

Landscape with a White Horse, (1912),
    24 x 18¼ .... (279)   2,750
Composition, 1917, 29 x 19¾ .... (258)   2,300
The Public Garden in Bordeaux, 1919,
    20½ x 23¼ .... (202)   3,500
Landscape, 1920, 15 x 18¼ .... (227)   350
Landscape in Lille, 19½ x 23¼ .... (179)   1,300
The Village, 13 x 21¾ .... (224)   800
The Old Farm, 1929, 11 x 18 .... (202)   950
The Black House, 1956, 17¾ x 21¼ .... (225)   900
Still Life with a Red Fan, 15 x 21¾ .... (233)   580
Boats at La Madrague, 1957, 21½ x 25¼ .... (225)   1,000
Landscape, the Cliff, oil on cardboard,
    10¾ x 13¾ .... (232)   226
Reclining Nude, ... (209)   720
Portrait of a Woman, 23¼ x 18¼ .... (255)   548
Woman in Her Kitchen, 23½ x 14¾ .... (315)   686
Family Life, 23¾ x 29 .... (303)   900

1964

Still Life, 21¼ x 25¾ .... (375)   780
The Studio, 21¾ x 18¼ .... (401)   500
Nude Leaning on Her Elbow, 10¾ x 18¼ .... (472)   380
Nude, 11 x 14 .... (372)   1,000
Bather, 1956, 28½ x 23¾ .... (418)   560
Seated Nude, 36½ x 29 .... (450)   900
Landscape with Houses, 10¾ x 14 .... (332)   440
Villeneuve-lès-Avignon, 13 x 21¾ .... (382)   620
Thouars, 1959, 25¾ x 21¼ .... (372)   1,500
Landscape of the Roussillon, 15 x 21¾ .... (401)   1,900

1965

Ville d'Avray, 21¼ x 25¾ .... (586)   1,700
Football, (1918), 19 x 21¼ .... (617)   1,808
Bordeaux Harbor, on cardboard, 27 x 32½ .... (632)   2,460
Seated Nude, 16½ x 13¼ .... (617)   283
Seated Nude, 25¾ x 21¼ .... (497)   560
Landscape, 15 x 21¾ .... (510)   760
Landscape, on panel, 12¼ x 9½ .... (561)   520
Still Life with a Book, 18¼ x 21¾ .... (561)   700
Still Life with an Easel, 1956, 21¾ x 18¼ ...... (599)   610

1966

Venice, 14 x 25¾ .... (672)   1,170
The Negro, (1912), 29¼ x 19½ .... (713)   1,700
Rugby, 1917, 25¾ x 21¼ .... (798)   3,752
Bust of a Woman, 23¾ x 18¼ .... (727)   1,200
Landscape, 21¼ x 25¾ .... (670)   760
St. Paul de Vence, 19 x 23¼ .... (819)   1,640

1967

The Castle, 1911, 26 x 21¾ .... (978)   3,300
A Street in Bergerac, 1912, 18 x 15 .... (963)   4,600
Rugby, 1917, on panel, 14 x 14 .... (888)   3,593
Still Life, (1917), 25¾ x 32 .... (978)   3,600
The Garden, Bordeaux, 1919, 21 x 23¾ .... (841)   3,500
Landscape of La Cadière, 12¾ x 15¾ .... (937)   700
Landscape of Marmande, 15 x 18¼ .... (934)   560
Landscape with a Church, 12¾ x 18¼ .... (1006)   1,941
At the Dance, on cardboard, 22 x 28½ .... (919)   1,808

The Steeple, 1933, 29 x 36½ . . . . (1000) $1,000
Composition with a Jug, 18¼ x 24 . . . . (950)   920
The Reapers, oil on paper laid down on canvas,
    23 x 31½ . . . . (893)   2,600
The Garden, 17¾ x 12½ . . . . (954)   4,000
Bather, 25¾ x 19¾ . . . . (911)   1,120
Seated Nude, 32 x 23½ . . . . (912)   1,360
Seated Nude, 32 x 23¾ . . . . (995)   1,400
Nude Resting, on board, 17 x 19¾ . . . . (870)   900

1968–July 1969

Rue d'Assas, (1907), 32 x 23¾ . . . . (1173)   7,820
Lovers, 1912, 25¼ x 21¾ . . . . (1121)   3,640
Miscellanea, (1920), on panel, 14¾ x 13 . . . . (1030)   1,600
The Two Friends, the Beach, 1922, 33¾ x 50¾ . . (1187)   2,360
Marseilles Harbor, 1923, 36¼ x 25¾ . . . . (1152)   4,000
Marseilles, 18¼ x 25¾ . . . . (1026)   1,120
The Harbor, 24½ x 32 . . . . (1117)   3,600
Landscape, 1933, 29 x 36½ . . . . (1066)   860
Bordeaux Harbor, 36½ x 25¾ . . . . (1057)   7,000
Landscape, 19¾ x 28 . . . . (1162)   2,240
The Animals of the Farm, 14¾ x 17½ . . . . (1116)   520
Young Woman with a Necklace, 36½ x 23¾ . . . . . (1189)   3,000
Nude with Red Cushions, 25¾ x 31½ . . . . (1043)   1,300
Woman of Algiers, 45¾ x 35¼ . . . . (1113)   2,740
Reclining Nude, 15 x 18¼ . . . . (1210)   1,080
The Rugby Players, 12¾ x 16 . . . . (1187)   3,304
The Countryside Around the River Drôme, 1958,
    29 x 36½ . . . . (1080)   3,300
View from the Terrace, 1958, 23 x 28 . . . . (1202)   1,400
Still Life, 21¾ x 18¼ . . . . (1060)   2,560
The Terrace, 21¼ x 25¾ . . . . (1220)   1,960
Woman in Profile, 21¼ x 14 . . . . (1222)   800
Country Party, 25¾ x 17¾ . . . . (1222)   880
Landscape, 14¼ x 25 . . . . (1222)   820
Figures in a Landscape, 7½ x 9½ . . . . (1222)   340
Still Life, 21¼ x 25¾ . . . . (1223)   1,520
View of Gordes, 15 x 21¾ . . . . (1224)   1,360
Mountainous Landscape at Marmande,
    25¾ x 32 . . . . (1225)   2,020
Rio de Janeiro: Houses and Gardens, 15 x 18¼ . . (1225)   960
Landscape, 1955, 21¼ x 25¾ . . . . (1230)   920
Harvesters, on paper mounted on canvas,
    23 x 31½ . . . . (1231)   2,600
The Judgment of Paris, 1928, 19¾ x 29 . . . . (1235)   3,750
Seated Young Woman, 1910, on paper laid down
    on board, 39½ x 31¼ . . . . (1243)   2,000
Who Are We?,[1] 1918, 36½ x 29 . . . . (1254)   5,200
Interior with a Woman, on panel, 14 x 10 . . . . (1254)   1,300
Tulips, 15¾ x 12¾ . . . . (1257)   1,100
Breakfast, 1914, 21¾ x 18¼ . . . . (1264)   2,710
Landscape, 1911, 26 x 17¾ . . . . (1268)   4,756
Nude Seated Before the Harbor, 46¼ x 35½ . . . . (1268)   3,248
Portrait of Madame Lhote, 14 x 14 . . . . (1268)   1,624

[1]A copy of the central part of Gauguin's work.

Gustave Loiseau

(1865–1935)

Birthplace: Paris, France. Soon becomes interested in reproducing etchings and lithographs. An inheritance later allows him to devote himself to painting, settle in Montmartre, and attend the Ecole des Arts Décoratifs, Paris. Meets Maufra.

1890   Stay in Pont-Aven. Participates in the Salon des Indépendants, Paris. Exhibits, with Maufra, in a shop in the Rue Le Pelletier.

1891-94   Exhibits at the Galerie Le Barc de Boutteville, Paris. Series of snowy landscapes. Exhibits at the Galerie Durand-Ruel, Paris.

1895   Settles at Moret-sur-Loing. Stays in Normandy and in the south of France.

1905-10   Series of river bank scenes.

1935   Died, Paris.

Sales

DRAWINGS

1961–1962

Landscape, 1912, pencil and watercolor, 6½ x 8 . . . . (9) $ 40

1963

Rouen, View of Lacroix Island, 1929, charcoal
    and India-ink wash, 8 x 10 . . . . (242)   32

1964

The River Seine in Rouen, 1929, charcoal,
    4½ x 9½ . . . . (404)   24

1966

Notre-Dame, charcoal with watercolor lights,
    7½ x 10¾ . . . . (798)   158

1967

Triel, 1917, black pencil and wash, 5 x 6¾ . . . . (1002)   76

1968–July 1969

Floods in Nantes, black chalk and watercolor,
    6 x 9½ . . . . (1059)   94
Pontoise, pencil, 1935, 7½ x 9½ . . . . (1253)   56

WATERCOLORS

1963

Notre-Dame of Vaudreuil, 1917, watercolor,
    5½ x 4½ . . . . (242)   60

1964

Les Martigues, watercolor, 7¼ x 9 . . . . (404)   22

1965

Fécamp Harbor, 1920, watercolor, 6¼ x 9 . . . . (617)   124
The Sea in Fécamp, 1920, watercolor, 8¼ x 10 . . . . (586)   146
Fécamp: The River, 1920, watercolor, 8¼ x 10 . . . . (497)   80
Auvers-sur-Oise, watercolor, 6½ x 8 . . . . (556)   180

1966

Landscape, watercolor, 9 x 13 . . . . (798)   181
Fécamp, 1930, watercolor, 8 x 11½ . . . . (781)   140
Les Martigues, watercolor, 7¼ x 9 . . . . (796)   240

1967

Fishing Harbor, watercolor, 11½ x 9½ . . . . (919)   271

1968–July 1969

The Flooded Road, watercolor, 6½ x 9½ . . . . (1179)   280
Landscape, pastel, 30½ x 19¾ . . . . (1174)   690

Fishing Boats, watercolor, 8¾ x 11 .... (1238) $ 270
Fécamp, 1924, watercolor, 6 x 8 .... (1253)   100
Fécamp, 1925, watercolor, 6½ x 8 .... (1253)   84
Sketch Sheet, drawing and watercolor,
  16¼ x 10 .... (1253)   22

PAINTINGS

1961–1962

Mist Over the River Oise, 10¾ x 18¼ .... (167)   900
White Frost, Banks of the River Oise, 1906,
  21 x 25¼ .... (161)   2,200
Mist Over the River Oise, 1907, 25¾ x 32 .... (116)   2,000
Sun Over the Snowy Village, 1907, 29 x 23¾ ...... (90)   2,240
St. John Cliffs, 1908, 25¾ x 36½ .... (34)   860
The Red-Roofed House, 1909, 21½ x 25¾ .... (6)   6,780
Moret-sur-Loing, Rain Effect, 21½ x 25¾ .... (9)   1,400
St. Jouin Cliffs, 1908, 25¾ x 36½ .... (124)   840
View of Fécamp, 21¼ x 25¼ .... (70)   3,792
The Small Bridge, 29 x 21¼ .... (32)   2,000
The Red House at Port-Marly, 21¾ x 25¾ .... (50)   2,000
St. Maclou at Pontoise, 29 x 21¼ .... (50)   3,200
Flooded River, 23¾ x 29 .... (30)   2,120
Black Rocks, 21¼ x 29 .... (30)   2,100
Notre-Dame and the Quays Under Snow,
  10¼ x 15 .... (90)   850
A Village and a Landscape, 19½ x 23¾ .... (64)   4,000
A Street in a Village, 18¼ x 21¾ .... (138)   5,600
Floods, 1912, 23¾ x 36¾ .... (114)   1,700
Flood, 23¾ x 36¾ .... (147)   1,300
The Cathedral, 25¾ x 21¼ .... (32)   2,300
Triel, Snow Effect, 1916, 24 x 24 .... (56)   2,000
Sablons Hill Under Snow, 23½ x 32 .... (160)   1,460
Landscape, 1919, 17½ x 21¾ .... (164)   467
The Bridge Over the Drôme, Brantôme, 1920,
  19¾ x 24 .... (168)   1,300
The Simounou Mill, Pont-Aven, 1927, 23¾ x 29 ... (53)   1,620
The Entrance of the Village, 18¼ x 21¾ .... (53)   2,100
Vase of Flowers, on cradled panel, 17¾ x 14¾ ..... (96)   2,940

1963

Moret Bridge, (1898), 19¾ x 23¾ .... (225)   3,500
Auxerre: The Cathedral, 25¾ x 21¼ .... (198)   4,800
The Cliff, 1902, 23¾ x 32 .... (291)   1,120
Port-Marly at Daybreak, 1905, 21¼ x 25¾ ...... (316)   3,000
A Factory by the Waterside, 1905, 23¾ x 32 ..... (306)   1,600
The Haystack, 1906, 21¼ x 25¾ .... (283)   2,825
Landscape, 23¾ x 29 .... (283)   4,068
Seascape, 1907, 23¾ x 32 .... (241)   2,100
Springtime in the Ile-de-France, 1916, 19¾ x 29 .. (242)   4,100
The Footbridge at Triel, 1917, 23¾ x 36½ .... (303)   2,820
The Suspension Bridge, 1917, 23¾ x 36½ .... (224)   1,960
Pontoise: la rue aux balais, 1923, 29 x 21¼ ...... (278)   2,300
Yport Cliffs, 1925, 21¼ x 32 .... (306)   2,000
The Sea Amid the Rocks, 15½ x 16¼ .... (262)   760
Jars Point at Cape Frehel, 29 x 36½ .... (259)   2,560
Landscape, 21¼ x 32 .... (232)   4,023

1964

Still Life with a China Doll, 18¼ x 15 .... (377)   1,672
Sunny Frozen Landscape, 1899, 23¼ x 28½ ..... (458)   4,353
Rainy Day, 21¾ x 18¼ .... (371)   1,440
The River in Winter, 1910, 21¼ x 28½ .... (405)   8,126

Dull Weather at Hédouville, 21 x 25¾ .... (405) $2,031
Floods, Auvers, 1912, 14¾ x 21½ .... (405)   3,192
Floods, Auvers, 1912, 14½ x 20¾ .... (441)   2,034
Quai St. Martin in Auxerre, 1912, 19¾ x 24 ..... (354)   4,800
The Cathedral, 21½ x 26 .... (454)   2,488
The Villa Julia at Pont-Aven, 1928, 21¼ x 25¾ ... (472)   1,540
The Orchard, 23¾ x 19 .... (456)   3,000

1965

Banks of the River Seine in Summer, Tournedos-
  sur-Seine, 1899, 23¾ x 32 .... (612)   6,900
Regattas on the River Seine, 23¾ x 32 .... (523)   5,000
The Barn, 1897, 15 x 18¼ .... (617)   3,164
Belle Isle: The Spit of Coton Harbor, 1901,
  23¾ x 29 .... (602)   4,204
The Harbor, 1903, 24 x 19¾ .... (564)   2,700
Willows Alongside the River Oise, 1908, 21 x 28 .. (583)   4,933
The Farm, 21¾ x 18¼ .... (619)   2,260
Landscape with a Cathedral, 20 x 29 .... (553)   2,720
At the Village, 1921, 18¼ x 21¾ .... (611)   4,000
Montmartre, 21¾ x 18¼ .... (494)   2,900

1966

The Cliff of Normandy, 1901, 23¾ x 28½ .... (681)   6,120
The Factory Alongside the River Oise, 1905,
  23¾ x 32 .... (749)   2,800
Sun Over the Snowy Village, 1907, 21 x 29¾ .... (648)   6,500
The Orchard, Pontoise, 21 x 25½ .... (689)   2,902
The Brook, 23 x 28 .... (753)   2,612
The River Oise at Parmain, 23¾ x 29 .... (809)   7,200
Yveport Cliffs, 1924, 21¼ x 25¾ .... (745)   5,650
Flowers, 24½ x 18 .... (784)   2,300

1967

Pont-Aven, 1922, 21¼ x 25¾ .... (901)   7,200
Entrance of a Village, Autumn, 1908, 25½ x 21 ... (985)   5,451
Shadows on the Sea, 1914, 21¼ x 25¾ .... (1000)   1,600
Snow at Triel, 1916, 19¾ x 24 .... (993)   3,000
Landscape, 21½ x 25¾ .... (918)   3,955
Landscape by the Waterside, 15½ x 18¾ .... (984)   4,500
The Sound, 18¼ x 22 .... (940)   813
The Fisherman's Boat, 1927, 18¼ x 23¾ .... (912)   4,100
Village and Orchard in Spring, 19¾ x 23¾ ...... (880)   6,910
A Street in a Village, 18¾ x 22 .... (911)   4,600
A Small Farm at Vaudreuil, 18¼ x 21¾ .... (849)   6,000
Yport Cliffs, 21¼ x 32 .... (850)   3,200
Dieppe Harbor, 18¼ x 21¾ .... (884)   6,400
Mist at St. Cyr, 18¼ x 21¾ .... (912)   2,700
The Rue Caulaincourt, 21¼ x 17 .... (912)   4,240
Moret-sur-Loing, 1934-35, 21¼ x 25¾ .... (912)   8,000
Vase of Flowers, on cardboard, 18¼ x 15 .... (926)   600

1968–July 1969

Flooding Near Nantes, 21¼ x 25¾ .... (1173)   4,140
The Harbor, 1903, 18½ x 21¾ .... (1184)   9,600
The River Oise at Auvers, 1912, ... (1037)   2,500
The River Oise in Pontoise, 21¾ x 25¾ .... (1018)   13,000
The Hills of the Hermitage, Pontoise, 21¼ x 29 .. (1187)   11,328
Triel, 1915, 19¾ x 24 .... (1189)   15,000
Paris: Banks of the River Seine at Notre-Dame,
  1919, 15 x 18¼ .... (1106)   3,200
The Kitchen Garden in Winter, 1921, 21¾ x 26 .. (1184)   10,500
The Cliffs, Yport, 1924, 21¼ x 25¾ .... (1060)   4,160
The Fish Auction, Fécamp, (1925), 19¾ x 23¾ ... (1208)   10,000

Dieppe Fairway, 1926, 23¾ x 29 . . . . (1200) $9,600
The Sound, 17¾ x 22 . . . . (1059)   2,106
A Country Road, 5¾ x 5¾ . . . . (1183)   760
The Poplars, 32 x 25¾ . . . . (1175)   9,000
Landscape, 5½ x 5¾ . . . . (1042)   600
Landscape, 24 x 29 . . . . (1181)   13,600
A River in the Woods, 23¾ x 29¾ . . . . (1018)   3,000
Lilies and Peonies, on cardboard laid down on
    cradled panel, 21¾ x 15 . . . . (1051)   600
Still Life, on paper laid down on canvas,
    19¾ x 24 . . . . (1061)   700
Etretat Cliffs, Porte d'Amont, 1902, 23¾ x 32 . . . (1224)   6,000
The Fisherman's House, 1927, 29 x 23¾ . . . . (1224)   12,400
*Still Life with a Decanter, a Jug, and a Vase of
    Roses,* 18¼ x 14¾ . . . . (1225)   960
Red Roses, on panel, 25¾ x 6¼ . . . . (1231)   220
Jug of Varied Roses, on board, 17½ x 14 . . . . (1241)   907
Flowers, 25¾ x 6½ . . . . (1252)   1,800
Houses by the River, 1903, 18½ x 21¾ . . . . (1255)   8,900
The Quai de l'Hôtel de Ville, Paris, 1918,
    24 x 19¾ . . . . (1258)   11,000
The Hermitage Hill, Pontoise, 1930, 21¼ x 29 . . . (1258)   12,000
Banks of the River Eure, 23¾ x 29 . . . . (1268)   11,368
Pontoise, 1924, 19¾ x 24 . . . . (1268)   11,368
Flowers, on cardboard, 21¾ x 15 . . . . (1268)   3,526

Bernard Lorjou

(1908–   )

Birthplace: Blois, France.

1911   His family settles in Paris.

1925   Works in the design studio of Francis Ducharne, a silk mercer.

1938–40   Visits the museums of Vienna and Madrid.

1948   With Bernard Buffet, wins the Prix de la Critique, Paris. Takes part in the exhibition "Hommes-Témoins" at the Galerie du Bac, Paris.

1949   Participates in the Salon des Indépendants, the Salon d'Automne, and the Salon des Tuileries, Paris.

1951   Exhibits his lithographs at the Galerie Urban, Paris.

1952   Given an award by the Venice Biennial.

1953   Exhibits at the Galerie Charpentier, Paris, and Wildenstein's, New York.

1957   Shows his works in a booth on the Esplanade des Invalides, Paris.

1959   Exhibits at the Galerie Wildenstein, Paris.

1963   One-man show at the Moulin Rouge, Paris.

Resident in Paris.

Sales

DRAWINGS

1961–1962

Major Thompson, colored chalk and colored ink,
    31½ x 25¾ . . . . (34) $ 200
The Injured Bull, pencil, 26½ x 40 . . . . (72)   150

1963

Study for the Atomic Age, ink, 23¾ x 19¾ . . . . (314)   80

1964

Sketch for the Portrait of Brigitte Bardot,
    colored pencil, 38¼ x 23¼ . . . . (343)   320
Studies, 1950, pencil, 24 x 18¼ . . . . (386)   3,000

1965

The Bargeman, on canvas, 36½ x 29 . . . . (547)   420

1966

Figure with a Hat, charcoal on canvas,
    36½ x 29 . . . . (756)   240

WATERCOLORS

1964

Nude, gouache on paper laid down on canvas,
    49¾ x 42¼ . . . . (472)   600

PAINTINGS

1961–1962

Fool with Birds, 39½ x 32 . . . . (71)   1,500
Harlequin, 45¾ x 31½ . . . . (80)   2,200
Vase of Flowers, 21¾ x 15 . . . . (120)   1,820
Cut Flowers, 18¼ x 21¾ . . . . (30)   2,100
Flowers, 40 x 26¼ . . . . (64)   3,250
Still Life with Fruit, 19¾ x 25¼ . . . . (162)   800
Duck and Flowers, oil on metal, 39¼ x 27¼ . . . . . . (96)   3,920

1963

The Guinea Hen, 1953, 21¼ x 29 . . . . (275)   1,250
The Tree in Winter, 1956, 31½ x 25¾ . . . . (254)   1,800
The Pheasant, 57¼ x 34¾ . . . . (293)   3,100
Reclining Nude, 49¾ x 42¼ . . . . (293)   520
Still Life with a Bunch of Flowers, 21¾ x 15 . . . . . . (233)   2,000
Landscape, with Houses, 29 x 21¼ . . . . (258)   2,020

1964

Still Life with a Pineapple, 1956, 32 x 25¾ . . . . (371)   2,400
Still Life with a Fish, 36¼ x 26 . . . . (354)   4,000
Flowers in a Vase, 36½ x 25¾ . . . . (340)   3,000
Angel Musician, 24 x 19¾ . . . . (409)   400
Bust of a Woman, 38¾ x 25¾ . . . . (337)   1,100
The Bird, 25 x 32 . . . . (366)   1,400

1965

The Boat, 1955, 29 x 39½ . . . . (561)   1,960
Wintry Landscape, 1956, 23¾ x 29 . . . . (561)   1,560
Still Life: Mushroom and Clog, 21¼ x 29 . . . . (561)   760
The Bullfight, 1954, on cardboard laid down on
    panel, 33½ x 38 . . . . (552)   1,080
The Bull, on cardboard laid down on canvas,
    32 x 25¾ . . . . (567)   1,356
Harlequin with a Guitar, 1958, 35¾ x 23½ . . . . (612)   720
Flowers in a Jug, 23¾ x 14¾ . . . . (575)   1,382
Vase of Flowers, 39½ x 29 . . . . (632)   1,500
Cathedral, 36½ x 23¾ . . . . (632)   1,760
Vase of Flowers, 39½ x 25¾ . . . . (564)   2,600

1966

Vase of Flowers on a Blue Background,
32 x 25¾ .... (742) $1,000
Charlemagne, 39½ x 29 .... (742)   320
Harlequin Wearing a Red Cap, oil on tin foil,
39 x 25¾ .... (810)   1,700
Still Life with a Bottle of Wine and Pears,
21¾ x 28½ .... (784)   2,250

1967

The Bull, 1954, 39 x 25¾ .... (976)   1,000
Wreck, 31½ x 39½ .... (963)   3,250
Before the Storm, 49½ x 35¼ .... (888)   967
Chartres Cathedral, 35½ x 23¾ .... (893)   1,250
Still Life with Flowers, 50½ x 35¼ .... (870)   5,000
Still Life with a Turbot, 31½ x 45¾ .... (911)   1,600
Bunch of Flowers, on cradled panel, 25¾ x 19¾ .. (967)   1,356
Seated Harlequin, 57¾ x 35¼ .... (870)   6,250
The Clown, 45¼ x 25 .... (841)   7,250

1968–July 1969

Harbor Scene, 19¾ x 25¾ .... (1030)   1,900
Lighters on the Canal, 21¼ x 25¾ .... (1026)   2,400
Harlequin, on copper, 40 x 65¾ .... (1121)   2,700
Harlequin, 57¾ x 35¼ .... (1080)   3,000
Still Life with Flowers, 60¼ x 50½ .... (1080)   3,750
Hen Pheasant, 25¼ x 32 .... (1196)   1,360
The Teal, 13 x 18¼ .... (1026)   800
The Sunflowers, 23¾ x 29 .... (1113)   1,460
Still Life, 19¾ x 21¾ .... (1117)   860
Bunch of Flowers, on paper laid down on canvas,
30 x 22 .... (1208)   1,500
Flowers on a Yellow Background, 32 x 23¾ ..... (1184)   2,220
Harlequin, 39½ x 25¾ .... (1225)   1,540
Summer Delights, 28¾ x 39¼ .... (1232)   3,250
Wine and Pears, 21¼ x 28½ .... (1232)   2,750
Still Life with a Bottle, 21¾ x 18¼ .... (1238)   1,200
Flowers and Onions, 29 x 23¾ .... (1243)   1,000
Still Life, on board, 11¾ x 8¾ .... (1248)   1,900
Vase of Flowers, 22½ x 30½ .... (1248)   2,200
The Great Green Tree, 32 x 24 .... (1258)   2,000
The House of the Noëls, 21¾ x 18¼ .... (1258)   1,160
Fruit and Flowers, 17½ x 21 .... (1273)   1,058

Laurence Stephen Lowry

(1887–   )

Birthplace: Manchester, England. Studies at the Manchester School of Art.

1920-30   Participates in local shows.

1932   Death of his father.

1939   A. J. McNeill Reid discovers his works. First one-man show at the McNeill Reid Gallery.

1941-51   Retrospective exhibitions at the Salford Art Gallery.

1959   Retrospective exhibition at the City Art Gallery, Manchester.

1962   Retrospective exhibition at the Graves Art Gallery, Sheffield.

1964   An exhibition entitled "Homage to Lowry" takes place at the Monks Hall Museum, Eccles, Lancashire.

1967   Retrospective exhibition at the Tate Gallery, London. Exhibits at the Crane Kalman Gallery, London.

Sales

DRAWINGS

1964

An Accident, 1925, pencil 10 x 14 .... (420) $ 189
Peel Park, 1920, charcoal and pastel, 8¾ x 14¾ ... (444)   290

1965

The Path, 1960, pencil and wash, 9 x 13 .... (643)   263

1966

Johnson's Building, 1930, pencil, 10¾ x 14¾ ..... (825)   691

1968–July 1969

Hulme Place, Salford, 1926, pencil, 9½ x 13¾ ... (1025)   471
The Newspaper Seller, 1930, pencil, 10¾ x 14¾ .. (1143)   743
The Stairs, 1932 .... (1206)   1,227
Landscape, 1942, pencil, 8¼ x 10¼ .... (1074)   354
The Lighthouse, 1956, pencil, 10 x 14 .... (1165)   446
The Walk, 1960, pencil, 13¾ x 9¾ .... (1141)   472

WATERCOLORS

1966

Seaside Scenes, 1920, two pastels, each
10¾ x 14¾ .... (761)   1,161

PAINTINGS

1963

The Sea, 1957, 9¾ x 11½ .... (268)   411

1964

The Children on the Beach, 1946, on panel,
13 x 24½ .... (364)   3,192
The Village Street, 1935, on panel, 14 x 19¾ ..... (444)   4,643
After the Match, 1944, 14 x 25 .... (356)   2,764
The Mill, 1959, 14 x 17¾ .... (421)   1,797

1965

Romantic Landscape, 1941, on board, 15 x 10½ ... (544)   2,031
News of the Elections, 1945, on board, 20 x 16¼ .. (506)   2,073
Glasgow, the Docks, 1947, 17¾ x 21¼ .... (506)   3,179
Head of a Young Girl, 1955, 19¾ x 23¾ .... (584)   829
Street of an Industrial Town, 1961, on board,
11¾ x 10 .... (522)   1,935

1966

Romantic Landscape, 1947, on board, 15 x 10¾ ... (693)   1,327
Street Scene, 1948, on panel, 11 x 20 .... (709)   4,643
The Meeting, 1949, 19½ x 23¾ .... (761)   8,845
Several Figures on a Square, 1950, 29¾ x 39½ .... (825)   8,292
Street Scene, 1961, on board, 10¾ x 8¾ .... (825)   2,488
Conversation in the Street, 1964, on board,
10 x 8 .... (825)   1,382

1967

Ambulance Drawn by an Old Horse, 1941, on
    panel, 15¾ x 23 . . . . (1003) $5,688
Winter Road, 1953, on panel, 8¼ x 15 . . . . (1003)   830
Old Houses, 1922, on panel, 9¾ x 4¾ . . . . (869)   719
The Quarrel, 1925, 14 x 10 . . . . (944)   1,045
Street Scene, 1927, 15½ x 11¾ . . . . (869)   3,593
The Football Match, 1932, on panel, 16¾ x 21¾ . . (959)   4,351
Old Berwick, 1936, on panel, 21 x 13 . . . . (959)   8,996
Street Scene, 1941, 11¾ x 15¾ . . . . (853)   8,706
Scene on a Beach, 1943, 17¾ x 25¾ . . . . (944)   10,737
Motherly Argument, 1950, 11¾ x 9 . . . . (944)   929
Sunday Afternoon, 1957, 45½ x 59½ . . . . (853)   21,753
Village at the Seaside, 1961, 18 x 24 . . . . (944)   4,643

1968–July 1969

Workers Coming Out of the Factory, 1929,
    17 x 25 . . . . (1165)   9,416
Industrial Town, 1922, on panel, 17 x 21 . . . . (1143)   10,903
The Bridge, 1931, 19 x 15½ . . . . (1025)   8,673
Several Figures in a Small Town, 1935,
    15½ x 19½ . . . . (1025)   13,629
The Blast Furnaces, 1941, on board, 18 x 24 . . . . . (1141)   7,080
Garden Place, Ancoats, 1944, 15½ x 19¾ . . . . (1206)   9,440
Sea and Sky, 1945, 15¼ x 19½ . . . . (1165)   1,858
The Estuary, 1944, 15¾ x 19¾ . . . . (1074)   8,968
Man Looking at Something, 1962, 11¾ x 8 . . . . . . (1143)   1,437
On the Beach, 1957, 19½ x 23½ . . . . (1143)   7,186
Seascape, 1964, 30¼ x 40¼ . . . . (1025)   2,478
Newbiggin by the Sea, 1966, 18 x 22 . . . . (1143)   6,443

Maximilien Luce

(1858–1941)

Birthplace: Paris, France.

1874   Serves his apprenticeship with an engraver. Studies
painting in the evening, chiefly at the Académie
Suisse, Paris—taught by Carolus Duran.

1877   Stay in London.

1884–85   After military service, attends the class of Carolus
Duran. Meets Pissarro, who converts him to Impressionism. Also meets Signac.

1887   Participates in the Salon des Indépendants, Paris,
where he exhibits annually.

1889   Turns to Neo-Impressionism and is soon regarded
as an important figure of the group. Participates
in the exhibition held by the XX, Brussels. He is
one of the chief contributors to anarchist periodicals: *La Révolte, Le Père Peinard, Les Temps
Nouveaux.*

1894   In a famous trial involving thirty anarchists, he is
incarcerated in the Prison Mazas, Paris, for four
months. Executes a series of lithographs showing
prison scenes, published with a preface by Jules
Vallès. Goes to Belgium after his discharge to escape from anarchist repression. Works on the
theme of the workman's life. Gradually reverts to
earlier Impressionism.

1899   Exhibits at the Galerie Durand-Ruel, Paris.

1904   Exhibits at the Galerie Druet, Paris.

1909   Exhibits at the Galerie Bernheim-Jeune, Paris.

1920–22   Exhibits at the Galerie Durand-Ruel, Paris.

1935   Becomes president of the Société des Indépendants,
Paris.

1941   Died, Paris.

1942   Retrospective exhibition at the Salon des Indépendants, Paris.

Sales

DRAWINGS

1962–1963

Meadow at Bessy, 1910, colored pencil, 8¾ x 12 . . (120) $ 260
The Bateau-Lavoir, pencil and pen, 3¾ x 5½ . . . . . (168)   50
Dieppe, 1922, wash, 12¼ x 18¾ . . . . (58)   320
Back from the Ploughed Land, colored pencil,
    15 x 21¼ . . . . (171)   200

1963

Country Scene, charcoal, 19 x 24½ . . . . (209)   80
The Gathering of Apples, charcoal, 15½ x 22 . . . . . (223)   180
Charing Cross Bridge, (1890), pencil, 6½ x 8½ . . . . (255)   658
The Circus Caravan; View of Lagny, two
    drawings, ink, 4½ x 5¾ and pencil, 5¾ x 8 . . . . (179)   175

1964

View of the Tuileries, pencil, 8 x 10½ . . . . (872)   150
The Rue Montorgueil, pencil and ink, 9 x 6½ . . . . . (331)   22
The Nurse, pen and pencil, 3¾ x 1¾ . . . . (384)   40
Studies of Men, 9 drawings arranged on a sheet of
    paper by the artist, 16¼ x 12¾ . . . . (323)   130
The House, pencil, 8 x 10¾ . . . . (357)   120
Two Fishing Scenes, India ink, each 5¼ x 8 . . . . . . (321)   225

1965

Resting on the Promenade, black stone,
    4¾ x 6½ . . . . (567)   45
Back from the Ploughed Land, colored pencil,
    15 x 21¼ . . . . (617)   283
The Cart in Front of the Farm House, India-ink
    wash, 11 x 15 . . . . (581)   120

1966

Mother and Child Walking, charcoal, 8 x 8 . . . . (819)   210
Woman Lacing Up Her Shoe, charcoal,
    10½ x 7½ . . . . (819)   230
Barns at Méricourt, wash, 10 x 16¼ . . . . (711)   166
Suburban Road, pen, 6¾ x 9¼ . . . . (781)   70
Military Man and Figures, 4 x 3¾ . . . . (691)   80
1914, India ink, 14 x 19¾ . . . . (655)   40
Landscape of the River Cure, charcoal, and
    India-ink wash, 12¾ x 19½ . . . . (668)   250
Landscape, charcoal, 4½ x 6 . . . . (788)   36
The Orchard, India-ink wash and charcoal,
    23¾ x 17¾ . . . . (721)   300

1967

Landscape, colored pencil, 12½ x 18 .... (855) $ 364

Portrait of Félix Fénéon, black lead, 10¾ x 7¾ ... (939)   415

Woman Sewing, charcoal, 11¾ x 8 .... (936)   84

1968–July 1969

The Rest, 8 x 9¾ .... (1042)   52

Harvesttime, wash and sepia, 11 x 16¾ .... (1213)   284

Village on the Bank of a River, pencil and wash,
    12¾ x 19¼ .... (1134)   260

Landscape with a Tower, pencil with wash lights,
    12¼ x 19¼ .... (1183)   250

Portrait of a Woman, black pencil, 6¾ x 4 ...... (1110)   122

Chess Players, India ink, 5 x 3¾ .... (1134)   94

The Two Trees, charcoal and wash, 8¼ x 11 ..... (1039)   58

In the Storeroom, three drawings on one sheet,
    pen .... (1089)   400

Landscape, charcoal and wash, 19½ x 25¼ ...... (1223)   360

Studies of a Young Boy, 6 drawings, ink and
    pencil .... (1223)   180

Studies, 4 drawings .... (1223)   140

Landscape, pencil and wash, 10 x 13½ .... (1231)   625

Studies of a Man, two drawings, pencil and
    charcoal, 3 x 5¾ and 3 x 5 .... (1231)   175

The Destroyed Chapel, charcoal and chalk,
    18¾ x 24 .... (1238)   60

The Convoy, 19 x 24 .... (1238)   38

Lost in the Tempest, 17½ x 24¾ .... (1238)   60

The Bateau-Lavoir, pencil and pen on gray-blue
    paper, 3½ x 5¼ .... (1241)   139

Ploughman and Soldiers, brush and black ink on
    buff paper, 14 x 21 .... (1241)   353

Houses, pencil, 3¼ x 5½ .... (1247)   52

Fields, wash, 8¼ x 11 .... (1253)   170

Family Scene at the Farm, charcoal, 13½ x 18¾ . (1256)   640

Gathering In Hay at the Farm, charcoal and
    wash, 21 x 29¼ .... (1256)   800

Landscape, Houses, and Figures, charcoal, and
    pastel, 15½ x 10¾ .... (1268)   464

Man with a Sword, black chalk, 2½ x 5½ .... (1273)   55

WATERCOLORS

1963

Landscape, pastel, 8¾ x 14 .... (196)   150

Riverside, watercolor, 12¾ x 19½ .... (190)   290

1964

Landscape at Eragny, pastel, 14¼ x 21¾ .... (341)   400

Seated Woman Sewing, pastel, 7 x 10 .... (331)   136

1965

Landscape, 1910, pastel, 9 x 12¾ .... (640)   220

The Thatch-Roofed Cottage, 1939, watercolor,
    8 x 9½ .... (572)   120

1966

Little Girl with a Blue Apron, pastel, 6½ x 3¾ .... (819)   400

Riverside, pastel, 11¾ x 8¾ .... (819)   2,800

The Ploughed Land, pastel, 14¾ x 21 .... (711)   360

Reclining Nude, 1889, pastel, 12¾ x 15½ .... (819)   3,000

1967

The Pont de Neuilly, watercolor, 5¾ x 8¼ .... (976)   240

Landscape, pastel, 10¾ x 15½ .... (967)   542

The Pond, pastel, 6¾ x 10 .... (886)   420

The Sheet of Water, watercolor, 7½ x 11 .... (841)   500

1968–July 1969

Landscape, pastel, 10 x 16¾ .... (1039) $ 280

The River Seine at Rolleboise, pastel, 7 x 10 ..... (1051)   760

PAINTINGS

1961–1962

The Fisherman, 18¼ x 25¾ .... (71)   2,040

A Lane Near Nantua, 1900, 31¾ x 39 .... (64)   11,000

The Sand Pit at Méricourt, 15¾ x 21 .... (171)   1,000

Rolleboise, 19¾ x 24 .... (160)   1,740

The Forge, 1895, 45¾ x 35¼ .... (47)   1,700

The Cow by the Pond, 20 x 26 .... (146)   360

Two Horses Before an Industrial Valley,
    10 x 14 .... (44)   900

Banks of the River Seine, 8 x 10 .... (30)   540

The Bridge, 9¼ x 12¾ .... (125)   2,700

Bathers, 19¾ x 25½ .... (96)   3,250

A Path Along the Riverside, 1936, 36½ x 29 ...... (119)   800

Le Tréport, 1937, 9½ x 13 .... (161)   190

Portrait of Signac, on cardboard, 10¾ x 8¾ ..... (114)   360

Lucie Cousturier in Her Garden, on panel,
    13 x 9½ .... (68)   1,320

1963

The Pond, on panel, 13 x 16 .... (241)   4,140

Harbor Scene, on cardboard, 23¼ x 28½ .... (241)   800

Portrait of Ludovic Pissarro, 1897, 18 x 14¾ ..... (202)   3,800

Charleroi, 1897, 15¼ x 20 .... (232)   1,243

Maternity, (1898), 64¼ x 31¼ .... (255)   1,782

Bather, (1899), 28½ x 36¾ .... (316)   3,250

Bathers, 21¼ x 25¼ .... (225)   3,600

The Leuvehaven, Rotterdam, 1908, 21¼ x 31¼ ... (202)   9,000

Bathing, 1908, 16¼ x 13 .... (318)   5,000

Bathing, 13 x 19¾ .... (209)   380

Riverside, on cardboard, 11¾ x 8¼ .... (254)   4,600

Landscape, 1917, 14¾ x 19½ .... (202)   1,750

Country Landscape, 15 x 18¼ .... (316)   2,250

A Lane in the Country, 6 x 7½ .... (257)   312

Harvesttime, 1927, 21¼ x 32 .... (306)   1,100

The River Seine at Rolleboise, 1935, on panel,
    6¼ x 7¼ .... (246)   138

Landscape at Rolleboise, 9¾ x 14 .... (233)   960

The Dock of Le Tréport, on paper laid down on
    canvas, 15¼ x 18¼ .... (291)   500

Buildings, 32 x 23¾ .... (234)   620

The Wheelbarrow, on panel, 11½ x 11¾ .... (179)   750

Scene on a Beach, on panel, 10 x 12¾ .... (300)   640

Bathing, 28 x 36½ .... (258)   1,400

Flowers in a Vase, on paper laid down on board,
    20¾ x 21 .... (316)   3,500

1964

Smoke Over the City, 1899, on cardboard,
    11¾ x 24 .... (331)   660

The Bridge, 1890, on a fan shaped panel,
    10½ x 23½ .... (453)   2,349

Landscape of the Beauce, (1903–05), on canvas
    laid down on cardboard, 10 x 17 .... (376)   820

Houses in the Trees, 18¼ x 21¾ .... (336)   700

Bathing, 1903–05, 29 x 36½ .... (416)   3,040

Rotterdam, 1907, on cardboard, 10 x 14½ .... (323)   740

Bathing, (1908), 16¼ x 13 .... (354)   1,500

The Creek, 23¾ x 29 .... (409)   1,200

Gardens at Auvers, 18¼ x 21¾ .... (472)   960

Riverside Under a Stormy Sky, 1911-12, 24 x 32¼ .... (475) $1,660

Landscape, on board, 10 x 14 .... (377) 475

The River Seine at St. Mamès, on cardboard, 15 x 18¼ .... (366) 600

Rouen Harbor, 35½ x 30½ .... (329) 2,400

Méricourt, 18¼ x 21¾ .... (465) 1,500

Lighters on the River Seine, 1925, on cardboard, 20¾ x 27 .... (450) 840

Housebreaking, 39 x 32 .... (454) 1,216

Dust Over the Town, on cardboard, 8¾ x 14 ..... (398) 920

Landscape of Paris, on cradled panel, 11¾ x 16¼ .... (394) 1,400

Notre-Dame, 14¾ x 23¾ .... (458) 2,077

Washerwomen, 18¼ x 21¾ .... (457) 960

Banks of the River Seine, 32 x 45¾ .... (399) 1,420

Flowers in a Vase, on paper laid down on canvas, 16¾ x 21 .... (354) 2,250

Charleroi, the Factories, 25¾ x 32 .... (397) 3,700

The Seasons, 4 oils on canvas, 52 x 52 .... (401) 4,000

1965

Blast Furnances, Charleroi, 1896, 39½ x 31 ...... (633) 3,000

Landscape, 1906, on cardboard, 16¾ x 22 .... (619) 2,320

Flowers in a Pot, 16¼ x 13 .... (632) 1,120

Dieppe Harbor, (1907), on panel, 8¾ x 14 .... (632) 1,360

Banks of the River Seine, 21¼ x 29 .... (632) 1,440

Landscape with High Trees, 1923, 25¾ x 32 ...... (523) 1,800

Bathing, 25¾ x 32 .... (491) 1,100

The Quiet River, 12¾ x 17½ .... (583) 1,393

The Valley, 1928, 6½ x 17½ .... (585) 493

The River Seine, Nieghborhood of Mantes, 1929, 12½ x 20 .... (539) 1,500

Banks of the River Seine at Rolleboise, 13 x 18¼ .... (511) 1,192

The River Seine at Méricourt, 19 x 25 .... (582) 1,520

Washerwoman in Normandy, on paper laid down on canvas, 18¼ x 21¾ .... (515) 960

Seascape, 1929, on paper laid down on canvas, 18¼ x 21¾ .... (577) 630

Coast of Brittany, on cardboard, 10¾ x 14 .... (545) 368

Horses and Children on the Beach, 5¼ x 8¾ ..... (494) 575

Trees Along the Seaside, Sunset, on cardboard, on canvas, 14 x 11 .... (611) 1,440

Bathing Horses on the Banks of the River Seine Near the Pont-Marie, 32 x 39½ .... (611) 1,160

The Edge of a Lake with Bathers, on panel, 11¾ x 15 .... (507) 1,000

Bunch of Flowers, 21¾ x 18¼ .... (494) 1,400

A Garden in Antwerp, 18¼ x 21¾ .... (619) 970

Landscape, 14 x 21 .... (522) 1,935

The Rest, 13 x 19¾ .... (530) 560

Harvesttime, on paper, 14¼ x 10½ .... (553) 1,080

1966

Seated Nude Combing Her Hair, 1890, 25¾ x 18¼ .... (819) 7,400

The Pont Neuf, 1889, on cardboard, 9¼ x 14¼ .... (819) 12,000

The Cart, 1889, on cardboard, 6¼ x 10¾ .... (819) 6,800

The Thames and Parliament in London, 1890-95, 19½ x 25¾ .... (727) 15,300

Banks of the River Seine at Herblay, 1892, 25¾ x 32 .... (819) 18,600

The Rue Réaumur, 1896, 24 x 19¾ .... (793) 4,200

Cutting of the Rue Réaumur, 1896, 18¼ x 15 ..... (797) $4,520

The Rue Réaumur, 1897, 23¼ x 29 .... (819) 8,400

The Road Works on the Avenue Junot, 21¼ x 25¾ .... (808) 2,467

A Boulevard Under the Rain, 1896, 15¾ x 13 ..... (819) 6,100

Poplars at Bois-le-Roi, 1899, 15¾ x 12¾ .... (755) 2,100

The Farm of Guerne, 10½ x 16½ .... (689) 553

Portrait of Félix Fénéon, 1902, 21¾ x 15 .... (752) 500

The Village of Bessy-sur-Cure (Yonne), 1906, 25¾ x 30½ .... (753) 5,514

Landscape at Rolleboise, 23¼ x 42 .... (655) 2,960

Bennecourt Village (Seine-et-Oise), on cardboard, 8¾ x 10¾ .... (824) 840

The River Seine Under Snow in Paris, 1917, 16¾ x 21¼ .... (724) 1,500

The River Seine at the Pont Mirabeau, 21¼ x 32 .... (726) 1,500

The Place St. Michel at Night, on cardboard, 6½ x 10¼ .... (720) 212

Banks of the River Seine, 15 x 11 .... (742) 600

Riverside, on cardboard, 8¼ x 11¾ .... (819) 5,600

The Rue Mouffetard, 32 x 25¾ .... (819) 16,000

Sunset, Honfleur, 1927, 18¼ x 21¾ .... (648) 900

Méricourt, on panel, 10 x 14 .... (772) 340

Harvesttime, 1929, 11¾ x 19¾ .... (665) 3,400

The River Seine Near Vétheuil, 1929, on cardboard, 4¾ x 20 .... (668) 560

Apple Trees in Blossom at St. Ay, Loiret, on paper laid down on canvas, 10 x 14¼ .... (811) 1,100

Landscape with a Bridge, on paper laid down on board, 6¾ x 13 .... (784) 700

Landscape, on paper laid down on canvas, 11½ x 15¾ .... (670) 960

A Family Seated Under a Willow, 21 x 25 .... (757) 1,244

The Workers, on cardboard, 23¼ x 28½ .... (798) 1,243

Workers in Front of a Blast Furnace, on cardboard, 14 x 19 .... (745) 2,260

In the Night, on board, 13 x 10 .... (784) 2,750

The Washerwomen, 12¾ x 16 .... (760) 1,219

The Stranded Boat, 16¾ x 21¼ .... (674) 1,880

Souvenir of Rotterdam, 23 x 31¼ .... (698) 2,720

The Orchard, 24½ x 31¾ .... (776) 7,500

1967

Bathers, (1899), 28½ x 36¾ .... (954) 3,250

Bathing, on panel, 9½ x 10¾ .... (949) 360

The Path of Le Pinet, St. Tropez, 1904, 25¾ x 36½ .... (976) 18,000

Maritime Landscape, on cardboard, 20½ x 25¾ ... (850) 1,500

Daybreak Over the Sea, 25¾ x 36½ .... (858) 11,000

A Lake in the Mountain, 10½ x 16 .... (858) 460

A River in Winter, 1905, 14¾ x 17¾ .... (1006) 2,115

Buffalo Bill's Circus, 1905, on cardboard, 6½ x 4¾ .... (876) 1,300

Bessy-sur-Cure, 1910, 25¾ x 32 .... (923) 18,800

Bathing Horses in the River Seine Near the Pont-Marie, 31½ x 39 .... (989) 2,750

The Quays in Rouen, 1912, 35½ x 30½ .... (988) 3,981

Maritime Landscape, on cardboard, 20½ x 25¾ ... (912) 2,600

The Towboat, oil on paper, 10¼ x 15¾ .... (911) 1,400

Perros-Guirec, on panel, 10½ x 14 .... (909) 1,400

Fluvial Landscape with a Bridge, 1920, 35½ x 47½ .... (870) 2,500

The Road at Moulineux, 23¾ x 32 .... (852) 3,100

The Halt of the Peasants, 13 x 19¾ .... (852) 900

Paris, the Place Dauphine Seen from the Quai du Louvre, on cardboard, 15 x 21¾ .... (984) $6,620

Riverside, 17½ x 25 .... (984)   1,600

Honfleur, 1928, on panel, 9 x 13 .... (911)   880

The Beach, on cardboard, 6 x 9 .... (874)   376

Landscape at Rolleboise, 29 x 34¾ .... (912)   2,700

The Plain of Bagneux, 17½ x 14 .... (888)   470

Landscape with a Farm, 14 x 26½ .... (841)   1,800

Landscape, 10 x 12¾ .... (870)   1,000

Landscape, 7 x 11 .... (831)   600

Bathers, 21¾ x 25¾ .... (989)   3,250

The River Seine in the Surroundings of Vétheuil, 6¾ x 14 .... (893)   900

Landscape by the Waterside, 19¾ x 25¾ .... (964)   1,200

The Scaffolding, 32 x 21¼ .... (978)   3,100

1968–July 1969

Montmartre, the House of Suzanne Valadon, 1895, 21¼ x 25¾ .... (1109)   16,200

Roofs Under Snow: The Rue Denfert, 1887, on cardboard, 11½ x 15¾ .... (1181)   4,300

The Chauffeur, 1888, 49½ x 40¾ .... (1181)   9,800

The Forge, (1890), 21¾ x 18 .... (1080)   4,250

Camaret II, 1894, on board, 11 x 14 .... (1061)   1,000

Village Along the Riverside, 1896, 19½ x 25¾ ... (1113)   6,600

The Rue Mouffetard, 1896, 25¾ x 32 .... (1152)   35,000

The Rue Réaumur, Paris, 1896, 18¼ x 15 .... (1068)   7,080

Gisors Church, 1898, 29 x 36¼ .... (1132)   24,780

Industrial City, 1899, on board, 11½ x 24 .... (1138)   2,106

St. Tropez, 1903, on cardboard, 7½ x 14¾ .... (1109)   1,760

Rouen Harbor, (1905), 28 x 35½ .... (1187)   9,440

The River Marne at Quinquangrogne, 1905, on paper mounted on cardboard, 10 x 14¾ ..... (1121)   1,200

Bathers, (1906), 51½ x 63¼ .... (1080)   4,000

The Harbor, (1912), on board, 26½ x 20½ .... (1126)   2,230

Rouen Harbor, 1913, 32¼ x 39½ .... (1152)   19,000

The Valley of the River Seine, Near Rolleboise, 1917, on cardboard, 16¾ x 21¼ .... (1117)   1,620

Fishermen at Rolleboise, on cardboard laid down on panel, 10½ x 15 .... (1178)   1,250

Surroundings of Rolleboise, 29 x 39½ .... (1219)   2,000

The Towboat, 15 x 21¾ .... (1039)   700

Lunch in the Country, 25¾ x 36½ .... (1116)   3,700

The Quai d'Ivry, Paris, on panel, 7¾ x 10¾ ..... (1187)   1,180

Road Works on the Pont d'Iéna, 25¾ x 31½ .... (1039)   1,360

Bathers on the Edge of a Lake, on paper laid down on canvas, 15¾ x 21¼ .... (1187)   1,652

The Rest on the Grass, on cardboard, 13 x 9½ ... (1051)   1,800

Bathing Horses in the River Seine Near the Pont-Marie, 31½ x 38¾ .... (1132)   3,068

The Vert-Galant, on board, 13 x 19½ .... (1203)   2,181

Honfleur, 1933, 15 x 21¾ .... (1210)   2,400

Sailboats Near the Coast, on board, 9¾ x 12¾ .. (1132)   1,180

The Approaches to the Village, 14 x 11 .... (1030)   1,200

Le Tréport, 1937, on paper laid down on canvas, 11¾ x 18¾ .... (1019)   840

On the Banks of the River Oise, on cardboard, 10 x 14 .... (1174)   2,645

The Goat Girl, 18¼ x 21¾ .... (1106)   2,200

Bathing, on panel, 9 x 13 .... (1089)   560

Riverside, on panel, 10¼ x 14 .... (1159)   1,900

A Horse Quenching Its Thirst in a River, 18½ x 22 .... (1088)   1,900

The Old Dock in Honfleur, 23¾ x 29 .... (1184)   4,060

Landscape of Méricourt, on panel, 10 x 14 ...... (1171) $1,000

Bessy-sur-Cure, on panel, 10¼ x 13½ .... (1154)   630

Threshing Wheat in Brittany, on paper, 10½ x 14½ .... (1049)   1,200

Wintry Landscape, on cardboard, 11¾ x 15¾ .... (1078)   330

The Locomotive, 18¼ x 25¼ .... (1125)   5,750

The Jousts, 18¼ x 25¾ .... (1200)   5,200

The Place St. Michel, at Night, on cardboard, 6½ x 10¼ .... (1026)   600

Portrait of Lucie Cousturier, 55½ x 31 .... (1181)   30,000

Bathing, 10¾ x 10 .... (1220)   920

Herd in a Meadow, 1909, 18¼ x 25¾ .... (1224)   4,800

The Unloaders, oil on paper laid down on cardboard, 23¾ x 29 .... (1225)   1,400

Bathing, on cardboard, 13¼ x 20 .... (1225)   1,720

Bank of the River Seine, 15 x 11 .... (1225)   840

The Fishermen with a Dog, 13 x 9½ .... (1227)   1,100

In the Country, two paintings, each 8 x 10¼ ..... (1231)   2,160

Church in a Meadow, 6 x 9 .... (1231)   800

By the Riverside, 10¼ x 16 .... (1231)   650

River Scene, on board, 9½ x 13 .... (1231)   1,200

The River Seine: Surroundings of Monts, 1929, 12½ x 10 .... (1231)   1,400

Banks of the River Seine, 9½ x 13½ .... (1231)   1,700

The Building, 39½ x 31¾ .... (1231)   4,000

Workers, on board, 16½ x 21 .... (1231)   1,800

Landscape, on cardboard, 10¾ x 13¾ .... (1238)   920

The Country, on cardboard, 8¾ x 10¾ .... (1238)   60

View of Méréville, on board, 1903, 19½ x 29½ ... (1239)   19,200

The Leuvehaven, Rotterdam, 1908, 21½ x 31¾ .. (1239)   19,200

The River Seine at Billancourt, (1910), 25 x 35¾ .... (1239)   9,600

The Sacré-Coeur Seen Through the Gardens of Montmartre, 15½ x 10 .... (1240)   2,520

The Smith's Hearth, (1890), 21¾ x 18 .... (1240)   4,080

The Return of the Fishermen, 17½ x 21¼ .... (1240)   1,008

River in the Valley, 12¾ x 17¾ .... (1240)   2,760

Lighters on the River, 15½ x 20½ .... (1241)   3,280

Demobilization, 1918, on cardboard, 6½ x 29¾ .. (1247)   700

Rouen Harbor, 36 x 30½ .... (1248)   6,500

River Scene, 32 x 45¾ .... (1248)   4,500

Bend of the River Seine, Rolleboise, on board, 20½ x 10¾ .... (1248)   6,000

The Excavation, 5¼ x 9½ .... (1248)   1,250

Varlin's Death, 19½ x 25¾ .... (1253)   450

Towboats and Barges, 9½ x 14 .... (1254)   2,300

The Navvies, 1908-12, 47½ x 39½ .... (1254)   5,200

The Rest Near the River with a Sailboat, on canvas laid down on cardboard, ... (1255)   1,900

Steamer on the River, 16¼ x 21¼ .... (1255)   4,040

The River Marne at Quinquancrogne, 1905, 14¾ x 10 .... (1255)   2,000

Rotterdam Harbor, on cradled panel, 19¾ x 25¾ .... (1256)   6,200

The Planer on the Works Site, on cardboard, 13½ x 13 .... (1256)   1,000

Sailboats in Rotterdam Harbor, 1908, 18¼ x 21¾ .... (1256)   7,220

Rotterdam Harbor, 1908, 18¼ x 21¾ .... (1256)   7,400

Washerwomen Near the Village, on cardboard, 10¼ x 13½ .... (1257)   1,960

Breton Harbor, on cardboard, 10¼ x 15½ .... (1258)   8,200

Landscape, 1907, 13½ x 16¾ .... (1262)   2,200

The Farm, 19¾ x 25¾ .... (1264)   1,100

Riverside in the Loiret, on panel, 14 x 19¾ ...... (1265) $2,600
Félix Fénéon with His Greatcoat On,[1] 1902,
    21¼ x 15 .... (1265)   2,200
Landscape, 1907, 19½ x 25 .... (1270)   13,200
Sea and Rocks, 1893, 21 x 25½ .... (1270)   15,600
Village by the River Bank, 1896, 19 x 25 .... (1270)   8,400
Portrait of the Artist's Mother Having Dinner,[2]
    (1882–83), 17½ x 14½ .... (1271)   3,120

Jean Lurçat

(1892–1966)

Birthplace: Bruyères, Vosges district, France.

1912   Goes to Paris. Attends the Ecole Nationale des Beaux-Arts and the Académie Colarossi, Paris.

1914   Serves his apprenticeship with Laffite, for whom he begins to execute frescoes. Wounded during World War I.

1915–17   Takes an increasing interest in tapestry.

1917   Exhibits his oils at the Tanner Gallery, Zurich. Executes his first tapestry.

1920   Participates in the Salon des Indépendants, Paris.

1922   First one-man shows in Paris at the Galerie Povolowski and the Galerie Vildrac.

1930   Exhibits his tapestries in New York.

1931   Settles at Vevey. First tapestries executed at the Manufacture d'Aubusson.

1933   Stay in the U.S.

1936   First tapestries executed at the Manufacture des Gobelins.

1939–40   The state commissions him to do an important tapestry entitled "Les Quatre Saisons." Settles in Aubusson. Works with Gromaire, Derain, and Raoul Dufy.

1944   Exhibition of his tapestries at the Galerie Louis Carré, Paris.

1945   Elected president of the Association des Peintres Cartonniers de Tapisserie.

1946   Participates in the exhibition "La Tapisserie Française du Moyen-Age à nos jours" at the Musée National d'Art Moderne, Paris. Writes three books in which he develops his theory of the revival of tapestry. Exhibits all over Europe.

1954   Exhibits at the Museum of Modern Art, Moscow. Executes a tapestry entitled "Hommage aux Morts de la Résistance et de la Déportation" for the Musée National d'Art Moderne, Paris.

1957   Designs his largest and most renowned tapestry "Le Chant du Monde."

1962   Trip to the U.S.S.R., Morocco, Switzerland, and other countries.

[1]Dedicated "A l'ami Gino."
[2]On the reverse, a little sketch of a sailboat.

1964   Becomes a member of the Académie des Beaux-Arts, Paris.

1966   Died. (Although he won fame mainly through his tapestries, Lurçat painted throughout his career, producing several oils and gouaches, as well as a number of etchings and lithographs intended for book illustrations.)

Sales

DRAWINGS

1965

Woman with Her Arms Raised, 1918, pen,
    10¾ x 7½ .... (530) $ 20
Provençal Village, 1918, pencil, 12¾ x 9½ .... (535)   124

1966

Cock, India ink and watercolor, 10¼ x 8¼ .... (745)   452

1968–July 1969

Still Life, 1927, pencil and pastel, ... (1240)   96
Untitled, 1925, pencil, 9 x 15 .... (1266)   64
Untitled, 1925, pencil, 9 x 20 .... (1266)   76

WATERCOLORS

1961–1962

Dancers, 1925, watercolor, 11¾ x 8¾ .... (68)   156
The Octopus, gouache, 23¾ x 35¼ .... (93)   237
Fruits éclatés, gouache, 11 x 15 .... (59)   250
Seeds and Fruit, 1925, watercolor, 9 x 13½ .... (59)   54
The Cock, gouache, 24½ x 19 .... (110)   400
Insect, 1948, gouache, 8¼ x 7¼ .... (105)   149

1963

The Fishermen's Nets, 1939, gouache,
    10¾ x 12¾ .... (238)   124
The Standard Bearers, gouache, 11¾ x 13¼ ...... (281)   316
Cliffs, 1947, gouache, 17½ x 28 .... (190)   174
Cock, gouache, 24½ x 19½ .... (181)   360

1964

The Water Carrier, pastel, 17½ x 14 .... (321)   275
The Standard Bearer, gouache, 11¾ x 13¼ .... (335)   220
Still Life with Grapes, 1922, gouache, 10 x 11½ ... (428)   197
Landscape and Fruit, 1935, gouache, 10 x 24¼ .... (328)   136

1965

Fruits éclatés, 1927, pastel, 10 x 20 .... (627)   280
Sun and Moon, gouache, 13 x 18¼ .... (597)   246
Seascape, 1952, gouache, 17¾ x 29¼ .... (567)   701

1966

The Cock, gouache, 58½ x 27¾ .... (744)   904
The Bullfighter, 1926, gouache, 18¾ x 11¾ .... (681)   280
Fabulous Landscape, 1931, gouache, 8¼ x 17½ ... (711)   230
The Beach, gouache, 9 x 15½ .... (815)   276
Butterflies, gouache, 19¾ x 15¾ .... (745)   339
Bathers, gouache, 18¾ x 10 .... (701)   225
Maritime Landscape, gouache, 7½ x 10 .... (670)   96
Still Life, 1948, watercolor, 14¾ x 29¾ .... (721)   300
Fancied Landscape, 1952, gouache, 17¾ x 29¾ ... (814)   560
The H Man, 1954, gouache, 22 x 15 .... (798)   384
The Cock, 1954, watercolor, 24 x 18¾ .... (706)   250
Local Flourish; The Poet and the Chair Keeper,[1]
    two gouaches, 21 x 27¼ and 21¾ x 27¾ ...... (784)   300

[1]Costumes for the ballet *Jardin Public.*

1967

The Hogfish, 1922, gouache, 15 x 21¼ .... (935) $ 220

The Cock, watercolor, 10¼ x 8¼ .... (971)   80

Apples in a Landscape, gouache, 9¼ x 12 .... (874)   220

Seaside, gouache, 9 x 15½ .... (926)   290

1968–July 1969

Boat on the Strand, gouache, 9¼ x 15½ .... (1161)   640

The Beauty of St. Tropez, gouache, 25 x 18¾ .... (1061)   150

The Siren, gouache, 14¾ x 10¾ .... (1128)   100

Still Life, 1953, gouache, 11½ x 21¾ .... (1162)   260

Bird, watercolor, 16 x 19½ .... (1059)   372

Fantasy, 1938, gouache, 22 x 29 .... (1231)   500

The Snake, watercolor, 13¾ x 10 .... (1231)   200

Cut Apples, pencil, pastel, and paint, 13 x 16½ .. (1245)   160

Butterfly and Turtle, 1950, watercolor,
     15¾ x 19¾ .... (1266)   128

PAINTINGS

1961–1962

Still Life, 1913, oil on cardboard, 20¼ x 26 .... (105)   904

Landscape: Nostromo, 1929-30, 25¾ x 39½ ...... (105)   588

Composition with Sailboats, 29 x 39½ .... (27)   520

Composition, 1925, 23¾ x 36½ .... (56)   560

Scotland, 1927, on board, 25¾ x 17 .... (128)   659

The Balcony, 1928, 32 x 45¾ .... (156)   550

Landscape, 1929, 36½ x 23¾ .... (59)   450

1963

Young Peasant, 1924, 45¾ x 28¾ .... (216)   548

Landscape at the Seaside, 1926, 21¼ x 32 .... (299)   230

Mythology, 1929, 12 x 24 .... (255)   466

The Wall, 1930, 23¾ x 29 .... (316)   700

Green and Blue Nudes, 45¾ x 23¾ .... (185)   250

1964

Seascape, 1926, 21¼ x 31½ .... (374)   425

Portrait of a Greek, 1927, 46¼ x 34½ .... (480)   280

Landscape, 1928, 35¼ x 46¼ .... (387)   498

Maritime Landscape, 1929, 25¾ x 39½ .... (375)   164

The Frost, 1929, 27¾ x 45 .... (454)   553

Two Men in the Nude, 1930, on panel,
     13½ x 10¾ .... (448)   600

Seaside, 9½ x 14 .... (341)   600

1965

The Fishwife, (1925), 45¾ x 28½ .... (559)   760

The Turk, 1926, 36 x 23½ .... (497)   280

Woman with an Amphora, 1926, 24 x 15 .... (524)   190

Smyrniote, 1926, 32 x 39½ .... (577)   290

Wintry Landscape, 1928, 31½ x 45½ .... (582)   829

Composition, 29 x 36½ .... (572)   520

Ship Ahoy, on panel, 9 x 13½ .... (624)   332

1966

Bathers, 1928, 18¼ x 25 .... (721)   200

The Sails, 1931, 51½ x 77¼ .... (741)   1,600

The Turk, 16 x 10 .... (784)   425

The Dance of Death, 12 x 15 .... (671)   218

Flowers, 15¾ x 13 .... (781)   200

Flowery Creek, 32 x 51½ .... (685)   2,000

1967

The Watermelons, 1927, 10¾ x 16¼ .... (971)   110

The Small Fort, 1928, 35 x 45¾ .... (985)   593

The Pink Sky, 1929, 35¼ x 45¾ .... (850)   340

The White Wall, 1930, on board, 11 x 21 .... (957)   553

Two Nudes, on panel, 20 x 10¼ .... (883) $ 200

Maritime Landscape, 31½ x 43½ .... (949)   370

1968–July 1969

Landscape, 1926, 25¾ x 39½ .... (1048)   770

Landscape, 1929, 36½ x 23¾ .... (1179)   540

A Boat on the Beach, 1930, on panel, 15¾ x 13 .. (1043)   130

Ship Ahoy, on panel, 9½ x 13¾ .... (1070)   283

Three Figures, 1930, on panel, 10 x 14 .... (1030)   350

The Coast, (1936), 12¾ x 23½ .... (1132)   590

The Bullfighter, 24 x 15 .... (1213)   180

Woman with Baskets of Fruit, 23¾ x 32 .... (1042)   600

Turkish Woman, 1925, 36½ x 23¾ .... (1230)   800

The Coast of Brittany, 1935, 48 x 60 .... (1231)   3,250

The Wreck, 1930, on panel, 21 x 14½ .... (1248)   300

The Zouave, 1925, on board, 15½ x 9½ .... (1266)   2,400

Nude in a Landscape, 27¾ x 21 .... (1268)   835

Stanton Macdonald-Wright

(1890–)

Birthplace: Charlottesville, Virginia, U.S. His family is of Dutch descent.

1907   Goes to Paris. Attends the Sorbonne University, the Académie Julian, and the Ecole des Beaux-Arts. Meets Morgan Russell.

1912   With Morgan Russell, founds Synchronism—a movement very close to Robert Delaunay's Orphism.

1913-14   Participates in the Salon des Indépendants, Paris. Synchronist exhibition at Bernheim's, Paris. Takes part in the Armory Show, New York.

1916   Returns to the U.S.

1917   One-man show at the Stieglitz Gallery 291, New York.

1919   Reverts to figuration.

1937   Stay in Japan.

1950   Retrospective exhibition at the Rose Fried Gallery, New York.

1952-53   Second stay in Japan.

1954   Reverts to abstraction.

1956   Important retrospective exhibition at the County Museum, Los Angeles.

Resident in Santa Monica, California.

Sales

PAINTINGS

1964

Return Sunlight, 1956, 30 x 24 .... (372) $1,500

Parting, 1956, 29¾ x 23¾ .... (324)   700

1967

Still Life, 1930, 35¼ x 27¼ .... (860)   3,250

August Macke

(1887-1914)

Birthplace: Meschede, Germany.

1904-06 Attends the Fine Arts School of Düsseldorf. Trip to Italy, the Netherlands, Belgium, and Great Britain.

1907 First trip to Paris. Discovers Impressionism.

1907-08 Stay in Berlin. Meets B. Koehler, his future dealer. Trip to Italy and to Paris. Discovers the works of Cézanne and Seurat.

1909 Marries Elizabeth Gerhardt. Trip to Switzerland and to Paris. Meets Karl Hofer.

1910 Meets Franz Marc and becomes very friendly with him; both men begin to keep up a correspondence. Visits the Matisse exhibition in Munich. Matisse's works make an impression upon him and exert a strong influence on his painting.

1911 Settles in Bonn. Participates in the first exhibition of the "Blaue Reiter" at the Tannhauser Gallery, Munich.

1912 Participates in the Sonderbund exhibition, Cologne. Trip to Paris with Marc, where he meets Delaunay and Le Fauconnier.

1913 Delaunay and Apollinaire call on him in Bonn. Organizes the exhibition "Rheinische Expressionisten" in Bonn. Participates in the first Herbstsalon at Der Sturm Gallery, Berlin.

1914 Trip to Tunis with Paul Klee and Louis Moilliet. Died, Champagne, France, during World War I.

Sales

DRAWINGS

1961-1962

Colored Composition I, charcoal, pencil, pastel, and watercolor, 15 x 12½ .... (106) $4,068

Drawer for Hats, charcoal, 7 x 4¼ .... (106) 633

The Man with a Horse, 1912, colored pencil, 10¾ x 12¾ .... (155) 340

In the Rain, 1913, pen, 5 x 3¼ .... (24) 148

Abstract Shapes XIV, colored pencil, 8 x 5¾ ..... (111) 600

1964

The Indian Wedding, 1913, colored India ink, 57¼ x 122½ .... (380) 2,460

Abstract Shapes VII, 1913, pencil and colored pencil, 8 x 6½ .... (374) 550

1965

Three Nudes, India ink, 10 x 13½ .... (638) 209

Walker in the Rain, 1909, pencil, 4½ x 5¾ .... (618) 394

1966

Abstract Shapes XVI, India ink and colored chalk, 8 x 6½ .... (738) 640

1967

Nude, Back View, 1912, pencil, 6½ x 4 .... (907) 148

Elizabeth, 1912, pencil, 11 x 8¼ .... (970) 541

Street Scene, 1912-13, black chalk, 7¼ x 5¼ ..... (930) 542

Shapes II, 1913, India ink, 19 x 14 .... (986) 738

Abstract Shapes XX, colored pencil, 8 x 5¾ ..... (1004) 750

1968-July 1969

A Suburban Street in Bonn, (1912), pencil, 10¾ x 12¾ .... (1209) $ 595

Abstract Shapes VII, 1913, colored chalk and black lead, 8 x 6½ .... (1209) 1,116

Landscape, 1912, pencil, 4 x 6½ .... (1105) 285

Elizabeth, 1913, pencil, 7¼ x 9 .... (1090) 422

Oberhofen; Flugelland, two drawings heightened with pastel, 8 x 6¼ and 6 x 8 .... (1030) 500

WATERCOLORS

1961-1962

Composition, 1913, watercolor, colored pencil and chalk, 14¾ x 12 .... (44) 3,000

Hot Summer,[1] 1911, tempera, 10¾ x 12¾ .... (94) 1,082

A Street in Tunis, 1914, watercolor, 11½ x 8¾ ..... (88) 9,840

1964

Scenes, 1910, watercolor, 14¼ x 10 .... (428) 590

Fishermen and Nets, 1908, watercolor, 11¾ x 9 ... (398) 420

1966

Study Sheet, 1910, watercolor, 14¼ x 10 .... (712) 836

Sunny Street with a Dog, 1911, gouache, 10¾ x 12¾ .... (792) 788

Before the Regattas, 1912, charcoal and watercolor, 14¾ x 17½ .... (735) 4,068

1967

Composition, watercolor, 11½ x 17½ .... (986) 2,460

1968-July 1969

Reclining Woman, 1914, watercolor, 10¾ x 8 .... (1085) 2,852

PAINTINGS

1961-1962

A Street with a Church, 1911, on cardboard, 40¾ x 31½ .... (88) 6,888

Woman Reading, on cardboard, 20¾ x 16½ .... (88) 1,771

Still Life with Apples, Pears, and Begonias, 1914, 19 x 22 .... (88) 12,423

1963

Bathers, on cardboard, 15 x 18¼ .... (284) 1,968

1965

Still Life, 1912, on cardboard, 32 x 38 .... (638) 11,562

Red Tulips in a White Vase, 1912, 27½ x 21 ...... (566) 12,204

1967

Suburban Street, 1911, oil, gouache, watercolor, and black chalk, 10 x 14¼ .... (930) 1,989

1968-July 1969

The Arab Storyteller, 1912, on paper, 15¼ x 16¾ .... (1094) 13,888

The Park, (1906), on panel, 29½ x 22¼ .... (1138) 4,708

Woman Reading, 1913, on board, 20¾ x 16¾ .... (1239) 15,600

[1] Interior with a reclining woman and a child.

Lucien Madeline

(1863–1920)

Birthplace: France.

1920   Died. His work consists chiefly of landscapes.

Sales

WATERCOLORS

1963
Fréjus Cove, gouache, 17¾ x 21¾ . . . . (209) $ 140

1968–July 1969
La Ronde, watercolor, 7 x 8¾ . . . . (1042)   70

PAINTINGS

1961–1962
Riverside, 18¼ x 21 . . . . (60)   150
Summer Light on Le Trieux, 32 x 39½ . . . . (139)   360
Banks of the Stream Le Trieux in Autumn,
   32 x 39½ . . . . (139)   530
October Light on the Sédelle, 30½ x 39½ . . . . (139)   420
Banks of the River Creuse in Summer,
   38½ x 51½ . . . . (160)   1,200
Landscape of the River Creuse, 1916,
   18¼ x 21¾ . . . . (115)   440
St. Karadec Chapel, 32½ x 39½ . . . . (139)   520
The Farm with Hydrangeas, 32 x 39½ . . . . (11)   600

1963
The Swing Bridge at Dieppe, 1906, 18¼ x 21¾ . . . . (190)   380

1964
Landscape . . . . (366)   200
Quay at Taillebourg, 21¼ x 25¾ . . . . (337)   440
The Bridge, 1904, on cardboard, 21¼ x 25¾ . . . . . . (355)   540
Longuivy, High Tide, (1919), 23¾ x 29 . . . . (371)   600

1965
Landscape of the South of France, 23½ x 29 . . . . . (503)   280
Landscape of the River Creuse, 1905,
   14¾ x 21¼ . . . . (607)   260
Landscape of the River Creuse in the Morning,
   1905, on board, 7¼ x 10¾ . . . . (545)   283
The Thatch-Roofed Cottages, 18¾ x 21¾ . . . . (538)   260
Low Tide, 18¼ x 21¾ . . . . (498)   420
The Wash House, 18 x 21½ . . . . (598)   270
The River Seine at Puteaux, 21 x 25½ . . . . (563)   380
Longuivy, High Tide, 1919, 23¾ x 29 . . . . (492)   560
Landscape Under Snow, 1919, on cardboard,
   10¼ x 13¼ . . . . (523)   184
Surroundings of Douarnenez, 32 x 39½ . . . . (553)   540

1966
Seaside, 32 x 29½ . . . . (672)   700
Breton Landscape, 21 x 25 . . . . (757)   663
Seascape, 25¾ x 32 . . . . (711)   400
Landscape, 15 x 18¼ . . . . (666)   440
Rocks at Low Tide, 23¾ x 28½ . . . . (772)   270
The Wash House, 18 x 21¼ . . . . (766)   220
La Daurade in Toulouse, 21 x 25¾ . . . . (692)   310
The Pines at Longuivy, 21¼ x 25¾ . . . . (718)   360
The River Creuse, on cardboard, 14¾ x 17¾ . . . . . (731)   260
Basteyron Village, Corrèze district, 21¼ x 25¾ . . . (817)   580

Surroundings of Crozant, 25¾ x 32 . . . . (663)   400
Village Street, on cardboard, 15¼ x 11 . . . . (674)   90
Drying Sheets in Saintonge, 21¼ x 25¾ . . . . (809)   700
Landscape of the River Creuse, 38¼ x 51½ . . . . . . (727)   860
Paris, 18¾ x 22 . . . . (788)   290

1967
Heather and Poplars, Creuse, 1903, 25¾ x 32 . . . . (873)   340
The Sunny Meadow, 1903, 19¾ x 25¾ . . . . (897)   300
The Bridge on the River, 21¼ x 25¾ . . . . (848)   400
Snowy Landscape, 18¼ x 21½ . . . . (875)   560
Breton Landscape, 13 x 18¼ . . . . (898)   100
Diben Rocks, 25¾ x 32 . . . . (926)   590
Mediterranean Landscape, 18¼ x 21¾ . . . . (935)   370
Houses of Saintonge by the Waterside, (1912),
   23¾ x 29 . . . . (912)   800
Landscape, 1914, on panel . . . . (894)   82
Seated Nude, 18¼ x 13 . . . . (855)   170

1968–July 1969
Breton Landscape, 1904, 15¾ x 19¾ . . . . (1051)   600
River and Washerwomen at Billiers, 1910,
   23¾ x 29 . . . . (1184)   1,020
Seascape, on panel, 13 x 16¼ . . . . (1040)   84
The Cove, Low Tide, 1913, 19¾ x 25¾ . . . . (1029)   420
Summer's End on Douarnenez Cove, 23¾ x 29 . . (1161)   720
Winter, 1917, 18¼ x 21¾ . . . . (1116)   500
The Pond, 11¾ x 16¼ . . . . (1179)   126
The Constance Tower, on cardboard, 15 x 18¼ . . (1042)   210
The River Seine at the Pont-Marie, 21¼ x 25¾ . . (1075)   200
Great Tide at Le Diben; Bouchardon Mill, two
   paintings, each 18 x 21¾ . . . . (1113)   1,700
The Bridge of La Folie, 21¼ x 25¾ . . . . (1015)   470
Washerwoman in the Shadow, 25¾ x 32 . . . . (1026)   660
Mediterranean Landscape, 31½ x 39½ . . . . (1210)   1,900
Fishing Boat in La Rochelle, (1910), 21¼ x 25½ . . (1227)   700
Bridge Over the Souvigne at Argentat,
   21¼ x 25¾ . . . . (1227)   800
Bathers, 21¼ x 25¾ . . . . (1227)   940
The Little Beach (Longuivy 1913), 28½ x 23¼ . . . (1238)   1,000
The Farm with Hydrangeas (Le Diben 1911),
   28½ x 38¾ . . . . (1238)   1,240
Nude, 17¾ x 13 . . . . (1245)   400
Holm Oaks, Noirmoutiers, (1911), 21¼ x 25¾ . . . (1254)   1,000
*Longuivy: The Harbor Seen from the Artist's
   House*, 1919, 25¾ x 32 . . . . (1255)   4,000
A Path by the Waterside, 1910, 25½ x 31¾ . . . . . (1255)   3,700
The Swing Bridge, 1906, 18¼ x 21¾ . . . . (1255)   2,600
Bouchardon Mill, 1907, 25¾ x 32½ . . . . (1255)   3,400
Fishing Boats in the Estuary, Morbihan, 1910,
   21¼ x 29 . . . . (1255)   3,000
Blaze of Dry Wood on the Path, 1905, 25½ x 32 . (1255)   3,400
Drying Sheets in Saintonge, 21¼ x 25¾ . . . . (1255)   2,500
The Old Church (Kermouster), (1914),
   21¼ x 25¾ . . . . (1260)   2,000

Alberto Magnelli

(1888-1971)

Birthplace: Florence, Italy. Studies art by himself and often goes to Paris.

1913   Stay in Paris. Meets the Futurists.

1914   Stay in Paris. Meets Apollinaire, Max Jacob, Picasso, Léger, and Gris. Paints figurative compositions. Returns to Italy.

1915   First series of colorful abstract pictures.

1917-33   Reverts to figuration.

1933   Returns to Paris. Reverts to abstraction. Takes part in the main Parisian salons of abstract art.

1947   One-man show at the Galerie Drouin, Paris.

1954   One-man show at the Palais des Beaux-Arts, Brussels. Exhibits at the Van Abbe Museum, Eindhoven.

1955   One-man show at the Musée d'Antibes, Antibes.

1971   Died, Meudon, near Paris.

Sales

DRAWINGS

1961-1962

Composition, 1937, pen and pencil, 9½ x 7¼ ..... (105) $ 169

WATERCOLORS

1961-1962

Composition, 1946, 25¾ x 19¾ .... (105)   1,130
Composition, watercolor, 15 x 11½ .... (13)   200
Composition, watercolor, 17½ x 14 .... (110)   120

1964

Composition, watercolor, 17½ x 14¼ .... (430)   240

1966

Composition, 1957, gouache and watercolor,
19½ x 25¼ .... (738)   369

PAINTINGS

1961-1962

Still Life with a Bottle and a Caldron, 1914,
27¾ x 21¾ .... (155)   1,400
Episode, 1946, 21½ x 18¼ .... (105)   1,627
Diffused Light, 1950, 51½ x 64 .... (88)   3,444
Composition, 1957, oil on paper laid down on
canvas, 25¾ x 19¾ .... (110)   210

1963

Composition, 1937, oil on slate, 9 x 12¾ .... (286)   360
Variations, 1957, 25¼ x 21¼ .... (273)   611

1964

Composition, 1948, collage, 29¼ x 18¾ .... (471)   1,266
Incorporated, 1956, 29 x 36½ .... (386)   620

1965

Composition, 1948, collage, 19¼ x 15 .... (566)   588
Action, 1957, 21¾ x 18¼ .... (545)   622

1966

On a Siena Background, 1963, 18¼ x 21¾ .... (802)   2,240
Composition, 1955, collage, 12¼ x 18¼ .... (745)   565

1967

Composition, 1949, collage, 29 x 28½ .... (851) $ 858
Composition, 1953, 21¾ x 18¼ .... (960)   739
Face au large No. 4, 1955, 36 x 28½ .... (892)   1,452

René Magritte

(1898-1967)

Birthplace: Lessines, Belgium.

1916-18   Attends the Academy of Fine Arts, Brussels. Takes a great interest in Futurism and in abstract art.

1920   First exhibition at the Galerie Le Centre d'Art, Brussels.

1922   Marries Georgette Berger. Discovers di Chirico through a reproduction of "The Song of Love" (1914), which helps to develop the trend of his painting.

1924   His works are closely akin to those of the Surrealists in Paris. Contributes to the *Dada Review.*

1925   Signs a contract with the Galerie Le Centaure, Brussels.

1927   First one-man show at the Galerie Le Centaure, Brussels.

1928   Goes to Paris. Makes friends with the Surrealists, especially André Breton and Paul Eluard. Contributes to *La Révolution Surréaliste, Le Minotaure,* and other reviews. Completes his own way of painting, distinguished by a strong desire to surprise that is meant to offer a new, unusual, and truly poetical vision of things—yet supported by the most traditional techniques in painting. Exhibits at the Galerie Goemans, Paris.

1930   Returns permanently to Brussels.

1930-40   Participates in all the important international exhibitions of Surrealism. Provides a number of accounts of his conception of art.

1936   First one-man show in the U.S. at the Julian Levy Gallery, New York.

1948   Exhibition at the Galerie du Faubourg, Paris.

1949   Exhibition at the Alexandre Iolas Gallery, New York.

1950   Participates in the International Exhibition at the Carnegie Institute, Pittsburgh.

1957   Designs a mural for the Palais des Beaux-Arts, Charleroi. Participates in the São Paulo Biennial.

1960   Retrospective exhibition at the Museum of Contemporary Arts, Dallas, Texas.

1961   Designs a mural for the Palais des Congrès, Brussels.

1967   Died.

1969   Retrospective exhibition at the Tate Gallery, London.

Sales

DRAWINGS

1964

The Vintage Month, 10¾ x 8¼ .... (379) $ 224

1967

Bust-Shaped Rocks, 1959, ball-point pen,
8 x 5½ .... (985)   154

Study Sheets, 5 drawings, 3¾ x 3¾, 3 x 5¼, 4 x 3,
3¼ x 4½, and 3¼ x 4 .... (939)   152

1968–July 1969

Two Variants of the Painting "Pure Reason,"
1959, pencil, 9 x 7¾ .... (1101)   552

Woman in an Armchair, red pencil, 12¼ x 8¼ ... (1174)   230

Nude, Adam and Eve, Abstraction, etc.,
7 drawings, 4 in India ink, 3 in pencil,
1924-25 .... (1096)   782

Flowers, black lead, double sided, 3¾ x 5¾ ...... (1161)   60

Composition with a Piano, double sided,
3¾ x 5¾ .... (1227)   78

Study for the Castle of the Pyrenees, pencil,
8 x 10¼ .... (1231)   350

Candles Grow in the Forest, ink and black lead,
7 x 5¼ .... (1268)   1,346

Study of a Rose, pencil, 3¾ x 4¾ .... (1273)   114

WATERCOLORS

1963

The Seducer, watercolor, 10¼ x 13¾ .... (249)   760

The Land of Osiris, gouache, 10¼ x 14 .... (249)   800

The Ovation, gouache, 10¾ x 14 .... (263)   1,200

1964

La Folie aux grandeurs, 1963, watercolor,
11½ x 16¾ .... (386)   1,040

Still Life with Eggs in a Nest, gouache,
6¾ x 5¼ .... (321)   575

Beautiful Realities, watercolor, 13 x 10¼ .... (471)   1,921

1966

Baucis Landscape, 1966, gouache, 10¾ x 8¼ ..... (751)   2,073

Sac à Malice, 1959, gouache, 13¾ x 10¼ .... (744)   2,712

The Smile, 1959, gouache, 13¾ x 10¼ .... (745)   2,260

1967

The Married Priest, 1959, gouache, 13¾ x 10¼ ... (918)   2,712

The Smile, 1959, gouache, 13¾ x 10¼ .... (919)   1,808

The Domain of Arnheim, gouache, 11¾ x 15 ..... (1001)   2,800

1968–July 1969

Still Life with a Candlestick, gouache, 14 x 18½ . (1125)   10,120

The Grove, gouache, 10¾ x 14 .... (1268)   9,048

The Prophet, (1947), 15½ x 22½ .... (1270)   14,400

PAINTINGS

1961–1962

Window and Ninepin, 29¼ x 25¼ .... (149)   3,002

The Chief Confidence, (1927-28), 45½ x 31½ ...... (21)   5,372

The Point of View, 21 x 28½ .... (3)   750

1963

Pure Reason, 1948, 23¾ x 29 .... (219)   2,938

A Plain Love Story, 18¼ x 15 .... (249)   2,200

The Vintage Months, 1959, 39½ x 64 .... (249)   6,000

1964

Blue Cinema, 1925, 25 x 20¾ .... (416) $1,244

The Pipes in Love with the Moon, 1928,
21¼ x 29 .... (416)   4,146

Obsession, 32 x 45¾ .... (474)   6,200

Facing the Whispers, (1930), 19¾ x 25¾ .... (471)   3,729

The Secret of the Procession, 29 x 39½ .... (427)   3,600

Pisa Night, 1953, 18¼ x 14 .... (439)   1,600

The Close Friend, 1958, 28¾ x 25¼ .... (354)   4,500

Farewell, 19¾ x 23 .... (368)   1,106

1965

The Knowing Tree, 25¾ x 29¾ .... (512)   4,000

Women by the Waterside, 14 x 18¼ .... (512)   1,400

The Glade, 1944, 21¼ x 32 .... (520)   3,800

The Apparition II, 21¼ x 28 .... (522)   1,797

The Legend of Centuries II, 1950, 31½ x 23¾ .... (526)   7,000

1966

Human Condition, 1935, 21¼ x 29 .... (753)   7,545

The Beautiful Prisoner, 1935, 18 x 25¾ .... (753)   8,706

Time, (1935), 22 x 23 .... (678)   7,250

The Resolving Recollection, 25¾ x 19½ .... (776)   7,000

Victory, 1939, 28¾ x 21¼ .... (776)   8,000

1967

The Mysterious Proof, 1929, 19¾ x 25¾ .... (962)   8,800

Secret Life, 1929, 21¾ x 18¼ .... (962)   8,000

1968–July 1969

Nocturne, (1927), India ink, watercolor, and
collage, 16¾ x 22 .... (1109)   4,800

The Future of Kings, 1927, 19¾ x 25¾ .... (1080)   11,000

The Voice of the Atmosphere, 1928, 10¼ x 7¼ ... (1187)   8,024

The Wizard Accomplices, 41½ x 55½ .... (1173)   34,040

You'll Never Know, collage, 15½ x 9 .... (1173)   7,590

A Face with Sky Eyes, 18¼ x 21¾ .... (1065)   10,000

Image in Itself, 1961, 25¼ x 19½ .... (1109)   12,600

Secret Life, 14 x 18½ .... (1125)   11,040

The Museum of the King, kama-mère,
25¾ x 19¾ .... (1189)   15,800

The Seducer, 1950, 19 x 23 .... (1239)   32,400

The Famous Man, 1926, 25½ x 31½ .... (1239)   28,800

Young Loves, 13 x 16¼ .... (1268)   20,880

Future, 1934, 21 x 25 .... (1270)   45,600

A Plain Love Story, 1959, 18 x 15 .... (1270)   22,800

Aristide Maillol

(1861–1944)

Birthplace: Banyuls-sur-Mer, France.

1881–82 Goes to Paris to devote himself to painting. Gains a scholarship and enters the Ecole Nationale des Beaux-Arts, Paris.

1884 Exhibits at the Salon des Indépendants, Paris.

1892–95 Meets Gauguin, who encourages him considerably. Starts to execute tapestries, ceramics, and sculptures. Participates in the Salon de la Société Nationale, Paris. Sets up a studio of tapestry at Banyuls. Marries Clotilde Narcisse. Meets Daniel de Monfreid. Participates in the Salon de la Libre Esthétique, Brussels.

1899 Settles at Villeneuve St. Georges. Meets Picasso and the Nabis. Because of failing sight, gives up tapestry and devotes himself to sculpture, which will finally bring him fame. Ambroise Vollard buys a series of statues—thanks to Vuillard's influence.

1902–03 Exhibits at the Galerie Berthe Weil, Paris. Successful one-man show at the Galerie Ambroise Vollard, Paris. Settles at Marly-le-Roi to remain close to his friends Maurice Denis, Vuillard, and K. X. Roussel.

1904 Participates in the Salon d'Automne, Paris.

1905 Auguste Rodin, full of admiration for his work, introduces him to Count Harry Kessler, who becomes his patron. Regarded as an innovator, he becomes very successful. Exhibits "The Mediterranean" at the Salon d'Automne, Paris.

1908 Trip to Greece. Produces "Night."

1910 Exhibits "Pomona." A Russian collector commissions a group entitled "The Seasons."

1911 Exhibits his tapestries at the Galerie Bernheim-Jeune, Paris. Produces "Flora."

1925 The state buys his monument to Cézanne. First one-man show in the U.S. at the Albright Art Gallery, Buffalo, New York.

1928 Exhibition at the Goupil Gallery, London. Exhibition at the Flechtheim Gallery, Berlin. Trip to Germany, where he meets Einstein.

1933 Major exhibition in New York at the Brummer Gallery. Retrospective exhibition at the Kunsthalle, Basel. Inauguration of the monument to Claude Debussy at St. Germain-en-Laye.

1937–39 Produces "The Three Nymphs." Participates in the Paris World's Fair. Illustrates works by writers such as Verlaine and Virgil. With Despiau, exhibits at the Institute of Modern Art, Boston.

1940 Begins "Harmony," his last statue.

1944 Died, Banyuls, after an automobile accident.

Sales

DRAWINGS

1961–1962

Study for Debussy, 1929, red chalk, 11¾ x 9 . . . . (8) $1,050

Reclining Nude, colored chalk on gray paper,
8 x 12½ . . . . (37) 650

Bathers, red chalk, 14 x 10 . . . . (111) 700

Bather, red chalk, 10¾ x 8 . . . . (152) 475

Standing Nude, red chalk, 12¼ x 7 . . . . (143) 904

Back View of a Nude, red chalk, 14 x 10 . . . . (109) 1,040

Reclining Nude, red chalk, 9 x 14¼ . . . . (168) $ 470

Standing Nude, Her Arms Raised, 15¼ x 5¼ . . . . . (106) 384

Back View of a Woman in the Nude, 12½ x 7¼ . . . (106) 350

Back View of a Woman, Conté pencil,
13¼ x 6¼ . . . . (76) 580

Back View of a Nude, charcoal, 13½ x 8 . . . . (102) 720

1963

Back View of a Nude, charcoal, 9½ x 7½ . . . . (312) 360

Seated Nude, Back View, red chalk, 21 x 14 . . . . . . (198) 1,000

Back View of a Nude, red chalk, 9 x 13¼ . . . . (232) 678

Reclining Nude, red chalk, 6 x 9½ . . . . (283) 1,876

Reclining Nude, Back View, charcoal, 9¾ x 12 . . . (255) 877

1964

Little Girl with Plaits, black and sepia pencil,
13½ x 11 . . . . (466) 300

Seated Nude, Three-Quarter View, black lead,
8½ x 12 . . . . (376) 260

Standing Nude, double sided, charcoal with white
lights, 14¾ x 8 . . . . (399) 320

Reclining Nude, red chalk, 6¾ x 9¾ . . . . (385) 429

Squatting Nude, red chalk, 13½ x 10¾ . . . . (368) 442

Standing Nude, red chalk, 13 x 8 . . . . (416) 1,382

Young Girl Drying Herself, red chalk,
11¾ x 7¼ . . . . (368) 553

Back View of a Nude, red chalk, 12¾ x 9¼ . . . . (423) 950

1965

Study of a Squatting Nude, red chalk,
10¼ x 13½ . . . . (523) 980

Nude, Her Arms Behind her Back, Conté pencil,
12¾ x 9 . . . . (564) 1,000

Lion (recto), *Standing Nude* (verso), red chalk,
21¼ x 13½ . . . . (629) 638

Back View of a Nude, pencil, 9 x 11¾ . . . . (494) 400

Back View of a Nude, red chalk, 13 x 8½ . . . . (545) 679

Reclining Nude, Back View, black pencil,
10 x 14¾ . . . . (577) 440

Two Bretons Before a Landscape, charcoal,
39¼ x 31¼ . . . . (640) 1,000

1966

Standing Nude, red chalk, 9 x 14¾ . . . . (745) 791

Standing Nude, pencil, 12¾ x 4¾ . . . . (735) 1,040

Front View of a Nude, (1920), charcoal
heightened with white, 46¼ x 16¾ . . . . (735) 2,938

Standing Woman in the Nude, red chalk,
8 x 4½ . . . . (667) 450

Squatting Nude, red chalk, 7½ x 8¼ . . . . (743) 220

Seated Nude, Front View, red chalk,
15½ x 10¾ . . . . (794) 320

Back View of a Nude, 10¾ x 10 . . . . (789) 240

Women in Front of a Landscape, (1895), charcoal
on paper laid down on canvas, 39½ x 32 . . . . . (672) 1,240

Two Standing Nudes, (1922), black-lead, 7½ x 6 . . (689) 829

Back View of a Nude, charcoal, 10¾ x 8 . . . . (815) 1,106

Reclining Model, red chalk, 10¾ x 14¾ . . . . (665) 700

Reclining Nude, red chalk heightened with white,
8¼ x 14 . . . . (703) 2,250

1967

Standing Nude, red chalk, 14¼ x 10 . . . . (965) 475

Nude Thinking, red chalk, 11¾ x 7¼ . . . . (898) 1,000

Study of a Nude, Back View, red chalk,
14 x 10½ . . . . (939) 608

Reclining Nude, red chalk, 8¾ x 14 . . . . (985) 593

Standing Nude, Her Hands Behind Her Neck,
   red chalk, 13¼ x 9 . . . . (984) $ 620
Lovers, charcoal, 7½ x 9 . . . . (881)   663
Nude, (1940), red chalk, 11½ x 15¼ . . . . (889)   1,600

1968–July 1969
Reclining Nude, red chalk, 9 x 13¼ . . . . (1050)   800
Reclining Nude, charcoal, 5¾ x 9 . . . . (1088)   750
Reclining Woman, (1910), red chalk, 11 x 15½ . . . (1134)   755
Reclining Nude, red chalk, 8¾ x 14¾ . . . . (1127)   966
Seated Nude, red chalk and pencil heightened
   with white, 14 x 9¼ . . . . (1080)   1,200
Seated Nude, red chalk, 12¾ x 8¾ . . . . (1221)   620
Front View of a Nude, charcoal, 15 x 8¾ . . . . (1221)   320
Standing Woman in the Nude, pencil,
   14¾ x 10¼ . . . . (1240)   1,080
Seated Young Lady, pencil heightened with white
   chalk, 8½ x 12¼ . . . . (1240)   1,320
Bather, pencil, 10¼ x 6½ . . . . (1240)   672
Standing Nude,[1] pencil and red chalk, 15 x 9¼ . . (1240)   1,008
Three Studies of Bathers, black chalk on buff
   paper, 9¾ x 8½ . . . . (1241)   1,108
Standing Nude, black pencil, 12¾ x 8½ . . . . (1241)   706
Woman's Head, pencil, 23 x 20 . . . . (1246)   1,300
Three Women, blue pencil, 8¼ x 10¼ . . . . (1246)   650
Seated Woman, red chalk, 10¼ x 7¼ . . . . (1246)   650
Squatting Nude, red chalk on tan paper,
   9¾ x 8¼ . . . . (1248)   425
Standing Nude, 7½ x 5¼ . . . . (1256)   640
Standing Nude, 15½ x 8 . . . . (1256)   780
Nude Seated on the Ground, charcoal heightened
   with white chalk, 11½ x 9¼ . . . . (1272)   960
Standing Nude, black pencil, 14¾ x 8½ . . . . (1272)   1,320
Nude with a Shawl, charcoal, 11¼ x 8¼ . . . . (1273)   554

WATERCOLORS
1966
Back View of a Nude, pastel, 12½ x 5½ . . . . (792)   984

1967
Back View of a Woman Walking, pastel,
   15 x 9¾ . . . . (898)   1,100

PAINTINGS
1963
Woman's Head in Profile, 10¾ x 8¾ . . . . (198)   2,400

1965
Olive Trees, on cardboard, 14¼ x 19½ . . . . (564)   1,400
Vase of Roses, on panel, 15¾ x 11½ . . . . (581)   920

[1]Dedicated "A Gustave Edouard, gentil mécène et ami des Arts."

Kasimir Malevitch

(1878–1935)

Birthplace: Kiev, Russia. Studies painting in Kiev and Moscow.

1907   Very much impressed by the first exhibition of Fauvism held in Moscow.

1911-12   Becomes a member of the group of artists "Jack of Diamonds" and participates in their exhibitions. Goes to Paris. Cubism and Futurism exert a strong influence on him.

1913   Exhibits in Moscow his famous "Black Square on White Background"—the starting point of his adherence to abstract art.

1915   With Maïakovski and Larionov, issues the manifesto "From Cubism to Suprematism."

1919   Exhibits his "White Square on White Background" in Moscow. Teaches at the Moscow Fine Arts School.

1921   Teaches at the Leningrad Fine Arts School.

1926   Goes to Germany to write the book *Die gegenstandslose Welt.*

1935   Died, Leningrad. (Very little is known about the last stages of his life.)

Sales

DRAWINGS
1965
Composition, (1915), pencil and gouache,
   8¾ x 7¼ . . . . (624) $1,520

PAINTINGS
1966
House and Garden, (1904), 17 x 20½ . . . . (757)   1,161

Mané-Katz

(1894–1962)

Birthplace: Krementchoug, Ukrainia, Russia.

1910   Enters the Kiev Fine Arts School.

1913   Goes to Paris, entering the Ecole Nationale des Beaux-Arts, where he meets Soutine.

1914   Makes a trip to London, then returns to his country.

1921   Settles permanently in Paris.

1923   One-man show at the Galerie Percier, Paris. (Catalog preface by Waldemar George.)

1925   Participates in the Salon d'Automne and the Salon des Indépendants, Paris. One-man show at the Galerie Percier, Paris.

1927   Becomes a French citizen.

1928   Trip to Palestine and Syria.

1930	His picture "Homage to Paris" creates a sensation at the Salon des Surindépendants, Paris.
1934	Retrospective exhibition at the Galerie Georges Petit, Paris.
1938	One-man shows at the Wildenstein Galleries, New York, and the Galerie Katia Granoff, Paris.
1940-45	Spends World War II in New York.
1942	Exhibits at the Wildenstein Galleries, New York. Also exhibits at the Chicago Arts Club.
1949	One-man show at the Georges Binet Gallery, New York.
1951	One-man show at the Galerie Charpentier, Paris.
1962	Died. (Mané-Katz won fame by devoting his work to the portrayal of life in the central European ghettos.)

Sales

DRAWINGS

1961-1962

Seated Arab, 1928, wash, 11¾ x 8¾ . . . . (127) $ 50

1963

Two Young Jews, sepia wash, 23 x 17½ . . . . (179)   450
Little Donkeys, charcoal, 19¾ x 25¾ . . . . (295)   84

1964

The Rabbi, sepia wash, 25 x 19 . . . . (472)   340
Portrait of a Young Woman, wash, 17 x 10¾ . . . . . (382)   110
The Wedding, India ink, 13 x 9¾ . . . . (374)   175

1965

The Rabbi, wash, 10 x 14 . . . . (627)   264
Jewish Boys, India-ink wash, 14 x 10¾ . . . . (541)   325
Seated Woman, wash, 24¾ x 19¼ . . . . (598)   180

1966

The Guiltless Rebellion, wash, 19¾ x 27 . . . . (711)   720

1967

Rabbi's Head, 1927, India ink, 19 x 14 . . . . (975)   560
The Rabbi, India ink, 13½ x 8¼ . . . . (855)   370
St. Francis, sepia wash, 23 x 16¾ . . . . (893)   600
The Dance, pen, 10¼ x 13½ . . . . (950)   116
The Clown, India ink, 16¾ x 11½ . . . . (1007)   120

1968-July 1969

Self-Portrait, pen, 14 x 11 . . . . (1088)   300
A Wedding Scene, India ink, 13¼ x 10 . . . . (1030)   450
Standing Nude, sepia wash, 23 x 17¼ . . . . (1088)   550
Study of a Woman, 1926, India ink, 14 x 19½ . . . . (1191)   330
Portrait of Rubin, pencil and watercolor, 11¾ x 10 . . . . (1127)   161
Faun in Profile, 1926, India-ink wash, 20½ x 14¾ . . . . (1228)   480
Study of a Woman, 1926, brush and India ink, 14 x 19½ . . . . (1240)   408
Nude, sepia wash on brown paper, 22¾ x 17¼ . . . (1248)   400
Young Lady, India ink and brush, 14¾ x 17½ . . . (1259)   520

WATERCOLORS

1961-1962

Man and Child, 1931, pastel, 36 x 18¼ . . . . (98)   240
Rabbi and Torah, watercolor, 12¼ x 8¾ . . . . (102)   400
Rabbi and Torah, gouache on board, 25¾ x 19½ . . . . (111)   500

1963

The Harbor, gouache, 19¼ x 25¼ . . . . (241) $ 440
The Reading of Scriptures, watercolor, 13½ x 9 . . . (181)   340
Japanese Dancer, watercolor, 32¼ x 21½ . . . . (208)   375
Three Rabbis and Three Boys, gouache, 25¾ x 19¾ . . . . (232)   1,672

1964

The Young Lady with a Donkey, 1926, pastel, 21¼ x 17¾ . . . . (404)   1,080
Storm Over the Adriatic, 1936, gouache, 18¼ x 24 . . . . (430)   380
A Rabbi Teaching Children, gouache, 19½ x 23½ . . . . (370)   660
Reclining Nude, gouache, 8 x 11 . . . . (445)   160
Mother and Child, gouache, 17¾ x 21 . . . . (450)   640
The Israeli Shepherd, gouache, 25¾ x 19¾ . . . . (377)   994

1965

Jews with the Torah, watercolor, 13½ x 10 . . . . (611)   500
The Talmudist Pupil, watercolor and gouache, 19¼ x 14 . . . . (494)   525
Jewish Musicians, gouache on board, 19½ x 25 . . . (507)   1,700
London, the Thames, watercolor, 15 x 20 . . . . (505)   260
Woman, Her Breast Bare, 1929, pastel, 27¾ x 22¾ . . . . (646)   370
The Fantastic Ride, gouache, 9½ x 12½ . . . . (503)   380

1966

The Thames in London, 1925, watercolor, 14¾ x 21 . . . . (702)   250
Rabbi's Head, watercolor, 10¾ x 8¼ . . . . (718)   520
Bathers, 1936, watercolor, 14½ x 23¾ . . . . (665)   275
A Wave on the Adriatic Sea, 1936, gouache, 19½ x 25¼ . . . . (681)   700
Boats at Sea, gouache . . . . (828)   560
The Siesta in a Kibbutz of Galilee, 1938, gouache, 18¼ x 24 . . . . (798)   2,147
Horse, gouache on blue paper mounted on canvas, 21 x 17¾ . . . . (665)   1,000
The Double-Bass Player, watercolor, 23¾ x 19¼ . . . . (772)   1,200

1967

Seascape, gouache and oil on paper laid down on canvas, 18¼ x 24 . . . . (976)   1,000
Bather, pastel, 23¾ x 18¾ . . . . (912)   600
Still Life, gouache, 25¾ x 19¼ . . . . (963)   1,300
Two Young Jews, gouache, 18¼ x 21¾ . . . . (999)   920
Jewish Musicians, gouache, 18¼ x 24 . . . . (923)   1,820

1968-July 1969

Rabbi, watercolor, 9 x 12¼ . . . . (1098)   400
The Man with a Hat, pastel, 19 x 13½ . . . . (1014)   960
The Beautiful Jew, 1929, gouache, 28 x 22½ . . . . . (1210)   1,000
The Bearded Violinist, gouache, 25¾ x 19¾ . . . . . (1127)   2,070
The Strolling Violinist, gouache, 25¾ x 19¾ . . . . . (1174)   2,070
Horses, watercolor, 9 x 24 . . . . (1138)   743
Mother and Child, varnished gouache, 18¼ x 21¾ . . . . (1116)   1,040
Father and Son, watercolor on rice paper, 17 x 13 . . . . (1030)   850
Nude, pastel, and gouache, 28 x 20 . . . . (1061)   1,100
Nude, pastel and gouache, 27¾ x 8 . . . . (1231)   850
Seascape, gouache on paper laid down on canvas, 17½ x 23½ . . . . (1240)   960
The Arabian Family, gouache, 17 x 25 . . . . (1240)   1,200
Three Sailors, 1926, gouache, 24½ x 18¾ . . . . (1254)   2,400
Violinist Wearing Boots, gouache, 25¾ x 19¾ . . . (1208)   2,204

PAINTINGS

1961–1962

The Child with a Blue Scarf, 1925, 36½ x 29	(155)	$1,700
The Teen-Agers, 1925, 36½ x 29	(73)	1,200
Landscape of Ukrainia, 16 x 10¾	(93)	994
Bust of a Man with a Green Hat On, 1929, 21¾ x 18¼	(133)	940
The Rabbi, 1933, 31½ x 23¾	(161)	900
Saturday Walk in Jerusalem, 21½ x 17¾	(37)	850
The Torah, 45¾ x 35¼	(18)	1,107
The Sailing Kings, 16¼ x 20	(19)	600
The Strolling Musicians, 36½ x 29	(57)	84
The Green Shawl, 1954	(26)	1,800
The Wedding, 32 x 39½	(71)	2,000

1963

Vase of Flowers, 32 x 21¼	(306)	2,020
The Clown's Dressing Room, 1927, 36½ x 23¾	(306)	3,000
Rabbi's Head, 1929, 29 x 21¼	(246)	620
Young Man Reading the Bible, 11¾ x 11¾	(281)	1,582
Vase of Flowers, 1935, 25¾ x 21¼	(254)	1,000
The Spaniard and the Red-Haired Woman, 36 x 29	(257)	760
Stranded Boat, 21¾ x 15	(254)	960
A Jewish Wedding, (1952), 35½ x 28¼	(202)	2,500
Self-Portrait, on canvas laid down on board, 15½ x 11½	(208)	600
Jewish Shepherd, on board, 24¾ x 18¾	(225)	1,000
The Student, 1960, 25¼ x 20¾	(202)	2,000
Musicians in Israel, 1962, 21¾ x 18¼	(190)	960

1964

The Red-Haired Jew, 1926, 36½ x 25¾	(404)	1,600
Still Life, 39½ x 57¼	(438)	6,000
An Arab at Prayers, (1929-31), 29¾ x 19½	(453)	2,764
Rabbi with a Green Coat, 1935, 32 x 23¾	(450)	1,700
Rabbi with a Brown Coat, 1935, 25¾ x 18	(450)	1,600
Landscape of Ukrainia, 10¾ x 16	(471)	1,672
Landscape, 8¾ x 12¾	(321)	750
The Heder, 21¾ x 18¼	(377)	1,808

1965

Portrait of a Jewish Peasant, 29¼ x 23¾	(629)	2,902
Pious Child in His Festal Costume, 14 x 8¾	(567)	1,627
Two Sheep, 8¾ x 10¾	(617)	904
The Thatch-Roofed House, 19¾ x 24	(516)	1,120
The Majorette, 24 x 19¾	(548)	720
The Sousaphonist, on cardboard, 22 x 15¼	(617)	1,695

1966

Jew's Head, 1927, 29 x 23¾	(648)	2,000
The Talmudists, 1930, 42¾ x 63¼	(689)	5,528
The Young Talmudist, 46¾ x 43½	(711)	3,220
The Pupil of the Talmud, 1940, 29¾ x 25	(665)	3,000
A Jew at Prayers, 24 x 19¾	(745)	3,955
The Wall of Lamentations, 1934, 25¾ x 22	(793)	2,700
A Jewish Orchestra, 14 x 10¾	(820)	1,260
A Jewish Musician, 10 x 8	(648)	600
The Violinist, 28½ x 23½	(689)	5,528
Seated Man, 46¼ x 32	(798)	4,294
Man and Child, 25¾ x 21¾	(811)	2,400
Woman with a Hat, 24 x 17¾	(767)	1,440
Flowers in a Vase, 45¾ x 35¼	(705)	3,040
Flowers, 16¼ x 10¾	(745)	2,825
Vase of Flowers, 34½ x 27¾	(757)	3,317

1967

Still Life, 1922, on cardboard, 18¼ x 16¼	(975)	$ 700
Portrait of a Rabbi, 1925, 36½ x 28½	(898)	2,400
Arab Woman, 1928, on board, 25¾ x 19¾	(989)	2,000
Young Lady, 1929, 39½ x 29	(993)	5,240
Seated Nude, 1942, 39½ x 30	(870)	1,850
The Refugee, 1941, 32 x 40½	(870)	4,250
Two Jewish Boys, 11¼ x 11¼	(939)	1,437
Young Talmudists, 36½ x 29	(976)	5,700
A Young Man Reading the Bible, 11¾ x 11¾	(918)	1,921
The Talmud Lesson, 18 x 21¾	(841)	3,500
Nude Lying on a Sofa, 13¾ x 13¾	(888)	967
Two Young Jews Standing, 17¾ x 12¾	(888)	2,626
Preaching Rabbi, 31½ x 25	(888)	3,593
The Young Violinist, 30 x 25	(982)	4,266
The Fire Rider, 20 x 24	(988)	2,737
Rhapsody in Blue, 36¼ x 25¾	(893)	3,500
Notre-Dame of Paris and the Quays, 26 x 32	(967)	3,729
Notre-Dame of Paris, 29 x 36½	(911)	3,200
Bunch of Flowers, 23¾ x 20	(919)	3,164
The Cart of Flowers, 18¼ x 21¾	(936)	1,900
Self-Portrait with a Red Tie, 21¾ x 18¼	(963)	4,250

1968–July 1969

Jew with an Umbrella, 1932, on canvas laid down on board, 24 x 18¼	(1070)	3,776
The Wall of Lamentations, (1947), 26 x 22	(1126)	3,469
Young Talmudists, 18¼ x 22	(1030)	2,250
The Rabbi, 46¼ x 35¼	(1113)	4,020
Hanukkah, 45¾ x 35¼	(1181)	8,400
Head of a Bearded Man, 7 x 5¾	(1030)	500
Fishermen on the Jordan, 18¼ x 21¾	(1174)	2,484
Figures, 17¾ x 21¾	(1127)	3,565
Arab Couple, 39¼ x 17¾	(1187)	1,888
Landscape, 21¼ x 25¾	(1127)	2,760
The Thatch-Roofed Cottage, 20¼ x 25	(1132)	1,227
Sailboats, 1941, on board, 21¾ x 27	(1138)	1,735
Little Fishermen, 13½ x 10¼	(1187)	1,298
Bunch of Flowers, 1917, 23¾ x 20¾	(1070)	3,068
Vase of Flowers, 1928, 25 x 19¼	(1030)	2,250
Flowers, 35½ x 23¾	(1183)	2,040
Bunch of Flowers, 23¾ x 20	(1060)	4,800
Old Jew with an Umbrella, 1930, 28¼ x 12¼	(1231)	2,400
Arab Riders, 27½ x 36½	(1231)	5,250
Quartet: One Did Not Show, 39½ x 32	(1231)	950
Two Horses, 1942, 35¾ x 27¾	(1240)	3,840
The Village, 17½ x 21	(1240)	2,280
The Violinist, 25½ x 19½	(1248)	3,000
Vase of Flowers, 29¼ x 21¼	(1265)	3,240
Rabbi with the Torah and a Young Boy, 30¼ x 25	(1268)	11,600

Alfred Manessier

(1911–   )

Birthplace: Saint-Ouen, Somme district, France.

1929 Goes to Paris and enters the Ecole Nationale des Beaux-Arts.

1933–35 Participates in the Salon des Indépendants, Paris. Attends the Académie Ranson, Paris, where he meets Bissière.

1937 Executes decorations for the Paris World's Fair.

1938 Takes part in the exhibition "Témoignages" at the Galerie Matières, Paris.

1939 Participates in the second Salon des Jeunes Artistes, Paris.

1940–41 Settles in the Lot district.

1942 Takes part in the exhibition "Vingt Peintres de tradition française" at the Galerie Braun, Paris. Participates—until 1949—in the Salon d'Automne, Paris.

1943 From now on, focuses a large part of his activity on the expression of his new faith, which he succeeds in depicting through the means of nonfigurative painting—thus opening a new approach to religious art in perfect harmony with modernism. Settles in Normandy.

1945 Participates in the exhibition "La Jeune Peinture française" at the Palais des Beaux-Arts, Brussels.

1946 One-man show at the Galerie Drouin, Paris.

1948 Participates in the Salon de Mai, Paris.

1949 Executes a tapestry entitled "Le Christ à la colonne." Exhibits a series of lithographs on the theme of Easter, at the Galerie Jeanne Bûcher, Paris.

1951 Participates in the exhibition "Peintres d'aujourd'hui, France-Italie," Turin.

1952 Participates in the International Exhibition at the Carnegie Institute, Pittsburgh.

1953 One-man show at the Galerie de France, Paris. Given an award by the Sâo Paulo Biennial.

1954 Participates in an exhibition at the Guggenheim Museum, New York.

1955 Exhibits at the Museum of Modern Art, New York, and the Palais des Beaux-Arts, Brussels.

1956–59 Participates in Documenta II, Kassel. Frequent stays at Moissac in Provence. Exhibitions at the Galerie de France, Paris.

Resident in Paris.

Sales

DRAWINGS

1966

Compositions, two drawings, wash, each
25 x 39¼ . . . . (776) $ 600

WATERCOLORS

1961–1962

Composition, pastel, 11¾ x 15 . . . . (75)   1,106
Composition, 1950, gouache, 6¾ x 6 . . . . (156)   1,080
Composition, gouache, 12¾ x 19½ . . . . (109)   1,800
Composition, 1953, pastel and watercolor,
11 x 9 . . . . (120)   700

Composition, 1956, gouache, 12¾ x 10 . . . . (149) $ 1,185
Composition, 1958, gouache, 21½ x 30¼ . . . . (143)   3,164
Composition, 1958, gouache, 10¼ x 21 . . . . (143)   1,356
Composition, 1958, watercolor, 10¼ x 29¾ . . . . (149)   1,738
Composition, 1958, gouache, 17¾ x 14 . . . . (156)   1,260
Composition, 1959, pastel, 12¾ x 10 . . . . (18)   1,243

1963

Composition, 1948, watercolor, 7 x 4½ . . . . (249)   200
Composition, 1943, gouache, 9 x 5¾ . . . . (249)   700
Composition, 1953, gouache, 11 x 9¼ . . . . (249)   740
Composition, 1953, watercolor, 11¼ x 9½ . . . . (283)   1,876
St. John of the Cross, gouache, 12 x 9 . . . . (283)   1,175
Composition, 1956, gouache, 12¾ x 10 . . . . (299)   700
Composition, 1958, gouache, 17¾ x 14 . . . . (249)   820

1964

Composition, 1943, watercolor, 12¼ x 9½ . . . . (472)   720
Composition, gouache and pastel, 7½ x 6½ . . . . (377)   678
Abstract Composition on a Yellow Background,
1957, tempera, 12¾ x 10 . . . . (385)   1,243
Composition, 1958, watercolor, 10 x 13 . . . . (386)   1,600
Composition in Orange, Green, and Yellow, 1959,
pastel, 10 x 12¾ . . . . (374)   225

1966

Composition, 1949, gouache, 12¾ x 9¾ . . . . (797)   904
Spiritual Hymn of St. John of the Cross, (1959),
gouache, 12¼ x 9½ . . . . (776)   1,800

1968–July 1969

Still Life, 1944, pastel, 12¾ x 9½ . . . . (1181)   1,220
Composition, 1959, pastel and stick of
greasepaint, 12¾ x 10 . . . . (1127)   1,196

PAINTINGS

1961–1962

The Circus, 24 x 19¾ . . . . (160)   3,020
Composition with a Mask, 1945, 29 x 21 . . . . (27)   4,800
Composition, 1947, 23¾ x 17½ . . . . (129)   3,021
1949, 13¾ x 10¾ . . . . (88)   2,952
Stigmata, 1951, 13 x 9½ . . . . (93)   3,164
The Drowsy Harbor, 1951, 64 x 38½ . . . . (71)   620
Composition (on a Green Background), 1953,
15¼ x 18¼ . . . . (88)   4,428
Mineral II, 1954, 22½ x 22½ . . . . (149)   3,634
The Appeal of Spring, 1956, 45 x 77¼ . . . . (93)   16,046
Lavender, 1959, 38½ x 51½ . . . . (88)   11,070

1963

Veronica, 19¾ x 19¾ . . . . (296)   2,200
Green Night, 1951, 10¾ x 8¾ . . . . (296)   700
Stigmata, 9½ x 13 . . . . (283)   2,825
In the Marais, 1954, 21¼ x 25¾ . . . . (254)   2,200
The Torrent, 1959, 38¼ x 51½ . . . . (279)   12,000

1964

Composition, 1958, 39½ x 19¾ . . . . (372)   1,400
The Bells of Victory, 10 x 13 . . . . (372)   700
Passion, Red-Blue, 1948, 10¾ x 8¼ . . . . (454)   1,161

1965

Objects and Transparency, 1950, 11¼ x 15 . . . . (569)   1,582
Red and Yellow Composition, 1953, 10¼ x 17¾ . . . (583)   1,219
Mercantile Harbor, 1956, 13 x 21½ . . . . (561)   1,300
Dernier Froid, 1957, 15 x 18¼ . . . . (553)   2,600

1966

Veronica, 1952, 19¾ x 19¾ . . . . (749) $1,440

Mercantile Harbor, 1956, 12½ x 21 . . . . (749) 1,110

Pour la Fête du Christ roi, 1952, 77¼ x 59¼ . . . . . . (678) 14,000

Little Dutch Landscape, 1956, 57¼ x 34½ . . . . (686) 3,040

Composition, 9½ x 16¼ . . . . (745) 1,356

A Tribute to the Holy Poet St. John of the Cross,
1958, 79 x 59¼ . . . . (776) 9,000

1967

Boats in the Morning, 1945, 14¾ x 23¾ . . . . (841) 2,000

Chronicle, 1952, 19¾ x 19¾ . . . . (993) 1,600

Night, 1963, 10¾ x 18¼ . . . . (935) 1,300

1968–July 1969

The Tree and the Night, 1951, 32 x 39½ . . . . (1117) 3,400

Gray Boats, 1955, 36½ x 29 . . . . (1174) 5,750

Study of a Spanish Landscape, 12¾ x 19¾ . . . . . . (1185) 1,020

Flowers and Foliage, single enamel with an
orange background, 13 x 9½ . . . . (1109) 1,400

The Crown of Thorns, 1955, 29 x 39½ . . . . (1117) 2,000

The Circus, 24 x 19¾ . . . . (1117) 3,000

The Night Light, 1946, 16¼ x 10¾ . . . . (1255) 2,900

The Dales, 19¾ x 37½ . . . . (1265) 4,800

Edouard Manet

(1832–1883)

Birthplace: Paris, France. (In an upper-middle-class family.) Drawing soon appeals to him.

1848-49 As his father refuses to let him study painting, he embarks for Brazil as an apprentice pilot. Executes a great number of sketches during the journey.

1850-56 Returning to Paris, he enters the studio of the painter Couture. Also studies the old masters at the Louvre Museum and improves his education by visiting the chief European museums, reproducing several masterpieces. Also attends the Académie Suisse, Paris.

1859 Like Courbet, he is exclusively interested in contemporary topics—such as his "Absinthe Drinker" (refused by the Salon).

1861 Exhibits for the first time at the Salon, Paris and even wins a medal for his "Guiterero." One-man show at the Galerie Martinet, Paris, includes "Lola de Valence" and "Music at the Tuileries." Although his pictures are disparaged by the public, they fire the future Impressionists, who immediately regard him as their master.

1863 His famous "Dejeuner sur l'herbe," refused by the Salon, creates a scandal at the Salon des Refusés, Paris. Marries the Dutch pianist Suzanne Leenhoff.

1865 "Olympia," accepted by the Salon, creates a still more terrible scandal. (Undoubtedly this hurt him—no one wished more eagerly to be accepted than he did. Playing the part of a revolutionary was against his inclination but he could not imagine challenging his own conception of art. The boldness of his subject matter, hardly offending us today, exasperated the public. Paradoxically, his dazzling technical simplifications, through which he truly revolutionized painting, comparatively escaped notice.) Trip to Spain, where he studies Velasquez and Goya.

1866 His "Fife" is refused by the Salon.

1867 Excluded from the Paris World's Fair, he sets up his own exhibition at the Place de l'Alma.

1868 Lightens his palette. Meets Berthe Morisot—his future sister-in-law. Exhibits his portrait of Zola at the Salon.

1869 Begins to work in the open.

1870 Series of landscapes of the Norman coast. Young artists gather around him at the Café Guerbois, Paris.

1872-73 Durand-Ruel buys a number of his pictures. Gradually gains success.

1874 Makes friends with Claude Monet. Although he does not participate in the Impressionist exhibitions, he is slightly influenced by the movement and again lightens his palette.

1880 One-man show at La Vie Moderne, Paris. A victim of a creeping paralysis, he works in colored pencils and pastel.

1882 Paints his last great picture—"The Bar at the Folies-Bergères."

1883 Died, Paris.

Sales

DRAWINGS

1961-1962

The Lady on a Sofa, ink and watercolor,
5¾ x 5¼ . . . . (84) $3,570

Study for "The Bar at the Folies-Bergères,"
wash, 8¾ x 10 . . . . (18) 9,718

1963

Bust of a Seated Woman, pencil, 7¼ x 4¾ . . . . (315) 302

1964

Woman Rowing, pen, 3¼ x 3½ . . . . (477) 1,180

Plainte moresque, wash, 12½ x 10¾ . . . . (396) 2,160

Four Figures on Theater Seats, India ink,
6¾ x 4¾ . . . . (359) 3,000

1965

A Glade with Figures, pen and pencil, 4½ x 6½ . . . (596) 246

1966

Study of Heads, Study of a Cat, double-sided
drawing, black lead and wash, 6½ x 4½ . . . . . . (706) 900

Young Woman Sewing in a Garden, pen,
7¼ x 6½ . . . . (712) 1,722

1967

Two Lemons on Brown Paper, colored chalk,
6 x 7 . . . . (913) 2,460

1968–July 1969

At Père Lathuille's, pen, 7 x 7½ . . . . (1092) 1,686

Bullfighter, pencil and watercolor, 3¾ x 4¾ . . . . . (1134) 1,770

Silentium, (1860), charcoal and red chalk,
10 x 7¾ . . . . (1224) 2,020

WATERCOLORS

1963

Bullfight Scene, fan-shaped watercolor, 23¼ x 8 .. (277) $4,936

1964

The Tub, 1878, gouache on canvas, 18 x 22 ...... (367) 27,640

Méry-Laurent au carlin, 1882, watercolor on
 ivory, 4 x 3¾ .... (416) 5,528

Bullfighters, watercolor, 9½ x 16¼ .... (405) 7,545

1967

Woman in a Broad-Brimmed Hat, (1882–83),
 pastel on canvas, 22 x 18½ .... (954) 75,000

PAINTINGS

1961–1962

Head of an Old Woman, (1856), 19¾ x 15¾ ...... (128) 13,730

Alice Lecouvé, Her Breast Bare, 1875,
 28 x 22½ .... (128) 32,952

Woman Reading,[1] (1878–79), 36½ x 29 .... (84) 63,158

1963

Street Decked with Flags, 13½ x 10 .... (298) 7,700

Oloron-Ste.-Marie, 1871, 24½ x 18¼ .... (277) 21,936

The Rue Mosnier and the Grinder, 1875,
 16 x 13¼ .... (279) 11,000

Alice Lecouvé, Her Breast Bare, 1875,
 28 x 22½ .... (247) 24,678

1964

Madame Manet in the Glasshouse, 31½ x 39½ ... (458) 11,028

The Omnibus, on board, 6½ x 10 .... (405) 2,902

1965

The Smoker (The Good Pipe), 1866, 39½ x 31½ .. (594) 450,000

Veiled Young Woman, Berthe Morisot, 1872,
 23¾ x 18¼ .... (522) 55,280

Bunch of Flowers, 11¾ x 14½ .... (576) 9,492

1966

Alice Lecouvé, Her Breast Bare, 1875,
 28 x 22½ .... (812) 44,500

The Meal at Simon's (After Veronese), 1853–56,
 11½ x 24 .... (753) 5,804

Chrysanthemums, 1881, oil on paper laid down
 on a fan-shaped canvas, 8¾ x 17 .... (750) 7,186

1968–July 1969

Basket of Flowers, sketch on canvas, 25¾ x 32 ... (1093) 122,000

The Black Boat at Berck, (1873), on cardboard,
 8 x 13¼ .... (1109) 94,000

The Absinthe Drinker, 16¼ x 12¾ .... (1200) 16,000

[1] Madame Jules Guillemet.

Henri Manguin

(1874–1949)

Birthplace: Paris, France.

1895 Enters the Ecole Nationale des Beaux-Arts, Paris, in Gustave Moreau's studio. Makes friends with Camoin, Matisse, Marquet, and Puy.

1899 Marries Jeanne Carette.

1900 Exhibits at the Société Nationale, Paris.

1902 Participates in the Salon des Indépendants, Paris.

1903 Exhibits at the Galerie Berthe Weil, Paris.

1904 Participates in the Salon d'Automne, Paris.

1905 Participates in the Salon d'Automne in the Fauvist room. Stay at St. Tropez with Signac.

1906 One-man show at the Galerie Druet, Paris. Meets H. E. Cross and Van Rysselberghe.

1914–18 Stay in Switzerland and in Brittany.

1920 Frequent stays in St. Tropez.

1943 Exhibits at the Galerie Paul Pétridès, Paris.

1949 Died, St. Tropez.

Sales

DRAWINGS

1964

Interior with a Nosegay, wash, 13½ x 9½ .... (414) $ 64

Cahors, 1922, pen, 10 x 14¼ .... (386) 300

1965

Reclining Nude, ink, 6 x 7½ .... (599) 90

1966

The Dockers, wash, 8¼ x 11 .... (689) 20

1967

St. Tropez Harbor, pen, 11½ x 8 .... (953) 600

Landscape of Provence, India ink, 8¼ x 10¾ ..... (921) 160

1968–July 1969

The Landing Stage, wash, 8¼ x 10¾ .... (1042) 200

Reclining Nude, pencil, 8 x 10¼ .... (1213) 120

The Tucked-Up Blouse, India-ink wash,
 17¼ x 19¾ .... (1031) 160

St. Tropez, Little Harbor, India ink, 8¼ x 10½ .. (1028) 176

Seated Nude, 11 x 8¾ .... (1245) 270

Young Woman in Front of Her Mirror, wash,
 9½ x 8 .... (1253) 560

Woman with a Mirror, red chalk, 20½ x 23¾ .... (1256) 1,500

The Farm, pen, 4½ x 8 .... (1262) 120

WATERCOLORS

1961–1962

Cavalaire, 1906, watercolor, 14½ x 11½ .... (114) 700

Fishing Boats, watercolor, 6¾ x 9 .... (119) 160

1963

Landscape, watercolor, 9¼ x 12 .... (241) 440

1964

The Vase of Roses, watercolor, 12¾ x 9¾ .... (393) 270

Bathers in Dieppe, 1927, watercolor, 12 x 18¾ .... (454) 216

1965

Grimaud, 1923, watercolor, 9½ x 13¼ .... (612) 620

1967

Marseilles, 1923, watercolor, 9 x 13½ . . . . **(874)** $ 350
Landscape, watercolor, 7 x 9½ . . . . **(967)** 554

1968–July 1969

St. Tropez, 1926, watercolor, 10 x 14 . . . . **(1051)** 640
Village at the Bottom of the Mountain,
    watercolor, 10½ x 16¾ . . . . **(1255)** 1,240
The Woman in Blue, gouache, 10¼ x 13½ . . . . **(1268)** 2,320

PAINTINGS

1961–1962

The Fisherman's House, 15 x 18¼ . . . . **(30)** 1,200
Interior with a Seated Woman, 36½ x 28¾ . . . . **(84)** 2,334
View of Ramatuelle, 1920, 23½ x 28¾ . . . . **(44)** 1,700
Conversation on the Rocks, 25¼ x 21 . . . . **(71)** 1,300
Woman with a Nosegay, 15 x 18¼ . . . . **(40)** 1,200
The Vase of Windflowers, 18¼ x 15 . . . . **(26)** 1,200
Nude, 21¾ x 18¼ . . . . **(27)** 980
Standing Nude, 13½ x 16¼ . . . . **(70)** 1,106
Nude, 19¾ x 24 . . . . **(71)** 5,000

1963

The Terrace on the Sea, 29 x 36½ . . . . **(293)** 1,400
St. Tropez: The Siesta, 21¼ x 25¾ . . . . **(303)** 1,440
Toulon Harbor, 25¾ x 21¼ . . . . **(306)** 1,260
A Vase of Carnations, on cardboard, 18¼ x 15 . . . . **(306)** 1,200

1964

Cavalière: The Red Rocks, 1906, 21¾ x 18¼ . . . . . **(399)** 7,200
Still Life with Melons, (1906), 25¾ x 21¼ . . . . **(471)** 3,390
Seated Nude, 17¾ x 14¾ . . . . **(454)** 884
The Sailboats, 15½ x 21¾ . . . . **(409)** 1,220

1965

Still Life with Fruit and a Jug, on paper laid
    down on canvas, 17 x 23¾ . . . . **(516)** 3,200
Vase of Flowers, 16¼ x 13 . . . . **(632)** 960
A Conversation on the Rocks, 25 x 20½ . . . . **(535)** 1,106
St. Tropez, 18¼ x 15 . . . . **(553)** 2,960

1966

A Vase of Flowers, 24 x 18¼ . . . . **(681)** 1,700
Tulips, 29¾ x 21¼ . . . . **(745)** 2,260
Carnations in a Vase, on board, 17¾ x 13½ . . . . . . **(808)** 2,177
Young Woman at Her Toilette, 16¼ x 13 . . . . **(795)** 800
Bather, (1908-10), 26 x 21¼ . . . . **(812)** 4,422
Landscape of St. Tropez, 15½ x 17¾ . . . . **(828)** 1,200
The Gulf of St. Tropez and the Vineyards,
    23¾ x 29 . . . . **(685)** 5,200

1967

St. Tropez at Sunset, (1937), 23¾ x 29 . . . . **(898)** 5,200
The Flower Girl, 1906, 36½ x 28½ . . . . **(857)** 5,000
Woman at Her Toilette, 25¾ x 21¼ . . . . **(857)** 860
Model Resting, (1906), 32 x 39½ . . . . **(918)** 7,232
Still Life with Fruit, 17 x 21¾ . . . . **(884)** 1,800
A Vase of Mimosas, 21 x 17¾ . . . . **(985)** 1,541
The Vase of Roses, 10¾ x 8¾ . . . . **(978)** 2,100
Carnations in a Vase, on cardboard, 26 x 15 . . . . . . **(912)** 2,920
Still Life with Cyclamens, (1912), 38½ x 47½ . . . . . **(912)** 7,000

1968–July 1969

Nude on a Sofa, 36½ x 29 . . . . **(1106)** 4,300
Still Life with Cyclamens, (1912), 38¾ x 51½ . . . . **(1057)** 15,500
Surroundings of St. Tropez, 1927, 28½ x 36 . . . . . **(1070)** 5,192

Still Life with Oysters, 16 x 12¾ . . . . **(1070)** $ 897
Honfleur, 18¼ x 15 . . . . **(1078)** 1,300
Reclining Model, 9½ x 13 . . . . **(1189)** 3,800
Woman Reading, Three-Quarter View,
    23¾ x 19¾ . . . . **(1060)** 3,200
Sinopolis, 32 x 25¾ . . . . **(1181)** 4,400
The West Indian Girl, (1936), 18¼ x 14¾ . . . . **(1208)** 4,000
Nudes in a Landscape, 24 x 19¾ . . . . **(1268)** 6,496
Interior with a Woman, (1899), 23½ x 19 . . . . **(1271)** 2,760
Still Life with Peaches, Plums, and Almonds,
    8¾ x 10¼ . . . . **(1271)** 1,632

Man Ray

(1890-   )

Birthplace: Philadelphia, Pennsylvania, U.S. At the age of seven, decides to become an artist.

1912   First one-man show.

1913   Marries A. Lacroix. Visits the Armory Show, New York, and discovers the European avant-garde.

1915   One-man show at the Daniel Gallery, New York. Makes friends with Marcel Duchamp

1916   Participates in the foundation of the Society of Independent Artists, New York. Participates in the Forum exhibition of Modern American Painters, New York.

1920   With Duchamp, Hudson, and Katherine Dreier, founds the Société Anonyme.

1921   With Marcel Duchamp, issues the single issue of *New York Dada.* Goes to Paris. First one-man show in Paris at the Librairie 6.

1922   Issues in Paris *Les Champs Délicieux,* an album of his photographs with a preface by Tristan Tzara. Participates in the first international Dada show, the Salon Dada, at the Galerie Montaigne, Paris.

1925   Participates in the first Surrealist exhibition at the Galerie Pierre, Paris.

1926   Issues "Revolving Doors," a series of color collages. Collaborates in several Surrealist motion pictures.

1932   Takes part in "Exposition Retrospective Dada 1916-1932" at the Galerie de l'Institut, Paris, and in the "Surrealist Exhibition" at the Julian Levy Gallery, New York.

1936-38   Participates in "International Surrealist Exhibition" at the New Burlington Gallery, London; in "Fantastic Art, Dada and Surrealism" at the Museum of Modern Art, New York; in "Trois Peintres Surréalistes" at the Palais des Beaux-Arts, Brussels; and in "Exposition Surréaliste Internationale" at the Galerie des Beaux-Arts, Paris.

1946   Exhibits "Objects of My Affection" at the Circle Gallery, Los Angeles. Marries Juliet Browner.

1951   Settles in Paris. Exhibits watercolors at the Galerie Bergrünn, Paris.

1959 Exhibition at the Institute of Contemporary Art, London. Participates in the international Surrealist exhibition at the Galerie Daniel Cordier, Paris.

1961 Awarded gold medal at the Venice Photography Biennial.

1962 Exhibits photographs and "rayographs" at the Bibliothèque Nationale, Paris.

1963 Exhibits paintings, drawings, rayographs, chess sets, books, and objects at Princeton University Art Gallery.

1964 Participates in the exhibition "Le Surréalisme" at the Galerie Charpentier, Paris.

1966 Participates in the Dada exhibition at the Musée National d'Art Moderne, Paris.

Sales

DRAWINGS

1963

Faces, 1943, India ink and watercolor,
18½ x 14¼ .... (286) $ 70

1965

Easel Painting, 1938, pen, 14 x 10¾ .... (491)   100

1968–July 1969

Reclining Woman, 1924, pointe d'argent, 7 x 9 ... (1134)   826

In the Light of the Moon, 1948, colored ink on
panel, 24 x 20 .... (1215)   1,200

WATERCOLORS

1963

Nude, 1912, gouache, 11 x 15½ .... (249)   330

Landscape, 1913, gouache, 10 x 11 .... (315)   274

1966

Still Life, 1914, gouache on black paper, 7 x 5 .... (665)   225

Landscape, 1913, gouache, 10 x 11 .... (757)   221

1967

Landscape, 1913, watercolor, 10 x 11¾ .... (841)   410

PAINTINGS

1963

Measure for Measure, 1948, 27 x 18¾ .... (249)   440

Anthony and Cleopatra, 1948, 30 x 24 .... (249)   1,700

Feminine Painting, 1954, 50¼ x 44¼ .... (249)   640

Romeo and Juliet, 1954, 32 x 23¾ .... (249)   600

1964

Composition, 1956, pavatex, 7½ x 9½ .... (377)   158

The Violoncellist, 1958, 47½ x 23¾ .... (401)   400

1965

Theater, 1916, collage, 23¾ x 17¾ .... (512)   1,100

Truth, 1957, 25¼ x 31½ .... (512)   140

1966

The Tempest, 1948, 18¼ x 24 .... (672)   630

Torso, 1964, plastic paint, 18¼ x 15 .... (751)   553

1967

Face, 1952, on cardboard, 10¾ x 9 .... (941)   260

Woman with a Harp, 1957, 63½ x 38 .... (912)   2,400

1968–July 1969

The Village, 1913, 20 x 16 .... (1208)   7,500

Society People, 1929, on panel, 74¼ x 39¼ ...... (1208)   2,000

Green Rose, on panel, 17½ x 14 .... (1215) $1,500

Face Vase, 1946, 18 x 14 .... (1215)   1,400

Modern Mythology III, 1956, 57¾ x 45 .... (1203)   545

Tulips, 21¾ x 17 .... (1226)   5,640

Souvenir of Paris, 1951, diameter 7 .... (1248)   625

Decoration of Rational Bodies, 1933, 15 x 22 .... (1268)   6,728

Franz Marc

(1880–1916)

Birthplace: Munich, Germany.

1900 Attends the Fine Arts Academy of Munich.

1903–04 Stay in Paris and Brittany. Discovers the Impressionists and Japanese prints.

1906 Trip to Greece.

1907 Second stay in Paris.

1908 First painting of the series "Lenggries Horses."

1909 Meets August Macke.

1910 Meets Kandinsky.

1911 Executes the series entitled "Three Red Horses." With Kandinsky, contributes to the book *Der Blaue Reiter.* Becomes a member of the New Association of Artists of Munich, but like Kandinsky and Münter, soon breaks from it. First exhibition of "Der Blaue Reiter" at the Tannhauser Gallery, Munich.

1912 Exhibition of "Der Blaue Reiter" at Der Sturm Gallery, Berlin. Second exhibition of "Der Blaue Reiter" at the Goltz Gallery, Munich. Third stay in Paris—with Macke. Meets Robert Delaunay.

1913 Participates in the first Herbstsalon at Der Sturm Gallery, Berlin. Turns to abstract painting.

1915 Executes his last work during World War I—"Abstract Sketchbook."

1916 Died, Verdun, France.

Sales

DRAWINGS

1963

Horses in the Meadow, 1910, India ink and
watercolor, 4½ x 6¾ .... (219) $1,356

Self-Portrait, 1914, pencil, 11 x 10¼ .... (297)   763

1964

Three Horses in a Landscape, (1910-11), pencil,
4½ x 7¼ .... (385)   1,040

1965

Back View of a Horse, pencil, 7¼ x 4½ .... (597)   763

Landscape with Fir Trees, 1910-11, pencil and
stump, 6¾ x 4¼ .... (618)   1,427

1966

Three Figures Seated at Table, pencil, 5 x 8¼ .... (712)   394

1967

Seated Cat, pencil and gouache, 6½ x 5¼ . . . . (930) $ 814
Three Horses, 1911, pencil and stump, 6¾ x 8¾ . . (970) 2,017
Three Bathers, 1909, pencil and wash, 8 x 4¾ . . . . (970) 935
A Horse in a Landscape, wash, 8¾ x 6½ . . . . (908) 2,460

1968–July 1969

A Horse in a Landscape, 1911, pencil, 4¼ x 7¼ . . (1114) 1,637

WATERCOLORS

1961–1962

Two Horses in a Landscape, watercolor,
 11 x 8¾ . . . . (106) 2,034

1963

Stag in a Landscape, 1910, watercolor, 7 x 9 . . . . . . (284) 738

1965

Fleeing Stag, 1905, watercolor, 4¾ x 6¼ . . . . (597) 657

1967

Two Gazelles, (1914), watercolor, 13 x 18 . . . . (914) 2,460

PAINTINGS

1961–1962

Two Horses in a Landscape, 1912, oil on glass,
 8¾ x 10 . . . . (88) 7,134

Louis Marcoussis

(1883–1941)

Birthplace: Warsaw, Poland.

1901 Attends the Academy of Fine Arts of Krakow.

1903 Settles in Paris. Attends the Académie Julian, where he meets de La Fresnaye.

1904 Paints in the Impressionist style.

1905 Contributes to reviews such as *La Vie Parisienne* and *L'Assiette au Beurre,* Paris. Participates in the Salon d'Automne, Paris.

1906 Participates in the Salon des Indépendants, Paris. Meets Degas.

1910 Meets Apollinaire, Braque, and Picasso. Changes his own name of Markous to Marcoussis. Executes his first Cubist pictures.

1912 Participates in the exhibition of the Section d'Or, Paris.

1913 Marries Alice Halicka.

1920–21 Participates in "Exposition internationale d'art moderne," Geneva. Exhibits at Der Sturm Gallery, Berlin.

1924–25 One-man show at the Galerie Pierre, Paris. (Catalog preface by Tristan Tzara.) Leads a very worldly life.

1927 Illustrates *L'indicateur des chemins du coeur* by Tristan Tzara. Stay in Brittany.

1929 One-man show at the Galerie Georges Bernheim and the Galerie Jeanne Bûcher, Paris.

1933 First one-man show in the U.S. at the Knoedler Gallery, New York.

1934 Illustrates *Alcools* by Apollinaire. Stay in the U.S. Exhibits engravings at the Chicago Arts Club.

1936 Retrospective exhibition of engravings at the Palais des Beaux-Arts, Brussels.

1941 Died, Cusset, France.

Sales

DRAWINGS

1965

Still Life with a Pear, (1920), pencil and gouache,
 9 x 9 . . . . (582) $1,106

1966

Sheet Anchors, 1930, pencil, 7¼ x 9 . . . . (742) 220
Presumed Portrait of Apollinaire, pencil,
 10 x 8¾ . . . . (811) 1,600
Still Life, 1929, charcoal, 18¾ x 24½ . . . . (703) 600

1968–July 1969

Nude, black lead, 10¼ x 7½ . . . . (1031) 360

WATERCOLORS

1961–1962

Still Life with a Pipe, gouache, 5¾ x 8 . . . . (155) 1,220
Still Life, 1920, gouache, 12¾ x 9 . . . . (88) 984
Abstraction, 1920, gouache, 5¾ x 11¾ . . . . (152) 675

1963

Composition with Musical Instruments;
 Composition with Musical Instruments, 1911,
 two gouaches, each 32 x 12¼ . . . . (283) 3,616
Composition with a Guitar, 1927, gouache,
 6¾ x 10½ . . . . (241) 1,120

1964

Still Life, 1919, chalk and tempera, 7½ x 10 . . . . . . (385) 1,017

1965

Honor and Resistance, gouache, 11½ x 14¼ . . . . . . (559) 640
Still Life, (1922), gouache, 10¼ x 18¾ . . . . (618) 2,952
Still Life with a Pipe, a Bottle, and Figs, (1925),
 charcoal, watercolor and gouache,
 10 x 16¼ . . . . (566) 1,062
Composition, gouache, 4 x 3¼ . . . . (589) 560

1966

Still Life, 1927, gouache, 10 x 17¾ . . . . (671) 871
Still Life, 1925, watercolor and gouache,
 22 x 13¼ . . . . (703) 1,300
Yesterday's and Today's Fashion, gouache,
 8¾ x 11¾ . . . . (796) 280

1968–July 1969

Still Life with a Guitar, gouache, 11¾ x 16¾ . . . . (1184) 760
The Stabbed Dove, 1927, gouache, 17½ x 22¼ . . . (1191) 1,888
Still Life with a Guitar, 1927, gouache on paper
 laid down on canvas, 12¼ x 17½ . . . . (1256) 2,000
Composition with a Glass, 1923, pencil and
 gouache on an oval paper, 7¾ x 6¾ . . . . (1272) 1,584

PAINTINGS

1961–1962

The Bar of the Porto, (1911-15), 13 x 18 . . . . (3) 1,800
Glass and Violin, 1921, oil and glass, 9½ x 19 . . . . . (140) 1,922

Lovers, 1926, oil on glass, 25¾ x 14 . . . . (140) $ 604
Kerety Harbor, 1927, on cardboard, 12¾ x 15¾ . . . . (59) 3,400
Still Life with a Shell, 1927, 21¼ x 32 . . . . (31) 3,844
Still Life with a Fruit Stand, on cardboard,
 12¾ x 29¾ . . . . (155) 3,000

1963
Still Life No. 3, 1920, 25¾ x 31½ . . . . (279) 4,500
Still Life with a Guitar, 1927, oil on glass,
 18¾ x 22 . . . . (210) 1,371
Still Life with Fish, 1927, 16¼ x 28 . . . . (299) 1,980
Knife, Bottle, and Breton Bread, 1929,
 23½ x 29 . . . . (247) 2,742
Morning Cries, 1939, 16¼ x 13 . . . . (200) 1,900
Squatting Woman, 1940, 36½ x 25¾ . . . . (299) 3,400

1964
Still Life with a Red Mullet, 1925, 23¾ x 29 . . . . . . (460) 3,200
Cubist Composition, 1921, oil on glass, 7½ x 6¼ . . (399) 640
Cubist Head, 28 x 35¼ . . . . (416) 2,211
Still Life with a Loaf, 1929, 23¾ x 29 . . . . (405) 755
Reclining Nude, 10¾ x 14 . . . . (408) 1,600

1965
Still Life with a Cup of Fruit, 1929, 13¼ x 16¼ . . . . (559) 1,020

1966
Still Life, 1914, oil and collage on canvas,
 21¾ x 18¼ . . . . (801) 6,000
"Byrrh" the Pyrogen, 1914, oil and collage on
 canvas, 16¼ x 10¾ . . . . (735) 5,424
Fruit Stand, 1922, 12¼ x 8¾ . . . . (801) 2,000
Object III, 1927, oil on glass placed on a plinth,
 28 x 22½ . . . . (776) 3,000
Rain, 1928, 29 x 39½ . . . . (776) 4,350
Antwerp, 1928, 57 x 37¼ . . . . (694) 20,000
Still Life with a Fruit Stand, 1929, 13¼ x 16¼ . . . . (666) 1,120
The Dead Bird on the Pedestal Table, 1930,
 13 x 16¼ . . . . (701) 2,100
Musical Instruments and Breton Bread, 1930,
 21¾ x 25¾ . . . . (753) 2,031
Composition with a Guitar, 15¼ x 18½ . . . . (711) 1,360
Composition, 1933, on canvas laid down on
 board, 4 x 2½ . . . . (701) 225
The Meeting, 1937, 25 x 31½ . . . . (694) 3,400
Reclining Nude, 10¾ x 14¼ . . . . (797) 1,808

1967
Composition, 1940, 6¼ x 8¾ . . . . (848) 760
Still Life, 1921, oil and collage on panel, 8 x 5¼ . . . (939) 1,382
The Absinthe Drinker, 1927, 19 x 11¾ . . . . (985) 1,541
The Audience, (1928), 25¾ x 32 . . . . (864) 2,750
Night II (Composition with a Frog), 1937,
 18 x 24 . . . . (870) 1,100
The Big Fly, 1937, 18 x 15 . . . . (893) 900
Pear, Glass, and Knife, oil on glass, 14¼ x 10¼ . . . (930) 1,989
Composition with a Guitar, 15¼ x 18½ . . . . (854) 1,600
Figures in a Landscape, 14¼ x 21¼ . . . . (888) 1,935

1968–July 1969
Still Life, 36 x 12¾ . . . . (1125) 9,200
Two Blue Figures, 24 x 19¾ . . . . (1125) 8,510
The Basket of Grapes, 1920, oil on glass,
 9¾ x 17½ . . . . (1187) 2,360
Two Figures, 1930, 21¾ x 18¼ . . . . (1043) 5,000
Faces and Anchor, 1930, 28 x 35½ . . . . (1193) 2,478

Interior with a Tuba and Stairs, 1930,
 18¼ x 25¾ . . . . (1068) $4,248
Still Life Before the Balcony, 1930, oil and sand
 on canvas, 21¾ x 18 . . . . (1208) 3,500
Surrealist Composition, 1933, on cardboard,
 24 x 19¾ . . . . (1129) 2,360
Cubist Composition, 1940, 6¼ x 8½ . . . . (1049) 1,200
Quinquina Composition, (1912), 13 x 16 . . . . (1231) 3,300
Fish on Newspaper, 1926, 8¼ x 10¼ . . . . (1262) 2,300
Musical Instruments and Breton Loaf, 1930,
 21¾ x 25¾ . . . . (1268) 6,612

John Marin

(1870–1953)

Birthplace: Rutherford, New Jersey, U.S.

1893 Establishes an architect's business.

1899–01 Decides to devote himself to painting. Attends the Philadelphia Academy of Fine Arts.

1901–03 Attends the Art Students League, New York.

1905 Trip to Paris. Executes several etchings.

1910 One-man show at the Stieglitz Gallery, New York. Participates in the Salon d'Automne, Paris. Trip to Austria.

1913 Participates in the Armory Show, New York.

1920 One-man show at the Daniel Gallery, New York.

1925–30 Stay in Mexico.

1936 Retrospective exhibition at the Museum of Modern Art, New York.

1950 Participates in the Venice Biennial.

1953 Died, Addison, Maine.

Sales

DRAWINGS

1963
Sunset, 1951, pencil and watercolor, 10 x 14 . . . . . . (189) $1,200

WATERCOLORS

1961–1962
Castorland, 1913, watercolor, 15¾ x 13½ . . . . (37) 2,500

1965
Landscape, 1911, watercolor, 13 x 16 . . . . (541) 3,100
Landscape, watercolor, 15¾ x 14 . . . . (489) 3,750

1966
Landscape, 1916, watercolor, 17¾ x 14¼ . . . . (790) 2,800
Clouds, 1908, watercolor, 10 x 8 . . . . (790) 1,200

1967
Berkshire Hills, 1912, watercolor, 14 x 16 . . . . (952) 3,500
Boats, Stonington, 1920, watercolor, 19¾ x 16 . . . . (952) 7,500

1968–July 1969

Springtime Landscape, 1918, pastel and
watercolor, 9 x 11¾ .... (1035) $2,750

Landscape, 1912, watercolor, 14 x 16¾ .... (1160) 4,500

Deer Isle, Maine, 1922, watercolor, 14¾ x 18¾ .. (1229) 9,000

Green Head, Deer Isle, Maine, 1924, charcoal
and watercolor, 17½ x 21¾ .... (1246) 10,000

Rustling Brook, 1923, watercolor and charcoal,
13¼ x 16½ .... (1246) 11,500

Dunescape, 1923, pencil and watercolor, 9 x 12 .. (1246) 3,500

PAINTINGS

1967

Movement in Gray, Green, and Red No. 2, 1949,
22 x 28¼ .... (952) 11,000

Marino Marini

(1901–   )

Birthplace: Pistoia, Italy.

1925–28 Studies painting and sculpture at the Academy of Fine Arts of Florence.

1929 Teaches at the School of Art of the Villa Reale, Monza—until 1940.

1930–37 Goes frequently to Paris, where he meets di Chirico, Magnelli, de Pisis, Kandinsky, Picasso, and Braque. Also goes to Germany, the Netherlands, and England.

1935 Awarded grand prize for sculpture by the Rome Quadriennale.

1940 Teaches sculpture at the Academia Brera, Milan.

1943–46 Stays in Switzerland, where he meets Germaine Richier and Giacometti. Settles in Milan.

1950 Trip to New York. One-man show at the Curt Valentin Gallery, New York. Trip to England, where he meets Henry Moore.

1952 Awarded grand prize of sculpture at the Venice Biennial.

1954 Given an award by the Academia dei Lincei, Rome.

1959 Executes a monumental work at The Hague.

1962 Retrospective exhibition at the Kunsthaus, Zurich.

Sales

DRAWINGS

1961–1962

Pomona, 1944, chalk and gouache, 13 x 9½ .... (151) $1,058

Rider on Horseback, 1952, India ink and pastel,
24¼ x 16¾ .... (152) 1,400

1963

The Acrobat on Horseback, 1952, India ink, pen,
and brush, 21¼ x 17 .... (219) $1,130

Horse and Rider, (1957), pen-scratched black
color, 7¼ x 4¾ .... (219) 147

Two Nudes, India ink and gouache, 13½ x 9½ .... (275) 300

1964

Study of a Horse, 1949, India ink and gouache
heightened with white, 15 x 19¼ .... (385) 848

Red Horse, ink and watercolor, 6¼ x 8 .... (467) 492

Seated Nude, India ink, 7½ x 12¼ .... (435) 320

1965

Horse and Rider, 1952, ink and gouache,
16¾ x 14 .... (606) 500

Study of Horses, 1953, pen and gouache,
25¾ x 18¼ .... (624) 1,161

The Acrobat, ink, 14¾ x 11 .... (535) 332

1966

Study of a Horse and Rider, colored pencil,
9¼ x 11¾ .... (802) 544

1967

Seated Nude, 1939, pen and watercolor,
10 x 7¾ .... (881) 498

Two Nudes, ink and gouache, 11 x 8¾ .... (841) 600

Seated Nude, ink and pencil, 15¼ x 11¼ .... (985) 427

Woman in the Nude, ink and watercolor,
7 x 5¾ .... (870) 350

Horse and Rider, 1952, India ink and pastel,
24½ x 17 .... (1004) 2,100

Composition, (1945), white drawing on a black
background, 15¼ x 11½ .... (919) 1,017

Horse and Rider, 1948, India ink, 13½ x 9½ ...... (889) 650

1968–July 1969

People in Chains, 1928, pen and watercolor,
21¼ x 16 .... (1214) 1,280

WATERCOLORS

1961–1962

The Rider, 1946, pastel, 11¾ x 14 .... (15) 190

Four Women, 1948, watercolor and pencil,
13 x 17 .... (88) 664

Cubist, 1945, gouache, 23¾ x 18¼ .... (149) 1,027

Red Horse, 1953, gouache, 24 x 16¾ .... (149) 1,106

The Green Horse, 1953, gouache and oil,
43 x 24¼ .... (44) 1,100

A Red Horse, 1955, gouache, 29¾ x 21¼ .... (156) 800

Rider on a Blue Background, 1956, gouache,
25 x 19 .... (88) 935

1963

Red Nude, gouache, 14¼ x 10 .... (236) 814

Rearing Horse, 1953, tempera, 23¾ x 16½ .... (208) 500

Red Horse, 1955, gouache, 29¾ x 21¼ .... (299) 640

1964

Horse and Rider, 1952, gouache and ink,
16¾ x 13¾ .... (387) 498

Study of a Horse and Rider, 1952, pastel,
watercolor, and ink, 24 x 16¾ .... (405) 319

An Acrobat Between Two Horses, tempera,
18¾ x 12¾ .... (374) 1,650

Rider, 1955, gouache, 29¾ x 18¼ .... (386) 1,400

1965

Donatella, 1956, pastel, 32¼ x 24¼ . . . . (545) $1,132

1966

Horse and Rider, tempera and collage on board,
19½ x 14¾ . . . . (713)   1,500
Horse and Rider, 1947, gouache and charcoal,
16 x 11¾ . . . . (721)   600
Horse and Rider, 1959, tempera and collage,
19½ x 14¾ . . . . (648)   1,050
Horse and Rider, gouache and oil on board,
20 x 19¾ . . . . (784)   1,000

1967

Studies of Nudes, 1928-38, gouache and ink,
14¼ x 11 . . . . (881)   1,714
Horse, 1949, gouache and India ink, 15¼ x 20¼ . . (908)   1,107
Horse and Rider, 1950, casein and gouache,
25 x 16¾ . . . . (893)   2,000
Horse, 1953, gouache, 24 x 16½ . . . . (930)   1,672
Horse, 1954, gouache, 24½ x 17 . . . . (910)   984
Horse and Rider, 1955, gouache and ink,
19¼ x 13 . . . . (957)   2,073
Donatella, 1956, pastel and pencil, 31½ x 24 . . . . . . (940)   813
The White Horse, gouache, 19 x 13 . . . . (935)   640

1968-July 1969

The White Horse, gouache, 19 x 13 . . . . (1013)   560
Horse, gouache and India ink, 6½ x 8½ . . . . (1127)   2,254
Horse and Rider, 1953, gouache, 34 x 24 . . . . (1191)   3,540
Horse, 1949, India ink and gouache, 15 x 20¼ . . . (1246)   2,750
Horse on a Blue Background, 1953, gouache,
17¼ x 24½ . . . . (1268)   4,176

PAINTINGS

1961-1962

Man on Horseback, 1944, 10¾ x 14 . . . . (75)   1,106
Horse, 1953, oil on paper, 24½ x 34 . . . . (164)   1,318
A Horse and a Brown and Black Rider, 1959, oil
and collage, 16 x 11½ . . . . (93)   678

1963

Horse and Rider, 1957, 33¾ x 24¾ . . . . (189)   1,800

1964

Horse and Rider, 1955, on paper laid down on
canvas, 32 x 23 . . . . (431)   4,750
Pongée, oil and collage on paper, 16 x 11¾ . . . . (448)   3,250
Horse and Rider, 1957, 31 x 22½ . . . . (437)   2,880

1965

Horse and Face, 1951, 39½ x 27¾ . . . . (616)   4,800
Horse, on paper, 16¾ x 12¾ . . . . (539)   1,000
Skin Diving, 1962, on paper laid down on panel,
16¾ x 13 . . . . (541)   2,400

1966

Black Horse, 1950, on cardboard laid down on
canvas, 39½ x 29¾ . . . . (802)   6,080
Horses, 1953, on cardboard, laid down on canvas,
26 x 18¾ . . . . (802)   2,560
Two Riders, 1953, 65 x 45½ . . . . (686)   11,056

1967

Composition, 1955, 43½ x 33½ . . . . (962)   7,200

1968-July 1969

Horse, 1953, oil and gouache, on paper,
24½ x 17 . . . . (1101)   1,840
The Rider, 1956, oil on paper, 10 x 7½ . . . . (1174)   4,370

Study of a Rider, 1960, 59¼ x 40½ . . . . (1176) $10,000
A Rider and a Horse, 1960, collage and gouache,
15½ x 11¾ . . . . (1145)   550
Composition in Black and Blue, 1961, 19 x 15 . . . . (1214)   512
Composizione di giocolieri, 1961, 59¼ x 59¼ . . . . (1057)   12,500
Horse, (1957), oil on paper mounted on canvas,
53¼ x 34½ . . . . (1235)   6,500

Albert Marquet

(1875-1947)

Birthplace: Bordeaux, France.

1890   Enters the Ecole des Arts Décoratifs, Paris, where he meets Matisse and becomes his friend.

1897   Enters the Ecole Nationale des Beaux-Arts in Cormon's studio and later in Gustave Moreau's. Meets Manguin, Rouault, and Camoin. Also attends the Academy Ranson.

1900   Participates in the Salon de la Société Nationale, Paris.

1901   Participates in the Salon des Indépendants, Paris—until 1910.

1902   Exhibits at the Galerie Weil, Paris.

1903-06   Fauve period. Participates in the Salon d'Automne, Paris, with his fellow Fauves. Trip to Normandy with Raoul Dufy.

1907   One-man show at the Galerie Druet, Paris.

1908-09   Starts a long series of travels to European and North African harbors. Trip to Naples and Hamburg.

1911   Stays in Honfleur and Tangier.

1912   Visits Norway. Trips to Le Havre, Rotterdam, Hamburg, and Tangier.

1913   Stays in Morocco with Matisse and Camoin.

1914   Trip to Rotterdam and to Collioure in the south of France.

1915-19   Settles in Marseilles.

1920   Stays in La Rochelle and in Algiers.

1923   Marries Marcelle Marty, a writer. Frequent stays in North Africa.

1925   Works mainly in watercolor.

1928   Stay in Egypt.

1933-34   Travels to Romania and the U.S.S.R.

1936-37   Stays in Switzerland.

1940   Settles in Algiers during World War II and meets Saint-Exupéry and Gide again.

1945   Returns to Paris.

1947   Died, Paris.

Sales

DRAWINGS

1961–1962

Reclining Nude, 1920, India ink, 6¼ x 8½ . . . . (106) $ 226
Porquerolles, 1934, pen, 4¼ x 6¼ . . . . (71) 600
Marseilles, the Old Harbor, pen, 8 x 10¾ . . . . (10) 700
Harbor, pen, 6¾ x 8¼ . . . . (57) 440
The Confidants, India ink, 5½ x 8¼ . . . . (53) 200
Landscape with Pine Trees, India ink, 5¾ x 7¼ . . . . (24) 113
*Sailboats, Fishermen, and Strollers in the
    Harbor,* pen, 11 x 6½ . . . . (53) 310
The Iceman and the Street Porter, pen, 5¾ x 4 . . . . (53) 68
Back View of a Nude, ink, 7 x 4½ . . . . (52) 160
Reclining Woman in the Nude, India ink,
    6¼ x 9½ . . . . (124) 250
*Seated Woman in the Nude, Turning to the
    Right,* India-ink wash, 12¾ x 9½ . . . . (158) 110
Woman Fastening Her Stockings, black pencil,
    8½ x 6¼ . . . . (114) 240

1963

Riders, pen, 3½ x 3¾ . . . . (209) 60
Seated Nude, India ink, 10¼ x 7½ . . . . (187) 110
Seated Nude with Legs Crossed, black pencil,
    8 x 4½ . . . . (221) 310
The Walkers, 1899, colored pencil, 6 x 7½ . . . . (243) 960
Young Woman, Her Right Hand Raised, ink,
    5¼ x 3 . . . . (312) 580
The Mother-in-Law, wash, 3¾ x 2½ . . . . (255) 137
Study of a Nude, (1905), pencil, 12 x 9½ . . . . (315) 165
Reclining Nude, India ink and pencil, double
    sided, 7¼ x 10¾ . . . . (283) 294

1964

Standing Nude, wash, 7 x 4¾ . . . . (466) 302
The Old Resident (recto), 1900, *Seated Man*
    (verso), India ink, 5¾ x 3¾ . . . . (454) 111
Reclining Nude, (1912), India ink, 7½ x 10¼ . . . . . (428) 258
Portrait of a Woman, black pencil, 5 x 3¾ . . . . (332) 120
The Transporter Bridge in Rouen, pen, 4 x 6¾ . . . (450) 276
The Lighters, charcoal, 16 x 20 . . . . (387) 498
The Rider, pen, 4¼ x 3½ . . . . (441) 249
Woman Walking, India ink, 5 x 3¾ . . . . (374) 200
Nude, pen, 8½ x 13 . . . . (386) 600
The Nanny, 1905, ink, 10¾ x 7¼ . . . . (368) 304

1965

A Horse and a Feminine Figure, pen, 6¾ x 8¾ . . . (588) 140
Landscape on the Waterside, pen, 11 x 8 . . . . (588) 370
Algerians and Europeans, pen, 6 x 4 . . . . (588) 70
Young Woman Writing, pen, 8 x 6 . . . . (577) 240
Nude, pen, 7½ x 5¾ . . . . (516) 200
Team, India ink and brush, 6½ x 10 . . . . (617) 633

1966

The Public Garden, pen, 4½ x 7 . . . . (718) 162
The Pont St. Michel and the Palais de Justice,
    ink, 10 x 12¼ . . . . (781) 900
Arabian Figures, India ink, 8¼ x 13½ . . . . (796) 160
Algiers, pen, 4 x 6 . . . . (714) 180
Boats, India ink, 3¾ x 6¾ . . . . (796) 300
Boats, India ink, 3¾ x 5½ . . . . (744) 339
Reclining Nude, India ink, 7¼ x 10 . . . . (670) 250
Seated Nude, India ink, 6¾ x 10¼ . . . . (824) 760
Landscape with Stone Pines, India ink, 8 x 10¼ . . (815) 553

1967

The Two Girl Friends, pen, 6¾ x 8¾ . . . . (919) $ 362
Back View of a Woman, charcoal, 4 x 5¾ . . . . (967) 339
Portrait of an Actor, India ink, 8 x 6 . . . . (921) 140
Sailboat, pen, 12¾ x 8¼ . . . . (909) 300
The Towboat; Window Opening on the Harbor,
    two drawings, pen, each 12¼ x 9½ . . . . (978) 1,000

1968–July 1969

A Boat in the Harbor, ink, 6¾ x 9½ . . . . (1167) 400
*Figures on the Harbor and Boat Alongside a
    Quay,* pen, 7 x 4¼ . . . . (1167) 220
Feminine Figure, India ink, 4 x 5¾ . . . . (1127) 299
View from the Window, Algiers, 1920, India ink,
    9¾ x 8 . . . . (1191) 188
Sidi Boussaïd, India ink, 5¼ x 7¼ . . . . (1174) 368
The Sailboat, pen, 4 x 5¾ . . . . (1014) 360
Bathers, ink, 4½ x 6½ . . . . (1051) 190
The Meeting, pen, 8 x 11 . . . . (1138) 545
Reclining Nude Reading, (1930), India ink,
    8 x 6 . . . . (1134) 165
Standing Nude, black lead, 11 x 7¼ . . . . (1227) 110
Triel, 1931, pen and ink, 4 x 5¼ . . . . (1231) 400
Algiers, 1941, pen and ink, 3½ x 5½ . . . . (1231) 325
Figures, India ink, double sided, 7¼ x 11 . . . . (1234) 300
Hendaye, pen, 3¾ x 6½ . . . . (1253) 360
Standing Nude, India ink, 7¼ x 4¾ . . . . (1268) 325

WATERCOLORS

1961–1962

Riverside, watercolor, 6¾ x 11 . . . . (32) 1,160
Riverside, watercolor, 8¾ x 11 . . . . (156) 1,700
The Market Place in Fez, watercolor, 8¼ x 11½ . . . (10) 1,160
Hendaye, 1926, watercolor, 6¼ x 9 . . . . (18) 1,695
Window with Flowers, gouache, 8½ x 6 . . . . (34) 1,260

1963

Landscape with a Dome, watercolor, 4¾ x 7¼ . . . . (222) 570
The Quays of the River Seine, pastel, 8¾ x 11 . . . . (311) 1,160

1964

The Sables-d'Olonne, 1932, watercolor, 6¾ x 10 . . (409) 2,020
The Factory, pastel, 5 x 7 . . . . (418) 400
Venice, 1936, watercolor, 7¼ x 8¾ . . . . (398) 1,500
Algiers, watercolor, 6¾ x 9¾ . . . . (401) 1,700

1965

In Algeria, 1928, watercolor, 6¾ x 9½ . . . . (523) 820
A Villa in Algiers, 1928, watercolor, 6¾ x 9½ . . . . (640) 900
Harbor Scene, watercolor, 8 x 11 . . . . (624) 930
The Harbor, watercolor, 8 x 11 . . . . (582) 1,050
The Factory, pastel, 5¼ x 7 . . . . (497) 390
Three Arabs, watercolor, 11½ x 8¾ . . . . (499) 1,500

1966

The Beach at Hendaye, 1926, watercolor,
    6¾ x 10 . . . . (741) 1,800
Algiers, 1932, watercolor, 9 x 11½ . . . . (685) 2,200
The Ledge Above the Sea, 1940, watercolor,
    11½ x 15½ . . . . (706) 1,420
Seascape, watercolor, 6½ x 8¼ . . . . (744) 1,808
A Bridge Over the River Seine, pastel, 8¾ x 11 . . . (815) 967

1967

The Louvre and the Pont-Royal, (1906), pastel
    and colored pencil, 9 x 11 . . . . (995) 830
A Villa in Algiers, 1928, watercolor, 6¾ x 10 . . . . . (984) 760

Landscape of the South of France, 1929,
    watercolor, 6½ x 10 . . . . (857) $1,240

The Basque Coast, 1933, watercolor, 6¾ x 9¾ . . . . (918)   2,034

The Bridge, pastel, 8¾ x 11 . . . . (897)   840

A Scene in Algeria, watercolor, 9½ x 12¼ . . . . (850)   760

1968–July 1969

Landscape, watercolor, 6½ x 9¾ . . . . (1174)   1,955

Landscape, pastel, 6½ x 10 . . . . (1171)   1,800

The Sailboats, watercolor, 6¾ x 10 . . . . (1183)   1,640

St. Etienne du Mont, pencil and pastel on gray
    paper, 6¼ x 9¾ . . . . (1246)   1,700

Seascape, watercolor . . . . (1250)   1,500

Crans-sur-Sierre, 1936, watercolor, 8¾ x 11 . . . . . (1254)   3,500

The Liner, watercolor, 4 x 4½ . . . . (1256)   900

Seascape, watercolor, 4½ x 5¾ . . . . (1256)   560

Audierne, 1928, 8¾ x 11 . . . . (1258)   3,000

Oran, watercolor, 6¾ x 9½ . . . . (1265)   1,140

PAINTINGS

1961–1962

St. Tropez, 1905, 19¾ x 24 . . . . (171)   10,000

A Street of Algiers, (1921), oil on cradled panel,
    8¼ x 6 . . . . (93)   3,797

Tunisian Landscape, 1923, 19¾ x 24 . . . . (6)   8,814

The Roadstead of Toulon, 1938, 19¾ x 24 . . . . (124)   8,000

Algiers Harbor, 21¾ x 15 . . . . (18)   9,718

A Harbor, 24½ x 32 . . . . (18)   13,108

Algiers Harbor: The Crane, 1942, 15¾ x 25¾ . . . . . (114)   7,000

View of Algiers, 10¾ x 16¼ . . . . (73)   3,100

Marseilles Harbor, 19¾ x 24 . . . . (73)   9,600

Marseilles, l'Estaque, 25¾ x 32 . . . . (10)   10,000

Poissy: The Lighter on the River Seine, oil on
    cardboard mounted on canvas, 7 x 9 . . . . (53)   1,560

Landscape of the River Rhône, 19¾ x 23¾ . . . . (155)   7,200

Banks of the River Seine, oil on cardboard
    mounted on canvas, 7¼ x 9½ . . . . (155)   840

St. Jean de Luz, October, 19¾ x 24 . . . . (124)   3,700

The White Boat in Venice, 15 x 21¾ . . . . (160)   9,300

1963

The River Seine at Méricourt, (1936),
    19¾ x 23¾ . . . . (194)   7,600

The River Seine at Poissy, on panel, 13 x 16¼ . . . . (293)   6,220

The Quay, 9 x 8 . . . . (255)   1,508

Algiers, 18¼ x 25¾ . . . . (318)   5,620

The Harbor, 21¼ x 29 . . . . (253)   6,800

La Frette: The Church and the Village,
    13 x 16¼ . . . . (198)   7,600

Landscape, 8 x 6¼ . . . . (232)   3,503

The Town Close to the Sea, 19¾ x 24 . . . . (224)   11,600

1964

Collioure Harbor, 1912, 18¼ x 21¾ . . . . (378)   9,040

The Old Harbor in Marseilles, 26½ x 29 . . . . (405)   13,059

The Landing Stage, 19¾ x 24 . . . . (347)   11,600

The Bay, 13 x 16¼ . . . . (337)   3,400

Triel, 32 x 25¾ . . . . (340)   12,000

The Bidassoa, 25¾ x 32 . . . . (340)   11,000

The Bidassoa, 13 x 16¼ . . . . (341)   3,600

The Tents, 1933, 19½ x 24 . . . . (416)   24,047

The Statue in the Garden, 23¾ x 19½ . . . . (458)   10,157

The Pont St. Louis, 1934, 23 x 28½ . . . . (453)   22,112

The End of the Season: La Frette, 1939, on panel,
    13 x 16¼ . . . . (401) $4,100

The Mediterranean, on canvas laid down on
    cardboard, 12¾ x 16¼ . . . . (401)   2,200

Tunisia: "Le Drapeau," on panel, 16¼ x 13 . . . . . . (398)   3,600

Algiers, Dull Weather, on canvas laid down on
    cardboard, 13 x 16¼ . . . . (347)   4,200

View of Algiers, 10¾ x 16¼ . . . . (471)   6,893

Seaside, Algeria, 25 x 31¼ . . . . (416)   27,640

1965

The Window at l'Estaque, 14¼ x 13 . . . . (564)   3,900

Docks in Hamburg, (1909), 25¾ x 31¾ . . . . (526)   21,000

The Transporter Bridge, Rouen, 1912,
    25¾ x 31½ . . . . (522)   13,820

The Stroller in the Mediterranean Harbor, 1916,
    12¾ x 16 . . . . (624)   6,634

Marseilles Harbor, (1916), 29¼ x 36¼ . . . . (583)   20,314

An Afternoon in Hesnes, on panel, 12¾ x 15¾ . . . . (515)   4,500

The Posters in Paris, (1921), 15¾ x 12½ . . . . (617)   9,040

The River Seine, Ile St. Louis, (1921), 25 x 31½ . . . (594)   18,000

The Harbor, (1925), 20 x 24 . . . . (594)   2,500

Workers on the Quay, 13 x 18¼ . . . . (617)   8,588

Boulogne-sur-Mer, the Town, on canvas laid
    down on cardboard, 12¾ x 16 . . . . (569)   7,684

Bidassoa, 1926, 21¼ x 25¾ . . . . (569)   9,944

Nuages-Fontarabie, 1926, 19¾ x 24 . . . . (619)   10,800

A Boat in Porquerolles, on panel, 13 x 16¼ . . . . . . (518)   5,400

The Terrace in Porquerolles, 1939, 19½ x 23¾ . . . . (522)   9,674

The Aloes, Algiers, 1944, 29 x 24 . . . . (633)   11,000

View from the Heights of Algiers, on panel,
    15 x 18¼ . . . . (552)   4,760

1966

Carnival on the Beach, 1906, 19¾ x 24 . . . . (776)   36,000

The River Seine at Poissy, 1908, on cardboard,
    6½ x 9½ . . . . (681)   5,000

The River Seine at La Frette, 23 x 19½ . . . . (719)   8,600

Marseilles, 1916, 23¾ x 29 . . . . (744)   16,950

The River Seine at Samois, (1917), 18¼ x 21¾ . . . . (744)   12,430

A Street at Bougie, 1925, 19¾ x 24 . . . . (798)   6,667

Davos Village, (1936), 25¾ x 21¼ . . . . (744)   13,560

Porquerolles, 1938, 25 x 32 . . . . (713)   13,000

Rough Sea, 8¾ x 10¼ . . . . (750)   4,146

Algiers, (1941), 14¾ x 21½ . . . . (750)   7,739

Algiers Harbor, on board, 8¾ x 10¾ . . . . (797)   4,972

Algiers, Mustapha Hills, on board, 13 x 16¼ . . . . . (830)   4,300

Landscape of Sidi-Bou-Saïd, 23¾ x 32 . . . . (809)   6,600

The Diving Board, 1945, on canvas laid down on
    board, 13 x 16 . . . . (757)   7,186

The Pont-Neuf, 24 x 19¾ . . . . (681)   10,800

1967

The Beach, on panel, 13 x 16¼ . . . . (852)   8,200

A Road at Canteleu, Fog, 12¾ x 15¾ . . . . (852)   3,620

Houses on the Water at Samois, on cardboard,
    10¾ x 14 . . . . (911)   3,800

Cargo Boats in the Harbor, on panel, 10¾ x 8¾ . . (916)   5,100

Poissy, the River Seine, on canvas laid down on
    cardboard, 9½ x 7½ . . . . (919)   2,486

The Transporter Bridge, Rouen, 1912,
    25¾ x 31½ . . . . (954)   16,000

View on the Quays of the River Seine, on canvas,
    12¾ x 15¾ . . . . (864)   10,000

The Dale, Jouy-en-Josas, on panel, 13 x 16¼ . . . . (857)   4,200

Sidi-Bou-Saïd, 16¼ x 13 .... (858) $4,120
Sidi-Bou-Saïd, 19¾ x 23¾ .... (923)   6,600
Sidi-Bou-Saïd, 1923, 19¾ x 24 .... (938)   15,478
A Street at Bougie, 1925, 19¾ x 24 .... (844)   7,980
Bougie Harbor, 1925, 25 x 31¼ .... (982)   13,035
Algiers Harbor, 1935, 19¾ x 25¾ .... (965)   13,108
A Harbor in Algeria, 15 x 18¼ .... (901)   7,400
Algiers Harbor, 1941, 19½ x 25¼ .... (880)   9,950
St. Jean de Luz, the Bridge, 25¾ x 32 .... (923)   18,600
An Impression of Winter in Paris, 15 x 18¼ ...... (987)   21,400

1968–July 1969
Surroundings of Paris, 1917, 14 x 10¾ .... (1173)   9,200
Seaside, Flamanville (Manche), 1901,
    19½ x 23½ .... (1068)   2,360
Boats in the Harbor, (1907), 12½ x 15½ .... (1045)   13,600
Banks of the River Seine at Poissy, 1908,
    7½ x 9 .... (1132)   2,832
Algiers Harbor, (1925), 25¾ x 32 .... (1152)   36,000
Algiers Harbor, 29 x 23¾ .... (1189)   15,200
The River Seine in Rouen, 25¾ x 32 .... (1051)   20,000
Boats in Marseilles Harbor, 23¾ x 29 .... (1051)   11,600
Le Havre Harbor, (1934), 19½ x 24 .... (1176)   17,000
Audierne Harbor, 25¾ x 32 .... (1053)   21,600
Crans-sur-Sierre, Snowy Landscape, 1936, on
    panel, 13 x 16¼ .... (1053)   8,400
Porquerolles 38: Pink Clouds, 19¾ x 24 .... (1189)   8,000
A Park with a Statue, 23¾ x 19½ .... (1126)   6,938
Surroundings of St. Jean de Luz in the Morning,
    13 x 16¼ .... (1109)   9,400
Harbor, 1941, 25¾ x 19¾ .... (1173)   18,400
Lighters on the River, 25¾ x 32 .... (1176)   20,000
The Studio in Algiers, 1942, on canvas laid down
    on cardboard, 6½ x 8 .... (1189)   3,000
Boats in Algiers Harbor, 25¾ x 32 .... (1200)   21,000
View of Algiers, 10¾ x 16¼ .... (1125)   7,130
View of Algiers, (1943), 8¾ x 10¾ .... (1173)   4,600
Algiers Harbor, 5¾ x 9½ .... (1181)   6,400
The Aloes, 1944, 29 x 23¾ .... (1053)   12,000
The Louvre, the Carrousel Courtyard, 25¾ x 32 . (1049)   14,400
Pont-Neuf, Springtime, on cardboard mounted
    on canvas, 10¾ x 14 .... (1109)   10,200
Porte de Versailles, 21¼ x 25¾ .... (1090)   11,160
Banks of the River Seine, in Winter, 23¾ x 29 ... (1125)   21,850
Vase of Flowers, 9¾ x 5¾ .... (1200)   6,200
The Quai des Grands Augustins, (1906),
    23¾ x 29 .... (1224)   34,000
Boats in Marseilles Harbor, 23¾ x 29 .... (1226)   15,600
The Balcony, 1945, 25½ x 19¾ .... (1235)   26,000
The Pont-Neuf, Paris, 21½ x 28¾ .... (1235)   24,000
La Rochelle Harbor, (1920), 19¾ x 24 .... (1239)   30,000
The Artist's House at Sidi-Bou-Saïd, on panel,
    16¼ x 13 .... (1239)   8,640
Pont St. Michel, Snow, 25½ x 31¾ .... (1241)   40,300
The River Seine at Notre-Dame, 19¾ x 24 ...... (1249)   13,000
The Pont-Neuf, 21¾ x 18¼ .... (1254)   32,400
*The River Seine in Paris (Quai des Grands
    Augustins)*, 25¾ x 32 .... (1256)   40,000
The Towboat, on cardboard, 8¼ x 6½ .... (1257)   4,640
Landscape, 12¾ x 16¼ .... (1258)   8,400
Edge of a Lake, 32 x 25¾ .... (1268)   30,160
Seascape, 21¼ x 25¾ .... (1268)   26,680
Hesnes, Norway, (1924), 13 x 16¼ .... (1268)   10,612
Le Pyla, 1935, 19¾ x 24 .... (1268)   17,400

Reginald Marsh

(1898–1954)

Birthplace: Paris, France.

1916-20   Studies painting at Yale University.

1920-24   Attends the Art Students League, New York. One-man show at the Whitney Studio Club, New York. Principally interested in city scenes.

1927   One-man show at the Curt Valentine Gallery, New York.

1928   One-man show at the Weyhe Gallery.

1930   Exhibits steadily at the Rehn Galleries, New York, until 1953.

1943   Works as a war correspondent for *Life* magazine. Given an award by the National Academy of Design, New York.

1953   One-man show at the Martha Jackson Gallery, New York.

1954   Died.

Sales

DRAWINGS

1966
The Witness, (1953), pen and wash, 8¾ x 15¾ .... (665) $ 550

1968–July 1969
Scene on a Beach, wash, 21¾ x 29½ .... (1035)   1,800
Nude Studies, ink, 8¾ x 11¾ .... (1229)   2,250
Nude Studies, 1932, red chalk, 11 x 15½ .... (1248)   475

WATERCOLORS

1963
New York Harbor, 1936, watercolor,
    13½ x 19¼ .... (272)   500
Industrial Landscape, watercolor, 13 x 19¾ ...... (208)   500
Dockside, New York, 1938, watercolor,
    13½ x 19¼ .... (272)   950

1964
The Acrobats at Tony Pastor's Theater, 1924,
    tempera, 25 x 20½ .... (363)   1,900

1965
The Walk, 1946, tempera on paper, 22½ x 31 ..... (610)   3,600

1966
Fishing Boats, watercolor and pen, 10 x 14¼ ..... (721)   400
Industrial Site, watercolor and charcoal,
    10 x 13 .... (805)   400

1967
The Stork Club, 1940, watercolor, 26½ x 39½ .... (889)   6,750
Locomotive No. 2, 1928, watercolor, 12¾ x 19¾ .. (969)   1,200
Manhattan Skyscrapers, 1930, watercolor,
    14 x 20 .... (969)   1,100

1968–July 1969
Scene in a Harbor, 1929, watercolor, 14 x 19¾ ... (1030)   850
Two Locomotives, 1927, pencil and watercolor,
    14 x 19¾ .... (1088)   650
Young Lady Drawing, 1939, watercolor,
    14¾ x 20¾ .... (1035)   1,800
Grand Central Terminal, 1942, watercolor and
    charcoal, 25¾ x 38¼ .... (1080)   1,100

Seaside, 1947, watercolor and India ink,
14 x 19¾ .... (1035) $3,000
The Locomotive, 1928, 13¼ x 19¼ .... (1160)   3,500
S. S. Bremen, 1938, watercolor, 14 x 20 .... (1229)   300

PAINTINGS

1961–1962
Broadway at 40th Street, 1952, on panel,
35½ x 11¾ .... (85)   1,600

1963
Coney Island, 1953, on panel, 8 x 10 .... (272)   1,200
Rustic Romance, on panel, 11¾ x 14¾ .... (272)   1,050

1966
The Display, on panel, 24 x 17¾ .... (790)   1,500

1968–July 1969
Woman in the Street, 1951, on panel, 10 x 8 ..... (1035)   4,250
Windy Day, 1939, on board, 14½ x 10½ .... (1229)   3,600

Henri Martin

(1860–1943)

Birthplace: Toulouse, France.

1879	Attends the Académie Julian, Paris.
1880	Participates steadily at the Salon, Paris.
1885	Gains a scholarship that enables him to make a trip to Italy. Comes under the influence of Neo-Impressionism.
(1890)	Frequently commissioned by the state. Executes murals for the Paris Hôtel de Ville. Promoted to the rank of Chevalier of the Legion of Honor.
1899	Executes decorations for the Paris World's Fair. Frequently exhibits at the Galerie Georges Petit, Paris, in the group known as "La Société Nouvelle."
1910	First one-man show at the Galerie Georges Petit, Paris.
1943	Died.

Sales

DRAWINGS

1963
Nude with a Rose, 1895, 15¾ x 9 .... (79) $ 30

1968–July 1969
The Shepherdess, charcoal and red chalk,
36½ x 18¾ .... (1212)   90

WATERCOLORS

1968–July 1969
Woman with a Lyre, pastel, 27 x 15½ .... (1231)   800

PAINTINGS

1961–1962
The Door Opening on the Garden, 21 x 37½ ..... (155) $ 540
Poplars, 25¼ x 38 .... (161)   900
Landscape, 19¾ x 36½ .... (124)   1,240
View of Paris, Snow Effect, on panel,
21¼ x 17¾ .... (120)   1,300
Collioure, 30½ x 36¾ .... (30)   1,520
Surroundings of Collioure, 31 x 39½ .... (72)   2,900
Fishing Harbor, 33½ x 37½ .... (71)   3,000
Seascape, 32 x 39½ .... (53)   760

1963
Self-Portrait, on panel, 21 x 17½ .... (293)   310
Marseilles, the Old Harbor, 1905, 32 x 25¾ ...... (306)   2,700
Paris, Snow Effect, 27¾ x 32½ .... (306)   1,900
The Child in the Garden of the Tuileries,
25¾ x 21¼ .... (192)   740
The Stone Pines on the Côte-d'Azur, 15 x 24 ..... (254)   300
The Flowery Portal, 25¾ x 32 .... (185)   620

1964
The Great Trees and the Church, 41½ x 23¾ ..... (440)   2,000
The Church in the Mountain, 39½ x 32 .... (345)   860
On the Terrace, 33¼ x 42 .... (454)   359
The Arbor, 39½ x 34 .... (466)   660
The Pergola, on panel, 26 x 28 .... (448)   2,000
The Door of the Garden, 25¾ x 32 .... (354)   1,600
Garden, 35½ x 45¾ .... (467)   3,690
Landscape with Poplars, 25¼ x 37½ .... (456)   1,600
Fields After the Harvest, 21 x 34¾ .... (395)   1,360
The Entrance Door at Marquaisol, 36½ x 29 ..... (405)   1,306
Flowers in a Vase, on cardboard, 21¾ x 18¼ ..... (401)   1,100

1965
The Duck Pond, 37½ x 45¾ .... (632)   5,400
Portrait of Laurens, 1903, on cardboard,
13 x 11¾ .... (612)   400
Bust of a Young Girl, 18¼ x 11¾ .... (518)   360
La Bastide du Vert (Lot), (1910), 32 x 33½ .... (516)   2,000
Trees in Bloom at La Bastide, 37½ x 27 .... (603)   2,660
Poplars in a Field, 25¼ x 36½ .... (585)   1,596
The Sower, 31½ x 31½ .... (539)   4,500
The Artist's Garden, 29 x 33½ .... (539)   4,000
Women by the Riverside, 25¾ x 21¾ .... (633)   3,500
The Orchard, 46¾ x 43½ .... (532)   1,500
Woman with a Basket, 38¾ x 23 .... (532)   840
Snowy Landscape, 25¾ x 19¾ .... (508)   600
Landscape, 19¾ x 36½ .... (512)   1,220
A Cup and a Coffeepot, on panel, 17½ x 14¾ ..... (582)   332
Marseilles Harbor, 27¾ x 41½ .... (553)   3,900

1966
The Park of Versailles, 1923, 116½ x 78 .... (727)   1,600
The Bridge Over the Stream Vert, 27 x 29¾ ...... (745)   3,164
St. Cirq-Lapopie, 31½ x 42¾ .... (814)   6,000
The Stream Lot, 40½ x 29¾ .... (749)   2,300
The Pergola, on panel, 26 x 28 .... (713)   3,000
The Terrace, 25 x 19¾ .... (784)   3,600
A Corner of the Terrace, 36¾ x 20½ .... (784)   6,250
View from the Balcony, 25¾ x 31¾ .... (776)   4,500
Paris, Snow Effect, on panel, 20 x 15¼ .... (772)   800
The Bridge, 19¾ x 13 .... (648)   500

Women in a Landscape, 23¾ x 32 . . . . (670) $1,760
Sailboats, on panel, 14 x 10¼ . . . . (757) 1,161
Vase of Flowers, on canvas . . . . (673) 920

1967
The Church, 36½ x 26½ . . . . (852) 2,200
Workmen: Place de La Concorde, triptych,
 central panel 26½ x 38¾, side panels
 26½ x 12¾ . . . . (993) 3,200
The Lovers, 32 x 19 . . . . (993) 1,400
Underwood, 29 x 49½ . . . . (978) 1,500
Landscape of the Lot, 29 x 36½ . . . . (984) 4,000
Apple Trees in Blossom, on cardboard,
 12¾ x 16¼ . . . . (929) 600
Harvesttime, 18¼ x 21¾ . . . . (995) 2,220
Ploughmen, 24 x 29¾ . . . . (841) 3,000
Marseilles Harbor, 18 x 21¾ . . . . (963) 4,250
A Bridge Over the River, 27 x 29¾ . . . . (919) 2,712

1968–July 1969
Composition with a Goat Girl, 79 x 187¾ . . . . (1049) 10,100
The Tree Looking Down Upon the Valley, on
 panel, 12¾ x 15¾ . . . . (1052) 1,000
The Ornamental Lake with Cypresses, 1900,
 25¼ x 35½ . . . . (1138) 7,434
The Bridge Over the Stream Vert, (1915),
 27 x 29¾ . . . . (1080) 4,500
Interior of a Farmhouse, 31½ x 51½ . . . . (1210) 4,800
The Village, 16¾ x 24¾ . . . . (1189) 1,800
Portal of a Church, 36½ x 29 . . . . (1175) 2,900
The Arbor, 23¾ x 29 . . . . (1113) 4,200
The Pines Near the Creek, on cardboard,
 15 x 18 . . . . (1184) 1,840
Le Basin fleurie, 35½ x 47½ . . . . (1200) 11,400
Ophelia, on board, 20½ x 14¾ . . . . (1070) 1,888
The Gipsy, 18¼ x 14¾ . . . . (1030) 1,300
Self-Portrait Before a Landscape,[1] on panel,
 21 x 14¾ . . . . (1212) 1,060
A Bride, 19½ x 13 . . . . (1231) 850
View of Sète, on panel, 11¾ x 19¼ . . . . (1239) 4,800
Sunny Village by the Waterside, (1904),
 31½ x 31½ . . . . (1239) 8,830
The Ornamental Lake in the Garden,
 26½ x 31½ . . . . (1240) 4,800
Red Flowers, on panel, 15½ x 12½ . . . . (1241) 1,490
Bathers, 10½ x 6½ . . . . (1241) 706
The Church, 22½ x 23 . . . . (1252) 4,620
Landscape, 1900, 49 x 29¾ . . . . (1252) 6,120
La Bastide du Vert in the Lot, in Spring,
 32 x 26½ . . . . (1258) 9,300
The Stream Lot at St. Cirq-Lapopie,
 35½ x 25¾ . . . . (1258) 4,200
The Vine Arbor in Blossom, 27¾ x 38¾ . . . . (1261) 10,000
The River Lined with Poplars, 40¼ x 29¼ . . . . (1261) 16,000
Landscape, 14¼ x 20¼ . . . . (1273) 1,386
Landscape, on panel, 18¼ x 11 . . . . (1273) 1,058

[1] On the reverse, a sketch with a woman in a garden.

André Masson

(1896–   )

Birthplace: Balagny-sur-Mer, Oise district, France.

1919 Settles in Paris. Enters the Ecole Nationale des Beaux-Arts, Paris.

1922 Cubist period. He is particularly influenced by Juan Gris.

1924 First exhibition is organized by Kahnweiler at the Galerie Simon, Paris.

1924-29 Meets Antonin Artaud, André Breton, Miró, and Max Ernst. Joins Surrealism and takes part in the first exhibition of the group at the Galerie Pierre, Paris. The works of William Blake, the Marquis de Sade, Kafka, and Nietzsche exert a great influence upon him.

1929-32 Trip to Germany and the Netherlands.

1933 Exhibits with Miró in New York.

1934-36 Stays in Tossa, Spain. Executes a large number of paintings portraying the Spanish Civil War.

1937 Returns to France. Starts his second Surrealist period.

1942-45 Stays in the U.S. Begins to turn to abstract painting, influenced by trends of the time: action painting and abstract expressionism.

1946 Returns to France. Issues *Bestiaire,* including twelve drawings and lithographs. Executes a stage decoration for *Morts sans sépulture* by Jean-Paul Sartre.

1947 Settles in Aix-en-Provence.

1949 Series of etchings for *Les Conquérants* by André Malraux.

1950 Retrospective exhibition in Basel.

1951 One-man show at the Galerie Leiris, Paris.

1957 Retrospective exhibition at the Galerie Leiris, Paris.

1964-65 Executes an important decoration for the ceiling of the Théâtre de France (the former Odéon), Paris.

Sales

DRAWINGS

1961-1962
The Three Symbolical Donkeys, (1937), pen,
 18¾ x 25¾ . . . . (140) $ 330

1963
Mismina V, India ink, 19 x 12¼ . . . . (185) 130
Costa Brava, colored ink, 12¾ x 16¾ . . . . (210) 2,194

1964
Four Nudes, 1933, colored pencil, 22 x 18¾ . . . . . . (368) 276

1965
The Fishermen, 1930, ink and watercolor,
 10¾ x 14¾ . . . . (606) 325
The Stars, ink, 12¼ x 9 . . . . (585) 261
Nude, 1954, India ink, 24 x 18 . . . . (598) 240
Composition, 1959, India ink, 26½ x 20½ . . . . (559) 110
Two Men, pen, 12¾ x 15 . . . . (567) 768

1966
Composition, India-ink wash, 17½ x 12¼ . . . . (731) 110
Nude, 1953, India ink, 25 x 17½ . . . . (738) 197
Bird Specter, 1956, India-ink wash, 19¾ x 25¾ . . . (720) 170

1967

Two Men, (1931), pen, 12¾ x 15 .... (919) $1,017

The Land of Metamorphosis, India ink,
18¾ x 24¾ .... (990)   935

A Figure on the Beach, India ink, 9¾ x 12¼ ...... (930)   163

1968–July 1969

Surrealist Composition, (1935), two drawings,
India ink, each 15¾ x 11¾ .... (1096)   483

The Spring, 1939, pen, 19 x 25 .... (1174)   1,035

Composition, India ink, 17½ x 12¼ .... (1029)   120

Summer Sorrow, colored chalk and charcoal,
18¾ x 24¾ .... (1138)   496

Metamorphosis, 1943, pen, 19 x 23 .... (1226)   500

WATERCOLORS

1961–1962

The Child with a Chameleon, India ink and pastel
on masonite, 18¼ x 14 .... (129)   824

Composition, watercolor, 23¾ x 17¾ .... (143)   1,030

1963

The Lovers, 1935, watercolor, 13 x 10 .... (210)   302

Composition, pastel, 17 x 24 .... (216)   274

Insects and Pollen, 1955, watercolor and gouache,
17¼ x 11¼ .... (232)   678

1964

Landscape, gouache, 9¾ x 12¾ .... (351)   400

Two Dancers, watercolor, 20 x 9½ .... (386)   300

Composition, pastel, 12¾ x 21¼ .... (460)   900

The Cock, 1930, pastel, 23¾ x 29 .... (460)   1,300

Dawn, 1946, pastel on canvas, 20 x 25¼ .... (460)   1,300

The Eagle's Night, 1957, tempera and oil,
29 x 36 .... (372)   1,700

Orris, 1960, tempera and oil, 32 x 25¾ .... (372)   1,600

1965

The Bath, pastel, 19¾ x 24 .... (510)   460

1967

Summer Dawn, pastel, 19 x 25 .... (975)   700

Heads of Hunger, pastel, 19 x 25 .... (975)   280

Composition, (1934), pastel laid down on canvas,
23¾ x 19½ .... (919)   1,356

Sun, (1935), gouache, 14¼ x 10¾ .... (967)   881

The Citadel, 1940, watercolor and gouache,
18¾ x 18 .... (939)   774

Kabuki 6, 1955, gouache, 6½ x 9¾ .... (985)   332

1968–July 1969

Kabuki 6, 1955, gouache, 6½ x 9¾ .... (1078)   480

Metamorphosis, 1959, pastel, 18¼ x 21¾ .... (1129)   420

Summer in Hell I, (1962), pastel on a black
background, 13 x 19¾ .... (1127)   782

Composition, pastel, 12¾ x 21¼ .... (1212)   240

Composition, gouache, 6¾ x 10 .... (1268)   673

Working Woman, 1944, 30½ x 22½ .... (1268)   1,856

Elk Skull in the Forest, (1945), watercolor,
24 x 17¾ .... (1268)   1,206

PAINTINGS

1961–1962

Bird and Fish Fight, 1927, 9½ x 25½ .... (164)   1,922

Animal Figure, (1933), sand and oil, 17¾ x 8½ .... (140)   2,059

West Indian, (1935), 16 x 13 .... (128)   840

Emblematical View of Toledo, 1933–39,
63¾ x 48¼ .... (164) $6,316

Niobe, 1947, 71¼ x 55½ .... (129)   7,140

Bather by a Torrent, 49½ x 25¼ .... (29)   2,800

La Fécundation des fleurs, 1955, 25¾ x 18¼ ...... (155)   1,400

Red Mullet and Chrysanthemums, 23¼ x 8 .... (37)   800

The Cockfight, 19 x 24 .... (164)   1,510

Blue and Green Panorama of the River Seine,
14 x 51 .... (40)   2,200

Forlornness, 1956, 19¾ x 23¾ .... (93)   2,712

1963

Tarragona, 1934, 21¼ x 28¾ .... (315)   1,645

The Miners, (1945), 9 x 22 .... (283)   2,034

Coming Out of the Bath, 1946, 33¼ x 27 .... (279)   3,500

Arch and Mausoleum, 1948, 21¾ x 18¼ .... (242)   800

Don Quixote and the Puppets, 13½ x 22½ ...... (210)   1,919

The Forum and the Stars, 32 x 39½ .... (258)   2,700

1964

Emblematical View of Toledo, (1933–39),
63¾ x 48¼ .... (354)   7,000

Still Life with Cards, 1923, 25¾ x 21¼ .... (378)   5,198

Blois, 1942, 25¾ x 36½ .... (472)   1,200

The Apple Eater, 1943, 24 x 20 .... (378)   1,930

The Tower and the Boats, (1946–47),
40¼ x 33¼ .... (460)   3,400

Summer's End, 1955, 32 x 39½ .... (372)   1,800

Fighting Chimeras, 1955, 29 x 21¼ .... (372)   1,500

Crossroads by Night, 1956, oil and tempera on
canvas, 36½ x 29 .... (471)   4,859

Little Bathers in Arcachon, 23¾ x 14¾ .... (458)   1,451

1965

La Repas de poissons, 1923, 29 x 23¾ .... (615)   4,000

Still Life in a Garden, 1924, 24 x 15 .... (566)   3,842

The Head, (1925), 29 x 23¾ .... (569)   4,746

The Crown, 1925, 36½ x 29 .... (615)   5,000

The Man in the Garden, 1930, 39½ x 29 .... (583)   2,031

The Man in the Garden, 1930, 39½ x 29 .... (617)   6,102

The Hired Mourners, 1932, 23¾ x 51½ .... (615)   3,000

Automatons' Hotel, 1942, 28½ x 36½ .... (485)   3,600

Conflict, 1955, sand and gouache, 25¾ x 19¾ ..... (617)   949

The Birds' Blood, 1956, sand and objects,
29¾ x 29¾ .... (615)   2,700

Tumulus I, 1957, oil, gouache and sand,
29¾ x 29¾ .... (485)   3,000

The Migration, 1957, 48 x 39½ .... (485)   4,500

In the Grass, 1960, 23¾ x 28½ .... (494)   650

1966

Insects' Engagement, 12 x 21¼ .... (808)   2,467

The Storm, 1924, 23¾ x 29 .... (801)   800

Young Lady at a Window, 1926, 29 x 19¾ .... (801)   2,900

Fish, Birds, 1926, 24 x 19¾ .... (811)   2,100

The Knight, 1927, oil and sand on canvas,
36½ x 20 .... (676)   4,200

The Sower, 1931, 36½ x 29 .... (801)   2,600

The Grave Diggers, 1934, 35 x 51 .... (707)   4,750

The Sun Through the Branches, 1950, 21½ x 18 ... (751)   1,161

On the Mountain, 1951, 10¾ x 14 .... (745)   1,130

Heavenly Body, 13 x 11½ .... (681)   400

1967

The Comet, 1926, 14 x 10¾ .... (975)   960

The Wrong Bull, 1937, 14¾ x 24 .... (880)   2,764

Hora de Toros, 1937, 29 x 39½ .... (975)   3,500

Nudes in a Room, 29 x 23¾ . . . . (975) $2,000

Composition, on cardboard, 17½ x 13¾ . . . . (990) 492

The Miners, 1945, 9 x 22 . . . . (918) 1,921

1968–July 1969

Andalusian Harvesters, (1935), 35¼ x 45¾ . . . . . . (1208) 3,500

Bullfight, 1936, 21 x 29 . . . . (1145) 2,700

Crossroads by Night, Tokyo, 1936, oil and
tempera on canvas, 36½ x 29 . . . . (1174) 5,750

The Land of Salt, (1939), oil and collage on
board, 16¼ x 20¼ . . . . (1125) 4,830

Caryatid, 1939, assembling, oil and sand on
board, 13½ x 6½ . . . . (1070) 1,180

Feast, 1956, 35½ x 31½ . . . . (1174) 6,440

Still Life with Fish, 19½ x 24 . . . . (1196) 1,060

Blois, (1947), 25¾ x 36½ . . . . (1224) 2,900

Nightly Germination, 1955, 25¾ x 21¼ . . . . (1268) 2,320

Georges Mathieu

(1921–   )

Birthplace: Boulogne-sur-Mer, France.

1942　Gives up the study of law and philosophy to devote himself to painting.

1944　Turns to nonfigurative painting.

1946–47　Participates in the Salon des Moins de Trente Ans, Paris. Settles in Paris. Sets up the group called "Non-Figuration Psychique." Its first exhibition, "L'Imaginaire," is held at the Galerie du Luxembourg, Paris. Participates in the Salon des Réalités Nouvelles and the Salon des Surindépendants, Paris.

1949–50　Issues his book *Analogie de la Non-Figuration.* Takes part in a group show at the Galerie René Drouin, Paris. Exhibits at the Perspective Gallery, New York. First one-man show at the Galerie René Drouin, Paris.

1951–52　Takes part in the exhibition "Signifiants de l'informel" organized by M. Tapié. One-man show at the Stable Gallery, New York, organized by Alexandre Iolas.

1953–54　Takes part in the exhibition "Younger European Painting" at the Guggenheim Museum, New York. One-man shows at the Kootz Gallery, New York; the Chicago Arts Club; and the Galerie Rive Droite, Paris.

1955–56　One-man shows at the Alexandre Iolas Gallery, New York; the Galerie Pierre, Paris; and the Institute of Contemporary Art, London.

1958–59　One-man shows at the Kunstmuseum, Basel, and the Musée des Beaux-Arts, Neuchâtel.

1960　One-man show at the Museum of Modern Art, São Paulo.

1962　One-man shows in Basel, Jerusalem, Munich, and Tel Aviv.

1963　One-man show at the Palais des Beaux-Arts, Brussels. Retrospective exhibition at the Musée National d'Art Moderne, Paris.

1964–65　One-man show at the Galerie Charpentier, Paris. Exhibits in Zurich, Düsseldorf, Copenhagen, Montreal, and Milan.

1966–67　Designs an important tapestry (executed by the Manufacture des Gobelins) for the Montreal World's Fair. Executes a series of posters for Air France.

Resident in Paris.

Sales

DRAWINGS

1961–1962

Composition, India ink, 19¾ x 25¾ . . . . (43) $ 144

Composition, 1949, India-ink wash, 32½ x 21 . . . . . (110) 140

1963

Composition, 1948, wash, 23 x 17¼ . . . . (280) 164

Composition, India ink and violet ink, 22½ x 30 . . (205) 560

Brown and Black, 1958, colored ink, 21 x 28¾ . . . . (216) 219

Composition, 1959, India ink and watercolor,
19¾ x 27¾ . . . . (299) 710

1964

Composition, 1948, India ink, 24½ x 17¾ . . . . (426) 76

Composition, 1954, India ink, 18¾ x 23¾ . . . . (374) 200

Composition, 1959, India ink and gouache,
19½ x 25¾ . . . . (351) 320

1965

Composition, 1958, India ink, 21¾ x 29¾ . . . . (512) 420

Composition in Violet and Black, 1959, colored
ink, 21½ x 29¾ . . . . (582) 387

1966

Black and White, 1948, ink, 23 x 17 . . . . (736) 140

Composition, 1959, ink and tempera, 27 x 18 . . . . . (815) 276

Composition in Violet and Black, 1959, colored
ink, 21½ x 29¾ . . . . (689) 249

Composition, India ink, 23¼ x 17¼ . . . . (809) 190

1968–July 1969

Composition, 1957, India ink on a red
background, 11¾ x 8¼ . . . . (1268) 410

WATERCOLORS

1961–1962

Composition, 1954, gouache, 16 x 19½ . . . . (106) 395

Composition, watercolor, 22 x 30 . . . . (109) 530

Composition, gouache, 22 x 29¾ . . . . (75) 664

Gouache No. 16, 19 x 27 . . . . (16) 506

Composition on a Black Background, 1958,
gouache, 25 x 19 . . . . (143) 565

Composition, watercolor, 23¾ x 19½ . . . . (160) 600

Composition, 1960, gouache, 19½ x 27¾ . . . . (143) 565

1963

Composition, 1954, gouache, 23¾ x 17½ . . . . (299) 300

Composition, 1954, gouache, 19 x 25 . . . . (262) 160

Composition, 1959, watercolor and ink,
21 x 28¾ . . . . (208) 225

Composition, 1959, gouache, 32½ x 25 . . . . (249) 670

Composition, 1960, watercolor, 19½ x 25¾ . . . . (224) 400

Composition, 1960, watercolor, 19 x 27 . . . . (224) 560

MATHIEU

1964

Composition, 1954, gouache on red paper,
18 x 24 .... (454) $ 498

Composition, 1954, gouache, 19¾ x 25¾ .... (372)   850

Composition, 1955, watercolor, 17½ x 23¾ .... (375)   310

Composition, 1959, watercolor and colored ink,
19¾ x 25¾ .... (375)   380

Graphisme Rose, 1958, gouache, 19¾ x 27 .... (441)   565

Composition in Yellow on a Black Background,
1959, gouache, 19 x 26½ .... (438)   250

Painting, 1959, gouache on black paper,
25 x 19½ .... (454)   719

Composition, 1960, watercolor, 19¾ x 26 .... (441)   260

1965

Composition on an Orange Background,
watercolor, 29¾ x 21¾ .... (519)   220

Composition, 1948, gouache, 25 x 19½ .... (497)   110

Composition, 1957, watercolor, 25 x 35½ .... (512)   340

Composition, 1958, watercolor, 9 x 12 .... (545)   170

Composition, 1963, watercolor, 30 x 22 .... (617)   791

1966

*Red and Yellow Composition on a White
Background,* 1957, watercolor and India ink,
13 x 21¼ .... (741)   320

Lyricism in Pink, 1958, gouache, 19½ x 29 .... (745)   475

Composition in Mauve and Black, 1958, gouache,
21¼ x 29¼ .... (759)   600

Composition, 1959, watercolor, 21 x 28½ .... (784)   300

Composition, 1959, gouache, and tempera,
27 x 18 .... (815)   387

Composition, 1960, gouache, 27 x 19 .... (751)   802

"If I Should Lose You," 1961, watercolor and
collage, 22 x 30½ .... (805)   250

1967

Composition, 1958, gouache, 21¼ x 29 .... (926)   344

Composition in White and Black, 1959, gouache,
19 x 27 .... (888)   332

1968–July 1969

Composition, 1960, watercolor, 17¾ x 25¾ ...... (1121)   560

Composition, 1960, watercolor, 17¾ x 25¾ ...... (1202)   600

Design of a Mural for a Villa at Castelaras,
gouache, 16¼ x 39¼ .... (1118)   320

Composition, black gouache on red paper,
19¼ x 25 .... (1273)   479

PAINTINGS

1961–1962

Abstraction, 1951, oil on paper on canvas,
21½ x 33½ .... (111)   200

Night, 1954, casein on board .... (129)   686

Composition, 1954, oil on paper, 52¼ x 25¾ ...... (124)   460

Composition, 25¾ x 19¾ .... (161)   190

Clement of Alexandria, 1956, 35¼ x 58 .... (116)   1,440

1963

Composition, 1949, 38 x 24 .... (200)   1,700

A Tribute to Death .... (299)   3,000

1964

Composition, 1955, oil, India ink, and gold on
cardboard, 19¾ x 25¾ .... (467)   541

Origen, 1956, 35¼ x 57¼ .... (351)   1,620

Composition, 1957, 32½ x 51½ .... (471)   1,898

The Wedding of Marie de Blois, 1960,
70½ x 118¼ .... (372)   5,250

1965

The First Campaign of Thierry d'Alsace, 1960,
49½ x 128½ .... (485) $5,500

Egregis, 1952, 64½ x 51½ .... (524)   980

Composition on a Black Background, 1961,
45 x 57¾ .... (519)   1,800

1966

Composition in Black, 1947, on panel,
47½ x 63¼ .... (678)   4,000

Philip II, the Conqueror, 1958, 32 x 51½ .... (681)   1,400

A Tribute to Eric, 32 x 51½ .... (727)   1,840

1967

Lothair's Mistake, 1954, 32¼ x 51½ .... (912)   1,000

Ptolemy Ratifies the Issue, 1958, 35¼ x 56½ ..... (870)   1,400

Composition in Red, Blue, and White, 1959,
35¼ x 57¾ .... (888)   967

Composition, 1964, 19¾ x 29 .... (838)   900

1968–July 1969

Scale on a Blue Background, 1956, 32 x 50¾ .... (1202)   2,800

Nudes and Architecture, 28½ x 36 .... (1235)   7,500

Night, 1954, casein on board, 19½ x 25 .... (1237)   650

Henri Matisse

(1869–1954)

Birthplace: Le Cateau, Nord district, France.

1891   Gives up his law studies to attend the Académie Julian, Paris.

1892   Enters the Ecole Nationale des Beaux-Arts, Paris, in the studio of Gustave Moreau, where he meets Rouault, Marquet, and Manguin. Also meets Raoul Dufy and Friesz.

1897-98   Meets Camille Pissarro and comes under the influence of Impressionism. Considerably lightens his palette. Buys Cézanne's "Bathers" from Ambroise Vollard. Discovers Provence and the Mediterranean light. Begins to use pure color.

1899   Attends the Académie Carrière, Paris, where he meets Derain. Executes his first sculptures.

1901   Participates in the Salon des Indépendants, Paris, where he meets Vlaminck.

1902   Takes part in a group show at the Galerie Berthe Weil, Paris.

1903   Participates in the first Salon d'Automne, Paris.

1904   First one-man show at the Galerie Ambroise Vollard, Paris. Spends the summer at St. Tropez with Signac. Briefly attracted by Neo-Impressionism.

1905   Participates in the Salon d'Automne, Paris, with Vlaminck, Van Dongen, Derain, Rouault, and the others, in the famous room derisively called "la cage aux fauves," where Fauvism is first shown to the indignation of the public. Matisse's painting "Luxe, Calme, et Volupté" is constructed by means of broad areas of pure color. Soon appears as the leader of the group, reasonably enough, since Fauvism—owing to the powerful color and bold simplifications it demands—perfectly squares with his understanding of life and art. He is the only Fauve whose concerns remain closely linked to Fauvism throughout his career.

1906 One-man show at the Galerie Druet, Paris. Trip to Biskra, Algeria. Meets Picasso. Discovers Negro art.

1907 Exhibits his "Blue Nude" at the Salon des Indépendants, Paris. Trip to Italy. Opens his own art school on the Boulevard des Invalides, Paris.

1908 First exhibition in New York at the Stieglitz Gallery. Issues "Notes d'un peintre" in *La Grande Revue,* Paris. Exhibits at the Cassirer Gallery, Berlin.

1910 Retrospective exhibition at the Galerie Bernheim-Jeune, Paris. Produces "Dance" and "Music."

1911-13 Trips to Morocco. One-man show at Bernheim-Jeune's, Paris.

1915 Exhibits at the Montross Gallery, New York.

1917 Settles in Nice and meets Renoir.

1920 First monograph on Matisse by Marcel Sembat. Executes stage decorations for Stravinsky and Diaghilev. Series of "Odalisques."

1924 Exhibits at the Brummer Gallery, New York. Retrospective exhibition at the Ny-Carlsberg Glyptothek, Copenhagen.

1927 Wins the first prize at the Carnegie International Exhibition, Pittsburgh.

1930 Appointed member of the Carnegie Jury.

1931-33 After a series of travels in Europe, goes to Tahiti. Executes an important mural for the Barnes Foundation. Retrospective exhibitions at the Galerie Georges Petit, Paris, and at the Museum of Modern Art, New York. Illustrates Mallarmé's *Poésies.*

1936 Exhibits his recent paintings at the Galerie Paul Rosenberg, Paris.

1938-39 First "papiers découpés." Settles at Vence, near Nice.

1941 Becomes seriously ill.

1944-45 Retrospective exhibitions at the Salon d'Automne, Paris, and the Victoria and Albert Museum, London. Illustrates *Pasiphaé* by Henri de Montherlant.

1948 Major retrospective exhibition at the Philadelphia Museum of Art. Illustrates *Amours* by Ronsard.

1950 Wins the first prize at the Venice Biennial. Executes the decoration of the Chapelle du Rosaire des Dominicaines de Vence.

1951 Exhibits at the Museum of Modern Art, New York.

1952 Inauguration of the Musée Matisse at Le Cateau, France.

1954 Died, Cimiez, near Nice.

1956 Retrospective exhibition at the Musée National d'Art Moderne, Paris.

Sales

DRAWINGS

1961-1962

Woman's Head, pen, 17 x 14 . . . . (26) $1,400
Portrait of a Woman, 1937, India ink, 24 x 16¼ . . . (106) 3,277

Seated Woman, 1939, India ink, 14¾ x 10¾ . . . . (68) $1,200
The Woman with a Veil, 1939, pen, 10¼ x 14 . . . . . . (32) 1,100
The Two Girl Friends, pen, 19¾ x 18¾ . . . . (109) 760
Woman's Head, 1942, pen, 15¾ x 20½ . . . . (6) 2,305
Young Nude, Her Hands Behind Her Head, pen,
9¾ x 7½ . . . . (125) 1,900
Flowers in a Tobacco Pot, 1942, pen, 12½ x 9¾ . . . (121) 370
Still Life with a Fruit Stand, pen, 1944,
20½ x 15¾ . . . . (32) 1,640
Reclining Man in the Nude, (1889-90), pencil,
6½ x 12 . . . . (128) 494
Standing Nude, black lead, 11¾ x 4¾ . . . . (106) 542
Reclining Nude, black lead, 9¾ x 13¾ . . . . (106) 1,672
Two Odalisques, pencil, 14¾ x 19½ . . . . (31) 5,767
Woman's Head, 1947, black pencil, 16¾ x 11 . . . . . . (8) 1,250
Head of a Young Lady, 1947, black lead,
20½ x 15½ . . . . (96) 1,500
Nude Model, pencil, 15½ x 10 . . . . (96) 1,900
Woman, Her Hand on Her Cheek, pencil,
16¼ x 10¾ . . . . (20) 3,792
Young Woman Reading, stick of greasepaint,
19¾ x 15¼ . . . . (95) 1,600
The West Indian, black lead, 15¾ x 11¾ . . . . (84) 1,785
Le Tabac Royal, Interior with a Seated Woman,
1940, pencil, 13 x 17½ . . . . (164) 2,334

1963

Seated Nude with Legs Crossed, 1920, pencil,
12 x 9 . . . . (219) 1,175
The Two Friends, 1928, ink, 19¾ x 15 . . . . (210) 2,879
Nude Facing the Mirror, 1937, ink, 11 x 14¾ . . . . . (179) 2,300
Portrait of Alexina Matisse, 1938, charcoal,
24 x 16 . . . . (210) 3,290
Portrait of C. Pallady, the Romanian Painter,
black lead, 15 x 10½ . . . . (314) 700
Seated Nude, 1937, black-lead, 20½ x 14¾ . . . . . . (179) 1,700
Maternity, 1939, India ink, 21¾ x 17½ . . . . (283) 2,147
Seated Woman, with Hands Crossed, 1940, Conté
pencil, 17½ x 13 . . . . (243) 1,320
Le Tabac Royal, 1942, ink, 12¾ x 9½ . . . . (265) 956
Head of a Young Lady in Left Profile, 1942,
pencil, 10¼ x 8 . . . . (219) 791
Woman with a Violet, 1942, India ink, 21 x 15¾ . . . (255) 686
Seated Woman, 1942, charcoal, 19 x 15 . . . . (206) 1,260
Portrait of a Woman, 1944, pen, 20 x 14¾ . . . . (208) 1,650
Theanor, 1945, charcoal, 20¼ x 15½ . . . . (316) 4,000
Boat Sailing Back into the Harbor, St. Tropez,
India-ink wash, 7¼ x 9¾ . . . . (254) 600
Portrait of a Woman, 1952, sepia on paper,
20½ x 15½ . . . . (299) 560

1964

Sailboats at Collioure, (1904), blue pencil,
12¾ x 8¼ . . . . (475) 320
Seated Man in the Nude, (1912), pencil,
11½ x 8 . . . . (453) 884
Mademoiselle Yvonne Landsberg in Profile, 1914,
pen, 25¾ x 13 . . . . (416) 3,593
Young Woman Reading, stick of greasepaint,
19¾ x 15 . . . . (472) 1,700
Marguerite Reading, charcoal, 12¼ x 13½ . . . . (405) 3,192
Self-Portrait, 1919, ink, 10¾ x 7¼ . . . . (454) 1,354
Reclining Nude, 1935, pen, 15 x 22 . . . . (340) 2,360
Blue Eyes, 1935, pencil, 11 x 14¾ . . . . (458) 4,933

Portrait of Alexina Matisse, 1938, charcoal,
24 x 16 .... (367) $3,040

Portrait of a Woman, 1938, charcoal,
23¾ x 15¾ .... (321) 1,000

Woman with Face Inclined, 1942, stick of
greasepaint, 20¼ x 16 .... (378) 1,898

*Bust of a Young Lady Before a Book, Her Arms
Resting on a Table*, stumped charcoal,
15¾ x 10¼ .... (378) 2,373

Young Woman with a Book, black pencil,
15¾ x 10¼ .... (336) 1,040

Young Woman Leaning on Her Elbow, 1942,
India ink, 15¾ x 20½ .... (409) 1,900

Reclining Odalisque, pencil, 6¼ x 14½ .... (385) 1,808

Reclining Nude, pen, 15 x 19¾ .... (429) 1,107

Fishing Boats, pen, 19½ x 12¼ .... (467) 1,476

Seated Woman, 1944, pen, 20¼ x 16 .... (416) 1,935

Portrait of a Seated Woman, 1944, pen,
21¼ x 15¾ .... (354) 1,800

Vase of Flowers, 1945, pencil, 20 x 15 .... (367) 2,902

Still Life with a Vase of Flowers, 1944, India ink,
15½ x 20½ .... (385) 1,876

The Virgin and the Child,[1] pen, 8¼ x 10½ .... (354) 1,600

Danièle, 1947, charcoal, 19 x 12¼ .... (354) 3,500

Siren, 1949, charcoal, 21¾ x 14¼ .... (416) 3,040

Bust of a Young Woman, 1950, India ink,
20¾ x 16¼ .... (471) 1,220

Portrait of a Woman, 1952, black pencil,
18¼ x 11 .... (416) 1,520

1965

Seated Nude, (1904-05), pencil, 12 x 8 .... (541) 1,500

Study of a Nude, (1905), India ink, 10¼ x 7¾ ..... (606) 1,350

The Venetian Dress, (1922-23), charcoal,
20 x 15½ .... (575) 6,910

Studies of an Odalisque, 1928, pencil, 14 x 18¼ ... (522) 6,357

Odalisque, charcoal, 18½ x 24 .... (632) 9,000

Nude with a Necklace, 1935, India ink, 15 x 20 ... (566) 3,629

The Melon, 1936, pen, 4¾ x 8 .... (535) 829

Woman Leaning on Her Elbow, 1941, India ink,
19¾ x 14¾ .... (569) 1,921

Study of a Reclining Nude, 1943, red chalk,
20½ x 15½ .... (594) 2,100

Fruit Stand, 1944, India ink, 20½ x 15¾ .... (529) 1,200

Portrait of a Young Woman, 1944, charcoal,
20 x 15½ .... (633) 3,000

Young Woman and Still Life, 1944, pen,
20½ x 15¾ .... (602) 2,667

*Portrait of Gérard Matisse, the Artist's
Grandson*, 1945, charcoal, 23 x 15¾ .... (512) 840

Portrait of Paul Léautaud, 1946, charcoal,
15½ x 11½ .... (624) 967

Woman's Head, Eve, 1948, drawing on canvas,
21 x 16¼ .... (616) 1,600

1966

Standing Nude, black lead, 11¾ x 9 .... (745) 1,492

Reclining Nude, 1929, pen, 10¾ x 17¾ .... (738) 1,968

Reclining Nude, 1935, pen, 12¾ x 16¼ .... (816) 3,198

Model Resting, (1935), pen, 17¾ x 20½ .... (751) 5,252

Two Women, 1938, ink, 15 x 20¼ .... (707) 5,500

Portrait of His Friend Pallady, pencil, 15 x 9¾ ... (666) 1,000

Woman Seated in an Armchair, pencil,
14 x 10¼ .... (686) 3,317

[1]Study for the Chapelle de Vence.

Interior with a Seated Nude, 1935, India ink,
9¼ x 12½ .... (735) $1,853

Odalisque, pencil, 6½ x 15 .... (665) 3,000

Reclining Odalisque, 1944, charcoal, 14¼ x 21½ .. (703) 7,500

Woman's Head, charcoal, 14 x 9½ .... (770) 3,124

Bust of a Young Woman, 1950, India ink,
20¾ x 16¼ .... (797) 5,650

Sailboats Before St. Tropez Harbor, India ink,
7¼ x 10 .... (784) 1,000

Self-Portrait, India ink, 15¾ x 10¼ .... (801) 5,000

1967

Seated Nude, (1904-05), pencil, 12 x 20 .... (841) 1,300

Study of a Man in the Nude, (1904), pencil,
12 x 8¾ .... (985) 806

St. James Lily, 1919, pen, 9¼ x 11 .... (985) 1,612

Vase of Flowers, (1935), black lead, 12¾ x 9½ .... (918) 2,667

Nude Seated in Front of the Mirror, 1937, pen,
14¾ x 11 .... (889) 4,500

Woman Sleeping on a Table Corner, 1939,
charcoal, 24 x 16 .... (1004) 15,000

Inclined Face, 1941, India ink, 15¾ x 21 .... (941) 3,800

Young Lady in an Armchair, 1942, India ink,
21 x 16¼ .... (889) 4,000

Woman's Head, 1945, ink, 16 x 21 .... (1004) 6,500

Peaches, pencil, 9¾ x 15¼ .... (930) 237

Portrait of Gil Marchex the Pianist, India ink,
18¾ x 12¼ .... (961) 440

Young Lady with a Mantilla, India ink,
19¾ x 15 .... (889) 5,000

1968–July 1969

Standing Nude, (1908), pencil, 12¼ x 8¼ .... (1068) 2,242

Sleeping Nude, black pencil, 8½ x 13¾ .... (1050) 1,380

Portrait of Gil Marchex the Pianist, India ink,
14½ x 12¼ .... (1134) 2,124

Nude with a Necklace, 1935, India ink, 15 x 20 .. (1101) 5,750

Seated Woman, pencil, 10½ x 7 .... (1101) 1,610

Warrior Costume for "Le Chant du Rossignol,"
pencil, 16¾ x 8¾ .... (1142) 5,192

Reclining Nude, 1941, India ink, 7¼ x 9¾ .... (1114) 2,480

Reclining Nude, Back View, pencil, 10¼ x 13 ... (1126) 3,221

Young Woman Leaning on Her Elbow, 1944, pen,
20¼ x 15½ .... (1191) 7,452

Portrait of André Rouveyre, 1944, charcoal,
15½ x 10¾ .... (1140) 400

Seated Nude with Legs Crossed, pencil,
21¾ x 16¾ .... (1216) 3,100

Doucia, 1951, black chalk, 20¾ x 16¼ .... (1134) 3,776

Flowers in a Vase, pencil, 21¾ x 17½ .... (1173) 9,430

Studies of Cows, India ink, 1912, 6¾ x 9¾ ...... (1240) 1,560

Le Nasturtimus, 1942, pencil, 7¾ x 10¼ .... (1240) 1,920

The Violinist, (1922), charcoal, 18¾ x 24¾ ...... (1246) 7,500

Woman Seated Before a Window, (1924),
charcoal, 12 x 18 .... (1246) 7,750

Portrait of His Grandson Gérard, 1945, charcoal,
23½ x 15¾ .... (1246) 3,250

Portrait of Madame Chanvin,[2] India ink,
19½ x 15½ .... (1265) 9,000

Portrait of a Little Girl, 1947, charcoal,
19¾ x 15¾ .... (1268) 7,656

Flowers, 1945, pencil, 15¾ x 20½ .... (1268) 6,032

[2]Dedicated "A Chanvin, cordialement."

Woman Reading, 1939, charcoal, 23¾ x 16 ...... **(1268)** $18,106
Portrait of a Woman, 1939, charcoal, 24¾ x 19 .. **(1268)** 14,848
Study of a Nude, (1906-08), 16¾ x 11¾ .... **(1272)** 6,720

WATERCOLORS

1961–1962
Odalisque on a Yellow Background, 1929, pastel,
13 x 20 .... **(84)** 16,476

1964
The Dancer, 1925, pastel, 17¾ x 24 .... **(367)** 42,013

1965
Woman Seated in Front of a Window, 1935,
pastel and gouache, 24 x 19¾ .... **(594)** 41,000

1966
The Pont St. Michel, 1907, pastel, 9½ x 10¾ ..... **(801)** 7,800
The Parakeet and the Siren, 1952-53, gouache
and cut-up papers, 133¼ x 305 .... **(750)** 88,448

PAINTINGS

1961–1962
The Thatch-Roofed Cottage,[3] 1897, 21¾ x 31 ...... **(71)** 3,600
Still Life with a Lemon, 1895, 18¼ x 23¾ .... **(116)** 15,600
Woman with a Green Parasol, 1920, 27¾ x 22½ .... **(83)** 87,872
Seated Nude, 1917-18, 11¾ x 15¾ .... **(70)** 13,430
Interior with a Young Woman, oil on cardboard,
16 x 12 .... **(93)** 25,990
Two Women on a Terrace, 1921, 27 x 21¼ .... **(8)** 62,500
Young Woman at the Window, Nice 1921,
25¾ x 21¼ .... **(96)** 40,000
Woman Facing a Mirror, 1935, 17¾ x 22 .... **(140)** 16,476
Landscape, oil on paper on board, 7½ x 11½ ...... **(96)** 3,000
Notre-Dame de Paris, 18½ x 22 .... **(125)** 24,400
*Interior with Engraved Floor, Woman Seated in a
Yellow Armchair,* 1940, 21 x 25¼ .... **(83)** 104,348

1963
The Garden of the Mill, Corsica, (1898), oil on
paper laid down on canvas, 10 x 12¼ .... **(279)** 9,500
Harbor Scene in Corsica, (1904-05), oil on paper,
7¾ x 8¾ .... **(247)** 7,678
A Cup of Oranges, 1916, 21¼ x 25¾ .... **(210)** 32,904
The Fishing Boats, 1918, oil on cardboard,
10¼ x 13½ .... **(206)** 7,000
Dancer Resting, 1942, 18¼ x 15 .... **(316)** 36,000
The Harbor, 12¼ x 15½ .... **(254)** 7,800

1964
Lemons and Mimosas, 1944, 21¼ x 29 .... **(454)** 60,808
The Black Cup, 1941, 15¾ x 12¾ .... **(458)** 23,216
Still Life, 14¼ x 17½ .... **(458)** 15,961
The Citadel of Belle-Ile, 13 x 16¼ .... **(397)** 7,000

1965
Still Life, 1896, 11¼ x 12¼ .... **(522)** 7,739
Still Life, the Table Set in the Garden, (1898), on
cardboard, 15 x 16½ .... **(613)** 19,200
Marseilles Harbor, the Fishing Boats, 1918, on
panel, 11 x 14 .... **(561)** 4,300
The Pont de Sèvres at St. Cloud, (1920),
18¼ x 21¾ .... **(526)** 27,500
Woman with a Green Parasol, (1920),
27¾ x 22½ .... **(526)** 72,500

The Gorges du Loup, (1922-23), 18½ x 22 .... **(526)** $62,000
Woman Seated in Front of Her Piano, 1924,
18¼ x 14¾ .... **(575)** 15,202
Seated Woman, on canvas laid down on board,
13 x 9½ .... **(526)** 23,000

1966
Landscape at Collioure, (1911), 36 x 25 .... **(694)** 42,000
The Mill, (1912), on cardboard, 14¾ x 12¾ .... **(801)** 10,020
The Woman by the Fountain, (1917), 32 x 25 ..... **(676)** 70,000
Park in the Rain, Nice, 1918, on board,
10 x 13¼ .... **(750)** 20,730
Woman Seated in an Armchair, Her Breast Bare,
(1919), 20¾ x 14¼ .... **(686)** 41,460
The Nets of Etretat, (1920-21), 17¾ x 16¼ .... **(812)** 27,640
The Chinese Vase, 1922, 13¼ x 22 .... **(808)** 78,354
The Violet Bolero, 1941, 28½ x 21 .... **(776)** 42,500
Nude with a Bathing Wrap, 1941, 19¾ x 24 .... **(744)** 48,816
*White Seaweed on an Orange and Red
Background,* 1952, cut-up paper,
20½ x 15¾ .... **(678)** 16,500
Nice, the Window Looking Out on the Sea,
13 x 21¾ .... **(685)** 11,000

1967
The Pont de Sèvres with Plane Trees, 1917,
10¾ x 14 .... **(930)** 14,916
Woman's Head, (1918), 14 x 10½ .... **(954)** 11,500
Seated Woman in Blue, 1937, 25 x 19 .... **(993)** 64,000
Seated Nude, on canvas laid down on cardboard,
17¾ x 14¼ .... **(987)** 33,500

1968–July 1969
Tempest at Belle-Ile, (1896), 21¼ x 26 .... **(1189)** 14,000
Belle-Ile sur Mer Harbor, oil on paper,
7¾ x 8¾ .... **(1132)** 15,340
The Yellow Flowers, 1902, 18¼ x 21½ .... **(1132)** 51,920
Notre-Dame from the Artist's Window, 1902,
18½ x 21¾ .... **(1187)** 60,180
The River Seine in Paris, (1911), on board,
10¼ x 14 .... **(1056)** 30,000
Fishing Boats, Marseilles Harbor, 1918, on
board, mounted on panel, 10¾ x 13½ .... **(1132)** 16,756
Arbre de neige, 1950-51, collage, 16 x 10¼ ...... **(1132)** 10,384
Still Life with a Tin Pot, on panel, 9 x 13 .... **(1053)** 15,800
Apollo, 1953, ceramics consisting of 16 squares,
128½ x 168¾ .... **(1187)** 80,240
Entrance of a Cabaret in Brittany, 1896,
14¾ x 18 .... **(1235)** 27,000

---

[3]Dedicated "A Madame Albert Legrand, hommage respectueux."

Echaurren Roberto Antonio Sebastian Matta

(1911-   )

Birthplace: Santiago, Chile.

1931	Finishes his studies in architecture.
1933-35	Goes to Paris, where he meets and works with Le Corbusier. Stay in Spain, where he meets Frederico Garcia-Lorca. Begins to take an interest in drawing and painting.
1936	Returns to Paris. Joins Surrealism and makes friends with André Breton and Miró.
1938	Participates in the illustration of *Les Chants de Maldoror* by Lautréamont.
1939	Goes to the U.S. with Tanguy and Duchamp. (Resident in the U.S. until 1945.)
1941	One-man show at the Pierre Matisse Gallery, New York.
1945	Returns to Europe and settles in Paris. Stay in Italy.
1946	One-man show at the Museum of Modern Art, New York.
1947	Takes part in a Surrealist exhibition at the Galerie Maeght, Paris.
1954	Travels to Chile and Peru.
1956	Executes a mural for UNESCO, Paris. One-man show at the Galerie du Dragon, Paris.
1957	Retrospective exhibition at the Museum of Modern Art, New York.
1959	Participates in Documenta II, Kassel, Germany.
1961-63	Travels to South America and Cuba. Exhibits at the Cordier Warrenin Gallery, New York.
1966	Trip to the U.S. Teaches at the Minneapolis School of Art.

Sales

DRAWINGS

1961-1962

Composition, colored pencil, 10¾ x 14¾ .... (111) $ 150

The Spherical Roof Around Our Tribe, chalk and pastel, 39 x 57 .... (37)   2,250

1963

Composition, pencil, 14¾ x 18¾ .... (286)   204

Abstraction, 1960, pencil and watercolor, 19¾ x 25¼ .... (208)   325

1964

Composition, pen, 14¾ x 22½ .... (377)   226

The Collective Man, 1955, colored pencil, 18¾ x 25 .... (375)   280

Abstraction in Green, Yellow, and Blue, 1960, pencil and watercolor, 19¾ x 25¾ .... (374)   150

1965

Composition, colored pencil, 15½ x 25 .... (547)   210

1966

Abstract Composition No. 8, (1961), colored pencil, 23¾ x 29¼ .... (805)   235

1967

Skiers, pencil, 19½ x 27¾ .... (889)   650

Surrealist Face, colored pencil, 58¾ x 25¾ .... (881)   995

1968-July 1969

Composition, chalks and collage, 14 x 18¾ ...... (1215) $ 500

Motion Pictures, 1961, colored chalk, 19½ x 25 .. (1114)   347

Surrealist Composition, black lead and colored pencil, 10 x 12¾ .... (1123)   170

Composition, 1960, pencil, pastel, and watercolor, 19½ x 25½ .... (1231)   625

Auditorium, India ink, 8 x 7¼ .... (1237)   325

WATERCOLORS

1961-1962

Composition, 1956, pastel, 13 x 19¾ .... (16)   158

1963

Portrait of a Man, 1959, pastel, 41½ x 29¾ .... (299)   600

Composition, 1961, pastel and colored chalk, 18¾ x 24½ .... (272)   325

1964

Composition, 1961, pastel, 22½ x 30½ .... (461)   480

Composition, tempera, 12¾ x 14¼ .... (321)   275

Composition, 1965, gouache, 14½ x 15¾ .... (329)   250

1965

S. T., 1961, pastel, 18¼ x 15 .... (616)   256

1966

Inner Landscape, (1947), pastel on paper laid down on canvas, 39½ x 59¼ .... (784)   1,200

1968-July 1969

Composition, pastel, 17 x 21 .... (1214)   448

Les Semeurs d'incendie au piège, pastel, 19½ x 25 .... (1268)   557

PAINTINGS

1961-1962

Composition No. 1, 25¾ x 29¾ .... (111)   625

Composition, 24½ x 28½ .... (75)   1,106

Composition, 33½ x 39½ .... (70)   1,580

Fantasia, 24½ x 30 .... (20)   1,738

Erupting Volcano, (1951), 17¾ x 19¾ .... (37)   1,000

Wise Earth, Rome 1952, 27 x 34½ .... (129)   961

Assicurteur, 1958, 45 x 57 .... (149)   2,370

Abstraction, 1958, 24¾ x 29¾ .... (85)   1,200

Space Conquest, 1961, 31½ x 39 .... (85)   1,600

1963

I Am Walking. . ., (1947), 41¾ x 42½ .... (202)   1,800

Havoc, (1948-50), 31¼ x 38½ .... (272)   1,900

Landscape, 1951, 26 x 30 .... (315)   1,261

To Die for Bread, 1953, 38½ x 48¼ .... (189)   2,500

The Full Light, 1955, 45½ x 57¼ .... (316)   3,850

Still Life, 45 x 57¾ .... (299)   1,900

1964

Composition, 1963, 33 x 40¾ .... (461)   1,200

The Absolute Unity, 1942, 28 x 35½ .... (453)   3,870

Max the Explorer, 32 x 39½ .... (439)   1,200

Landscape, 1951, 26 x 29¾ .... (454)   1,382

Composition, 1955, 31¼ x 38¾ .... (329)   1,200

1965

Composition, (1958-59), 46¼ x 42¾ .... (539)   1,850

Wise Earth, on canvas laid down on panel, 27 x 34 .... (541)   1,800

Panarea, 1961, 23 x 30 .... (616)   1,200

1966

Composition, 25¼ x 29¾ . . . . (802)	$ 1,360
The Remainer, (1945), 45½ x 32 . . . . (707)	4,100
Composition, 25 x 19¾ . . . . (745)	1,469
Dawn, 1954, 45 x 57¼ . . . . (776)	4,750
Composition, 23¾ x 29 . . . . (810)	800
Neither Yesterday Nor Later, 1965, 21¾ x 18¼ . . . (751)	1,161

1967

Composition, 45 x 57¾ . . . . (995)	2,200
Composition, 26¼ x 18¼ . . . . (990)	787
Composition, 1964, 45½ x 57¾ . . . . (963)	2,700

1968–July 1969

Crucifixion, 19¾ x 25¾ . . . . (1202)	840
Morning Beckons, 1954, 44½ x 55½ . . . . (1080)	2,500
The Bed of Spring, 55½ x 78 . . . . (1018)	4,400
Composition, 1953, 47 x 71¼ . . . . (1208)	4,900
Apollo, 1954, 28¾ x 23¾ . . . . (1240)	2,160
Machine Age, (1952), 46¼ x 70½ . . . . (1268)	9,976
Chilean Marshland, (1953), 59¼ x 78¼ . . . . (1268)	5,336

Maxime Maufra

(1861–1918)

Birthplace: Nantes, France.

1881	Goes to England on business but soon begins to paint. Discovers Turner, Constable, Bonnington, and the Dutch masters.
1883-84	First trip to Scotland. Returns to Nantes and keeps on painting in his leisure hours.
1886	Exhibits "The Flood at La Haute-Isle" at the Salon, Paris.
1888-94	Participates in the Salon des Indépendants, Paris.
1890	Gives up business to devote himself entirely to painting. Has a strong liking for landscapes. Participates in the Salon des Champs-Elysées, Paris. Makes a trip to Brittany, where he meets Gauguin and Sérusier. Stays a few months at Pont-Aven. Executes his first drawings, watercolors, engravings, and lithographs.
1890-94	Participates in the Salon du Champ de Mars and the Salon de la Société Nationale, Paris. First one-man show at the Galerie Le Barc de Boutteville, Paris. Durand-Ruel buys most of his work.
1896	Exhibits his landscapes of Scotland at Durand-Ruel's, Paris and New York.
1898	Executes a series of landscapes and seascapes at St. Guénolé.
1907	One-man show at the Galerie Durand-Ruel, Paris.
1913	Trip to Algeria.
1918	Died, Poncé-sur-le-Loir, Sarthe district.

Sales

DRAWINGS

1963

The Square at Baud de Bretagne, 1908, pencil and watercolor, 9¾ x 11¾ . . . . (240)	$ 202
The Cliff, colored chalk, 4½ x 5¾ . . . . (255)	82

1964

Seaside, pencil, 7½ x 12¼ . . . . (336)	32

1965

Trégastel, charcoal, 4 x 6½ . . . . (617)	68

1968–July 1969

The Rocks, 6¾ x 10 . . . . (1227)	60

WATERCOLORS

1961–1962

Rocks at the Seaside, watercolor, 7¾ x 9¾ . . . . (43)	220
Surroundings of Le Havre, 1905, watercolor, 10 x 14 . . . . (119)	160

1963

Boulogne: Sailboats in the Bay, watercolor and gouache, 8¾ x 11 . . . . (318)	360
A Beach in Brittany, watercolor, 9 x 11¾ . . . . (186)	350
Hilly Landscape, 1904, watercolor, 9½ x 14 . . . . . . (234)	320
Surroundings of Le Havre, (1905), watercolor, 14 x 10 . . . . (281)	350
Flotilla at Sunrise, watercolor, 7½ x 10¼ . . . . (222)	104

1964

Boats in the Creek, watercolor and gouache, 9½ x 12¼ . . . . (332)	100
The Ornamental Lake at the Tuileries, pastel, 9 x 11½ . . . . (463)	340

1965

Surroundings of Pont-Aven, 1894, watercolor and charcoal, 9¼ x 11½ . . . . (503)	200

1966

The Road, 1912, watercolor, 11¾ x 19 . . . . (718)	164
Landscape, watercolor, 9 x 12 . . . . (655)	176
Notre-Dame de la Clarté, (1894), watercolor, 12 x 15¼ . . . . (794)	240

1967

Sailboats Leaving the Harbor, watercolor, 8 x 9½ . . . . (879)	150
Landscape of Brittany, watercolor and stick of greasepaint, 9 x 12 . . . . (967)	294

1968–July 1969

Landscape, 1894, watercolor, 9 x 11¾ . . . . (1042)	400
A House on the Edge of the Cliff, watercolor, 9½ x 11½ . . . . (1019)	200
Landscape, watercolor and gouache, 8¾ x 11 . . . . (1026)	240
The Lighthouse on the Pier, watercolor and gouache, 12¼ x 13 . . . . (1226)	500
Ile de Ré, pencil and watercolor, 12 x 9¼ . . . . (1248)	300

PAINTINGS

1961–1962

Banks of the River Elorn, 1897, 24 x 29 . . . . (50)	2,040
Helburn Head Cliffs, 1895, 32 x 40 . . . . (143)	407
Pinkish Haze in Scotland, 1895, 18¼ x 21¾ . . . . (9)	180
Misty Evening in Douarnenez, 1897, 21¼ x 25¾ . . . (72)	1,300

The Cap de la Chèvre, 1899, 23¾ x 29 . . . . (155) $1,100

The Pier at the Sables d'Olonne, 1905,
29 x 36½ . . . . (50)   1,300

Rocks by the Seaside, 23¾ x 29 . . . . (155)   1,600

Low Tide at Le Havre, Dull Weather,
19¾ x 25¾ . . . . (109)   1,400

Beig-Meil, Morning, 1900, 23¾ x 29 . . . . (56)   840

L'Estérel, 1912, 24¾ x 30¾ . . . . (67)   1,813

1963

The Fairy Town, 1900, 26 x 32 . . . . (316)   2,600

Sailboats, 1900, 18¼ x 21¾ . . . . (190)   600

Beig-Meil: Seaweed in Bloom, 1900, 23¾ x 29 . . . . (278)   1,700

Low Tide in Le Havre, 1905, 19¾ x 25¾ . . . . (241)   1,700

Landscape, on panel, 11¾ x 17¾ . . . . (241)   300

Loch Eteve (Scotland), 1905, 19½ x 25¾ . . . . (306)   1,100

Rough Sea at Belle-Ile, 1907, 20½ x 31½ . . . . (286)   1,200

Burning Seaweed at the Seaside, 21¼ x 25¾ . . . . . (194)   800

Lavardin Castle, 1908, 29 x 23½ . . . . (210)   960

The Pont-Neuf, 1909, 25½ x 31¼ . . . . (225)   3,500

Pontivy Harbor (Morbihan), 1909, 23¾ x 31¾ . . . . (316)   5,000

Sauzon Harbor, Belle-Ile sur Mer, 15 x 18¼ . . . . . (254)   2,400

Rosporden Pond, 1911, 25¾ x 36½ . . . . (306)   1,600

La Napoule Cove, 1916, 23¾ x 29 . . . . (278)   2,300

The Bridge at Auray, Morbihan, 1918,
23 x 28½ . . . . (255)   1,316

1964

The River Seine in Winter, 1888, 10½ x 14 . . . . (321)   750

The Mill, 1889, 19½ x 32 . . . . (472)   1,320

The Road, 1901, 15 x 18¼ . . . . (399)   800

Sunset at Morgat Cove, 1900, 25¾ x 32 . . . . (399)   1,200

A Beach in Brittany, 23 x 34¾ . . . . (405)   2,031

A Bay in Brittany, 15 x 18¼ . . . . (466)   1,080

The High Cliff, Vaucottes sur Mer, 23 x 28 . . . . . . (454)   1,106

The Willows at Minds (Eure), 1903, 21 x 25¼ . . . . (416)   884

Sandscape, 14¼ x 17½ . . . . (411)   1,060

The Steamer (Dieppe), 21¼ x 25¾ . . . . (371)   1,400

Brig Alongside the Quay at Auray, 13 x 16¼ . . . . . (347)   2,420

1965

The Banks of the Stream Elorn, 1897, 23¾ x 29 . . . (564)   3,800

November Sea, Cap de la Chèvre, 1899,
25¾ x 32 . . . . (553)   1,600

The Sardine Boats, 1900, 18¼ x 21¾ . . . . (632)   1,160

Light Swell, Douarnenez Bay, 23¾ x 32 . . . . (611)   1,240

The Cliff, 18¼ x 25¼ . . . . (583)   1,161

A Beach in Brittany, 23 x 34¾ . . . . (583)   1,886

Sailboats, Sunset, 1915, 23¼ x 28 . . . . (624)   1,603

The Thatch-Roofed Cottage, 10 x 13 . . . . (523)   196

*The Old Bridge of St. Goustan at Auray, in the
Fog,* 1918, 21¼ x 25¾ . . . . (602)   2,893

1966

Auray Harbor, 23¾ x 29 . . . . (814)   2,500

Snowy Landscape in the Loir-et-Cher, 1918,
18¼ x 21¾ . . . . (814)   2,320

Stormy Night, Morgat, 1901, 21¾ x 25 . . . . (784)   1,900

The Thatch-Roofed Cottage, 1901, 15 x 18¼ . . . . . (726)   1,500

The Harbor, 1889, 13 x 16¾ . . . . (795)   620

Douarnenez, from the Sea, 15 x 21¾ . . . . (809)   1,660

Loch Eteve (Scotland), 1892, 19½ x 25¾ . . . . (756)   1,280

November Sea (Cap de la Chèvre), 1899,
25¾ x 32 . . . . (702)   1,900

Etretat Cliffs, 21 x 25 . . . . (757)   1,935

Palue Dunes, Finistère, 1902, 21¼ x 29 . . . . (681) $1,400

The Footbridge in the Fog, 1917, 21¼ x 25¾ . . . . . (670)   2,500

Marly, Springtime, 17 x 20 . . . . (808)   2,177

1967

Le Pô Harbor (Quiberon Bay), 1909, 23¾ x 32 . . . (901)   3,400

Gray Sea in Brittany, 1895, 18¼ x 21¾ . . . . (1000)   1,700

The Tempest, 1896, 21¼ x 29 . . . . (857)   600

A Storm on Batz Pier, 1897, 23¾ x 29 . . . . (850)   1,500

Evening Impression, Brittany, 1884, 31 x 34¾ . . . . (985)   1,185

Pouliguen Cove, 1887, 21 x 17½ . . . . (912)   1,400

Cliff Corner, 1895, 23¾ x 29 . . . . (941)   820

Cap de la Chèvre, 1899, 23¾ x 29¾ . . . . (870)   1,200

Lavardun in the Evening, 1907, 25¾ x 32 . . . . (849)   2,600

The Flood at the Quai de la Rapée, 1910,
17½ x 21¼ . . . . (880)   4,422

In the Mountains, 21¼ x 25¾ . . . . (1000)   400

The Sardine Boats in Concarneau, 18¼ x 21¾ . . . . (919)   1,243

The Waves, Brittany, 25¾ x 32¼ . . . . (989)   2,750

The Cliffs, 18¾ x 25¾ . . . . (967)   1,582

Yellow Cliffs, Quiberon Bay, 23¾ x 29 . . . . (912)   1,640

The Artist's Studio at Kerhostin, 25¾ x 32 . . . . (861)   1,680

1968–July 1969

The Coast of Brittany Near Pont-Aven, 1893,
22½ x 33 . . . . (1109)   3,500

The Lock at Veston Near Nantes, 1889,
18¾ x 31¼ . . . . (1070)   3,776

Heavy Weather at Le Pouldu, 1891, 17 x 29 . . . . . . (1051)   1,000

The Strand, 1894, on panel, 7½ x 9½ . . . . (1210)   840

Pinkish Haze in Scotland, 1895, 18¼ x 21¾ . . . . . . (1026)   600

A Cliff in Quiberon, (1895), 23¾ x 29 . . . . (1053)   2,200

La Romanche Valley, the Snowy Torrent, 1904,
25¾ x 32 . . . . (1051)   2,040

Paris: The Pont du Louvre After the Storm,
(1909), 25¾ x 32 . . . . (1189)   5,400

*Before the Rain, Water Mill Near Auray
(Morbihan),* 1911, 23¼ x 28½ . . . . (1184)   5,560

White Cliffs, 21¼ x 25½ . . . . (1184)   1,200

Landscape with a Church, 23¾ x 29 . . . . (1060)   4,800

White Cliffs, 21¼ x 25¾ . . . . (1113)   1,400

The Cove, 1893, 29 x 23¾ . . . . (1224)   1,200

Lighthouses, 1905, 23¾ x 29 . . . . (1224)   3,100

Quiberon: A Place with Cliffs, (1895), 23¾ x 29 . . (1225)   2,300

Seaport in Brittany, 1900, 23¾ x 29 . . . . (1225)   1,620

The Old Mill, Les Andelys, 1902, 23 x 28 . . . . (1239)   11,040

Sortie d'un transport, Le Havre, 1905, 23 x 28 . . . (1240)   9,840

The Breakwater at Villerville, 21 x 25 . . . . (1248)   2,500

White Cliffs, 21¼ x 25¾ . . . . (1255)   1,500

Sunset, 1899, 18½ x 21¾ . . . . (1255)   1,600

Landscape at Pont-Aven, 1890, 16¼ x 28½ . . . . . . (1256)   4,800

Breton Harbor, on panel, 12¾ x 16¼ . . . . (1256)   2,900

Pont-Aven in the Rain, 1890, 17½ x 14 . . . . (1261)   4,600

Rough Weather, 1891, 17 x 29 . . . . (1268)   1,276

Open Sea, 1891, 21¾ x 39¼ . . . . (1271)   3,840

Les Andelys in the Morning, 1902, 17¾ x 21¼ . . . (1271)   8,160

The Old Tower at Houdon, 1896, 18 x 21½ . . . . . . (1273)   3,530

Alfred Maurer

(1868–1932)

Birthplace: New York, U.S.

1897-14 Goes to Europe and settles in Paris.

1901 Awarded first prize and gold medal by the Carnegie Institute, Pittsburgh.

1907 One of the first Americans in Paris to embrace Fauvism. Introduces his closest friend, the American abstractionist Arthur Dove, to the movement.

1909 One-man show at the Stieglitz Gallery, New York.

1914 Returns permanently to the U.S. and begins to lead an almost hermitlike existence.

1932 Died, New York, a suicide.

Sales

DRAWINGS

1963
Standing Nude, India ink, 13½ x 9 . . . . (275) $ 125

WATERCOLORS

1963
Woman's Head, (1924), tempera on paper,
20¾ x 17 . . . . (179)   850

1964
Two Young Girls, gouache and watercolor,
20½ x 17½ . . . . (329)   800

PAINTINGS

1961–1962
Seated Woman, 24 x 19½ . . . . (85)   400

1968–July 1969
Two Women, on masonite, 21½ x 18 . . . . (1229)   4,500

Jean Metzinger

(1883–1956)

Birthplace: Nantes, France.

1900 Arrives in Paris. Comes under the influence of Neo-Impressionism.

1905 Briefly attracted to Fauvism.

1908 Meets Picasso, Braque, and their friends. After Braque and Picasso, he is the third artist to embrace Cubism.

1910 Exhibits "Portrait of André Rouveyre," his first Cubist work.

1911 Participates in the Salon des Indépendants and the Salon d'Automne, Paris, in the Cubist rooms—along with Delaunay, Gleizes, Le Fauconnier, Léger, Juan Gris, Jacques Villon, and Marcel Duchamp.

1912 Participates in the first exhibition of the movement known as La Section d'Or, at the Galerie de La Boétie, Paris. Also participating are Léger, Juan Gris, Delaunay, Herbin, Gleizes, Roger de La Fresnaye, and Jacques Villon. With Gleizes, issues an important book entitled *Du Cubisme.*

1930 End of his Cubist period. Reverts to a more representational art until the end of his career.

1956 Died, Paris.

Sales

DRAWINGS

1961–1962
Cubist Still Life, charcoal, 15 x 11¾ . . . . (102) $ 136

1963
Dance, pencil, 13½ x 18½ . . . . (275)   375

1964
Portrait of a Young Lady, pencil, 19 x 18¼ . . . . (405)   1,161

1965
Composition with a Fruit Stand, black lead,
9 x 12¼ . . . . (490)   170
Still Life, pencil, 12 x 8¾ . . . . (541)   425

1967
Seated Nude, pencil on pink paper, 16 x 12 . . . . . (1004)   400

1968–July 1969
Still Life, pencil, 7½ x 9 . . . . (1129)   260
Still Life with Pears, pencil, 7¾ x 10¾ . . . . (1203)   793
Allegory, India ink, 13½ x 9 . . . . (1110)   150
Seated Nude, pencil on pink paper, 16 x 12 . . . . . (1145)   375
The Circus, 1914, pen and India ink, heightened
with white gouache, 9¼ x 8 . . . . (1240)   2,040
Cubist Landscape, charcoal, 24 x 19 . . . . (1268)   3,944

WATERCOLORS

1961–1962
Interior with a Seated Woman in the Nude,
gouache, 11½ x 8 . . . . (164)   522

1963
A Young Lady Dancing with a Bear, watercolor
and gouache, 15¾ x 12½ . . . . (262)   380

1965
Woman: Clown with a Bear, watercolor,
12¼ x 9¼ . . . . (577)   120

1966
The Dance of the Bear, watercolor, 11¾ x 9 . . . . . . (648)   375

1967
Dance, gouache, 9½ x 17½ . . . . (935)   200
Interior with a Seated Woman, (1920), gouache,
11½ x 8¼ . . . . (939)   1,050
Bather with a Dove, gouache, 10¾ x 14 . . . . (929)   520

1968–July 1969
Woman with a Fan, watercolor, 7½ x 5¾ . . . . (1104)   300

PAINTINGS

1961–1962
Still Life, 32 x 23¾ . . . . (143)   1,695
Still Life, 25¾ x 36½ . . . . (30)   1,020
The Fruit Stand, 1916, 29 x 21¼ . . . . (120)   2,560
Still Life with a Bottle of Rum, 1917, 23 x 31½ . . . . (140)   2,179

The Fruit Stand, 1918, 31¼ x 20¾ .... **(140)** $1,922
The Village, 14¾ x 17¾ .... **(129)**   961
The Poplars, 1917 .... **(68)**   1,600
Cubist Composition, 25¾ x 21¼ .... **(33)**   1,420
Roulette, 38 x 57¼ .... **(13)**   2,400
Harbor Scene, 21¼ x 17¾ .... **(64)**   4,750
The Sphinx, 45¾ x 35¼ .... **(133)**   1,220
Still Life with Flowers, (1929), 23½ x 31½ .... **(37)**   2,850

1963

Summer Landscape with Sailboats (recto), *Nude*
  (verso), (1910), 18½ x 25 .... **(309)**   4,285
Landscape, 1919, 32 x 39¼ .... **(247)**   3,565
The Village, 1919, 21¾ x 18¼ .... **(188)**   1,120
Landscape, 1919, 18¼ x 21¾ .... **(299)**   2,160
Roulette, Cubist Composition, (1921),
  37½ x 56¼ .... **(225)**   3,000
The Gray Cat, 14 x 10¾ .... **(251)**   320
The Sphere and the Banjo, 1930, 25¾ x 36½ ..... **(306)**   1,460
The Sea, 25¼ x 36¼ .... **(275)**   950

1964

Pears and Grapes, 1903, 18¼ x 25¾ .... **(346)**   900
Still Life with a Cat, 21¼ x 17¾ .... **(374)**   1,050
Still Life, 21¾ x 18½ .... **(374)**   1,700
Fluvial Landscape, 1907, on cardboard,
  14½ x 18¼ .... **(380)**   1,353
The House in the Trees, 36 x 23 .... **(416)**   3,317
The Field of Flowers, 18¼ x 24 .... **(474)**   1,200
A Face in a Landscape, 25¼ x 21 .... **(329)**   1,500
Village Street, 18¼ x 24 .... **(401)**   2,400
Still Life with Melons and Eggs, 1924,
  23¾ x 31½ .... **(405)**   1,364
The Roofs, 21¾ x 15 .... **(393)**   500
The Equestrienne, 39½ x 29 .... **(379)**   460
The Acrobat and the Horse, 39½ x 29 .... **(335)**   580
Arts, 1928, 55 x 40¼ .... **(465)**   1,440
The Ship, 25¾ x 19¾ .... **(386)**   2,100

1965

Pointillist Landscape, 21¼ x 29 .... **(561)**   4,400
La Rochelle Harbor, 28½ x 39¼ .... **(575)**   4,146
Still Life with a Coffeepot, 1916, 21 x 28½ .... **(594)**   6,250
Harlequin, (1917), 64 x 61¾ .... **(526)**   3,000
The Day, Still Life, 16 x 13 .... **(624)**   1,520

1966

Portrait of Robert Delaunay, 1906, 25 x 20½ ..... **(808)**   7,835
Landscape, 28 x 14 .... **(805)**   1,500
Landscape, (1925), 18¼ x 21¾ .... **(735)**   949
Reclining Woman, (1926), 28½ x 39¼ .... **(757)**   3,179
Nude with a Boat, 14 x 10¾ .... **(784)**   1,800
Red Flowers, 10½ x 16¼ .... **(723)**   500
A House on the Edge of a Lake, 12¾ x 15¾ .... **(648)**   2,300
Navigation, 47½ x 71¼ .... **(749)**   1,500

1967

Landscape, 1921, 23¾ x 32 .... **(930)**   1,130
Woman, 1917, 36½ x 29 .... **(990)**   4,428
Blue Vase, (1930), 21¾ x 14¾ .... **(864)**   3,000
Still Life, 19¾ x 24 .... **(963)**   4,250
The Pink House, 14 x 10¾ .... **(894)**   390
A Village Through the Trees, on cardboard,
  10 x 8 .... **(929)**   560
Navigation, 47½ x 71¼ .... **(839)**   320
Bathers, 10¾ x 14 .... **(923)**   1,300

Two Bathers, on panel, 13½ x 9¼ .... **(912)** $1,100
Seated Nude with a Green Bathing Wrap,
  14 x 10¾ .... **(850)**   652
Harlequinade, 18¾ x 25¾ .... **(841)**   3,250
Young Woman with Palms, 25¾ x 21½ .... **(858)**   7,600
Sculpture or Painting, painted relief, 13 x 18¼ .... **(911)**   2,100

1968–July 1969

Flowers and Fruit, 18¼ x 21¾ .... **(1049)**   1,600
Landscape, 1920, 21¼ x 28½ .... **(1208)**   5,750
The Village, 1920, 21¼ x 29 .... **(1121)**   2,700
Woman Powdering Herself, (1920), 39½ x 29 .... **(1060)**   4,480
Still Life, 1924, 23¾ x 32 .... **(1026)**   3,020
Still Life, 13 x 18 .... **(1080)**   2,850
Still Life, 18 x 21½ .... **(1057)**   7,500
Siren in a Boat, 44¾ x 63½ .... **(1059)**   3,097
The Dance of Harlequins, 17¾ x 24¼ .... **(1193)**   4,213
The Boats, on cardboard, 9 x 11 .... **(1125)**   4,370
The Village, 25¾ x 36 .... **(1117)**   3,800
Portrait of a Woman, 24 x 18 .... **(1080)**   3,000
Young Woman with Palms, 25¾ x 21¼ .... **(1113)**   7,800
La Statue du sémaphore, 46 x 35¼ .... **(1224)**   2,700
Still Life, 8½ x 10¾ .... **(1248)**   4,000
The Village, 32 x 23¾ .... **(1252)**   4,020
The Snowy Roofs, (1921), 15 x 21¾ .... **(1271)**   4,320
Landscape by a Lake, 35½ x 23 .... **(1273)**   4,670

Jacob Isaac Meyer De Haan

(1852–1895)

    Birthplace: Amsterdam, Netherlands.

1870   Begins to study painting.

1880   Exhibits at the Salon, Paris. Makes friends with Camille Pissarro and comes under the Impressionist influence. Meets Gauguin and greatly admires his work.

1888   Stay at Pont-Aven.

1889–90   Stays at Le Pouldu and becomes Gauguin's closest friend. Bad health and lack of money prevent him from following Gauguin to Tahiti.

1890–91   Meets the Nabis in Paris.

1895   Died, the Netherlands.

Sales

PAINTINGS

1968–July 1969

Peasants Hackling Hemp, 1889, 52½ x 78¼ ..... **(1270)** $ 62,400

Joan Miró

(1893–   )

Birthplace: Barcelona, Spain.

1907 Enters the Barcelona Fine Arts School.

1912 Attends the Gali School of Art, Barcelona.

1918 First exhibition at the Dalmau Gallery, Barcelona.

1919 First trip to Paris, where he meets Picasso.

1920 Meets Reverdy, Tzara, Max Jacob, and Masson. From now on, spends winters in Paris and summers in his house at Montroig, Spain. Executes a series of still lifes under the influence of Cubism.

1921 First one-man show at the Galerie de la Licorne, Paris. (Catalog preface by Maurice Raynal.)

1923-24 Participates in the Salon d'Automne. Meets Aragon, André Breton, and Eluard.

1925 Exhibition at the Galerie Pierre, Paris. Participates in the first exhibition of Surrealism at the Galerie Pierre, Paris, and appears as one of the most important Surrealists. Deeply impressed by Klee's work.

1928-30 Trip to the Netherlands. Exhibits at Bernheim's, Paris. Series of his "Fancied Portraits." Executes his first collages and takes part in an exhibition of collages at the Galerie Goemans, Paris. (Catalog preface by Aragon.) One-man show at the Valentine Gallery, New York.

1931 One-man show at the Chicago Arts Club. Birth of his daughter Dolores.

1932 Exhibits at the Galerie Pierre, Paris, and the Pierre Matisse Gallery, New York. Participates in the Salon des Surindépendants, Paris.

1934-53 "Wild period" (période sauvage).

1937 Executes a mural for the Paris World's Fair.

1940 Settles in Spain during World War II. Executes his first ceramics in 1944.

1947 First trip to the U.S. Executes a mural for the Plaza Hotel, Cincinnati. Gradually moves toward abstraction.

1948 Returns to Paris. Important exhibition at the Galerie Maeght, Paris.

1949-50 Retrospective exhibition at the Kunsthalle, Bern and Basel. Settles in Barcelona but makes frequent trips to Paris. Illustrates *Parler seul* by Tristan Tzara.

1953 One-man show at the Galerie Maeght, Paris, on his sixtieth birthday.

1954 Participates in the Venice Biennial.

1955-59 Devotes himself to ceramics.

1956 Retrospective exhibitions at the Palais des Beaux-Arts, Brussels; at the Kunsthalle, Basel; and in Amsterdam.

1957-58 Executes two important ceramic murals for UNESCO, Paris.

1958 Participates in the exhibition "Cinquante Ans d'art moderne" at the Brussels World's Fair. Exhibits his "Wild Paintings" at the Pierre Matisse Gallery, New York.

1959 Second trip to the U.S. Retrospective exhibition at the Museum of Modern Art, New York, and the Museum of Los Angeles. Given an award by the Guggenheim Foundation.

1960 Executes an important ceramic mural for Harvard University.

1961 Exhibits recent paintings at the Galerie Maeght, Paris.

1962 Major retrospective exhibition at the Musée National d'Art Moderne, Paris.

Sales

DRAWINGS

1961–1962

Standing Nude,[1] (1917), pencil, 8¼ x 6 . . . . (31) $ 192

Model, 1937, pencil, 8 x 10¾ . . . . (70)   553

Seated Nude, charcoal and pastel on mauve paper, 8¾ x 10 . . . . (31)   686

The Paraffin Lamp, 1924, pencil, white chalk and gouache on canvas, 31½ x 39¼ . . . . (129)   30,206

"And the Bosoms Died," 1927, India ink, 18½ x 24½ . . . . (29)   1,140

Composition, India ink, 18¼ x 23¾ . . . . (96)   1,000

Picadors, 1949, India ink, 18¼ x 24½ . . . . (149)   948

Composition, 1949, pencil and gouache, 20 x 13 . . . (164)   2,059

1963

Standing Nude, (1917), pencil, 8 x 6 . . . . (225)   400

Figures, India ink and watercolor, 22½ x 29¾ . . . . (202)   3,750

Composition, 1930, pencil, 24½ x 18¼ . . . . (232)   452

The Hat, 1930, pencil, 23 x 18 . . . . (255)   686

A Figure, 1937, black pencil, 28½ x 41 . . . . (299)   1,220

Composition, charcoal and wash, 18¼ x 24½ . . . . . (249)   1,500

Women with Furs, pencil and watercolor lights, 22 x 17½ . . . . (194)   980

A Woman and a Star, 1961, colored chalk, 11 x 9 . . . . (216)   96

1964

Composition, 1930, stick of greasepaint, 24 x 17¾ . . . . (377)   1,492

Figure, 1934, black chalk and colored pencil, 28½ x 42¾ . . . . (405)   2,612

The Man with the Tissue Paper, 1934, drawing and collage, 24½ x 18¼ . . . . (460)   2,000

Signs and Figurations, 1935, India ink and watercolor, 12 x 17 . . . . (385)   836

The Rape, 1937, pencil, 9 x 12 . . . . (454)   498

The Cat (Figure Before the Star), (1949), pen and watercolor, 10 x 13 . . . . (448)   1,300

Fancied Figure II, (1956), pencil and watercolor, 11¾ x 9 . . . . (374)   1,000

Faces, India ink and watercolor, 18¼ x 25 . . . . (372)   2,200

Composition, India ink, 18½ x 24½ . . . . (354)   1,200

Composition, charcoal and wash, 24½ x 18¼ . . . . . (401)   960

1965

Woman, (1927), India ink and pastel, 5¼ x 6½ . . . . (535)   636

Constellations of a Seated Woman, (1940–41), brushed ink, 24½ x 19 . . . . (624)   2,764

Composition, 1950, India ink on a lithograph, 14½ x 20 . . . . (566)   588

Cat, 1962, colored chalk, 12¾ x 21 . . . . (638)   590

Star, charcoal, 29 x 41½ . . . . (512)   800

1966

Women with Furs, colored pencil and watercolor, 22 x 17¾ . . . . (666)   1,400

Figures, 1937, India ink and gouache, 12 x 12 . . . . . (735)   3,390

[1] Dedicated "A l'ami Ricart."

The Beauty and the Beast, 1962, colored pencil, 13¾ x 22 .... (711) $ 560

Composition, 1962, black ink and watercolor, 24½ x 35½ .... (808)   4,063

Woman Surrounded by a Couple of Birds, 1964, black ink and watercolor, 25¼ x 34¾ .... (808)   8,706

The Terror of the Bad-Luck Bird, 1965, colored pencil and watercolor, 34¾ x 25¾ .... (753)   9,867

1967

Composition, 1935, pen, 11¾ x 8¼ .... (967)   791

Signs and Symbols, 1938, chalk and gouache, 27¼ x 41½ .... (957)   7,739

Composition, 1947, India ink, 9 x 6½ .... (930)   881

The Women with Furs, ink, pencil, and watercolor, 14¾ x 11 .... (889)   3,000

Composition, colored pencil, 14¾ x 11 .... (962)   1,280

Composition, colored pencil and ink, 9¼ x 14¾ .. (1005)   1,185

Composition, wash and colored pencil, 11¾ x 9½ .... (996)   1,000

Composition, pencil, 12¾ x 10 .... (841)   850

1968–July 1969

Seated Nude, 1917, pencil, 6 x 8¼ .... (1068)   637

Figure, 1917, pencil, 6¾ x 5¾ .... (1214)   1,280

Nude, 1937, black lead, 11¾ x 8¾ .... (1106)   760

Composition, 1951, colored chalk, 6 x 8¾ .... (1194)   893

Constellation of a Seated Woman, India ink, 24 x 19½ .... (1018)   640

The Little Prince, ball-point pen, 8¾ x 7¼ ...... (1191)   236

Figure, pencil, 18 x 24½ .... (1240)   5,760

Composition, black lead and paint on gray cardboard, 9¾ x 13¾ .... (1268)   2,204

WATERCOLORS

1961-1962

Two Figures and a Dragonfly, 1926, gouache, 16¼ x 12¾ .... (84)   6,590

Bird Flying Toward the Sun, pastel, 12¾ x 18½ .... (70)   1,264

To the Escape Ladder, watercolor, 26 x 19¾ ...... (18)   6,441

Composition, watercolor, 19¾ x 18¼ .... (30)   2,820

Face, (1934–36), gouache and watercolor, 14¼ x 11 .... (96)   4,500

Rebelling Women, 1938, gouache, 22½ x 29¾ ..... (149)   2,212

Women with Furs, watercolor, 22 x 17½ .... (26)   1,720

Man Looking at the Moon, 1942, watercolor, 19 x 25 .... (69)   7,110

Object-Painting, gouache on board, 24 x 28 ...... (129)   4,119

Composition, watercolor and colored ink, 12 x 15¾ .... (143)   1,898

1963

The Shooting Star, 1929, watercolor, 19 x 24¾ ... (283)   2,260

Faces in the Night, gouache and watercolor, 17½ x 23¼ .... (202)   3,500

Figures on a Red Background, 1937, gouache, 30 x 21¾ .... (299)   3,000

The Rebelling Woman, 1938, gouache, 22 x 29¾ .. (200)   4,200

1964

Woman Walking, 1931, gouache, 24½ x 18¼ ..... (387)   2,211

Object-Painting, 1932, gouache on board, 19 x 30¾ .... (368)   2,073

A Woman Walking in the Street, 1935, gouache, 23¾ x 17¾ .... (386)   2,000

Figures, gouache and collage, 29¾ x 21¼ .... (371)   2,700

The Parrot, gouache and collage, 35½ x 29 ...... (460) $4,600

Composition, 1964, watercolor, 29¼ x 10¾ ...... (386)   3,800

1965

The Grasshopper, 1953, watercolor, 13½ x 19½ ... (637)   3,800

A Woman and Birds, 1962, gouache and oil, 19 x 24 .... (539)   8,750

Composition, 1965, gouache, 25¼ x 16½ .... (574)   920

1966

A Vase of Flowers and a Butterfly, 1922-23, egg tempera on panel, 32 x 25¼ .... (686)   35,379

Woman, Bird, and Stars, 1942, watercolor, gouache and India ink, 18¾ x 13¾ .... (678)   15,000

Composition, 1951, watercolor, 12¼ x 9 .... (798)   1,672

Composition, gouache and watercolor, 25¾ x 19¾ .... (744)   5,876

1967

Signs and Figuration, 1935, India ink and watercolor, 12 x 17 .... (930)   1,107

Black Sun and Figures, 1949, watercolor, 9¾ x 12½ .... (975)   1,900

A Page of Music, gouache, watercolor, and collage, 22 x 30½ .... (975)   6,600

Composition, watercolor and pencil, 15¾ x 12¾ .. (893)   1,250

Composition, watercolor, 14½ x 21¾ .... (918)   3,480

A Figure in a Landscape, gouache, 27¾ x 39½ .... (896)   6,000

1968–July 1969

The Cat (Figure Before the Star), (1949), pen and watercolor, 10 x 13 .... (1088)   1,250

Head and Bird, gouache and oil on paper, 39½ x 27¾ .... (1057)   9,000

Woman, Birds, Stars, (1950-55), gouache, 18 x 23 .... (1018)   8,500

Composition, watercolor, 14¾ x 21¾ .... (1113)   3,000

Composition, gouache, India ink, and collage, 9 x 4¾ .... (1080)   1,400

Red Abstract, 1960, watercolor, 17½ x 21¾ ...... (1059)   942

Figures, 1963, pastel, 28½ x 39¼ .... (1125)   12,650

Composition, watercolor and gouache, 10¾ x 16½ .... (1226)   2,400

Man's Head and Bird, gouache, 35¼ x 25¾ ..... (1268)   17,632

Composition, gouache, 22 x 17¼ .... (1268)   4,060

PAINTINGS

1961-1962

Cambrils Beach, 1917, 14¾ x 18¼ .... (18)   4,068

Still Life with a Flowerpot, 27¾ x 23¼ .... (30)   7,000

Man and Woman Together, 1931, oil and gouache on paper, 24 x 18 .... (105)   3,729

Head of a Young Woman, 1932, 14 x 11 .... (129)   7,140

Tenderness of the Moonbeam Meeting a Beautiful Bird at Dawn, 1954, 9½ x 6¾ ..... (149)   7,900

Women, Birds, and Constellations, triptych on board, 54¾ x 69¾ .... (129)   15,103

1963

Snake and Bird in Space, (1930), 14¼ x 11 ...... (279)   6,500

Painting, 1953, 76¾ x 38¼ .... (279)   7,000

1964

The Sign of Death, 1927, 29 x 36½ .... (460)   8,400

Painting, 1927, 8¾ x 10½ .... (453)   4,975

The Star, 1927, 25¼ x 31 .... (367)   12,162

Collage, 1929, drawing and collage, 40¾ x 28 ..... (453)   3,731

Composition, 1933, on cardboard, 14¼ x 14¼ ..... (367) $3,040
Composition, 1934, oil and collage, 12¼ x 8¾ ..... (378)   1,898
The Comet-Bird and the Flowery Parasol, 1947,
    23½ x 31½ .... (367)   35,932

1965
Le Porrides, Prades, 1917, 20 x 24¼ .... (573)   27,640
The Catalan, 1925, 39½ x 32 .... (615)   24,000
The Steward of the Music Hall, 1925,
    39½ x 30¾ .... (637)   9,500
The King's Fool, 1926, 45¾ x 57¾ .... (615)   20,000
Painting, 1927, 8¾ x 10¾ .... (637)   3,500
Circus Horse, 1927, 76¾ x 110½ .... (526)   57,500
Blue Star, 1927, 45¾ x 35¼ .... (615)   26,000
Composition, 1933, 5½ x 38½ .... (615)   34,000
Metamorphosis, 1936, pencil and collage,
    24½ x 17¾ .... (539)   2,600
Children, Kites, and Star, 1945, oil and gouache,
    10¼ x 19¾ .... (539)   6,750
The Flower Stem Is Growing Toward the Moon,
    1952, 36½ x 28 .... (561)   36,000
*The Disheveled Hair and the Flight of
    Constellations,* 1954, 50½ x 70¾ .... (575)   49,752

1966
Seated Woman in the Nude, with a Bird, (1917),
    31¼ x 25 .... (694)   37,000
The Heart, 1925, 25¾ x 19¾ .... (776)   10,500
Composition, 1926, 45¾ x 35¼ .... (801)   32,000
Birds, 1927, 38¼ x 51½ .... (801)   10,000
Figure, 1927, 36½ x 29¼ .... (808)   29,020
Woman with a Red Hat, 1927, 51½ x 38½ .... (776)   30,000
Portrait, 1927, 57½ x 45¼ .... (694)   22,000
Nude Twin Sisters in the Forest at Sunset, 1931,
    23¾ x 25¾ .... (801)   16,400
Murals No. 1, 1933, fresco, 22 x 97¾ .... (678)   40,000
Murals No. 2, 1933, fresco, 22 x 97¾ .... (678)   35,000
Mother and Son, 1934, oil and gouache on board,
    25¾ x 18¼ .... (753)   13,059
Self-Portrait II, 1938, 50½ x 77¼ .... (678)   85,000
Women and Birds in the Night, (1944), on canvas
    laid down on canvas, 15½ x 14¼ .... (694)   28,000
Hallowe'en, 1953, on panel, 42 x 23 .... (678)   57,500
Two Figures, 1965, 32 x 21¼ .... (747)   18,020
The Opera Singer, 1966, 32 x 21¼ .... (751)   18,519

1967
The Bird, 1926, 29 x 36½ .... (975)   15,200
Collage, 1929, 28 x 42¾ .... (880)   9,950
The Dancer, 1929, collage, 39¼ x 27 .... (880)   9,950
Composition, 1934, on board, 10½ x 7¾ .... (864)   6,000
Children's Games, on cardboard, 19¾ x 31¼ ..... (857)   3,600
Man and Woman in a Landscape, 1960, oil and
    gouache, 29¾ x 41 .... (941)   10,000

1968–July 1969
Painting, 1933, 50¾ x 63¼ .... (1018)   13,000
Woman, 1936, oil on paper mounted on board,
    54 x 39¼ .... (1064)   9,440
Women in the Night, 1966, oil and gouache on
    paper, 35¼ x 26 .... (1132)   9,912
Seated Woman, 1967, 14 x 8¾ .... (1057)   8,500
At the Jardin du Luxembourg, on cardboard,
    6½ x 9¼ .... (1233)   380
Group of Figures, 1938, 28¾ x 36¼ .... (1239)   72,000
Painting, 1927, 38¼ x 51¼ .... (1239)   57,600

Paula Modersohn-Becker
(1876–1907)

Birthplace: Dresden, Germany. (Née Paula Becker.)

1888   Her family moves to Bremen.

1896   Goes to Berlin to study art.

1897   Trip to Worpswede, near Bremen, with her friend Clara Westhoff—sculptress and future wife of Rilke.

1899   Stay in Worpswede, where she elaborates her own style among a group of artists including Mackensen, Vogeler, Modersohn, and Clara Westhoff.

1900   First trip to Paris.

1901   Marries Otto Modersohn and settles in Worpswede.

1903   Trip to Paris. Rilke, Rodin's secretary, introduces her to the sculptor.

1905-06   Stay in Paris, where she works by herself. Greatly admires the French masters, especially Cézanne, Gauguin, and Van Gogh.

1907   Died, Worpswede, a few weeks after the birth of her first child. (One of Rilke's poems, "Requiem," [1908], is dedicated to her memory.)

Sales

DRAWINGS

1961–1962
Portrait of an Old Man, charcoal, 29¼ x 15¾ ..... (24) $ 295
The Fruit Trees, chalk, 9 x 12¾ .... (107)   271

1964
Mother and Child, 1907, charcoal, 9½ x 12½ ..... (385)   260

1966
A Tree, chalk, 10¼ x 12 .... (716)   344

1967
The Haystacks, charcoal, 8¾ x 11¾ .... (990)   443
Woman, Her Breast Bare, charcoal, 30½ x 16½ .. (910)   615
Portrait of a Man, colored chalk, 22 x 17 .... (970)   344

1968–July 1969
Children in the Hen House, (1900), chalk,
    11¼ x 15¾ .... (1114)   942
Mother and Child, charcoal, 7¼ x 10¾ .... (1209)   496

PAINTINGS

1961–1962
Three Children Playing with Sand, 1902, oil on
    cardboard, 18 x 27¾ .... (88)   2,066
Alte Armenhauslerin mit Ziege, 1903, on
    cardboard, 21 x 27¾ .... (88)   4,059

1963
Landscape, 1904, on paper, 17¾ x 15¼ .... (230)   1,033

1964
Still Life, 1907, 18½ x 22 .... (467)   6,396
Landscape with a House and a Child, on
    cardboard, 19¼ x 20 .... (380)   1,722

1965
The Tree Trunk, on cardboard, 29 x 14¾ .... (566)   1,989
Thatch-Roofed Cottage on the Hill, 1923, on
    cardboard, 15½ x 21¼ .... (638)   935
Half-Length Portrait of a Young Girl, (1904), on
    board, 19¼ x 14 .... (618)   5,166

1966

Half-Length Portrait of an Old Woman, (1897),
on cardboard, 25¾ x 17¾ .... (792)   2,706

1967

Night Festival, 1903, on cardboard, 23½ x 28¼ ... (930)   3,277
A Child in the Nude, (1904), 27¼ x 23 .... (930)   4,633

1968–July 1969

Portrait of a Young Lady, (1898), on cardboard,
17½ x 19¼ .... (1114)   1,488

Amedeo Modigliani

(1884–1920)

Birthplace: Leghorn, Italy.

1895   Attacked by the tuberculosis from which he never recovers.

1898-03   Attends the fine arts schools of Leghorn, Florence, and Venice.

1905-06   Goes to France and settles permanently in Montmartre, Paris.

1908-10   Participates in the Salon des Indépendants, Paris.

1909-10   Meets Brancusi and devotes himself to sculpture for a time. Starts a long series of portraits that include Brancusi, Picasso, Max Jacob, Lipchitz, Paul Guillaume, and Soutine.

1913   Settles in Montparnasse. Makes friends with Kisling and Soutine.

1914-15   Becomes intimate with the British actress Beatrice Hastings. Meets Leopold Zborowski. The dealer Paul Guillaume buys some of his paintings.

1917   Becomes involved with Jeanne Hébuterne, a young Frenchwoman. Produces most of his masterpieces between 1917 and 1919, asserting his exceptional mastery and his absolute independence of contemporary movements in painting.

1918   First one-man show, at the Galerie Berthe Weil, Paris, creates a scandal.

1918-19   Paints his "Self-Portrait" (collection F. Matarazzo Sobrinho, Sâo Paulo). Stay in Nice. Birth of his daughter Jeanne.

1920   Died, Paris, exhausted by illness and alcohol. (Jeanne Hébuterne commits suicide the following day.)

Sales

DRAWINGS

1961-1962

Portrait of Simon Lévy, pencil, 13¼ x 10½ .... (18) $ 1,989
Portrait of a Woman, pencil, 11¾ x 7½ .... (26)   800
A Woman, pencil, 10¼ x 6¼ .... (20)   3,476
Seated Nude, pencil, 21½ x 17¼ .... (20)   4,108

Portrait of Leopold Zborowski, (1919), pencil,
14 x 8 .... (31) $ 769
Nude, black lead, 14¾ x 9½ .... (32)   960
Young Nude, pencil, 12¾ x 9¾ .... (34)   800
Bust of a Young Man, pencil, 16 x 10½ .... (34)   1,300
Portrait of a Young Woman, pen, 14¼ x 10 ...... (37)   1,500
Don Quixote, pencil, 16¼ x 9¾ .... (44)   1,800
Study of a Woman, pencil, 16¼ x 10 .... (44)   1,300
Portrait of a Woman, pencil, 11¾ x 7½ .... (53)   900
Nude Model, blue pencil, 15¼ x 10 .... (64)   1,764
Leopold Zborowski Playing the Violin, pencil,
16½ x 10½ .... (84)   2,472
Nude, 1917, pencil, 14¾ x 8¾ .... (85)   1,800
Portrait of the Painter Schwansen, black lead,
10½ x 8 .... (106)   701
Portrait of Madame Zborowska, black lead,
14 x 10¼ .... (114)   1,000
Bust of a Nude, pencil, 8 x 5 .... (111)   425
Portrait of a Woman, pencil, 14¾ x 9½ .... (119)   640
Head of a Caryatid, charcoal, 16½ x 10 .... (128)   2,059
Portrait of Kisling, pencil, 16½ x 10 .... (152)   2,200
Portrait of Jeanne Hébuterne, pencil,
15¼ x 9½ .... (164)   1,922

1963

Caryatid, pencil, ink, and wash, 14¾ x 10 .... (202)   5,250
Nude, 1917, pencil, 13¼ x 8¾ .... (208)   1,350
Self-Portrait, pencil, 16½ x 10 .... (210)   1,920
Jeanne Hébuterne, pencil, 15¾ x 10 .... (210)   1,371
Seated Nude, 1914, black and blue pencil,
10¼ x 13¾ .... (232)   2,938
Portrait of Madame Kisling, pencil, 16½ x 8¾ .... (219)   1,605
Nude, blue pencil, 12½ x 9¾ .... (225)   500
Portrait of a Woman, pencil on gray paper,
11½ x 8 .... (225)   2,500
Head of Jeanne Hébuterne, pencil, 13¼ x 10 ..... (255)   394
A Legionnaire Smoking, pencil, 15¾ x 10 .... (277)   823
A Figure, black lead, 16 x 11¾ .... (283)   4,181
Portrait of Simon Lévy, pencil, 12¾ x 10 .... (309)   1,121
Portrait of the Painter Henri Ramey, black lead,
7¾ x 5 .... (298)   1,000
Woman's Head, pencil, 18¾ x 12½ .... (316)   3,750

1964

Head of a Woman Wearing a Hat, 1917-18,
pencil, 12¾ x 9½ .... (367)   3,870
Bust of a Young Lady, black lead, 13¼ x 10 ...... (366)   600
Caryatid, pencil and pen, 25¾ x 18¾ .... (354)   1,950
Harlequin, 1910-12, pencil, 16½ x 9½ .... (385)   1,944
Front View of a Young Girl, pencil, 12 x 8½ ...... (385)   1,876
Portrait of Soutine, pencil, 17½ x 11½ .... (385)   2,260
Jeanne Hébuterne, black lead, 9½ x 6½ .... (372)   2,000
Maternity, black lead, 18¼ x 10¼ .... (371)   2,020
Portrait of Simon Lévy, pencil, 12 x 10 .... (387)   608
Woman's Head, blue pencil, 16½ x 10 .... (416)   2,488
Maria Emma, 1914, pencil, 10½ x 8½ .... (416)   1,935
Portrait of Moïse Kisling, 1915, pen and wash,
8 x 4¾ .... (416)   1,382
Portrait of Kisling, pencil, 15¾ x 9¾ .... (448)   1,300
Portrait of Blaise Cendrars, 1917, pencil,
16½ x 11 .... (435)   2,560
Nude, 1918, pencil, 11¾ x 8¼ .... (433)   1,695
Portrait of a Man, pencil, 15¾ x 9½ .... (453)   1,659
Woman's Head, pencil, 17¼ x 10½ .... (454)   1,990
A Caryatid in Red, pencil and watercolor,
27 x 17¼ .... (460)   13,000

1965

Portrait of a Woman, 1917, pencil, 17¾ x 11¾ . . . . (516) $1,260
Woman in Profile, pencil, 20 x 16½ . . . . (512)   2,560
Seated Woman, pencil, 16½ x 10¼ . . . . (526)   3,750
Caryatid, pencil and colored pencil, 16½ x 10 . . . . (538)   210
Nude, pencil, 16½ x 10 . . . . (538)   1,300
Caryatid, colored chalk, 22 x 16¾ . . . . (575)   9,122
Portrait of Jean Cocteau, pencil, 15¾ x 10½ . . . . . (553)   2,000
Bust of a Woman, pencil, 16¼ x 9½ . . . . (561)   700
Portrait of Leopold Zborowski, pencil,
   16½ x 11½ . . . . (582)   2,212
A Figure, black lead, 16½ x 10¼ . . . . (617)   2,327
Portrait of a Young Lady, pencil, 16 x 9½ . . . . (633)   1,600
Back View of a Nude, pen and ink, 13 x 9½ . . . . . . (624)   1,382
Woman's Head, blue pencil and black lead,
   20 x 13¼ . . . . (624)   3,594
Portrait of Soutine, pencil, 16½ x 10½ . . . . (633)   4,750

1966

Portrait of a Man, black lead, 16¾ x 10 . . . . (658)   4,500
Portrait of the Publisher Bernouard, pen,
   7 x 4¾ . . . . (670)   740
Seated Nude, pencil, 18¼ x 10¾ . . . . (666)   3,020
A Soldier, black lead, 16½ x 9¾ . . . . (703)   3,500
Seated Man, black lead, 15¾ x 9¾ . . . . (703)   2,500
Hermaphrodite, black lead on paper laid down on
   board, 15¾ x 9¾ . . . . (703)   2,600
Portrait of a Man, pencil, 16¾ x 10½ . . . . (711)   1,800
Seated Woman, pencil and black lead, 16½ x 10 . . (744)   3,729
Standing Woman, pencil, 16½ x 9¾ . . . . (770)   3,408
Nude, pencil, 16½ x 9¾ . . . . (805)   2,400
Portrait of a Man, pencil, 16½ x 9¾ . . . . (770)   3,408

1967

Portrait of Moïse Kisling, 1915, pencil, 11 x 8¼ . . . (881)   2,156
Seated Nude, pencil, 9 x 11¾ . . . . (873)   1,500
The Fedinan Family, pencil, 16½ x 10¼ . . . . (889)   3,000
Model Resting, black lead, 12½ x 9½ . . . . (901)   1,100
Bust of a Young Woman, Her Hands Crossed,
   pencil, 18¾ x 13¾ . . . . (923)   2,900
Portrait of Moïse Kisling, 1915, sepia wash,
   8½ x 5¼ . . . . (930)   1,628
Head of Leopold Zborowski, pencil, 16 x 11 . . . . . . (939)   2,212
Nude, black lead, 16 x 11¾ . . . . (918)   2,147
Jeanne Hébuterne Seated, pencil, 12¾ x 9 . . . . (985)   2,607
Portrait of A. Lagar, 1919, pencil, 16½ x 9½ . . . . . (975)   4,000
Portrait of Soutine, black lead, 15¾ x 9 . . . . (965)   3,955
Caryatid, black lead, 15¾ x 10¼ . . . . (965)   3,955
Bust of a Nude, pencil, 10½ x 7½ . . . . (978)   910
Young Nude, Her Hands on Her Breast, pencil,
   12 x 9½ . . . . (1004)   2,000
The Man with the Pipe, pencil, 16½ x 10¼ . . . . . . (1004)   1,700
Head of a Young Lady, pencil, 18¼ x 11½ . . . . . . (1004)   2,100

1968–July 1969

Standing Nude, 1909-10, pencil, 17 x 10¾ . . . . . . (1214)   5,920
Seated Woman, black lead, 21 x 14¼ . . . . (1125)   8,855
Portrait of a Young Girl, (1915-16), pencil,
   16¼ x 10 . . . . (1030)   1,800
Little Girl Seated, pencil, 15 x 10 . . . . (1068)   4,130
Reclining Nude, pencil, 11 x 14 . . . . (1030)   2,700
Caryatid, pencil and watercolor, 25¼ x 19½ . . . . . (1193)   30,975
Caryatid, (1914), pencil on gray paper,
   24½ x 19 . . . . (1056)   14,000
Caryatid, black lead and red pencil, 21¼ x 17 . . . . (1200)   8,000

Portrait of a Bearded Man, pencil, 18 x 11¾ . . . . (1080) $3,000
Portrait of Soutine, black lead, 15¾ x 9 . . . . (1125)   4,025
Portrait of Kisling, 1915, pencil, 15¾ x 9½ . . . . . (1214)   7,040
Presumed Portrait of Paul Guillaume, pencil,
   15¾ x 10 . . . . (1119)   680
Portrait of Zborowski, black lead, 10 x 7½ . . . . . . (1183)   3,400
Christ on the Cross, black lead, 16¾ x 9½ . . . . . . (1106)   1,600
Presumed Portrait of Paul Guillaume, black lead,
   15¾ x 9½ . . . . (1225)   1,020
Presumed Portrait of Kikoïne, Young, black lead,
   16 x 10½ . . . . (1233)   850
Caryatid, pencil and red pencil, 21 x 17 . . . . (1239)   15,600
Portrait of a Man, black pencil, 15½ x 10¾ . . . . . (1268)   7,888
Seated Woman, (1916), pencil, 17 x 10½ . . . . (1268)   6,264
Young Man with a Hat, pencil, 18¾ x 11¾ . . . . . . (1272)   19,200

WATERCOLORS

1961–1962

Caryatid, gouache, 27½ x 19½ . . . . (64)   21,000
Pink Nude, 1917, watercolor, 16¾ x 20 . . . . (145)   26,860

1964

Portrait of a Young Lady, tempera and pastel on
   board, 18 x 11½ . . . . (354)   12,000

1965

Caryatid, watercolor and colored pencil laid
   down on canvas, 24¾ x 15¼ . . . . (553)   8,600

1967

Caryatid, pastel and red chalk, 20 x 16¾ . . . . (975)   16,000

PAINTINGS

1961–1962

Portrait of Beatrice, 31¾ x 20 . . . . (6)   48,590
Nude, oil, watercolor and pencil on board,
   25½ x 19¼ . . . . (21)   31,180
The Man with the Glass of Wine, 37¼ x 21½ . . . . . . (84)   101,602
Portrait of the Engraver Gosvel, 9½ x 7½ . . . . (88)   10,578
Young Lady on a Blue Background, 23½ x 19½ . . . (128)   38,444
Head of a Young Lady, Nice 1918, 23½ x 17¾ . . . . (128)   49,428
The Italian Woman, 1919, 16 x 12½ . . . . (128)   17,849

1963

Portrait of a Man, 28¼ x 20 . . . . (202)   27,500
A Boy in Red, 35½ x 23¼ . . . . (210)   65,808
Young Woman with a Fur-Collared Coat, 1916,
   26¼ x 21¾ . . . . (285)   18,080
Portrait of the Poet Rouveyre, 1915, 25½ x 16½ . . (309)   24,720
Portrait of Jeanne Hébuterne, 18¼ x 13 . . . . (309)   23,072

1964

Portrait of a Young Peasant, oil on paper laid
   down on canvas, 28¾ x 18¾ . . . . (431)   62,500
Marthe, 1918, 16 x 12¾ . . . . (458)   24,667
Head of a Young Lady, oil on paper laid down on
   panel, 13¾ x 10¼ . . . . (448)   8,000
The Redhead, on cardboard, 20 x 16½ . . . . (460)   26,800

1965

Portrait of Morgan Russell, 1918, 39 x 24¾ . . . . . . (522)   87,066
Head of a Young Lady, 12¾ x 10¼ . . . . (539)   9,250
Woman's Head, on board, 18¾ x 14 . . . . (539)   8,500
Portrait of a Woman, 1918, 21¾ x 12¾ . . . . (564)   6,000
Portrait of a Woman, 16 x 13 . . . . (553)   21,200
Red-Haired Woman, on panel, 13½ x 10½ . . . . (583)   20,314
The Woman in Blue, on board, 41½ x 29½ . . . . (583)   43,530

The Common Girl, 1918, 40¾ x 25½ . . . . (615) $ 240,000
Louise, 21¾ x 18¼ . . . . (615)   80,000
The Servant, 31¾ x 18¼ . . . . (615)   54,000
Portrait of Max Jacob, 1916, 28¾ x 23½ . . . . (615)   100,000
Portrait of the Poet André Rouveyre,[1] 1915,
   25½ x 16½ . . . . (637)   40,000
Portrait of a Young Woman, 20½ x 14½ . . . . (629)   14,510
The Opera Singer from Nice, 16¾ x 12¾ . . . . (637)   28,000

1966

Woman with a Blue Scarf, 12½ x 9½ . . . . (694)   19,000
Woman with a Hat, 23¾ x 18 . . . . (694)   40,000
A Young Lady of Montmartre, 24¾ x 17½ . . . . (713)   60,000
Portrait of Jeanne Hébuterne, 18½ x 14¾ . . . . (753)   23,216
Woman's Head, on paper, 15¾ x 11¼ . . . . (801)   42,000
Caryatid, 31¾ x 17¾ . . . . (801)   11,800

1967

Portrait of the Engraver Weil, 1910, 28¼ x 23¼ . . . (880)   22,665
Portrait of Marie Wassilieff, 28¼ x 20¾ . . . . (954)   40,000

1968–July 1969

Portrait of Beatrice Hastings, (1915–16), on
   board, 18½ x 11¼ . . . . (1132)   42,480
Middle-Class Woman, Madame C., 1917,
   23¾ x 18¼ . . . . (1057)   55,000
The Common Girl, (1917), 32 x 21¼ . . . . (1176)   80,000
Portrait of Madame C.D., 1918, on cradled panel,
   31½ x 19½ . . . . (1056)   92,000
The Blond with Earrings, (1918–19), 18 x 11¾ . . . (1056)   87,000

[1] Sold in London in 1963 for $24,720.

Laszlo Moholy-Nagy

(1895–1946)

Birthplace: Bacsbarsod, Hungary. Studies law in Budapest.

1914–18 Wounded during World War I, he begins to design portraits. The Russian avant-garde appeals to him.

1920 Paints as an abstractionist and never reverts to figuration.

1922 With the Hungarian poet Kassak, publishes *Buch Neuer Künstler*—the first anthology of the art of the international avant-garde.

1922–28 Teaches at the Bauhaus at Weimar and Dessau, playing an important part.

1934 Stay in Amsterdam.

1935 Stay in London. Starts the painting-sculptures that he calls "space modulators."

1937 Journey to the U.S., where he founds his own successful school of design. Several retrospective exhibitions in the U.S.

1946 Publishes *The New Vision,* New York. Died, Chicago.

1947 *Vision in Motion* is published in Chicago.

Sales

DRAWINGS

1964

Abstraction, (1940), pencil and watercolor on
   board, 26 x 19 . . . . (448) $ 1,100

1967

Composition, 1946, colored pencil and India ink,
   17½ x 11¾ . . . . (970)   884

1968–July 1969

Perpetuum Mobile, (1919), India ink and
   watercolor, 23 x 18½ . . . . (1114)   2,232

WATERCOLORS

1961–1962

Abstraction, gouache and collage on blue paper,
   19¼ x 14½ . . . . (101)   655
Motion, 1920, watercolor, India ink, and collage,
   23½ x 17 . . . . (88)   787

1967

Constructivist Composition, 1923, pencil and
   watercolor, 17¼ x 14 . . . . (930)   994

PAINTINGS

1961–1962

Q I, 1923, 37¾ x 37¾ . . . . (88)   5,904

1967

Composition, collage on black paper,
   24½ x 16½ . . . . (908)   1,230
Sil 3, 1933, oil and gouache on a silvered panel,
   19¾ x 24 . . . . (864)   2,400
Construction, 1940, oil on plastic, 8 x 14¾ . . . . (870)   1,100

1968–July 1969

Composition, (1922), collage, 11 x 8¾ . . . . (1096)   1,380

Piet Mondrian

(1872–1944)

Birthplace: Amersfoort, the Netherlands. (As Pieter Cornelis Mondriaan.)

1888 Executes his first drawings.

1892–97 Enters the Amsterdam Academy of Fine Arts.

1897–07 Paints landscapes and still lifes in a naturalistic style.

1908–10 Settles at Domburg. Participates in an exhibition at the Stedelijk Museum, Amsterdam. Takes part in the foundation of Moderne Kunst Kring, Amsterdam. Deeply impressed by Matisse's works, he begins to use pure color.

| **1911** | Participates in the Salon des Indépendants, Paris—until 1914. First stay in Paris. Greatly admires the Fauves, but is soon attracted by Cubism—influenced by Delaunay, Léger, Picasso, and Survage. |

1913 Participates in the first Herbstsalon, Berlin. Elaborates his first abstract paintings based on vertical and horizontal lines.

1914 Returns to the Netherlands.

1917 With Van Doesburg, founds the review *De Stijl.* Contributes to this review until 1924.

1919 Returns to Paris and settles in Montparnasse.

1920 Provides an account of his theories in the book *Le Néo-Plasticisme.* (Published by Léonce Rosenberg, Paris.)

1922 Retrospective exhibition at the Stedelijk Museum, Amsterdam, on his fiftieth birthday.

1925 Writes *Die Neue Gestaltung* for the Bauhaus at Dessau.

1927 Participates in the Salon des Tuileries, Paris.

1930 Participates in the exhibition "Cercle et Carré" at the Galerie 23, Paris.

1932 Becomes a member of the group known as "Abstraction-Création," Paris.

1938 Settles in London.

1940 Goes to the U.S. and settles in New York during World War II. Produces the series called "Boogie-Woogie."

1942-43 One-man shows at the Valentin Dudensing Gallery, New York. Participates in the exhibition "Artists in Exile" at the Pierre Matisse Gallery, New York.

1944 Died, New York.

1945 Retrospective exhibition at the Museum of Modern Art, New York.

1946 Retrospective exhibition at the Stedelijk Museum, Amsterdam.

Sales

DRAWINGS

1961–1962

A Sturdy Tree with an Entanglement of Gnarled Branches, charcoal, 12¾ x 19½ .... (64) $5,500

Chrysanthemums and Poppies, charcoal, 14 x 9¼ .... (64)   1,500

1965

The Park, pencil and wash, 6¼ x 8 .... (545)   509

1966

A Forest Near Oele, (1907), charcoal and gouache, 23 x 16¾ .... (686)   4,422

1968–July 1969

Landscape with a Church, wash, 37½ x 23 ...... (1138)   1,041

Chrysanthemums and Poppies, (1908), charcoal on buff paper, 14 x 9½ .... (1246)   6,000

WATERCOLORS

1966

The Dahlia, watercolor, 11¾ x 7½ .... (698)   1,795

1967

A Canal in Holland, (1905-07), watercolor and charcoal, 15¾ x 23¼ .... (982) $4,503

Landscape, (1907), watercolor and gouache, 10 x 14 .... (893)   1,750

1968–July 1969

Park Scene, watercolor, 5 x 6 .... (1246)   600

PAINTINGS

1961–1962

Kerktoren, Zoutelande, Isle of Walcheren, 1910, 35¼ x 24¼ .... (64)   47,000

1963

The Mill, (1900-05), on canvas laid down on board, 9¼ x 11¾ .... (202)   5,500

Fluvial Landscape, (1905), on board, 21¼ x 28¾ .. (225)   4,000

Landscape, (1909-10), 14 x 24¼ .... (225)   1,600

Grazing Cows, on panel, 12¾ x 14¾ .... (202)   3,250

1964

Portrait of Egbert Knipers, (1902), 31½ x 19 ...... (416)   1,658

The Mill by the Lake, (1905), on board, 11¾ x 12 .... (367)   3,317

The Water Mill, (1906), on board, 14 x 21½ ...... (454)   3,040

Composition with Faces, (1912), 20 x 28 .... (416)   6,910

1965

Composition in Blue, Red, and Yellow, 1921, 22 x 19½ .... (485)   42,000

Landscape with Mills, 1893, 10 x 12¼ .... (616)   880

The Mill, on canvas, 12½ x 16¾ .... (591)   2,394

1966

Two Cows Under the Trees, (1905), 19¾ x 25 ..... (753)   1,596

The Corn Field, 33 x 58 .... (698)   5,984

The Little Goat, on canvas, 10¼ x 14¼ .... (822)   1,142

Composition in Red, Blue, and Yellow, 1928, on panel, 48¼ x 31¼ .... (676)   60,000

1967

Landscape, on canvas laid down on board, 12¼ x 15 .... (870)   2,500

Landscape with a Thatch-Roofed Cottage, (1903), oil on paper laid down on board, 12¾ x 14¾ .... (870)   2,750

Fishing Boat, (1906), 12¾ x 17½ .... (864)   3,250

Still Life with Sunflowers, (1907), 21¼ x 22½ ..... (864)   5,250

The White Thatch-Roofed Cottage, on board, 16¾ x 23¼ .... (988)   3,234

Barges at Their Moorings, 1905, on board, 17½ x 24¼ .... (982)   1,304

1968–July 1969

Landscape with a Mill, (1897), on board, 10¼ x 14¼ .... (1070)   4,484

Snowy Landscape with a Farmhouse and a Peasant, (1900), 19½ x 23¾ .... (1132)   5,900

Landscape with Haystacks, (1900), 18¼ x 23¼ ... (1132)   5,900

Landscape, 1905, 10¾ x 14 .... (1018)   2,000

Landscape with a Mill, (1907), 14¼ x 19¾ .... (1069)   4,795

Haystacks, on panel, 10 x 14 .... (1204)   822

Landscape with a Farm, on panel, 9 x 13½ ...... (1218)   480

Boerderij waarvoor een waterpomp, on cardboard, 12½ x 14 .... (1248)   3,000

Composition I, 1920, 29½ x 25½ .... (1270)   64,800

Claude Monet

(1840–1926)

Birthplace: Paris, France.

1845 His family settles in Le Havre.

1855-58 Meets Eugène Boudin, who interests him in painting in the open.

1859 Attends the Académie Suisse, Paris, where he forms a friendship with Camille Pissarro.

1862 Returns to Normandy, where he meets Jongkind. Enters the Ecole Nationale des Beaux-Arts, Paris, in Gleyre's studio, where he meets Bazille, Renoir, and Sisley. They lighten their palettes.

1863 The four friends are terribly impressed by Manet's "Déjeuner sur l'herbe," exhibited at the Salon des Refusés, Paris.

1864 Long stay in Normandy, at the "Ferme Saint-Siméon," with Bazille, Jongkind, and Boudin.

1865 Participates in the Salon, Paris. Paints his own "Déjeuner sur l'herbe" (now partly destroyed). Gradually approximates future "Impressionism."

1866 Meets Manet. Paints "Women in the Garden" and "The Green Dress."

1868-69 Paints his first landscapes of the banks of the river Seine.

1870 Marries Camille Doncieux, his model. His works are refused by the Salon. Stays in London, where he meets Pissarro and Sisley again. They discover Turner's works. Charles Daubigny introduces them to Paul Durand-Ruel, their future dealer.

1872 Returns to Paris. Arranges his studio on a boat at Argenteuil, near Paris. Meets Gustave Caillebotte.

1873 Paints "Boulevard des Capucines."

1874 Paints "Argenteuil Bridge." Participates in the foundation of the "Société Anonyme des Artistes Peintres, Sculpteurs, et Graveurs," which includes Pissarro, Sisley, Renoir, Berthe Morisot, Guillaumin, Degas, and Cézanne. The first exhibition of the group, held at Nadar's, Paris, creates an unprecedented outburst of hilarity. Monet's work "Impression, Rising Sun" impels a critic to call the group "impressionistic" in mockery. Monet soon appears as the leader of the group. (In actual fact, only Monet, Pissarro, and Sisley should be regarded as genuine Impressionists.)

1876-79 Participates in the exhibitions of the Impressionist group, Paris. Paints the series entitled "La Gare Saint-Lazare." Death of his wife.

1878-80 Paints "Snow Effect at Vétheuil."

1883 Settles at Giverny, Eure district. With Renoir, visits Cézanne at l'Estaque. Amateurs and dealers begin to take an interest in his work.

1888 Stay in Antibes.

1892 Paints about forty views of Rouen Cathedral in order to render the shifts and vibrations of light.

1895 Trip to Norway. Starts the brilliant series entitled "Nymphéas."

1900 Trip to London.

1905-09 Continues to paint his "Nymphéas," which are exhibited at Durand-Ruel's, Paris. (Bequeaths them to the state in 1923.)

1908 Trip to Venice.

1926 Died, Giverny.

Sales

WATERCOLORS

1961–1962

Sailboats, pastel, 16¾ x 10¾ .... (42) $3,620

Ste. Adresse, 1861, pastel, 11 x 18¼ .... (128)   6,865

1963

The Tableland of the Caux, pastel, 6¾ x 11½ ..... (303)   1,900

1967

A Bridge in London, pastel, 11¾ x 18¾ .... (852)   6,200

1968–July 1969

Landscape, Sunset, pastel, 5¼ x 10¼ .... (1113)   2,360

The Manne Porte at Etretat, (1883-85), pastel,
   9 x 13 .... (1235)   13,000

PAINTINGS

1961–1962

Jean Monet in His Cradle, 1867, 45¼ x 35½ ...... (37)   80,000

Zaandam, (1871-72), 17½ x 28¾ .... (83)   109,840

Drift Ice Breaking Up, 1880, 23¾ x 38¾ .... (137)   47,500

Customs Officer's Hut, 1882, 23½ x 28¾ .... (64)   55,000

Pourville, 1882, 23¼ x 30½ .... (164)   13,730

Cliffs at Varangeville, 1882, 23¾ x 31¾ .... (64)   37,500

Tempest, Dieppe Pier, (1882-83), 21¼ x 29 .... (140)   27,460

The Shady Road, on panel, 36 x 19 .... (76)   21,000

The Garden Door, 23¾ x 29 .... (29)   33,200

The Flowery Arches, 32¼ x 36¾ .... (159)   92,288

Sandbar at Port-Villez, 1886, 25¾ x 32 .... (169)   29,020

Nymphéas, 40¼ x 79 .... (29)   54,000

Nymphéas, 51½ x 79 .... (31)   54,920

*The Blue Boat, Madame Blanche Monet, and
   Madame Jean Monet,* (1887), 43 x 51 .... (112)   153,776

The River Seine at Port-Villez, 1894,
   25¾ x 41½ .... (156)   15,400

A Cliff Near Dieppe, 1897, 25½ x 38¾ .... (64)   38,000

Sunset at Pourville, 1897, 39¼ x 25 .... (128)   24,714

The River Near Moret, 1900, 24 x 32 .... (145)   28,440

Venice: Palazzo Dario, 1908, 32 x 26 .... (140)   50,800

Still Life with Eggs, (1910), 28¾ x 36¼ .... (64)   37,500

The Flowery Arches, 1913, 31½ x 36¼ .... (64)   65,000

1963

The Railway Bridge at Argenteuil, (1874-75),
   23 x 38½ .... (245)   211,134

A Lane at Pourville, 1882, 29 x 23¾ .... (316)   105,000

Fishingboats off Pourville, 1882, 21¼ x 26 .... (210)   82,260

The Fir Trees at Varangeville, 1882, 23¾ x 29 .... (316)   51,000

Etretat Cliff, 1883, 23¾ x 31¾ .... (316)   25,000

The Meadow at Giverny, Haze Effect, 1884,
   25 x 36¼ .... (277)   24,678

Etretat Cliff, (1886), 22 x 32½ .... (316)   10,500

Etretat Peak, 1886, 31½ x 25¼ .... (316)   26,000

Tulips, 1891, 20 x 14¾ .... (258)   11,000

The Customs Officer's House, 1897, 26 x 36¾ .... (293)   33,200

The Water Lilies, (1918), 59¾ x 79 .... (279)   137,500

The River, 32¾ x 23 .... (206)   14,000

1964

La Heve Spit, Honfleur, 1864, 15½ x 28½ .... (405)   58,040

The Wooden Bridge at Argenteuil, 1873,
   21¼ x 29 .... (367)   132,672

Argenteuil, 23¾ x 32 .... (458)   110,276

Epinay Road: Snow Effect at Argenteuil, 1874,
21½ x 29¼ . . . . (367) $ 93,976

Vétheuil, (1878), 19¾ x 23¾ . . . . (448)   26,000

The River in Autumn, 1878, 21¼ x 27 . . . . (416)   52,516

The River, 32¾ x 23 . . . . (471)   27,120

Blue and Yellow Windflowers, (1878-80),
6½ x 15½ . . . . (416)   31,786

Riboudet Mount, 22 x 29¼ . . . . (399)   33,000

Apple Trees in Blossom, 25¾ x 21¼ . . . . (399)   26,000

The Valley of the Stream Scie, Pourville, 1882,
23¼ x 31¼ . . . . (416)   46,988

Meadow at Giverny, 1886, 36 x 31½ . . . . (458)   34,824

The Lane on the Cliff at Varangeville, 23¾ x 29 . . . (397)   6,000

The Garden Door, 29 x 23¾ . . . . (340)   28,000

Charing Cross Bridge, Westminster,
1899, 25¾ x 32 . . . . (458)   63,844

1965

Landscape: Vétheuil, 25 x 34½ . . . . (512)   41,000

Ste. Adresse, (1867), 22½ x 31½ . . . . (613)   140,000

Zaandam,[1] (1871-72), 17½ x 28¾ . . . . (575)   93,976

Spring at Argenteuil, 1872, 20 x 25 . . . . (522)   66,336

On the Cliff: Madame Monet and Her Son Jean,
1875-78, 39½ x 32 . . . . (562)   504,000

The Lane on the Cliff at Varangeville,
23¾ x 29¼ . . . . (583)   8,706

The Cliffs at Pourville, 1882, 21¼ x 32 . . . . (575)   69,100

The Stream Epte at Giverny, 1884, 23¾ x 29 . . . . . (628)   29,020

Landscape at Vétheuil, (1885-88), 29 x 29 . . . . (575)   24,876

Small Haystacks, 1887, 26 x 39½ . . . . (583)   60,942

Poplars, 1891, 36¼ x 32 . . . . (526)   95,000

Dawn Over the River Oise, 1894, 25¾ x 39½ . . . . . (594)   42,500

Landscape in the Rain, 24 x 29¼ . . . . (539)   28,000

The Cliffs at Pourville, Heavy Weather, 1896,
25¼ x 39½ . . . . (583)   55,138

A Cliff Near Dieppe, 1897, 25¾ x 39½ . . . . (594)   3,500

Young Woman Knitting, two studies on the same
canvas, 22½ x 17 . . . . (559)   9,600

The Customs Officer's Hut, 1897, 25¾ x 36 . . . . . . (583)   29,020

Waterloo Bridge, Dull Weather, 1901,
25¾ x 29¾ . . . . (629)   55,138

San Giorgio Maggiore Church, Venice, 1908,
25¾ x 36½ . . . . (594)   64,000

Nymphéas, 39½ x 79 . . . . (526)   112,500

1966

Honfleur Harbor, 1866-67, 17¾ x 21½ . . . . (750)   35,932

Cliffs at Pourville, 1882, 22½ x 31¼ . . . . (686)   89,830

The Lane at Varangeville, 1882, 23 x 28¾ . . . . (750)   19,348

The River Seine at Jeufosse, Near Vernon, 1884,
23¾ x 29 . . . . (814)   90,000

Falaise Vale, 1885, 30¼ x 23¾ . . . . (704)   43,166

The Cliffs at Etretat, (1885-86), 23 x 31½ . . . . (694)   40,000

Port-Domois Grotto, Belle-Isle, 1886, 25¾ x 32 . . . (713)   72,500

Rocks of the River Creuse, 1889, 25¾ x 32 . . . . (750)   38,696

Haystack in the Sunset, Hoarfrost Weather,
1891, 25¾ x 36½ . . . . (812)   66,336

Rouen Cathedral, 1894, 42 x 29¼ . . . . (808)   168,316

Nymphéas, (1924), 51¾ x 79 . . . . (713)   55,000

The River Seine at Les Andelys, 32 x 36¾ . . . . (797)   52,432

Kolsaas Mount, 29¾ x 36½ . . . . (811)   10,220

Giverny: Falaise Hamlet in the Fog, 29 x 36½ . . . . (727)   22,000

Fog Effect No. 2 on a Sound of the River Seine,
21¾ x 29¼ . . . . (727)   15,600

[1] Sold in London in 1962 for $109,840.

1967

The River Seine at Argenteuil, 1872, 18¾ x 37¼ . . (901) $190,000

Le "14 Juillet," 1872, 23¾ x 32 . . . . (988)   87,080

Amsterdam Harbor, (1873), 24 x 40 . . . . (864)   95,000

The Banks of the River Seine, 1874, 21¼ x 29 . . . . (901)   67,000

Winter at Argenteuil, 1875-76, 24½ x 40½ . . . . (938)   320,624

Olive-Tree Grove, 1884, 25¼ x 31½ . . . . (938)   41,460

The Cliffs at Pourville, Rough Sea, 1882,
25¾ x 39½ . . . . (880)   41,460

The Bridge at Bordighera, 1884, 24½ x 31½ . . . . . . (880)   38,696

The Garden at Giverny, (1910-20), 29 x 36 . . . . (988)   54,736

The Beach at Ste. Adresse, 1867, 23¼ x 31½ . . . . . (938)   113,324

The Terrace at Ste. Adresse, 38¾ x 51½ . . . . (988)   1,393,280

1968–July 1969

Louveciennes, Snow Effect, (1869-74),
22 x 25¾ . . . . (1151)   250,000

Portrait of Jean Monet, (1871), 16 x 12¾ . . . . (1132)   122,720

Portrait of Madame Camille Monet, (1875-78),
45½ x 35¼ . . . . (1151)   500,000

The Road at Vétheuil, 1878, 19¾ x 24 . . . . (1151)   180,000

The River Seine at Lavacourt, (1878-80),
18¼ x 24 . . . . (1057)   47,000

The Vale of the Stream Scie, Pourville, 1882,
23¼ x 31¼ . . . . (1132)   90,860

The Coast of Normandy, 1882, 23 x 31¼ . . . . (1126)   66,906

Cliffs at Pourville, Low Tide, 1882, 23 x 31½ . . . (1068)   44,840

The River Seine Near Vernon, 1883, 29 x 35½ . . . (1126)   104,076

The Vale of Falaise, 1885, 25 x 31¼ . . . . (1132)   118,000

The Road at Giverny, 1885, 23¾ x 32 . . . . (1176)   60,000

Springtime at Giverny, 1886, 25¾ x 21¼ . . . . (1068)   70,800

Landscape at Moret, 23¾ x 32 . . . . (1125)   40,940

Villers Cliffs, Rough Sea, (1887), 25½ x 32¼ . . . . (1176)   62,500

View of the River Creuse, 1889, 29 x 36 . . . . (1187)   56,640

The Poplars on the Banks of the Stream Epte,
1891, 39½ x 25¾ . . . . (1181)   130,000

Cliffs Near Dieppe, (1897), 25 x 39 . . . . (1187)   56,640

Charing Cross Bridge, Westminster, 1899,
25¾ x 32 . . . . (1126)   70,623

Kolsaas Mount, 24½ x 35½ . . . . (1193)   59,472

White Frost, 21½ x 29 . . . . (1053)   74,200

The Icicles, 1888, 23¾ x 39½ . . . . (1224)   75,000

Kolsaas Mount, Norway, 1895, 25¾ x 39½ . . . . . . (1235)   40,000

The Waters of the River Somme, Sun Effect,
1889, 28½ x 35¾ . . . . (1239)   60,000

Kolsaas Mount, Norway, (1895), 25¾ x 36½ . . . . (1268)   41,760

Pierre Montezin

(1874–1946)

Birthplace: Paris, France.

1893 Participates in the Salon des Indépendants, Paris.

1903 Participates in the Salon des Indépendants, Paris. Most of his pictures are landscapes painted under the influence of the Impressionist manner.

1919 Participates in the Salon des Artistes Français, Paris. Works at Dreux and Moret-sur-Loing.

1923 Promoted to the rank of Chevalier of the Legion of Honor.

1941 Appointed member of the Académie des Beaux-Arts, Paris.

1946 Died, Moëlan-sur-Mer, Brittany.

Sales

WATERCOLORS

1961–1962

On the Terrace, gouache, 8¾ x 14¼ . . . . (76) $ 980

The Pond Before the Farm, gouache, 14¾ x 21¼ . . . . (123) 620

Haymaking Time,[1] gouache, 14 x 12¾ . . . . (177) 300

1964

The Banks of the River Seine, pastel, 10 x 16½ . . . (335) 540

The Walk, gouache, 8¼ x 11 . . . . (374) 764

1965

Sailboats, gouache, 10¾ x 9 . . . . (603) 440

1966

Barges Along the Waterside, gouache, 10¼ x 13 . . (685) 1,360

Venice, gouache, 10¾ x 15½ . . . . (669) 820

The Fishing Boats, gouache laid down on canvas, 19 x 27 . . . . (711) 440

1967

The Meeting Place of the Hunters, gouache, 8 x 11¾ . . . . (852) 1,120

Sunday by the Waterside, pastel with gouache lights, 15¾ x 19½ . . . . (858) 1,560

A Landscape with Willows, pastel and gouache, 15 x 20¾ . . . . (858) 960

Landscape with Fir Trees, gouache, 6 x 9¾ . . . . (976) 400

Two Figures in a Landscape, watercolor and gouache, 4½ x 6 . . . . (955) 150

1968–July 1969

The Town of Soissons, in 1918, gouache, 5¾ x 7½ . . . . (1089) 136

The Boat, 1923, gouache and pastel on paper laid down on canvas, 23 x 31¼ . . . . (1113) 2,740

The Light Cart, 1930, gouache, 19 x 25 . . . . (1219) 1,300

Landscape with Willows, pastel and gouache, 15 x 20½ . . . . (1116) 840

Riverside, gouache, 9 x 14¼ . . . . (1261) 2,400

Orchards in Blossom, gouache, 23¼ x 28½ . . . . . . (1261) 4,300

The Trees in Blossom, gouache, 23¾ x 29 . . . . (1261) 4,100

PAINTINGS

1961–1962

Fall at Neuilly, 29 x 23¾ . . . . (34) 4,120

Haymaking Time, 48 x 21¾ . . . . (30) 1,240

[1] Dedicated "Affectueux souvenir à l'ami Verdier."

Haymaking Time, 19¾ x 29 . . . . (68) $2,000

Banks of the River Seine, 21¾ x 21¾ . . . . (30) 820

The Road at Bessé, 21¾ x 21¾ . . . . (18) 497

The Flower Market in Paris, 15 x 21¾ . . . . (70) 1,264

The Meadow in Normandy, 23¾ x 29 . . . . (155) 1,040

The Yard of a Breton House, on panel, 5 x 8 . . . . . (150) 102

Oxen in a Meadow, 29 x 36½ . . . . (156) 1,670

Barges Under Snow, 19½ x 19 . . . . (175) 847

1963

Oxen in a Meadow, 29 x 36½ . . . . (260) 880

Oxen in a Meadow, 29 x 36½ . . . . (206) 1,220

Landscape of the River Creuse, 24 x 29 . . . . (320) 1,344

Riverside, 21¼ x 25¾ . . . . (215) 900

Haymaking Time, 29 x 36 . . . . (306) 1,120

A Park in Spring, 23¾ x 29 . . . . (299) 800

Little Girl in a Garden, 21¼ x 26 . . . . (246) 310

Riverside, 18¼ x 21¾ . . . . (246) 560

Summer Landscape, 23¾ x 29 . . . . (215) 640

Still Life with Flowers, 18¼ x 21¾ . . . . (241) 800

The Riding Alley of the Bois de Boulogne, 23¾ x 29 . . . . (293) 1,700

The "Promenade des Anglais," 29 x 36½ . . . . (198) 3,300

The Walk Along the Road, 21¼ x 29 . . . . (318) 5,600

1964

A River Lined with Poplars, 23¾ x 29 . . . . (474) 1,100

Riverside, 19¾ x 29 . . . . (450) 1,480

The Road Along the River, 29 x 36 . . . . (393) 840

Landscape . . . . (424) 1,600

The Sunny Farm, 17¾ x 21¼ . . . . (333) 1,020

Country Scene, 29 x 36½ . . . . (440) 1,920

Harvesttime, 11¾ x 18¼ . . . . (382) 400

The Orchard, 23¾ x 32 . . . . (341) 1,920

The Tedder, 47½ x 21¾ . . . . (401) 1,800

The Pond, End of the Day, 21¼ x 25¾ . . . . (325) 760

The Water Lilies, 29 x 27¾ . . . . (335) 1,900

Figures by the Riverside, 24 x 29 . . . . (398) 3,000

The Rue de Seine at Veneux, 29 x 23¾ . . . . (399) 3,000

1965

Moret-sur-Loing, 18¼ x 21¾ . . . . (564) 1,620

A Heron by the Waterside, 27 x 17¾ . . . . (571) 200

Back to the Farm, 18¼ x 21¾ . . . . (571) 1,160

Monthulet Mill in Autumn, 18¼ x 25¾ . . . . (607) 1,600

A Walk by the Waterside, 19¾ x 25¾ . . . . (647) 2,760

The Bridge Over the River Seine, at St. Mammès, 29¼ x 36½ . . . . (408) 2,600

The Banks of the River Loing Near St. Mammès, 19½ x 29 . . . . (547) 2,500

The River Loing at Moret, 23¾ x 29 . . . . (612) 4,100

Springtime Landscape, 13 x 21¾ . . . . (621) 1,700

The Riverside in Autumn, 18¼ x 21¾ . . . . (548) 840

A Gondolier in Venice, on cardboard, 10¾ x 14 . . . (516) 400

The Bunch of Flowers . . . . (570) 540

1966

Rowing, 29¾ x 36½ . . . . (664) 2,200

Riverside with Poplars, 21¼ x 25¾ . . . . (659) 800

The Road Along the Edge of the Pond, 19½ x 28½ . . . . (666) 3,740

The Road to Bessé in the Rain, 21¾ x 21¾ . . . . . . (749) 1,400

Moret-sur-Loing, 18¼ x 21¾ . . . . (731) 1,000

Landscape of the River Loing, 15¾ x 29¼ . . . . (702) 1,600

The Banks of the River Loing, 24 x 29 . . . . (726) $1,700
The Road Along the River Loing, 23¾ x 29 . . . . (727) 2,300
Cows at the Watering Place, 21¾ x 25¾ . . . . (793) 520
Harvesttime, 46¾ x 21 . . . . (689) 1,106
Venice, oil on cork . . . . (799) 3,900
Landscape of Venice, oil on paper, 19¾ x 17¾ . . . . (745) 2,486
Water Lilies, 23¾ x 29 . . . . (809) 2,400
Sunday on the Banks of the River Seine,
    23¾ x 29 . . . . (804) 3,000
A Bunch of Roses, 19¾ x 24 . . . . (758) 500
Still Life with a Bunch of Flowers, 17¾ x 21 . . . . . . (760) 1,161
The Garden Barrier, 29¼ x 24 . . . . (753) 3,773

1967
Nice: Before the Casino de la Jetée, 25¾ x 32 . . . . (901) 7,000
Bicycles by the Waterside, 21¼ x 29 . . . . (977) 3,000
Fishermen on the Banks of the River Loing,
    19¾ x 24 . . . . (1007) 1,300
The Lake, 10¼ x 15¾ . . . . (968) 340
Poplars by the Waterside in Springtime,
    19¾ x 25¾ . . . . (923) 3,500
Landscape, on cardboard, 19 x 23¾ . . . . (926) 800
Lighters on the River Seine, 23¼ x 28½ . . . . (985) 4,266
Landscape, on panel, 9½ x 7¼ . . . . (874) 280
The Merry-Go-Round, 21¼ x 25¾ . . . . (935) 1,640
Harvesttime, 25¾ x 36½ . . . . (987) 4,200
Haymaking Time, 1933, 29 x 36½ . . . . (912) 2,800
The Turkey Cocks, on cardboard, 29 x 36½ . . . . . . (993) 1,240
Bathing, 35¼ x 45¾ . . . . (912) 2,100
Still Life, 19¾ x 24 . . . . (968) 1,200
Vase of Roses, 24 x 31½ . . . . (832) 620

1968–July 1969
Harvesttime, 15 x 24 . . . . (1200) 2,400
Harvesting in the Creuse, 1942, 29 x 36½ . . . . (1060) 4,160
The Pond in the Creuse, 23¼ x 28½ . . . . (1039) 2,900
The Lake and the Great Trees, on panel,
    9½ x 7½ . . . . (1179) 520
The Village in Springtime, 18¼ x 24 . . . . (1053) 840
Riverside, 23¾ x 32 . . . . (1051) 1,800
The Tree in Blossom, 11¾ x 15¼ . . . . (1138) 843
The Virginia Creeper, 18¼ x 21¾ . . . . (1015) 560
Harvesttime, 23¾ x 32 . . . . (1113) 5,900
The Village Under Snow, 20¼ x 25¾ . . . . (1184) 4,220
The Lake, 21¼ x 25¾ . . . . (1184) 3,400
The Alley of Poplars, 21¾ x 18¼ . . . . (1117) 2,500
Still Life, 20 x 24 . . . . (1196) 600
A Bunch of Roses, 32¼ x 25¾ . . . . (1161) 84
Landscape, 23¾ x 29 . . . . (1222) 3,900
Banks of the River Loing, 21¼ x 25¾ . . . . (1226) 2,700
Riverside, 35½ x 51½ . . . . (1226) 9,000
Bunch of Gillyflowers, 33½ x 19 . . . . (1227) 620
Fisherman by the Riverside, 28 x 28 . . . . (1241) 7,560
Roses, 23¾ x 29 . . . . (1252) 3,000
The Turkey Cocks, on paper, 28 x 35½ . . . . (1256) 2,200
Riverside, 29 x 36½ . . . . (1258) 4,400
Poplars, 29 x 36½ . . . . (1258) 3,000
Fashionable Ladies by the Waterside, 29 x 36¾ . . (1261) 13,000

Henry Moore

(1898–   )

Birthplace: Castleford, Yorkshire, England.

1919-21 Enters the Leeds School of Art. A scholarship enables him to attend the Royal College of Art, London.

1923 First stay in Paris.

1924 Appointed instructor of sculpture at the Royal College of Art, London.

1925 Trip to France and Italy.

1928 First one-man show at the Warren Gallery, London. Commissioned to execute an important carved relief for the London underground station at St. James's Park.

1929 Marries Irina Radetzky.

1932 Moves from the Royal College of Art to the Chelsea School of Art.

1934 First monograph on his work by Herbert Read.

1936 Participates in the international Surrealist exhibition at the New Burlington Galleries, London.

1940 Settles in Hertfordshire.

1941 First retrospective exhibition at Temple Newsam, Leeds.

1947 Gives up teaching.

1948 Given an award by the Venice Biennial.

1951 Retrospective exhibition at the Tate Gallery, London. Trip to Greece.

1953 Trip to Mexico. Given an award by the São Paulo Biennial.

1960 One-man show at the Whitechapel Gallery, London.

1963 Executes an important sculpture for Lincoln Center, New York.

1968 Major retrospective exhibition at the Tate Gallery, London, on his seventieth birthday.

Sales

DRAWINGS
Studies for a Sculpture, 1936, black chalk and
    gray wash, 21¼ x 14 . . . . (74) $1,510
Standing, Seated, and Reclining Figures, India
    ink, colored chalk and watercolor,
    15 x 21¾ . . . . (106) 2,147
Two Women, 1947, India ink, chalk, watercolor,
    and tempera, 15 x 22 . . . . (106) 2,599
The Underground Shelter, 1942, pen, colored
    chalk and gray wash, 10¾ x 8 . . . . (74) 2,746
Women Winding Wool, 1948, pen, pencil, black
    chalk, and watercolor heightened with white,
    20½ x 23½ . . . . (118) 4,119
Baptism, pencil, pen, black chalk, and watercolor
    with white lights, 8¾ x 6¾ . . . . (118) 2,746
Study for Sculpture, pencil, ink, and wash,
    44 x 10¾ . . . . (148) 1,236

1963
Reclining Nude, 1927, pencil and black ink,
    15½ x 12 . . . . (213) 824
Idea for a Sculpture, 1928, orange and black
    chalk heightened with white, 9¾ x 4¾ . . . . (268) 384
Mother and Child, 1928, ink and gray wash,
    11½ x 14 . . . . (207) 877

Mother and Child, pen and wash, 14¾ x 10¾ ..... **(202)** $2,500

A Sheet with 9 Compositions, 1940, pen and
India-ink wash with white lights, 10 x 13¾ ... **(219)** 1,853

Ideas for a Sculpture, 1940, pen, colored chalk,
and watercolor, 10 x 16¾ .... **(207)** 2,194

Studies of a Wrapped Figure, 1942, pen, charcoal,
and watercolor, 22½ x 17½ .... **(207)** 2,879

Studies for a Sculpture, 1950, pen and gray wash,
11 x 8¾ .... **(304)** 2,468

1964

Studies for a Sculpture, 1938, pencil,
19½ x 15½ .... **(461)** 2,240

Nude, 1928, India ink wash, 16¾ x 11¾ .... **(421)** 553

Standing Nude, 1926, India ink and wash,
16¼ x 6½ .... **(385)** 542

Two Figures Surrounded by 21 Sketches, 1932,
India ink, colored ink, and wash, 22 x 15¼ ... **(385)** 2,079

Study of Figures, pen and watercolor,
6½ x 11¼ .... **(354)** 900

Three Studies of Reclining Figures, 1944, pencil
and watercolor, 21 x 14¼ .... **(364)** 3,482

1965

Seated Nude, 1928, pen and watercolor,
12¾ x 12¾ .... **(545)** 1,018

Reclining Figures, 1942, India ink, colored chalk
and white lights, 23 x 17½ .... **(566)** 2,893

Portrait of the Artist's Mother, 1926, pen, wash,
and white lights, 10¾ x 7 .... **(605)** 1,045

Ideas for a Sculpture, 1956, ink, colored chalk,
and watercolor, 10¾ x 7½ .... **(584)** 1,603

Seated Figure, black chalk, ink, and wash,
14¾ x 10¾ .... **(643)** 2,349

1966

Reclining Nude, 1928, pen and wash, 13 x 16¾ ... **(693)** 719

Standing Nude, 1931, wash, 20½ x 14 .... **(825)** 995

Studies for a Sculpture, 1932, pen and wash on
paper laid down on board, 22 x 15 .... **(760)** 2,902

Drawings for a Sculpture, 1932, ink and wash,
10 x 7¼ .... **(648)** 1,100

Two Women and a Child, 1940, ink, colored
chalk, and watercolor heightened with white,
13 x 15¾ .... **(825)** 6,910

Seated Figures, 1941, pen, black chalk and
watercolor, 10¾ x 14¾ .... **(751)** 3,317

Sleeping Figures, 1941, black chalk and
watercolor heightened with gouache,
12 x 18¼ .... **(761)** 11,056

Ideas for a Sculpture, 1956, ink, colored chalk,
and watercolor, 11 x 7¾ .... **(693)** 1,797

1967

Young Lady, wash, 16 x 10 .... **(944)** 1,161

Reclining Nude, 1928, pencil and
wash, 11¼ x 16¼ .... **(889)** 1,600

Studies for a Sculpture, 1936, India ink and
colored chalk heightened with gouache,
15 x 22 .... **(914)** 3,567

Studies for a Sculpture, 1937, black chalk and
watercolor, 10 x 8 .... **(1003)** 1,422

Ideas for a Sculpture, 1938, pencil, black chalk,
and wash, 14¾ x 21¾ .... **(853)** 4,063

Study of Reclining Figures for a Sculpture, 1940,
ink, pencil, colored chalk, and watercolor,
10 x 16¾ .... **(945)** 5,804

Standing and Reclining Figures, 1940, India ink
and colored chalk heightened with white,
14¾ x 21¾ .... **(990)** 4,428

Miner Drilling, 1942, ink, colored chalk and
watercolor, 11¾ x 8¼ .... **(1003)** $3,318

Seated Figures, 1949, pencil, ink, watercolor, and
white lights, 11¾ x 10 .... **(869)** 2,902

Ideas for a Sculpture, 1951, colored chalk,
15¾ x 22 .... **(957)** 3,040

1968–July 1969

Seated Nude, 1925, brush and India-ink wash,
16 x 11¾ .... **(1206)** 1,652

Study, 1932, India ink and wash, 21½ x 15 ...... **(1127)** 4,370

Ideas for a Sculpture (recto), 1943, *Reclining
Figures* (verso), red and black chalk, pen, and
wash, 6¾ x 10 .... **(1074)** 3,894

A Group, 1944, pen and wash, heightened with
white, 12¼ x 11¾ .... **(1149)** 10,500

Studies of Figures, pencil, pen, colored chalk, and
watercolor, 10 x 6¾ .... **(1141)** 2,596

WATERCOLORS

1961–1962

Two Frieze Figures, 1951, pencil and watercolor,
11½ x 9½ .... **(88)** 1,304

1963

Tower, A Study for a Sculpture, (1961), special
watercolor appearing recto and verso,
11¾ x 9½ .... **(232)** 678

1964

Seascape, 1874, watercolor, ... **(468)** 56

1965

Sleeping Shelters, 1941, watercolor, 15 x 22 ...... **(616)** 2,080

Study for a Sculpture, watercolor and gouache,
9 x 6¾ .... **(541)** 1,500

Mother and Child Under a Shelter, watercolor
and colored pencil, 10¾ x 8¼ .... **(643)** 4,353

1968–July 1969

Composition, 1944, watercolor, 10¾ x 7¼ .... **(1141)** 897

Nine Heads of Animals, 1954, pencil and
watercolor, 11½ x 9½ .... **(1101)** 2,760

Three Reclining Figures, watercolor, pencil, and
collage, 8¾ x 4½ .... **(1080)** 850

Composition, 1966, watercolor, 11½ x 9¼ .... **(1173)** 3,335

Seated Figure, gouache, 6¾ x 5¾ .... **(1268)** 4,060

PAINTINGS

1963

A Study for Sculptures, 1951, grisaille on paper,
11½ x 9 .... **(316)** 2,250

1964

Studies of Sculptures, 1951, grisaille, tempera on
paper, 11½ x 9 .... **(372)** 2,300

Giorgio Morandi

(1890–1964)

Birthplace: Bologna, Italy.

1909 Attends the Academy of Fine Arts, Bologna.

1914 Comes under the influence of Cézanne and Cubism. Mainly paints still lifes.

1917-20 Joins di Chirico's "Metaphysical Painting." Participates in the exhibitions of the group called "Valori Plastici."

1925 Participates in the exhibition "Novecento," Milan.

1939 One-man show in Rome.

1946 One-man show in Milan.

1948 Given an award by the Venice Biennial.

1950 Participates in the exhibition of Italian art at the Musée National d'Art Moderne, Paris.

1957 Given an award by the São Paulo Biennial.

1964 Died.

Sales

DRAWINGS

1961-1962

Landscape, 10¼ x 13	(14)	$ 253
Landscape, 9 x 11¾	(69)	411
Still Life, watercolor, 8 x 11¾	(69)	1,264
Still Life, 1945, 11¾ x 15¾	(75)	664
Still Life, 1953, 8¾ x 11¾	(75)	474
Still Life, pencil, 8¼ x 10¼	(149)	411

1964

Bottles, 1946, pencil, 6½ x 8	(453)	636
Still Lifes, three drawings, 7½ x 11, 6½ x 9½, and 7½ x 10¾	(386)	820

1965

Still Life with Bottles, pencil, 7 x 4	(566)	520
Landscape, 9½ x 13	(616)	960

1966

Still Life, 1943, 8 x 7¼	(802)	1,360
Still Life, 1954, pencil, 6½ x 8¾	(784)	800

1967

Still Life, 1948, pencil, 8¼ x 22	(882)	1,200

1968-July 1969

Still Life, 1940, pencil, 6½ x 9½	(1214)	1,280

WATERCOLORS

1961-1962

Landscape, 1915, watercolor, 9¾ x 7½	(106)	972
Hilly Landscape, 1915, watercolor, 8¾ x 6¾	(106)	972
Grizzena, watercolor, 6 x 8¾	(15)	569
Landscape, watercolor, 6½ x 8¼	(14)	664
Still Life, watercolor, 10¼ x 14	(145)	1,580
Still Life, 1960, watercolor, 9½ x 13	(164)	824

1964

Landscape, 1958, watercolor, 8 x 12	(453)	1,216

1967

Still Life, 1959, watercolor, 9 x 11	(889)	3,600

PAINTINGS

1961-1962

Landscape, 1936, 21 x 23¾	(149)	$8,848
Still Life with Shells, 1938, 8 x 11	(20)	6,636
Still Life, 10 x 11¾	(70)	6,004
Still Life, 14 x 15¾	(14)	4,740
Landscape, 1940, 10¾ x 17	(164)	5,217
Landscape, 1943, 13¼ x 15¾	(88)	6,642
Still Life with Bottles, 1953, 13½ x 17	(88)	8,241
Still Life, 1955, 10 x 14	(149)	6,320
Still Life, 1959, 11¾ x 10	(164)	4,668

1963

Still Life, 1943, 10¾ x 11¾	(249)	3,800
Still Life, 13 x 18¼	(200)	4,800

1964

Still Life, 1948, 12¼ x 15½	(461)	11,200
Still Life, 1948, 11½ x 15½	(453)	5,804
Still Life, (1952), 11¾ x 15½	(372)	9,500
Landscape, 1956, 9½ x 8	(453)	3,870
Still Life, 1960, 10 x 11¾	(435)	7,520
Still Life, 10 x 12¼	(437)	7,680

1965

Self-Portrait, 1925, 24½ x 19	(616)	12,400
The Cortile of the Via Fondazza, 1956, 14 x 20	(522)	9,121
Still Life with a Coffeepot, (1961), 12 x 14¼	(617)	13,334
Still Life, 1962, 15¾ x 14	(616)	9,600
Landscape, 1963, 15¾ x 14	(616)	10,400

1966

Still Life, 1941, 12 x 18¼	(802)	14,400
Still Life, 1956, 15¾ x 18	(802)	14,400
Flowers, 1947, 6½ x 8	(802)	7,680

1967

Still Life, 1949, 10¾ x 14	(962)	13,600
Still Life, 1947, 19 x 12¼	(962)	16,800
Still Life, 10 x 14	(954)	14,000

1968-July 1969

Still Life, 12¼ x 19	(1125)	20,240

Henri Moret

(1856–1913)

Birthplace: Cherbourg, France. Enters the Ecole Nationale des Beaux-Arts, Paris.

1876 Takes a trip to Brittany, during his military service, where he meets Maurice Denis, Sérusier, Emile Bernard, and Gauguin.

1880-86 Participates in the Salon des Champs-Elysées, Paris. Trip to the Netherlands.

1888	Stay in Pont-Aven.
1889	Stay at Le Pouldu. Paints mainly seascapes. Signs a contract with Durand-Ruel. Participates in the Paris World's Fair with Gauguin and Emile Bernard.
1894-95	Participates in the Salon des Indépendants, Paris.
1898	One-man show at the Galerie Durand-Ruel, Paris.
1900-02	Exhibits at the Durand-Ruel Gallery, New York—with d'Espagnat, Loiseau, and Maufra.
1903-08	Participates in the Salon d'Automne, Paris. One-man show at the Galerie Le Barc de Boutteville, Paris.
1913	Died, Paris.

Sales

DRAWINGS

1968–July 1969

The Road, 1885, charcoal on brown paper, 4¾ x 8 .... (1138) $ 104

WATERCOLORS

1966

Rocks, watercolor, 10 x 13 .... (671)   232

PAINTINGS

1961–1962

A Valley in Nevez, 1909, 21 x 25½ .... (85)   800
The Water Mill, 15 x 21¾ .... (155)   1,600
Working in the Fields, 21¼ x 25¾ .... (155)   1,180
Autumn Landscape, 23¾ x 29 .... (122)   1,356
Belle-Ile en Mer, 23¾ x 29 .... (160)   1,340
Haymaking Time, 21¾ x 18¼ .... (52)   1,310
Landscape of Brittany, 19¾ x 24 .... (52)   1,920
Le Dalmani, Finistère, 1913, 29 x 24 .... (50)   2,440
Seaside in the Finistère, 12¼ x 25¾ .... (162)   1,620
Goulphar Cliffs, 32 x 25¾ .... (162)   840

1963

The Coast of Brittany in the Sun, 1902, 25¾ x 36½ .... (291)   1,800
Berg-O-Morg Signal Station, Finistère, 1904, 25¾ x 36½ .... (258)   1,000
Women on the Heath .... (212)   640
Trees Along a River, 32 x 23¾ .... (306)   2,700

1964

The Creek, 18¼ x 24 .... (335)   860
Sailboats in the Creek, 18¼ x 24 .... (370)   1,100
Evening at Ouessant, 23 x 27¾ .... (454)   1,244

1965

Armor, 15 x 18¼ .... (556)   400
The Coast of Brittany in the Sun, 1901, 25¾ x 36½ .... (553)   2,180
Les Aiguilles, Belle-Ile en Mer, 1904, 31½ x 25¾ .... (624)   1,658
The Mill at Riec, 1904, 25¾ x 32 .... (602)   2,034
Goulphor Cliff, 32 x 25¾ .... (539)   3,000
The Signal Station, Finistère Coast, 1909, 25 x 35½ .... (522)   3,870

1966

Maritime Landscape, 15 x 18¼ .... (819)   1,800
A Creek in Brittany, 1903, 18¼ x 24 .... (670)   1,820

The Signal Station, Finistère Coast, 1909, 25 x 35½ .... (689) $1,520
Landscape of Brittany, 21¾ x 26 .... (727)   1,760

1967

Cherbourg, 1890, 15 x 18¼ .... (967)   2,486
The British Graveyard, 1901, 20½ x 28 .... (885)   1,741
Seaside, 16¼ x 23 .... (893)   2,500
Evening at Ouessant, 23¾ x 29 .... (1000)   2,100
Two Breton Women at Pont-Aven, 14¾ x 19¾ ... (919)   2,147
Landscape of the Finistère, Autumn, 1909, 28½ x 23¾ .... (888)   2,902
The Signal Station, Finistère Coast, 1909, 25 x 35½ .... (1006)   2,488
Misty Weather, Brittany, 29 x 36½ .... (864)   4,500
The Red Sail, 21¾ x 25¾ .... (870)   3,000
Red Rocks, 15 x 18¼ .... (912)   2,000

1968–July 1969

Brigneau Signal Station, 1900, 23¾ x 32 .... (1189)   7,000
Setting Sun at Doelant, 1896, 25¾ x 21¼ .... (1166)   2,360
Les Aiguilles, Belle-Ile en Mer, 1904, 32 x 25¾ .. (1059)   2,726
Evening at Raguenez, 1905, 19¾ x 25¾ .... (1189)   3,800
Maria Lake in Quimper in Winter, 1909, 12¾ x 16 .... (1132)   4,012
Misty Weather, Brizellec, Finistère, 1911, 21¾ x 18¼ .... (1189)   7,400
The River Bellon, 23¾ x 32 .... (1113)   4,300
A Path in the Heather, 21¼ x 29 .... (1210)   4,600
The Evening at Ouessant, 24 x 29 .... (1080)   2,750
Landscape, 19¾ x 25¾ .... (1194)   4,216
Seascape, 1896, 21¼ x 25¾ .... (1225)   1,600
Sailboats at Douëlan, 1906, 12½ x 17¾ .... (1273)   5,040

Berthe Morisot

(1841–1895)

	Birthplace: Bourges, France.
1860	Meets Corot.
1863	Takes a trip to Antwerp, where she works in the open.
1864	Participates in the Salon, Paris.
1868	Sits for Manet's "Balcony."
1872	Trip to St. Jean de Luz and Spain.
1870-73	Participates in the Salon, Paris.
1874	Participates in the first exhibition of Impressionism, at Nadar's, Paris. Marries Manet's brother, Eugène.
1876-77	Participates in the second and third exhibitions of Impressionism, Paris.
1882	Trip to Italy.
1885	Trip to Belgium and Holland.

1886	Participates in the eighth exhibition of Impressionism, Paris. Stay at Jersey, Channel Islands.
1887	Exhibits at the Galerie Georges Petit, Paris. Stay in the Sarthe district.
1892	Death of her husband. Private exhibition at the Galerie Boussod et Valadon, Paris.
1894	Participates in the exhibition "La Libre Esthétique," Brussels.
1895	Died, Paris.

Sales

DRAWINGS

1961–1962

The Haymaker, red chalk, 10¾ x 7	(93)	$ 701

1963

Seated Young Lady, brown chalk, 9 x 6½	(219)	463

1964

Suns, colored pencil, 10½ x 7½	(398)	620
Seated Young Lady, blue pencil, 7½ x 5¼	(416)	1,050
Sunflowers in a Garden, colored pencil, 13½ x 10	(405)	929
Women's Heads, black lead, 9 x 7¾	(329)	300
Portrait of Madame Paul Valéry as a Child, charcoal heightened with white, 15¾ x 12¾	(399)	700

1965

Picking Cherries, 1891, red chalk, 28¾ x 19	(624)	8,016
Gathering Fruit, pencil, 12¾ x 8	(511)	640
Portrait of a Young Lady in Left Profile, charcoal heightened with white, 15¾ x 13	(494)	1,800

1966

Lorient Harbor, 1869, pencil and watercolor, 6¼ x 8	(750)	6,081
Study for "The Bath," black pencil and red chalk, 21 x 15½	(689)	2,764
Reclining Nude, pencil heightened with white, 14¼ x 23¼	(731)	900

1967

Portrait of Jeanine Gobillard, black lead, 7½ x 5½	(921)	560
Portrait of Julie Manet, 1890, charcoal and red chalk, 20½ x 16¾	(1004)	6,000

1968–July 1969

A Young Woman, red chalk, 21¾ x 15¾	(1106)	1,440
Young Lady Holding a Fishing Rod, pencil, 9 x 5	(1138)	1,041
The Haymaker, 13¼ x 9	(1254)	4,000
Study for "The Bath," 1894, red chalk and black pencil on tracing paper, 18¼ x 23¼	(1258)	4,000
Young Lady Embroidering, pencil, 7½ x 9	(1272)	960
Recollection of the Carnival of Nice, Louise Riesener in Domino, pastel, 18¾ x 24½	(1272)	3,840

WATERCOLORS

1961–1962

The Forest of Fontainebleau, watercolor, 11½ x 8¾	(102)	920
Nice, Seen from Cimiez, 1888, pastel, 17 x 23¼	(84)	3,844
In the Vineyards, Bougival, watercolor, 6 x 8½	(109)	1,100
Underwood, watercolor and gouache, 11 x 8¾	(93)	1,785

1963

Landscape, watercolor, 9¾ x 8	(258)	$2,400
Two Women, pastel, 17¾ x 14	(283)	2,373
Little Girl in a Garden, watercolor, 14 x 10¼	(241)	2,200
Underwood, 1894, watercolor, 11 x 8	(202)	1,000

1964

Portrait of Blanche Pontillon, 1872, pastel, 13 x 10	(354)	700
Reclining Nude, 1891, pastel, 18¼ x 24	(367)	2,902

1965

Little Girl with a Blue Hat, watercolor and gouache, 8¼ x 6¾	(567)	2,034
Skating, 1879, pastel on gray paper, 17½ x 14	(575)	2,073
Gorey Bridge, 1886, watercolor, 7¼ x 9¼	(582)	1,935
Nice, Seen from Cimiez, from the Villa Ratti, 1888, pastel, 17 x 15½	(553)	6,500

1966

Nice, Seen from Cimiez, 1888, pastel, 17 x 15½	(711)	6,000

1967

View of Cimiez, 1888, pastel, 17 x 23¼	(965)	5,085
The Kite, watercolor, 10¾ x 7½	(987)	4,200

1968–July 1969

Little Girl Seated, watercolor, 8 x 4¾	(1183)	3,300
Surroundings of Nice Seen from the Garden of Cimiez, watercolor, 8¼ x 11	(1225)	2,800
Skating, (1879), pastel on gray paper, 17½ x 14	(1246)	3,000
Child in Bed, (1885), pastel, 12 x 16	(1270)	10,080

PAINTINGS

1961–1962

Landscape of the South of France, (1890), 10¼ x 15	(18)	6,215
The Lake of the Bois de Boulogne, Boats and Swans, 17½ x 21¾	(31)	15,927
Little Girls and Horses in the Country, 25½ x 30	(109)	11,000

1963

Angèle the Nurse, Suckling Julie Manet, 1880, 19¾ x 24	(258)	25,000
On the Cliff at Portrieux, 1894, 15 x 21¾	(245)	17,000

1964

Miss Reynolds and Julie Manet, 1884, 27¼ x 23	(416)	33,168
Young Lady Fixing Her Skate, 1893, oil sketch, 13¼ x 10¼	(416)	9,674
Full-Length Portrait of Little Marcelle,[1] 1895, 15¾ x 12½	(416)	8,845

1965

Landscape (Bougival), 1882, 14 x 17	(575)	14,373
Little Girls in the Garden, the Basket, 1885, 23¾ x 29	(575)	40,078
Young Lady with a Green Coat, 1894, 7½ x 29	(624)	17,966

1966

Still Life with Flowers, 21¼ x 12	(698)	2,339
Mezy in Autumn, 1890, 25¾ x 21¼	(742)	13,000

1968–July 1969

Fécamp Harbor, 1874, 18¼ x 21¾	(1106)	124,000
On the Beach, 1873, 9½ x 19¾	(1132)	108,560
Three Children in a Park, on paper laid down on canvas, 21¼ x 25¾	(1045)	10,400

[1] This is the artist's last work.

The Pier, 1875, 9½ x 20½ . . . . (1187) $ 47,200
The Small Boat,[2] 11 x 14 . . . . (1224) 36,600
Compiègne Forest, (1885), 20¾ x 25 . . . . (1235) 26,000
Seascape at Cowes, Isle of Wight, 1875,
 17 x 25½ . . . . (1270) 38,400

Robert Motherwell

(1915-   )

Birthplace: Aberdeen, Washington, U.S.

1932 Enters Stanford University, California.

1935 Enters Harvard Graduate School.

1938-39 Trip to Paris. Spends the summer at the University of Grenoble.

1940 Enters the department of art history and archeology at Columbia University, New York.

1941 Takes a great interest in Surrealist theories. Decides to devote himself to painting—particularly fond of collages.

1942 First exhibition in the international Surrealist exhibition at the Whitelaw Reid Mansion, New York.

1944 Appointed director of *Documents of Modern Art,* Wittenborn and Co., New York—until 1951. First one-man show at Peggy Guggenheim's Art of This Century Gallery, New York. Teaches at Black Mountain College, North Carolina—until 1951.

1946 Exhibits at the Kootz Gallery, New York (again in 1948, 1949, and 1953); the San Francisco Museum of Art; the Chicago Arts Club; and the Galerie Jeanne Bûcher, Paris. Participates in "Fourteen Americans" at the Museum of Modern Art, New York.

1947 Participates in the exhibition "Trois Américains" at the Galerie Maeght, Paris.

1948 With Baziotes and Rothko, founds the school called "Subjects of the Artists."

1949 Opens his own school of fine arts, New York.

1951 Participates in "School of New York" at the Frank Perls Gallery, California; "Abstract Painters and Sculptors in America" at the Museum of Modern Art, New York; "Forty American Painters 1940-1950" at the University of Minnesota, Minneapolis; and the São Paulo Biennial. Teaches at Hunter College, New York.

1952 Participates in the International Exhibition at the Carnegie Institute, Pittsburgh—and again in 1955 and 1958.

1955 Participates in "Cinquante Ans d'art aux Etats-Unis" at the Museum of Modern Art, Paris.

1957 Exhibits at the Sidney Janis Gallery, New York—and again in 1959.

1958 Participates in "New American Painting" at the Museum of Modern Art, New York.

1959 Participates in Documenta II, Kassel.

1961 Retrospective exhibition at the Museum of Modern Art, New York. Exhibits his collages at the Galerie Berggruen, Paris.

1965 Commissioned to execute a mural for the John F. Kennedy Federal Office Building, Boston. Exhibition, "Robert Motherwell, Works on Paper," at the Museum of Modern Art, New York.

Resident in New York.

Sales

WATERCOLORS

1965
Abstraction, tempera and oil on board, 14 x 11 . . . (494) $ 425

1968-July 1969
Composition, ink and gouache on paper,
 11 x 14 . . . . (1237) 900

PAINTINGS

1963
Bull No. 2, on panel, 14 x 22¼ . . . . (272) 1,000
Composition in Black and Gray, on panel,
 21 x 15¾ . . . . (179) 500

1964
Abstraction on a Green Background, 1945, on
 canvas, 15¾ x 11¾ . . . . (372) 1,100
Abstraction, 1946, 18¼ x 14 . . . . (372) 1,000

1965
In Black with Yellow Ocher, 1960, oil on paper,
 30 x 23 . . . . (526) 3,500
Before the Italian Mediterranean, 1961, oil on
 paper, 53 x 42¾ . . . . (526) 4,500
Diary of a Painter, 1958, 70½ x 100¼ . . . . (526) 11,000

1966
Bull No. 2, 1958, on board, 14 x 23 . . . . (651) 1,100
Full Liberty, 1965, oil on paper, 9 x 11 . . . . (729) 150

1967
No. 10, 1958, oil and red pencil on paper,
 11¼ x 14¼ . . . . (889) 375
Beside the Sea No. 36, 1962, oil on paper,
 29 x 23 . . . . (864) 2,250
The Sun, 1944, oil and collage on board,
 32 x 29¾ . . . . (870) 2,400

[2]Sailing on the river Seine near Mallarmé's house.

Otto Müller

(1874–1930)

Birthplace: Liebau, Germany.

1894-96 Attends the Dresden Academy of Fine Arts.

1896-97 Trip to Switzerland and Italy.

1898-99 Stay in Munich.

1903-04 Meets Paula Modersohn-Becker.

1908-09 Meets Rilke.

1910 Meets Kirchner, Schmidt-Rottluff, and Nolde, and becomes a member of "Die Brücke."

1919-30 Teaches at the Academy of Breslau.

1930 Died, Breslau.

Sales

DRAWINGS

1961-1962

Reclining Woman, colored chalk, 14¾ x 22 . . . . (107) $ 492

1964

Self-Portrait with Two Women, India ink and watercolor, 10¾ x 7½ . . . . (428) 984

Young Nude, (1928), blue and yellow chalk, 23 x 17¾ . . . . (385) 1,853

1965

Two Standing Nudes, black and yellow chalk, 27 x 19¾ . . . . (638) 1,107

1966

Gipsy and Children Close to Their Caravan, blue pencil, 26¼ x 19½ . . . . (735) 4,520

1968–July 1969

Seaside, colored pencil and watercolor, 19¾ x 13½ . . . . (1114) 1,984

WATERCOLORS

1961-1962

A Clump of Trees, (1918), chalk and watercolor, 19¾ x 13½ . . . . (24) 1,181

Nude, watercolor and colored chalk, 24¼ x 18¼ . . . (88) 1,058

1963

Young Nude by the Waterside, watercolor, 26¾ x 19¾ . . . . (284) 1,353

1967

Underwood, pastel and colored chalk, 19¾ x 13½ . . . . (998) 1,476

PAINTINGS

1966

Nude Seated in the Underwood, 1924-25, 43½ x 33½ . . . . (792) 12,300

1968–July 1969

Underwood, (1924), 39¼ x 33¼ . . . . (1114) 9,920

Edvard Münch

(1863–1944)

Birthplace: Løten, Norway.

1881-84 Attends the School of Arts and Crafts and Christian Krohg's school of painting, Oslo.

1885 First stay in Paris.

1889 First one-man show in Oslo. A scholarship enables him to spend the winter in Paris.

1890 Enters the studio of Bonnat, Paris. Sees paintings by Pissarro, Seurat, Toulouse-Lautrec, Gauguin, and Van Gogh. First trip to Germany.

1891 Trip to the French and Italian Rivieras. Works under the influence of Neo-Impressionism.

1892 Participates in the exhibition held at the Architektenhaus, Berlin.

1894-96 First engravings, lithographs, and woodcuts. Contributes to the review *Pan,* Berlin. Stage decoration for *Peer Gynt* by Ibsen, at the Théâtre de L'Oeuvre, Paris. Exhibits at the Galerie de l'Art Nouveau, Paris.

1897 Exhibits the "Frieze of Life" at the Salon des Indépendants, Paris.

1898 Goes to Germany. Starts a series of full-length portraits.

1902 Meets Max Linde, who becomes his friend and patron. Executes a book of etchings and lithographs entitled *Aus dem Hause Linde.* Exhibits the "Frieze of Life" at the Secession, Berlin. Exerts a strong influence on the formation of German Expressionism.

1906 Stays at Count Harry Kessler's, Weimar.

1908-09 Leaves Germany. Experiences a period of psychical and nervous trouble and has to spend some time in a Copenhagen hospital. Lightens his colors.

1912 Participates in the Sonderbund exhibition, Cologne.

1915 Executes murals for Oslo University.

1920-22 Trips to Berlin, Paris, and Italy. Exhibition at the Kunsthaus, Zurich.

1927 Exhibits at the National Gallery, Oslo.

1937 Participates in the Paris World's Fair. In Germany, his works are exposed as "degenerate" by the Nazis.

1940 Series of self-portraits.

1944 Died, Norway.

Sales

DRAWINGS

1961-1962

The Sick Young Lady, 1896, colored chalk, 14 x 21 . . . . (106) $7,006

1963

Pegase, India ink, 8¼ x 6½ . . . . (284) 369

1967

May I Come?, (1919), pencil on board, 15¼ x 9½ . . . . (951) 1,016

1968–July 1969

Woman Seated on the Stairs, (1895), pencil and ink, 10¾ x 6½ . . . . (1068) 2,014

WATERCOLORS

1964

Two Young Ladies, 1910, watercolor, 20 x 27¼ ... **(385)** $ 9,605

1967

Seated Young Lady Dressing, (1900), watercolor,
19 x 12¾ .... **(930)**   6,554

PAINTINGS

1961–1962

Bewachsenes Haus, 1902, 36½ x 43½ .... **(88)**   51,660
Autumn Landscape, 1910, 16¾ x 26 .... **(88)**   37,638

1963

Young Lady, 1935, 19¾ x 13 .... **(243)**   4,400

1964

The Public Baths, 1907, 44¼ x 35¼ .... **(367)**   15,478

1965

Young Bather, 1908, 79 x 39¼ .... **(566)**   22,600
Portrait of Ibsen in a Café .... **(579)**   866
Portrait of Colonel Georg Stang, 1889,
35½ x 23¾ .... **(522)**   19,348
Inspiration, 1914, 27 x 35½ .... **(522)**   17,137

1967

Snowy Landscape, 1880, on panel, 5¾ x 7¼ ...... **(985)**   9,480
Woman by the Riverside, 1880, on panel,
8¼ x 6½ .... **(985)**   10,665
Landscape, 1916, 25¾ x 31½ .... **(880)**   27,087

1968–July 1969

Children on the Beach, (1908-09), 22¾ x 27 ..... **(1101)**   22,540
Woman in Greenery,[1] 36 x 28¾ .... **(1232)**   57,000

Gabriele Münter

(1877–1962)

Birthplace: Berlin, Germany.

1897-01   Studies painting in Düsseldorf and Munich.

1902   Attends the "Phalanx," Munich, and meets Kandinsky, its president.

1903-08   Makes a series of trips with Kandinsky.

1909-10   With Kandinsky and Jawlensky, participates in the foundation of the New Association of Artists, Munich, and in the first exhibition of this group.

1911-12   Participates in the first and second exhibitions of "Der Blaue Reiter," Munich.

1913   Participates in the first Herbstsalon, Berlin.

1914   Trip to Switzerland with Kandinsky.

1918-28   Stay in Copenhagen.

1929-30   Trip to France.

[1] Portrait of Miss Maria Agathe Meier.

1931   Settles in Murnau.
1956   Given an award by the city of Munich.
1962   Died.

Sales

WATERCOLORS

1961–1962

A Bunch of Flowers, 1958, watercolor and oil,
11 x 8 .... **(151)** $ 192

1964

Hilly Landscape, 1955, gouache, 23 x 16½ .... **(392)**   640

1966

Flowers, 1947, watercolor, 24 x 17 .... **(805)**   850
Still Life with Flowers, watercolor, 25 x 18¼ ..... **(712)**   836

1968–July 1969

A Bunch of Flowers, 1942, gouache, 25¾ x 18 .... **(1030)**   650

PAINTINGS

1963

Still Life with Flowers, 1961, oil on paper,
23¾ x 17¾ .... **(284)**   369
Mountain Brook, 1909, on board, 12¾ x 17½ ..... **(225)**   1,700
The Country in Blossom, 1910, on board,
13 x 17½ .... **(316)**   3,000
Kandinsky in His Garden, 1912, on board,
13 x 17¾ .... **(316)**   4,000
Hilly Landscape, 1956, oil on cardboard,
16¾ x 21½ .... **(228)**   640

1965

Portrait of a Child, 1940, 25¾ x 21¼ .... **(545)**   679
Hilly Landscape with Houses, on cardboard,
17¾ x 23 .... **(638)**   984
The Basset Hound, oil on paper, 12 x 17¼ .... **(638)**   172
Tutzing (The Red House), 1908, on board,
14 x 18¾ .... **(637)**   3,500
The Blue Garden, 1909, on board, 21¾ x 19 ...... **(539)**   3,500
Still Life, 1910, on cardboard, 20¾ x 15 .... **(566)**   1,040
Landscape, Murnau, 1956, oil on paper, ... **(597)**   590
Vase of Flowers, 1959, oil on paper, 10¼ x 12¼ ... **(618)**   167

1966

Winter Landscape at Murnau, oil on paper,
16¾ x 23¼ .... **(712)**   886
Still Life, (1911), on board, 34 x 19¼ .... **(753)**   4,933
Mountain Village, oil on bister paper,
12¼ x 18¾ .... **(753)**   1,596
Two Trees in a Marshy Landscape, 1934, on
panel, 16 x 13 .... **(784)**   2,250
Winter Landscape, (1955), oil on paper,
23¾ x 17¾ .... **(716)**   886
Landscape at Murnau, 1960, oil on paper,
12½ x 9¾ .... **(775)**   369

1967

Flowers, 1942, oil on paper, 25¾ x 17¾ .... **(870)**   550
A Street in Murnau, (1908-09), on board,
10 x 15¼ .... **(963)**   2,500
Still Life, (1911), on board, 34 x 19¼ .... **(940)**   2,902
Still Life, on cardboard, 10 x 14 .... **(970)**   1,033
Still Life, on board, 8¾ x 12¼ .... **(841)**   1,300
Still Life, on cardboard, 16¼ x 12¾ .... **(910)**   787
Yellow Flowers in a Blue Vase, oil on paper,
24 x 17 .... **(885)**   377

Alpine Village, oil on paper, 12¼ x 18¾ .... **(885)** $1,393

Wintry Landscape, on cardboard, 16¾ x 23¾ ..... **(990)**   590

Flowers, 1951, on cardboard, 28 x 19¾ .... **(930)**   678

1968–July 1969

Mountain Brook, 1909, on board, 13 x 17¾ ...... **(1080)**   3,000

Interior with a Red Table, 1908, on board,
20 x 26½ .... **(1057)**   5,250

Sunset, 1909, on cardboard, 13 x 16¼ .... **(1101)**   2,875

Still Life, on board, 15 x 20 .... **(1208)**   2,750

Kandinsky and Erma Bossi, (1910), 19½ x 27½ .. **(1114)**   3,968

Landscape, 1961, on cardboard, 14¾ x 18½ ..... **(1114)**   496

Pfangasse, Murnau, 1908, on board, 13 x 16 ..... **(1232)**   7,500

Village Church at Murnau, (1946–47), on board,
15 x 18¼ .... **(1232)**   5,750

Dark Still Life with Statuettes, 1910,
17½ x 23¾ .... **(1232)**   3,500

Staffelsee, (1924), on board, 13 x 17½ .... **(1232)**   4,000

After the Storm, 1932, 29 x 36½ .... **(1232)**   5,000

Stilleben mit Vogeldecke, (1911), on board,
26 x 19 .... **(1241)**   3,020

Tanwetter in Moos, oil on paper, 23¼ x 16¼ .... **(1241)**   1,108

Yellow Flowers in a Blue Vase, oil on paper,
24 x 16¾ .... **(1241)**   655

Ben Nicholson

(1894–   )

Birthplace: Denham, Buckinghamshire, England.

1910-11   Attends the Slade School of Art, London.

1912-18   Travels abroad. Meets the Cubists in Paris. Spends a year in Pasadena, California.

1932-33   Trip to France. Joins the group "Abstraction-Création," Paris—until 1935.

1934   Calls on Mondrian in his Paris studio. Participates in the Venice Biennial.

1935   Participates in the exhibition "Thèse, Antithèse, Synthèse," Lucerne.

1936   Participates in the exhibition "Cubist and Abstract Art" at the Museum of Modern Art, New York.

1939   Settles in Cornwall, England.

1952   Given an award by the Carnegie Institute.

1954   Retrospective exhibition at the Venice Biennial, where he wins the Ulissi prize.

1955   Retrospective exhibition at the Tate Gallery, London, and the Musée National d'Art Moderne, Paris.

1956   Given an award by the Guggenheim Foundation, New York.

1957   Given an award by the São Paulo Biennial.

1958   Executes murals for UNESCO, Paris. Settles in Switzerland.

1959   Participates in Documenta II, Kassel.

1966   Retrospective exhibition at the Crane Kalman Gallery, London.

Sales

DRAWINGS

1961–1962

Fresco, 1958, pencil and gouache, 8 x 4¾ and
10 x 7¼ .... **(149)** $ 790

Still Life (Newlyn), 1948, pencil and oil on board,
31 x 19½ .... **(118)**   6,041

Still Life, 1930, pencil and oil on board,
19¼ x 29½ .... **(118)**   4,119

Composition with a Still Life, 1930, pencil and oil,
12 x 14 .... **(74)**   2,197

Painting, 1945, pencil and oil on board,
10 x 15½ .... **(148)**   1,236

Composition with a Still Life, 1948, pencil and oil
on board, 13¾ x 9¾ .... **(74)**   3,295

1963

Still Life, 1945, pencil and oil, 21 x 26¼ .... **(207)**   4,113

Corinth, 1954, pencil, 14¾ x 7½ .... **(268)**   1,042

Assisi, 1955, pencil, 14½ x 18¾ .... **(268)**   658

1964

Still Life, 1952, India ink and pencil .... **(1011)**   1,968

Still Life, 14¼ x 19 .... **(386)**   500

From Red to Black, 1955, pencil and oil, 5¾ x 9 .. **(356)**   1,106

April 1959, pencil on a pink background,
18¾ x 24 .... **(385)**   904

View of Locarno, black lead, 11¾ x 11 .... **(329)**   500

1965

Sutton Veny, 1925, pencil, 14 x 20 .... **(643)**   249

Newlyn Harbor, 1939, pencil, 9 x 14¼ .... **(506)**   719

Rhodes, 1959, pencil and wash, 14 x 18¾ .... **(605)**   813

April 59 (Kos), pencil, 22¼ x 17¼ .... **(566)**   1,017

Menalon Brown, 1962, pencil and wash,
14 x 14¼ .... **(541)**   1,050

1966

White Jug, 1962, pencil, 14½ x 19 .... **(735)**   260

View of St. Ives, 1954, black lead and colored
pencil, 12¾ x 18¾ .... **(681)**   520

Chinese Bottle, 1955, pencil on paper laid down
on canvas, 19¾ x 15¾ .... **(825)**   1,520

A Chapel at Porto San Jacobo, 1956, pencil,
14¾ x 18 .... **(784)**   425

1967

Menalon Brown, 1962, pencil and wash,
14 x 14¼ .... **(889)**   650

Prince and Princess, 1932, pencil and oil on
board, 14¾ x 21¼ .... **(957)**   7,186

Still Life, 1945, pencil and oil on board,
19½ x 20 .... **(957)**   4,422

Snowy Landscape, Yorkshire, 1953, pencil and
wash, 15 x 22 .... **(1003)**   1,422

Still Life, (1956), pencil and yellow wash,
19¾ x 14 .... **(957)**   1,244

1968–July 1969

View from the Window, St. Ives, 1954, pencil and
watercolor, 12¾ x 18¾ .... **(1206)**   2,242

View from a Balcony, pencil, 12 x 11 .... **(1165)**   942

Still Life, 1955, pencil and oil wash, 12¼ x 15 .... **(1074)**   1,369

WATERCOLORS

1967

Composition, 1940–47, gouache, 10 x 10 ....(866) $1,382

Composition, Seen from St. Ives, 1954,
    watercolor, pen, and charcoal, 13 x 19 ....(919)   904

PAINTINGS

1961–1962

Composition, 1933, oil and pencil, 19¾ x 15½ .....(38)   2,334

Painting, 1937, on board, 15¾ x 21¼ ....(118)   1,922

Abstract Composition, (1945), 47 x 35½ ....(118)   3,844

Still Life, Blue, 1949, 52½ x 39¼ ....(118)   7,688

Tuscany (Red-Blue), 1951, cardboard on a
    painted background, 9 x 11 and 13 x 14½ .....(149)   3,318

Off Brown and Off Yellow, 1951, oil and pencil
    on canvas, 37½ x 25¾ ....(149)   4,108

Gwithian, 1955, 41¾ x 41½ ....(38)   7,688

1963

Still Life with a Landscape,[1] 1946, 15½ x 19¼ ....(268)   3,976

Still Life with Jugs, 1929, 15 x 21¾ ....(304)   3,565

Villandry, 1930, on panel, 12¾ x 17¾ ....(207)   1,590

Composition in Red, Yellow, and Blue, 1933,
    pencil and oil on board, 11¾ x 15 ....(304)   2,742

White Relief, 1934, 10 x 7 ....(268)   1,042

Off Brown and Off Yellow, 1951, 38 x 26 ....(200)   3,100

Pavane, 1955, 24 x 24 ....(279)   6,500

Abstract Landscape, 1959, oil and collage on
    board, 21¼ x 23 ....(189)   3,750

Porthcurno, 1960, 42¾ x 59 ....(268)   7,678

1964

Still Life, 1949, on canvas laid down on board,
    32¾ x 18¼ ....(448)   6,000

Still Life, 1951, on board, 20 x 32 ....(461)   6,400

June 1956, relief collage on panel, 19½ x 8¾ .....(431)   2,600

April 1957, on panel, 48¼ x 41¾ ....(431)   14,000

1965

Composition, 1939, 21 x 27¾ ....(643)   2,764

Gwithian, 1955, 42 x 42 ....(637)   15,000

March 1960, oil and pencil on board, 17¾ x 14 ...(584)   3,593

1966

March 1956, relief oil and pencil on panel,
    26¾ x 18¾ ....(735)   3,842

Painting, 1935, 27¾ x 35½ ....(693)   3,455

Painted Relief, 1939, on board, 14¾ x 25¾ ....(693)   2,764

White Relief, 1939, on panel, 34½ x 38¾ ....(678)   8,000

Still Life, 1945, oil and pencil on canvas laid
    down on board, 22½ x 21 ....(709)   7,632

Signal, 1954, oil on paper, 22¾ x 15½ ....(811)   840

Pink Goblets, 1959, 17¾ x 20¾ ....(802)   4,160

February 1962, oil and pencil on board, 24 x 24 ...(751)   6,081

1967

September 4th 1953, oil and pencil on canvas,
    56½ x 26 ....(930)   3,955

June 1959, colored relief, 11 x 11 ....(930)   1,718

The Daily, 1933, on panel, 27 x 17½ ....(940)   4,351

Landscape, 1923, on board, 14 x 21¾ ....(853)   2,757

Composition, 1933, 15 x 22 ....(914)   3,567

Painting, 1934, 27¼ x 39½ ....(853)   4,933

Painting, 1937, 16 x 21¾ ....(869)   4,975

[1]Towednack, Cornwall.

Cornish Port, Still Life, 1944, on panel, 9 x 11 ....(944) $4,208

Tumblers, 1952, collage, oil, and pencil,
    10¾ x 10¼ ....(841)   1,700

1968–July 1969

Aegean Landscape, 1961, engraved panel,
    29 x 70 ....(1057)   16,000

Sidney Nolan

(1917–   )

Birthplace: Melbourne, Australia.

1934   Attends the art school of the National Gallery of Victoria, Melbourne.

1938   Marries Elizabeth Patterson. Exhibits his abstract works at the Contemporary Art Society, Melbourne.

1939   The first exhibition of modern European painting held at the Melbourne Town Hall exerts a great influence on him.

1940   First one-man show in Melbourne. Works under the influence of Klee and Miró.

1942–45   Reverts to representational painting.

1943   Exhibits his landscapes of Wimmera at the Contemporary Art Society, Melbourne.

1947   One-man show in Brisbane, Queensland. Marries Cynthia Hanser and settles in Sidney.

1948   Stage decorations and costumes for *Orphée* by Jean Cocteau, at Sidney University.

1951   Visits France, England, Spain, Portugal, and Italy. One-man show at the Redfern Gallery, London.

1954   Participates in the Venice Biennial.

1955–56   Visits Greece, Turkey, India, Japan, Mexico, and the U.S.

1957   Major retrospective exhibition at the Whitechapel Gallery, London. Studies engraving and lithography in Paris.

1958–60   Stay in the U.S.

Sales

WATERCOLORS

1964

The Goat, watercolor, 10 x 11¾ ....(356) $ 719

1966

Landscape of the Alps, watercolor and gouache,
    10 x 11¾ ....(693)   608

PAINTINGS

1963

Dust Storm at Darwin, 1951, on panel,
    29 x 41¼ ....(207)   1,645

Ned Kelly on Horseback, 1955, on board,
    11¾ x 8 ....(268)   1,042

1964

Crucifixion, on panel, 35½ x 47½ .... (329) $1,200
George Black, 1949, oil on glass, 11¾ x 10 .... (364) 450

1965

Leda and the Swan, oil on paper, 10 x 11¾ .... (643) 691
Leda and the Swan, 1960, on board, 47½ x 35½ ... (584) 1,327

1966

Leda and the Swan, 1959, oil on paper, 11¾ x 9 ... (751) 829
African Study, 1963, oil on paper, 20 x 24½ ...... (709) 638

1967

Landscape, 1952, oil, pastel, and watercolor on
   paper, 8 x 10 .... (853) 696
Ned Kelly, 1956, 48¼ x 36¼ .... (869) 1,797
African Study, 1962, oil on paper, 20 x 24½ ...... (945) 1,327

1968–July 1969

Landscape in the Moonlight, 1960, on board,
   48¼ x 60 .... (1025) 3,221
Tivoli, (1955), oil on paper, 10 x 12 .... (1074) 708
Leda and the Swan, oil on paper, 12 x 10 .... (1206) 755
Leda and the Swan, 1960, on board, 48¼ x 59¼ .. (1206) 4,484
Landscape of Australia, 1950, on board,
   30½ x 24 .... (1130) 5,452

Emil Nolde

(1867–1956)

Birthplace: Tonden, Schleswig-Holstein, Germany.
His family name is Hanssen.

1884–88 Attends the School of Wood Sculpture, Flensburg.

1889 Enters the School of Arts and Crafts, Karlsruhe.

1892 Professor at the Musée de l'Industrie et des Métiers,
St. Gall.

1899 Trip to Paris, where he attends the Académie
Julian.

1901–03 Stays in Berlin, Copenhagen, and Flensburg.
Marries Ada Vilstrup.

1904–05 Impressionist period. Changes his name, Emil Hanssen, to Emil Nolde.

1906 Becomes a member of "Die Brücke." First woodcuts. Paints with Schmidt-Rottluff at Alsen.

1907 Participates in the exhibition of "Die Brücke" in
Dresden-Löbtau, but later breaks away from this
group. First lithographs.

1910 Participates in the exhibition of the "New Secession," Berlin.

1911 Trip to Belgium and Holland. Deeply impressed by
Van Gogh's works. Meets Ensor.

1912 Series of religious paintings. Meets Macke and Jawlensky. Participates in the exhibition of "Der
Blaue Reiter" at the Goltz Gallery, Munich.

1913 Takes part in a scientific expedition in the Pacific.

1927 Jubilee exhibition in Dresden.

1931–34 Issues *Das Eigene Leben* and *Jahre der Kämpfe.*

1937 His works are designated as "degenerate" by the
Nazis.

1941 The German government forbids him to paint.

1952 Participates in the Venice Biennial, where he wins
the engraving prize.

1956 Died, Seebüll, Schleswig-Holstein.

1956–57 Retrospective exhibitions in Bremen, Munich, and
Hamburg.

Sales

DRAWINGS

1964

Giants and Men, 1901, pencil and ink, 4½ x 6 .... (385) $ 240

1965

Weissig Near Dresden, Stormy Weather, pen and
   wash, 9¼ x 11¾ .... (566) 452

1966

Opera Singer, 1909, India ink, 10¼ x 4½ .... (735) 384
Two Calves, India ink, 17¾ x 23¾ .... (775) 517
Village at the Seaside, pen, wash, and watercolor,
   13 x 18¾ .... (808) 3,482

1967

The Couple, India ink, 11¾ x 7½ .... (908) 689
Standing Boy in the Nude, pen and watercolor,
   10 x 5¾ .... (881) 1,520

1968–July 1969

Two Fishermen, 1910, ink and watercolor,
   14 x 19¾ .... (1030) 3,500
The Street, 1920, India ink and watercolor,
   10 x 16 .... (1191) 5,428
Theater Stage, 1910–11, colored ink, 11¾ x 8¾ .. (1209) 1,339
Peasant in a Field, charcoal, 6 x 10¾ .... (1145) 425

WATERCOLORS

1961–1962

The Neighbors, (1910–11), watercolor, 5¾ x 9 ..... (24) 640
Narcissus and Red Amaryllis, watercolor,
   11¼ x 9¼ .... (24) 1,132
Exotic Moon Flowers, watercolor, 18½ x 14 .... (64) 3,000
Windflowers, watercolor, 13½ x 17¾ .... (64) 2,250
Moonflowers, watercolor, 12¾ x 17¾ .... (37) 1,600
The Couple, (1911), watercolor, 8¾ x 11¾ .... (151) 394
Herode et Marianne, 1919, watercolor,
   10¼ x 7¾ .... (151) 517
Quiet Sea, watercolor, 13½ x 18¾ .... (151) 3,444
Two Boats, watercolor, 13 x 18¼ .... (151) 3,075
Sailboats, watercolor and India ink, 6¾ x 6½ ..... (106) 701
Landscape with a Mill, watercolor, 6¾ x 9 .... (106) 746
Rittersporn, watercolor, 13½ x 9¼ .... (106) 1,672
Northern Landscape, 1920, watercolor,
   14 x 19½ .... (69) 3,081
The Steamer in the Open Sea, (1920), watercolor,
   9 x 10¾ .... (88) 1,304
Stor und Pfeilschwanze, (1925), watercolor,
   14 x 18¾ .... (149) 1,580
Japanese Theater, 1927, watercolor, 8¼ x 11¾ ... (107) 787

Sunset at the Seaside, (1930), watercolor,
14½ x 21 .... **(88)** $4,526

A Farmyard in the Sunset, watercolor,
12¾ x 17¾ .... **(94)**   1,279

1963

Landscape Full of Figures, watercolor,
17¾ x 10 .... **(179)**   300

Nude with Red Hair, watercolor, 18 x 11½ ...... **(239)**   1,444

Still Life with Orchids, watercolor, 13¼ x 18¾ ... **(228)**   2,337

Still Life with Flowers, (1940), watercolor,
13¼ x 18 .... **(297)**   1,673

Stormy Clouds, watercolor, 7¼ x 5¾ .... **(284)**   394

Aquarium, watercolor, 14¼ x 18¾ .... **(249)**   1,000

1964

Sailboat, (1913-14), watercolor, 10½ x 13½ ...... **(428)**   1,181

Two Natives, 1913-14, watercolor, 19¼ x 14 ..... **(385)**   1,266

Still Life with Flowers, 1920, watercolor,
13¼ x 18 .... **(385)**   3,390

Seaside, (1920), watercolor, 13¼ x 18 .... **(349)**   2,660

Recumbent Tiger, watercolor, 13¼ x 18¼ .... **(380)**   1,722

The Viking, (1930), watercolor, 7¼ x 12¾ .... **(385)**   2,531

Flowers, watercolor, 18¾ x 13¾ .... **(454)**   1,935

Nude, gouache, 10 x 8 .... **(354)**   1,500

The Sunflowers, watercolor, 17¼ x 12 .... **(392)**   2,214

The Parrot, watercolor, 18¾ x 14 .... **(470)**   3,444

1965

The Towboat in Hamburg Harbor, watercolor
and India ink, 11 x 16½ .... **(545)**   2,403

Yellow Flowers, watercolor, 18¾ x 13½ .... **(545)**   4,809

Flowers, watercolor, 13½ x 18¾ .... **(637)**   2,300

Sunflowers, watercolor, 17¾ x 14 .... **(637)**   5,500

Two Fish, (1914), watercolor, 14 x 18¾ .... **(541)**   1,800

Landscape, 1918, watercolor, 13¾ x 18¾ .... **(616)**   2,240

Gondolas in Venice, 1925, watercolor, 13 x 18¾ ... **(618)**   2,706

Native and Child, watercolor, 19 x 13 .... **(597)**   1,107

Landscape with Thatch-Roofed Cottages,
watercolor, 13 x 18½ .... **(522)**   5,390

Woman Seated at a Table, watercolor,
14 x 18¾ .... **(549)**   3,444

Alpine Lake, watercolor on blotting paper,
13¼ x 17½ .... **(561)**   1,000

The Actor, watercolor, 11¾ x 9 .... **(638)**   1,033

1966

Portrait of a Native, watercolor, 19½ x 15 .... **(712)**   2,583

Native's Head, watercolor, 20 x 15½ .... **(775)**   1,476

Boats, (1914), watercolor, 9¼ x 11 .... **(735)**   2,712

Portrait of a Spaniard, watercolor, 19¼ x 13¾ .... **(716)**   738

Head of a Little Girl, watercolor, 14¾ x 12 .... **(665)**   2,100

Vase of Flowers, watercolor, 14 x 18¾ .... **(784)**   2,100

Woman and Flowers, (1920), watercolor,
17¾ x 13 .... **(784)**   3,750

April Moon, (1925-30), watercolor, 13½ x 19 ... **(792)**   3,690

Fleur de Lys, watercolor, 14¾ x 12¼ .... **(792)**   2,952

Still Life with Flowers, watercolor, 6 x 9 .... **(739)**   1,722

Red Clouds, watercolor, 12¾ x 19½ .... **(739)**   2,214

Rapperswill-bei-Zürich, watercolor, 18¼ x 13 .... **(753)**   2,612

The Windmill, watercolor and pastel, 6¾ x 9¼ .... **(689)**   1,520

1967

A Bridge in Dresden, watercolor, 13 x 18¼ .... **(908)**   3,444

Double Portrait, watercolor, 13 x 17¾ .... **(908)**   3,444

Portrait of a Dancer of the South Seas,
watercolor, 20 x 15 .... **(930)**   1,808

Two Figures, (1913-14), watercolor, 13½ x 19½ ... **(889)** $1,900

Dusk, watercolor, 13¼ x 18¼ .... **(910)**   4,059

Landscape, (1908), watercolor and pen, 6¾ x 11 .. **(910)**   738

Red Roses, watercolor, 13½ x 10 .... **(1004)**   3,000

Dahlias, watercolor, 10¾ x 9 .... **(970)**   2,091

The Schooner, watercolor, 10¾ x 8 .... **(990)**   2,952

Rapperswill-bei-Zürich, watercolor, 18¼ x 13 .... **(951)**   2,031

The Windmill, watercolor and pastel, 6¾ x 9¼ .... **(985)**   1,185

1968–July 1969

A Boat on the Beach, watercolor, 14 x 18¾ .... **(1188)**   3,800

Landscape, 1908, watercolor, 14 x 19 .... **(1134)**   2,242

A Boat Under an Orange-Yellow Sky, (1912),
watercolor, 9 x 10¾ .... **(1114)**   3,720

Flowers, watercolor, 10¼ x 9 .... **(1114)**   3,920

The Old Windmill, watercolor, 14 x 19 .... **(1114)**   2,976

The Young Couple, 1913, watercolor on a
lithograph .... **(1114)**   9,920

Self-Portrait with a Hat, (1917), watercolor and
India ink, 8¼ x 6¼ .... **(1194)**   1,984

Marshy Landscape, (1920), watercolor,
12 x 18¼ .... **(1068)**   5,428

Child's Head, watercolor, 10¾ x 7¼ .... **(1101)**   782

Head of a Little Girl, watercolor, 10¾ x 8¾ ..... **(1101)**   1,150

Landscape, watercolor, 12 x 18¼ .... **(1101)**   4,255

Still Life with Flowers, watercolor, 18¾ x 13¼ ... **(1101)**   3,450

Flowers, watercolor, 14 x 18¾ .... **(1080)**   2,900

Steamers, watercolor, 6½ x 10 .... **(1030)**   4,500

Seaside, in the Evening, watercolor, 14 x 18¾ ... **(1018)**   3,500

Native's Head, watercolor and India ink,
19½ x 14¼ .... **(1090)**   2,133

Landschaft mit Korndiernen, (1912), watercolor,
12¾ x 18¼ .... **(1232)**   4,000

Orris and Buddha Statuette, (1930), watercolor,
14¼ x 19 .... **(1232)**   8,000

Vase of Flowers, (1930), watercolor, 15 x 18 ..... **(1246)**   6,250

The Red House, (1920), watercolor, 13¼ x 18 .... **(1246)**   5,500

Zwei Huernacheren, watercolor, 13¾ x 18½ ..... **(1248)**   4,750

Salome's Dance of the Veils, (1908), watercolor,
12¾ x 10 and 13½ x 10 .... **(1268)**   3,480

PAINTINGS

1961–1962

Palm Trees, 29 x 34¾ .... **(88)**   13,038

The Flower Garden, 1926, 29 x 34¾ .... **(88)**   24,846

White Dahlias, 1948, 35½ x 27 .... **(88)**   15,006

Man and Woman, 1910, 14¼ x 19 .... **(70)**   7,900

1963

Russian II, (1913), 27 x 24 .... **(279)**   18,000

***Landscape with Two Thatch-Roofed Cottages at
Nightfall,*** (1925), 27 x 27½ .... **(228)**   4,920

1964

Clouds, 24 x 18¼ .... **(470)**   9,348

Landscape, 13½ x 19 .... **(461)**   2,400

Head, 1913, 30½ x 26¾ .... **(385)**   4,294

The Two Cossacks, 1914, 29¼ x 35 .... **(385)**   21,696

Portrait of Gustav Schiefler, 1915, 32¾ x 29 ...... **(385)**   14,916

1965

Ada Nolde Sewing, 1906, 22 x 22 .... **(566)**   12,204

The Mill, (1924), on panel, 16¾ x 12¾ .... **(637)**   6,000

Landscape, 18¾ x 25¼ .... **(517)**   1,065

1966

Horsewoman on a Red Horse, on cardboard,
   16 x 14 .... (739) $ 3,444
Seaside, (1910), 27¾ x 31¾ .... (686)   11,609
Summer Clouds, 1913, 29 x 35 .... (735)   19,888
Face and Flowers, (1915), 24 x 18¾ .... (776)   9,000
The Holy Virgin and the Child, 35½ x 29 .... (770)   21,300
Landscape with Red Clouds, 31 x 31½ .... (816)   14,760
D Sea, (1930), on panel, 28½ x 39½ .... (750)   17,966

1967

View of Etna, 1905, 15¾ x 22 .... (970)   4,551
Seaside, (1910), 29 x 34¾ .... (970)   13,776
Vase of Flowers and Statuette, 24 x 18¾ .... (940)   7,545
Clouds, 1918, 24 x 18¼ .... (982)   9,480

1968–July 1969

The Alchemist, (1911-13), 24 x 16¾ .... (1132)   35,872
Still Life E, (1914), 28¾ x 31¼ .... (1232)   32,500
The Three Wise Men, (1911), 20¼ x 16¾ .... (1232)   30,000
Tropengut, (1915), 29 x 34½ .... (1232)   45,000

Georgia O'Keeffe

(1887–   )

Birthplace: Sun Prairie, Wisconsin, U.S.

1904-05 Attends the school of the Chicago Art Institute.

1907-08 Attends the Art Students League, New York.

1912-16 Devotes herself to teaching.

1917 First private exhibition—of abstract works—at Stieglitz' "291" Gallery, New York. Marries Alfred Stieglitz.

1920 Reverts to representational painting.

1923 Retrospective exhibition at the Anderson Gallery, New York.

1927-29 One-man show at Stieglitz' Intimate Gallery, New York.

1931 Exhibits at An American Place Gallery, New York—until 1950.

1937 Exhibits at the Downtown Gallery, New York—until 1961.

1943 Retrospective exhibition at the Chicago Art Institute.

1946 Retrospective exhibition at the Museum of Modern Art, New York.

1947 Elected member of the National Institute of Arts and Letters.

1953 Retrospective exhibition at the Dallas Museum of Fine Arts, Texas.

Sales

WATERCOLORS

1967

Goat's Horn with Red, 1945, pastel, 27¾ x 31½ ... (952) $14,000

PAINTINGS

1967

The Dune, 1930, 10 x 24 .... (952) $ 8,000
Coxcomb, (1931), 20 x 17 .... (952)   6,000

José Clemente Orozco

(1883–1949)

Birthplace: Ciudad Guzman, Mexico.

1908-14 Attends the National Academy of Fine Arts.

1910 First exhibition—of drawings—at the Academy of Fine Arts.

1916 First one-man show in Mexico.

1917-18 First trip to the U.S.

1922-27 Executes his first murals for the National Preparatory School.

1923 Marries Margarita Valladares.

1925-26 One-man show in Paris.

1927-32 Second trip to the U.S.

1929-31 Exhibits in Paris, Vienna, New York, and Los Angeles. Murals for the School of Social Research, New York.

1932-34 Murals for the Palace of Fine Arts, Mexico.

1940 Murals for the Supreme Court of Justice and for the old church of the Hospital of Jesus, Mexico.

1946-47 Wins the National Prize in Arts and Sciences. Exhibition at the Palace of Fine Arts, Mexico.

1947-48 Murals for the open-air theater of the National School of Teachers, Mexico, and for the Chamber of Deputies, Guadalajara.

1949 Died.

Sales

DRAWINGS

1961-1962

Study for a Fresco, charcoal on green paper,
   17¾ x 23¾ .... (44) $ 450

1966

Victory, 1944, India ink, 14¾ x 10¾ .... (784)   1,300

1968–July 1969

Flamenco Dancers, ink, 12 x 15 .... (1246)   1,100

WATERCOLORS

1967

Five Heads, gouache, 11 x 15¾ .... (1004)   3,250

PAINTINGS

1963

Self-Portrait, 1938, 28¾ x 23¾ .... (225)   8,000

1964

The Coming of Quetzalcoatl, (1932-34), study for
a fresco, 20 x 26 . . . . (354) $7,000

1968-July 1969

Street Corner, 22¼ x 16 . . . . (1231)   6,000

Amédée Ozenfant

(1886-1966)

Birthplace: St. Quentin, France.

1906   Attends the Académie de la Palette, Paris.

1915   Founds the review *L'Elan,* to which such artists as
Dunoyer de Segonzac, Picasso, Max Jacob, and
Apollinaire contribute.

1918   With Le Corbusier, issues *Après le Cubisme,* the first
manifesto of Purism.

1920-25   With Le Corbusier, sets up the review *L'Esprit
Nouveau.*

1928   Issues his famous book *Art* (Paris).

1931   Issues *Leben und Gestaltung* (Potsdam and Berlin)
and *Foundations of Modern Art* (London and New
York).

1932   Sets up his own school of art, the Académie Ozenfant, Paris.

1935-38   Stays in London, where he founds a second Ozenfant Academy.

1936-37   Teaches art history and aesthetics at the French Institute and at the French Lycée, London.

1938   Goes to the U.S. and settles in New York. Delivers
lectures in American universities such as Yale,
Columbia, Cornell, and Harvard—until 1955.

1939   Founds the Ozenfant School of Art, New York.
Teaches at the New School, New York—until
1945.

1949   Promoted to the rank of Officer of the Legion of
Honor.

1952-53   Re-issue of *Foundations of Modern Art.*

1955   Returns to France. Founds the Atelier Ozenfant in
Cannes.

1956-61   Participates in the São Paulo Biennial and in several
international exhibitions.

1966   Died.

Sales

WATERCOLORS

1968-July 1969

*Still Life: Bottles and Decanters on a Black
Background,* 1926, gouache and charcoal,
25¼ x 19½ . . . . (1255) $1,240

PAINTINGS

1961-1962

Still Life: Bottles, 1926, 28½ x 23¼ . . . . (140) $3,570

Jug on a Gray Background, (1926-28), on panel,
15 x 19 . . . . (164)   357

Still Life with a Jug, 19¾ x 29 . . . . (114)   760

1963

Still Life: Bottles and Glasses, 1927, 31½ x 25¼ . . (210)   1,097

Still Life with a Violin, 20½ x 17 . . . . (216)   356

1964

Sailboats, on panel, 10 x 13 . . . . (375)   180

1965

The Regattas, 13 x 16¼ . . . . (547)   160

1966

The Violin, 18¼ x 15 . . . . (811)   1,220

Composition, on panel, 10 x 13 . . . . (655)   164

Geometrical Objects, 1916, 28¾ x 35½ . . . . (689)   3,731

1967

Still Life, 1926, 29 x 23¾ . . . . (995)   2,220

White Jug on a Gray Background, on panel,
15 x 19½ . . . . (995)   820

Window, 28½ x 36½ . . . . (941)   640

1968-July 1969

Sailboats, on panel, 13 x 10 . . . . (1018)   425

Autumn in the Mountains, 18 x 15 . . . . (1018)   1,250

Julius Pascin

(1885-1930)

Birthplace: Widdin, Bulgaria. (Born Julius Pincas.)

1891-92   His family settles in Bucharest.

1902   Studies painting in Vienna.

1903   Stays in Munich, where he contributes to such reviews as *Jugend* and *Simplicissimus.*

1905   Decides to sign his name Pascin instead of Pincas.
Goes to Paris and settles in Montparnasse.

1907   Meets Hermine David, his future wife. First one-
man show at the Paul Cassirer Gallery, Berlin.

1908   Attends the academies of Montparnasse. Participates in the Salon d'Automne, Paris—until 1912.

1910   Commissioned by Cassirer to illustrate a book by
Heinrich Heine.

1911   Participates in the Secession exhibition, Berlin.

1912-13   Participates in the Sonderbund exhibition, Cologne,
and in the Armory Show, New York. Exhibits at
the Galerie Berthe Weil, Paris.

1914   Goes to London and then to New York.

1914-20   Settles in the U.S. during World War II. Visits the
southern states and Cuba.

1918   Marries Hermine David.

1920	Becomes an American citizen. Returns to Paris, where he exhibits at Berthe Weil's, Georges Bernheim's, and the Salon des Indépendants. Meets Lucy Krohg.
1921	Visits North Africa—and again in 1924.
1923	Exhibits at the Brummer Galleries, New York.
1925	Trip to Italy. Exhibits at the Flechtheim Gallery, Düsseldorf.
1926	Travels to Egypt, Palestine, and Tunisia.
1927-28	Returns to New York for a while, followed by Lucy Krohg.
1929	Trip to Spain and Portugal. Signs a contract with the Galerie Bernheim, Paris.
1930	Exhibits at the Knoedler Galleries, New York. Died, a suicide, on the opening day of his exhibition at the Galerie Georges Petit, Paris.
1931	Memorial exhibition at the Downtown Gallery, New York, and the Galerie Lucy Krohg, Paris.

Sales

DRAWINGS

1961–1962

The Three Women,[1] charcoal, 18¾ x 23¼ .... (71) $2,600

Reclining Woman, charcoal and watercolor, 10 x 14 .... (164)   686

Seated Woman in the Nude, charcoal with pastel lights, 12¾ x 9¾ .... (36)   920

Figures, pen and watercolor, 11½ x 16¾ .... (114)   1,200

A Scene in a Brothel, watercolor, 18¾ x 21¾ ...... (41)   2,100

Seated Young Woman, 1904, pencil and watercolor, 11¾ x 10 .... (37)   1,500

Women Meeting, pencil, wash, and watercolor, 6¾ x 9½ .... (80)   800

(I Hope You'll) Enjoy Your Dinner!, pen and pencil, 10¾ x 7¾ .... (152)   425

In a Park, India ink, 9 x 11¼ .... (128)   357

A Lively Place in the Casbah, heightened wash, 8¼ x 8¼ .... (27)   700

The Siesta, wash with watercolor lights, 6½ x 9 .... (27)   640

Reclining Nude, black lead, 3½ x 6¾ .... (106)   181

Portrait of a Young Woman, black lead, 9 x 11½ .... (168)   180

Riverside, black lead, 4¼ x 6¾ .... (154)   240

Model Resting, black pencil, 17 x 22 .... (171)   640

Reclining Nude, black lead, 8¼ x 7½ .... (171)   320

1963

Interior with Figures, ink with watercolor lights, 8½ x 9 .... (247)   1,782

Interior with a Couple,[2] charcoal and India ink, 14½ x 19½ .... (220)   1,175

Country Party, pen, 4 x 6 .... (234)   142

Group of Women, pencil, 7½ x 9½ .... (179)   375

Reclining Nude, Back View, charcoal, 16¼ x 21¾ .... (220)   746

Nude, Back View, pen, 9 x 5½ .... (269)   133

Nude, pen and watercolor, 8¾ x 8½ .... (179)   500

Reclining Nude, India ink, pastel, and watercolor, 13 x 10¼ .... (224)   900

Seated Nude, pencil, 13½ x 7¼ .... (309)   461

Girls Resting, pen, 9½ x 19¼ .... (315) $ 439

The Market (recto), *Reclining Nude* (verso), pen and gouache, 12¼ x 19 .... (315)   2,084

A Scene in Cuba, pencil, 6½ x 9¼ .... (283)   509

Havana, pen heightened with watercolor, 15 x 18¼ .... (198)   1,700

The Ladies . . . , India ink, 12 x 15 .... (254)   280

Parisians Walking, 1923, 7½ x 10 .... (254)   320

Girl Friends, pencil and watercolor, 8 x 7 .... (208)   375

The Happy Family, (1925), pencil and ink heightened with watercolor, 13½ x 16¾ ..... (202)   1,000

1964

Reclining Nude, (1920), India ink and black lead, 15¾ x 21 .... (385)   859

Mother and Child, India ink heightened with watercolor, 11¾ x 7¼ .... (385)   610

The Whisperers, 1926, India ink on gray paper, 10 x 12¾ .... (354)   900

Rebecca Standing, 1928, charcoal, 19½ x 9 .... (416)   553

Job, India ink, 10¼ x 6½ .... (346)   240

A Village, Panama, pen and wash, 9½ x 12¼ ..... (416)   498

Road Works in Panama, pencil and watercolor, 7½ x 10¼ .... (368)   774

The Crew in Cuba, colored pencil, 6¼ x 8 .... (378)   814

The Public Garden, colored pencil, 8 x 10 .... (441)   610

The Gossips, pencil, 10 x 7 .... (374)   525

The Girls, pen, India-ink wash, and colored-pencil lights, 6 x 7¼ .... (399)   500

Figures, ink, 11½ x 18¾ .... (329)   450

Seated Young Woman, pen and wash, 14¾ x 10½ .... (329)   650

Seated Nude, charcoal and chalk, 17½ x 12¼ .... (362)   296

Figures, pen, 11 x 7½ .... (394)   840

The Three Women, charcoal, 18¾ x 23¼ .... (340)   2,100

1965

Interior with Figures, (1917), ink and watercolor, 8¾ x 9 .... (494)   1,200

Meetings, 1918, two drawings on one sheet, 8 x 8¼ and 3 x 4 .... (566)   418

The Two Girl Friends, pen, 16¾ x 21¾ .... (277)   560

The Family Picture, pen, 9½ x 11 .... (627)   520

Seated Young Girl, pencil, 17¾ x 12¾ .... (696)   1,000

Figures, ink and pencil, 11¾ x 7¾ .... (606)   600

A Scene in a Park in Panama, charcoal, 7½ x 9½ .... (624)   636

A Group of Nudes, pen and wash, 20¾ x 16¾ .... (522)   1,106

Hermine David and Her Friends, India-ink wash, 9½ x 12¾ .... (617)   949

Putney Night, pen, 12¾ x 14¾ .... (567)   565

Putney Night; Portofino Club Night,[3] 12¾ x 14¾ and 12½ x 15¼ .... (491)   720

The End of a Watercolor Painter, 5¾ x 4½ ...... (625)   380

Long Live Mr. Rodo, (1926), India ink on gray paper, 10 x 12¾ .... (539)   900

The Quays, colored pencil, 6½ x 8 .... (523)   410

Figures in a Park, charcoal and colored pencil, 6½ x 11 .... (582)   332

The Café, ink heightened with watercolor, 9 x 16¾ .... (535)   1,106

---

[1]Presumed portraits of Hermine David, Lucie Krohg, and an unknown person.

[2]Katherine Dudley and the painter Ganso.

[3]Two drawings intended for the book *Fermé la nuit* by Paul Morand.

1966

Seated Woman, pencil and charcoal, 23¾ x 23 ... (790) $2,275

Reclining Nude, pencil, 9½ x 11¾ .... (670) 360

Three Women on a Bench, pen and watercolor,
8 x 8 .... (815) 608

Les Trois Grâces chez Vénus, pen, 19 x 25¼ ..... (824) 820

Young Nude Holding Back Her Tunic, pencil and
sepia, 19½ x 15 .... (824) 370

The Prostitutes, pencil, 19 x 23¾ .... (757) 719

A Scene in a Brothel, pen, 8 x 11¾ .... (784) 500

Women, ink with watercolor lights, 19½ x 24½ ... (784) 1,500

Three Girls, pen, 6½ x 4½ .... (735) 678

Street Scene in Havana, pen and colored pencil,
7¼ x 12¼ .... (741) 1,600

A Scene in a Brothel, pencil and watercolor,
8 x 8¾ .... (702) 1,100

Finetti, (1906-07), ink and pencil, (No. 36),
11¾ x 8 .... (665) 375

Christmas 1907: Big Hit—The "Mahlzeit" Toy,
pen and wash heightened with red pencil ... (706) 200

Seated Young Woman in the Nude, black chalk,
13¾ x 9½ .... (677) 380

*Georges Kars Playing the Violin Beside Hermine
David,* India ink with pastel lights,
10¼ x 8¼ .... (743) 440

Die Meister vom Stuhle, pen, 10¾ x 6¾ .... (743) 320

Die Brüder von Stuhle, 10 drawings, pen
heightened with watercolor and colored
pencil, 8¼ x 5½ .... (743) 2,000

The Reprobation, pen, watercolor, and varnish,
6 x 8 .... (726) 900

Portrait of Wilhelm Uhde, pencil, 11¾ x 9½ ...... (798) 262

Morocco, pen, 17¾ x 23¾ .... (665) 1,500

Gestwicki's Trial (recto), *Portrait of the Artist*
(verso), pencil and pen, 13 x 8 .... (648) 400

Study of a Nude, pencil, 12¼ x 10 .... (757) 525

The Pub, pencil, 6¾ x 8¾ .... (691) 400

The Moulin-Rouge, pen and wash, 7¼ x 9 .... (805) 475

Hermiette and Madeleine, 1929, charcoal,
25¼ x 19½ .... (689) 1,658

The Greedy Children (recto), *Study of a Girl*
(verso), pencil and watercolor, 15 x 19 ...... (689) 884

1967

Two Reclining Nudes, pencil and watercolor,
10 x 13½ .... (931) 1,130

Reclining Nude, pencil and watercolor,
10 x 12¾ .... (987) 2,100

Reclining Woman in the Nude, pencil, 12 x 18¼ .. (857) 560

Seated Nude, pencil, 6¾ x 6¾ .... (876) 120

Seated Nude, India ink, 13 x 8¾ .... (1004) 950

Nude, pencil and colored chalk, 11 x 16¾ .... (970) 664

Standing Nude, ink and watercolor, 12½ x 9¼ .... (889) 950

Standing Nude, Back View, black lead,
18¾ x 12¼ .... (919) 904

The Two Girl Friends, stick of greasepaint,
19 x 24 .... (911) 1,900

The Two Girl Friends, India ink and watercolor,
12¾ x 12¾ .... (919) 1,085

Two Young Ladies Seated on the Floor, pencil
and watercolor, 7¼ x 7¼ .... (1004) 2,200

Lively Interior, pencil and watercolor, 9 x 11 .... (1004) 1,700

A Seaman with Two Prostitutes, pencil and
watercolor, 7½ x 5¼ .... (939) 608

At the Café, 5¼ x 7¼ .... (978) 600

A Scene in a Night Club, India ink and
watercolor, 6 x 7¼ .... (967) $1,130

At the Bar, 1922, pencil, 8 x 10¼ .... (978) 920

At the Bal Tabarin, (1927), pencil, 7½ x 10 .... (870) 425

The Public Garden, pen, 7½ x 9½ .... (934) 300

The Light Cart, colored pencil, 6¾ x 8¼ .... (883) 840

A Peasant Asleep in His Cart, Panama, pen and
colored pencil, 5¾ x 9 .... (881) 774

Afternoon in the Park, pen, 6½ x 9 .... (881) 498

Two Peasants in Panama, pen and watercolor,
10 x 7½ .... (985) 450

Figures in a Park in Panama, pen and wash,
8¼ x 7½ .... (985) 427

A Walk in Cuba, stick of greasepaint, 8 x 10 ..... (965) 814

A Scene in Cuba, pencil and watercolor, 5¾ x 5 . (1004) 900

At the Horse Races, India ink, 6¾ x 6½ .... (883) 960

The End of the Watercolor Painter, India ink,
5¾ x 4½ .... (859) 171

1968–July 1969

Three Young Girls, pencil and watercolor,
diameter 8, ... (1145) 950

Berthe, (1909), pencil, 6¼ x 9 .... (1145) 325

The Girl Friends, pencil, 16½ x 13¼ .... (1113) 1,640

Reclining Nude, pencil and watercolor,
9½ x 12¾ .... (1193) 2,726

Reclining Nude, pen and watercolor lights,
7¼ x 11 .... (1078) 440

Seated Nude, charcoal, 10 x 9½ .... (1043) 640

Back View of a Nude, 1930, charcoal, 23¼ x 17 .. (1068) 708

A Study of a Reclining Nude, black lead and
colored chalk, 12¼ x 9¾ .... (1191) 708

Reclining Nude, pen and watercolor, 6¼ x 14.... (1030) 1,000

Seated Nude, pen and watercolor, 17¾ x 13¾ ... (1030) 1,900

Studies of a Woman, sepia ink, 14¾ x 23 .... (1134) 590

La Chemise relevée, pen and wash, 11¾ x 8¼ ... (1134) 519

Nude in an Armchair, charcoal and pastel,
19¾ x 15 .... (1026) 3,300

Beauty Care, ink, 11 x 14¼ .... (1116) 380

Women at the Bar, ink with watercolor lights,
6½ x 9 .... (1134) 1,180

A Scene in Cuba, black lead, 8¾ x 11¾ .... (1174) 448

A Scene in the Caribbean Islands, pen and
watercolor, 10 x 13¼ .... (1080) 1,900

At the Café, black lead, 6½ x 8¼ .... (1127) 552

Portofino Night, pen, 12½ x 15¼ .... (1127) 920

At the Tuileries, pencil, 4½ x 6¾ .... (1051) 280

Family Wrangles, pen, 4¾ x 7 .... (1030) 450

The Entrance of the Village, pencil, 7½ x 10 ..... (1051) 660

Music Party, pen and watercolor, 10 x 14 .... (1191) 708

The Departure, India ink, 7½ x 10¾ .... (1191) 826

Caricature of Charles Laborde, pen, 14 x 10 ..... (1231) 250

Seated Man, 1912, wash, 8 x 10¼ .... (1238) 320

Otto Feldmann, 10½ x 8 .... (1238) 380

Conversation in the Street, pencil, 8½ x 6½ ..... (1240) 528

At the Bar, India ink, 7¾ x 8½ .... (1240) 576

The Conversation, India ink and watercolor,
5 x 6¼ .... (1240) 1,248

The Payment, India ink, 8½ x 7½ .... (1240) 624

Afternoon on the Coast, black pencil and
watercolor, 9 x 11¾ .... (1240) 912

Two Arab Women and a Man with a Cigar,
pencil and watercolor, 6 x 7½ .... (1240) 912

Reclining Woman, green chalk, 12½ x 9½ .... (1241) 403

Standing Nude, pencil, 9 x 6¾ . . . . (1241) $ 240

Old Piedre Market, New Orleans, pencil and
wash, 7½ x 10 . . . . (1246) 1,200

Wind Blowing, ink and wash, 7¾ x 9¼ . . . . (1246) 1,200

Seated Young Girl, pencil and wash, 10¼ x 7¾ . . (1246) 2,000

Seated Woman, India ink and wash, 13½ x 10¼ . (1248) 1,750

Smiling Seated Man, black lead, 10¾ x 8 . . . . . . (1260) 350

Nude, black lead, 9¼ x 7¼ . . . . (1268) 1,276

Reclining Woman, India ink and stick of
greasepaint, 10¾ x 8 . . . . (1268) 974

Driving to Panama in a Cart, pencil, 6½ x 8 . . . . . (1272) 768

Study of a Prostitute (recto), 10 x 7, *Three
Women Seated at Table* (verso), 5½ x 9½,
brush and ink . . . . (1272) 480

Two Women Lying on a Bed, pencil, 14½ x 19½ . (1272) 1,248

The Conversation, pencil, 15 x 18¾ . . . . (1272) 864

The Animals of the Farm, pencil, 7¾ x 9¾ . . . . . . (1273) 428

WATERCOLORS

1961–1962

Young Lady with a Bunch of Flowers, 1919,
watercolor, 5¾ x 3½ . . . . (26) 220

Cendrillon, watercolor, 18¾ x 24½ . . . . (32) 1,100

The Family, watercolor, 8¼ x 11 . . . . (119) 800

The Conversation, watercolor, 8 x 6 . . . . (73) 620

The Loan Office, watercolor, 9 x 9½ . . . . (155) 560

A Scene in Havana, watercolor, 10¼ x 8 . . . . (160) 880

A Scene in a Street in Havana, watercolor,
6½ x 11 . . . . (171) 1,400

The Young Designer, watercolor, 17 x 12¼ . . . . . . (171) 1,200

Reclining Woman in the Nude, watercolor,
10 x 9 . . . . (116) 1,140

On the Bench, watercolor, 6 x 8 . . . . (102) 700

Intimacy, pastel, 11 x 8½ . . . . (143) 1,311

1963

Scenes in Havana, two watercolors, each
6 x 8¾ . . . . (276) 1,100

Studies of Negroes, South Carolina, (1915),
watercolor, 10 x 9¼ . . . . (315) 768

Disheveled Nude, pastel, 17¾ x 21¾ . . . . (210) 2,057

Women, gouache and India ink, 11¾ x 17 . . . . (246) 260

Woman and Child, pastel, 21½ x 14¼ . . . . (283) 4,633

The "Ladies" in the Drawing Room, watercolor,
11¾ x 15¾ . . . . (298) 2,760

1964

The Flower Girls, watercolor, 11 x 8¼ . . . . (398) 1,760

Three Girls in a Park (recto), gouache, *Woman
and Child* (verso), ink, 9½ x 9 . . . . (416) 1,161

Dancers in Havana, watercolor, 7½ x 6½ . . . . (399) 700

Landscape of Havana, watercolor, 8 x 10¼ . . . . . . (409) 1,100

Street Scene in Havana, watercolor, 7¼ x 9 . . . . . . (340) 1,300

The "Ladies" in the Drawing Room, watercolor,
10 x 8 . . . . (377) 1,356

Seated Young Woman, round-shaped watercolor,
diameter 3¼ . . . . (450) 330

Women, watercolor, 8 x 8¼ . . . . (471) 1,469

Seated Woman, pastel, 24 x 18¼ . . . . (399) 2,500

1965

Cuba, 1924, watercolor, 10¼ x 14¼ . . . . (518) 3,400

Women Seated at a Table, watercolor, 7½ x 6¾ . . (611) 960

The Flower Girls, watercolor, 10¾ x 8¼ . . . . (586) 1,360

Monologue, watercolor, 14 x 10½ . . . . (632) 1,300

1966

The Couple, watercolor, 29 x 24½ . . . . (717) $2,200

A Scene in Tunisia, watercolor, 15 x 18 . . . . (742) 2,400

1967

Seated Woman, pastel, 20 x 16¾ . . . . (952) 4,500

A Scene in Cuba, watercolor, 9 x 10¾ . . . . (952) 800

Loan Office, watercolor, 9½ x 10 . . . . (858) 580

Entertainment, watercolor, 4 x 6½ . . . . (934) 600

1968–July 1969

Study of a Man, 1913–14, gouache and ink on
board, 21¾ x 14 . . . . (1018) 2,000

In a Public Garden, watercolor, 8 x 5¾ . . . . (1039) 800

Cuba, watercolor, 8¼ x 11¾ . . . . (1051) 880

Street Scene in Winter, watercolor, 8 x 5¾ . . . . . (1191) 1,227

The Family Party, watercolor, 4¾ x 6¾ . . . . (1026) 1,200

Szep No. 496, watercolor, 16¾ x 11 . . . . (1216) 2,500

In the Drawing Room, Marseilles, (1930), pen
and watercolor, 17½ x 22 . . . . (1246) 5,750

Woman in a Pink Bodice, watercolor,
17½ x 21¾ . . . . (1252) 3,420

Scene in Havana, watercolor, 13 x 16¼ . . . . (1256) 4,900

Woman, watercolor, 11¾ x 11½ . . . . (1268) 1,276

Harbor, watercolor, 9½ x 7½ . . . . (1268) 1,114

PAINTINGS

1961–1962

Little Girl with a Pink Bodice, on cardboard,
18¼ x 15 . . . . (18) 11,878

Young Lady, on cradled cardboard, 24½ x 20 . . . . . (18) 16,498

Young Lady with a Green Chair, (1922),
34½ x 28¾ . . . . (88) 17,220

The Two Women, 24 x 18¼ . . . . (109) 6,600

Seated Young Lady, 25¾ x 21¾ . . . . (160) 8,220

1963

The Dark-Haired Woman, 32 x 25 . . . . (316) 17,000

Young Woman Seated in an Easy Chair, (1924),
31½ x 25¼ . . . . (247) 13,162

Seated Nude, Back View, 1924, 25¾ x 21¼ . . . . . . (255) 8,774

The Two Young Girls, 1926, 31¾ x 25¾ . . . . (210) 19,194

The Toilette, 25¾ x 21¼ . . . . (232) 3,842

The Toilette, 25¾ x 21¼ . . . . (306) 7,300

*Seated Woman, a Black Ribbon Around Her
Neck,* 25¾ x 21¼ . . . . (293) 12,400

1964

Seated Nude, 1907, 28½ x 21 . . . . (335) 7,000

Seated Nude, 25¼ x 20½ . . . . (458) 13,930

Nude on a Bed with a Dressing Gown, on board,
16¾ x 21¼ . . . . (454) 9,674

Nudes: One Seated, the Other Standing,
28½ x 23 . . . . (458) 8,706

Two Nudes, 25¾ x 32 . . . . (340) 12,200

Reclining Nude, 19¾ x 24 . . . . (340) 7,100

Reclining Nude, 20 x 26½ . . . . (453) 2,488

Seated Woman, 1912, on canvas laid down on
panel, 25¼ x 19½ . . . . (416) 16,584

Seated Young Woman, 36 x 29 . . . . (448) 13,500

Seated Woman, 36½ x 29 . . . . (448) 14,000

The Blue Bodice, on cardboard laid down on
canvas, 14¾ x 14¼ . . . . (371) 4,000

A Jew in Green, 1920, 25 x 20¼ . . . . (416) 4,975

Seated Woman, 25¾ x 21¼ . . . . (471) 7,684

Nude on a Lounge Chair, 29¼ x 25 . . . . (454) 13,820

The Two Girl Friends, on cradled panel,
19¾ x 15 .... (341) $4,000

Woman with a Blue Bodice, on cardboard,
16 x 11½ .... (401)   6,000

1965

Recling Nude, 20 x 25¼ .... (516)   10,900

Reclining Nude, 18¼ x 22 .... (582)   2,211

Standing Red-Haired Woman, Her Breast Bare,
on board, 12¾ x 8 .... (494)   2,400

The Two Girl Friends, on board, 19¾ x 14¾ ...... (633)   8,500

Portrait of a Seated Woman, 25¾ x 21¼ .... (583)   3,192

Seated Woman, 29 x 23¾ .... (628)   12,188

Seated Nude, 35½ x 31½ .... (569)   9,718

1966

Two Seated Young Women, on board,
25¾ x 21¼ .... (776)   14,500

Nude in an Armchair, on board, 24 x 21¾ .... (776)   8,500

Woman Resting, 23¼ x 31 .... (776)   11,000

Portrait of a Woman, 24 x 18¼ .... (672)   5,820

A Jew in Green, 1920, 25 x 20½ .... (689)   3,040

Portrait of an Englishwoman, 18¼ x 15 .... (809)   5,000

Reclining Model, 32 x 25¾ .... (793)   14,420

Woman Lying in an Armchair, 29 x 22¼ .... (727)   14,600

Portrait of John Barber, 1925, 40 x 30½ .... (776)   16,000

1967

Half-Nude Woman, 25¾ x 21¾ .... (901)   12,000

Young Nude in an Armchair, 32 x 25¾ .... (918)   14,012

Standing Nude, 25 x 20¾ .... (940)   5,804

The Model with a Stool, 25¾ x 21¼ .... (938)   9,674

Nude, 1922, on board, 16¾ x 21¼ .... (988)   5,474

Seated Nude with Black Stockings, 25¾ x 20¾ ... (921)   3,620

Young Lady with a Flowery Hat, (1927),
31½ x 25 .... (954)   27,000

Seated Young Lady, on cradled panel,
24¾ x 21¼ .... (864)   13,500

Portrait of Hermine David, on canvas laid down
on board, 17¾ x 13½ .... (954)   10,500

Seated Woman, 25¾ x 21¼ .... (965)   10,170

1968–July 1969

Portrait of a Woman, (1905–08), 29 x 24 .... (1056)   15,000

The Café-Concert, 1908, on board, 28¼ x 23¼ ... (1176)   29,000

Seated Young Lady, Half Nude, (1924–25),
36½ x 29 .... (1152)   36,000

Marietta, 1927, 36½ x 29 .... (1051)   22,200

The Lady in Green, (1927), 36½ x 25¾ .... (1152)   30,000

Portrait of a Seated Young Lady, (1928),
32 x 25¾ .... (1057)   25,000

Nude Leaning on Her Elbow, on cardboard,
17¾ x 21¾ .... (1117)   9,300

Girl Seated in an Easy Chair, 32 x 25¾ .... (1126)   17,346

The Two Friends,[4] 25¾ x 32 .... (1106)   18,000

The Two Girl Friends, peinture à l'essence,
25¾ x 19¾ .... (1225)   9,600

The Toilette, 25¾ x 21¼ .... (1226)   18,600

Hermine in a Large Blue Hat, 1923, 29 x 23½ ... (1232)   23,500

Jew in Green, 1920, 25½ x 21 .... (1248)   7,000

Nude Lying on a Sofa, 32 x 23¾ .... (1268)   29,000

[4]Sold in Paris in March 1964 for $12,200.

Max Pechstein

(1881–1955)

Birthplace: Zwickau, Germany.

1900–02 Attends the Dresden Academy of Fine Arts.

1906 Meets the artists of "Die Brücke" and becomes a member of the group. Spends the summer with Kirchner at Goppeln near Dresden.

1907 Trip to Italy. Meets Van Dongen in Paris.

1908 Stays in Berlin.

1909 Spends the autumn with Heckel and Schmidt-Rottluff at Dangast.

1910 His works refused by the Berlin Secession, he contributes to the foundation of the New Secession.

1911 With Kirchner, sets up the MUIM Institute, Berlin. Second trip to Italy.

1912 Leaves "Die Brücke."

1919 Travels in Switzerland, Italy, and the south of France.

1923 Becomes a member of the Preussischen Akademie der Künste, Berlin.

1933 Excluded from the Preussischen Akademie der Künste. Not allowed to exhibit his works nor to go abroad.

1945 Teaches at the Hochschule für Bildende Künste, Berlin.

1955 Died, Berlin.

Sales

DRAWINGS

1961–1962

Reclining Woman in the Nude, Back View, 1910,
pen and watercolor, 18¼ x 23¼ .... (151) $ 234

Bathers, 1913, India ink and watercolor,
8¾ x 15 .... (106)   203

A Summer Day in Montreux, 1923, colored chalk,
24½ x 19¾ .... (106)   203

Nude, India ink, 19 x 14½ .... (100)   228

Dancer, colored chalk, 8 x 6½ .... (101)   90

The Windmill, India ink and brush, 6½ x 8 .... (24)   84

1963

Woman with a Cigarette, (1913), India ink,
3¾ x 5¼ .... (211)   42

Seated Nude, pen, 13¼ x 15½ .... (228)   135

Seated Nude, colored chalk, 21 x 15¾ .... (284)   221

1964

Fishing Harbor, 1913, pencil and watercolor,
14¼ x 18¼ .... (448)   1,100

Portrait of a Man, 1918, pencil and watercolor,
15½ x 11¾ .... (448)   750

Head of a Young Lady, 1920, pencil, 13½ x 10¾ .. (385)   113

1965

Seaside and Sailboats, 1911, colored chalk,
6½ x 8 .... (566)   271

Seated Nude, 1918, pen and watercolor,
17¼ x 13½ .... (545)   255

1966

The Tussle, (1910), pencil and India ink, 6½ x 8 .. (677)   84

Bathers on the Beach, 1912, pen, 10¾ x 14¼ ..... (739)   295

Nidden Beach, pen and watercolor, 8 x 8 .... (735)   362

Seated Nude, charcoal and wash, 23¾ x 17½ . . . . . **(712)** $ 308

Still Life with Flowers and a Snail, 1927, pen,
25¾ x 20 . . . . **(775)** 221

1967

Bathers, 1910, pencil and watercolor, 13 x 17 . . . . . **(931)** 384

Bather, 1912, black chalk and watercolor,
16¾ x 13 . . . . **(908)** 221

Head III, 1919, India ink and watercolor,
21¼ x 17 . . . . **(910)** 394

Mother and Child on the Beach, 1919, charcoal
and watercolor, 12¾ x 16 . . . . **(881)** 359

Circus Scene, 1920, India ink and watercolor,
11¼ x 8¾ . . . . **(931)** 305

1968–July 1969

Two Nudes, 1917, India ink, 13¾ x 17¼ . . . . **(1090)** 298

Bather, 1912, India ink, 10¼ x 14 . . . . **(1134)** 236

Woman with a Fur Coat, 1917, pen, 22 x 15¾ . . . . **(1209)** 1,017

The Boat, 1911, colored chalk, 4½ x 5¾ . . . . **(1114)** 211

Portrait of a Young Lady, 1920, pencil and sepia,
14 x 10¾ . . . . **(1203)** 396

The Viaduct, colored pencil and India ink, 5 x 6 . **(1030)** 325

Gymnastics Time, pencil and ink, 5½ x 8¼ . . . . . . **(1094)** 37

WATERCOLORS

1961–1962

Clouds in the Rain, 1923, watercolor,
19½ x 25¾ . . . . **(131)** 418

Landscape with Houses and Gardens, (1925),
watercolor, 19½ x 23¾ . . . . **(88)** 517

Die Negerin, watercolor, 4½ x 6½ . . . . **(128)** 110

Fishermen Unloading Their Catch, 1930,
watercolor and gouache, 19¾ x 24½ . . . . **(94)** 295

1963

Clown, 1910, watercolor, 10¾ x 8 . . . . **(208)** 360

Landscape with a Sailboat, 1917, watercolor and
pencil, 17½ x 24 . . . . **(220)** 124

Reclining Nude, Back View, watercolor and India
ink, 17½ x 23¼ . . . . **(197)** 456

1964

Still Life with Red Poppies, 1917, watercolor,
19½ x 15 . . . . **(385)** 192

Landscape, 1918, watercolor and pencil,
14¾ x 18½ . . . . **(354)** 2,000

Fishermen's Boats Out at Sea, 1920, watercolor,
20¾ x 28¼ . . . . **(392)** 1,230

1965

Bather, 1911, watercolor and India ink,
11½ x 15½ . . . . **(566)** 316

Landscape, 1922, watercolor, 19½ x 25½ . . . . **(587)** 760

Mountainous Landscape, 1925, watercolor,
18¾ x 28 . . . . **(624)** 415

Sailboats, 1931, watercolor, 19 x 24 . . . . **(624)** 525

Seated Nude, watercolor and pencil, 17 x 13½ . . . **(514)** 247

Monte Rosso al Mare, watercolor and India ink,
17 x 24½ . . . . **(545)** 622

1966

Fishermen's Village, 1933, watercolor,
17½ x 24¼ . . . . **(712)** 1,009

The Village Street, 1932, gouache and watercolor,
21 x 29¾ . . . . **(713)** 3,250

1967

Two Bathers, (1910), India ink and watercolor,
11¼ x 8¾ . . . . **(906)** $ 418

Harvesters, 1924, India ink and watercolor,
15¾ x 19½ . . . . **(908)** 369

View of Montreux, 1925, black chalk and
watercolor, 15¾ x 19½ . . . . **(908)** 640

Fluvial Landscape, 1930, watercolor and gouache,
18¾ x 24 . . . . **(889)** 1,400

Nude at the Seaside, India ink and watercolor,
11 x 17¾ . . . . **(990)** 492

Heavy Sea, 1935, watercolor and gouache,
20½ x 27 . . . . **(990)** 1,033

Wintry Landscape, watercolor, 23½ x 29 . . . . **(1004)** 1,600

1968–July 1969

Fisherman No. 2, 1911, tempera, 12¾ x 16 . . . . . . **(1145)** 1,000

Three Bathers, 1913, watercolor, 15 x 14¼ . . . . . . **(1114)** 422

Nude Combing Her Hair, 1924, watercolor,
24¾ x 19½ . . . . **(1114)** 694

Head of a Young Lady, 1922, watercolor and
tempera, 26½ x 19¾ . . . . **(1146)** 836

Village Street, 1925, watercolor, 19½ x 29 . . . . **(1080)** 2,100

View of Positano, 1925, pen and watercolor,
23 x 29 . . . . **(1209)** 1,860

Coastal Scene, 1923, watercolor, 17¾ x 22¾ . . . . **(1246)** 2,100

Landscape with a Sailboat, pencil and watercolor,
17 x 23¼ . . . . **(1246)** 1,900

PAINTINGS

1961–1962

In the Morning: Fishermen's Houses at Nidden,
1909, 19¾ x 25¾ . . . . **(106)** 2,531

Noon in Summer, 1911, 29¾ x 39½ . . . . **(106)** 2,215

Still Life with Orris and Lilies, 1918, 27¾ x 25¾ . . **(106)** 1,266

Fishing Fleet, (1919), 35½ x 45 . . . . **(37)** 5,000

A Castle at Collioure, 1931, 19¼ x 24½ . . . . **(4)** 1,230

The Bathers, (1912-14), 31¾ x 27 . . . . **(37)** 2,750

Still Life with Fruit, 1913, 35½ x 35½ . . . . **(31)** 2,334

The Javanese Shawl, 48½ x 36 . . . . **(88)** 4,772

1963

Seegang, 1921-30, 31¼ x 39 . . . . **(202)** 2,750

The Storm, 31½ x 39 . . . . **(225)** 2,000

1964

The Rescuers' Boat, 17¾ x 23¾ . . . . **(470)** 2,706

Portrait of a Man with an Opera Hat, 1912,
23¾ x 15¾ . . . . **(385)** 678

Landscape with a Dune (recto), *Seated Young
Lady* (verso), 32½ x 40 . . . . **(385)** 3,729

The Sunflowers, 1912, 31¼ x 27 . . . . **(448)** 6,250

Still Life, 1913, 38½ x 29¾ . . . . **(410)** 787

Landscape, 1919, 31 x 38¾ . . . . **(354)** 8,000

Still Life, 1920, 27¾ x 31½ . . . . **(380)** 1,427

Fishing Boats in the Sunset, 1923, 31½ x 38½ . . . . **(380)** 2,583

Nude, 32¾ x 24¼ . . . . **(428)** 1,230

Reclining Nude, 29 x 38¾ . . . . **(368)** 967

Landscape, on board, 16¾ x 22½ . . . . **(354)** 3,000

1965

Sunrise at the Seaside, 1921, 39½ x 31½ . . . . **(566)** 1,672

Red Houses, with a Mill, (1910), 27 x 32 . . . . **(637)** 5,000

Still Life with African Statuettes, 1918,
26¾ x 35½ . . . . **(618)** 4,428

Nude, 32 x 25 .... (539) $ 1,750
Dusk Over the Village, 1930, 27¾ x 31½ .... (507) 4,000
Springtime, 27¾ x 31½ .... (637) 5,500

1966
Four Nudes, the Evening, on the Beach, 1911,
   27¾ x 31½ .... (735) 7,684
Vase of Flowers, 1912, 31½ x 28 .... (753) 5,804
Still Life, 1913, 58 x 41 .... (686) 4,699
Still Life, 1913, 58 x 41 .... (776) 4,200
The Reeds, 1921, 39½ x 31¼ .... (808) 5,224
Evening, 31½ x 39½ .... (739) 3,936

1967
Child's Head, (1920), 21¼ x 20 .... (915) 2,460
Young Woman at Her Dressing Table, 1921,
   40 x 31¾ .... (970) 9,840
Bather, 1922, 27¾ x 31½ .... (998) 1,599
Fishing Boats, 26½ x 30¼ .... (963) 3,500

1968–July 1969
Sea Tale, 1920, 47½ x 35¾ .... (1173) 16,100
The Boy with a Balloon, 1917-19, 23¾ x 19½ .... (1208) 4,500
Portrait of a Woman, 1919, 31½ x 27¼ .... (1114) 3,968
Ripe Corn, (1922), 19¾ x 22½ .... (1126) 6,443
Fishing Boats on the Strand, (1925), 31¾ x 38¾ . (1085) 3,720
Still Life with Fruit, 1946, on cardboard,
   19¼ x 25¼ .... (1090) 1,042
Still Life, 22½ x 19¾ .... (1105) 1,216
Seated Nude, 32 x 24 .... (1070) 3,304
After the Bath, 1921, 30½ x 39 .... (1232) 12,000

Constant Permeke

(1886–1952)

Birthplace: Antwerp, Belgium. (Attends the Academies of Bruges and Ghent.)

1909 Settles at Laethem-St. Martin.

1912-14 Lives in Ostend. Impressionist period. Gradually turns toward Expressionism—under the influence of the painter Servaes. Seriously wounded during World War I, he is taken to England.

1916 Settles at Chardstock, Devonshire.

1918-25 Returns to Belgium. Lives successively in Antwerp and Ostend.

1925 Series of seascapes. Settles permanently at Jabbeke, near Bruges. Becomes the most famous Flemish Expressionist of his generation.

1936 Starts to sculpt.

1940-45 Series of nudes.

1947 Retrospective exhibition at the Musée d'Art Moderne, Paris.

1950-52 Participates in the Venice Biennial.

1952 Died, Jabbeke.

Sales

DRAWINGS

1961–1962
The Young Man, stumped charcoal, 24½ x 18¾ .... (73) $ 600

1964
Standing Nude, pencil and charcoal, 7¼ x 5½ .... (368) 193
Back View of a Nude, black chalk and wash,
   17¾ x 7¾ .... (368) 304

1965
Seated Nude, (1928), charcoal, 13¼ x 9 .... (566) 231
Seated Nude, 1940, red chalk, 25¾ x 19¾ .... (589) 500
Peasant, 31 x 23 .... (636) 960

1966
Peasant Working, charcoal, 14¼ x 13 .... (782) 680
Nude, 1925, 59¼ x 45½ .... (700) 3,000
Portrait of Sam Saltz, 1928, 19¾ x 17¾ .... (708) 1,100

1967
Reclining Nude, 26½ x 38¾ .... (846) 1,600
Young Peasant in a Field, 59¾ x 34 .... (867) 4,800
Standing Nude, 59¼ x 36¾ .... (867) 4,400
Reclining Nude, 1951, stick of greasepaint,
   9¾ x 12¾ .... (919) 124

1968–July 1969
Portrait of a Woman, 13½ x 10 .... (1022) 600
Nude, 39½ x 29¾ .... (1065) 3,200
The Wrestlers, charcoal .... (1218) 640

WATERCOLORS

1961–1962
Nude, pastel, 63¼ x 47½ .... (80) 320

1965
The Woman with a Basket, pastel and charcoal,
   62 x 39½ .... (636) 18,500

1968–July 1969
Reclining Nude, pastel on board, 29¾ x 38 ...... (1134) 2,360

PAINTINGS

1961–1962
The Farmyard, 25¾ x 31½ .... (20) 6,952
Interior of a Cattle Shed, 31½ x 39½ .... (21) 5,372
Seascape .... (54) 4,728
Head of a Fisherman, on panel, 23 x 17 .... (116) 780
The Willows, on cardboard, 12¾ x 18¾ .... (73) 3,240
The Cow, 21½ x 28½ .... (164) 604

1964
The Farmyard, 25¾ x 31¾ .... (461) 5,120
Undulating Sky, 19¾ x 27¾ .... (427) 2,000
Fluvial Landscape, 21 x 26¼ .... (479) 2,122

1965
Yellow and Blue Seascape, 23 x 29¼ .... (636) 2,200
Moonrise, 21 x 30 .... (636) 4,000
The Cloud, 38¾ x 50¾ .... (636) 12,400
Summer Daybreak, 65 x 70½ .... (636) 16,000
A Scene on a Farm, 25½ x 31½ .... (486) 2,992
Flemish Winter Landscape, 22 x 31¼ .... (645) 5,059
Seascape, 19¾ x 27¾ .... (536) 1,200
A Farm in Flanders, 19½ x 27¾ .... (589) 2,400
Red Roofs, 25¾ x 30 .... (636) 5,400

1966

The Farmyard, 19½ x 23½ .... (823)	$ 2,992
A Horse in a Farmyard, 25¼ x 29¼ .... (823)	4,080
Seascape, 15¼ x 23¼ .... (698)	2,938
The Man with a Sickle, 20½ x 31¼ .... (753)	2,031
Flemish Landscape, 19¾ x 27¾ .... (767)	2,400
Boerenkop, 23¼ x 19½ .... (782)	3,600
Autumn Landscape, 31½ x 39½ .... (680)	8,000

1967

Seascape, 1924, on board, 20 x 24 .... (962)	3,200
Jabbeke Village, 25¾ x 31½ .... (871)	6,400
Wintry Landscape, 21¼ x 29¼ .... (1001)	3,400
Young Peasant in a Field, 59¾ x 34 .... (871)	4,800
Seascape, 23¾ x 29¾ .... (949)	700

1968–July 1969

The Farm, 29¾ x 39½ .... (1065)	7,800
Fishing Harbor, 29 x 41½ .... (1065)	4,800
Seascape, 23¾ x 31½ .... (1150)	4,800
Old Barn, 21¾ x 31½ .... (1150)	7,600

Henri Person

(1876–1926)

Birthplace: Amiens, France. (Attends the Ecole Nationale des Beaux-Arts, Paris, in the studio of Cormon.)

1905   Enters the Société des Artistes Français, Paris.

1907   Makes a trip to Turkey with Signac.

1909   Participates in the Salon des Indépendants, Paris.

1922   Gathering works by painters who worked at St. Tropez (such as Signac, Camoin, Cross, and Dunoyer de Segonzac), he succeeds in exhibiting them in a municipal building—the future Musée de l'Annonciade.

1926   Died, Paris.

1961   An important retrospective exhibition—with a catalog preface by Dunoyer de Segonzac—at the Galerie de Paris, Paris, secures wider public recognition of this hitherto little-known painter.

Sales

DRAWINGS

1968–July 1969

Sailboats Alongside a Quay, India ink, 8¾ x 11 .. (1242)	$ 220

WATERCOLORS

1963

Port-Cros, 1904, watercolor, 14 x 9¾ .... (281)	678

1966

Sailboats in the Harbor, watercolor, 9 x 41 .... (741)	$ 600
The Harbor, watercolor, 5¾ x 7¾ .... (803)	320
The Harbor, watercolor, 8¼ x 11¾ .... (663)	320

1968–July 1969

Antibes, watercolor, 10 x 15¾ .... (1162)	270
Maritime Landscape, 1908, watercolor, 10 x 15½ .... (1089)	360
Harbor of the South of France, watercolor, 5¼ x 7½ .... (1242)	400
St. Sophia, watercolor, 8 x 6¾ .... (1242)	280
Antibes Cove, 8¼ x 1¼, watercolor .... (1242)	320
The Departure of the Cargo, watercolor, 7¼ x 1¼ .... (1242)	170
St. Tropez Lighthouse, watercolor, 7¼ x 10 ..... (1242)	240
Les Martigues, watercolor, 7¼ x 10 .... (1242)	520
The Tartans, watercolor, 7½ x 10¼ .... (1242)	560
Grimaud, watercolor, 16 x 22 .... (1242)	1,200
Istanbul Harbor, watercolor, 8 x 10 .... (1242)	180
Village in Provence, watercolor, 8¼ x 10 .... (1242)	460
Sailboats in Istanbul, watercolor, 9 x 6¼ .... (1242)	540
The Bosporus, watercolor, 8 x 10 .... (1242)	280
Provence, watercolor, 14 x 15¾ .... (1242)	200
Notre-Dame de la Garde, Marseilles, watercolor, 8¼ x 8 .... (1242)	180
Toulon Harbor in the Morning, watercolor, 7½ x 10 .... (1242)	640
Sails Aground, watercolor, 8¼ x 11¾ .... (1242)	230
The Red Sailboat, watercolor, 8¼ x 10¼ .... (1242)	500
The Golden Horn in Istanbul, watercolor, 8¾ x 10¼ .... (1242)	240
Sky Effect, watercolor, 8¼ x 10¼ .... (1242)	220
The Boulevard des Batignolles, (1913), watercolor, 9 x 12¾ .... (1242)	400
St. Tropez Gulf in the Evening, watercolor, 8¾ x 11¾ .... (1242)	300
The Mine, watercolor, 8¼ x 14 .... (1242)	120
Boats Alongside a Quay, watercolor, 12¼ x 8¼ .. (1242)	960
Sunset Over the Sea, watercolor, 9 x 14 .... (1242)	400
Montauban: The Musée Ingres, watercolor, 9½ x 14¼ .... (1242)	280
The Provençal Mas, watercolor, 9½ x 14 .... (1242)	400
Grimaud, watercolor, 9½ x 14 .... (1242)	240
Istanbul: The Bosporus, watercolor, 10¼ x 15¾ . (1242)	800
The Valentri Bridge in Cahors, watercolor, 10¼ x 14 .... (1242)	900
Albi, watercolor, 10 x 14 .... (1242)	800
The Storm, watercolor, 10¼ x 14 .... (1242)	640
The Calanque, watercolor, 9½ x 14 .... (1242)	800
The Pink Sky, watercolor, 9½ x 14 .... (1242)	260
The Vineyards, watercolor, 10¼ x 16 .... (1242)	720
The Fountain, watercolor, 8¼ x 14 .... (1242)	260
Poissy, watercolor, 8¼ x 10¾ .... (1242)	340
Sun Breaking Through the Clouds, watercolor, 9½ x 14 .... (1242)	300
St. Tropez: Boats Alongside a Quay, watercolor, 8¼ x 11¾ .... (1242)	450
Provençal Village, watercolor, 10¼ x 16¼ .... (1242)	1,320
Creek at Sunrise, pastel, 8¼ x 11¾ .... (1242)	260
Riverside, watercolor, 10¼ x 15¾ .... (1242)	500
River Lined with Trees, watercolor, 10¼ x 15¾ .. (1242)	640
The Parasol Pines, pastel, 30½ x 37¼ .... (1242)	1,240
Antibes, pastel, 30½ x 37¼ .... (1242)	1,800
Constantinople, watercolor, 10 x 15¾ .... (1262)	320

PAINTINGS

1963

Sailboats in Antibes Harbor, 29 x 36½ . . . . (198) $1,240

1965

Mediterranean Landscape, 32½ x 47 . . . . (580)   260

1968–July 1969

The White Sail, on panel, 7¼ x 10 . . . . (1242)   600

Mediterranean Village, 13½ x 17½ . . . . (1242)   500

Marseilles Harbor, 11 x 15½ . . . . (1242)   800

Sailboats in the Harbor, 17½ x 25¼ . . . . (1242)   660

Chapel Ste. Anne, 17½ x 25¼ . . . . (1242)   1,000

Morning Haze Over Antibes, 17½ x 25¼ . . . . (1242)   910

Les Canoubiers Cove, 21 x 25¾ . . . . (1242)   1,600

The Tartans, 13 x 17½ . . . . (1242)   2,400

St. Tropez, 13 x 17½ . . . . (1242)   600

The Red Rock, 13 x 17½ . . . . (1242)   600

The Fishing Boats, on panel, 13 x 17½ . . . . (1242)   800

Surroundings of Ste. Maxime, on panel,
    14¾ x 17½ . . . . (1242)   700

Paris, on panel, 13 x 17½ . . . . (1242)   1,160

Morning Over Toulon Harbor, (1913), 29 x 36 . . . (1242)   9,200

"14 Juillet" at St. Tropez, on panel, 13 x 17½ . . . (1242)   760

The Lighthouse, 13 x 17½ . . . . (1242)   420

The Tartan, on panel, 17½ x 13 . . . . (1242)   560

The Fishing Boats, 29¾ x 36¾ . . . . (1242)   3,300

St. Tropez: The East Wind, on panel, 13 x 17½ . . (1242)   640

The Stranded Boat, 13 x 15¾ . . . . (1242)   480

St. Tropez Harbor, 10¾ x 15¾ . . . . (1242)   560

La Garoupe, 17½ x 23¾ . . . . (1242)   900

Harbor of the South of France in the Morning,
    20½ x 29¼ . . . . (1242)   800

The White Sailboat, 35½ x 45½ . . . . (1242)   5,000

Les Andelys, 17½ x 25¼ . . . . (1242)   400

Country in Spring, 17½ x 23¾ . . . . (1242)   600

La Ponche, 26½ x 32½ . . . . (1242)   3,600

Les Canoubiers Cove, 25¾ x 32 . . . . (1242)   2,700

The Outer Harbor, 23¾ x 29 . . . . (1242)   3,400

The Fishermen's District at St. Tropez,
    23¾ x 29 . . . . (1242)   1,600

Ste. Maxime Seen from St. Tropez, 29¼ x 36¾ . . (1242)   2,000

Boulevard des Batignolles, 29¾ x 36¾ . . . . (1242)   3,200

St. Tropez, 35½ x 45¾ . . . . (1242)   3,200

St. Tropez: The Fishermen's Harbor, on panel,
    7¼ x 10 . . . . (1242)   1,240

Sunset Over the Garrigue, on panel, 7¼ x 10 . . . . (1242)   360

The Flower Bed in Blossom, on panel, 7¼ x 10 . . (1242)   880

Sunset Over St. Tropez Harbor, on panel,
    7¼ x 10 . . . . (1242)   600

St. Tropez, on panel, 7¼ x 10 . . . . (1242)   400

Village Beneath the Mist, on panel, 7½ x 10 . . . . . (1242)   800

The Beach, on panel, 7¼ x 10 . . . . (1242)   700

The Tempest, on panel, 7½ x 10 . . . . (1242)   720

Antibes, on panel, 7¼ x 10 . . . . (1242)   1,000

The Sailboat, on panel, 7¼ x 10 . . . . (1242)   400

The Parasol Pines, 7¼ x 10 . . . . (1242)   2,400

Grimaud Gulf, 35¾ x 46¾ . . . . (1242)   4,600

St. Tropez: La Ponche, 30 x 39½ . . . . (1242)   3,200

Meadow at Daybreak, 24 x 29 . . . . (1242)   310

The Harbor, 13 x 17½ . . . . (1242)   1,600

Village by the Waterside, 21¼ x 25¾ . . . . (1242)   700

Landscape Near St. Tropez, 24½ x 29 . . . . (1242)   560

The Great Trees, 17½ x 23¾ . . . . (1242)   1,000

The Citadel, 26½ x 33¼ . . . . (1242)   800

Jean Peske

(1870–1947)

Birthplace: Golta, Russia.

1885–86   Attends the Fine Arts School of Odessa.

1887   Goes to Warsaw, where his master Gerson advises him to study in Paris.

1892   Attends the Académie Julian, Paris. Meets Albert André, Louis Valtat, Paul Sérusier, and Félix Fénéon. Admires Toulouse-Lautrec above all. Exhibits with the Nabis at the Galerie Le Barc de Boutteville, Paris.

1913   One-man show at the Galerie Devambez, Paris.

1947   Died.

Sales

DRAWINGS

1967

The Hut at the Seaside, India-ink wash,
    19¾ x 25¾ . . . . (919) $ 407

The Great Tree, India ink, 10¼ x 8 . . . . (876)   36

1968–July 1969

Landscape, India ink and watercolor,
    15½ x 11½ . . . . (1038)   70

Seascape, India ink, 19¾ x 25¾ . . . . (1060)   384

Notre-Dame from the Quays, India-ink wash,
    18¾ x 22½ . . . . (1122)   90

The Net Menders, colored pencil, 9½ x 12¼ . . . . (1247)   102

WATERCOLORS

1961–1962

Riverside, 1917, watercolor, 11¾ x 17¾ . . . . (90)   80

Favière Beach (Var), watercolor, 8½ x 13¾ . . . . (36)   64

1963

Trees by the Waterside, watercolor, 14¾ x 12¼ . . . (278)   36

1964

Marseilles: The Old Harbor, 1916, watercolor,
    11½ x 15 . . . . (336)   66

1966

Provençal Village, 1912, watercolor, 11¾ x 18½ . . . (769)   170

The Boat, watercolor, 8¾ x 14 . . . . (781)   96

1967

The Thatch-Roofed Cottage, watercolor,
    18¾ x 25¼ . . . . (1007)   280

The Great Trees Near the Pond, watercolor,
    31½ x 25 . . . . (850)   360

The Great Trees, watercolor, 31½ x 25 . . . . (926)   600

1968–July 1969

Surroundings of Amiens, watercolor, 25 x 19 . . . . (1072)   120

Landscape of Vendée, watercolor, 23 x 15½ . . . . . (1087)   180

The Beautiful Tree, watercolor and gouache,
    25¾ x 32 . . . . (1171)   340

Olive Tree at the Seaside, watercolor,
    6½ x 10¼ . . . . (1213)   130

The Vineyards in Winter, watercolor, 10 x 14 . . . . (1078)   210

The Farm Near the Bridge, watercolor and wash,
    18¼ x 24 . . . . (1211)   250

Riverside, watercolor, 23¾ x 18¼ . . . . (1154)   400

Landscape with a River, watercolor, 24 x 18¼ . . . (1119)   400

La Favière Beach (Var), watercolor, 8¼ x 13½ . . (1220)   280

The Fisherman's House, 1945, watercolor,
14 x 17½ .... (1227) $ 400
The Trees, watercolor, 25¼ x 19½ .... (1227) 220
Breton by the Brookside, watercolor,
17¾ x 14¾ .... (1230) 500
The Shepherd, watercolor, 11¾ x 18¼ .... (1230) 150
Autumn Landscape, watercolor, 9 x 14¾ .... (1253) 300
Street of Paris, watercolor, 21¼ x 14 .... (1265) 1,020

PAINTINGS

1961–1962
A Brook in the Var, on panel, 14¾ x 17¾ .... (81) 80

1963
A Bunch of Flowers in a Vase, on cardboard,
18¼ x 21 .... (264) 70
The Grande Bastide, 1923, 19¾ x 25¾ .... (286) 42

1964
The Grande Bastide, 19¾ x 25¾ .... (472) 104
Landscape of the South of France, on panel,
22 x 26½ .... (333) 250

1965
Banks of the Brook, on panel, 14¾ x 17¾ .... (492) 82

1966
The Rocks at Le Lavandou, on panel, 14 x 10¾ ... (804) 310
Landscape, 15 x 18¼ .... (796) 136
Maritime Landscape, 51¾ x 77½ .... (670) 800

1967
Pastoral Scene, on panel, 25¾ x 32 .... (876) 500
The Burnt Slope, on panel, 21¼ x 25¾ .... (996) 580
Landscape, on panel, 14¾ x 18¼ .... (838) 330
The Apple Tree, 15 x 18¼ .... (934) 260
The River Seine at Vétheuil, 32½ x 40 .... (949) 1,360

1968–July 1969
Mother and Child, on panel, 13 x 9¾ .... (1026) 760
Landscape with a Bridge, 32 x 39½ .... (1042) 640
Still Life, 1916, on panel, 10¾ x 14 .... (1042) 86
Flowers, 15 x 18¼ .... (1078) 340
Flowers, 15 x 21¾ .... (1154) 220
Vase of Windflowers, on cardboard, 15 x 21¾ ... (1078) 440
Bunch of Flowers, 1946, 15 x 18½ .... (1161) 200
The Vase of Peonies, 14 x 10¾ .... (1122) 122
Old Chestnut Trees at Collobrières, 25¾ x 32 ... (1117) 1,240
Interior with the Artist's Family, 32 x 40 .... (1113) 1,800
The Trees by the Brook, 17¾ x 23¼ .... (1227) 560
The Tree by the Seaside, 1929, 32 x 73¼ .... (1227) 600
The Wintry Vineyard, 13¼ x 21¾ .... (1245) 320
The Tree, 39½ x 32 .... (1253) 600
Landscape, 19¾ x 25¾ .... (1256) 1,500
Vase of Flowers, 21¼ x 14 .... (1265) 800
Reading in the Garden, 15 x 18¼ .... (1256) 4,000

Hippolyte Petitjean

(1854–1929)

Birthplace: Mâcon, France.

1872 A scholarship enables him to enter the Ecole Natio-nale des Beaux-Arts, Paris.

1884 Makes friends with Seurat and comes under the influence of Neo-Impressionism.

1891 Participates in the Salon des Indépendants, Paris.

1892 Exhibits at the Galerie Le Barc de Boutteville, Par-is, with Signac, Cross, Luce, Pissarro, Gauguin, and Cézanne.

1929 Died, Paris.

1954 Retrospective exhibition at the Galerie de l'Institut, Paris, on his centenary.

Sales

DRAWINGS

1964
The Artist Near His Easel,[1] 1897, charcoal,
24½ x 19 .... (411) $ 220
Pastoral, colored pencil, 10¼ x 8 .... (394) 220

1965
The Great Trees, 1894, colored pencil,
11¼ x 5¼ .... (503) 80

1966
Bather at the Fountain, black pencil, 9 x 11½ .... (723) 116

1968–July 1969
Seated Woman, 9 x 6 .... (1121) 320
The Park, 1928, colored pencil, 12¼ x 8¼ .... (1121) 100
Bather, charcoal, 12¼ x 18¾ .... (1117) 600
Back View of a Reclining Nude, red chalk,
10¾ x 14¼ .... (1202) 200
Country Road Seen from the Dale, pencil,
6¾ x 10¾ .... (1225) 220
Landscape, red chalk, 11¾ x 18¼ .... (1253) 280

WATERCOLORS

1961–1962
The Conversation in the Park, watercolor,
11¾ x 8¾ .... (155) 760
The Garden in Blossom, watercolor, 11¾ x 17 ..... (33) 620
The Flower Garden, watercolor, 15 x 12¾ .... (30) 640
Landscape of the South of France, watercolor,
11½ x 16¾ .... (44) 875
Landscape with Red Roofs, watercolor,
9½ x 7¼ .... (71) 720

1963
Angling by the River Seine, watercolor,
10½ x 17 .... (232) 904
Nude in a Landscape, watercolor, 10 x 14 .... (190) 640
Woman with a Jar, watercolor, 18¼ x 11¾ .... (306) 400
Mountainous Landscape, watercolor, 7¼ x 11½ .. (206) 740

1964
Nude on the Edge of a Lake, gouache and
watercolor, 9 x 12¼ .... (321) 700
The Vine, watercolor, 12 x 19½ .... (329) 1,050

[1]Self-portrait.

1965

Study of a Man, watercolor, 11 x 7½ . . . . (599) $ 220
Woman with a Jar, watercolor, 17½ x 11 . . . . (582)   442

1966

Young Nude Combing Her Hair, varnished
  gouache, 12½ x 6¾ . . . . (711)   560
Standing Nude, (1895–1900), watercolor,
  16¾ x 9 . . . . (735)   1,763
Landscape of Provence, watercolor, 14 x 17 . . . . . . (784)   800
The Tree, watercolor, 9½ x 12 . . . . (671)   160

1967

Standing Woman in the Nude, varnished
  gouache, 12¼ x 6½ . . . . (898)   400
Nude with a Jar, watercolor, 17¾ x 11 . . . . (934)   700
Sailboats, watercolor, 11¾ x 19¾ . . . . (931)   1,582

1968–July 1969

Seated Woman, watercolor, 9½ x 6½ . . . . (1121)   550
Landscape, watercolor, 9½ x 6½ . . . . (1121)   220
Children in a Landscape of Provence, watercolor,
  12¾ x 16¾ . . . . (1068)   2,478
Children in a Landscape of Provence, (1890),
  watercolor, 12¼ x 16¾ . . . . (1174)   4,140
Rest on the Hill, 1894; ***Landscape,*** 6¼ x 9 and
  6¾ x 9½ . . . . (1183)   640
Still Life, watercolor, 11 x 14 . . . . (1088)   700
Conversation in the Park, watercolor,
  12¾ x 8¾ . . . . (1030)   1,500
Daphnis and Chloe, pastel, 24 x 17¾ . . . . (1116)   800
View of Notre-Dame, (1896), watercolor,
  18¾ x 12½ . . . . (1240)   4,560
Banks of the River Seine, watercolor,
  14½ x 20¾ . . . . (1246)   3,000
Woman with an Amphora, watercolor,
  18¼ x 11¾ . . . . (1268)   1,044
Path in a Park, watercolor, 15¾ x 12 . . . . (1272)   2,400

PAINTINGS

1961–1962

Bathers in a Woody Landscape, 1901,
  28¼ x 38½ . . . . (91)   577
Nude on the Edge of a Lake, 1903, 31½ x 21¼ . . . . . (64)   3,700
Vase of Flowers, 16¼ x 13 . . . . (30)   1,000

1964

Nude, 18½ x 24 . . . . (354)   2,200
Back View of a Nude, 10¾ x 18¼ . . . . (448)   1,800
Standing Nude, oil on paper laid down on canvas,
  12½ x 6½ . . . . (450)   760

1965

Women in a Landscape, on cardboard,
  8¾ x 10¾ . . . . (588)   960
Landscape with a River, on cardboard, 6¾ x 8¾ . . (492)   450

1966

Women in a Landscape, on panel, 7½ x 10 . . . . (797)   2,712
Well in a Village Street, 18¼ x 25¾ . . . . (829)   92
Landscape of Burgundy, 15 x 21¾ . . . . (655)   280
Rue de Donzy, Le Perthuis (Saône-et-Loire),
  1911, 15 x 21¾ . . . . (781)   460
Bathers, on panel, 7¼ x 10 . . . . (726)   1,780
Still Life with Flowers, 15¾ x 13 . . . . (648)   1,100

1967

Gathering Oranges, 1894, on a semicircle-shaped
  canvas, 14 x 27¾ . . . . (1002)   500
Compassion, (1901–02), 25¾ x 19¾ . . . . (893)   4,000

Donzy-le-Perthuis, 1911, 14 x 21¾ . . . . (898) $ 420
Picking Flowers, 1913, 25¾ x 32 . . . . (911)   9,000
Jaunt at the Seaside, on panel, 7½ x 10 . . . . (939)   2,073
Allée du Parc Montsouris, 22 x 18 . . . . (870)   2,750

1968–July 1969

Seated Woman, 32 x 25¾ . . . . (1110)   1,220
By the Waterside, 1895, 23¾ x 29 . . . . (1132)   12,980
Three Women in a Landscape, on board,
  8¼ x 10 . . . . (1187)   1,670
Bathers, on panel, 7¼ x 10 . . . . (1039)   1,520
Portrait of Madame Petitjean, 1898, 16 x 13 . . . . . (1187)   10,620
Bathers in the Evening, 1902, 29 x 39½ . . . . (1106)   2,300
Portrait of the Artist's Wife Seated, 1914,
  39¼ x 31½ . . . . (1208)   7,000
Bathing, on cardboard, 10¼ x 15 . . . . (1202)   800
Young Woman Seated on a Red Pedestal Table,
  17½ x 21 . . . . (1117)   1,200
The Country Church, on panel, 10¼ x 15¾ . . . . . . (1051)   840
The Storyteller, on cardboard, 13 x 17 . . . . (1121)   1,800
The Spring, After Ingres, on panel, 16¾ x 8¾ . . . (1121)   3,200
Landscape, 1923, on board, 5¼ x 9¼ . . . . (1240)   504
Bathers, 18 x 21¾ . . . . (1249)   7,000
The Village, 15 x 21¾ . . . . (1253)   840
Women Bathing, 10¾ x 8¾ . . . . (1255)   4,160
Women at the Fountain, 19¾ x 24 . . . . (1257)   8,020
Riverside . . . . (1263)   280
Seascape, the Mouth of the River Escaut . . . . . . (1263)   720
The Vision, 1896, on board, 19¼ x 14¾ . . . . (1271)   2,880

Francis Picabia

(1878–1953)

Birthplace: Paris, France.

1897   Enters the Ecole Nationale des Beaux-Arts, Paris, in the studio of Cormon. Meets Pissarro and paints under the influence of Impressionism until 1908.

1903   Participates in the Salon des Indépendants, the Salon d'Automne, and the Salon des Artistes Français, Paris.

1905   One-man show at the Galerie Haussmann, Paris.

1909   Comes under the influence of Cubism.

1911–12   Contributes to the foundation of the Section d'Or, Paris—with Villon, Gleizes, Metzinger, Léger, La Fresnaye, Apollinaire, and others.

1912–13   Paints "Udnie" and a series of abstract paintings. First stay in the U.S. Participates in the Armory Show, New York. One-man show at Stieglitz' "291" Gallery, New York.

1915   Second trip to the U.S.

1917   Goes to Barcelona. Publishes the first issue of the review *391*. Returns to the U.S., exhibits with the Independent Artists, New York, and continues his review *391* with Marcel Duchamp.

1918 Stay in Lausanne. Issues his book *Poèmes et dessins de la fille née sans mère.* Meets the Dada group of Zurich.

1919 Issues *391* in Zurich and Paris. Participates in the exhibition "The Evolution of French Art" at the Arden Gallery, New York. Exhibits at the Kunsthaus, Zurich.

1920 Issues the review *Cannibale.* Organizes an important Dada festival in Paris, but breaks away from the Dada movement the following year.

1924 Contributes to René Clair's film *Entracte.* Also Contributes to the Surrealist reviews and participates in their exhibitions.

1926 Reverts to figurative painting.

1930 First retrospective exhibition at the Galerie Rosenberg, Paris.

1936 Participates in the international exhibition of Surrealism at the Museum of Modern Art, New York.

1940-45 Spends World War II in the south of France.

1945 Returns to Paris and starts to work in abstract painting again.

1949 Important retrospective exhibition at the Galerie Drouin, Paris.

1950 Exhibits with Marcel Duchamp at the Rose Fried Gallery, New York.

1953 Died, Paris.

Sales

DRAWINGS

1961–1962

La Chienne de Baskerville, 1927, India ink and charcoal, 25¼ x 19 .... (85) $ 500

Woman's Head, 1936, pencil, 14¾ x 10¼ .... (161)   150

Portrait of the Author, pen, 9½ x 7½ .... (102)   400

1963

Man and Woman, 14¾ x 10¾ .... (193)   180

Woman's Head, Transparency, sepia, 16¾ x 11¾ .... (237)   32

The Young Lady and the Owl, 1940, charcoal, 10 x 14 .... (315)   178

1964

Portrait of a Woman, 1946, stick of greasepaint, 15¾ x 11¾ .... (379)   100

Nude, pencil, 7¼ x 4¾ .... (393)   40

Two Women's Heads, pencil and watercolor, 14 x 9 .... (455)   276

1965

Young Negro, pencil heightened with watercolor, 11 x 16¾ .... (564)   90

1966

Tono, Tono, Nino y cante, 1932, ink and gouache, 29¼ x 21¼ .... (751)   2,902

Boldini at the Bois, pencil, 7½ x 5¼ .... (804)   140

Wistiti, wash, 13 x 9½ .... (769)   34

1967

Landscape, 1909, colored pencil, 9½ x 12¾ .... (921)   260

1968–July 1969

Allegory, 11 x 7¼ .... (1042)   100

Allegory of the Horsewoman, India-ink wash, 7¼ x 9¼ .... (1077)   190

Circle and Five, black ink, 6½ x 4 .... (1059) $ 644

The Negro, 1932, black pencil, 11 x 6¾ .... (1180)   300

The Wrestlers, black lead, 12 x 9¼ .... (1179)   320

Portrait of a Bald Man, pencil and watercolor on board, 3¼ x 3 .... (1068)   240

Mechanical Composition I, 1919, pen and colored wash, 15 x 10 .... (1203)   1,487

Cannes: Sunbath, black pencil, 10½ x 8¼ .... (1131)   140

Women's Heads, ink heightened with watercolor, 9 x 7 .... (1051)   260

Portrait of Boldini, black lead, 7¼ x 4¾ .... (1161)   38

Seaside, 1905, charcoal, 9½ x 8 .... (1234)   190

Three Studies of a Nude, India ink and wash, 14 x 12¼ .... (1241)   806

Two Figures, ink and charcoal, 24 x 18¼ .... (1246)   1,300

Ship at Sea, charcoal, 11¾ x 9 .... (1267)   360

WATERCOLORS

1961–1962

Landscape, 1905, watercolor, 9½ x 13½ .... (49)   190

The Spanish Girl, watercolor, 24½ x 17½ .... (46)   110

Bullfighter,[1] watercolor, 17½ x 14¼ .... (115)   100

Bather with a Green Costume, watercolor, 10¾ x 14¾ .... (158)   36

Banks of the River Seine at the Bois de Boulogne, watercolor, 9 x 12¾ .... (51)   160

Springtime, 1937, gouache, 25¾ x 21¼ .... (149)   980

1963

Portrait of a Woman, 1920, watercolor, 18¾ x 14¾ .... (280)   100

1964

Crystal Lamp, 1922, watercolor, 23¾ x 29 .... (405)   1,451

Teen-Ager's Dream, 1943, watercolor, 11½ x 9 ... (346)   150

Loving Thoughts, pastel, charcoal, and India ink, 23¾ x 21¼ .... (341)   1,000

1965

The Spanish Girl, watercolor, 24 x 18¼ .... (508)   120

The Spanish Girl, watercolor, 27¾ x 19¾ .... (561)   760

Transparency, watercolor and black lead, 12¾ x 10 .... (632)   300

1966

The Andalusian, watercolor, 24½ x 18¼ .... (711)   440

La Loye Fuller, pastel, 11 x 7½ .... (726)   240

Hell, (1923), watercolor, 19¾ x 24 .... (721)   900

Walking Nude, watercolor, 9 x 7¼ .... (826)   130

The Sea Gulls, pastel, 4¾ x 6½ .... (670)   200

Nude, watercolor, 9 x 7 .... (718)   280

Adam and Eve, gouache, 21¾ x 19 .... (809)   1,220

1967

Aviation, (1917–20), India ink and watercolor, 29¾ x 21½ .... (889)   3,500

Hell, (1923), watercolor, 19¼ x 24 .... (963)   1,100

Portrait of Jean Cocteau, watercolor and wash, 18¾ x 12¾ .... (875)   500

The Spanish Girl, watercolor, 23¾ x 18¼ .... (857)   280

At the Theater, watercolor and gouache, 8¼ x 5¾ .... (949)   240

1968–July 1969

Landscape, 1909, pastel, 9½ x 11¾ .... (1168)   400

Portrait of a Woman, gouache, 15¾ x 13 .... (1026)   1,200

[1] Inscribed "Barcelone."

Woman Smoking a Cigar, watercolor and
gouache, 25¾ x 19¾ ....(1081) $ 620

Iodanis, watercolor, 15¼ x 19½ ....(1184)   1,260

The Circus, (1940), gouache, 24 x 19¾ ....(1080)   3,000

Allegory, watercolor, 10 x 7¼ ....(1221)   250

Mechanical Drawing, 1919, pen and watercolor,
12 x 9½ ....(1241)   2,020

Mechanical Drawing, 1919, pen and watercolor,
10½ x 6½ ....(1241)   957

The Blue Man, watercolor, 9½ x 7½ ....(1265)   600

PAINTINGS

1961–1962

Moret-sur-Loing, 1902, on panel, 6½ x 9½ ....(136)   200

Landscape with Olive Trees, 1902, 21¼ x 25¾ .....(34)   800

St. Tropez and the Harbor from the Citadel, 1903,
29 x 36½ ....(114)   1,700

Group of Bathers, (Fauve period), 21¾ x 18¼ ....(132)   700

Martigues, 1905, 29 x 39½ ....(84)   549

On the Banks of the River Yonne, 1907,
36 x 23¾ ....(84)   1,373

That's Clear..., oil on board, 13 x 17¾ ....(31)   1,098

Villejuif, 24 x 19¾ ....(123)   800

Surrealist Composition, 24 x 19¾ ....(35)   290

The Woman with Mimosa, 46 x 35¼ ....(109)   500

Bust of a Young Woman in the Flowers,
64 x 51½ ....(110)   1,540

Lovers, (1925-27), 35¾ x 28¼ ....(152)   650

The Torrent, 29 x 36½ ....(173)   940

Adam and Eve, on panel, 41½ x 29¾ ....(161)   44

Face, 1936, 29 x 36½ ....(75)   2,212

Abstract Composition, 1947, oil on cardboard,
24½ x 20 ....(105)   1,198

1963

St. Tropez, the Sailboat, 29 x 23¾ ....(258)   2,200

Berre Pond, 1905, 13 x 18¼ ....(303)   240

The Banks of the River Loing, 1908, 29 x 39½ ....(258)   3,100

Flowers in a Vase, 1909, 25¾ x 21¼ ....(318)   900

Composition, 1931, Villejuif, 24 x 19¾ ....(249)   800

Witch of Time, 1946, on cardboard, 28½ x 23¼ ...(299)   320

Composition, 1949, on board, 21¼ x 25¼ ....(208)   450

The Sky, 1949, on panel, 30 x 25¾ ....(249)   860

A Figure, 42 x 29¾ ....(249)   1,400

Witch of Time, 29 x 23¾ ....(180)   270

The Ages of Woman, 29¼ x 36½ ....(232)   2,712

Portrait of Danielle Darrieux, 29¾ x 21 ....(254)   200

Maritime Landscape, 18¼ x 15 ....(190)   380

Composition with Fish, on panel, 19¾ x 23¾ .....(262)   600

I Wait for You, on panel, 39½ x 32 ....(249)   1,300

Halia, 64 x 51½ ....(206)   1,500

1964

Path of the Sablons at Moret, 1904, 18¼ x 21¾ ...(341)   1,400

Notre-Dame de Paris, 1906, 29 x 36½ ....(397)   3,620

Victory Over Evil (recto), *Head of a Young
Spanish Lady* (verso), on cardboard,
19½ x 14 ....(335)   600

The Bunch of Flowers, 1909, 35¼ x 45½ ....(321)   1,000

Church in a Landscape, 1910, 29 x 36½ ....(325)   600

The Mountain Lake, 29 x 36½ ....(399)   1,100

Bridges Over the River Creuse, on cardboard,
25¼ x 21 ....(401)   1,400

Woman with a Jug, oil on paper laid down on
canvas, 21¾ x 18¼ ....(450) $ 302

Cows in Pasture, 35¼ x 46¼ ....(408)   1,000

Orphens, 24 x 19¾ ....(370)   160

The Philosopher, 1946, 39½ x 32 ....(401)   1,020

The Chapel, 39½ x 32 ....(351)   1,560

Sea Bed, 32 x 39½ ....(371)   2,000

1965

Figure, on cardboard, 42 x 29¾ ....(512)   900

Walking Along a Stream, 1905, 14¾ x 20¾ ....(624)   2,349

Landscape, (1907), 29 x 36½ ....(567)   6,102

Vase of Flowers, 1909, 28½ x 23¾ ....(611)   1,200

Landscape, 21¼ x 25¾ ....(516)   960

Transparency, 41½ x 29¾ ....(617)   3,164

Mademoiselle Bonicelli, 24 x 19¾ ....(512)   840

Spanish Surrealist Composition, on cardboard,
27 x 21 ....(512)   1,100

Surrealist Portrait of a Woman, double-sided
cardboard, 18¾ x 13½ ....(538)   400

Myrte (Four Heads), (1934), on panel,
47¾ x 37¼ ....(535)   1,935

Surrealist Nude, 36½ x 29 ....(553)   2,900

1966

Portrait of "L," on board, 18 x 12 ....(784)   1,900

The Small Bridge, 1902, 15¾ x 12¾ ....(683)   480

The Mill, 1905, 29¼ x 36½ ....(681)   2,300

The Bridge at Villeneuve-sur-Yonne, Sun Effect,
1906, 26 x 36¾ ....(749)   3,000

Castle and Ornamental Lake, 1909, 25¾ x 32 .....(808)   3,482

Martigues Tower, on panel, 9½ x 5¾ ....(655)   140

The Couple, on panel, 41½ x 29¾ ....(672)   1,000

Recollection of Nothing, on board, 20½ x 14¾ ....(665)   3,500

1967

Adam and Eve, on cardboard, 21¾ x 19 ....(934)   960

The Old Mill, 1905, 21¼ x 29 ....(858)   1,960

The Mills, 1907, 36½ x 29 ....(919)   5,650

Fishing Boats, on cardboard, 15½ x 19¾ ....(977)   500

Antibes, on canvas laid down on cardboard,
10¾ x 13½ ....(977)   640

The Clown, on panel, 33¼ x 27¾ ....(996)   840

The Zebra, 23¼ x 28½ ....(884)   1,600

Apollo and His Horses, 63¼ x 53½ ....(921)   3,000

Woman with a Snake, 31 x 24½ ....(967)   1,356

Portrait of Danielle Darrieux, on cardboard,
29¾ x 21 ....(912)   1,000

Head, (1939), 20½ x 18¼ ....(888)   884

Young Woman in Profile, 21¼ x 18¼ ....(973)   420

Bust of a Woman, on panel, 17¾ x 14¾ ....(971)   130

Still Life with Fish, 23¾ x 29 ....(909)   800

Still Life, 29¼ x 36½ ....(978)   1,240

Bird Flight, 1949, on cardboard, 15¾ x 14¾ ......(918)   3,164

Bird, 1949, on cardboard, 15¾ x 14¾ ....(965)   1,627

Bather, 23¼ x 28½ ....(876)   1,600

Landscape, 21¾ x 25¾ ....(870)   2,750

1968–July 1969

*Morning Effect in Winter, Banks of the River
Yonne,* 1905, 15½ x 21¾ ....(1049)   3,600

Cannes, the Central Street and the Suquet, on
panel, 12¾ x 9 ....(1120)   1,200

The Pines, Sun Effect, St. Tropez, 1909,
23¾ x 29 ....(1053)   3,500

Myrte (Four Heads), (1934), on panel,
47½ x 37¼ . . . . (1018) $4,750
Suzanne's Dream, 1949, on board, 29 x 20 . . . . . . (1059)   991
The Peasant, on cardboard, 24 x 20½ . . . . (1161)   260
The Peasant with a Hat, on board, 21¾ x 18 . . . . (1070)   153
Black Face,[2] on cardboard, 18¼ x 15 . . . . (1075)   580
Portrait of a Young Woman, on cardboard,
28 x 24½ . . . . (1116)   300
Nude, Transparency, 96¼ x 51 . . . . (1053)   3,800
Figure on the Beach, on cardboard, 29¾ x 40 . . . . (1125)   5,060
The River Seine at Vernon, the Mill, 21¼ x 29 . . (1113)   2,320
The Red Trees Before the Church, 29 x 23¾ . . . . (1113)   3,540
Still Life with a Tureen, 29 x 36½ . . . . (1026)   1,600
The Pink Granite Rocks Near Ploumanach, 1910,
29 x 36½ . . . . (1265)   4,400
The Dolls, (1911-12), 20 x 29 . . . . (1270)   8,880
A Figure on the Beach, (1924), on board,
29 x 40 . . . . (1270)   7,200

Pablo Picasso

(1881–   )

Birthplace: Málaga, Andalusia, Spain. José Ruiz Blasco is his father's name and Maria Picasso his mother's.

1895   His family settles in Barcelona, where he attends the school of fine arts. Sets up his first studio the following year.

1897   First exhibition at "Els 4 Gats," Barcelona. Makes a trip to Madrid and enters the Academia San Fernando.

1900   Executes illustrations for the review *Joventut.* First trip to Paris.

1901   Stay in Madrid. Signs his name Picasso instead of Pablo Ruiz Picasso. Second trip to Paris. Exhibits at Vollard's. Meets Max Jacob. Beginning of the Blue period.

1904   Settles permanently in Paris, at the "Bateau-Lavoir," Montmartre.

1905   Meets Guillaume Apollinaire. Beginning of the Rose period. A Russian amateur buys about fifty paintings from him over the next nine years. Executes a series of etchings entitled "Les Saltimbanques" (Vollard, Paris).

1906-07   Meets Juan Gris and Matisse. Paints the portrait of Gertrude Stein. Paints his famous work "Les Demoiselles d'Avignon," often regarded as the first Cubist painting. Apollinaire introduces him to Georges Braque. Signs a contract with D. H. Kahnweiler.

1909   Beginning of analytical Cubism. Exhibits at the Tannhäuser Gallery, Munich.

1912   Beginning of synthetic Cubism. First collages.

[2]On the reverse, portrait of a woman.

1917   Stage decorations and costumes for Diaghilev's ballet *Parade,* with music by Erik Satie. Stay in Rome.

1918   Paul Rosenberg becomes his principal dealer. Marries Olga Koklova.

1920   Beginning of his neoclassic period.

1921   Paints "The Three Musicians."

1925-27   Participates in the first Surrealist exhibition at the Galerie Pierre, Paris. Distorts and dislocates his figures under the influence of Surrealism.

1929-31   Series of "Metamorphoses." Executes a series of etchings intended for Ovid's *Metamorphosis* (Skira, Geneva). Given an award by the Carnegie Institute, Pittsburgh.

1932   Important retrospective exhibition at the Galerie Georges Petit, Paris.

1934   Stay in Spain. Series of "Tauromachies."

1935   Jaime Sabartès becomes his secretary.

1936   Backs the Republicans during the Spanish Civil War.

1937   Paints "Guernica"—lent to the Museum of Modern Art, New York, by the artist.

1938   Series of "expressionist" heads.

1939-45   Exhibits at the Museum of Modern Art, New York. Spends World War II in Paris. Paints "Le Crâne de Boeuf" in 1942. Participates for the first time in the Salon d'Automne, Paris, with eighty works. Exhibits at the Victoria and Albert Museum, London.

1946   Revives ceramics at Vallauris in the south of France.

1947-50   Devotes himself to lithographs, discovering new processes.

1953   Paints "War and Peace." Retrospective exhibitions in Rome, Milan, and Lyons.

1955   Settles in Cannes. Retrospective exhibition at the Musée des Arts Décoratifs, Paris.

1957   Retrospective exhibition at the Museum of Modern Art, New York.

1967   Important retrospective exhibition at the Grand Palais, Paris.

Resident in the south of France.

Sales

DRAWINGS

1961–1962

Portrait of Lola, the Artist's Sister, (1899-1900),
colored chalk, 17½ x 8½ . . . . (137) $18,000
Fashionable Lady Going to the Café, 1901,
12¼ x 16¼ . . . . (26)   11,600
The Horse, Barcelona 1901, pen and colored
pencil, 3¾ x 5½ . . . . (120)   2,300
Olympia, Barcelona 1901, pen and colored pencil,
6¼ x 9 . . . . (120)   7,600
Nude Man Squatting, (1902-03), pencil,
8¼ x 6¾ . . . . (164)   439
Seated Man,[1] sepia ink, 11½ x 8½ . . . . (140)   6,041
The Horse, (1905), India ink, 8½ x 12¾ . . . . (37)   850
Nude Combing Her Hair, 1905, pen, 9½ x 6¼ . . . . (149)   4,582
The Woman with a Dog, black pencil, 13 x 9½ . . . . (141)   2,400

[1]Dedicated "Al amigo Pablo Gargallo, Paris, 6 mayo 1904."

The Harlequin, pencil, 12 x 7½ ....(141) $3,700
Reclining Nude, 1906, ink and brush, 12¾ x 16 ...(128)   4,119
Portrait of Guillaume Apollinaire, pen, 11½ x 9 ....(20)   2,270
The Headwaiter; Man in a Bowler Hat; Two Coachmen, three drawings, 7¼ x 12¾ ....(70)   4,740
Standing Nude, 1917, India ink and brush, 11¾ x 4 ....(106)   3,345
Three Sketches of Women's Heads, 1917, pencil, 8 x 5¾ ....(37)   1,100
Reclining Nude,[2] 1919, pencil, 8 x 10¾ ....(84)   3,570
Neapolitan Girl with a Fish, 1919, pencil, 12¼ x 8¼ ....(140)   5,767
Three Heads of Spanish Dancers,[3] 1919, three drawings, pen and watercolor, each 5¾ x 4½ ....(164)   1,922
Women Bathing, 1920, black pencil, 8¾ x 12¾ ...(171)   1,800
Vera Savina Dancing, (1922), pen, 6½ x 5¾ ......(164)   769
Four Models, 1925, India ink, 14 x 10 ....(140)   5,492
Seated Nude, 1931, black lead, 18¾ x 25¼ ....(105)   5,876
Head, 1937, pencil, 3¾ x 5¾ ....(44)   600
Reclining Nude, 1938, pen, 10¾ x 14 ....(129)   2,471
A Satyr Near a Sleeping Young Nude, 1940, pen, 14¾ x 18 ....(64)   2,750
Faun's Head,[4] 1945, pen, 12¾ x 9½ ....(100)   950
The Centaurs, 1946, pen, 19 x 25 ....(164)   1,098
Sleeping Woman, 1952, India ink, 20 x 26 ....(149)   6,636
The Dove of Peace, blue pencil, 8¾ x 12¼ ....(26)   900
Portrait of a Young Lady, 1953, pencil and charcoal, 10 x 8 ....(124)   1,640
Mother and Child,[5] 1953, India ink, 10¼ x 8¼ ....(94)   2,165
Standing Young Woman and Seated Man, 1953, India ink, 13¾ x 10¼ ....(94)   1,624
Bust of a Faun, 1953, ball-point pen, 5¾ x 4¾ .....(57)   150
Nude and Masked Cupid, 1954, India ink, 12 x 9 ....(8)   2,250
Young Woman with a Monkey, 1954, ink and brush, 12¾ x 9½ ....(31)   2,609
The Centaurs' Fight, pen, 23¾ x 19¾ ....(31)   3,844
Bullfight, 1958, colored pencil, 8 x 10 ....(68)   1,400
Flowerpot, 1958, colored pencil, 26 x 19¾ ....(167)   1,800
Bunch of Flowers, 1958, colored pencil, 25 x 19½ ....(93)   8,814
The Grand Duke, wash and colored pencil, 7 x 6¼ ....(71)   600
Flowers, 1958, colored pencil, 9 x 8¾ ....(71)   800
Centaurs' Fight, India ink, 19¾ x 25¼ ....(71)   2,620
Bullfight, 1958, colored chalk, 7 x 10¼ ....(129)   2,059
Bullfight, India ink and watercolor, 11 x 14 ....(69)   2,212
Avant La Pique II, 1959, India ink and brush, 10¾ x 15 ....(151)   4,920
The Bullfight, 1960, wash, 9½ x 12 ....(143)   2,486
Picador with a Girl, 1960, No. 15, black wash, 18¾ x 12¼ ....(129)   4,394
Bullfight Scene, wash, 7 x 9 ....(29)   2,100
The Picador, India ink, 10¾ x 8¼ ....(29)   1,220
Bullfight, charcoal, 7¼ x 12¾ ....(39)   1,400
La Nana, Spanish Dancer, pencil, 4¼ x 3 ....(18)   2,260
Madame Alacrou, pencil, 13½ x 20 ....(21)   18,960

[2]Dedicated "A mon ami cher H. Pierre Roché."
[3]Make-up design for Diaghilev's ballet *Le Tricorne.*
[4]Dedicated "Pour Pierre Massot-Picasso."
[5]Jacqueline and Claude.

The Woman with a Large Hat, watercolor, 5¾ x 5½ ....(26) $3,000
Colomba, 6 x 8 ....(15)   664
Face, pen, 11 x 8¾ ....(171)   640
Composition, colored pencil, 5¼ x 4¼ ....(66)   1,600
The Goat, colored pencil, 10¼ x 8 ....(49)   760
Still Life with Fruit, colored pencil, 7¼ x 8¼ .....(162)   1,020

1963

Cancan Dancer, (1900), 18¾ x 12¼ ....(220)   7,458
Dancer with a Young Boy, 1903, ink, 6¾ x 4½ ....(316)   2,400
The Equilibrist, 1904, India ink, 8 x 3¼ ....(220)   3,164
Apples and Teapot, 1909, ink, 11¾ x 19¾ ....(277)   2,468
This is Your Portrait, Mademoiselle, (1910), pen, 9 x 3 ....(299)   580
The Family, (1914), charcoal, 24 x 18¾ ....(247)   5,484
Harlequin Holding a Mask, (1916-17), pencil, 10¾ x 6¾ ....(220)   2,486
Still Life in Front of a Window, 1919, pencil, 19½ x 11¾ ....(277)   3,016
Musician and Sleeping Woman, 1921, India ink, 9 x 12 ....(202)   2,000
Pan's Flute, 1923, pencil and colored chalk on gray paper, 9 x 7¾ ....(279)   18,000
Minyas' Daughters Refusing to Recognize the God Bacchus, 1930, pencil, 12¾ x 9½ ....(220)   1,944
Composition, 10¼ x 8¼ ....(215)   400
The Painter and His Model, 1933, charcoal, 10¾ x 10 ....(277)   3,290
The Flower Woman, colored pencil, 25¼ x 19 ....(205)   1,400
Woman's Head, 1936, black lead, 15½ x 11¾ ....(204)   780
The Family, colored chalk, 14¾ x 10¼ ....(255)   1,097
The Fallen Horse, 1941, pen, 8¼ x 10¾ ....(254)   1,260
Reclining Woman in the Nude, 1941, black pencil, 8 x 10½ ....(254)   1,540
Seated Nude, 1942, pen, 24½ x 17 ....(316)   7,500
Variation II Upon the Flower Woman, 1948, colored pencil, 25¼ x 19½ ....(306)   1,600
Sleeping Woman, 1952, wash, 19¾ x 25¾ ....(206)   2,700
Satyr's Head, 1954, colored chalk, 25¼ x 18½ ....(277)   1,234
The Dove, 1957, blue pencil, 11¾ x 9½ ....(258)   640
Fauns and Faun Women, 1956, colored pencil, 19½ x 15¾ ....(258)   1,800
Flowers and Hands, 1958, pencil, 25 x 19½ ....(283)   8,927
Bullfight Scene, 1960, India-ink wash, 7¼ x 9½ ...(232)   2,486

1964

Red-Haired Woman in Profile, ink and colored pencil, 5½ x 3¾ ....(378)   2,034
Portrait of a Woman, (1899), oval drawing, charcoal, 11¾ x 8¼ ....(335)   3,900
The Wounded Bullfighter, 1901, ink and colored chalk, 3¾ x 5¼ ....(420)   1,103
Maternity, (1903), pencil and India ink, 9½ x 7¼ ....(335)   4,800
The Beggar, (1903), pencil and pen, 12¼ x 4¾ ....(354)   4,100
The Toilette, 1905, pen and pencil on gray paper, 7¼ x 11¾ ....(405)   7,545
Back View of a Woman and Child, 1905, charcoal, 8¾ x 4 ....(385)   2,305
Apple, 1909, bister ink, 4½ x 5¼ ....(385)   2,034
The Grand Duke, India-ink wash and colored pencil, 7 x 6¼ ....(401)   600
Study, Paris, Springtime, 1912, pen, 7½ x 3¼ ....(405)   1,103
Seated Man, pen and colored pencil, 5¼ x 3 ......(378)   2,599
Nude, (1920), pencil, 7¾ x 4¼ ....(378)   904

Woman and Child, 1920, pencil, 10¾ x 8¼ .... **(401)** $2,320

Seated Young Lady, 1921, pencil, 10¾ x 8¼ ...... **(385)**   3,842

At the Café,[6] 1922, pen, 7¼ x 6¾ .... **(377)**   2,599

Nude with a Mirror and Flute Players, 1923,
India ink, 9¾ x 12¾ .... **(367)**   6,634

Head of an Old Man, India ink, 12¼ x 9½ .... **(465)**   2,100

Head of a Man Writing, colored pencil, 4¼ x 4 ... **(418)**   240

Seated Woman, 1926, pen and wash, 10½ x 9 ..... **(454)**   4,975

Portrait of Max Jacob, 1928, 11 x 8 .... **(460)**   2,420

Man's Head, colored pencil, 5¾ x 4¼ .... **(351)**   1,220

Seated Nude, 1943, pencil, 20 x 25¾ .... **(416)**   6,910

Back View of a Couple, colored pencil,
6½ x 4½ .... **(340)**   5,000

Dora Maar, wash, 12¼ x 9½ .... **(340)**   2,000

Sun, 1948, pen, 6½ x 5¾ .... **(329)**   800

Masks, 1954, India ink, 9¼ x 12½ .... **(399)**   1,400

Satyr's Head, 1958, colored pencil, 15½ x 10 ..... **(329)**   1,100

Satyr's Head, India-ink wash, 10 x 6¾ .... **(368)**   1,658

Flowers, 1958, colored pencil with pastel lights,
8 x 15½ .... **(401)**   710

The Bunch of Flowers, India-ink wash,
25¾ x 20 .... **(471)**   4,520

Centaurs' Fight, 1959, black chalk, 19½ x 25¾ .... **(385)**   4,972

War and Peace, 1959, colored pencil,
14¼ x 10¼ .... **(458)**   1,016

Study, 1959, charcoal and India ink, 10¼ x 11 .... **(347)**   3,800

Bather, 1961, pencil, 13 x 19¾ .... **(392)**   4,428

Head with a Bear, 1963, colored chalk,
14¾ x 10¾ .... **(385)**   791

1965

Portrait of a Woman, (1899), charcoal,
8½ x 11¾ .... **(617)**   5,650

*Title Page of "Los viejos cafés de Barcelona" by
Tomas Caballé y Clos,* 1901, black pencil,
12¾ x 11½ .... **(564)**   4,800

Figures Under a Bridge, 1901, ink and colored
pencil, 5¼ x 3½ .... **(633)**   3,500

Junyer in Majorca, 1901, colored pencil on paper
laid down on canvas, 13½ x 10½ .... **(624)**   3,593

Bust of a Woman, 1901, ink and colored pencil,
4¾ x 3¼ .... **(522)**   1,382

Man in Evening Dress, 1902, ink and blue pencil,
5 x 3½ .... **(522)**   1,106

The Hair Style, (1902), ink and blue pencil,
12 x 9 .... **(624)**   1,327

The Showman, (1903), pencil and blue chalk,
14 x 10 .... **(633)**   11,000

Portrait of Leo Stein, 1905, pen, 6¾ x 4½ .... **(624)**   1,327

Woman with a Mandolin, 1910, charcoal and
India ink, 12½ x 6½ .... **(566)**   3,729

The Violin, (1910-11), charcoal, 24 x 18¼ .... **(522)**   3,870

The Fisherman, 1919, pencil, 18¼ x 11¾ .... **(624)**   2,211

Bathers, 1921, pencil, 9½ x 13¾ .... **(624)**   9,950

Seated Nude, 1923, ink, 25¼ x 18 .... **(582)**   7,186

Squatting Woman, 1925, ink, 16 x 20 .... **(582)**   8,845

Face, 1934, India-ink wash, 25¾ x 20 .... **(564)**   3,400

The Beggar, colored chalk, 11 x 7½ .... **(629)**   4,353

The Centaurs, pen, 19¾ x 25¼ .... **(512)**   2,800

Head of a Woman Wearing a Hat, with a Fish,
1938, pen, 17½ x 9¼ .... **(624)**   4,975

Reclining Nude, 1941, pen, 8 x 10¾ .... **(545)**   705

[6]Dedicated "A mon vieux Utrillo qui n'a pas l'air vieux encore."

Seated Nude, 1943, pencil, 25¾ x 19½ .... **(539)** $8,000

Primitive Arts, 1943, ink, 10 x 14 .... **(539)**   1,100

Woman and Cat, 1954, pen, 12 x 8¾ .... **(629)**   3,773

Flying Bull, 1956, colored pencil, 14¼ x 10¼ ..... **(637)**   1,800

The Visit, 1959, ink and wash, 14¾ x 22½ .... **(637)**   3,400

The Human Comedy: Figures, 1959, pen,
15½ x 22¼ .... **(624)**   5,804

Picador and Women, 1960, India-ink wash,
14¾ x 10¼ .... **(569)**   8,362

The Bunch of Flowers, 1961, colored pencil,
10¼ x 8 .... **(507)**   1,000

The Clown, 1962, colored pencil, 24½ x 19½ ..... **(637)**   6,500

The Smoker, 1964, colored pencil, 29 x 20½ ...... **(609)**   7,600

1966

A Group of Artists, (1901), charcoal, 10 x 12¼ .... **(707)**   6,000

A Study of a Head, (1902-03), pen, 5½ x 6½ ..... **(689)**   1,935

Spanish Beggar, (1902-03), pen, 6 x 3¾ .... **(703)**   1,400

Woman's Head, (1907), Conté pencil,
25¼ x 18¾ .... **(801)**   13,200

Face, (1912-13), ink, pencil, and collage,
16½ x 11 .... **(694)**   9,500

Carnival, colored pencil, 13½ x 10¼ .... **(670)**   620

Head, (1919), pencil, 10½ x 7¾ .... **(815)**   1,327

Head, (1926), black lead, 25 x 18¾ .... **(703)**   3,000

Women on the Beach, 1934, India ink, 10 x 14 .... **(784)**   3,500

Woman's Head, 1936, black lead, 16½ x 12½ ..... **(668)**   1,300

The Talking Pencil, 1936, ink, colored pencil,
watercolor, and collage, 13¼ x 20 .... **(751)**   7,186

Femme hurlant sa douleur, 1937, black chalk,
11½ x 8 .... **(753)**   5,804

Woman's Head, 1941, pencil, 10¼ x 8 .... **(703)**   2,700

*A Standing Young Woman in the Nude and a
Seated Man,* 1953, India ink, 13¾ x 10¼ ..... **(712)**   2,829

At the Circus, 1954, pen and wash, 9½ x 11¼ ..... **(808)**   3,773

The Bullfight, 1957, India-ink wash, 20 x 26 ...... **(801)**   8,020

The Conversation, 1959, charcoal, 15¼ x 22 ...... **(812)**   5,804

The Reproof, 1959, India ink and gouache on
paper laid down on canvas, 14 x 20 .... **(811)**   5,300

Toreador and Picador, 1959, India-ink wash,
19½ x 24¼ .... **(689)**   3,870

Torero, 1960, India-ink wash, 17½ x 27¾ .... **(686)**   9,398

Picador and Figures, 1960, India ink and wash,
20 x 25¾ .... **(753)**   11,608

Picador with a Woman, 1960, pen and wash,
25¾ x 20½ .... **(808)**   5,514

The Luncheons, 1961, pencil, 10¼ x 16¾ .... **(798)**   4,068

Picnic, 1961, pencil, 10¾ x 16¾ .... **(751)**   3,317

Man's Head, 1963, colored pencil on a printed
sheet of the Editions du Rocher, 14¾ x 11 .... **(665)**   1,300

1967

Barcelona, fuente en el parque, 1895, pen,
11 x 7¾ .... **(881)**   1,327

*Three Heads of Women and a Woman Leaning
on a Table,* (1900), colored chalk, 8 x 5¾ ..... **(982)**   4,977

The Beggar, (1903), pencil and ink, 12¼ x 4¾ ... **(1004)**   6,250

Two Men, 1905, pen, 9 x 12 .... **(841)**   3,100

The Absinthe Drinker, pencil, 6 x 4½ .... **(857)**   1,760

Suzanna and the Old Man, pencil, 9¾ x 6½ ...... **(857)**   700

Peasant's Head, 1906, pen, 8¼ x 5¼ .... **(889)**   6,000

The Fruit Stand, 1909, charcoal, 24½ x 18½ ...... **(975)**   20,800

Landscape with a Fan, Céret 1911, pen and wash,
11½ x 9 .... **(982)**   7,110

Seated Nude, black lead, 6½ x 3¾ .... **(980)**   280

The Centaur, 1920, one-line drawing, 10½ x 8 .... **(975)** $2,700

"The Four Zodiacal Signs" in "Mercure," 1924,
   pencil, 8 x 9¾ .... **(922)**   829

Woman, 1927, pen, 10¾ x 8¾ .... **(975)**   2,600

Sleeping Woman, 1931, India ink, 9¾ x 12¾ ..... **(975)**   4,800

Composition with a Man, ink, 6½ x 8 .... **(889)**   1,500

Portrait of Dora Maar, 1940, pencil, 12 x 9¼ ..... **(982)**   4,266

Reclining Woman in the Nude, 1941, 8¼ x 11 ..... **(976)**   2,160

Bust of a Woman, 1941, India ink, 10¾ x 8¼ ..... **(931)**   1,130

Head, 1950, pen, 7 x 7 .... **(910)**   443

Head of a Bearded Man, 1951, colored chalk,
   13½ x 10 .... **(990)**   1,107

Santa Claus, 1953, colored pencil and gouache,
   14¼ x 10 .... **(939)**   553

Fight Between a Centaur and a Man, 1959,
   charcoal, 20 x 26 .... **(938)**   3,870

Figure with a Palm Tree, 1959, colored pencil,
   17 x 12¾ .... **(911)**   2,400

La Pique III, 1959, wash, 20 x 26¼ .... **(940)**   6,965

Corrida, 1941, India ink, 10¼ x 13 .... **(918)**   2,486

Bullfight Scene, 1963, India-ink wash,
   11¾ x 9¾ .... **(993)**   2,100

1968–July 1969

Barcelona, the Fountain in the Park, 1895, pen,
   11 x 8 .... **(1030)**   1,000

Antonio Gelaber, Rusinol, Miguel, and Utrillo,
   (1902), ink and colored pencil, 5½ x 3½ ..... **(1068)**   7,080

The Tavern, Barcelona, colored pencil,
   4¾ x 6¾ .... **(1121)**   7,200

The Two Giants, (1905), India ink, 12¾ x 8¾ .... **(1173)**   10,350

The Toilette: Study for the Hair Style, 1905–06,
   ink and pencil on gray paper, 7¼ x 11¾ ..... **(1126)**   21,063

The Blue Vase, 1906, pen and blue pencil,
   12 x 8½ .... **(1068)**   18,880

Two Standing Women, 1906, pencil, 24½ x 17¾ .. **(1056)**   25,000

Composition with the Ace of Clubs, 1914, pencil,
   9 x 11½ .... **(1064)**   12,980

Woman with a Zither, 1914, pencil, 25¼ x 18¾ .. **(1068)**   8,260

The Family, (1914), charcoal, 24 x 18¾ .... **(1132)**   21,240

Pierrot, (1916), pencil, 11¾ x 9 .... **(1080)**   2,100

Woman Playing the Guitar in an Armchair, 1916,
   pencil and watercolor, 6 x 5 .... **(1057)**   23,000

Diaghilev, 1917, green ink, 7½ x 6¼ .... **(1142)**   7,788

Bathers, 1921, pencil, 9½ x 13¾ .... **(1064)**   21,240

Nude on the Beach, 1923, pen, 9 x 11¼ .... **(1198)**   7,300

The Sculptor, 1932, pen, 10¼ x 11¾ .... **(1138)**   1,858

Woman's Head,[7] pencil, 12 x 9¼ .... **(1080)**   7,500

Head of a Woman Wearing a Hat, with a Fish,
   1938, pen, 17½ x 9¼ .... **(1064)**   9,440

Minotaur, 1940, pencil, 12 x 9¼ .... **(1064)**   6,136

Nude, 1941, pen, 8 x 10¼ .... **(1032)**   2,200

Portrait of a Woman, 1943, India ink, 12¾ x 9½ . **(1191)**   5,900

Portrait of Florence, 1947, pencil, 9 x 5¼ .... **(1080)**   3,250

Faun's Head, 1954, colored chalk, 10¼ x 8 ...... **(1085)**   843

Faun's Head, 1958, colored chalk, 14¾ x 11 ..... **(1146)**   836

The Palm Tree, Cannes, 1958, colored chalk,
   12¾ x 9½ .... **(1203)**   1,041

Study for a Bather, 1959, ink, 9½ x 19¾ .... **(1173)**   4,025

The Centaurs' Fight, 1959, 19½ x 25¼ .... **(1117)**   5,000

War and Peace, 1959, colored pencil,
   14¼ x 10¼ .... **(1127)**   1,380

Head, 1960, colored pencil, 9 x 6¼ .... **(1191)**   1,180

Bathers, 1961, pencil, 12¾ x 19½ .... **(1216)** $9,000

The Lunch, 1961, black lead and colored pencil,
   10¾ x 16¾ .... **(1018)**   9,000

Nestor's Account of the Trojan War, pencil,
   13 x 10¼ .... **(1101)**   3,680

El Toro, 1963, pen and watercolor, 8 x 8¼ ...... **(1101)**   2,116

Woman, Child, and Musketeer, 1966, bister
   pencil, 21¾ x 18¼ .... **(1173)**   11,040

Two Nudes, 1967, 19½ x 24 .... **(1185)**   6,100

The Couple, 1967, India-ink wash, 14¾ x 21 ..... **(1125)**   11,040

Head, 1967, India ink, 29¾ x 22¼ .... **(1173)**   15,410

The Man with a Lamb, Eating Watermelons,
   1967, pen and wash, 24 x 19½ .... **(1064)**   9,440

Nude, 1928, ink, 7 x 4¼ .... **(1235)**   12,000

At the Café, black and colored chalk, 4½ x 6½ .. **(1241)**   5,540

Harlequin, (1926), charcoal with heightening,
   19½ x 12 .... **(1241)**   15,120

Falcon, 1946, pen and ink with wine wash on a
   paper tablecloth, 17½ x 10¾ .... **(1241)**   1,008

Study: Back View of a Woman, 1906, charcoal,
   23 x 17 .... **(1246)**   14,000

Old Romeu,[8] wash and watercolor, 8 x 6 .... **(1258)**   7,600

Nonell, Catalan Painter, matches and watercolor,
   7¾ x 6 .... **(1258)**   5,600

Pompollo Jener, Catalan Writer, pen and
   watercolor, 7¾ x 5¾ .... **(1258)**   6,600

Flower, blue pencil, 14¾ x 7¾ .... **(1260)**   390

Faun's Head,[9] 1957, colored pencil, 12½ x 8¾ ... **(1262)**   1,500

Man with a Cigarette, 1964, colored pencil,
   29¾ x 21 .... **(1268)**   14,384

Bust, 1941, India ink, 7¾ x 10½ .... **(1268)**   4,640

The Bather, 1959, India ink, 9½ x 11½ .... **(1268)**   4,872

Woman's Head, 1943, India ink, 12¾ x 9½ ...... **(1268)**   8,120

Composition, India-ink wash, 10¾ x 8½ .... **(1268)**   2,413

The Swallows, 1934, colored pencil, 10¾ x 10 .... **(1268)**   9,280

The Rescue, 1932, pencil, 13¼ x 20 .... **(1272)**   17,280

Lunch, 1961, pencil, 10 x 16¼ .... **(1272)**   5,280

Composition, 1933, pen and black ink,
   15¼ x 19½ .... **(1273)**   5,040

WATERCOLORS

1961–1962

Young Woman with a Hat, Barcelona 1901,
   pastel, 8¾ x 5¼ .... **(120)**   6,000

Junyer and Picasso, pastel, 10 x 13 .... **(18)**   8,814

Picasso and Junyer in the Tavern, Barcelona,
   1903, pastel, 10 x 13 .... **(120)**   4,400

Celestine, 1903, pastel, 11 x 9¼ .... **(18)**   15,594

The Death of Harlequin (recto), 1905, *Woman
   Seated in a Garden* (verso), 1901, gouache on
   board, 25¾ x 37½ .... **(83)**   219,680

Front and Side View of a Nude, 1906, gouache on
   paper on canvas, 22¾ x 16¾ .... **(8)**   46,000

Bottle and Guitar, gouache, 5½ x 4¼ .... **(171)**   900

Face, 1955, pastel, 8¾ x 12¼ .... **(75)**   1,422

Figure, 1957, pastel, 11 x 14¼ .... **(14)**   1,738

1963

Bullfight, 1899, watercolor, 10¼ x 8¼ .... **(210)**   10,420

The Hair Style, 1899, pastel and watercolor,
   18¾ x 11¾ .... **(316)**   18,500

Les Saltimbanques, (1901), watercolor, 14 x 10 ... **(316)**   7,500

---

[7] Dora Maar.

[8] Els 4 Gats.

[9] Executed on the review *Verve.*

Junyer and Picasso in a Night Club, 1903, pastel,
10 x 13 . . . . (283) $9,718

The Guitar,[10] 1920, gouache, 5 x 2 . . . . (247) 1,426

Seated Man, watercolor and gouache,
24½ x 18¼ . . . . (224) 13,600

1964

The Toilette, 1901, pastel, 10½ x 11 . . . . (367) 17,966

Still Life, 1915, watercolor, 8 x 7 . . . . (354) 6,500

Guitar Upon a Fireplace, 1920, pastel,
11¼ x 8¼ . . . . (460) 6,400

Bathers, 1921, watercolor, 9 x 13 . . . . (378) 9,944

The Hand, 1921, watercolor, 4¾ x 6¼ . . . . (460) 2,100

Still Life, gouache, 12½ x 9¾ . . . . (474) 3,600

Woman's Head, watercolor, 12¼ x 9½ . . . . (460) 15,600

The Yellow Nude, watercolor, 23¾ x 16¼ . . . . (460) 26,500

The Rape of the Sabines, 1955, watercolor and
pastel, 19½ x 25 . . . . (435) 1,760

1965

Bullfight, 1899, watercolor, 10½ x 8¼ . . . . (526) 14,000

Woman's Red Head, 1906-07, gouache,
25 x 18¾ . . . . (615) 57,000

Guitar, 1920, tempera, 5 x 2 . . . . (566) 3,028

The Banjo Player, 1921, watercolor and gouache,
10¾ x 8¼ . . . . (615) 6,600

Composition, watercolor, 11 x 8¾ . . . . (567) 429

Woman Lying Before a Window, 1934, watercolor
and India ink, 10 x 12¾ . . . . (583) 7,545

Portrait of Dora Maar, 1939, gouache,
18¼ x 15 . . . . (615) 17,000

Faun Playing the Diaule, 1947, gouache and oil
on paper on canvas, 25¾ x 19¾ . . . . (526) 12,000

Faun on a Gray Background, 1947, gouache on
paper laid down on canvas, 26 x 20 . . . . (539) 11,500

"Pour Sapone," 1959, watercolor, 21¾ x 14¾ . . . . . (541) 750

The Smoker, 1964, pastel, 25¼ x 19¾ . . . . (561) 8,600

The Painter at His Work, 1964, gouache,
38½ x 29¾ . . . . (616) 14,400

1966

A Scene of Bohemian Life, Barcelona, 1898,
pastel, 9½ x 11¾ . . . . (742) 7,500

Le Repas du pauvre, 1903, watercolor, 9½ x 13 . . . (801) 24,000

The Beggar, 1904, watercolor, 14¼ x 10¼ . . . . (801) 25,200

Harlequin on Horseback, 1906, ... (801) 18,000

Nude Man with Hands Crossed, 1907, gouache,
24½ x 18½ . . . . (694) 25,000

Woman's Head, 1907, watercolor, 12¼ x 10 . . . . . . (703) 13,500

Study for "Nude with Drapery" II, 1907, gouache,
11¾ x 9¼ . . . . (694) 12,500

Glass and Fruit on a Table, (1910), watercolor,
6¼ x 6½ . . . . (739) 6,050

The Smoker, 1964, pastel, 25¼ x 20 . . . . (808) 8,706

Absinthe (Portrait of the Painter Cornuty), 1902,
watercolor, 12¼ x 9 . . . . (801) 32,000

1967

Portrait of the Artist's Father, 1895, watercolor,
11 x 7¾ . . . . (881) 4,008

Bullfight, 1900, pastel, 14 x 15¾ . . . . (938) 116,088

At the Café (Angel de Soto), pastel, 18¼ x 11½ . . . (988) 67,176

The Clowns of Mercury, 1924, pastel and pencil,
7¾ x 8½ . . . . (1004) 4,750

Reclining Head, 1942, gouache, 12 x 15¾ . . . . (918) 7,232

Head of a Woman, 1943, gouache, 25¾ x 19¾ . . . . (975) 8,000

*Model for the Poster: Exposition de Peinture,
Vallauris,* 1956, watercolor, 20¾ x 15 . . . . (889) 2,500

[10]Dedicated "Pour Gontcharova."

1968–July 1969

Study for the Picture "The Embrace," watercolor,
4¾ x 7 . . . . (1109) $ 8,400

Still Life, 1906, gouache, 13½ x 15 . . . . (1068) 29,500

Bottle and Guitar, 1912-13, pastel, 18¾ x 24½ . . . (1068) 9,676

Guitar on a Table, 1920, pastel, 10¼ x 8 . . . . (1057) 11,000

Man and Woman, 1921, pastel and charcoal,
41 x 28 . . . . (1064) 70,800

Seated Nude, 1939, gouache, 10¼ x 8 . . . . (1181) 8,400

Seated Nude, 1939, gouache, 10¾ x 8¼ . . . . (1064) 11,800

Flowers, 1948, watercolor, and pastel,
25¼ x 19½ . . . . (1125) 7,130

Woman Picking a Flower, pastel on lithographic
paper, 10¾ x 8¼ . . . . (1127) 2,576

Man's Head, 1964, pastel and gouache,
13¾ x 10¼ . . . . (1216) 6,000

Portrait of a Man, 1964, pastel, 21¼ x 14¾ . . . . . . (1125) 8,510

The Artist at His Work, 1964, gouache on a
lithograph, 38¼ x 29¼ . . . . (1064) 30,680

The Artist at His Work, 1964, gouache on a
lithograph, 38¼ x 29¼ . . . . (1173) 23,000

Flowers in a Vase, 1961, watercolor and gouache,
16¾ x 10¼ . . . . (1226) 7,600

*Poster Design for the Play "Hotel de l'Ouest,
chambre 22,"* 1904, 21½ x 17¼ . . . . (1239) 76,800

The Nurse and the Soldier, pastel, 18¾ x 15½ . . . (1254) 23,600

Man's Head, 1964, pastel, 21¼ x 14¾ . . . . (1268) 12,760

Glass, Ace of Clubs, and Cut Pear, 1914,
13 x 7¾ . . . . (1270) 50,400

Scene in a Park, (1901), pastel, 18½ x 25 . . . . (1272) 12,480

Flowers and Jug, 1906, watercolor, pen, and sepia
ink, 15¾ x 11¾ . . . . (1272) 7,200

Woman Seated in an Armchair, 1914, pen, India
ink, and watercolor, 10½ x 7½ . . . . (1272) 20,400

PAINTINGS

1961–1962

Interior of a Café, Barcelona, 1897, on canvas laid
down on cardboard, 7½ x 9¾ . . . . (120) 7,500

Café de la Rotonde, 1900, 18¼ x 32¼ . . . . (8) 81,000

Pots and Lemons, 1907, Paris, 21¾ x 18¼ . . . . (129) 19,222

The Bathers, 1907-08, 36 x 36 . . . . (140) 79,634

Young Woman Seated on a Sofa, 6 x 4 . . . . (125) 10,840

Fruit Stand with Pears and Apples, 1908,
8¼ x 9 . . . . (145) 22,120

Bottle and Glass, 1912, collage on canvas,
23¾ x 17¾ . . . . (129) 24,714

Our Future Is in the Air, 1912, oval-shaped
canvas, 15 x 21¾ . . . . (140) 49,428

*Clarinet, Violin, Fruit Stand with Fruit, Music
Sheet, Pedestal Table,* 1912-14, 39 x 31¼ . . . . . (37) 70,000

Glass and Fruit, 1921, 12¾ x 15 . . . . (84) 20,595

The Greek Girl, 1924, 72 x 29¼ . . . . (83) 82,380

Dance, 1929, 13 x 16¼ . . . . (171) 5,400

Woman's Face, 1934, oil on paper, 25¼ x 19½ . . . . (114) 3,500

Still Life with Fish, 1936, 19½ x 23¾ . . . . (31) 28,009

Seascape, Juan-les-Pins 1937, 14¾ x 18¼ . . . . (31) 25,263

Woman's Face, on paper laid down on canvas,
1940, 25¼ x 18¼ . . . . (32) 23,000

Woman with a Hat, 1941, 24 x 15 . . . . (106) 30,510

Woman with a Bodice, Portrait of Dora Maar,
1944, 23¾ x 36½ . . . . (70) 33,180

Woman in a Studio, 1956, 29 x 36½ . . . . (88) 30,504

La Pique, 1960, oil on cardboard, 10¼ x 8¼ . . . . . . (93) 3,616

1963

Scene in a Park, 1901, pastel, 18½ x 25¼ .... (202) $ 11,000
Seated Girl in the Nude, 1908, 29 x 23¾ .... (127) 100,000
The Fruit Stand, 1910, 21 x 17¾ .... (247) 50,727
Decanters and Books, 1910-11, 15 x 18¼ .... (210) 30,710
Pipe, Glass, and Cut Pear, 1914, collage and oil
   on board, 15¼ x 15¼ .... (210) 23,307
The Toilette, Dinard 1922, 8¾ x 6½ .... (277) 35,646
The Hair Dressing, Three Women, 1923,
   39½ x 32 .... (210) 38,388
Bust of a Woman, June 1940, oil on paper,
   25 x 17¾ .... (277) 19,194
Still Life with a Candle, 1944, 23¾ x 36½ .... (247) 38,388
Leisure Hours, 1956, 39½ x 32 .... (283) 25,764
Reclining Woman (Red Background), 1960,
   23¾ x 29 .... (316) 33,000
The Musician, 14¾ x 17¾ .... (241) 13,600
Seated Woman and Her Shadow, 29 x 23¾ ...... (263) 24,020

1964

Still Life with Fruit, 1895, 39¾ x 27½ .... (367) 9,674
The Man with a Hood, 1895, 17½ x 10¾ .... (416) 7,739
Mother and Child, 1898, on panel, 3¾ x 5¾ ...... (448) 3,750
The Workers, 1898, on panel, 3¾ x 5¾ .... (448) 2,750
The Guitar, 1917, 28¾ x 23¼ .... (453) 41,460
Glass, Bunch of Flowers, Guitar, and Bottle,
   1919, 39½ x 32 .... (431) 117,500
Teapot on a Starry Background, on paper laid
   down on canvas, 26 x 20 .... (399) 6,420
The Young Lady, 1929, 21¾ x 18¼ .... (460) 9,000
Guitar, collage, 24¼ x 15½ .... (460) 26,000
Woman's Head, 29 x 21¾ .... (480) 12,200
Faces and Plants, 1932, on panel, 7¼ x 9 .... (405) 16,832
Still Life with a Jug, 1939, 10¾ x 17½ .... (454) 20,730
Woman with a Blue Body, 1941, 36½ x 23¾ ...... (460) 34,600
Man's Head, 1941, 21¾ x 13 .... (465) 11,200
The Arlesian Girl, 21 x 15 .... (340) 12,000
Glass and Lemon, 1944, 10¾ x 8¾ .... (340) 62,000
Skull, Lamp, Leeks, and Vase, 1946, 32 x 45¾ .... (458) 36,275
Bust of a Faun, 1946, oil and India ink on paper,
   26 x 20 .... (385) 9,605
The Chinese Chest of Drawers, 1953, on panel,
   58¼ x 45 .... (454) 46,988
The Bullfight (recto), oil, pastel and charcoal,
   Toreador and Picador (verso), charcoal on
   paper, 4¾ x 7¼ .... (454) 15,202
Woman Seated in an Armchair, 1960,
   51¼ x 38¼ .... (367) 52,516
Seated Nude, 1960, 57¾ x 45¼ .... (453) 63,572
The Old Musician, 1960, 21 x 25¼ .... (458) 15,961
The Painter and His Model, 1963, 17¾ x 21¼ .... (458) 21,766

1965

Interior of a Tavern, 1897, on canvas laid down
   on board, 9 x 11¼ .... (522) 35,932
The Old Woman, (1903), 13 x 7¼ .... (526) 7,000
A Young Lady of Avignon, 1907, 25¾ x 23 .... (615) 70,000
Sleeping Woman, 1908, 32 x 25¾ .... (615) 124,000
The Pont Neuf, 1911, 13 x 9½ .... (566) 22,600
Woman with a Mandolin, 1911, 15 x 9½ .... (615) 23,000
Our Future Is in the Air, 1912, oval canvas,
   8¾ x 5¾ .... (615) 15,000
"Ma Jolie," 1914, 17¾ x 15¾ .... (615) 80,000
Pipe, Glass, and Tobacco Pack, 1918, 7½ x 9½ ... (624) 8,016

Still Life with a Pipe, 1920, 10¾ x 8¾ .... (569) $20,340
Still Life with a Guitar, 1921, 39½ x 25¾ .... (615) 35,000
Fruit Stand, Bottle, Guitar, 1925, 39½ x 61¼ ..... (594) 35,000
Girl Thinking, 1928, 14 x 7½ .... (594) 11,000
Fruit Stand and Guitar, (1927-29), on board,
   38½ x 51½ .... (526) 70,000
The Rescue, 1932, 14 x 10¾ .... (539) 16,000
Woman Seated on a Chair, 1937-38, 64 x 51½ .... (573) 138,200
Woman's Head, 1938, 21¾ x 18¼ .... (526) 22,000
Woman in a Blue Bodice, 1941, 45¾ x 35¼ .... (526) 115,000
Still Life with an Ox Skull, 1942, 51½ x 38½ ..... (615) 130,000
Glass and Jug, 1944, 10¼ x 13½ .... (594) 19,000
Woman in an Armchair, 1949, 23¾ x 19½ .... (575) 17,966
Portrait of Mademoiselle D. (Sylvette), 1954,
   34½ x 25¾ .... (561) 18,000
Arlesian Girl on a Yellow Background, 1958,
   21½ x 15 .... (522) 20,730
Squatting Nude, 1959, 57¼ x 44¾ .... (637) 52,500
Still Life with a Great Vase, 1959, 34½ x 39½ ..... (561) 20,000
Lunch on the Grass, 1961, 25¾ x 34½ .... (561) 16,200
Great Woman's Head, 1961-62, 39½ x 32 .... (637) 45,000
Woman in an Armchair, 1963, 45¾ x 29 .... (561) 56,000
The Painter and His Model in the Studio, 1963,
   25¾ x 34½ .... (561) 31,000
Self-Portrait, white paper stuck on glass,
   15¾ x 11½ .... (539) 3,100

1966

Interior of "Els 4 Gats" in Barcelona, 1899,
   16¼ x 11 .... (694) 40,000
The Coffeepot with a Starry Background, on
   paper laid down on canvas, 25¼ x 19½ ...... (753) 13,059
Vase of Flowers, 1901, 19½ x 15½ .... (750) 43,948
Boy's Head, (1906), 14 x 8½ .... (694) 40,000
Woman with a Mandolin, 1908, 39¼ x 31½ .... (676) 100,000
Still Life, Glass and Apple, 1911, 11 x 6½ .... (694) 10,500
Head, 1929, 28½ x 23¾ .... (676) 55,000
The Lady with a Flower, 1932, 64 x 51½ .... (678) 92,500
Three Bathers, (1920-23), on board, 31½ x 39¼ ... (676) 115,000
Dark-Haired Young Lady (Dora Maar), 1939, on
   panel, 23½ x 17½ .... (678) 52,500
Woman with a Yellow Hat, 1941, 29¼ x 23¾ .... (776) 30,000
Woman in an Armchair, 1941, 51½ x 38½ .... (801) 50,000
Woman's Head, 1943, peinture à l'essence, laid
   down on canvas, 25¾ x 19¾ .... (801) 10,400
Still Life with Cherries, 1943, 31½ x 51 .... (678) 75,000
Still Life with a Lemon, 1944, 13 x 16¼ .... (724) 14,200
The Faun with a Violet Coat, 1946, oil on paper
   laid down on canvas, 25¾ x 20 .... (801) 17,000
Seated Woman,[11] 1953, on panel, 39½ x 32 .... (808) 37,726
The Studio, 1956, 18¼ x 21½ .... (750) 17,966
Arlesian Girl on a Green Background, 1958,
   16 x 13 .... (784) 8,000
Man's Head, 1965, 25¾ x 21¼ .... (747) 14,000

1967

Man with a Lamp,[12] 39½ x 25¾ .... (988) 49,760
*Mother and Child in Profile (Maternity at the
   Seaside),* 1902, 32¾ x 23¾ .... (880) 525,160
The Old Woman, 12¾ x 7¼ .... (931) 13,560
Landscape, 1908, on panel, 10¼ x 8 .... (982) 14,694

[11] Françoise Gilot.
[12] Portrait of Cardona.

Card, Glass, Bottle on a Pedestal Table, 1916,
  peinture à l'essence and sand on board,
  10¾ x 14 .... (975) $ 37,000
Still Life, 1919, 14 x 10¾ .... (993)   26,400
Portrait, 24 x 19¾ .... (965)   32,544
Reclining Woman, 1937, 29 x 23¾ .... (975)   30,000
Soles, 1940, 23¾ x 36½ .... (880)   42,782
Glass and Apple, (1944), oil on paper laid down
  on canvas, 13 x 10 .... (940)   4,643
Woman's Head, 1945, 25¾ x 21 .... (940)   23,216
Woman in an Armchair, 1946, 21½ x 18¼ .... (982)   34,365
The Nymph, 1946, on paper laid down on canvas,
  19¼ x 25¼ .... (864)   11,000
The Cock, 1951, fresco laid down on panel,
  27 x 35½ .... (911)   13,000
Woman Dressing, 1953, 18¼ x 15 .... (975)   18,400
Landscape with a Pine Tree, 1953, 14¾ x 21¼ .... (940)   15,090
The Chinese Chest of Drawers, 1953, on panel,
  58¼ x 45 .... (954)   37,500
The Man with a Striped Costume, 1956,
  64 x 51½ .... (954)   42,500
Portrait of a Woman, 1962, 28¾ x 21½ .... (1005)   30,810

1968–July 1969

Interior of a Tavern, 1897, on canvas laid down
  on panel, 9 x 11½ .... (1018)   7,750
The Nude with Stockings, 1901, 26¼ x 20½ ..... (1132)   186,440
The Embrace, 1905, on cardboard, 21 x 27¾ ..... (1109)   200,000
Landscape of Gossol, 1906, 27¾ x 39¼ .... (1151)   430,000
Nude on a Bed, 1907, on panel, 14½ x 14¾ ...... (1057)   72,500
Landscape, Paris, Summer, 1908, on panel,
  10¾ x 8¼ .... (1125)   23,000
The Pedestal Table, 1911, 11 x 6¾ .... (1176)   26,000
The Injured Bird (The Pigeon), 1912, 18½ x 11 .. (1056)   57,000
The Arlesian Girl, 1912, 30 x 21¾ .... (1068)   106,200
The Tip of the Ile de la Cité, 1912, oval-shaped
  canvas, 35½ x 28 .... (1064)   295,000
The Cup of Coffee, 1912, collage, charcoal, and
  gouache, 24 x 14 .... (1064)   47,200
Glass and Reverse of Playing Cards, 1914, on
  board, mounted on cradled panel, 10 x 6½ .. (1057)   40,000
*"Ma Jolie," Guitar, Bottle, Cluster of Grapes,
  and Glass,* 1914, oil, sand, and sawdust,
  20¼ x 26¾ .... (1064)   231,280
Glass, 1914, on canvas laid down on panel,
  9 x 11½ .... (1064)   20,060
Man with a Guitar, Montrouge,[13] 1918,
  51½ x 35¼ .... (1109)   103,200
Still Life in a Landscape, 1915, 24 x 29½ .... (1064)   136,880
Tobacco Pack and Newspaper, 1919, 11¾ x 5¼ .. (1187)   18,880
Still Life with a Pipe, 1920, 10¾ x 8¾ .... (1187)   28,320
Stage Curtain for "Le Train Bleu,"[14] 1924,
  distemper, 268 x 316 .... (1141)   162,840
Woman's Head, (1929), 8¾ x 5¾ .... (1126)   19,824
Still Life with a Sheep's Skull, 1939, 19½ x 23½ .. (1064)   30,680
Still Life with Flowers, 1941, 36½ x 29 .... (1189)   56,000
Squatting Nude, 1959, 57¼ x 45 .... (1064)   40,120
Reclining Woman with a Cat, 1964, 44¾ x 76¼ .. (1068)   66,080
Little Boy, Front View, 1964, 14 x 10¾ .... (1125)   33,120
Reclining Nude, 1964, 25¼ x 39½ .... (1064)   49,560
Landscape, Mougins, 1965, 21 x 25¾ .... (1064)   22,420

[13]Wedding present from Picasso to Apollinaire.
[14]Dedicated to Diaghilev.

Man's Head, 1965, 25¾ x 21¼ .... (1125) $ 30,820
Mougins, 1965, 21¼ x 25¾ .... (1173)   36,800
The Bathers,[15] 1918, plaster mounted on canvas,
  51½ x 68 .... (1126)   7,434
Head of a Reclining Woman, 21¼ x 25¾ .... (1268)   34,800
The Pack of Tobacco, 1919, 11¾ x 5¼ .... (1268)   25,560

Edouard Pignon

(1905–   )

Birthplace: Bully, France.

1920   Begins to work as a miner, but soon gives up this job to become a house painter.

1927   Goes to Paris and works at Citroën's. Attends evening classes at the Ecole de Montparnasse and the Ecole des Arts Décoratifs.

1932   Participates in the Salon des Indépendants, Paris.

1934   Participates in the exhibition organized by the Association des Artistes et Ecrivains Révolutionnaires, Paris, where he meets Léger, Lhote, and Vieira da Silva.

1936-37   Devotes himself entirely to painting. Exhibits at Durand-Ruel's, Paris.

1939   First one-man show at the Galerie d'Anjou, Paris.

1941   Takes part in the exhibition "Vingt Peintres de tradition française" at the Galerie Braun, Paris. Also exhibits at the Galerie Jeanne Bûcher, Paris.

1942   Takes part in the exhibition "Douze Peintres d'aujourd'hui" at the Galerie de France, Paris—together with Bazaine, Estève, Lapicque, Le Moal, Manessier, and others.

1944-45   Contributes to the foundation of the Salon de Mai, Paris. Stay at Collioure in the south of France.

1946-47   One-man show at the Galerie de France, Paris. Trip to Ostend and Sweden.

1948   Stage decorations for *Shéhérazade* by Jules Supervielle.

1949-50   One-man show at the Galerie de France, Paris. Settles at Sanary.

1951   Given an award by the São Paulo Biennial.

1952   Stage decorations for *Mother Courage* by Berthold Brecht, at the TNP, Paris.

1953   Takes a great interest in ceramics.

1958   One-man show at the Perls Gallery, New York.

1960   Exhibits at the Galerie de France, Paris. Retrospective exhibitions at the Musée de Metz and the Musée du Luxembourg, Paris.

1962   One-man show at the John Lefebvre Gallery, New York.

1964   Retrospective exhibitions at the Nuova Milano Gallery, Milan, and the Musée d'Art et d'Histoire, Geneva.

1966   Retrospective exhibition at the Musée d'Art Moderne, Paris.

[15]Decoration made for Blaise Cendrars' bedroom.

Sales

DRAWINGS

1961–1962

Bust of a Woman in the Nude, 1944, black lead,
17¾ x 12¼ ....(117) $ 44
The Olive Tree, 1953, pen, 18¾ x 24½ ....(124)   50

1963

The Woman with a Bowl, 1946, charcoal,
24 x 18¼ ....(296)   120
The Diggers, 1952, charcoal and watercolor,
12¼ x 18¾ ....(241)   580

1964

Maternal Scene, 1939, charcoal, 18¾ x 24¾ ......(377)   384
Harvest Scene, 1958, wash, 17 x 25¾ ....(436)   80
The Cocks, 1959, felt pen, 14 x 20¼ ....(476)   160

1965

The Cocks, 1959, felt pen, 14 x 20 ....(497)   150

1967

The Cock, 1960, colored pencil, 10 x 12¾ ....(934)   64
Landscape, India-ink wash, 12¾ x 18¼ ....(919)   192
The Three Musketeers, 1960, ink, 13 x 19½ ......(956)   72

1968–July 1969

The Fishermen at Ostend, 1945, pen, 12¾ x 19 ..(1147)   90
Harlequin, 1956, 13 x 10¼ ....(1129)   66
The Cock, 1960, colored pencil, 9 x 11¾ ....(1078)   100
The Meeting, India ink, 1950, 7¼ x 10½ ....(1225)   202

WATERCOLORS

1961–1962

Fish and Sails, 1948, watercolor, 18¼ x 24 ....(80)   300
Still Life, watercolor, 14 x 10 ....(13)   300
Landscape, 1957, watercolor, 19 x 25¼ ....(18)   678
The Thresher, 1958, watercolor, 22½ x 30½ ......(124)   320
Threshing Corn at Vilighiano, Italy, 1959,
gouache, 22 x 31 ....(124)   130

1963

Boats in the Harbor, watercolor, 11¾ x 15¾ .....(281)   147
The Boat, 1946, gouache, 10¼ x 16¾ ....(296)   340
Landscape, watercolor, 19½ x 25 ....(185)   200
Back from Fishing, Ostend, 1947, gouache,
19 x 24½ ....(299)   350
The Telegraphists, 1953, watercolor, 18¾ x 24½ ..(280)   800

1964

Fishing Boats, 1953, watercolor, 18¼ x 24 ....(333)   200
Landscape, 1956, watercolor, 21¾ x 29¼ ....(375)   320
Olive Trees, 1957, watercolor, 19½ x 25 ....(335)   420
Travaux champêtres, 1959, 12¾ x 18¾ ....(377)   203
Composition, 1960, watercolor, 22½ x 30 ....(386)   640

1965

Woman Under the Trees, 1944, watercolor,
7¾ x 10 ....(538)   820
Composition, 1947, watercolor and gouache,
19½ x 25¼ ....(552)   140
The Vine Harvest, watercolor, 12¾ x 17 ....(599)   240
Olive Trees, 1956, watercolor, 21¾ x 29¼ ....(627)   360
Chioggia, 1956, gouache, 18¾ x 25 ....(541)   325

1966

Still Life with a Coffeepot, 1938, watercolor and
gouache, 8¾ x 11 ....(681) $ 220
The Couple, 1945, gouache, 14¼ x 19 ....(795)   240
The Olive Tree, 1949, watercolor, 9½ x 11¾ ......(652)   120
Yellow Landscape, 1956, gouache, 21¼ x 29¾ ....(741)   800
The Creek, 1957, watercolor, 19½ x 25 ....(706)   500

1967

The Couple, 1945, gouache, 14¼ x 19 ....(848)   270
Ostend, 1947, watercolor, 19 x 25 ....(845)   480

1968–July 1969

Seated Woman, 1945, gouache, 12¾ x 7¼ ....(1147)   180
Seated Woman, 1945, gouache, 12¾ x 7¼ ....(1072)   140
Ostend, 1949, watercolor, 19 x 25¼ ....(1043)   280
The Picking, 1952, watercolor, 12¼ x 19 ....(1167)   720
Olive Trees, 1957, watercolor, 19½ x 25 ....(1043)   520
The Cock, 1959, watercolor, 37¼ x 25 ....(1075)   156
Olive Trees, 1963, gouache, 22½ x 30½ ....(1153)   640
The Spinney, 1962, watercolor, 21¾ x 29¼ ......(1230)   720

PAINTINGS

1961–1962

Nude, 39½ x 47½ ....(30)   1,600
The Card Players, 1938, 38½ x 51½ ....(114)   1,400
Woman Musing, 1945, 29 x 23¾ ....(116)   840
Trees in the Country, 1951, 23¾ x 29 ....(114)   620
Peasants in the Fields, 1952, on panel, 26 x 32 ....(110)   400
Gathering Olives, 1953, 19 x 25 ....(155)   560

1963

The Card Players, 1938, 39½ x 51½ ....(318)   1,900
Still Life with Plaster, (1943), 23¾ x 29 ....(232)   1,718
Trees, 1951, 23¾ x 29 ....(249)   500
Ship on the Stocks, 1953, 21¼ x 25¾ ....(254)   340
The Masts, 1953, 29 x 36½ ....(296)   720
Vendanges, 1954, 14¾ x 17¾ ....(315)   548
Cock Fight, 1959, 32½ x 39½ ....(254)   420
Catalan, 19½ x 10¾ ....(180)   400

1964

The Net Menders at Collioure, 1946, 20 x 26 .....(350)   240
Composition, 1948, 25¾ x 32 ....(394)   1,050
Lively Scene with Figures, 1955, 14 x 10¾ ....(393)   260
Still Life, 23¾ x 29 ....(377)   1,469
Cock Fight, 1960, 13 x 18¼ ....(335)   700

1965

Nude in a Landscape, 1953, on panel,
40¾ x 48½ ....(553)   1,400
Landscape, 1955, 14 x 9½ ....(567)   791
Fighting Cock, 1958, 25¾ x 21¼ ....(609)   800

1966

Portrait of a Young Woman, 1945, 29 x 23½ ......(816)   738
Figures, 1952, 28 x 35½ ....(815)   3,317
Landscape at Vallauris, 1956, 29 x 41 ....(815)   8,292
The Red Cock, 1958, 16¼ x 12¾ ....(805)   275
Landscape, 1959, 31½ x 25¾ ....(802)   1,440
Threshing, 1959, 10¼ x 17½ ....(778)   356
Travaux des champs, 14¾ x 21¼ ....(669)   400
Travaux des champs, 13 x 18¼ ....(672)   520
Vendanges vertes, 23¾ x 32 ....(814)   6,400

1967

The Fish, 1944, 15 x 18¼ . . . . **(911)** $ 360
Catalan Peasant, 1946, 63¾ x 38½ . . . . **(982)**   5,214
The Gatherer of Jasmine, 23¾ x 36½ . . . . **(1007)**   360
Landscape with a Hill, 1956, 35¼ x 46 . . . . **(880)**   8,016
Threshing, 1962, 17¾ x 21 . . . . **(939)**   498

1968

The Cock Fight, 1959, 51½ x 63¼ . . . . **(1068)**   2,360
Woman Drinking, 1946, 18¼ x 22 . . . . **(1150)**   920
Still Life with Mask and Lemon, 29 x 23¾ . . . . . . **(1210)**   700
Old Woman Seated at Table, 1946, 28¾ x 36½ . . **(1240)**   2,880
Young Woman Seated at Table, 1946, 18 x 21¾ . . **(1240)**   1,560

Filipo de Pisis

(1896–1956)

Birthplace: Ferrara, Italy. (Real name is Luigi Tibertelli.)

1914   Studies at the University of Bologna.

1916   Meets di Chirico. Corresponds with Tzara, Apollinaire, Breton, and Cocteau. Comes under the influence of Metaphysical painting.

1919   Takes a great interest in Buddhist philosophy. Meets Giorgio Morandi. Issues *Pittura Moderna* (Ferrara).

1925   Settles in Paris.

1927   Takes part in the exhibition "Les Italiens de Paris," Paris. Meets Matisse and Picasso.

1929   Participates in the exhibition "Un Groupe d'Italiens de Paris" at the Galerie Zach, Paris.

1930   Participates in the Rome Quadrennial. Trip to Amsterdam.

1931   Exhibits at the Galeria d'Arte Moderna, Rome. Also exhibits with di Chirico at the American Club, and at the Galerie Jacques Benjean (catalog preface by François Mauriac), Paris.

1932   The Venice Biennial assigns an entire room to his work. Exhibits at the Galerie Bernheim, Paris. Makes friends with Leonor Fini.

1933   Stay in London.

1937   Takes part in the exhibition "Epoque Métaphysique" at the Galerie Rive Gauche, Paris.

1939   Returns to Italy.

1947   One-man show at the Palma Gallery, Rome.

1948   Affected by nervous trouble.

1956   Died, Milan.

Sales

DRAWINGS

1964

Sleeping Girl, pencil, 16¼ x 10 . . . . **(435)** $ 144

1966

The Boxers, 1933, pencil and watercolor,
7¼ x 5½ . . . . **(802)**   176

1968–July 1969

Portrait of Giorgio Morandi, stick of greasepaint,
12¾ x 8¾ . . . . **(1214)**   224

WATERCOLORS

1961–1962

Figure, pastel, 8 x 8 . . . . **(14)**   158

1966

Flowers, 1950, tempera, 19 x 13 . . . . **(802)**   512

1967

Gaston Gerad, Paris, 1956, watercolor, 9 x 12 . . . . **(882)**   288
Flowers in a Glass, watercolor, 13 x 9 . . . . **(881)**   263

1968–July 1969

Wrestlers, watercolor, 10¼ x 17 . . . . **(1214)**   512
Still Life with a Fish, 1931, watercolor, 7¾ x 10 . . **(1214)**   272
Vase of Flowers, watercolor, 24 x 18¼ . . . . **(1134)**   944
Flowers, watercolor, 24½ x 18¾ . . . . **(1174)**   1,196

PAINTINGS

1961–1962

Still Life with a Book and a Pipe, (1923), oil on
cardboard, 13 x 16¼ . . . . **(149)**   948
The Violet Flowers, 1926, 21¾ x 18¼ . . . . **(149)**   4,108
Flowers, 1926, on board, 18¼ x 15 . . . . **(164)**   934
Landscape, 1927, 14 x 19¾ . . . . **(14)**   948
Flowers, 24 x 18¾ . . . . **(147)**   820
Still Life, 1929, 15 x 18¼ . . . . **(14)**   1,106
Vase of Flowers, 23¾ x 31½ . . . . **(14)**   2,370
Landscape, 1930, 8 x 11¾ . . . . **(69)**   822
Fruit, 1935, 24 x 24 . . . . **(31)**   1,648
Piazza di Parigi, 10 x 14 . . . . **(14)**   758
Folies-Bergères, 15¾ x 19¾ . . . . **(15)**   1,106
Venice, 1946, 18¼ x 21¼ . . . . **(149)**   3,002

1963

Flowers, 35¼ x 23 . . . . **(315)**   3,290
Bathing in the Mountain, 1926, 23¾ x 32 . . . . **(246)**   720
Fruit, 1935, on board, 24 x 24 . . . . **(255)**   2,331
Sea Food, 1942, 17½ x 22½ . . . . **(210)**   1,234
Landscape, 31½ x 23¾ . . . . **(216)**   1,234
Venice, 20 x 12¾ . . . . **(315)**   1,371

1964

Still Life with a Fish, 1925, 16¼ x 21 . . . . **(461)**   4,480
Carnations in a Landscape, 1924, 25¾ x 18¼ . . . . . **(435)**   3,200
Still Life with Flowers, 1925, 22 x 28½ . . . . **(439)**   3,840
Flowers, on panel, 23¼ x 15¾ . . . . **(365)**   638
A Spot in Paris, 36½ x 23¾ . . . . **(351)**   2,900
Street Scene, 1931, on cardboard, 23 x 17 . . . . **(416)**   1,244
Still Life with a Vase of Flowers, 1940-42, on
cardboard, 25 x 19 . . . . **(461)**   2,400
Still Life with Fruit and Vegetables, 31 x 38½ . . . . **(401)**   1,500
Flowers, 1946, 26 x 20 . . . . **(454)**   1,382
Venice, 1947, 31½ x 23¾ . . . . **(368)**   967

1965

Still Life, 1925, 21¼ x 25¾ .... (616) $ 4,480
Bunch of Flowers, 1947, 32 x 23¾ .... (567)   4,068
Still Life, on panel, 11½ x 21¼ .... (583)   1,219

1966

Still Life with a Fish, 1926, 17 x 26 .... (802)   5,440
Still Life with a Bottle and a Vase of Flowers,
    1932, 25¾ x 18¼ .... (802)   4,480
La Table des souvenirs, 1932, 24 x 32½ .... (802)   6,720
Bunch of Flowers, 1947, 32 x 23¾ .... (745)   3,729

1967

Nude, (1940), on board, 11¾ x 9 .... (882)   768
Flowers, 1950, 9¼ x 6 .... (962)   880
Still Life on the Beach, (1928), on cardboard,
    17¾ x 29 .... (962)   3,840

1968–July 1969

Vase of Flowers, 21½ x 12¾ .... (1187)   1,652
The Lady in a Blue Hat, 13 x 8¾ .... (1243)   1,800
Vase of Flowers, 21¾ x 15 .... (1267)   1,760
Still Life, 19¾ x 25¾ .... (1268)   4,640
Greek Shepherd, 23¾ x 19¾ .... (1268)   3,480
Flowers, 28 x 25¼ .... (1268)   4,640
Street Scene, Place Richelieu, Paris,
    25½ x 19¾ .... (1273)   5,800
Place Vendôme, 28 x 20½ .... (1273)   5,800

Camille Pissarro

(1830–1903)

Birthplace: St. Thomas, West Indies.

1841   Sent to France to be educated in Paris. Starts to draw.

1855   Second trip to Paris. Meets Corot, who leads him to landscape painting. Attends the Académie Suisse, Paris.

1859   Exhibits at the Salon, Paris. Meets Claude Monet.

1861   Refused by the Salon, Paris. Meets Cézanne and Guillaumin.

1863   Participates in the Salon des Refusés, Paris, with Manet, Jongkind, Guillaumin, Cézanne, Fantin-Latour, and others. As the oldest of the future Impressionists, he exerts an influence on the group.

1864   Exhibits two landscapes at the Salon, Paris, as "pupil of Corot."

1868   Exhibits two views of Pontoise at the Salon, Paris.

1870–71   Stays in London, where he meets Paul Durand-Ruel. During the war, German soldiers occupy his studio at Louveciennes and destroy a great number of his works.

1873   Settles in Pontoise.

1874   Takes part in the first Impressionist exhibition, at Nadar's, Paris, and in its organization. (Exhibits with the Impressionists until 1880.) Executes engravings with Degas and Mary Cassatt.

1883   One-man show at Durand-Ruel's, Paris. Trip to Rouen, where he meets Gauguin. Durand-Ruel organizes a series of Impressionist exhibitions in Boston, Rotterdam, London, and Berlin.

1885   Meets Seurat and Signac, who convert him to Neo-Impressionism. Participates in the exhibition organized by Durand-Ruel in Brussels.

1886   Participates in the great Impressionist exhibition organized by Durand-Ruel in New York.

1887   With Seurat, exhibits with the "Groupe des Vingts," Brussels.

1888   Breaks away from Neo-Impressionism.

1892   One-man show at Durand-Ruel's, Paris. Spends half his time in Eragny, near Paris.

1903   Died, Paris.

Sales

DRAWINGS

1961–1962

Landscape (Petites Dalles), 1893, colored pencil,
    6½ x 8 .... (18) $1,695
Landscape of the West Indies, pencil, 11 x 13½ .... (18)   249
*Landscape with Factory Chimneys in the
    Background,* pencil and colored chalk,
    4½ x 5¾ .... (74)   69
Man's Head, pen and wash on checked paper,
    5¾ x 4 .... (147)   100
The Village Path, black lead, 5¾ x 7½ .... (68)   90
The Ploughman, black lead, 6¾ x 4¾ .... (68)   210
Peasants Talking, charcoal, 18¼ x 24 .... (128)   1,373
Conversation Under the Apple Tree, colored
    pencils, 11½ x 8¾ .... (73)   1,840
The Hay Carriers, charcoal, 8 x 12 .... (73)   900

1963

Portrait of a Young Man, pencil; *Landscape with
    a Rock,* India ink; two drawings on a double
    sheet, 1877, 6½ x 8¾ .... (220)   452
Antel Near La Roche-Guyon, 1889, pencil,
    12¾ x 19 .... (232)   588
Landscape (Petites Dalles), 1893, colored pencil,
    6½ x 8 .... (232)   1,356
The Market, ink and chalk, 10 x 8 .... (316)   3,500
The Hay, pen and colored pencil, 9 x 6¼ .... (311)   1,360
The Sower, black lead, 5¾ x 3¾ .... (218)   140
Place du Grand-Martroy, black pencil, 6 x 8 ..... (179)   400
La Roche-Guyon, black lead, 9 x 12¼ .... (242)   130
La Roche-Guyon, pencil, 9 x 12¼ .... (315)   302
In the Garden, pencil, 11¾ x 18 .... (202)   1,100
The Wild Apple Tree, pencil, 15¼ x 22½ .... (255)   1,974
The Bridge, stick of greasepaint, 3¾ x 6 .... (243)   400
Horse, charcoal, 10 x 14¾ .... (275)   475

1964

Study of a Tropical Plant, (1853), pencil on
    brown paper, 14¾ x 10 .... (321)   400
Seated Old Woman (recto), 1854, *Hilly
    Landscape* (verso), black lead, 11½ x 10 ..... (469)   300
Portrait of Doctor Freedenberg (West Indies
    period), black lead, double-sided drawing,
    13 x 11 .... (469)   170

Rue St. Vincent, Montmartre, 1860, charcoal
with white lights, 5¾ x 8 . . . . (420) $ 900

Le Père Melon au repos, (1879), charcoal,
9 x 11 . . . . (368)   967

Mother and Child Sleeping Under a Tree, 1891,
sepia, 9 x 11¾ . . . . (340)   2,500

The Walk, 1895, pencil, 4 x 6½ . . . . (416)   1,106

Landscape, pencil, 7¼ x 11½ . . . . (321)   750

Landscape of La Roche-Guyon, pencil, 9 x 12¼ . . (377)   497

Banks of the River Seine at La Roche-Guyon,
black lead, 4¾ x 8 . . . . (376)   210

A Peasant Picking Up Cabbages, colored pencil,
12¼ x 9¼ . . . . (401)   1,800

A Man Playing the Flute, pencil, 11¾ x 15½ . . . . (448)   2,300

Seated Peasant, black lead, 23 x 15¾ . . . . (448)   3,400

Ludgate Hill, London, black pencil, 7¼ x 5¾ . . . . (404)   540

1965

Young Woman, Her Hands Behind Her Back,
(1888), charcoal and colored chalk, 20 x 14 . . . (526)   17,500

Young Lady Reading, charcoal heightened with
white, 8¾ x 7½ . . . . (582)   774

Hay Market, black lead, 8½ x 14 . . . . (503)   750

Cows, pencil, 6½ x 7¼ . . . . (606)   450

Market Scene, pencil, 8 x 6½ . . . . (526)   2,300

Peasant Leaning on His Fork, charcoal,
6¼ x 3¾ . . . . (504)   300

The Sower, pen, 9¼ x 7¼ . . . . (526)   4,100

Peasant on a Donkey, pencil and ink, 8 x 9½ . . . . (535)   829

Landscape at St. Thomas (West Indies), double-
sided drawing, 9 x 11 . . . . (612)   200

Young Boy, Study of Hands, pencil, 20 x 15¾ . . . (561)   560

Bust of a Man, pen and black lead, 6¼ x 4¼ . . . . (567)   396

Small Seated Nude, pen and pencil, 7 x 5 . . . . . . (617)   655

1966

The Kitchen Garden, pen, fan-shaped drawing,
10 x 14 . . . . (772)   560

Landscape of Eragny, (1885–88), chalk, 6¾ x 10 . . (773)   886

Little Girl Seated, charcoal on blue paper,
12¼ x 9½ . . . . (712)   1,624

The New Idolaters, pencil and ink, 11 x 8¾ . . . . . (721)   1,250

Young Boy and Study of Hands, 1888, charcoal,
colored chalk, and pastel, 20 x 15¾ . . . . (808)   2,902

Working Woman, pencil, 3¼ x 5¾ . . . . (648)   275

Seated Peasant, charcoal, 18¾ x 10¾ . . . . (757)   3,593

1967

The Farmyard, charcoal, double-sided drawing,
9½ x 15¾ . . . . (912)   1,600

A Street in Mâcon, 6½ x 9¼ . . . . (1004)   5,000

The Black Woman, 1867, charcoal with white
lights, 12 x 9¼ . . . . (1004)   4,750

The Artist's Family, (1895), pen, 8¾ x 7 . . . . (1004)   2,600

Steep Road (recto), 1853, *Study of an Indian*
(verso), pencil, 10¾ x 7¼ . . . . (913)   615

A Scene in Caracas, 1854, sepia wash and
watercolor, 9½ x 12¾ . . . . (881)   1,382

The Young Shepherdess, pen and black lead,
5¼ x 3¾ . . . . (929)   160

Harvesters, pencil, 9 x 14 . . . . (940)   1,741

Troyes, Town Center, pencil and watercolor,
9 x 7¼ . . . . (881)   2,211

Seated Woman, black and brown pencil,
11¼ x 8½ . . . . (985)   1,232

1968–July 1969

Landscape, charcoal, 6½ x 9½ . . . . (1127) $1,610

Women, black lead, 8 x 5¾ . . . . (1127)   874

The Farmyard (recto), (1880), *The Tree* (verso),
black chalk, 9½ x 15¾ . . . . (1126)   1,982

The Farmyard,[1] (1880), charcoal, 9½ x 15½ . . . . (1174)   3,220

The Water Carrier, (1874), black lead,
11½ x 7½ . . . . (1085)   868

Peasant Working, pencil, 18¼ x 12¾ . . . . (1134)   1,770

The Potato Crop, black pencil, 6¾ x 4¾ . . . . (1137)   1,040

The Fish Market in Dieppe, black pencil,
6½ x 4 . . . . (1019)   580

Two Peasants in a Landscape Near Eragny,
charcoal, 9½ x 11½ . . . . (1207)   5,208

Giverny, pencil, 7¾ x 6½ . . . . (1080)   1,100

Osny, the Feast, pencil and watercolor, 7¼ x 6 . . (1030)   1,150

Back View of a Sower (recto), (1895), *Front View
of a Sower* (verso), pencil and India ink,
8 x 5 . . . . (1191)   2,124

Peasants in the Fields, pen, fan-shaped drawing,
8 x 14 . . . . (1026)   660

Rue des Arpents in Rouen, pen, 6½ x 6½ . . . . . . (1199)   1,100

Back View of a Peasant, charcoal, 18½ x 11 . . . . . (1068)   5,192

Cabbage Sorters, (1883), pencil, 8 x 6½ . . . . (1068)   2,242

Seated Peasant, 10½ x 8 . . . . (1026)   900

Baby's Lunch, black pencil, 10¼ x 7 . . . . (1104)   740

View of Paris, fan-shaped drawing with
watercolor, 11¾ x 23¼ . . . . (1224)   1,960

Study of a Woman in the Nude, pencil,
6¾ x 4¾ . . . . (1225)   700

Osny Near Pontoise, pencil, 8 x 4¾ . . . . (1231)   475

Gathering Hay, 5 x 6½ . . . . (1231)   550

Study of a Tree, pencil, 7 x 11 . . . . (1240)   480

La Ronde, (1884), 18 x 23¾ . . . . (1240)   7,680

Village Street, pencil, 4½ x 7 . . . . (1240)   216

Haystacks, black pencil, 4¾ x 6½ . . . . (1240)   336

Landscape at Pontoise, black pencil, 4 x 6¼ . . . . (1240)   336

*Underwood Landscape at the Hermitage,
Pontoise,* pencil, 8¼ x 10¾ . . . . (1246)   650

Picking Peas (recto), watercolor and charcoal,
9 x 11¾, *Portrait of Georges* (verso),
watercolor and pencil, 8½ x 11½ . . . . (1246)   7,000

Charigny, pencil, 4¼ x 6¼ . . . . (1248)   700

A Peasant; A Peasant and Her Horse, two
drawings, Conté pencil, 4¾ x 33½ . . . . (1254)   400

The Thatch-Roofed Cottage, colored pencil,
11¾ x 9 . . . . (1262)   1,160

Anatomical Study, Back View, charcoal, 8 x 8¼ . (1267)   30

Studies of a Head and Figures, black lead,
double-sided drawing, 6½ x 4 . . . . (1267)   84

Portrait of Monsieur Alfred Isaacson, charcoal,
11 x 10 . . . . (1268)   4,640

Men Working in the Fields, 6¼ x 11 . . . . (1268)   824

Peasant at Work, colored pencil on ceramic tile,
8 x 8 . . . . (1272)   3,480

WATERCOLORS

1961–1962

Peasant's Head, 1883, gouache on cardboard on
board, 16¾ x 18½ . . . . (64)   10,000

*Gardeuse de vaches, effet de brouillard, Eragny
1890,* watercolor, 12¼ x 25 . . . . (164)   1,785

[1]On the reverse, *The Tree.*

Eragny, watercolor, 8¼ x 11 . . . . (30) $ 640
Landscape, watercolor, 6 x 7¼ . . . . (93)   2,260
Landscape of Eragny, 1890, watercolor,
  6½ x 9½ . . . . (114)   2,000
Landscape of Eragny, 1890, watercolor,
  4¾ x 6¾ . . . . (143)   1,492

1963
Landscape at Azincourt, watercolor, 8½ x 11½ . . . (293)   1,500
Morning at Eragny, watercolor, 8 x 10¼ . . . . (318)   1,360
Sunset, (1871), pastel, 6½ x 10 . . . . (277)   950
The Market Gardeners, fan-shaped watercolor,
  4½ x 13 . . . . (258)   640
Two Peasants, 1889, gouache, 13½ x 9½ . . . . (225)   8,000

1964
La Gardeuse de vaches, watercolor, 8¾ x 6½ . . . . . (466)   3,000
Young Peasants Talking, (1884), pastel,
  22¼ x 15¾ . . . . (431)   15,000
Vachère tricotant, 1885, fan design, watercolor,
  11½ x 23 . . . . (405)   3,482
A Peasant and Cows in a Meadow, in the
  Morning, 1886, watercolor, 16¼ x 20½ . . . . . . (474)   6,000
The Two Shepherdesses, 1888, watercolor and
  gouache, 4¾ x 6½ . . . . (351)   1,900
The Shepherd, 1890, fan-shaped gouache,
  10 x 21¼ . . . . (340)   1,900
Landscape of Eragny, 1890, watercolor,
  6¼ x 9¼ . . . . (394)   930
The Two Peasants, (1890), gouache, 6¾ x 10 . . . . . (416)   9,674
The Fish Market, watercolor, 11½ x 8¾ . . . . (481)   3,000
The Pig Market, watercolor and gouache,
  8¼ x 6½ . . . . (325)   1,300
St. Martin's Fair at Pontoise, watercolor,
  6 x 7¾ . . . . (409)   1,560
Chatillon-sur-Seine, watercolor, 8¾ x 6¾ . . . . (377)   2,893
Versailles Road at Louveciennes, watercolor and
  pencil, 7¾ x 10 . . . . (453)   5,804

1965
Portrait of Old Papeille, Pontoise, (1874), pastel,
  21¾ x 18¼ . . . . (561)   620
English Landscape, 1872, gouache, 11¾ x 9 . . . . . . (633)   4,750
Young Shepherdess on the Bank of a Brook,
  gouache, 6½ x 8¼ . . . . (553)   3,760
Study for "The Washerwomen," pastel, 17 x 9 . . . . (526)   7,500
Haymaking Time, pastel and colored chalk,
  18¼ x 24 . . . . (545)   7,778
Landscape, Eragny, 1890, watercolor, 6½ x 9½ . . . (617)   2,848
Woman with a Parasol, pastel, 14¾ x 10 . . . . (632)   5,100

1966
Landscape, fan-shaped gouache, 6 x 21¼ . . . . (744)   6,667
Potato Market, Boulevard des Fossés, Pontoise,
  1882, gouache, 10¼ x 8 . . . . (812)   16,584
The Market, Boulevard des Fossés, Pontoise,
  1885, gouache, 23¼ x 18¾ . . . . (812)   33,997
Landscape of Eragny, (1886), watercolor,
  4¾ x 8 . . . . (686)   7,186
The Pea Crop, 1887, gouache on paper laid down
  on board, 20½ x 25¼ . . . . (750)   38,696
Landscape of Eragny, 1890, watercolor, 8½ x 11 . . (815)   995
Landscape at Eragny, 1890, watercolor,
  4¾ x 6¾ . . . . (814)   1,120
The Washerwoman, (1898), gouache on canvas,
  6½ x 5½ . . . . (750)   8,292

Peasant Fixing Her Kerchief, pastel, 11½ x 8¼ . . . (750) $5,528
Shepherdess at the Watering Place, gouache,
  8 x 7 . . . . (797)   8,136
Les Gardeuses de vaches, watercolor, 7¼ x 9½ . . . (685)   1,220
Gardeuse de vaches à Pontoise, gouache,
  20 x 13½ . . . . (685)   6,000

1967
View of Bazincourt, Fog, pastel, 19½ x 25 . . . . (940)   7,545
The Market Place, 1883, gouache, 12 x 23 . . . . (965)   15,820
The Artist's Mother, Light Effect, 1888,
  watercolor, 4¾ x 6¾ . . . . (985)   1,849
Gardeuse de vaches, Bazincourt, (1890), pencil
  and gouache, round paper, diameter 4¾ . . . . . (931)   1,808
Landscape at Eragny, 1892, watercolor, 8¾ x 11 . . (857)   1,860
The Corn Field, pastel, 10½ x 14¾ . . . . (993)   2,600
Landscape with a Barrier, watercolor, 4¾ x 7¾ . . . (839)   860

1968–July 1969
Landscape, pastel, 10¾ x 14¾ . . . . (1113)   4,400
Sunset, pastel, 7¼ x 10¼ . . . . (1053)   2,800
Gardeuse de vaches, effet de brouillard, Eragny,
  1890, pencil and watercolor, fan-shaped
  paper, 12¼ x 25¼ . . . . (1111)   5,208
Cows at the Pond Near Osny, 1886, gouache on
  silk, 10¼ x 15½ . . . . (1106)   6,200
Morning Light Over Pontoise; Landscape of
  Eragny, two watercolors, 6 x 9½ and
  6½ x 9½ . . . . (1202)   4,000
Tedders at Eragny, watercolor, 6 x 7¾ . . . . (1200)   5,200
Interior, 1882, gouache, 13 x 10 . . . . (1125)   25,300
View of Bazincourt, Fog Effect, pastel on canvas,
  20¼ x 25¾ . . . . (1057)   10,000
Bridge at Caracas, Venezuela, 1854, watercolor
  and pencil, 9½ x 12 . . . . (1240)   5,040
La Causette, pastel, (1892) . . . . (1252)   40,000
Spring Effect, 1890, watercolor, 8¼ x 11 . . . . (1252)   3,100
The Road, pastel, 10¼ x 15½ . . . . (1262)   6,040
Springtime at Eragny, 1890, watercolor and
  gouache, 8¾ x 11¼ . . . . (1262)   3,400
Jeanne and Paul-Emile Pissarro Playing,[2] (1890),
  8¾ x 10¾ . . . . (1270)   25,920
Flood of the River Oise, Pontoise, 1873, pencil
  and watercolor, 7 x 10 . . . . (1272)   5,880

PAINTINGS
1961–1962
St. Germain Road at Louveciennes, 1870,
  15 x 18 . . . . (137)   40,000
Wintry Landscape in England, 1871, 16¾ x 20¾ . . (137)   42,500
The Snow at Louveciennes, 1871, 21¼ x 17 . . . . . . (83)   71,396
The Railway Barrier at Le Patis Near Pontoise,
  (1873–74), 25¾ x 32 . . . . (88)   37,146
Moonlight, (1877), 18½ x 14¼ . . . . (116)   2,900
Fog at the Hermitage, Pontoise, 1879,
  18¼ x 21¾ . . . . (140)   26,087
La Roche-Guyon, 15 x 19½ . . . . (164)   4,943
Old Path in Autumn, Pontoise, 1887, 25 x 21¼ . . . (128)   21,968
Chelsea Bridge, 1890, 23¼ x 28½ . . . . (37)   70,000
White Frost at Giverny, 1891, 18¼ x 15 . . . . (176)   18,000
Sunset with Fog at Eragny, 1891, 19¾ x 23¾ . . . . . (18)   18,758
The Plain: Haymaking Scene, 11½ x 23 . . . . (32)   13,000
The Fagot Gatherers, (1892–94), 7¾ x 5½ . . . . (164)   4,805

[2]Dedicated "A ma chère nièce Alice."

Woman Pulling On Her Stocking, 1895,
15 x 18¼ .... (29) $12,420

Quai St. Sever in Rouen, 1896, 29 x 36½ .... (83) 76,888

The Carrousel, Autumn Morning, 1899,
29 x 36½ .... (112) 49,428

The Louvre, Wintry Morning Sun, 1901,
29 x 36¼ .... (137) 70,000

Dieppe Outer Harbor, 1902, 21½ x 25¾ .... (128) 41,190

1963

The Path, 1858, on panel, 5¼ x 7 .... (221) 1,800

La Varenne-St. Hilaire, 1863, 14 x 17¾ .... (255) 1,645

St. Stephen's Church, Lower Norwood, 1870,
17 x 21 .... (245) 74,034

The Goose Girl at Montfoucault, 1875,
23¾ x 29 .... (316) 50,000

Charity, 1876, 22¼ x 18¼ .... (316) 20,000

Uphill Road, Surroundings of Pontoise, 1876,
18¼ x 21¾ .... (210) 35,646

Peasant with a Donkey, Pontoise, the Manure,
1876, 18¼ x 21¾ .... (277) 23,307

The Quarry at the Hermitage, Pontoise, 1878,
21¼ x 17¾ .... (283) 21,357

Portrait of Georges,[3] 1880, 17½ x 14¾ .... (245) 41,130

Charing Cross Bridge, London, 1890, 23¼ x 36 ... (245) 128,874

Bazincourt Meadows, 1893, on board,
7¼ x 11½ .... (277) 5,484

Red Sky at Bazincourt, 1893, 18¼ x 22 .... (277) 26,049

The Louvre, the River Seine, Misty Morning,
1901, 29 x 36 .... (259) 49,000

The Entrance of Dieppe Harbor, 8¾ x 10¾ ...... (306) 6,400

1964

A Walk in the Forest, 1856, on panel, 5¼ x 7¼ ... (395) 1,200

Surroundings of Paris, 1857, 11¾ x 18¼ .... (369) 2,698

The Road, (1870), 15¾ x 12¼ .... (278) 12,430

Osny Road, Pontoise, 1872, 18¼ x 22 .... (458) 101,570

The River Seine at Port-Marly, 1872,
18¼ x 21¼ .... (367) 46,988

The Railway Barrier Near Pontoise, 1873,
25¾ x 32 .... (367) 88,448

Eragny in November, on panel, 13¼ x 16¼ .... (459) 10,170

The Chat, Valhermeil Path, 1874, 23 x 28¾ ...... (453) 46,988

The Beggars' Track, Pontoise, Snow Effect, 1874,
19¾ x 24 .... (347) 23,200

Landscape with a Peasant and a Cow, (1876),
18¼ x 21¾ .... (378) 27,120

Banks of the River Oise, Pontoise, 1876,
14¾ x 21 .... (416) 22,112

Portrait of Paul-Emile, (1894), 14 x 10¾ .... (347) 7,200

Quay in Rouen, Sunset, 1896, 18¼ x 21¾ .... (399) 25,000

Portrait of Jeanne, (1898), 21 x 18¼ .... (454) 20,730

Eragny Garden, 1898, 29 x 36½ .... (463) 65,000

Landscape at Varangeville, 1899, 25 x 21¼ .... (367) 55,280

Summer Morning, Underwood, 1901, 21 x 17¾ ... (416) 27,640

A Walk in the Orchard, 1901, 12¼ x 10¾ .... (474) 16,000

1965

*Two Women Chatting by the Seaside, St.
Thomas*, 1856, 10 x 15½ .... (624) 8,292

The Gleaners, 1868-70, 14 x 21¾ .... (512) 8,000

Riverside, 1871, 10¼ x 15½ .... (522) 17,966

*A June Morning, View from the Heights of
Pontoise*, 1873, 21 x 35¼ .... (522) 77,392

Landscape with Rocks, Montfoucault, 1874,
25¾ x 36½ .... (613) $77,000

The Beggars' Track, Pontoise, 1878, 29 x 23¾ .... (629) 49,334

The Brook at Osny, 1883, 25¾ x 21¼ .... (628) 75,452

Busagny Castle, 1884, 21¼ x 25¾ .... (628) 37,726

Gardeuse de vaches, Eragny, 1887, oil on paper,
21¼ x 25¾ .... (594) 35,000

Gardeuse de vaches, 1892, 28¾ x 23½ .... (633) 26,000

Back Garden at Eragny, Dull Weather, Morning,
1901, 25¾ x 32 .... (594) 50,000

The Washerwomen at Eragny, 36½ x 29 .... (569) 90,400

*The Willows in the Meadows, Dull Weather,
Eragny*, 1903, 20½ x 25 .... (575) 24,876

The Chestnut Seller .... (493) 55,000

1966

Harvesttime, 1857, on panel, 5¾ x 10¾ .... (749) 2,000

The Avenue Under the Woods, 1859, 16¼ x 13 .... (742) 7,000

Louveciennes Road, Snow Effect, 1872,
18 x 21¾ .... (686) 77,392

Versailles Road at St. Germain, Louveciennes,
1872, 12¾ x 18¼ .... (750) 66,336

A Place in Louveciennes, 18¾ x 15½ .... (753) 49,334

The Hermitage Lane, Pontoise, 1874, 18¼ x 15 ... (686) 34,550

Winter at Montfoucault, Snow Effect, 1875,
45 x 43½ .... (812) 102,268

Poultry Yard in Pontoise, 1877, 13 x 16¼ .... (797) 19,210

The Hermitage, Neighborhood of Pontoise, 1877,
26 x 21¼ .... (812) 80,156

Landscape at Osny, View of the Faun, (1883),
27 x 49¼ .... (686) 44,224

The Ornamental Lake at the Tuileries, 1900,
21¼ x 25¾ .... (812) 40,078

1967

Tempest at St. Thomas, 1854, 9½ x 13 .... (880) 2,764

Self-Portrait, (1854), 11¾ x 10½ .... (880) 3,870

A Corner of a Village, 1863, 15¾ x 20½ .... (864) 60,000

The Pond at Ennery, 1874, 21¼ x 25¼ .... (938) 88,448

Underwood Landscape at Pontoise, 1875,
21¼ x 25¾ .... (901) 42,000

Gisors Hills, Dull Weather, 1885, 17¾ x 21½ ..... (938) 30,404

The Hermitage Road, Pontoise, 1877,
25¾ x 21¾ .... (864) 57,500

Shepherd Caught in a Shower, 1889, distemper,
23¼ x 28½ .... (978) 12,700

Flood, Morning Effect, Eragny, 1892, 21¼ x 26 ... (880) 51,134

Wintry Landscape, Bazincourt, 1893, on panel,
9½ x 12¾ .... (954) 22,000

View of Berneval, 1900, 29 x 35¼ .... (938) 66,336

The Ornamental Lake at the Tuileries, Mist,
1900, 21¼ x 25¾ .... (965) 50,398

The Meadow at Moret, 1901, 21¼ x 25¼ .... (938) 52,516

Statue of Henry IV, Trees in Blossom, 1901,
18¼ x 15½ .... (954) 32,500

1968–July 1969

Domont Lane at Montmorency, on panel,
6¾ x 8¾ .... (1180) 10,020

Landscape at the Hermitage, Pontoise, 1874,
23¾ x 29 .... (1151) 145,000

The Duck Pond at Montfoucault, 1875,
18 x 21½ .... (1068) 66,080

Bunch of Flowers, 1876, 28 x 23 .... (1151) 90,000

Banks of the River Oise at Auvers, 1878,
21¼ x 25 .... (1132) 56,640

---

[3] Third son of the artist.

Poultry Yard, Pontoise (recto), 1878, ***Washer-
women on the Banks of the River Oise,
Pontoise*** (verso), 1878, 12¾ x 15¾ .... **(1187)** $ 61,360
View of Ennery Road, 1879, 21¼ x 25¾ ....**(1173)**   93,380
The Chou Hill at Pontoise, 1882, 32 x 25¾ ......**(1056)**   92,500
The Brook, Osny, 1883, 25¾ x 21¼ ....**(1176)**   91,575
Corn Market, 1884, distemper, 18¾ x 23 ....**(1187)**   54,280
Sunrise in Rouen, 1898, 25¾ x 32 ....**(1126)**   161,070
The Tuileries Garden on a Springtime Morning,
    1899, 29 x 36¾ ....**(1151)**   260,000
The Cart of Wood, 6½ x 9¾ ....**(1026)**   6,260
Underwood Alley, 16¼ x 13 ....**(1113)**   10,800
Apple Trees, Sinking Sun, Eragny, 1893,
    18¼ x 21¾ ....**(1109)**   52,000
Portal of St. Jacques Church in Dieppe, 1901,
    30½ x 25¾ ....**(1151)**   130,000
Haymaking Time at Eragny, 1901, distemper on
    paper on canvas, 18½ x 23 ....**(1187)**   49,560
The Pont-Neuf, Paris, 1902, 21¾ x 25¾ ....**(1151)**   210,000
The Statue of Henry IV, Trees in Blossom, 1901,
    18 x 15¼ ....**(1235)**   42,000
Landscape at Valhermeil, (1878), 14½ x 21 ......**(1239)**   48,000
Peasants and Haystacks, 1878, 21¼ x 25½ ......**(1239)**   110,400
View of Pontoise, 1873, 20¾ x 31¾ ....**(1241)**   215,000
Harvesttime, 1892, 18½ x 20½ ....**(1270)**   91,200
Gathering Potatoes, 1893, 18¼ x 21¾ ....**(1270)**   120,000

Lucien Pissarro

(1863–1944)

Birthplace: Paris, France. (The eldest son of Camille Pissarro, he receives part of his training
from his father.)

1883   Studies painting in London.

1885   Meets Seurat and Signac and joins Neo-Impressionism, like his father. Contributes to periodicals
such as *La Revue Illustrée,* Paris.

1890   Settles permanently in England and breaks away
from Neo-Impressionism.

1916   Becomes a British citizen.

1921   Exhibits at the Leigh Gallery, London.

1924   Exhibits at Bernheim-Jeune's, Paris.

1934   Exhibits at Bernheim-Jeune's, Paris.

1944   Died, Hewood, Somerset.

Sales

DRAWINGS

1963

The Hill, 1916, ink, wash, and colored chalk,
    5 x 8½ ....**(268)** $ 165

1964

Richmond, 1935, pencil, pen, and watercolor,
    4¼ x 6 ....**(356)** $ 111

1965

"Aux Indépendants," 1889, black chalk, 8 x 6½ ...**(643)**   691

1966

Orange Trees in Le Lavandou, 1922, ink, colored
    chalk, and watercolor, 10 x 7½ ....**(761)**   276
View of Colchester, ink and watercolor, 8 x 10 ....**(825)**   221
The River, Youlgreave, 1928, pen, pencil, and
    watercolor, 6¾ x 7¾ ....**(693)**   166

1968–July 1969

The Road, 1915, pen, colored chalk, and
    watercolor, 5¼ x 8 ....**(1025)**   161
The Chalets, La Frette, 1924, pencil, pen, and
    watercolor, 6¼ x 8 ....**(1141)**   448

WATERCOLORS

1968–July 1969

Old Houses, pastel, 20 x 15¾ ....**(1116)**   800
The Park, watercolor, 11 x 8¾ ....**(1074)**   212
Eragny Church, 1887, gouache, 7¼ x 9 ....**(1252)**   2,100

PAINTINGS

1961–1962

Kew Gardens, 1920, 16¾ x 20 ....**(31)**   577

1963

Landscape at Hastings, 1918, 16¾ x 20¾ ....**(213)**   659
The Water Tower, Kew Gardens, 1920,
    16 x 20½ ....**(309)**   330
The Water Tower, 1920, 16 x 20½ ....**(268)**   411
A Lane at Colignac, 1934, 20½ x 24¾ ....**(304)**   877

1964

View of Cline Vale, Hastings, 1918, 16¾ x 20¾ ...**(364)**   493
The Fishermen's Village, 17¾ x 20¾ ....**(420)**   247

1965

Gunville Pond, Sedgehill, 1916, 20½ x 25 ....**(584)**   1,161
View of Milton, 1917, 8 x 10¾ ....**(487)**   166
Landscape, 1923, 10 x 6¾ ....**(584)**   166

1966

The Village, 1890, 25¾ x 32 ....**(819)**   4,400
The Towpath, 1892, 19 x 17½ ....**(793)**   1,000
Bramble Hill, 1917, 20½ x 16¾ ....**(825)**   608

1967

Landscape, 1909, 17 x 21 ....**(1003)**   3,081
Sicié Mountain, Le Brusq, 1925, 23 x 28¼ ....**(945)**   2,488
The Fishermen's Village, 1925, 17¾ x 21¼ ....**(944)**   1,886
Hewood Hamlet, Somerset, 1940, 17¾ x 21¼ ....**(869)**   829

1968–July 1969

Meriden Valley, Coldharbour, 1916, 21¼ x 25 ...**(1143)**   5,699
Landscape of Les Brusq, 1925, on board, 9 x 13 ..**(1025)**   2,230
After the Rain, Bazincourt, 1893, 18 x 21½ ......**(1241)**   6,800
Blackpool, Devon, 1921, 25 x 21 ....**(1248)**   2,500

Serge Poliakoff

(1906–1969)

Birthplace: Moscow, Russia.

1919 Goes to Istanbul following the outbreak of the Russian Revolution.

1923 Arrives in Paris after extensive travel in Europe.

1930 Starts to paint and attends the Académie Frochot and the Académie de la Grande Chaumière, Paris. Supports himself by playing the guitar in the Russian cafés of Paris.

1935–37 Stays in London, where he attends the Slade School of Arts. His favorite painters are Klee and Juan Gris.

1937 Returns to Paris. Meets Kandinsky and turns to abstraction. Makes friends with Robert and Sonia Delaunay.

1938 Participates in the Salon des Indépendants, Paris—until 1945.

1946 First one-man show at the Galerie de l'Esquisse, Paris. Participates in the Salon des Réalités Nouvelles and in the Salon de Mai, Paris.

1947 Wins the Kandinsky prize. One-man show at the Galerie Denise René, Paris.

1948 One-man show at Tokanten Gallery, Copenhagen.

1952 Signs a contract with the Galerie Bing, Paris. Very much impressed by Malevitch.

1955 One man show at the Knoedler Gallery, New York.

1959 One man show at the Knoedler Gallery, Paris. Participates in Documenta II, Kassel.

1962 The Venice Biennial assigns an entire room to his work. Becomes a French citizen.

1963 Exhibits at the Guggenheim Museum, New York, and the Tate Gallery, London.

1965–66 Given an award by the Tokyo Biennial and by the Menton Biennial.

1967–68 Participates in the exhibition "Painting in France 1900–1967" at the Metropolitan Museum of Art, New York.

1968 Exhibits at the Lefebvre Gallery, New York.

1969 Died, Paris.

Sales

DRAWINGS

1968–July 1969

Composition, pencil and watercolor, 10¾ x 8 .... (1061) $ 325

WATERCOLORS

1961–1962

Abstract Composition, gouache, 25¾ x 15½ .... (29) 900
Abstract Composition, gouache, 17½ x 23½ ...... (120) 460
Composition (Series of the Postage Stamps),
 watercolor, 3¼ x 2¾ .... (155) 180
Composition, gouache, 10½ x 7¾ .... (168) 210
Composition, watercolor, 24 x 18 .... (168) 840
Composition, gouache, 19¾ x 25¾ .... (69) 948
Composition, gouache, 17¾ x 23¾ .... (143) 768
Composition, 1955, gouache, 18¾ x 24½ .... (149) 474
Green and Yellow Composition, gouache,
 13 x 21¼ .... (64) 1,250
Composition, gouache, 15 x 21 .... (30) 800

1963

Composition, 1946, gouache, 9½ x 7¼ .... (287) $ 490
Yellow Composition, gouache, 18¼ x 23¾ .... (224) 560
Composition, double-sided gouache, 20 x 15¾ .... (299) 480
Composition (Series of the Postage Stamps),
 watercolor, 2¾ x 3¼ .... (187) 80
Composition, gouache, 23¾ x 17¾ .... (234) 320
Composition, (1958), gouache, 24½ x 19 .... (220) 678

1964

Composition, gouache, 18¾ x 24½ .... (351) 600
Composition, 1944, watercolor and black chalk,
 17½ x 23¾ .... (470) 197
Abstraction, watercolor, 17¾ x 23¾ .... (438) 650
Composition, gouache and watercolor,
 17¾ x 23¾ .... (438) 1,000
Red Glints, gouache, 10 x 12¾ .... (480) 140
Composition, gouache, 23¾ x 17¾ .... (465) 480
Composition, gouache, 19¾ x 25¼ .... (413) 960
Composition, gouache laid down on canvas,
 18½ x 24 .... (401) 340

1965

Composition, (1950), watercolor, 25 x 19 .... (568) 475
Composition, 1960, gouache, 24 x 18¼ .... (561) 600
Composition in Red, gouache, 10 x 12¾ .... (580) 56
Composition, watercolor, 9½ x 12¾ .... (609) 260

1966

Composition, 1965, gouache, 17 x 23¾ .... (721) 950
Composition, gouache, 17 x 23 .... (718) 300
*Abstract Composition in Red, Blue, Green, and
 Gray,* 1959, gouache, 25¼ x 19 .... (735) 1,446
Composition, gouache, 19 x 25 .... (814) 600
Red and Yellow, 1961, gouache, 24 x 18½ .... (792) 1,525

1967

Composition in Four Colors, gouache,
 17½ x 23¼ .... (976) 600
Russian Dancers, gouache .... (834) 330
Composition, 1953, gouache, 23¼ x 17½ .... (996) 620
Composition in Red, Blue, Black, and Yellow,
 1958, gouache, 18¾ x 25 .... (1005) 427
Composition, 1959, gouache, 23¾ x 17¾ .... (998) 935
Composition, gouache and watercolor, 18¼ x 24 .. (963) 650
Abstract Composition, gouache, 15¾ x 21¾ ...... (960) 436

1968–July 1969

Composition, watercolor, 24 x 19½ .... (1043) 400
Composition, 1948, gouache, 17½ x 24 .... (1200) 960
Composition, 1953, watercolor and gouache,
 23¾ x 17¾ .... (1129) 360
Composition, 1953, gouache, 17 x 23 .... (1177) 600
Yellow, Red and Black in the Center, 1957,
 tempera, 18¾ x 24½ .... (1102) 713
Composition in Red, Black, and White II,
 gouache, 18¾ x 25 .... (1203) 446
Composition, gouache, 18¾ x 24¾ .... (1030) 725
Composition on a Yellow Background, gouache,
 17 x 23 .... (1072) 640
Composition in Black, White, and Yellow,
 gouache, 24 x 18 .... (1183) 500
Composition, gouache, 10¼ x 8 .... (1191) 307
Composition, watercolor, 10¾ x 7¼ .... (1202) 320
Composition, gouache, 14¾ x 21 .... (1213) 700
Composition, gouache, 25 x 19½ .... (1049) 600

Composition, 1964, gouache, 25 x 18¾ .... (1114) $ 1,339
Composition in Blue, 1965, gouache, 17½ x 24 ... (1138)   322
Composition, tempera, 25½ x 19¾ .... (1240)   1,080
Composition in Black, Red, and Blue, gouache,
    12¼ x 9¼ .... (1240)   672
Composition in Red, Blue, Black, and Yellow,
    1958, gouache, 18¾ x 24¾ .... (1240)   960
Abstract Composition, watercolor, 18¼ x 24 .... (1241)   706

PAINTINGS

1961–1962

Composition, 1949, 10¾ x 16¼ .... (75)   1,027
Composition, 1950, 32 x 39½ .... (149)   2,528
Composition, 1955, 26 x 31½ .... (145)   3,634
Composition in Red, Blue, and Orange, (1955),
    45½ x 35¼ .... (88)   3,542
Composition in Green and Blue, 1954–55,
    29 x 23¾ .... (88)   2,460
Composition, 1958, on panel, 25 x 31½ .... (85)   1,800
Composition, 1958, 45¾ x 35¼ .... (149)   2,212

1963

Composition, 1948, 35½ x 28 .... (208)   850
Composition, 1953, 32 x 25¾ .... (309)   1,318
Composition, (1955), on panel, 29 x 23½ .... (220)   1,627
Composition, 13 x 18¼ .... (287)   500
Composition, 29 x 23¾ .... (299)   1,200
Composition, 32 x 25¾ .... (249)   1,700
Composition, on panel, 51½ x 38½ .... (299)   2,200

1964

Composition in Black, Red, and Yellow, 1954,
    35¼ x 46 .... (431)   3,100
Composition, 45½ x 35¼ .... (465)   820
Blue Abstract, 39½ x 31½ .... (386)   1,800
Green and Gray, 1962, 29 x 36½ .... (380)   1,845

1965

Abstract Diptych No. 1, 1954, 45 x 35¼ .... (485)   2,750
Diptych No. 2, 1954, 45 x 35¼ .... (485)   2,750
Composition, 25¾ x 21¼ .... (618)   2,952
Composition, 1954, 29 x 23¾ .... (507)   1,450
Composition, 1958, 29¾ x 23¾ .... (606)   2,200
Composition, 26 x 18¾ .... (524)   412
Composition, 50¾ x 37½ .... (637)   4,250

1966

Composition No. 2, 1952, 50¼ x 38¼ .... (678)   8,250
Dyptich, 1953, on board, 24 x 17¾ .... (686)   2,626
Composition, 1956, on panel, 29¼ x 23¾ .... (805)   1,050
Composition, Blue Background, 51¼ x 38 .... (701)   2,000
Composition, 39½ x 32 .... (798)   2,124

1967

Composition, (1952), 39½ x 32 .... (931)   3,955
Composition in Blue, (1954), 45¾ x 35¼ .... (967)   2,260
Composition in Red, Brown, and Black,
    25¾ x 21¼ .... (908)   1,722
Didi, 35¼ x 50½ .... (989)   1,750
Composition, 1958, 29¼ x 23¾ .... (893)   1,300
Composition in Green and Gray, 1962, 28 x 36¼ .. (888)   1,658
Composition, 1965, 39¼ x 31¾ .... (864)   2,500

1968–July 1969

T-648, 38¼ x 51½ .... (1018)   1,750
Composition, 25¾ x 18¼ .... (1129)   760

Red Composition, 36 x 28½ .... (1117) $ 1,000
Composition, 40 x 32 .... (1043)   1,180
Composition, on panel, 45½ x 35 .... (1187)   3,068
Composition, 1954, 45½ x 35¼ .... (1088)   3,250
Composition, 45¾ x 34¾ .... (1127)   3,220
Composition, 1954, 45¾ x 35 .... (1237)   3,000
Composition, oil on panel, 35½ x 28 .... (1237)   3,000
Composition, 36½ x 25¾ .... (1268)   2,900

Jackson Pollock

(1912–1956)

Birthplace: Cody, Wyoming, U.S. (Studies painting and sculpture at the Manual Arts High School, Los Angeles.)

1929   Goes to New York, where he attends the Art Students League. Is taught by Thomas Hart Benton—until 1931.

1930–34   Makes several stays in the West. Very much impressed by the art of the American Indians and by Mexican artists such as Orozco, Rivera, and Siqueiros.

1935   Settles in New York. Admires Picasso and Miró above all.

1938–42   Works on the Federal Art Project.

1940   Turns to abstract Expressionism.

1941–42   Learns the Dadaist technique of automatic creation from his friend Robert Motherwell.

1943   First one-man show at Peggy Guggenheim's Gallery, Art of This Century, New York. Exhibits here until 1947.

1944   Marries Lee Krasner.

1946   Settles permanently at East Hampton, Long Island, New York.

1948   Exhibits at the Betty Parsons Gallery, New York— and again in 1951.

1950   First one-man show in Europe at the Museo Correr, Venice—organized by Peggy Guggenheim.

1951   Reverts partly to representational painting. Paints mainly in black and white. Participates in the São Paulo Biennial.

1952   Exhibits at the Sidney Janis Gallery, New York— and again in 1955. Participates in the exhibition "The New Decade" at the Whitney Museum of American Art and in "Fifteen Americans" at the Museum of Modern Art, New York. Also participates in the International Exhibition of the Carnegie Institute, Pittsburgh.

1956   Participates in the Venice Biennial. Died, Southampton, New York. Retrospective exhibition at the Museum of Modern Art, New York. (Pollock appears as the principal figure of the American movement known as "action painting," which soon won international appreciation.)

Sales

DRAWINGS

1964

Composition, 1944, colored ink, 18¾ x 24½ ...... (454) $ 5,528

1966

Composition, (1946), ink and watercolor,
15¾ x 12 .... (651) 2,400

1967

Wishes, 1946-47, pen and colored pencil,
5¾ x 3¼ .... (985) 379

Seated Nude, pen, 7½ x 5½ .... (985) 521

1968–July 1969

Composition, 1941, charcoal and colored pencil,
17¾ x 13¼ .... (1237) 900

WATERCOLORS

1965

Composition, 1950, gouache, oil, and stones,
21¾ x 39½ .... (489) 7,000

1967

Composition, 1944, gouache on panel, 18¾ x 60 ... (864) 9,000

1968–July 1969

Untitled, 1941, mixed media, 18 x 13¾ .... (1237) 900

Composition, watercolor and India ink,
18¾ x 24½ .... (1268) 9,048

PAINTINGS

1961–1962

Landscape, 1937, 12¾ x 18¾ .... (84) 357

Number Three, 1949, 31½ x 62 .... (31) 60,412

1963

Horizontal White, (1941-47), 22 x 36¾ .... (316) 15,000

Water Figure, 1945, 76¼ x 29¼ .... (247) 13,162

Comet, 1947, 37¼ x 18¼ .... (247) 13,170

1964

No. 19, 1948, 34 x 38¼ .... (367) 24,876

Horizontal White, 22 x 36¾ .... (367) 5,528

1965

Untitled Composition, 1943, 35¼ x 44¼ .... (522) 9,674

Composition, 1944, on board, 18¾ x 60 .... (522) 6,081

Blue Unconscious, 1946, 84½ x 56½ .... (526) 45,000

*Composition in Black, Blue, and Red on a White
Background,* 1948, oil on paper laid down on
panel, 22¾ x 30½ .... (485) 14,000

Abstraction, 1949, oil and enamel on canvas laid
down on panel, 27 x 12¾ .... (485) 12,000

1966

Sun-Scape, 1946, on panel, 19¾ x 23¾ .... (651) 4,250

Composition, 1941, 28 x 50¼ .... (678) 24,000

Composition No. 16, 1949, enamel paint on paper
laid down on panel, 31 x 22¼ .... (678) 32,000

1968–July 1969

The Vase of Flowers, oil and gouache on paper,
9 x 10 .... (1117) 2,600

Ritual, 1953, 92 x 42¼ .... (1057) 44,000

Abstract Composition in Blue, 35¼ x 28¼ ...... (1241) 2,770

Jean Pougny

(1894–1956)

Birthplace: Konokkala, Russia.

1910 First stay in Paris, where he attends the Académie Julian.

1912 Participates in the exhibition "Union of Youth," Petrograd.

1913-14 Second stay in Paris. Participates in the Salon des Indépendants, Paris. Comes under the influence of Cubism and abstract art.

1915 Sets up the exhibition "Tramway W," Petrograd, which includes Malevitch and Tatlin. With Malevitch, signs the manifesto of "Suprematism."

1917-19 Appointed teacher at the Academy of Fine Arts of Petrograd.

1920-22 Leaves the U.S.S.R. for Berlin. One-man show at Der Sturm Gallery, Berlin. Writes a book on modern art. Paints "The Musician," which shows a synthesis between abstract and representational painting.

1923 Settles permanently in Paris. Meets Léger, Marcoussis, Ozenfant, and Severini. Elaborates his final style, inspired partly by Bonnard and Vuillard.

1924 Participates in the first Salon des Tuileries, Paris.

1925 First one-man show in Paris at the Galerie Barbazanges.

1933 One-man show, organized by Paul Guillaume, at the Galerie Jeanne Castel.

1940 Settles in Antibes with Robert Delaunay.

1943 One-man show at the Galerie Louis Carré, Paris.

1946 Becomes a French citizen.

1947 One-man show at the Galerie de France, Paris.

1949 One-man show at the Knoedler Gallery, New York—and again in 1951.

1956 Died, Paris.

1958 Important retrospective exhibition at the Musée National d'Art Moderne, Paris.

1966 His wife donates fifty-four works to the Musée National d'Art Moderne, Paris.

Sales

DRAWINGS

1965

The Billiard Players, charcoal, 16¾ x 20 .... (547) $ 200

Harlequin with a Violoncello, 7¼ x 4¾ .... (609) 200

1966

Circus Scene; Equestrian Acrobatics, two
drawings, pencil, each 25 x 19 .... (731) 500

1967

The Country on Sunday, 5¾ x 12¾ .... (1007) 110

1968–July 1969

Abstract Composition, 1916, pen, 21¼ x 15½ .... (1193) 2,478

Blue House, Vitebsk 1917, brush with India ink,
pencil, blue pencil, and wash, 12¼ x 8 ...... (1273) 1,210

The Little Path, black and gray washes, 10½ x 8 . (1273) 428

WATERCOLORS

1961–1962

The Open Window, gouache, 16¾ x 11¾ .... (102) $ 800
The Rendezvous, 1900, gouache, 19 x 24½ .... (98) 400
Interior, pastel, 8¾ x 12¾ .... (93) 768
Interior, watercolor, 14¼ x 19½ .... (123) 400
The Garden, watercolor and gouache,
    18¼ x 25¾ .... (120) 640
A Street in Montmartre, gouache, 16¾ x 12½ ..... (34) 820

1963

Still Life with Fish, gouache, 12¾ x 18¼ .... (293) 880
"14 Juillet," gouache, 18¾ x 10¼ .... (206) 1,700
A Street in Montmartre, gouache, 19 x 13¾ ...... (288) 1,500

1965

In the Street, gouache, 11½ x 18¼ .... (409) 124
Mask and Palette, double-sided gouache,
    13 x 13 .... (386) 280
Seated Woman, at a Café, gouache, 6¾ x 6¾ .... (346) 470

1965

The Orchestra, gouache, 17 x 18¾ .... (567) 859
Jug of Flowers on a Chair, watercolor,
    21¼ x 16¾ .... (599) 410
Still Life, gouache, 6¾ x 8¾ .... (538) 600
The Young Woman with a Violin, gouache,
    12¾ x 7½ .... (523) 1,200

1966

The Lovers' Dance, watercolor, 14¾ x 19¾ ...... (711) 560
The Orchestra, gouache, 17 x 18¼ .... (798) 1,017
Still Life with Fruit, gouache and oil on paper,
    6¼ x 11½ .... (809) 1,620
The Cab, gouache, 3¾ x 5¾ .... (742) 620
The Street, gouache, 18¾ x 13¼ .... (745) 2,260

1967

The White Chair, gouache, 22 x 8¾ .... (976) 1,280
The Open Window, gouache, 21¾ x 16¾ .... (995) 500
Landscape, watercolor, 19 x 24 .... (912) 700
On the Beach, gouache, 5¾ x 4¾ .... (934) 312
The Beach, gouache, 7¼ x 14¼ .... (912) 1,760
The Banks of the River Seine, gouache,
    17¾ x 23 .... (978) 2,000

1968–July 1969

White Pot and Bread, 1922, gouache,
    23¾ x 17½ .... (1203) 1,189
The Bridge, 1923, gouache, 16¾ x 12¾ .... (1191) 1,062
Stage Costume for a Woman, 1923, gouache,
    18¾ x 11¾ .... (1142) 519
Still Life with a Pipe and a Glass, 1924, gouache,
    11¼ x 15½ .... (1134) 425
Woman in an Armchair, 1940, gouache,
    8¼ x 7¾ .... (1203) 446
Glasses and Chair, gouache, 10¼ x 14¾ .... (1180) 160
The Fish, gouache, 12¾ x 18¼ .... (1043) 400
The Chair, gouache and distemper on paper laid
    down on canvas, 19¾ x 14 .... (1043) 1,700
The Café, 1926, gouache, 16¾ x 22 .... (1240) 360
Jug and Books, (1922), gouache, 17 x 23¾ ...... (1273) 1,108
White Pot and Loaf, 1922, gouache, 23½ x 17½ .. (1273) 1,386

PAINTINGS

1961–1962

Porte de St. Cloud, 21¼ x 25¾ .... (30) 2,820
Landscape, oil on cradled canvas, 13 x 9¾ .... (143) 1,265
Still Life with Hat and a Stick, 20 x 31 .... (143) 1,492

1963

The Public Garden, 21¼ x 25¾ .... (293) $ 2,600
La Rue aux autobus, Paris, 21¼ x 25¾ .... (198) 1,400
Still Life with Fruit, 13 x 18¼ .... (288) 1,000
Interior, (1938–39), 11¾ x 13½ .... (314) 2,200
Still Life with a Chair, 34½ x 30¾ .... (298) 6,400

1964

The Painter, 5¾ x 3¾ .... (471) 588
Figures on the Beach, 8¾ x 11 .... (368) 2,902
Landscape of the South of France: Canoës, on
    cardboard, 13½ x 17 .... (371) 3,960
Glass and Mask, 10¾ x 14 .... (466) 340
The Carriage, on cardboard, 8¾ x 10¾ .... (471) 1,808
Harlequin, oil on paper, 5¼ x 2¾ .... (355) 190
Studio Corner, on cardboard, 20 x 7¼ .... (371) 2,800

1965

The Conversation, on cardboard, 8¼ x 10¼ ...... (503) 2,600
Woman Seated in a Garden Armchair, on
    cardboard, 6¾ x 5¾ .... (581) 380
Still Life, on canvas laid down on panel, 6 x 8 .... (611) 700
Composition with a Chair, on canvas laid down
    on panel, 5¾ x 3¼ .... (598) 780
The White Horse, on canvas laid down on panel,
    4 x 5¾ .... (548) 380
Interior of a Studio, 7¼ x 10¾ .... (547) 1,600
The Public Garden, 21¼ x 25¾ .... (523) 2,500

1966

The Bridge, 15 x 18¼ .... (797) 4,972
Interior, oil on paper, 12¼ x 6¾ .... (670) 1,000
Plate of Fruit, 18¼ x 13 .... (798) 1,695
The Black Pedestal Table, on cardboard,
    22¼ x 19 .... (798) 1,618

1967

Woman in an Armchair, on panel, 7½ x 6½ ...... (919) 1,808
The Cab at the Race Course, on cardboard,
    10¾ x 13½ .... (987) 1,400
Still Life with a Chair, oil on paper, 21 x 8 .... (911) 1,400
Embarking in Marseilles, on cardboard,
    5¾ x 7¼ .... (967) 1,356
A Street in Paris, 18¼ x 21¾ .... (857) 2,300
Harnessed Horse, on panel, 5¾ x 8½ .... (943) 520
Seated Woman, oil on paper laid down on
    canvas, 11½ x 8¾ .... (911) 1,300
The Harbor, on cardboard, 14¾ x 15 .... (996) 1,510
The Bus, on cardboard, 10½ x 4¾ .... (912) 1,220
The Bus, 13 x 9 .... (919) 2,712

1968–July 1969

Oriental Interior, 11½ x 8¾ .... (1127) 1,610
Woman in an Armchair, on panel, 7¾ x 6¾ ..... (1127) 1,932
Interior with an Easel, (1947), on panel,
    14 x 10¼ .... (1127) 3,795
Abstract Composition, 1915, 34½ x 22 .... (1113) 8,600
Sultans, on cardboard, 20 x 16 .... (1113) 3,800
Green Sculpture, 1915, painted wood, metal, and
    cardboard mounted on panel, 19¾ x 15½ ...... (1193) 8,921
Landscape, (1942), on cardboard, 9 x 5¾ .... (1174) 2,070
The Painter on the Beach, on panel, 7¼ x 10¼ .. (1043) 3,240
The Fun Fair, on cardboard laid down on cradled
    panel, 11 x 10½ .... (1049) 2,020
The Bus, 12½ x 9 .... (1132) 826
Still Life with a Violin, 49¾ x 31¾ .... (1184) 2,400

Still Life, 35½ x 51¾ . . . . (1184) $ 2,800
The Fruit Stand, 6¾ x 6¾ . . . . (1202) 1,000
Still Life, on cardboard, 25¼ x 19½ . . . . (1213) 660
Table and Plate of Fruit, on panel, 17 x 21 . . . . . . (1200) 1,700
Figures on the Beach, 1955, oil on paper,
    5¾ x 14 . . . . (1203) 1,784
The Quai de la Râpée, 4¼ x 9¼ . . . . (1225) 2,000
Masks and Easel, on panel, 10¾ x 24¾ . . . . (1238) 1,400
Still Life with Fruit, on cardboard, 7¾ x 19¾ . . . . (1238) 1,000
Still Life with a Pipe, 22¾ x 11¾ . . . . (1238) 1,000
Seated Woman, on canvas laid down on
    cardboard, 75 x 33½ . . . . (1258) 1,600
Pink Vase, (1917), 25¼ x 19¼ . . . . (1273) 9,570

PAINTINGS

1964
St. Malo Beach, 1907, 17¾ x 21 . . . . (431) $ 21,000
Still Life with Fruit, 1913, 16 x 21 . . . . (431) 18,000

1968–July 1969
Evening Walk, 10¼ x 13¾ . . . . (1235) 31,000

Maurice Prendergast

(1859–1924)

Birthplace: St. John's, Newfoundland. (His family
    soon moves to Boston.)

1884–87 Goes to Europe with his brother Charles. Attends
the Académie Julian and the Académie Colarossi,
Paris. On returning, Maurice and Charles settle in
Winchester, Massachusetts.

1898 Returns to Europe. Comes under the influence of
Neo-Impressionism and of the Nabis.

1908 Participates in the exhibition of "The Eight" at the
Macbeth Gallery, New York.

1910–12 Stays in Italy.

1913 Paints "The Promenade." Participates in the Armory Show, New York.

1914 Settles in New York with Charles, who is also a
painter.

1924 Died, New York. (Prendergast may be regarded as
the first modern American painter.)

Sales

WATERCOLORS

1965
The Gardens of the Luxembourg, 1909,
    watercolor, 10¾ x 8¼ . . . . (610) $3,250

1966
St. Malo, the Rocks, (1910-12), watercolor,
    13½ x 19¼ . . . . (707) 12,500

1967
Notre-Dame de Paris (recto), 11 x 9, *The "Grands
Boulevards"* (verso), 7½ x 8, watercolor . . . . . (889) 4,250

1968–July 1969
Woman on the Cliff, 1909, watercolor, 12¾ x 14 . . (1035) 4,250
Early Beach, (1897), 13¾ x 12¼ . . . . (1229) 20,000
Woman in a Garden, watercolor, 11 x 6¾ . . . . (1229) 7,500
Woman in Blue, watercolor, 8¼ x 5½ . . . . (1246) 6,500

Pierre Prins

(1838–1913)

Birthplace: Paris, France. (Very little is known
    about him.)
Starts to paint in the manner of Corot, but later
    meets Edouard Manet and comes under the influence of the Impressionists. Like them, he is interested mostly in landscape painting.

1913 Died, Paris.

Sales

WATERCOLORS

1961–1962
Banks of the River Seine at Triel, 1887, pastel,
    14¼ x 19¾ . . . . (169) $ 860

1963
March Morning at Le Guichet, (1890), pastel,
    14 x 23 . . . . (302) 490

1964
Marly-le-Roi: A Path in the Forest, pastel,
    12¼ x 17½ . . . . (350) 66
Springtime in Seine-et-Oise, 1878, pastel,
    17 x 20½ . . . . (401) 520
The Orchard at Seucy-en-Brie, 1880, pastel,
    17 x 22½ . . . . (399) 1,120

1965
The Lane, pastel, 12¾ x 18¼ . . . . (567) 294
Cloud on Colombel, 1886, pastel, 14¼ x 20 . . . . . . (561) 420
Parc des Fortifications d'Auteuil à La Muette,
    1912, pastel, 17¾ x 14¾ . . . . (564) 500
Trees in Bloom, pastel, 15¼ x 24¼ . . . . (550) 226
Springtime in Seine-et-Oise, 1878, pastel,
    17½ x 20½ . . . . (518) 1,600

1966
In the Islands of the Old Meudon, pastel,
    17 x 23 . . . . (683) 160
The Orchard, pastel, 12¾ x 21¾ . . . . (817) 70

1967
Parc des Fortifications d'Auteuil à La Muette,
    1912, pastel, 17¾ x 14¾ . . . . (987) 700
Landscape at Le Guichet (Seine-et-Oise), pastel,
    24½ x 18¼ . . . . (950) 480

1968–July 1969
The Thatch-Roofed Cottage, pastel, 12¼ x 17½ . . (1026) 300

PAINTINGS

1961–1962

Toghao Mountains, the Road to Chad,
19½ x 29 . . . . (53) $ 520

1963

The Sea at St.-Valéry-sur-Somme, 1891,
21¼ x 25¾ . . . . (299)   960

1965

Flowery House, Bougival, (1880), 21¼ x 29 . . . . . . (564)   900

Washerwomen in the Forest of Fontainebleau,
13 x 18¼ . . . . (491)   560

1967

Farm at Sucy-en-Brie, (1895), 14¾ x 21¾ . . . . (852)   2,200

After the Storm, on cardboard, 6¾ x 10 . . . . (955)   320

1968–July 1969

The River Seine at Triel, 1910, 16¾ x 19½ . . . . . . (1106)   4,000

Jean Puy

(1876–1960)

Birthplace: Roanne, France. (Studies architecture at the Fine Arts School of Lyons.)

1898   Settles in Paris. Turns to painting and attends the Académie Julian.

1899   Leaves this academy to enter the studio of Eugène Carrière, Paris. Meets Matisse, Derain, and Laprade.

1901   With Matisse and Marquet, participates in the Salon des Indépendants, Paris.

1905   Participates in the Salon d'Automne, Paris, with the Fauves—Matisse, Marquet, Van Dongen, Derain, Vlaminck, Manguin, Rouault, Friesz, Valtat, and others.

1906-21   The dealer Ambroise Vollard buys a large part of his work.

1939   Executes an important decoration for the Lycée du Parc, Lyons.

1949   Exhibits at the Musée de Mulhouse and at the Galerie Lorenceau, Paris.

1950   Exhibits in his native town.

1960   Died, Roanne.

1963   Retrospective exhibition at the Musée des Beaux-Arts, Lyons.

Sales

DRAWINGS

1961–1962

Landscape, black lead, 9½ x 12¼ . . . . (168) $ 18

1963

Talloires, 1910, 9½ x 12¼ . . . . (209) $ 64

Reclining Woman, pencil and watercolor,
5¾ x 8¼ . . . . (251)   42

1965

Washing, 6½ x 9 . . . . (538)   60

1966

Standing Nude, 21¼ x 8 . . . . (672)   30

A Study of Two Nudes, black lead, 23 x 18¾ . . . . . (798)   316

Hilly Landscape, colored pencil, 5½ x 7¾ . . . . (798)   41

1967

Standing Nude, charcoal, 15 x 7½ . . . . (999)   80

1968–July 1969

Needlework, colored pencil, 11 x 17 . . . . (1110)   400

Back View of a Standing Nude, 1906, pen and
charcoal, 18¾ x 11½ . . . . (1031)   100

The Harbor, colored pencil, 9 x 12¼ . . . . (1154)   176

Fishing Boat in the Harbor, black pencil
heightened with pastel, 8¾ x 11¾ . . . . (1225)   280

WATERCOLORS

1966

Dolls, gouache, 19¾ x 23¼ . . . . (745)   542

In the Studio, 1911, pastel, 12¾ x 9 . . . . (731)   210

Bust of a Woman, 1944, pastel, 23 x 14¾ . . . . (781)   84

1967

The Doll, gouache, 12¾ x 9¾ . . . . (926)   640

1968–July 1969

In the Public Garden, watercolor, 4½ x 6¾ . . . . . . (1051)   260

Boats, 1919, pastel, 8¼ x 10 . . . . (1174)   207

The Bather, gouache, 14¼ x 10¼ . . . . (1233)   220

Baby with Ducks, gouache, 14 x 9¾ . . . . (1245)   156

PAINTINGS

1961–1962

Still Life with Apples, on panel, 10 x 13½ . . . . (68)   200

The Doll, 18¼ x 21¾ . . . . (117)   260

Woman in the Grass, oil on cardboard,
15 x 21¼ . . . . (156)   1,040

Boats at Bénodet, 21¼ x 36½ . . . . (109)   1,200

The Village Through the Trees,[1] 14¾ x 17 . . . . (177)   410

1963

Belle-Ile-en-Mer Harbor, 1901, 39½ x 59¼ . . . . (306)   1,160

Nude and Still Life, 1910, 38½ x 51½ . . . . (221)   400

Nude in a Studio, 1914, 32½ x 39½ . . . . (246)   400

The Painter and His Model, 31¼ x 38¾ . . . . (286)   500

The Reading, 31½ x 39½ . . . . (192)   400

The River, on panel, 18¼ x 21¾ . . . . (314)   330

The Bunch of Tulips and Windflowers,
19¾ x 24 . . . . (254)   380

1964

The Pedestal Table Before the Window,
23¾ x 29 . . . . (399)   760

Woman Seated in a Garden, on cardboard,
14¾ x 21 . . . . (404)   320

The Schooner, 11¾ x 17½ . . . . (407)   678

The Basket of Fruit, on panel, 13 x 18¼ . . . . (335)   600

[1]On the reverse, bust of a woman.

Still Life with Fruit, on cardboard, 8¼ x 10¾ ..... (366)	$ 400
Still Life, double-sided painting, 19¾ x 24 .... (359)	800
The Artist and His Model, 29¼ x 24 .... (394)	1,100

1965

Sunset Over the Sea, 1898, 21¼ x 29 .... (617)	4,407
Great Underwood, 19¾ x 37½ .... (613)	840
Boats, "The Blaze," 1901, on cardboard, 15½ x 22¾ .... (613)	1,400
Woman at the Window, 1905, 19¾ x 25¾ .... (632)	1,800
Woman at the Balustrade, 19¾ x 32 .... (538)	630
Half-Length Portrait of a Woman, on cardboard, 18¼ x 15 .... (492)	150
Village with Red Roofs, (1906), 28½ x 32½ .... (569)	3,503
The Seated Model, 25¾ x 18¼ .... (508)	116
The Model, 32 x 23¾ .... (532)	1,500
The Village, 12¾ x 21¼ .... (581)	160
The Forest, 21¼ x 25¾ .... (511)	244
Sun Bath, 1938, 21¼ x 25¾ .... (632)	1,300

1966

Still Life with Red Carnations, 25¾ x 21¼ .... (795)	960
Tempest at Belle-Ile-en-Mer, 1901, 35¼ x 51½ ... (726)	2,000
Nude on a Pink Sofa, 26 x 34½ .... (669)	1,000
Woman Seated Under the Trees, 1907, 36½ x 29 .... (669)	2,400
Terrace at the Seaside, 19¾ x 31½ .... (657)	600
Seaside, on canvas laid down on board, 19¾ x 24 .... (721)	400
Boats in a Creek, 23¾ x 32 .... (741)	1,700
A Beach with Figures, 29 x 41 .... (727)	2,240
Vase of Flowers, (1908–10), 24 x 19½ .... (750)	2,211
Sculpture in the Studio, on cardboard laid down on canvas, 25¾ x 32½ .... (794)	170
The Reading, 25¾ x 36½ .... (724)	1,000
Reclining Woman, 29 x 36½ .... (745)	4,294

1967

Belle-Ile-en-Mer, Little Sauzon Harbor, 23¾ x 36½ .... (852)	2,000
Clouds on St. Malo, 13 x 29 .... (897)	480
Fishermen's Wives on the Beach, 11¾ x 14 ...... (1007)	280
Village Through the Trees, 24 x 19¾ .... (900)	680
Portrait in the Forest, 36½ x 31 .... (987)	2,000
Portrait of a Woman, 25¾ x 21¼ .... (855)	820
Reclining Woman with a Pink Sofa, 29 x 36½ .... (912)	2,000
Nude with a Sofa, 29 x 23¾ .... (935)	1,420
Young Ladies Picking Flowers, 25¾ x 32 .... (919)	678
Vase of Flowers, oil on paper, 17½ x 11¾ .... (923)	760
Still Life, on board, 15½ x 21¾ .... (974)	650
The Artist's Studio, 25¾ x 32 .... (950)	280
The Studio, 32 x 25¼ .... (984)	1,700

1968–July 1969

Woman with a Parasol by the Seaside, 1900, 18 x 24 .... (1106)	2,700
Stranded Boats (The Blaze), 1901, on cardboard laid down on canvas, 15½ x 22½ .... (1200)	1,620
Sailboats Alongside a Quay, 1903, 19¾ x 24 ..... (1113)	1,800
Sailboats, 18¼ x 21¾ .... (1045)	580
Belle-Ile-en-Mer, 19¾ x 25¾ .... (1060)	3,200
Landscape by the Waterside, oil on paper laid down on canvas, 21¼ x 25¾ .... (1053)	1,500
The Doll, 1919, 20½ x 12¼ .... (1053)	220
View of a Village, 28½ x 35¼ .... (1213)	3,040

The Glade Beneath a Blue Sky, on paper laid down on canvas, 14¾ x 14¾ .... (1202)	$ 340
Interior, 26 x 19¾ .... (1039)	720
Young Woman with a Blue Beret, on cradled panel, 17 x 14¾ .... (1084)	84
Folk Dance, 13 x 18¼ .... (1128)	250
Basque Dances, 12¾ x 17¾ .... (1066)	220
Doll and Toys, 24 x 19¾ .... (1161)	280
Still Life with Grapes, on panel, 15 x 21¼ .... (1219)	1,500
Tulips, on panel, 20½ x 24½ .... (1202)	1,560
Country Dance, 13 x 18¼ .... (1225)	280
Woman Seated in the Park, (1906), 24 x 19¾ .... (1232)	5,000
The Doll with a Shawl, 24 x 19¾ .... (1245)	300
Boats on the River, 1911, 21¼ x 25½ .... (1248)	2,000
Woman on a Red Sofa, 25¾ x 36½ .... (1258)	2,700
The Harbor, Belle-Ile, 1912, on cardboard, 5¾ x 9¼ .... (1262)	220
Seascape, on board, 15 x 17¾ .... (1268)	1,382

Odilon Redon

(1840–1916)

Birthplace: Bordeaux, France.

1855	Decides to devote himself to painting. Meets the botanist Clavaud, who helps him discover Delacroix, Flaubert, Baudelaire, and Poe.
1857	Goes to Paris to enter the Ecole Nationale des Beaux-Arts but fails the entrance examination.
1858	Enters the studio of Gérôme, Paris. Very much impressed by the work of Gustave Moreau.
1863	The engraver Bresdin initiates him in etching and lithography.
1867	Participates for the first time in the Salon, Paris, with an etching entitled "Landscape."
1868	Writes art criticism for the review *La Gironde.*
1870	Settles in Montparnasse, Paris. Meets Corot and Fantin-Latour. Trip to the Netherlands.
1879	Executes an album of lithographs entitled "In the Dream."
1880	Marries Camille Fargue.
1881–82	Exhibits at "La Vie Moderne" and "Le Gaulois." Works mainly in charcoal.
1883–89	Devotes himself to black and white engraving. Birth of his son Ary.
1884	Participates in the first Salon des Indépendants, Paris.
1885	Participates in the exhibition of the Impressionist group.
1889	Exhibits at Durand-Ruel's, Paris. Meets A. Mellerio.
1891	Meets Gide, Valéry, and Mallarmé.

1899   Exhibition, "Hommage à Odilon Redon," at Durand-Ruel's, Paris. Gives up engraving and turns to pastel and oil. Executes pictures presenting unusual and refined visions derived from the deepest strata of mind—qualities that will attract the Surrealists to his work. Shows a strong liking for religious subject matters.

1909   Settles in Bièvres and lives in retirement.

1916   Died, Paris. (His work is closely linked to modern art.)

Sales

DRAWINGS

1961–1962

Bust, 20 x 14¼ .... (71) $1,220

Crowned Christ, pencil, 8 x 5 .... (152)   325

1963

Dante and Virgil in a Landscape, (1865–70), charcoal, 12½ x 9¾ .... (202)   1,900

1964

The Battle, 1865, charcoal, 25¼ x 44¼ .... (378)   5,650

Woman's Head, (1887), charcoal, 10¾ x 10¾ ..... (367)   2,764

Head in the Foliage, pen, 8½ x 7½ .... (368)   967

Musing, black lead, 10¼ x 8¼ .... (483)   1,040

1965

Ecstasy, (1885–95), charcoal, 19¾ x 14¾ .... (568)   1,740

Nude in the Forest, charcoal, 21¼ x 14¾ .... (504)   2,400

Terror, black lead, 7¼ x 9 .... (504)   400

Perseus, pencil, 5¾ x 3¾ .... (582)   608

Allegory, 10½ x 8 .... (511)   164

1966

St. Michel, pencil and watercolor, 8½ x 4½ ...... (798)   904

Roland at Roncevaux, (1865), pen and black ink, 13½ x 10 .... (808)   5,804

1968–July 1969

The Heights, charcoal .... (1236)   4,000

Nude in Chains, India ink, 3 x 4 .... (1245)   80

Eve Lamenting Abel's Death, black lead, 7½ x 6½ .... (1268)   3,016

WATERCOLORS

1961–1962

Salome, pastel, 23 x 15½ .... (125)   7,800

1963

Geraniums, pastel, 19 x 16¼ .... (258)   15,000

Cain's Flight, (1865), watercolor, 6½ x 10 .... (202)   1,000

The Yellow Sail, pastel, 23 x 18¾ .... (279)   19,000

Butterflies, (1912), watercolor, 10¼ x 8½ .... (277)   5,758

Girl in Red, Reading, pastel, 14¼ x 11 .... (254)   6,020

1964

Child's Head, pastel, 10¼ x 8¾ .... (463)   7,800

Cain and Abel, pastel, 31¼ x 23 .... (398)   3,000

Mystic Flowers, pastel on gray paper, 19¾ x 12 ... (354)   8,000

The Holy Women, (1897), pastel, 24 x 20 .... (416)   15,478

1965

Woman in an Orange Veil, pastel, 12¾ x 9¼ ..... (512)   1,160

Cain and Abel, pastel, 31½ x 23 .... (575)   6,910

The Fisherwoman, 1900, pastel, 23¾ x 17¾ .... (522)   11,608

1966

Geraniums, pastel, 19 x 16¼ .... (748) $16,272

Composition with a Horse's Head, pastel, 10¼ x 9 .... (741)   2,000

Shell, pastel on canvas, 14¾ x 9 .... (812)   1,382

Study of a Bunch of Flowers, chalk and watercolor, 6¾ x 5 .... (735)   2,712

The Monsters, pastel, 12 x 9½ .... (750)   3,593

1967

The Yellow Sail, pastel, 23 x 18¾ .... (864)   22,000

The Blond Child, 1899, pastel, 15 x 12¾ .... (982)   10,902

Madame Sabouraud, 1907, pastel, 31 x 36 .... (982)   48,585

Woman with a Flower, pastel, 21 x 14¾ .... (970)   1,181

1968–July 1969

The Holy Women, pastel, 24¼ x 20 .... (1176)   30,000

Flowers and Butterfly on a Blue Background, (1905), pastel, 11 x 9½ .... (1235)   22,500

Thoughts on Hamlet, (1910), watercolor and pencil, 9½ x 7 .... (1272)   2,040

PAINTINGS

1961–1962

The Red Angel, (1890), 20½ x 15 .... (18)   12,769

The White Horse, on panel, 9½ x 12¾ .... (95)   1,200

Landscape Near Peyrelevade, 18¼ x 21¾ .... (26)   4,900

The Sailboat, (1900), 24½ x 31¼ .... (164)   7,963

At the Bottom of the Sea, (1905), 22¾ x 18¾ ...... (64)   22,000

1963

Icarus, 1900, 20½ x 15 .... (210)   4,387

Icarus, on board, 7½ x 10 .... (277)   2,331

The Boat, 21¾ x 18¼ .... (198)   6,000

Boats, 25¾ x 32 .... (206)   8,200

The Ferryman on the River Bank, 35½ x 31½ .... (306)   10,000

1964

Allegory in Red, on panel, 12¼ x 9½ .... (471)   4,407

The Geranium Pot, (1905), 19¾ x 12¾ .... (367)   56,662

St. Georges Mill, 1905, 10¾ x 16¼ .... (399)   980

Poppies in a Blue Vase, (1905–10), on canvas laid down on board, 15½ x 15¾ .... (416)   42,842

The Warrior, on board, 12¾ x 9 .... (454)   2,211

Prometheus in Chains, 25¾ x 19¾ .... (371)   6,800

1965

Marine Divinity, 13 x 18¼ .... (569)   12,656

Gothic Window, 1900, 25 x 19 .... (594)   40,000

Flowers, Red Background, (1905), 22 x 18¼ ...... (594)   50,000

St. Georges Mill, 1905, 10¾ x 16¼ .... (617)   5,424

The Geranium Pot, (1908–10), 25 x 19½ .... (522)   45,606

The Lonely Tree, 8½ x 12¾ .... (645)   4,760

Poet's Dream, on board, 20 x 10¼ .... (526)   10,500

1966

Allegory in Red, on cradled panel, 12¼ x 9½ ..... (797)   6,780

Ophelia's Death, (1905), on board, 27¾ x 21¼ .... (750)   15,202

The Breton Woman, gray paint on cardboard, 20½ x 14¾ .... (823)   7,072

1967

Flowers in a Vase, 32 x 25¾ .... (988)   47,272

1968–July 1969

Bunch of Flowers, 21¼ x 29 .... (1109)   19,000

The Warrior, on board, 12¾ x 9 .... (1208)   7,000

Vase of Flowers, 21¾ x 15¼ . . . . **(1093)** $ 102,000
Christ and the Snake, (1910), on board,
26½ x 20½ . . . . **(1235)** 26,000
Portrait of Madame Violette Heymann, 1909,
11½ x 8¼ . . . . **(1239)** 16,320
Butterflies, 25¾ x 19¾ . . . . **(1258)** 50,020
Couple in Profile, on cardboard . . . . **(1263)** 22,220

Pierre-Auguste Renoir

(1841–1919)

Birthplace: Limoges, France.

1845   His family settles in Paris.

1854   Starts to decorate china and later, in 1858, fans.

1862   Enters the Ecole Nationale des Beaux-Arts, Paris, in the studio of Gleyre, where he meets Monet, Sisley, and Bazille.

1866-67   Works are refused by the Salon, Paris.

1868   Participates for the first time in the Salon, Paris.

1869   Works with Monet at "La Grenouillère."

1870   Exhibits at the Salon, Paris.

1873   Meets Paul Durand-Ruel. Paints with Monet at Argenteuil.

1874   Participates in the first exhibition of the Impressionist group, at Nadar's, Paris. Makes friends with Caillebotte.

1876   Paints "Le Moulin de la Galette," "La Balançoire," and "Portrait of Monsieur Choquet." Takes part in the second exhibition of the Impressionist group, Paris.

1877   Participates in the third exhibition of the Impressionist group, Paris.

1879   Participates in the Salon and in the fourth exhibition of the Impressionist group, Paris.

1881   Paints "Luncheon of the Boating Party." Visits Algeria and Italy.

1882   Executes a portrait of Wagner. Works with Cézanne at L' Estaque. From now on, spends almost every summer in the south of France. Participates in the seventh exhibition of the Impressionist group, Paris.

1883   One-man show at Durand-Ruel's, Paris.

1884-85   Gradually breaks away from Impressionism. Birth of his son Pierre.

1886   Participates in the important Impressionist exhibition organized in New York by Durand-Ruel.

1888   Stays at Cézanne's, at the Jas de Bouffan. Attacked by facial paralysis.

1890   Beginning of his "période nacrée" (pearly period).

1892   One-man show at Durand-Ruel's, Paris.

1894   Birth of his son Jean, the future film director.

1896   One-man show at Durand-Ruel's, Paris.

1901-03   Birth of his son Coco. Settles in the south of France, first at Le Cannet and then permanently at Cagnes.

1904   Retrospective exhibition at the Salon d'Automne, Paris.

1905-09   His illness grows worse.

1912   Has to have his brushes fixed to his fingers to be able to paint again.

1913   One-man show at Bernheim-Jeune's, Paris.

1915   Death of his wife.

1919   Died, Cagnes.

Sales

DRAWINGS

1961–1962

Madame Renoir and Her Son Pierre, 1885, red and white chalk on gray paper . . . . **(112)** $27,460
The Great Bather, red chalk heightened with white, 36 x 27¾ . . . . **(112)** 14,279
Mother Suckling Her Child, red chalk, 28 x 23 . . . . **(20)** 8,216
Mesdemoiselles Lerolle at the Piano, 1890, charcoal on white paper, 19¼ x 25 . . . . **(84)** 31,579
Study for Mesdemoiselles Lerolle at the Piano, 18¾ x 23¾ . . . . **(167)** 1,900
Nude, 1892, black lead, 13½ x 8¾ . . . . **(117)** 1,000
Gabrielle Dressing, red chalk, 29¼ x 22½ . . . . **(29)** 5,200
The Two Bathers with Hats, pencil and pen, 11 x 9 . . . . **(76)** 2,200
The Two Bathers with Hats, Conté pencil and pen, 10¾ x 9 . . . . **(138)** 3,028
The Pinned-Up Hat, pen, 5¼ x 3¾ . . . . **(125)** 3,000
Nude with a Tambourine, pencil, 18¼ x 11¾ . . . . . . **(71)** 1,740
The River Rhône and the River Saône, (1910), red chalk on white paper, 23¼ x 18½ . . . . **(112)** 13,730
Nude, (1911-12), pen, 11¾ x 8¾ . . . . **(96)** 900
Berthe Morisot and Her Daughter, pencil, 11¾ x 9 . . . . **(31)** 1,510

1963

A Sketch Album of Travels Through Algeria and Italy, (1881), approximately 20 figures and 10 landscapes . . . . **(312)** 4,000
Judgment of Paris, red chalk heightened with chalk, 25¼ x 35½ . . . . **(318)** 14,800
The Nurse, charcoal and chalk, 25¾ x 19 . . . . **(318)** 3,400
Portrait of a Child, charcoal, 16¼ x 13½ . . . . **(271)** 300
Rosita Mauri, (1881-83), charcoal, 11½ x 12¾ . . . . **(277)** 1,919
The Woman with a Muff, (1880-83), pencil and sepia ink, 18¼ x 11 . . . . **(277)** 14,258
The Folk Dance, red chalk, 11¾ x 8¾ . . . . **(208)** 3,100
Study of Plants and Trees, ink with watercolor lights, 7 x 6 . . . . **(247)** 3,290
Nude Drying Her Foot, charcoal and red chalk, 17 x 11¼ . . . . **(277)** 2,194
Young Lady Seated on a Chair, red and black chalk with white lights, 12 x 9¼ . . . . **(277)** 6,581

1964

Seated Young Lady, (1880), pencil, 11¾ x 9 . . . . . . **(335)** 7,400
Bust of a Woman, charcoal, 17¾ x 13½ . . . . **(464)** 3,200
Woman with a Muff, (1880-83), pencil and sepia, 18¼ x 11 . . . . **(378)** 16,950
Two Young Ladies Walking, (1883-85), red and black chalk with white lights, 23¾ x 15¾ . . . . . **(416)** 39,249

Madame Renoir and Her Son Pierre, (1885-86),
ink, 28 x 21 .... (454) $8,292

Madame Renoir and Her Son Jean, 1886, red and
white chalk on canvas, 35½ x 20½ .... (367)   4,975

Harvest: Woman and Child, red chalk on paper
laid down on canvas, 45½ x 15¼ .... (401)   10,400

Young Boy Playing Croquet, black lead,
8¾ x 11¾ .... (321)   1,000

Coco Drawing, Conté pencil, 23¾ x 17¾ .... (340)   14,000

Study for the Pastel "Child with an Apple," 1915,
pencil heightened with red chalk on tracing
paper, 21¾ x 30½ .... (378)   8,588

A Page of Sketches for "King Oedipus," black
lead, 19 x 11½ .... (471)   3,842

Portrait of the Bourgeois-Gentilhomme, charcoal,
17¾ x 11½ .... (335)   1,200

1965

Mesdemoiselles Lerolle at the Piano, 1890,
charcoal, 19¼ x 25 .... (575)   26,258

The Apple Seller, (1890-93), pencil on paper laid
down on canvas, 19 x 21¼ .... (522)   4,146

Musicians, charcoal, 19½ x 15 .... (624)   1,520

Seated Young Lady, chalk, 16¾ x 11½ .... (596)   1,230

Little Girl in Profile, stick of greasepaint,
15½ x 15 .... (569)   4,068

Young Lady and Child, red chalk, 14 x 10 .... (568)   2,712

Woman Sewing, black pencil and red chalk on
tracing paper, 24½ x 19¾ .... (518)   1,040

Judgment of Paris, red chalk with chalk lights,
25¼ x 35½ .... (551)   8,600

1966

Madame Renoir and Her Son Pierre, red chalk
and white chalk on bister paper, 27¾ x 23 .... (753)   8,706

The Apple Seller, (1890-93), pencil on paper laid
down on canvas, 19 x 21¼ .... (815)   4,008

The Declaration of Love, red chalk on paper laid
down on canvas, 31¼ x 25 .... (750)   9,674

Bather, red chalk, 10 x 7¼ .... (815)   2,488

The Guitar Player, (1900), charcoal, 22¼ x 18¼ ... (797)   12,430

Peasant, pencil and watercolor, 14¾ x 8½ .... (703)   2,700

1967

Dancing Nude with a Veil, Back View, pencil,
7¾ x 6½ .... (912)   600

*La Promenade en barque (Madame Renoir and
Pierre),* 1886, pencil and watercolor, 11 x 9 .. (982)   23,700

Nude with a Tambourine, 1912, pencil,
17¾ x 11¾ .... (965)   4,520

Back View of a Nude, pencil, 11¾ x 7¼ .... (981)   2,240

Bather, red chalk, 19 x 12 .... (889)   2,300

1968–July 1969

Young Woman Reclining, red chalk and charcoal
on paper laid down on canvas, 17½ x 21 .... (1199)   30,600

Gabrielle with a Red Bodice, red chalk and
charcoal, 21 x 17¼ .... (1199)   19,600

Gabrielle, Her Breast Bare, (1890), red chalk,
16 x 13½ .... (1187)   18,880

Madame Renoir and Her Children, black lead,
11¾ x 18¼ .... (1125)   2,990

Study of Bathers, (1885), red chalk with white
lights, 12¾ x 17 .... (1187)   16,520

Woman's Head, 1893, pencil, 6 x 4½ .... (1088)   2,300

Study of a Bather and of a Woman's Face, black
pencil, 17½ x 11½ .... (1137)   1,300

Portrait of a Woman, pencil, 11¾ x 8¼ .... (1078) $1,200

*Page of Studies Including Two Self-Portraits and
Other Figures,* (1910), pencil and pen,
18¼ x 12¼ .... (1085)   2,480

Nude with Her Right Arm Raised, black lead,
9 x 6½ .... (1255)   2,500

Seated Woman, blue pencil, 15 x 11 .... (1256)   620

Study for King Oedipus, charcoal and red chalk,
16¾ x 11½ .... (1268)   1,879

WATERCOLORS

1961–1962

Young Nude, Back View, (1885-90), pastel,
29¼ x 18 .... (140)   21,968

Young Woman with Drapery, pastel, 21¼ x 14¾ .. (123)   3,900

Landscape Near Cagnes, (1908-10), watercolor,
6½ x 8¾ .... (164)   2,471

1963

Seated Bather, pastel, 24½ x 19 .... (210)   79,518

Portrait of Mademoiselle Dieterle, (1890), pastel,
19¾ x 15½ .... (241)   17,020

Bathers, pastel, 16¾ x 13½ .... (309)   7,910

1964

Landscape at Cagnes, (1895), watercolor,
4 x 2¾ .... (338)   230

Pimientos and Tomatoes, pastel, 7¼ x 9½ .... (454)   2,211

1965

Little Bérard, (1879-80), pastel, 19½ x 12¼ .... (624)   7,186

The Croquet Game, pastel, 23¾ x 17¾ .... (518)   2,200

Mademoiselle Dieterle, pastel, 15¾ x 20 .... (617)   24,408

Nude, pastel, 20 x 14¼ .... (569)   8,136

1967

Woman with a Blue Bodice, pastel, 24 x 18 .... (864)   35,000

*Young Lady with a Hat Adorned with Roses,
Charlotte,* pastel, 24½ x 20 .... (981)   33,200

Green Landscape, with a Little House,
watercolor, 7¼ x 9 .... (981)   1,520

1968–July 1969

Interior with a Seated Young Woman, (1879-80),
pastel, 24¼ x 18¼ .... (1132)   132,160

The Road, Overcast Weather, (1890), watercolor,
8¼ x 10½ .... (1092)   2,852

Young Lady with an Orange Kerchief, (1895),
pastel, 22 x 17½ .... (1187)   89,680

Bathers with a Crab, (1897), pastel, 17¾ x 20 .... (1126)   42,126

Portrait of Jean Renoir, 1895, pastel, 21¼ x 16 .. (1068)   44,840

Cap Martin, watercolor, 4¾ x 6¼ .... (1241)   3,020

PAINTINGS

1961–1962

Trees Lining a River, (1875-80), 5¾ x 7¾ .... (128)   4,394

Argenteuil, 1880, 21¾ x 25¾ .... (29)   80,000

Bathers, 1885, 18¾ x 15 .... (32)   38,000

Reclining Nude, (1885), 12 x 16¾ .... (164)   12,357

Woman with a Hat, 1885, 8 x 10¾ .... (69)   15,800

Three Young Ladies Walking, (1885), 25¼ x 21 .... (83)   131,808

Girl with Red Stockings, (1885), 12¾ x 9½ .... (64)   21,000

Seated Nude, 16¼ x 13½ .... (83)   24,714

The Young Lady in Pink, 11¾ x 6 .... (98)   6,200

Boats in Argenteuil, 1888, 21 x 25¾ .... (83)   131,808

Young Nude, (1888-90), 17 x 13½ .... (84)   98,856

Bust of a Little Girl, 2¾ x 3 .... (160) $ 580
Young Ladies by the Waterside, (1893),
   12¼ x 16½ .... (112)   115,332
Back View of a Nude, 1894, 8 x 8¼ .... (53)   6,600
The Meadow, 1895, 8¼ x 12¾ .... (156)   3,820
Portrait of a Young Woman, (1895), 18¾ x 14 ..... (84)   52,174
Studies of Figures, 11½ x 9½ .... (26)   6,400
Christine Lerolle,[1] 1897, 22¾ x 21¼ .... (128)   68,650
Portrait of Pierre, Son of Alfred Sisley,
   10¼ x 8¼ .... (128)   24,714
Young Boy Looking at His Album, 11 x 9½ .... (76)   24,400
The Guitar Player, 1897, 14 x 12 .... (164)   8,238
Woman Seated on the Grass, 8½ x 9½ .... (76)   12,000
Les Martigues, 7¼ x 10¾ .... (160)   7,500
Figure on the Beach, 1898, 10 x 15¾ .... (18)   11,074
Still Life with Apples, (1898), 8¼ x 14¾ .... (143)   18,532
Still Life with Fruit, 8¾ x 14 .... (18)   16,950
Still Life, Figs, and Peaches, 13 x 18¼ .... (29)   28,000
Three Apples, 6¾ x 13½ .... (97)   7,200
Landscape After Corot, 1898, 15½ x 21¼ .... (156)   8,600
Landscape at Cagnes, 1900, 8¾ x 13 .... (18)   11,978
Landscape of Cagnes, 1900, 9½ x 14 .... (145)   18,960
Landscape, (1900), 8¾ x 13 .... (93)   9,944
Bunch of Roses, 18¼ x 15 .... (143)   24,634
Young Lady in the Fields, (1900), 18¼ x 22 .... (31)   90,618
Studies of Heads, Flowers, and Landscape,
   13 x 6¼ .... (17)   4,400
View of Morillon, 18 x 21¼ .... (128)   31,579
Landscape at Cagnes, 1905, 8¾ x 13 .... (70)   11,060
Landscape, Cagnes, 1905, 12¾ x 16¾ .... (64)   31,000
Landscape at Cagnes, 5¾ x 8 .... (150)   4,294
Landscape of the South of France, 10¼ x 13 ...... (71)   13,800
Underwood, (1905), 14¾ x 10¼ .... (93)   12,882
Study of a Landscape, 2¾ x 4 .... (47)   312
Landscape, 1905, 8¼ x 12¾ .... (167)   4,300
Wind Blowing, 1906, 6½ x 11¼ .... (167)   2,800
Landscape at Cagnes, 1909, 12¾ x 21¼ .... (71)   33,600
Landscape of Cagnes, 9½ x 14 .... (93)   21,470
Landscape, Cagnes, 1910, 11¼ x 19½ .... (156)   8,600
Bend of the Road, 11 x 14¾ .... (29)   5,800
Landscape at Cagnes, 11 x 16¼ .... (93)   16,498
Seated Nude, (1913), 16¼ x 13½ .... (83)   24,714
The Blond Lady, 17½ x 14¼ .... (160)   12,000
The Greek, 10 x 8¾ .... (64)   3,750
Bather with a Fountain, 1914, 21¾ x 18¾ .... (112)   28,833
Young Woman with a Pink Body, 1914, 13 x 9½ .. (138)   16,950
Landscape of the South of France, 1914,
   11 x 15¾ .... (71)   4,100
Landscape at the Seaside, 1914, 6½ x 12¾ .... (71)   5,600
Mountainous Site, 1914, 9½ x 12 .... (156)   4,600
Study of Cows in the Meadow, 19¾ x 24 .... (124)   7,100
Windflowers, 20 x 16½ .... (29)   51,000
Roses in a Vase, 18¼ x 21¾ .... (76)   55,800
Still Life, 4½ x 8½ .... (143)   3,277
Still Life with Fruit, 6¾ x 11 .... (120)   7,000
Dorados, 12¾ x 20½ .... (114)   14,000
The Pimientos, 11 x 17¾ .... (164)   7,414
Festival of Pan, 24¼ x 28¾ .... (163)   100,000

[1] Inscribed "Au petit diable Christine Lerolle."

1963

Portrait of a Young Woman in Black, (1875-76),
   12½ x 9¼ .... (245) $ 126,032
*Portrait of Monsieur and Madame Benjamin
   Godard*, 1877, 13¾ x 10¼ .... (245)   65,808
Peaches, 1878, 7¼ x 13½ .... (206)   11,000
Young Lady with a Chignon, 1882, 21¼ x 17½ .... (247)   71,292
Seated Man Leaning on a Table, Back View,[2]
   (1885), 16¼ x 13 .... (279)   17,000
Little Girl with a Hat, 1890, 21¼ x 17¾ .... (245)   167,262
Madame Renoir and Her Son Pierre, 1890,
   15½ x 11¾ .... (245)   49,356
Nude in a Landscape, (1890-95), 12 x 15¾ .... (261)   27,968
Gabrielle Reading, 15½ x 12 .... (261)   23,307
The Reading, 16¼ x 13 .... (199)   48,600
Heads of Two Children, 1892, oil on canvas laid
   down on panel, 2¾ x 5¼ .... (295)   900
Portrait of Madame Cézanne, 1898, 8 x 5¾ ...... (241)   5,600
The Man in Black Seated on the Beach, 1898,
   10 x 14¾ .... (241)   4,000
Children's Heads, 1900, 21¼ x 14¾ .... (316)   46,000
Gulf of Brittany, Houses and Trees on the Cliff,
   1902, 11 x 14¾ .... (245)   21,388
Landscape Near Cagnes, (1900-10), 10 x 15 ...... (210)   7,678
Landscape of Cagnes, 8 x 10¼ .... (232)   9,266
At the Seaside, (1905), 21¼ x 25¾ .... (316)   20,000
Essoyes. 1905, 18¼ x 17¾ .... (247)   23,307
Head of a Young Lady, (1905), 7¼ x 7½ .... (316)   9,500
The Farm at Essoyes, 1913, 21½ x 25¼ .... (316)   35,000
Sketch of a Landscape, Seated Woman in Red,
   1916, 11¾ x 14 .... (254)   7,600
Little Girl Reading, 7¼ x 5¼ .... (223)   4,900
*Sleeping Woman, Her Hands Crossed on Her
   Head*, 1919, 13½ x 17½ .... (247)   24,678
Woman Wearing an Arabian Blouse, Reading,
   1919, 15½ x 16¼ .... (277)   24,678
Portrait of a Woman, 6½ x 6 .... (223)   2,160
Nude Dressing, 7¾ x 4¾ .... (199)   4,920
Nude, 11¾ x 7 .... (254)   5,200
Back View of a Nude, 8 x 4¼ .... (233)   4,000
Nude with Roses, 15 x 10 .... (258)   5,600
Bust of a Young Lady, 15¾ x 12¾ .... (312)   39,000
Bather and Fountain, 21¼ x 18¼ .... (194)   46,200
Vase of Flowers, 13 x 11 .... (194)   11,600
Roses, 8 x 18½ .... (243)   14,000
Vase of Roses, 18¼ x 15 .... (232)   21,470
Roses, 7½ x 11¾ .... (283)   10,170
Cup of Fruit, 10¾ x 14¼ .... (245)   21,936
Cup and Sugar Pot, 6½ x 10¼ .... (254)   7,000
Landscape, on canvas laid down on panel, 4 x 6 .. (318)   1,160
Landscape of the South of France, 4¾ x 6½ ...... (258)   1,700
Landscape of the South of France, 7¾ x 10¾ ..... (243)   4,400
Aix-en-Provence, 8 x 11½ .... (283)   8,136
Rowing, 12¾ x 17¾ .... (293)   25,086
The Lane in the Country, 12¼ x 21¾ .... (318)   20,400
Mirror Frame, oil on cement, 78¼ x 48¼ .... (198)   1,120

1964

The Young Soldier, (1877-80), 21 x 12½ .... (367)   127,144
Portrait of an Old Woman, 1878, 17¾ x 14¾ ..... (454)   66,336
The Vase of Chrysanthemums, (1880-82),
   31½ x 25 .... (367)   154,784

[2] Presumed portrait of Frédéric Bazille.

Roses in a Vase, 21¾ x 17¾ . . . . (458) $ 50,786
Portrait of a Woman, (1883), 19 x 14¼ . . . . (335) 67,000
Blond Woman Combing Her Hair, 1886,
 25¾ x 21¼ . . . . (367) 174,132
Young Boy in a Sailor Suit, (1887), 16¼ x 13 . . . . . (347) 10,400
Boy's Head, (1887), 16¼ x 12¾ . . . . (448) 11,500
Aix-en-Provence, (1890), 8 x 11½ . . . . (335) 4,600
Aix-en-Provence, (1890), 8 x 11½ . . . . (450) 5,700
Roses, (1890–95), 6½ x 11¾ . . . . (354) 8,000
Landscape, Cagnes, 1893, 8¾ x 10¾ . . . . (435) 11,200
Apples, 1892, 6½ x 12¾ . . . . (416) 8,845
Lunch on the Grass, 1893, 12¾ x 15¾ . . . . (416) 32,062
Peaches, 1895, 15 x 21½ . . . . (453) 31,786
Still Life with Apples, (1898), 8¼ x 14¾ . . . . (450) 15,020
Still Life with Apples, (1898), 9 x 13 . . . . (471) 11,074
Apples and Pears, 8 x 12¾ . . . . (458) 20,314
Landscape, (1898), 10¾ x 13½ . . . . (378) 11,978
Landscape of Cagnes, (1900), 9½ x 14 . . . . (378) 18,080
Study of Boats, 5 x 8 . . . . (351) 2,160
Two Women in a Landscape, (1903), 21¼ x 25¼ . . (450) 56,000
Woman with a White Blouse, 19½ x 14¾ . . . . (471) 60,116
Gabrielle in the Garden, 10 x 15½ . . . . (347) 14,600
*Madeleine with a White Bodice and Bunches of
 Flowers*, 22 x 19¾ . . . . (399) 104,000
The Beach at Cagnes, (1903), 4¾ x 11½ . . . . (354) 6,500
Les Collettes Garden at Cagnes, 1905,
 9½ x 19¼ . . . . (464) 9,800
The Terrace: Madame Renoir at Cagnes, 1908,
 13¼ x 10¾ . . . . (367) 38,696
Mediterranean, 6 x 11½ . . . . (380) 5,412
Coco with a Pink Hat, 7½ x 8¼ . . . . (367) 19,901
Portrait of Dédée, 10 x 9½ . . . . (407) 8,136
Riverside with Figures, (1905), 12¾ x 21¼ . . . . (459) 16,950
Cup of Tea, Spoon, and Lemon, 1909, 8¾ x 13 . . . (416) 10,503
The Collarette, 1909, 16¼ x 13 . . . . (474) 64,000
After the Bath, 16¼ x 12 . . . . (367) 26,534
Farmyard at Essoyes, 1910, 17½ x 21¼ . . . . (416) 30,404
Banks of the River Seine at Argenteuil,
 21¾ x 25¾ . . . . (340) 8,000
Landscape with Two Figures, 12¼ x 16¼ . . . . (340) 17,200
Regattas, 5 x 8 . . . . (418) 2,820
Summer Landscape, 14¾ x 17¾ . . . . (458) 15,090
Portrait of a Little Girl, 4½ x 3½ . . . . (398) 2,620
Bust of a Young Lady, 1913, 11½ x 9½ . . . . (416) 16,584
Trees Before a House, 6¾ x 5¾ . . . . (416) 3,593
Woman Leaning Her Chin on Her Hands, 1917,
 10 x 9¼ . . . . (401) 14,600

1965

In the Forest of Fontainebleau, 1866, 32 x 25¾ . . . (583) 26,432
On the Road, 1872, 18¼ x 15 . . . . (522) 30,404
Bouquet in a Vase, 1878, 18¾ x 13 . . . . (594) 125,000
Portrait of a Young Woman, (1885), 15 x 11¾ . . . . (575) 30,404
In Love (Young Lady's Head), 1888, 16¼ x 13¼ . . (526) 32,500
Two Young Ladies, (1888), 13 x 10 . . . . (539) 30,000
The Farm, 1892, 23¼ x 31 . . . . (624) 33,168
Young Ladies by the Waterside,[3] (1893),
 13 x 16½ . . . . (633) 57,500
Still Life with Pomegranates, 1893, 14½ x 18½ . . . (522) 58,044
Pomegranates, 8 x 13 . . . . (569) 10,396
Landscape with Figures, (1895), 23¼ x 28¾ . . . . . . (624) 66,336

[3]Sold in London in 1962 for $115,332.

Landscape of Provence, (1895), 17½ x 21 . . . . (569) $16,046
Woman's Head in Left Profile, 12¾ x 10¾ . . . . (569) 38,872
Study for "The Woman with a Guitar," 1898,
 10 x 9 . . . . (629) 13,930
Young Lady in the Fields, 1900, 22 x 18¼ . . . . (575) 77,392
Young Woman, Her Arms Folded, 22 x 18½ . . . . . (617) 88,140
Apples and Pears, 1901, 8 x 12¾ . . . . (629) 17,412
Apples, 8½ x 14¾ . . . . (617) 13,560
Melon and Tomatoes, 18¼ x 21¾ . . . . (617) 29,380
Bust of a Young Child Wearing a Hat, 8¾ x 8 . . . . (518) 6,800
Gabrielle, (1908), 18¾ x 13¼ . . . . (526) 40,000
Reclining Nude, 4 x 7 . . . . (569) 6,328
Landscape of Grasse, 1913, 11 x 14¾ . . . . (561) 8,600
The Reading, 19¾ x 16¾ . . . . (518) 41,400
Landscape and Stream Seen from Mourillon,
 18¾ x 22 . . . . (617) 50,624
Bust of a Young Lady with a Straw Hat, 1917,
 8 x 6¾ . . . . (624) 8,568
Reclining Woman, 1918, 10 x 7¾ . . . . (624) 11,885
Vase of Chrysanthemums, 16 x 13 . . . . (575) 33,168
Bunch of Roses in a Vase, 16¼ x 13 . . . . (553) 26,200
Unfinished Landscape, 14¾ x 18 . . . . (640) 30,000

1966

Woman Musing, (1875), 18¼ x 15 . . . . (749) 290,000
Three Partridges, (1880), 12¼ x 15¾ . . . . (808) 49,334
The Church and the Cliffs at Varangeville, (1880),
 21¼ x 29 . . . . (797) 30,284
Aix-en-Provence, (1890), 8 x 11¼ . . . . (819) 4,920
Apples, (1892), 6½ x 12¾ . . . . (797) 10,396
Landscape, (1893), 8¾ x 14¼ . . . . (686) 9,950
Pierre Renoir's Head, (1894–96), 6½ x 5¾ . . . . (694) 9,000
The Music, (1895), 51½ x 16¼ . . . . (744) 39,550
The Dance, (1895), 51½ x 16¼ . . . . (744) 39,550
Silenus, 1900, 12¾ x 7¾ . . . . (814) 5,600
*House and Trees with Mountains in the
 Background*, 1904–10, 7¼ x 11¾ . . . . (814) 12,400
White Roses, 1907, 10¼ x 11¾ . . . . (741) 40,000
Geraniums, 11¾ x 10 . . . . (713) 22,000
Still Life with Flowers, 8 x 19¾ . . . . (776) 15,000
The Post Office at Cagnes, 12¾ x 18¼ . . . . (744) 34,352
An Alley at Les Collettes Garden, Cagnes, 1907,
 9 x 12¼ . . . . (741) 71,000
Red Mullets, (1914), 8¼ x 12¼ . . . . (689) 3,317
Young Lady with a Pink Bodice, (1914),
 16¼ x 13 . . . . (694) 13,000
Tobacco Pot, (1915), 6½ x 5½ . . . . (694) 3,500
Windflowers, (1916), 12¾ x 12 . . . . (694) 11,000

1967

Nude Combing Her Hair, 14¼ x 9½ . . . . (901) 31,000
*The Croquet Game (Children in Montmartre
 Garden)*, 18¼ x 21¾ . . . . (901) 50,000
Vase of Lilacs, (1873–75), 21¼ x 25¾ . . . . (988) 69,664
The Horsewoman, (1878), 15 x 12¼ . . . . (918) 36,160
The Gondola in Venice, 1881, 23½ x 29¾ . . . . (880) 35,932
Flowers in a Vase, 1881, 26 x 21½ . . . . (864) 100,000
Childhood, 1891, 25¾ x 19¾ . . . . (880) 152,020
Pont-Aven Calvary, 1892, 15½ x 18¼ . . . . (988) 33,588
The Spring, (1895), 25 x 17½ . . . . (982) 47,400
Young Lady in Profile, (1895), 11 x 7½ . . . . (923) 123,600
Coco's Head, 3¼ x 2¾ . . . . (976) 2,500
Seated Woman with a Hat, 26½ x 21½ . . . . (954) 71,400

The Fountain, (1895), 18¼ x 11½ .... **(982)** $ 40,290
Mother and Child, (1900), 25¾ x 21¾ .... **(954)** 105,000
The River Seine at Argenteuil, 16¼ x 24½ .... **(978)** 8,200
Dancing Silenus, 1900, 12¾ x 7½ .... **(935)** 7,000
Provençal Landscape, 3½ x 8¼ .... **(987)** 2,700
Study of Windflowers, (1906-10), 9½ x 7¼ .... **(888)** 3,731
Three Young Ladies Seated on the Grass,
   11¾ x 14¾ .... **(880)** 37,314
Roses in a Vase, 15½ x 13 .... **(954)** 25,000
Landscape, 11¾ x 12¾ .... **(911)** 11,000
Mountainous Landscape, 5¾ x 10 .... **(940)** 12,769
Landscape, 12¼ x 10 .... **(981)** 6,060
Still Life with Apples on a White Tablecloth,
   8¾ x 12¼ .... **(909)** 15,000
Woman with a Rose, 22 x 18½ .... **(965)** 85,880

1968–July 1969
The Pont des Arts, Paris, (1868), 24½ x 40¾ .... **(1151)** 1,550,000
Portrait of Alfred Sisley's Son Pierre, (1873-75),
   10¼ x 8¼ .... **(1193)** 47,082
The Woman with a Cat, (1876-78), 13 x 10 ...... **(1187)** 141,600
Reclining Woman in the Nude, (1888),
   59¾ x 23¼ .... **(1017)** 144,000
Young Lady Carrying a Basket of Flowers, 1888,
   32½ x 24½ .... **(1109)** 140,000
Young Lady in Profile, (1888), 12¾ x 9¼ .... **(1050)** 214,000
Two Nudes in a Niche, (1890), 12¼ x 16¼ .... **(1176)** 90,000
The Spring, 1895, 25 x 17½ .... **(1173)** 64,550
Still Life, Three Lemons and a Bowl, (1895),
   7½ x 11 .... **(1187)** 20,296
Reclining Woman, Back View, (1897), 10 x 18 ... **(1068)** 49,560
Christine Lerolle, 1897, 22¾ x 21¼ .... **(1126)** 89,208
Figures, Trees, Bottom of the Sea, Sketch of a
   Head, 1898, 9½ x 12¼ .... **(1187)** 23,600
Landscape of Cagnes, 1900, 10 x 14 .... **(1173)** 29,900
Washerwomen and Bathers at Essoyes, 1900,
   17½ x 21¼ .... **(1068)** 63,720
Nude with Drapery, (1908), 18¾ x 15 .... **(1176)** 40,000
The Washerwomen at Cagnes, (1912),
   17½ x 21¼ .... **(1125)** 78,200
The Washerwomen at Le Béal, Cagnes, 1912,
   17½ x 21¼ .... **(1068)** 51,920
King Oedipus, (1912), 11 x 11½ .... **(1132)** 8,260
Bather, (1916-18), 11¾ x 10¼ .... **(1056)** 37,500
Young Lady with a Rose, 1917, 20 x 15¾ .... **(1049)** 112,000
Woman with a Blue Bodice, 21¾ x 18¼ .... **(1109)** 69,000
Head of a Young Woman with a Rose, 10 x 8¼ .. **(1173)** 26,220
Woman in Profile, 16¼ x 13 .... **(1157)** 52,000
Portrait of Vera Sergine, 19½ x 23½ .... **(1049)** 62,000
Studies of Heads, 12¾ x 12¾ .... **(1183)** 29,200
Portrait of a Child, 3¾ x 3 .... **(1026)** 1,400
Reclining Young Lady in the Nude, oil on fan-
   shaped straw laid down on canvas, 6¾ x 15 . **(1184)** 4,400
Landscape in the Neighborhood of Cagnes,
   6½ x 13 .... **(1113)** 9,600
Les Collettes, 18¼ x 20 .... **(1049)** 84,000
Landscape of the South of France, 8 x 12¼ ..... **(1092)** 16,120
Landscape, 8¾ x 11 .... **(1183)** 5,500
Landscape, 7¾ x 17¼ .... **(1109)** 13,000
La Rochelle Gunpowder Factory, 12¾ x 15½ .... **(1125)** 35,420
Study for "The Folk Dance," 18 x 10 .... **(1126)** 91,686
The Angler, 7½ x 17¾ .... **(1189)** 7,100
Flowers, 8 x 21¼ .... **(1173)** 33,350
Still Life with Apples and a Flower, 8¾ x 12¼ ... **(1126)** 18,585

Roses, 7½ x 5¼ .... **(1199)** $ 8,400
Roses, 12¾ x 11 .... **(1106)** 24,400
The Cup, 7½ x 11½ .... **(1106)** 10,200
Still Life with Plums and Peaches, 8 x 12 .... **(1058)** 10,416
Still Life with China and Lemons, 6¼ x 14½ ..... **(1058)** 8,680
Cauliflower and Pomegranate, 14 x 18½ .... **(1126)** 27,258
Still Life, 5½ x 13¼ .... **(1173)** 16,560
Fish, 13 x 21¾ .... **(1173)** 32,660
Apples, Sketch of a Landscape, 7¼ x 5½ .... **(1109)** 7,400
Head of a Fair-Haired Woman, 1908, 9¾ x 7¼ .. **(1224)** 55,000
Head of His Son Coco, (1905), 8¼ x 7½ .... **(1235)** 22,500
The Pear Tree, 17¼ x 14½ .... **(1235)** 85,000
Woman Reading, (1880-85), 15½ x 12½ .... **(1235)** 215,000
Decorated Crockery, (1916), 7¼ x 12½ .... **(1235)** 10,000
The Glade, (1908), 13 x 16½ .... **(1235)** 30,000
King Oedipus, 13¾ x 13¾ .... **(1239)** 18,000
The Italian Woman, (1890), 9 x 8 .... **(1239)** 21,600
Rose in a Vase, Landscape and Chairs in a
   Room, 14¾ x 11½ .... **(1239)** 52,800
Landscape, on canvas laid down on panel,
   2½ x 5¾ .... **(1240)** 1,968
Landscape, 3¾ x 4½ .... **(1240)** 2,400
Young Lady Carrying a Basket of Fruit,
   31¾ x 24¼ .... **(1241)** 105,800
Head of a Little Girl, on board, 2¾ x 2¾ .... **(1241)** 1,058
Landscape of the South of France, (1896),
   11¾ x 15 .... **(1252)** 30,400
Boats on the River, (1898), 6¾ x 11 .... **(1252)** 19,000
Landscape, 8¾ x 13 .... **(1254)** 16,000
Bust of a Woman, 9¼ x 7 .... **(1254)** 13,500
Allegory, 1860, 18¼ x 15 .... **(1254)** 22,200
Landscape of Provence, 6¾ x 9 .... **(1255)** 8,800
Two Little Girls, 3½ x 3½ .... **(1255)** 2,000
Portrait of Mademoiselle Rivière,[4] 1907,
   21¾ x 18¼ .... **(1258)** 110,000
Still Life, 9½ x 14¾ .... **(1258)** 14,000
Flowers, 7¼ x 11¾ .... **(1268)** 19,952
Roses, 9 x 13 .... **(1268)** 18,560
Flowers, 8¾ x 13 .... **(1268)** 17,400
Bust of a Young Woman, 8¾ x 7¼ .... **(1268)** 24,360
Nude .... **(1268)** 15,776
Farmyard at Essoyes, 18½ x 21¼ .... **(1268)** 55,680
Flowers, 8 x 21¼ .... **(1268)** 30,624
Seed Bed for Flowers, 7¼ x 9 .... **(1268)** 13,920
Landscape, 8¾ x 12¾ .... **(1268)** 13,688
Landscape of Cagnes, 7½ x 11¼ .... **(1268)** 18,560
Landscape of Cagnes, 13 x 16¾ .... **(1268)** 43,616
Windflowers, 1901, 13 x 15¼ .... **(1270)** 88,800
The Farm, 1892, 23¼ x 30¾ .... **(1270)** 33,600
Houses in a Landscape of the South of France,
   7¾ x 11 .... **(1270)** 21,600
Strawberries on a White Tablecloth, 9½ x 14¼ .. **(1270)** 31,200
Landscape Near Cagnes, 10 x 14 .... **(1270)** 22,800

[4]Dedicated "A Renée Rivière."

Jean-Paul Riopelle

(1924-   )

Birthplace: Montreal, Canada.

1940 Contributes to the foundation of the group called "Automatisme."

1944 Executes his first abstract paintings.

1946 Visits the U.S. and Italy. Settles in Paris. Takes a great interest in Surrealism.

1947 One-man show at the Galerie Nina Dausset, Paris. Takes part in the international exhibition of Surrealism at the Galerie Maeght, Paris. Participates in the exhibition "L'Imaginaire" at the Galerie du Luxembourg, Paris, together with Wols, Mathieu, and Hartung.

1951 Participates in the São Paulo Biennial—and again in 1955.

1952 One-man show at the Galerie Pierre, Paris.

1953 Participates in the exhibition "Younger European Painters" at the Guggenheim Museum, New York.

1954 One-man show at the Galerie Rive Droite, Paris. Participates in the Venice Biennial—and again in 1962.

1956 One-man show at the Galerie Dubourg, Paris.

1959 Participates in Documenta II, Kassel.

1963 Exhibits at the Phillips Collection, Washington, and at the Quebec Museum. One-man show at the Pierre Matisse Gallery, New York.

Resident in Paris.

Sales

WATERCOLORS

1963

Composition, 1953, watercolor, 29¾ x 41½ .... (232)	$1,017
Composition, 1953, watercolor, 29¾ x 41½ .... (283)	1,130

1965

Abstraction, 1954, watercolor, 19½ x 23¾ .... (494)	750
Abstract Composition, watercolor, 17½ x 23¼ .... (507)	250
Murmurs, gouache, 19¾ x 25¾ .... (518)	460

1966

Composition, 1948, watercolor, 9½ x 13½ .... (826)	160

PAINTINGS

1961–1962

Abstraction, 1952, 31½ x 38¾ .... (85)	3,250
Composition, 1957, 25¾ x 21¼ .... (88)	2,239
Composition, 14 x 10¾ .... (80)	760
Composition, 25¾ x 32 .... (143)	2,260
Composition, 19¾ x 23¾ .... (16)	711
Composition, 1958, 16¼ x 13 .... (149)	2,212
Composition, 1958, 23¾ x 29 .... (18)	2,260
Composition, 1958, 19¾ x 25¾ .... (110)	940
Composition, 1959, 33½ x 45¾ .... (145)	3,476

1963

Composition, 1952, 79 x 60 .... (279)	12,000
Composition, 32 x 39½ .... (232)	3,616
Le Ventoux, 1958, 31¾ x 39 .... (315)	3,153
Composition, 1959, oil on paper laid down on canvas, 23 x 31 .... (299)	960

1964

Red Cap, 1953, 25¾ x 32¾ .... (431)	$4,500
"Je sais le bas," 25¼ x 31½ .... (329)	2,000
By the Spring, 1958, 23¼ x 28¾ .... (454)	1,327
Weathercock, 1958, oil on paper laid down on canvas, 23 x 31 .... (431)	1,200
Composition, 23¾ x 23¾ .... (377)	1,672

1965

Abstract Composition, 1949, 37½ x 50¾ .... (583)	6,384
Composition, 25¾ x 32 .... (617)	2,373
Composition, 13 x 18¼ .... (567)	316
Composition, (1956–57), 29 x 36 .... (606)	1,500
Composition, 1956–57, 28¼ x 35½ .... (535)	1,271
Sentry, 1957, 21¼ x 25¾ .... (638)	2,337
Blue Composition, 1957, 38 x 51¼ .... (624)	2,488
Counterscarp, 14¾ x 23¾ .... (541)	1,400
Slope, 1958, 31¼ x 38¾ .... (583)	1,886

1966

Composition, 1949, 38 x 51½ .... (686)	4,146
Rift in the Clouds, 1956, 39¼ x 28¾ .... (751)	3,040
Composition, 1958, oil on paper, 19¾ x 25¾ ...... (648)	1,100
Composition, 1959, oil on paper laid down on canvas, 29¾ x 41½ .... (681)	560

1967

Composition, 1953, 25¾ x 36¼ .... (870)	1,100
Night Copper, 1953, 25¾ x 36½ .... (963)	2,500
Composition, 1953, 38½ x 57¼ .... (965)	3,503

1968–July 1969

Composition, 13 x 18¼ .... (1127)	1,610
Composition, 39½ x 28½ .... (1208)	5,500
Composition, 1958, oil on paper laid down on canvas, 19¾ x 25¾ .... (1145)	693
Advent, 25½ x 31¾ .... (1132)	2,596
Composition, 1956, 32 x 39½ .... (1268)	4,872

Diego Rivera

(1886–1957)

Birthplace: Guanajuato, Mexico.

1898 Attends the evening classes of the Academy San Carlos, Mexico.

1907 Trip to Spain, where he studies painting.

1909 Visits Paris, where he settles until 1920. Meets Picasso, Juan Gris, Modigliani, and Apollinaire. Comes under the influence of Cubism.

1920–21 Visits Italy, then returns to Mexico.

1921–22 Executes his first murals for the Preparatory School, Mexico.

1922–29 Murals for the Ministry of Public Education, Mexico.

1928	Murals for the House of the Red Army, Moscow.
1930-31	Murals for the Institute of Arts, Detroit.
1933	Murals for the Worther School, New York, and for the California School of Arts.
1934	Murals for the Palace of Fine Arts, Mexico.
1957	Died, Mexico.

Sales

DRAWINGS

1961-1962

Woman and Children Praying, pencil, 6 x 4 .... (45) $ 250

1963

Mexican Peasant, 1940, pencil, 14¾ x 10 .... (272) 450

Portrait of a Child, charcoal and sepia,
19 x 12¼ .... (286) 500

1964

Mother and Child, pencil, 10¾ x 12¾ .... (321) 425

1965

Market Scene, India ink, 15 x 11 .... (494) 450

1966

The Porter, 1946, black chalk on rice paper,
14¾ x 10¾ .... (671) 435

1967

The Glass Blower, India ink on rice paper,
15¼ x 10¾ .... (889) 550

Study of a Fresco, 1932, red chalk, 9 x 44½ ..... (1004) 550

Portrait of a Woman, 1947, ink and watercolor,
23¾ x 17¾ .... (893) 2,250

1968-July 1969

Woman and Death, 1906, black chalk and wash
with white lights, 7¼ x 14 .... (1203) 793

Cantero (The Stone Hewer), charcoal,
10¼ x 14¾ .... (1134) 708

The Glass Blower, India ink on rice paper,
15¼ x 10¾ .... (1145) 500

Mother and Child, charcoal and watercolor,
11¾ x 8¼ .... (690) 675

Scene in a Mexican Village, 1906, pen and wash,
4 x 6 .... (1203) 545

The Arrest, 1930, India ink, 12¼ x 10 .... (1030) 425

WATERCOLORS

1961-1962

Mexican Girl Reading, 1941, gouache and
watercolor, 15 x 10¾ .... (44) 1,900

Banana Man, watercolor, 14¾ x 10½ .... (152) 1,600

1963

Mother and Child, 1934, tempera on board,
30¾ x 22¾ .... (275) 4,100

Woman with a Bunch of Flowers, 1938, pastel and
pencil, 24 x 18¾ .... (286) 660

Tobacco and Cotton,[1] watercolor, 16¾ x 12¾ .... (179) 400

Indio, watercolor on rice paper, 10¾ x 14¾ ...... (179) 1,000

1965

Little Girl in Profile, watercolor, 14¾ x 10¾ ...... (541) 1,750

1966

Jungle Scene, 1908, gouache, 12¾ x 14¾ .... (757) 442

[1] Ballet costumes.

1967

Suburban Houses, 1918, watercolor and pencil,
13½ x 19½ .... (1004) $ 1,800

1968-July 1969

Market Scene, 1935, watercolor on canvas,
12¾ x 19¼ .... (1030) 3,300

The Volcanic Mountain, watercolor, 11¾ x 17½ . (1138) 1,858

Woman Seated in a Green Armchair, watercolor,
13 x 10¼ .... (1117) 2,200

Young Mexican, pastel, 19½ x 12 .... (1080) 2,100

Portrait of Ramon Beteta's Son, pastel,
51½ x 25¾ .... (1018) 1,500

El Official de la Marina, 1930, pencil and
watercolor, 16½ x 12½ .... (1246) 1,500

Landscape with Figures, (1940), 18 x 22 .... (1246) 6,000

Factories in Green and Red Tones, 1928,
watercolor, 18 x 26 .... (1246) 4,250

Street Scene, pencil and watercolor, 19 x 16¼ ... (1273) 2,150

PAINTINGS

1961-1962

Still Life with a Demijohn, 1915, 34½ x 27¾ .... (96) 3,500

The Bottle of Anise, 1915, 27¾ x 25¾ .... (140) 2,883

1963

The Wounded Soldier, 1931, oil on zinc,
11¾ x 13¾ .... (225) 1,750

1964

Mexican Peasants, Man and Woman, 1925,
35¼ x 26½ .... (368) 2,902

1965

Landscape of Toledo, 1912, 43½ x 35½ .... (539) 5,000

Portrait of a Woman, (1917), 31½ x 25¾ .... (539) 12,500

Portrait of Ilya Ehrenburg, 1915, 43½ x 35¼ ..... (539) 21,000

Peasant Holding a Pig, 1935, on board,
31¼ x 23½ .... (535) 1,603

The Child with Toys, 1949, 30 x 40 .... (637) 6,500

1966

Portrait of Ramon Gomez de la Serna, 1915,
43 x 35½ .... (753) 14,510

Still Life, 1915, 31½ x 25¼ .... (776) 12,000

Basket of Peaches, 1917, on panel, 26½ x 32 ..... (776) 10,000

Oranges, 1917, 21½ x 25½ .... (808) 5,224

1967

Still Life with Lemons, 1916, 23¾ x 28¾ .... (864) 16,500

Still Life: Orange and Two Glasses, 1917,
29 x 21¼ .... (954) 9,500

Seated Young Woman, 1944, on canvas laid down
on panel, 48¾ x 59¼ .... (841) 12,500

1968-July 1969

Portrait of Mr. Best, 1913, 90 x 62¾ .... (1080) 19,000

Portrait of a Spaniard, 1912, 78 x 64½ .... (1080) 13,000

The Old Peasant with a Blue Overall,
31½ x 29¼ .... (1208) 9,000

Cosecha de Herro, 1920, 18 x 21½ .... (1235) 19,000

Still Life with an Orange, and Two Glasses, 1917,
28¾ x 21¼ .... (1235) 8,000

Larry Rivers

(1923-   )

Birthplace: New York, U.S.

1930 First attracted to music and becomes a jazz saxophonist.

1947 Starts to paint at Hans Hofmann's school.

1949 One-man show at the Jane Sheet Gallery, New York.

1950 Spends a year in Europe. Greatly admires Bonnard and Soutine.

1951 Exhibits at the Tibor de Nagy Gallery, New York— until 1962.

1954 Exhibits his sculptures at the Stable Gallery, New York, and at the Whitney Museum of American Art, New York.

1956 Participates in the exhibition "Twelve Americans" at the Museum of Modern Art, New York.

1957 Participates in the São Paulo Biennial.

1960 Exhibits his sculptures at the Martha Jackson Gallery and at the Dwan Gallery, Los Angeles.

1962 One-man show at the Galerie Rive Droite, Paris. Takes part in the Seattle World's Fair.

1963 Exhibits at the Pennsylvania Academy of Fine Arts, Philadelphia.

Resident in Southampton, New York.

Sales

DRAWINGS

1968–July 1969

Composition, pencil and pastel, 8 x 10 . . . . (1018) $ 350
To Mike for Birth, pencil, 10 x 11 . . . . (1237) 350

WATERCOLORS

1968–July 1969

Bathers, 1922, pastel and gouache, 13 x 16 . . . . . . (1088) 475

PAINTINGS

1961–1962

Portrait of an Artist (Howard Kanovitz), 1960, on canvas laid down on board, 20¾ x 18¾ . . . . . . (111) 600

1965

Southampton Backyards, 1956, 29¾ x 44¾ . . . . (489) 3,750
Valentine Painting, 1959, 52¼ x 50¾ . . . . (583) 2,332
The Fish, 1961, 70½ x 61 . . . . (512) 2,600
French Money III, 35¼ x 59¼ . . . . (512) 3,800
Vocabulary III (Human Body), 1962, 83½ x 48¼ . . . . (592) 4,500
"Dutchmasters Blunts," 1963, 55¼ x 41½ . . . . (489) 5,000

1966

Valentine Painting, 1959, 50¾ x 50¾ . . . . (651) 4,250
Young Blood, 1962, oil on paper, 14 x 16¼ . . . . (651) 275
Washington Crossing the Delaware, 1960, 85 x 108¾ . . . . (707) 7,500

1968–July 1969

Steel Plant, 1958, 17¾ x 18¾ . . . . (1088) 775
"17" Portrait of Vicky Hochberg, 1960, 48¼ x 43¾ . . . . (1080) 2,750
Landscape, 1961, 20 x 16 . . . . (1138) 1,165
Composition, on board, 12¼ x 14¼ . . . . (1237) 1,300

Christian Rohlfs

(1849-1938)

Birthplace: Niendorf, Holstein, Germany.

1888 Executes his first Impressionist paintings.

1897 Sees pictures by Claude Monet for the first time.

1909 Exhibits at the Volkwang Museum, Hagen.

1910 Exhibits at the Grossherzogliches Museum, Weimar. First exhibition at the National Gallery, Berlin.

1910-12 Visits Munich and the Tyrol.

1925 Second exhibition at the National Gallery, Berlin.

1927 Spends nine months in Ascona, Lake Maggiore.

1929 Exhibits in Frankfurt, Berlin, Basel, and Zurich.

1933 Exhibits in Paris. The Louvre Museum acquires one of his paintings.

1936 Exhibits at the Detroit Institute of Arts.

1938 Died, Hagen, Germany.

Sales

DRAWINGS

1963

Clouds on the Northern Sea, 1932, watercolor, 20 x 28 . . . . (220) $1,130
Monte Gambarogno, 1933, watercolor, 6¾ x 9½ . . (220) 176

1964

Woman's Head, 1915, black chalk and tempera, 5¾ x 5¾ . . . . (385) 122

1965

The Edges of Lake Maggiore, 1933, colored chalk, 17½ x 23¼ . . . . (568) 1,424

1966

Boats on Lake Maggiore, colored chalk and watercolor, 9½ x 13¼ . . . . (735) 294

1967

Erfurt Cathedral, 1924, black chalk, 13 x 10 . . . . . . (931) 305

1968–July 1969

By the Strand of the Northern Sea, 1926, India ink, 14 x 20 . . . . (1090) 136

WATERCOLORS

1961–1962

Tulpen im Beet, 1910, watercolor, 21¾ x 14¼ . . . . . . (24) 787
Flowers in a Vase (Red Moon), 1919, watercolor, 19¾ x 26 . . . . (88) 1,845
Self-Portrait with a Woman, 1920, watercolor and charcoal, 21¼ x 17½ . . . . (88) 836
Clematis and Calla, 1920, watercolor, 22¼ x 15¾ . . . . (149) 822
Blue Flowers, 1920, watercolor and tempera, 22 x 15¾ . . . . (107) 861
Red Tulips, (1925), watercolor, 10½ x 14¾ . . . . (107) 369

1963

Standing Nude, 1919, gouache, 19½ x 13½ . . . . . . (308) 950

1964

Landscape, 1902, pastel, 9½ x 11¾ . . . . (470) 2,952
Standing Nude, 1909, watercolor and India ink, 19 x 13¼ . . . . (470) 1,722
Young Lady's Head (recto), *The Snake Charmer* (verso), gouache, 11 x 8½ . . . . (454) 180

1965

The Steeple of Soest Church, (1905-06),
watercolor, 15¼ x 22 .... (545) $1,554

Adam and Eve, 1919, watercolor, 16¾ x 20½ ..... (568)   904

Woman's Head, on the Left, 1921, watercolor,
19½ x 17 .... (638)   689

Still Life, 1924, watercolor, 20 x 28½ .... (638)   2,952

1966

Standing Nude, Back View, charcoal, watercolor,
and India ink, 25½ x 17½ .... (712)   1,624

Meadow in Bloom, 1931, watercolor and colored
pencil, 7 x 10 .... (716)   344

Yellow Flowers with a Blue Vase, 1918,
watercolor, 19¼ x 26 .... (739)   1,589

Monte Tamaro, 1932, watercolor and colored
chalk, 9½ x 13 .... (735)   746

1967

Red Flowers, chalk and watercolor, 7¼ x 5½ ..... (915)   123

Still Life with Flowers, 1923, tempera, 27 x 19½ ... (970)   2,706

Harlequin, 1923, tempera, 22 x 17½ .... (970)   689

Adam and Eve, watercolor and India ink,
8¾ x 9¾ .... (906)   342

Couple in the Street, watercolor, 25¼ x 19 .... (908)   689

Reclining Nude, watercolor, 13½ x 21 .... (990)   984

Cactus Flowers, watercolor and India ink,
21 x 17½ .... (990)   1,722

Landscape, (1924), tempera, 15¼ x 22 .... (910)   2,091

1968–July 1969

The Pine Grove, 1910, watercolor, 20 x 27¾ ..... (1090)   1,240

Fleurs-de-Lis, 1919, watercolor and gouache,
22½ x 17½ .... (1076)   1,240

Tulips, (1920), tempera, 25¼ x 19 .... (1114)   2,604

Reclining Nude, watercolor, 25¾ x 19½ .... (1094)   521

Mountain with a Chapel, 1931, watercolor,
11¾ x 9 .... (1232)   3,250

Red Tulips, (1905), watercolor, 11¾ x 8½ .... (1232)   2,750

Village in the Evening, (1922), watercolor,
10 x 13½ .... (1232)   2,500

PAINTINGS

1963

The Farm with a Mirror, 1928, 31½ x 24 .... (297)   2,017

1964

Goethe's Garden in Weimar, 1902, 22½ x 29 ..... (385)   2,373

Reclining Nude, 1902, on cardboard, 19 x 27¾ .... (392)   2,214

A Street in Soest, 1907, 23¼ x 31 .... (470)   5,412

A Couple in the Moonlight, 1912, 39½ x 48¼ ..... (470)   3,198

Three Women, 31½ x 23¾ .... (380)   4,920

1965

The Forest, 25¾ x 19 .... (583)   726

1966

Haystacks, 1907, 39½ x 23¾ .... (775)   2,263

Nude, 1918, 27¼ x 17½ .... (716)   1,082

Kiefern, 23 x 18¾ .... (815)   332

1967

Underwood, 22½ x 18¼ .... (990)   689

Woman Reading, 1905, 31½ x 20½ .... (970)   2,362

1968–July 1969

Standing Nude, 1910, 31½ x 20 .... (1090)   1,736

The Grape Eaters, (1910), 25½ x 20 .... (1114)   794

Portrait of a Peasant, 1928, 32 x 17½ .... (1114)   2,356

Hugellandschaft, 1907, 20 x 28 .... (1232)   8,500

Tower Amid the Trees, (1910), 19¾ x 25¼ ...... (1232)   11,000

Mark Rothko

(1903–1970)

Birthplace: Dvinsk, Russia.

1913   His family leaves Russia and settles in Portland, Oregon.

1921-23   Studies art at Yale University.

1925-26   Settles in New York and attends the Art Students League in Max Weber's class.

1929   Exhibits at the Opportunity Gallery, New York.

1933   First one-man shows at the Museum of Portland and the Contemporary Arts Gallery, New York.

1935   Member of "The Ten."

1936-37   Works on the Federal Art Project.

1940   One-man show at the Neumann-Willard Gallery, New York.

1945   One-man show at Peggy Guggenheim's Gallery: Art of This Century, New York. Turns to abstraction. Exhibits in the group shows held at the Whitney Museum of American Art, New York—until 1950.

1946   Exhibits at the Betty Parsons Gallery, New York.

1947   Creates his first series of rectangular forms floating in space.

1947-49   Teaches at the California School of Fine Arts.

1948   Sets up the group called "Subjects of the Artists," New York, with Motherwell, Barnet Newman, and Baziotes.

1950   Visits England, France, and Italy.

1951-54   Teaches at Brooklyn College. Participates in "Abstract Painting and Sculpture in America" and in "Fifteen Americans" at the Museum of Modern Art, New York. Participates in the São Paulo Biennial. Exhibits at the Sidney Janis Gallery, New York.

1955   Participates in "Cinquante Ans d'art moderne aux Etats-Unis" at the Musée National d'Art Moderne, Paris.

1958   Participates in the International Exhibition at the Carnegie Institute, Pittsburgh, and in the Venice Biennial.

1959   Trip to Europe. Participates in "The New American Painting" at the Museum of Modern Art, New York, and in Documenta II, Kassel.

1961   One-man show at the Museum of Modern Art, New York, and at the Whitechapel Gallery, London.

1962   Retrospective exhibition at the Musée National d'Art Moderne, Paris.

1970   Died, a suicide.

Sales

WATERCOLORS

1964

Composition, 1947, gouache on gray paper,
25¾ x 19½ .... (372) $ 700

PAINTINGS

1961-1962

Composition, 1959, 25 x 38½ .... (70)   5,688

1964

Composition, 1941, 29 x 24½ . . . . (372) $ 2,500

Two Dark Rectangles on a Red Background, (No.
44), 1955, 8¾ x 42¼ . . . . (372)   10,000

Red and Yellow, 1958, on board, 29¾ x 21¾ . . . . . . (458)   5,804

1965

Red Number 22, 1957, 80¼ x 69¾ . . . . (592)   15,500

1966

Composition, (1942), 11¾ x 15¾ . . . . (651)   550

Georges Rouault

(1871–1958)

Birthplace: Paris, France.

1885   Serves his apprenticeship at a stained-glass maker's, while attending the evening classes of the Ecole Nationale des Arts Décoratifs, Paris.

1891   Decides to become a painter and enters the Ecole Nationale des Beaux-Arts, Paris, in the studio of Elie Delaunay—soon to be replaced by Gustave Moreau. Starts a long series of religious paintings.

1893   Meets Matisse in Gustave Moreau's studio.

1895   Participates for the first time in the Salon, Paris.

1898   Death of Gustave Moreau. Rouault is appointed curator of the Musée Gustave Moreau, Paris.

1902   Takes a great interest in the movement which will later be called Fauvism.

1903   Stays at l'Abbaye du Ligugé with a group of Catholic artists. With Matisse and Marquet, participates in the first Salon d'Automne—until 1908. Executes a series of works expressing the misery of the world and his rebellion against society.

1905   Participates in the Salon d'Automne, Paris, and the Salon des Indépendants—until 1912.

1906   Exhibits at Berthe Weil's, Paris.

1908   Marries Marthe Le Sidaner. Starts his series of judges and tribunals.

1909   First one-man show at the Galerie Druet, Paris.

1916   Vollard becomes his sole dealer and advises him to execute engravings for the illustration of several books.

1921   Michel Puy issues the first monograph on Rouault.

1924   Retrospective exhibition at the Galerie Druet, Paris.

1926   Issues *Souvenirs Intimes,* Paris. Investigates material and color.

1929   Stage decorations and costumes for Diaghilev's ballet *Le Fils Prodigue,* with music by Prokofiev.

1937   Participates in the Salon des Indépendants, Paris. Executes a few tapestries.

1938   The Museum of Modern Art, New York, shows his graphic work.

1940   Lionello Venturi issues a monograph on Rouault in New York. Devotes himself to religious painting.

1945   Retrospective exhibition at the Museum of Modern Art, New York.

1946   Braque-Rouault exhibition at the Tate Gallery, London.

1948   Retrospective exhibition at the Kunsthaus, Zurich, and at the Venice Biennial. Executes stained glass for the church of Assy, Haute-Savoie.

1951   The exhibition "Hommage à Georges Rouault" is held at the Palais de Chaillot, Paris, on his eightieth birthday.

1952–54   Retrospective exhibitions in Paris, Amsterdam, Brussels, Cleveland, New York, Los Angeles, Tokyo, Osaka, and Milan.

1958   Died, Paris. (Rouault is one of the very few French masters endowed with an Expressionist temper.)

Sales

DRAWINGS

1961–1962

The Circus I, black wash with white lights,
16 x 14 . . . . (64) $2,500

The Circus II, Portrait of an Acrobat, black wash with white lights, 11½ x 8 . . . . (64)   3,250

The Circus III, A Chubby Clown, black wash with white lights, 14 x 10 . . . . (64)   2,250

Old Mrs. Gautron, 1916, India ink, 9 x 6¼ . . . . (109)   1,300

1964

Three Faces, India-ink wash, 4¾ x 8¼ . . . . (341)   700

Von Krapot Is Quite Learned, wash, 9 x 6 . . . . (474)   700

1965

Young Lady with a Red Ribbon, 1913, colored chalk and watercolor, 10½ x 7½ . . . . (583)   3,482

The Vagrant, 1923, wash and gouache, 9½ x 7½ . . (564)   1,320

1967

Master of the Cask: Ubu, 1918, wash, 9 x 6¾ . . . . (1004)   1,500

L'Homme au doigt pointé, 1917, India ink with watercolor lights, 13 x 8¼ . . . . (1134)   4,248

Study for "Hideous Woman," India ink and chalk on an aquatint by the artist, 10¼ x 6½ . . . . . . (1191)   3,304

WATERCOLORS

1961–1962

Figures, 1908, watercolor, 12¾ x 8¼ . . . . (18)   5,537

The Wrestler, (1912-13), gouache, 15½ x 11¾ . . . . . (8)   6,500

The Man with a Jacket, 1915, watercolor, 15½ x 10¼ . . . . (171)   1,900

Official Figure, watercolor, 12½ x 8¼ . . . . (93)   4,520

Place de la Concorde, 1929, gouache, 19¾ x 14 . . . . (96)   7,000

1963

Landscape, 1901, watercolor, 6¼ x 8½ . . . . (202)   2,100

Dancer, watercolor with pastel lights, 9 x 5¼ . . . . . (299)   2,220

Bust of a Woman, 1915, watercolor, 11¾ x 8½ . . . . (210)   1,645

The Judge, 1939, tempera on paper, 13 x 10 . . . . . . (210)   10,420

Portrait of a Man, watercolor . . . . (311)   1,360

1964

Bust of a Woman, 1905, double-sided watercolor, 8½ x 6¼ . . . . (401)   5,600

Pierrot, (1908), gouache, 13¼ x 11¼ . . . . (367)   8,845

The Officer, (1912), watercolor, 13¾ x 8¼ . . . . (448)   3,000

Bust of a Woman, 1915, watercolor, 12 x 5 .... (368) $ 1,244

Portrait of a Man, 1930, gouache and ink,
10 x 7¾ .... (367) 4,975

Woman's Head, 1930, gouache and ink, 10 x 7¾ .. (367) 6,081

Neptune, 1930, gouache, 9½ x 7½ .... (448) 3,750

The Blacksmiths, watercolor and gouache,
8¾ x 7½ .... (401) 2,300

The Artists, watercolor, 11¾ x 8 .... (378) 3,842

1965

Woman's Head, (1915), gouache, 12¾ x 9¼ ..... (624) 4,146

Pierrot, gouache, 6½ x 5¾ .... (522) 6,910

The Holy Face, gouache, 19 x 12¾ .... (553) 12,200

"Hector" the Manager, gouache, 15¾ x 11½ ..... (569) 9,266

1966

Rolling Wrestler, 1906, watercolor and gouache,
27¼ x 21¾ .... (801) 24,400

The Wrestler, (1913), watercolor, 14¾ x 11 ...... (686) 4,975

Roc the Bird (Cock), 1918, watercolor, 9 x 12¾ ... (745) 1,898

Caricature of President Wilson, 1918, watercolor
and colored pencil, double-sided watercolor,
14 x 9½ .... (753) 1,886

Suburban Scene, 1930, gouache and pastel, and
ink, 13 x 11 .... (694) 8,000

Landscape, gouache, 7½ x 12½ .... (797) 4,068

Circus Scene, gouache, 14¼ x 16¾ .... (750) 18,242

1967

Figures in a Landscape, 1917, watercolor,
11¾ x 7½ .... (901) 2,000

The Artists, watercolor, 11¾ x 8 .... (918) 3,842

Landscape of Palestine, 1901, gouache,
5¼ x 8¾ .... (987) 800

Acrobat, watercolor and gouache, 15 x 11½ ..... (1000) 2,400

King Ubu in the Colonies, 1931, gouache on the
title page of "Les Réincarnations du Père
Ubu," 17 x 12¾ .... (940) 6,384

1968–July 1969

The Great Rock, 1906, watercolor, 14 x 17½ ..... (1125) 7,590

The Clown with a Rose,[1] 1908, watercolor and
gouache, on paper mounted on canvas,
39½ x 25¾ .... (1189) 87,000

The Rustic Family, 1911, watercolor and gouache,
oval work, 11½ x 11 .... (1132) 4,248

Discord, 1915, tempera, 14 x 9½ .... (1068) 8,260

The Burial of Hope, 1929, pastel on a lithograph,
13 x 8¾ .... (1126) 1,015

Two Clowns, watercolor, 14¾ x 23¼ .... (1126) 14,868

Gentilly: Sad Slum, 1929, gouache, watercolor,
and India ink, 14 x 20 .... (1057) 8,000

*Landscape with a Black Woman Carrying a Jug
on Her Head,* 1931, gouache, 17 x 12¾ ..... (1018) 6,700

Front View of a Nude with Her Arm Raised,
watercolor and colored ink, 11¼ x 7 .... (1026) 2,500

Roc the Bird, 1918, brush, ink, and watercolor,
8¾ x 13 .... (1241) 1,159

Versailles, gouache and oil wash on paper
mounted on canvas, 7¼ x 12 .... (1246) 2,000

Nude in a Blue Coat, (1912), watercolor and
gouache, 11¾ x 7½ .... (1268) 7,424

Landscape, 1912, gouache, 10¼ x 7¼ .... (1268) 7,888

Portrait of a Man, 1930, gouache and ink on
paper, 10 x 7¾ .... (1270) 7,200

The Burial of Hope, 1929, pastel on lithograph,
13 x 8¾ .... (1273) 1,008

[1] Signed Jacques Piot.

PAINTINGS

1961–1962

Nude with a Rose in Her Hair, 1909,
16½ x 19½ .... (84) $ 35,698

Two Peasants, (1909), 35¼ x 24 .... (128) 23,890

Two Peasants, 25¾ x 18¼ .... (128) 19,222

Landscape, (1912), peinture à l'essence and
pencil, 10½ x 7½ .... (18) 6,780

Composition, (1912), peinture à l'essence and
pencil, 6¾ x 11¾ .... (18) 5,876

Nude, 1912, oil on paper on canvas, 11 x 10¼ ..... (88) 5,412

Equestrienne, 17 x 13 .... (93) 17,176

Clown with a Collarette, 1919, collage on canvas,
25¾ x 18¾ .... (37) 25,000

Christ Crucified, (1922), oil on paper on canvas,
26 x 19¾ .... (83) 17,849

Two Clowns, (1930), 18¾ x 11 .... (84) 32,952

The Dog, 11 x 16¼ .... (124) 4,000

The Box, oil on paper laid on panel, 8¼ x 6 ...... (164) 2,746

Christian Intimacy, (1935), 21¾ x 27¾ .... (164) 14,279

Christ and St. John, oil on paper, 25 x 19¾ ..... (164) 13,730

Biblical Scene, oil on paper, 6¾ x 5¼ .... (18) 7,684

The Solitary Disciple, 15 x 12 .... (31) 8,238

Nocturne (Biblical Landscape), 1938, 6¾ x 8¾ .... (8) 8,000

Head of Christ, 1939, oil on paper laid down on
canvas, 21¾ x 17¾ .... (29) 14,300

Pierrette, 1939, on canvas on board, 19 x 14¾ ..... (8) 23,000

Bathers, oil on paper laid down on canvas,
5½ x 11 .... (114) 3,200

Nude, 31½ x 23½ .... (8) 60,000

War, 15¼ x 11¼ .... (116) 5,600

The Red-Haired Boy, 1947, oil on paper laid
down on canvas, 18¼ x 13 .... (29) 15,000

The Asian, oil on cradled panel, 14¾ x 9 .... (155) 28,000

Flowers, design for a stained glass of Assy
Church, on paper laid down on canvas,
16¾ x 9½ .... (32) 12,000

1963

The Galerie Druet, (1906), peinture à l'essence on
paper laid down on canvas, 23¼ x 19½ ...... (247) 12,339

Man's Head, 1906, oil on paper laid down on
canvas, 18¾ x 12¾ .... (277) 6,855

The Wrestler, 1906, peinture à l'essence,
16¾ x 11 .... (254) 10,000

The Clown, (1907), on board, 8¾ x 6½ .... (210) 8,226

The Acrobat, oil on paper laid down on canvas,
28½ x 19¾ .... (316) 7,500

The Equestrienne, 9 x 6½ .... (190) 4,000

Bacchanalia, 26¼ x 18¾ .... (277) 13,710

Clown, (1920-25), oil on cardboard, 6½ x 4¾ ..... (254) 2,600

Maritime Landscape (recto), *Father and Son*
(verso), 1927, oil on paper, 10¾ x 8¼ .... (232) 7,571

Woman's Head, 1930, oil on paper laid down on
canvas, 17 x 12 .... (255) 18,097

Bust of a Young Woman, peinture à l'essence on
paper, 11¾ x 8¼ .... (258) 3,100

"Qui donc se connait?" 1930, 13¾ x 11 .... (225) 6,000

Pierrot, (1937-38), on panel, 17 x 13¼ .... (247) 24,678

The King, (1937-38), 17 x 13 .... (210) 20,565

Interior with Christ and Three Figures, 1937-38 .. (206) 13,820

Jesus with Simon-Peter at Capernaum,
10¼ x 7½ .... (194) 12,000

Head of Christ .... (224) 17,000

Le Christ aux outrages, oil on paper, 5¼ x 4 ..... (254) $1,360

Miserere (Lord, It Is Thou I Know), 1939, oil on tracing paper laid down on canvas, 25¼ x 20 .... (254) 15,600

The Red-Haired Boy, oil on paper mounted on canvas, 17½ x 12½ .... (277) 13,710

Maternity, au vieux faubourg des Longues-Peines, (1950–53), on panel, 19½ x 14 .... (210) 21,388

1964

Character of Molière, (1912), on panel, 21½ x 18¾ .... (367) 8,292

Clown, on cardboard, 9 x 6½ .... (378) 9,944

The Clown, oil on paper laid down on canvas, 4½ x 4½ .... (401) 3,100

Clown, (1920–25), on cardboard, 6½ x 4¾ .... (351) 2,100

Woman with a Green Hat, (1929–30), oil on paper laid down on canvas, 25 x 19 .... (405) 18,863

Flowers in a Vase, (1930–40), 28 x 23¼ .... (431) 46,000

Head of Pierrot, (1937–38), 24 x 17¾ .... (416) 41,460

Head of Pierrette, oil on paper, 19¾ x 13 .... (378) 27,572

"Qui ne se grime pas?" oil and gouache, 25¾ x 19¾ .... (465) 17,000

Darkness, 14¾ x 22 .... (471) 19,549

War, oil on paper laid down on canvas, 15¼ x 11¼ .... (401) 7,300

Le Christ aux outrages, oil on double-sided paper, 5¼ x 4 .... (351) 2,020

Christ and the Fishermen, on board, 12¾ x 17¾ .. (454) 11,609

The Baptism of Christ, oil on paper laid down on canvas, 25 x 19 .... (458) 13,059

Miserere (De Profundis), (1945), 17½ x 23¾ ..... (453) 13,820

Interior with a Fireplace, on paper laid down on canvas, 25 x 19½ .... (399) 12,200

The Station, 16¾ x 13 .... (368) 6,357

The Suburb, 13½ x 19 .... (368) 9,674

Vase of Flowers, oil on paper laid down on canvas, 25¾ x 19¾ .... (340) 46,000

1965

Clown's Head, (1919), oil on paper laid down on board, 8½ x 6½ .... (624) 6,081

The Clown, on panel, 11 x 8¾ .... (559) 5,700

Christ and the Fishermen, 1930, 19½ x 25 .... (522) 29,022

The Way to Calvary, 1934, 26½ x 20 .... (561) 13,520

Woman with a Flowery Hat, (1938), 22 x 16¾ .... (573) 35,103

Seated Figure, peinture à l'essence, 12¼ x 7½ .... (617) 4,746

The Oriental Woman, 1938, 6 x 11½ .... (561) 3,100

The Fountain of Cézanne, design for a monument dedicated to Cézanne, 41½ x 29¾ .... (561) 18,400

A Scene After the Passion, 1938, 15½ x 12¼ ..... (526) 10,500

Small Suburb, 1939, oil on paper laid down on canvas, 20 x 15½ .... (594) 18,000

Clown's Head, on panel, 14 x 11 .... (569) 18,080

The Judges, 7½ x 6¾ .... (569) 9,153

Clown's Head,[2] (1952), on cradled panel, 15¾ x 10¾ .... (594) 25,000

"Hector" the Manager, oil on paper, 15¾ x 11½ .... (617) 9,040

Matutina, oil on paper laid down on canvas, 29 x 21 .... (617) 38,420

Equestrienne, oil on paper laid down on panel, 9½ x 11½ .... (553) 7,200

[2]*Castaprince guérisseur, vieux cirque forain.*

1966

Biblical Scene, 13 x 16¾ .... (685) $10,000

White-Haired Woman, 1929, oil on paper, 8¾ x 11 .... (797) 9,040

Circus Scene, 1934, 16¼ x 11½ .... (776) 18,000

The Breton Wedding, 1937, 27¼ x 47¼ .... (686) 38,696

Small Suburb, 1939, oil on paper laid down on canvas, 19¾ x 15 .... (808) 11,318

The Way to Calvary, 1939, oil on paper, 26½ x 20 .... (744) 24,860

Biblical Landscape, oil on paper, 11 x 7¾ .... (744) 5,424

Holy Face, oil on paper laid down on canvas, 25¼ x 19¾ .... (819) 16,000

1967

Flowers of Evil (Les Fleurs du Mal), 29 x 22½ .... (923) 38,000

The Galerie Druet, (1906), peinture à l'essence and oil on paper laid down on canvas, 24½ x 20 .... (982) 9,954

Punchinello, (1906), oil on paper laid down on canvas, 26 x 19 .... (954) 12,000

Girl with Two Figures, 1910, oil on paper laid down on canvas, 15¾ x 13 .... (985) 4,503

Bathers, (1910), oil on paper laid down on canvas, 17½ x 24½ .... (988) 24,880

The Refugees, 1912, oil on paper, 11¼ x 7½ ..... (864) 4,500

The Auguries, 1923, oil on paper laid down on canvas, 23¾ x 20 .... (940) 10,737

The Judge, 4½ x 9 .... (965) 9,492

Le Sindon, (1925), oil on paper laid down on canvas, 28½ x 23¾ .... (864) 32,500

Le Sindon, (1937), 26 x 20½ .... (954) 20,000

Biblical Landscape, 7½ x 11½ .... (965) 11,978

Biblical Landscape with Three Porches, 14 x 10¼ .... (918) 22,600

Miserere ("Solitaire en cette vie d'embûches et de malices"), 1939, oil on paper laid down on canvas, 25¾ x 19¾ .... (938) 20,730

The Holy Face, oil and gouache on paper, 9½ x 8 .... (940) 8,706

The Holy Face, oil on paper laid down on canvas, 24 x 21 .... (938) 30,404

Landscape, peinture à l'essence and stick of greasepaint, 7¾ x 12¼ .... (995) 4,000

1968–July 1969

Figure, oil on paper, 11¾ x 7¼ .... (1173) 7,360

Adam and Eve, 17¾ x 13 .... (1173) 18,400

Circus, 1905, oil on paper, 8¼ x 9¾ .... (1183) 5,000

Man's Head, 1909, oil on paper laid down on panel, 21¼ x 15 .... (1132) 7,552

Nudes, (1916), on cradled cardboard, 18¼ x 21¾ .... (1125) 19,550

The Judge, 1924, 4¾ x 9 .... (1183) 10,000

Landscape, (1935), oil on paper, 14¼ x 9 .... (1125) 9,200

Circus Man, 1936, oil on paper laid down on canvas, 23¼ x 15¾ .... (1056) 45,000

Landscape in the Moonlight, (1937), 10 x 12¾ ... (1173) 25,760

The Chinese, 1937, oil on paper laid down on canvas, 41 x 28½ .... (1056) 92,500

Clown with Three Buttons, 1937, 12¾ x 10 ...... (1018) 10,500

Le Sindon, (1937–38), 23 x 16¾ .... (1068) 25,960

Clown with a Bass Drum, (1939), 27 x 19¾ ...... (1176) 37,500

Man's Head, (1941), oil on paper laid down on canvas, 18¾ x 12¾ .... (1018) 9,000

Solange, 1949–58, on panel, 18¾ x 14 .... (1132) 40,120

Circus Queen, (1952), on panel, 23¼ x 16¼ ..... **(1068)** $ 35,400

Biblical Landscape, (1955), 19 x 24¾ .... **(1132)** 35,400

Biblical Landscape, 6¾ x 5½ .... **(1113)** 10,220

Head of Christ, 25 x 19½ .... **(1173)** 25,300

Head of Christ, on cardboard, 10 x 8¼ .... **(1173)** 4,600

Biblical Landscape, 10¾ x 7½ .... **(1125)** 17,595

Landscape with Figures, on cardboard laid down
on cradled panel, 11½ x 8 .... **(1049)** 11,600

Christ on the Cross, oil on paper laid down on
canvas, 24½ x 19 .... **(1106)** 21,000

*Miserere No. 36 ("Ce sera la dernière petit
père"),* oil on an etching, 23¾ x 17 .... **(1106)** 6,600

Woman with a Green Hat, oil on paper mounted
on canvas, 25 x 19 .... **(1235)** 56,000

The Apparition: "Au pressoir le raisin fut foule,"
on canvas mounted on board, 16 x 21½ .... **(1235)** 18,000

Clown's Head, (1920), 4¼ x 4¼ .... **(1239)** 4,560

Nude, (1931-39), 15½ x 11¼ .... **(1239)** 15,840

Figure, (1926), 14 x 10¾ .... **(1255)** 18,000

Biblical Landscape, 13 x 8¾ .... **(1268)** 19,720

Side View of a Figure, 1934, 16¾ x 12¼ .... **(1268)** 18,106

Biblical Landscape, 27¾ x 21 .... **(1268)** 75,400

Biblical Landscape, 10¾ x 7½ .... **(1268)** 27,840

Odalisques, 1924, gouache and oil on paper,
11 x 8¾ .... **(1270)** 6,720

Henri Rousseau
(Le Douanier Rousseau)

(1844–1910)

Birthplace: Laval, Mayenne, France.

1864-68   Enlists in the army. (There are no facts to support the rumor that he took part in the Mexican Campaign.)

1869   Marries Clémence Boitard. Settles in Paris, where he works at l'Octroi (customs house). Starts to paint in his leisure hours.

1880   Executes his first signed works.

1884-86   Executes a series of copies at the Louvre Museum, Paris. Participates for the first time in the Salon des Indépendants, Paris, where he exhibits until the end of his life. Gives up his job, living on a scanty retirement pension, violin lessons, and portraits.

1890   Meets Gauguin, Odilon Redon, Seurat, and Camille Pissarro.

1891   Introduces an exotic setting into one of his pictures, "The Tempest in the Jungle."

1895   Achieves a monumental painting entitled "War" (Louvre Museum).

1899   Marries Rosalie-Joséphine Nourry.

1906   Meets Robert Delaunay, Picasso, Vlaminck, Max Jacob, Apollinaire, and Maurice Raynal.

1907   Forms friendships with the American painter Max Weber and the German critic Wilhelm Uhde, who buys some of his pictures.

1908   Picasso organizes a banquet in his honor at the Bateau-Lavoir. Paints "The Snake Charmer."

1909   Paints "The Poet and His Muse."

1910   Paints "The Dream" and "The Wedding." First exhibition of his works in New York at Stieglitz's gallery, "291." Died, Paris. (Henri Rousseau is the first and certainly the most remarkable of a brilliant series of artists going by such names as naïves and modern primitives—because of their unconcern about intellectual vistas of painting and their ever freshly poetical vision of the world. They include Vivin, Bombois, Bauchant, Kane, Hirshfield, and Aristide Caillaud.)

1911   Wilhelm Uhde writes the first monograph on Rousseau.

Sales

PAINTINGS

1961–1962

Riverside, 1886, on board, 10¼ x 13½ .... **(26)** $12,000

Monsieur Frumence Biche in Plain Clothes,
(1890-91), 18¼ x 15 .... **(156)** 8,000

The Lake of the Bois de Boulogne, 7½ x 11 .... **(90)** 4,100

*Maréchal des Logis Frumence Biche du 35ème
d'Artillerie,* (1893), 36½ x 29 .... **(156)** 20,000

The Walk of the Park Montsouris, (1895),
24½ x 21 .... **(164)** 19,222

View of the Fortifications,[1] (1896), 18¼ x 24 .... **(84)** 38,444

1963

View of the River Bièvres, at Gentilly, 1895,
15 x 18¼ .... **(210)** 21,936

The Holy Family, 1905, 35¼ x 25 .... **(277)** 19,194

1964

Monsieur Frumence Biche in Plain Clothes,
18¼ x 15 .... **(399)** 5,000

*Maréchal des Logis Frumence Biche du 35ème
d'Artillerie,*[2] (1893), 36½ x 29 .... **(340)** 14,000

1965

*View of the Fortifications, Boulevard Gouvion St.
Cyr,* (1896), 18¼ x 24 .... **(594)** 44,000

Landscape,[3] 7¼ x 11 .... **(617)** 10,622

Landscape with a Cow, 1909, 13 x 18¼ .... **(615)** 25,000

1966

Village Street Near a Stream, 1886, on an oval
canvas, 14¾ x 18¼ .... **(686)** 27,640

Landscape with an Angler, (1886), 9¼ x 14½ ..... **(686)** 30,404

The Outer-Circle Railway, Snow Effect,
15 x 18¼ .... **(741)** 13,000

1967

Portrait of an Old Woman in Profile,
12¾ x 10¼ .... **(912)** 13,200

1968–July 1969

Castle on the Riverside, 18¾ x 25¾ .... **(1202)** 18,200

The Industrial Town, 18¼ x 21¾ .... **(1106)** 13,000

The Lock, 18¼ x 21¾ .... **(1106)** 14,000

[1] Boulevard Gouvion St. Cyr.
[2] Sold in Paris in 1962 for $20,000.
[3] Bois de Boulogne.

The Park Montsouris, 25¾ x 21¼ . . . . (1113) $ 10,000
Study for "The Park Montsouris, the Kiosk,"
   1910, on paper, 8 x 10¼ . . . . (1226)   7,600
Still Life with Glasses and Crockery, on panel,
   11¾ x 19¾ . . . . (1255)   12,700
Little Girl with a Carnation, 1915, 14¾ x 10¾ . . . (1255)   10,000
Old Woman in Profile with a Black Cap,
   12¾ x 10¼ . . . . (1255)   3,000

Ker-Xavier Roussel

(1867–1944)

Birthplace: Lorry-lès-Metz, Lorraine, France. (His family moves to Paris, where he later forms a friendship with Edouard Vuillard at the Lycée Condorcet.)

1888   Roussel and Vuillard meet Bonnard, Maurice Denis, Ranson, and Sérusier at the Académie Julian, Paris.

1890   Contributes to the foundation of the Nabis group.

1891   Participates in the first exhibition of the Nabis at the Galerie Le Barc de Boutteville, Paris—and again in 1893.

1893   Marries Vuillard's sister.

1894   Exhibits his pastels at the Revue Blanche, Paris.

1896   Exhibits stained-glass designs at the Galerie l'Art Nouveau, Paris.

1897–98   Exhibits with the Nabis at Vollard's, Paris.

1899   One-man show at Bernheim-Jeune's, Paris. Participates in the Nabis exhibition at Durand-Ruel's, Paris. Settles at L'Etang-la-Ville.

1905   Makes a trip to the south of France with Maurice Denis; they visit Cézanne.

1930   Exhibits with Bonnard and Vuillard at the Seligmann Gallery, New York.

1944   Died, L'Etang-la-Ville.

Sales

DRAWINGS
1964
Self-Portrait, 1928, pencil, 7¾ x 5¼ . . . . (418) $ 140
Squatting Nudes, red chalk with white lights,
   9 x 11 . . . . (483)   200
1965
Resting, 8¼ x 11¼ . . . . (578)   40
1966
Nymph and Satyr, India ink, 4½ x 5 . . . . (742)   70
The Two Trees, black lead, 4½ x 8 . . . . (654)   64
Seated Nude, charcoal heightened with chalk,
   8¼ x 12¼ . . . . (781)   124
Draped Nude, charcoal heightened with chalk,
   8¼ x 12¼ . . . . (718)   160

1968–July 1969
Seated Nude, charcoal heightened with white,
   15 x 10 . . . . (1019) $ 240
Seated Nude in Left Profile, charcoal and white
   lights on buff-colored paper, 14¾ x 18 . . . . . . (1031)   130
The Grief of Europa, 1915, red chalk, 8¾ x 11 . . . (1121)   140
The Nymph, India ink, 7¼ x 12 . . . . (1262)   60

WATERCOLORS
1961–1962
The Dance Near the Willow, pastel, 19 x 25 . . . . . . (171)   900
Landscape, pastel, 10 x 13¼ . . . . (116)   400
Nude, pastel 12¾ x 9½ . . . . (143)   316

1963
Bathers, pastel, 33 x 49¾ . . . . (296)   9,200
Bather at the Seaside, pastel on tracing paper
   laid down on cardboard, 30½ x 42¾ . . . . (259)   120
The Bend of the Road, pastel, 12¼ x 18¾ . . . . (259)   580
Landscape, pastel, 13½ x 19¾ . . . . (281)   644

1964
Nausicaa and Ulysses, Seaside, pastel,
   11¾ x 18 . . . . (348)   640
Nude, 1904, pastel, 7¾ x 11¼ . . . . (408)   240
Landscape, 1933, pastel, 12¼ x 19 . . . . (465)   400
Gathering Apples, pastel, 17¾ x 21¾ . . . . (411)   320
Landscape at L'Etang-la-Ville, pastel on gray
   paper, 11¾ x 17¾ . . . . (404)   420
Summer Landscape, pastel, 19 x 24½ . . . . (407)   1,130
The Spring, pastel, 16¾ x 25 . . . . (333)   1,340

1965
Landscape with Figures, (1900),
   pastel, 8¾ x 14¼ . . . . (568)   1,040
Nude in the Studio, (1905), pastel, 25 x 19 . . . . (575)   1,106
Bacchanalia, pastel, 14¼ x 16¾ . . . . (564)   460
The Couple, pastel, 11¾ x 19½ . . . . (490)   184
Landscape at Franconville, pastel, 8¾ x 20½ . . . . . (624)   387
Etnay-la-Ville, pastel, 14¾ x 19¾ . . . . (512)   360
Landscape, pastel, 4¾ x 8 . . . . (640)   160
The Beach, pastel, 5 x 8 . . . . (523)   124

1966
Pastoral, tempera (curved top), 38¾ x 25¼ . . . . (741)   1,200
The Cuiseaux, 1906, pastel, 14¼ x 21¼ . . . . (741)   2,000
Meadow, pastel, 8 x 17 . . . . (691)   300

1967
Women in a Landscape, (1900), pastel, 8 x 13¼ . . . (931)   1,130
Children in a Landscape, pastel, 12¾ x 16¾ . . . . . . (923)   580
Landscape with a Haystack, pastel, 10¼ x 12¾ . . . (839)   760
Self-Portrait, 1911, pastel, 12½ x 10 . . . . (839)   1,620
Landscape, pastel, 7¼ x 16¾ . . . . (926)   264
Landscape, pastel, 10¼ x 14¼ . . . . (987)   500
Daphnis and Chloe, pastel, 14¾ x 9 . . . . (919)   701
Ruins of Chevreux (Jura), 1906, pastel,
   14¼ x 21¾ . . . . (970)   1,599
Daphnis and Chloe, pastel, 14¾ x 9 . . . . (970)   590
Bacchus, Fauns, and Nymphs, pastel, 12¼ x 28 . . . (911)   1,300

1968–July 1969
Fauns and Nymphs, pastel, 15 x 19¾ . . . . (1159)   1,240
Landscape, 1897, pastel, 22 x 31 . . . . (1066)   360
Figures in a Landscape, pastel, 10¼ x 13½ . . . . . . (1174)   1,035

Two Figures in the Country, pastel, 32 x 39½ .... **(1180)** $1,800
Summer Landscape, (1920), pastel, 10¾ x 23¾ ... **(1127)** 1,150
Landscape, 1933, pastel, 12 x 18¾ .... **(1088)** 250
Bather, pastel, 9¼ x 11¾ .... **(1061)** 350
Bathers, pastel on paper laid down on board,
  30½ x 42¾ .... **(1191)** 897
The Hamlet, pastel, 7¼ x 11½ .... **(1180)** 440
Landscape, pastel, 8 x 11¾ .... **(1222)** 10
Fauns and Nymphs, tempera, 9½ x 17¾ .... **(1225)** 1,700
An Afternoon on the Grass, pastel, 19 x 25 ...... **(1241)** 1,760
Couple Embracing Under a Tree, pastel on bister
  paper .... **(1263)** 1,560
Faun and Nymph, pastel, 5¼ x 7½ .... **(1265)** 480

PAINTINGS

1961-1962
Sleeping Nymph, peinture à la colle on
  cardboard, 28 x 37 .... **(171)** 900
Acis and Galatea, 27¾ x 14¾ .... **(147)** 600
Faun and Nymphs, 34½ x 83 .... **(30)** 860
Maternity, 13 x 16¼ .... **(25)** 272

1963
Bathers, on cardboard, 10 x 16¾ .... **(235)** 164
Bather Resting, 19¾ x 25 .... **(259)** 500
Nymphs in the Glade, 10 x 11¾ .... **(185)** 170
Landscape of the Yonne, 8 x 10¾ .... **(298)** 520
Riders and Nymphs in a Wooded Landscape, on
  board, 19¾ x 25¾ .... **(308)** 380

1964
Figures in the Country, oil on paper laid down on
  canvas, 43½ x 63¼ .... **(399)** 1,600
Bathing, on cardboard, 10 x 16¾ .... **(366)** 500
Faun and Nymph, on cradled cardboard,
  31 x 39½ .... **(474)** 1,000
Nymph with a Rock, on an oval canvas,
  31½ x 21 .... **(394)** 1,040
Autumn Landscape, 28¾ x 18¾ .... **(321)** 750
Mother and Children in a Garden, 11¾ x 17 ...... **(348)** 400
Pastoral, 68 x 30 .... **(340)** 1,360

1965
Bacchanalia in Front of the God Pan,
  34¾ x 83¾ .... **(553)** 1,000
Fauns and Nymphs at the Bottom of a Tree,
  26½ x 20 .... **(515)** 840
Faun and Nymphs, 17½ x 25¼ .... **(574)** 1,500
Bathing, on cardboard, 9½ x 16¾ .... **(619)** 610
Faun in Ambush, 35 x 37 .... **(522)** 1,797
The Afternoon of a Faun, 1919, 67¼ x 87 .... **(614)** 2,750

1966
Sleeping Nymph, on cardboard, 28 x 37 .... **(685)** 1,500
Faun, Nymph, and Children, on cradled panel,
  16¾ x 22 .... **(741)** 1,600

1967
The Triumph of Bacchus, 12¼ x 28 .... **(1002)** 760
Bucolic Scene, on cardboard, 39½ x 26 .... **(933)** 1,200
Theater Scene, on cardboard, 19¾ x 25¾ .... **(898)** 500
Faun and Nymphs, (1925), on cardboard,
  29¼ x 43½ .... **(918)** 5,650

1968-July 1969
Eurydice piquée, 45½ x 64 .... **(1180)** 8,000
Fauns and Nymphs, 17¾ x 25¼ .... **(1051)** 2,400

Bacchanalia, 1912, on cardboard, 28½ x 30½ .... **(1180)** $2,600
Mythological Scene, by the Mediterranean, on
  board, 25¾ x 32¼ .... **(1187)** 2,006
The Birth of Venus, on panel, 8 x 14 .... **(1187)** 1,652
The Rape of Leucippus' Daughters, on board,
  with curved pediment, 8½ x 5 .... **(1138)** 768
Bathing, 13 x 16¼ .... **(1115)** 310
Tree in Bloom, 17¾ x 13¼ .... **(1106)** 1,220
Venus Resting, 39½ x 70 .... **(1225)** 8,000
The Plain, distemper on canvas laid down on
  cardboard, 15 x 21¾ .... **(1254)** 1,040
Venus and Adonis, 68½ x 29½ .... **(1270)** 5,760

Luigi Russolo

(1885-1947)

Birthplace: Portogruaro, near Venice, Italy. (Studies painting by himself and also takes a great interest in music.)

1909 Marinetti issues his Futurist manifesto in Paris. Russolo meets Boccioni and Carrà at Marinetti's.

1910 Signs the manifesto of the Futurist painters in Milan—with Ballà, Boccioni, Carrà, and Severini.

1911 Paints "The Rebellion."

1913 Signs the manifesto "L'Arte dei Rumori."

1917 Seriously wounded during World War I.

1919 Settles in Paris. Reverts to a clearer representational painting.

1947 Died.

Sales

PAINTINGS
1961-1962
Self-Portrait, 1913, 18¼ x 15 .... **(149)** $3,476

Théodore van Rysselberghe

(1862–1926)

Birthplace: Ghent, Belgium. (Studies painting at the local fine arts school.)

1884 Contributes to the foundation of the group of the XX, Brussels.

1886 Visits Paris and is immediately won over to Neo-Impressionism. Meets Seurat and makes friends with Signac, Henri-Edmond Cross, and Luce. With his friend the poet Verhaeren, makes Brussels the second center of the movement.

1894 Appears as a leading figure in the new Brussels group called "La Libre Esthétique."

1898 Settles in Paris. Also spends a lot of time in the south of France.

1905 Exhibition at the Galerie Druet, Paris—and again in 1911.

1908 Exhibition at the Galerie Bernheim-Jeune, Paris.

1922 Retrospective exhibition at Giroux's, Brussels.

1926 Died, St. Clair, in the south of France.

Sales

DRAWINGS

1961–1962

Seated Nude, red chalk, 17½ x 14¾ . . . . (154) $ 110
Portrait of a Woman, charcoal, 11½ x 8¾ . . . . (63) 104

1963

Self-Portrait in Right Profile, black chalk on green paper, 19¼ x 17¾ . . . . (220) 373
Nude with a Bathing Wrap, 1910, wash, 25¼ x 13¼ . . . . (235) 40

1965

Portrait of Madame Francis Vielé-Griffin (1897), charcoal, 12¾ x 11½ . . . . (568) 407

1966

Elizabeth van Rysselberghe, 1909, black chalk, 12¼ x 16¼ . . . . (735) 949

1967

La Mortola, pencil and watercolor, 14 x 17½ . . . . . (931) 610
Seated Nude Combing Her Hair, charcoal, 14¾ x 10 . . . . (913) 394
Portrait of Mademoiselle Augustine de Rothmaler, charcoal, 8½ x 8¾ . . . . (939) 276
Madame Monnon, 1899, 13¾ x 10½ . . . . (931) 791
Seated Young Woman, red chalk, 22 x 17½ . . . . . . (886) 110
The Stairs, black chalk and watercolor, 13½ x 17½ . . . . (940) 871

1968–July 1969

In the Train, black pencil, 10¼ x 14 . . . . (1110) 340
Portrait of Emil Verhaeren, Conté pencil, 8 x 9 . . (1104) 260
Landscape, black lead and colored pencil, 11½ x 9 . . . . (1191) 850
Standing Nude, 1910, red chalk, 24¼ x 12 . . . . (1102) 264
Nude, red chalk, 21¼ x 15¾ . . . . (1174) 276
Woman with a Tub, red chalk, 8¾ x 7¼ . . . . (1246) 750
Maritime Landscape, charcoal, 11½ x 16¼ . . . . . . (1253) 220
Study of Nudes, red chalk, 21¾ x 11 . . . . (1262) 200

WATERCOLORS

1961–1962

The Dunes: St. Tropez, 1896, watercolor, 6¾ x 9 . . . . (164) $ 137
Bust of a Young Lady, 1913, pastel, 25 x 19 . . . . (49) 600

1963

Seascape, 1896, watercolor, 9 x 12¾ . . . . (232) 1,107
Volendam, watercolor, 9 x 12¾ . . . . (182) 500

1964

Aquarium at Naples, 1909, watercolor, 11½ x 8¾ . . . . (409) 132
St. Tropez, 1896, watercolor, 6¾ x 9 . . . . (394) 550

1965

Young Woman by the Sea, watercolor, 11½ x 8¾ . . . . (577) 342

1966

Seated Young Woman in the Nude, 1912, pastel, 33½ x 23¾ . . . . (798) 2,260
Villa d'Este, watercolor and pencil, 8¾ x 11 . . . . . . (721) 600
Garden in Summer, watercolor and gouache on paper mounted on canvas, 14 x 19¾ . . . . (665) 800

1967

Boats at Kortoene, watercolor, 7½ x 9½ . . . . (1007) 300
Reclining Young Woman, watercolor, 10¾ x 7½ . . (911) 460
Garden, gouache and watercolor, 14¾ x 7½ . . . . . . (963) 600

1968–July 1969

Flowers, watercolor, 10¼ x 13 . . . . (1110) 260
Landscape, 1906, watercolor, 8¼ x 10¾ . . . . (1110) 400
The River Seine at Le Petit-Andelys, watercolor, 6¾ x 10 . . . . (1191) 1,416
Underwood, watercolor, 8¾ x 11½ . . . . (1140) 230
A Mill in Holland, 1905, pencil and watercolor, 10¼ x 7½ . . . . (1102) 253
Portrait of Marguerite, (1905–10), pastel, 22½ x 16¾ . . . . (1208) 2,250
Young Lady with a Green Hat, watercolor, 10¾ x 8¼ . . . . (1171) 500
Elizabeth Sleeping, pastel, 14¾ x 8¼ . . . . (1104) 900
Portrait of Jeanne Pissarro, pastel, 29 x 23¾ . . . . (1200) 3,400
Scene in the Garden, gouache and watercolor, 13½ x 16 . . . . (1231) 300
Boats Alongside a Quay at Kortoene, pencil and watercolor, 7½ x 9½ . . . . (1240) 720
View on the Sea, watercolor, 16½ x 12¼ . . . . (1246) 500
Le Lavandou, watercolor, 9¼ x 12¾ . . . . (1246) 550

PAINTINGS

1961–1962

Farmyard, on panel, 10¼ x 14 . . . . (96) 3,000
Young Woman, Her Breast Bare, 13 x 16¼ . . . . . . (120) 1,020
Les Baumelles Seen from a Provençal Hill, 1924, 17¾ x 21½ . . . . (64) 1,750

1963

Elizabeth van Rysselberghe Reading on a Balcony, (1897), 24 x 19¾ . . . . (316) 7,000
Sunset at Ambleteuse, 1899, 25¾ x 32 . . . . (283) 14,577
Three Little Girls, 1901, 20¾ x 24¾ . . . . (202) 5,000

1964

Landscape, (1895), 15 x 18¼ . . . . (448) 2,000
Fishing Boats, 1900, on panel, 12½ x 16 . . . . (378) 9,040
The Rocky Creek, 1906, 18¼ x 21¾ . . . . (332) 2,920

Landscape, 1908, on cardboard, 15¼ x 22 .... (471) $2,938
Portrait of a Woman, on cardboard, 8¾ x 9 ...... (471)   1,130
Nude at Her Toilette, on cardboard, 19¾ x 9½ ... (371)   2,300
Draped Nude, oil on paper, 16¼ x 9½ .... (366)   1,120
Two Bunches of Windflowers, 1910, 18¼ x 22 ..... (427)   1,480
Seaside, 1914, 18¼ x 21¾ .... (342)   2,060

1965

The Parasol Pine, 1914, oil on paper laid down
  on canvas, 18¼ x 21¾ .... (564)   2,300
Three Little Girls, 1901, oil on paper laid down
  on canvas, 21¼ x 25 .... (633)   3,500
Bodenhausen Children, (1908), on cardboard laid
  down on canvas, 27¼ x 23¾ .... (580)   1,040
Reclining Nude, 1914, 35½ x 57¼ .... (617)   7,910
Back-Lighted Nude, on panel .... (567)   3,729
Landscape, 16¼ x 21¼ .... (567)   2,825
Rock, 1919, on cardboard, 15¾ x 12½ .... (617)   1,582
The Fountain, 96¼ x 63¼ .... (561)   2,300
Notre-Dame de Paris, on panel, 8¼ x 11½ ...... (575)   1,797
Nude with a Blue Bathing Wrap, oil on paper laid
  down on cardboard, 15¾ x 9¼ .... (547)   1,240
Young Woman Sleeping, 14¾ x 17¾ .... (612)   2,200

1966

Landscape, 1906, 16¾ x 22 .... (798)   3,955
The Knitter, 1882, 13 x 19 .... (767)   600
The Church, 19½ x 25 .... (698)   2,176
Portrait of the Artist's Mother, 1900,
  46¼ x 34¾ .... (808)   8,126
Portrait of a Woman, on cardboard, 10 x 8 ...... (772)   520
Vase of Flowers, 1910, 19¾ x 15¾ .... (749)   1,300
The Balustrade, 32 x 46¼ .... (776)   2,000
Shoal of Fish, 1917, 25 x 39¼ .... (813)   967
Paquita, 1919, 38 x 63¼ .... (808)   2,612
Landscape, 1926, 19¾ x 23¾ .... (648)   2,250

1967

Portrait of Alice Sethe, 1888, 76¾ x 38¼ .... (912)   18,000
Breakwaters at Heyst, 1888, 21 x 25 .... (939)   2,764
Portrait of Madame van Rysselberghe, 1911,
  46¼ x 35¼ .... (978)   3,400
Eucalyptus at Cavalière, 1905, 39½ x 32 .... (912)   11,700
Vase of Flowers, 1912, 32 x 26 .... (995)   2,900
Cap Bénat, 1914, 18¼ x 21¾ .... (918)   4,520
Reclining Nude, on board, 10 x 19¾ .... (841)   1,300
Back View of a Woman, 18¼ x 15 .... (904)   1,100
Portrait of a Woman, 1923, 42¾ x 37½ .... (967)   904

1968–July 1969

Cap Bénat, 1914, oil on paper laid down on
  canvas, 18¼ x 21¾ .... (1173)   6,210
Breakwaters at Heyst, 1888, 21 x 25 .... (1070)   2,360
Portrait of Elizabeth, the Artist's Daughter,
  (1890), on board, 21¼ x 15½ .... (1187)   3,422
Garden and Arcade, (1900), 31¾ x 33¼ .... (1208)   6,000
Flowery Landscape, 63¼ x 45¼ .... (1106)   2,840
Seated Bather, Her Foot in the Water, (1905), on
  cardboard, 24 x 14¼ .... (1102)   1,196
Reclining Nude, on board, 10 x 19¾ .... (1061)   1,000
Vase of Flowers, 1907, on panel, 17¾ x 20½ ..... (1113)   2,100
The Pot of Zinnias, 1907, on panel, 14¾ x 19½ .. (1187)   2,714
Shoal of Fish, 1917, 25 x 39¼ .... (1070)   1,133
Child in a Sailor Suit, 1919, 67¼ x 39½ .... (1026)   4,200
View of Le Lavandou, 1925, 17 x 27 .... (1051)   1,500

The Statue, 51¾ x 38 .... (1116) $ 460
The Stairs, 63¼ x 51½ .... (1110)   1,260
Palm Trees and Arums, 34¼ x 25¾ .... (1200)   3,400
Woman at Her Dressing Table, 34¼ x 25¾ ..... (1053)   13,000
Landscape with Houses, 19¾ x 30½ .... (1150)   16,400
Cockatoo in the Garden, mixed media on paper
  mounted on canvas, 14½ x 17½ .... (1231)   850
Elizabeth, the Artist's Daughter, Rome, 1909, on
  panel, 17½ x 13¾ .... (1231)   2,750
Mediterranean Seaside, 1919, on board, 13 x 16 . (1231)   1,200
Seated Woman in the Nude, 1916, 20 x 14 ...... (1231)   1,200
Woman with a Pink Necklace, 1907, 37½ x 32½ . (1232)   3,000
Grapes on the Vine, (1908), on board, 23¼ x 18 .. (1235)   2,000
Portrait of Madame Paul Dubois,[1] 1888,
  75½ x 37¼ .... (1239)   48,000
The Rocks, Belle-Ile, (1888–90), 19¼ x 23½ ..... (1239)   16,800
Elizabeth van Rysselberghe with Her Fox Terrier,
  1910, 24 x 19¾ .... (1240)   1,560
Seated Nude, 1912, 46 x 27¾ .... (1258)   2,000
The Garden, 63¾ x 51½ .... (1258)   4,000
Landscape with Cypresses, Côte des Maures,
  (1903), 63½ x 44½ .... (1270)   6,720
Portrait of Emile Verhaeren, 1915, 25½ x 27½ ... (1270)   3,840
Roger Martin du Gard at Home, 45½ x 31½ .... (1273)   706

Egon Schiele

(1890–1918)

Birthplace: Tulln, near Vienna, Austria-Hungary.

1906 Enters the Vienna Academy of Arts. Meets Oskar Kokoschka.

1907 Meets Gustav Klimt, president of the Vienna Secession, who exerts a great influence upon him until 1909.

1908 With a group of local artists, exhibits for the first time at Klosternneuburg, near Vienna.

1909 Leaves the Vienna Academy. Exhibits at the second Wiener Kunstschau, Vienna. With other artists, sets up the "Neukunstgruppe Wien."

1911 Participates in the Hagendbund exhibition, Vienna. P. von Gutersloh writes the first monograph on Schiele.

1912 Involved with the police on morals charges. Exhibits with the Munich Secession. Participates in the Sonderbund exhibition, Cologne.

1913 One-man show at the Goltz Gallery, Munich. Exhibits with the Secession in Vienna and Düsseldorf. One-man shows in The Hague, Hamburg, Breslau, Stuttgart, and Berlin.

1914 Exhibits with the Munich Secession—and again in 1917.

[1] Born Alice Sethe.

1915 Marries Edith Harms. One-man show at Arnot's, Vienna.

1916 Exhibits with the Berlin Secession.

1918 Important and very successful exhibition of his works is held at the Vienna Secession. Participates in "100 Years of Viennese Painting" at the Kunsthaus, Zurich. Died, like his wife, in an influenza epidemic.

Sales

DRAWINGS

1961–1962

Half-Dressed Woman, 1913, pencil and
  watercolor, 19 x 12 . . . . (88) $ 886

Young Lady in the Nude, black chalk and
  watercolor, 16¼ x 6 . . . . (106) 1,356

Mother and Child, black lead, 17½ x 11¾ . . . . (106) 588

Man's Head, charcoal, 12¾ x 4¾ . . . . (106) 610

1963

Seated Nude, India ink and pencil, 11¾ x 10¾ . . . (225) 450

Study of a Nude, 1908, colored pencil, 10 x 7½ . . . (269) 144

Blond Young Lady in a Blue Chemise, 1913,
  pencil and watercolor, 15½ x 9½ . . . . (220) 2,034

Kneeling Nude, 1914, pencil, 18¾ x 12½ . . . . (220) 678

1964

Young Lady Undressing, 1910, pencil, 17 x 9½ . . . (385) 3,661

Nude Removing Her Chemise, 1916, pencil,
  17¾ x 12¾ . . . . (428) 984

Young Lady Seated, 1918, black chalk,
  18¼ x 11¾ . . . . (349) 950

Portrait of a Man of 314 (Heger), chalk,
  18¼ x 11¾ . . . . (423) 760

1965

Squatting Nude, Wearing a Necklace, 1912,
  pencil, 19 x 12¾ . . . . (568) 1,153

Reclining Nude, 1912, pencil and watercolor,
  12¾ x 19 . . . . (568) 2,034

Kneeling Man in the Nude, 1908, black chalk,
  10¼ x 9½ . . . . (587) 418

Lovers, 1912, pencil, 19 x 12½ . . . . (542) 836

Seated Nude, 1913, pencil, 11½ x 18¼ . . . . (625) 2,470

Reclining Nude, 1918, pencil and charcoal,
  17¾ x 11 . . . . (624) 2,266

Reclining Nude, charcoal, 10¾ x 15¾ . . . . (606) 1,400

Nude Removing Her Chemise, 1913, pencil and
  watercolor, 19 x 12¾ . . . . (597) 1,230

Back View of a Nude, pencil, 16¾ x 12 . . . . (535) 498

Two Nudes, 1918, pencil, 12¾ x 18¾ . . . . (583) 1,596

1966

Portrait of a Young Man, pencil and watercolor,
  17 x 11¾ . . . . (665) 2,500

Kneeling Nude, 1912, pencil, 18¾ x 12¾ . . . . (757) 498

Self-Portrait with Raised Arms, 1913, charcoal
  and watercolor, 19 x 12½ . . . . (677) 2,280

Nude with Long Hair, black chalk, 18¼ x 11¾ . . . . (677) 1,900

Young Lady with a Hat (recto), 1913, *Standing
  Nude* (verso), pencil, 19 x 12¾ . . . . (763) 1,140

Reclining Nude, black chalk, 10½ x 18¼ . . . . (735) 1,537

Man's Head, 1916, charcoal, 18 x 11¾ . . . . (712) 1,033

Portrait of Arthur Roessler, charcoal, 11¾ x 8½ . . (735) 723

1967

Reclining Nude, 1914, pencil, 12½ x 19 . . . . (906) $2,280

Reclining Nude, 11¾ x 19 . . . . (859) 608

Reclining Nude, 1918, black chalk, 20 x 17½ . . . . . (931) 1,401

Seated Nude, charcoal and watercolor,
  17¾ x 12¼ . . . . (1004) 2,300

Standing Nude, 1918, charcoal, 18¼ x 11½ . . . . (889) 2,100

Back View of a Reclining Woman, 1915, pencil,
  10¾ x 17½ . . . . (882) 720

1968–July 1969

Reclining Nude, black chalk, 11½ x 18¼ . . . . (1102) 2,990

Reclining Young Lady, 1918, charcoal,
  11¾ x 17¾ . . . . (1146) 2,090

Front View of a Nude, 1918, black chalk,
  18¼ x 11½ . . . . (1041) 2,090

The Shy Little Girl, (1910), chalk and watercolor,
  17¾ x 11¾ . . . . (1105) 3,040

Reclining Woman, black chalk, 10 x 17½ . . . . (1105) 1,900

WATERCOLORS

1961–1962

Young Lady Dancing, 1913, watercolor and
  pencil, 19 x 12¾ . . . . (100) 950

Moa, Reclining Nude, 1911, pencil and
  watercolor, 18¼ x 12 . . . . (106) 2,599

Teen-Ager Running (Study of the Nude),
  watercolor, 4¼ x 12½ . . . . (1) 380

Nude, 1917, watercolor and colored chalk,
  16¼ x 11¾ . . . . (61) 836

1963

Standing Young Lady, Her Face in Her Hands,
  1911, watercolor and pencil, 17¾ x 6 . . . . (220) 1,469

Self-Portrait, 1912, watercolor and pencil,
  19 x 9 . . . . (220) 1,921

Lovers, 1913, gouache, watercolor, and pencil,
  19¼ x 12¾ . . . . (220) 2,328

1965

Portrait of Silvia Koller, 1918, watercolor,
  18¼ x 11¾ . . . . (514) 3,420

Back View of a Man in the Nude, 1910,
  watercolor, 17¾ x 12¼ . . . . (514) 950

Standing Child in the Nude, 1915, pencil and
  watercolor, 19¼ x 12¾ . . . . (568) 2,396

1966

Nude with Green Stockings, 1918, watercolor and
  black chalk, 18¼ x 11½ . . . . (740) 3,230

Red-Haired Nude, watercolor, gouache, and
  charcoal, 14¾ x 10 . . . . (735) 1,582

1968–July 1969

Young Lady in a Blue Dress, 1911, watercolor,
  18¾ x 12 . . . . (1064) 12,980

The Embrace, 1913, watercolor and tempera,
  12¾ x 19 . . . . (1064) 10,620

PAINTINGS

1964

Chrysanthemums, (1909–10), oval canvas,
  24½ x 36¾ . . . . (462) 2,470

The Lady with a Black Hat, 1909, 39½ x 39½ . . . . . (349) 14,440

1965

Reclining Women, 1907, on cardboard,
  21 x 10¾ . . . . (616) 5,920

Oskar Schlemmer

(1888–1943)

Birthplace: Stuttgart, Germany.

1906	Enters the School of Fine Arts of Stuttgart, where he studies until 1910.
1910	Stay in Berlin.
1914	Short trip to Paris with Baumeister.
1919	With Baumeister, exhibits at Der Sturm Gallery, Berlin.
1920	Teaches at the Bauhaus at Weimar.
1931	Executes murals for the Volkwang Museum, Essen.
1932–33	Teaches at the Academy of Berlin, but is soon dismissed by the Nazis.
1934	Settles at Eichberg in Bavaria.
1938	Participates in the exhibition "Bauhaus 1918-28" at the Museum of Modern Art, New York.
1938–41	Works in a color factory in Stuttgart.
1943	Died, Baden-Baden.

Sales

DRAWINGS

1964

Head in Profile, 1922, India ink, 14½ x 7¼ .... (385) $ 452

WATERCOLORS

1961–1962

Four Heads, 1928, watercolor, 17½ x 12¾ .... (88)   6,396

A Group of Red-Haired Boys, 1932, watercolor, 13 x 9½ .... (106)   3,616

1965

The Colt, 1938, watercolor, 10¾ x 7 .... (638)   984

1966

Woman in Profile, 1931, watercolor, 11 x 8 .... (735)   3,729

1967

Head in Profile and Four Figures, (1928), 22 x 16¾ .... (931)   7,684

1968–July 1969

Before the Mirror, (1931), watercolor, 10¼ x 6½ .... (1173)   5,290

Four Side Views, 1932, watercolor, 17½ x 12¾ ... (1114)   7,936

Head in Left Profile, 1925, watercolor, 9¾ x 7¾ . (1059)   793

Figures in a Room, (1932), pastel, 8½ x 11 .... (1232)   4,000

PAINTINGS

1961–1962

Vierergruppe, Breslau 1931, 18½ x 15 .... (88)   11,070

At Table (Dark) II, 1937, oil on paper on cardboard, 25½ x 18¾ .... (88)   9,840

1963

Woman's Head, 1942, oil on paper, 11¾ x 8¼ .... (297)   1,058

1964

The Awakening, 1940, oil on paper, 15 x 10¾ ..... (385)   1,356

1968–July 1969

Group, 1941, oil on paper, 15¾ x 12¾ .... (1102)   4,830

Karl Schmidt-Rottluff

(1884–   )

Birthplace: Rottluff, near Chemnitz, Germany.

1905	Settles in Dresden and starts to study architecture. Meets Heckel, Kirchner, and Bleyl; with them, sets up the group "Die Brücke" in Dresden.
1906	Meets Nolde, who joins "Die Brücke." First and second exhibition of the group in Dresden-Löbtau.
1909	Creates the album of "Die Brücke."
1910	Participates in the exhibitions of the New Secession, Berlin. Participates in the exhibitions of "Die Brücke" at the Arnold Gallery, Dresden.
1911	Spends the summer in Norway. Contributes to the review *Der Sturm,* Berlin. Meets Otto Müller and Lyonel Feininger.
1912	Participates in the Sonderbund exhibition, Cologne, and the exhibition of the "Blaue Reiter" at the Goltz Gallery, Munich. First Berlin exhibition of "Die Brücke" at the Gurlitt Gallery.
1913	Dissolution of "Die Brücke."
1915	Exhibition at the Goltz Gallery, Munich.
1917	Series of religious etchings.
1918–19	Settles permanently in Berlin.
1923–24	Visits Italy and Paris.
1931	Becomes a member of the Berlin Academy of Fine Arts—until his exclusion by the Nazis.
1935	Exhibits at the Buchholtz Gallery, Berlin.
1936	Exhibits at the Westerman Gallery, New York.
1937	Forfeits his works, which are regarded as "degenerate" by the Nazis.
1941	Forbidden to paint.
1946	Appointed professor at the Berlin School of Fine Arts.
1948	Exhibits at the Kunsthalle, Bern.
1950	Participates in the retrospective exhibition of "Die Brücke" at the Venice Biennial. (Regarded as one of the most renowned German Expressionists.)

Sales

DRAWINGS

1964

Autumn Landscape, India ink and colored chalk, 15¾ x 21¼ .... (428) $ 664

Reclining Nude, colored chalk, 12¾ x 16¾ .... (385)   373

Still Life with an African Statue, 1951, India ink and wash, 18¾ x 25¾ .... (385)   249

1965

The Poplars, 1946, colored chalk and India ink, 15¾ x 21¼ .... (638)   787

Bathers on the Beach, black chalk, 15¼ x 19¾ ... (638)   418

1966

Autumn Landscape, colored chalk and India ink, 15¾ x 21¼ .... (712)   1,427

Seaside with a Lighthouse, 1926, black chalk, 15 x 20 .... (735)   429

Still Life with Flowers, India ink and watercolor, 27¾ x 19¾ .... (735)   768

1967

Nude, black chalk, 13½ x 18¾ ....(931) $ 475

A Village by the River Rhône, (1940), India ink,
16½ x 12¾ ....(970)   443

Beach by the Northern Sea, 1921, pencil,
16¼ x 19½ ....(908)   295

1968–July 1969

Marine Landscape, 1919, pencil, 11 x 15¾ ......(1114)   347

WATERCOLORS

1961–1962

Partie an der Ostsee, watercolor, 19¾ x 27¾ ......(94)   959

Still Life with Flowers, watercolor, 27½ x 19¾ ....(151)   517

1963

The Bridge, watercolor, 19¾ x 27¾ ....(308)   950

Summer Landscape, watercolor and colored
chalk, 10½ x 15½ ....(228)   861

1964

Landscape with a Town, watercolor, 19¾ x 27½ ..(470)   1,476

Landscape, watercolor, 15¼ x 20½ ....(392)   787

Landscape, tempera, 10¼ x 15¾ ....(349)   684

View of Lake Maggiore, 1953, watercolor,
17¾ x 26 ....(385)   588

1965

Young Woman with a Basket of Fruit, 1908,
watercolor, 26½ x 19¾ ....(568)   3,480

Still Life with Flowers, watercolor and India ink,
27 x 18¾ ....(638)   886

Bunch of Flowers, watercolor, 19½ x 27¾ ....(545)   849

1966

Still Life with Flowers and Fruit, watercolor,
19 x 26½ ....(712)   1,353

Poppies, watercolor, 19¼ x 26½ ....(739)   1,845

1967

Reclining Nude, Back View, 1913, watercolor and
India ink, 14¾ x 19¾ ....(908)   1,181

Fishing Boats, watercolor and colored chalk,
10¾ x 15 ....(908)   984

Boats, 1935, watercolor and colored chalk,
10¾ x 15 ....(990)   1,107

Dinkelsbuhl, (1937), watercolor, 19¾ x 27¼ ......(910)   1,599

1968–July 1969

Still Life with Flowers, watercolor and India ink,
15¾ x 21¼ ....(1194)   893

Red Flowers, pen and pastel, 10¼ x 15½ ....(1203)   793

Landscape with Birch Trees, 1905, watercolor,
11 x 14½ ....(1232)   4,250

PAINTINGS

1961–1962

The Small House, 1904–06, 19¾ x 26 ....(88)   11,562

1964

Roses, 25¾ x 29 ....(328)   3,500

Woman in a Red Dress, 1920, 40 x 34¾ ....(385)   4,746

1965

Summer Landscape, 1935, 25½ x 29 ....(545)   4,809

Landscape with a Great Tree, 1948, 30 x 35½ .....(638)   8,364

1967

Three Women by the Seaside, Nightfall, 1919,
38¾ x 44¼ ....(931)   14,238

1968–July 1969

Summer Day, 1907, 24 x 26¼ ....(1209) $15,376

Washerwomen at the Seaside, (1921),
38½ x 44¼ ....(1232)   35,000

Claude-Emile Schuffenecker

(1851–1934)

Birthplace: Fresnes-St.-Mamès, Haute-Saône, France.

1871   Meets Gauguin, who works at a stockbroker's firm in Paris, and becomes very friendly with him.

1872   Exhibits at the Salon, Paris, until 1882.

1884   Participates in the Salon des Indépendants with his friend Dubois-Pillet. Makes friends with Luce, Emile Bernard, Pissarro, Van Gogh, Guillaumin, and Odilon Redon.

1886   Takes part in the eighth Impressionist exhibition, Paris.

1889   Sets up the Impressionist and Synthetic group, which holds its exhibition at the Café Volpini, Paris.

1890   Undergoes a period of depression during which he isolates himself from his fellow painters.

1926   Participates in the Salon des Indépendants, Paris, on its fiftieth birthday.

1934   Died, Paris.

1935   Retrospective exhibition at the Salon des Indépendants, Paris.

Sales

DRAWINGS

1965

Concert at the Tuileries, ink, 9 x 13 ....(539) $1,750

The Evening, pencil, 11½ x 9 ....(624)   221

1966

Etretat, colored pencil with pastel heightening,
6¼ x 8½ ....(793)   180

1967

Portrait of Paul Gauguin, pencil, 7¼ x 6¼ ....(931)   452

Village Road, pencil, 8½ x 7¼ ....(881)   41

1968–July 1969

The Boulevard de Port-Royal Under Snow,
charcoal heightened with gouache,
15 x 12¾ ....(1026)   420

Cliffs, colored chalk, 7¼ x 4¾ ....(1203)   136

WATERCOLORS

1961–1962

Sceaux Castle, pastel, 9½ x 12¾ ....(119)   90

1963

Presumed Portrait of His Daughter, pastel,
15¾ x 12¼ .... (276) $ 120
In the Park of Sceaux, pastel, 9½ x 12¾ .... (291) 120

1964

At the Edge of the Pond, pastel, 11¼ x 15 .... (370) 180
Tunnel at the Bois, pastel, 16¾ x 21¾ .... (438) 325
Child Coming Out of School, pastel, 23¾ x 17¾ .. (377) 904

1965

The Dale, pastel, 17½ x 22½ .... (503) 400
The Rocks, pastel, 5¼ x 8¼ .... (607) 100
Cliffs, two pastels, each 8 x 10¼ .... (541) 350

1966

Etretat, pastel, 4½ x 7¼ .... (692) 120
The Coast at Sanary, pastel, 9 x 12 .... (720) 144
Seaside, pastel, 4¾ x 7¼ .... (772) 114
Cliffs, pastel, 5 x 7½ .... (796) 130

1967

Landscape, pastel, 4½ x 8¼ .... (949) 80
The Village, watercolor and blue pencil,
12 x 13¼ .... (985) 213

1968–July 1969

Ile de France, pastel, 4¾ x 7 .... (1055) 110
The Pond, pastel, 13 x 18¼ .... (1087) 250
Underwood, pastel, 17 x 21¾ .... (1030) 500
Seaside, pastel, 4¾ x 7¼ .... (1048) 130
Landscape, pastel, 5 x 7¼ .... (1161) 100
Springtime in the Valley, pastel, 14¾ x 18¾ ..... (1077) 260
Red Roofs, pastel, 14 x 18¼ .... (1140) 180
Three Little Girls in a Landscape, pastel,
18¾ x 22½ .... (1114) 744
The Monastery, pastel, 6 x 9 .... (1134) 189
Landscape, pastel, 12¾ x 18¼ .... (1243) 240
Coast of Normandy, pastel, 5¼ x 8 .... (1243) 110
Cliffs, pastel, 9½ x 12¼ .... (1265) 200
Village by the Seaside, pastel, 16¼ x 21¾ .... (1265) 620
The Ballerina, (1887), pastel, 23¾ x 14¼ .... (1265) 1,800

PAINTINGS

1961–1962

Snow: Rue Boulard, 1884, 21¾ x 19 .... (80) 640

1963

Seascape in Brittany, 13 x 16¼ .... (204) 820

1964

Fishermen at the Bottom of the Cliffs, 1887,
19¾ x 24 .... (371) 1,600
Notre-Dame and the Quays, 17 x 23¾ .... (459) 1,401

1965

Young Woman Reading in a Meadow, 1886,
25¾ x 32 .... (511) 10,000
Riverside, 18¼ x 21¾ .... (529) 400
Seaside, 1886, 12½ x 16 .... (624) 1,327

1966

Rocks at the Seaside, 1886, 13 x 16¼ .... (819) 2,160
The Heights of Meudon, 18¼ x 22 .... (737) 1,000
Snowy Scene, 1884, 26½ x 18¼ .... (818) 755
Wintry Landscape, 6¾ x 8¾ .... (665) 450
Notre-Dame de Paris Under Snow, 19¾ x 23¾ ... (648) 1,200
The Harbor, 17½ x 23 .... (753) 4,063
Road Lined with Trees, (1888), 28½ x 23 .... (784) 2,500

1967

Sailboats at Dieppe Beach, (1885), 15 x 18 .... (963) $1,000
The Seaweed Gatherers, 1887, 19¾ x 24 .... (911) 1,700
The Seaweed Gatherers, 1887, 15 x 21¾ .... (852) 800
Etretat, (1895), 15¼ x 18¾ .... (841) 1,500
The Cliffs at Pantin, 1904, 31 x 37½ .... (985) 1,422
View of Notre-Dame, 16¾ x 23 .... (985) 2,015
Notre-Dame de Paris, 17 x 23¾ .... (870) 1,000

1968–July 1969

Still Life with a Jug. (1889), 13 x 9 .... (1026) 820
Dunkirk Beach, 14¾ x 18 .... (1203) 694
Landscape with an Old Bridge, 25 x 31¼ .... (1070) 1,463
Landscape, 23¾ x 29 .... (1139) 700
Etretat, the Cliffs, 1887, 19¾ x 24 .... (1138) 2,106
A Corner of the Beach at Concarneau, 1887,
15 x 22 .... (1231) 4,250
Landscape, 25½ x 21 .... (1231) 1,500
Portrait of the Painter Fernand Quignou, (1892),
31½ x 25½ .... (1239) 9,600
Seated Nude, on board, 17 x 14¾ .... (1241) 353
Harbor Scene at Etretat Yport, (1895),
15¼ x 18½ .... (1248) 1,100
Village Street, 1895, 25 x 28¼ .... (1271) 1,440
View of a Church on the Outskirts of a Wood,
21¼ x 25½ .... (1273) 2,770

Kurt Schwitters

(1887–1948)

Birthplace: Hanover, Germany.

1908-14 Studies at the Hanover School of Arts and Crafts
and then at the Academy of Dresden.

1915 Marries Helma Fisher. Settles in Hanover. Turns to
Expressionism.

1918 Comes under the influence of Cubism and then of
abstract painting.

1919 Executes his first "Merz" pictures, consisting of dis-
parate elements merged into a work of art. Exhib-
its at Der Sturm Gallery, Berlin.

1920 Exhibits at the Société Anonyme, New York. Begins to arrange his "Merzbau" in Hanover.

1922 Meets Van Doesburg.

1923 Publishes his review *Merz*—closely related to the
Dada movement.

1929 Takes part in "Abstract and Surrealist Painting" at
the Kunsthaus, Zurich.

1930 Takes part in the exhibition of "Cercle et Carré" at
the Galerie 23, Paris.

1932 Joins the "Abstraction-Création" group, Paris.

1933 Trip to Norway.

1936	Participates in "Cubism and Abstract Art" and in "Fantastic Art, Dada, and Surrealism" at the Museum of Modern Art, New York.
1941	Settles in England.
1947	Executes his collage "For Käte," which is regarded as a Pop prototype.
1948	Died, Ambleside, England.

Sales

DRAWINGS

1961–1962

Z 100 Hochgebirge, 1918, black chalk, 9¾ x 5¾ ... (106) $ 362

Aq. 13, 1919, India ink and watercolor, 7¾ x 5½ .. (105) 678

Abstract Composition, 1935, black lead,
 10 x 4¾ .... (106) 146

1964

Landscape, pencil and watercolor, 8 x 6½ .... (385) 181

1966

Composition, 1918, black pencil, 6¼ x 4¼ .... (805) 350

1967

Village Church, 1917-18, black chalk, 7¾ x 5¾ ... (970) 713

1968–July 1969

"Für Jan Tschichold," 1935, pencil, 10¼ x 9¼ ... (1088) 200

WATERCOLORS

1967

The Sweepers, 1914, watercolor and black chalk,
 21 x 16¾ .... (990) 590

Abstraction, 13, 1919, pen and watercolor,
 8 x 5¾ .... (931) 678

1968–July 1969

Composition, watercolor and collage, 8 x 6¼ .... (1173) 1,610

Composition, watercolor and collage, 8 x 6¼ .... (1268) 2,088

PAINTINGS

1961–1962

Asinet, collage, 10¾ x 8 .... (106) 2,034

The Violin, 1926, collage, 4¾ x 3¾ .... (106) 1,085

Collage, 1928, 6 x 4½ .... (88) 1,255

Do Not Vote..., collage, 17 x 12¾ .... (20) 2,844

In the Kitchen, collage, 24 x 20 .... (20) 9,164

Composition, 1930, collage, 4½ x 3¾ .... (49) 280

A Tribute to Van Gogh, 1936, on board,
 21 x 24½ .... (145) 3,792

Composition, collage .... (16) 790

Collage, 1944, 7¼ x 10 .... (129) 961

High Mountains, 1947, 7¼ x 8 .... (75) 1,264

1963

Dammerstock, 1929, collage, 12¼ x 9½ .... (255) 960

1964

Trade and Bank, 1930, collage, 6¾ x 5¼ .... (461) 1,920

Painting No. Mz 478, 1922, collage, 7¼ x 5¾ ..... (453) 1,161

Composition, 1943, collage, 8½ x 6 .... (372) 1,100

Katzenjammer Kids, 1947, collage, 6 x 4½ .... (372) 425

1965

Aerial Painting, 1917, oil and collage on paper
 laid down on board, 18½ x 24 .... (594) 8,000

Composition with Labels, 1922, collage,
 7¼ x 5¾ .... (501) 1,400

Composition with a Letter, 1921, collage,
 7 x 5¾ .... (501) $1,600

Still Life with Flowers, 1945, on board,
 12¾ x 15½ .... (545) 1,271

Basel, 1947, collage, 10 x 8 .... (568) 1,356

1966

Points 106, 47, collage, 8 x 6¼ .... (784) 1,900

Wol, 1920, collage No. Mz 123, 9 x 5¾ .... (676) 800

Herz-Klee, 1920, collage No. Mz 79, 5¾ x 4½ .... (676) 3,500

Collage, 1947, collage, 11 x 9½ .... (751) 1,714

Springtime, collage, 19 x 15 .... (686) 2,764

Ade Mz 26.46, 1926, collage, 7¼ x 5½ .... (676) 2,750

1967

Goldkaro, 1921, collage on newsprint, 7¼ x 5¾ ... (915) 1,033

Collage, 1920, 6¾ x 5¾ .... (985) 1,422

March 1927, collage, 6½ x 4¾ .... (889) 950

Composition, (1945-46), collage, 6¼ x 5 .... (1004) 1,200

Untitled, 1946, collage, 5 x 3¾ .... (931) 768

Collage, 1947, collage, 8½ x 7¼ .... (881) 884

1968–July 1969

Fluvial Landscape, 1915, on panel, 5½ x 6½ ..... (1090) 446

Picture Mz 478, 1922, collage, 7¼ x 5¾ .... (1102) 2,300

Merz-Drawing, 1930, collage, 8 x 5¾ .... (1059) 991

Composition, 1930, collage, 8 x 5¾ .... (1138) 694

Composition, collage and gouache, 6¾ x 5¾ ..... (1125) 2,553

Yellow, Red, and Blue Collage, 6 x 4½ .... (1191) 1,888

Blue, Yellow, and Red Composition, (1945),
 collage, 8 x 6¼ .... (1070) 944

Collage, 1930, 4 x 2¾ .... (1241) 856

Composition, 1947, collage, 8½ x 7 .... (1272) 1,468

Giovanni Segantini

(1858–1899)

Birthplace: Arco, Italy. (Studies painting at the Academia Brera, Milan.)

1878-81	Joins the group called "Scapigliatura," Milan.
1882	Retires to the country, where he devotes himself to painting in the open.
1886	Embraces Italian Divisionism. Retires to the mountains.
1891	Meets Greviati—another Italian Divisionist—whose work he highly appreciates.
1899	Died, at the Chalet du Schafberg, Haute-Engadine, Switzerland. (One of the most renowned Italian Divisionists, he exerted a strong influence upon the Futurists at the beginning of their career.)

Sales

DRAWINGS

1961–1962

Love at the Spring of Life, 1897, 19 x 20 .... (94) $ 763

1963
Interior with Three Seated Women, colored
    chalk, 9½ x 15 ....(307) $ 520
1964
Myriam in the Desert, 1898, charcoal,
    31¼ x 23¼ ....(403)   1,130
The Goat, colored pencil, 4½ x 7¾ ....(428)   369
1967
The Widow, black chalk, 12¼ x 7¼ ....(990)   246
1968–July 1969
Edelweiss, 1898, charcoal, 25¼ x 14¾ ....(1126)   2,726

WATERCOLORS

1967
The Sick Child, 1877, watercolor on gray paper,
    21¼ x 14½ ....(940)   1,219
1968–July 1969
The Hero, pastel, 15 x 10½ ....(1107)   230

PAINTINGS

1965
Still Life, on cardboard, 18 x 24 ....(617)   6,780
1967
Children Fishing, 17¾ x 10½ ....(991)   1,211
1968–July 1969
Peasant in a Winter Landscape, 29¼ x 39½ .....(1182)   11,500

Séraphine de Senlis

(1864–1934)

Birthplace: Assy, Oise, France. (Called Séraphine
Louis. Spends her childhood tending flocks. Later
moves to Senlis where she works as a
charwoman.)

1912   Becomes the housemaid of German critic Wilhelm
Uhde, who is amazed by her natural gift for painting. He buys some of her pictures and encourages her to keep on painting.

1930   She experiences a mental breakdown.

1934   Died, in the mental hospital of Clarmont-de-l'Oise.
(Her work consists exclusively of pictures of flowers, fruits, and leaves.)

Sales

PAINTINGS

1964
An Apple, 9½ x 14 ....(351) $ 300
Foliage, 19¾ x 25¾ ....(351)   1,200
Water Lilies, 45¾ x 32 ....(351)   1,000

1967
Cherry-Tree Branch, on panel, 8 x 10 ....(888) $ 415
Orange, 9½ x 14 ....(898)   400
1968–July 1969
Bunch of Flowers, 31½ x 23¾ ....(1043)   5,000
Flowers, 31½ x 23¼ ....(1256)   5,600

Paul Sérusier

(1863–1927)

Birthplace: Paris, France.

1888   Attends the Académie Julian, Paris. Spends the
summer at Pont-Aven, where he meets Gauguin.
Under his guidance, he paints the famous "Talis-
man," which amazes his fellow students in Paris—the future Nabis.

1889-90   Sets up the Nabis group—with Bonnard, Vuillard,
Roussel, Maurice Denis, and Ranson. Stay at Le
Pouldu in Brittany, with Gauguin and Meyer de
Haan. Paints "La Mer au Pouldu."

1891   Exhibits with the Nabis at the Galerie Le Barc de
Boutteville, Paris.

1892   Stay at Pont-Aven with Verkade, Ranson, and
others.

1895   Makes a trip to Italy with Maurice Denis—and
again in 1904. Discovers the frescoes of the
Quattrocento.

1897   Travels in Central Europe. Stay at the Couvent de
Beuron, where his friend Verkade has become a
monk. Visits him again in 1899 and 1903.

1903   Buys a house at Chateauneuf-du-Faou.

1908   With Maurice Denis, teaches painting at the Académie Ranson, Paris.

1912   Marries one of his pupils and spends his honey-
moon in Florence.

1914   Retires to Brittany. Takes an increasing interest in
medieval art. Decorates his house and the Church
of Chateauneuf.

1921   Issues *ABC de la Peinture* (Paris).

1927   Died, Morlaix, Brittany.

Sales

DRAWINGS

1963
The Wood Gatherer, Brittany, India-ink wash,
    5¾ x 3¾ ....(222) $ 66
1964
Landscape with a Little Wood, charcoal with
    color heightening, 6¼ x 16¼ ....(441)   131

1965

Breton Woman, with a Coif, charcoal and chalk,
22½ x 16¼ .... (547) $ 460

Pont-Aven, stick of greasepaint, 6¼ x 7¼ .... (631) 116

1967

Figures in a Landscape, 9 x 11½ .... (995) 160

1968–July 1969

The Bretons, black pencil, 6 x 8 .... (1180) 130

Breton Peasants' Heads, pen, 4¾ x 4¾ .... (1178) 70

The Dead Tree, charcoal and black lead,
15½ x 10¾ .... (1244) 104

The Three Trees, India-ink wash on gray paper,
12¾ x 8¼ .... (1244) 122

House in the Country, black lead, 5½ x 7¼ ...... (1244) 32

Brook Under the Woods, charcoal, 10½ x 12¼ .. (1267) 300

Three Landscapes, sepia wash, 9 x 15½ .... (1267) 210

Little Breton Girls, two drawings, charcoal,
7 x 4¼ and 3¼ x 4 .... (1267) 290

WATERCOLORS

1967

Landscape with an Ancient Bridge, pastel,
23¾ x 18¼ .... (897) 620

1968–July 1969

The Washerwomen, watercolor, 6 x 6¾ .... (1219) 220

Studies of Breton Women, pencil, India ink, and
watercolor, 10½ x 9¼ .... (1272) 432

PAINTINGS

1961–1962

Still Life with a Fruit Stand, (1890), 21 x 28½ ...... (31) 2,471

Farmyard in Pont-Aven, 25¾ x 23¾ .... (157) 5,800

The Reading, 18¼ x 21¾ .... (97) 940

Blond Young Girl, 20½ x 15¾ .... (171) 600

Still Life with a Jug, 1891, 10 x 14 .... (93) 1,446

The Mountain Road, 1893, 28½ x 23¼ .... (159) 13,184

The Witches' Cavern, 21 x 25¾ .... (173) 1,110

The Fields, Two Peasants on the Right,
21¼ x 25¾ .... (50) 400

Brook Under the Woods, 21¾ x 17 .... (80) 1,040

1963

*Breton Woman Carrying a Burden; Back from
the Fountain,* two paintings, each 44¼ x 27 .. (312) 2,000

Breton Peasant, 1890, 16¾ x 12¾ .... (210) 4,661

Still Life, 1891, 10¾ x 14 .... (283) 1,627

Breton Farm, 1891, on board, 23¼ x 17¾ .... (309) 4,944

Young Lady's Head, (1900), 27 x 16¼ .... (255) 603

The Dreaming Girl, 1925, 25¾ x 19¾ .... (306) 1,800

Jug with Windflowers and a Plate of Plums, 1926,
23¾ x 14¾ .... (306) 1,400

The Criticism, 20 x 13 .... (298) 740

Apples and Lemons, 15½ x 21 .... (198) 1,600

Autumn in Pont-Aven, 36½ x 29 .... (283) 5,424

1964

The Fagot Gatherers, (1890–92), 28½ x 35½ ...... (416) 4,422

Peasant and Her Donkey, 1907, 34 x 20½ .... (398) 2,600

Banana, Orange, and Lemon, on board, 10 x 13 .. (454) 1,382

Autumn in the Dale, on cardboard, 10½ x 13 ..... (404) 540

The Green Pears, 23 x 16¾ .... (471) 1,808

Morning Haze, 23 x 15½ .... (471) 1,537

Washerwomen, Le Bas-Pouldu, on paper laid
down on canvas, 20½ x 12¾ .... (343) 1,220

1965

Landscape, 1890, 28½ x 36 .... (617) $ 8,588

Breton in a Meadow, 1894, 19¾ x 24 .... (553) 3,700

Landscape at Pont-Aven, 13½ x 15¾ .... (624) 2,349

Ship at Her Moorings, on canvas laid down on
panel, 19¾ x 12¾ .... (583) 2,322

Landscape of Brittany, 1906, 36½ x 29 .... (532) 2,500

Young Lady with a Blue Veil, on cardboard,
17½ x 13½ .... (577) 560

The Yellow Poplars, 1920, 18¼ x 25¾ .... (547) 1,500

Still Life Under the Arbor, 1921, 23¾ x 33½ ...... (640) 1,640

1966

Still Life with Pears, 1923, 14 x 21 .... (685) 1,100

Landscape, 22 x 15½ .... (655) 1,040

Green Landscape, Chateauneuf-du-Faou Valley,
1919, 17¾ x 25¾ .... (653) 1,400

Pont-Aven Landscape, 1892, 24 x 16¾ .... (744) 7,910

1967

Landscape of Pont-Aven, 1903, 19¾ x 29 .... (901) 1,000

The Fountain, (1892), 43½ x 54½ .... (982) 6,636

Woman's Head, 18¼ x 13¾ .... (855) 900

Still Life, on panel, 21¾ x 15 .... (912) 1,220

Bretons in the Valley, 29 x 36 .... (993) 1,980

1968–July 1969

Autumn in Pont-Aven, (1900), 36½ x 29 .... (1173) 20,930

Devotion to Saint Herbot, 1893, 29 x 36½ .... (1189) 10,000

The Threshing, 1896, 17½ x 20½ .... (1113) 2,400

The Lesson of Botany, 1918, 35¼ x 57¼ .... (1068) 8,968

Green Landscape, 1920, 18¼ x 26½ .... (1051) 1,400

Apples and Lemons, 15½ x 21 .... (1184) 2,220

Landscape, 19¾ x 24 .... (1078) 1,000

Women at the Spring, 43½ x 27 .... (1138) 1,536

Still Life, 23¼ x 23½ .... (1113) 2,400

Corn Reaper, 1889, 18¼ x 15 .... (1239) 12,480

Landscape, 18¼ x 15 .... (1268) 1,392

Georges Seurat

(1859–1891)

Birthplace: Paris, France.

1875   Forms a friendship with Aman-Jean at the Ecole Municipale de Dessein, Paris.

1877   Frequently visits museums, where he executes many copies after painters such as Holbein, Poussin, and Raphael. Admires Ingres above all.

1878   With Aman-Jean, enters the Ecole Nationale des Beaux-Arts, Paris—in the studio of Henri Lehmann, a pupil of Ingres. Becomes passionately fond of Chevreul's scientific treatise *De La Loi du contraste simultané des couleurs et de l'assortiment des objets coloriés*—which exerts a decisive influence on the development of his painting.

1879-80   Enlists in the army and spends a year at Brest in Brittany, where he discovers the sea.

1881   Devotes himself to drawing and succeeds in creating his own style. Carefully studies Delacroix' colors.

1882   Executes a first series of pictures painted in thin separate strokes.

1883   Exhibits his drawing "Portrait of Aman-Jean" at the Salon, Paris. Paints his first work based on the contrast of color—"The Bathers: Asnières" (Tate Gallery, London). (Had executed dozens of studies for this painting and continues to work as painstakingly and methodically.)

1884   "The Bathers" is refused by the Salon, Paris, but is exhibited at the first Salon des Indépendants, Paris. Sets up the Société des Artistes Indépendants—with Redon, Angrand, Dubois-Pillet, Signac, and Cross.

1885   On Signac's advice, goes to Grandchamp, near Le Havre, where he paints his first seascapes. Meets Pissarro, who joins his group until 1889. Paints "A Sunday Afternoon at the Ile de la Grande-Jatte" (Art Institute, Chicago), the chief masterpiece of Neo-Impressionism—then called "Divisionnisme" or "Pointillisme."

1886   Thanks to Pissarro, he and Signac are reluctantly admitted by the Impressionists to show in their last exhibition, Paris, where "La Grande-Jatte" creates a scandal.

1887   Takes part in the exhibition of the XX, Brussels—and again in 1889.

1888   Exhibits "Circus Parade" and "The Model" at the fourth Salon des Indépendants, Paris.

1889   Paints a series of seascapes at Le Crotoy.

1890   Stays at Gravelines, near Dunkirk.

1891   Participates in the famous Symbolist banquet that includes Mallarmé, Anatole France, André Gide, Gauguin, and Odilon Redon. While organizing the Indépendants' exhibition, he is attacked by a sudden chill and dies after three days, aged thirty-one. (Seurat's genius is regarded as typically representative of French culture.)

Sales

DRAWINGS

1961–1962

Un Bonhomme, pen, 4¾ x 1¾ .... (32) $ 440

The Girders, Conté pencil, 9½ x 11¾ .... (20)   10,270

Two Horses, charcoal, 8¾ x 11¾ .... (29)   13,000

1963

Woman Moving Off, pencil, 6 x 4½ .... (198)   2,400

Boats at Sunset, charcoal, 6¾ x 9¼ .... (284)   640

1964

Coachman with His Horse, pencil, 6½ x 4¼ ...... (471)   1,921

Drum, Soldiers, and a Woman, 1879-80, colored pencil, 6 x 9½ .... (367)   691

The Closed Sunshade, Conté pencil, 6 x 4 .... (398)   1,020

1965

Back View of a Seated Woman, (1881), charcoal, 7 x 4½ .... (596)   2,460

Monsieur Loyal, 1890, Conté pencil, 12 x 5¼ .... (575)   1,106

Man Seated on a Bench, Conté pencil, 5¾ x 4¼ .... (553)   1,800

Parthenon: Fragment of the Frieze, 1875, Conté pencil, 14¼ x 20 .... (640)   800

1966

L'Estacade de Port-en-Bessin, Conté pencil, 8¾ x 11½ .... (744) $6,102

Study of a Leg, pencil, 9½ x 6 .... (671)   813

Standing Nude in Left Profile, pencil, 12¼ x 9 .... (671)   987

Standing Woman Wearing a Chignon, black lead, 6½ x 3¾ .... (797)   1,356

The Orange Seller, (1881), Conté pencil, 10¾ x 8½ .... (797)   3,277

1967

Soldier Reading, Seated on a Bench, (1879-80), black lead and colored pencil, 5¾ x 9¼ ...... (881)   1,797

Woman Seated on a Bench, (1881), charcoal, 6¾ x 4 .... (985)   2,963

Figure of a Seated Woman, 12¼ x 9½ .... (976)   3,800

1968–July 1969

Two Heads, a Bust and a Figure, After Plasters, (1876-78), pencil, 9¼ x 5¾ .... (1068)   425

Seated Woman Turned Toward the Left, black lead, 4 x 2¾ .... (1174)   690

Seated Woman Turned Toward the Right, black lead, 6½ x 4¼ .... (1053)   1,240

Landscape, (1881), Conté pencil, 10 x 11¾ ..... (1053)   17,920

L'Estacade de Port-en-Bessin, 1888, pencil, 8¾ x 11¼ .... (1239)   12,000

Outline of Houses and Trees, Rays, Roofs at Sunrise, (1883), 9½ x 12¾ .... (1256)   11,000

PAINTINGS

1961–1962

By the Riverside, on panel, 6¼ x 9¾ .... (137)   24,000

1963

Figure in a Meadow, (1883), on panel, 6 x 9¾ .... (245)   93,228

Clothes, Hat, Study for "The Bathers," (1883), on panel, 7 x 10¼ .... (245)   76,776

1965

Houses and Garden, 1882, 11 x 18¼ .... (629)   92,864

Meadows in the Summertime, 1883, on panel, 6½ x 10 .... (629)   104,472

1966

Peasants at Montfermeil, (1882), on panel, 6¼ x 9¾ .... (750)   99,504

To the Market Town, (1883), on panel, 6½ x 10 ... (808)   58,040

Gino Severini

(1883–1966)

Birthplace: Cortona, Italy.

1901-03 Goes to Rome, where he meets Boccioni and Ballà.

1906 Goes to Paris and meets Modigliani, Max Jacob, Suzanne Valadon, Utrillo, Braque, and Dufy.

1910 Signs the manifesto of the Futurist painters in Milan—with Ballà, Boccioni, Carrà, and Russolo. Paints his first important works. Meets Picasso.

1911 Paints "The Milliner."

1912 Takes part in the Futurist exhibitions held in cities such as Paris, London, and Berlin.

1913 Marries Paul Fort's daughter.

1914 His manner gets very close to abstraction.

1915-21 Cubist period—series of still lifes with musical instruments.

1917 One-man show at Stieglitz' Gallery "291," New York.

1918-20 Takes a great interest in mathematics.

1921 Issues his book *Du Cubisme au Classicisme.*

1922 Series of "Harlequins."

1925 Executes frescoes and mosaics for churches of Switzerland, notably in Fribourg and Lausanne.

1929 Decorates the house of Léonce Rosenberg.

1933 Executes mosaics for the Palazzo della Triennale, Milan.

1935 Given an award by the Rome Quadrennial.

1946 Issues the first volume of his memoirs *Tutta la vita di un pittore* (Garzanti, Rome).

1950 Participates in the Venice Biennial. Settles at Meudon, near Paris.

1956 Takes part in the exhibition "Oeuvres Futuristes et Cubistes" at the Galerie Berggruenn, Paris.

1966 Died.

Sales

DRAWINGS

1964

Pierrot with a Guitar, ink, 21 x 14¾ . . . . (454) $ 276
The Acrobat, India-ink wash, 26 x 13½ . . . . (447) 180
Dancers, 1955, ink and colored chalk, 9½ x 11¾ . . (435) 320

1965

Pierrot Playing the Guitar, (1923-24), ink, 17½ x 12¾ . . . . (582) 276
The Jockey, ink and watercolor, 19 x 25¼ . . . . (494) 775
Maternity, pencil, 11½ x 9 . . . . (599) 60
Composition, India ink, 8¾ x 11 . . . . (627) 140

1966

Still Life (Cubist Composition), pencil, 6 x 4¾ . . . . (739) 738
Still Life, 8¼ x 11¾ . . . . (655) 98
Punchinello Playing the Guitar, pen, 22 x 15¼ . . . . (802) 960
Harlequin with a Guitar, ink, 21 x 14¾ . . . . (671) 377

1967

Dancer, 1913, India ink, 11¼ x 7½ . . . . (931) 836
Self-Portrait, 1915, chalk and wash, 21¼ x 15¾ . . (1004) 5,250
Still Life with a Pedestal Table, 10¾ x 8¼ . . . . (926) 280

1968–July 1969

Figures, 1924, pencil, 11 x 14¾ . . . . (1116) $ 200
Face, pen, 25¾ x 18¾ . . . . (1061) 300
Dancer, pen, 25 x 17¾ . . . . (1088) 1,100
Still Life, pencil, 9 x 12¾ . . . . (1088) 550
Still Life with a Coffeepot and a Fruit Stand, pencil, 9 x 12¾ . . . . (1028) 32
Futurist Fantasy, 1962, black chalk and blue ink, 26½ x 19¾ . . . . (1126) 991
Young Lady with a Guitar, 12¾ x 8¼ . . . . (1230) 700
Dance Rhythm,[1] 1912, pencil heightened with white, 6¼ x 5½ . . . . (1232) 1,700
Still Life,[2] pen and India ink, 8¾ x 11 . . . . (1240) 408
Fantasia Futurista, 1962, black chalk and blue ink, 26½ x 19¾ . . . . (1273) 1,260

WATERCOLORS

1961–1962

Bus (Dynamic Rhythm of a Head in a Bus), 1912, pastel, 24¼ x 18¼ . . . . (88) 5,166
Dancer Amid the Tables, 1912, tempera, pastel, and charcoal, 19¾ x 14 . . . . (149) 5,688
Tramway on a Boulevard, 1913, pastel, 11 x 14¾ . . . . (69) 4,740
Trolley, 1913, pastel on a sandy background, 19¾ x 25¾ . . . . (88) 5,412
Figure, 1913, pastel, 18½ x 15 . . . . (85) 1,600
Woman and Autumn, 1919, watercolor, 13 x 20½ . . . . (70) 632
Harlequin, 1921, gouache, 11¾ x 9 . . . . (131) 760
Harlequin, 1948, pastel, 14 x 18¾ . . . . (75) 2,054
The Dancer, (1957), gouache, 25¼ x 19½ . . . . (111) 1,200
Still Life with a Lily of the Valley, gouache, 25¾ x 17½ . . . . (158) 720

1963

Harlequins, 1921, gouache, 11¾ x 9 . . . . (269) 684
Dancers, watercolor, 25¼ x 18¾ . . . . (306) 560

1964

Dancer, pastel and India ink, 20½ x 14¼ . . . . (458) 3,773
Portrait of a Man, 1904, pastel, 19½ x 25½ . . . . . . (404) 900
Composition, (1951), gouache, 11¼ x 8¾ . . . . (387) 387
Composition, gouache, 8¼ x 6¾ . . . . (405) 580

1965

Composition, 1913, gouache, 15½ x 7½ . . . . (616) 2,400
Composition, 1930, gouache, 22 x 15 . . . . (637) 2,200
Composition, (1951), gouache, 11¼ x 8¾ . . . . (582) 498
Figure, watercolor, 11¾ x 8¾ . . . . (627) 400
The Open Window, pastel, 18¼ x 12¾ . . . . (640) 600

1966

Ballerina, 1912, pastel and India ink on gray paper, 20½ x 14¼ . . . . (808) 3,482
Composition, watercolor, 8 x 10 . . . . (670) 300
Harlequin, gouache, 15 x 11 . . . . (805) 1,400
Ballet, gouache, 16 x 11 . . . . (815) 498
Movement, 1960, watercolor, 31½ x 18¾ . . . . (665) 1,200

1967

Portrait of a Woman, 1911, oval pastel, 25 x 20½ . . . . (981) 2,100
Dancers, (1912), pastel, 17¾ x 23¾ . . . . (1004) 4,750

[1]Inscribed on the reverse "Ce dessin est fait par moi en 1912."
[2]Inscribed "Al vecchio e caro amico Mario Marionelli, affetuoso ricordo di Gino Severini, Parigi, Decembre 1962."

Harlequin, and His Love, gouache, 12¾ x 8 ...... **(939)** $ 884
Composition, 1945, pastel, 15¾ x 10 .... **(962)** 608
Study, gouache, 14¾ x 11 .... **(963)** 2,000
Movement, 1960, watercolor, 32 x 19 .... **(940)** 1,451
Still Life with Fish, 1964, pastel, 19 x 25¼ .... **(881)** 691

1968–July 1969
Newspaper, Guitar, and Ace of Hearts, (1918),
  gouache, 11 x 7½ .... **(1191)** 3,776
Composition with a Bottle of Rum, (1922),
  gouache, 14¾ x 9¾ .... **(1173)** 1,656
Ballerina, gouache, 25¾ x 19¾ .... **(1134)** 1,534
Still Life, watercolor, 10 x 14 .... **(1213)** 800
Guitar and Fruit, Rome, oval gouache,
  14¼ x 22½ .... **(1109)** 1,700
Futurist Fantasy, (1960), gouache, 25 x 18 .... **(1061)** 1,050
Red Dancer, 1960, tempera, 25¾ x 18½ .... **(1214)** 2,880
Still Life, 1964, watercolor, 8 x 10 .... **(1061)** 450
Composition, 1964, pastel, 11 x 14¾ .... **(1129)** 380
Bottles, Fruit Stand, and Guitar, watercolor,
  10½ x 14½ .... **(1240)** 1,560
Composition, gouache, 20 x 14½ .... **(1268)** 3,595

PAINTINGS

1961–1962
Portrait of Cravan,[3] 1912, collage and drawing,
  21¾ x 17¾ .... **(149)** 15,010
Dynamism of Shapes, 1912, 29 x 39½ .... **(145)** 17,380
The Guitar, (1920), 45 x 36¼ .... **(84)** 1,648
Still Life with Fish, 21 x 29 .... **(96)** 2,000
Motorcyclist Riding Through the Country,
  19¾ x 25¾ .... **(15)** 3,160
Light and Movement, 1958, 25½ x 19½ .... **(37)** 2,300

1964
Harlequin, 11½ x 8¼ .... **(405)** 1,074
Still Life with a Violin, 19¾ x 25¾ .... **(375)** 860
Still Still with a Mandolin, 36½ x 23¾ .... **(439)** 2,880

1965
Mandolin on the Pedestal Table, 1917,
  29 x 21½ .... **(616)** 8,000
Pink Dancer, 1941, 25¾ x 18¾ .... **(539)** 2,000
Light and Movement, 21 x 25¾ .... **(503)** 860

1966
Still Life with a Violin, 19¾ x 26 .... **(656)** 1,200
Composition, 24 x 19¾ .... **(730)** 2,000

1967
Springtime, 1950, on panel, 21¾ x 18 .... **(870)** 1,200
The Ballet of the Thirteen Dances, 36½ x 25¾ .... **(883)** 3,220

1968–July 1969
Hilly Landscape, 1904, 13¼ x 29½ .... **(1187)** 2,478
Composition with a Dove, oil and collage,
  10¾ x 14 .... **(1173)** 2,875
Still Life with a Fruit Stand, 15 x 18¼ .... **(1028)** 3,100
Instruments and Ceramic Vase, 7 x 26½ .... **(1177)** 1,460
Portrait of a Man, 31½ x 23 .... **(1213)** 270
The Springtime, 1950, on panel, 21¾ x 18 .... **(1145)** 1,700
Still Life with a Coffeepot, 1917, 21¼ x 15½ ..... **(1226)** 8,000
The Clown Painter, 1937, on paper mounted on
  canvas, 14 x 10 .... **(1231)** 1,000

[3]Inscribed on the reverse "Portrait géométrique d'Arthur Cravan 1912."

René Séyssaud

(1867–1952)

Birthplace: Marseilles, France. (Enters the Fine
Arts School of Marseilles.)

1875 Enters the Fine Arts School of Avignon.
1897 First exhibition at the Galerie Le Barc de Boutteville, Paris, where Ambroise Vollard notices his
works and proposes a contract that Séyssaud refuses to sign. Owing to his colorful manner, he
later appears as a precursor of Fauvism.
1899 Exhibits at Ambroise Vollard's, Paris.
1903 Contributes to the foundation of the Salon d'Automne, Paris. Some of his paintings are bought by
the Musée de Luxembourg, Paris.
1932 Takes part in "Paysages de France" at the Galerie
Charpentier, Paris. Exhibits at the Georges Binel
Gallery, New York.
1947 Promoted to the rank of Officer of the Legion of
Honor.
1951 Given an award by the Menton Biennial.
1952 Died, St. Chamas.
1956 Retrospective exhibition at the Musée Galliéra,
Paris.

Sales

WATERCOLORS
1966
Landscape, watercolor, 11½ x 14¾ .... **(723)** $ 136

1968–July 1969
Village of the South of France, gouache, 24 x 15 **(1033)** 204
The Valley, watercolor wash, 13 x 16¼ .... **(1072)** 180

PAINTINGS
1961–1962
Dusk at Aix, (1896), 29 x 4½ .... **(53)** 1,500
Boats on the Strand, 15 x 24 .... **(53)** 500
St. Chamas in the Summer, 23¾ x 19¾ .... **(30)** 1,040
Landscape of Provence, 18¼ x 21¾ .... **(33)** 1,300
Lavender Gatherer, 15 x 21¾ .... **(26)** 1,400
The Red Rocks at the Seaside, 13¾ x 20¼ .... **(125)** 1,180
Still Life, 17¾ x 13 .... **(25)** 250
Reclining Nude, 17¾ x 21¼ .... **(175)** 968

1963
Still Life with a Plate of Fruit, 1947, on
  cardboard, 46 x 32 .... **(258)** 1,120
Landscape of Mont Ventoux, 25¾ x 39½ .... **(215)** 800
Flowers and Fruit of Provence, 1947, 46 x 32 ..... **(190)** 1,240
Poplars at St. Chamas, 39½ x 29 .... **(306)** 1,800
Work in the Fields, oil and gouache on
  cardboard, 12¾ x 19¾ .... **(227)** 560
Le Vallon du Galloux, 15¾ x 24 .... **(194)** 1,500
Les Alpilles, 18¼ x 21¾ .... **(319)** 1,260
Ploughing, 15 x 24 .... **(229)** 2,000

1964
Seascapes, two paintings, each 6¾ x 13 .... **(409)** 400
The Cliffs and the Sea, 18¼ x 25¾ .... **(418)** 760
Landscape, 21¾ x 18¼ .... **(466)** 500

Toulouse Rocks, 15 x 24 .... (401) $1,300
March Morning, 1903, on panel, 24 x 15 .... (334) 1,400
Landscape of Provence, 15 x 24 .... (331) 1,620

1965
Seascapes, two paintings, each 6¾ x 13 .... (492) 500
Springtime, Almond Trees in Blossom .... (595) 1,360
Peasants in the Fields, 15 x 24 .... (508) 900
Landscape, 17½ x 39½ .... (572) 1,100
Haymaking Time, 21¾ x 18¼ .... (588) 860
Harvesters, 19¾ x 24 .... (590) 2,100
The Estérel, on cardboard, 10¾ x 13½ .... (563) 340
Bunch of Gillyflowers, 18¼ x 15 .... (516) 580
Still Life with Bottles .... (601) 2,800

1966
Mediterranean Landscape, 21¼ x 25¾ .... (829) 1,600
Landscape, 21¼ x 29 .... (828) 800
The Way to the Grotte Rouge, (1900), on board,
    14½ x 23¼ .... (818) 580
Underwood, 29 x 36½ .... (778) 540
Autumn Landscape, 15 x 23¾ .... (779) 1,000
Hilly Landscape, 31½ x 45 .... (691) 1,000
The Red Slopes at Agay, 13½ x 20 .... (660) 2,300
The Gatherers of Potatoes, 6½ x 10¾ .... (818) 247
Old Street of Provence, on cardboard, 24 x 15 .... (672) 380
Almond Trees in Blossom in the Alpilles,
    39½ x 25¾ .... (649) 1,680
Fishing Boats, 57½ x 110½ .... (681) 200
The Way to the Grotte Rouge, 1900, 15 x 24 ...... (697) 2,220
The Path of Blackberry Bushes, 1905, 15 x 23¾ ... (684) 2,100

1967
Boats on the Strand, 15 x 24 .... (886) 440
Return from the Fields at Villes-sur-Auzon, on
    panel, 15 x 24 .... (874) 960
The Valley of the Touloubre, 12¼ x 19¾ .... (895) 1,400

1968–July 1969
Still Life with a Fruit Stand, on cardboard,
    23¾ x 32 .... (1110) 900
Still Life with Books, 26 x 36½ .... (1110) 170
Seascapes, 29¼ x 36¾ .... (1110) 1,020
Mediterranean Coast, 25¾ x 32 .... (1109) 1,000
Vineyards, 18¼ x 21¾ .... (1197) 4,600
Cap Canaille at Cassis, 14¾ x 21¼ .... (1197) 4,800
Landscape of Provence, 15 x 21¾ .... (1212) 920
*Landscape of the South of France, with a Red
    Field, Harvesttime,* 23¾ x 36½ .... (1053) 2,200
The Harbor, (1895), 21¼ x 25¾ .... (1200) 3,800
Bunch of Flowers, 22½ x 18¼ .... (1121) 400
Cypresses on the Edge of a Pond, on cardboard,
    11¾ x 22 .... (1110) 200
Seascape, 19¾ x 29 .... (1254) 2,500
Flowers in a Vase, 21¾ x 18¼ .... (1262) 1,760

Ben Shahn

(1898–1969)

Birthplace: Kowno, Lithuania.

1906 His family emigrates to the U.S. and settles in Brooklyn, New York.

1922–25 Studies art in New York.

1927 Trip to Europe and North Africa.

1930 First one-man show at the Downtown Gallery, New York.

1931–32 Executes his famous series on "The Passion of Sacco and Vanzetti"—typical of social realism.

1936 Becomes a member of the Artists' Congress, dedicated to propagandizing antifacism.

1940 One-man show at the Julian Levy Gallery, New York.

1940–42 Executes murals for the Social Security Building, Washington, D.C.

1944 One-man show at the Downtown Gallery, New York—and again in 1949, 1952, 1955, 1959, and 1961.

1947 Teaches at the Boston Museum Summer School. Retrospective exhibition at the Mayor Gallery, London.

1947–48 Retrospective exhibition at the Museum of Modern Art, New York.

1951 Teaches at the Brooklyn Museum Art School.

1954 Participates in the São Paulo Biennial and the Venice Biennial.

1956–57 Trip to Europe. Teaches and exhibits at Harvard University. Exhibition, "The Graphic Work of Ben Shahn," at the American Institute of Graphic Arts, New York. Retrospective exhibition at the Institute of Contemporary Art, Boston.

1961–62 Retrospective exhibition at the Stedelijk Museum, Amsterdam.

1969 Died.

Sales

DRAWINGS

1964
Bird Resting, wash, 8½ x 10¾ .... (329) $ 600

WATERCOLORS

1967
Horizon, Ohio, 1945, tempera, 10 x 25¾ .... (952) 5,000
Two Angels, watercolor and ink, 10¾ x 12¾ ...... (893) 850
Chicago, 1955, gouache and watercolor,
    25 x 39½ .... (952) 13,000

1968–July 1969
Demonstrators on Behalf of Sacco and Vanzetti,
    (1931), gouache on paper laid down on panel,
    14¼ x 10 .... (1035) 8,250

PAINTINGS

1961–1962
Cybernetic Studies, gouache and oil on panel,
    13½ x 21½ .... (85) 2,100

1967
Portrait of Anna Linder, 1926, on canvas on
    board, 19¾ x 15¾ .... (860) 850

Charles Sheeler

(1883-1965)

Birthplace: Philadelphia, Pennsylvania, U.S.

1900-03 Attends the School of Industrial Art, Philadelphia.

1903-06 Enters the Pennsylvania Academy of Fine Arts, taught by William Chase.

1909 With Chase, visits England, Holland, and Spain. Also visits Italy.

1913-16 Attracted successively by Cézanne and by Cubism.

1917-18 Devotes a large part of his time to photography and exhibits his photographs at the Modern Gallery, New York. Like Demuth and Shamberg, he proceeds from Cubism to create a simplified and stylized style later called Precisionism or Cubism-Realism. Later declares: "In these paintings I sought to reduce natural forms to the borderline of abstraction."

1919 Settles in New York.

1920 One-man show at the De Zayas Gallery, New York.

1922 One-man show at the Daniel Gallery, New York.

1924 One-man show at the Whitney Studio Club, New York.

1926 Exhibits at the Neumann Gallery, New York.

1927 Makes a trip to River Rouge, where the Ford Motor factory inspires him to do a series of paintings akin to photography.

1932 One-man show at the Chicago Arts Club.

1940 Reverts to his Precisionist manner of 1818. Participates in the International Exhibition at the Carnegie Institute, Pittsburgh.

1965 Died.

Sales

WATERCOLORS

1967

Steel-Croton, No. 2, 1953, tempera, 6¼ x 9¼ ..... (952) $4,500

PAINTINGS

1967

Improvisations on a Mill Town, 1949, 29¾ x 24 ... (952) 14,000

Walter Richard Sickert

(1860-1942)

Birthplace: Munich, Germany.

1868 His family moves to Great Britain.

1881 Attends the Slade School, London, taught by Whistler.

1883 Makes a trip to Paris, where he meets Degas.

1884 Exhibits at the Royal Society of British Artists until 1888.

1885 Stays in Dieppe, to which he often returns.

1888 Becomes a member of the New English Art Club—until 1917.

1889 Organizes the Impressionist exhibition held at the Goupil Galleries, London, showing works by English artists painting in the Impressionist manner.

1895 Visits Venice—and again in 1900 and 1904.

1905 Settles in London. Becomes a member of the Salon d'Automne, Paris.

1927-29 Presides over the Royal Society of British Artists.

1938 Settles at Bathampton.

1942 Died, Bathampton, Somerset.

Sales

DRAWINGS

1961-1962

Interior with Two Women, black chalk, pen, and blue wash, 10¾ x 14½ .... (148) $1,098

1963

Hubby, charcoal and wash with white lights, 13½ x 12¾ .... (207) 192

1964

The Tree, pen and watercolor, 7 x 10 .... (417) 145

1965

Degas in Orléans (or in New Orleans), ink and black and white chalk, 15 x 12¾ .... (584) 1,244

The Rose Window of St. Jacques Church at Dieppe, black and white chalk, 11¾ x 9 ...... (584) 111

The Old Bedford, blue, black, and white chalk, 27¾ x 12¾ .... (506) 553

1967

Study of a Nude, ink and pencil, 11¾ x 8 .... (945) 387

Stitch, Stitch, Stitch, pen, 9 x 7 .... (1003) 356

St. Jacques, Dieppe, pen and watercolor, 10 x 7½ .... (869) 442

Rue du Mortier d'Or, Dieppe, charcoal, 11¾ x 9 .... (853) 551

Quai Voltaire, pen and charcoal heightened with white, 11 x 8 .... (959) 871

1968-July 1969

The Rue St. Jean at Dieppe, pencil, charcoal, and green wash heightened with white, 10 x 11¾ .... (1074) 142

PAINTINGS

1961-1962

The Horse Race at Dieppe, on board, 7½ x 9¾ .... (74) 824

Good Night, God Protect You... , 20½ x 15¾ ..... (67) 1,252

Christine Bathing, (1932), 24¼ x 25¼ .... (118) 2,471

1963

The Gallery of the Old Mogul, 23¾ x 28¾ .... (309) 2,966

View of the Basilica of St. Mark and the Clock Tower, (1903), 14¾ x 17½ .... (309) 9,558

Portrait of Conchita Supervia, 22¾ x 14½ .... (213) 857

The Grande Rue at Dieppe, 11¾ x 14¾ .... (207) 494

A Square at Dieppe, (1900), 12¾ x 15½ .... (304) 4,113

1964

La Giuseppina, (1904), 17¾ x 14¾ .... (356) 3,317

Landscape Near Dieppe, on board, 8 x 10 .... (356) 1,244

Reclining Nude, (1908), 14¾ x 17¾ .... (356) 3,593

The Teahouse at Dieppe, on panel, 9 x 5¾ .... (364) 2,031

1965

The Livestock Market, 1885, on panel, 9 x 14¾ ... (584)	$ 774
The Young Venetian, (1901), 18¾ x 14¾ .... (584)	3,870
Hilda Spong in "Trelawny of the Wells," on panel, 13 x 10 .... (605)	2,757
The Orchestra, 29¾ x 17¾ .... (643)	332
The Quai Duquesne and the Rue Notre-Dame at Dieppe, 1900, 15¾ x 12¾ .... (643)	1,880
St. Jacques Church at Dieppe, 1902, 17 x 14¾ .... (584)	4,008
Miss Hilda Glyder, 23¾ x 19¾ .... (506)	719
Seated Nude, (1905), 19¾ x 14¾ .... (506)	2,709

1966

St. Mark's, Venice, 1901, 23¾ x 19¾ .... (693)	3,317
Woman in a Red Dress, 15¾ x 19¼ .... (693)	2,764
Romeo and Juliet, 19¾ x 27¾ .... (693)	387
St. Jacques Church, Dieppe, (1905), 21 x 18¼ .... (825)	4,146
Munster Square by Night, (1907), 18¼ x 20 ...... (825)	553
Portrait of Maurice Asselin, (1914), 19¾ x 15¾ ... (693)	1,106

1967

Horses of St. Mark's, 21¼ x 17¾ .... (944)	6,384
The Seafood Sellers, Dieppe, 1900, 12¾ x 15¾ ... (944)	2,322
Reclining Nude, (1905), 15¾ x 19½ .... (869)	2,626
The Russian, (1905), 19¾ x 15½ .... (869)	2,764
Munster Square by Night, (1907), 18 x 20 .... (1003)	593
The Obelisk Near Bath, (1916), 14¾ x 15 .... (869)	829
Street Scenes, Dieppe, 18 x 14¾ .... (853)	3,482

1968–July 1969

The Old Bedford, (1887), on panel, 13½ x 9½ ... (1025)	1,363
The Yellow Skirt, 10¾ x 14 .... (1143)	1,982
St. Jacques Church at Dieppe, (1905), 21¾ x 17¾ .... (1074)	3,068
Notre-Dame de Paris Seen from the River Seine, 12¾ x 15¾ .... (1074)	1,298
The Eldorado, Paris, (1906), 19¼ x 23¼ .... (1074)	5,192
The Casino of Dieppe, 1907, 17¾ x 21¼ .... (1141)	3,540
Portrait of a Man in Profile, 17¾ x 14 .... (1141)	690
Reclining Woman in the Nude, 18¼ x 20 .... (1109)	4,200

Paul Signac

(1863–1935)

Birthplace: Paris, France.

1880   Though his parents want him to be an architect, he decides to devote himself to painting when he sees Monet's works at "La Vie Moderne." Meets Guillaumin, who encourages him to paint.

1884   Participates in the first Salon des Indépendants, Paris, where he meets and makes friends with Cross and Seurat. Immediately won over to Seurat's theories. Unlike Seurat, an austere and secretive character, he is endowed with an exuberant and passionate temper that soon leads him to serve as a link between Seurat and the other painters of the group. Meets Chevreul. Participates in the foundation of the Société des Artistes Indépendants, Paris.

1886   First visit to the south of France, at Collioure.

1888   Exhibits with the XX, Brussels.

1889   Calls on Van Gogh in Arles.

1891   Seurat's sudden and untimely death induces him to assume the full leadership of Neo-Impressionism.

1892   Fascinated by the sea, he sails extensively in the Mediterranean and off the Breton coast. (Uses 32 yachts in his lifetime.) As a sailor, discovers St. Tropez, to which he attracts a number of painters. Settles in a villa of his own called "La Hune" at St. Tropez, where he stays every year. Leaves strict Pointillism to paint in square, mosaiclike brushstrokes. At this time, he also feels attracted by brighter and even violent colors—this is why he will be called a Pre-Fauve.

1896   Trip to Holland—and again in 1898 and 1906.

1898   Becomes president of the Salon des Indépendants, Paris.

1899   Issues his treatise "D'Eugène Delacroix au Néo-Impressionism," Paris, a basic work on the theory of color. Exhibits at Durand-Ruel's, Paris.

1903   Exhibits at the Cassirer Gallery, Berlin. Exhibits at Bernheim-Jeune's, Paris.

1904   Trip to Italy—and again in 1905, 1907, and 1908.

1907   Trip to Constantinople.

1935   Died, Paris. (As well as his paintings, his watercolors are regarded as being among the most admirable in modern art.)

Sales

DRAWINGS

1961–1962

Constantinople, Sails Aground, 1907, charcoal and India ink, 28¾ x 36¼ .... (31)	$2,334
Constantinople, India ink heightened with watercolor, 31½ x 25 .... (56)	940
Towboats on the River Seine, black lead with color lights .... (158)	64

1963

Sannois, Seine et Oise, 1900, pencil and watercolor, 5¾ x 8¾ .... (275)	900
The Golden Horn, 1902, pencil and India ink, 16¾ x 21 .... (210)	877
Constantinople: Sails Aground, 1907, charcoal and India ink, 28¾ x 55¼ .... (210)	1,645
The Three-Master in St. Tropez, 1911, wash, 11 x 15¾ .... (198)	800
St. Tropez, pencil and watercolor, 6½ x 9½ ...... (179)	800
Quai de Suffren, St. Tropez, pencil and watercolor, 6½ x 9¼ .... (202)	2,300
Sailboats in the Harbor, pencil, 4¾ x 6¾ .... (255)	548
Fishing Boat, Port-Louis, 1922, India ink, 10¾ x 17 .... (232)	1,017
Seascape, colored pencil, 3¼ x 7 .... (179)	200
Landscape at Lézardrieux, Côtes du Nord, 1924, pencil and watercolor .... (202)	2,700
Lézardrieux, pencil and watercolor, 6 x 8½ ...... (208)	1,400

Viviers, 1928, colored pencil and watercolor,
11 x 16¾ . . . . **(225)** $1,750

The Pont des Arts, pencil and watercolor,
9 x 11¾ . . . . **(277)**   1,097

Notre-Dame de Paris, charcoal, 10¼ x 16¼ . . . . . . **(311)**   1,420

1964

Antibes, (1900), India ink, 9 x 6¾ . . . . **(385)**   373

Boats in the Harbor of St. Tropez, sepia wash,
8½ x 11½ . . . . **(377)**   1,695

Constantinople, 1907, pencil and watercolor,
11¾ x 17½ . . . . **(212)**   2,600

Fort St. Jean in Marseilles, pencil and wash,
7½ x 10 . . . . **(456)**   480

Constantinople, India-ink wash, 31½ x 44¾ . . . . . . **(366)**   1,480

Harbor Scene, pencil and watercolor with white
lights, 9 x 12¾ . . . . **(374)**   1,700

Stranded Boat at St. Tropez, 1930, pencil, pen,
and reed, 4½ x 6¾ . . . . **(377)**   633

Barfleur Harbor, sepia wash, 9¾ x 17 . . . . **(394)**   760

St. Malo Harbor, 1933, pencil and sepia wash,
11 x 17 . . . . **(454)**   1,106

The Harbor, pencil, 27¾ x 34½ . . . . **(471)**   2,034

1965

Antibes, 1910, pencil and watercolor,
11½ x 16¾ . . . . **(583)**   2,089

Le Havre Harbor, 1923, pencil and watercolor,
8 x 10 . . . . **(606)**   1,600

Constantinople, wash, 30½ x 44¾ . . . . **(503)**   1,240

View of Constantinople, pencil and ink, 17 x 21 . . . **(638)**   1,230

The Pont des Arts and the Louvre, 1933, ink,
17 x 21 . . . . **(638)**   520

La Rochelle Harbor, charcoal, pen, and wash,
4½ x 5¾ . . . . **(568)**   339

Sailboat Alongside the Quay, wash, 4¼ x 6¾ . . . . . **(516)**   550

The Pont des Arts, pencil and watercolor,
9 x 11¾ . . . . **(575)**   1,880

1966

St. Tropez, wash, 11 x 14¼ . . . . **(718)**   600

Portrieux, the Harbor, 1925, wash, 11 x 17 . . . . **(829)**   780

Santa Maria della Salute, Venice, pencil and
gouache, 7¾ x 10 . . . . **(815)**   1,161

St. Malo, 1930, black chalk and watercolor,
11¼ x 17¼ . . . . **(808)**   3,192

The Rue de Lhomond, 1930, wash, 8¾ x 14¾ . . . . . **(798)**   1,311

Constantinople, wash and India ink, 30¼ x 44¼ . . **(744)**   2,260

Sailboats in the Harbor, Ile de Croix, pencil
heightened with watercolor, 8½ x 11 . . . . **(757)**   2,073

Sailboat in the Harbor, pencil and India ink,
12¼ x 18 . . . . **(775)**   2,558

1967

Sannois, 1900, pencil and watercolor, 5¾ x 8¾ . . . **(870)**   600

The Cruiser, 1915, India ink with colored pencil
and watercolor lights, 6½ x 10 . . . . **(984)**   280

The Pont-Neuf, India-ink wash, 11½ x 17½ . . . . . . **(965)**   859

1968–July 1969

The River Seine at Les Andelys, (1921), black
pencil and gouache, 11½ x 16½ . . . . **(1134)**   2,950

Riverside, charcoal, 10 x 17 . . . . **(1114)**   4,960

The Suspension Bridge, sepia wash, 11½ x 17½ . . **(1066)**   940

Santa Maria della Salute, Venice, pencil and
gouache, 7¾ x 10 . . . . **(1068)**   1,935

St. Malo, sepia wash, 11 x 17½ . . . . **(1117)**   1,700

View of Antibes, pencil, pen, and wash,
35¼ x 28¾ . . . . **(1138)** $3,965

The Lighthouse, India ink, 10¾ x 7½ . . . . **(1060)**   640

Quimperlé Cathedral, (1900), pencil and
watercolor, 6¼ x 4¼ . . . . **(1231)**   1,700

The Tower and the Lighthouse, Sunset,[1] 7¾ x 8   . **(1240)**   960

Boats on the River Seine, pencil and watercolor,
4¼ x 5¾ . . . . **(1240)**   1,200

The Pont-Neuf, India-ink wash, 11 x 17½ . . . . . . **(1268)**   1,160

WATERCOLORS

1961–1962

St. Tropez, the Harbor, 1899, watercolor,
7¼ x 10 . . . . **(143)**   2,170

Sun in St. Tropez, watercolor, 7 x 10 . . . . **(30)**   1,200

Venice, watercolor, 7½ x 10 . . . . **(30)**   1,400

Fishing Boats, Marseilles, 1907, watercolor,
4 x 4½ . . . . **(177)**   360

Constantinople: The Golden Horn, St. Sophie,
1907, watercolor, 4 x 4½ . . . . **(177)**   350

Constantinople, The Golden Horn, watercolor,
5¼ x 6¾ . . . . **(156)**   840

The White Mosque at Stamboul, watercolor,
5¼ x 6¾ . . . . **(156)**   940

"14 Juillet" at St. Tropez, 1907, watercolor,
4¾ x 4 . . . . **(158)**   700

Venice, 1908: La Salute in Pink, watercolor and
India ink, 6¼ x 8 . . . . **(167)**   1,360

View of Notre-Dame, 1910, watercolor,
10¾ x 16¾ . . . . **(167)**   1,000

The Lighters, watercolor, 4½ x 6 . . . . **(25)**   440

Sailboats in the Harbor, 1910, watercolor and
charcoal, 12¼ x 18¼ . . . . **(106)**   1,808

Sailboats in the Harbor, watercolor, 4½ x 7½ . . . . . **(12)**   360

St. Tropez, Sunset, watercolor, 4¾ x 6¾ . . . . **(156)**   1,220

Antibes Harbor, watercolor, 9 x 11¼ . . . . **(76)**   2,000

Les Andelys, pencil and watercolor, 9½ x 14¾ . . . . . **(94)**   3,321

Les Andelys, the Church, 1923, pencil and
watercolor, 10¼ x 15 . . . . **(156)**   1,400

La Rochelle, watercolor, 10¾ x 16½ . . . . **(71)**   3,000

La Rochelle, 1926, watercolor, 10¾ x 16¼ . . . . **(88)**   1,919

La Rochelle, the Harbor and the Town, 1926,
watercolor, 9½ x 15¾ . . . . **(141)**   2,300

Pont des Arts, 1926, watercolor, 11 x 17½ . . . . **(141)**   2,000

Towboat on the River Seine, watercolor,
8¼ x 11 . . . . **(141)**   1,800

Boats at Concarneau, watercolor, 9½ x 7¼ . . . . . . **(141)**   1,200

Moissac, 1926, watercolor, 10 x 16¾ . . . . **(156)**   1,360

Lézardrieux Suspension Bridge, watercolor,
5¼ x 8 . . . . **(26)**   786

St. Gingolf, watercolor, 6¼ x 9¼ . . . . **(26)**   640

Grimaud Village, watercolor, 7¼ x 10 . . . . **(18)**   2,215

Le Puy-en-Valay, pencil and watercolor,
14¼ x 10½ . . . . **(156)**   1,200

Sailboat, 1927, watercolor, 6 x 4½ . . . . **(143)**   644

Avignon Castle from the River Rhône, 1928,
watercolor, 11½ x 17¾ . . . . **(119)**   2,600

St. Malo, Three-Master Alongside the Quay,
1928, watercolor, 10¾ x 17½ . . . . **(114)**   1,900

The Liner, watercolor, 6 x 10 . . . . **(5)**   510

Pont St. Esprit, 1928, watercolor, 11½ x 17 . . . . . . **(120)**   1,160

Columbus Day Parade, watercolor, 19¾ x 25¾ . . . **(143)**   6,667

Landscape, gouache, 10 x 13 . . . . **(143)**   3,051

[1] Inscribed "Entendu. Amitiés. P. S."

1963

Sunset at Samos, 1900, watercolor, 4½ x 6 . . . . . . (284) $ 886

St. Tropez, the Bay, 1902, watercolor, 6¼ x 7¾ . . . (254) 1,220

Monikendam Bridge, watercolor, 10¼ x 16¼ . . . . . (186) 960

Venice, La Salute in Pink, 1908, watercolor and
India ink, 6¼ x 8 . . . . (254) 1,440

St. Tropez, the Garden, 1909, watercolor and
India ink, 5¼ x 6¾ . . . . (254) 900

La Rochelle, 1900, watercolor, 10¾ x 13½ . . . . (224) 1,600

Le Petit Andelys, 1923, watercolor, 10 x 14½ . . . . . (210) 2,194

Landscape, watercolor, 5 x 7¼ . . . . (258) 380

Pont des Arts in Paris, 1924, watercolor,
7¼ x 9¾ . . . . (283) 1,153

Vannes Harbor, 1925, watercolor, 11 x 15¼ . . . . . . (299) 2,000

Pont d'Austerlitz, 1925, watercolor, 11 x 13½ . . . . . (231) 1,648

Landscape, Donzère, 1926, watercolor,
10¾ x 16¾ . . . . (232) 2,486

Pont des Arts, 1927, watercolor, 10½ x 17½ . . . . . . (198) 2,020

Sailboats at St. Servan, 1930, watercolor,
11½ x 17¾ . . . . (283) 3,300

1964

Flessingue Harbor, 1899, watercolor, 8 x 10¾ . . . . (354) 1,050

Back-Light Effect at Sannois, 1900, watercolor,
6¾ x 10 . . . . (371) 2,500

St. Tropez Harbor, 1901, watercolor, 16 x 11½ . . . (401) 2,400

St. Tropez Harbor, (1906), watercolor, 9 x 10¾ . . . (377) 1,931

The Harbor, watercolor and gouache, 8½ x 11 . . . . (474) 3,500

Marseilles: The Harbor, 1907, watercolor and
gouache, 11 x 15¾ . . . . (341) 1,360

Constantinople: The Golden Horn, St. Sophie,
1907, watercolor, 4 x 4½ . . . . (351) 580

The Golden Horn, watercolor, 10¼ x 16¾ . . . . (458) 1,306

The Lighter on the River Seine, 1910, watercolor
and pencil, 10 x 12¼ . . . . (374) 900

Antibes, 1910, watercolor, 11¾ x 16½ . . . . (475) 1,620

Two Sailboats Alongside the Quay, black chalk
and watercolor, 7½ x 10 . . . . (380) 1,230

Pantin, L'Ourcq Canal, 1927, watercolor,
11 x 16¾ . . . . (378) 2,712

Audierne, 1927, watercolor, 10¾ x 16¾ . . . . (473) 1,460

Seascape at Honfleur, 1931, watercolor,
10¼ x 16¾ . . . . (401) 2,400

St. Raphael Harbor, 1931, watercolor,
11½ x 17¼ . . . . (340) 3,740

Pont des Arts, watercolor, 4¾ x 8 . . . . (382) 700

Venice, watercolor, 8 x 11¾ . . . . (340) 2,040

Villefranche, watercolor, 10¼ x 16¼ . . . . (416) 2,764

Fishing Boats, charcoal and watercolor,
11½ x 17 . . . . (367) 2,349

Boats in the Harbor, 1934, watercolor, 11 x 16¾ . . (418) 2,800

Boats at Sables-d'Olonne, watercolor and
gouache, 11 x 16¾ . . . . (359) 1,840

La Rochelle, watercolor, 11 x 16½ . . . . (377) 2,825

1965

St. Tropez, 1901, watercolor, 15¾ x 11½ . . . . (631) 2,700

Rotterdam Harbor, 1906, watercolor, 10¼ x 16 . . . (582) 1,244

Constantinople, (1907), watercolor and India ink,
6½ x 8 . . . . (567) 1,514

Constantinople: The Golden Horn, watercolor,
6¼ x 8 . . . . (512) 900

Boats in the Harbor, 1920, watercolor, 7¼ x 10 . . . (587) 1,520

Lomalo Harbor, 1922, watercolor, 10 x 15½ . . . . . . (548) 1,440

Sailboats in the Harbor, 1922, watercolor,
8¼ x 11¾ . . . . (597) $1,599

The Towboat, watercolor, 7¼ x 9¾ . . . . (617) 2,441

St. Andéol, 1926, watercolor, 11 x 17½ . . . . (553) 1,600

Bourg St. Andéol, 1926, watercolor, 11 x 17¾ . . . . (586) 2,000

Seascape, 1926, watercolor, 16¾ x 11 . . . . (567) 2,260

Venice, Haze, watercolor, 5½ x 6¾ . . . . (503) 800

Le Gouin Church, 1927, watercolor, 10¼ x 17½ . . . (530) 1,100

St. Malo, 1928, watercolor, 10½ x 16¾ . . . . (553) 1,960

St. Vaast Harbor, 1931, watercolor and pencil,
11 x 17½ . . . . (624) 2,764

1966

Cap Gris-Nez, 1903, watercolor, 5¾ x 8¾ . . . . (745) 768

View of St. Sophie, Constantinople, 1907, pencil
and watercolor, 5 x 7½ . . . . (735) 949

Lézardrieux, Côtes du Nord, 1924, watercolor
and black lead, 11¾ x 18¼ . . . . (681) 2,600

Concarneau, 1925, watercolor, 10¾ x 15 . . . . (685) 2,500

Landernau, watercolor, 10¼ x 15½ . . . . (702) 2,700

St. Malo, 1927, watercolor and charcoal,
10½ x 16¾ . . . . (792) 1,968

La Turbuele, Entrance of the Harbor, 1929,
watercolor, 8 x 17 . . . . (744) 2,147

The River Seine in Paris, watercolor, 11 x 17¼ . . . (744) 4,191

The River Seine in Paris, watercolor and pencil,
11¾ x 15¾ . . . . (648) 1,500

Boats in the Roadstead, watercolor, 9 x 11½ . . . . . (796) 1,340

St. Malo, 1931, watercolor, 11 x 17 . . . . (670) 1,820

The Towboat at Sannois, watercolor, 6 x 6¾ . . . . (741) 760

1967

The Entrance of Marseilles Harbor, charcoal and
watercolor, 4 x 7¼ . . . . (931) 859

The Dike at Volendam, Holland, 1890,
watercolor, 8 x 10¾ . . . . (901) 760

Rotterdam Harbor, 1906, watercolor,
10¼ x 16¼ . . . . (905) 1,400

Boats at Groix, 1923, watercolor, 10¾ x 15 . . . . . . (923) 1,700

Sailboats at Paimpol, 1924, watercolor,
10¾ x 17 . . . . (852) 2,800

Roscoff Harbor, watercolor, 6¾ x 13 . . . . (909) 1,700

Concarneau, the Bridge, 1925, watercolor and
gouache, 11 x 15½ . . . . (935) 2,200

Concarneau, 1925, watercolor, 4¼ x 6¼ . . . . (995) 1,000

St. Servan, 1927, watercolor, 11 x 17½ . . . . (918) 2,667

Paimpol, Boats in the Harbor, 1927, watercolor,
11¾ x 17½ . . . . (984) 2,800

St. Malo, 1927, watercolor and pencil, 10½ x 16 . (1004) 3,250

Lézardrieux, watercolor, 4 x 6½ . . . . (842) 600

St. Malo Harbor, 1928, pencil and watercolor,
10¼ x 17½ . . . . (982) 4,503

Cancale Harbor, 1929, watercolor, 14¾ x 10¾ . . . . (857) 1,620

Audierne Bay, 1930, watercolor, 11½ x 17½ . . . . . . (901) 3,800

St. Tropez, watercolor, 11 x 10¼ . . . . (915) 3,075

St. Paul de Vence, charcoal and watercolor,
11¾ x 17½ . . . . (998) 2,017

The River Seine and the Institut, watercolor,
5¼ x 8¾ . . . . (911) 1,160

1968–July 1969

Dusk, 1900, watercolor, 4½ x 6 . . . . (1094) 620

St. Tropez, 1906, watercolor, 10 x 15½ . . . . (1082) 1,620

View of Antibes, 1913, pencil, watercolor, and
gouache, 9½ x 11¾ . . . . (1134) 1,770

Concarneau Harbor, 1921, watercolor,
10¾ x 17½ .... **(1126)** $4,213

Fishing Boat, pencil and watercolor, 8 x 10¾ .... **(1102)** 2,576

Croix Harbor, 1923, black pencil and watercolor,
11 x 16¾ .... **(1134)** 6,136

Fishing Boats, La Rochelle, 1926, watercolor,
10 x 15¾ .... **(1157)** 2,400

Pont des Arts, 1925, watercolor, 4¾ x 8 .... **(1162)** 1,400

Pont des Arts, 1925, watercolor, 10¾ x 16¾ ..... **(1113)** 2,500

Paimpol, 1925, watercolor, 10¾ x 17 .... **(1213)** 5,300

Concarneau, 1925, watercolor, 10 x 14¼ .... **(1183)** 3,400

Boats in the Harbor, watercolor, 11 x 15¾ ...... **(1116)** 2,120

Vase of Flowers, 1926, watercolor, 24 x 19 ...... **(1180)** 4,520

Bourg St. Andéol, 1926, watercolor, 7¼ x 9½ .... **(1137)** 2,000

La Rochelle: Fishing Boats, watercolor,
7½ x 11½ .... **(1137)** 1,100

Sailboat in the Harbor, watercolor, 11 x 17¼ .... **(1026)** 2,160

St. Servan Harbor, 1927, pencil, watercolor, and
gouache, 11 x 17½ .... **(1191)** 6,136

Binic Harbor, 1929, pencil and watercolor,
10¼ x 16¾ .... **(1134)** 4,012

Lézardrieux Harbor, 1929, watercolor,
10¾ x 17 .... **(1068)** 5,192

Paimpol, watercolor, 11 x 17½ .... **(1189)** 5,600

The Anchorage of the Pointe du Séran,
watercolor and gouache, 9¾ x 7¾ .... **(1049)** 1,160

Sand Barges at Portrieux, watercolor,
5¼ x 17¾ .... **(1127)** 1,472

Adour Stream, Bayonne, 1925, watercolor,
7¼ x 9½ .... **(1224)** 3,900

Seascape, 1894, lampshade-shaped watercolor,
8¾ x 35½ .... **(1224)** 2,100

The Towboat, Sannois, 1900, watercolor,
5¾ x 6½ .... **(1230)** 1,700

Sailboats Aground at St. Tropez, (1900), pencil
and watercolor, 9½ x 6 .... **(1240)** 1,920

Three-Master at Anchor at Lézardrieux, 1927,
9¾ x 18 .... **(1240)** 8,400

View of Granville, watercolor, 10¾ x 14¾ .... **(1254)** 4,000

Hennebont, watercolor, 6½ x 4 .... **(1256)** 2,300

The Pink Sail, watercolor, 10 x 10¼ .... **(1256)** 2,560

Pont St. Esprit, watercolor .... **(1263)** 2,240

The Sailboat, watercolor, 4 x 6 .... **(1265)** 960

La Rochelle, 1920, watercolor, 11½ x 8¼ .... **(1265)** 1,500

Les Martigues: Sailboats in the Harbor, 1930,
watercolor, 11 x 16¼ .... **(1265)** 5,000

Sailboat on the Stocks at St. Tropez, 1902,
gouache, watercolor, and pencil, 9½ x 6½ ... **(1272)** 3,120

*View of Notre-Dame from the Pont des Saints-
Pères,* 1911, black pencil and watercolor,
10¼ x 15¾ .... **(1272)** 5,040

Concarneau Harbor, 1929, black pencil and
watercolor, 10½ x 17 .... **(1272)** 2,880

PAINTINGS

1961–1962

Flessingue Pier, 1896, 23¼ x 31½ .... **(164)** 17,574

Dressed Ships at Groix Lighthouse, 29 x 36½ ..... **(80)** 26,000

The Entrance of Honfleur Harbor, 1899,
15½ x 20 .... **(159)** 14,832

Antibes, Five O'Clock, 1905, on board,
10¾ x 14 .... **(164)** 3,707

Eucalyptus in Antibes, 1907, 36½ x 29 .... **(18)** 23,052

Constantinople: The Golden Horn, Mist, 1907,
26 x 32 .... **(31)** 31,579

1963

Suburb of Paris, 1883, 28½ x 35¾ .... **(225)** $ 30,000

View of Les Andelys,[2] 1886, 18¼ x 25¾ .... **(277)** 8,774

Le Bateau lavoir à Asnières (recto), *Paris, Quai
de la Tournelle* (verso), 1886, 23½ x 36¼ ..... **(210)** 32,904

The River Loire, 1889, oil on silk, 12¾ x 27 ...... **(245)** 9,597

Garden in St. Tropez, 1909, 25¾ x 31½ .... **(279)** 43,000

Entrance of the Harbor, 1927, 18¼ x 21¾ .... **(316)** 25,000

The River Near the Institut, 14¾ x 21 .... **(258)** 10,000

1964

*Portrait of Félix Fénéon on the Enamel of a
Rhythmic Background of Measures and
Angles, of Shades and Tints,* 1890, op. 217,
29 x 36½ .... **(416)** 58,044

Landscape, 1883, 18¼ x 25¾ .... **(471)** 16,724

Flessingue Pier, 1896, 23 x 31½ .... **(416)** 33,168

La Rochelle Harbor, 27¾ x 35½ .... **(402)** 32,000

Venice, 10¾ x 14¼ .... **(378)** 7,458

1965

Suburb of Paris, 1883, 29 x 36½ .... **(522)** 30,404

The Rainbow, Breton Harbor, 1893, 16 x 19¾ .... **(522)** 26,258

1966

Low Tide at St. Briac, 1884, 18¼ x 25¾ .... **(819)** 10,400

A Garden at St. Tropez, 1909, 25¾ x 31½ .... **(808)** 40,628

Place des Lices, St. Tropez, on panel,
7½ x 10¾ .... **(819)** 3,600

1967

Argenteuil Bridge, by Day and by Night, (1886),
on a fan-shaped canvas, 24½ x 12¾ .... **(938)** 4,699

Suburban Garden at Asnières, 1883, 18¼ x 24 .... **(988)** 11,942

Cannes Harbor, 1902, 10¾ x 13 .... **(982)** 14,220

1968–July 1969

Suburb of Paris, (1883), 29 x 36¼ .... **(1053)** 32,600

*Portrait of Félix Fénéon on the Enamel of a
Rhythmic Background of Measures and
Angles, of Shades and Tints,*[3] 1890, op. 217,
29 x 36½ .... **(1176)** 110,000

Flessingue Pier, 1896, 23 x 31½ .... **(1068)** 61,360

Rainbow in Venice, 1905, 29 x 39¼ .... **(1189)** 104,000

Venice in the Morning, 1908, 29 x 36½ .... **(1132)** 92,040

Anchorage at La Giudecca, Venice, 1908,
29 x 36½ .... **(1152)** 110,000

La Salis, Antibes, 1916, 36¾ x 29¼ .... **(1152)** 95,000

Pont des Arts, (1925), 35¼ x 45½ .... **(1152)** 125,000

Notre-Dame de la Garde, Marseilles, 1931,
29 x 36¾ .... **(1152)** 92,500

Portrieux Harbor, 1888, 18¼ x 21¾ .... **(1224)** 110,200

The Fountain of the Lices, St. Tropez, 1895, on
panel, 7½ x 10¾ .... **(1239)** 10,800

Antibes: The Tower, 25¾ x 32 .... **(1254)** 79,000

Riverside, 1885, 13 x 18¼ .... **(1270)** 10,320

St. Briac: The Sailors' Cross, 1885, 13 x 18½ .... **(1270)** 21,600

Antwerp, on panel, 9¾ x 6¼ .... **(1273)** 3,910

---

[2]This work could be the last non-Pointillist picture by the artist.
[3]Sold in London in 1964 for $58,044.

Gustave Singier

(1909-   )

Birthplace: Warneton, Belgium.

1919 Goes to Paris and becomes a French citizen.

1923 Starts to paint from nature. Attends the Ecole Boulle, Paris. Later works as a commercial artist—until 1936.

1936 Meets Charles Walch, who encourages him to devote himself to painting. Gradually turns to abstraction.

1937 Participates in the Salon d'Automne, Paris.

1939 Participates in the Salon des Tuileries, Paris.

1941 Takes part in "Vingt Peintres de tradition française" at the Galerie Braun, Paris.

1943 Takes part in "Douze Peintres d'aujourd'hui at the Galerie de France, Paris.

1945 Participates in the Salon de Mai, Paris.

1946 Exhibits with Le Moal and Manessier at the Galerie Drouin, Paris.

1952 One-man show at the Galerie de France, Paris—and again in 1955, 1957, and 1959.

1954 Participates in the Venice Biennial.

1955-56 Participates in Documenta I, Kassel. Executes tapestries and stained-glass designs for *Orpheo* by Monteverdi, held at the Festival of Aix-en-Provence.

1957 One-man show at the Hamburg Museum.

Resident in Paris.

Sales

DRAWINGS

1961-1962

Composition, 1946, India ink, 10 x 6¾ . . . . (110) $ 100

1967

Composition with Horizontal Lines and a Circle,
1957, India ink, 8¾ x 11 . . . . (908)   123

WATERCOLORS

1961-1962

Still Life, 1943, watercolor, 18¼ x 11¾ . . . . (93)   565

Refraction—Dazzling, 1953, watercolor, 15 x 11 . . . (88)   590

Migration, watercolor, 17¾ x 21¾ . . . . (153)   400

Composition, 1959, watercolor, 17¾ x 22 . . . . (93)   814

1963

Abstraction, 1950, watercolor, 9¾ x 7¼ . . . . (208)   350

Composition, 1951, watercolor, 14¾ x 10¾ . . . . (296)   240

1964

Marine Garden, 1959, watercolor, 18¼ x 22 . . . . . . (455)   415

Escape and Return to St. Tropez, 1962,
watercolor, 18¼ x 21¾ . . . . (386)   700

1965

Composition, 1952, gouache and black chalk,
10¾ x 8 . . . . (618)   133

Allegory on the Crafts, watercolor and gouache,
20 x 13 . . . . (580)   130

1966

Composition, 1948, gouache, 9½ x 12¾ . . . . (829)   280

1967

Composition, 1956, watercolor, 17½ x 21½ . . . . (985)   569

Composition, 1954, watercolor and gouache,
19½ x 12¾ . . . . (835)   270

1968-July 1969

Composition, 1954, watercolor, 25 x 17½ . . . . (1177) $ 680

Composition, 1956, watercolor, 18¼ x 21¾ . . . . . . (1264)   600

PAINTINGS

1961-1962

La Muleta, 1946, 29 x 23¾ . . . . (88)   1,476

Bergamasque, 1951, 24 x 19¾ . . . . (88)   2,239

Springtime in Paris, 1952, 51¾ x 38½ . . . . (88)   3,247

Inspired Traveler, 27¼ x 16¾ . . . . (143)   1,085

Migration, 1960, 17¾ x 21¾ . . . . (153)   400

1963

The Garden Table, 1944, 32 x 25¾ . . . . (296)   520

1964

Terraced Town, 1956, 9½ x 5¾ . . . . (377)   113

1965

Motorway, 1951, 7½ x 9 . . . . (638)   738

Composition, 11¾ x 14¾ . . . . (507)   175

Flemish Portrait, 1963, 39½ x 32 . . . . (512)   1,020

1966

Village by the Waterside, 1950, 18¼ x 15 . . . . (802)   960

The Picadors,[1] 1953, 15 x 21¾ . . . . (811)   600

Navigable Space, 1954, 51½ x 38½ . . . . (745)   2,712

1967

Composition, 1954, 51½ x 38½ . . . . (919)   2,034

Roman Ruins, on panel, 9 x 11½ . . . . (950)   64

1968-July 1969

Composition with a Red Sun, 1964, on panel,
17½ x 17½ . . . . (1118)   360

The Tub, 1946, 39½ x 32 . . . . (1043)   480

David Alfaro Siqueiros

(1896-   )

Birthplace: Chihuahua, Mexico.

1908 His family settles in Mexico.

1911 Attends the Academy of San Carlos, Mexico, where he meets Orozco.

1914 Participates in the Mexican revolution.

1919-22 Goes to Europe. Meets Diego Rivera in Spain. Murals for the Preparatory School, Mexico.

1932 Goes to the U.S.

1937 Goes to Spain and takes part in the Civil War with the republicans.

1939 First one-man show in New York at the Pierre Matisse gallery.

1940 Murals for the Palace of Fine Arts, Mexico.

1950 Given an award by the Venice Biennial.

Resident in Mexico.

[1]Sold with a lithograph of the painting, No. 9/75.

Sales

WATERCOLORS

1967
Nude, 1932, gouache and watercolor, 18¼ x 25 ..(1004) $2,400

PAINTINGS

1961–1962
Portrait of a Woman, 1931, on board,
33½ x 24¾ ....(152) 875

1966
Portrait of the Artist's Wife, 1931, 35½ x 26 ......(776) 4,250

1967
The Fight, on panel, 14¾ x 25¾ ....(990) 2,460

Mario Sironi

(1885–1961)

Birthplace: Sassari, Sardinia, Italy.

1914-15 Meets Ballà and Boccioni and comes under their influence for a time.

1917 Meets di Chirico and embraces his Metaphysical painting.

1922 Contributes to the foundation of the movement know as "Novecento."

1924 Participates in the Venice Biennial—and again in 1928, 1930, and 1932.

1931 Given an award by the Carnegie Institute, Pittsburgh. Participates in the Rome Quadrennial—and again in 1935, 1948, and 1955.

1961 Died, Milan.

1962 Retrospective exhibition at the Venice Biennial.

Sales

DRAWINGS

1964
Composition, pen and wash, 6½ x 9 ....(582) $ 138

1968–July 1969
Truck, pencil, 8 x 8¼ ....(1214) 560
Seated Nude, India ink, 10¼ x 5¾ ....(1070) 118

WATERCOLORS

1961–1962
Landscape with Mountains, tempera on paper on board, 18¼ x 25¾ ....(164) 934
Figure with a Tree, 1919, tempera, 7¼ x 9½ ....(15) 316
Mountain, tempera, 14 x 20 ....(14) 569
The Ship, 1931, tempera, 29¼ x 40 ....(15) 948

Horse's Head, tempera, 9 x 11¾ ....(14) $ 395
Woman's Head, tempera, 10 x 15¾ ....(14) 411
Two Figures, 1948, tempera on paper on canvas,
26¾ x 19½ ....(149) 916
Colored Composition, tempera, 15 x 20½ ....(69) 1,659
Multiplication, (1950), gouache, 13½ x 20 ....(88) 1,033

1964
Three Masks; Architectural Fantasy, two watercolors, 9 x 11¾ and 13 x 13 ....(438) 775
The Harbor, gouache on paper laid down on canvas, 10 x 13 ....(454) 691
Half-Length Portrait of a Man, 1944, tempera, 7¼ x 8 ....(329) 300
Stormy Landscape, tempera, 10¼ x 7¼ ....(435) 576
Composition, 1914, tempera, 9½ x 14¼ ....(461) 2,080

1965
The Harbor, gouache on paper laid down on canvas, 10 x 13 ....(624) 387
The Church, gouache, 15½ x 19 ....(502) 871

1966
Landscape, gouache and tempera on paper, 13¾ x 25 ....(815) 1,050

1967
Composition with a House and a Manikin, 1942, tempera, 18 x 14 ....(882) 1,760
Composition with a Motorcar, (1914–17), watercolor, 4 x 3 ....(889) 500

1968–July 1969
The Harbor, gouache on paper laid down on canvas, 10 x 13 ....(1191) 708
Composition, gouache and watercolor, 8¾ x 13¼ ....(1231) 525

PAINTINGS

1961–1962
The Cyclist, 1915, 28 x 38 ....(21) 13,430
Metaphysical Interior, 1917, 29 x 34½ ....(70) 5,530
Family in an Urban Landscape, 1919, 8¼ x 12¾ ...(14) 1,738
The Rocky Violence of a Landscape, 19¾ x 27¾ ....(70) 3,318
Young Lady with Her Dog, 1929, 31½ x 27¼ .....(149) 11,060
Il Porto, 1930, 19¾ x 25¾ ....(20) 6,636
Composition, 1939, 35½ x 47½ ....(145) 8,690
Composition in Black and Green, 15¾ x 19¾ ......(69) 1,580
Woman at Her Balcony, 40 x 33 ....(20) 9,875
Viandante, 12¾ x 18¾ ....(69) 1,106
The Three Phantasms, 1950, 19¾ x 15¾ ....(149) 4,424
Multiplication, 1951, oil on cardboard, 31½ x 39½ ....(88) 5,412

1964
Urban Landscape, (1945), on panel, 10¾ x 15¾ ...(461) 4,480
Man Seated Between Two Standing Nudes, (1930), 37½ x 36½ ....(461) 10,400
Meditation, 23¾ x 19¾ ....(437) 5,120
Colored Architecture, 21¾ x 17¾ ....(435) 2,080
Landscape, oil, pencil, and ink on paper laid down on board, 14¾ x 18¾ ....(454) 967

1965
Landscape with a Mountain, oil on cardboard laid down on canvas, 11¾ x 17 ....(525) 2,560
Composition, 1949, on board, 27¾ x 21¾ ....(616) 6,400
The Sailor, 1928, 23¾ x 17½ ....(616) 3,200
La Coupole, 22 x 16¾ ....(535) 746

1966

Landscape, (1950), 13½ x 19½ .... (802) $3,200
Composition, 1948, 30½ x 34½ .... (802)   6,400
Composition, 1948, 25 x 21¾ .... (802)   8,800
The Myth, 1928, 31½ x 27¾ .... (802)   14,400
Composition, 1932, 14¾ x 19¼ .... (665)   1,500

1967

Suburb, (1947), 11¾ x 10 .... (962)   6,080
Houses and Horse, 1921, 17 x 18¾ .... (962)   8,000
Urban Landscape with Horse and Manikin,
    (1924), 43½ x 47½ .... (882)   15,520
Composition, (1940), on cardboard laid down on
    canvas, 28½ x 40¾ .... (962)   5,760
Mountainous Landscape, (1952), 19¾ x 27¾ ..... (962)   5,440
Urban Landscape with Two Riders, (1953),
    23¾ x 27¾ .... (870)   1,500
Composition with a Landscape, by Night, (1955),
    15¾ x 19¾ .... (882)   3,040

1968–July 1969

Composition, 27 x 35¼ .... (1126)   2,354
Mountainous Landscape, oil on paper laid down
    on canvas, 11½ x 17 .... (1127)   1,955

Alfred Sisley

(1839–1899)

Birthplace: Paris, France. (His family is of English descent.)

1857   Stays in London and learns the English language.

1862   Enters the Ecole Nationale des Beaux-Arts, Paris, in the studio of Gleyre, where he meets Monet, Renoir, and Bazille.

1865   Paints in the forest of Fontainebleau and the surroundings of Paris. Works in a desultory way like an amateur until 1870–72.

1866   Participates in the Salon, Paris.

1870–71   Like Monet and Pissarro, settles in London during the war of 1870. Meets Paul Durand-Ruel, who buys some of his paintings.

1872   Returns to France to find his family ruined by the war—lives the rest of his life in a state of near destitution. Exclusively attracted by landscapes, he paints most of his masterpieces in the Ile-de-France between 1872 and 1880. No other painter will capture the limpid pearly atmosphere of the Ile-de-France as beautifully as he does in his oils, which look even fresher than watercolor.

1874   Participates in the first exhibition of the Impressionists held at Nadar's, Paris—and again in 1876 and 1877.

1879   Settles permanently at Moret-sur-Loing, near Paris.

1883   Major one-man show at the Galerie Durand-Ruel, Paris. His work does not attract notice.

1899   Died, Moret-sur-Loing.

Sales

DRAWINGS

1961–1962

A Lane in the Country, colored pencil, 3¾ x 6½ .. (177) $ 650
Peasant; Peasant, colored pencil, each 3¾ x 2¾ .. (177)   520

1964

Little Girl with a White Apron, colored pencil,
    4¼ x 2¾ .... (398)   440

1965

The Geese, colored pencil, 5½ x 4½ .... (612)   440
The Thistles, colored pencil, 5½ x 4½ .... (612)   240

1966

Studies of Barges and of a Horse, colored pencil,
    7½ x 9½ .... (685)   620
The Flood at Moret, 1889, pencil, 6 x 7½ .... (811)   500

1967

The Fishermen; The Dog, two drawings, colored
    pencil, 3¾ x 4¾ and 12½ x 3 .... (1002)   640

1968–July 1969

Three Studies of Barges, colored chalk,
    7¼ x 9½ .... (1241)   2,150

WATERCOLORS

1961–1962

*Goose Girls on the Banks of the River Loing;
Banks of the River Loing,* pastel, 11½ x 15½
    and 11½ x 12¾ .... (76)   13,000

1964

Banks of the River Seine at La Roche-Guyon,
    1888, pastel, 15 x 21½ .... (416)   15,202
The Approaches of a Railway Station in Winter,
    (1880), pastel, 15 x 20½ .... (347)   12,200

1965

An Orchard, (1885), pastel, 6½ x 9½ .... (624)   1,658

1966

The River Loing at St. Mammès, (1880), pastel
    and charcoal, 11½ x 15½ .... (750)   11,056
The Goose Girl, pastel, 10 x 12¾ .... (819)   10,400
The Duck Pond, pastel on bister paper laid down
    on canvas, 11½ x 15¾ .... (694)   7,000

1967

Banks of the River Seine, (1880), pastel,
    8¼ x 13 .... (938)   4,146
The Geese, 1895, pastel, 10 x 12¾ .... (965)   19,436

1968–July 1969

Sunny Snowy Landscape, pastel, 14¾ x 17½ .... (1132)   26,432
Banks of the River Seine at La Roche-Guyon,
    (1888), pastel, 15 x 21½ .... (1176)   15,000
The Little Goose Girl, pastel, 10¼ x 14 .... (1183)   16,400
Farm by the Riverside, (1880), pastel, 11 x 15¼ .. (1239)   12,000

PAINTINGS

1961–1962

Bougival Bridge, 1871, 18 x 14¾ .... (176)   54,000
The Chemin des Grès at Belleville, 1873,
    23¾ x 19½ .... (137)   52,500
The Thames at Hampton Court, 1874,
    18¼ x 21¾ .... (31)   72,769
Last Ray of Sun, Louveciennes, 1873, 15 x 21¾ ... (140)   31,579
Winter at Louveciennes, 1876, 23¼ x 28¾ .... (64)   72,500

Along the Railway Near Sèvres, 1879, 18¾ x 25 ... **(164)** $ 12,357

The River Loing at Moret, Dull Weather, 1880,
25¼ x 36 .... **(83)** 82,380

Winter at Veneux-Nadon, Les Bruyères, 1880,
21¼ x 29 .... **(37)** 48,000

Old Houses at Veneux-Nadon: Snow Effect,
(1880–81), 21½ x 27 .... **(64)** 55,000

The River Loing at Moret, 1883, 19¾ x 25¾ ...... **(128)** 79,634

Moret Bridge, Flood Time, 29¼ x 36½ .... **(29)** 126,000

The Canal of the Loing at St. Mammès, 1885,
15 x 21¾ .... **(32)** 51,000

Moret-sur-Loing, 15 x 18¼ .... **(32)** 54,400

*Idle Barges on the Canal of the Loing at St.
Mammès,* 1885, 15 x 22 .... **(114)** 42,000

The Banks of the River Loing, 1886, 20¾ x 28¼ ... **(64)** 60,000

Moret in the Morning, 1888, 14¾ x 21¼ .... **(84)** 41,190

The "Faubourg du Pont" at Moret, 1892,
17 x 21¾ .... **(114)** 23,600

1963

Riverside at St. Mammès, 15 x 21¾ .... **(312)** 45,000

Snow Effect at Louveciennes, (1872),
17½ x 21¼ .... **(277)** 54,840

The River Seine at Bougival, 1873, 20 x 28 ...... **(245)** 98,712

October Morning (The River Seine), 1876,
17¾ x 21¼ .... **(210)** 24,678

Entrance of the Village, 1876, 19½ x 25 .... **(245)** 67,179

Landscape, Near Louveciennes, 1876,
24¼ x 18¼ .... **(316)** 48,000

Autumn Sun, 1879, 29 x 21¼ .... **(259)** 29,000

The River Seine at Suresnes, 1880, 17¾ x 25 ..... **(247)** 48,808

The Banks of the River Loing Near Moret, 1883,
19¾ x 29 .... **(277)** 60,324

An Orchard, 1885, 18¼ x 21¾ .... **(210)** 57,582

The Lane to Veneux-Nadon in the Springtime,
1885, 21¼ x 29 .... **(210)** 63,066

The Dam on the River Loing, Barges, 1885,
18¼ x 21¾ .... **(277)** 41,130

*View of Moret and of the Banks of the River
Loing,* (1888), 25¾ x 16 .... **(210)** 38,388

Banks of the Canal at Moret, 1894, 15 x 18¼ ..... **(243)** 39,200

A Bend of the River Loing, 1896, 21¼ x 25¾ ..... **(210)** 60,324

1964

Bunch of Flowers,[1] 1872, 25¾ x 20 .... **(458)** 98,668

A Suburb of Paris, 1877, 12¾ x 16 .... **(459)** 22,600

The Swallows' House, 1878, 18 x 25¾ .... **(347)** 54,000

Barges on the River Seine, Autumn Effect, 1879,
10¾ x 16¼ .... **(347)** 29,000

The Canal of the Loing in Moret, 1882,
15 x 21¾ .... **(463)** 31,600

St. Mammès Dam, 1885, 15¼ x 22 .... **(458)** 69,648

The River Loing at Moret, 1885, 18¼ x 22 ...... **(458)** 78,354

Moret Bridge in Autumn, 1888, 20¾ x 28 .... **(367)** 82,920

The Chevrueil Pond Near Moret, 1888,
19½ x 26 .... **(463)** 48,200

Plum Trees and Walnut Woods in the Springtime,
1889, 24 x 29 .... **(453)** 55,280

Langland Bay, 1897, 25 x 31½ .... **(453)** 44,224

1965

The Thames at Hampton Court, 1874, 14 x 23¾ .. **(594)** 50,000

The Clover Field, 1874, 21¼ x 29 .... **(575)** 62,190

The Banks of the River Loing at Moret, (1883),
14¾ x 23¾ .... **(617)** $ 63,732

Poplar-Lined Walk, 29¼ x 23¾ .... **(617)** 51,528

Lighters on the River Loing, 1884, 15 x 21¾ ...... **(522)** 55,280

The Banks at St. Mammès, (1884), 21¼ x 29 ..... **(629)** 34,824

The Dam at St. Mammès, (1885), 15 x 21¾ .... **(617)** 68,930

The River Loing at Moret, in the Summertime,
1891, 29 x 36½ .... **(628)** 92,864

Moret-sur-Loing, (1891), 14¾ x 18¼ .... **(583)** 34,824

The River Seine at the Bas-Meudon, 19¾ x 24 ... **(613)** 62,000

1966

Veneux Plain, 15½ x 21 .... **(797)** 51,980

The Dam at St. Mammès, 1885, 15 x 21¾ .... **(797)** 79,100

The Low Tide, Afternoon, 1897, ... **(713)** 48,000

Along the Railway, 1879, 18¼ x 25¼ .... **(808)** 20,314

*Hunters on the Outskirts of Marly Forest, in
Autumn,* 1873, 18¼ x 25¾ .... **(812)** 91,212

1967

Winter at Veneux-Nadon, 1881, 20¾ x 28 .... **(938)** 102,268

Beneath the Bridge of Moret in the Morning,
1891, 21 x 25¼ .... **(938)** 71,864

Landscape at St. Mammès, 1881, 13½ x 19 ..... **(864)** 65,000

A Street in Louveciennes, 1875, 19 x 12¾ .... **(901)** 44,000

The Waterside Near Port-Marly, 1873,
13 x 18¼ .... **(978)** 51,000

Hoarfrost, (1873–74), 18¾ x 15¼ .... **(864)** 50,000

A Works Site at St. Mammès, 1880, 21¼ x 28¾ ... **(982)** 85,320

Road at the Entrance of the Village, 12¾ x 18¼ .. **(940)** 69,648

The Lane to the Fields in the Morning, 1890,
15 x 18¼ .... **(988)** 37,320

*The Stream Orvanne and the Canal of the Loing
in Winter,* 29 x 23¾ .... **(965)** 48,590

Sunset, Road from Versailles to Chaville,
19¾ x 25¾ .... **(981)** 51,000

1968–July 1969

Study of a Lock at Hampton Court, 1874, on
panel, 3¾ x 2¾ .... **(1183)** 11,000

Banks of the River Seine, Near St. Cloud, 1879,
15 x 18 .... **(1187)** 70,800

A Works Site at St. Mammès, 1885, 21¾ x 29 ... **(1117)** 104,000

The Dam at St. Mammès, 1885, 15 x 21¾ .... **(1125)** 74,750

Landscape in the Springtime, Morning Effect,
15 x 18¼ .... **(1007)** 28,000

The Lane in the Fields in the Morning, 1890,
15 x 18¼ .... **(1117)** 44,000

Storr Rock, Ladies Cove, in the Evening, 1897,
25¾ x 32 .... **(1053)** 36,000

A Path at Les Sablons, (1883), 18¼ x 22 .... **(1235)** 77,500

The Flood, St. Germain Road,[2] 17½ x 23½ ...... **(1239)** 144,000

Barges on the River Loing, 1896, 21 x 25¾ ...... **(1239)** 117,600

Banks of the River Seine at Port-Marly, 1875,
21¼ x 25¾ .... **(1258)** 200,000

An Inn at Hampton Court, 1874, 20 x 27¼ ...... **(1258)** 140,000

Landscape at Louveciennes, 1873, 20¾ x 28½ ... **(1270)** 93,600

On the Outskirts of the Wood, Les Sablons,
1884, 9 x 11 .... **(1270)** 132,000

Ebb Tide, Ladies Cove, Langland Bay, 1897,
25½ x 32 .... **(1270)** 76,800

Springtime Landscape, Morning Effect, 1890,
15 x 18 .... **(1270)** 43,200

---

[1]These flowers are, as far as we know, the only ones ever painted by the artist.

[2]This painting was bought from the artist by Durand-Ruel in January 1880 for 300 francs.

Gustave de Smet

(1877–1943)

Birthplace: Ghent, Belgium. (His brother Léon is also a painter.)

1888–95 Enters the Royal Academy of Fine Arts of Ghent.

1897 Marries Augusta van Hoorebeke.

1901–13 Settles at Laethem-St.-Martin, where he founds the second group of Laethem with Van der Berghe and Permeke. Impressionist period.

1914 Escapes to the Netherlands at the beginning of the war. Discovers German Expressionism and meets the French painter Le Fauconnier. Darkens his palette and starts to elaborate a new way of painting.

1922 Returns to his country. Goes to Ostend with Permeke and then settles near Laethem. Signs a contract with the Galerie Le Centaure, Brussels. One-man show at the Galerie Giroux, Brussels.

1927 After a short Cubist period, he settles permanently at Deurle-sur-Lys. Lightens his palette. With Permeke, Servaes and Van der Berghe, he forms the nucleus of Flemish Expressionism.

1929 Retrospective exhibition at the Galerie Giroux, Brussels.

1931 One-man show at the Galerie de France, Paris.

1936 Retrospective exhibition at the Palais des Beaux-Arts, Brussels—and again in 1942.

1940 Reverts to a more realist style.

1943 Died, Deurle-sur-Lys.

Sales

WATERCOLORS

1967

La Salle de danse, 1921, gouache, 25¼ x 21 ...... (867) $7,000

PAINTINGS

1961–1962

The Farm at Sunset, 16¾ x 20 .... (20) 3,002

In the Woods, 1917, 30¾ x 33½ .... (21) 2,686

Borderij met zon, on cardboard .... (103) 788

1964

Dressing, 24 x 20 .... (427) 2,200

Fisherman's Wife, 1917, 19¾ x 26½ .... (427) 3,200

1965

Village at Laren, 21¾ x 25 .... (589) 3,000

Fishermen's Village, on cardboard, 9 x 12¾ ...... (589) 740

Young Lady in Pink, 34 x 27¼ .... (520) 4,200

Interior, 31½ x 39½ .... (520) 800

Seaside, 37¼ x 39¼ .... (645) 4,134

1966

Nude with Goldfish, 57¾ x 45 .... (700) 8,400

Flowers at the Window, 25¾ x 31½ .... (700) 2,000

The River Meuse Near Liége, on cardboard, 20½ x 27¾ .... (767) 3,000

Landscape with Birds, 20½ x 20½ .... (767) 2,400

The Goat Girl, 1910, 40¼ x 56 .... (700) 2,800

Landscape, on cardboard, 10¾ x 14 .... (782) 720

Peasant Dressing, 21¼ x 26½ .... (680) 3,000

The River Meuse at Liége, on cardboard, 20 x 27 .... (698) 1,588

1967

Sheaves of Corn Near the Farm, 15½ x 22 .... (871) $3,000

Landscape with a Train, 23¾ x 19¾ .... (947) 5,000

Village Fair in Ghent, 18¼ x 32 .... (871) 2,400

The Dancing Room, 1921, 25¼ x 21 .... (871) 7,000

Sheaves of Corn Near the Farm, 15½ x 22 .... (867) 3,000

1968–July 1969

View of a Village with a Church, (1921–23), 12¼ x 10¾ .... (1091) 1,000

The Hunter, on cardboard, 17 x 15 .... (1150) 5,600

The Fiancés, 1922, 21¾ x 26½ .... (1150) 6,800

Flowers, 25¼ x 21¼ .... (1150) 2,000

Fisherman .... (1065) 4,800

The Poplars Along the Stream Lys, (1922–23), on board, 11½ x 13¼ .... (1126) 2,106

Sir Matthew Smith

(1879–1959)

Birthplace: Halifax, Yorkshire, England.

1900–04 Enters the Manchester School of Art.

1905–07 Attends the Slade School of Art, London.

1908–09 Stays at Pont-Aven and then at Etaples.

1910–12 Stays in Paris, where he attends Matisse's school. Participates in the Salon des Indépendants, Paris. Marries Gwendolen Salmond. Makes frequent trips to France until the outbreak of World War I.

1920 Becomes a member of the "London Group."

1926 First one-man show at the Mayor Gallery, London.

1929 Retrospective exhibition at the Tooth Gallery, London.

1930 Stays in Aix-en-Provence.

1938 Retrospective exhibition at the Venice Biennial—and again in 1950.

1953 Retrospective exhibition at the Tate Gallery, London.

1954 Knighted by the Queen.

1959 Died, London.

1960 Memorial exhibition at the Royal Academy, London.

Sales

DRAWINGS

1968–July 1969

Still Life, colored chalk, 14¾ x 18¾ .... (1025) $ 421

Portrait of Elizabeth Townsend, (1941), two studies, pen, each 11¾ x 8¾ .... (1141) 260

Still Life, colored chalk, 19¾ x 15¼ .... (1074) 260

WATERCOLORS

1961-1962
Still Life with Flowers, watercolor, 16¾ x 13½ .... (148) $ 439

1964
Flowers in a Vase, watercolor, 19¾ x 13 .... (364)   319

1966
Daffodils in a Vase (recto), *Study of Tulips*
  (verso), watercolor, 19¾ x 13 .... (825)   608

1968-July 1969
Study of Tulips, 1943, watercolor, 20¼ x 17¼ .... (1206)   236
Landscape, watercolor, 9 x 12 .... (1025)   186

PAINTINGS

1961-1962
Red Roses in a Green Vase and Two Apples on a
  Table, 21 x 17½ .... (38)   3,021
Mauve Blouse, Villa Brune, Paris, 1924,
  20¾ x 28 .... (148)   1,318

1963
Landscape Near Aix, Springtime, 1935, 10 x 8 .... (268)   877

1964
Landscape Near Aix-en-Provence, 15 x 17¾ ..... (444)   2,322

1965
Woody Landscape with a Church, 1922, on panel,
  8¾ x 10¾ .... (506)   1,603
White Roses, (1930), 19 x 23¾ .... (643)   1,106
Young Lady with a Flower, 34¾ x 27 .... (584)   1,797

1966
Reclining Nude, 23 x 31¼ .... (694)   2,600
Portrait of Loretta Hugo, 16 x 14 .... (818)   1,393
The Flowerpot, 1926, 31½ x 17¾ .... (818)   1,973
Vase of Red Roses, 17¾ x 21 .... (825)   3,040
Vase of Flowers, 23 x 19¾ .... (693)   1,327
Dahlias, 20 x 24 .... (776)   1,800
Nude with a Rose, 1944, 39½ x 29¾ .... (693)   2,211
The Beach, Dieppe, 25¾ x 31½ .... (760)   2,264

1967
Seated Woman, 1920, 29¾ x 25 .... (869)   2,211
The Woman with a Rose, 25 x 21¼ .... (944)   696
Lilacs and Roses, 21¾ x 17¾ .... (1003)   1,896
Still Life with Pears, (1936), 12¾ x 17¾ .... (959)   3,192
Reclining Nude, 21 x 28¼ .... (944)   3,192
Nude with a Red Chair, 39½ x 29 .... (853)   2,175
Portrait of a Young Lady, 24 x 20 .... (853)   522

1968-July 1969
Still Life, (1930), 23¾ x 29 .... (1208)   2,500
Vase of Flowers, 25¾ x 19¾ .... (1165)   3,221
Vase of Flowers, (1930), 25 x 20¾ .... (1074)   2,242
Still Life, 1930, 17¾ x 14¾ .... (1206)   4,720
Vera, (1924), 17¾ x 14¾ .... (1206)   637

Pierre Soulages
(1919-   )

Birthplace: Rodez, Aveyron, France. (As a child, he is fascinated by prehistoric and Romanesque arts and starts to paint very early.)

1927 Makes a trip to Paris, where he sees works by Cézanne and Picasso at the Galerie Rosenberg. Attends the Fine Arts School of Montpellier for two years.

1938 Stay in Paris.

1940-46 Spends World War II in his native countryside.

1946 Settles in Paris and devotes himself entirely to painting. Starts his series of black and brown abstractions.

1947 Participates in the Salon des Surindépendants, Paris.

1949 First one-man show at the Galerie Lydia Conti, Paris. Participates in the Salon de Mai, Paris.

1950 Exhibits at the Sidney Janis Gallery, New York.

1951 Stage decorations and costumes for Graham Greene's *The Power and the Glory,* directed by Louis Jouvet, Paris.

1953 Given an award by the São Paulo Biennial. Takes part in "Younger European Painters" at the Guggenheim Museum, New York.

1954 First one-man show in New York at the Kootz Gallery—and again in 1955, 1956, and 1957.

1955 Exhibits at the Gimpel Gallery, London—and again in 1958. Takes part in "The New Decade" at the Museum of Modern Art, New York, and in Documenta I, Kassel—and in Documenta II in 1959. Participates in the International Exhibition of the Carnegie Institute, Pittsburgh.

1956 One-man show at the Galerie de France, Paris—and again in 1959.

1957 Given an award at the international exhibition of painting in Tokyo.

1958 Participates in the Brussels World's Fair.

1964 Wins the Carnegie Prize, Pittsburgh.

1967 Retrospective exhibition at the Musée National d'Art Moderne, Paris.

Resident in Paris.

Sales

DRAWINGS

1961-1962
Composition, 1949, pen on paper on canvas,
  25¼ x 19½ .... (129) $ 494

1964
Composition in Black, India ink, 19¾ x 12¾ ...... (368)   221

1965
Composition, 1949, India ink, 25¾ x 19¾ .... (568)   1,537

1968-July 1969
Composition, blue and black ink, 39½ x 29 ...... (1070)   566
Abstract Composition, 1961, pen and wash,
  25¾ x 19½ .... (1138)   471

WATERCOLORS

1961-1962
Composition, tempera, 19¾ x 25¾ .... (75)   1,580
Composition (Black), (1958), gouache,
  25¾ x 19¾ .... (88)   984

1963

Composition, 1951, gouache and India-ink wash,
25 x 19½ .... (220) $ 949

Composition, (1960), gouache, 21 x 29 .... (283)   1,130

1967

Composition, (1951), gouache and oil on paper,
25¾ x 19¾ .... (970)   1,845

1968–July 1969

Black, Blue, and Green Composition, brush,
India ink, and watercolor, 25½ x 19½ .... (1272)   600

PAINTINGS

1961–1962

Composition, 1950, oil on paper on board,
25¾ x 19½ .... (129)   1,373

Vertical Composition, 1951, 25 x 19½ .... (85)   2,100

Horizontal Composition, 1951, 16 x 21½ .... (85)   1,600

Composition, 1958, 36 x 25¾ .... (88)   3,936

Composition (Red Background), 1959,
36½ x 25¾ .... (149)   2,950

1963

Untitled, 1951, 51½ x 77½ .... (277)   2,742

"28 Juillet 1953," 76 x 50½ .... (189)   7,000

Composition, 1960, 63½ x 51¾ .... (131)   6,000

1964

"10 Octobre 1952," 35¼ x 45½ .... (431)   7,000

1965

Red on Black, 1954–55, 36¼ x 25¾ .... (624)   2,349

"7 Février 1957," 77¼ x 61¾ .... (637)   9,000

Painting "4 Juillet 1957," 28½ x 21¼ .... (539)   1,000

Painting "7 Mai 1958," 63¼ x 38½ .... (485)   5,500

Blue Strikes, 51½ x 38 .... (583)   3,192

1966

Composition, 1953, 39½ x 29 .... (791)   2,500

Painting, 1957, 76¾ x 51¾ .... (686)   7,186

Composition, 1958, 63¾ x 45 .... (776)   5,500

1968–July 1969

Composition, 1954, 36½ x 25¾ .... (1176)   5,500

Abstract Composition, 1949, oil on paper laid
down on canvas, 25¾ x 17¾ .... (1208)   1,750

Composition, 35¾ x 28½ .... (1187)   3,540

Painting, 1958, 63 x 38 .... (1235)   5,500

"10 October 1952," 33 x 45½ .... (1235)   9,500

Composition in Blue, Yellowish, and Black,
20 x 24 .... (1241)   2,520

Chaim Soutine

(1894–1943)

Birthplace: Smilovitch, Lithuania.

1910   Goes to Vilno and spends three years at the local art school while working at a photographer's.

1911-13   Arrives in Paris and settles at "La Ruche" in Montparnasse. Enters the Ecole Nationale des Beaux-Arts, Paris, in Cormon's studio. Meets several foreign artists—Zadkine, Lipchitz, Chagall, Laurens, and Kremegne. Forms a profound friendship with Modigliani.

1919   Modigliani introduces him to the dealer Leopold Zborowski, who buys some of his paintings and suggests that he spend some time in the south of France at Céret.

1920-22   Stays at Céret, where he paints about two hundred pictures in a strong Expressionist manner, using subdued precious color applied with a full brush. Terribly affected by Modigliani's death. Returns to Paris.

1923   Doctor Barnes buys about one hundred of his pictures.

1925   Trip to Cagnes.

1927   Paints the series of "Altar Boys."

1929   Stays with Monsieur and Madame Castaing at the Chateau de Lèves, Chatel-Guyon.

1943   Takes refuge at Champigny-sur-Veude, Touraine. Died, Paris, after an operation.

1944   Retrospective exhibition at the Salon d'Automne, Paris.

Sales

PAINTINGS

1961–1962

*View of the Studio of Oscar Miestchaninoff, Cité
Falguière,* 1914, 25¾ x 19½ .... (128) $8,238

The Red Viaduct at Céret, 1919, 21¾ x 15 .... (120)   18,500

Landscape at Cagnes, 24 x 17¾ .... (114)   11,000

Landscape, (1922), 17½ x 21 .... (128)   12,357

Le Boeuf écorché, 1923, 29 x 23¾ .... (18)   36,838

Portrait of a Child Dressed in Red, 25¼ x 19¾ .... (37)   22,000

Red Thatch-Roofed Cottages, 25¾ x 36½ .... (26)   10,000

Mouton à l'étal, 25 x 15½ .... (30)   15,000

Calf with Red Curtain, (1924), 30¾ x 19 .... (64)   17,000

The Pastry Cook, (1927), 25 x 19½ .... (112)   76,888

Valet, 1928, 28 x 16¾ .... (8)   76,000

Woman with a Chair, (1930), 31½ x 17½ .... (31)   21,968

*The Artist's Palette with Several Colors, in Its
Box,* 5¾ x 14¼ .... (149)   221

1963

Reclining Woman, (1918), 21½ x 32 .... (247)   12,339

Red Sword Lily, 1918–19, 25¼ x 21 .... (306)   13,600

The Road to Céret, (1920–21), 25¾ x 31½ .... (210)   13,710

Sleeping Woman, (1926), 15¾ x 13 .... (279)   13,500

Clamart Wood, 1927, 31½ x 19½ .... (255)   9,323

The Young Bull, 22½ x 15¾ .... (255)   10,968

Hanging Chicken on a Blue Background,
40 x 30 .... (254)   14,000

The Castle, 18¼ x 21¾ .... (232)   14,464

1964

The Dwarf, (1917), 32 x 23½ .... (450) $ 6,400
The Red Castle at Céret, (1919), 21 x 30½ .... (454)   22,112
The Hen, 1921, 40 x 29¾ .... (354)   20,000
Portrait of a Woman, 1925, 25 x 19½ .... (453)   34,550
Young Woman in Red on a Blue Background,
   (1927-28), 29 x 21¼ .... (431)   42,500
Surroundings of Chartres, 1930, 19½ x 22 .... (401)   13,300
The Poplars, 25¾ x 31½ .... (465)   28,000
Young Lady with a Doll, (1932) .... (367)   36,485
Portrait of a Woman, Her Head Leaning on Her
   Left Hand, 22 x 13 .... (474)   6,800
Red Flowers, 24 x 21 .... (378)   9,718
Vase of Sword Lilies, 16¼ x 9¾ .... (464)   4,220
Still Life with Sweet Red Peppers, 25¼ x 17½ .... (472)   17,000
Le Boeuf écorché, 30½ x 20 .... (339)   12,800
Bag, 23 x 14¼ .... (471)   12,656
The Cock, 32 x 14 .... (347)   9,000
Self-Portrait, 21¾ x 15¾ .... (404)   10,600

1965

The Cock, 32 x 14 .... (561)   8,020
The Red Castle at Céret, 1919, 21½ x 31½ .... (616)   19,200
Landscape at Cagnes, (1920), 25½ x 17½ .... (617)   19,210
Suburban Landscape, (1920), 25¾ x 21¼ .... (637)   16,000
Alley Lined with Trees, 31½ x 19 .... (583)   20,314
Woman's Head, (1920), 13½ x 10¾ .... (594)   14,000
Portrait of a Young Lady, 18¾ x 16¼ .... (628)   20,894
Landscape of Céret, (1921-22), 20½ x 27¼ ...... (583)   17,412
Landscape, (1922), 17½ x 21 .... (575)   10,503
Woman Knitting, (1923), 32½ x 23¼ .... (583)   21,765
Young Woman Leaning on Her Hand, 21¾ x 13 .. (512)   11,200
Sword Lilies, 16¼ x 9½ .... (569)   7,910
Woman's Head, 1931, 14 x 15¾ .... (616)   21,600
Landscape at Céret, (1941), 27¾ x 21½ .... (617)   37,742

1966

Sword Lilies in a Blue Vase, 21¾ x 15 .... (666)   7,200
Sword Lilies, (1917-18), 25 x 20¾ .... (776)   9,500
Trees at Céret, (1919), 21¼ x 29 .... (686)   23,494
A Boy in Blue, 1926, 32 x 23¾ .... (676)   50,000
Two Children, 9½ x 16¼ .... (744)   8,701
Young Lady in Red, 1928, 31¼ x 23¾ .... (713)   47,500
The Young Valet, (1929), on canvas laid down on
   board, 25¾ x 21½ .... (686)   19,348
The Woman with a Chair, (1930), 31½ x 17½ ..... (750)   27,916
Portrait of a Woman, 25 x 19½ .... (797)   38,420
Landscape at Champigny, with a Reclining
   Figure, (1942), 29 x 25¾ .... (686)   23,494
Beef with Red Curtain, 31½ x 19 .... (808)   15,671
Still Life, 25¼ x 17¾ .... (811)   14,400

1967

Still Life with a Loaf and a Fish, 1924,
   21¾ x 29¼ .... (993)   12,000
Woman with a Black Dress, on panel,
   25¼ x 19¾ .... (965)   39,098
Restless Landscape, (1919), 20¼ x 29 .... (864)   27,500
Child in Blue, 16¾ x 10¾ .... (954)   13,500
Self-Portrait,[1] 21¾ x 15¾ .... (901)   17,000

1968–July 1969

The Trees, (1920-23), 18¼ x 24 .... (1176)   24,000
Skinned Veal, (1924), 32 x 19½ .... (1176)   20,000

[1]Sold in Paris in 1964 for $10,600.

Still Life with Fish, 15 x 18 .... (1193) $ 12,390
Woman on a Red Sofa, (1918), 21¼ x 32 .... (1235)   46,000
Chickens on a White Tablecloth, (1930),
   19¾ x 24 .... (1235)   17,000
The Pheasants, 22½ x 14¼ .... (1268)   25,288
Woman in a Red Bodice, 28 x 18¼ .... (1268)   26,680

Raphael Soyer

(1899–   )

Birthplace: Tombov, Russia. (His brothers Isaac and Moses are also painters.)

1912   His family emigrates to the U.S.

1919-21   Enters the Art Students League, New York, taught by Guy Pène du Bois.

1929   One-man show at the Daniel Gallery, New York.

1932   One-man show at l'Elan Gallery, New York.

1933   Exhibits at the Curt Valentine Gallery, New York—and again in 1938.

1944   One-man show at the Weyhe Gallery, New York. Takes an interest in European Expressionists and in American painters such as Kuniyoshi, Weber, Marsh, and Levine.

1951-52   Exhibits at the National Academy of Design, New York.

1960   One-man show at the ACA Gallery, New York.

1964   One-man show at the Forum Gallery, New York.

Resident in New York.

Sales

DRAWINGS

1961–1962

Seated Model, colored chalk and pencil,
   14¾ x 10½ .... (111) $ 150

1963

Model Undressing, pencil and watercolor,
   18½ x 11½ .... (179)   250
The Bath, charcoal, 16¾ x 13½ .... (218)   220

1964

Heads, black lead, 12¾ x 10 .... (321)   150
Studies of Nudes, 1957, sepia ink and wash,
   14 x 8¾ .... (374)   175

1965

Reclining Nude, ink, 15¾ x 11¾ .... (489)   350

1968–July 1969

Standing Nude, charcoal and watercolor,
   23 x 13 .... (1164)   700

WATERCOLORS

1966

Reclining Nude, watercolor and charcoal,
14 x 22 ....(805) $ 400

Nudes, two watercolors, each 8 x 5¾ ....(805) 350

1968–July 1969

East Houston Street, New York, 1927,
watercolor, 9 x 13 ....(1062) 650

Seated Girl, pastel, 13 x 16½ ....(1248) . 600

Woman Undressing, pencil and watercolor,
16 x 16 ....(1248) 400

PAINTINGS

1961–1962

Window Shopping, 35½ x 23¾ ....(85) 2,700

1963

Two Dancers, 19¾ x 15¾ ....(272) 950

The Young Italian Girl, 10¾ x 8 ....(275) 400

1965

The Subway Corridor, 1946, 41½ x 25¾ ....(489) 4,750

Woman's Head, 10 x 8¼ ....(507) 650

1966

Reclining Nude, 8 x 10 ....(721) 500

Young Lady Putting On Her Petticoat, 1962,
42¾ x 88 ....(707) 7,250

1967

Dancer, 11¾ x 8¾ ....(2088) 950

Nudes, two pictures on canvas laid down on
cardboard, each 21 x 8¼ ....(989) 2,000

1968–July 1969

Seated Nude, 14 x 10 ....(1035) 2,000

Reclining Nude, 20 x 24 ....(1088) 2,100

Young Girl Sleeping, 12 x 16 ....(1062) 1,800

Portrait of Ernest Fiene, 25¾ x 20 ....(1160) 2,000

Portrait of a Girl, 16 x 12 ....(1229) 2,250

Nicolas de Staël

(1914–1955)

Birthplace: Petrograd, Russia. (He is the great-grand-nephew of Madame de Staël, the French writer.)

1919 His family flees to Poland to escape the Russian revolution.

1921-22 Death of his parents. Sent to Brussels.

1932-33 Enters the Académie Royale des Beaux-Arts, Brussels. Trip to the Netherlands, where he discovers Rembrandt and Vermeer. Executes his first watercolors. Visits Paris, where he becomes acquainted with a great number of works by Cézanne, Matisse, Braque, and Soutine.

1934-35 Stays in Spain and Italy. Returns to Brussels.

1936-37 Stay in Morocco, where he meets Jeannine Guilloux, his future wife. Short trip to Algeria and to Naples. Returns to Paris, where he attends the Académie Léger. Copies Chardin's paintings at the Louvre.

1939 Enlists in the French Foreign Legion and is sent to Tunisia.

1940 Settles in Nice with Jeannine.

1942 Meets Magnelli, Delaunay, Arp, and Le Corbusier. Turns to abstract art.

1943 Settles in Paris, where the dealer Jeanne Bûcher encourages and assists him.

1944 Forms a friendship with Georges Braque, whom he admires very much, and with his fellow countryman André Lanskoy. Takes part in an abstract group show at the Galerie de l'Esquisse, Paris. One-man show at the Galerie de l'Esquisse, Paris. Participates in the Salon d'Automne, Paris.

1945 Successful one-man show at the Galerie Jeanne Bûcher, Paris. Participates in the Salon de Mai, Paris. Sells his pictures to the dealers Dubourg, Drouin, and Louis Carré.

1946 Death of Jeannine. Becomes associated with the Galerie Louis Carré, Paris. Marries Françoise Chapouton.

1947 Moves to a spacious studio near Braque's. Executes a series of very large paintings. Meets by chance the American dealer Theodore Schempp, who introduces his works to the U.S.

1948 Jacques Dubourg becomes his exclusive dealer—until De Staël's death. Becomes a French citizen.

1950 First one-man show in New York at the Theodore Schempp Gallery. The Musée National d'Art Moderne, Paris, buys one of his paintings. First monograph on De Staël by Georges Duthuit. One-man show at the Galerie Dubourg, Paris—and again in 1954 and 1955.

1952 Series of his "Football Players." One-man show at the Mathiesen Gallery, London.

1953 Visits Italy and the U.S. One-man show at the Knoedler Gallery, New York. Paul Rosenberg becomes his exclusive dealer in America. Buys a castle at Manerbes, Vaucluse. Gradually reverts to a simplified representational painting.

1954 Settles in Antibes.

1955 Commits suicide by throwing himself out of his window.

1956 Retrospective exhibition at the Musée National d'Art Moderne, Paris.

Sales

DRAWINGS

1961–1962

Composition, 1943, charcoal, 9¼ x 12¼ ....(120) $ 600

Composition, 1951, India ink, 27 x 21¾ ....(143) 1,220

1963

Seascape, 1951, India ink, 21 x 27¾ ....(287) 1,200

Composition, charcoal, 9 x 12¼ ....(188) 320

1964

Abstract Composition, 1943, black chalk,
12 x 29 ....(392) 2,337

1966

Composition, 1949, charcoal, 11¾ x 9¼ .... (689) $ 553

1967

Composition, 1945, charcoal, 19 x 12½ .... (970) 1,476

Composition, 1945, charcoal and white chalk,
    20¼ x 16 .... (870) 1,500

Composition, India ink, 29¾ x 21 .... (996) 800

Composition, 1951, India ink, 8¼ x 11½ .... (933) 300

Composition, India ink, 9½ x 12 .... (857) 720

1968–July 1969

Composition, 1945, charcoal, 18¾ x 11¾ .... (1080) 600

Composition, India ink, 28¼ x 41½ .... (1080) 1,200

The River Escaut, 1951, India ink, 8 x 11 .... (1264) 900

WATERCOLORS

1963

Composition in Gray, watercolor and gouache,
    15 x 10¾ .... (316) 1,300

Composition in Gray and Sepia, watercolor and
    gouache, 14¾ x 10¾ .... (225) 1,250

Abstract Composition, watercolor, 13½ x 8¼ ..... (255) 686

1965

Abstract Composition, 1949, gouache,
    8¾ x 11½ .... (583) 1,886

1966

Seascape, (1953), watercolor, 5 x 6¾ .... (648) 800

1967

Composition, 1949, gouache, 9 x 11¾ .... (1004) 2,750

1968–July 1969

Composition, 1944, pastel, 18¾ x 12 .... (1125) 1,485

Composition, gouache and collage, 6 x 6¾ ...... (1256) 2,500

PAINTINGS

1961–1962

Composition, 1943, 26 x 18¼ .... (88) 6,888

Composition, 1943, 24 x 18¼ .... (110) 6,000

Composition, 1946, 21¼ x 25¾ .... (171) 7,200

The Space at Crans, 1948, 18½ x 24½ .... (129) 10,984

Composition, 1948, 41 x 84 .... (31) 31,304

Seascape, 1951, 34¾ x 51 .... (31) 15,103

Landscape, 25¾ x 32 .... (29) 11,000

Composition in White, Blue, and Red, 13 x 16¼ ... (29) 7,800

Villerville-sur-Mer,[1] 4¾ x 8¾ .... (50) 2,400

Composition, 19¾ x 25¾ .... (50) 9,000

Composition, 19¾ x 29 .... (50) 11,500

Composition with a Dark Blue Background, 1953,
    collage on cardboard, 12¾ x 8¼ .... (149) 1,501

The Lighthouse at Gravelines, 1954, 23¼ x 31½ ... (129) 19,771

Composition, 18¼ x 25¾ .... (97) 10,400

Composition, 23¾ x 32 .... (97) 12,000

Composition, 23¾ x 32 .... (97) 16,000

1963

A Harbor, on cardboard, 15 x 21¾ .... (306) 5,400

Composition, 1944, 10¾ x 18¼ .... (249) 7,200

Composition, 1946, 28 x 23 .... (247) 6,855

The Storm, (1946–47), 51½ x 35½ .... (279) 25,000

Gray Composition, 1948, 58¾ x 27 .... (247) 29,065

[1]Inscribed on the reverse "Noël 52."

Composition, 1950, 10¼ x 13¼ .... (210) $7,678

An Apple, 1952, 9½ x 14 .... (210) 6,581

Composition on a Blue Background I, (1953),
    collage, 24½ x 18¾ .... (202) 2,750

Under the Snow, 1954, 23¾ x 32 .... (232) 22,148

The Precious Stone, collage and gouache,
    13 x 9½ .... (255) 1,097

1964

Composition, ... (341) 5,200

Composition, 1944, 51½ x 28 .... (471) 15,820

Composition, 1944, 51½ x 28 .... (405) 2,322

Landscape with a Gray Sky, on board, 4¾ x 8¾ .. (458) 4,063

Brown Composition, 1946, 10¾ x 8¾ .... (458) 5,514

Composition, 1946, 25 x 21¼ .... (378) 7,910

Landscape, 1952, 19½ x 23¾ .... (416) 22,112

Composition on a Red Background, 1953, collage,
    22½ x 17½ .... (454) 3,317

Composition on a Blue Background II, 1953,
    collage, 22½ x 19 .... (454) 4,284

Grignan, 1953, 26 x 31¾ .... (431) 27,500

Decanter, 1953, 32 x 25¾ .... (431) 33,000

1965

Abstraction, 21¾ x 15 .... (539) 5,500

Composition, 1943, 25¾ x 18¼ .... (561) 2,300

Music in Mind, 1948, 32 x 23¾ .... (573) 22,112

Composition, 1948, 10 x 16¾ .... (594) 7,000

Volume of Things, 1949, on panel, 76½ x 39¼ .... (526) 45,000

Flowers, (1951–52), 58¼ x 38¾ .... (485) 68,000

Landscape, Honfleur, 1952, 25¾ x 31½ .... (485) 30,000

Landscape, La Ciotat, 1952, 25¾ x 31½ .... (485) 34,000

Still Life, (1952), 31¾ x 25¾ .... (485) 20,000

Collage in Blue, 1953, collage, 25 x 19 .... (624) 2,488

1966

Village, 5¾ x 9 .... (744) 3,051

Village, on panel, 5¾ x 9 .... (793) 4,000

Composition, 1943, 25¾ x 18¾ .... (749) 3,300

Composition in Gray and Yellow, 1946,
    38¾ x 25 .... (686) 13,820

Green and Yellow Rectangles, 1950, 51¼ x 38¼ ... (678) 42,000

Composition, 1950, 18¼ x 24 .... (750) 9,950

Composition, (1951), 11 x 16¾ .... (812) 16,584

Still Life with Pears, 1953, 31¾ x 35½ .... (678) 26,000

Composition, Black Background, 1953, collage,
    20½ x 16¼ .... (776) 3,250

Composition, Light Green, 1953, collage,
    12¾ x 9 .... (776) 1,750

The Walking Men, (1954), collage, 13¾ x 5¼ ..... (815) 967

Sicily, 1954, 25½ x 36½ .... (776) 26,000

Mediterranean, (1954), 8¾ x 13 .... (776) 4,000

Standing Nude, (1954), 57¾ x 38¾ .... (776) 40,000

1967

Composition, 1951, 28½ x 36½ .... (938) 20,730

Composition on a White Background, 1953,
    collage, 18¼ x 20½ .... (880) 4,422

Composition, Dark Green Background, 1953,
    collage, 12 x 9 .... (938) 2,349

Collage, 1953, collage, 23¼ x 19 .... (982) 2,370

Composition, 1953, collage, 25 x 18¾ .... (893) 1,500

Collage on a Mauve Background, collage,
    21 x 16¾ .... (987) 2,100

1968–July 1969

Old Houses of the Village, 1942, 24 x 18¼ ...... (1173) $ 8,050
Seascape, 35¼ x 51 .... (1173)   50,600
Abstract Composition, 1946, 21¾ x 25¾ .... (1176)   10,000
Composition, 1948, on board, 41 x 84 .... (1057)   46,000
Composition, 1950, 39½ x 29 .... (1193)   42,126
Composition in Blue and Gray, 1950, 9¼ x 13¼ .. (1068)   10,620
An Apple, 1951-52, 9½ x 14 .... (1053)   9,200
"Les Indes Galantes," 1953, 63¾ x 45 .... (1068)   89,680
Composition, 15 x 18¼ .... (1125)   11,040
Composition, 31½ x 51½ .... (1125)   50,600
Composition, 18¼ x 24 .... (1125)   11,500
Composition, collage, 8¾ x 12¾ .... (1126)   1,982
Composition, 1948, on panel, 19¾ x 24 .... (1239)   14,400
Composition, 29 x 21¼ .... (1268)   20,880
Composition, 1944, 32 x 25¾ .... (1268)   8,352
Composition, 1950, 18 x 24 .... (1270)   24,000
Collage, 1953, 24½ x 19 .... (1270)   3,840
Collage, 1953, 23½ x 19 .... (1270)   3,120

WATERCOLORS

1964

Seated Woman, gouache, 39½ x 26½ .... (438) $ 850

1967

Still Life, pastel, 24 x 17 .... (870)   300

1968–July 1969

Abstraction, pastel, 14 x 18¼ .... (1035)   3,500

PAINTINGS

1966

Deposizione, 19¾ x 23¾ .... (701)   900

1967

Funerals, 20 x 24 .... (893)   550

1968–July 1969

Tropical Flowers, 33¾ x 14 .... (1160)   2,500

Joseph Stella

(1877–1946)

Birthplace: Muro Lucano, Italy.

1896   Goes to the U.S., where he first studies medicine and pharmacology.

1897   Enters the Art Students League, New York.

1898– 1900   Attends the New York School of Arts, taught by William Chase.

1909   Goes to Europe, where he becomes aware of the Italian Futurist movement and is strongly influenced by it.

1910   First one-man show at the Carnegie Institute, Pittsburgh.

1913   One-man show at the Italian National Club, New York. Participates in the Armory Show, New York.

1915–18   Period of industrial subjects. Starts his famous series on Brooklyn Bridge, which is for him "The shrine containing all the efforts of the new civilization."

1926   Exhibits at the Curt Valentine Gallery, New York.

1930   One-man show at the Galerie Sloden, Paris.

1932   Exhibition at Washington Place, Paris.

1942   One-man show at the Knoedler Gallery, Paris.

1946   Died, New York.

Sales

DRAWINGS

1964

Head of a Young Man, (1905), red chalk, 10 x 4 ... (363) $ 175

1968–July 1969

Still Life with Apples, colored pencil, 10 x 12¼ .. (1035)   375
Study for "The Brooklyn Bridge," ink, 8 x 5 ..... (1235)   400

Clifford Still

(1904–   )

Birthplace: Grandin, North Dakota, U.S. (Studies at Spokane University, Washington.)

1933–41   Teaches at Washington State College.

1941   Exhibition at the Museum of Art, San Francisco. Elaborates his own abstract style and appears as one of the most inventive figures of his time in American painting.

1946   Participates in the exhibition "Art of This Century" at the Betty Parsons Gallery, New York.

1949–50   Teaches at the California School of Fine Arts. Regarded as a pioneer of mural-scale painting.

1952   Takes part in the exhibition "Fifteen Americans" at the Museum of Modern Art, New York.

1955   Participates in the exhibition "Cinquante Ans d'art aux Etats-Unis" at the Musée National d'Art Moderne, Paris.

Resident in New York, where he teaches at Hunter College and Brooklyn College.

Sales

PAINTINGS

1961–1962

Untitled, (1946), 45½ x 33½ .... (164) $9,886

1965

Painting, 1951, 94¾ x 76 .... (592)   29,000

1968–July 1969

Painting, 1951, 68½ x 58 .... (1057)   26,000
1948-H, 1948, 76 x 70 .... (1235)   43,000

Léopold Survage

(1879–1968)

Birthplace: Moscow, Russia. (His family name is Sturzwage. Attends the Moscow Academy of Fine Arts.)

1908 Settles in Paris.

1911-12 Participates for the first time in the Salon des Indépendants, Paris—in the Cubist room—and in the Salon d'Automne.

1917 First one-man show at the Galerie Bongarg, Paris. (Catalog preface by Apollinaire.)

1919 Contributes to the foundation of the Section d'Or, Paris, and becomes the secretary of the movement.

1920-22 One-man shows at the Galerie Léonce Rosenberg, Paris, and the Galerie l'Effort Moderne, Brussels. Marries the pianist Germaine Meyer. Produces the stage decorations and costumes for Diaghilev's *Mavra* with music by Stravinsky, Paris.

1925 One-man shows at the Chicago Arts Club and at the Galerie Percier, Paris.

1927 One-man shows at the Galerie Granoff, Paris; the Kraushaar Gallery, New York; and the Chester Gallery, Chicago. Becomes a French citizen.

1928 Wins the gold medal at the Milan Triennial. Participates in the exhibition of the Vienna Secession.

1929 One-man show at the Knoedler Gallery, New York. Takes part in several group shows held in Paris, Chicago, São Paulo, and New York.

1934 Participates in "International Theater Art" at the Museum of Modern Art, New York.

1937 Executes important decorations for the Paris World's Fair, where he wins a gold medal.

1939 Starts to paint in a casein emulsion. The Museum of Modern Art, New York, buys a series of his works.

1949-50 One-man shows at the Galerie des Deux-Iles, Paris, and at the San Fedele Gallery, Milan. Participates in "L'Art abstrait, ses origines, ses premiers maîtres," at the Galerie Maeght, Paris.

1955 One-man show at the Galerie Drouant-David, Paris.

1958 Participates in the Brussels World's Fair, where he wins a silver medal. Executes an important mural entitled "Pax" for the Palais des Congrès, Liége.

1959 One-man show at the Obelisk Gallery, London.

1960 Wins the Guggenheim prize for his work "Maternity."

1961 One-man shows at the Galerie Bellechasse and the Galerie Lucie Weil, Paris.

1966 Retrospective exhibition at the Palais Galliéra, Paris.

1968 Died.

Sales

DRAWINGS

1961-1962

Study of a Man in the Nude, pen, 12¼ x 9½ . . . . . . (154) $ 38

1963

Beauty of Collioure, 1957, 5¾ x 3¾ . . . . (209)   18

1964

Composition, 1957, pencil and watercolor, 19½ x 12¾ . . . . (321)   125

1966

Figures, pen and wash, 12¼ x 9¼ . . . . (815) $ 111

Composition, 1962, pencil and charcoal, 15 x 18¾ . . . . (692)   220

1967

Composition, India ink, 8¾ x 11½ . . . . (926)   320

1968–July 1969

Composition, wash, 16¾ x 10¼ . . . . (1213)   414

"Attributs de la Musique,"[1] pen, 8¼ x 6¾ . . . . . . (1244)   76

Athlete, 1932, pencil, 13¼ x 10 . . . . (1266)   50

WATERCOLORS

1961-1962

La Celle St. Cloud, 1911, watercolor, 9 x 11¾ . . . . (102)   250

Figure and Houses, 1917, watercolor, on paper laid down on canvas, 23¾ x 18¾ . . . . (117)   320

Buildings, 1920, gouache, 10¼ x 9 . . . . (161)   100

The Earth, gouache, 14¾ x 18¾ . . . . (82)   500

The Fire, gouache, 15 x 18¾ . . . . (82)   500

Figure and Houses, 1957, watercolor, 10¾ x 6¾ . . (110)   320

1963

Landscape of the South of France, 1911, watercolor, 9 x 13 . . . . (300)   160

The Village, 1918, watercolor, 8¼ x 14 . . . . (190)   170

The Roofs, 1921, watercolor, 6 x 9 . . . . (280)   130

Women of Collioure, watercolor and gouache, 18¾ x 13 . . . . (205)   360

1964

Houses, 1920, watercolor and India ink, 8¼ x 6¾ . . . . (333)   84

Composition for "Mavra," 1922, watercolor and India ink, 12¼ x 10 . . . . (333)   196

Composition, 1935, watercolor, 14¼ x 19 . . . . (366)   460

Composition, pastel, 20½ x 14¼ . . . . (413)   280

The Dove, 1949, watercolor, 14 x 15¾ . . . . (346)   420

The Bathers, Palermo, (1960), watercolor, 15½ x 19½ . . . . (375)   200

1965

Blue and Yellow Landscape, 10 x 13¾ . . . . (563)   480

Landscape, watercolor, 9½ x 13 . . . . (581)   64

The Red Roof, 1920, watercolor, 6 x 9 . . . . (529)   280

Women of Collioure, 1932, watercolor, 18¾ x 13 . . . . (503)   400

Women of Collioure, 1932, watercolor, 18¾ x 13 . . . . (640)   230

Composition, 1938, gouache, 14 x 10 . . . . (523)   250

Taormina, 1954, pastel, 13 x 9½ . . . . (631)   220

1966

Colored Rhythms, 1913, watercolor, 12¾ x 12¼ . . . (670)   180

Colored Rhythm, 1913, watercolor, 11¾ x 10¼ . . . (809)   240

Blue and Yellow Landscape, 1914, watercolor, 10 x 13¾ . . . . (655)   310

Cubist Composition, 1921, watercolor, 6½ x 6¾ . . . (745)   249

Composition for "Mavra," 1922, gouache, 25 x 19½ . . . . (731)   400

Composition, 1938, gouache, 9 x 4¾ . . . . (798)   384

1967

Colored Rhythm, 1913, watercolor, 11¾ x 10 . . . . . (854)   240

Chromatic Disk, Colored Rhythm, 1913, gouache, 11¾ x 10¼ . . . . (973)   230

Composition, watercolor, 5¾ x 5¾ . . . . (950)   80

[1]Program for *Le Triptyque.*

1968–July 1969

The Song of Songs, 8 gouaches, ... (1202) $1,600
Landscape, 1921, watercolor, 9 x 6 . . . . (1154) 156
Composition, 1939, gouache, 8¾ x 7 . . . . (1042) 240
Naples, 1952, watercolor, 20½ x 14 . . . . (1212) 420
Men and Horses, watercolor, 21½ x 29 . . . . (1185) 400
Landscape, watercolor, 9 x 11¾ . . . . (1230) 300
The City, watercolor, 9 x 9¼ . . . . (1232) 800
Fire and Water, watercolor, 27 x 19½ . . . . (1234) 170
The Orange Carrier, 1961, watercolor,
   15½ x 19½ . . . . (1243) 400
The Sleeping Town, gouache, 15½ x 9½ . . . . (1247) 1,240
Landscape of the South of France, 1950,
   watercolor, 19¾ x 25¾ . . . . (1247) 400
*Composition with a Figure Wearing a Bowler
   Hat,* gouache, 8 x 10¾ . . . . (1255) 1,200
Village Street, 1930, two watercolors, each
   9½ x 12¼ . . . . (1264) 960
View of St. Job, 1934, watercolor, 11¾ x 19 . . . . . (1266) 320
Fall of Icarus, 1937, gouache, 17¾ x 11¾ . . . . (1268) 766
Cubist Composition, 1917, watercolor, 25 x 19 . . . (1268) 3,016

PAINTINGS

1961–1962

Vase of Flowers, 1921, 15½ x 10 . . . . (174) 110
Cubist Landscape, 39½ x 32 . . . . (39) 920
Woman with a Dove, 1930, 25¾ x 21¼ . . . . (9) 350
The Twins, 1945, 29 x 21¼ . . . . (114) 900

1963

Young Woman by the Seaside, 1930, 13 x 16¼ . . . . (257) 320
Swallow, Black Bird, 1927, 13 x 28 . . . . (255) 384
The Table, collage, 10 x 9½ . . . . (205) 420

1964

Landscape with a Leaf, (1926), 32 x 25¾ . . . . (354) 2,250
Portrait, 1934, 14 x 10¾ . . . . (375) 290
The Village Amid the Trees, 19¾ x 24 . . . . (328) 220
Charity, 1943, on panel, 39¼ x 27¼ . . . . (401) 940

1965

Composition, 1927, 21¼ x 25¾ . . . . (503) 760
Composition, 1927, 21¼ x 25¾ . . . . (599) 590

1966

The Town, 1927, 21¼ x 25¾ . . . . (670) 760

1967

The Entrance of the Town, 39½ x 32 . . . . (976) 2,600
Still Life with a Fruit Stand, 1919, oil on paper,
   11¾ x 16 . . . . (1006) 398
Treboul, 1922, on panel, 9½ x 13 . . . . (949) 340
The Bird in the City, (1927), 21¼ x 25¾ . . . . (850) 660
Landscape with Houses, 39¼ x 52½ . . . . (973) 870
Woman with a Bird, (1948), on panel, 6¼ x 5 . . . . . (980) 120
Seaside, 1948, on board, 36½ x 25¾ . . . . (962) 1,600
View of Douarnenez, 19¾ x 23¾ . . . . (884) 400
The Couple, 1964, 25¾ x 21¼ . . . . (857) 260

1968–July 1969

Composition, (1917), 29 x 23¾ . . . . (1125) 5,750
Young Lady with a Basket of Fish, 1924,
   31½ x 29 . . . . (1145) 1,000
The Farm with a Fountain, 1925, 35¼ x 45¾ . . . . . (1201) 2,500
Water Carrier on a Blue Background, 1926,
   25¾ x 21¼ . . . . (1121) 1,000

The Road, 1926, peinture à l'essence on panel,
   10 x 13 . . . . (1140) $ 210
Landscape with Leaves, 1928, 31½ x 39½ . . . . (1080) 2,000
Woman with a Fish, 1936, 16¼ x 13 . . . . (1118) 520
The Water Carrier, 1939, 24 x 15½ . . . . (1129) 360
Chimera, 1954, casein paint on panel, 7¼ x 9½ . . (1202) 500
Douarnenez, 17 x 21 . . . . (1192) 170
Fisherman, 32 x 23¾ . . . . (1042) 400
Composition, 29 x 23¾ . . . . (1029) 2,240
Composition, and Black Figure, 15½ x 21¾ . . . . . . (1173) 4,140
The House, 1927, 21¼ x 25¾ . . . . (1230) 1,580
Fish and Figures, 1956, 25¼ x 21¼ . . . . (1230) 1,200
Composition with Flowers, 32 x 23¾ . . . . (1230) 3,600
Perrette, 1934, 18¼ x 21¼ . . . . (1254) 1,400
*"L'Apprentissage se fait journellement, tissé de
   l'angoisse, et du désir quotidien,"* 1945,
   21¼ x 28¾ . . . . (1258) 760
The Fish, 1955, on panel, 11¾ x 16¼ . . . . (1258) 700
Composition, 1966, 21¾ x 18¼ . . . . (1268) 1,438

Rufino Tamayo

(1899–   )

Birthplace: Oaxaca, Mexico. (His family later settles in Mexico City.)

1917 Attends the Academy of San Carlos, Mexico City, for a short time. Discovers successively Impressionism, Cubism, Picasso, and Braque in French reviews. Also takes a great interest in the Mexican artistic tradition.

1926 Exhibits in New York and Mexico City.

1933 Executes a mural for the National Conservatory of Music, Mexico City. Appointed professor at the National School of Fine Arts, Mexico City.

1938 Settles in New York. From now on, spends only the summer in Mexico.

1943 Mural for the library of Smith College, Northampton.

1948 Retrospective exhibition entitled "Twenty Years of Painting" at the National Institute of Fine Arts, Mexico City.

1950 Goes to Europe. Participates in the Venice Biennial and exhibits at the Galerie des Beaux-Arts, Paris.

1951 Retrospective exhibition at the Palais des Beaux-Arts, Brussels.

1952 Participates in the exhibition of Mexican art at the Musée National d'Art Moderne, Paris. Exhibits at the Kunsthalle, Bern.

1957-58 Stay in Paris.

Sales

DRAWINGS

1961–1962

Mexican Woman, charcoal, 24¼ x 20¾ . . . . (44) $ 775
The Workman, pencil, 11¾ x 8½ . . . . (111) 100

1963
Figure in the Doorway, 1956, pencil, 23½ x 18 . . . . (272) $ 750

1964
Nude Model, pencil, 13½ x 10¼ . . . . (321)   375

1968–July 1969
Two Faces, 1947, pencil, 9 x 6½ . . . . (1145)   200
Still Life, 1953, pencil, 8¼ x 11½ . . . . (1216)   800

WATERCOLORS

1961–1962
Clown, gouache, 14¾ x 21¾ . . . . (85)   1,750
Mexican Girl, 1945, watercolor, 16¾ x 12¾ . . . . . . (152)   1,200

1963
The Man with a Haystack, watercolor, 16 x 12 . . . (179)   1,700
A Ranchero, 1931, gouache and watercolor,
    3¼ x 4 . . . . (208)   375
Woman's Head, 1939, watercolor, 15¾ x 12¾ . . . . (179)   1,050

1965
Woman with a Red Blouse, pastel and watercolor,
    14 x 10¾ . . . . (644)   500

1967
Nina, watercolor, 10¼ x 8 . . . . (870)   1,300
Dancer, 1927, gouache and watercolor,
    9¾ x 6¾ . . . . (841)   550
The Apple Seller, watercolor, 23¾ x 17¾ . . . . (952)   3,000

1968–July 1969
Women of Oaxaca, 1938, watercolor, 18 x 13½ . . (1216)   1,800
The Soldiers, 1924, watercolor, 6½ x 5½ . . . . (1231)   1,600
A Man and a Woman, 1926, watercolor, 10 x 7 . . (1231)   1,600
Portrait of a Young Girl, 1927, watercolor,
    10 x 7 . . . . (1231)   1,600
Los Obreros, 1935, watercolor, 11 x 8¼ . . . . (1246)   2,700
Domingo en Chapultepec, 1934, gouache,
    12½ x 10 . . . . (1246)   2,300
El Trabajador, 1934, watercolor, 8¼ x 10¾ . . . . . . (1246)   2,700

PAINTINGS

1961–1962
Portrait of a Seated Child, 1928, 28¾ x 24¾ . . . . (96)   2,600
Mujer Morida, 1931, 33¼ x 49 . . . . (64)   3,250
Ghostly Bird, 1956, 31½ x 39 . . . . (85)   3,600
The Lovers, 1958, 51½ x 38½ . . . . (149)   4,424

1963
"La Perla," 1950, 77¾ x 50 . . . . (272)   7,000
The Pursued Man, 1956, on panel, 39 x 31¼ . . . . . . (272)   3,250
Toast to Joy, 1956, 39 x 31¼ . . . . (247)   4,387
Facing the Sun, 1957, 39 x 31¼ . . . . (202)   5,250
Head, 1958, 20½ x 17 . . . . (279)   3,100

1964
The Shadow of a Man, 1961, 32 x 39½ . . . . (405)   493
"La Perla," 1956, 96 x 50¾ . . . . (405)   4,353
Still Life with Watermelons and a Bottle, 1956,
    31 x 39½ . . . . (431)   4,250

1965
The Pipe Smoker, 1945, 30½ x 23¼ . . . . (526)   7,000
Woman in the Night, 1947, 40 x 30 . . . . (539)   7,500
"La Perla," 1950, 78¾ x 50¾ . . . . (539)   9,250

1968–July 1969
Fantasy, 1961, 18¼ x 22 . . . . (1035)   3,250
Portrait of Olga, 1935, 41½ x 32¼ . . . . (1080)   6,500

Yves Tanguy

(1900–1955)

Birthplace: Paris, France. (Works in the maritime service, traveling to England, Spain, Africa, and South America.)

1922   Returns to Paris. (Decides to devote himself to painting upon seeing one of di Chirico's paintings at the Galerie Paul Guillaume.)

1925   Meets the Surrealists and joins the group. Contributes to "La Révolution Surréaliste." Takes part in all the Surrealist exhibitions in France and abroad.

1939   Goes to the U.S.

1940   Visits Reno, San Francisco, and Los Angeles.

1942   Trip to Canada and Washington. Settles in Woodbury, Connecticut.

1948   Becomes an American citizen.

1952   Exhibits at the Galerie Renou, Paris.

1955   Died, Woodbury, Connecticut.

Sales

DRAWINGS

1963
Still Life, (1930), pencil, 12½ x 9½ . . . . (179) $ 250
Two Still Lifes, (1930), two drawings, pencil, each
    12½ x 9½ . . . . (275)   650
Fantastic Landscape, (1951), India ink,
    9½ x 7¼ . . . . (220)   283
Composition, 1951, India ink, 11 x 16½ . . . . (208)   400

1964
Two Compositions, two drawings, India ink, each
    12¾ x 9½ . . . . (321)   325
Composition, 1935, pen, 7¾ x 6 . . . . (328)   180

1965
Composition, 1926, pen, 10¾ x 9 . . . . (541)   225
Composition, pencil, 10 x 12¾ . . . . (494)   150
Undefined Divisibility, 1943, black ink,
    15½ x 9½ . . . . (585)   406
Surrealist Composition, 1945, pen and watercolor,
    8¾ x 5 . . . . (568)   814

1966
Surrealist Landscape, 1926, pen and India ink,
    11 x 9 . . . . (818)   696

1967
Surrealist Composition, 1926, India ink and
    watercolor, 3½ x 2¼ . . . . (931)   407
Composition, 1939, India ink, 9½ x 6¾ . . . . (931)   904
Composition, 1950, pen, 10¾ x 8¼ . . . . (870)   1,200
Compositions, two drawings, ink, 5 x 3 . . . . (893)   550
Exquisite Corpse,[1] (1935), pencil and collage,
    10 x 6½ . . . . (970)   1,427

1968–July 1969
Figure, 1931, pencil, 10¾ x 8 . . . . (1215)   1,200
Composition, (1937), pen, 7½ x 2½ . . . . (1191)   519
Composition, pen and yellow wash, 15¾ x 9 . . . . . (1123)   140

[1] In collaboration with Jacques and Victor Brauner.

WATERCOLORS

1963

Surrealist Outline, 1947, gouache, 18½ x 12½ .... (277) $ 2,879
Surrealist Landscape, 1944, gouache, 5¼ x 10¾ ... (277)   1,097
Shapes, gouache, 12 x 5 .... (316)   3,000

1964

Untitled, 1936, gouache, 3¾ x 11 .... (454)   1,410
I See Only Her, 1950, gouache, 25 x 19½ .... (453)   2,764

1965

Untitled, 1946, gouache, 14 x 11 .... (583)   4,353

1966

Composition, tempera, 3½ x 11¾ .... (678)   6,500
Marine Tower, (1953), gouache, 21 x 3¾ .... (776)   3,000

PAINTINGS

1961–1962

L'Empalmage, 1935, oil on canvas on board,
13¼ x 10¼ .... (129)   6,590
Composition, (1936), 18½ x 24½ .... (84)   8,238
Tomorrow, 1936, 21½ x 17½ .... (140)   8,238

1964

Untitled, 1928, 35½ x 25 .... (454)   11,747
Surrealist Composition, 1929, 19¾ x 25¾ .... (474)   4,000
Finis par mordre, 1935, 25¾ x 21 .... (453)   7,739
Certainty, 1939, 10 x 13¼ .... (454)   6,081
The Chance Corners, 1942, 23 x 31½ .... (416)   19,348
Les Transparents, 1951, 39¼ x 32 .... (367)   22,112

1965

Toilette de l'air, 1937, 39¼ x 31½ .... (522)   19,348
La Cage des temps, 1951, on panel, 9 x 10 .... (539)   6,000

1966

Sunny Hello, 1929, 25¼ x 35½ .... (753)   11,608
Untitled, 1931, 12¾ x 21¾ .... (750)   10,503
I Am Waiting for You, 1934, 28¾ x 45 .... (686)   36,485

1967

Composition, 1927 .... (923)   11,600

 Turns to abstract painting. Trip to New York. First one-man show in New York at the Martha Jackson Gallery. Exhibits in Stockholm, Düsseldorf, Basel, Munich, Milan, Paris, and Chicago.

1956 First one-man show in Paris.

1958 Wins the first Carnegie prize, Pittsburgh. Given an award by the Venice Biennial. Series of one-man shows in Europe.

Sales

DRAWINGS

1963

The Bride, pencil and ink, 13 x 16¾ .... (281) $ 588

1964

Composition, 1963, India ink, 25¾ x 19¾ .... (441)   362

PAINTINGS

1963

White Sand, 51½ x 77¼ .... (299)   2,620

1964

Composition, 1962, oil on fabric, 41½ x 29¼ ...... (386)   1,000
Composition, 23¼ x 20½ .... (480)   520
Composition in Black, oil and marble background
on canvas, 25¾ x 32 .... (372)   1,700
Superposition of Gray Matter, 1961,
77¼ x 102¾ .... (471)   6,441

1965

Composition (The Two Trays), 1959, collage on
black paper, 13 x 8¾ .... (545)   1,556

1966

Composition No. 9, oil and sand on canvas,
51¼ x 63½ .... (678)   4,000
"CC 92 Barna 7," 32 x 51½ .... (729)   1,000
Half-Relief in Black, 1965, 32 x 25¾ .... (751)   1,216

1967

Composition, 1958, 75 x 51½ .... (923)   2,600
Bottle (1966), oil and sand on canvas,
18¼ x 15¼ .... (963)   1,000
Composition, 25¾ x 32 .... (918)   1,921

1968–July 1969

Great Relief with a Lateral X, 1961, oil, sand, and
plaster on canvas, 76¼ x 119¾ .... (1080)   10,000
Beige with a Gray Rectangle, 1960, oil and sand
on canvas, 20 x 24 .... (1088)   3,300
Ocher with Red Tracks, oil and sand on canvas,
33½ x 21¾ .... (1088)   2,300
Composition, 5 B, 1960, collage, 27 x 19¾ .... (1173)   920

Antonio Tapiès

(1923-   )

Birthplace: Barcelona, Spain.

1946 Gives up his law studies to devote himself entirely to painting. His favorite painters are the Surrealists—Miró and Dubuffet above all.

1948 Sets up the group "Dau al set," Barcelona. Exhibits for the first time at the October Show, Barcelona.

1950-51 A scholarship enables him to spend some time in Paris. First one-man show in Barcelona. Visits Belgium and Holland.

Georg Tappert

(1880–1957)

Birthplace: Berlin, Germany.

1900-04	Attends the Karlsruhe Academy of Fine Arts.
1906	First one-man show at the Paul Cassirer Gallery, Berlin.
1907-09	Settles in Worpswede and teaches with artists living there.
1910	Returns to Berlin. Contributes to the foundation of the New Secession—with a group of young artists including "Die Brücke."
1911	Invites Kandinsky, Marc, and other members of "Der Blaue Reiter" to participate in the third exhibition of the New Secession, Berlin. One-man show at the Kunsthalle, Bremen.
1912	Invited by Kandinsky and Marc to take part in the second exhibition of "Der Blaue Reiter," Munich. Participates in the Sonderbund exhibition, Cologne.
1913	Participates in "Neue Kunst," Vienna.
1918	With Pechstein and Klein, sets up the "November Gruppe." Takes part in all the exhibitions of this group.
1919	Appointed professor at the Berlin Academy of Fine Arts.
1920	Exhibits his graphic works at Neumann's, Berlin.
1929	Participates in the Salon d'Automne, Paris.
1933	Undergoes a series of confrontations with the Gestapo.
1937	Dismissed from his teaching post at the Berlin Academy.
1945	Commissioned by the American Military Government to direct the reconstruction of an art college in Berlin.
1957	Died.
1959	Retrospective exhibition at Documenta II, Kassel.

Sales

PAINTINGS

1963

The Box, 1907, 21¼ x 33 . . . . (316) $2,600

1964

Musing, 1904, 39½ x 28 . . . . (448) 1,700

1968–July 1969

Betty Seated with a Fan, (1910), 43 x 36 . . . . (1232) 8,000
"La Belle Hélène," (1924), on board, 28¼ x 40 . . . (1232) 3,250
Duet from "La Belle Hélène," (1924), 26 x 23¾ . . (1232) 2,750
Garden of Hesperides, (1904), 31½ x 30 . . . . (1232) 3,250

Kostia Terechkovitch

(1902–   )

Birthplace: Metcherskoe, near Moscow, Russia.

1907	His family settles in Moscow.
1913	Decides to devote himself to painting upon seeing an important exhibition of French painting.
1917	Attends the Academy of Fine Arts of Moscow for three months. Leaves Russia.
1920	Arrives in Paris.
1925	Exhibits for the first time at the Salon d'Automne, Paris. Exhibits with Tchelitchev and Lanskoy at the Galerie Henry, Paris.
1926	Exhibits with Roland Oudot at the Galerie Girard, Paris. Meets Brianchon and Legueult.
1928	First monograph on him by F. Fels (Editions du Triangle, Paris).
1935	Marries Yvette Le Mercier.
1936	Paints his portrait of Soutine.
1939	Enlists in the French army.
1942	Becomes a French citizen.
1946	Executes two tapestry designs for the Manufacture d'Aubusson.
1950	Trip to Finland.
1951	Participates in the first exhibition of "Les Peintres témoins de leur temps" at the Musée d'Art Moderne, Paris, and in all the following exhibitions of this group.
1955	Stay in North Africa.
1957	Exhibits his still lifes at the Galerie Bernier, Paris.
1958	Trip to Spain. Important monograph on him by J.P. Crespelle (Cailler, Geneva).

Resident in Paris.

Sales

DRAWINGS

1961–1962

Meditation, Conté pencil, 24 x 17¾ . . . . (168) $ 110

1964

Young Lady, pencil, 20 x 15¾ . . . . (346) 140
Portrait of the Wife of the Artist, 1932, pencil, 21¼ x 16½ . . . . (374) 150

1966

Musing, black pencil heightened with colored pencil, 24 x 18¼ . . . . (683) 140

1967

Seated Young Woman, 1929, pencil, 21¾ x 16¼ . (1007) 70

1968–July 1969

Portrait of a Woman, 1929, pencil, 21¾ x 16¼ . . . (1042) 140
Portait of a Woman, 1929, pencil, 21¾ x 16¼ . . . . (1084) 76

WATERCOLORS

1961-1962

The Young Lady and the Soldier, watercolor, 12¾ x 10 . . . . (102) 300
The Beach, gouache, 11¾ x 18¼ . . . . (71) 520
"Les petits rats de l'Opéra," watercolor and gouache, 15¾ x 14 . . . . (155) 210
Suzanne, watercolor, 24½ x 18¾ . . . . (98) 260

1963

The Guingette on the Bank of the River Marne,
  watercolor, 17½ x 21¼ .... (179) $ 375

The Skier, watercolor, 25¼ x 18¾ .... (209)   120

Young Lady in the Bloom of Youth, pastel,
  22 x 18½ .... (222)   300

Dancers, two watercolors heightened with
  gouache, 23¼ x 9½ and 22½ x 9 .... (258)   720

The Woman in a Red Hat, 1931, watercolor,
  23¼ x 14¼ .... (293)   440

1964

On the Beach, 1960, watercolor, 20 x 15¼ .... (335)   600

The Sitting, watercolor, 15¾ x 21 .... (409)   700

1965

Racehorse and His Jockey, oval watercolor
  heightened with gouache, 17 x 15½ .... (613)   104

The Paddock, 1961; ***Race Course,*** 1961, two
  watercolors, each 11 x 12¾ .... (559)   900

Little Girls Playing on the Beach, watercolor,
  14¾ x 12¾ .... (621)   150

Figure, watercolor, 12¾ x 10 .... (567)   328

1966

Seated Young Lady, watercolor, 23¾ x 18¾ ...... (824)   520

The Landing Stage, watercolor, 18¼ x 24 .... (828)   290

On the Edge of the Lake at Montreux, 1931,
  watercolor, 25¼ x 19½ .... (794)   360

Portrait of Georges Rouault, gouache,
  10¾ x 8¼ .... (729)   660

1967

The Moorish Servant, Sidi Boussaïd, 1964,
  watercolor and gouache, 23¼ x 17½ .... (995)   800

Sidi Boussaïd, 1964, watercolor, 23¾ x 17¾ ...... (919)   949

1968–July 1969

The Paddock, 1961, two watercolors, each
  11 x 12¾ .... (1181)   760

PAINTINGS

1961–1962

The Shady Walk, 32 x 39½ .... (39)   1,000

The Crossroads, 18¼ x 21¾ .... (90)   560

On the Terrace at Antibes, 1949, 28½ x 21¼ ..... (156)   1,800

Menton, 1950, oil on panel, 25¾ x 32 .... (156)   1,500

Young Lady in the Garden, 35¾ x 25¼ .... (152)   450

Figures in a Boat, 21 x 26 .... (128)   522

The Sideboard, 39½ x 29 .... (143)   2,034

1963

The Vase of Carnations, 25¾ x 36½ .... (276)   1,000

Little Girl with Cherries, 1943, on cardboard,
  25 x 17¾ .... (296)   1,500

Waterfall, 1957, 21¾ x 43¾ .... (258)   2,000

Young Lady on the Terrace, 1958, 39½ x 29¾ .... (241)   1,220

Young Lady on the Terrace, 39½ x 29¾ .... (311)   1,400

Garden in Bloom at Avallon, 19 x 23¾ .... (232)   904

Garden in Bloom at Avallon, 19¾ x 24 .... (281)   972

Landscape, on cardboard, 21¼ x 25¾ .... (299)   1,440

Landscape at the Seaside, on board, 19¾ x 25¾ .. (275)   500

Woman, Her Breast Bare, 24 x 19¾ .... (293)   1,570

Woman with a Hat, 25¾ x 21¼ .... (242)   4,200

1964

Tree with Birds, 1953, 25¾ x 19¾ .... (370)   660

In the Garden, on cardboard, 14¼ x 10½ .... (393)   560

Vase of Flowers, 18¼ x 15 .... (351) $ 440

Banks of the River Marne, 23¾ x 32 .... (475)   700

Still Life, 21 x 31½ .... (409)   1,200

Fish, oil on panel, 11¾ x 25¼ .... (480)   360

Village Under Snow, 21¼ x 29 .... (337)   700

Model with Ballet Shoes, 32 x 18¼ .... (335)   760

Bust of a Woman in the Nude, 24 x 19¾ .... (472)   1,300

Morning in Menton, 51½ x 38½ .... (399)   3,200

Nana After Manet, 45¾ x 32 .... (399)   2,020

1965

Seated Young Woman, 1939, on cardboard,
  41½ x 23 .... (567)   2,396

Portait with a Red Dress, 31½ x 23¼ .... (628)   813

Young Dancer, 1945, on cardboard, 21¼ x 14¾ ... (547)   760

Landscape, Le Croisic, 1953, 23¾ x 28½ .... (567)   1,808

Morning in Menton, 51½ x 38½ .... (512)   3,260

Recollection of Ghardaja, 1955, on panel,
  32½ x 26 .... (547)   1,260

Flowers, 21 x 31¼ .... (535)   1,050

Children in the Doorway, 25¾ x 21¼ .... (518)   2,000

1966

Still Life, 19¾ x 25¾ .... (681)   1,220

Walk on the Pier at Roscoff, 1927, on cardboard,
  12¾ x 15¼ .... (793)   740

Garden in the South of France, 23¾ x 33¾ .... (741)   1,800

Rider, pavatex, 33 x 14¼ .... (798)   1,853

Young Lady in a Straw Hat, oil on paper laid
  down on canvas, 25 x 15 .... (701)   1,700

Young Woman in a Blue Hat, on cardboard,
  29 x 17 .... (745)   1,582

1967

Restaurant "Ledoyen," 21¼ x 29 .... (923)   1,300

Portrait of a Woman, on cardboard, 25 x 22 ...... (974)   620

Veiled Woman, on cardboard, 24 x 19¾ .... (905)   340

The Deer, 25¾ x 32 .... (901)   2,000

1968–July 1969

Still Life with Vegetables of Provence,
  32 x 25¾ .... (1049)   2,000

Still Life with a Sideboard, 39½ x 29 .... (1127)   2,760

At the Jardin des Plantes, 21¼ x 29 .... (1180)   1,160

Portrait of a Woman, on cardboard, 9 x 6½ ...... (1098)   480

Birds Under a Globe, on cardboard, 26½ x 14¼ .. (1178)   300

Cannes, 29 x 23¾ .... (1061)   1,800

Bagatelle Park, 25¾ x 36½ .... (1224)   1,600

Little Girl Seated at Table, 25¼ x 19¾ .... (1268)   3,480

Mark Tobey

(1890–   )

Birthplace: Centerville, Wisconsin, U.S.

1911 — Goes to New York.

1917 — First exhibition at the Knoedler Gallery, New York.

1922 — Discovers Cubism. Settles in Seattle, Washington, where he teaches at the Cornish School—until 1925.

1923 — Meets the Chinese painter Teng Kuei, who introduces him to Chinese brushwork.

1925 — Goes to Europe and settles in Paris. Visits Barcelona, Greece, Istanbul, Beirut, and Haifa.

1927 — Returns to Seattle.

1930 — Moves to Great Britain, where he teaches at the Dartington Hall School—until 1937.

1931 — Trip to Mexico.

1932 — Travels in Europe and visits Palestine.

1934 — Stay in China and Japan with Teng Kuei.

1935 — First "White Writings." Paints "Broadway Norm." Completes the elaboration of his style.

1939 — Returns to Seattle.

1944 — One-man show at the Willard Gallery, New York.

1948 — Participates in the Venice Biennial—and again in 1956 and 1958. Exhibits at the Otto Seligman Gallery, Seattle.

1951 — Participates in "Abstract Painting and Sculpture in America" at the Museum of Modern Art, New York. Retrospective exhibition at the Whitney Museum of American Art, New York. Participates in the São Paulo Biennial—and again in 1955.

1952 — Participates in the International Exhibition at the Carnegie Institute, Pittsburgh—and again in 1955 and 1958.

1954–55 — Spends one year in Europe. One-man show at the Institute of Contemporary Art, London. Retrospective exhibition at the Art Institute of Chicago. One-man show at the Galerie Jeanne Bûcher, Paris.

1956 — Returns to Seattle.

1959 — Murals for the Washington State Library of Olympia. Participates in Documenta II, Kassel.

1960–62 — Retrospective exhibitions at the Museum of Pasadena, California, and at the Musée des Arts Décoratifs, Paris. Settles in Basel. Retrospective exhibitions at the Whitechapel Art Gallery, London; the Museum of Modern Art, New York; the Cleveland Museum of Art; and the Art Institute of Chicago.

1966 — Exhibits at the Beyeler Gallery, Basel.

1968 — Exhibits at the Hanover Gallery, London.

Sales

DRAWINGS

1961–1962

Four Faces, 1954, pen, 10¾ x 5¼ . . . . (164) $ 412

1963

Composition in Black and White, India ink, 23¼ x 34¾ . . . . (249)   900

Faces, 1954, India ink, 10¾ x 5¼ . . . . (299)   560

1966

Composition, 1954, ink and gouache on gray paper, 6¼ x 8¼ . . . . (784) $1,300

1967

Market Rhythms, 1958, India ink with white lights, 18¾ x 16¾ . . . . (931) 2,441

1968–July 1969

Flight, 1957, sumi ink on rice paper, 23¼ x 34¼ . . (1246) 1,500

WATERCOLORS

1961–1962

Composition, 1954, tempera, 10¾ x 8¼ . . . . (149) 1,738

Within Itself, 1959, tempera, 11 x 8 . . . . (129) 2,197

1963

Milk Glass, 1954, watercolor, 17 x 11½ . . . . (189) 3,250

1964

Undersea Flora, 1954, tempera, 11 x 7¼ . . . . (461) 2,880

Cosmic Tension, 1959, tempera on cardboard, 9¾ x 12¾ . . . . (461) 3,840

Blaze of the Century, 1947, tempera on paper, 25¼ x 19½ . . . . (431) 4,500

Invitation to Space, 1961, gouache, 27 x 18¼ . . . . . (386) 4,600

1965

"The Bride and His Tree," 1943, tempera, 10 x 12 . . . . (507) 2,400

Abstraction, 1946, watercolor, 7¼ x 11 . . . . (494)   300

Beach Fragment, 1955, gouache, 35¼ x 25 . . . . (526) 8,000

Composition in Blue, Pink, Brown, and Dark Gray, 1958, tempera on paper laid down on panel, 44¼ x 34¾ . . . . (485) 10,500

Wild Field, 1959, tempera, 24 x 27¾ . . . . (592) 14,000

Little Party, 1960, gouache, 5¼ x 6½ . . . . (527) 1,400

The Two Images, 1960, gouache, 6¾ x 5 . . . . (624) 1,161

Composition, 1961, gouache, 7 x 8 . . . . (617) 1,684

Composition, 1961, tempera on paper on canvas, 43½ x 33¼ . . . . (485) 8,500

1966

Landscape with a Yellow House, 1912, watercolor, 15¾ x 13 . . . . (790)   425

Skylines, 1933, gouache, 12¾ x 19¾ . . . . (707) 1,500

Composition, 1954, watercolor and pencil, 7¼ x 14 . . . . (651) 2,000

Advance of History, 1964, tempera on paper laid down on board, 25½ x 19½ . . . . (751) 6,910

Composition, 1965, gouache, 9¼ x 6 . . . . (798) 1,808

Composition, gouache, 11 x 9 . . . . (749)   740

1967

Composition, 1958, tempera on black paper, 6¼ x 20 . . . . (931) 1,311

Released, (1949), tempera on paper, 15½ x 19½ . . . (864) 3,250

Beach, 1943, gouache and tempera, 5 x 6½ . . . . (919)   633

Gray World, 1959, tempera, 10 x 6¼ . . . . (1004) 1,700

New York, 1959, tempera, 8¼ x 16 . . . . (1004) 2,700

Composition, 1958, gouache, 4 x 11 . . . . (1004) 1,200

Composition, 1962, gouache, 16¾ x 11¾ . . . . (939) 2,211

Composition, 1962, watercolor, 3 x 4 . . . . (919)   260

Composition, 1964, tempera, 6 x 15 . . . . (963) 1,750

1968–July 1969

Abstraction, gouache and watercolor on board, 27 x 7½ . . . . (1208) 1,100

Blue Composition, gouache, 8½ x 7¼ . . . . (1174)   828

Self-Portrait, 1948, tempera on board, 14 x 7¼ .. **(1061)** $ 650
Small Universe, 1959, tempera and ink, 9 x 11 ... **(1187)** 3,304
 # 8, 1966, watercolor, 8¼ x 7¼ .... **(1231)** 425
 # 3, 1966, watercolor, 11½ x 8 .... **(1231)** 600
 # 4, 1966, watercolor, 12 x 8¼ .... **(1237)** 750
XI, 1950, pencil and tempera, 11¼ x 8½ .... **(1237)** 550
Bunch of Flowers, 1965, mixed media on paper,
13 x 9½ .... **(1237)** 1,150
Composition, 1954, mixed media on rice paper,
16 x 12½ .... **(1237)** 2,500
Meditative Series, (1954), tempera, 14 x 17¾ .... **(1268)** 5,614
Garden, 1956, 24¼ x 36¾ .... **(1272)** 4,560

PAINTINGS

1961-1962

Composition, 1955, oil on paper laid down on
canvas, 13½ x 17¾ .... **(167)** 1,120

1963

Composition, 1954, gouache, 10¾ x 8 .... **(299)** 350

1965

Saintly Fires, 1960, 6¾ x 4¾ .... **(489)** 800
Plane of Poverty, 1960, 77¼ x 44¾ .... **(485)** 15,000

1968-July 1969

Rhythms, 1961, on board, 25 x 18¾ .... **(1187)** 10,856
Spiral, 1963, oil on paper, 4¾ x 6¾ .... **(1129)** 320
The Bather, 1927, 24 x 18 .... **(1229)** 1,200

WATERCOLORS

1963

The Gathering, watercolor, 6½ x 8¾ .... **(246)** $ 42

PAINTINGS

1961-1962

Native Woman, 1928, 18¾ x 41½ .... **(152)** 1,000
The Village, 28½ x 43 .... **(96)** 2,500
Still Life, 1920, on panel, 17¾ x 24 .... **(161)** 320

1963

Still Life, 1920, on panel, 17½ x 23¼ .... **(275)** 700
The Hôtel de Ville of Paris, 1927, 14¾ x 17¾ ..... **(179)** 275

1966

Composition, 1931, on board, 15 x 11½ .... **(678)** 2,600

1967

Composition, 1930, 27 x 19 .... **(975)** 760
Composition, 1931, 29 x 17¾ .... **(975)** 1,900
Street Scene, New York, 1920, 18 x 25¾ .... **(963)** 1,100

1968-July 1969

Construction Composition, 1931, 23¾ x 19½ .... **(1145)** 6,250
Rhythm, 1932, 25¾ x 21¼ .... **(1145)** 3,250
Street Scene, New York, 1920, oil on paper laid
down on panel, 18 x 25¾ .... **(1018)** 3,500
Still Life, 1920, on cradled panel, 17¾ x 23½ .... **(1231)** 1,400
Retrato, 1940, 13¾ x 10 .... **(1248)** 275
The Village, 28½ x 43½ .... **(1248)** 3,500

Joaquin Torres-Garcia

(1874-1949)

Birthplace: Montevideo, Uruguay.

1891 Goes to Barcelona, where he studies mural painting.
1910 Trip to Paris and Brussels. Discovers Futurism, which exerts a strong influence upon him.
1917 Devotes himself entirely to painting.
1920-22 Stay in the U.S. and in Europe.
1924-32 Settles in Paris. Sets up his theory of "Constructivism." Contributes to the review *Cercle et Carré*.
1930 Participates in the exhibition "Cercle et Carré" at the Galerie 23, Paris—a major survey of abstract art organized by M. Seuphor.
1934 Returns to Montevideo, where he founds the Association of Constructivist Art and where he gradually wins fame.
1944 Issues "Universalismo Constructivo."
1949 Died.

Sales

DRAWINGS

1967

Composition, 1932, India ink, 9 x 7¼ .... **(870)** $ 575

Henri de Toulouse-Lautrec

(1864-1901)

Birthplace: Albi, France. (His family, descended from the Comtes de Toulouse, is one of the oldest in the French aristocracy.)

1878-79 As a result of two accidents, his legs are broken and become stunted. Executes many drawings displaying a natural and exceptional talent. (His entire work is based on drawing.) Horses are his favorite subject matter. Decides to become a painter.
1882-86 Enters the Ecole Nationale des Beaux-Arts, Paris, in the studio of Bonnat, and then in the studio of Cormon, where he meets Van Gogh. Impressed by Manet and above all by Degas. Settles in Montmartre, spending his time in the cabarets, at the circus, or at the Moulin de la Galette. Meets Pissarro, Gauguin, Seurat, and Degas.
1889 Exhibits for the first time at the Salon des Indépendants, Paris.
1891 Executes his first poster for the Moulin Rouge.

1892	Exclusively interested in depicting human beings, he portrays the singers and dancers of Montmartre: Aristide Bruant, Jane Avril, Yvette Guilbert, La Goulue, Valentin le Désossé, and Chocolat—and includes them in several of his works. First lithographs. Starts his series of brothel scenes.
1893	Exhibits at the Goupil Gallery, Paris—and also in 1898 in London.
1894-96	Trip to Brussels and London, where he meets Oscar Wilde and Whistler. Participates in the first exhibition of "La Libre esthétique," Brussels. Visits Holland, Spain, and Portugal.
1899	Undermined by alcohol, he has to be hospitalized. Produces his album *Au Cirque*.
1901	Died, in the castle of Malromé, Gironde.
1902	Retrospective exhibitions at the Salon des Indépendants and the Galerie Durand-Ruel, Paris.
1922	Inauguration of the Musée Toulouse-Lautrec, Albi.

Sales

DRAWINGS

1961–1962

Studies of Horses, Dogs, and Riders, pen,
8 x 11 . . . . (121) $ 920

Studies, 23 x 17¾ . . . . (71)   1,700

The Last Salutation,[1] 1887, India ink and
gouache, 23¾ x 17½ . . . . (128)   16,476

*Portrait of Charles de Toulouse-Lautrec Reading
"Le Figaro,"* charcoal, 23¾ x 17½ . . . . (128)   10,435

Horsewoman, double-sided drawing, 5½ x 8¼ . . . . (143)   3,616

Trot attelé, pen, 6 x 10 . . . . (143)   2,667

The Horse, wash, 6 x 4½ . . . . (71)   380

Two Jockeys, pen, 4¾ x 7¾ . . . . (64)   1,700

Bust of a Man, 8 x 4¾ . . . . (30)   600

Women and Men in Profile, 5 x 8¼ . . . . (68)   300

Caricatures and Heads, double-sided drawing,
pencil, 5 x 8¼ . . . . (128)   549

The Woman Gardener, pencil, 10 x 6½ . . . . (44)   700

Studies of Heads, pencil, 4¾ x 8 . . . . (152)   370

*Two Women, One Smoking, the Other Lying
Down,* colored pencil, 5¾ x 8¾ . . . . (152)   450

In the Sitting Room, colored pencil, 6½ x 10 . . . . . . (33)   1,100

In the Sitting Room, colored pencil, 6½ x 10 . . . . . (109)   800

Prostitute, pen, 4¾ x 3¾ . . . . (102)   440

Yvette Guilbert, 1898; *La Goulue; C'est Margot,*
three little drawings, pencil . . . . (85)   1,300

1963

Landscape, pencil, 5¾ x 9 . . . . (179)   425

Peasant Man and Woman, ink, 4 x 7 . . . . (290)   700

Sketch of Horses and Figures, double-sided
drawing, pencil, 8¾ x 5¼ . . . . (283)   1,017

The Team, black lead, 6 x 9½ . . . . (314)   1,130

Study of Cocks, Sowers, etc..., double-sided
drawing, pencil, 5 x 8½ . . . . (208)   600

Ox, Dog, Cat, pencil, 6¼ x 8 . . . . (305)   375

The Rider, pencil, double-sided drawing, 6 x 10 . . . (232)   1,672

The Horse, pencil, 10 x 5¾ . . . . (283)   791

Circus Scene, sepia ink, 8 x 5 . . . . (225)   800

A Man and His Dog, ink and wash, 12¾ x 24¾ . . . (265)   659

Study: Figures and Heads, double-sided drawing,
pen, 9 x 14 . . . . (316)   850

[1]Signed Treclau.

Portrait of a Man, pencil, 8 x 4¾ . . . . (255) $ 823

Figures at a Café, India-ink wash, 8¼ x 11½ . . . . . (206)   520

The Admiral, wash, 8¼ x 25¼ . . . . (185)   600

Studies Including a Pipe Smoker, double-sided
drawing, black lead and watercolor,
8¾ x 5¼ . . . . (318)   500

*Bust of a Woman in Profile; Men and Women in
Profile,* double-sided drawing, pencil,
4½ x 8¼ . . . . (241)   400

Bust of a Woman, pen, 6½ x 4½ . . . . (275)   600

Bust of Valentin le Désossé in Profile, India ink,
6½ x 4½ . . . . (307)   339

1964

Jockey on Horseback, (1882), ink, 5¾ x 9¾ . . . . . . (454)   2,488

The Waltzing Girls, (1896), colored pencil,
12¾ x 8¼ . . . . (454)   5,390

The Ball of the Moulin de la Galette, 1889, ink
and blue pencil, 33¾ x 37½ . . . . (416)   69,100

Edward VII, 1896, pencil, 3¾ x 3½ . . . . (392)   615

The Tightrope Dancer, 1899, colored pencil and
pastel, 18¼ x 12¾ . . . . (448)   23,000

The Milk of Masters, ink, 14 x 9 . . . . (453)   1,603

The Horsewoman, ink, 14 x 8¾ . . . . (453)   1,327

The Death of the Pig, ink, 8½ x 13 . . . . (453)   691

Lamartine, ink, 14 x 8¾ . . . . (453)   774

Peasant Man and Woman, ink and pencil, 4 x 7 . . (374)   725

Portrait of Michael, Bicycle Racer, black lead,
4¾ x 7¾ . . . . (350)   230

Seated Woman, 8¼ x 6 . . . . (366)   520

The Wasp-Waisted Corset, double-sided drawing,
10 x 6½ . . . . (366)   560

The Team, black lead, 8¾ x 12¾ . . . . (399)   2,600

1965

Study of a Man Walking, (1883), pencil,
8¼ x 5¼ . . . . (624)   691

Into the Saddle (recto), *Three Studies of Riders*
(verso), pencil, 7¼ x 9 . . . . (624)   2,073

Harnessed Horse, pencil, 6 x 9 . . . . (611)   700

Dogs and Wild Boars (recto), *Studies of Knights
in Armor, Stag and Dogs' Heads* (verso),
black lead, 8 x 11¾ . . . . (580)   500

*Horse and Feminine Face, Feminine Face in
Profile; Boat,* two drawings, black lead, each
6½ x 10 . . . . (564)   300

Study of a Coachman and Horse's Head, pen,
8¼ x 12¾ . . . . (530)   340

Horses, double-sided drawing, pencil, 6¼ x 10 . . . . (617)   2,102

Drinking Soldier, black lead, 9 x 6¾ . . . . (617)   1,017

The Troika (recto), *Rider and Dog* (verso), black
lead, 6¼ x 7½ . . . . (561)   1,000

The Bathers, pen, 5¼ x 8¾ . . . . (624)   1,327

Portrait of a Man, pencil and ink, 6¾ x 4½ . . . . . . (541)   600

Seated Woman, pencil heightened with white,
8¼ x 6 . . . . (606)   550

Self-Caricature, pencil, 3¾ x 2 . . . . (582)   1,327

Excursion Out at Sea, wash and pen,
14¾ x 12¾ . . . . (518)   2,300

Standing Nude, India ink, 6 x 3¾ . . . . (567)   1,130

1966

Studies of Horses and Riders, (1883), pen,
8½ x 14 . . . . (812)   2,349

A Horse and Its Jockey, (recto), (1884), *Study of
Horses' Heads,* (verso), pencil and ink,
6 x 9¼ . . . . (750)   1,382

Grazing Horse, pencil, 6½ x 10¼ . . . . (741)   900

La Ronde, blue and red pencil, 6½ x 10¼ . . . . (741) $ 820

A Japanese Looking at a Woman, 1889, pen,
7½ x 5½ . . . . (773)   2,460

Bird on a Branch, After Hokusaï's Manner,
(1894), pen and wash, 7½ x 4¾ . . . . (686)   1,244

Duck After Hokusaï's Manner, (1894), pen and
wash, 7½ x 4¾ . . . . (686)   1,382

Polecat Heads, pencil, 6¾ x 10½ . . . . (798)   565

Figures, pencil, 7 x 8¾ . . . . (798)   486

Dasiré Dihau (recto), *Buste Lauré* (verso), pencil,
7¼ x 4½ . . . . (768)   1,382

Réjane Playing Madame Sans-Gêne (recto), 1894,
Bust of a Woman (verso), pencil, 4½ x 7 . . . . (768)   1,327

Eros Vanné, 1894, pen, 6½ x 4¼ . . . . (768)   967

Debauchery, 1896, pen, 4 x 5½ . . . . (768)   2,211

The Barmaid, pen, 7½ x 4½ . . . . (768)   1,935

Woman with a Tub, blue pencil, 6¼ x 4 . . . . (768)   415

Woman in Front of a Mirror, black lead, 6 x 7¼ . . (741)   780

*Half-Length Portrait of Maurice Guilbert in
Profile,* black lead, 6¾ x 4½ . . . . (681)   1,020

Promenade of the Poodle, wash on a fan,
13 x 25 . . . . (753)   2,177

Paddock: The Jockey, pen, 8 x 5 . . . . (768)   3,317

Self-Portrait, pen, 5¾ x 4¾ . . . . (768)   2,488

Caricature of Doctor Gabriel Tapié de Céleyran,
pen, 8 x 5 . . . . (768)   1,658

Portrait of Gabriel Tapié de Céleyran, black lead,
12¼ x 8¼ . . . . (681)   2,040

Cheval se rendant à l'entrainement, black lead,
6¾ x 8¾ . . . . (681)   1,360

Clown with a Hoop, black lead, 6¾ x 8¾ . . . . (681)   2,500

Draft Horse, black lead, 6¾ x 4¾ . . . . (681)   360

Clown in a Dunce's Cap, black lead, 8¾ x 6¾ . . . . (681)   1,700

*The Circus Wings: Equestrienne, Clown, and
Horse,* black lead, 8¾ x 6¾ . . . . (681)   10,100

Lautrec Painting, in Left Profile (recto), *Figure
and Studies of Men's Heads* (verso), black
lead, 7 x 9 . . . . (681)   7,600

1967

*Bust of a Woman Wearing a Great Hat, and
Three Women's Heads* (recto), *Three
Horses* (verso), (1880), pencil, 10¼ x 6½ . . . . (881)   1,161

Woman's Toilette, wash, 23¾ x 18¾ . . . . (981)   16,400

The Soldier, pen, 5¼ x 3¾ . . . . (911)   1,420

Presumed Portrait of Charles Tapié de Céleyran,
pencil, 6½ x 9½ . . . . (911)   1,100

Woman's Head, (1894), pen, 8¾ x 5¾ . . . . (841)   1,200

*The Trainer and His Dog, and Two Other Circus
Characters,* pencil, 7¼ x 9 . . . . (881)   608

Cyrano de Bergerac in Procession (recto), *Three
Men* (verso), pencil, 7¼ x 9 . . . . (881)   663

Stag-Hunting Scene, black lead, 7½ x 11½ . . . . (857)   600

The Paddock, pencil, 7½ x 11¼ . . . . (857)   5,400

The Waiter at Maxim's, pencil, 4¼ x 7 . . . . (870)   500

At the Piano, pencil, 20½ x 10 . . . . (931)   4,746

Men's and Women's Heads, black lead,
6¾ x 8¾ . . . . (857)   270

Man Wearing a Bowler Hat, Back View (recto),
4¾ x 6½, *Study of a Woman* (verso), pencil,
8½ x 4½ . . . . (985)   616

Reclining Woman, pencil, 4½ x 7 . . . . (923)   600

Study of Riders and Figures, double-sided
drawing, pencil, 5¾ x 7¼ . . . . (923)   1,160

Notebook, including 38 pages of drawings and
inscriptions, pencil, 5¾ x 3¾ . . . . (939)   1,658

1968–July 1969

The Jockey, (1899), pencil, 6¾ x 10¼ . . . . (1085) $2,232

Back View of a Man (Oscar Wilde ?), pencil,
5¾ x 3¼ . . . . (1134)   3,304

Presumed Portrait of the Artist Brandes, pencil,
6¼ x 4½ . . . . (1174)   368

*Théâtre de l'Oeuvre, Bust of a Woman and
Bearded Gentleman,* pen, 6¼ x 3¾ . . . . (1191)   1,180

The Couple, pen, 5¾ x 3¾ . . . . (1088)   900

Hue, Hioup, Hin!, 4 x 6¾ . . . . (1089)   480

The Vine Harvester, charcoal stump and varnish
on canvas, 32 x 25¾ . . . . (1113)   10,800

The Bastinado, wash, 8¾ x 17½ . . . . (1222)   660

Sescau at the Moulin Rouge, 1894, India-ink
wash, 8¼ x 6¼ . . . . (1224)   3,440

At the Circus, in the Wings, (1896), 9 x 7 . . . . (1239)   10,800

Two Women, pen, 6¾ x 4¼ . . . . (1240)   1,680

Riders, Studies of a Head (recto), *Figures* (verso),
pencil, 5¼ x 7¼ . . . . (1240)   1,440

In the Street, (1879), pen, 7 x 5½ . . . . (1240)   480

At School, (1879), pen, 7 x 5½ . . . . (1240)   576

Woman and Monkey, pencil, 6 x 9½ . . . . (1241)   1,159

The Winner (recto), *Horses* (verso), pencil,
5½ x 7 . . . . (1241)   1,008

*Nude with a Washtub, Monsieur Cantenat,
Bordeaux,* two drawings, pencil, 6½ x 3½
and 6½ x 4 . . . . (1248)   2,400

The Artist Brandes, pencil, 6½ x 4½ . . . . (1254)   370

Study of Nudes, black lead, 6¼ x 8 . . . . (1265)   340

Study of Horses, pen, 7¼ x 10¾ . . . . (1265)   440

Study of Horses and Figures, four drawings,
4 x 6¾ . . . . (1265)   1,600

WATERCOLORS

1961–1962

Angling,[2] 1899, watercolor on paper laid down on
canvas, 11¾ x 24 . . . . (167)   5,600

La Goulue, watercolor, 6½ x 4¾ . . . . (37)   5,750

The Two Legendary Sisters, watercolor and
gouache, 12 x 10 . . . . (137)   6,500

Design for the Cover of the "Motographe,"
watercolor on a photograph, 10½ x 12¾ . . . . . (57)   250

1963

Seated Dancer with Pink Stockings, pastel,
21¼ x 17¾ . . . . (254)   188,600

The Clown; Two Studies, double-sided pastel,
pastel, charcoal, and colored pencil,
10¼ x 6½ . . . . (316)   7,250

1965

Cavalry Drill, (1880), watercolor, 6 x 10 . . . . (575)   1,935

1967

Rolande of the Rue des Moulins, gouache,
18¾ x 13¾ . . . . (857)   16,000

1968–July 1969

The Stairs of the House in the Rue des Moulins,
1899, pastel, 27 x 16¾ . . . . (1193)   11,151

Monk Seated in a Church, (1880), watercolor,
10 x 7¼ . . . . (1193)   4,956

The Falconer, watercolor, 9 x 5¾ . . . . (1224)   2,100

[2]Dedicated "A mon amie Renée Albert."

PAINTINGS

1961–1962

The Pier, on panel, 5½ x 9	(32)	$2,200
The Girl Clown, 18¾ x 12¾	(125)	58,000
In the Sitting Room of the Rue des Moulins, 1894, 23¾ x 15¾	(140)	54,920
The Polisher, (1887), 25¾ x 32	(83)	74,142

1963

The Milliner, oil on cardboard, 12¼ x 9	(259)	26,400
The Dog, on panel, 12¾ x 16¼	(206)	3,000
The Pier, on panel, 5½ x 9	(250)	400
Huntsman Tightening His Girth, 1879, on panel, 8 x 6¼	(225)	10,500
The Hunter,[3] (1880–81), on panel, 14 x 10	(245)	18,097
Ballet Scene, Seen from the Wings, 1886, 17½ x 33½	(245)	95,970

1964

Raoul Tapié de Céleyran Riding a Donkey, 1881, 23¾ x 19¾	(401)	50,400
Bulldog in Front of a Mouse Trap, on panel, 5¼ x 8¾	(465)	2,300
The Pier, on panel, 5½ x 9	(345)	540
Spartan Showing a Drunken Helot to His Son, (1883), on panel, 8¾ x 6½	(378)	3,164
Jane Avril, Back View, on cradled cardboard, 19 x 13	(464)	20,000
The Jockeys, 18¼ x 13	(340)	15,600
The Ball at the Opéra, peinture à l'essence on cardboard, 25¼ x 20½	(340)	80,000

1965

Study of a Bust, 1883, 9 x 11	(583)	2,322
Dancer in Her Dressing Room, 1885, peinture à l'essence, 45 x 39½	(594)	105,000
Woman Seated in a Garden, (1888–91), on board, 21¾ x 17¾	(594)	105,000
Study of a Man in the Nude, peinture à l'essence on tracing paper, 23¾ x 17½	(553)	4,400
Nude Combing Her Hair, 1896, peinture à l'essence, 22 x 16	(575)	22,112
The Man with a Boater,[4]	(493)	90,000

1966

The Polisher,[5] (1887), 25¾ x 32	(713)	30,000
Cabriolet, on panel, 6¾ x 9	(811)	8,200
Study of a Man in the Nude, (1883), 31¼ x 25	(686)	26,258
The Ball at the Opéra, (1894), on board, 25¼ x 21	(713)	100,000

1967

On the Stairs of the Rue des Moulins, 1893, on board, 26 x 21	(880)	55,280
Jockeys on Horseback, 25¾ x 17¾	(911)	60,000
Boat Drawing Near a Pier (recto), 1880, *Study of a Figure on a Beach* (verso), on panel, 5½ x 9	(888)	1,520

1968–July 1969

Yvette Guilbert, 1895, ceramic made at Ivry at Emile Mueller's, 20 x 11	(1109)	9,400
Palette, one of the artist's palettes,	(1224)	620

---

[3]Presumed portrait of the artist's father.
[4]Portrait of Jean Grenier.
[5]Sold in London in 1962 for $74,142.

Maurice Utrillo

(1883–1955)

Birthplace: Paris, France. Son of the artist Suzanne Valadon.

1891	Adopted by Miguel Utrillo, a Spanish painter.
1899	Works in a bank, from which he is soon dismissed owing to his immoderate drinking.
1900	Has treatment for alcoholism—and again in 1912, 1917, 1918, and 1921.
1902	Starts to paint at Montmagny, near Paris.
1903–04	Lives in Montmartre with his mother. Comes under a slight Impressionist influence. Executes a great number of paintings, mostly of Montmartre.
1905	Signs his work Maurice Utrillo V.
1907–14	"White period"—his most appreciated series of paintings.
1909	Exhibits for the first time at the Salon d'Automne, Paris. Francis Jourdain, Elie Faure, and Octave Mirbeau take an increasing interest in his work.
1913	First one-man show at the Galerie Eugène Blot, Paris.
1917	Zborowski, Modigliani's dealer, buys some of his pictures.
1919	Exhibits at the Galerie Lepoutre, Paris.
1921	Exhibits with Valadon at the Galerie Berthe Weil, Paris—and again in 1922. First monograph on him by Francis Carco.
1923	Exhibits with Valadon at the Galerie Bernheim-Jeune, Paris.
1924	Settles in the Avenue Junot in Montmartre with his mother and the painter André Utter.
1926	Stage decorations for Diaghilev's ballet *Birabeau.* Gradually wins fame.
1927	"Multicolored period." Produces a large number of paintings.
1930	Receives the Legion of Honor.
1936	Marries Madame Pauwels (Lucie Valore).
1938	Death of Suzanne Valadon.
1948	Retrospective exhibition at the Salon d'Automne, Paris.
1953	Retrospective exhibition at the Galerie Pétridès, Paris.
1955	Died, Dax.
1959	Retrospective exhibition at the Galerie Charpentier, Paris.

Sales

DRAWINGS

1961–1962

The Moulin de la Galette, pencil, 12¼ x 9½	(84)	$ 549
The Moulin de la Galette, 1938, colored pencil, 8 x 10¼	(124)	400

1963

Rue de l'Abreuvoir, pencil, 9¾ x 13¼	(232)	689

1964

The House, 1923, pencil on paper laid down on canvas, 7 x 8	(329)	850
Suburban Spot, 1923, colored pencil, 3¾ x 4	(409)	400
Street in Montmartre, wash, 7¾ x 10¼	(327)	240

The Moulin de la Galette, 1933, colored pencil,
22½ x 17½ .... (335) $ 700

Rue Ste. Rustique at Montmartre, pencil,
11¾ x 15½ .... (471) 1,096

Rue de l'Abreuvoir, pencil, 9¾ x 13¼ .... (471) 1,288

Church of St. Bernard, Ain, 1937, colored pencil,
14¼ x 9 .... (335) 1,600

1965

A Street of Montmartre, black lead and colored
pencil, 9 x 12¼ .... (548) 340

Street Scene, 1924, charcoal heightened with
pastel and colored pencil, 9 x 12¼ .... (582) 1,658

1966

The Moulin de la Galette, colored pencil,
11¾ x 15 .... (653) 2,040

The Mills at Montmartre, colored pencil,
6½ x 9½ .... (668) 600

Houses, black lead, 9½ x 12 .... (801) 800

Rue de l'Abreuvoir, pencil, 9¾ x 13¼ .... (798) 2,260

1967

Sunday at Montmartre, 1955, colored pencil,
15¾ x 21¾ .... (935) 2,300

A Street in Montmartre, colored pencil,
17½ x 16¾ .... (918) 5,198

Village Church, colored pencil, 12¾ x 10 .... (886) 960

Village Church, colored pencil, 12¾ x 10 .... (858) 1,160

Self-Portrait, 1955, ink and pencil, 15½ x 12 ..... (951) 755

1968–July 1969

Figures by the Seaside, colored pencil, 4¼ x 5¾ . (1121) 1,500

Church of St. Bernard, Ain, colored pencil,
9½ x 11 .... (1113) 2,000

The Lapin Agile, black lead and colored pencil,
7 x 11 .... (1053) 900

Fantastic Sonnet, colored pencil, 8 x 6¼ .... (1088) 350

The Sacré-Coeur,[1] colored chalk, 17½ x 16¾ .... (1273) 6,300

WATERCOLORS

1961–1962

Church of St. André, Angoulême, 1920, gouache,
18¾ x 25¼ .... (69) 7,584

L'Impasse, 1922, gouache, 9 x 13 .... (71) 7,000

The Farm, watercolor and gouache, 11¾ x 11 ...... (95) 2,600

The Windmill, gouache, 9½ x 9½ .... (138) 3,300

St. Roch, Château de Chavannes, 1928, gouache,
10¾ x 13½ .... (143) 4,158

*Rue Ravignan and the Sacré-Coeur at
Montmartre,* (1935), gouache, 18¾ x 25 .... (88) 5,658

The Pont Neuf, watercolor, 9 x 12¼ .... (30) 2,100

Avenue Junot at Montmartre, gouache,
9 x 12¼ .... (29) 4,200

The Church of Domrémy, 1936, gouache,
19 x 23¾ .... (18) 3,074

Country Church, pastel, 9½ x 12¼ .... (15) 1,264

1963

*The Barracks of Lourcine, Boulevard de Port-
Royal,* 1923, gouache, 10 x 13 .... (202) 4,500

A Walk, 1933, pastel, 11¾ x 17½ .... (232) 2,622

Montreval Church, Ain, gouache, 11½ x 8¼ ...... (232) 1,017

The Cour du Dragon, Rue de Rennes, 1934,
gouache, 17 x 12¾ .... (210) 4,387

Street Scene, gouache and watercolor,
12 x 18¾ .... (316) 3,000

The Street, gouache, 12¾ x 19½ .... (283) $8,814

The Moulin de la Galette, gouache on a menu,
5¼ x 3¾ .... (238) 1,040

Place Jean-Baptiste Clément, in Montmartre,
gouache, 25¾ x 19 .... (232) 6,441

1964

The Rue des Abbesses, 1922, gouache, 10 x 34 .... (368) 4,146

Two Women, 1923, watercolor and gouache,
11 x 10 .... (346) 930

The Hoardings, 1923, watercolor, 9½ x 12¼ ...... (465) 1,960

The Moulin de la Galette, 1925, round
watercolor, diameter 7¾ .... (471) 1,763

Royan Harbor, 1936, gouache, 18¾ x 24 .... (354) 4,500

The Lapin Agile in Montmartre, 1938, gouache,
12¼ x 9½ .... (399) 3,400

The Sacré-Coeur, gouache, 15 x 11½ .... (335) 3,200

Notre-Dame, gouache, 12¾ x 9 .... (340) 1,600

The Eiffel Tower, gouache, 11¾ x 9 .... (340) 1,600

Montmartre, gouache on a menu, 4½ x 3¾ .... (409) 1,560

1965

Street in Montmartre, 1922, gouache, 8 x 10½ ... (553) 4,000

The Rue des Abbesses, 1923, gouache, 15¾ x 21 .. (518) 5,200

The Garden in Montmartre, gouache, 9¾ x 13½ .. (567) 8,701

The Moulin de la Galette, 1925, watercolor,
10 x 14 .... (561) 2,620

Suburban Street, gouache, 14 x 21¼ .... (638) 4,920

Suburb Under Snow, gouache, 19¾ x 25¼ .... (561) 9,600

1966

Villa at Ecouen, 1923, gouache, 15 x 18¾ .... (686) 6,910

Still Life, 1928, watercolor and gouache,
20 x 14¾ .... (665) 1,900

Portrait of Maurice de Vlaminck, watercolor,
13½ x 10 .... (743) 1,700

*Sacré-Coeur de Montmartre and St. Pierre
Square,* 1933, gouache, 8¾ x 13 .... (743) 4,120

The Moulin de la Galette, 1933, gouache,
18¼ x 12 .... (694) 7,500

The Lapin Agile, pastel, 7½ x 11¾ .... (656) 860

Rue de l'Abreuvoir, 1933, gouache, 11½ x 17¾ .... (701) 5,500

The Lapin Agile, 1938, gouache, 12¼ x 9 .... (741) 4,800

Suburb, tempera, 7¼ x 10¼ .... (802) 4,480

Montmartre, gouache, 19 x 25¼ .... (744) 10,170

Rue du Mont Cenis, gouache, 18¼ x 21¼ .... (797) 9,040

The Grande Rue at Marly-le-Roi, gouache,
25 x 19¾ .... (797) 9,718

1967

The Moulin de la Galette, 1922, gouache,
10 x 14 .... (923) 3,920

St. Eloi Mill, 1923, watercolor and gouache,
14¾ x 19 .... (899) 5,904

The White Villa, 1924, gouache on paper laid
down on board, 9½ x 12 .... (940) 2,322

A Street at Marly-le-Roi, 1925, gouache,
25 x 19¾ .... (965) 9,718

The Chapel of Le Puy at Bourganeuf, 1927,
gouache, 19¾ x 14¾ .... (852) 3,820

A Corner of the Rue de Seine Near the Institut,[2]
1927, watercolor and gouache, 12¼ x 9½ .... (923) 4,200

Landscape at Chamelet, Rhône, 1930, gouache,
13 x 19½ .... (898) 4,020

Rue Auguste Schenk, Ecouen, 1935, gouache,
18¾ x 24½ .... (864) 11,250

---

[1]Dedicated "Au Docteur Laforêt."

[2]Dedicated "A Chéron, Roi de la Brocante."

*The House Where Joan of Arc Was Born at
    Domrémy*, 1935, gouache, 18¾ x 25 .... **(987)** $ 6,000

The Tower of Philippe-Auguste in Rouen, 1936,
    gouache, 25 x 18¾ .... **(989)**   4,500

Lively Street, gouache, 12¼ x 15½ .... **(978)**   3,400

A Street of Paris, Near the Eiffel Tower,
    gouache, 25 x 18¾ .... **(993)**   7,500

The Rue du Mont-Cenis, gouache, 12¾ x 15½ ... **(1004)**   7,000

1968–July 1969

The Rue des Abbesses, 1922, gouache,
    9½ x 13¼ .... **(1193)**   12,390

St. Bernard Church, 1925, gouache, 22 x 25¾ .... **(1125)**   10,350

Menu: Shrove Tuesday, 1926, watercolor,
    10½ x 8 .... **(1202)**   4,100

A Corner of the Rue de Seine Near the Institut,
    1927, watercolor and gouache, 12¼ x 9½ .... **(1109)**   7,200

The Porte Neuve, Vézelay, 1932, gouache,
    13 x 16 .... **(1216)**   7,500

Castle of Ganay, Côte d' Or, 1933, gouache,
    14¾ x 20 .... **(1049)**   6,500

*The House Where Joan of Arc Was Born and the
    Church of Domrémy*, gouache, 14¾ x 19½ .. **(1132)**   8,732

The Lapin Agile, pastel, 7¾ x 9¾ .... **(1006)**   2,400

The Lapin Agile, gouache, 18¾ x 11¾ .... **(1137)**   8,000

The Lapin Agile, gouache, 13 x 20 .... **(1108)**   7,590

Montmartre, gouache, 10 x 12¾ .... **(1173)**   7,360

Montmartre in Winter, gouache on paper laid
    down on canvas, 15½ x 22¾ .... **(1080)**   7,000

The Rue St. Vincent, gouache, 18¼ x 23¾ ...... **(1117)**   9,900

Place Jean-Baptiste Clément in Montmartre,
    gouache, 19½ x 25 .... **(1176)**   17,500

The Eiffel Tower, gouache, 12¾ x 9 .... **(1018)**   3,500

Figures in the Square, 1923, gouache, 9¼ x 12½ . **(1224)**   10,000

*Sacré-Coeur of Montmartre and St. Pierre
    Square*, 1935, 7½ x 6¼ .... **(1226)**   9,000

"Au Consulat d'Auvergne," Rue Norvins, 1938,
    19 x 25 .... **(1235)**   14,500

View of Montmartre,[3] gouache, 10¾ x 8½ .... **(1258)**   6,400

Alfortville, 1924, gouache, 9 x 12¼ .... **(1261)**   9,200

PAINTINGS

1961–1962

Street at Montmagny, 1908, 21¼ x 29 .... **(29)**   25,200

The Church of Montmagny, (1908-09), on panel,
    19¾ x 28¾ .... **(8)**   36,500

A Street at Conquet in Brittany, (1911), 24 x 32 .... **(83)**   30,206

The Moulin de la Galette, (1911), 8¾ x 13 .... **(90)**   1,440

Church St. Jacques du Haut-Pas, (1911-12),
    25¾ x 19¾ .... **(8)**   28,000

The Wall of the Garden, 1912, 21¾ x 28¾ .... **(128)**   15,103

The Walk, 9½ x 13 .... **(30)**   2,160

Place Ravignan, (1912-13), on cardboard,
    10¾ x 14 .... **(93)**   12,204

The Abbey of Breuil, 18¼ x 21¾ .... **(141)**   4,700

The Cathedral of St. Claude, 18¾ x 24½ .... **(141)**   6,200

Lighthouse in Brittany, 1912, 18¼ x 25 .... **(164)**   7,140

The Rue Cortot, (1913), on cardboard,
    17¾ x 13½ .... **(73)**   8,400

Fontainebleau, 1913, on cardboard, 12¾ x 16¾ ... **(171)**   11,400

Montmartre, the Moulin de la Galette, 15 x 22 ... **(171)**   6,060

The Moulin de la Galette, 8½ x 12¾ .... **(26)**   1,800

[3] In the same frame, *Flowers*, a gouache by Lucie Valore, 1953.

Montmartre, the Gardens of the Sacré-Coeur,
    1914, on cradled cardboard, 16¼ x 20 ... **(32)** $7,000

The Moulin de la Galette, (1914-16), on board,
    23¾ x 19¾ .... **(96)**   9,500

Rue de l'Abreuvoir, 11¾ x 14¼ .... **(18)**   6,328

Villa with a Park, (1913-15), on panel,
    15½ x 18¾ .... **(96)**   6,000

Rue de Sannois Under Snow, 19½ x 23¾ .... **(71)**   7,200

The White Church, 19¾ x 24½ .... **(71)**   10,600

*Chapel of the Sisters of St. Vincent de Paul at
    Clichy-sur-Seine*, 1915, on cardboard,
    20½ x 29¼ .... **(88)**   12,792

The Mill of Sannois, 1915, 21 x 29¼ .... **(145)**   14,220

A la Belle Gabrielle, (1918-19), on panel,
    24 x 19 .... **(84)**   6,590

St. Bernard Church, Ain, 1924, 9 x 11¾ .... **(143)**   6,554

Bassieux Castle at Anse, Rhône, 1925, on
    cardboard, 11 x 14¾ .... **(116)**   4,600

*The Church and the Rue St. Jacques at Cosne,
    Nièvre*, 1925, 29¼ x 40 .... **(18)**   18,306

Landscape, 17¾ x 21 .... **(93)**   10,848

The Church of Villiers-le-Bel, Seine-et-Oise,
    25¾ x 21¼ .... **(124)**   4,200

The Church of Verderonne, Oise, 1927,
    25¾ x 32 .... **(76)**   6,400

Limas, Rhône, 1929, 25¼ x 35¾ .... **(64)**   16,000

Montmartre, 1932, 110½ x 67¼ .... **(93)**   22,600

*Montmartre with the Sacré-Coeur in the
    Background*, 17¾ x 23½ .... **(31)**   5,492

La Clayette Castle, Saône-et-Loire, 1934 .... **(76)**   7,600

The Boulevard, 19¾ x 24 .... **(6)**   12,204

A Street at Bourg-la-Reine, on cardboard,
    19¾ x 25¾ .... **(6)**   8,814

The Sacré-Coeur, 20 x 16¼ .... **(20)**   18,960

The Moulin de la Galette, 1937, 20¾ x 16¾ .... **(67)**   3,626

View of the Castle of Bussy, St. Julien,
    14¾ x 17¼ .... **(67)**   7,251

Beauvallon, the Gulf, on cardboard, 15½ x 19¾ ... **(114)**   6,400

Rue Norvins, oil on cardboard, 12¼ x 8¼ .... **(29)**   2,040

The Rue Norvins, 15 x 18¼ .... **(68)**   7,300

Bunch of Flowers, 1940, on cardboard,
    10¾ x 8¾ .... **(68)**   1,800

The Eiffel Tower, 17¾ x 54¼ .... **(64)**   10,500

A Street at Auteuil, (1941-42), 21¾ x 18¼ .... **(167)**   12,000

1963

The Factory at Aubervilliers, (1908), on panel,
    22 x 28¾ .... **(210)**   15,904

Near the Moulin de la Galette, 23¾ x 29 .... **(243)**   10,400

Suburban Landscape, 18¼ x 21¾ .... **(243)**   7,400

Landscape, 19¾ x 25¾ .... **(506)**   7,840

The Lapin Agile at Montmartre, 1913, 23¼ x 31 .. **(316)**   33,000

Garden in Montmartre, 1914, oil on cradled
    panel, 15¾ x 20 .... **(283)**   13,108

Groslay Church, (1914), on panel, 21¾ x 29 ...... **(225)**   11,000

Village Road Under Snow, 12½ x 17½ .... **(203)**   6,000

Village Road Under Snow, on cardboard,
    12½ x 17½ .... **(306)**   4,220

Street at Sannois, 1915, 23½ x 31½ .... **(247)**   21,388

The House of Berlioz, 1916, 20¾ x 28½ .... **(202)**   7,750

The Barracks at Compiègne, (1916), on
    cardboard, 14¾ x 21 .... **(232)**   20,792

The Castle of Chillon, (1916), on board,
    20½ x 25¼ .... **(210)**   10,420

[4]The house of Berlioz.

[5]The house of Berlioz.

The Red House, 19¾ x 24½ .... (637) $ 13,000
A Street in Montmartre, 12¾ x 15½ .... (583) 6,965
Montmartre, on cradled panel, 26 x 25¾ .... (503) 6,700
Flowers, Christmas, 1954, on cardboard,
   10 x 7¾ .... (616) 4,160

1966

Thatch-Roofed Cottages in a Garden in Bloom,
   9½ x 12¾ .... (682) 3,500
Notre-Dame and the River Seine, (1905-06), on
   cardboard, 8¼ x 11 .... (745) 11,978
Suburban Church, (1909), on board mounted on
   cradled panel, 21¾ x 29 .... (707) 16,000
Street of Montmartre, (1910), 25¾ x 36½ .... (801) 20,400
The Castle, (1911), 23 x 31½ .... (750) 18,795
Corte, Corsica, (1912), 24 x 32½ .... (776) 16,000
Rue Ravignan, Paris, (1913), on board,
   21¼ x 29¼ .... (776) 23,000
Suburban Street, 13 x 16¼ .... (808) 6,965
The Lapin Agile, (1914), on board, 22 x 30¾ ...... (750) 38,696
The Abbey of Breuil, (1916), on panel, 15 x 21½ .. (689) 5,528
Rue du Mont-Cenis,[6] (1920), 35½ x 27¾ .... (797) 12,204
The Moulin de la Galette, 8¾ x 11¾, *The Tile-
   Roofed House,* 1922, 8¾ x 11½, two pictures
   on cardboard .... (685) 20,000
A Street in Montmartre, 18¼ x 21¾ .... (681) 9,820
The Lapin Agile, 19¾ x 25¾ .... (681) 15,700
The Lapin Agile, on cardboard, 21¼ x 14¼ .... (792) 11,562
The Church of Villetanneuse, (1923),
   18¼ x 21¼ .... (819) 11,000
Restaurant at Robinson, 1924, 13½ x 18¾ .... (812) 13,820
The Moulin de la Galette, 1925, 4¾ x 7¼ .... (677) 2,280
Bassieux Castle, 1927, on cardboard,
   11½ x 15½ .... (802) 7,680
A Flowerpot, 1928, on cradled panel, 7½ x 5¾ .... (784) 1,600
Church and Castle of Pont-à-Mousson, 1928,
   39½ x 29 .... (724) 13,000
Church, Notre-Dame de Royan, 39½ x 25¾ ...... (749) 10,800
Basilica of Ars, 1929, 25¾ x 32 .... (713) 13,500
Ouroux Church, 1930, 25¾ x 32 .... (745) 6,554
"La Rue Jeanne d'Arc prolongée à Paris," 1934,
   on canvas, laid down on panel, 23 x 31¼ ..... (812) 13,820
A Street at Auteuil, 1936, on cradled panel,
   22½ x 26½ .... (814) 17,000
The Moulin Rouge, on board, 21¼ x 17¾ .... (753) 10,157
Church Under Snow, 1937, 21¼ x 25¾ .... (819) 12,000
Street Under Snow, on cardboard, 18¼ x 21¾ .... (656) 10,000

1967

A Mill at Sannois, (1910), 23¼ x 31½ .... (940) 13,059
Red House at Sannois, (1922), 23 x 31½ .... (938) 37,314
The Lapin Agile, 1912, 20½ x 27¼ .... (858) 18,800
*The Philosopher Tower and the Moulin de la
   Galette,* 1912-14, on cardboard, 20½ x 29 .... (965) 27,120
The Enclosure, 1915, 13¼ x 16¼ .... (995) 8,800
Shanty on the Outskirts of a Wood, 9¾ x 13¾ .... (909) 6,000
Church, (1916), on canvas laid down on board,
   23¾ x 19¾ .... (963) 9,000
The Portal of the Entrance of the Church,
   24 x 19¾ .... (995) 12,240
The Bridge and the Church, Yonne, 1920,
   21¼ x 25½ .... (962) 12,000
The Church of Villetanneuse, 1920, 20 x 26¾ ..... (857) 9,600
The Castle, (1920), on panel, 9 x 12¼ .... (923) 3,000

[6]The house of Berlioz.

The Moulin de la Galette, 1920-21, on cardboard,
   12¾ x 15 .... (857) $ 6,600
The Moulin de la Galette, on cardboard,
   14 x 10¾ .... (931) 11,752
The House of Berlioz, (1920), 35½ x 27¾ .... (844) 14,200
A Street in Montmartre, 14 x 18¼ .... (923) 8,400
Church and Castle of Pont-à-Mousson, 1928,
   38¾ x 28½ .... (988) 3,636
Arbresle Castle, Rhône, 1928, 23¾ x 29 .... (954) 19,000
Church of St. Germain des Prés, 1935, 29 x 23¾ .. (938) 13,820
St. Bonnet Chapel at Montmélias, 1935,
   23¾ x 32 .... (935) 2,900
The Rue Lepic in Montmartre, 1938, 19¾ x 24 .... (987) 12,200
Portrait of Madame Utrillo, 1938 .... (993) 4,500
The Sacré-Coeur, 21¾ x 18¼ .... (882) 10,400
The Moulin de la Galette and the Sacré-Coeur,
   17¾ x 21¼ .... (938) 7,739
Groslay Church, (1940-45), 14¾ x 18 .... (963) 10,500
The Mill, on cradled cardboard, 15 x 21¾ .... (901) 12,000
The Church at Puteaux, 24 x 19¾ .... (901) 11,000
The Bridge of St. Ouen, 19¾ x 25¾ .... (923) 10,400
The White Hat .... (993) 2,900

1968–July 1969

Castle of Montmartre, (1906), on panel,
   14 x 21¼ .... (1039) 3,200
Rue de l'Abreuvoir, (1909), 19¾ x 25¾ .... (1199) 35,800
Pontoise Church, 24 x 19¾ .... (1173) 19,320
The Mill of Sannois, (1910), 23¾ x 31½ .... (1173) 26,450
Boulevard Arago, (1910), 25¾ x 32 .... (1125) 24,150
Rue de Montmartre, (1911), 21 x 28¾ .... (1126) 69,384
Montguichet Castle, (1911), 23¾ x 31½ .... (1132) 30,680
The Rue du Mont-Cenis, (1911-15), on board
   mounted on panel, 25 x 32¾ .... (1193) 64,428
The Square with Palms, (1912), 26½ x 42¼ ...... (1200) 25,000
Groslay Church, (1912), 22 x 30 .... (1132) 23,600
The Moulin de la Galette and the Sacré-Coeur,
   on cradled panel, 9½ x 13 .... (1113) 9,000
The Mill at Montmartre and the Sacré-Coeur,
   (1915), on cardboard, 12¾ x 13½ .... (1026) 10,000
The Apse of Chaucouin, Seine-et-Marne, (1916),
   on board, 20½ x 29 .... (1057) 15,000
The Church Square at Pontoise, (1916),
   23¾ x 29 .... (1125) 18,400
Snowy Landscape, (1917), on board, 19¾ x 25¾ . (1193) 29,736
The Gobelins, (1922), 19¾ x 25¾ .... (1069) 10,960
The Castle of La Pierre, on cardboard,
   18¼ x 26½ .... (1202) 14,000
Andorri Church, 1922, 23¾ x 19¾ .... (1202) 16,000
"Aux Marronniers" at Robinson, 1922-23, on
   cardboard, 19¾ x 25¾ .... (1199) 22,200
A Street at Ivry, 1924, 21 x 27¾ .... (1152) 30,000
Longpont Basilica, Seine-et-Oise, 19¼ x 14 ..... (1126) 12,390
*Sunday in the Village: The House of Joan of Arc
   at Domrémy,* 1926, 25¾ x 36½ .... (1183) 20,000
The Sacré-Coeur of Montmartre, 1926,
   39½ x 32 .... (1152) 60,000
The Rue St. Vincent, 1930, on board mounted on
   panel, 24½ x 31 .... (1068) 21,240
A Street in Montmartre, (1930), on canvas laid
   down on panel, 14¾ x 17¾ .... (1187) 11,800
Church of Conflans d'Albertville, Savoie, 1934,
   23¾ x 17¾ .... (1187) 14,160
Place du Tertre in Winter, (1937), 13 x 16¼ ..... (1018) 6,500

The Flowers of the "14 Juillet," 1937, 18¾ x 15 .. **(1049)** $ 8,000
Paris, Hôtel Scipion, 21¾ x 29 .... **(1049)** 15,600
Montmartre "A la Belle Gabrielle," 18¼ x 21¾ .. **(1049)** 11,200
A Street of Montmartre, 18 x 21½ .... **(1176)** 30,000
The Bateau-Lavoir, on board, 12¾ x 17½ .... **(1145)** 6,750
The Thatch-Roofed Cottage, 8¼ x 12¾ .... **(1067)** 2,800
The Mill of Sannois, 23¼ x 32 .... **(1117)** 14,600
Landscape Near Montmagny, 8¾ x 11¾ .... **(1162)** 8,400
The Lapin Agile, on cradled panel, 14¼ x 21 .... **(1208)** 20,500
The Lapin Agile, 13 x 16¼ .... **(1125)** 11,730
Bunch of Lilies of the Valley,[7] 12¾ x 16¼ .... **(1125)** 8,050
Groslay Church, on cardboard laid down on
   canvas, 23 x 30½ .... **(1226)** 17,700
Barracks, 9¾ x 13¼ .... **(1231)** 8,000
A Street at Bourg-la-Reine, Seine, Rue Robierre
   de Vallaire, (1923), 19¾ x 25½ .... **(1235)** 32,500
Suburban Street, 19¾ x 9½ .... **(1235)** 25,000
The Bridge of the Avenue de St. Ouen, (1913-14),
   21½ x 28¾ .... **(1235)** 51,000
St. Pierre Church and the Sacré-Coeur, 18 x 22 . **(1235)** 19,000
A Street in Montmartre, (1915), on board laid
   down on panel, 19¼ x 28 .... **(1239)** 18,000
Dourdan: View of the Castle and the Church,
   28¾ x 23¾ .... **(1241)** 21,500
Rue de Limas, Rhône, 1929, 25 x 36 .... **(1241)** 29,000
The "Café Briard," Paris, 24 x 19½ .... **(1241)** 22,700
A la Belle Gabrielle, on board, 9¼ x 7½ .... **(1248)** 8,000
The Stream Bièvres at the Gobelins, (1920),
   10¾ x 13 .... **(1252)** 12,800
Marolles Church, 21¼ x 27¾ .... **(1254)** 20,400
The House in the Forest, 8½ x 12½ .... **(1258)** 7,200
Montmartre: The Rue du Mont-Cenis,
   15 x 23¾ .... **(1258)** 20,000
The Abbey of the Pointe St. Mathieu, 23 x 32 ... **(1268)** 30,160
Rue du Mont-Cenis with the House of Berlioz,
   1914, 25¾ x 36½ .... **(1268)** 58,000
Flowers and Poems,[8] on cardboard, 25¼ x 19 .... **(1268)** 12,992
Groslay Church, (1912-14), on cardboard,
   23 x 30½ .... **(1268)** 47,120
Landscape with a Mill, on cradled panel, 3 x 4 ... **(1268)** 2,784
The Mill, 8¾ x 11½ .... **(1268)** 9,976
The Church Square at Poissy, 22 x 29¾ .... **(1268)** 17,169
The Mill of Sannois, 15 x 21¾ .... **(1268)** 20,880
Rue St. Rustique, (1920), 22 x 18 .... **(1270)** 25,200
Works Site at the Gobelins, 1922, 17¾ x 23¾ .... **(1270)** 33,600
A Church in Provence, (1925), 19¾ x 25½ .... **(1270)** 36,000

[7] Dedicated to Lucie Valore.
[8] Dedicated "A Jojo Poulbot, Paris, Montmartre, an 1928."

Suzanne Valadon

(1865–1938)

Birthplace: Bessines-sur-Gartemps, Limousin, France. (As Marie-Clémentine Valadon.)

1880   Becomes a professional model, sitting for Puvis de Chavannes, Renoir, Toulouse-Lautrec, and Degas.

1883   Starts to draw. Birth of her son, the future Maurice Utrillo.

1894   Thanks to Degas, who encourages her to paint, she exhibits at the Salon de la Société Nationale des Beaux-Arts, Paris.

1896   Marries Paul Moussis. Devotes herself entirely to painting. Sells some of her works to Le Barc de Boutteville and to Ambroise Vollard.

1909   Divorces Paul Moussis to live with the painter André Utter.

1910   Participates in the Salon d'Automne, Paris.

1911   First one-man show at Clovis Sagot's, Paris.

1913   Participates in a group show at the Galerie Berthe Weill, Paris.

1914   Marries André Utter.

1915   One-man show at the Galerie Berthe Weil, Paris.

1920   Takes part in "La Jeune Peinture française" at the Galerie Manzy-Joyant, Paris.

1921   Exhibits with Utrillo and Utter at Berthe Weil's, Paris—and again in 1922.

1923   Exhibits with Utrillo at Bernheim-Jeune's, Paris.

1926   Retrospective exhibition, including "Les Lanceurs de filets," at the Salon des Indépendants, Paris.

1927   Retrospective exhibition at the Galerie Berthe Weil, Paris.

1931   Major retrospective exhibition at the Galerie Le Centaure, Brussels. Private exhibition at the Galerie Le Portique, Paris—and again in 1932.

1932   Retrospective exhibition at the Galerie Georges Petit, Paris.

1938   Died, Paris.

Sales

DRAWINGS

1961–1962

Utrillo Aged Nine,[1] pencil, 9 x 11¾ .... **(141)** $4,200
The Try-On, heightened charcoal, 23¾ x 18½ .... **(141)** 1,640
The Sleeping Model, heightened charcoal,
   16¾ x 21¼ .... **(141)** 1,000
The Model, pencil, 7½ x 7½ .... **(141)** 2,000
Woman at Her Toilette, 1909, charcoal with
   gouache lights, 14 x 10¾ .... **(32)** 900
Nude Putting On Her Stockings, colored pencil,
   14¾ x 11¾ .... **(68)** 1,500
Bathers, charcoal on tracing paper, 16¼ x 22½ .... **(35)** 320
Reclining Young Woman in the Nude, red chalk,
   17¾ x 23¾ .... **(155)** 360
Woman in the Nude, Conté pencil, 11¾ x 7 .... **(76)** 130
The Bath, pencil and pastel, 10¼ x 11½ .... **(125)** 2,460
Study of a Seated Woman in the Nude, 1922,
   charcoal heightened with pastel, 18¼ x 15 ..... **(80)** 800

[1] Inscribed "Mon Utrillo à 9 ans."

Study of a Man in the Nude, black lead,
12 x 4¼ . . . . (58) $ 140
The Court of St. Bernard Castle, black lead,
6¾ x 7¾ . . . . (177) 66
Still Life with Fruit, three drawings, Conté
pencil, 6½ x 4, 7¼ x 4½, 10 x 7¾ . . . . (76) 860

1963

Nude with a Sofa, 1894, India ink, 8 x 8¾ . . . . (254) 360
After the Bath, (1895), charcoal, 7¼ x 6 . . . . (255) 1,097
Woman at Her Toilette, 1909, charcoal,
13 x 10½ . . . . (241) 780
Nude Sponging Her Back, black pencil,
5¾ x 4¾ . . . . (232) 949
Bathers, charcoal on tracing paper, 16¾ x 23¼ . . . (238) 420
Study of a Nude, charcoal, 23 x 14¼ . . . . (293) 240

1964

Reclining Nude with Raised Arms, 1904, charcoal,
11¾ x 15½ . . . . (371) 1,100
Nude with a Mirror, charcoal, 8 x 6 . . . . (340) 1,200
Nude with Red Hair, (1909), charcoal and red
chalk, 23 x 10¾ . . . . (401) 760
Nude, 1909, 13 x 10¾ . . . . (471) 949
Seated Woman in the Nude, 1916, Conté pencil,
15¾ x 11½ . . . . (408) 260
Woman in the Nude, pencil, 11¾ x 7¼ . . . . (384) 132
Reclining Young Woman on a Sofa, red chalk,
7¼ x 8¾ . . . . (398) 800
Young Nude on a Sofa, 8¼ x 11½ . . . . (445) 5,000
Tub Time, red chalk, 13 x 16¾ . . . . (452) 5,200

1965

Standing Nude, 1900, black pencil, 23 x 10¾ . . . . . (631) 600
Preparations for the Bath, 1910, pencil,
12¾ x 14¼ . . . . (624) 3,040
Nude in an Armchair, red chalk, 18 x 14 . . . . (529) 520
Nude Combing Her Hair, 1920, 19½ x 12¾ . . . . . . (503) 260
Seated Nude, Back View, charcoal, 18 x 14¼ . . . . . (638) 221
Standing Nude, 1921, charcoal and pastel,
14¼ x 10½ . . . . (624) 1,382
The Road, pencil, 4 x 6 . . . . (581) 56
Study of Roses, red chalk, 13¼ x 10¾ . . . . (563) 380

1966

Young Woman Combing Her Hair, 9 x 5 . . . . (711) 550
Kneeling Nude, 1895, Conté pencil, 9½ x 12¼ . . . . (800) 460
Louise in the Nude on the Sofa, 1895, black
pencil on onionskin paper, 8¼ x 7¼ . . . . (668) 1,000
Nude in an Armchair, red chalk, 18¼ x 14 . . . . (721) 725
Standing Nude, Front View, 1915, charcoal,
31½ x 17¾ . . . . (829) 220
After the Bath, red chalk, 10¼ x 8 . . . . (809) 1,700
Nude, 1920, charcoal, 19½ x 12¾ . . . . (692) 200
Woman Thinking, 1920, pencil, 14½ x 11 . . . . (793) 540
Long-Haired Nude, 1928, charcoal and colored
pencil, 19 x 13 . . . . (689) 1,935
Woman with a Tub, black lead, 9½ x 6½ . . . . (745) 1,266

1967

The She-Ass, 1902, charcoal and red chalk,
7¾ x 10¼ . . . . (879) 110
Montmartre, the Rue St. Vincent, pencil,
10¾ x 8¾ . . . . (943) 284
Seated Woman, 1920, charcoal, 21¾ x 15½ . . . . . . (978) 800
Portrait of a Young Lady, red chalk, 10 x 8 . . . . . . (939) 498
The Bath, black lead, 9 x 11 . . . . (1004) 1,600
Landscape, 8¼ x 11¾ . . . . (1007) 120

1968–July 1969

Portrait of Maurice Utrillo, (1902), black lead,
8¼ x 5¾ . . . . (1127) $2,070
Standing Nude, 1896, black pencil and red chalk,
11 x 5½ . . . . (1174) 2,944
Front View of a Nude, 1915, charcoal, 24 x 18 . . . (1026) 780
Standing Nude, Back View, charcoal, 10¼ x 7¼ . (1191) 472
Landscape, 8¼ x 11¾ . . . . (1042) 112
The Garden, charcoal, 8 x 6½ . . . . (1172) 184
Study of Roses, black chalk, 13¼ x 10¾ . . . . (1134) 142
Reclining Nude Turned Toward the Left,
charcoal, 15½ x 24 . . . . (1224) 900
Seated Model, 7½ x 6½ . . . . (1253) 710
Young Woman with Raised Arm, 10¼ x 8 . . . . (1253) 610
Standing Woman in the Nude, 1915, charcoal,
23¾ x 17¾ . . . . (1255) 800
Reclining Nude, black pencil, 19¾ x 25¾ . . . . (1265) 800
The Baker, black lead, 9 x 6½ . . . . (1268) 2,320
Le Bon Lait, pencil, 6¼ x 7 . . . . (1273) 96

WATERCOLORS

1961–1962

Nude in a Pink Chemise, pastel, 18¼ x 9¾ . . . . (141) 2,300
Back View of a Nude, pastel, 15¾ x 10¼ . . . . (141) 1,360

1963

Nude in a Bathing Wrap, pastel on gray paper,
10 x 7¼ . . . . (247) 1,234

1964

Leda with the Swan, pastel, 17 x 28½ . . . . (394) 3,040

1965

The Dancer with a Tutu, pastel, 16¾ x 10 . . . . (553) 2,600

1966

Woman with a Little Girl on the Waterfront,
pastel and gouache, 20½ x 12¾ . . . . (743) 1,120

1968–July 1969

Back View of a Nude on an Armchair, 1905,
pastel, 24½ x 20½ . . . . (1224) 12,000

PAINTINGS

1961–1962

The House by the River, 1917, on cardboard,
19¾ x 25¾ . . . . (114) 6,200
Marigolds and Violets, 1919, 18¼ x 15 . . . . (171) 6,200
Nude Draping Herself, 1919, 31½ x 23¼ . . . . (78) 5,200
The Red-Haired Woman, 1919, on cardboard . . . . . (68) 3,200
Reclining Nude, 1921, 23¾ x 32 . . . . (27) 7,000
The Bunch of Flowers, 1921, 21¼ x 25¾ . . . . (29) 5,200
Flowers in a Vase,[2] 1922, 21¼ x 15 . . . . (71) 7,200
Young Woman in a Red Bodice, 1922, 24 x 18¾ . . . (93) 5,311
St. Bernard Castle, 1927, 32 x 23¾ . . . . (32) 2,200
Portrait of a Woman, 24 x 18¼ . . . . (26) 4,800

1963

Vase of Flowers, 1916, 29 x 22½ . . . . (232) 5,424
The Country House, 1918, 21 x 16¼ . . . . (318) 2,700
Red-Haired Woman, 1919, on cardboard,
18¼ x 15 . . . . (206) 2,020
The Blue Ribbon, 1921, 21¾ x 18¼ . . . . (210) 3,016

[2]Dedicated "Amicalement à Maurice Raynal."

Landscape at St. Bernard Castle, 1922,
32 x 23¾ . . . . (232) $ 5,763
The Blue Vase with Lilacs, 21¾ x 15 . . . . (276) 5,600
Nude on a Sofa, 32 x 47½ . . . . (198) 9,400
Reclining Nude with Yellow Drapery, 1921,
23¾ x 32 . . . . (306) 4,400

1964
Reclining Nude on a Red Sofa, 1918, 15¾ x 21 . . . (465) 1,420
Portrait of a Woman, 1919, on cardboard,
19½ x 16¼ . . . . (377) 2,938
Bust with a Blue Ribbon, 1921, 21¾ x 18 . . . . (340) 1,800
Seaside, on cardboard, 21 x 25¾ . . . . (340) 6,600
Portrait of a Young Lady, 1925, 39½ x 32 . . . . (340) 6,900
Bunch of Flowers, 1926, 12¾ x 9 . . . . (471) 6,554
Back View of a Bather, 1929, 21¼ x 25¾ . . . . (340) 6,000
Nude with a Blue Shawl, 1930, 25¾ x 21¼ . . . . (399) 5,000
Young Lady Seated in a Park, 1930, 36½ x 29¼ . . (399) 4,000
André Utter and His Dogs, 1932, 63½ x 51½ . . . . . (354) 7,000
Flowers in a Vase, 1933, on cardboard,
21 x 15½ . . . . (378) 5,763

1965
The House, on cardboard, 15 x 21 . . . . (564) 2,300
The Tree of Montmagny Quarry, (1910),
21¼ x 29 . . . . (526) 13,000
Standing Nude, 1916, 34½ x 23¾ . . . . (640) 3,480
Reclining Nude on a Red Sofa, 1918, 15¾ x 21 . . . (567) 1,808
Landscape of Corsica, 1918, 21¼ x 25¾ . . . . (611) 5,300
Woman with a Blue Ribbon, Her Breast Bare,
1921, 21 x 17½ . . . . (583) 2,322
St. Bernard Tower, 1927, 31½ x 23¼ . . . . (522) 3,317
Nude with a Blue Shawl, 1930, 25¾ x 21¼ . . . . (490) 4,400
Roses and Hydrangeas in a Vase, 1933, on
cardboard, 21 x 15½ . . . . (617) 7,797
Portrait of the Artist, 1934, 16 x 13 . . . . (633) 3,750

1966
Woman with a Little Girl, 36½ x 23¾ . . . . (711) 8,400
Self-Portrait, 1893, 15¾ x 10½ . . . . (743) 12,000
Nudes at Their Toilette, 1908, 41¼ x 23¾ . . . . (743) 11,000
Winter Afternoon, 1917, on cardboard,
20½ x 14 . . . . (793) 2,500
Grigny Church, Rhône, 1918, 24 x 19¾ . . . . (743) 4,000
Reclining Woman, 1918, 15¾ x 21 . . . . (798) 2,486
Cows Grazing, 13 x 16¼ . . . . (685) 800
Still Life, 19¾ x 25¾ . . . . (776) 5,500
Nude with a Mirror, 1928, 29 x 21¼ . . . . (814) 8,000

1967
Standing Nude, 1916, 34¼ x 23¾ . . . . (912) 4,000
The Woman with a Small Dog, 1919, 36½ x 25¾ . . (993) 3,300
Still Life with a Candle Stick, 1921, 36½ x 25¾ . . . (987) 8,000
La Vachère, 1922, 23¼ x 28¾ . . . . (940) 5,804
Self-Portrait . . . . (993) 7,200

1968–July 1969
Belgodère Church, Corsica, 1913, 29 x 36½ . . . . . (1159) 13,360
Flowers, 1916, on cardboard, 20 x 27¾ . . . . (1125) 8,740
The Hairdressing, 1916, on canvas laid down on
board, 41½ x 29¾ . . . . (1187) 6,608
The Hill of Meyzieux Church, 1917, 29 x 36½ . . . (1049) 6,600
Woman with Her Breast Bare, 1917, 23¾ x 19¾ . (1045) 3,200
The Woman with a Small Dog, 1919, 36½ x 25¾ . (1200) 3,600
Reclining Nude, 1921, 23¾ x 24 . . . . (1060) 10,400
The Blue Ribbon, 1921, 21¼ x 18 . . . . (1018) 4,500

Great Nude with a Picture, 1922, on cardboard,
39½ x 28½ . . . . (1049) $ 6,200
Daybreak in the Meadow, 1922, 21¼ x 21¼ . . . . . (1127) 4,140
Nude with a Bunch of Flowers, 1925,
35½ x 39½ . . . . (1158) 14,200
Germaine Utter at Her Window, 1926, 32 x 25¾ . (1202) 16,000
Young Lady in Front of Her Window, 1930,
35¾ x 28¼ . . . . (1187) 8,968
Bunch of Flowers, 19 x 13 . . . . (1173) 11,040
Seated Model, 25¾ x 21¼ . . . . (1103) 5,800
St. Bernard Terrace, 1927, 32 x 23¾ . . . . (1224) 3,620
The Woman Painter, 1927, oil and gouache,
53¼ x 36¼ . . . . (1225) 3,400
The White Rose, 1936, 14 x 10¾ . . . . (1226) 3,500
André Utter and His Dogs, 1932, 64¼ x 51¼ . . . . (1232) 5,250
Vase of Flowers, 1922, 18½ x 13¾ . . . . (1235) 10,500
Portrait of Lily Walton, 1923, 24 x 18 . . . . (1235) 12,000
White Rose, 1936, 14 x 10¾ . . . . (1268) 8,816

Félix Vallotton

(1865–1925)

Birthplace: Lausanne, Switzerland.

1882 Goes to Paris and attends the Académie Julian and the Ecole Nationale des Beaux-Arts for a short time. Executes a great number of copies at the Louvre Museum.

1885 Exhibits for the first time at the Salon, Paris.

1887 His portrait of Jasinsky creates a scandal at the Salon, Paris. Works at a picture restorer's.

1889 Visits Vienna and Venice. Makes friends with Toulouse-Lautrec.

1890-95 Becomes a specialist in woodcuts. Contributes as an art critic to the *Gazette de Lausanne.*

1891 Participates for the first time in the Salon des Indépendants, Paris. Contributes to the *Revue Blanche* until 1894—and again from 1901 to 1909.

1893 Participates in the Salon des Indépendants, Paris. Exhibits with the Nabis at the Galerie Le Barc de Boutteville, Paris.

1896 Illustrates *La Maîtresse* by Jules Renard and *Le Livre des Masques* by Rémy de Gourmont.

1900 Becomes a French citizen.

1903 Participates in the Salon d'Automne, Paris.

1904 Four of his statues are cast by Hebrard. Turns from small canvases to larger compositions.

1906-10 Series of nudes.

1908 Stays in Honfleur, Lausanne, and Winterthur.

1913 Trip to Russia, Italy, and Germany.

1921-22 Stays in Cagnes in the south of France. Series of landscapes.

1925 Died, Paris.

Sales

DRAWINGS

1963
Scene in a Classroom, ink and watercolor,
10¼ x 8 .... (255) $ 55

1964
Study of a Nude, pencil, 10¾ x 5 .... (441)   124
Nude with a Chair, India-ink wash, 9 x 4½ .... (366)   72

1965
Seated Nude, black lead, 11½ x 7 .... (567)   102
Standing Nude, Back View, black pencil,
11½ x 6¾ .... (603)   50
Two Nudes, pencil, 11 x 7½ .... (624)   50

1966
Reclining Woman in the Nude, pencil,
8¾ x 12¼ .... (742)   200

1967
Reclining Nude, 8¼ x 12¼ .... (911)   340
Reclining Nude, charcoal, 8¾ x 13½ .... (964)   300
Two Nudes, charcoal, 11 x 7½ .... (881)   116
The Arrest, ink, 10¾ x 8¾ .... (939)   152

1968–July 1969
Seated Woman, pencil, 6¾ x 5¼ .... (1174)   115
Seated Nude, black lead and charcoal, 7½ x 4¾ . (1161)   100
Back View of a Nude, 7½ x 4¾ .... (1078)   152
Landscape at Dax, 1917, black chalk, 6½ x 8 .... (1102)   368

WATERCOLORS

1968–July 1969
Houses of Provence, pastel, 14 x 16¾ .... (1070)   1,038

PAINTINGS

1961–1962
Cagnes: The Palm Tree, 1924, 29 x 23¾ .... (120)   900
The Little Bather, on cardboard, 7¼ x 4¾ .... (57)   310
Blond Nude Stepping into the Water,
19¾ x 25¾ .... (70)   1,264
Still Life, 32 x 25¾ .... (93)   2,599
Bunch of Roses, 27 x 21¼ .... (143)   2,124

1963
Woman with Yellow Drapery, 1913, 32 x 25¾ ..... (318)   1,100
Young Woman with a Blue Scarf, 24 x 19¾ ...... (198)   900
Orpheus Tortured by the Maenads, 1914,
21¾ x 17¾ .... (258)   320
Honfleur Pier, 1920, 21¼ x 25½ .... (225)   2,500
Bather, 1925, 29 x 23¾ .... (310)   588

1964
Nude in a White Chemise, 1902, on panel,
29¾ x 22½ .... (440)   4,200
Still Life with Flowers, 1906, on cardboard,
24¾ x 25 .... (406)   4,520
Still Life, 1912, 32½ x 34¾ .... (347)   2,400
Bust of a Model, 32 x 25¾ .... (397)   760
Flood Tide at Houlgate, 1913, 29¾ x 39½ .... (406)   4,746
The River Seine at Mantes, 1917, 20½ x 35¼ ..... (385)   1,921
The Roman Road at Cagnes, 1920, 29 x 23¾ ..... (341)   1,600
Honfleur Pier, 1920, 21 x 25 .... (453)   4,422
The Stream Eure at Pacy-sur Eure, 1924,
32 x 21¼ .... (347)   2,300

1965
Still Life, Metal Dish, 25¾ x 32 .... (632) $ 2,820
Landscape of the Leman, 1889, on panel,
10½ x 14 .... (569)   2,034
Wild Flowers in a Jug, 1911, 32 x 23¾ .... (564)   1,600
Portrait of a Woman, 1920, 35¼ x 45¾ .... (619)   1,240
First Rays of Sun, 1921, 32 x 23¾ .... (532)   2,240
Seated Nude, 1922, 36½ x 29 .... (598)   1,240

1966
Flowers, 1921, 21¾ x 18¼ .... (798)   1,808
Nude, 1918, 18¼ x 21¾ .... (798)   3,209
Nude Holding Back Her Shirt, 1904,
51½ x 38½ .... (819)   5,800
Back View of a Nude, 1909, 23¾ x 19 .... (808)   2,902
The Woman with a Mantilla, 1909, 24 x 19¾ ..... (808)   2,902

1967
Squatting Nude with a Cat, 1919, 40 x 32¼ .... (919)   4,068
Sunset, 1915, 21¼ x 28½ .... (985)   2,489
Still Life with Daffodils, 25¾ x 21¾ .... (932)   4,746
Interior: Mother and Child, on board,
19¼ x 19¾ .... (982)   9,480

1968–July 1969
Women and Children on the Edge of a Lake,
1900, on cardboard, 11 x 19 .... (1180)   8,000
Bust of a Woman, 1906, 25¾ x 32 .... (1109)   2,800
The Lady with a Green Veil, 1907, 39½ x 32 ..... (1125)   5,750
Nude with a Mirror, 1909, 36½ x 29 .... (1174)   3,450
African Woman with a Turban, 1910, 39½ x 32 .. (1093)   6,000
Nude Seated on the Waterfront, 1911,
21¼ x 25¾ .... (1060)   7,680
Wooded Hill on the Edge of Lake Leman, 1911,
29 x 39½ .... (1181)   7,300
Landscape, 1922, 32 x 25¾ .... (1045)   2,800
Houses on the Bank of the River, 10¼ x 10¾ .... (1045)   980
Seated Young Woman, Front View, 1924,
31½ x 25 .... (1187)   3,540
Landscape, 1925, 17½ x 13 .... (1014)   440
The Palm Tree, 1924, 29 x 23¾ .... (1224)   2,600
Orpheus Attacked by the Maenads, 1914,
21½ x 18 .... (1231)   850
Interior with a Woman, 1897, on cardboard,
10½ x 17 .... (1268)   3,712
Bather, 1915, 32 x 23½ .... (1271)   1,920
The Path, 1922, 23½ x 28¾ .... (1273)   4,280

Georges Valmier

(1885–1937)

Birthplace: Angoulême, France.

1905–09 Attends the Ecole Nationale des Beaux-Arts, Paris, in the studio of O. Merson. From the influence of Cézanne proceeds gradually to Cubism—just like Braque and Picasso (whom he has not yet met).

1911–12 Paints portraits and still lifes in dark shades. Participates in the Salon des Indépendants, Paris, together with Braque, Léger, Picasso, and Delaunay.

1913 Period of colored Cubism.

1919 Signs a contract with Léonce Rosenberg.

1921 Participates in the Salon des Indépendants, Paris. First one-man show at Léonce Rosenberg's, Paris. Series of collages.

1922–23 Stage decorations for *Isabelle et Pantalon* by Max Jacob, for *Cyprien ou l'Amour à 18 Ans* by Pillement, and for a number of other plays.

1926 Takes part in the Société Anonyme's "International Exhibition of Modern Art" at the Brooklyn Museum, New York.

1927 One-man show at Léonce Rosenberg's and at the Galerie Briant-Robert, Paris.

1930 Alters his style, introducing curves and black outlines into his paintings. Designs playing cards.

1932 Participates in "25 Ans de Peinture Abstraite" at the Galerie Braun, Paris. Joins the group "Abstraction-Création" and takes part in its exhibitions.

1935 Exhibits at the Galerie des Beaux-Arts, Paris. Takes part in "Les Créateurs du Cubisme" at Wildenstein's, Paris.

1937 Participates in "Les Maîtres de l'art indépendant" at the Petit Palais, Paris. Executes three decorations for the Paris World's Fair. Died, Paris.

Sales

WATERCOLORS

1963

Reclining Nude, watercolor and collage,
6½ x 9½ .... (205) $ 212

1964

Cubist Composition, gouache, 5¾ x 8 .... (393)   210

1965

The Unwonted Hour, gouache on collage,
9½ x 7¼ .... (612)   310

Composition, gouache, 12¼ x 9½ .... (598)   356

1966

"L'Effort Moderne," 1919, gouache, 8¼ x 5¾ ..... (784)   550

Composition, watercolor, 8 x 10¾ .... (730)   344

1967

Composition with Flowers, gouache and collage,
10¾ x 8¾ .... (870)   275

1968–July 1969

Still Life with a Pot, gouache, 8 x 12 .... (1088)   225

The Woman with a Headband, 1924, gouache,
7½ x 4½ .... (1162)   300

Composition, 1931, gouache, ink, and collage,
8 x 10¾ .... (1061)   475

Cubist Composition: Man in a Landscape,
gouache, 12¾ x 17¾ .... (1196)   800

Le Bal Musette, gouache, pen, and India ink,
7½ x 15½ .... (1240) $ 600

The Three Gossips, gouache, 18¾ x 12¼ .... (1244)   1,020

Composition, 1918, gouache and collage,
10 x 7½ .... (1266)   860

PAINTINGS

1961–1962

The Street, 1912, 25¾ x 21¼ .... (153)   520

Woman with an Armchair, 1923, 29¾ x 18¼ ...... (110)   1,160

Composition with Figures, 1924, 24 x 18¼ .... (155)   640

The Bunch of Flowers, 1925, 25 x 19 .... (140)   879

1964

The Street, 1912, 21¼ x 25¾ .... (472)   550

View of the Roofs, Springtime, 1922,
15½ x 21¾ .... (328)   460

1965

The Village, 23¼ x 29 .... (559)   604

1967

Cubist Composition, 29 x 23¾ .... (967)   1,695

Composition, 1920, collage, 8 x 6 .... (848)   180

The Village, 1924, 29 x 36½ .... (867)   1,800

Composition, 1925, 36 x 25¾ .... (870)   1,000

Landscape, 19¾ x 24 .... (875)   620

1968–July 1969

Cubist Figures, 1923, 23½ x 36 .... (1106)   2,800

The Village, 1925, 27¾ x 37½ .... (1125)   4,600

The Houses, 1925, 27¼ x 37¼ .... (1029)   2,000

Still Life, 1927, 26¼ x 35½ .... (1173)   4,370

Composition, 1931, 39½ x 29 .... (1181)   3,800

Figures, 24 x 18¼ .... (1167)   970

The Unwonted Hour, collage and gouache,
9 x 6½ .... (1178)   360

The Basket of Fruit, 1925, 19¾ x 25¾ .... (1255)   1,820

Louis Valtat

(1869–1952)

Birthplace: Dieppe, France.

1887–91 Attends the Ecole Nationale des Beaux-Arts, in the studio of Gustave Moreau, and the Académie Julian, Paris.

1889 Participates in the Salon des Indépendants, Paris.

1894–95 Stays in the south of France at Banyuls and Collioure, where he meets Maillol. Visits Spain.

1897 Contributes to the review *L'Omnibus de Corinthe.*

1899 Has a house built in Anthéor in the south of France, where he spends a lot of time until 1914.

1900	Marries Suzanne Noël. Works with Renoir in the south of France. Signs a contract with Ambroise Vollard.
1903	Achieves a series of paintings anticipating Fauvism. Leaves this manner when Fauvism begins. Participates in the Salon d'Automne, Paris. Stays at Signac's in St. Tropez.
1905	Participates in the Salon d'Automne, Paris. Does some sculpture with Renoir.
1913	Makes friends with Paul Valéry.
1914	Settles permanently in Paris. Stay at Les Andelys.
1918	Executes a statue of St. Martin for the church of Ver-sur-Mer.
1927	Trip to the Pyrenees and to Arles.
1928-31	Stay in Ouistreham, where he paints several pictures.
1939	Stay at the Lac du Bourget.
1948	Loses his sight.
1952	Died, Paris. Major retrospective exhibition at the Salon d'Automne, Paris.

Sales

DRAWINGS

1961–1962

The Nurse, charcoal with pastel lights, 17½ x 12¾ .... (158) $ 38

The Letter, charcoal with pastel lights, 17 x 13 ... (161) 52

1963

Bust of a Nude (recto), *Woman's Head* (verso), black lead, 4¾ x 3¼ .... (222) 42

The Fisherman's Wife; The Oyster Shellers, 9½ x 11½ and 9 x 11¾ .... (202) 2,000

Seated Woman, (1910), India ink, 11¾ x 9¾ ...... (208) 450

Head of a Little Girl, ink, 9 x 6¼ .... (305) 290

The Big Tree, pencil and watercolor, 11¾ x 15½ .... (275) 800

1964

Woman and Child, India ink and pastel, 8¾ x 7¾ .... (366) 140

Mother and Child, black pencil and pastel, 8¾ x 6½ .... (411) 216

Walk, 1922, pencil, 6 x 4 .... (357) 65

Woman Seated in an Armchair, pencil and watercolor, 11½ x 8¼ .... (454) 498

The Ironer, pencil and watercolor, 10 x 8 .... (374) 725

Seated Woman, pencil and watercolor, 10 x 8 .... (438) 900

1965

The Laundress, pencil, 7 x 5 .... (494) 200

Child's Head, red chalk, 10¾ x 9 .... (488) 100

Child on His Knees, red chalk, 10 x 8 .... (492) 120

Two Seated Women, pencil and watercolor, 11 x 9 .... (507) 700

Seated Nude, pencil, 12½ x 11 .... (516) 84

The Farm, ink, 6 x 8¼ .... (541) 175

1966

Standing Woman, pencil and watercolor, 11¾ x 8 .... (665) 275

Sketch of Children, red chalk, 8 x 10¼ .... (663) 62

In the Kitchen, wash, 9½ x 12¼ .... (692) 130

Oriental Woman; Mother and Young Lady, pencil and ink, 9 x 7 and 10 x 7 .... (648) 275

Bretons in Their Coifs, drawing heightened with pastel, 8¼ x 10 .... (711) $ 160

Rustic House, ink, 9¼ x 11¼ .... (653) 190

Young Woman Thinking, colored pencil, 11¾ x 9 .... (711) 400

1967

Young Lady in a Boat, colored pencil, 9½ x 12¾ .... (926) 190

Bust of a Young Lady, red chalk, 10 x 7¼ .... (897) 100

Young Woman Weeping, pencil, 10¾ x 7¼ .... (865) 72

The Soap Bubbles, black pencil, 12¼ x 9 .... (833) 116

Child's Head, red chalk, 8 x 9½ .... (948) 110

Child Writing, stick of greasepaint, 15 x 11 .... (919) 339

Bust of a Young Woman, red chalk, 10 x 7¼ .... (845) 76

Women's Heads, red chalk, 8 x 11¾ .... (841) 200

The Cup of Tea, black pencil with watercolor lights, 10 x 7½ .... (909) 440

1968–July 1969

The Estérel, 1898, pencil, 12¾ x 19½ .... (1060) 800

Michaella, 1898, colored pencil, 9½ x 12¾ .... (1117) 640

The Red Rocks at Anthéor, 1901, colored pencil, 9¾ x 12¾ .... (1183) 380

Young Woman with a Hat, black lead, 12½ x 10 . (1127) 207

The Woman with a Hat, 10 x 6½ .... (1153) 160

The Sleeping Child, red chalk and Conté pencil, 18¼ x 21¾ .... (1225) 560

Rocks at Anthéor, colored pencil, 9¾ x 12¾ .... (1225) 500

Three Women, pencil, 4 x 5½ .... (1231) 110

The Tree, pencil, 6¾ x 4¾ .... (1231) 75

The Oriental Palace, India ink on buff paper, 9 x 8 .... (1231) 75

Rocks at Anthéor, (1901), colored pencil, 9¾ x 12¾ .... (1233) 540

Little Girl Running, ink, 6 x 4¾ .... (1233) 64

Seamstress, pencil and colored chalk, 9½ x 11½ . (1241) 605

Seamstress, pencil and watercolor, 10 x 7¾ ..... (1241) 504

Trees, pencil, 4¾ x 7¾ .... (1248) 60

Study of Figures, pencil, 3¼ x 5¼ .... (1248) 50

Three Women, green and red ink, 11¾ x 8 ...... (1248) 800

The Young Draftsman, red chalk, 21¼ x 17½ .... (1255) 1,700

Little Girl with a Croissant, black pencil heightened with pastel on tracing paper, 10 x 11¾ .... (1258) 1,000

Landscape, pen, 9 x 12¾ .... (1262) 240

Woman Sewing, black pencil and watercolor, 7½ x 10 .... (1262) 410

WATERCOLORS

1961–1962

The Red Rocks, watercolor, 9¾ x 12¾ .... (144) 200

1963

Group of Figures, watercolor, 9½ x 12¼ .... (188) 200

The Red Rocks, watercolor, 10 x 12¾ .... (254) 360

1964

Mountains, 1903, watercolor, 9 x 12¾ .... (374) 275

Anthéor, 1906, watercolor, 16½ x 18¾ .... (418) 1,000

The Ball, watercolor, 9¼ x 12½ .... (379) 360

Women Sewing and Washing, two watercolors, each 10¼ x 8¼ .... (354) 1,400

At the Races, pastel, 23¾ x 19 .... (341) 3,000

1965

The Bar of the Moulin Rouge, 1893, pastel,
29 x 21¾ . . . . (612) $ 8,020

The Village on the Hill, 1894, watercolor,
9½ x 11¾ . . . . (559)   380

Study of Little Girls, 1898, watercolor, 10 x 7¾ . . . (586)   120

Young Woman in Red, watercolor, 8 x 10 . . . . (617)   633

At the Hairdresser's, watercolor, 10 x 7¾ . . . . (604)   270

Woman with a Red Umbrella, watercolor,
4¾ x 3½ . . . . (604)   140

Woman's Figure, watercolor, 9¾ x 7½ . . . . (630)   152

Reclining Nude, pastel, 10 x 8 . . . . (503)   190

Children on the Beach, pastel, 6 x 10 . . . . (563)   220

Portuguese Boats, watercolor, 9¾ x 12½ . . . . (612)   340

1966

The "Gendarme," watercolor, 12¾ x 10 . . . . (706)   370

Seated Woman with a Green Dress, watercolor,
10 x 7¼ . . . . (819)   580

The Seamstress, watercolor, 8½ x 6½ . . . . (711)   220

A Seamstress, watercolor, 10 x 7½ . . . . (726)   320

Woman Combing Her Hair, watercolor,
10 x 7½ . . . . (781)   280

Woman and Child, watercolor, 5¾ x 7½ . . . . (824)   186

Landscape with Figures, watercolor and gouache,
19 x 25 . . . . (713)   5,000

Vase of Flowers, watercolor, 22½ x 19 . . . . (772)   600

Plums and Peaches, watercolor, 9½ x 14¼ . . . . (796)   1,400

1967

Beach of Normandy, (1908), watercolor,
12¼ x 19¾ . . . . (912)   2,000

Nude Combing Her Hair, watercolor, 10 x 7¼ . . . . (934)   220

The Alley in the Park, watercolor, 10¾ x 14 . . . . . . (852)   360

The Landing Stage, pastel, 11¾ x 15 . . . . (898)   340

Needlework, watercolor, 9½ x 7¼ . . . . (911)   1,200

1968–July 1969

At the Cabaret, (1895), pastel, 26½ x 22 . . . . (1116)   8,000

Woman in a Green Dress, watercolor,
10½ x 7¾ . . . . (1116)   400

Woman in a Fur Coat, watercolor, 6½ x 3¾ . . . . . (1026)   170

Woman with a Hat, watercolor, 4¾ x 3¾ . . . . (1029)   136

Seated Woman, pencil and watercolor,
9¼ x 7½ . . . . (1138)   186

Woman with a Red Umbrella, watercolor,
5 x 3½ . . . . (1026)   160

Seated Woman, watercolor, 9¾ x 7½ . . . . (1196)   130

Young Woman Under the Lamp, watercolor,
10 x 7½ . . . . (1183)   1,040

Woman Putting On Her Gloves, pencil and
watercolor, 11 x 7½ . . . . (1088)   350

Haute Couture, watercolor, 10 x 7¼ . . . . (1174)   609

The Hairdressing, watercolor, 10 x 7¾ . . . . (1026)   340

At the Theater, watercolor, 11 x 8¾ . . . . (1053)   700

Beach of Normandy, 1914–16, watercolor,
11¾ x 18¼ . . . . (1060)   2,240

Bathing Huts on the Beach, 1916, watercolor,
9 x 11¾ . . . . (1118)   400

The Landing Stage, pastel, 11¾ x 15½ . . . . (1051)   420

Still Life, watercolor, 11 x 16¼ . . . . (1030)   1,500

Teatime, pastel, 13 x 17¾ . . . . (1225)   1,800

Woman with a Hat, pastel, 15 x 11 . . . . (1225)   1,800

Seated Woman in a Flowery Kimono, watercolor,
7½ x 10 . . . . (1244)   720

Couple of Dancers, watercolor, 10 x 19 . . . . (1244) $ 660

Woman on a Staircase, watercolor, 10 x 7½ . . . . . (1244)   600

Woman in Yellow Lying on a Sofa, watercolor,
7½ x 10 . . . . (1244)   640

Entrance of La Rochelle Harbor, watercolor,
5¼ x 7¼ . . . . (1244)   620

La Rochelle Harbor, watercolor, 4¾ x 7½ . . . . . . (1244)   420

Village of Brittany, watercolor, 3¾ x 6½ . . . . (1244)   340

Sailboats in Brittany, watercolor, 4 x 5½ . . . . (1244)   520

The Orchestra, watercolor, 4½ x 6½ . . . . (1244)   680

The Orator, watercolor, 4¼ x 5¼ . . . . (1244)   400

The Skaters, watercolor, 5¼ x 4¼ . . . . (1244)   240

Still Life with Shells, pencil, pen, and pastel,
7½ x 10¼ . . . . (1248)   350

The Beach Huts, watercolor, 9 x 11½ . . . . (1253)   860

Two Seamstresses, watercolor, charcoal, and
pastel, 11¾ x 18¼ . . . . (1255)   1,680

Young Boy Reading in an Armchair, pastel,
10¾ x 14 . . . . (1258)   1,600

Mountainous Landscapes, two watercolors, each
3¾ x 5¾ . . . . (1258)   1,000

Landscapes, two watercolors, each 4 x 5¼ . . . . . . (1258)   900

The Cut Corn, watercolor, 14¼ x 20 . . . . (1265)   1,200

Seascape with a Lighthouse, watercolor,
3¾ x 6¾ . . . . (1267)   380

Village by the Waterside, watercolor, 4¼ x 5½ . . (1267)   340

Woman with a Red Umbrella, watercolor,
5 x 3¾ . . . . (1268)   232

PAINTINGS

1961–1962

Cyclamens, 1908, 15 x 18¼ . . . . (119)   1,440

Flowers, (1909), 17½ x 31½ . . . . (93)   5,424

Flowers in a Vase, 21 x 28½ . . . . (96)   6,750

Orris with an Empire Vase, 32 x 18¼ . . . . (32)   2,200

Tulips and Windflowers, 21¼ x 25¾ . . . . (76)   2,700

Vase of Tulips, 21¾ x 19 . . . . (123)   1,800

Back View of a Woman, (1910), peinture à
l'essence, gouache and varnish on
cardboard laid down on canvas,
18¼ x 23¾ . . . . (58)   2,600

Women with a Sofa, on panel, 22½ x 29½ . . . . (64)   10,000

Woman at Her Embroidery, 9 x 7¼ . . . . (162)   840

The Child with a Hoop, 25¾ x 32 . . . . (168)   2,960

The Sailboats, 13 x 16¼ . . . . (116)   3,300

The Red Rocks at Belle-Ile, 32 x 25¾ . . . . (29)   2,100

Landscape at Asnelle, (1916), 13 x 16¼ . . . . (102)   1,400

The Pont du Carrousel, 21¼ x 25¾ . . . . (156)   3,100

Landscape of the South of France, 10¼ x 15¾ . . . . (161)   600

1963

Woman and Child, 32 x 25¾ . . . . (254)   2,700

The Artist's Garden at Anthéor, 1901, 25¾ x 32 . . . (254)   8,000

The Windflowers, 1903, oil on cardboard,
22¼ x 31¼ . . . . (232)   7,910

Feast in Marseilles, (1905), oil on paper,
16¾ x 23¼ . . . . (279)   4,250

Child with a Wooden Horse, (1907), 31½ x 39 . . . . (225)   4,000

The Ironer, (1908), 15 x 18¼ . . . . (316)   5,500

Arrangement of Flowers, (1907), 18¾ x 28½ . . . . . . (202)   3,500

Flowers, 32 x 25¾ . . . . (283)   9,040

Still Life with Flowers, 18¼ x 10¾ . . . . (241)   760

Child with a Hoop, 1912, 32 x 25¾ . . . . (278)   2,500

The Merry-Go-Round, 35¼ x 45¾ . . . . (306)   2,800

The Pink Child,[1] 1916, 19¾ x 19¾ . . . . (278) $ 840

Seated Woman with a Red Kerchief, 32 x 25¾ . . . . (224)   2,120

Still Life with Colocynths, (1920), on cardboard,
9½ x 22½ . . . . (254)   1,640

Scene in a Street of Brittany, 12¾ x 32 . . . . (247)   1,645

The Carrousel, 1930, 10 x 13½ . . . . (247)   1,645

Bois de Boulogne: Boats on the Lake, on canvas
laid down on cardboard, 10¾ x 14 . . . . (318)   1,500

Vase of Tulips, 21¾ x 19 . . . . (224)   2,000

Vase of Flowers, 24 x 19¾ . . . . (204)   2,500

Still Life with Fruit, 10½ x 15¾ . . . . (179)   3,000

Still Life, 11¾ x 11¾ . . . . (314)   1,762

The Mistletoe, 10¾ x 12¾ . . . . (275)   500

Seated Woman, 18¼ x 15 . . . . (293)   1,000

The Reading, 32 x 25¾ . . . . (258)   2,620

Madame Valtat Sewing, 36½ x 29 . . . . (276)   6,000

1964

The Ball, 1895, oil on paper laid down on canvas,
70½ x 85¾ . . . . (473)   13,600

The Studio, 1890, 68 x 87 . . . . (473)   9,200

The Parisian, 1892, 87 x 68 . . . . (473)   7,000

In Front of the Mirror, 25¾ x 32 . . . . (341)   3,700

The Forlorn Farm, 25¾ x 32 . . . . (355)   1,460

Anthéor Gardens, (1903), 25¾ x 32 . . . . (371)   6,500

The Village, on cardboard, 9 x 12¼ . . . . (366)   1,200

Near the Village, 13 x 16¼ . . . . (355)   1,620

Woman in a Garden, (1904), on canvas laid down
on board, 12¾ x 13½ . . . . (448)   5,750

Cargo at Ouistreham, 15½ x 22 . . . . (340)   4,020

The Rocks, on cardboard, 16¾ x 20½ . . . . (340)   3,100

At the Ball, 25¾ x 32 . . . . (340)   2,320

Boats in the Harbor, 10¾ x 14 . . . . (359)   1,420

The Vase of Flowers, on cardboard, 18 x 12½ . . . . (393)   1,000

Flowers in a Chinese Vase, 36½ x 29 . . . . (399)   3,020

La Calanque, 1907, 25¾ x 32 . . . . (399)   1,560

Still Life with a Watermelon, (1910), 14¼ x 23¼ . . (472)   640

Flowers in a Pot and Marigolds, 25¾ x 21¼ . . . . . (408)   1,100

Still Life with a Clock, 19¾ x 24 . . . . (335)   1,400

Vase of Flowers, 21¾ x 18¼ . . . . (337)   1,500

Maritime Landscape, 21¼ x 25¾ . . . . (337)   2,600

Vase of Flowers with Red Drapery, 18¼ x 15 . . . . (340)   2,400

The Cascade of the Bois de Boulogne, 11 x 14 . . . . (352)   1,520

Riders at the Bois, 9½ x 13 . . . . (371)   2,000

The Model, 21¾ x 18¼ . . . . (448)   1,100

Woman Knitting, 8 x 7¾ . . . . (329)   1,250

The Woman with a Yellow Scarf, on panel,
7¼ x 4 . . . . (370)   326

Woman Sewing, 10 x 14 . . . . (366)   1,360

Young Woman Reading, 32 x 25¾ . . . . (378)   4,068

The East Wind, 23 x 31½ . . . . (454)   4,146

A Plate of Strawberries, on panel, 11½ x 11 . . . . . (323)   640

The Apple Trees, on canvas laid down on panel,
10¾ x 14 . . . . (443)   900

Flowers, 10½ x 18¼ . . . . (354)   1,600

Two Women on a Sofa, on cardboard, 13¼ x 10 . . (377)   1,537

Vase of Flowers, 21¾ x 17¼ . . . . (465)   3,400

1965

The Reading, (1903), 19¾ x 24 . . . . (553)   3,200

Park of Versailles, 1906, on cradled panel,
7¼ x 9½ . . . . (613)   1,800

[1] The artist's son.

Seaside, (1907), on panel, 7¼ x 9½ . . . . (567) $ 2,034

The Rape of Europa, 51½ x 32½ . . . . (516)   5,000

Landscape of Auvergne, 19¾ x 24¼ . . . . (503)   3,000

Rustic Landscape, 15¼ x 18½ . . . . (588)   1,400

Dancers at the Folies-Bergères, (1919),
39½ x 32 . . . . (526)   7,250

Seated Woman, 5¾ x 11 . . . . (507)   600

The White Dress, 32 x 40 . . . . (640)   580

Seated Woman, 18¾ x 14¾ . . . . (538)   1,000

Three Young Ladies, on canvas laid down on
board, 10 x 8 . . . . (606)   1,700

Floral Composition, 18¼ x 18¼ . . . . (612)   1,460

Vase of Flowers, on panel, 17 x 12¾ . . . . (575)   1,244

Vase of Flowers, 16 x 13 . . . . (539)   3,750

Vase of Flowers, 21¼ x 25¾ . . . . (561)   2,700

Tulips in a Vase, 18¼ x 15 . . . . (524)   1,100

Windflowers, 15 x 18¼ . . . . (539)   2,400

Flowers, 21¾ x 25¾ . . . . (637)   6,500

Vase of Flowers, 21¾ x 15 . . . . (492)   2,200

Great Vase of Flowers, 36¼ x 28¾ . . . . (575)   4,699

Landscape of Provence, 25¾ x 32 . . . . (633)   5,750

Landscape, 18¼ x 21¾ . . . . (567)   5,198

The Beach, 15 x 21¾ . . . . (532)   3,200

The Swans in the Bois de Boulogne, 11 x 14 . . . . . (503)   2,020

Carrousel Court, on canvas laid down on
cardboard, 10¾ x 13½ . . . . (552)   1,460

Tapestry, 25¾ x 32 . . . . (518)   1,920

1966

Riverside, 16¾ x 22 . . . . (745)   4,520

Landscape, on cardboard, 7¼ x 25¾ . . . . (744)   6,780

Garden, 13 x 10 . . . . (797)   3,119

Outskirts of the Wood, 21¼ x 25¾ . . . . (648)   4,500

Woman Seated in Her Garden, 15 x 17¾ . . . . (824)   2,800

The Obstacle, 9½ x 11½ . . . . (737)   1,400

Mixed Flowers, (1906-07), 14 x 14¾ . . . . (808)   2,177

Still Life, the Studio, (1908), 32 x 25 . . . . (776)   6,750

Yellow Roses, Blue Background (1905), on canvas
laid down on board, 18¼ x 15½ . . . . (776)   5,250

Windflowers with a Red Curtain, 13 x 16¼ . . . . . . (742)   2,020

Tulips, 18¾ x 22 . . . . (784)   2,800

Flowers in a Vase, 18¼ x 15 . . . . (758)   1,560

Tulips, 14¼ x 13 . . . . (711)   1,200

Vase of Flowers and Grapes, 20 x 24 . . . . (681)   3,060

The Blond Child, (1910), 15 x 9 . . . . (750)   3,317

The Woman in Blue, 24 x 19¾ . . . . (725)   2,200

The Seamstress, on canvas laid down on
cardboard, 8 x 7¼ . . . . (672)   920

Women's Orchestra, on cradled cardboard,
19¾ x 25¾ . . . . (727)   2,520

Reflection, 12 x 10¾ . . . . (784)   2,200

Café Concert Dancer, on panel, 7¼ x 5¼ . . . . (819)   7,200

1967

The Mediterranean Pine Grove, 1903,
38½ x 51¼ . . . . (954)   20,000

Madame Valtat Under the Olive Tree, 1903, on
cardboard, 15 x 21 . . . . (978)   3,800

Mediterranean Landscape, 25¾ x 32 . . . . (901)   4,400

Country Landscape, 1904, 7¼ x 8¾ . . . . (976)   1,300

Landscape, 18¼ x 21¾ . . . . (967)   4,520

The Fruit Stand, 1905, 9½ x 13 . . . . (978)   3,600

Still Life with Apples, 15 x 18¾ . . . . (989)   7,000

Port-en-Bessin, 1906, 18¼ x 21¾ .... (911) $ 10,000
Landscape of the South of France, 1907,
18¼ x 21¼ .... (978) 8,800
The Red House, (1910), 7½ x 9 .... (976) 1,200
Vase of Flowers with Two Carrots, 1920,
21¼ x 29 .... (989) 7,500
The Vase of Windflowers, on panel, 8½ x 10¾ .... (852) 2,100
Vase of Mimosa and Still Life, 21¼ x 29 .... (926) 3,000
Still Life, on panel, 11 x 8¾ .... (963) 2,500
Flowers in a Vase, 13 x 16¼ .... (897) 3,000
Red Flowers, on board, 10¾ x 9 .... (870) 2,000
Flowers in a Green Vase, 21¾ x 15 .... (935) 1,980
Flower Bed, on cardboard, 15¾ x 12¾ .... (850) 1,500
Vase of Flowers, 25¾ x 21¼ .... (912) 3,800
Bunch of Flowers, 29 x 23¾ .... (911) 7,000
Still Life with a Basket of Fruit, 14¾ x 17¾ ...... (985) 3,318
*The Vine Arbor, in Front of the Thatch-Roofed
Cottage,* 15 x 18¼ .... (923) 9,600
Boats at Ouistreham, 15 x 18¼ .... (987) 6,800
Stag Hunting, 25¾ x 32 .... (912) 7,200
Underwood with Figures, 35¼ x 27¾ .... (893) 6,500
The Orchard, 15 x 18¼ .... (978) 3,900
La Coiselle, Valley of Chevreuse, 57¾ x 34¾ ..... (918) 6,328
Nudes with a Blue Armchair, 63¾ x 51½ .... (912) 4,600
The Woman with a Cat, 18¼ x 15 .... (912) 3,100
Woman with a Necklace, 31½ x 25¼ .... (864) 10,000
Home Life, 25¾ x 32 .... (857) 3,620
Dancers, on cradled panel, 5¾ x 5 .... (967) 972
Seated Woman Holding a Cat, 36¼ x 29 .... (963) 7,000
The Musicians, on panel, 9 x 5¾ .... (870) 1,600
Self-Portrait, 32 x 39½ .... (901) 1,500

1968–July 1969

The Bateau-Mouche, (1895), 21 x 25¼ .... (1132) 20,060
The Oyster Shellers, 1896, 21 x 25 .... (1187) 16,520
Anthéor Rocks, (1899), 26 x 32½ .... (1117) 8,000
Seaside Landscape, (1903), 21¼ x 25¾ .... (1173) 13,800
Women in Hats, (1904), 11 x 10¼ .... (1125) 6,900
Vase of Flowers with Two Carrots, 1920,
21¼ x 29 .... (1080) 4,250
The Bathers, (1919), on cardboard laid down on
canvas, 16¾ x 21¼ .... (1116) 2,700
Rocks by the Seaside, 1909, 25¾ x 32¼ .... (1176) 11,500
The Merry-Go-Round, 1908, 35¼ x 45¾ .... (1060) 12,000
Still Life, (1905), 18¼ x 24 .... (1173) 8,740
Seascape, 1924, 10¾ x 14 .... (1174) 2,760
Still Life with Grapes, 1937, on panel, 6¾ x 9 .... (1061) 1,500
The Flowerpot, on canvas laid down on board,
6¾ x 6¼ .... (1187) 1,652
Flowers in a Vase, 21¾ x 18¼ .... (1049) 3,300
Tulips and Anemones, 21¾ x 18¼ .... (1200) 10,000
Vase of Flowers, 14¾ x 31½ .... (1200) 7,000
Roses, 16¾ x 41 .... (1109) 2,500
The Bouillabaisse, 18¼ x 32 .... (1113) 1,480
The Young Partridges, 9½ x 14¼ .... (1104) 560
The Corn, 5 x 7 .... (1051) 340
Landscape, 18¼ x 21¾ .... (1075) 3,000
Springtime in the Ile-de-France, 21¼ x 9 .... (1109) 7,000
The River Seine Near Paris, 25¾ x 32 .... (1109) 6,400
View of a Harbor, 19¾ x 24 .... (1053) 7,000
The Flower Beds, Choisel, 21¼ x 29 .... (1117) 7,000
Fréjus, 9½ x 13 .... (1019) 1,000

Bois de Boulogne, 11¾ x 8¼ .... (1189) $ 3,040
Bois de Boulogne, 9½ x 12¾ .... (1113) 2,000
The Three Graces, 32 x 25¾ .... (1106) 2,800
Seated Man Reading, oil on paper laid down on
cradled panel, 19¾ x 12¾ .... (1117) 4,400
The Seamstress, 14¾ x 11 .... (1174) 4,485
The Caress, on cradled panel, 13½ x 8 .... (1174) 2,300
Portrait of a Little Girl, 10 x 11½ .... (1132) 1,298
Two Women, 7¼ x 6½ .... (1061) 850
Dancer, on cradled panel, 5¾ x 3¼ .... (1038) 150
Children's Games, 9 x 36½ .... (1189) 33,600
The Windflowers, 13 x 9½ .... (1221) 1,700
Wild Flowers, 11 x 19¾ .... (1224) 1,700
The Bluets, 10¼ x 19¾ .... (1224) 1,000
The Lake of the Bois de Boulogne, 9½ x 13 ..... (1224) 3,100
Underwood, 13 x 16¼ .... (1224) 2,160
Portrait of a Seated Woman, (1925), 36½ x 29 ... (1225) 7,200
Le Perron fleuri, 16¼ x 21½ .... (1226) 3,600
Lily of the Valley, on canvas laid down on
cardboard, 12¾ x 9 .... (1226) 2,800
Chrysanthemums and Grapes, 19½ x 11½ .... (1226) 6,000
Tulips, Daffodils, and Windflowers, 9½ x 27¾ ... (1226) 5,800
Portrait of a Young Lady, (1890), on cradled
panel, 16 x 12½ .... (1231) 4,100
Windflowers, 15 x 18 .... (1231) 2,400
Seated Woman, 1933, 7 x 5¼ .... (1231) 1,200
Moulin Rouge, (1900–01), on panel, 12¼ x 16¾ .. (1235) 10,000
Bowl of Peaches, (1906), 14¾ x 18 .... (1239) 14,880
The Forest, 1938, 10 x 13 .... (1240) 2,760
Epaves roulées par les vagues, 7¼ x 8¾ .... (1240) 1,440
Roses, 18 x 23 .... (1241) 13,860
The Pot of Lilies of the Valley, 15 x 18 .... (1241) 5,540
Flowers .... (1250) 2,000
Flowers, on panel, 14 x 10¾ .... (1252) 3,160
Flowers, 6¾ x 7½ .... (1253) 1,040
Carteret, Brittany, 21¼ x 25¾ .... (1254) 10,400
Sailboats and Rocks, 10¾ x 13¾ .... (1255) 3,200
Fair-Haired Young Woman Sitting, in Profile,
25¾ x 19¾ .... (1255) 3,000
Sailboats Near the Coast, 10½ x 13½ .... (1255) 2,600
Young Women on the Rocks, 11 x 14 .... (1256) 13,800
The Cup of Fruit, 9½ x 13 .... (1256) 5,000
The Sweet Williams, 16¼ x 14 .... (1256) 5,000
The Belle-Epoque, on paper laid down on canvas,
17 x 14¾ .... (1256) 5,400
Young Lady Doing Up Her Bodice, on paper laid
down on panel, 14 x 10¼ .... (1258) 7,900
Flowers, 21¾ x 15 .... (1258) 7,100
Sunny Landscape, 15 x 21¾ .... (1258) 6,400
Fauve Landscape, 13 x 18¼ .... (1258) 4,000
Flowers in a Vase, 18¼ x 14 .... (1258) 3,000
Basket of Cherries, on paper laid down on
canvas, 9½ x 12¾ .... (1258) 3,600
Woman in a Green Bodice, on panel,
diameter 3 .... (1265) 162
The Painted Lips, on panel, diameter 3 .... (1265) 160
The Two Friends, on panel, diameter 10 .... (1265) 320
Woman with a Chignon, on panel, diameter 4 ... (1265) 160
Portraits of Women on an Orange Background,
on panel, diameter 4¼ .... (1265) 150
Diana and Cupid, on panel, oval, 3¼ x 2½ ...... (1265) 110
Zeus and Diana, on panel, oval, 3½ x 2¾ .... (1265) 140

Woman in a Bedizened Dress, on panel,
diameter 4¼ .... (1265) $ 220

Portraits of Women, on panel, diameter 6 .... (1265)   600

Fashionable Ladies, on panel, diameter 4¼ ...... (1265)   540

Mythological Scene, on panel, oval, 2¾ x 2½ .... (1265)   110

Diana and Jupiter, on panel, oval, 3¼ x 2¼ ..... (1265)   142

Diana, on panel, diameter 3 .... (1265)   100

Young Lady with a Yellow Cap, on panel,
diameter 3 .... (1265)   140

The Abduction of Diana, on panel, oval,
3¼ x 2½ .... (1265)   370

Woman in a Red Bodice, on panel,
diameter 4¼ .... (1265)   420

Women Seen from the Back, on panel,
diameter 4¼ .... (1265)   120

The Laundress, on canvas laid down on panel,
8 x 6 .... (1265)   780

Flowers, 13 x 10¾ .... (1268)   4,060

Flowers, 21¾ x 18¼ .... (1268)   9,164

Seated Woman, 13¼ x 10 .... (1268)   1,972

Flowers, 8¾ x 6½ .... (1268)   2,111

Landscape of Normandy, 11½ x 10¾ .... (1268)   2,506

Cherry Laurels, 20 x 15½ .... (1268)   6,844

The Wild Apple Tree, (1908), 23 x 28 .... (1270)   11,520

*Young Woman Reading, with an Azalea on the
Table,* 23 x 28 .... (1270)   13,200

Claude Venard

(1913–   )

Birthplace: Paris, France. (Attends the Ecole Nationale des Beaux-Arts, Paris, for two days, and then works at Chauffrey's, a restorer, until the outbreak of World War II.)

1936   Takes part in the first exhibition of the group "Forces Nouvelles" at the Galerie Billet-Worms, Paris.

1942   First one-man show at Barrero's, Paris.

1958   Contributes to the foundation of the Salon de Mai, Paris.

1959   One-man show at the Galerie Charpentier, Paris.

1967   One-man show at the Galerie Félix Vercel, New York. Vercel becomes his exclusive dealer.

1969   One-man show at the Galerie Félix Vercel, Paris.

Resident in the south of France.

Sales

WATERCOLORS

1965

The Harbor, watercolor, 16¾ x 25¼ .... (563) $ 82

Composition, watercolor, 16¼ x 25¼ .... (530)   20

1967

Still Life with Fruit, Flowers, and a Pipe,
gouache, 11¾ x 9 .... (920) $ 130

Composition, watercolor, 16¼ x 25 .... (968)   66

1968–July 1969

Composition, gouache, 17½ x 26¼ .... (1245)   62

PAINTINGS

1961–1962

Spheres and Shapes, 23½ x 23½ .... (44)   1,200

The Lesson of Geometry, 18¼ x 14¾ .... (164)   494

Composition, 29¾ x 29¾ .... (173)   600

The Bathing Huts, oil on board, 39½ x 39½ .... (93)   1,311

Still Life with Sea Urchin, 16¾ x 32 .... (146)   310

Seascape and Road, 31 x 38½ .... (37)   1,500

1963

Landscape, 8¾ x 10¾ .... (287)   144

Still Life with a Guitar, 31¼ x 15½ .... (315)   686

Nature Morte à la Cornue, 32 x 23¾ .... (234)   200

The Chairs, 1956, 38¾ x 38¾ .... (225)   1,000

The Towers of Paris, 1956, 15 x 50¼ .... (315)   823

The Buildings, 27¾ x 15¾ .... (222)   150

Landscape of the South of France, 29¼ x 29¼ .... (275)   550

Still Life with Fruit, 20½ x 29 .... (233)   170

Composition, 23¾ x 23¾ .... (180)   280

Basket of Fruit, 29¼ x 29¼ .... (275)   650

The River Seine in Paris, 18¼ x 21½ .... (255)   658

The Sacré-Coeur of Montmartre, 57 x 44¼ ...... (202)   1,750

1964

Glass, 14 x 10¾ .... (470)   271

The Engine, 29 x 36½ .... (449)   216

Bridges Over the River Seine, 35¼ x 45¾ .... (484)   580

Clown's Head, 12¾ x 9½ .... (374)   225

The Rowboat, 1955, 14 x 27¾ .... (393)   160

Scene in a Harbor, 17¾ x 21¾ .... (438)   1,000

Jeu de poissons, 17¾ x 21 .... (329)   350

Still Life with a Fish, 37½ x 37½ .... (329)   850

The Avenue des Batignolles, 1959, 45 x 57¾ ...... (448)   3,100

Still Life, 23¾ x 29 .... (355)   300

1965

Still Life with Avocados and Cherries, 21¼ x 25 .. (535)   498

Notre-Dame de Paris, 1954, 77¼ x 44¾ .... (541)   2,300

Still Life, 29¾ x 29¾ .... (599)   190

Interior, 18¼ x 13 .... (598)   90

Bottle and Fruit, 1956, 28 x 23 .... (582)   498

Composition, 27¾ x 16¼ .... (50)   500

1966

Landscape, 13 x 18¼ .... (721)   350

Still Life, 23¾ x 29 .... (809)   500

Vase of Flowers, 18¼ x 13 .... (692)   240

Harbor Scene, 23¾ x 23¾ .... (665)   600

The Red Sails, 13 x 16 .... (805)   350

Composition, 8¾ x 6½ .... (745)   203

Composition, 8¾ x 6½ .... (798)   226

Abstract Composition, 14¼ x 17½ .... (671)   522

1967

The Studio, 39½ x 29 .... (989)   200

Industrial Landscape, 29¼ x 29¼ .... (985)   427

The Artist's Studio, 1942, 39½ x 32 .... (855)   1,540

1968–July 1969

Unloading the Boat, 1953, 29 x 39½ . . . . (1026) $ 460

The Paddle Boat, 14 x 27¾ . . . . (1177)   500

Stranded Boat, 15 x 18¼ . . . . (1012)   116

Marine Composition, 29 x 29 . . . . (1187)   519

The Mills of the Butte (Montmartre),
39½ x 39½ . . . . (1030)   900

Houses of Brittany, 26½ x 34½ . . . . (1042)   240

Two Nuns in a Garden, 21 x 28½ . . . . (1132)   472

Still Life, 29¼ x 29¼ . . . . (1132)   330

Still Life with Cherries, 1958, 20½ x 25 . . . . (1070)   543

Still Life with a Green Wardrobe, 31½ x 38¾ . . . . (1059)   347

Still Life with a Ewer, 29 x 23¾ . . . . (1179)   340

Young Woman with a Pack of Cards,
50¼ x 63¼ . . . . (1048)   200

Irma La Douce, 50½ x 39 . . . . (1145)   750

Fun Fair, 39¼ x 39¼ . . . . (1231)   900

The Mistral; The Piano at the Sacré-Coeur, two
paintings, 29½ x 29½ . . . . (1231)   1,300

Aquatic Festival, 39½ x 39½ . . . . (1234)   560

The Empty Street, 17¼ x 12¼ . . . . (1241)   215

The Blue Jug, 39½ x 39½ . . . . (1245)   300

Four Fruits, 1964, 39¼ x 39¼ . . . . (1248)   950

The Guitar at Notre-Dame, 39¼ x 39¼ . . . . (1248)   700

Fields of Lavender, 29¾ x 29¾ . . . . (1260)   340

Composition, 29¾ x 29¾ . . . . (1260)   420

Reclining Nude, 38½ x 51½ . . . . (1268)   2,784

Maria-Elena Vieira da Silva

(1908–   )

Birthplace: Lisbon, Portugal.

1928   Goes to Paris, where she studies sculpture with Despiau and Bourdelle; painting with Dufresne, Léger, and Friesz; and engraving with Hayter.

1930   Marries the Hungarian painter Arpad Szenès.

1931-33   Participates in the Salon d'Automne and the Salon des Surindépendants, Paris. Attends the Académie Ranson, Paris. First private exhibition at the Galerie Jeanne Bûcher, Paris.

1935-36   Lives in Lisbon.

1937   Private exhibition at the Galerie Jeanne Bûcher, Paris. Executes tapestry designs for Madame Cuttoli.

1938   Takes part in the exhibition "Ecole de Paris" at the Galerie Jeanne Bûcher, Paris.

1939   Private exhibition at the Galerie Jeanne Bûcher, Paris.

1940-47   Settles in Rio de Janeiro.

1942   Private exhibition at the Museum of Fine Arts, Rio de Janeiro.

1946   Private exhibition at the Marian Willard Gallery, New York. Participates in the UNESCO exhibition at the Musée d'Art Moderne, Paris, and in the Salon des Réalités Nouvelles.

1947   Returns to Paris. (Soon becomes a French citizen.) Participates in the Salon d'Automne and in the Salon des Surindépendants, Paris—and again in 1948 and 1949. Private exhibition at the Galerie Jeanne Bûcher, Paris—and again in 1951 and 1957.

1949   Private exhibition at the Galerie Pierre, Paris—and again in 1951 and 1955.

1950   Exhibits with Reichel at La Hune, Paris. Participates in the Venice Biennial—and again in 1954.

1951   Takes part in "Peintres d'aujourd'hui, France-Italie" in Turin—and again in 1959.

1952   Stage decorations for *Parodie* by Adamov. Participates in the International Exhibition at the Carnegie Institute, Pittsburgh—and again in 1955 and 1958.

1953   Given an award by the São Paulo Biennial.

1955   Participates in the "New Decade" at the Museum of Modern Art, New York, and in Documenta I, Kassel—and in Documenta II in 1959.

1958   Given an award by the Carnegie Institute, Pittsburgh, and by the Guggenheim Foundation, New York. Participates in "Cinquante Ans d'art moderne" at the Brussels World's Fair.

Resident in Paris. (She seems to be the most creative woman artist in modern painting.)

Sales

DRAWINGS

1961–1962

Composition, charcoal . . . . (59) $ 276

The Birds, colored pencil, 4½ x 5¾ . . . . (58)   120

1963

Composition, 1960, charcoal, 10¾ x 8¾ . . . . (287)   190

1966

Composition, India ink, 11½ x 8¾ . . . . (730)   220

1967

Composition, 1957, India ink and watercolor,
10 x 12¾ . . . . (919)   215

1968–July 1969

Composition, 1957, India ink and gouache,
9¾ x 12¾ . . . . (1102)   287

WATERCOLORS

1961–1962

Rio, gouache, 16¾ x 19 . . . . (160)   1,620

The Conversation, 1939, gouache, 6½ x 11½ . . . . (98)   320

City, 1948, watercolor, pen, and typewriting,
9 x 12¾ . . . . (149)   1,580

Composition, 1949, watercolor, 7½ x 5¾ . . . . (80)   960

Composition, 1952, gouache, 14 x 19 . . . . (93)   949

Rue de Lisbonne, 1955, watercolor, 10 x 12¼ . . . . . (149)   1,106

Composition, 1956, watercolor, 20½ x 13½ . . . . (167)   1,020

Composition, 1956, gouache, 27¾ x 27¾ . . . . (149)   3,160

The Fire Bird, gouache, 5 x 6 . . . . (86)   310

Arborescent City, gouache, 8 x 19¼ . . . . (93)   1,763

Street of Paris, gouache, 9½ x 6 . . . . (156)   540

Composition, gouache, 8 x 13½ . . . . (75)   1,659

1963

Rue de Paris, gouache, 9½ x 6 . . . . (249) $ 540

Street, gouache, 16¼ x 9½ . . . . (200) 2,000

The Swallow, gouache, 14¾ x 11½ . . . . (263) 1,100

The Façade, 1963, gouache and tempera on
    paper . . . . (270) 600

1964

Composition, 1956, gouache, 14¼ x 18¼ . . . . (386) 1,200

Composition, 1952, watercolor, 11¾ x 9 . . . . (377) 859

Landscape, 1956, gouache, 13¼ x 18¼ . . . . (471) 1,763

Composition, gouache, 27 x 27 . . . . (413) 2,600

1965

The Golden City, 1951, watercolor, 13½ x 18½ . . . (507) 900

Composition, 1954, tempera, 12¼ x 15 . . . . (564) 1,000

Composition, 1955, gouache, 8½ x 14¾ . . . . (609) 760

Composition, 1956, gouache, 13½ x 18¼ . . . . (617) 1,356

Abstract Composition, 1957, gouache,
    13½ x 9½ . . . . (485) 1,000

1966

Composition, 1958, gouache on paper laid down
    on board, 20 x 25¾ . . . . (776) 1,450

Composition, 1958, gouache, 27 x 14¼ . . . . (689) 1,520

Composition, 1962, gouache, 26 x 26½ . . . . (757) 1,658

Composition, gouache, 11 x 14¾ . . . . (745) 904

1967

Composition, 1952, gouache, 12¼ x 9 . . . . (852) 640

Composition, 1956, gouache, 10¾ x 9½ . . . . (939) 691

The Boats in the Harbor, 1957, gouache,
    13¾ x 27 . . . . (938) 1,382

Composition, gouache, 26 x 26 . . . . (919) 2,260

1968–July 1969

Interior with a Still Life, 1947, watercolor,
    13¾ x 10½ . . . . (1102) 874

Composition in White and Blue, gouache,
    7¼ x 11 . . . . (1138) 273

Two Blues, gouache, 7¼ x 11 . . . . (1059) 446

The Houses, gouache and watercolor, 10 x 18¾ . . (1255) 2,500

Composition, gouache, 15 x 12 . . . . (1268) 2,598

PAINTINGS

1961–1962

Banks of the Thames, 16 x 29¾ . . . . (164) 2,334

Rio de Janeiro, 1947, 12¾ x 15½ . . . . (164) 1,043

The Houses, 1948, 6 x 10¼ . . . . (129) 961

The Warriors, 1949, 21¼ x 29 . . . . (149) 3,160

Composition, 1951, 28 x 22½ . . . . (29) 5,160

Composition, 1953, 16¾ x 20½ . . . . (143) 3,164

The Elevated Subway, 1955, 62½ x 87 . . . . (88) 20,910

Composition, 32 x 39½ . . . . (168) 5,600

1963

Banks of the Thames, 16¼ x 29¾ . . . . (200) 2,700

Composition, 1946, 13 x 9½ . . . . (299) 860

Composition, 1951, 21 x 25¼ . . . . (247) 4,113

Composition, 1951, 29 x 23¾ . . . . (299) 3,500

Composition, 1953, 16¾ x 20½ . . . . (283) 3,164

Noon, 1957, 31½ x 51½ . . . . (299) 3,700

Rio de Janeiro, 13 x 16¼ . . . . (200) 2,400

1964

The Birds, 1952, 29 x 36½ . . . . (469) 2,500

The Fowler, 13 x 21¼ . . . . (375) 940

Composition, 1956, 32 x 39½ . . . . (378) 6,780

1965

Composition: Battle of the Reds and Blues, 1953,
    51½ x 63¾ . . . . (573) $ 16,584

The Hard Way, 1956, 31½ x 31½ . . . . (522) 2,764

Small Town, 21¾ x 13 . . . . (617) 3,277

1966

The Ballet, 1939, 23 x 31½ . . . . (812) 3,317

Rio de Janeiro, 12¾ x 15½ . . . . (749) 1,100

1967

The City, 1951, 25 x 20½ . . . . (938) 5,804

The City, 1948, collage and gouache, 11¾ x 7½ . . . (870) 325

Station, 1951, 28½ x 23¾ . . . . (857) 2,900

The Hard Way, 1956, 31½ x 31½ . . . . (880) 3,870

Villeneuve, 1960, 25¾ x 59½ . . . . (896) 7,800

1968–July 1969

Composition, 21¼ x 17¾ . . . . (1127) 4,600

The Ballet, 1939, 24 x 32¼ . . . . (1145) 2,500

Composition, 1955, 18¼ x 25¾ . . . . (1117) 4,400

Composition, 1958, 36½ x 29 . . . . (1181) 6,600

Landscape, 32 x 39½ . . . . (1117) 7,200

The Rue des Chevaliers, 13 x 8¼ . . . . (1237) 1,000

City Composition, 1949, 17½ x 14½ . . . . (1271) 2,520

The Blue City, 1955, on board, 15¾ x 12¼ . . . . . . (1237) 1,450

The Hanging Gardens of Semiramis, 1958,
    25¼ x 36 . . . . (1237) 4,100

Jacques Villon

(1875–1963)

Birthplace: Damville, Eure, France. (Born Gaston Duchamp, he is the eldest brother of sculptor Raymond Duchamp-Villon and painters Marcel Duchamp and Suzanne Duchamp.)

1894   Enters the Faculty of Law, Paris, but soon gives up his studies to begin an artistic career.

1895   Enters Cormon's studio, Paris. Changes his name to Jacques Villon. Contributes until 1910 to Parisian reviews such as *Le Rire, L'Assiette au Beurre, Quartier Latin,* and *Le Courrier Français.*

1898   Settles in Montmartre. Meets Toulouse-Lautrec at the Moulin Rouge.

1903   Participates in the first Salon d'Automne, Paris.

1906   Settles in Puteaux, a suburb of Paris, where he spends the rest of his life.

1910   Devotes himself exclusively to painting.

1912   As the originator of the "Section d'Or" group, takes part in its first exhibition at the Galerie La Boétie, Paris—with Raymond Duchamp-Villon, Marcel Duchamp, La Fresnaye, Metzinger, Picabia, Léger, Herbin, and Delaunay.

1913   Participates in the Armory Show, New York.

1919	Returns to engraving to make a living. First abstract period.
1921–30	Executes a series of color prints from paintings by contemporary masters (Bernheim-Jeune, Paris).
1922	Takes part in the exhibition of the Société Anonyme, New York.
1925	Last exhibition of the Section d'Or at the Galerie Vavin-Raspail, Paris.
1928	One-man show at the Brummer Gallery, New York.
1930	Devotes himself entirely to painting.
1931–33	Second abstract period. One-man show at the Chicago Arts Club—and again in 1953.
1935	Trip to the U.S.
1939	Participates in the first Salon des Réalités Nouvelles, Paris.
1940	Leaves Paris and goes to Normandy and Tarn.
1942	Important exhibition at the Galerie de France, Paris, with Raymond Duchamp-Villon.
1944	One-man show at the Galerie Louis Carré, Paris—and again in 1948 and 1955.
1949	Wins the grand prize for engraving at the international exhibition of Lugano. One-man show at the Galerie Louis Carré, New York, and at the Institute of Contemporary Art, Boston.
1950	The Venice Biennial assigns an entire room to his work.
1951	Participates in "L'Ecole de Paris 1900–50" at the Royal Academy of Arts, London. Retrospective exhibition at the Musée National d'Art Moderne, Paris.
1952	Participates in "L'Oeuvre du XXème siècle" at the Musée National d'Art Moderne, Paris, and at the Tate Gallery, London.
1955	One-man show at the Musée Toulouse-Lautrec, Albi. Participates in Documenta I, Kassel.
1956	Wins the grand prize of the Venice Biennial.
1963	Died.

Sales

DRAWINGS

1961–1962

The Corporal's Toilette, 1898, charcoal and watercolor, 11¾ x 9 .... (149) $ 284

Women's Work, 1901, wash, 10 x 8 .... (115) 290

Nude with a Tub, 1907, 7¼ x 6¾ .... (49) 156

Little Girl in a Tub, 1907, pencil and charcoal, 7¼ x 6¾ .... (164) 275

The Equestrienne, 1914, pen, 6¾ x 12 .... (119) 160

Composition, 1914, pen, 2¾ x 2¾ .... (102) 164

Study for a Self-Portrait, 1940, pen and pencil, 16¼ x 11¼ .... (149) 1,185

Nude, black lead, 7½ x 4¾ .... (154) 140

The Barricades, pen, 3¾ x 7¼ .... (26) 290

Illustration for "Dents de Lait, Dents de Loup," India ink on tracing paper .... (168) 600

1963

Two Parrots, 1904, pencil and watercolor, 9 x 7¼ .... (255) 548

Sculpture in the Studio, wash and black lead .... (238) 200

The Reveler, India ink and watercolor, 15 x 20½ .... (254) 960

Little Girl Seated, 1907, on tracing paper, 16¾ x 14 .... (254) $ 600

The Man with a Split Ear, 1911, charcoal, 20½ x 16 .... (299) 640

The Cabman, pencil and watercolor, 6½ x 5¼ .... (311) 380

Dominique Bonnaud, ink, 8 x 5 .... (305) 200

The Magi, pen, 10¼ x 7¼ .... (258) 320

Plane Engine, India ink, 12¼ x 10 .... (205) 560

Cubist Figures, pen, 9¾ x 6½ .... (232) 1,130

Study for "Prométhée Délivré," 1958, ink and watercolor, 12½ x 9¾ .... (208) 475

1964

Yon Lug après une nuit d'orgie, (1895), India-ink wash and black lead, 5¼ x 7¾ .... (436) 120

Village Street, pen, 7¾ x 10¾ .... (436) 220

Lacing Up a Corset, 1900, India ink, 4 x 4 .... (377) 215

The Good Customer, 1901, pencil and watercolor heightened with white, 10 x 8 .... (329) 850

Soldier at a Café, pencil and watercolor, 8 x 4¾ .. (398) 480

The Dove, pencil and watercolor, 10¼ x 7¼ .... (378) 1,311

Dove, drawing with watercolor lights, 9½ x 6¾ ... (443) 1,060

Composition, pencil, 9½ x 11¾ .... (483) 360

Baby Sleeping, 1940, double-sided drawing, India ink, 6¾ x 10 .... (366) 156

The Introduction, 1947, pencil and watercolor, 11¾ x 7¾ .... (346) 136

The Call in the Studio, India ink and watercolor, 9½ x 25¼ .... (441) 1,243

1965

The "Bistro," 1895, ink and pencil, 7¼ x 4¾ .... (541) 375

Portrait of a Man, 1902, wash, 7 x 5 .... (561) 120

Still Life with a Parrot, 1932, pencil and black and red ink, 11¼ x 17½ .... (567) 2,102

Composition, 1934, India ink and black lead, 9 x 10½ .... (567) 429

Harvesttime, black lead, 7¼ x 15½ .... (508) 330

Brothel, 1943, on tracing paper, double-sided drawing, 10 x 8 .... (627) 230

Studies of Women in the Nude, pen and watercolor, 11½ x 21¾ .... (585) 871

Horses, pen heightened with watercolor, 9¼ x 12 .... (559) 1,000

The Sleeping Baby, 1952, pen, 7¼ x 10 .... (559) 840

Virgin, Children, St. Bernard Dogs, 1952, ink, watercolor, and gouache, round drawing, diameter 15½ .... (485) 2,250

1966

Young Woman with a Wolf, 1897, black pencil and wash with watercolor lights, 7½ x 5 .... (758) 280

Women on a Merry-Go-Round, 1901, pen, India ink, and blue wash, 14 x 11¾ .... (811) 280

The Cow, pen, 6 x 10 .... (829) 84

Figures, pen, double-sided drawing, 8½ x 6¼ .... (718) 206

Spirals, India ink, 10¾ x 17 .... (810) 380

The Halt, pen, 5½ x 8 .... (711) 200

The Cab, pencil, 10¼ x 8¼ .... (737) 230

Seated Young Lady, 1939, India ink, 10¼ x 8 .... (770) 696

Portrait of a Man, 1940, pen, 11½ x 9 .... (718) 300

The Pasha, pencil and watercolor, 8 x 5½ .... (726) 150

Doctor C . . . , pen, 10 x 8 .... (648) 425

The Violinist, 1903–60, India ink heightened with pastel, 16¼ x 9 .... (687) 300

1967

The Love Letters, (1902), India-ink wash and blue pencil, 15¾ x 13 .... (929) $ 220
The Team, pen, 8¼ x 6¾ .... (929) 280
The Nun, pen and wash, 6¾ x 3¾ .... (897) 220
The Doll, India ink, 13 x 10¼ .... (897) 120
"You Are Going to Despise Me...," wash heightened with watercolor, 16¼ x 14¼ ...... (961) 320

1968–July 1969

The Soldier, colored pencil, 7½ x 4½ .... (1134) 106
Portrait of a Woman in a Hat, 1902, black chalk, 13¼ x 8¾ .... (1102) 241
Composition, 1914, pencil, 12¼ x 10 .... (1174) 1,840
Study of Figures, pen on checked paper, 5¾ x 8¼ .... (1075) 180
Study for a Self-Portrait, 1940, India ink, 16¼ x 11¼ .... (1080) 1,500
Two Children, black stone, 6½ x 4½ .... (1073) 100
The Doll, India ink, 13 x 10¼ .... (1140) 110
Study for Stained Glass, charcoal, ink, and gouache, 9½ x 15½ .... (1134) 142
Study for Stained Glass, colored pencil and pen on paper laid down on canvas, 9¾ x 16¼ ... (1187) 340
Reclining Nude, 1953, pen, 6¾ x 9¾ .... (1026) 380
Study for the Portrait of Joseph Pulitzer, Jr., 1954, India ink, 14 x 10¼ .... (1061) 500
Seated Woman Dressing, pencil, 9 x 7¼ .... (1221) 420
The Cab, 10¼ x 8¼ .... (1227) 150
Young Girl Seated, 1907, pencil, 11 x 6½ .... (1248) 550
The March Past, India ink on tracing paper, 12¼ x 9 .... (1256) 520
Composition, India ink, colored pencil, and watercolor, 7½ x 15¾ .... (1268) 1,740

WATERCOLORS

1961–1962

La Rôtie, 1901, gouache, 13¾ x 19¾ .... (3) 1,550
The Conversation, 1901, watercolor, 10¼ x 8¼ .... (53) 260
"Monsieur Le Comte," 1901, watercolor, 22½ x 17¾ .... (98) 580
La Montique de Paille, 1940, watercolor and pen, 8 x 12 .... (149) 395
Sleeping Baby, 1940, gouache and ink, 6¼ x 4¾ .. (143) 1,130
Composition, 1957, watercolor, 13½ x 19½ .... (93) 3,051
Branch of an Apple Tree in Blossom, watercolor, 10 x 8 .... (59) 900
The Sitting, gouache, 9 x 6½ .... (116) 640

1963

Good Day from the UUF, 1897, watercolor, 11¾ x 8 .... (295) 70
Daphné, watercolor on a lithograph, 9 x 19¾ ..... (205) 1,640
Illustration for "The Bucolics," watercolor, 8¾ x 10¾ .... (249) 1,700
Still Life with a Wedding Globe, watercolor, 19¾ x 14¾ .... (205) 2,000

1964

Aviation, gouache, 10 x 6 .... (399) 320
The Horse, 1914, watercolor, 9½ x 12¼ .... (399) 360
The Conquest of the Air, watercolor and gouache, 9¾ x 24 .... (471) 1,243
Creation of the World and Lights, 1954, watercolor, 11½ x 7¾ .... (376) 490
The Conquest of the Air, 1960, watercolor and gouache, 9 and 3¾ x 24 .... (376) 410

1965

The Horse, 1914, watercolor, 9½ x 12¼ .... (491) $ 600
The Grisette and the Little Dog, watercolor, 4½ x 3¼ .... (505) 400
Composition, 1932, gouache, 8¼ x 12¼ .... (612) 800
Christ, watercolor and pen, 10 x 8 .... (632) 560
Composition, watercolor, 4¾ x 9¼ .... (561) 320
The Olympus, 1957, watercolor, 10¾ x 20 .... (516) 800

1966

The Wedding Globe, watercolor, 6½ x 4¾ .... (74) 1,040
Composition, 1916, watercolor, 19½ x 12¾ .... (811) 1,420
Cubist Composition, 1924, watercolor, 10 x 6¾ ... (759) 700
Clown, 1925, watercolor and ink, 7½ x 4½ .... (784) 425
Bust of a Woman, watercolor, 5¾ x 4 .... (826) 360

1967

The Pasha, watercolor, 8 x 5½ .... (850) 180
The Grisette and the Little Dog, 1897, watercolor, 4½ x 3 .... (996) 420
Olympus, 1957, watercolor, 11¾ x 20½ .... (857) 440

1968–July 1969

Zodiac Signs: The Bull, The Twins, 1937, watercolor, 7½ x 12¾ .... (1202) 3,000
The Horses, watercolor, 9½ x 11¾ .... (1119) 1,000
Two Normans Seated on a Bench, watercolor, 4 x 5¾ .... (1073) 560
At the Café, watercolor and India ink, 7¼ x 5¼ .. (1073) 340
At the Café, watercolor and gouache, 14¾ x 11¾ .... (1127) 1,035
The Harbor, 1959, watercolor, 10 x 7¼ .... (1026) 3,000
The Parrot, watercolor, 8¼ x 6½ .... (1221) 600

PAINTINGS

1961–1962

Portrait of a Man, 1912, 36 x 28½ .... (18) 16,950
Village, 1926, 32 x 25¾ .... (149) 8,848
Forsaking, 36½ x 29 .... (149) 11,376
Stool with Papers, 1926, 31½ x 21½ .... (84) 1,510
Caliban, 25¾ x 21¼ .... (160) 8,000
Flowers in a Blue Vase, 1926, 39½ x 27¾ .... (76) 9,000
Portrait of a Woman, 1929, 16¼ x 13 .... (76) 600
The Dove, 1947, 8¾ x 13 .... (53) 5,200
The Dove, 8¾ x 13 .... (30) 5,800
Prehistory, 1957, 25¾ x 36½ .... (149) 14,220
The Frogs Asking..., 16¼ x 13 .... (143) 6,328
"Les Gars de Batterie," 1947, 35¼ x 57¾ .... (149) 31,600

1963

Bust of a Young Woman, 1932, on cardboard, 14 x 10¾ .... (287) 2,840
Seated Boy, 1932, 12¾ x 9½ .... (190) 3,400
Eve, 1938, 45¾ x 32 .... (249) 10,200
Portrait of a Chansonnier, 14 x 9½ .... (263) 3,120
Summer Rest, 16¼ x 22 .... (200) 3,800
Our Friend Colette, 1939, 14 x 9½ .... (232) 5,424
Seated Nude, oil on cardboard, 14 x 10¾ .... (232) 904
Sleeping Baby, 1952, 10¾ x 5¾ .... (283) 6,554
The Spring, 1957, 21¾ x 15 .... (232) 6,780
Nude, 15 x 19 .... (258) 4,000

1964

Portrait of Yvonne, 1927, 16 x 12¾ .... (448) 2,500
Portrait of a Man, 18¼ x 15 .... (366) 2,000
Under the Tent, 1929, 17½ x 23½ .... (454) 11,056

Landscape, 1931, on canvas laid down on
cardboard, 14 x 10¾ . . . . (399) $1,300

Composition, 1932, on canvas laid down on
board, 16 x 10 . . . . (354)   2,750

Nude, 1936, 10¾ x 8¾ . . . . (408)   2,700

The Spring, 1957, 21½ x 15 . . . . (416)   7,739

1965

The Picnic (After Manet), on paper, 18¼ x 23¾ . . (624)   3,870

Stool, 1926, 32 x 25¾ . . . . (569)   3,729

Stool with Papers, 1926, 32 x 25¾ . . . . (640)   3,800

Portrait of a Woman, 1932, on cardboard,
14 x 10¾ . . . . (561)   1,600

Portrait of a Woman, 1933, 18¼ x 13 . . . . (564)   1,800

Portrait of a Woman, 1945, 11½ x 9¼ . . . . (632)   980

From Wheat to Straw, 1946, 25 x 55½ . . . . (633)   35,000

Chantilly, the Horses' Walk, 1950, 20 x 58¼ . . . . . (573)   31,786

"Portrait of Rose Selavy" (Marcel Duchamp),
1953, 32 x 23¾ . . . . (485)   23,000

Study for the Portrait of Mr. Pulitzer, 1954,
15½ x 11¾ . . . . (637)   2,500

The Vulture Flies Away, 1956, 36 x 29 . . . . (485)   11,000

Still Life, 15 x 18¼ . . . . (512)   5,700

1966

Half-Length Portrait of a Woman, 1932, on
cardboard, 14 x 10¾ . . . . (727)   1,500

The Shark Plane, 1954, 9½ x 12¾ . . . . (797)   3,209

Palette on Parchment, 9 x 11¾ . . . . (829)   180

1967

Self-Portrait, 1909, 15¾ x 10 . . . . (989)   1,950

Head, 1919, 12¾ x 8½ . . . . (880)   2,764

Landscape, 1923, 8¾ x 6½ . . . . (909)   1,100

Under the Tent, 1923, 17½ x 23¾ . . . . (988)   2,488

Adam, 1938, 13 x 9½ . . . . (976)   2,320

Study for Beaugency Castle, 1940, 18¼ x 15 . . . . . . (901)   6,600

Threshing in Normandy, 11 x 25¾ . . . . (901)   9,000

Landscape of the Lot-et-Garonne, 1941,
21¼ x 28½ . . . . (911)   9,200

Study for the Portrait of a Man, 1954, 15 x 11¾ . . (870)   1,800

1968–July 1969

The Haulers, 1908, 25½ x 36½ . . . . (1176)   22,000

Portrait of Claude Méran, 1923, 28¾ x 23½ . . . . . (1176)   15,000

The Model, 1930, 21¾ x 15 . . . . (1117)   5,400

Portrait of a Woman, 1932, on cardboard,
14 x 10¾ . . . . (1053)   1,920

The Alms, (1943), 8½ x 10½ . . . . (1125)   6,900

The Flight, (1945), 18¼ x 21¾ . . . . (125)   7,820

Young Woman with a Green Bodice, 1947,
16¼ x 13 . . . . (1109)   5,600

A Plane, 1954, 7½ x 10¾ . . . . (1026)   3,800

The Vulture Flies Away, 1956, 36 x 29 . . . . (1132)   14,160

The Vineyards, 8 x 9 . . . . (1026)   1,800

The Quays of the River Seine, Paris,
18¼ x 21¼ . . . . (1193)   2,230

Flowers . . . . (1250)   3,200

Flowers . . . . (1250)   4,200

Flowers . . . . (1250)   3,700

The Garden, 1941, 25¾ x 36½ . . . . (1258)   20,000

Threshing in Normandy, 11 x 25¾ . . . . (1258)   9,000

Woman, 1930, 21¾ x 18¼ . . . . (1258)   2,900

The Fund Holder, 1932, 21¾ x 16¼ . . . . (1258)   3,400

Laziness, (1947), 21¼ x 25¾ . . . . (1268)   19,024

Louis Vivin

(1861–1936)

Birthplace: Hadol, Vosges, France.

1879   Enters the Direction Centrale des Postes, Paris, as supernumerary. Starts to paint.

1889   Participates in the Salon des Employés des Postes, Paris. Also exhibits at the "foire aux croûtes" near the Sacré-Coeur, Montmartre.

1904   Exhibits at the Hôtel des Postes, Paris.

1910   Appointed principal inspector of the postal services.

1920   The dealer Bing takes some interest in his work.

1922   Retires and devotes himself exclusively to painting.

1923   First attack of hemiplegia. Paints "Reims Cathedral" (Musée National d'Art Moderne, Paris).

1925   German critic Wilhelm Uhde takes a great interest in his work, buys some of his pictures, and encourages him to keep on painting. Series of his monuments.

1936   Second attack of hemiplegia. Died, Paris.

1937   Included in "Les Maîtres populaires de la Réalité," Paris.

Sales

PAINTINGS

1961–1962

Seaside, 18¼ x 21¾ . . . . (30) $2,000

Notre-Dame de Paris, 1925, 18¼ x 21¼ . . . . (44)   1,450

Tigers and Their Prey, 18¾ x 23¼ . . . . (174)   934

1963

Garden in Bloom, on cardboard, 6¼ x 10 . . . . (215)   320

Garden in the Springtime, on an oval board,
9½ x 4¾ . . . . (215)   160

Joan of Arc at Domrémy, 15 x 14 . . . . (201)   690

1964

The Washerwomen, 15 x 21¾ . . . . (472)   3,200

Wintry Landscape, 15 x 17¾ . . . . (385)   972

1965

Wintry Landscape, 15 x 17¾ . . . . (568)   1,266

Fishing Harbor, 15 x 21¾ . . . . (511)   800

1966

Place de la Bastille, (1932-35), 24 x 19¾ . . . . (784)   2,250

Interior of a Church, 15 x 18¼ . . . . (805)   700

1967

Les Buttes-Chaumont, 15 x 21¾ . . . . (978)   3,400

The Painter at Montmartre, 13 x 18¼ . . . . (978)   2,620

1968–July 1969

The Sacré-Coeur, 8¼ x 12¾ . . . . (1030)   725

Village in Winter, 15 x 22¾ . . . . (1145)   2,000

Mother and Child in a Park, 1882, 14 x 10¼ . . . . . (1043)   360

The Meal at the Farm, 15 x 18¼ . . . . (1043)   1,440

The Garden of the Country House, 18¾ x 25¾ . . (1255)   5,660

Maurice de Vlaminck

(1876–1958)

Birthplace: Paris, France.

1894 Marries.

1895 Becomes passionately fond of bicycling. Studies drawing with Robichon and Rigal. Takes a great interest in Impressionism.

1899–1900 Teaches music to support himself. Meets Derain and moves resolutely toward painting. Both friends share the same studio on the isle of Chatou, near Paris. Meets Claude Monet at Durand-Ruel's.

1901–02 Immensely impressed by the Van Gogh exhibition he visits with Derain at Bernheim's, Paris. Derain introduces him to Matisse. Makes an increasing use of pure color. Issues his first novel, illustrated by Derain.

1905 Meets the artists of the "Bateau-Lavoir" in Montmartre—Picasso, Van Dongen, Max Jacob, and Guillaume Apollinaire. Takes part in a group show at the Galerie Berthe Weil, Paris. Participates for the first time in the Salon des Indépendants and in the Salon d'Automne, Paris, in the famous room derisively called "la cage aux fauves." Owing to his violent temper, fully expressed in his work, Vlaminck is generally regarded as the typical Fauve painter.

1906 Executes his most brilliant series of Fauve paintings, including "Les Bateaux-Lavoir," "Country House," and "Fishermen at Nanterre." Ambroise Vollard buys all his work.

1908 Abandons pure color to devote himself to new investigations under the influence of Cézanne's work.

1914–15 Takes a stand against Cubism. Elaborates an original manner tinged with Expressionism. Chiefly attracted by landscapes, he also paints flowers and some still lifes and portraits.

1918 Meets Zborowski, André Salmon, and Francis Carco.

1919 Important one-man show at the Galerie Druet, Paris.

1920 Settles at Auvers-sur-Oise.

1925 Settles at Rueil-la-Gadelière, Eure-et-Loir, for the rest of his life.

1933 One-man show at the Galerie Bernheim-Jeune, Paris, and at the Palais des Beaux-Arts, Brussels.

1936 Wins the Carnegie prize—and again in 1939.

1939 One-man show at Wildenstein's, New York.

1955 Becomes a member of the Académie Royale de Belgique.

1956 Major retrospective exhibition at the Galerie Charpentier, Paris.

1958 Died, Rueil-la-Gadelière.

Sales

DRAWINGS

1961–1962

Landscape, India ink, 8 x 10½ . . . . (124) $ 800
Flowers in a Vase, pen, 13½ x 10¼ . . . . (32)   560
La Potinière, India ink, 10¼ x 14 . . . . (93)   1,763

1963

Landscape, (1917), sepia wash, 17 x 21 . . . . (255) $1,508
Landscape, ink, 16¾ x 21¾ . . . . (210)   960
Wintry Landscape, wash, 8 x 10 . . . . (188)   220

1964

Landscape, India ink, 7½ x 9½ . . . . (377)   994
The Hamlet, India ink, 8 x 12¼ . . . . (399)   460
The Farm, ink, watercolor, and gouache, 13¼ x 17 . . . . (387)   2,626

1965

La Potinière, India ink, 10¼ x 14 . . . . (569)   1,537

1966

Village Behind the Corn Field, (1925), wash, 14½ x 18 . . . . (655)   1,200
Village Behind the Corn Field, (1925), wash, 14½ x 18 . . . . (727)   1,080
Landscape of the River Orne, 8 x 10½ . . . . (764)   640
The Village, ink and gouache, 17¾ x 21½ . . . . (686)   6,081
Houses Amid the Trees, 1914, charcoal, 19¾ x 25½ . . . . (798)   3,390

1967

Village Street, India-ink wash, 10 x 8¼ . . . . (996)   1,140
Landscape, India ink, 7½ x 9½ . . . . (967)   701
Village Street, pen, 10 x 14 . . . . (985)   2,270
Landscape, India ink, 14¾ x 21 . . . . (975)   2,800
Self-Portrait, 1955, pen, 15½ x 12 . . . . (951)   1,596
Street of a Little Town, ink and watercolor, 14 x 18¼ . . . . (940)   3,773
The Water Mill, ink and watercolor, 17 x 23 . . . . . (1004)   6,000

1968–July 1969

Pontoise, India-ink wash, 14 x 17½ . . . . (1026)   1,200
Landscape, India ink, 11¾ x 15½ . . . . (1127)   1,840
Village Street, (1930), pen, 10 x 12¾ . . . . (1085)   744
House in a Landscape, wash, 15 x 18¼ . . . . (1139)   2,700
Landscape, charcoal, 6 x 9 . . . . (1248)   1,100
Landscape, India ink, 11 x 16¼ . . . . (1256)   2,000

WATERCOLORS

1961–1962

Landscape in the Surroundings of Paris, watercolor, 15½ x 20 . . . . (141)   3,200
Landscape with an Enclosure, watercolor, 9½ x 12¼ . . . . (141)   1,800
Landscape, watercolor, 18½ x 21¾ . . . . (106)   4,565
Landscape, watercolor, 14¾ x 21¾ . . . . (20)   6,636
Landscape, gouache, 17¾ x 21¼ . . . . (62)   3,600
Village Street in Winter, (1935), gouache, 17¾ x 21¼ . . . . (88)   4,477
Village Street, watercolor, 17½ x 21¼ . . . . (32)   3,000
Scene in a Village, gouache and watercolor, 19½ x 25¼ . . . . (64)   6,500
Thatch-Roofed Cottages on the Edge of the Road, gouache, 14¾ x 18 . . . . (124)   3,300
The Road, watercolor and gouache, 17½ x 21 . . . . . (18)   4,972
The Fisherman, watercolor, 17¾ x 21½ . . . . (93)   4,972
The Bridge at Rueil, watercolor, 13½ x 16¾ . . . . . . (171)   2,100

1963

The Tree by the Riverside, (1922), watercolor and gouache, 17 x 21 . . . . (225)   3,000
Landscape, watercolor, 17½ x 20¾ . . . . (208)   3,200
Landscape, watercolor, 13½ x 16¾ . . . . (232)   3,390

Landscape: The Pond, gouache, 17½ x 21 . . . . **(258)** $1,800

Landscape, Snow Effect, gouache, 14¾ x 17½ . . . . **(299)**   530

The Village, gouache and paint on paper,
9½ x 12¾ . . . . **(224)**   4,600

Still Life with Fruit and a Decanter, watercolor,
17½ x 23¾ . . . . **(283)**   6,554

1964

Vase of Flowers, 1906, gouache, 22 x 23¼ . . . . **(405)**   3,192

The "Buvette," watercolor and gouache,
18 x 21¼ . . . . **(354)**   5,000

Street Under Snow, gouache, 17¾ x 21¾ . . . . **(443)**   3,440

Village Street, gouache, 18¼ x 21¾ . . . . **(378)**   6,780

Village Path, watercolor, 15 x 20 . . . . **(458)**   871

The Village, gouache, 13¼ x 17 . . . . **(454)**   2,626

Suburban Scene, watercolor and gouache,
17½ x 20½ . . . . **(448)**   3,250

The Farm, watercolor, 11¾ x 15 . . . . **(409)**   1,750

Landscape, watercolor, 17¾ x 21¼ . . . . **(372)**   5,100

Landscape, gouache, 17½ x 21 . . . . **(408)**   6,600

1965

Landscape, (1924), gouache, 17¾ x 21¼ . . . . **(549)**   5,166

The Rustic House, gouache, 17¾ x 21¼ . . . . **(516)**   2,800

Village Street Under Snow, gouache,
14¼ x 18¼ . . . . **(567)**   4,407

Village Street, watercolor, 20 x 21 . . . . **(581)**   2,020

The Grocer's, watercolor and gouache,
17¾ x 23¼ . . . . **(600)**   2,600

The Fisherman, watercolor and India ink,
17½ x 21¾ . . . . **(545)**   2,546

The Haystacks, watercolor, 15 x 18¼ . . . . **(632)**   4,000

1966

Landscape, (1910), gouache and watercolor,
17½ x 22¼ . . . . **(689)**   5,528

Hilly Landscape, watercolor, 16¾ x 20¼ . . . . **(698)**   2,774

Village Crossed by a River, (1925), watercolor
and India ink, 18¼ x 21¾ . . . . **(735)**   4,068

Outskirts of the Wood, watercolor, 13 x 16½ . . . . . **(739)**   1,845

Snow Effect, gouache, 18¾ x 22 . . . . **(811)**   5,420

Brown Landscape, watercolor, 17¾ x 21 . . . . **(784)**   3,750

1967

Banks of the River Oise, (1920), watercolor and
gouache, 18¾ x 24 . . . . **(889)**   3,850

Landscape, watercolor and India ink,
12¾ x 15¾ . . . . **(918)**   5,650

Bunch of Flowers, gouache, 24 x 19¾ . . . . **(928)**   7,006

Landscape, gouache, 17½ x 21 . . . . **(912)**   3,300

House on the Edge of the Road, watercolor,
17¾ x 21¼ . . . . **(901)**   4,400

The Village Street, watercolor and gouache,
15½ x 18¼ . . . . **(995)**   7,300

The Watering Place in the Village, watercolor
and gouache, 17¾ x 21¾ . . . . **(987)**   4,400

Riverside, watercolor, 9 x 11¾ . . . . **(841)**   1,800

1968–July 1969

Autumn Landscape, watercolor, 14¼ x 18¾ . . . . . **(1183)**   6,200

Landscape, watercolor, 24 x 18½ . . . . **(1125)**   11,500

The Path to the Farm, gouache, 13½ x 17½ . . . . . **(1125)**   4,025

Village Street, watercolor and gouache,
18 x 21¼ . . . . **(1113)**   6,200

Landscape, watercolor and gouache, 17¾ x 21¼ . . **(1113)**   6,000

Moonlight Landscape, watercolor and gouache,
16¾ x 20 . . . . **(1145)**   4,000

Village Street, gouache and watercolor,
17¾ x 20½ . . . . **(1018)** $5,750

View of a Village, gouache, 17 x 20¾ . . . . **(1132)**   7,552

Street Under Snow, gouache, 17¾ x 21¼ . . . . **(1193)**   9,912

The Mill, watercolor and gouache, 17½ x 21 . . . . **(1189)**   8,000

The Canal, watercolor, 14¾ x 18¾ . . . . **(1213)**   8,200

Village in the Fields, 1907, watercolor,
15½ x 20¾ . . . . **(1109)**   18,400

The "Poisson Frit," Street at Valmondois,
varnished gouache on paper laid down on
canvas, 18¼ x 21¾ . . . . **(1224)**   9,200

The Blue Hour in the Suburbs, watercolor,
17¾ x 21¾ . . . . **(1268)**   9,976

Farmyard, gouache, 17¾ x 21 . . . . **(1272)**   9,840

Village Church, watercolor, 19½ x 25 . . . . **(1273)**   9,570

PAINTINGS

1961–1962

Landscape of Chatou, (1903), 21½ x 25¾ . . . . **(128)**   43,936

Still Life, 1904, 29 x 36½ . . . . **(84)**   32,952

Bunch of Roses, (1905), peinture à la colle,
20 x 23 . . . . **(71)**   4,200

Mont Valérien, (1908), 25¾ x 32 . . . . **(128)**   49,428

Landscape of Normandy, 1910, 29¼ x 33 . . . . **(145)**   28,440

The Flood at Le Pecq, 1910, 19½ x 23¾ . . . . **(64)**   11,500

Still Life with a Jug, (1911), 18¼ x 21¾ . . . . **(32)**   7,600

Still Life with a Jug, (1911), 18¼ x 21¾ . . . . **(114)**   6,400

The Roofs of the Village, (1910–12), 21¼ x 21¼ . . . . **(96)**   20,000

Landscape, (1912), 21¼ x 25¾ . . . . **(143)**   19,210

The Great Bunch of Flowers, (1913–14),
25¼ x 21¼ . . . . **(88)**   10,086

The Castle, 1916, 23¼ x 28 . . . . **(164)**   8,238

The Teapot, 1920, 32 x 42 . . . . **(71)**   13,200

Still Life, 1920, 21¾ x 25¼ . . . . **(20)**   11,850

Bunch of Flowers, (1921), 24 x 18¼ . . . . **(93)**   14,690

Country Church, 23¾ x 29 . . . . **(29)**   8,400

The Flood, 1926, 25¾ x 32 . . . . **(29)**   8,800

Village Street, 1928 . . . . **(30)**   9,700

Still Life with a Pike, 19¾ x 25¾ . . . . **(106)**   3,978

After the Storm, (1935), 19½ x 23¾ . . . . **(64)**   12,500

Vase of Flowers, 18¼ x 15 . . . . **(32)**   6,400

Flowers, 18¼ x 15 . . . . **(18)**   11,074

Flowers in a Vase, 21¾ x 15 . . . . **(116)**   11,400

Peonies, 23¾ x 19 . . . . **(84)**   11,533

Still Life with Bread, 15¼ x 18½ . . . . **(30)**   5,400

Still Life, 21¼ x 29 . . . . **(71)**   5,260

The Dahlias, 32 x 23¾ . . . . **(114)**   20,000

Haymaking Near the Village, 29 x 36½ . . . . **(114)**   9,600

Haymaking Near the Village, 29 x 36½ . . . . **(141)**   16,400

Country Road, 19½ x 25 . . . . **(96)**   18,000

Village Street Under Snow, 21¼ x 25¾ . . . . **(171)**   7,620

Landscape of the River Eure, 19½ x 24¾ . . . . **(164)**   7,689

Snowy Landscape, 19¾ x 24 . . . . **(69)**   6,636

Landscape, 15 x 21¾ . . . . **(168)**   5,700

Landscape with Red Roofs, 29 x 36½ . . . . **(80)**   16,000

The Castle, 21¼ x 32 . . . . **(6)**   15,820

Church and Graveyard, 18¼ x 24 . . . . **(109)**   3,900

The Hôtel de la Truite, 29 x 36½ . . . . **(120)**   8,100

The Hôtel de la Gare, 29¾ x 36½ . . . . **(26)**   8,000

Entrance of the Harbor, 21¼ x 25¾ . . . . **(18)**   16,950

A Cliff by the Seaside, 25¾ x 32 . . . . **(124)**   1,880

The Towboats Alongside the Quay, 29 x 32 . . . . . . **(116)**   15,200

1963

My House Near the Great Trees, 18¾ x 22 ...... (254) $8,000

Bunch of Flowers, (1905), peinture à la colle, 19½ x 23 .... (210)   5,484

The Docks at Le Havre, (1906), 32 x 36 .... (247)   54,840

Chatou, 1908, 23¾ x 29 .... (283)   26,894

The River Seine at Triel, (1908), 20½ x 24 .... (241)   12,000

Hérouville Village, 29 x 36½ .... (241)   14,000

Walk at the Entrance of a Castle, (1909), 12¾ x 16 .... (225)   8,000

London Bridge, (1910), 20 x 24 .... (293)   14,000

House by the Waterside, 14¾ x 21¼ .... (317)   7,200

The Flood at Ivry, 1910, 36½ x 29 .... (312)   21,000

Banks of the River Seine, 1911, 25½ x 31½ ...... (210)   24,678

Cassis Harbor, (1911), 37¼ x 45½ .... (202)   22,500

Flowers, (1913), 28½ x 23¾ .... (316)   6,000

Bougival Bridge, 1914, 15 x 22 .... (210)   9,597

Flowers, (1919), 18¼ x 15 .... (283)   11,300

Flowers in a White Vase, 25¼ x 19¾ .... (254)   9,000

Bend of the Road, (1920), 17¾ x 21½ .... (277)   7,678

Still Life with Books and a Candle, (1920), 21¼ x 28¾ .... (225)   12,000

Village Street,[1] (1922-24), 26 x 32 .... (316)   10,000

The Park of Versailles, 29 x 23¾ .... (190)   6,000

The River Oise Near Mériel, 1923, 15 x 21½ ..... (315)   6,581

Snowy Landscape, 25¾ x 32 .... (258)   10,000

White Flowers in a Gray Pot, 25¾ x 19¾ .... (258)   10,000

Street Under Snow, 25¾ x 32 .... (215)   5,160

Wintry Landscape, (1925-30), 25¾ x 32 .... (316)   16,000

Village Under Snow, 31½ x 45½ .... (293)   15,600

Farm on the Edge of a Pond, 29 x 36½ .... (318)   11,000

The Forest on Fire, 23¼ x 28½ .... (232)   9,040

The Torrent, 21¼ x 29 .... (206)   4,800

Landscape, 12¾ x 15¾ .... (202)   7,500

Still Life with Pears, 17¾ x 21½ .... (202)   5,000

Flowers in a Vase, 18¼ x 15 .... (224)   5,220

Chrysanthemums, 21¼ x 18¼ .... (296)   16,400

1964

Landscape, 1900, 29 x 23¾ .... (464)   2,640

Still Life, 1908-09, 28 x 35¼ .... (454)   29,022

The Fishing Boats and the Lighthouse, (1909-10), 35¼ x 45½ .... (454)   22,112

The Fishing Boat, 17¾ x 21 .... (458)   9,577

Trees Alongside a River in Autumn, 25 x 31¼ .... (416)   18,795

Riverside, 29 x 36½ .... (37)   17,620

The Bridge, 1912, 19 x 28 .... (453)   16,584

Barge and Towboat on the River Seine, 23¾ x 29 .... (340)   15,600

Village Under Snow, 23¾ x 29 .... (340)   9,000

The Café, (1912-14), 21 x 25 .... (416)   11,056

The Village Road, 21¼ x 25¾ .... (340)   8,000

Portrait of a Woman, (1914), 25¾ x 19¾ .... (354)   12,500

Vireille Halt, (1915), 31 x 36½ .... (354)   14,000

The Hamlet, 21¼ x 25¾ .... (399)   5,000

Landscape, (1918), 18¼ x 21¾ .... (354)   9,000

Flowers, (1919), 18¼ x 15 .... (378)   10,622

Bunch of Flowers, 21¾ x 15 .... (464)   8,000

Landscape, (1920), 15 x 18¼ .... (448)   9,500

Entrance of the Forest, 1923, 31½ x 39 .... (416)   13,820

The Village Street, 21¼ x 25¾ .... (398)   7,420

---

[1]The red house.

1965

The Road, 23¾ x 29 .... (347) $14,000

The Road, 23¾ x 28¾ .... (465)   9,200

Landscape, 29 x 36½ .... (465)   23,700

Restless Sea, 1932, 20 x 26 .... (416)   4,146

Le Havre Harbor, 20½ x 26½ .... (405)   14,365

Still Life, 23¾ x 29¼ .... (405)   15,090

Still Life with a Fruit Stand, 23¾ x 29 .... (378)   17,854

The Farm with a Red Field, 18¼ x 21¾ .... (347)   9,200

Landscape with a Red House, (1935), 20 x 24 ..... (385)   8,814

Still Life with Flowers, (1935), 22 x 18½ .... (385)   10,396

Flowers in a Pot, 29¾ x 19¾ .... (347)   14,200

The Park of Versailles, 29 x 23¾ .... (398)   6,000

Barge at Triel, 20 x 24 .... (471)   17,289

Stormy Landscape, 28 x 35½ .... (453)   14,926

Storm, (1945), 21¼ x 25¾ .... (378)   7,006

Autumn Landscape, 21¼ x 25¾ .... (470)   8,364

The House with an Apple Tree, 24½ x 31¼ ...... (458)   14,510

Path in the Snow, 25¾ x 32 .... (347)   9,400

Wintry Landscape, 31½ x 39½ .... (471)   15,142

Palette .... (451)   90

1965

My Father's House, (1904), 21¼ x 25¾ .... (594)   45,000

Still Life with Copper Tumblers, (1908-09), 24½ x 19 .... (575)   9,674

The Old Harbor, (1910-11), 31¾ x 39¼ .... (575)   16,584

The Village Street, 1911, 25¾ x 32 .... (594)   21,000

The Village, 15 x 18¼ .... (590)   6,700

Still Life, (1911), 18¼ x 21¾ .... (553)   9,600

Still Life with Fruit, 29 x 36¾ .... (553)   12,200

London Bridge, 1911, 20 x 24 .... (583)   8,706

Suburban Street, (1912), 25¾ x 31½ .... (522)   12,438

The Village Street, 21¼ x 25¾ .... (545)   8,497

The Outlet of the Village, 19¾ x 24 .... (564)   6,600

The House Among the Trees, 21¼ x 28 .... (637)   14,500

Banks of the River Rhône, 1914, 28 x 35¼ ...... (628)   26,118

The "14 Juillet" at Chatou, (1915), 19¾ x 25¾ .... (637)   17,000

Bridge at Chatou, 28½ x 36¾ .... (564)   31,866

Fishermen Close to a Bridge, 29 x 36½ .... (552)   12,900

Landscape of the River Oise, 25¾ x 32 .... (640)   9,220

Landscape with Sailboats, 23¾ x 29 .... (640)   7,760

Road to Beaune, (1920-25), 17¾ x 21½ .... (624)   7,186

Flowers in a Tin Pot, (1922), 21¾ x 18¼ .... (617)   9,718

The White and Green Bouquet, 21 x 14¾ .... (637)   11,000

La Sologne, (1922-25), 25¾ x 31½ .... (624)   11,609

Garden by the River, (1925), 23½ x 28¾ .... (526)   17,500

Landscape, 21¾ x 25¾ .... (594)   10,000

Landscape of Hérouville, (1928), 23¾ x 28½ ..... (561)   8,000

Vireille Halt, 27¾ x 36½ .... (602)   9,040

The Road to Brest, 25¾ x 32 .... (547)   9,000

Landscape of the Beauce, 18¼ x 21¾ .... (539)   6,500

Snow Effect, 21¼ x 25¾ .... (526)   21,000

The Storm, 21¼ x 25¾ .... (633)   21,000

The Tempest, 25¾ x 32 .... (512)   7,800

Wild Flowers, 21¾ x 15 .... (512)   7,400

Flowers in a Vase, 21¾ x 18¼ .... (564)   9,000

The Vase of Flowers, 18¼ x 15 .... (561)   7,400

Village Street in Winter, 25¼ x 31¼ .... (583)   10,157

The Village Under Snow, 23¾ x 29 .... (515)   8,600

Wintry Landscape, 32 x 45¾ .... (569)   11,074

Landscape, 19¾ x 24 .... (539)   11,500

Underwood, 21¼ x 25¾ .... (617) $ 20,792

Bunch of Flowers, on cradled panel, 22 x 18½ .... (526)   11,000

The Church, 18¼ x 21¾ .... (561)   5,800

Still Life After Cezanne, 25¾ x 34½ .... (561)   29,000

1966

The River, 29¼ x 36½ .... (744)   33,900

Houses at Bougival, 1914, 15½ x 19½ .... (685)   11,000

Vase of Flowers, 25¾ x 19¾ .... (776)   19,000

Still Life with a Fruit Stand, 25¾ x 32½ .... (742)   17,000

Bunch of Wild Flowers, 18¼ x 15 .... (800)   11,000

Still Life, (1920), 23 x 28¾ .... (689)   8,707

Still Life with a Tin Pot, 1923, 18¼ x 21½ ...... (686)   11,056

Field of Red Poppies, 21 x 25 .... (808)   12,188

Still Life with a Pipe and Books, (1928),
21¼ x 29¼ .... (776)   14,000

Still Life with a Fish and a Bowl of Cherries,
32½ x 45¾ .... (753)   12,188

Flowers with a Blue Vase, 15 x 18¼ .... (797)   13,108

Bunch of Flowers, 20½ x 27¾ .... (797)   16,272

Poissy, (1909), 23¾ x 32 .... (797)   32,544

The House, 10¾ x 14 .... (666)   1,800

The Road, 18¼ x 21¾ .... (685)   8,600

After the Storm, (1920), 18½ x 21¾ .... (713)   12,000

The Farm, 18 x 22 .... (784)   6,500

The Mill, (1910), 29 x 36¼ .... (750)   20,730

The Hamlet Under Snow, (1938), 23½ x 29 ...... (776)   16,000

The White Church, 15 x 18½ .... (713)   10,000

The Church, 18½ x 24 .... (745)   10,622

The Mill at Meslay-le-Vidame (Eure-et-Loir),
21 x 25¼ .... (689)   6,357

Wintry Landscape, 32 x 45¾ .... (744)   12,656

1967

Village Street, 15½ x 20 .... (923)   8,200

Still Life, 1908–09, 28 x 35¼ .... (982)   29,625

Village by the Riverside, (1909), 25¼ x 31½ ...... (864)   32,500

Landscape, 1909, 28½ x 23¾ .... (988)   36,076

Landscape with a Bridge, (1910), 27¾ x 35¼ ..... (982)   21,330

The River, (1910), 29¼ x 36¼ .... (918)   32,544

The Gray House, 19¾ x 25¾ .... (918)   11,300

View of Meulan, (1911), 23 x 29 .... (938)   11,609

Landscape by the Waterside, 1911, 29 x 23¾ ..... (984)   15,000

The Farm, 23¾ x 29 .... (962)   15,200

The House Around the Corner, (1920),
12¾ x 15¾ .... (963)   9,500

Hôtel du Laboureur, Rueil-la-Gadelière, (1925),
35½ x 45¾ .... (954)   30,000

Tillières-sur-Avre, 23¾ x 29¾ .... (864)   12,000

Village Under the Storm, 21½ x 25¾ .... (857)   8,800

The Boat, 9½ x 13 .... (911)   6,200

Castle by the Riverside, 32 x 39½ .... (935)   10,420

The Entrance of the Village, 23 x 28 .... (905)   11,000

City Street Under Snow, 35¼ x 46 .... (940)   29,020

Entrance of the Village, 23¾ x 26 .... (954)   21,000

Village in the Ile-de-France, 25¾ x 32 .... (965)   24,860

Landscape of Beauce, 1945, 23½ x 29¾ .... (864)   18,250

Banks of the River Oise, 25¾ x 32 .... (978)   16,040

Seascape, 29 x 36½ .... (987)   15,800

The Harbor, 29 x 36½ .... (901)   15,000

Flowers in a Vase, 18¼ x 13 .... (901)   14,400

Vase of Flowers, 22 x 15½ .... (954)   21,000

Flowerpot, 24 x 18¼ .... (965)   12,430

Bouquet in a White Vase, 21¼ x 17¾ .... (965) $ 22,600

Still Life with Figs, a Bowl, and a Knife, on
panel, 17¾ x 21¼ .... (940)   5,804

Still Life with Onion, 19¾ x 24 .... (852)   8,000

1968–July 1969

Landscape, (1903), 25¼ x 19¾ .... (1125)   27,600

Barges on the River Seine at Chatou, (1907–08),
25¼ x 30¾ .... (1132)   59,000

The Dish of Apples, 1908, 23¾ x 29 .... (1187)   30,680

Barges at Chatou, (1908), 25 x 31½ .... (1068)   27,140

*Little Sailboat and a Barge on the River Seine at
Chatou,* (1908–09), 29 x 36½ .... (1132)   54,280

The Floods, Banks of the River Seine, 1910,
35½ x 28 .... (1068)   33,276

Flood on the Bank of the River Seine, 1910,
35½ x 28 .... (1173)   43,700

The River Oise at Auvers, (1910), 25¼ x 31¾ .... (1070)   4,400

Houses by the Waterside, (1910), 23¾ x 35¼ .... (1176)   35,000

Bunch of Chrysanthemums, (1910–12), 28¾ x 23   (1068)   22,420

Path Alongside a River, (1912), 25 x 31¾ .... (1132)   35,400

Still Life with Fruit, (1916), 15¼ x 18¼ .... (1018)   14,000

Landscape of the Valmondois, (1917),
25¾ x 32¼ .... (1152)   40,000

La Carouge (Valmondois), 29¼ x 36¼ .... (1193)   52,038

"Au Poisson Frit" (Valmondois), oil on paper laid
down on canvas, 18¼ x 21¾ .... (1109)   7,200

Street at Valmondois, 13 x 16 .... (1090)   9,424

Sailboats, Honfleur, (1918), 23 x 28¾ .... (1132)   35,400

Landscape, (1920), 21¼ x 25¾ .... (1125)   21,620

Still Life with a Leg of Mutton and a Cockade,
1922, 19¾ x 25¾ .... (1126)   4,460

Village Under Snow, (1923–24), 32 x 39½ .... (1152)   45,000

Street Under Snow, 32 x 40 .... (1189)   55,000

Riverside, 22 x 26 .... (1189)   15,200

Bel-Ami (Portrait of M. Itasse), (1924),
25¾ x 19¾ .... (1152)   16,000

The Corn, 1925, 23¾ x 29 .... (1148)   24,000

Favière Church (Eure-et-Loir), 15 x 18¼ .... (1109)   14,000

La Bauche (Savoie), (1926), 29¼ x 36½ .... (1152)   27,000

House on the Edge of the Road to Brezolles,
(1926), 21¼ x 29 .... (1152)   23,500

Still Life with Artichokes, (1926–28), 32½ x 46¼ . (1152)   27,000

Village Under Snow, (1927), 29¼ x 36¾ .... (1152)   43,000

Church and Corn Field (Near Chartres), (1928),
32 x 39½ .... (1152)   52,000

Vase of Flowers, (1930), 24 x 18¼ .... (1217)   24,000

The Kitchen Table, (1932), 32 x 46¼ .... (1152)   19,000

Wintry Landscape Near Rueil-la-Gadelière,
(1932), 19¾ x 24 .... (1125)   16,100

Great Bunch of Flowers, (1933), 32 x 23 .... (1152)   3,600

Riverside, 18¼ x 24 .... (1109)   16,000

The Roofs, 32¼ x 39½ .... (1176)   63,000

Village Under Snow, 23¾ x 29 .... (1200)   27,000

The Village Road, 21½ x 26 .... (1057)   19,000

Lively Village Street with Figures, 21¼ x 25¾ ... (1202)   22,600

Village Under Snow, 21¼ x 25¾ .... (1049)   16,400

Landscape and House, 18¼ x 21¾ .... (1113)   10,000

Riverside, 29 x 36½ .... (1106)   25,000

The Trawler, 23¾ x 32 .... (1199)   12,000

The Bunch of Flowers, 18¾ x 15 .... (1106)   13,200

Vase of Flowers, 16¾ x 13½ .... (1117)   10,000

Still Life with a Watermelon, 23¾ x 29 .... (1045)   16,000

Flowers, 18¼ x 13 . . . . (1173) $ 14,490

Vase of Flowers, 21¾ x 15 . . . . (1176)   17,000

The Poet Fritz Vanderpyl, 25¾ x 21¼ . . . . (1224)   17,200

Bunch of Flowers, (1920), 21¾ x 18¼ . . . . (1225)   18,000

The Hamlet Under Snow, 21¼ x 25¾ . . . . (1226)   24,000

Hôtel du Centre, 18¼ x 21¾ . . . . (1226)   16,200

Landscape, 13 x 16¼ . . . . (1226)   10,000

Two Houses and a Corn Field, (1925), 23¾ x 29 . (1235)   21,000

Vase of Flowers, (1925), 24 x 19½ . . . . (1235)   29,000

Auvers-sur-Oise, the Railway Station, (1923),
     18½ x 22 . . . . (1235)   17,000

The Rib of Beef, (1930), 21¼ x 28¾ . . . . (1235)   10,000

The Road to Mantes, (1923), 29 x 36½ . . . . (1235)   35,000

The Church, (1930), 8½ x 13 . . . . (1235)   15,000

Wintry Landscape, (1925), 21½ x 25¾ . . . . (1235)   28,000

Breteuil Castle, (1920), 23¾ x 29 . . . . (1235)   21,000

The Viaduct, (1914), 25½ x 31½ . . . . (1235)   32,500

The Harvest, 21½ x 25½ . . . . (1235)   20,000

Bateau-Lavoir, Barge, and Bridge on the River
     Seine, (1908), 28¾ x 21¼ . . . . (1239)   45,600

Snowy Village, (1930), 21 x 25¼ . . . . (1239)   38,400

Riverside, (1930), 13 x 16¼ . . . . (1239)   19,200

Vase of Flowers, 18 x 15 . . . . (1239)   22,800

Woody Alley, 1924, 21¾ x 18¼ . . . . (1239)   11,040

Fishing Boats, in the Harbor, Sunset,
     23¼ x 28¼ . . . . (1241)   18,900

Landscape, the Farm, 15 x 18¼ . . . . (1254)   16,200

Vase of Flowers, 18¼ x 13 . . . . (1254)   10,400

The Hotel Beside the Woody Alley, 29 x 36½ . . . (1255)   28,000

Storm Over the Sea, 29 x 36½ . . . . (1258)   11,000

Vase of Flowers, 21¾ x 18¼ . . . . (1268)   20,416

Landscape, 23¾ x 29 . . . . (1268)   25,520

The Bridge Over the River Seine at Chatou,
     (1906), 26½ x 37¼ . . . . (1270)   208,800

The Old Bridge at Mantes (Seine-et-Oise),
     (1909-10), 21¼ x 25¾ . . . . (1270)   48,000

Vase of Flowers, (1914), 31 x 25 . . . . (1270)   36,000

The Farm and the Poplars, (1910), 25 x 31 . . . . . (1270)   36,000

White and Blue Flowers, 10¼ x 8 . . . . (1270)   18,720

Bunch of Asters, (1951), 25 x 19 . . . . (1270)   14,440

Corn Field and Village, 21 x 25½ . . . . (1270)   28,800

Houses and Fields, 21 x 25 . . . . (1270)   16,320

Edouard Vuillard

(1868–1940)

Birthplace: Cuiseaux, Saône-et-Loire, France.

1877   His family settles in Paris.

1883   Death of his father. Forms a friendship with K.X. Roussel, who marries his sister Marie in 1893.

1886   Influenced by Roussel, he moves toward painting. Both friends attend several Parisian ateliers. They meet Maurice Denis.

1888   Enters the Académie Julian, Paris. Meets Bonnard. Briefly attends the studio of Gérôme at the Ecole Nationale des Beaux-Arts, Paris.

1889   Joins the Nabis group, which includes Sérusier, Maurice Denis, Roussel, Bonnard, and Ranson.

1890   Simplifies forms under the influence of Japanese art.

1891   First exhibition at "La Revue Blanche," Paris. With the Nabis, participates in the Salon des Indépendants, Paris. Shares a studio with Bonnard and Maurice Denis.

1892   Participates in the Nabis' exhibition at the Galerie Le Barc de Boutteville, Paris. Paints "Sous la Lampe," in which his new passion for black shades appears. Meets Verlaine and Mallarmé.

1893   Stage decorations for Ibsen's *Rosmersholm* for the opening of the Théâtre de l'Oeuvre, Paris.

1894   Starts a series of great decorative compositions.

1899   Executes "Interieur," a painting which is considered to be among the most representative of his style.

1903-14   Stays in Normandy with the dealer Hessel. Trip to London and Holland with Bonnard.

1908   Teaches at the Académie Ranson, Paris, with Roussel and Maurice Denis.

1918-20   Turns toward a more realistic painting.

1928   Death of his mother.

1930   Trip to Spain with Prince Bibesco.

1932   Important Bonnard-Vuillard exhibition at the Kunsthaus, Zurich. Begins the series of society portraits that include the Comtesse de Polignac, Madame de Noailles, and Elvire Popesco.

1937   Executes important decorations for the Palais de Chaillot, Paris.

1938   Bonnard-Vuillard exhibition at the Art Institute of Chicago.

1939   Decorations for the Palais de la Société des Nations, Geneva.

1940   Died, La Baule.

Sales

DRAWINGS

1961–1962

The Trees of the Place Vintimille, (1912), pencil,
     8¼ x 5 . . . . (93) $ 339

Tristan Bernard in the Park of Sceaux, India ink,
     11¾ x 7½ . . . . (156)   700

Madame Vuillard in Profile, (1920), pencil,
     8½ x 5¼ . . . . (164)   714

1963

Madame Lucie Hessel, (1905), pencil, 6¾ x 4 . . . . . (208)   450

Ambroise Vollard Sitting at a Table, pencil,
     3 x 4½ . . . . (255)   439

Madame Vuillard's Bedroom, (1920), pencil,
     4 x 6 . . . . (281)   158

View of Bonnard's House in Cannes, 1920,
     charcoal and pastel, 12¾ x 18¼ . . . . (315)   2,742

Smiling Woman, black chalk, 9½ x 11¾ . . . . (179)   750

Interior, pencil, 4½ x 7½ . . . . (179)   225

Design for a Poster, drawing laid down on
     canvas, 51½ x 114 . . . . (283)   949

1964

The Vuillard Family, 26 Rue de Calais, (1918),
     pencil, 6½ x 5 . . . . (416)   3,870

Interior, pencil, 4½ x 8 . . . . (377)   328

Portrait of Madame Wertheimer, charcoal,
27 x 34½ .... (335) $ 800
The Lawyer, charcoal and pastel, 9 x 11¾ .... (329)   825
The Soup Kitchen, black pencil, 11¾ x 14¼ ...... (340)   1,700
Nurse at the Jardin du Luxembourg, pencil and
pastel, 23¾ x 16¾ .... (448)   3,250

1965
Mother and Child in a Garden, charcoal and
pastel, 9¼ x 9½ .... (624)   4,975
The Artist's Mother, pencil heightened with
white and pastel, 11¾ x 9 .... (624)   1,105

1966
Tristan Bernard in the Park of Sceaux, India-ink
wash, 11¾ x 7½ .... (749)   800
Interior with a Lamp Shade (Madame Hessel),
pencil, 6¾ x 3¾ .... (742)   280
Two Dancers, pencil and pen, 7 x 11¾ .... (783)   200
Portrait of a Gentleman (After Lebrun), pencil,
8 x 4¾ .... (783)   600
The Artist's Mother, pencil, 15 x 11¼ .... (689)   1,382

1968–July 1969
Portrait of Madame Wertheimer, charcoal,
27¾ x 35¼ .... (1125)   1,955
Interior, charcoal, 15 x 21 .... (1125)   3,910
Portrait of the Comtesse de Polignac, pencil,
8 x 5 .... (1214)   1,600
Tristan Bernard in the Park of Sceaux, 1895, pen
and wash, 11½ x 7¼ .... (1069)   1,096
In the Garden, pencil and watercolor, 7½ x 4½ .. (1134)   1,133
Landscape, black pencil and pen, 5¾ x 4 .... (1131)   220
The Grandmother, black lead, 6¾ x 3¾ .... (1127)   690
*Les Coquelins in "Le Barbier de Séville": Don
Basilio and Figaro,* wash and watercolor,
9½ x 7½ .... (1222)   1,020
The Glimpse, pencil, 9 x 6¾ .... (1240)   2,040
Sketches, two drawings, 6 x 3¾ .... (1253)   400
Interior, two drawings, 6¾ x 4 .... (1253)   400
The Cavalier Bernin at Versailles, pencil,
7¾ x 4½ .... (1272)   480
The Cook, black pencil, 6¼ x 8¾ .... (1272)   1,080
The Viewer, pencil, 7 x 4½ .... (1272)   288
View of an Interior, pencil, 8¼ x 4¾ .... (1272)   1,008
Woman and Young Lady Seated at Table, pencil,
8 x 4½ .... (1272)   840
*Madame Hessel at the Clos Cézanne at
Vaucresson,* (1920), 8 x 4½ .... (1272)   1,008

WATERCOLORS
1961–1962
Village Beneath a Stormy Sky, pastel, 25 x 18¼ .. (155)   5,200
Landscape, Les Clayes Castle, pastel, 9 x 11¾ .... (49)   1,800
Cannes, 1914, pastel, 12¾ x 23 .... (143)   2,893
Portrait of Rosengert, pastel, 9½ x 12¼ .... (32)   1,300
Portrait of a Man, pastel, 9½ x 9½ .... (93)   1,311
Portrait of Nina, pastel, 19 x 25 .... (114)   4,000
The Square Louis XVI, pastel, 10½ x 14¼ .... (86)   700
Open Window on the Square Vintimille, pastel
and colored pencils, 12¾ x 9¾ .... (80)   1,000

1963
Landscape, pastel, 10¼ x 14 .... (241)   1,720
*A Sketch for the Library of the Princesse
Bassiano,* 1906, gouache and tempera,
20½ x 15¾ .... (243)   1,700
Landscape, (1915), pastel on brown paper,
12¾ x 9½ .... (279)   2,500

Interior, (1920), pastel, 13 x 10 .... (279) $ 6,000
Interior, pastel, 38 x 45¾ .... (232)   6,328
Interior with a Child, pastel, 29 x 27¾ .... (202)   5,000
The Two Friends, pastel, 11 x 11¼ .... (247)   3,016
The Bridge Game, pastel on board, 7½ x 10¼ .... (247)   6,855
The Café Wepler, pastel, 20½ x 28 .... (258)   4,400
Flowery Landscape, (1930), pastel on paper
mounted on canvas, 37½ x 21¼ .... (316)   8,500
The Street, pastel, 12¾ x 9½ .... (315)   1,289
Clayes Castle, pastel, 9 x 11½ .... (194)   1,460
Portrait of Nina, pastel, 18¾ x 24½ .... (202)   6,000

1964
The Fat Fisherwoman, (1910), pastel, 19 x 25 ..... (416)   4,146
The Big Tree, pastel, 10½ x 14 .... (378)   1,582
Landscape at Home, pastel, 23¾ x 19 .... (341)   1,800
Place Vintimille, pastel, 12¾ x 9 .... (394)   1,660
Madame Hessel at Home, pastel on paper laid
down on canvas, 24½ x 26 .... (458)   15,961
The Lounge, in the Evening at Vaucresson, pastel
and distemper on paper, 25 x 17½ .... (405)   16,541
The Woman on a Sofa, pastel, 12½ x 10 .... (398)   1,180
Interior, pastel, 11½ x 10¼ .... (377)   1,808
Madame Gaborie, pastel on gray paper, 9 x 12 .... (354)   3,000
Women, pastel, 12½ x 9½ .... (471)   3,435
The Masseur, pastel, 12¾ x 16¾ .... (380)   1,600
Standing Woman in a Red Dress, pastel,
12¾ x 9½ .... (399)   2,200
Woman Writing, pastel, 7½ x 6 .... (371)   3,400

1965
The Woman with a Veil, (1902), pastel,
43½ x 28½ .... (633)   23,000
Young Woman Getting Out of Bed, (1905), pastel,
28 x 40¼ .... (522)   23,494
Pola the Mad, 1908, pastel, 17½ x 18¼ .... (559)   1,620
Place Vintimille, (1908-09), tempera on cardboard
laid down on canvas, 29¾ x 39½ .... (616)   16,000
Interior with a Woman, pastel, 25¼ x 19¾ ...... (564)   2,800
Portrait of a Man in an Interior, pastel,
24 x 18¼ .... (564)   1,820
Portrait, pastel, 9½ x 12¾ .... (567)   2,260
Le Parc Monceau, pastel, 21¼ x 32 .... (569)   4,407
Portrait of Marie Vuillard, pastel, 7½ x 8 .... (541)   725
Interior (Woman and Child), pastel laid down on
canvas, 20½ x 21¾ .... (569)   12,091
The Jardin des Tuileries, tempera on paper laid
down on canvas, 30 x 29¾ .... (594)   16,000
In Les Clayes Park, pastel, 35½ x 58 .... (633)   22,000
Landscape, pastel, 13 x 9½ .... (617)   3,842
The Basket, pastel, 15¾ x 30 .... (539)   1,000
Two Women by the Waterside in Normandy,
pastel, 40 x 28¾ .... (575)   13,820

1966
Madame Vuillard Seated at Table, pastel,
10¾ x 6 .... (744)   3,616
The Square Louis XVI, (1890), pastel, 10¾ x 14 ... (689)   1,244
The Bank of Pouligny, (1905-10), tempera and
charcoal on paper laid down on canvas,
35¼ x 42 .... (686)   14,373
Landscape, pastel, 13 x 10 .... (648)   1,500
Little Girl, pastel, 29¾ x 28 .... (694)   11,000
Madame Hessel in the Garden at Ouistreham,
pastel on paper laid down on canvas,
24 x 45¾ .... (797)   22,600

1967

Interior with a Seated Woman, pastel on paper
on canvas, 39½ x 27¾ .... (942) $6,100

The Vido Game, pastel, 24 x 18¼ .... (942)   6,800

The Children at Villerville, 1908, gouache,
23¼ x 17¾ .... (938)   9,950

Landscape, pastel, 9¼ x 12¼ .... (967)   3,390

The Comedian, pastel, 10 x 10¾ .... (852)   1,620

The Square Louis XVI, pastel, 10¾ x 14½ .... (857)   1,280

Interior, pastel on gray paper, 9 x 12¾ .... (870)   1,750

Squint-eyed person at His Desk, pastel,
21 x 17¾ .... (942)   5,000

Singer in Red, pastel, 21¼ x 8 .... (1004)   6,500

Woman at Her Toilette, pastel, 25 x 24½ .... (938)   20,730

1968–July 1969

Pola the Mad, 1908, pastel, 19 x 25 .... (1183)   5,200

*Yvonne Printemps on Stage, Seen from the
Wings,* 1917, tempera on paper laid down on
canvas, 67¼ x 58 .... (1113)   10,700

The Fireplace, 1919, pastel, 14 x 22¾ .... (1174)   6,900

Portrait of Two Women, pastel, 12½ x 9½ ...... (1174)   3,450

Little Girl at the Piano,[1] pastel, 16¾ x 12¼ ...... (1117)   6,300

Woman and Child, pastel, 36 x 30½ .... (1125)   12,420

Landscape, pastel and oil on cardboard,
11¾ x 5¾ .... (1125)   3,680

Vuillard's Bedroom at Les Clayes, (1930), pastel,
9½ x 12¾ .... (1036)   3,300

Portrait in Blue, pastel on brown paper,
27 x 21¾ .... (1057)   20,000

*Portrait of the Princesse Antoine Bibesco Born
Asquith,* (1936-38), pastel, 19½ x 24 .... (1191)   8,260

Woman in a Landscape, tempera on paper laid
down on canvas, 38¾ x 61¾ .... (1126)   9,416

Reclining Woman, pastel on gray paper,
10 x 12¾ .... (1080)   1,850

The Avenue, tempera, 15 x 23 .... (1106)   3,300

At the Café, pastel, 18¼ x 25 .... (1126)   3,965

The Open Window, pastel heightened with
gouache, 10¼ x 6¾ .... (1221)   1,220

Madame Rosengart and Her Daughter, pastel,
30 x 34¾ .... (1226)   12,800

The Garden, gouache on board, 7¾ x 10¼ ...... (1240)   1,680

Les Clayes Castle, pastel, 8½ x 10 .... (1246)   2,500

Country Road, pastel, 11½ x 8¼ .... (1246)   1,500

The Spa Establishment at Vichy, pastel,
38¾ x 56¼ .... (1252)   12,600

The Pines, (1914), pastel, 11¾ x 8 .... (1255)   800

The Workmen's Meal, pastel, 19 x 25¼ .... (1258)   4,000

The Alley of Les Clayes, pastel on paper laid
down on canvas, 9½ x 12¼ .... (1265)   4,500

The Market, pastel, 12¾ x 10 .... (1268)   4,640

The Dog, pastel, 11¾ x 9 .... (1268)   5,714

The Shop Window, pastel, 37½ x 45½ .... (1268)   10,440

View of a Garden from a Window, pastel and
charcoal, 12¼ x 9¼ .... (1272)   4,320

PAINTINGS

1961–1962

Portrait of the Artist with a Mirror, (1888),
17½ x 21 .... (137)   45,000

Landscape, 1890, oil on paper laid down on
canvas, 30¼ x 17½ .... (143)   8,136

Sleeping Baby, on cardboard, 14¾ x 13 .... (143)   13,560

[1]Madame Hessel and Lulu.

Women on a Bench at the Tuileries, 1895, on
cardboard, 12¼ x 15½ .... (93) $15,820

Cyprien Godebski and Misia Playing the Piano,
(1895), oil on paper on panel, 25 x 22 .... (112)   64,531

Godebski Talking .... (32)   3,200

Interior with a Lamp,[2] 1896, on panel, 13¾ x 14 .... (93)   16,046

Portrait of Madame Bonnard, peinture à
l'essence and oil on board, 15½ x 12 .... (112)   46,682

The Dining Room, (1900), on board, 4½ x 17¾ .... (164)   5,492

Interior, (1906), 10½ x 14 .... (8)   11,000

Interior, Woman Sewing, (1908-12), distemper on
gray board, 17½ x 17 .... (84)   13,181

Madame Hessel Reading, peinture à l'essence on
paper mounted on canvas, (1917),
42 x 24½ .... (37)   5,250

"14 Juillet," on panel, 10¼ x 4 .... (106)   2,305

Interior with Two Figures, distemper, 27 x 29 ..... (114)   6,200

Woman Sewing, 10 x 6½ .... (125)   8,600

The Hall, distemper on paper laid down on
canvas, 17¾ x 19¾ .... (80)   6,400

Maxim's, on cardboard, 19¾ x 19¾ .... (18)   12,430

1963

Fishermen in Brittany, (1891-92), on board,
10¼ x 13¼ .... (210)   8,226

The Shirt, distemper on cardboard, 14¼ x 12¼ ... (210)   5,484

Portrait of a Man, (1895), 10½ x 8½ .... (247)   11,516

Two Seated Women, (1896), on panel,
9¼ x 12¾ .... (279)   9,500

Self-Portrait, (1899), 30¾ x 19½ .... (279)   57,500

Night Feast, (1900), on panel, 14¾ x 17 .... (232)   5,198

The Table, on cardboard, 15 x 10¾ .... (206)   4,200

The Subway, Villiers Station, 18¾ x 22¾ .... (206)   3,200

The Subway Carriage, peinture à la colle on
paper, 22½ x 19¾ .... (258)   4,200

The Lamp, 1905, distemper on paper laid down
on canvas, 12¼ x 8¼ .... (210)   7,403

Two Figures, on panel, 8 x 11 .... (202)   2,000

Woman in the Kitchen, 15½ x 12½ .... (306)   12,000

Portrait of Madame Tristan Bernard,
50¾ x 43½ .... (190)   3,220

Portrait of Madame Tristan Bernard,
50¾ x 43½ .... (309)   16,480

The Sea, peinture à l'essence on cardboard laid
down on canvas, 9 x 14¾ .... (255)   3,839

Tennis, oil on cardboard, 10¾ x 9 .... (259)   12,000

The Balustrade, distemper on cardboard,
61 x 25¾ .... (283)   16,724

1964

Landscape, 1890, on panel, 9¼ x 11½ .... (367)   8,845

The Sick Person, (1892), 9½ x 12¾ .... (348)   5,400

The Breakfast,[3] (1893), peinture à l'essence on
cardboard, 6½ x 7½ .... (348)   3,420

Misia and Thadée Nathanson, Rue St. Florentin,
(1896), 19½ x 21 .... (416)   45,606

Stage Front of the Théâtre Antoine, 1896, on
board, 12¾ x 19½ .... (416)   13,820

Interior with Madame Vuillard, (1897), on board,
17 x 25 .... (454)   22,112

Interior with a Woman, oil on paper, 24 x 19¾ ... (471)   16,272

Mother and Child, on cardboard, 30½ x 29½ ..... (471)   26,442

[2]Nathanson at his desk.
[3]Madame Vuillard.

The Bare Arms,[4] (1898-1900), on board,
18½ x 22 .... (454) $ 24,876

View of Cannes, 1901, 30 x 25¾ .... (347) 12,000

Inside of the Factory of Thadée Nathanson in Lyons, 1915, India ink and distemper on canvas, 19¾ x 25¾ .... (347) 3,300

Portrait of Madame Nathanson, distemper on paper laid down on board, 22 x 18¼ .... (458) 6,965

Landscape of the Ile-de-France, (1904), on board, 22½ x 30 .... (367) 6,910

Banks of the River Seine in the Suburbs of Paris, on cardboard, 20 x 24½ .... (459) 19,888

The Roussel Children, Rue de Calais, (1908), peinture à la colle on paper laid down on canvas, 19 x 23¾ .... (405) 9,286

The Balustrade, distemper on canvas laid down on panel, 55½ x 25¾ .... (458) 22,055

Woman Seated Near a Lamp, (1908-10), 28 x 27 .... (367) 55,280

The Meeting Under the Parasol, on cardboard, 14¼ x 20½ .... (473) 11,000

Interior with a Seated Woman, oil and distemper on cardboard, 14 x 11¾ .... (473) 10,040

Madame Vuillard Sewing, Place Vintimille, (1910), peinture à la colle, 25 x 19 .... (405) 8,126

Salle Wagram, on cardboard, 11 x 8¼ .... (340) 2,100

Sketch for the Portrait of the Princesse de Polignac, on paper laid down on canvas, 33½ x 27¼ .... (340) 3,100

Madame Hessel, Rue de Naples, 1913, on board, 12¼ x 8¾ .... (416) 18,242

The Antiques at the Louvre, Enameled Stained Glass in the Background, 1920, peinture à la colle, colored chalk and charcoal, 37¾ x 44¼ .... (367) 8,292

The Walk, peinture à la colle on board, 9¼ x 11½ .... (458) 12,188

Neighborhood of Paris, on board, 10¾ x 14 ...... (448) 6,250

Landscape, on panel, 16½ x 14½ .... (465) 14,000

Seated Nude, on cardboard, 22½ x 13 .... (394) 13,000

Woman at the Telephone, 24½ x 18¼ .... (371) 22,000

The Drawing Room of Madame Gillou, 29 x 36½ .... (463) 47,000

1965

At the Window, 14 x 11¾ .... (526) 32,500

Young Woman in Black, (1895), on board, 8½ x 6½ .... (624) 2,488

Portrait of a Man, (1895), 11 x 9 .... (633) 9,500

The Estérel: View of Cannes,[5] (1896), on panel, 11½ x 14 .... (526) 18,000

Standing Nude, (1906), on panel, 15¾ x 11½ ..... (526) 25,000

Summer Residence, on cardboard, 25¾ x 19¾ .... (617) 7,458

Interior with Madame Vuillard, (1897), on board, 17 x 25 .... (633) 19,000

The Manicurist, (1897), on panel, 13¼ x 11 .... (522) 15,202

Vase of White Roses, (1900-05), on panel, 11 x 10½ .... (522) 20,454

The Flowers of the Lounge, on board, 24½ x 18¾ .... (526) 25,000

Chestnut Trees in Bloom, peinture à la colle, 25 x 19 .... (518) 2,500

Still Life with a Flowery Vase, on cardboard, 9¼ x 10 .... (553) 2,600

[4]Misia in her apartment.
[5]Garden in front of the sea.

Café Concert, 1904-05, 16¼ x 21¼ .... (616) $ 17,600

Mademoiselle Jacqueline Fontaine, 1910, peinture à l'essence, 62¾ x 45¾ .... (569) 33,674

The Lunch, on cardboard, 5¾ x 8¼ .... (516) 2,200

A Horse in the Rue de Rivoli, (1910), peinture à l'essence, 19½ x 16¾ .... (617) 7,345

The Hessels' Green Lounge, ... (493) 83,000

Madame Hessel and Her Friends, 1918, distemper on paper, 42 x 51½ .... (561) 5,400

Theater Stage, on cardboard, 12 x 20 .... (553) 4,800

Zacharie, 10¼ x 8 .... (564) 600

The Conversation, on cardboard, 8 x 12¾ .... (559) 2,600

Seated Nude, on cardboard, 22½ x 13 .... (553) 13,200

Landscape, on panel, 7¼ x 7½ .... (640) 3,800

Portrait of the Comtesse de Noailles, (1930), 44 x 50½ .... (526) 74,000

1966

The Artist's Mother in Her Kitchen, 15½ x 12½ .. (753) 23,216

The Artist's Mother, (1903-04), on canvas laid down on canvas, 11½ x 9½ .... (750) 4,975

First-Class Coach, peinture à l'essence on paper laid down on canvas, 23 x 19¾ .... (797) 7,458

Interior with Two Women, (1917), oil on paper laid down on canvas, 19¾ x 28½ .... (713) 19,000

Landscape, 59¼ x 24½ .... (744) 13,560

Madame Hessel and Her Friends, 1918, oil on paper laid down on canvas, 42¼ x 51½ ...... (744) 18,080

Under the Lamp, Madame Hessel's Lounge, Rue de Naples, (1924), 19 x 29 .... (808) 34,824

The Apple Tree, 16¼ x 22 .... (808) 5,514

Reclining Woman, on cardboard, 10¾ x 14 .... (797) 14,012

Lucie Belin at Home, on cardboard, 15¾ x 12¾ ... (814) 12,000

The Hay Cart, on cardboard, 19 x 23¾ .... (811) 13,200

Interior, oil on paper, 15¼ x 21½ .... (686) 20,730

1967

Interior, peinture à la colle on paper laid down on canvas, 23¾ x 18¾ .... (923) 14,800

Two Feet, (1893), on panel, 4½ x 8¼ .... (957) 3,040

Two Women by the Seaside in Normandy, (1907), oil on paper laid down on canvas, 40 x 28½ .. (918) 19,436

Madame Vuillard and Her Grandchildren: Jacques and Annette Roussel, (1908), 23¼ x 32 .... (918) 42,940

Madame Vuillard Sewing, Place Vintimille, (1910), oil on paper, 25¾ x 19¾ .... (864) 7,000

Woman Reading Before Her Desk, 39½ x 32½ ... (901) 56,000

Home Life, 78¼ x 63¾ .... (858) 24,000

In the Library, oil on paper, 21 x 16¾ .... (909) 1,800

Interior, oil on paper laid down on canvas, 24 x 19¾ .... (965) 19,888

Portrait of Madame Nathanson, oil on paper laid down on canvas, 23 x 19½ .... (965) 14,464

Woman with a Flowery Hat in a Landscape, distemper on paper laid down on canvas, 62½ x 39½ .... (942) 8,000

Portrait of Madame Fontaine, distemper, 51¾ x 38½ .... (942) 15,200

Mallarmé's House, distemper, 18¼ x 15¾ .... (987) 4,800

Reclining Nude, on cardboard, 10 x 25¾ .... (978) 6,600

First-Class Coach in the Subway, peinture à la colle, 22¾ x 21½ .... (954) 9,500

Vase of Flowers, on cardboard, 7½ x 6½ .... (976) 4,100

1968–July 1969

Madame Vuillard Sewing, 1895, on board,
12¾ x 14¼ . . . . (1132) $ 63,720

Madame Vuillard on Her Balcony, (1899), on
panel, 15 x 13½ . . . . (1132) 36,580

The Artist's Mother, 1903, 10 x 10 . . . . (1181) 9,600

The Horse of the Rue de Rivoli, 1910, on
cardboard, 19¾ x 17 . . . . (1183) 7,600

Arms Factory at Lyons: The Forge, 1916-17,
distemper, 29¾ x 61 . . . . (1053) 3,200

*Professor H. Vaquès and His Assistant Dr.
Parvon Working in Hospital with the
Sphygmomanometer,* (1917), peinture à la
colle heightened with pastel, 25¼ x 19½ . . . . (1187) 21,712

Madame Hessel and Her Friends, (1918),
peinture à l'essence on paper laid down on
canvas, 38¼ x 51½ . . . . (1176) 30,000

Interior: At Madame W.'s, (1924), peinture à la
colle on cardboard heightened with pastel,
23¼ x 20½ . . . . (1125) 15,640

*Portrait of Madame Fontaine Seated in Her
Lounge,* oil on paper laid down on panel,
21¼ x 10 . . . . (1117) 2,600

Entrance of a Village, on cardboard laid down on
canvas, 16¾ x 14 . . . . (1176) 13,000

Model Resting, 14 x 15¼ . . . . (1125) 16,100

The Road, on cardboard laid down on canvas,
25¼ x 16¾ . . . . (1125) 9,660

The Restaurant, peinture à la colle on paper laid
down on canvas, 23¼ x 15½ . . . . (1187) 9,440

Portrait of Madame Hélène Nathanson, oil on
paper laid down on canvas, 23 x 19½ . . . . (1187) 11,800

Woman Combing Her Hair, on cardboard,
23 x 17¾ . . . . (1049) 3,500

Garden, on cardboard, 15 x 10¾ . . . . (1173) 19,780

Mallarmé's House, distemper, 18¼ x 15¾ . . . . (1168) 6,000

Vase of Flowers, 19 x 16¾ . . . . (1199) 28,000

Woman Seated in a Meadow in Normandy,
(1905), 15 x 26¼ . . . . (1239) 16,800

*A Corner of the Place Vintimille Seen from the
Artist's Window,* (1905), 15¾ x 10 . . . . (1239) 14,400

Painter Ker-Xavier Roussel in His Studio,
(1925-30), 29 x 28¼ . . . . (1239) 14,400

The Garden at La Jacanette, (1906), peinture à la
colle on board, 21¼ x 21 . . . . (1239) 14,880

Interior with a Seated Woman, on board,
21¾ x 10½ . . . . (1239) 9,600

Interior with Madame Vuillard, (1897), on board,
17 x 25 . . . . (1241) 42,800

Madame Hessel at the Telephone, 19¼ x 19¼ . . . (1241) 20,200

Portrait of Mademoiselle X, (1912), 18¾ x 18¼ . . (1254) 7,400

Family Portrait, 75 x 65¼ . . . . (1258) 12,400

Roses in a Vase, 11¾ x 17 . . . . (1268) 19,256

The Square Vintimille, (1908-09), on cardboard,
29¾ x 39½ . . . . (1268) 26,680

Nude, on cardboard, 11¼ x 8¼ . . . . (1268) 9,976

The Family on the Terrace, distemper on canvas,
21¼ x 33¼ . . . . (1268) 10,904

The Hen House at l'Etang-la-Ville, on cradled
cardboard, 17¾ x 21¼ . . . . (1268) 11,600

Mallarmé's House, on cardboard, 15½ x 17¾ . . . . (1268) 15,080

Misia and Thadée Nathanson, Rue St. Florentin,
19½ x 20¾ . . . . (1270) 81,600

Little Glade in a Forest, 8½ x 10¼ . . . . (1270) 8,160

Honfleur Harbor, on paper laid down on canvas,
20¾ x 26 . . . . (1270) $ 13,440

Nude Seated on a Sofa, 32 x 25¾ . . . . (1270) 24,000

Landscape with Little Girls, a Goat, and a Dog,
(1910), peinture à la colle on paper laid down
on panel, 54¾ x 25¾ . . . . (1270) 9,600

Max Weber

(1881–1961)

Birthplace: Bialystok, Russia.

1891 His family emigrates to the U.S.

1898-01 Attends the Pratt Institute, taught by Arthur Dow.

1905-08 Goes to Paris, where he attends the Académie Julian, the Académie Colarossi, and the Académie
de la Grande-Chaumière. Meets Matisse. Greatly
admires Fauvism. Participates in the Salon des
Indépendants and the Salon d'Automne, Paris.

1908 Returns to the U.S.

1909 First one-man show at the Haas Gallery, New
York.

1911 One-man show at Stieglitz's "291" Gallery, New
York. Cézanne and Cubism exert a determinant
influence upon him.

1912-16 Series of semi-abstract works, such as "Chinese
Restaurant" (1915). Exhibits at the Murray Hill
Gallery, New York.

1913 Retrospective exhibition at the Newark Museum,
New Jersey.

1917-18 Reverts to figuration. Series of colored woodcuts.

1924-37 Has several one-man shows at the Neumann Gallery, New York.

1926 Retrospective exhibition at the Galerie Bernheim-
Jeune, Paris.

1930 Retrospective exhibition at the Museum of Modern
Art, New York.

1943 One-man show at the Carnegie Institute, Pittsburgh.

1942-47 Several one-man shows at the Paul Rosenberg Gallery, New York, including a retrospective exhibition in 1944.

1961 Died, Great Neck, New York.

1962 Memorial exhibition at the American Academy of
Art, New York.

Sales

WATERCOLORS
1965

Wooded Landscape, watercolor on board,
10¾ x 8¾ . . . . (489) $1,400

1966

Seated Model with Left Arm Raised, 1949,
    watercolor, 5 x 4 . . . . **(665)** $ 400

1967

Still Life, watercolor and gouache, 8¾ x 8¾ . . . . . . **(860)**   1,600
Still Life with a Flowery Tablecloth, pastel,
    8 x 10 . . . . **(952)**   1,200

1968–July 1969

Still Life, watercolor and gouache, 8¾ x 8¾ . . . . . **(1018)**   1,200
Bathers, 1912, watercolor, 12½ x 9½ . . . . **(1229)**   2,100
Bathers, 1910, watercolor, 3¾ x 5¼ . . . . **(1246)**   850
Morning, 1911, watercolor, 11½ x 9 . . . . **(1246)**   2,200
Seated Figure, 1918, gouache and watercolor,
    5 x 4¼ . . . . **(1248)**   1,100

PAINTINGS

1965

The Park, 1910, 10¾ x 8 . . . . **(494)**   1,600
The Sculptress, 1951, 19¾ x 23¾ . . . . **(489)**   4,000

1966

Woman Playing with a Bird, 1953, 36¼ x 27 . . . . . . **(707)**   7,500

1967

The Reading, (1942), 25 x 20 . . . . **(860)**   7,000

1968–July 1969

Standing Nude, 1911, on board, 9¼ x 5¾ . . . . **(1035)**   2,300
Reclining Nude, 10 x 14 . . . . **(2664)**   3,250
The Lake, (1911), on board, 10 x 12¾ . . . . **(1160)**   1,600

Otto Wols

(1913–1951)

Birthplace: Berlin, Germany. (Born Otto Alfred
Schultze-Battmann. Attends the Bauhaus at
Dessau.)

1932   Settles in Paris, where he meets the Surrealists.

1933   Trip to Spain. Becomes a photographer to earn his
living.

1936   Exhibits his photographs in a bookshop called "Les
Pléïades," Paris, under the name of Wols.

1937   Appointed official photographer of a pavilion of the
Paris World's Fair.

1939–40   As a German citizen he is imprisoned for a year.

1940   Settles near Marseilles and works very hard.

1942   Exhibits his gouaches at the Betty Parsons Gallery,
New York.

1945   Returns to Paris. Important one-man show at the
Galerie Drouin, Paris—and again in 1947.

1948–49   Executes a great many illustrations intended for
works by Jean-Paul Sartre, Kafka, Artaud, and
Paulhan. Exhibits at the Galleria del Milione,
Milan.

1950   One-man show at the Hugo Gallery, New York.

1951   Died, Paris. (Having produced a number of outstanding works since 1945, he is generally regarded
now as one of the most creative abstract painters
of his generation.)

1958   Important retrospective exhibition at the Venice
Biennial.

Sales

DRAWINGS

1961–1962

Profile, (1948), pen and watercolor, 8¼ x 6 . . . . **(24)** $1,599
Composition, (1949), pen and watercolor, 8 x 6 . . . **(107)**   1,845
Composition, 9½ x 6½ . . . . **(68)**   270
The Bridge, India ink, 8 x 5½ . . . . **(106)**   972
Composition, India ink and watercolor, 6 x 7¾ . . . . **(93)**   1,311

1963

Composition, (1941), pencil and watercolor,
    10 x 7¼ . . . . **(279)**   2,500
The Barred Windows, pencil and watercolor,
    10½ x 7¼ . . . . **(232)**   994
Composition, India ink with heightening,
    5¾ x 8¼ . . . . **(299)**   700
The Trees, India ink with heightening, 5½ x 7½ . . **(299)**   720

1964

Balloons, (1942), India ink and watercolor,
    16¼ x 12¾ . . . . **(385)**   1,243
Composition, India ink, 10 x 6½ . . . . **(379)**   500
Vegetation, 1947, pen and wash, 9¼ x 4¾ . . . . **(453)**   608

1965

Gloomy Sunday, pen and watercolor, 8¾ x 7¾ . . . **(606)**   1,350

1966

Composition, pen heightened with watercolor,
    9½ x 6 . . . . **(751)**   884
The Blue Hills, pen and watercolor, 10¾ x 14¾ . . . **(808)**   2,177
Building in the Storm, 1951, pen and watercolor,
    7¾ x 5¾ . . . . **(808)**   2,902
Guitar Player, ink and watercolor, 15¾ x 12 . . . . . . **(703)**   525
The Hammer Thrower, ink and watercolor,
    11¾ x 15 . . . . **(703)**   450

1967

Composition, (1950), pen and watercolor,
    11¾ x 9 . . . . **(982)**   1,067
Threatening Claws, 1939, India ink and
    watercolor, 10½ x 14½ . . . . **(910)**   1,230
Janus Sleeping, 1941, pen, 10¾ x 7¼ . . . . **(990)**   886
Gloomy Sunday, (1949), pen and watercolor,
    8½ x 8¼ . . . . **(881)**   967

1968–July 1969

Compositions I, II, and III, 1946–47, pencil,
    5¾ x 4½, 5¼ x 4, and 8 x 5¼ . . . . **(1134)**   425
Pullulation, (1941), India ink, 12¾ x 11 . . . . **(1114)**   5,208
Surrealist Composition, 1940, India ink and
    watercolor, 12½ x 9½ . . . . **(1114)**   3,472
Scarlet Image, 1947, ink and watercolor,
    10½ x 6½ . . . . **(1134)**   1,227
Desires for Freedom, pen and watercolor,
    12 x 9 . . . . **(1068)**   2,006
Orchestra, pen, black and red pencil, 10¼ x 7¼ . . **(1226)**   1,000
Strange People on the Sofa, 1940, pen, India ink,
    and watercolor, 7 x 10½ . . . . **(1272)**   912
Homo Sapiens, 1947, pen and India ink, brown
    chalk, and gray wash, 9¼ x 6 . . . . **(1272)**   720
Composition, 1939, pen, India ink, and
    watercolor, 10½ x 7¼ . . . . **(1272)**   360

WATERCOLORS

1961–1962

Bateau ivre, 1945, gouache, 8 x 6 . . . . (149) $1,359

Landscape, 1944, watercolor, 7¼ x 9½ . . . . (70)   1,343

Composition, 1945, watercolor and pen,
9¾ x 7½ . . . . (88)   1,525

Abstract Composition in Blue and Pink,
(1948-50), watercolor, 9½ x 6¾ . . . . (88)   1,009

The Dream, watercolor, 9¼ x 12¼ . . . . (20)   1,817

Composition, watercolor and pen, 12 x 9¼ . . . . (106)   1,243

Composition, watercolor, 7½ x 5 . . . . (156)   800

Composition, watercolor, 12¾ x 10¼ . . . . (153)   1,300

Composition, watercolor, 13½ x 17½ . . . . (129)   1,373

Composition, gouache, 10 x 8 . . . . (89)   700

Composition, gouache and ink, 6¼ x 9¾ . . . . (143)   1,130

1963

Lost Surprise, (1949), watercolor and India ink,
4½ x 7¼ . . . . (277)   768

Rouen, watercolor, 9 x 6 . . . . (190)   820

Composition, watercolor, 7½ x 5 . . . . (249)   960

Composition, 1944, watercolor, 6 x 9 . . . . (249)   1,040

The City, watercolor, 6 x 9 . . . . (299)   1,140

1964

Composition, 1948, watercolor and India ink,
9½ x 7 . . . . (380)   1,230

1965

The City, 1939, watercolor, 14 x 11¾ . . . . (616)   5,440

Desires for Freedom, watercolor and India ink,
12 x 9 . . . . (619)   1,600

1966

Composition with Houses, watercolor and ink on
board, 12¼ x 9 . . . . (648)   1,300

Composition, watercolor, 4¾ x 6½ . . . . (749)   520

Number 3, watercolor, 10¼ x 14¾ . . . . (678)   3,000

Composition, watercolor and pen, 8¼ x 11¾ . . . . . (745)   1,808

Ghost Ship, (1949), watercolor, 9 x 6½ . . . . (744)   3,277

Banjo, India ink and watercolor, 12½ x 9 . . . . (735)   3,277

Composition, watercolor, 5¾ x 4½ . . . . (816)   1,845

1967

Surrealist Construction, (1940), watercolor,
18¼ x 14¾ . . . . (982)   1,896

Pink and Blue, watercolor, 8 x 5½ . . . . (967)   904

Lighting, 1943, watercolor, 5¼ x 8 . . . . (967)   2,486

1968–July 1969

A Street of Rouen, watercolor, 9¼ x 6¼ . . . . (1127)   2,760

Earth, watercolor, 8¾ x 5¾ . . . . (1127)   2,185

Flowers, watercolor, 6¾ x 10¼ . . . . (1117)   1,620

The Hammer Thrower, pen and watercolor,
12¼ x 15¾ . . . . (1209)   1,290

The House by the Cliff, 1938, pen and watercolor,
14¾ x 10¾ . . . . (1209)   1,885

Voilier Courage, watercolor, 8 x 5¾ . . . . (1174)   3,450

Mechanical Composition, watercolor, 8¼ x 11¼ . (1225)   2,020

Figures, watercolor, 12¼ x 9½ . . . . (1226)   1,700

Figures and Fabulous Animals, watercolor,
9 x 12¼ . . . . (1258)   1,700

Fantastic Landscape, watercolor, 11½ x 9 . . . . (1258)   1,500

PAINTINGS

1967

Composition, 1947, 12¾ x 17¾ . . . . (982)   1,896

Andrew Wyeth

(1917–   )

Birthplace: Chadds Ford, Pennsylvania, U.S. (Son of the painter Newell Convers Wyeth.)

1937   First one-man show at the Macbeth Gallery, New York—and again in 1941.

1948   Paints "Christina's World."

1953   One-man show at the Knoedler Gallery, New York.

1958   Participates in the Brussels World's Fair.

Resident in Chadds Ford.

Sales

DRAWINGS

1964

The Broken Ear, pencil, 13½ x 20¾ . . . . (363) $1,000

1966

Study of a Landscape, pen and wash, 17 x 21¾ . . . (790)   3,250

WATERCOLORS

1965

Snowy Landscape, 1962, watercolor, 17½ x 22¾ . . (489)   6,000

1966

The Corn Field, (1945), watercolor, 21 x 29¾ . . . . . (710)   8,000

The Iron Age, (1950), watercolor, 21 x 29¾ . . . . . . (790)   12,000

Fields in Winter, 1942, tempera on panel,
17 x 41½ . . . . (707)   34,000

1967

Landscape of Maine, (1940), watercolor,
17¾ x 21¾ . . . . (860)   12,000

The Afternoon, 1939, watercolor, 17¾ x 21½ . . . . . (889)   8,250

Seaside, 1939, watercolor, 17¾ x 21¾ . . . . (889)   6,500

Teel's Island, (1945), watercolor, 21¾ x 29¾ . . . . . (969)   12,500

Rocking Chair in a Landscape, 1965, watercolor,
18¾ x 23¾ . . . . (969)   17,500

1968–July 1969

Morning Light, Martinsville, (1939), watercolor,
17¾ x 22 . . . . (1035)   9,000

Barnacles, watercolor, 17½ x 12½ . . . . (1229)   8,000

PAINTINGS

1968–July 1969

Martinsville Lobstermen, (1940), watercolor,
19 x 29 . . . . (1229)   18,000

Zao-Wou-Ki

(1920–   )

Birthplace: Peking, China.

1934-40 Enters the National School of Fine Arts of Hang-Tcheou.

1941-47 First exhibition in Shanghai. Teaches drawing at the National School of Fine Arts of Hang-Tcheou.

1948 Goes to France and settles in Paris. Learns to speak French, visits the museums and galleries. Becomes better acquainted with European masters. Meets Klee, whom he admires above all.

1950 Participates in the Salon de Mai, Paris.

1951 First one-man show at the Galerie Pierre, Paris.

1952-54 Exhibits at the Cadly-Birch Gallery, New York.

1953 One-man show at the Galerie Gérard Cramer, Geneva.

1953-56 Exhibits his watercolors and lithographs at "La Hune," Paris.

1955 Given an award by the Carnegie Institute, Pittsburgh.

1956 One-man show at the Kleemann Gallery, New York.

1957-60 Exhibitions at the Galerie de France, Paris.

1958-59 Exhibits at the Kootz Gallery, New York.

Resident in Paris.

Sales

DRAWINGS

1964

Landscape, 1953, ink and watercolor, 11¾ x 19½ .... (372) $ 600

1965

A City Located on a Broken Ground, 1955, ink and watercolor, 10 x 15 .... (541)   600

1968–July 1969

The Bathers, 1952, 12 x 19 .... (1237)   250

WATERCOLORS

1961–1962

Composition, 1957, watercolor, 13 x 16¼ .... (93)   768

1963

Composition on a Blue Background, 1959, gouache, 16 x 22 .... (80)   588

Composition, watercolor, 14¼ x 15¾ .... (283)   407

1964

Composition, 1957, gouache, 21 x 14¼ .... (377)   429

PAINTINGS

1963

My Country, 36¾ x 23¾ .... (235)   76

1964

Abstraction, 44¾ x 57¼ .... (372)   1,600

1965

My Country, 1957, 23¾ x 36 .... (507)   1,900

The Flower, 1952, 31½ x 20½ .... (583)   755

1967

Composition, 51½ x 38½ .... (963)   2,750

1968–July 1969

Tracks in the City, 1954, 51½ x 63¼ .... (1080) $ 1,600

Abstraction, 1958-59, 25½ x 21¾ .... (1237)   750

The Bathers, 15 x 18 .... (1237)   275

Gabriel Zendel

(1906–   )

Birthplace: Paris, France. (Soon develops a passion for drawing and painting.)

1925-28 Attends the Institut d'Esthétique Contemporaine, Paris. Visits the Netherlands.

1929 Exhibits for the first time at the Salon des Vrais Indépendants, Paris.

1934 First one-man show at the Galerie de Paris, Paris. Participates in the principal Parisian salons.

1939 Marries Agathe Schneider.

1940 Arrested by the Nazis, he succeeds in escaping to the unoccupied part of France. Settles in Cannes until the end of World War II.

1947 Issues *Cirque,* a book including a text by Léon-Paul Fargue and 25 illustrations by Zendel.

1948-49 First trip to the U.S. One-man show at Durand-Ruel's, New York.

1950 One-man show at Durand-Ruel's, Paris. Participates in the international exhibition of engraving at the Musée National d'Art Moderne, Paris.

1951 Durand-Ruel closes his New York gallery, where Zendel was to exhibit each year. Included in the first show of the yearly exhibition "Les Peintres témoins de leur temps" at the Musée d'Art Moderne, Paris. Takes part in this exhibition every year.

1952 One-man show at the Galerie Drouant-David, Paris. Several stays in Burgundy. P. Descargues writes a monograph on him (PLF, Paris).

1953 Does ceramics in the studio of Henri Plisson, Paris. Participates in the second International Art Exhibition, Tokyo.

1954 Takes part in the exhibition "L'Ecole de Paris" at the Galerie Charpentier, Paris—and again in 1955.

1955 Takes part in the exhibition "Regards sur la peinture contemporaine" at the Musée Galliéra, Paris. Exhibition at the Obelisk Gallery, Washington, D.C.

1956 One-man show at the Galerie Drouant-David, Paris. (Catalog preface by Waldemar George.) Monograph in the collection *Documents* (Pierre Cailler, Geneva).

1958-59 One-man show at the Galerie Carlier, Paris—and again in 1960. Visits Venice.

1960 Buys a country house in Burgundy.

1964-65   Executes two series of illustrations for *Les Céliba-taires* by Henry de Montherlant and for *Nuits de Princes* by Joseph Kessel (Lidis, Paris).

1966   Second trip to U.S.

1968   Wins the first prize at the Trouville Biennial.

Resident usually six months in his Paris studio and six months in his house in Burgundy.

Sales

PAINTINGS

1961-1962

Landscape, 19¾ x 29 .... (12) $ 160

Still Life with Fruit, 13 x 21¾ .... (2)   230

Still Life with Flowers, and a Fruit Stand, 1945, on panel, 29 x 23¾ .... (9)   100

1963

The Lighthouse, 19¾ x 24 .... (314)   320

1964

The Yellow Chair, 1954, on panel, 17 x 16¼ ...... (430)   80

1965

Bunch of Flowers, 10 x 7¾ .... (606) $ 75

The Cliffs, 19¾ x 25¾ .... (538)   60

The Chapel, on cardboard, 12¾ x 16¾ .... (578)   40

1966

Still Life, 19¾ x 23¾ .... (648)   175

Meudon, 18¼ x 24 .... (824)   70

The Goose, 1953, 23¾ x 29 .... (674)   84

1967

Still Life with Cherries, 9½ x 16¼ .... (996)   26

Still Life with a Fruit Stand, 11¾ x 24 .... (937)   100

Vase of Flowers, 23¾ x 6 .... (941)   150

1968-July 1969

Etretat, 1956, 54 x 65 .... (1089)   44

The Village Path, 19¾ x 24 .... (1221)   120

Still Life with Sunflowers, 1955, 35¼ x 45¾ ..... (1247)   360

Still Life with a Coffeepot, 1948, on masonite, 25½ x 31¾ .... (1248)   150

The Studio, 1962, 35¼ x 46¾ .... (1266)   2,100

INDEX OF SALES

KEY NUMBER	DATES	AUCTIONED BY	IN
	May '62		
87	2–3	Kunsthallen	Copenhagen
88	3–4	Stuttgarter Kunstkabinett	Stuttgart
89	6	P. Martin, Hôtel des Chevau-Légers	Versailles
90	9	G. Blache, Hôtel Rameau	Versailles
91	9	Sotheby & Co.	London
92	10	E. Ader, Hôtel Drouot	Paris
93	12	Galerie Motte	Geneva
94	14–16	Karl & Faber	Munich
95	14	C. Robert, Hôtel Drouot	Paris
96	16	Parke-Bernet Galleries	New York
97	17	Crédit Municipal	Paris
98	18	M. et P. Rheims, Hôtel Drouot	Paris
99	21	E. Ader, Hôtel Drouot	Paris
100	22–25	Dorotheum	Vienna
101	23	Klipstein & Kornfeld	Bern
102	23	G. Blache, Hôtel Rameau	Versailles
103	23	Palais des Beaux-Arts	Brussels
104	23	M. et P. Rheims, Hôtel Drouot	Paris
105	24	Klipstein & Kornfeld	Bern
106	25	Klipstein & Kornfeld	Bern
	June '62		
107	2	Dr Ernst Hauswedell	Hamburg
108	4	M. Boscher, Hôtel Drouot	Paris
109	5	P. Martin, Trianon-Palace	Versailles
110	6	G. Blache, Hôtel Rameau	Versailles
111	7	Parke-Bernet Galleries	New York
112	14	Sotheby & Co.	London
113	15	C. Robert, Hôtel Drouot	Paris
114	18	E. Ader et C. Robert, Palais Galliéra	Paris
115	18	R. P. Oury, Hôtel Drouot	Paris
116	19	M. et P. Rheims, Palais Galliéra	Paris
117	20	P. Renaud, Hôtel Drouot	Paris
118	20	Sotheby & Co.	London
119	21	P. Martin, Hôtel des Chevau-Légers	Versailles
120	22	R. P. Oury, Palais Galliéra	Paris
121	22	M. et P. Rheims, Hôtel Drouot	Paris
122	26–30	Galerie Fischer	Lucerne
123	27–28	G. Blache, Hôtel Rameau	Versailles
124	28	M. et P. Rheims et Laurin, Palais Galliéra	Paris
125	29	R. G. Laurin, Palais Galliéra	Paris
	July '62		
126	3	M. et P. Rheims, Hôtel Drouot	Paris
127	4	E. Ader, Hôtel Drouot	Paris
128	4	Sotheby & Co.	London
129	5	Sotheby & Co.	London
130	19	P. Martin, Hôtel des Chevau-Légers	Versailles
	Sept. '62		
131	18	Dorotheum	Vienna
132	24–25	A. Baussy, Villa Rêve-d'Or	Cannes
	Oct. '62		
133	14	G. Blache, Hôtel Rameau	Versailles
134	15	Boisgirard, Hôtel Drouot	Paris
135	26–27	Helmut Tenner	Heidelberg
136	29	R. P. Oury, Hôtel Drouot	Paris
137	31	Parke-Bernet Galleries	New York
138	30	Hôtel Beau-Rivage	Lausanne
	Nov. '62		
139	4	G. Blache, Hôtel Rameau	Versailles
140	7	Sotheby & Co.	London
141	8	E. Ader, Hôtel Drouot	Paris
142	9–10	Parke-Bernet Galleries	New York
143	10	Galerie Motte	Geneva
144	11	G. Blache, Hôtel Rameau	Versailles
145	13–15	Galleria Brera	Milan
146	18	P. Martin, Hôtel des Chevau-Légers	Versailles
147	19	E. Ader, Hôtel Drouot	Paris
148	21	Sotheby & Co.	London
149	21–23	Finarte	Milan
150	23–26	Galerie Fischer	Lucerne
151	24	Dr Ernst Hauswedell	Hamburg
152	24	Parke-Bernet Galleries	New York
153	25	G. Blache, Hôtel Rameau	Versailles
154	26	C. Robert, Hôtel Drouot	Paris
155	27	P. Martin, Trianon-Palace	Versailles
156	29	M. et P. Rheims, Palais Galliéra	Paris
157	29	R. P. Oury, Hôtel Drouot	Paris
158	30	M. et P. Rheims, Hôtel Drouot	Paris
159	30	Christie, Manson & Woods	London
	Dec. '62		
160	2	G. Blache, Hôtel Rameau	Versailles
161	3	P. Renaud, Hôtel Drouot	Paris
162	5	Palais Galliéra	Paris
163	5	Parke-Bernet Galleries	New York
164	5	Sotheby & Co.	London
165	9	J. P. Chapelle, Hôtel des Chevau-Légers	Versailles
166	9	R. Allaire, Hôtel des Ventes	Enghien
167	10	M. et P. Rheims, Palais Galliéra	Paris
168	10	C. Robert, Hôtel Drouot	Paris
169	11	M. et P. Rheims, Palais Galliéra	Paris
170	11	R. G. Boisgirard, Hôtel Drouot	Paris
171	12	E. Ader, Palais Galliéra	Paris
172	16	G. Blache, Hôtel Rameau	Versailles
173	17	R. P. Oury, Hôtel Drouot	Paris
174	19	Sotheby & Co.	London
175	19–20	Courchet et Japhet, Galerie Robioni	Nice
176	20	Crédit Municipal	Paris
177	21	M. et P. Rheims, Hôtel Drouot	Paris
	1963		
	Jan. '63		
178	13	P. Martin, Hôtel des Chevau-Légers	Versailles
179	24	Parke-Bernet Galleries	New York
180	28	M. Boscher, Hôtel Drouot	Paris

KEY NUMBER	DATES	AUCTIONED BY	IN
277	23	Sotheby & Co.	London
278	30	R. P. Oury, Hôtel Drouot	Paris
279	30	Parke-Bernet Galleries	New York
Nov. '63			
280	1	P. Martin, Hôtel des Chevau-Légers	Versailles
281	1	Galerie Motte	Geneva
282	2	Galerie Rudolf Manuel-Cadror	Bern
283	2	Galerie Motte	Geneva
284	6–8	Karl und Faber	Munich
285	8	Koller Gallery	Zurich
286	13	M. et P. Rheims et P. Renaud, Hôtel Drouot	Paris
287	17	G. Blache, Hôtel Rameau	Versailles
288	18	C. Robert, Hôtel Drouot	Paris
289	20	J. Dubourg, Hôtel Drouot	Paris
290	21	Parke-Bernet Galleries	New York
291	22	E. Ader, Hôtel Drouot	Paris
292	22	Parke-Bernet Galleries	New York
293	25	P. Martin, Trianon-Palace	Versailles
294	25	Courchet et Japhet, Hôtel Negresco	Nice
295	27	M. et P. Rheims, Hôtel Drouot	Paris
296	28	R. G. Laurin et Le Mouel, Palais Galliéra	Paris
297	30	Dr Ernst Hauswedell	Hamburg
Dec. '63			
298	1	G. Blache, Hôtel Rameau	Versailles
299	2	M. et P. Rheims, Palais Galliéra	Paris
300	2	P. Renaud, Hôtel Drouot	Paris
301	2	M. Charpentier, Hôtel Drouot	Paris
302	3	Morelle et Daussy, Hôtel Drouot	Paris
303	4	E. Libert, Palais Galliéra	Paris
304	4	Sotheby & Co.	London
305	5	Parke-Bernet Galleries	New York
306	6	R. P. Oury, Palais Galliéra	Paris
307	6	Galerie Fischer	Lucerne
308	3–6	Dorotheum	Vienna
309	6	Christie, Manson & Woods	London
310	7	Galerie Fischer	Lucerne
311	8	P. Martin, Moulin de Vauboyen	Bièvres
312	9	R. G. Laurin, Palais Galliéra	Paris
313	10	P. Couturier, Hôtel Drouot	Paris
314	11	C. Robert, Hôtel Drouot	Paris
315	11	Sotheby & Co.	London
316	11	Parke-Bernet Galleries	New York
317	12	Palais des Beaux-Arts	Brussels
318	14	E. Ader, Palais Galliéra	Paris
319	14	Hôtel des Ventes	Marseilles
320	30	Courchet et Japhet, Galerie Robioni	Nice
1964			
Jan. '64			
321	9	Parke-Bernet Galleries	New York
322	12	P. Martin, Hôtel des Chevau-Légers	Versailles
323	29	R. G. Laurin, Hôtel Drouot	Paris
324	29	Parke-Bernet Galleries	New York
325	31	E. Ader, Hôtel Drouot	Paris
Feb. '64			
326	12	E. Ader, Hôtel Drouot	Paris
327	16	G. Blache, Hôtel Rameau	Versailles
328	19	M. et P. Rheims, Hôtel Drouot	Paris
329	20	Parke-Bernet Galleries	New York
330	23	P. Martin, Hôtel des Chevau-Légers	Versailles
331	25	R. G. Laurin, Hôtel Drouot	Paris
332	27	E. Ader, Hôtel Drouot	Paris
333	28	P. Renaud, Hôtel Drouot	Paris
Mar. '64			
334	1	Hours, Hôtel des Ventes	Aix-en-Provence
335	5	P. Martin, Trianon-Palace	Versailles
336	6	Ribault-Menetière, Hôtel Drouot	Paris
337	8	G. Blache, Hôtel Rameau	Versailles
338	11	M. et P. Rheims, Hôtel Drouot	Paris
339	11	R. G. Laurin, Hôtel Drouot	Paris
340	12	E. Ader, Palais Galliéra	Paris
341	13	E. Ader, Palais Galliéra	Paris
342	15	J. P. Chapelle, Hôtel des Chevau-Légers	Versailles
343	15	Maison et Savot, Hôtel des Ventes	Orléans
344	16	Delorme, Hôtel Drouot	Paris
345	16	M. Boscher, Hôtel Drouot	Paris
346	16	C. Robert, Hôtel Drouot	Paris
347	18	M. et P. Rheims, Palais Galliéra	Paris
348	18	E. Ader, Hôtel Drouot	Paris
349	18	Dorotheum	Vienna
350	19	E. Ader, Hôtel Drouot	Paris
351	20	M. et P. Rheims, Palais Galliéra	Paris
352	23	Lemée, Hôtel Drouot	Paris
353	25	Parke-Bernet Galleries	New York
Apr. '64			
354	8	Parke-Bernet Galleries	New York
355	12	G. Blache, Hôtel Rameau	Versailles
356	15	Sotheby & Co.	London
357	15	Parke-Bernet Galleries	New York
358	15	Kunsthaus Lempertz	Cologne
359	20	P. Renaud, Hôtel Drouot	Paris
360	21–22	Courchet et Japhet, Galerie Robioni	Nice
361	22	Bivort, Hôtel Drouot	Paris
362	22	Helmut Tenner	Heidelberg
363	23	Parke-Bernet Galleries	New York
364	24	Christie, Manson & Woods	London
365	27	Christie, Manson & Woods	London
366	29	G. Blache, Hôtel Rameau	Versailles
367	29	Sotheby & Co.	London
368	30	Sotheby & Co.	London
May '64			
369	1–13	Arne Bruun Rasmussen	Copenhagen
370	3	P. Martin, Hôtel des Chevau-Légers	Versailles

KEY NUMBER	DATES	AUCTIONED BY	IN
561	15	M. et P. Rheims, Palais Galliéra	Paris
562	15	M. et P. Rheims, Palais Galliéra	Paris
563	16	G. Blache, Hôtel Rameau	Versailles
564	17	E. Ader, Palais Galliéra	Paris
565	17	Kornfeld und Klipstein	Bern
566	18	Kornfeld und Klipstein	Bern
567	18	Galerie Motte	Geneva
568	19	Kornfeld und Klipstein	Bern
569	19	Galerie Motte	Geneva
570	21	Picard, Hôtel Drouot	Paris
571	22	M. et P. Rheims, et R. G. Laurin, Palais Galliéra	Paris
572	22	R. G. Boisgirard, Hôtel Drouot	Paris
573	22	Sotheby & Co.	London
574	23	M. et P. Rheims, Hôtel Drouot	Paris
575	23	Sotheby & Co.	London
576	25	Galerie Fischer	Lucerne
577	30	E. Ader, Hôtel Drouot	Paris
578	30	G. Blache, Hôtel Rameau	Versailles
579	30	Arne Bruun Rasmussen	Copenhagen

July '65

KEY NUMBER	DATES	AUCTIONED BY	IN
580	1	M. et P. Rheims, Hôtel Drouot	Paris
581	2	P. Renaud, Hôtel Drouot	Paris
582	8	Sotheby & Co.	London
583	9	Christie, Manson & Woods	London
584	14	Sotheby & Co.	London
585	20	Christie, Manson & Woods	London
586	25	P. Martin, Moulin de Vauboyen	Bièvres

Sept. '65

KEY NUMBER	DATES	AUCTIONED BY	IN
587	15	Dorotheum	Vienna

Oct. '65

KEY NUMBER	DATES	AUCTIONED BY	IN
588	3	P. Martin, Hôtel des Chevau-Légers	Versailles
589	5	Campo Brothers	Antwerp
590	5-7	Courchet et Japhet, Galerie Robioni	Nice
591	5-18	S. J. Mak van Waay	Amsterdam
592	13	Parke-Bernet Galleries	New York
593	13-15	Palais des Beaux Arts	Brussels
594	14	Parke-Bernet Galleries	New York
595	15	Hôtel des Ventes	Marseilles
596	19	Karl und Faber	Munich
597	20	Karl und Faber	Munich
598	24	G. Blache, Hôtel Rameau	Versailles
599	25	Loudmer, Hôtel Drouot	Paris
600	25	Couturier, Hôtel Drouot	Paris
601	25	Hours, Hôtel des Ventes	Aix-en-Provence
602	28	Pequignot, Hôtel Beau-Rivage	Lausanne

Nov. '65

KEY NUMBER	DATES	AUCTIONED BY	IN
603	3	E. Ader, Hôtel Drouot	Paris
604	7	P. Martin, Moulin de Vauboyen	Bièvres
605	12	Christie, Manson & Woods	London
606	12	Parke-Bernet Galleries	New York

KEY NUMBER	DATES	AUCTIONED BY	IN
607	15	Couturier et Renaud, Hôtel Drouot	Paris
608	16-17	Courchet et Japhet, Galerie Robioni	Nice
610	18	Parke-Bernet Galleries	New York
611	19	Loudmer, Hôtel Drouot	Paris
612	21	P. Martin, Trianon-Palace	Versailles
613	23	E. Ader, Delorme et Champetier de Ribes, Palais Galliéra	Paris
614	24	Parke-Bernet Galleries	New York
615	25	E. Ader et Ribault-Menetière, Palais Galliéra	Paris
616	25	Finarte	Milan
617	27	Galerie Motte	Geneva
618	27	Dr Ernst Hauswedell	Hamburg
619	28	G. Blache, Hôtel Rameau	Versailles
620	28	J. P. Chapelle, Hôtel des Chevau-Légers	Versailles
621	29	R. G. Boisgirard, Hôtel Drouot	Paris
622	30	Paul Brandt	Amsterdam
623	30	Arne Bruun Rasmussen	Copenhagen

Dec. '65

KEY NUMBER	DATES	AUCTIONED BY	IN
624	1	Sotheby & Co.	London
625	1	Dorotheum	Vienna
626	2	E. Ader et Picard, Hôtel Drouot	Paris
627	3	Loudmer, Hôtel Drouot	Paris
628	3	Christie, Manson & Woods	London
629	3	Christie, Manson & Woods	London
630	5	P. Martin, Hôtel des Chevau-Légers	Versailles
631	6	C. Robert, Hôtel Drouot	Paris
632	7	M. Rheims, R. G. Laurin et P. Rheims, Palais Galliéra	Paris
633	8	Parke-Bernet Galleries	New York
634	8	Kunsthaus Lempertz	Cologne
635	8-9	Audap, Godeau et Solanet, Hôtel Drouot	Paris
636	8-9	Palais des Beaux-Arts	Brussels
637	9	Parke-Bernet Galleries	New York
638	9	Kunsthaus Lempertz	Cologne
639	10	Rosset, Hôtel Beau-Rivage	Lausanne
640	12	G. Blache, Hôtel Rameau	Versailles
641	13	Maringe, Hôtel Drouot	Paris
642	15	M. Rheims, R. G. Laurin et P. Rheims, Hôtel Drouot	Paris
643	15	Sotheby & Co.	London
644	15	Parke-Bernet Galleries	New York
645	16	S. J. Mak van Waay	Amsterdam
646	19	G. Blache, Hôtel Rameau	Versailles
647	20	Loudmer, Hôtel Drouot	Paris

1966
Jan. '66

KEY NUMBER	DATES	AUCTIONED BY	IN
648	13	Parke-Bernet Galleries	New York
649	24	Hours, Hôtel des Ventes	Aix-en-Provence
650	25	Albinet, Hôtel Drouot	Paris
651	27	Parke-Bernet Galleries	New York

KEY NUMBER	DATES	AUCTIONED BY	IN
743	17	C. Robert, Palais Galliéra	Paris
744	17	Galerie Motte	Geneva
745	18	Galerie Motte	Geneva
746	19	P. Martin, Hôtel des Chevau-Légers	Versailles
747	20	M. Rheims, R. G. Laurin, et P. Rheims, Palais Galliéra	Paris
748	20	Ledoux-Lebard et Lissilour, Hôtel Drouot	Paris
749	21	M. Rheims, R. G. Laurin, et P. Rheims, Palais Galliéra	Paris
750	22	Sotheby & Co.	London
751	23	Sotheby & Co.	London
752	24	Loudmer, Hôtel Drouot	Paris
753	24	Christie, Manson & Woods	London
754	24	Galerie Fischer	Lucerne
755	25	J. P. Chapelle, Hôtel des Chevau-Légers	Versailles
756	26	Martinot, Hôtel des Ventes	Pontoise
757	30	Sotheby & Co.	London
July '66			
758	1	E. Ader et Picard, Hôtel Drouot	Paris
759	7	P. Martin, Hôtel des Chevau-Légers	Versailles
760	15	Christie, Manson & Woods	London
761	20	Sotheby & Co.	London
762	25	P. Martin, Hôtel des Chevau-Légers	Versailles
Sept. '66			
763	14	Dorotheum	Vienna
764	25	P. Martin, Hôtel des Chevau-Légers	Versailles
765	27	S. J. Mak van Waay	Amsterdam
Oct. '66			
766	2	G. Blache, Hôtel Rameau	Versailles
767	4–5	Campo Brothers	Antwerp
768	6	Sotheby & Co.	London
769	9	P. Martin, Hôtel des Chevau-Légers	Versailles
770	10	Arne Bruun Rasmussen	Copenhagen
771	11	Arne Bruun Rasmussen	Copenhagen
772	16	G. Blache, Hôtel Rameau	Versailles
773	18	Karl und Faber	Munich
774	19	M. Rheims, R. G. Laurin, et P. Rheims, Hôtel Drouot	Paris
775	19	Karl und Faber	Munich
776	20	Parke-Bernet Galleries	New York
777	23	P. Martin, Hôtel des Chevau-Légers	Versailles
778	24	R. G. Boisgirard, Hôtel Drouot	Paris
779	24	Hours, Hôtel des Ventes	Aix-en-Provence
780	25	Paul Brandt	Amsterdam
781	26	Loudmer, Hôtel Drouot	Paris
782	27	Palais des Beaux-Arts	Brussels
Nov. '66			
783	2	Parke-Bernet Galleries	New York
784	3	Parke-Bernet Galleries	New York

KEY NUMBER	DATES	AUCTIONED BY	IN
785	4	Christie, Manson & Woods	London
786	5	Verleyen, Galerie Brugeoise	Bruges
787	7	Lemaire, Hôtel Drouot	Paris
788	13	G. Blache, Hôtel Rameau	Versailles
789	13	J. P. Chapelle, Hôtel des Chevau-Légers	Versailles
790	17	Parke-Bernet Galleries	New York
791	18	Audap, Hôtel Drouot	Paris
792	19	Dr Ernst Hauswedell	Hamburg
793	20	P. Martin, Trianon-Palace	Versailles
794	24	M. Rheims, R. G. Laurin, et P. Rheims, Hôtel Drouot	Paris
795	25	E. Ader et Picard, Hôtel Drouot	Paris
796	25	P. Renaud, Hôtel Drouot	Paris
797	25	Galerie Motte	Geneva
798	26	Galerie Motte	Geneva
799	28	Buzot, Hôtel Drouot	Paris
800	28	Champetier de Ribes, Hôtel Drouot	Paris
801	29	E. Ader et Ribault-Menetière, Palais Galliéra	Paris
802	29	Finarte	Milan
803	30	C. Robert, Hôtel Drouot	Paris
804	30	Loudmer, Hôtel Drouot	Paris
805	30	Parke-Bernet Galleries	New York
806	30	Dorotheum	Vienna
Dec. '66			
807	2	Bondu, Hôtel Drouot	Paris
808	2	Christie, Manson & Woods	London
809	4	G. Blache, Hôtel Rameau	Versailles
810	5	C. Robert, Hôtel Drouot	Paris
811	6	M. Rheims, R. G. Laurin, et P. Rheims, Palais Galliéra	Paris
812	7	Sotheby & Co.	London
813	7	Sotheby & Co.	London
814	8	E. Ader et Picard, Palais Galliéra	Paris
815	8	Sotheby & Co.	London
816	8–9	Kunsthaus Lempertz	Cologne
817	9	M. Rheims, R. G. Laurin, et P. Rheims, Hôtel Drouot	Paris
818	9	Christie, Manson & Woods	London
819	10	Loudmer, Palais Galliéra	Paris
820	11	P. Martin, Hôtel des Chevau-Légers	Versailles
821	11	Martinot, Hôtel des Ventes	Pontoise
822	13	Paul Brandt	Amsterdam
823	13	S. J. Mak van Waay	Amsterdam
824	14	Loudmer, Hôtel Drouot	Paris
825	14	Sotheby & Co.	London
826	16	Loudmer, Hôtel Drouot	Paris
827	19	C. Robert, Hôtel Drouot	Paris
828	21	R. G. Boisgirard, Hôtel Drouot	Paris
829	22	E. Ader et Picard, Hôtel Drouot	Paris
830	22	Crédit Municipal	Paris
1967			
Jan. '67			
831	19	Parke-Bernet Galleries	New York
832	25	P. Renaud, Hôtel Drouot	Paris

KEY NUMBER	DATES	AUCTIONED BY	IN
833	29	P. Martin, Hôtel des Chevau-Légers	Versailles
834	30	Loudmer, Hôtel Drouot	Paris

Feb. '67

KEY NUMBER	DATES	AUCTIONED BY	IN
835	1	E. Ader, Picard, et A. Ader, Hôtel Drouot	Paris
836	1	Sotheby & Co.	London
837	2	M. Rheims, R. G. Laurin, et P. Rheims, Hôtel Drouot	Paris
838	5	G. Blache, Hôtel Rameau	Versailles
839	15	M. Rheims, R. G. Laurin, et P. Rheims, Hôtel Drouot	Paris
840	15	E. Ader, Picard, et A. Ader, Hôtel Drouot	Paris
841	16	Parke-Bernet Galleries	New York
842	20	R. G. Boisgirard, Hôtel Drouot	Paris
843	26	P. Martin, Hôtel des Chevau-Légers	Versailles
844	26	J. P. Chapelle, Hôtel des Chevau-Légers	Versailles

Mar. '67

KEY NUMBER	DATES	AUCTIONED BY	IN
845	1	Loudmer, Hôtel Drouot	Paris
846	1	Palais des Beaux-Arts	Brussels
847	2	Parke-Bernet Galleries	New York
848	3	E. Ader, Picard, et A. Ader, Hôtel Drouot	Paris
849	6	Lemée, Hôtel Drouot	Paris
850	8	Loudmer, Hôtel Drouot	Paris
851	8	Arne Bruun Rasmussen	Copenhagen
852	9	E. Ader, Picard, et A. Ader, Palais Galliéra	Paris
853	10	Christie, Manson & Woods	London
854	12	P. Martin, Hôtel des Chevau-Légers	Versailles
855	12	G. Blache, Hôtel Rameau	Versailles
856	13	Champetier de Ribes, Hôtel Drouot	Paris
857	14	M. Rheims, R. G. Laurin, et P. Rheims, Palais Galliéra	Paris
858	15	P. Martin, Trianon-Palace	Versailles
859	15	Dorotheum	Vienna
860	16	Parke-Bernet Galleries	New York
861	19	Martinot, Hôtel des Ventes	Pontoise
862	20	C. Robert, Hôtel Drouot	Paris
863	30–31	Courchet, Galerie Robioni	Nice

Apr. '67

KEY NUMBER	DATES	AUCTIONED BY	IN
864	6	Parke-Bernet Galleries	New York
865	9	P. Martin, Hôtel des Chevau-Légers	Versailles
866	10	E. Ader, Picard, et A. Ader, Hôtel Drouot	Paris
867	11–13	Campo Brothers	Antwerp
868	11–15	Stads Auktionverket	Stockholm
869	12	Sotheby & Co.	London
870	12	Parke-Bernet Galleries	New York
871	13–14	Campo Brothers	Antwerp
872	18	Christie, Manson & Woods	London

KEY NUMBER	DATES	AUCTIONED BY	IN
873	19	E. Ader, Picard, et A. Ader, Hôtel Drouot	Paris
874	19	G. Blache, Hôtel Rameau	Versailles
875	20	G. Blache, Hôtel Rameau	Versailles
876	24	Loudmer, Hôtel Drouot	Paris
877	25	P. Renaud, Hôtel Drouot	Paris
878	26	Jozon, Hôtel Drouot	Paris
879	26	M. Rheims, R. G. Laurin, et P. Rheims, Hôtel Drouot	Paris
880	26	Sotheby & Co.	London
881	27	Sotheby & Co.	London
882	27	Finarte	Milan
883	28	Loudmer, Hôtel Drouot	Paris
884	28	R. G. Boisgirard, Hôtel Drouot	Paris
885	28	Christie, Manson & Woods	London
886	30	P. Martin, Hôtel des Chevau-Légers	Versailles

May '67

KEY NUMBER	DATES	AUCTIONED BY	IN
887	3	E. Ader, Picard, et A. Ader, Hôtel Drouot	Paris
888	3	Sotheby & Co.	London
889	4	Parke-Bernet Galleries	New York
890	9	Arne Bruun Rasmussen	Copenhagen
891	10	Courchet, Galerie Robioni	Nice
892	10	Arne Bruun Rasmussen	Copenhagen
893	11	Parke-Bernet Galleries	New York
894	17	G. Blache, Hôtel Rameau	Versailles
895	22	Hours, Hôtel des Ventes	Aix-en-Provence
896	24	M. Rheims, R. G. Laurin, et P. Rheims, Palais Galliéra	Paris
897	24	Loudmer, Hôtel Drouot	Paris
898	25	P. Martin, Hôtel des Chevau-Légers	Versailles
899	26–27	Leo Spik	Berlin
900	29	Robin, Hôtel Drouot	Paris
901	30	E. Ader, Picard, et A. Ader, Palais Galliéra	Paris
902	30	Champetier de Ribes, Palais Galliéra	Paris
903	30	Deurbergue, Palais Galliéra	Paris
904	30	Palais des Beaux-Arts	Brussels
905	31	P. Renaud, Hôtel Drouot	Paris
906	31	Dorotheum	Vienna

June '67

KEY NUMBER	DATES	AUCTIONED BY	IN
907	1	Kunsthaus Lempertz	Cologne
908	2	Kunsthaus Lempertz	Cologne
909	5	J. P. Chapelle, Hôtel des Chevau-Légers	Versailles
910	5	Dr Ernst Hauswedell	Hamburg
911	6	Loudmer, Palais Galliéra	Paris
912	7	G. Blache, Hôtel Rameau	Versailles
913	7	Karl und Faber	Munich
914	7	A. Weinmüller	Munich
915	8	Karl und Faber	Munich
916	9	Bivort, Hôtel Drouot	Paris
917	9	R. G. Boisgirard, Hôtel Drouot	Paris
918	9	Galerie Motte	Geneva
919	10	Galerie Motte	Geneva

KEY NUMBER	DATES	AUCTIONED BY	IN
920	11	P. Martin, Hôtel des Chevau-Légers	Versailles
921	12	C. Robert, Hôtel Drouot	Paris
922	13	Sotheby & Co.	London
923	14	M. Rheims, R. G. Laurin, et P. Rheims, Palais Galliéra	Paris
924	14	Solanet, Palais Galliéra	Paris
925	14	Kornfeld und Klipstein	Bern
926	15	G. Blache, Hôtel Rameau	Versailles
927	15	Kornfeld und Klipstein	Bern
928	15–16	Galerie Fischer	Lucerne
929	16	M. Rheims, R. G. Laurin, et P. Rheims, Hôtel Drouot	Paris
930	16	Kornfeld und Klipstein	Bern
931	17	Kornfeld und Klipstein	Bern
932	17	Galerie Fischer	Lucerne
933	19	P. Renaud, Hôtel Drouot	Paris
934	21	Loudmer, Hôtel Drouot	Paris
935	23	E. Ader, Picard, et A. Ader, Hôtel Drouot	Paris
936	26	Loudmer, Hôtel Drouot	Paris
937	28	M. Boscher, Hôtel Drouot	Paris
938	28	Sotheby & Co.	London
939	29	Sotheby & Co.	London
940	30	Christie, Manson & Woods	London

July '67

KEY NUMBER	DATES	AUCTIONED BY	IN
941	5	M. Rheims, R. G. Laurin, P. Rheims, et Loudmer, Hôtel Drouot	Paris
942	6	Lemée, Hôtel Drouot	Paris
943	9	P. Martin, Hôtel des Chevau-Légers	Versailles
944	14	Christie, Manson & Woods	London
945	19	Sotheby & Co.	London

Sept. '67

KEY NUMBER	DATES	AUCTIONED BY	IN
946	13	Dorotheum	Vienna

Oct. '67

KEY NUMBER	DATES	AUCTIONED BY	IN
947	3–5	Campo Brothers	Antwerp
948	8	P. Martin, Hôtel des Chevau-Légers	Versailles
949	11	Loudmer, Hôtel Drouot	Paris
950	15	G. Blache, Hôtel Rameau	Versailles
951	17	Christie, Manson & Woods	London
952	19	Parke-Bernet Galleries	New York
953	25	E. Ader, Picard, et A. Ader, Hôtel Drouot	Paris
954	26	Parke-Bernet Galleries	New York
955	27	Loudmer, Hôtel Drouot	Paris

Nov. '67

KEY NUMBER	DATES	AUCTIONED BY	IN
956	1	P. Martin, Hôtel des Chevau-Légers	Versailles
957	1	Sotheby & Co.	London
958	2	Arne Bruun Rasmussen	Copenhagen
959	3	Christie, Manson & Woods	London
960	3	Arne Bruun Rasmussen	Copenhagen
961	6	E. Ader, Picard, et A. Ader, Hôtel Drouot	Paris
962	7	Finarte	Milan

KEY NUMBER	DATES	AUCTIONED BY	IN
963	9	Parke-Bernet Galleries	New York
964	10	C. Robert, Hôtel Drouot	Paris
965	10	Galerie Motte	Geneva
966	11	P. Martin, Hôtel des Chevau-Légers	Versailles
967	11	Galerie Motte	Geneva
968	12	G. Blache, Hôtel Rameau	Versailles
969	15	Parke-Bernet Galleries	New York
970	18	Dr Ernst Hauswedell	Hamburg
971	22	Loudmer, Hôtel Drouot	Paris
972	22	Pescheteau, Hôtel Drouot	Paris
973	22	R. G. Boisgirard, Hôtel Drouot	Paris
974	24	P. Renaud, Hôtel Drouot	Paris
975	24	E. Ader et Ribault-Menetière, Hôtel Drouot	Paris
976	26	P. Martin, Trianon-Palace	Versailles
977	27	Champetier de Ribes, Hôtel Drouot	Paris
978	28	Loudmer, Palais Galliéra	Paris
979	28	Paul Brandt	Amsterdam
980	29	M. Rheims, R. G. Laurin, et P. Rheims, Hôtel Drouot	Paris
981	29	Crédit Municipal	Paris
982	29	Sotheby & Co.	London
983	29	Dorotheum	Vienna
984	30	Morelle, P. Renaud, Daussy, et Delorme, Palais Galliéra	Paris
985	30	Sotheby & Co.	London
986	30	Kunsthaus Lempertz	Cologne

Dec. '67

KEY NUMBER	DATES	AUCTIONED BY	IN
987	1	E. Ader, Picard, et A. Ader, Palais Galliéra	Paris
988	1	Christie, Manson & Woods	London
989	1	Parke-Bernet Galleries	New York
990	1	Kunsthaus Lempertz	Cologne
991	1	Galerie Fischer	Lucerne
992	2	Galerie Fischer	Lucerne
993	3	M. Rheims, R. G. Laurin, et P. Rheims, Palais Galliéra	Paris
994	3	M. Boscher, Palais Galliéra	Paris
995	3	G. Blache, Hôtel Rameau	Versailles
996	4	Loudmer, Hôtel Drouot	Paris
997	5	Karl und Faber	Munich
998	6	Karl und Faber	Munich
999	10	P. Martin, Hôtel des Chevau-Légers	Versailles
1000	11	Loudmer, Hôtel Drouot	Paris
1001	12–13	Palais des Beaux-Arts	Brussels
1002	13	E. Ader, Picard, et A. Ader, Hôtel Drouot	Paris
1003	13	Sotheby & Co.	London
1004	13	Parke-Bernet Galleries	New York
1005	14	Sotheby & Co.	London
1006	15	Christie, Manson & Woods	London
1007	18	Loudmer, Hôtel Drouot	Paris
1008	19–20	Courchet, Galerie Robioni	Nice
1009	21	M. Rheims, R. G. Laurin, et P. Rheims, Hôtel Drouot	Paris

KEY NUMBER	DATES	AUCTIONED BY	IN
1098	13	G. Blache, Hôtel Rameau	Versailles
1099	13	Kornfeld und Klipstein	Bern
1100	13	Arne Bruun Rasmussen	Copenhagen
1101	14	Kornfeld und Klipstein	Bern
1102	15	Kornfeld und Klipstein	Bern
1103	17	Dernis, Hôtel Drouot	Paris
1104	19	M. Rheims, R. G. Laurin, et P. Rheims, Hôtel Drouot	Paris
1105	19	Dorotheum	Vienna
1106	20	E. Ader, Picard, et A. Ader, Palais Galliéra	Paris
1107	21	Galerie Fischer	Lucerne
1108	22	Galerie Fischer	Lucerne
1109	24	M. Rheims, R. G. Laurin, et P. Rheims, Palais Galliéra	Paris
1110	24	C. Robert, Hôtel Drouot	Paris
1111	24	Dr Ernst Hauswedell	Hamburg
1112	24	Dr Ernst Hauswedell	Hamburg
1113	25	G. Blache, Hôtel Rameau	Versailles
1114	25	Dr Ernst Hauswedell	Hamburg
1115	26	R. G. Boisgirard, Hôtel Drouot	Paris
1116	26	P. Martin, Palais des Congrès	Versailles
1117	27	Loudmer, Palais Galliéra	Paris
1118	27	E. Ader, Picard, Ribault-Menetière, et A. Ader, Hôtel Drouot	Paris
1119	27	G. Blache, Hôtel Rameau	Versailles
1120	27	Courchet, Galerie Robioni	Nice
1121	28	C. Robert, Palais Galliéra	Paris
1122	28	P. Renaud, Hôtel Drouot	Paris
1123	28	M. Rheims, R. G. Laurin, et P. Rheims, Hôtel Drouot	Paris
1124	28	Morelle, Hôtel Drouot	Paris
1125	28	Galerie Motte	Geneva
1126	28	Christie, Manson & Woods	London
1127	29	Galerie Motte	Geneva
1128	30	P. Martin, Hôtel des Chevau-Légers	Versailles

July '68

KEY NUMBER	DATES	AUCTIONED BY	IN
1129	2	Loudmer, Hôtel Drouot	Paris
1130	2	Christie, Manson & Woods	London
1131	3	E. Ader, Picard, et A. Ader, Hôtel Drouot	Paris
1132	3	Sotheby & Co.	London
1133	4	Morel d'Arleux, Hôtel Drouot	Paris
1134	4	Sotheby & Co.	London
1135	5	C. Robert, Hôtel Drouot	Paris
1136	5	Loudmer, Hôtel Drouot	Paris
1137	5	E. Ader, Picard, et A. Ader, Hôtel Drouot	Paris
1138	5	Christie, Manson & Woods	London
1139	9	Michaud et Maringe, Hôtel Drouot	Paris
1140	10	Loudmer, Hôtel Drouot	Paris
1141	17	Sotheby & Co.	London
1142	18	Sotheby & Co.	London
1143	19	Christie, Manson & Woods	London
1144	21	P. Martin, Hôtel des Chevau-Légers	Versailles

Sept. '68

KEY NUMBER	DATES	AUCTIONED BY	IN
1145	18	Parke-Bernet Galleries	New York
1146	18	Dorotheum	Vienna
1147	22	P. Martin, Hôtel des Chevau-Légers	Versailles
1148	25	Courchet, Galerie Robioni	Nice
1149	25	Parke-Bernet Galleries	New York

Oct. '68

KEY NUMBER	DATES	AUCTIONED BY	IN
1150	1-2	Campo Brothers	Antwerp
1151	9	Parke-Bernet Galleries	New York
1152	10	Parke-Bernet Galleries	New York
1153	13	P. Martin, Hôtel des Chevau-Légers	Versailles
1154	14	Loudmer, Hôtel Drouot	Paris
1155	15	Arne Bruun Rasmussen	Copenhagen
1156	18	Morelle, Hôtel Drouot	Paris
1157	22	P. et J. P. Couturier, Libert, de Nicolay, Pillias, Lemée, Palais Galliéra	Paris
1158	22	P. Couturier, de Nicolay, J. P. Couturier, Palais Galliéra	Paris
1159	23	Dernis, Hôtel Drouot	Paris
1160	24	Parke-Bernet Galleries	New York
1161	27	G. Blache, Hôtel Rameau	Versailles
1162	28	R. G. Boisgirard, Hôtel Drouot	Paris
1163	31	Parke-Bernet Galleries	New York

Nov. '68

KEY NUMBER	DATES	AUCTIONED BY	IN
1164	6	Parke-Bernet Galleries	New York
1165	8	Christie, Manson & Woods	London
1166	9	Martinot, Hôtel des Ventes	Pontoise
1167	10	P. Martin, Hôtel des Chevau-Légers	Versailles
1168	12	E. Ader, Picard, et A. Ader, Hôtel Drouot	Paris
1169	12	Parke-Bernet Galleries	New York
1170	12	Galerie Koller	Zurich
1171	13	P. Renaud, Hôtel Drouot	Paris
1172	15	Loudmer, Hôtel Drouot	Paris
1173	15	Galerie Motte	Geneva
1174	16	Galerie Motte	Geneva
1175	18	Thullier, Hôtel Drouot	Paris
1176	20	Parke-Bernet Galleries	New York
1177	22	Loudmer, Hôtel Drouot	Paris
1178	22	Rheims, R. G. Laurin, et P. Rheims, Hôtel Drouot	Paris
1179	24	G. Blache, Hôtel Rameau	Versailles
1180	25	J. P. Chapelle, Palais des Congrès	Versailles
1181	27	Loudmer, Palais Galliéra	Paris
1182	30	Galerie Fischer	Lucerne

Dec. '68

KEY NUMBER	DATES	AUCTIONED BY	IN
1183	1	P. Martin, Trianon-Palace	Versailles
1184	1	G. Blache, Hôtel Rameau	Versailles
1185	3	M. Rheims, R. G. Laurin, et P. Rheims, Hôtel Drouot	Paris
1186	4	P. Couturier, Libert, de Nicolay, et J. P. Couturier, Palais Galliéra	Paris
1187	4	Sotheby & Co.	London
1188	4	Dorotheum	Vienna

BIBLIOGRAPHY

Barr, Alfred H., Jr. *Cubism and Abstract Art*. New York: Arno Press, 1968.

———. *Fantastic Art, Dada, Surrealism*. (Museum of Modern Art: Publications in Reprint Ser). New York: Arno Press, 1970.

Dorival, Bernard. *Les Étapes de la Peinture Française Contemporaine*. 3 vols. Paris: Gallimard, 1943-46.

Focillon, Henri. *La Peinture aux XIXème et XXème Siècle*. 2 vols. Paris: Renouard, 1928.

Humbert, Agnès. *Les Nabis et Leur Époque*. Geneva: 1954.

Huyghe, René. *Dialogue avec le Visible*. Paris: Flammarion, 1955.

Karpel, Bernard. *Art of the Twentieth Century: a Bibliography*. New York: George Wittenborn, Inc.

Leymarie, Jean. *French Painting of the Nineteenth Century*. 3 vols. Geneva: Skira, 1962.

Malraux, André. *Voices of Silence*. limited ed. New York: Doubleday & Co., Inc., 1953.

Moulin, Raymonde. *Le Marché de la Peinture en France*. Paris: Editions de Minuit, 1967.

Muller, Joseph-Emile. *Fauvism*. (World of Art Ser). Translated by Shirley Jones. New York: Praeger Publishers, 1967.

———. *L'Art Moderne*. Paris: Librairie Générale Française, 1963.

Myers, Bernard S. *Expressionism*. London: Thames and Hudson, 1957.

Nacenta, Raymond. *School of Paris*. 2nd ed. Greenwich, Conn.: New York Graphic Society, 1965.

———. *Nouveau Dictionnaire de la Peinture Moderne*. collective work. Paris: Hazan, 1963.

Ponente, Nello. *Modern Painting: Contemporary Trends*. New York: World Publishing Co., 1960.

Raynal, Maurice. *Modern Painting*. New York: World Publishing Co., 1956.

Read, Herbert. *A Concise History of Modern Painting*. (World of Art Ser). rev. ed. New York: Praeger Publishers, 1968.

Rewald, John. *The History of Impressionism*. New York: Museum of Modern Art, 1946.

Rheims, Maurice. *La Vie Étrange des Objets*. Paris: Plon, 1959.

Rose, Barbara. *American Art Since 1900*. (World of Art Ser). New York: Praeger Publishers, 1967.

Rouir, Eugène. *L'Estampe, Valeur de Placement*. Paris: Guy le Prat, 1970.

Seuphor, Michel. *L'Art Abstrait, Ses Origines, Ses Premiers Maîtres*. Paris: Galerie Maeght, 1949.

———. *Dictionnaire de la Peinture Abstraite*. Paris: Hazan, 1957.